THE BOOK OF COMMON PRAYER

THE *Book of Common Prayer* formed the order of service of the established church in England for 400 years from 1549 onwards, and is still in use today. Originally a primary instrument (along with the English Bible) of religious change at the Reformation, it was revised to fit new ideas of doctrine and ritual over the next hundred years. The violent reversals of religious history led to it being banned under the Catholic rule of Mary I between 1553 and 1558, and again under the puritan regime of Parliament from 1645 to 1660. Attempts to introduce the book in Ireland and in Scotland were equally controversial. In between these reversals, it was officially sanctioned by Elizabeth I and the Stuart monarchs, and its regular use was enforced by law. Morning and Evening Prayer on Sundays became the staple of everyday life. When the monarchy returned in 1660, the restoration of the *Book of Common Prayer* was the central symbol of cultural uniformity and religious settlement, and the text was revised once again. The 1662 edition then remained the standard form of liturgy up to the middle of the twentieth century, and as the British Empire spread around the globe, the *Book of Common Prayer* evolved into one of the most widespread books in history, with versions used in the USA and elsewhere. As well as the standard Sunday services, the orders for baptism, marriage, and burial have entered deep into the English language and provide a key to cultural history over a vast domain.

BRIAN CUMMINGS is Anniversary Professor at the University of York in the Department of English and Related Literature. He was previously Fellow of Trinity College, Cambridge, and Professor of English at the University of Sussex, and has also held Visiting Fellowships at the Huntington Library, California, and the Center for Advanced Studies at Ludwig-Maximilians Universität in Munich. His publications include *The Literary Culture of the Reformation: Grammar and Grace* (2002).

OXFORD WORLD'S CLASSICS

For over 100 years Oxford World's Classics have brought
readers closer to the world's great literature. Now with over 700
titles—from the 4,000-year-old myths of Mesopotamia to the
twentieth century's greatest novels—the series makes available
lesser-known as well as celebrated writing.

The pocket-sized hardbacks of the early years contained
introductions by Virginia Woolf, T. S. Eliot, Graham Greene,
and other literary figures which enriched the experience of reading.
Today the series is recognized for its fine scholarship and
reliability in texts that span world literature, drama and poetry,
religion, philosophy, and politics. Each edition includes perceptive
commentary and essential background information to meet the
changing needs of readers.

—

The Book of Common Prayer

The Texts of
1549, 1559, and 1662

—

Edited with an Introduction and Notes by
BRIAN CUMMINGS

OXFORD
UNIVERSITY PRESS

OXFORD

UNIVERSITY PRESS

Great Clarendon Street, Oxford OX2 6DP
United Kingdom

Oxford University Press is a department of the University of Oxford.
It furthers the University's objective of excellence in research, scholarship,
and education by publishing worldwide. Oxford is a registered trade mark of
Oxford University Press in the UK and in certain other countries

First published 2011

First published as an Oxford World's Classics paperback 2013

Impression: 11

British Library Cataloguing in Publication Data

Data available

ISBN 978-0-19-964520-6

Printed in Great Britain
on acid-free paper by
Clays Ltd., Elcograf S.P.A

PREFACE

SISYPHUS, it may be assumed, knew nothing of Christian liturgy. If I had known what was in store when Judith Luna of Oxford University Press invited me to prepare an edition of the *Book of Common Prayer* for the World's Classics, I might have thought twice. That it has appeared after all is largely down to her encouragement, enthusiasm, and gentle cajoling in seeing it through. In more material terms, I am grateful to the British Academy and the Huntington Library for the award of a Fellowship, which enabled me to spend a summer using the James R. Page Collection of early copies of the *Book of Common Prayer*, the largest collection of its kind in the world. Andreas Höfele gave me the opportunity to develop some of the issues at the stimulating seminars on religious pluralization at the Ludwig-Maximilians-Universität in Munich. A Major Research Fellowship with the Leverhulme Trust enabled me to finish the edition. Like anyone working on the *Book of Common Prayer*, I owe more than I can say (as my notes will bear witness) to the extraordinary scholarship it has inspired, especially of J. H. Blunt, Frank Brightman, Wickham Legg, and Francis Procter and W. H. Frere; and the more recent industry and insight of Geoffrey Cuming and Diarmaid MacCulloch. In more personal ways, Henry Woudhuysen has been a model of editorial meticulousness as well as a patient and sympathetic source throughout of bibliographical advice. Peter Blayney gave generously of his incomparable knowledge of early printing history, and especially of the *Book of Common Prayer*'s first godparents, Edward Whitchurch and Richard Grafton. On historical and doctrinal issues, Euan Cameron, Eamon Duffy, and Alex Walsham offered dazzling learning and intuition in reading versions of the Explanatory Notes; to Eamon I owe a much older debt as well, in that it was his lectures on the 1549 and 1552 editions that first alerted me to the ritual richness and inheritance of the *Book of Common Prayer* when I was an undergraduate. Margaret Aston and James Simpson also read parts of the edition with exacting care. Paul Luna, the designer, has responded to the challenges of the book with marvellous textual flair. I would also like to thank Sylvia Adamson, Sara Beckwith, Bernard Capp, Pat Collinson, Simon Ditchfield, Ian Green, Arnold Hunt, Gabriel Josipovici, Peter Lake, Seth Lerer,

Diarmaid MacCulloch, Peter Marshall, Dick Pfaff, Beth Quitslund, Bill Sheils, Bill Sherman, Abi Shinn, Céline Surprenant, and Ramie Targoff, for imaginative responses to more specific enquiries, for lending books and articles, and other gifts of friendship. Adrian Butterfield talked me through the life of the *Book of Common Prayer* from the point of view of a musician. Freya Sierhuis provided a new perspective in my thinking on this topic as on others. My colleagues Andrew Hadfield, John Lowerson, Femke Molekamp, Naomi Tadmor, Jenny Taylor, and Norman Vance helped with all kinds of request and cheered me up when the glass looked dark. Ardis Butterfield, Daniel Cummings, and Thomas Cummings watched me at work and blessed rather than cursed; my children are always my boldest teachers. Another kind of inspiration, less tangible, has come from seeing the liturgy in action, especially at the hands of Robert Atwell, Brother Anselm SSF, Jonathan Draper, Dana English, Giles Fraser, Donald Gray, and Rowan Williams. For help with hundreds of old copies and as many problems in identifying them, I would like to thank the staff of many libraries: the Bodleian in Oxford; All Souls' College, Oxford; New College, Oxford; the Cambridge University Library; St John's College, Cambridge; Trinity College, Cambridge; Trinity College, Dublin; of Canterbury Cathedral, Durham Cathedral and University, and Lambeth Palace; the Houghton Library at Harvard University and the Pierpont Morgan Library in New York; and especially the Huntington Library in San Marino, California, and the British Library, most hospitable and voluminous of all.

The late Stephen Medcalf has been the presiding spirit over all my efforts, almost as much once he was gone as in his wonderful conversation while alive; his memory breathes through everything here. The book is dedicated to him, *in societate mortuorum*.

London
Feast of St Enurchus, 2010

CONTENTS

INTRODUCTION

THE *Book of Common Prayer* is one of the most extraordinary books in history. From the Reformation to the Beatles, with some interruptions and alterations, it formed the order of service in the established church in England. It has been said, with some justice, that it has reached more listeners, via its daily offices, than the works of Shakespeare.[1] Human life in the English imagination is mediated through its idiom: in loving a partner, we promise to 'love her, comfort her, honour and keep her in sickness and in health'; in saying farewell to the dead, we come to terms with our own mortality, 'Earth to earth, ashes to ashes, dust to dust'. In the breadth of this practical influence, Prayer Book prose has seeped into the collective consciousness more profoundly than that of any other book written in English, even the Bible. Millions of English-speaking people, godly, wicked, or indifferent, have been baptized, married, or buried to its words.

Moving beyond England, the *Book of Common Prayer* is almost as commonplace: it has travelled around the world wherever there have been English colonists, traders, or missionaries. A version in Welsh appeared as early as 1567; independent editions in English (although to great opposition) were prepared in Ireland and in Scotland. In America, while many settlers preferred alternative forms of worship, versions of the book have remained in continuous use since before Independence, right up to our own lifetimes, with 4 July replacing the monarch's birthday in the thanks given unto God. The earliest surviving independent American version dates from New York in 1710, the latest adaptation was made in 1979. The *Book of Common Prayer* has been used from Canada to Brazil, from the West Indies to Nigeria, from Kenya to Bangladesh, from Sri Lanka to New Zealand. Translations have been made into Gaelic, Hindi, Urdu, Tamil, Maasai, and Hausa; into Latin, French, Dutch, and Italian; into Cantonese, Japanese, Spanish, and Arabic; and into Persian, Burmese, Fijian, Vietnamese, and three types of Inuit.[2]

---

[1] Diarmaid MacCulloch, *A History of Christianity* (London: Allen Lane, 2009), 631.

[2] Examples from David N. Griffiths, *The Bibliography of the Book of Common Prayer* (London: British Library, 2002), 469–588 ('Bibliography of Prayer Books in Other Languages').

The *Book of Common Prayer* is also one of the most frequently reprinted works in the worldwide history of the book. From the beginnings of printing to the dawn of the digital age—with two notable interruptions, between 1553 and 1558 under the Catholic Mary I, and from January 1645 (when the Puritan parliament banned it) to the royal restoration of 1660—barely a year has gone by without some new imprint, a book never out of print in nigh on 500 years. In 1587 the 'Orders concerning Printing' of the Stationers' Company exempted the *Book of Common Prayer* (along with statutes and proc- lamations, and catechisms and primers) from the official limit of print runs to 1,250 to 1,500 copies.[3] There were over 500 editions of the *Book of Common Prayer* between 1549 and the 1730s; an estimated average print run of 2,500 to 3,000 suggests well over a million copies in circulation in this period.[4] With new technology these numbers increased dramatically. At its height, for example in the decade from 1836 to 1846, the three official printers were producing nearly half a million copies between them per year. By any standard the book is a global publishing phenomenon. It was the first printed book in Ireland in 1551, and in several other countries later in the history of the British empire: a liturgy based on the *Book of Common Prayer* appeared as one of the first books in Mohawk in 1715, transplanting prayers at the oncoming of nighttime from Kentish smokefall to the forest wilderness by Lake Ontario.

Yet this very familiarity, while it makes the importance of the book easy to convey, also works to conceal its true significance. Sometimes the ubiquity of the *Book of Common Prayer* can make it seem bland, beckoning to a treasured Englishness as stereotyped as rain or hedgerows, dry-stone walls or terraced housing, *Brief Encounter* or *Wallace and Gromit*. The book has become part of the detritus of cultural memory, like the copies piled up in church pews or laid aside (whether battered with use or pristinely and reverently unread) on living-room bookshelves or bedside tables. Paradoxically, it is the fans of the Prayer Book who have been most at fault in this regard, in claiming for its prose a kind of stately majesty which hides its urgency and nervous energy; or in admiring in it a universality that preserves

[3] *Transcript of the Registers of the Company of Stationers of London 1554–1640*, ed. E. Arber, 5 vols. (London, 1875–94), ii. 43.

[4] Ian Green, *Print and Protestantism in Early Modern England* (Oxford: Oxford University Press, 2000), 182–3.

the past in amber, rather than allowing the vibrant and often controversial history of its composition and dissemination to appear in all its variety. The aim of this edition, then, is not only to make widely available to a general reader, and with all the aids of commentary and glossary a general reader deserves, a true classic among the world's classics. It is also to bring alive a new conception of that book, in ways which (it is hoped) will only add to a sense of its complexity, mystery, and wonder.

There are two primary misconceptions that this edition wishes to wrestle with. One is the thought that this is a narrowly religious book. Its writers obviously wished that they could make the peoples of the world more devout, but as well as being a book of 'prayer' this is a book of 'common prayer'. Until recently, churchgoing was a matter of everyday experience; even now, statisticians point out, more people go to church on Sundays than go to football stadiums on Saturdays. The *Book of Common Prayer* is a set of words to accompany everyday life, a way of coming to terms with pain, pleasure, and sorrow as well as a means to worship a creator. If our first mental impression of this book is of a minister in dark robes kneeling on a footstool, Samuel Pepys's lazy London Sunday on 13 November 1664 may be closer to a general Prayer Book norm:

This morning to church, where mighty sport to hear our Clerke sing out of tune, though his master sits by him that begins and keeps the tune aloud for the parish. Dined at home very well. And spent all the afternoon with my wife within doors—and getting a speech out of *Hamlett*, "To bee or not to bee', without book. In the evening, to sing psalms; and in came Mr Hill to see me, and then he and I and the boy finely to sing; and so anon broke up after much pleasure. He gone, I to supper and so to prayers and to bed.[5]

Pepys refers here to both Morning and Evening Prayer, the services which most sum up both the originality and the ordinariness of the *Book of Common Prayer*. These services were based on the medieval hours said every day in monasteries, but translated into a vernacular, post-Reformation context they became the staple of unexceptional life, a verbal (and musical) rhythm repeated once a week, a background to the thought processes by which a person addresses the trials of work or family. The previous year, for months in 1663 his visits to church are tormented by the fancy that his wife is leering during

[5] *The Diary of Samuel Pepys*, ed. Robert Latham and William Matthews, 11 vols. (London: Bell & Hyman, 1970–83), v. 320–1.

the service at Mr Pembleton, the dancing-master. Churchgoing is full of mental distractions. Pepys's prayers inhabit the same world as his other daily distresses and diversions.

As well as the regular services of Evensong or Communion, the *Book of Common Prayer* contains a series of 'occasional services', the rites of christening, wedding, and funeral. More than a book of devotion, then, this is a book to live, love, and die to. This is no other-worldly or unworldly book of the spirit removed from the body, but a book of the daily experience of the body, and of ordinary routine temporarily endowed with a quality of the eternal. Nor is it a book only of prayer, narrowly conceived. It is a book of ritual, of practices and performances used to transform the activities of a life. Rituals, anthropologists now tell us, are what make the human animal different. Mankind is a 'ceremonial animal', Wittgenstein said.[6] Ritual is the social act basic to humanity, the means by which we draw our lives together into a mutual practice. The rituals of the *Book of Common Prayer*, while special to the Christian tradition of one particular church, help us to understand the wider processes by which human beings communicate with each other and incorporate their lives in structures beyond the individual self or a single lifetime. But they also give a precise historical window onto the complex initiations and rites of passage which have filtered the experience of a broad cross-section of the world's populations through several centuries. Why do people bless themselves, or kiss each other in a gesture of peace, or give each other rings, or lay hands on their children's heads, or throw soil or herbs or flowers onto the coffin of a friend? These questions, and ones like them, punctuate this edition as a record of human memory and meaning which shows the depth of ritual influence on everyday life. The purpose of this edition is to present a religious book to the common reader. In the process, religion is revealed as a much bigger, less private, and less sanctimonious phenomenon than many modern secular readers assume.

The other misconception which this edition works to transform is the sense that this is a single book. The version of the *Book of Common Prayer* from which Pepys sang psalms in 1664 may well be one from the year commonly quoted, as if the book stood still for all time in one condition: 1662. In fact, the *Book of Common Prayer*

---

[6] *Philosophical Occasions, 1912–1951*, ed. James Klagge and Alfred Nordmann (Indianapolis: Hacket, 1993), 129.

has one of the most complicated textual histories of any printed book anywhere in the world. While distinct editions and impressions are hard to enumerate exactly, there were more than 350 different imprints before the date often referred to as the 'first' edition of 1662. This has far more than textual significance. For over a hundred years after its first appearance in 1549 under the artful eye of Archbishop Thomas Cranmer (1489–1556), the *Book of Common Prayer* was transformed several times over. While it was proclaimed by parliament to constitute an 'Act of Uniformity', its real effect was anything but. It came into being as a physical embodiment of a revolution in religious practice and in the politics of religion which we know as the Reformation, although even that term is a ragged shorthand for the domino of personal, communal, and national transformations which it provoked. The Reformation came to mean a rupture in the fabric of life as deep as any in European history, affecting anything from breakfast to sex. It divided families and even individuals against themselves, in the fight of conscience and conversion; it made people kill and die for their religion; yet it also created the conditions for extraordinary kinds of piety, literary creativity, and philosophical originality. The first *Book of Common Prayer* is thus a quintessential Reformation book: an engine of change, imposed on congregations and causing riots through its perverse assumption of doctrinal oddity and destruction of the old ways of experiencing the divine; yet also at the same time a vehicle for new forms of religious devotion and a brilliant literary achievement in its own right.

The second coming, as it were, of the *Book of Common Prayer* is a very different story. In 1660 a king returned to British shores from exile in France and the Netherlands, eleven years after his father, Charles I, had been executed outside his own royal palace in Whitehall. The restoration of the *Book of Common Prayer* was almost as important a symbolic act as the restoration of monarchy itself. The twenty years of Civil War and Commonwealth represent the last tragic scene of the English Reformation. Parliamentarians went to war over motives which included the establishment of the church in terms of royal supremacy and bishops; the elaborate ceremonies of worship and rituals of kneeling and crossing which were considered by many to be a remnant of Catholicism; and the use of the *Book of Common Prayer* itself, which was abolished in 1645. The *Book of Common Prayer*, which a hundred years before had been the object of the overthrow of old Catholicism, was now the iconic instrument of the traditional wing of the Church of England, known—after Archbishop William Laud (1573–1645)—as Laudians. This movement stood for ceremonial intricacy and sacramental seriousness, for priests called priests and dressed in vestments, for silver chalices and carved wooden kneelers. It was this that the Puritans wished to tear down in an iconoclasm as fierce as that which destroyed the statues and stained glass in the medieval stone jewel-box of the Lady Chapel of Ely Cathedral. In a grim but brilliant pun, the Puritans took up the cry, 'We know the devil must have little laud';[7] Laud was imprisoned on a charge of treason and executed in 1645, the year his precious *Book of Common Prayer* was thrown out of Eden into infamy.

The book now went into exile along with its owners. A Paris bookplate of 1651 marks the ownership of a 1637 quarto (small-size) edition as belonging to Mary Evelyn, the wife of John, that other great seventeenth-century diarist. Further engraved plates mark off the main sections of the book, indicating its practical employment as the family book of worship banished from its own churches but even now in hiding in Catholic France. Bound in at the end are three manuscript pages of 'Evening Prayer for this Family'.[8] Another Parisian survival is just as remarkable. It is one of the very few copies in existence of a quarto edition dated from the first year of the reign of Elizabeth I, 1559. It was rebound in Paris around 1650 for John Evelyn's father-in-law, Sir Richard Browne, the French ambassador for the king-in-waiting, and bears his coat of arms.[9] The copy indicates a royalist habit of collecting antiquarian prayer books as precious relics during the Interregnum. Two other copies were made for Browne with similar bindings and used in his Paris chapel as a way of preserving the English rite in exile.[10]

When theologians and divines assembled to revise the *Book of Common Prayer* for new use under Charles II after 1660, they did so with contradictory energies. Their number included presbyterians like Richard Baxter (1615–91), who had fought to replace the

---

[7] *Mercuries message, or, The coppy of a letter sent to William Laud, late Archbishop of Canterbury, now prisoner in the Tower* (London: [s.n.], 1641), A3ᵛ.

[8] *Book of Common Prayer* (London: Robert Barker, 1639), BL Eve.a.131.

[9] *The Booke of Common Praier* (London: Richard Jugge and John Cawood, 1559), Pierpont Morgan Library, New York, Bindings Collection Call No. 005421.

[10] *The Booke of Common Prayer* (London: Robert Barker, 1632), Lambeth Palace Library, class mark: H5145.A4 1632; marginal marks emphasize the prayers for the royal family.

episcopacy with a new system of church government, and the *Book of Common Prayer* with new forms of longer, improvisatory, and enthusiastic prayer. But they also included newly installed bishops who had once been thrown out of their parishes and lost their incomes, and even more importantly, lost their very means of staying in touch with salvation through the medium of a book which they held sacred. Bringing back the book was thus not just an ecclesiastical restoration but an act of cultural renewal or even a cleansing of the turbulent past. All of the eight bishops commissioned by Convocation on 21 November 1661 to meet daily in Ely House by Holborn in London, at 5 o'clock in the afternoon, to complete the work of revision, had been born in the reign of Elizabeth, and all but one was old enough to remember her as queen. The 1662 edition is a book of self-conscious nostalgia, like Browne's reverently rebound copy of 1559. Indeed, the first instinct of many of the revisers, especially John Cosin, bishop of Durham (1594–1672), was to restore the 1549 edition intact, and free it from the puritanized revisions which had taken place since that time. They failed in this aim: the book they gave us is more conservative in accommodating the desire to appease the presbyterians, and thus contains a fascinating mixture of what may loosely be called the 'Catholic' and 'Protestant' strains in the emerging Anglicanism that was to enjoy its high age in the eighteenth and nineteenth centuries. Yet the 1662 edition is still a consciously backward-looking book, using the by-now antique appearance of 'black-letter' or gothic script, and preserving the ornamental initial letters of the sixteenth-century editions. While it modernized some aspects of grammar and vocabulary, more often, with a linguistic historical consciousness that is remarkable, it preserved and even revelled in the archaic feel of an English language now a hundred years old. While the Gospels and Epistles were altered to the newer English of the King James Version of 1611, the Psalter was left in Miles Coverdale's version of 1540, because better loved in that state. This attachment to the familiarity of old wording is one of the prime ways in which the book has come to embody a site of deep social memory.

The great stages of the *Book of Common Prayer* are thus marked by paradox and even contradiction. Its first incarnation in 1549 was revolutionary, a brand-new book for an age which was self-consciously overturning the past. Yet in making this book Cranmer also preserved the vestiges of a thousand years of tradition, since much of it was translated from the Latin liturgy. Indeed, the text even preserves elements of the vernacular used in responses in the Latin rite. The words with which I began, from the service for Matrimony, are taken from a medieval York manual, where the husband promises to 'love her and kepe her in syknes and in helthe'; whereas the resonant English phrase, 'Earth to earth, ashes to ashes, dust to dust', translates directly the Latin 'terram terrae: cinerem cineri: pulverum pulveri'.[11] 'Erthe unto erthe' is a phrase in a very commonly copied medieval lyric, and is a stock citation. Rather than a newly coined book, the 1549 text can be seen as a kind of sacred parody or even travesty (in the strict sense) of old ritual. The new incarnation of 1662, by contrast, was a deliberate enactment of cultural recuperation, a mending of the torn leaves of the past through textual conservation and meticulously woven emendation. Yet, in its turn, it was to have the longest life of any *Book of Common Prayer*. Once revised in this form, it was left alone, and even an attempted revision in 1928 never officially replaced it. Indeed, in an old City church like St Bartholomew the Great in Smithfield, you can go along any Sunday now and hear psalms, the *Magnificat*, and *Nunc dimittis* sung to its everlasting words at Evensong.

This edition of the *Book of Common Prayer* attempts to reflect between its covers these strange twists of religion and ritual, incorporating both conflict and a journey of the imagination. It does not present the book as a single unchanging artefact, but instead as something volatile and dynamic, a moving object in time. It presents three distinct texts: the first of 1549; the great new edition of 1662; and in between, as if to mediate, the Elizabethan version of 1559, which incorporated (with some modifications) Cranmer's revised text of 1552, and which, with some further changes in 1604, lasted up to 1660 as the basic form of the text. The 1559 text is preferred to 1552, since the latter was withdrawn almost as soon as it was issued. Each version presented here is related to the others, but nonetheless holds its own place in a quite different political, intellectual, and social context. In this sense, the *Book of Common Prayer* is a wonderful example of a book which contains a whole history within it. It is, in addition, an exemplary instance of the history of the book as an object, an object which survives and is revised and reinterpreted over time. Holding this book in our hands is a way of coming to terms

---

[11] *Manuale ad usum percelebris ecclesie Sarisburiensis*, ed. A. Jefferies Collins, Henry Bradshaw Society, vol. 91 (1960), 158–9 ('Inhumatio defuncti').

with the past. However, it is important to realize this not only in the sense of a precious heritage, but also of a history which encompasses division and controversy as part of our collective memory. British history, and its interaction with the globe, is not one of seamless flow, but one of swift changes of sympathy and vertiginous paradoxes of perspective. The *Book of Common Prayer* is a vivid demonstration of that passionate and visceral sense of historical process.

The making of the Book of Common Prayer: medieval liturgy and the Reformation

A narrative history of the *Book of Common Prayer* from 1549 to 1662 is in some ways identical with a history of the British Reformations, and at the same time a history of British politics in its most violent and unpredictable period, from the Tudor succession crises through the regicide of 1649 and beyond. However, this is not a conventional historical narrative involving context and analysis. The *Book of Common Prayer* is also a major protagonist in these conflicts: it is like a character in a novel, rather than a theme in a history; it changes personality over time and affects the people around it.

The *Book of Common Prayer* was both a symptom of the Reformation and a major catalyst for further change. However familiar it has become, the very idea of it was in its time startling and even provocative. When the first edition was ordered to be placed in every parish church by Whitsunday, 9 June 1549, a majority of the people told to use it probably thought any prayer book written in English was incapable of enacting the prayers within it. The book was the heir (although, it needs to be emphasized, the bastard heir) to several hundred years of Latin liturgical tradition in England based on the Roman rite. The sources of the 1549 edition are very often directly taken from the Catholic tradition that was being supplanted; but comparing the English text with the Latin can be misleading, since it needs to be recalled that every omission and alteration from these sources, including the use of the vernacular at all, was noticed by its original users, and felt as a disturbance of the old ritual. This was a yearly cycle of procession, feast, and penitence, visual as well as verbal, bodily as well as doctrinal, theatrical as well as pious. It was centred in the spectacle of the Mass, the making anew of the redemption of Christ on the cross, offered once again on the altar in the form of his body and blood in the corporeal form of bread and wine. This was the vital action of the late medieval church, for laity as well as clergy, an action as much communitarian and social as it was devotional.[12] It took its place alongside a larger body of offices designed both for the life-span of the individual and for the seasons of the year. Perhaps the most striking of these is the medieval Office for the Dead, an elaborate sequence of actions which includes burial but which is also an act of incorporation in which the living conceived themselves as in community with the dead. The living actively prayed for the dead, said Masses for them, and asked for their intercession in turn in their own lives. Memorial offices and Masses for members of the family took their part in a year-long sequence interplaying with the cult of the saints: the continuing presence of the aid and intervention of the people of the past in the daily experience of the field or the workshop, of harvest or town guild.

Medieval life was highly liturgical. In terms of a literature, this liturgy was collected in a number of books for the use of clergy: primarily the missal, breviary, manual, pontifical, and processional. The missal contained the Ordinary and Canon of the Mass (the invariable framework of the rite); also the *Temporale*, portions proper to Sundays, other days, and special days; and the *Sanctorale*, portions proper to saints' days. The breviary was a compilation of the daily offices needed for an entire year; it was necessarily a fat and baggy book, and often divided in two. This included the various forms of the medieval 'hours'—originally the eight sequences of prayers and readings which divided day and night in the medieval monastery into a continuous form of devotion, from lauds to compline. The manual was a collection of rites in continuous pastoral use, such as baptism, marriage, visitation of the sick, and burial. The pontifical was a liturgical book for bishops, and contained services for which his presence was required—including confirmation, ordination, and the dedication of churches. Processionals were collections of chants used at processions throughout the liturgical year, and especially at major feasts and in the season of Rogation just before Ascension.

There is no such thing as 'the' medieval liturgy, however, or even 'the' liturgy used in England. There was a variety of practices, for which surviving manuscripts provide an often beautiful but

[12] Eamon Duffy, *The Stripping of the Altars: Traditional Religion in England 1400–1580* (New Haven and London: Yale University Press, 1992), 91–130.

intricately complex form of evidence. One important aspect of this is regional—or perhaps more properly diocesan—variation. In addition to the variation between the practice in the different religious orders (Benedictine, Cistercian, Carthusian, and so on, as well as the orders of friars), different cathedrals—for instance, York, Exeter, Hereford, Lincoln, London, Wells—developed distinctive liturgical traditions which in turn influenced parishes within their purview.[13] These are now known as the various liturgical 'uses'. While practice in the north of England took its lead from York (although Durham was jealous of its own independence), in the province of Canterbury—which contained fourteen cathedral churches—by the fourteenth century the dominant use in south-east England was that of Salisbury—known by its Latin name, Sarum. Somewhat disingenuously, the Act of Uniformity in 1549 begins by lamenting the 'diverse formes of commen prayer commonlie called the service of the Churche'.[14] Tudor politics disliked 'diversity'. Yet the Act was not quite telling the truth. Sarum by the early sixteenth century was very widely distributed, if not in any way standard as we might understand now. Parliament fully understood the significance of introducing a new order, but this was a matter of breaking the hold of the old, not of clearing up local inconsistencies.

When Henry VIII broke with Rome in 1534 in the Act of Supremacy, the effect on liturgical life was hardly foreseeable. Once his divorce was seen through, Henry himself remarried according to the old rite, and continued to use the liturgy of his childhood without a second thought. The inventory of his own books made at his death includes three Mass books, three ordinals, one pontifical, twenty-four processionals, and sixteen graduals (which contained collections of musical settings for the Proper of the Mass).[15] As for any late medieval Catholic, Henry enjoyed personal touches in his devotional books. One of his Latin Psalters has an illumination of his own fool, William Sommers, alongside the verse, 'The fool doth know in his heart there is no God'. Later in life he did also collect vernacular religious books: his copy survives of a 1542 English Psalter, printed by Edward Whitchurch, with his own handwritten comments. At Psalm

[13] Richard W. Pfaff, *The Liturgy in Medieval England: A History* (Cambridge: Cambridge University Press, 2009), chs. 12–14.

[14] 2 & 3 Edw. VI c.1, *Statutes of the Realm*, iv.37.

[15] James P. Carley, *The Books of King Henry VIII and his Wives* (London: British Library, 2004), 23–4.

55, next to 'hyde not thy selfe from my depe desyre', Henry makes an approving doodle in red.[16]

Henry's book-owning reflected his personal wealth and educated tastes, but it was very common in the late middle ages to own a Primer or Book of Hours which contained large elements of the liturgy with a Psalter and personal prayers.[17] In this material, the vernacular worked hand in hand with Latin material, although the liturgy itself was always in Latin. When Henry's Archbishop Cranmer began to consider the implications of an independent religious polity for everyday religious practice, it was this kind of material that provided both a model and a warning. Cranmer was a former Cambridge don (where he probably first read Martin Luther), a determined but temperamentally unzealous Reformer. His career began as a negotiator in the royal divorce, and the rest of his life was intertwined with royalty's deep desires. On one of these missions in Nuremberg in 1532, in a sudden moment of Lutheran conviction at odds with his priestly vow of celibacy, he married the niece of Andreas Osiander, the leading Lutheran theologian of that city.[18] Returning home, he found be had come so much into the king's favour that he had been made archbishop. He kept quiet about the wedding, left his wife Margarete in Germany, and set about the king's business with discreet efficiency. Increasingly, Cranmer came under continental influences in his theology, especially German and Swiss, entering into a twenty-year correspondence with Martin Bucer, the Strassburg Reformer, who also influenced Jean Calvin in Geneva.

It was in Nuremberg in Lent 1532, in company with Sir Thomas Elyot, the ambassador to the emperor Charles V, that Cranmer first experienced the Lutheran liturgy at first hand; in a letter Elyot described it (as foreigners tend to when attending church) as 'a long process'.[19] Luther had produced a prototype form of liturgy, the *Formula Missae et Communionis*, in 1523. It was in Latin but already attacked the central aspects of the Mass, and offered Communion in both kinds. It was followed by a plethora of vernacular forms of

---

[16] *The Psalter of David in English* ([London: Edward Whitchurch, 1542?]), BL C.25.b.4 (2), Ps.55.

[17] Eamon Duffy, *Marking the Hours: English People and Their Prayers 1240–1570* (New Haven and London: Yale University Press, 2006), 111.

[18] Diarmaid MacCulloch, *Thomas Cranmer: A Life* (New Haven and London: Yale University Press, 1996), 72.

[19] G. J. Cuming, *A History of Anglican Liturgy* (London: Macmillan, 1969), 40.

liturgy, beginning with the *Deutsche Messe* of 1526. Luther himself made metrical translations of the *Sanctus* and *Agnus Dei*. Luther's daily office consisted now of two Sunday services, Matins and Vespers; there were also weekday services for schools comprising psalms and passages from the Bible in Latin and German. Luther also brought out two versions of the Catechism, for instruction in Christian values and basic texts such as the Ten Commandments, in 1529. Zwingli in Zurich, and Bucer in Strassburg, also produced new liturgies, and Calvin was trying some of these forms in French in Geneva by 1540. By this time there were over a hundred different types of *Kirchenordnung* extant in Germany, one for every princedom and sometimes different ones for each city. In Cologne in 1542–3 Hermann von Wied, the prince-archbishop, attempted to regularize the Reformed versions into a single unified practice. Bucer was invited to help, and Luther's colleague Philipp Melanchthon provided doctrinal advice. The effort failed, and Hermann was deposed. The English effects of Hermann's aborted reforms were considerable, however: they appeared in an English translation, *A Simple and Religious Consultation* (1547), and Cranmer used the Latin text in preparing the *Book of Common Prayer*.[20]

Meanwhile, liturgical reform was in the air in Catholic Europe, too. Cardinal Francesco de Quiñones produced a revised breviary in 1535 commissioned by Pope Clement VII. Although this version was severely criticized at the Sorbonne in Paris, a second version acquired considerable popularity, and the Roman liturgy was in due course completely overhauled in 1570 after the Council of Trent.[21] Simplification and regularization of practice were favoured everywhere, along with new attitudes to musical performance and visual spectacle.

In England, a revised and edited version of the Sarum breviary was produced in 1541. Following the principles of the Henrician Reformation, it omitted any mention of the pope or of St Thomas Becket, the archbishop-martyr of Canterbury. New Reformed material enjoyed only a crabbed progress, however. An English Psalter of 1530 used Bucer as its basis. In 1534, William Marshall produced a Reformed Primer, with Protestantized expositions of the Creed, Lord's Prayer, *Ave Maria*, and Ten Commandments, while excluding the Litany and the Office of the Dead, problematic because of their inclusion of invocations of the saints and prayers for the departed. Meanwhile, in 1537, Edward Lee, Archbishop of York, ordered that the liturgical Epistles and Gospels should be read in English, and editions of the Sarum Primer appeared which included them in the Matthew's Bible version (ironically enough, using the New Testament text of William Tyndale, who was strangled and burned as a heretic in 1536).[22] The English Reformation was showing more determined efforts to transform daily life in parish churches. The 1538 Injunctions (which also forbade the use of candles before images) directed that the Bible be placed in every church and that the Creed, Lord's Prayer, and Ten Commandments should be recited in English in turn. No one was to be admitted to Communion who could not recite them. Some saints' names were omitted from the Litany.

More systematic attempts were now in hand to create a Reformed, and vernacular, liturgy. Cranmer commissioned two manuscript drafts (British Library Royal MS 7B.IV). They manifest all the vitiating and topsy-turvy momentum of religious change in these tumultuous years. Before the fall of Thomas Cromwell in 1540, the evangelical wing of the new church was in the ascendant; after that, Henry VIII drew back from supporting doctrinal novelty. Thus Cranmer's first draft liturgy, made in 1538–9, was radical and confident; the second, in the mid-1540s, was more conservative and hesitant.[23] The first, made around the time of serious negotiations with the Lutheran states, which culminated in the unhappy marriage to Anne of Cleves, is a revision of the breviary with a Lutheran air: there are three psalms at each service; three lessons work through the Bible throughout the year, chapter by chapter, starting with Genesis, Isaiah, and Matthew at Matins, and Genesis and Romans at Evensong. All of this is to be read from the pulpit, not the chancel. Collects are appointed for whole seasons (as in the German Brandenburg–Nuremberg order), not for single weeks. Only the Lord's Prayer and lessons are in English in the manuscript, the rest in Latin, although it is quite possible that Cranmer intended to take the plunge with the rest. Around 1545 he returned to make a new draft liturgy, copied out in his secretary Ralph

[22] Cuming, *History of Anglican Liturgy*, 49–50.
[23] MacCulloch, *Cranmer*, 221–6 and 332–4.

Morice's hand. Reflecting the way that Henry VIII's Reformation had now moved somewhat into reverse gear, the second draft is less adventurous: instead of reducing the medieval hours to the two services of Morning and Evening Prayer, as in 1538–9 and the eventual text of 1549, this version is more closely based on Quiñones's revised Roman breviary and has versions of all the hours.

As for a public Reformed liturgy, the only development which saw the light of day before the death of Henry VIII was a *Litany* published in 1544. Under the cover of the king's proposed war with France, Cranmer gambled correctly that his master would look favourably on an English service to be used in processions throughout the province of Canterbury, with plentiful prayers for the royal person and dire warnings against dissent or rebellion. This was the kind of liturgy kings liked best, but although a modest beginning, this was the start of the *Book of Common Prayer* proper, since it was reprinted with only minor alterations in 1549. In 1545, the 'King's Primer' was produced, attempting to impose uniformity; it includes English versions of the *Te Deum* and of the Canticles, which had been tried out in various versions since George Joye's *Hortulus animae* (1530), and which form the basis for the texts of those hymns used in 1549.

Yet despite the still limited presence of such liturgical texts in Primers designed for the populace, still less in parish life, there was little sign of receptivity for such innovations among ordinary people. In 1543 in Kent, Cranmer's agents, investigating whether the king's orders to use the vernacular were being observed, found people refusing to say the Lord's Prayer in English because they were uncertain whether it would work.[24] This should not be dismissed as superstition: all ritual (whether tossing a coin or signing a contract or promising to stay faithful to someone) involves saying the right words in the right order and in the right place and circumstances. The Reformation, among other things, involved an intense anxiety about how to do things with words. Do our words have the power to change the world we live in, or what happens inside us, or what will go on in the future? Religious prayer affected the state of the soul in this life and the next; but it also impinged on whether the crops would survive the winter, whether the plague would come next year, if it was

[24] The 'Prebendaries' Plot' affair; documents in *Letters and Papers, Foreign and Domestic, of the Reign of Henry VIII*, ed. J. S. Brewer, J. Gairdner, and R. H. Brodie (London: HMSO, 1862–1932), xviii/2, no. 546 [1543].

safe to hold a meeting of town elders next week or go on a journey tomorrow.

When Henry died in January 1547 it was not clear how far Reform would succeed, but the infancy of the new king Edward VI gave resolution to a generation of radical evangelicals who had been frustrated by the last decade of a Reformation more political than doctrinal. On Ash Wednesday, in a sermon at court, Nicholas Ridley (*c.* 1500–55) repudiated the images of the saints and the sacramental value of the water in the font as empty idols.[25] On his ascent to become bishop of Rochester in 1547, he directed that the stone altars in the churches of his diocese should be removed and wooden tables put in their place to celebrate the Lord's Supper. Such actions were not ornamental: an altar that was not stone was not an altar. The Injunctions of 1547 abolished processions, naming as especially offensive the procession that initiated the Mass on Sundays and major feasts.[26] Instead, priest and choir were to sing, kneeling, the new English litany in the central aisle of the church; a revised litany now removed the saints. Liturgy in the vernacular was a leading arm of the second Reformation of Edward's reign. At Easter, Compline was said in English in the Chapel Royal, presumably from the King's Primer. During May 1548 Matins, Mass, and Evensong were being said in English at St Paul's in London; the Mass for the anniversary of Henry's death was sung in English in Westminster Abbey in January 1549.[27]

At the heart of the 1547 Injunctions is a kind of revulsion towards a certain view of ritual, what we might call the religion of material things: 'casting holy water upon his bed, upon images, and other dead things; or bearing about him holy bread, or St John's Gospel, or making crosses of wood upon Palm Sunday in time of reading of the passion, or keeping of private holy days, as bakers, brewers, smiths or shoemakers, and such others do; or ringing of holy bells, or blessing with the holy candle.'[28] The new religion conceived of itself as a religion of the word, of scriptural texts and morally edifying preaching. Of course there is no absolute distinction between the two, and the

---

[25] Duffy, *Stripping of the Altars*, 449.

[26] Royal Injunctions of Edward VI, 1547; *Visitation Articles and Injunctions of the Period of the Reformation* [henceforth *VAI*], ed. W. H. Frere, 3 vols., Alcuin Club, 14–16 (London: Longmans, 1910), ii. 124.

[27] C. Wriothesley, *A Chronicle of England*, ed. W. D. Hamilton, 2 vols., Camden Society, NS nos. 11 and 20 (1875 and 1877), ii. 2.

[28] *VAI*, ii. 126.

Latin liturgy was by definition verbal and was supported by frequent sermons. But the new intellectual divisions often exaggerated such distinctions in increasingly violent ways.

By late 1547 the circumstantial accidents of European politics added to this new Protestant opportunity. Refugees from the religious wars were welcomed with open arms by Cranmer: they included the Italian Pietro Vermigli Martire, the Polish Jan Łaski, and the German Bucer. Vermigli was offered the chair in divinity at Oxford and Bucer the same in Cambridge. Almost as significantly, Charles V's persecution of Protestants in the Low Countries, which intensified in 1546, led to Antwerp printers fleeing to England.[29] This was the trigger for a flood of new and more professionally produced books in a still culturally backward England. The English *Book of Common Prayer* is as much a feature of this literary revivalism as it is of liturgical reform. The prelude was *The Order of the Communion*, which was brought into being on Easter Day, 1 April 1548. It was not a fully fledged vernacular Mass: this was still regarded as too risky a step. It contains only those parts of the service which it was felt demanded popular understanding of the meaning of words: for instance, the exhortations, and the administration of the elements of bread and wine. It must have been a strange experience: the priest conducted everything in Latin until communicating himself, and then broke into English. But it does contain the general confession, more or less in the form which has come down through the centuries: 'We do earnestly repent, and be heartily sorry for these our misdoings; the remembrance of them is grievous unto us; the burthen of them is intolerable.'

The content of Cranmer's Book of Common Prayer

The House of Commons began debating the bill for the introduction of the *Book of Common Prayer* on 19 December 1548. The prelude was something even more extraordinary, even unique, for an English parliament: a debate on the theology of the Eucharist, and the meaning of the Latin words *Hoc est corpus meum*, 'This is my body'.[30] Over the centuries these four words of Christ in the gospels had attracted a more fearsomely complex commentary than perhaps any words in history. Even university philosophers struggled with the more intricate strands in this. Jesus on his last night in Palestine seemed to mean

---

[29] MacCulloch, *Reformation*, 256–7.   [30] MacCulloch, *Cranmer*, 404.

two things at once: that in offering to break bread with his apostles he also left his body with them. The Mass in Christian liturgy was more than a celebration or memory of this: it was a re-enactment, in which Christ's body and blood miraculously reappeared and were sacrificed again and again every week. That this could be so was a matter of intense belief for many; for philosophers it was also a way of explaining some of the most fundamental problems in the universe. In the thirteenth century Thomas Aquinas, a Dominican professor of theology in Paris, used concepts from Aristotle to make fine distinctions both in the nature of things and in the nature of language. He distinguished between the 'substance' of a thing—what makes it what it is—and its 'accidents'—what it happens to be like in the world as we know it. In the Mass the substance of the bread changes and it becomes the body of Christ. But the accidents remain the same—it is still physically bread. Aquinas used the term *transubstantiatio* for this process, a word already made part of official church doctrine at the Fourth Lateran Council in 1215.[31] After Aquinas, philosophers moved into different explanations of reality and of how words relate to reality, but the doctrine did not change; meanwhile, at a less rarefied level of society the popular theory of what happened to bread and wine in the Mass was rather different. The common denominator was that Christ was bodily present in the Mass; but this 'real presence' could mean anything from a highly abstract argument to a magical belief in a change in the properties of everyday objects and their power to make further changes in the world around them: holy bread was carried on the person or scattered on the ground in order to protect the person or invigorate the crops.

Aquinas himself poured scorn on such notions, but in the heat of the Reformation high theology mixed explosively with popular belief and polemic often paid little attention to niceties. In any event, controversy over the Mass touched the deepest nerves in society. Luther took a traditional view on the real presence itself, but he denied that the Mass was a sacrifice, and he insisted that it should be administered to the laity in both kinds, both bread and wine. Huldrych Zwingli, the Swiss Reformer, took a more radical line on meaning and sacrament. It made no sense to interpret Christ's words literally, he must have meant something figurative by saying the bread was his body; and a sacrament in any case is not a physical action on a thing,

[31] MacCulloch, *Reformation*, 25–6.

but a form of covenant between God and man, a promise fulfilled by faith. These were profound arguments about meaning and literary interpretation as well as about ritual and performance. They were not easy to resolve; but a cruder form of the polemic belittled all ritual actions as forms of 'hocus pocus'. Indeed, a seventeenth-century English clergyman believed the words 'hocus pocus' to be a juggling corruption of the phrase *hoc est corpus*.

Cranmer himself increasingly followed the Swiss line in Eucharistic theology. In the debate in parliament he argued that the phrase *Hic calix* ('this cup') must be taken figuratively. A metaphor is just a metaphor. It was equally clear that several bishops could not accept the new formulations, including Edmund Bonner, bishop of London, but politics was favouring Cranmer. This controversy now carried over into the key decisions in formulating the new English liturgy. The broad outlines of a proposed liturgy were clear: the draft plan to simplify the breviary into two services, one for morning and one for evening, was accepted. The Litany was already in place from 1544. This version had by now excised most of the portions dependent on the cult of the saints. A similar exercise in censorship of the saints was carried out with the Calendar, which set out the liturgical year in the initial section of the book; and it also affected the programme of feast days in the central body of the Collects, Epistles, and Gospels which were provided for all the services through the year. There were now twenty-five major festivals in the year: alongside the central feasts of Christmas and Easter, there is a scriptural logic to the choice—the days celebrating apostles, evangelists, other major New Testament figures, along with Holy Innocents, All Saints', St Michael, and just two (the Purification and the Annunciation) of the many medieval feasts devoted to the Virgin Mary. This was nonetheless a drastic cutting-back on the liturgical year, with no room for some of the greatest feasts of the Virgin, such as the Assumption, still less for highly popular cults of medieval saints such as St Anne or even St George, who was nonetheless adopted for a more secular form of national identity.[32] The Calendar also left out a host of other celebrations of Catholic doctrine such as Corpus Christi and Holy Cross ('Holyrood'), although many of these latter days were mentioned in the Calendar as worthy of marking in lesser ways. Yet just in having a Calendar at all Cranmer was breaking with the trend in the

[32] Pfaff, *Liturgy in Medieval England*, 438–9.

continental Reformation. He also paid enormous attention to the writing of Collects for the regular Sundays in the year and for feast days. This is the writing for which he has won most lasting fame. Although many are direct translations from the Sarum Latin Collects, Cranmer's English versions have become buried deep in social memory.

Of the remainder of the book, much was taken from the medieval manual, those services now known in the Anglican church as 'occasional'. The service for Matrimony followed the Latin closely, as did largely Confirmation (taken from the pontifical). Catechism was also a simple matter for a Reformed mindset, as Protestant values placed a strong emphasis on doctrinal teaching, verbal repetition of the moral lessons of the Ten Commandments, and so forth. Visitation of the Sick was retained in a simplified form. Baptism proved more troubling. It was clearly scriptural, and was retained by all the Reformers as one of the two remaining of the seven Catholic sacraments. However, the Roman rite contained a number of physical actions and gestures of precisely the type that evangelicals considered superstitious. The 1549 *Book of Common Prayer* placed a central emphasis on the verbal promises of faith, but also involved physical actions such as the signing of the forehead and exorcism, and incorporated the sacred intervention of material things such as the chrisom (white cloth), the oil of unction, and the blessing of the water in the font.

However, by far the most visible and controversial transformations took place in the treatment of the Mass and the Office for the Dead.[33] The treatment of the dead was highly sensitive to Protestants, because of the association with the cult of the saints, and also because of the doctrine of purgatory, which was taken to be unscriptural. Purgatory had come under vociferous attack in the literary campaigns of the 1530s and 1540s. The new service cut out any implied reference to it, even though in places it created the impression that the dead person must already be in heaven. Prayers for the dead person are also cut, although at the moment of committal itself the priest addresses the corpse. This is a moment of continuing balance in the service, which also allowed for some processional use of psalms and even a form of Requiem Mass, although it took the heart out of this by excluding intercession for the dead.

Such details suggest more than one agenda was in play in the

[33] Duffy, *Stripping of the Altars*, 474–5.

formation of the 1549 *Book of Common Prayer*, both in the way that it had to pass Convocation, which (despite the exclusion of Stephen Gardiner, the bishop of Winchester and opponent of further Reform, in the Tower of London) included traditionalist bishops as well as the new-fangled zeal of Ridley and Hugh Latimer; and perhaps also in Cranmer's desire to allow for gradual revolution. Cranmer's role is sometimes hard to fathom, and he has easily been caricatured as vacillating or temporizing. It is more accurate to see him as doctrinally adventurous and tenacious in his will to enact change, but only at a pace which would allow for successful completion of long-term aims. He was also wisely cautious in relation to politics. There is a wonderful story in John Foxe's *Actes and Monuments*—the English Protestant martyrology—where Cranmer has his secretary Ralph Morice write some notes on doctrine and then tells him not to allow the notes to leave his person. Morice then gets into a terrible comic disaster as he crosses the Thames by water-ferry and is attacked by a bear running loose from the animal shows on the South Bank. The papers are soaked and then fall into the hands of an agent opposed to the new heresies. Cranmer escapes investigation by the skin of his teeth.[34]

Cranmer's doctrinal subtlety and literary skill combine in his masterly service for Communion. Yet to call it masterly may seem perverse, since it perhaps satisfied nobody fully: for traditional Catholics it was a mockery, refusing the elevation of the host and suppressing the bodily presence of Christ in the elements of the Mass. For the Reforming party, on the other hand, it retained more of the ritual spectacle than was comfortable. The Eucharistic prayer at least follows the form of the Canon of the Mass, and at one point, in the Visitation of the Sick, Cranmer even used the word 'Canon' himself. Is this carelessness? The alternative point of view is that it is a sign of Cranmer's sensitivity to opinions different from his own, a distinctly rare quality in the Reformation. Doctrinally, Cranmer's public position in debates at this period, and his alliances with European theologians, show that he did not believe the Mass to be a form of sacrifice. Christ made his sacrifice once and for all; what humans do in Communion is quite distinct, however sacred a devotion it is. Also, different people receive the Communion differently. At the debate in the House of Lords in December 1548, Cranmer is reported as saying that the bread is only

[34] Foxe, *Actes and Monuments*, 2 vols. (London: John Daye, 1570), ii. 1355–6.

the body of Christ for those 'that are members of his body'.[35] Those
that are not regenerate in Christ do not consume the body of Christ.
This denied the full Catholic doctrine of real presence, since it made
the place of transformation not the sacrament itself but the heart of
the believer.

Yet it may be that Cranmer's scrupulous care with words allowed
room in 1549 for more than one literal interpretation. In the Sarum
Canon there are six sections; Cranmer reduced these to three. At the
centre, he left the words:

O God heavenly father, which of thy tender mercie, diddest geve thine only
sonne Jesu Christ to suffre death upon the crosse for our redempcion, who
made there (by his one oblacion once offered) a full, perfect, and sufficient
sacrifyce, oblacion, and satysfaccyon, for the sinnes of the whole world,
and did institute, and in his holy Gospell commaund us, to celebrate a perpetuall memory of that his precious death, untyll his comming again.

The Latin Mass at this point leads on to compare the offering on the
cross with the offering of the elements of the Mass as a sacrifice made
by the Eucharistic rite. Cranmer leaves instead a piece of punctuation, a silent colon. He then continues:

Heare us (o merciful father) we besech thee: and with thy holy spirite and
worde, vouchsafe to bl✠esse and sanc✠tifie these thy gyftes, and creatures of bread and wyne, that they maie be unto us the bodye and bloude of
thy moste derely beloved sonne Jesus Christe. (p. 30)

In the silence between the words Cranmer left enough space for his
radical evangelical critics to feel that he was endorsing the sacrifice of
the Mass. The residue of the typographical indicators of a holy action
(✠) seem to confirm this by making the priest perform manual acts
of blessing. Yet a literal reading would have to say that the sacrifice is
not there. A true traditionalist was left unsatisfied, if he could follow
carefully enough the full nuance of the change. Reactions among con-
temporaries were confused. Bishop Thomas Thirlby recalled that he
thought that it had been agreed that the sacrifice of the Mass had been
confirmed, but then was taken away; the Spanish Protestant Enzinas
said that on this point 'the book spoke very obscurely'. Cranmer's
obscurity is powerfully moving, as the effort of literary care is traced
word by word over these transcendent meanings.

---

[35] MacCulloch, *Cranmer*, 405.

The official inauguration at Whitsun in St Paul's Cathedral was planned to put an end to arguments. Nonetheless, the new-fangled English *Book of Common Prayer*, and above all the Communion service, was dismissed by some as a 'Christmas game' or a 'Christmas play', a party trick no more able to save souls than a jester with a cap and bells. There were protests at the new book in Devon on the first day it was used. These derogatory descriptions appear in the articles formulated by the rebels, who took political control of Devon and Cornwall for a while, and besieged the city of Exeter. The government reacted with ferocity to this insurrection: 4,000 died in the south-west. Closer to London response was more measured, but further rebellion spread in July through the north and East Anglia. Bucer, newly arrived in Cambridge to begin his professorial duties, had to escape to Ely the very next day. Although not all the rioting was caused by the changes in religion, this was a Prayer Book rebellion in the sense that the promulgation of the book seems to have ignited a whole set of grievances like a tinderbox. Rebels demanded the proper use of holy bread and water, the restoration of processions and of the Lent ceremonies of ashes and palms, and prayers for the souls in purgatory by name, 'as oure forefathers dyd'.[36] The third article of the commoners of Devon and Cornwall was to 'have the Mass in Latin as was before'; the fourth, 'to have the sacrament hang over the high altar and there to be worshipped as it was wont to be'.[37]

Certainly, the idea of a new national religious consensus was a complete fiction. Indeed, the first person that the Privy Council found themselves having to deal with for contravening the king's new uniform religious orders of service was the king's own sister. The Lord Protector's agents passed information on Mary's devotions in her house to the Council on 16 June, reporting that she was 'refusing to have there celebrat the Servyce of the Communyon'.[38] The bishop of London, Edmund Bonner, failed to introduce the new service book until he was reminded in August, and did so then 'sadly and discreetly'.[39] Even when they used the book, priests often disguised it with the old forms of ritual, a 'Communion of our Lady'. Throughout

---

[36] Anthony Fletcher, *Tudor Rebellions* (1973), 135–6.
[37] *Troubles Connected with the Prayer Book of 1549*, ed. N. Pocock, Camden Society, NS no.37 (1884), 153–4.
[38] *Acts of Privy Council*, II (1547–1550), 291 [16 June 1549].
[39] *Chronicle of the Gray Friars of London*, ed. J. G. Nichols, Camden Society, OS no. 53 (1852), 62.

1550 the Council intervened in a series of cases involving nobles and gentry who were covertly saying or singing Masses in their private houses. Politics threatened to submerge the new order, but the reaction was more revolution. John Hooper, a virulent opponent of traditional religion, led a campaign against elements in the new service as too compromising. He called the *Book of Common Prayer* 'manifestly impious', dismissed the use of vestments by clergy in it as Judaizing, and refused to swear using the oath by the saints provided in the new *Ordinal*, the book of services for ordaining ministers introduced in 1550 to accompany the Prayer Book.[40] This was the prelude to a wider review of the *Book of Common Prayer*. Cranmer welcomed the opportunity to clarify his liturgical aims. Bucer produced a lengthy commentary on the 1549 edition, and the exiled Italian Reformer Peter Martyr also provided his views on a Latin translation, as his English was not good enough to read the original. Bucer's analysis represents the most incisive theological contribution to the *Book of Common Prayer* ever made, full of learning and insight. Yet it reflects also a personal leaning; it has been said that he 'was possessed with an unreasoning horror of the benediction of material objects'.[41] This was the green light for the radical faction, and spelt the end for many of the ritual elements left over from the medieval liturgy. Visitation articles in London forbade the priest from kissing the Lord's Table; blessing his eyes with the paten (the Communion plate); shifting the Prayer Book from one place to another; laying down and licking the chalice; ringing the sacring bell (a small bell rung at the elevation of the host); or putting any light in front of the sacrament.[42]

The result was the 1552 version, much more radically Protestant, eliminating the need to bless the water at the font or to bow to the host at Communion or to pray for the dead in any circumstances, all of them fundamental aspects of belief in most parts of the community a few years before. It was this second *Book of Common Prayer*, even more than the first, which attempted to eradicate Catholic England for good. Something of the controversial passion attached to physical actions can be seen in the 'Black Rubric', an addendum to the

[40] Hooper to Bullinger, 27 December, 1549, *Original Letters Relative to the English Reformation*, ed. H. Robinson, 2 vols. (Cambridge: Parker Society, 1846–7), 79; Hooper to Ridley, 20 October 1550, ibid. 573.

[41] F. Procter and W. H. Frere, *A New History of the Book of Common Prayer* (London: Macmillan, 1901), 573.

[42] Ridley's Injunctions for London Diocese, 1550; *VAI* ii. 241–2.

Communion introduced late to some copies of the revised version, allowing kneeling (which some wished to ban altogether) but attempting to control the emotions worshippers felt while kneeling, forbidding any adoration of the bread and wine (see Appendix A). Some of the changes were structural—in the Communion there were crucial changes in the order of the offertory and consecration, and the Gloria was moved to the end. There were many cuts of material now considered as smacking of old ritual, such as in the radical dismantling of any residual form of the Canon of the Mass which Cranmer had allowed in 1549. There were also large bodies of new material, such as the penitential introduction to both Morning and Evening Prayer. The version of 1552 embodies a new ideal of Christian worship, which combines both an aversion to the sacramental and ritual elements of the old and a positive emphasis on repentance and thanksgiving. It is undeniably more verbal and less visual, and in this way catches a new aesthetic of religious devotion. And yet this edition, while doctrinally of great importance, barely saw the light of day. The strange vicissitudes of Reformation history intervened once more. On 6 July 1553, at the age of 15, Edward VI died of a bacterial pulmonary infection. Although the Protestant elite attempted to prevent it, his sister Mary I came to the throne, and one of her first acts was to repeal the new Prayer Book; the Sarum Mass was re-established in 1554, and altars, roods, and statues were reinstated. The *Book of Common Prayer* went into exile, following its users, to Frankfurt and to Geneva, where local religious licensing required interesting alternative versions with fewer responses and a greater emphasis on the sermon.

But another untimely royal death changed everything again. The new queen, Elizabeth I, reversed religious policy once more, and in 1559 a new Act of Uniformity (effectively the fourth in a decade) provided for a new, moderately revised, *Book of Common Prayer* based on the 1552 version. This was a classic compromise. Some, encouraged by the return of the Latin liturgy, hoped to make England Catholic in practice if not in politics; while the exiles returned from Geneva clamoured for a more Genevan form of liturgy to prevail. The queen probably favoured a conservative form of liturgy along the lines of 1549, but her advisers, including William Cecil, urged 1552 as the least difficult political choice, with some alterations to placate enemies. References to 'the detestable enormities' of the pope were removed from the Litany; the words of administration of the elements at Communion were restored to the 1549 version, thus bringing back a reference to the real presence which had been rigorously excised in 1552.[43] The 'Black Rubric', with its tortuous reference to kneeling, was removed. The increasingly visible anxiety over the remaining ceremonies and ornaments in church services, and especially over vestments used by the clergy, was supposedly put to rest by a clause prescribing the orders made 'in the second year of the reign of Edward VI'. By fudging the issue, this clause was merely the framework for tensions which vexed the English church for the next 400 years.

The Elizabethan Book of Common Prayer:
ritual and performance

In one sense, the Elizabethan *Book of Common Prayer* can be said to represent the idea of 'religious settlement' that is generally attributed to that queen's reign. While there was some alteration in 1604, especially to the Baptism service, the 1559 text held sway until the tumult of the Civil Wars of the 1640s. Unlike its more famous siblings, 1549 and 1552, which were revolutionary books consigned to history almost as soon as they were created, 1559 moulded hearts over several generations. To understand this new book, we have to look beyond the text. The words are only the beginning, the outline; to understand the book in its fullness, we have to see it as a form of life. The *Book of Common Prayer* is a performative book, more like a play-text than like a novel in the way that we must approach it as readers. This edition pays respect to this by marking the rubrics which bring it into social reality, a little like the stage-directions in a Shakespeare play: with the difference that here the rubrics are authorized by the original writer. These rubrics, which were argued over in controversy for centuries, frequently take us to the heart of religious devotion. Religion is not only a matter of the right words, but the right words said in the right way using the right objects in the right order.

The title-page of the *Book of Common Prayer* presents itself as authorizing the 'Administration of the Sacraments, and other Rites and Ceremonies of the Church, According to the Use of the Church of England', yet as well as being voluminously exact about

---

[43] Edward Cardwell, *A History of Conferences Connected with the Revision of the Book of Common Prayer 1558–1690* (Oxford: Oxford University Press, 1861), 52–4.

these matters, it is often deliberately circumspect or even maintains an oracular silence. Much of the history of the book has thus been between the lines: either in passionate argument about what the true style of performance should be; or in the quieter truth-telling of ritual itself, in the frequently varied ways the book has been interpreted in individual churches or communities. One aspect of Elizabethan performance that is often only obliquely referred to in the text is the presence of music. This was partly due to the direct patronage (and taste) of the queen herself. In January 1575 she granted a twenty-one-year monopoly for printing polyphonic music 'either in churche or chamber' to Thomas Tallis and his younger colleague William Byrd.[44] Tallis had by now seen it all: he was around 70 years old, had first written music in Benedictine and Augustinian monasteries, and had served as Gentleman of the Chapel Royal for four successive monarchs of different religious persuasions. Byrd was an even more peculiar case for a royal Protestant commission, since it was about this time that he began to show clear associations with English Catholics. The first work using the monopoly was in fact a set of thirty-four Latin motets called the *Cantiones sacrae*. This includes a setting of part of the medieval Office for the Dead. Yet the work is dedicated to the queen, and while Byrd was by 1584 a 'recusant' who refused the sacraments in the English rite, he also took on commissions for the Chapel Royal which include settings for the new services of Morning and Evening Prayer and English anthems. These are for that very special survival of the English church, the great medieval cathedrals and collegiate churches recast in Reformed robes.

In ordinary parish churches music was of a plainer variety, at first in unison. But new forms of chant devised for the Psalms, based on medieval plainsong, began to be adapted in simple harmonized parts which crossed from one side of the church to the other. A complete version of metrical Psalms by Thomas Sternhold and John Hopkins, mostly in a popular form of 'ballad metre', was first issued by the printer John Day in 1562, and despite its association with Geneva this book was frequently bound with copies of the *Book of Common Prayer* for the next century. Harmonized singing of the Psalms has been part of the English church for 400 years, giving rise to this eulogy in the words of another hybrid Christian of the Elizabethan church, John

[44] Peter Le Huray, *Music and the Reformation in England* (Cambridge: Cambridge University Press, 1978), 193–4.

Donne, who converted in the opposite direction from Byrd, from Catholic to Protestant: 'And, O the power of Church-musick! that harmony added to this Hymn has raised the Affections of my heart, and quickned my graces of zeal and gratitude; *and I observe*, that I always return from paying this publick duty of *Prayer* and *Praise* to God, with an inexpressible tranquillity of mind, and a *willingness* to leave this world.'[45] In the eighteenth century these traditions gave way to a trend for a more modern form of church music, the familiar church hymn, which transposed itself into harmony with the liturgy without any need for textual revision; organ music, beginning with the offertory at Communion in Elizabethan times, also flourished in increasingly wider parts of the divine service.

The 'Ceremonies of the Church', that innocuous-seeming phrase, were the new dividing-line in religion, perhaps more so than doctrine or belief. Uniquely among Protestant churches, England retained bishops to rule church order and ordain ministers. For the most part in Elizabeth's reign these bishops accepted Calvinist theology, including predestination, even while their Calvinist cousins in Scotland or the Netherlands felt horror at the very idea of episcopacy under a royal sanction of supremacy. Many Calvinists in England agreed, and wished to move to a presbyterian form of church government. From the 1580s Archbishop John Whitgift imposed severe sanctions against those who refused to accept the Act of Uniformity, whether Catholic or Puritan, including a total endorsement of the *Book of Common Prayer*, and the state adopted brutal measures to enforce this message.[46] Outright opposition to the bishops became tantamount to sedition against the monarch, so increasingly what now seem arcane questions of church furniture and dress and custom became pointed scenes of dissent.

The appearance of the interior of an English church was now transformed from what a parishioner would have seen in 1530. A Royal Order of 1561 replaced the rood-screens (just restored by Mary I), generally with a royal coat of arms. The walls were usually whitewashed, and the Ten Commandments were placed on a wooden board, ousting the commonplace images of saints. Although Elizabethan

---

[45] Izaak Walton, *The Lives of John Donne, Sir Henry Wotton, Richard Hooker, George Herbert, and Robert Sanderson*, World's Classics (Oxford: Oxford University Press, 1927), 62.

[46] Patrick Collinson, *The Elizabethan Puritan Movement* (London: Jonathan Cape, 1967), 244–6.

injunctions allowed stone altars, many were ripped out; now there was a wooden table instead, in the body of the chancel, wrapped 'with a carpet, silk, or other decent covering'.[47] Inside the *Book of Common Prayer*, a short essay by Cranmer of 1549, 'Of Ceremonies', had been devised to limit further disagreement. This writing is full of balanced clauses, sitting on the fence as if on communion rails. It justified the origins of church ceremonies as 'of godly intent', while pusillanimously bewailing the later descent into 'undiscreet devotion' and zeal (p. 214). Some, which 'have much blinded the people', are 'to be cut away, and clean rejected'; others are to be kept, 'because they pertain to edification'. Yet which was which? Bishop Grindal, in his visitation in the diocese of London in 1565, noted a plethora of different practices: 'Some say the service and prayers in the chancel; others in the body of the church. Some say the same in a seat made in the church; some in the pulpit with their faces to the people. Some keep precisely the order of the book; others intermeddle Psalms in metre. Some say with a surplice; others without a surplice.'[48] The church was left to agonize, and the bitterness fed into the divisions which led eventually to Civil War and threatened the existence of the *Book of Common Prayer*, even as its authority was appealed to in discriminating between them.

In its everyday life the church was full of local compromise or lone stands by individual ministers, both equally to the distress of bishops' visitations. While the *Book of Common Prayer* provided for copes at Communion, in 1566 it was accepted this might only happen in cathedrals, and in parish churches a surplice would suffice.[49] Yet in practice, the *Book of Common Prayer* at times seemed to please almost no one. Many Elizabethans were still Catholic at heart, and conformed only reluctantly to a church now bereft of spiritual comfort and external signs. Puritans, on the other hand, mocked even the use of the surplice; rejected the wafer in favour of ordinary bread; objected to the sign of the cross in baptism, kneeling for Communion, the ring in marriage, the veil in 'churching' (the purification of women after childbirth), and bowing at the name of Jesus. While Catholics lamented the loss of their religion in the *Book of Common Prayer*, Puritans thought they might as well be 'papists' by using it at all. In 1604, after Elizabeth's long life ended, they hoped to persuade the new king from Scotland, James I, who had been brought

[47] *VAI*, iii. 108–10.   [48] BL, Lansdowne MS 8, fo. 16.   [49] *VAI*, iii. 171–80.

up a presbyterian (despite having a Catholic martyr for a mother), to take their side at a new conference on church order at Hampton Court. Yet James became the first English monarch for a century not to alter his country's religion, and apart from changes involving baptism by women, and baptism and confirmation for infants, the *Book of Common Prayer*, too, stayed the same.

Once again, change came not through the text of the divine services so much as in the externals that accompanied them. A new religious culture was emerging, associated at first with an older generation of clerics around Lancelot Andrewes (1555–1626), who had bided his time under the Calvinist bishops under Elizabeth I, and now rose to favour under James, who admired his ornate and learned style of preaching. In fact, Andrewes, who became bishop of Chichester and later Winchester, disliked the Puritan emphasis on sermons, and dedicated significance instead to reverence in worship, at the centre of which he placed the Communion.[50] Inner devotion became associated with outward reverence: chapels and cathedrals were enriched with more elaborate furniture. Some of this ornament owed its motivation to social snobbery: the early seventeenth century sees a growth in numbers of enclosed pews for the well-to-do, with locks on them and even roofs, which made them look like elaborate bedsteads. Satirists (and clerics) wondered at what their occupants did inside them. Yet attention to furnishings was also the sign of an affective pietism. Much of this surrounded the Communion. Church plate, especially chalices and patens, survives in abundance from Elizabeth's reign, but in the 1630s there is a revival of the medieval chalice, with its wide rim and base, in place of the Elizabethan conical shape; Laud's cup of 1635 is still in Lambeth Palace.[51] John Overall, one of Andrewes's associates and now dean of St Paul's in London, returned to the question of the sacrifice of the Mass, rejected a generation before. In his own practice he began to interpolate parts of the 1549 rite in place of its successors, in using the prayer of oblation at the consecration, as in Cranmer's Canon. Andrewes, too, referred to the sacrament as a 'sacrifice', and made his congregation bring their offerings to the altar rail after the Creed. The people remained in the chancel until the end of the Gloria after Communion.[52] Vestments were restored

---

[50] Peter Lake, *Anglicans and Puritans?* (London: Unwin Hyman, 1988), 227–8.

[51] J. C. Cox and A. Harvey, *English Church Furniture* (London: Methuen, 1907), 37.

[52] Cuming, *History of Anglican Liturgy*, 141.

in their formality and ritual distinction. Ministers now dressed in a fashion unlike anywhere in Reformed Europe.

This form of piety became associated above all, especially by his enemies, with the name of Laud, bishop of London from 1628 and archbishop of Canterbury from 1633. Laud was accused of tampering with the wording of the *Book of Common Prayer*, substituting the requirement to kneel 'at the name of Jesus' rather than 'in'.[53] Yet his innovation, too, was more in things than words: he ordered the altar to be placed against the east wall of the chancel rather than in the middle, and to be surrounded with rails, so that the congregation came to kneel before the altar both for the consecration and to receive the Communion.[54] These rails came sometimes to be ornately carved, and the floor of the chancel paved in finer churches with marble in black-and-white squares. Matthew Wren (1585–1667), a former chaplain of Andrewes, rebuilt the chapel at Peterhouse, Cambridge, combining the Baroque with a form of early Gothic revival, including stained-glass windows.[55] The sacramental furniture conceals a lacuna, for the fact was throughout this period that most people took Communion only rarely, and Morning and Evening Prayer were the standard forms of worship. In addition, in the seventeenth century as before, a variation in the weekly use of liturgy between small and large churches, and between parish and cathedral, always needs to be borne in mind, whether in the acceptable form of ceremonies, or music, or dress. Nevertheless, for Laud and his followers ceremonies are not an ornament or a mere external expression of the life of the church, but 'a vital means of expressing the beauty of holiness, which placed them at the centre of the spiritual life of the Christian'.[56]

It has been argued that there was more in common between the Laudians and the Puritans than they wished to acknowledge.[57] While the cliché says that the Laudians were the upholders of the sacraments, as opposed to Puritans favouring long and punishing sermons, both sides encouraged frequent attendance at Holy Communion.

---

[53] *Conferences*, 236.

[54] Kenneth Fincham and Nicholas Tyacke, *Altars Restored: The Changing Face of English Religious Worship, 1547–c.1700* (Oxford: Oxford University Press, 2007), 211–13.

[55] Ibid. 230.

[56] Anthony Milton, *Catholic and Reformed: The Roman and Protestant Churches in English Protestant Thought* (Cambridge: Cambridge University Press, 1995), 496.

[57] Arnold Hunt, 'The Lord's Supper in Early Modern England', *Past and Present*, 161 (1998), 39–83.

In truth, despite the brave new words about regular attendance and receiving in both kinds, most people still took Communion only once a year. Church attendance meant Morning and Evening Prayer, even though the bishops responded as early as Elizabeth's reign by proposing a long composite divine service with Matins, Litany, and Communion continuing without a break. Both wings of the church also attempted to impose moral discipline by limiting Communion to those of sincere godliness. But Laudianism also had a theological and political edge. Andrewes, as dean of the Chapel Royal, had instructed the new king Charles I in an anti-Calvinist theology opposed to pre-destination, and Charles combined this with emotional attachment to vestments and ornament. The Arminians (so dubbed after the distinguished Dutch anti-Calvinist divine, Jacobus Arminius) were known as a political faction as much as a doctrinal camp: 'What do the Arminians hold?' it was asked; 'All the best deaneries and bishoprics.' This was a piquant feature of anti-Laudian polemic.[58] By the time the political divisions of the 1630s widened into the Civil War which broke out in 1642, the *Book of Common Prayer* had become the badge of the royalist party, and church ceremonies were its cultural clothing as much as cavalier hats and lace.

The Root and Branch Petition of 1640—signed by 15,000 Londoners and presented to parliament a year later by Oliver Cromwell and Henry Vane—called for the elimination of episcopacy, 'root and branches', and singled out the *Book of Common Prayer* for opprobrium: the 'Liturgy for the most part is framed out of the Romish Breviary, Rituals and Mass-Book'.[59] But the response suggests that it was more ideology than demography that made out the *Book of Common Prayer* to be so partisan. The book had by now settled into the national consciousness. There were counter-petitions in favour of the liturgy in 1641, and contrary to the view that the *Book of Common Prayer* was imposed from above and was the creature of the aristocracy and gentry, support was said to come from 'hedgers at the hedge, plowmen at the plow, threshers in the barns'.[60] The abolition

---

[58] William Prynne, *Canterburies doome, or, The first part of a compleat history of the commitment, charge, tryall, condemnation, execution of William Laud* (London: John Macock, 1646), 529.

[59] S. R. Gardiner, *Constitutional Documents of the Puritan Revolution* (Oxford: Clarendon Press, 1906), 141.

[60] Judith Maltby, *Prayer Book and People in Elizabethan and Early Stuart England* (Cambridge: Cambridge University Press, 1998), 225.

of the *Book of Common Prayer* in 1645 was equally as political an act as its imposition had been in 1549. John Evelyn's plangent account of the suffering of 'Prayer Book Protestants' under the Puritan commonwealth is a testimony not only to the continued controversy the book provoked but also to the love it by now inspired, as a devotional object of familiar use, now considered ancient, precious, and venerable:

25 December 1657. I went with my Wife to London to celebrate *Christmas day* ... Sermon Ended, as he [the minister] was giving us the holy Sacrament, the Chapell was surrounded with Souldiers: All the Communicants and Assembly surprised & kept Prisoners by them, some in the house, others carried away ... These wretched miscreants, held their muskets against us as we came up to receive the Sacred Elements, as if they would have shot us at the Altar.[61]

For fifteen years in the seventeenth century, as under Mary for five years in the sixteenth century, but for opposite reasons of theological politics, the *Book of Common Prayer* disappeared from view. An alternative book, *A Directory for the Public Worship of God*, was published in its place, much more in line with continental Protestantism. Some clandestine use of the *Book of Common Prayer* continued, although usually in abridged form, while clergymen such as Jeremy Taylor experimented with some of the newly discovered ancient liturgies to create new English forms.[62] For others the book's exile provided a spur to reflect for the first time in a serious way on its history and provenance. Hamon L'Estrange, who collected old copies as a bibliophile, created a parallel-text edition, with the 1604 text in one column and the variants from the 1549, 1552, and 1559 editions, along with the 1637 Scottish liturgy, in a second column.[63] Matthew Wren, imprisoned in the Tower of London, spent his eighteen years of enforced leisure embarking on emendations to the 1604 version.

The Book of Common Prayer *and the Restoration of 1660*

Perhaps it seemed that the *Book of Common Prayer* was receding into the past. Presbyterians certainly hoped so, especially those who

[61] *The Diary of John Evelyn*, ed. E. S. de Beer, 6 vols. (Oxford: Clarendon Press, 1955), iii. 203–4.

[62] F. E. Brightman, *The English Rite*, 2 vols. (London: Rivingtons, 1915), vol. i; p. cxc.

[63] *The alliance of divine offices, exhibiting all the liturgies of the Church of England since the Reformation* (London: Henry Broom, 1659).

welcomed back the king. That it did not was due to the determined efforts of returning bishops from the old generation, like Wren himself, and most of all John Cosin, who now became a second father (after Cranmer) to the English Prayer Book. Cosin's career is an epitome of the vicissitudes of liturgical life over the last sixty years. He was John Overall's librarian and secretary, and later became a literary aide in the Arminian controversies of the 1620s. Moving to a benefice in Durham, he oversaw visitations with a punctilious eye for detail of ritual. It has been exactly said that Cosin's love for uniformity of performance of divine service went hand in hand with his 'love of beautifully carved woodwork'.[64] In this he was a devout Laudian. He was asked by the king to provide some private prayers for the use of the French queen Henrietta Maria and her ladies-in-waiting; in printed form it was a bestseller. In 1628 he was accused by a fellow cleric of popery in disguise: 'our young Apollo, [who] repaireth the Quire and sets it out gayly with strange Babylonish ornaments', he was charged with having erected glittering angels round the choir in Durham Cathedral, burning 220 candles at Candlemas, and having the Creed sung to the accompaniment of 'Organs, Sackbuts, and Cornets'.[65] He was also said to have cast a stern eye on members of the congregation who showed less devotion than they should: were the gentlewomen of Durham such 'lazy sows' that they could not stand up at the right moment in the service?

Cosin attracted more notice as master of Peterhouse, where the decoration of the notorious chapel became more opulent than ever, as he installed two huge new candlesticks, a flying cherub, and a stained-glass window over the altar based on Rubens's *Le coup de lance*. It was hardly surprising that he was brought before the Long Parliament soon after it was called in 1640. He bowed to his opponents and then, when told 'Heere is no Altar, Dr Cosin', showed another side to him, a self-knowing sharpness of wit: 'Why then, I hope there shall be no Sacrifice.'[66] He was ejected from Peterhouse in 1644, escaping to France dressed as a miller. There he became the focus of the exiled royalist forms of devotion, initially in the Louvre and then in Sir Richard Browne's residence, where he used the chapel to perform

---

[64] Cuming, *Godly Order*, 124.

[65] Anthony Milton, 'Cosin, John (1595–1672)', *Oxford Dictionary of National Biography* [henceforth *ODNB*], online edn., Oxford University Press <http://www.oxforddnb.com/view/article/6372>, accessed 17 Aug. 2010.   [66] Ibid.

the divine services in his own inimitable style. In exile his position became, interestingly, more complex. He showed more sympathy to continental Protestantism and more hostility to Catholicism, especially because of the sometimes-aggressive tactics to promote conversion among the exiles, including his own son. He devoted himself to further and deeper scholarship in liturgy, holy orders, sacraments, and ceremonies.

Charles II returned from The Hague to England in May 1660, entering London on his birthday, thus ending eleven years of government without a king and without an established church. After the restoration of the monarchy Cosin was perfectly placed to be at the centre of moves to revive the old *Book of Common Prayer* and bring it up to date. Indeed, Cosin initially had higher ambitions, although not so much in the direction of creating a new book as of an even bolder form of restoration, bringing back much of what had been excised since 1552 of the original book of 1549. At the heart of this ambition lay a sacramental ideal, which had been nurtured all the more strongly by years of exile from the altars of his youth, and by the historical researches of his Paris years in justifying the Anglican rite and holy orders in the face of possible extinction.[67] Appointed bishop of Durham, the diocese he most loved, and charged with a central role in revising the *Book of Common Prayer*, he now put forty years of liturgical devotion, knowledge, and energy into the task. Into a 1619 copy of the Jacobean text he wrote in his own hand a host of suggested emendations, based on his own notes dating back to the 1620s and those of Wren and other interested parties, including the Scottish liturgy of 1637. He was assisted by William Sancroft (1617–93), his domestic chaplain (later archbishop of Canterbury), both as amanuensis and collaborator. Known to history as the 'Durham Book', this trial effort was vigorously Laudian in its aims.

As events turned out, however, it was a political settlement that determined the appearance of the 1662 *Book of Common Prayer*, rather than religion alone. The prime mover was the earl of Clarendon, lord chancellor, and a group of ecclesiastics such as Gilbert Sheldon, bishop of London, who like Clarendon had been part of the Great Tew circle, the royalist intellectual elite before the Civil War. Clarendon was a latitudinarian in religion, his attitude to liturgy

[67] *Godly Order*, 130–1.

rather non-committal; ceremony for him was not of 'that important value . . . to be carried on with that passion'. While no friend of the Puritans, he wished to avoid further conflict over religion. Thus the resulting Savoy Conference of 1661, entrusted with the wording of the new Prayer Book, was composed of twelve commissioners of each persuasion: twelve bishops, matched by the same number of presbyterian divines. The traditionalists among the bishops included Cosin and Robert Sanderson (1587–1663), the new bishop of Lincoln, who had used a modified version of his own of the *Book of Common Prayer* during the Commonwealth. Presbyterians included the vocal leadership of Richard Baxter, and also Edward Reynolds (1599–1676), who had enough sympathies on both sides of the argument to have been made bishop of Norwich. The delegates were all expected to observe moderation, and while they viewed each other with suspicion, Sheldon took the initiative and divided the opponents in a move of calculated equilibrium, proposing as little change to the existing *Book of Common Prayer* as possible. This was as damaging to Cosin's dream of reviving the 1549 Canon of the Mass as it was to Baxter's hope of a new form of more enthusiastic prayer based on the Puritan *Directory*. The presbyterians were asked to draw up their objections (called the *Exceptions*) to the old book; these varied from large matters of principle to tiny issues of wording.[68] They revived the old resistance to four kinds of ceremonial, kneeling during Communion, the surplice, the cross in baptism, and the wedding ring. Godparents had been abolished in 1645 and should stay that way. The text should not assume that all the congregation will attain salvation; and throughout the presbyterians disapproved of the use of responses by the people, believing that prayer should be heartfelt rather than by rote. The Collects as a whole were disliked and should be rewritten. The minister should never be called 'priest'; Sunday should be the 'Lord's Day'; none of the readings should be from the Apocrypha.

This went far beyond the remit of the royal warrant for the conference, and as a whole the *Exceptions* clearly pointed in the direction of the Genevan service book. The bishops conceded just seventeen points out of ninety-six, of which only one was really substantial— and this was the use of the King James Version of the Bible for the readings, something the bishops themselves wanted. From early in its proceedings the Savoy Conference, which lasted from April to

[68] *Conferences*, 303–35.

July, drifted into inertia, like many academic committees and political summits since. Parliament was looking to take a coach and horses halfway between the parties and leave the text in the state of 1604, to remove any memory of Laud. Sancroft in the meantime worked on the 'Durham Book' a second time, improving rubrics and restoring the text in points of detail. He also worked on the Ordinal, the order for ordination, which was not included in the 'Durham Book'. With some persuasion, this work now began to be the basis of a revision, with Sheldon's approval. All of the corrections made by Sancroft were now transferred into a clean 1634 copy of the *Book of Common Prayer*, a matter now simply practical as the manuscript margins of the 'Durham Book' had become a muddy river of annotation and crossings-out. While this new 'Fair Copy' (as it was known) incorporated well over a hundred points of revision large and small, it also went back in a more conservative direction on some points, especially a crucial compromise on the Communion. This was a final conciliatory gesture to the dissenters, with Sheldon's approval; Cosin's opinion is not recorded.

The book presented to parliament has been estimated to involve 4,500 words removed from the old edition and 10,500 added. A copy was annexed to the Act of Uniformity, and then corrected. The carefulness of the operation is shown by the fact that it was these specially prepared copies with handwritten alterations, 'sealed' and then lodged in the House of Lords and the great cathedrals, that represented the 'true' copy of the text. While there were significant changes in key services such as Baptism, Confirmation, and Communion, and more so in the service for the Burial of the Dead, the new version was much closer to the old than might have been supposed by either wing of the political divide in 1660. The Collects were revised in many places, and the General Thanksgiving, by Reynolds, provided a new kind of prayer influenced by Puritan modes of feeling.[69] On the other hand, the Ordinal and the state services for the martyrdom of Charles I and the safe return of Charles II gave voice to Laudian sentiment. The new preface, usually attributed to Sanderson although no doubt approved in committee, sums up the 1662 *Book of Common Prayer*, which, with the Act of Uniformity, received the royal assent on 19 May 1662 and was prescribed for use from St Bartholomew's Day, 24 August: 'Our general aim therefore in this undertaking was, not to

[69] *Godly Order*, 161.

gratify this or that party in any their unreasonable demands; but to do that, which to our best understandings we conceived might most tend to the preservation of Peace and Unity in the Church' (pp. 210–11).

The Book of Common Prayer *past and future*

The 1662 version was concocted in a spirit of compromise and even with a limited notion of religious tolerance (that is, tolerance for those who agreed to conform). The key factor here was that it excluded Roman Catholics: not only as a matter of fact, but even of design, as a pact between all English-speaking Protestants in order to exclude Rome. It thus satisfied in its moment of appearance the desire for a national religious book. Yet even its most enthusiastic proponent would have been surprised to find that it was now to remain in force for more than 300 years. Indeed, almost from the outset there were efforts to revise it. During the reign of Charles II several texts became attached to it, including the Articles of Religion as well as the more ephemeral service to celebrate the salvation of London during the Great Fire (all the texts which appeared before 1685 are included in this edition in Appendix B). Large-scale proposals for revision first began in 1689, after the 'Glorious Revolution' which deposed the Roman Catholic James II. This reform contained many ameliorations in the direction of nonconformists, but it was not adopted. *A Form of Consecrating Churches* was published in 1714; in 1751 revised Tables and Rules were introduced.

After 1833, with the emergence of the Oxford Movement, there were assiduous efforts to bring the *Book of Common Prayer* more in line with Roman Catholic ritual and ceremonial, and widespread use of candles, incense, and vestments grew among those influenced by the *Tracts for the Times* of John Henry Newman and others. The 'Tractarians', led by Newman, John Keble, and Edward Pusey, heralded the integrity of the *Book of Common Prayer* against the low-church adherence to religious services in accordance with scripture alone. In 1874 the Public Worship Regulation Act attempted to regularize ritual practice and at the same time to shore up conformity among Anglicans after Newman's celebrated conversion to Rome. During this period the text of 1549 once again came into prominence, as the focus of desires to make the *Book of Common Prayer* more like the Sarum rite than 1662. Yet even following a Royal Commission in

1906, the version of 1662 suffered no real threat of demise until 1928. In this year a full-scale new version was finally published. It caused protests in the House of Commons, however, where many MPs from a nonconformist background were astonished to find themselves being asked to vote in favour of a revived doctrine of transubstantiation, and defeated the bill on 14 June. The bishops nonetheless approved the book as an alternative to 1662 for use in worship. The services for baptism and marriage found a good deal of local approval, and many vicars felt more comfortable marrying their parishioners without reference to 'men's carnal lusts and appetites, like brute beasts that have no understanding'; some couples rather liked the old wording and took equal pleasure in discomforting their relatives. But the main outcome was a renewed life for the 1662 *Book of Common Prayer*, until movements for a modern liturgy took shape in the 1960s. A series of alternative patterns were then adopted, until in 1980 a text with the rather uninspired title of *Alternative Service Book* appeared. In 2000, to mark the millennium, *Common Worship* finally marked the real end for 1662, although in many churches diehards and enthusiasts are still allowed their regular dosage of sixteenth-century prose at least once a week.

In the course of the great age of the *Book of Common Prayer*, from 1662 to 1966, its original purpose was stretched to and even beyond its limits. From the eighteenth century, the numbers of those who felt themselves excluded by it grew and grew, first on the dissenting side, and then among the increasing numbers of English Roman Catholics in the nineteenth and twentieth centuries. These factors only became more pronounced with the growth of the British empire, in two simultaneous dimensions, expansion abroad matched by retrenchment at home. The one effect was caused by the exportation of the *Book of Common Prayer* to the farthest points in the globe, as the book became the central sign of the Anglican communion in its worldwide mission; the other through immigration, as exiled communities of Catholics and dissenters found themselves shut off from the national church and its national ritual.

Although these movements would have astonished Cranmer as the original author of the book, they began in his lifetime with the authorization of an Irish form of the Prayer Book in 1551. This has a special place in history as the first book printed in Ireland, but it is also an exemplary moment of colonization. Even more than in

England, this was a book of civil imposition, with prayers against the pope in a country which had experienced no Reformation whatsoever. The book contained a special prayer for the governor of Ireland and the Irish people, simultaneously (and somewhat oddly) including the name of a commoner in the divine service: 'We most humblie beseche thee, that thou wilt so lighten the herte of thy servaunt (Sir James Croft) now governour over this realme . . .'[70] In a somewhat similar spirit, Charles I attempted to impose the English *Book of Common Prayer* in Scotland in the 1620s onwards, a country as unused to bishops as Ireland was to Protestants. The 1637 book led to riots, just as the English book had in 1549. Jenny Geddes threw her stool at the minister as he began to read the Collects in the Kirk of St Giles in Edinburgh: '*daur ye say Mass in my lug?*' The book was quietly dropped. In terms of its content, however, it was an influential and important edition, since it represented a substantial revision of 1604, including a seriously reconceived version of the Communion which greatly influenced Cosin.

Wherever empire spread, the *Book of Common Prayer* went with it. In this way it became the most internationally representative book in the language, and a symbol of power and cultural prestige, until, as this power waned, it became supplanted in this respect by that other leather-bound icon, the *Works of Shakespeare*. Yet while this began as an expression of anglophone monopoly, by a curious reverse process the *Book of Common Prayer* also encouraged a benign form of linguistic multiculturalism. In the desire to evangelize new peoples and cultures, missionary ministers became evangelists for global languages, notably assisting the recording, understanding, and printing of hundreds of tongues, including several which have since disappeared. This began as a European diaspora in Tudor and Stuart times: an edition appeared in Welsh in 1567 and in Irish in 1608; in French (for use in Calais) in 1553, and in Dutch (for the stranger churches) in 1645. Indeed, while the Commonwealth government forebade the printing of the *Book of Common Prayer* in England, it appeared in Rotterdam in two editions in the 1650s; and in English it was promoted in the colony of Virginia and the island of Barbados, the last living outposts of the book during the reign of Oliver Cromwell. As empire spread, the linguistic diversity grew decade by decade: the

[70] *The boke of the common praier* (Dublin: Humfrey Powell, 1551), S4ᵛ (inserted on the verso of the colophon).

Book of Common Prayer appeared in Algonquin in North America in 1715; in Tamil in southern India in 1802; elsewhere on the subcontinent in Urdu in 1814 and in Bengali in 1840; further afield in Maori in 1830; Cantonese in 1855; Malay in 1856; in Africa its spread began with a southern dialect of Swahili in 1876. In many cases, as well as encouraging knowledge of world languages the book had a profound educational as well as religious legacy.

These influences in fact outlasted empire. The Episcopal Church separated itself from the Church of England in the United States of America in 1789, a decade after Independence. While an independent Prayer Book was proposed in Philadelphia in 1785 (a radically shortened version), it was not well liked. Instead, the American Prayer Book published in 1790 consciously did not deviate far from 1662: while the Declaration of Independence of 1776 is asserted as an act of divine providence, 'this Church is far from intending to depart from the Church of England in any essential point of doctrine, discipline, or worship . . . further than local circumstances require'.[71] It took on its own life thereafter, with major revisions in 1892 and 1928, including an epiclesis (the blessing of the elements) in the Communion, and prayers for the dead, making it closer to Sarum than even to 1549; yet any user today will see the proximity to Cranmer. Above Golden Gate Bridge in San Francisco there is a sandstone cross commemorating the continuous presence of the *Book of Common Prayer* in America since Sir Francis Drake's chaplain first used it in California in 1579. In similar ways, the independent churches in Canada after 1918, in south India after 1947, and in Australia after 1961 each adopted a form of service book initially based very closely on 1662. Such influence extended beyond the Anglican communion. John Wesley, the founder of Methodism, declared that 'I believe there is no Liturgy in the world, either in ancient or modern language, which breathes more of a solid, scriptural, rational piety than the Common Prayer of the Church of England'.[72]

If the *Book of Common Prayer* tests the ordinary sense of history and language invested in a single book, in another sense it traverses historical sense altogether. For liturgy, even more than any other form of literary history, suspends the ordinary rules of temporality. The

---

[71] *The Book of Common Prayer* (Philadelphia: Halls & Sellers, 1790), A4ᵛ.
[72] *The Sunday Service of the Methodists in North America* (1784), 1.

Book of Common Prayer reaches back as much as it reaches forward. Indeed, it does so even beyond the knowledge of its own creators, never mind its everyday users. Cranmer was ambiguously aware that he was translating the Sarum rite of the medieval church even as he radically reformed it. By the time of Cosin, this knowledge of sources had become much more historically conscious. In the seventeenth century a sense of the antiquity of textual origins informed many of the decisions of the revisers. Yet still they did not fully know what it was they were dealing with. Indeed, in 1661 it was the presbyterians who pressed for a more accurate scholarship to authorize the new text according to the oldest possible models of liturgy. They did this because they suspected that the Roman liturgy could not be proved to go back so far, and certainly not to the early Christian centuries of Christ and his apostles. At a time when scriptural authority was the only proof of age that mattered, they hoped to prove that the text of the *Book of Common Prayer* could only be measured to medieval times.

In fact, in this they were both right and wrong. Wrong, in that many of the sources have turned out to be older than once thought. There is material in the *Book of Common Prayer* that certainly goes back to the sixth century, and links can be shown back to practices that are much older still. Yet right, in that the exact lineage of words cannot be traced back fully or with absolute certainty; we are at the mercy of the manuscript tradition, and manuscripts (even ones on papyrus or vellum rather than fragile modern paper) decay more quickly than words themselves.

Even here, though, the history of the *Book of Common Prayer* has much to tell us. By a curious accident of history, modern knowledge of medieval liturgy in England originates with nineteenth-century scholars of the Anglican rite.[73] These scholars—beginning with William Maskell, and continuing with Henry Bradshaw, W. H. Frere, and J. Wickham Legg, among others—wished to show a line of continuity between the medieval past and the Anglican present which was unbroken—apostolic, as it were. This aspiration was doctrinal as well as scholarly: it would serve to show the Church of England as truly Catholic. Whereas the original Reformers had been accused of destroying the medieval rite, their Victorian successors were arduous and ardent in their arguments that 1549 was as close as possible to the

[73] Pfaff, *The Liturgy in Medieval England*, 8–12.

Sarum use. This was something of an Anglo-Catholic myth. But in the process their historical delving did more than had ever been done before to unearth the original manuscripts of the liturgical traditions. They combined this with an increasingly formidable scholarship of non-Latin liturgies, the rituals of the Greek and Coptic and other early churches. Modern scholars of liturgy have a more nuanced and complex view of these histories. Not only is the line of descent now revealed to be less than apostolic, but the very notion of a unified 'liturgy' has broken down. Yet every modern effort at understanding these matters is influenced by the nineteenth-century pioneers. And the resulting picture is perhaps even richer than anything originally imagined. Liturgy is like a vast cognitive tapestry, in which text reaches within and around to meet other texts; in which one human experience is grafted onto another. The words of Morning Prayer or of Baptism in the seventeenth century, or for that matter in the twenty-first, contain the words of all previous centuries back to the time of the first years of the Roman empire, and in some cases hundreds of years earlier, back to the rituals of Jewish communities at the beginning of recorded meaning.

This edition thus creates an emotional palimpsest of history, in its very form, by presenting the text in three different states. There is no single liturgy, and there is no single *Book of Common Prayer*. The reader is presented with three different moments: the moment of origin, in 1549, a text of great influence but with almost no life of its own; then the text of 1559, with which Shakespeare and Milton were both familiar, although neither perhaps paid any allegiance to it; and finally the master-text of 1662, which saw out Jonathan Swift, Charles Dickens, and T. S. Eliot. No text of the *Book of Common Prayer* is a word set in stone. I do not offer the texts here as definitive, but as moments frozen in time, the state of the text at three points in history, which interact with the text in all its other years.

For, to frame our imagination of this record, we have to reconceive the forms of memory itself. It has often been tempting to create a history of ritual as a kind of genealogy, in which one text borrows from another. But liturgy is not, at root, a text; it is a form of speech. It is, more than any other, a living language suspended in time. Furthermore, as the liturgical historian Gregory Dix has said, rite is not speech alone. It is 'primarily something done', not said.[74]

[74] *The Shape of the Liturgy*, 2nd edn. (Westminster: Dacre Press, 1945), 12.

This is one of the ways that makes it hardest to judge liturgy as a form of writing like others. A good deal in the past has been said about Cranmer as a literary artist. This has sometimes missed the mark. Cranmer in the *Book of Common Prayer*, like other of its greatest creators, like Cosin and Sanderson, was not an author like any other. His best work is often precisely in recomposing rather than in composing. He translates and adapts rather than imagines freely. Yet this shows the poverty of our ways of describing literary skill, rather than any lack on his part. All acts of language, including the most exquisitely literary, participate in a dialogue or even communion with the rest of the language, from its beginnings to the present. Cranmer did not coin the words 'In the midst of life we are in death'; but he knew them from the inside, and he allowed them to live in others after him. Perhaps the greatest writers have admired this most of all in the language of the *Book of Common Prayer*. Some of the praise of the book, of the glories of its language, have been misplaced. It is not a special form of language; it is the ordinary language of its time, the vocabulary of the mid-sixteenth century, overlaid with the rhythm of the mid-seventeenth. Yet it is a language with an unmistakeable power, employed freely by all other users of the English language, whatever their religious affiliation or whether they have one at all. Winnie, in Samuel Beckett's *Happy Days*, contemplates the absurdity and futility of her life in the jetsam of her handbag, all the odds and ends spread out before her. 'For Jesus Christ sake Amen,' she says: 'World without end Amen.'[75]

---

[75] *Happy Days* (1961), in Samuel Beckett, *Complete Dramatic Works* (London: Faber, 1986), 138.

NOTE ON THE TEXTS

THERE is no easy way to edit the *Book of Common Prayer*. Up to 1662 it exists in five substantive versions—1549, 1552, 1559, 1604, and 1662. There is the additional complication of the Scottish version of 1637, which while never commonly used as a liturgy was one of the sources of the 1662 revision; and the 1928 Revised Edition, which while commonly used was never officially authorized. Yet even these substantive editions were reprinted with variations year on year; and with every new reign, and even with the birth, marriage, or death of members of the royal family, small alterations of text were being made all the time.

The principle behind this edition has been to present the text in three different states, the editions of 1549, 1559, and 1662. The reasons for this choice are set out in the Introduction. Yet even such a simple sentence hides a multitude of sins. The *Book of Common Prayer* was a large undertaking in 1549—necessitating a copy for every church in the realm—and was an enormous enterprise for the two printers involved in its production for England. In practice, they hired some of their work out to jobbing printers and compositors to help them. To meet the deadline of Whitsun, printing began in March, but the book was being reissued by May, and the *Short-Title Catalogue* (STC) lists five different states of the text even among surviving 1549 folio copies.

The printing history of the book

The main actors in 1549 were Richard Grafton, the King's Printer, and his business partner Edward Whitchuch. They had already worked on editions of the English Bible, and Grafton also on *The Order of the Communion* (1548). They continued to work in tandem on the 1552 revised version of the *Book of Common Prayer*. In 1553 Grafton lost his warrant as royal printer under Queen Mary I, but when Elizabeth I's reign restored the prospect of a vernacular prayer book, Grafton (and perhaps Whitchurch too) entertained schemes of reviving their business via this handsome monopoly. However, Elizabeth instead soon continued with Mary's official printer, John

Cawood, in collaboration with Richard Jugge. In any event, the printing of the new edition was both complex and hurried, and once again there are three different editions all of which bear the date of 1559.

Cawood died in 1572, and Jugge in 1577; Christopher Barker then succeeded as royal printer, and for the next 132 years the Barker family was involved in printing the *Book of Common Prayer* with a variety of business partners and assigns. Robert Barker (who also printed the first edition of the King James Version of the Bible) took over in 1603. Later Stuart editions bear the names of Bonham Norton and John Bill, to whom Barker sold shares in his monopoly. They survived to share in the new venture of 1662.

In 1549 printing of the *Book of Common Prayer* for Wales and the Marches was entrusted to John Oswen of Worcester; Peter Blayney has recently discovered that he may have produced one in 1552. However, after this date no edition was printed outside London until 1629. At this point the press of Cambridge University was given permission by the Privy Council to print the Prayer Book. However, to protect the privileges of the existing printers, the licence was limited to copies bound with the Bible and the metrical Psalms, and only in smaller formats. Oxford University gained the same rights in 1636, yet only exercised them in 1675. This demonstrates an increasing diversification of formats for Prayer Books, and of private use. Whereas the earliest editions show the need to provide books for church services, smaller formats either for the pew or for devotional use at home became increasingly common from the mid-Elizabethan period onwards. Quartos were produced alongside folios already in 1549; the first octavo edition was in 1553; and the first in sextodecimo in 1570. This latter book uses a tiny fount—the minuscule letters are around 1 mm in size. It may have been designed to be carried as a 'jewel book' (a devotional object) rather than read. However, it contained a full text, including Gospels and Epistles, and a 1575 printing of similar size (which survives in the Huntington Library in California) was certainly used, including to record family marriages and deaths from 1596 to 1628. These editions show the passage of the *Book of Common Prayer* from liturgy to private devotion.

Even after 1662 the *Book of Common Prayer* is far from a uniform entity. The printing was initially undertaken by the royal printers Bill and Barker and, in an octavo, John Field at Cambridge; but in the early eighteenth century John Baskett, who was not only royal printer but also a printer for Oxford University, began to transform the trade. Roman type had been used as an alternative to black-letter since Elizabethan times; Baskett championed its use and made other reforms of orthography and style. Later in the eighteenth century John Baskerville was similarly influential as an innovator in Cambridge Prayer Books. In the nineteenth century the royal printers gave over to the publishing firm Eyre & Spottiswoode, who with the two university presses dominated the industry down to modern times. Printing the *Book of Common Prayer* is still by royal prerogative to this day, and is permitted only by licence.

In the seventeenth century a historical sense of the book began to emerge and serious collecting of early editions began. Since the nineteenth century there have been a number of scholarly editions of the early texts. Notable among these are those of the publisher William Pickering in 1844, who produced six folio-sized facsimile editions of texts from 1549 to 1662; William Keeling's *Liturgiae Britannicae* (1842); J. H. Blunt's *Annotated Book of Common Prayer* (1866); several editions of the two Edwardian Prayer Books, including the Everyman edition by E. C. S. Gibson (1910); F. E. Brightman's *The English Rite*, 2 vols. (1915), which compares the versions of 1549, 1552, and 1662; John Booty's *The Book of Common Prayer, 1559* (1976); and Diarmaid MacCulloch's *The Book of Common Prayer: 1662 Version* (1999). I have made grateful use of all of these and other editions in preparing my own. The fullest account of the printing history is David N. Griffiths, *The Bibliography of the Book of Common Prayer 1549–1999* (2002).

The form of this edition

While the aim of this edition is to represent the book in multiple states, what is offered here is strictly a snapshot of the book in the three years chosen. A full text of all three editions would have necessitated a wheelbarrow to carry it, so a compromise has been made. The edition here of 1662 is comprehensive, and includes everything printed within its covers in that year, including the State Services ('Gunpowder Treason and Plot', etc.) which had formerly only been loosely inserted. In fact, the *Book of Common Prayer* varied considerably in its extent up to this point. The Psalter and the Ordinal were not formally part of the book before 1662, although they were printed in parallel editions and often bound together (along with a bible, and Sternhold and Hopkins's edition of the Metrical Psalms) for the convenience of users. The editions presented here of 1549 and of 1559 therefore exclude the Psalter and Ordinal on principle; but they also exclude, for reasons of space, several elements which were part of the original. The Calendar of the church year (which appeared before Morning Prayer in 1549 and 1559) is represented here only in the form of 1662. This part of the *Book of Common Prayer* varied considerably throughout the period; some account of this history is provided in the Explanatory Notes (see pp. 751–4). The Collects, Epistles, and Gospels also appear only in the version of 1662. These were placed before Communion in the texts of 1549 and 1559. The text of the scriptural lessons in those editions followed the Great Bible of 1540. In 1662 this was changed to the text of the King James Version (1611). This is the version represented here, although the actual lectionary of readings is almost entirely the same as in 1549 and 1559. The Collects of 1549 are also largely repeated in 1662 although they were slightly revised, and a small number added (the changes are recorded in the Explanatory Notes).

An ideal edition of the *Book of Common Prayer* would include all this material in its varieties, and also those of 1552, 1604, and 1928. This edition is not that ideal. However, it does present the divine services complete for 1549 and 1559, along with the Preface in its 1549 form, and Certain Notes, which is unique to 1549. Other elements originally included in the 1549 and 1559 texts, such as Of Ceremonies and the Order How the Psalter is Appointed to be Read (1549), and various Tables (1559) are represented in the 1662 text. In the appendices to this edition several other items have been included. These are, first, the 'Black Rubric' (Appendix A), the only revision of 1552 which was cut from 1559. This enables the reader to gain a sense of the full scope of the revised Edwardian Prayer Book. Secondly, Appendix B includes four texts which were commonly bound in with Prayer Books within the lifetime of Charles II. Two of these were ephemeral, but two (the Articles of Religion and the Table of Kindred and Affinity), while never properly speaking part of the *Book of Common Prayer*, have been so frequently printed with it that many people assume they are.

The texts are printed throughout in the order in which they originally appeared, rather than in a parallel-text edition, such as in

Brightman's *The English Rite*, the most obvious precedent for this edition. Brightman made the 1662 text his standard, and printed the corresponding passages from 1549 and 1552 in parallel columns, along with another column for Sarum and other sources. If my edition in any way lives up to his model I will be well pleased, but I have preferred to allow the original texts to speak entire in their own voice rather than chopping them up to indicate patterns of revision. The Explanatory Notes will, I hope, help to guide the reader in the complex process of revision.

An immediate consequence of presenting the three texts entire in this way was to make complete modernization of the text illogical. Although not every accident of spelling is significant, the English language changed considerably over the century between the editions, and respecting the original forms of the texts makes manifest this process. This is as striking in the case of 1662 as it is of the earlier texts. Modern versions said to be of '1662' in fact present the text as it became fossilized by the mid-nineteenth century. This nineteenth-century text contained enough archaic matter to make the text feel old ('thee', 'wilt', and so on). Yet it is not in fact the 'text' of 1662; indeed, the presence of the birthday of the current sovereign makes this obvious. Moreover, while the 1662 revisers made some changes in favour of clarity for their 'modern' readers, they were linguistically conservative in other respects, including orthography. They wished to make the text correspond to an idea of inherited tradition, and therefore used black-letter (or 'gothic') founts, by now decidedly out of date. Restoring the text to its 1662 orthography reveals this preservation of the consciously archaic all the more remarkably.

Each of the versions here has therefore been freshly edited. Original spelling is very largely retained, though some moderate modernization has been made to aid the reader (explained in detail below), and errors have been corrected. A full Glossary has also been provided which identifies older meanings as well as recording oddities of spelling. Punctuation, too, has largely been respected in its original form. These are oral texts, and punctuation in the sixteenth and seventeenth centuries was more rhetorical than logical in intention. The Psalter is specifically stated to be punctuated in order to aid singing, and to a lesser extent the punctuation elsewhere also aids reading aloud. Although readers will feel some unfamiliarity, the versions here enable the sound of the original to be recovered more naturally, although of course it is not possible to do this any more than imaginatively. The most controversial aspect of this will (to some readers) be the absence of apostrophes. I have agonized long about this question. Apostrophes are quite out of place in the text of 1549, where the '-es' form retains the genitive case of Middle English. In the text of 1662 they could be argued reasonably to be a help to a modern reader. However, the apostrophe was a novelty of the later seventeenth century, and is not found in 1662 except in one case of new text (the curious can seek it out below). Apostrophes began to appear on the title-pages and in the preliminary matter and some-times the rubrics of the *Book of Common Prayer* in around 1715 in Baskett's reformed editions. Yet even here they do not appear within the spoken forms of the divine services themselves. This occurs for the first time (to my knowledge) in 1743 in a Cambridge edition (in a small format). My conclusion is that the apostrophe does not belong in the 1662 *Book of Common Prayer*. For those who believe the apostrophe to be the epitome of grammatical and moral probity this may be a surprise, but the truth is that it was a mark never used by either Shakespeare or Milton (although they did use elisions, which the 1662 *Book of Common Prayer* also almost entirely eschews, again showing its textual conservatism). I trust my readers will forgive me on this small point, and I remind them also that this is an oral text and that the apostrophe, however noble, is completely inaudible.

The texts used in this edition

Orthography and punctuation, however, varies from imprint to imprint as well as from edition to edition. The 'Elizabethan Prayer Book' changes greatly in orthography and punctuation from 1559 to 1603; the text of 1662, even more so, as it was gradually transposed over the centuries. My aim, more modestly, is to represent in each case a single issue from each year. A full collation was beyond the scope of this edition. While I have consulted hundreds of copies in the preparation of this text, the base texts are the individual copies indicated here.

1549

THE | booke of the common | prayer and admi- | nistracion of | the | Sacramentes, and other | rites and ceremonies of | the Churche: after the |

ꝩꞩe of the Churche | of England. | LONDINI IN OFFICINA | *Edouardi Whitchurche.* | *Cum priuilegio ad imprimendum solum.* | ANNO DO. 1549. *Mense* | *Martii.*

The Act of Uniformity of 21 January 1549 ordered that the new *Book of Common Prayer* be in place by Whitsunday, 9 June. Cranmer gave the sermon at its first use in St Paul's Cathedral. At least four editions were in print by this stage, two of them produced early in March and two in May. It sold for two shillings unbound and three shillings and fourpence bound in paste boards. The 7 March 1549 imprint by Whitchurch (STC 16267) is the basis of this edition, using the British Library copy (shelf mark: C.25.l.14). Whitchurch's text is preferred to Grafton's as the latter misplaces the Litany and contains a number of other errors. I have compared Whitchurch's edition with the others printed in 1549, and whenever I have departed from the base text I have used one of these witnesses. Whitchurch printed three editions of the 1549 text in London, as did Grafton. In addition, Oswen produced an edition for Wales in Worcester, and in 1551 Humphrey Powell produced a separate Irish edition in Dublin. All of these editions are folio. Oswen also produced a quarto edition at Worcester in 1549.

1559

The Boke of | common praier, and ad- | ministration of the | Sacramentes, | and other | rites | and Ceremonies in | the Churche of | Englande. | *Londini, in officina Ri-* | *chardi Graftoni.* | Cum privilegio Regie | Maiestatis. | *Anno.* 1559.

It is not clear which of the three texts surviving of the *Book of Common Prayer* in 1559 is the earliest in production. The imprint of 1559 bearing the name of Grafton is an oddity, since he lost his licence to print in 1553 and later in 1559 gave up his press and type (some to his son-in-law Richard Tottel (see *ODNB*)). Perhaps this edition represents an attempt to get back into business; if so, he may have acted as an agent for Jugge and Cawood, and attached his name. Although one early copy has a cancel slip pasted in with the names of Jugge and Cawood, Peter Blayney has established that Grafton was responsible for its printing. Some of the decorated initials are from Grafton's shop, and some idiosyncrasies of the text are in line with his 1552 editions (see Explanatory Notes, p. 725). It was the last printed book of a distinguished *Book of Common Prayer* printer. Grafton's text (STC 16291) is the basis of the text prepared here, using the British Library copy (C.25.l.9), compared with the Bodleian Library copy (CP. 1559 d.1). It is preferred to STC 16292 (by Jugge and Cawood) since, although their status as royal printers might otherwise give them precedence, the Litany is imperfect in their edition and an incorrect 'State prayer' is included. A third edition (STC 16292a) by Jugge and Cawood is dated on the title-page 1559, but the Almanack begins at 1561 and the book as a whole may date from 1560.

1662

THE BOOK | *OF* | Common-Prayer | And Administration | Of the | SACRAMENTS, | AND OTHER | *RITES & CEREMONIES* | Of the 𝕮𝕳𝖀𝕽𝕮𝕳, | According to the Use | Of the | CHURCH of ENGLAND, | Together with the | *PSALTER or PSALMS* | of | 𝕯𝕬𝖁𝕴𝕯, | *Pointed as they are to be Sung* | *or Said in CHURCHES*: | And the | FORM & MANNER | OF | *Making, Ordaining, & Consecrating* | OF | *BISHOPS, PRIESTS,* | AND | *DEACONS.* | LONDON | Printed by His Maties Printers. | *Cum Privilegio* | MDCLXII

The case of 1662 is somewhat simpler, and the basis of the text in this edition is the full-sized folio edition (40 cm) of the royal printers (Wing B3622) using the copy in the British Library (shelf mark: 7.f.10). This particular copy has a royal coat of arms by Wenceslaus Hollar and is a presentation copy, with handsome engravings tipped in. However, the text officially approved for 1662 is not any printed version but the 'Sealed Book', that is, copies of this impression corrected in manuscript and certificated by the bishops' own signatures under the Great Seal. The printed copy of 1662 has therefore been compared with a copy of the 'Sealed Book' in Lambeth Palace Library (shelf mark: H5145.A4 (1662)), and another (in this case a fair copy of the 'Sealed Book' prepared for Lord Ellesmere) in the Huntington Library (shelf mark: HN 108701). The corrections of the 'Sealed Book' have been incorporated in the text established here.

Editorial principles

SPELLING

While this is an original-spelling edition, it has been moderately modernized. The use of i/j and u/v has been regularized; initial and medial 'long s' are modernized; abbreviations ('mm', 'nn', etc.) and some numerals ('.i.') have been silently filled out, as have contractions such as 'the' for 'yᵉ' and 'which' for 'wᶜʰ'. The names of biblical books in scriptural citations have been modernized and standardized (e.g. *Isa.* 1), although where a name of a book appears in the text proper it is retained in its original form (e.g. 'Esaie'). Where there is a clear error, I have emended in line with another text of the same year. I have also occasionally emended the orthography where modern usage would create obvious confusion; wherever possible I have again followed a contemporary text. Examples of this are the use of 'the' for 'thee' in Grafton's 1559; and the practice of eliding the initial definite article, common in 1549 and frequent in 1559 (e.g. 'thende' = 'the ende'; 'thepiphanie' = 'the epiphanie', etc.). Very exceptionally, where a glaring grammatical error is found in all contemporary editions I have emended without a contemporary witness. The spelling in 1662, while more regularized than in the sixteenth-century texts, is also inconsistent. I have allowed these inconsistencies to remain, in line with the rest of the edition. Variations likely to trouble a reader are recorded in the Glossary.

CAPITALIZATION

In the nineteenth century the capitalization of the *Book of Common Prayer* was standardized in line with contemporary religious belief. Thus the 'holy ghost' became the 'Holy Ghost', and the 'word' always 'the Word'. In general, capitalization is used in this edition out of bibliographical rather than pietistic zeal. When God is 'god', as often in 1549, I leave him that way, and only call him 'Him' when the text requires me to do so. When, however, capitalization is used to indicate direct speech (as in scriptural passages in 1662), I have emended where this has been changed through the carelessness of the compositor.

PUNCTUATION

In general, the original punctuation is retained. In the case of the texts of the Psalms used in 1549, Whitchurch's first impression does not, as his later ones did, normalize the mid-verse rhythmic hiatus [:]. I have emended according to the practice in his June edition. I have also normalized punctuation in the responses in antiphonal sequences, in line with what I have judged to be the standard for that edition. In the case of the 1559 text, the Jugge and Cawood editions clear up some ambiguities and confusions of punctuation in the Grafton text, especially in the saying of responses; and most of all in the Communion. This usually involves substituting a [:] for a [,] or a [.] for a [:]. In all texts, I have attempted to alter punctuation in line with a contemporary edition. In the case of 1662, as with orthography, there is an argument for modernizing punctuation more readily, in line with later practice, but once again I have respected the original text of 1662, except where an error has been made which is corrected in a subsequent edition. Occasionally I have made such emendations in punctuation in 1662 where the sense is otherwise confused.

LAYOUT

In other matters of layout, it should be borne in mind that this is not a facsimile edition; it does not follow every aspect of the originals. Some early editions, following medieval practice, used red ink (the origin of the word 'rubric') to indicate aspects of the text such as in the Calendar; this practice continued up to 1662. It is not used here. Nor is this edition, after all, a service book; it is therefore incorrect for it to imitate a service book in style. However, I have tried to indicate, by a number of typographical procedures, something of the *mise-en-page* of the originals, and have attempted some consistency of practice to give the reader a sense of this (see 'Rubrics', below).

One general matter of style is that the body of all the original texts is in black-letter. I have reproduced that here where it was used in headings to the individual services, to render some sense of the original appearance. However, while black-letter was also used for the spoken parts in all the versions from 1549 to 1662, in this edition roman type is used. Black-letter had a different significance in the different versions. In 1549 and 1559 black-letter was the standard typeface in use in all English print-houses. Later, in the Elizabethan period, roman type began to gain some favour, as it always had in learned and humanist books on the continent (outside the Germanic countries). Some editions of the *Book of Common Prayer* in smaller sizes (but not the majority) were printed in a roman fount. However, major new editions such as 1604 were still printed in black-letter. In 1662 black-letter was again chosen, just one feature that is consciously old-fashioned. It may in one respect reflect a Restoration nostalgic chic. But above all it shows the consciousness of the Caroline bishops that they were preserving a tradition, which deserved to be venerated and which also conveyed authority. The old look reinforced this sense of visible tradition, as perhaps did the fondness for antique orthography and vocabulary. This continues as part of the appeal of the book to this day, with the preference of people (who never use the word outside church) for the 'reverential' sound of 'thou', even though (originally) calling God 'thou' had a quite different meaning.

RUBRICS

The *Book of Common Prayer* has something of the character of a play-text, and some of the resources of the tradition of editing plays are used here. In this edition rubrics are centred if they are 'stage directions' for the saying of the liturgy; aligned left and justified if they indicate a more general ordination of church discipline or some other matter. There is some ambiguity between these types of rubric, of course.

Rubrics in the Roman breviaries and missals were always in red, an impression emphasized by the sheer number of priestly instructions. In the 1549 and 1559 original texts, while red ink was sometimes used, rubrics tend to be in black in a smaller gothic fount; in 1662 a roman fount was used in contrast to the habitual black-letter used for spoken text. All rubrics in this edition are given in italics. The lineation of versicles and responses ('Priest', 'Answer', etc.) has been standardized, so that the identity of the respondent (in italics) is on the same line as the response. Identifications ('Priest', 'Minister') are always given here in italics; in the original they are usually in a smaller fount on the line above.

INITIALS

All the editions from 1549 to 1662 are marked by an elaborate and even mannered use of decorated initials. These have been registered here by the use of large dropped capitals. I have only used such large capitals where there is either a decorated or an enlarged capital in the original text. The early editions also use several signs (including pointed leaves with blades, and printers' fists (or manicules), as well as paraphs) to mark out significant points in the text. These have been regularized here to the use of ¶, except in the case of headings, which also use, where appropriate, ornamental leaves. Where space allows, printers' flowers are used, as in the original editions, to indicate divisions in the text.

OTHER MARKS

The Greek cross (✠) is used at moments of sacred ritual at several points in the 1549 text, including Communion, Baptism, and Matrimony, and is reproduced here; it will be noted that these are all removed from the 1552 text, and thus do not appear in the 1559 version. This is discussed in the Explanatory Notes.

Using this edition

Inevitably, in preparing a text in different states I have produced a book which can be used in a number of ways. The Explanatory Notes, in particular, work cumulatively. The Explanatory Notes for 1549 reflect on how the text first came to be prepared, and therefore make general remarks on the evolution of liturgy and on the particular state of medieval ritual which formed the context for Cranmer's edition (and was often its primary source). The Explanatory Notes for 1559 comment specifically on how the text of 1549 was subsequently revised, both in 1552 and in 1559. The Explanatory Notes for 1662 describe how further revisions took place, which include in some cases the restoration of elements of 1549 in preference to 1552 and later editions. It will be obvious that not all of this information could be repeated from one section of Explanatory Notes to the next; but it will also be obvious that much of the information given in one context will be relevant elsewhere. Readers looking for elucidation on, say, the sign of the cross in Baptism, may wish to use all three sets of Notes in tandem. A finding Index of Services and Orders is included to aid this. In addition, I have used the Glossary not only to indicate specific meanings of words but to comment on terms of general use, as in a theological dictionary. Where appropriate, I have also cross-referenced entries in the Glossary with the Explanatory Notes. The different parts of the edition will work best when interconnected in this way.

. The existence of a note at the back of the book is indicated by a degree sign in the text. Notes describing the general nature of each version of an order of service are also provided at the relevant headword, without a cue.

NOTE ON MUSIC

MEDIEVAL liturgy had a rich musical heritage, and many surviving manuscripts contain notation, including ones for smaller churches as well as large foundations and monasteries. The *Book of Common Prayer* in 1549 contains many rubrics which indicate singing by a choir, and music was obviously permitted, if not encouraged, at Matins and Evensong. Yet it contained not one note of music, or any signal as to how music was to be performed. This partly reflected the complexity of the project—there were many other matters to be attended to; it also reflected concerns among Reformers about the use of music in divine services. As on other matters of ceremonies, some Protestants regarded music as distracting or even idolatrous. However, Luther wrote music as well as encouraging its use for devotional purposes; and Calvin allowed for metrical versions of psalms while disapproving of elaborate ceremonial music. As for Cranmer, in his notes on processions he did not reject music, but he did suggest that the words in liturgy should be sung (as far as possible) 'for every syllable a note', that is, so that the meaning could be articulated with the sound. This concurred with widespread anxiety—also expressed at the Council of Trent—that polyphony detracted from piety.

In 1550 Richard Grafton published *The Booke of Common Praier Noted* by John Merbecke, with the permission of Cranmer. Merbecke was sympathetic to the Reformation and had studied Calvin. He produced plainsong settings for all sections of Morning and Evening Prayer, and for Communion and some of the occasional offices as well. These followed the system of eight tones found in Sarum, already familiar to choirs. Merbecke's work did not go beyond this single edition, and the revised *Book of Common Prayer* of 1552 showed much less sympathy to music, omitting in many of the rubrics to mention the possibility of singing or the presence of the choir. In some churches, organs were destroyed.

However, as in other aspects of the performance of the *Book of Common Prayer*, this silence was not prescriptive in effect. Part-music survives from Edwardian years which shows settings of the Canticles and of the Ordinary of the Mass, along with anthem compositions for use with vernacular material. Under Elizabeth, the attitude to music seems to have been permissive. At the Queen's Chapel Royal composers such as Thomas Tallis and William Byrd were employed throughout the reign to train the choir as well as to write new music (for instance, settings of the *Magnificat* and *Nunc dimittis*) for divine services. This was not uncontroversial. Clergy, up to the level of convocation, often objected to complex choral music, as they might object to vestments or other ornaments. In cathedrals and collegiate churches choirs were employed on a regular basis, and accounts refer typically to six or eight lay musicians, and the same number of choristers, throughout the Elizabethan period and up to the Civil Wars. Some choir accounts survive for parish churches, such as Ludlow, which had a choir of twelve singers in the late sixteenth century, although this may not be typical.

Thus, while the stereotyped view of Protestant worship is that it rejected music, the *Book of Common Prayer*, as always, shows different motives converging. Yet the music was most often simple. After Merbecke, Thomas Morley produced versions of psalm chant in 1597, using the eight Sarum tones in four-part harmonizations. There are also chant-books from the reign of Charles I and, after the 1662 edition, in James Clifford's *The Divine Services and Anthems* (1664), which contained four special forms of harmonized chant, including 'Canterbury tune' and 'Christ Church tune'. This material was suitable for a trained choir. For everyday churches, the metrical Psalms of Thomas Sternhold and John Hopkins were published in a full edition by John Day, *The Whole Booke of Psalmes, Collected into English Meter* (1562). This was reprinted as many times as the *Book of Common Prayer* itself, and the two books are very often found bound together throughout the seventeenth century. They used the simplest form of musical setting, the 'ballad meter', for most psalms. John Jewel reported congregations joining in with singing psalms in Morning and Evening Prayer in his diocese of Salisbury as commonplace in the 1560s, adding: 'You may now sometimes see at St Paul's Cross [outside the cathedral in London], after the service, six thousand persons, old and young, of both sexes, all singing together and praising God.' Jewel may have been exaggerating, and others disapproved. But even the punctuation of the Psalter included in the various editions of the Elizabethan and Stuart *Book of Common Prayer* was designed to help singers by suggesting rhythm and pauses in chant. Choirs to this day use the comma and other marks as well as the medial colon (which separates each verse into two antiphonal halves) to determine how to sing.

SELECT BIBLIOGRAPHY

The Book of Common Prayer

Brightman, F. E., *The English Rite*, 2 vols. (London: Rivingtons, 1915).

Griffiths, David N., *The Bibliography of the Book of Common Prayer* (London: British Library, 2002).

Maltby, Judith, *Prayer Book and People in Elizabethan and Early Stuart England* (Cambridge: Cambridge University Press, 1998).

The Oxford Guide to the Book of Common Prayer: A Worldwide Survey, ed. Charles Hefling and Cynthia Shattuck (New York: Oxford University Press, 2006).

Procter, Francis, and W. H. Frere, *A New History of the Book of Common Prayer* (London: Macmillan, 1901).

Shepherd, M. H., *The Oxford American Prayer Book Commentary* (New York: Oxford University Press, 1950).

Further Reading

Aston, Margaret, 'Segregation in Church', in W. J. Sheils and Diana Wood (eds.), *Women in the Church*, Studies in Church History (Oxford: Blackwell, 1990), 242–81.

Cameron, Euan, *The European Reformation* (Oxford: Clarendon Press, 1991).

Cox, J. C., and A. Harvey, *English Church Furniture* (London: Methuen, 1907).

Clark, Francis, SJ, *Eucharistic Sacrifice and the Reformation* (London: Darton, Longman & Todd, 1960).

Collinson, Patrick, *The Birthpangs of Protestant England* (London: Macmillan, 1988).

—— *The Religion of Protestants: The Church in English Society 1559–1625* (Oxford: Clarendon Press, 1982).

Cressy, David, *Birth, Marriage and Death: Ritual, Religion and the Life-Cycle in Tudor and Stuart England* (Oxford: Oxford University Press, 1997).

—— *Bonfires and Bells: National Memory and the Protestant Calendar in Elizabethan and Stuart England*, rev. edn. (London: The History Press, 2004).

Cuming, G. J., *A History of Anglican Liturgy* (London: Macmillan, 1969).

Duffy, Eamon, *The Stripping of the Altars: Traditional Religion in England 1400–1580* (New Haven and London: Yale University Press, 1992).

Fincham, Kenneth, and Nicholas Tyacke, *Altars Restored: The Changing Face of English Religious Worship, 1547–c.1700* (Oxford: Oxford University Press, 2007).

Green, Ian, *The Christian's ABC: Catechisms and Catechizing in England c.1530–1740* (Oxford: Clarendon Press, 1996).

—— *Print and Protestantism in Early Modern England* (Oxford: Oxford University Press, 2000).

Hunt, Arnold, 'The Lord's Supper in Early Modern England', *Past and Present*, 161 (1998), 39–83.

—— 'The Debate on Lay Baptism in Early Modern England', *Past and Present* (forthcoming, 2011).

Hutton, Ronald, *The Rise and Fall of Merry England: The Ritual Year 1400–1700* (Oxford: Oxford University Press, 1994).

—— *The Restoration: A Political and Religious History of England and Wales 1658–1667*, rev. edn. (Oxford: Clarendon Press, 1993).

Kim, Hyun-Ah, *Humanism and the Reform of Sacred Music in Early Modern England: John Merbecke the Orator and The Booke of Common Praier Noted (1550)* (Farnham: Ashgate, 2008).

Lake, Peter, *Anglicans and Puritans?* (London: Unwin Hyman, 1988).

Le Huray, Peter, *Music and the Reformation in England 1549–1660* (Cambridge: Cambridge University Press, 1978).

MacCulloch, Diarmaid, *Reformation: Europe's House Divided, 1490–1700* (London: Allen Lane, 2003).

—— *Thomas Cranmer: A Life* (New Haven and London: Yale University Press, 1996).

—— *Tudor Church Militant: Edward VI and the Protestant Reformation* (London: Allen Lane, 1999).

Marshall, Peter, *Beliefs and the Dead in Reformation England* (Oxford: Oxford University, 2002).

Milton, Anthony, *Catholic and Reformed: The Roman and Protestant Churches in English Protestant Thought* (Cambridge: Cambridge University Press, 1995).

Pfaff, Richard W., *The Liturgy in Medieval England: A History* (Cambridge: Cambridge University Press, 2009).

Quitslund, Beth, *The Reformation in Rhyme: Sternhold, Hopkins and the English Metrical Psalter, 1547–1603* (Farnham: Ashgate, 2008).

Spinks, Bryan D., *Sacraments, Ceremonies and the Stuart Divines: Sacramental Theology and Liturgy in England and Scotland 1603–1662* (London: Ashgate, 2002).

Targoff, Ramie, *Common Prayer: The Language of Public Devotion in Early Modern England* (Chicago: University of Chicago Press, 2001).

Wabuda, Susan, *Preaching During the English Reformation* (Cambridge: Cambridge University Press, 2002).

Walsham, Alexandra, *Providence in Early Modern England* (Oxford: Oxford University Press, 1999).

CHRONOLOGY

1503 William Warham Archbishop of Canterbury.

1509 Accession of Henry VIII.

1515 Thomas Wolsey appointed Lord Chancellor.

1517 Martin Luther's 95 Theses.

1521 Luther's excommunication published in St Paul's Cathedral by Wolsey.

1523 *Formula missae et communionis* (publication of Luther's mass in Germany); also of Zwingli's in Zurich.

1524 Martin Bucer's service for 'Lord's Supper' in Strassburg.

1526 William Tyndale's New Testament in English printed in Germany.

1527 Divorce crisis begins.

1529 Fall of Wolsey; Thomas More Lord Chancellor.

1530 Augsburg Confession regularizes German Protestantism; George Joye's English Psalter; *Hortulus animae*, Protestant Book of Hours.

1532 Thomas Cranmer Archbishop of Canterbury; More resigns.

1533 Henry marries Anne Boleyn; birth of Princess Elizabeth; Brandenburg–Nuremberg Order of liturgy issued.

1534 Act of Supremacy; William Marshall, *A Goodly Primer in English*.

1535 Miles Coverdale's Bible in English; revised Roman Breviary by Francisco Quiñones.

1536 Dissolution of the Monasteries; Pilgrimage of Grace against Reformation; *Ten Articles* set out theology of the Church of England.

1537 *The Bishops' Book* (with expositions of the Creed, sacraments, and Ten Commandments).

1538 Royal Injunctions on religion, including condemnation of the cult of saints, images, and 'superstition'.

1539 *Six Articles* reverse some of the directions of the Protestant Reformation in England; the 'Great Bible' in English becomes official Bible for use in church.

1541 *Ordonnances ecclésiastiques* inaugurates Jean Calvin's reform movement in Geneva; Calvin's French liturgy introduced.

1543 *King's Book*, book of doctrinal explanation; Clément Marot, *Cinquante Pseaumes* (revised later by Théodore de Bèze).

1544 Hermann von Wied's liturgical reform published in Cologne (written by Bucer with Philip Melanchthon); English *Litany*.

1545 Council of Trent begins; the *King's Primer* regularizes liturgical materials in English.

1547 Accession of Edward VI; ascendancy of Protector Somerset; Royal Injunctions inaugurate 'second Reformation', including ban on processions, and ordering destruction of images; *Certain Homilies* published; Peter Martyr Vermigli refugee in England.

1548 *Order of the Communion*; exiles return, including Coverdale and Hooper.

1549 Act of Uniformity; first *Book of Common Prayer*; 'Prayer Book' rebellion; fall of Somerset; Bucer professor in Cambridge.

1550 *The form and manner of making, ordaining and consecrating of Bishops, Priests and Deacons* (Ordinal); John Hooper attacks use of vestments; reply by Nicholas Ridley.

1551 Peter Martyr Vermigli and Martin Bucer write commissioned comments on the 1549 *Book of Common Prayer*; *Book of Common Prayer* in Ireland.

1552 Second, revised *Book of Common Prayer*.

1553 42 Articles of Religion; death of Edward VI and accession of Mary I; repeal of Act of Uniformity and Common Prayer.

1554 Reunion with Rome; Act abolishing *Book of Common Prayer*; Sarum missal, etc., reintroduced in new printings.

1555 Persecution of Protestants begins; Ridley and Latimer burned in Oxford; Peace of Augsburg in Germany.

1556 Reginald Pole Archbishop of Canterbury; burning of Cranmer.

1558 Accession of Elizabeth I.

1559 Act of Uniformity; third *Book of Common Prayer*; Royal Injunctions on religion, including orders on furnishings, altars, and music; Matthew Parker Archbishop of Canterbury; final edition of Calvin's *Institutio christianae religionis*; John Knox's Genevan *Book of Common Order* issued in Scotland.

1560 Geneva Bible published, with verse numbers and marginal annotations.

1562 Thomas Sternhold and John Hopkins, *The Whole Booke of Psalmes, Collected into English Meter*.

1563 39 Articles of Religion; John Foxe's *Actes and Monuments* ('Book of Martyrs').

1566 Beginnings of Dutch Revolt; iconoclastic riots in the Netherlands; Archbishop Matthew Parker's *Advertisements*.

1568 Eighty Years' War, Dutch war of independence from Spain, begins; The 'Bishops' Bible' revises the Great Bible for use in churches.

1569 Northern Rebellion by Roman Catholic nobles against Elizabeth I.

1570 Elizabeth I excommunicated by papal Bull; Tridentine Missal published.

1572 Thomas Wilcox and John Field, *Admonition to Parliament*; massacre of Huguenots in Paris on feast of St Bartholomew.

1576 Edmund Grindal Archbishop of Canterbury; Geneva Bible reprinted in England, becoming the best-selling English Bible of the sixteenth century.

1577 *Formula of Concord* regularizes Lutheran confession in Germany.

1580 Jesuit mission in England begins.

1583 John Whitgift Archbishop of Canterbury.

1584 *A Book of the Form of Common Prayers* (Puritan alternative service book based on Knox's Genevan order).

1587 Reissue of the Geneva Bible with Tomson's notes to the NT.

1588 Martin Marprelate controversy begins, a Puritan attack on the bishops and the established church; Spanish Armada.

1594 Richard Hooker, *Laws of Ecclesiastical Polity*, later expanded.

1595 Lambeth Articles on predestination upheld by Whitgift but not officially promoted.

1603 Accession of James VI of Scotland as James I; Millenary Petition of the Puritans.

1604 Hampton Court Conference; fourth *Book of Common Prayer*; ecclesiastical *Canons* of the Church of England; Richard Bancroft Archbishop of Canterbury.

1605 Gunpowder Plot.

1606 Puritan *Survey of the Book of Common Prayer*.

1607 Jamestown colony in Virginia founded.

1609 Ulster Plantation by English and Scottish Protestants.

1610 Remonstrance to the States of Holland by the Dutch Arminians outlining five articles in disagreement with the Calvinist doctrine of predestination.

1611 Authorized Version of the Bible (King James Version); George Abbot Archbishop of Canterbury.

1618 Outbreak of Thirty Years' War; Synod of Dordt begins.

1620 Pilgrim Fathers begin religious migrations to New England.

1622 Directions to Preachers quelling religious controversy, especially on predestination.

1625 Accession of Charles I; he marries the Catholic Henrietta Maria.

1626 Final version of Lancelot Andrewes, *Preces privatae*.

1627 John Cosin, *Collection of Private Devotions*.

1628 William Laud Bishop of London; Duke of Buckingham bans teaching on predestination in Cambridge.

1629 Charles I dissolves parliament.

1630 Samuel Harsnett, Archbishop of York, bans sale of Calvinist writers in north of England.

1633 Laud Archbishop of Canterbury; Act of Privy Council replaces altars at east end of parish churches.

1637 Scottish *Book of Common Prayer*; causes unrest.

1640 Long Parliament begins; new ecclesiastical *Canons*; thirteen bishops impeached by Parliament.

1642 Civil War begins.

1645 *Book of Common Prayer* abolished by Parliament; *Directory of Worship* in its place; Laud executed; New Model Army formed.

1646 King surrenders to the Scots; bishops and archbishops abolished; presbyterian church established; regulations for exclusion from sacrament.

1648 Second Civil War.

1649 Trial and execution of Charles I.

1653 Oliver Cromwell dissolves Rump Parliament and becomes Lord Protector.

1658 Death of Oliver Cromwell; protectorate of his son Richard.

1659 Rump Parliament restored.

1660 Restoration of Charles II; William Juxon Archbishop of Canterbury (office vacant since 1645); Cosin Bishop of Durham and begins compilation of 'Durham Book' with Matthew Wren; review of *Book of Common Prayer* proposed by Earl of Clarendon, Lord Chancellor.

1661 Savoy Conference to revise *Book of Common Prayer*; presbyterian *Exceptions* printed; Baxter's reformed presbyterian liturgy.

1662 Act of Uniformity; revised *Book of Common Prayer*.

BIBLICAL ABBREVIATIONS

Old Testament

Gen.	Genesis	Ecc.	Ecclesiastes
Ex.	Exodus	Song	Song of Solomon
Lev.	Leviticus	Isa.	Isaiah
Num.	Numbers	Jer.	Jeremiah
Deut.	Deuteronomy	Lam.	Lamentations
Josh.	Joshua	Ezek.	Ezekiel
Judg.	Judges	Dan.	Daniel
Ruth	Ruth	Hos.	Hosea
1 Sam.	1 Samuel	Joel	Joel
2 Sam.	2 Samuel	Amos	Amos
1 King.	1 Kings	Obad.	Obadiah
2 King.	2 Kings	Jonah	Jonah
1 Chr.	1 Chronicles	Mic.	Micah
2 Chr.	2 Chronicles	Nah.	Nahum
Ezra	Ezra	Hab.	Habakkuk
Neh.	Nehemiah	Zeph.	Zephaniah
Esth.	Esther	Hagg.	Haggai
Job	Job	Zech.	Zechariah
Ps.	Psalms	Mala.	Malachi
Prov.	Proverbs		

New Testament

Matt.	Matthew	2 Thess.	2 Thessalonians
Mark	Mark	1 Tim.	1 Timothy
Luke	Luke	2 Tim.	2 Timothy
John	John	Tit.	Titus
		Philem.	Philemon
Acts	Acts of the Apostles	Heb.	Hebrews
Rom.	Romans	Jas.	James
1 Cor.	1 Corinthians	1 Pet.	1 Peter
2 Cor.	2 Corinthians	2 Pet.	2 Peter
Gal.	Galatians	1 John	1 John
Eph.	Ephesians	2 John	2 John
Phil.	Philippians	3 John	3 John
Col.	Colossians	Jude	Jude
1 Thess.	1 Thessalonians	Rev.	Revelation

Apocrypha

Tob.	Tobit	Sus.	Susanna
1 Esd.	1 Esdras	Bar.	Baruch
1 Macc.	1 Maccabees	Bel &	Bel and the Dragon
Wisd.	Wisdom	Dragon	
Ecclus.	Ecclesiasticus		

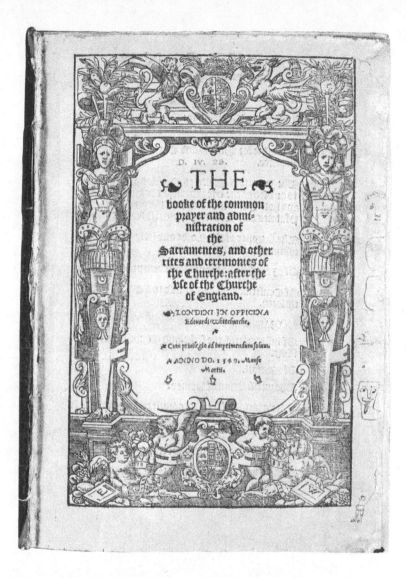

The booke of the common prayer (London: Edward Whitchurch, 1549),
STC 16267 (7 March 1549), Title page. Bishop Cosin's Library, Durham
University (shelf mark: SB+ 0851/1). Reproduced with permission. This
copy was probably owned by John Cosin.

THE CON-
tentes of this Booke.

THE PREFACE.

THERE was never any thing by the wit of man so well devised, or so surely established, which (in continuance of time) hath not been corrupted:° as (among other thinges) it may plainly appere by the common prayers in the Churche, commonlye called divine service: the firste originall and grounde whereof, if a manne woulde searche out by the auncient fathers, he shall finde that the same was not ordeyned, but of a good purpose, and for a great advaunce-ment of godlines: For they so ordred the matter, that all the whole Bible (or the greatest parte thereof) should be read over once in the yeare, intendyng thereby, that the Cleargie, and specially suche as were Ministers of the congregacion, should (by often readyng and meditacion of Gods worde) be stirred up to godlines themselfes, and be more able also to exhorte other by wholsome doctrine, and to confute them that were adversaries to the trueth. And further, that the people (by daily hearyng of holy scripture read in the Churche)° should continuallye profite more and more in the knowlege of God, and bee the more inflamed with the love of his true religion. But these many yeares passed this Godly and decent ordre of the auncient fathers, hath been so altered, broken, and neglected, by planting in uncertein stories, Legendes, Respondes, Verses, vaine repeticions, Commemaracions, and Synodalles, that commonly when any boke of the Bible was begon: before three or foure Chapiters were read out, all the rest were unread. And in this sorte, the boke of Esaie was begon in Advent, and the booke of Genesis in Septuagesima: but they were onely begon, and never read thorow. After a like sorte wer other bokes of holy scripture used. And moreover, whereas S. Paule would have suche language spoken to the people in the churche, as they mighte understande and have profite by hearyng the same: the service in this Churche of England (these many yeares) hath been read in Latin to the people, whiche they understoode not,° so that they have heard with theyr eares onely: and their hartes, spirite and minde, have not been edified thereby. And furthermore, notwithstandyng that the auncient fathers had devided the psalmes into seven porcions, wherof every one was called a nocturne:° now of late tyme a fewe of them have been dailye sayed (and ofte repeated) and the rest utterly omitted.

Moreover, the nombre and hardnes of the rules called the pie,° and the manifolde chaunginges of the service, was the cause, that to turne the boke onlye, was so hard and intricate a matter, that many times, there was more busines to fynd out what should be read, then to read it when it was founde out.

These inconveniences therfore considered: here is set furth suche an ordre, whereby the same shalbe redressed. And for a readines in this matter, here is drawen out a Kalendar° for that purpose, whiche is plaine and easy to be understanded, wherin (so muche as maie be) the readyng of holy scripture is so set furthe, that all thynges shall bee doen in ordre, without breakyng one piece therof from another. For this cause be cut of Anthemes, Respondes, Invitatories, and suche like thynges, as did breake the continuall course of the readyng of the scripture. Yet because there is no remedy, but that of necessitie there must be some rules: therfore certein rules are here set furth, whiche as they be fewe in nombre: so they be plain and easy to be understanded. So that here you have an ordre for praier (as touchyng the readyng of holy scripture) muche agreable to the mynde and purpose of the olde fathers, and a greate deale more profitable and commodious, then that whiche of late was used. It is more profitable, because here are left out many thynges, whereof some be untrue, some uncertein, some vain and supersticious: and is ordeyned nothyng to be read, but the very pure worde of God, the holy scriptures, or that whiche is evidently grounded upon the same: and that in suche a language and ordre, as is moste easy and plain for the understandyng, bothe of the readers and hearers. It is also more commodious, bothe for the shortnes thereof, and for the plaines of the ordre, and for that the rules be fewe and easy. Furthermore by this ordre, the curates shal nede none other bookes for their publique service, but this boke and the Bible: by the meanes wherof, the people shall not be at so great charge for bookes, as in tyme past they have been.

And where heretofore, there hath been great diversitie in saying and synging in churches within this realme: some folowyng Salsbury use,° some Herford use, some the use of Bangor, some of Yorke, and some of Lincolne: Now from hencefurth, all the whole realme shall have but one use.° And if any would judge this waye more painfull, because that all thynges must be read upon the boke, whereas before by the reason of so often repeticion, they could saye many thinges by heart: if those men will waye their labor, with the profite in knowlege, whiche dayely they shal obtein by readyng upon the boke, they will not refuse the payn, in consideracion of the greate profite that shall ensue therof.

And farsomuche as nothyng can, almoste, be so plainly set furth, but doubtes maie rise in the use and practisyng of the same: to appease all suche diversitie (if any arise), and for the resolucion of all doubtes, concernyng the maner how to understande, do, and execute the thynges conteygned in this booke: the parties that so doubt, or diversly take any thyng, shall alwaye resorte to the Bishop of the Diocese, who by his discrecion shall take ordre for the quietyng and appeasyng of the same: so that the same ordre be not contrary to any thyng conteigned in this boke.

¶ *Though it be appointed in the afore written preface, that al thinges shalbe read and song in the churche, in the Englishe tongue, to the ende that the congregacion maie be therby edified: yet it is not meant, but when men saye Matins and Evensong privatelye, they maye saie the same in any language that they themselves do understande. Neither that anye man shalbe bound to the saying of them, but suche as from tyme to tyme, in Cathedrall and Collegiate Churches, Parishe Churches, and Chapelles to the same annexed, shall serve the congregacion.*

❧ AN ORDRE ❧
for Mattyns dayly through the yere.

The Priest beeyng in the quier° shall begynne with a loude voyce the Lordes prayer, called the Pater noster.°

OURE father whiche arte in heaven, hallowed by thy name.° Thy kyngdom come. Thy wyll be done in earth as it is in heaven. Geve us this daye oure dayly bread. And forgeve us oure trespasses, as we forgeve them that trespasse agaynst us. And leade us not into temptacion. But deliver us from evell. Amen.

Then lykewyse he shall saye.

O Lorde, open thou my lyppes.°

Aunswere.

And my mouthe shall shewe forth thy prayse.

Priest.

O God, make spede to save me.

Aunswere.

O Lorde, make haste to helpe me.

Priest.

Glory be to the father, and to the sonne, and to the holye ghost. As it was in the begynning, is now, and ever shalbe world without ende. Amen.

Prayse ye the Lorde.

And from Easter to Trinitie Sondaye,

Alleluya.°

Then shalbe saied or song without any Invitatori° this Psalme, Venite exultemus,° *etc. in Englishe, as foloweth:*

OCOME lette us syng unto the Lorde: lette us hartely rejoyce in the strengthe of oure salvacion.   *Ps.* 95

Let us come before his presence with thankesgeving: and shewe ourselfe glad in hym with Psalmes.

For the Lord is a great God: and a great kyng above all goddes.

In his hande are all the corners of the yearth: and the strength of the hylles is his also.

The sea is his, and he made it: and his handes prepared the drye lande.

O come, let us worship and fall downe: and kneele before the Lorde oure maker.

For he is (the Lord) oure God: and we are the people of his pasture, and the shepe of his handes.

To daye, yf ye wyll heare his voyce, harden not your hartes: as in the provocacion, and as in the daie of temptacion in the wildernes.

When your fathers tempted me: proved me, and sawe my workes.

Fourtye yeares long was I greved with this generacion, and sayed: it is a people that do erre in their hartes: for they have not knowen my wayes.

Unto whom I sware in my wrath: that they shoulde not entre into my rest.

Glory be to the father, and to the sonne: and to the holy ghost.

As it was in the beginnyng, is nowe, and ever shalbe: worlde without end. Amen.

¶ *Then shal folow certaine Psalmes in ordre as they been appointed in a table°*
made for the purpose, except there be propre Psalmes appointed for that day.
And at the ende of every Psalme throughout the yeare, and lykewyse in the
ende of Benedictus, Benedicite, Magnificat, *and* Nunc dimittis, *shalbe*
repeated.

Glory be to the father and to the sonne, &*c.*

¶ *Then shalbe read ii. lessons distinctely with a loude voice,° that the people*
maye heare. The fyrst of the olde testament, the second of the newe. Like as
they be appoynted by the Kalender, excepte there be propre lessons assigned
for that daye: The ministre that readeth the lesson standing and turnyng hym
so as he maye beste be hearde of all suche as be present. And before every
lesson, the minister shal saye thus.

The fyrste, seconde, .iii. *or* .iiii. Chapter of Genesis, *or* Exodus, Matthewe, Marke,

or other lyke as is appoynted in the Kalender. And in the ende of every
Chapter, he shall saye.

¶ Here endeth suche a Chapter of suche a booke.

¶ *And (to the ende the people may the better heare) in such places where they doe syng, there shall the lessons be songe in a playne tune after the maner of distincte readyng:° and lykewyse the Epistle and Gospell.*

¶ *After the fyrste lesson shall folowe* Te Deum laudamus *in Englyshe,° dayly throughout the yeare, excepte in Lente, all the whiche tyme in the place of* Te Deum *shalbe used* Benedicite omnia opera Domini Domino, *in Englyshe as foloweth:*

Te Deum Laudamus.

W E praise thee, O God, we knowlage thee to be the Lorde.
    All the earth doeth wurship thee, the father everlastyng.
To thee al Angels cry aloud, the heavens and all the powers therin.
To thee Cherubin, and Seraphin continually doe crye.
Holy, holy, holy, Lorde God of Sabaoth.
Heaven and earth are replenyshed with the majestie of thy glory.
The gloryous company of the Apostles, praise thee.
The goodly felowshyp of the Prophetes, praise thee.
The noble armie of Martyrs, praise thee.
The holy churche throughout all the worlde doeth knowlage thee.
The father of an infinite majestie.
Thy honourable, true, and onely sonne.
The holy gost also beeyng the coumforter.
Thou art the kyng of glory, O Christe.
Thou art the everlastyng sonne of the father.
Whan thou tookest upon thee to delyver manne, thou dyddest not abhorre the virgins wombe.
Whan thou haddest overcomed the sharpenesse of death, thou diddest open the kyngdome of heaven to all belevers.
Thou sittest on the ryghthande of God, in the glory of the father.
We beleve that thou shalt come to be our judge.
We therfore praye thee, helpe thy servauntes, whom thou haste redemed with thy precious bloud.
Make them to be noumbred with thy sainctes,° in glory everlastyng.
O Lorde, save thy people: and blesse thyne heritage.
Governe them, and lift them up for ever.
Day by day we magnifie thee.
And we wurship thy name ever world without ende.
Vouchsafe, O Lorde, to kepe us this daye without synne.
O Lorde, have mercy upon us: have mercy upon us.
O Lorde, let thy mercy lighten upon us: as our trust is in thee.

O Lorde, in thee have I trusted: let me never be confounded.

Benedicite° omnia opera domini domino.

O ALL ye workes of the Lorde, speake good of the Lorde: prayse hym, and set hym up for ever.

O ye Angels of the Lorde, speake good of the Lorde: prayse hym, and set hym up for ever.

O ye heavens, speake good of the Lorde: prayse hym, and set him up for ever.

O ye waters that be above the fyrmamente, speake good of the Lorde: prayse hym, and set hym up for ever.

O all ye powers of the Lord, speake good of the Lord: prayse hym, and set hym up for ever.

O ye Sonne and Moone, speake good of the Lorde: prayse him, and set hym up for ever.

O ye sterres of heaven, speake good of the lorde: prayse him, and set him up for ever.

O ye showers, and dewe, speake good of the lord: praise him, and set him up for ever.

O ye windes of God, speake good of the Lord: praise him, and set him up for ever.

O ye fier and heate, prayse ye the Lorde: praise him, and set him up for ever.

O ye winter and summer, speake good of the Lorde: praise him and set him up for ever.

O ye dewes and frostes, speake good of the Lord: praise him, and set him up for ever.

O ye frost and colde, speake good of the Lorde: prayse him, and set him up for ever.

O ye yse and snowe, speake good of the Lorde: prayse him, and set him up for ever.

O ye nyghtes and dayes, speake good of the Lorde: prayse him, and set him up for ever.

O ye light and darkenes, speake good of the Lorde: prayse him, and set him up for ever.

O ye lighteninges and cloudes, speake good of the Lord: prayse him, and set him up for ever.

O let the yearthe speake good of the Lord: yea, let it prayse him, and set him up for ever.

O ye mountaynes and hilles, speake good of the Lord: prayse him, and set him up for ever.

O all ye greene thynges upon the earth, speake good of the Lorde: praise him, and set him up for ever.

O ye welles, speake good of the Lorde: praise him, and set him up for ever.

O ye seas, and floudes, speake good of the Lord: praise him, and set him up for ever.

O ye whales, and all that move in the waters, speake good of the Lorde: prayse hym, and set hym up for ever.

O all ye foules of the ayre, speake good of the lorde: prayse him, and set him up for ever.

O all ye beastes, and catell, speake ye good of the Lord: prayse him, and set him up for ever.

O ye children of men, speake good of the lorde: prayse him, and set him up for ever.

O let Israel speake good of the lorde: prayse him, and set him up for ever.

O ye priestes of the Lorde, speake good of the Lorde: prayse him, and set him up for ever.

O ye servauntes of the Lord, speake good of the Lord: prayse him, and set him up for ever.

O ye spirites and soules of the righteous, speake good of the Lorde: prayse him, and set him up for ever.

O ye holy and humble men of heart, speake ye good of the Lorde: prayse ye him, and set him up for ever.

O Ananias, Asarias, and Misael,° speake ye good of the Lorde: prayse ye him, and set him up for ever.

Glory be to the father, and to the sonne: and to the holy gost.

As it was in the beginning, is now, and ever shalbe: worlde without ende. Amen.

¶ *And after the seconde lesson, throughout the whole yere, shalbe used* Benedictus dominus deus Israel,° *&c. in Englishe as foloweth:*

Benedictus.

BLESSED be the lorde God of Israel: for he hath visited and redemed his people.   *Luke* 1

And hath lyfted up an horne of salvacyon to us: in the house of his servaunt David.

As he spake by the mouth of his holy Prophetes: which hath bene syns the world began.

That we shoulde be saved from our enemies: and from the handes of all that hate us.

To perfourme the mercy promised to our fathers: and to remember his holy covenaunt.

To perfourme the othe whiche he sware to our father Abraham: that he would geve us.

That we being delivered out of the handes of our enemies: might serve him without feare.

In holynesse and ryghteousnes before him all the dayes of our lyfe.

And thou childe, shalte bee called the prophete of the highest: for thou shalte goe before the face of the Lord, to prepare his wayes.

To geve knowledge of salvacion unto his people: for the remission of their sinnes.

Through the tender mercie of our god: whereby the daye spryng from an hygh hath visited us.

To geve lighte to them that sitte in darkenes, and in the shadowe of death: and to guide our fete into the way of peace.

Glory be to the father *&c.*

As it was in the beginnyng *&c.*

Then shalbe said dailye through the yere, the praiers folowing, as well at evensong as at Matins, all devoutely kneelyng.

Lorde have mercie upon us. Christe have mercie upon us. Lorde have mercie upon us.°

Then the minister shal say the Crede *and the Lordes praier*° *in englishe, with a loude voice, &c.*

Answere.

But deliver us from eivill. Amen.

Prieste.

O Lorde, shewe thy mercie upon us.°

Answere.

And graunt us thy salvacion.

Prieste.

O Lorde save the kyng.

Answere.

And mercifully heare us, when we cal upon thee.

Prieste.

Indue thy ministers with righteousnesse.

Answere.

And make thy chosen people joyfull.

Prieste.

O Lorde, save thy people.

Answere.

And blesse thyne inheritaunce.

Prieste.

Geve peace in oure time, O Lorde.

Answere.

Because there is none other that fyghteth for us, but only thou, O God.

Prieste.

O God, make cleane our hartes within us.

Answere.

And take not thyne holye spirite from us.

Prieste.

The lorde be with you.

Answere.

And with thy spirite.

Then shall dayly folowe three Collectes.° The firste of the day, which shalbe the same that is appointed at the Communion. The seconde for peace. The thirde for grace to lyve wel. And the two laste Collectes shall never alter, but dailye bee saide at Matins throughout al the yere, as foloweth. The priest standyng up and saiyng,

Let us praye.

¶ *Then the Collect of the daie.*

¶ *The second Collect: for peace.*

O GOD, which art author of peace, and lover of concorde, in knowledge of whome standeth oure eternall life, whose service is perfect fredome: defende us, thy humble servauntes, in al assaultes of our enemies, that wee surely trustyng in thy defence, maye not feare the power of any adversaries: through the myght of Jesu Christ our lorde. Amen.

The thyrde Collecte: for grace.

O LORDE oure heavenly father, almightye and everlivyng God, whiche haste safelye brought us to the beginning of this day: Defend us in the same with thy mighty power, and graunt that this daye wee fall into no synne, neyther runne into any kinde of daunger, but that al our doinges may be ordred by thy governaunce, to do alwaies that is righteous in thy sight: through Jesus Christe our lorde. Amen.

❧ AN ORDRE ❧
For Evensong through-out the yeare.

The prieste shall saye.

O URE FATHER, *&c.*
        Then likewise he shall saye.
O God, make spede to save me.

Answere.
O Lorde, make haste to helpe me.

Prieste.
Glory be to the father, and to the sonne: and to the holy ghost.
As it was in the beginning, is now: and ever shall be, worlde without ende. Amen.
Prayse ye the lorde.

And from Easter to Trinitie Sonday.
Alleluya.

As before is appointed at Matins.

Then Psalmes in ordre as they bee appointed in the Table° for Psalmes, except
there be proper psalmes appointed for that daye. Then a lesson of the olde
testamente as is appointed likewise in the kalender, except there be proper les-
sons appointed for that daye. After that, Magnificat anima mea dominum
in Englishe, as foloweth.

Magnificat.°

M Y soule doth magnifie the lorde.   *Luke* 1
    And my spirite hath rejoysed in God my savioure.

For he hathe regarded the lowelinesse of hys handemaiden.

For beholde, from henceforth all generacions shal cal me blessed.

For he that is mightye hath magnified me, and holy is his name.

And his mercie is on them that feare him throughoute all
generacions.

He hath shewed strength with his arme, he hath scatered the
proude in the imaginacion of their hartes.

He hath put down the mightie from their seate: and hath exalted
the humble and meeke.

He hathe filled the hungrye, with good thynges: and the riche he
hath sente awaye emptye.

He remembring his mercie, hath holpen his servaunt Israel: as he
promised to oure fathers, Abraham and his seede for ever.

Glory be to the father and to the sonne and to the holy gost.

As it was in the beginning, and is now, and ever shall be worlde
without ende. Amen.

Then a lesson of the newe testamente. And after that Nunc dimittis
servum tuum *in Englishe as foloweth.*

Nunc Dimittis.°

L ORDE, nowe lettest thou thy servaunte departe in peace, accordyng
   to thy woorde.   *Luke* 2

For myne iyes have sene thy salvacion.

Whiche thou haste prepared, before the face of all thy people.

To be a lyght for to lighten the Gentiles: and to bee the glorye of
thy people of Israel.

Glorye be to the father *&c.*

As it was in the beginnyng *&c.*

Then the suffrages before assigned at Matins, the clerkes kneelyng likewise,
with three Collectes. Fyrst of the daye: Seconde of peace: Thirde for ayde

agaynste all perilles, as here foloweth. Whiche .ii. laste collectes shall bee
daylye saide at Evensong without alteracion.

The seconde Collecte at Evensong.°

O GOD from whom all holy desyres, all good counsayles, and all
juste workes do procede: Geve unto thy servauntes that peace,
which the world cannot geve, that both our hartes maye be sette to
obey thy commaundementes, and also that by thee, we being defended
from the feare of oure enemies, may passe oure time in rest and quietnesse, throughe the merites of Jesu Christe our saviour. Amen.

The thirde Collect° for ayde agaynste all perils.

L YGHTEN our darkenes we beseche thee, O lord, & by thy great
mercy defende us from all perilles and daungers of thys nyght, for
the love of thy onely sonne, our saviour Jesu Christ. Amen.

In the feastes of Christmas, The epiphanie, Easter, The ascencion,
Pentecost, *and upon* Trinitie *Sonday, shalbe song or sayd immediatly° after*
Benedictus, *this confession of our christian fayth.*

Quicunque vult,° &c.

W HOSOEVER will be saved: before all thinges it is necessarye that
he holde the Catholyke fayth.

Whiche fayth except every one dooe kepe holy and undefyled:°
without doubt he shal perishe everlastingly.

And the Catholike faith is this: that we wurship one God in Trinitie,
and Trinitie in unitie.

Neyther confounding the persones: nor devidyng the substaunce.

For there is one persone of the father, another of the sonne: and an
other of the holy gost.

But the godhead of the father, of the sonne, and of the holy Goste,
is all one: the glorye equall, the majestie coeternall.

Such as the father is, suche is the sonne, and suche is the holy gost.

The father uncreate, the sonne uncreate: and the holy gost uncreate.

The father incomprehensible, the sonne incomprehensible: and
the holy gost incomprehensible.

The father eternall, the sonne eternall: and the holy gost eternall.

And yet they are not three eternalles: but one eternall.

As also there be not three incomprehensibles, nor three uncreated:
but one uncreated, and one incomprehensible.

So lykewyse, the father is almyghtie: the sonne almightie, and the holy gost almightie.

And yet are they not three almyghtyes: but one almightie.

So the father is God, the sonne God: and the holye gost God.

And yet are they not three Goddes: but one God.

So lykewise the father is Lord, the sonne Lord: and the holy gost Lorde.

And yet not three Lordes: but one Lorde.

For like as we be compelled by the christian veritie: to acknowlege every persone by hymselfe to be god and lord:

So are we forbidden by the Catholike religion: to say there be three goddes, or three lordes.

The father is made of none: neyther created nor begotten.

The sonne is of the father alone: not made nor created, but begotten.

The holy gost is of the father and of the sonne: neyther made nor created, nor begotten, but proceding.

So there is one father, not three fathers, one sonne, not three sonnes: one holy gost, not three holy gostes.

And in thys trinitie, none is afore nor after other: none greater nor lesse then other.

But the whole three persones: be coeternall together and coequall.

So that in all thinges, as it is aforesayd: the unitie in trinitie, and the trinitie in unitie, is to be wurshipped.

He therefore that will bee saved: must thus thinke of the trinitie.

Furthermore, it is necessary to everlasting salvacion: that he also beleve ryghtly in the incarnacion of oure Lorde Jesu Christe.

For the ryght fayth is that we beleve and confesse: that our Lorde Jesus Christe the sonne of God, is God and man.

God of the substaunce of the father, begotten before the worldes: and man of the substaunce of his mother, borne in the worlde.

Perfecte God and perfecte man: of a resonable soule, and humayne fleshe subsisting.

Equall to the father as touchyng his Godhead: and inferior to the father touchyng his manhoode.

Who although he be God and man: yet he is not two, but one Christe.

One, not by conversion of the Godhead into flesh: but by takyng of the manhoode into God.

One altogether, not by confusion of substaunce: but by unitie of person.

For as the reasonable soule and fleshe is one man: So God and man is one Christe.

Who suffered for oure salvacion: descended into hell, rose agayne the third daye from the dead.

He ascended into heaven, he sytteth on the right hand of the father, God almighty: from whence he shall come to judge the quicke and dead.

At whose commyng all men shall ryse agayne with theyr bodyes: and shall geve accompte of theyr owne workes.

And they that have done good, shall goe into life everlastyng: and they that have done evyll, into everlastyng fyre.

This is the Catholyke fayth: whiche excepte a man beleve faythfully, he cannot be saved.

Glory be to the father and to the sonne &c.

As it was in the begynnyng &c.

Thus endeth the ordre of Matyns and Evensong,° through the whole yere.

❧ THE SUPPER ❧
of the Lorde, and the holy Communion, commonly called the Masse.

*S*O many as intende to bee partakers of the holy Communion, shall sygnifie
their names to the Curate,° over night: or els in the morning, afore the beginning of Matins, or immediatly after.

¶ And if any of those be an open and notorious evill liver,° so that the congregacion by hym is offended, or have doen any wrong to his neighbours, by worde,
or dede: The Curate shall call hym, and advertise hym, in any wise not to
presume to the lordes table, untill he have openly declared hymselfe, to have
truly repented, and amended his former naughtie life: that the congregacion
maie thereby be satisfied, whiche afore were offended: and that he have recompensed the parties, whom he hath dooen wrong unto, or at the least bee in
full purpose so to doo, as sone as he conveniently maie.

¶ The same ordre shall the Curate use, with those betwixt whom he perceiveth
malice, and hatred to reigne, not suffering them to bee partakers of the Lordes
table, untill he knowe them to bee reconciled.° And yf one of the parties so
at variaunce, be content to forgeve from the botome of his harte, all that the
other hath trespaced against hym, and to make amendes for that he hymself
hath offended: and the other partie will not bee perswaded to a godly unitie,
but remaigne still in his frowardnes and malice: The Minister in that case,
ought to admit the penitent persone to the holy Communion, and not hym that
is obstinate.

¶ Upon the daie and at the tyme appoincted for the ministracion of the holy
Communion, the Priest that shal execute the holy ministery, shall put upon
hym the vesture appoincted for that ministracion, that is to saye: a white
Albe plain, with a vestement or Cope.° And where there be many Priestes, or
Decons, there so many shalbe ready to helpe the Priest, in the ministracion, as
shalbee requisite: And shall have upon them lykewise the vestures appointed
for their ministery, that is to saye, Albes, with tunacles. Then shall the Clerkes
syng in Englishe for the office, or Introite, (as they call it) a Psalme appointed
for that daie.

*The Priest standing humbly afore the middes of the Altar,° shall saie the
Lordes praier, with this Collect.°*

ALMIGHTIE God, unto whom all hartes bee open, and all desyres
knowen, and from whom no secretes are hid: clense the thoughtes
of our heartes, by the inspiracion of thy holy spirite: that we may
perfectly love thee, and worthely magnifie thy holy name: Through
Christ our Lorde. Amen.

Then shall he saie a Psalme appointed for the introite:° *whiche Psalme
ended, the Priest shall saye, or els the Clerkes shal syng.*

> Lorde have mercie upon us.°
> Lorde have mercie upon us.
> Lorde have mercie upon us.
>
> Christ have mercie upon us.
> Christ have mercie upon us.
> Christ have mercie upon us.
>
> Lorde have mercie upon us.
> Lorde have mercie upon us.
> Lorde have mercie upon us.

Then the Prieste standyng at Goddes borde° shall begin.

Glory be to God on high.°

The Clerkes.

And in yearth peace, good will towardes men.

We praise thee, we blesse thee, we worship thee, we glorifie thee,
wee geve thankes to thee for thy greate glory, O Lorde GOD heavenly
kyng, God the father almightie.

O Lorde the onely begotten sonne Jesu Christe, O Lorde God,
Lambe of GOD, sonne of the father, that takest awaye the synnes of
the worlde, have mercie upon us: thou that takest awaye the synnes of
the worlde, receive our praier.

Thou that sittest at the right hande of GOD the father, have mercie
upon us: For thou onely art holy, thou onely art the Lorde. Thou
onely (O Christ) with the holy Ghoste, art moste high in the glory of
God the father. Amen.

Then the priest shall turne hym to the people° and saye.

The Lorde be with you.

The Aunswere.

And with thy spirite.

The Priest.

Let us praie.

Then shall folowe the Collect of the daie, with one of these two Collectes folowyng, for the Kyng.°

ALMIGHTIE God, whose kingdom is everlasting, and power infinite, have mercie upon the whole congregacion, and so rule the heart of thy chosen servaunt Edward the sixt, our kyng and governour: that he (knowyng whose minister he is) maie above al thinges, seke thy honour and glory, and that we his subjectes (duely consydering whose auctoritie he hath) maye faithfully serve, honour, and humbly obeye him, in thee, and for thee, according to thy blessed word, and ordinaunce: Through Jesus Christe oure Lorde, who with thee, and the holy ghost, liveth, and reigneth, ever one God, worlde without ende. Amen.

ALMIGHTIE and everlasting GOD, wee bee taught by thy holy worde, that the heartes of Kynges are in thy rule and governaunce, and that thou doest dispose, and turne them as it semeth best to thy godly wisedom: We humbly beseche thee, so to dispose and governe, the hart of Edward the sixt, thy servaunt, our Kyng and governour, that in all his thoughtes, wordes, and workes, he maye ever seke thy honour and glory, and study to preserve thy people, committed to his charge, in wealth, peace, and Godlynes: Graunt this, O mercifull father, for thy dere sonnes sake, Jesus Christ our Lorde. Amen.

The Collectes ended, the priest, or he that is appointed, shall reade the Epistle, in a place assigned for the purpose, saying.

The Epistle of sainct Paule, written in the [   ] Chapiter of [   ] to the [   ].

The Minister then shall reade the epistle. Immediatly after the Epistle ended, the priest, or one appointed to reade the Gospel,° shall saie.

The holy Gospell written in the [   ] Chapiter of [   ].

The Clearkes and people shall aunswere.

Glory be to thee, O Lorde.

The priest or deacon then shall reade the Gospel: after the Gospell ended,
the priest shall begin.

I beleve in one God.°

The clerkes shall syng the rest.

The father almightie, maker of heaven and yearth, and of all thinges visible, and invisible: And in one Lorde Jesu Christ, the onely begotten sonne of GOD, begotten of his father before all worldes, God of GOD, light of light, very God of very God, begotten, not made, beeyng of one substaunce with the father, by whom all thinges were made, who for us men, and for our salvacion, came doune from heaven, and was incarnate by the holy Ghoste, of the Virgin Mary, and was made manne, and was Crucified also for us under Poncius Pilate, he suffered and was buried, and the thirde daye he arose again according to the scriptures, and ascended into heaven, and sitteth at the right hande of the father: And he shall come again with glory, to judge both the quicke and the dead.

And I beleve in the holy ghost, the Lorde and gever of life, who procedeth from the father and the sonne, who with the father and the sonne together, is worshipped and glorified, who spake by the Prophetes. And I beleve one Catholike and Apostolike Churche. I acknowlege one Baptisme, for the remission of synnes. And I loke for the resurreccion of the deade: and the lyfe of the worlde to come. Amen.

After the Crede ended, shall folowe the Sermon or Homely,° or some porcion of
one of the Homelyes,° as thei shalbe herafter devided: wherin if the people
bee not exhorted to the worthy receivyng of the holy Sacrament of the bodye
and bloude of our savior Christ: then shal the Curate geve this exhortacion,°
to those that be minded to receive the same.

DERELY beloved in the Lord, ye that mynde to come to the holy Communion of the bodye and bloude of our savior Christe, must considre what S. Paule writeth to the Corinthians, how he exhorteth all persones diligently to trie and examine themselves, before they presume to eate of that breade, and drinke of that cup: for as the benefite is great, if with a truly penitent heart,° and lively faith, we receive that holy Sacrament: (for then we spiritually eate° the fleshe of Christ, and drinke his bloude, then we dwell in Christ and Christ in us, wee bee made one with Christ, and Christ with us) so is the daunger great, yf wee receyve the same unworthely, for then wee become gyltie of the body and bloud of Christ our savior, we eate

and drinke our owne damnacion, not considering the Lordes bodye.
We kyndle Gods wrathe over us, we provoke him to plague us with
diverse dyseases, and sondery kyndes of death. Therefore if any
here be a blasphemer, advouterer, or bee in malyce or envie, or in
any other grevous cryme (excepte he bee truly sory therefore, and
earnestly mynded to leave the same vices, and do trust him selfe to
bee reconciled to almightie God, and in Charitie with all the worlde)
lette him bewayle his synnes, and not come to that holy table, lest
after the taking of that most blessed breade: the devyll enter into him,
as he dyd into Judas, to fyll him full of all iniquitie, and brynge him
to destruccion, bothe of body and soule. Judge therfore yourselfes
(brethren) that ye bee not judged of the Lorde. Let your mynde be
without desire to synne, repent you truely for your synnes past, have
an earnest and lyvely faith in Christ our savior, be in perfect charitie
with all men, so shall ye be mete partakers of those holy misteries.
And above all thynges: ye must geve moste humble and hartie thankes
to God the father, the sonne, and the holy ghost, for the redempcion
of the worlde, by the death and passion of our savior Christ, both
God and man, who did humble him self even to the death upon the
crosse, for us miserable synners, whiche laie in darknes and shadowe
of death, that he myghte make us the children of God: and exalt us
to everlasting life. And to the end that wee should alwaye remembre
the excedyng love of our master, and onely savior Jesu Christe, thus
diyng for us, and the innumerable benefites (whiche by his precious
bloud shedyng) he hath obteigned to us, he hath lefte in those holy
Misteries, as a pledge of his love, and a continuall remembraunce of
the same his owne blessed body, and precious bloud, for us to fede
upon spiritually, to our endles comfort and consolacion. To him
therfore, with the father and the holy ghost, let us geve (as we are
most bounden) continual thankes, submittyng our selfes wholy to hys
holy wil and pleasure, and studying to serve hym in true holines and
righteousnes, al the daies of our life. Amen.

*In Cathedral churches or other places, where there is dailie Communion, it shall
be sufficient to read this exhortacion above written, once in a moneth. And in
parish churches, upon the weke daies it may be lefte unsayed.*

¶ *And if upon the Sunday or holy daye the people be negligent to come to the
Communion: Then shall the Priest earnestly exhorte his parishoners, to dispose themselfes to the receiving of the holy communion more diligently, saiyng
these or like wordes unto them.*

DERE frendes, and you especially upon whose soules I have cure
and charge, on [   ] next, I do intende by Gods grace, to offre to
all suche as shalbe godlye disposed, the moste comfortable Sacrament
of the body and bloud of Christ, to be taken of them, in the remembraunce of his moste fruitfull and glorious Passyon: by the whiche
passion we have obteigned remission of our synnes, and be made
partakers of the kyngdom of heaven, whereof wee bee assured and
asserteigned, yf wee come to the sayde Sacrament, with hartie repentaunce for our offences, stedfast faithe in Goddes mercye, and earnest
mynde to obeye Goddes will, and to offende no more. Wherefore our
duetie is, to come to these holy misteries, with moste heartie thankes
to bee geven to almightie GOD, for his infinite mercie and benefites
geven and bestowed upon us his unworthye servauntes, for whom he
hath not onely geven his body to death, and shed his bloude, but also
doothe vouchesave in a Sacrament and Mistery, to geve us his sayed
bodye and bloud to feede upon spiritually. The whyche Sacrament
beyng so Divine and holy a thyng, and so comfortable to them whiche
receyve it worthilye, and so daungerous to them that wyll presume to
take the same unworthely: My duetie is to exhorte you in the meane
season, to consider the greatnes of the thing, and to serche and examine your owne consciences, and that not lyghtly nor after the maner of
dissimulers with GOD: But as they whiche shoulde come to a moste
Godly and heavenly Banket, not to come but in the mariage garment
required of God in scripture,° that you may (so muche as lieth in you)
be founde worthie to come to suche a table. The waies and meanes
thereto is.

First, that you be truly repentaunt of your former evill life, and
that you confesse with an unfained hearte to almightie God, youre
synnes and unkyndnes towardes his Majestie committed, either by
will, worde or dede, infirmitie or ignoraunce, and that with inwarde
sorowe and teares you bewaile your offences, and require of almightie
god, mercie, and pardon, promising to him (from the botome of your
hartes) the amendment of your former lyfe. And emonges all others,
I am commaunded of God, especially to move and exhorte you, to
reconcile yourselfes to your neighbors, whom you have offended, or
who hath offended you, putting out of your heartes al hatred and
malice against them, and to be in love and charitie° with all the
worlde, and to forgeve other, as you woulde that god should forgeve
you. And yf any man have doen wrong to any other: let him make

satisfaccion, and due restitucion of all landes and goodes, wrongfully
taken awaye or withholden, before he come to Goddes borde, or at
the least be in ful minde and purpose so to do, assone as he is able,
or els let him not come to this holy table, thinking to deceyve God,
who seeth all mennes hartes. For neither the absolucion of the priest,
can any thing avayle them, nor the receivyng of this holy sacrament
doth any thing but increase their damnacion. And yf there bee any of
you, whose conscience° is troubled and greved in any thing, lackyng
comforte or counsaill, let him come to me, or to some other dyscrete
and learned priest, taught in the law of God, and confesse and open
his synne and griefe secretly, that he may receive suche ghostly counsaill, advyse, and comfort, that his conscience maye be releved, and
that of us (as of the ministers of GOD and of the churche) he may
receive comfort and absolucion, to the satisfaccion of his mynde, and
avoyding of all scruple and doubtfulnes: requiryng suche as shalbe
satisfied with a generall confession, not to be offended with them that
doe use, to their further satisfiyng, the auriculer and secret confession
to the Priest:° nor those also whiche thinke nedefull or convenient,
for the quietnes of their awne consciences, particuliarly to open their
sinnes to the Priest: to bee offended with them that are satisfied, with
their humble confession to GOD, and the generall confession to the
churche. But in all thinges to folowe and kepe the rule of charitie,
and every man to be satisfied with his owne conscience, not judgyng
other mennes myndes or consciences: where as he hath no warrant of
Goddes word to the same.

¶ *Then shall folowe for the Offertory,° one or mo, of these Sentences of holy*
scripture,° to bee song whiles the People doo offer, or els one of them to bee
saied by the minister, immediatly afore the offeryng.

L ET your light so shine before men, that they maye see your good
woorkes, and glorify your father whiche is in heaven.   *Matt.* 5

Laie not up for your selfes treasure upon the yearth, where the rust
and mothe doth corrupt, and where theves breake through and steale:
But laie up for your selfes treasures in heaven, where neyther ruste
nor mothe doth corrupt, and where theves do not breake through nor
steale.   *Matt.* 6

Whatsoever you would that menne should do unto you, even so do
you unto them, for this is the Lawe and the Prophetes.   *Matt.* 7

Not every one that saieth unto me, lorde, lorde, shall entre into the kyngdom of heaven, but he that doth the will of my father whiche is in heaven. *Matt.* 7

Zache stode furthe, and saied unto the Lorde: beholde Lord, the halfe of my goodes I geve to the poore, and if I have doen any wrong to any man, I restore foure fold. *Luke* 19

Who goeth a warfare at any tyme at his owne cost? who planteth a vineyarde, and eateth not of the fruite thereof? Or who fedeth a flocke, and eateth not of the milke of the flocke? 1 *Cor.* 9

If we have sowen unto you spirituall thinges, is it a great matter yf we shall reape your worldly thynges? 1 *Cor.* 9

Dooe ye not knowe, that they whiche minister aboute holy thinges, lyve of the Sacrifice? They whiche waite of the alter, are partakers with the alter? even so hath the lorde also ordained: that they whiche preache the Gospell, should lyve of the Gospell. 1 *Cor.* 9

He whiche soweth litle, shall reape litle, and he that soweth plenteously, shall reape plenteously. Let every manne do accordyng as he is disposed in his hearte, not grudgyngly, or of necessitie, for God loveth a cherefull gever. 2 *Cor.* 9

Let him that is taught in the woorde, minister unto hym that teacheth, in all good thinges. Be not deceived, GOD is not mocked. For whatsoever a man soweth, that shall he reape. *Gal.* 6

While we have tyme, let us do good unto all men, and specially unto them, whiche are of the housholde of fayth. *Gal.* 6

Godlynes is greate riches, if a man be contented with that he hath: For we brought nothing into the worlde, neither maie we cary any thing out. 1 *Tim.* 6

Charge them whiche are riche in this worlde, that they bee ready to geve, and glad to distribute, laying up in stoare for themselfes a good foundacion, against the time to come, that they maie attain eternall lyfe. 1 *Tim.* 6

GOD is not unrighteous, that he will forget youre woorkes and labor, that procedeth of love, whiche love ye have shewed for his names sake, whiche have ministred unto the sainctes, and yet do minister. *Heb.* 6

To do good, and to distribute, forget not, for with suche Sacrifices God is pleased. *Heb.* 13

Whoso hath this worldes good, and seeth his brother have nede, and shutteth up his compassion from hym, how dwelleth the love of God in him? 1 *John* 3

Geve almose of thy goodes, and turne never thy face from any

poore man, and then the face of the lorde shall not be turned awaye
from thee.   *Tob.* 4

Bee mercifull after thy power: if thou hast muche, geve plenteously,
if thou hast litle, do thy diligence gladly to geve of that litle: for so
gathereste thou thy selfe a good reward, in the daie of necessitie.

Tob. 4

He that hath pitie upon the poore, lendeth unto the Lorde: and
loke what he laieth out, it shalbe paied hym again.   *Prov.* 19

Blessed be the man that provideth for the sicke and nedy, the lorde
shall deliver hym, in the tyme of trouble.   *Ps.* 41

*Where there be Clerkes, thei shall syng one, or many of the sentences above
written, accordyng to the length and shortenesse of the tyme, that the people
be offeryng.*

*In the meane time, whyles the Clerkes do syng the Offertory, so many as are
disposed, shall offer unto the poore mennes boxe° every one accordynge to
his habilitie and charitable mynde. And at the offeryng daies appointed:
every manne and woman shall paie to the Curate, the due and accustomed
offerynges.*

*Then so manye as shalbe partakers of the holy Communion, shall tary still in
the quire, or in some convenient place nigh the quire, the men on the one side,
and the women on the other syde.° All other (that mynde not to receive the
said holy Communion) shall departe out of the quire, except the ministers and
Clerkes.*

*Than shall the minister take so muche Bread and Wine, as shall suffice for the
persons appoynted to receive the holy Communion, laiyng the breade upon the
corporas,° or els in the paten,° or in some other comely thyng, prepared for
that purpose. And puttyng the wyne into the Chalice, or els in some faire or
conveniente cup, prepared for that use (if the Chalice wil not serve) puttyng
therto a litle pure and cleane water: And settyng both the breade and wyne
upon the Alter: Then the Prieste shall saye.*

The Lorde be with you.
Aunswere. And with thy spirite.
Priest. Lift up your heartes.°
Aunswere. We lift them up unto the Lorde.
Priest. Let us geve thankes to our Lorde God.
Aunswere. It is mete and right so to do.

The Priest.

IT is very mete, righte, and our bounden dutie that wee shoulde at all
tymes, and in all places, geve thankes to thee, O Lorde, holy father,
almightie everlastyng God.

¶ *Here shall folowe the proper preface, accordyng to the tyme (if there bee
any specially appoynted) or els immediatly shall folowe. Therefore with
Angelles. &c.*

PROPRE
Prefaces.°

¶ *Upon Christmas Daie.*

BECAUSE thou diddeste geve Jesus Christe, thyne onely sonne, to
bee borne as this daye for us, who by the operacion of the holy
ghoste, was made very man, of the substaunce of the Virgin Mari his
mother, and that without spot of sinne, to make us cleane from all
synne. Therefore &c.

¶ *Upon Easter daie.*

BUT chiefly are we bound to praise thee, for the glorious resurreccion of thy sonne Jesus Christe, our Lorde, for he is the very
Pascall Lambe, whiche was offered for us, and hath taken awaie the
synne of the worlde, who by his death hath destroyed death, and
by his risyng to life againe, hath restored to us everlastynge life.
Therefore &c.

¶ *Upon the Assencion Day.*

THROUGH thy most dere beloved sonne, Jesus Christ our Lorde,
who after his moste glorious resurreccion, manifestly appered to
all his disciples, and in their sight ascended up into heaven, to prepare a place for us, that where he is, thither mighte we also ascende,
and reigne with hym in glory. Therfore &c.

¶ *Upon Whitsondaye.*

THROUGH Jesus Christe our Lorde, accordyng to whose moste
true promise, the holy Ghoste came doune this daye from heaven,
with a sodain great sound, as it had been a mightie wynde, in the
likenes of fiery toungues, lightyng upon the Apostles, to teache them,
and to leade them to all trueth, gevyng them bothe the gifte of diverse
languages, and also boldnes with fervent zeale, constantly to preache

the Gospell unto all nacions, whereby we are brought out of darkenes and error, into the cleare light and true knowlege of thee, and of thy sonne Jesus Christ. Therfore &c.

¶ *Upon the feast of the Trinitie.*

IT is very meete, righte, and oure bounden duetie, that we should at al tymes, and in al places, geve thankes to thee O Lorde, almightye everlasting God, whiche arte one God, one Lorde, not one onely person, but three persones in one substaunce: For that which we beleve of the glory of the father, the same we beleve of the sonne, and of the holy ghost, without any difference, or inequalitie: whom the Angels &c.

After whiche preface shall folowe immediatly.

Therfore with Angels and Archangels, and with all the holy companye of heaven: we laude and magnify thy glorious name, evermore praisyng thee, and saying:

¶ Holy, holy, holy,° Lorde God of Hostes: heaven & earth are full of thy glory: Osanna in the highest.° Blessed is he° that commeth in the name of the Lorde: Glory to thee O lorde in the highest.

This the Clerkes shall also syng.

¶ *When the Clerkes have dooen syngyng, then shall the Priest, or Deacon, turne hym to the people and saye.*

Let us praie for the whole state of Christes churche.

¶ *Then the Priest turnyng hym to the Altar, shall saye or syng,° playnly and distinctly, this prayer folowyng.*

ALMIGHTIE and everlivyng GOD, whiche by thy holy Apostle haste taught us to make prayers and supplicacions, and to geve thankes for al menne: We humbly beseche thee moste mercyfully to receive these our praiers, which we offre unto thy divine Majestie, beseching thee to inspire continually the universal churche, with the spirite of trueth, unitie, and concorde: And graunt that al they that do confesse thy holy name, maye agree in the trueth of thy holye worde, and live in unitie and godly love. Speciallye we beseche thee to save and defende thy servaunt, Edwarde our Kyng, that under hym we maye be Godly and quietly governed. And graunt unto his whole counsaile, and to all that he put in aucthoritie under hym, that they maye truely and indifferently minister justice, to the punishemente of wickednesse and vice, and to the maintenaunce of Goddes true religion and vertue. Geve grace (O hevenly father) to all Bishoppes, Pastors, and Curates, that thei maie bothe by their life and doctrine, set furthe thy true and lively worde, and rightely and duely administer thy holy Sacramentes, and to al thy people geve thy heavenly grace, that with meke heart and due reverence they may heare and receive thy holy worde, truely servyng thee in holynes and righteousness, all the dayes of their life: And we most humbly beseche thee of thy goodnes (O Lorde) to coumfort and succour all them, whyche in thys transytory life be in trouble, sorowe, nede, syckenes, or any other adversitie. And especially we commend unto thy mercifull goodnes, this congregacion which is here assembled in thy name, to celebrate the commemoracion° of the most glorious death of thy sonne: And here we do geve unto thee moste high praise, and hartie thankes for the wonderfull grace and vertue, declared in all thy sainctes,° from the begynning of the worlde: And chiefly in the glorious and moste blessed virgin Mary, mother of thy sonne Jesu Christe our Lorde and God, and in the holy Patriarches, Prophetes, Apostles and Martyrs, whose examples (O Lorde) and stedfastnes in thy fayth, and kepyng thy holy commaundementes, graunt us to folowe. We commend unto thy mercye (O Lorde) all other thy servauntes, which are departed° hence from us, with the signe of faith, and nowe do reste in the slepe of peace: Graunt unto them, we beseche thee, thy mercy, and everlasting peace, and that at the day of the generall resurreccion, we and all they which bee of the misticall body of thy sonne, may altogether be set on his right hand, and heare that his most ioyfull voyce: Come unto me, O ye that be blessed of my father, and possesse the kingdom, whiche is prepared for you, from the begynning of the worlde: Graunt this, O father, for Jesus Christes sake, our onely mediatour and advocate.

O God heavenly father, which of thy tender mercie, diddest geve thine only sonne Jesu Christ, to suffre death upon the crosse for our redempcion, who made there (by his one oblacion once offered) a full, perfect, and sufficient sacrifyce, oblacion, and satysfaccyon,° for the sinnes of the whole worlde, and did institute, and in his holy Gospell commaund us, to celebrate a perpetuall memory of that his precious death, untyll his comming again: Heare us (o merciful father) we besech thee: and with thy holy spirite and worde, vouchsafe to bl✠esse and sanc✠tifie° these thy gyftes, and creatures of bread and wyne, that they maie be unto us the bodye and bloude of thy moste derely beloved sonne Jesus Christe.

Who in the same nyght that he was betrayed: tooke
breade, and when he had blessed, and geven thankes:
he brake it, and gave it to his disciples, saiyng: Take,
eate, this is my bodye which is geven for you, do this in
remembraunce of me.

*Here the priest
must take the
bread into his
handes.°*

Likewyse after supper he toke the cuppe, and when
he had geven thankes, he gave it to them, saiyng:
drynk ye all of this, for this is my bloude of the newe
Testament, whyche is shed for you and for many, for
remission of synnes: do this as oft as you shall drinke it in remembraunce of me.

*Here the priest
shall take the
Cuppe into his
handes.*

*These wordes before rehersed are to be saied, turning still to the Altar,
without any elevacion, or shewing the Sacrament to the people.°*

WHERFORE, O Lorde and heavenly father, accordyng to the
Instytucyon° of thy derely beloved sonne, our saviour Jesu
Christ, we thy humble servauntes do celebrate, and make here before
thy divine Majestie, with these thy holy giftes, the memoryall whyche
thy sonne hath wylled us to make, havyng in remembraunce his
blessed passion, mightie resurreccyon, and gloryous ascencion, ren-
deryng unto thee most hartie thankes, for the innumerable benefites
procured unto us by the same, entierely desiryng thy fatherly goodnes,
mercifully to accepte this our Sacrifice of praise and thankes geving:
most humbly besechyng thee to graunt, that by the merites and death
of thy sonne Jesus Christ, and through faith in his bloud, we and al
thy whole church, may obteigne remission of our sinnes, and all other
benefites of hys passyon. And here wee offre and present unto thee (O
Lorde) oure selfe, oure soules, and bodies, to be a reasonable, holy,
and lively sacrifice unto thee: humbly besechyng thee, that whosoever
shalbee partakers of thys holy Communion, maye worthely receive
the most precious body and bloude of thy sonne Jesus Christe: and
bee fulfilled with thy grace and heavenly benediccion, and made one
bodye with thy sonne Jesu Christe, that he maye dwell in them, and
they in hym. And although we be unworthy (through our manyfolde
synnes) to offre unto thee any Sacryfice: Yet we besech thee to
accepte thys our bounden duetie and service, and commaunde these
our prayers and supplicacions, by the Ministery of thy holy Angels,
to be brought up into thy holy Tabernacle° before the syght of thy
dyvine majestie: not waiyng our merites, but pardonyng our offences,

through Christe our Lorde, by whome, and with whome, in the unitie of the holy Ghost, all honour and glory, be unto thee, O father almightie, world without ende. Amen.

Let us praye.

A S our saviour Christe hath commaunded and taught us, we are bolde to saye. Our father whyche art in heaven, halowed be thy name. Thy Kyngdome come. Thy wyll be doen in yearth, as it is in heaven. Geve us this daye our dayly breade. And forgeve us our trespaces, as wee forgeve them that trespasse agaynst us. And leade us not into temptacion.

The aunswere. But deliver us from evill. Amen.

Then shall the priest saye.

The peace of the Lorde be alwaye with you.
The Clerkes. And with thy spirite.

The Priest.

C HRIST our Pascall lambe is offred up for us, once for al, when he bare our sinnes on hys body upon the crosse, for he is the very lambe of God, that taketh away the sinnes of the worlde: wherfore let us kepe a joyfull and holy feast with the Lorde.

Here the priest shall turne hym toward those that come to the holy Comniunion, and shall saye.

Y OU that do truly and earnestly repent you of your synnes to almightie God, and be in love and charitie with your neighbors, and entende to lede a newe life, folowyng the commaundementes of God, and walkyng from hencefurth in his holy wayes: drawe nere and take this holy Sacrament to your comforte, make your humble confession to almightie God, and to his holy church here gathered together in hys name, mekely knelyng upon your knees.

Then shall thys generall Confession° bee made, in the name of al those that are minded to receive the holy Communion, eyther by one of them, or els by one of the ministers, or by the prieste hymselfe, all kneling humbly upon their knees.

A LMYGHTIE GOD, father of oure Lord Jesus Christ, maker of all thynges, judge of all men, we knowlege and bewaile our manyfold synnes and wyckednes,° which we from tyme to tyme, most grevously have committed, by thought, word and dede,° agaynst thy divine majestie, provokyng moste justly thy wrath and indignacion against us, we do earnestly repent and be hartely sory for these our misdoinges, the remembraunce of them is grevous unto us, the burthen of them is intollerable: have mercye upon us, have mercie upon us, moste mercifull father, for thy sonne our Lorde Jesus Christes sake, forgeve us all that is past, and graunt that we may ever hereafter, serve and please thee in newnes of life, to the honor and glory of thy name: Through Jesus Christe our Lorde.

Then shall the Prieste stande up, and turnyng himselfe to the people, say thus.

ALMIGHTIE GOD our heavenly father, who of his great mercie, hath promysed forgevenesse of synnes to all them, whiche with hartye repentaunce and true fayth, turne unto him: have mercy upon you, pardon and delyver you from all youre sinnes, confirme and strengthen you in all goodnes, and bring you to everlasting lyfe: through Jesus Christ our Lord. Amen.

Then shall the Priest also say.

Heare what coumfortable woordes° our saviour Christ sayeth, to all that truely turne to him.

Come unto me all that travell and bee heavy laden, and I shall refreshe you. So God loved the worlde that he gave his onely begotten sonne, to the ende that al that beleve in hym, shoulde not perishe, but have lyfe everlasting.

Heare also what saint Paul sayeth.

This is a true saying, and woorthie of all men to bee received, that Jesus Christe came into thys worlde to save sinners.

Heare also what saint John sayeth.

If any man sinne, we have an advocate with the father, Jesus Christ the righteous, and he is the propiciacion for our sinnes.

Then shall the Priest, turnyng him to gods boord, knele down,° and say in the name of all them, that shall receyve the Communion, this prayer folowing.

WE do not presume° to come to this thy table (o mercifull lord) trusting in our owne righteousnes, but in thy manifold and great mercies: we be not woorthie so much as to gather up the cromes under thy table, but thou art the same lorde whose propertie is always to have mercie: Graunt us therefore (gracious lorde) so to eate the fleshe of thy dere sonne Jesus Christ, and to drynke his bloud in these holy Misteries, that we may continuallye dwell in hym, and he in us,° that oure synfull bodyes may bee made cleane by his body, and our soules washed through hys most precious bloud. Amen.

¶ *Then shall the Prieste firste receive the Communion in both kindes° himselfe, and next deliver it to other Ministers, if any be there presente (that they may bee ready to helpe the chiefe Minister) and after to the people.*

¶ *And when he delivereth the Sacramente of the body of Christe, he shall say to every one these woordes.*

The body of our Lorde Jesus Christe whiche was geven for thee, preserve thy bodye and soule unto everlasting lyfe.°

And the Minister delivering the Sacrament of the bloud, and geving every one to drinke once and no more, shall say.

The bloud of our Lorde Jesus Christe which was shed for thee, preserve thy bodye and soule unto everlastyng lyfe.

If there be a Deacon or other Priest, then shal he folow with the Chalice: and as the priest ministereth the Sacrament of the body, so shal he (for more expedicion) minister the Sacrament of the bloud, in fourme before written.

In the Communion tyme the Clarkes shall syng.

O lambe of god,° that takeste away the sinnes of the worlde: have mercie upon us.

O lambe of god, that takeste away the sinnes of the worlde: have mercie upon us.

O lambe of god, that takeste away the synnes of the worlde: graunt us thy peace.

Beginning so soone as the Prieste doeth receyve the holy Communion: and when the Communion is ended, then shall the Clarkes syng the post Communion.°

¶ *Sentences of holy Scripture, to be sayd or song every daye one, after the holy Communion, called the post Communion.*

If any man will folowe me, let him forsake hymselfe, and take up his crosse and folowe me. *Matt.* 16

Whosoever shall indure unto the ende, he shalbe saved. *Mark* 13

Praysed be the Lorde god of Israell, for he hath visited and redemed hys people: therefore let us serve hym all the dayes of our lyfe, in holines and righteousnes accepted before hym. *Luke* 1

Happie are those servauntes, whome the Lord (when he cummeth) shall fynde waking. *Luke* 12

Be ye readye, for the sonne of manne will come, at an hower when ye thinke not.   *Luke* 12

The servaunte that knoweth hys maisters will, and hath not prepared himself, neither hath doen according to his will, shalbe beaten with many stripes.   *Luke* 12

The howre cummeth and now it is, when true woorshippers shall wurship the father in spirite and trueth.   *John* 4

Beholde, thou art made whole, sinne no more, lest any wurse thing happen unto thee.   *John* 5

If ye shall continue in my woorde, then are ye my very disciples, and ye shall knowe the truth, and the truth shall make you free.   *John* 8

While ye have lighte, beleve on the lyght, that ye may be the children of light.   *John* 12

He that hath my commaundementes, and kepeth them, the same is he that loveth me.   *John* 14

If any man love me, he will kepe my woorde, and my father will love hym, and wee will come unto hym, and dwell with hym.   *John* 14

If ye shall byde in me, and my woorde shall abyde in you, ye shall aske what ye will, and it shall bee doen to you.   *John* 15

Herein is my father gloryfyed, that ye beare much fruite, and become my disciples.   *John* 15

This is my commaundement, that you love together as I have loved you.   *John* 15

If God be on our syde, who can be agaynst us? which did not spare his owne sonne, but gave him for us all.   *Rom.* 8

Who shall lay any thing to the charge of Goddes chosen? it is GOD that justifyeth, who is he that can condemne?   *Rom.* 8

The nyght is passed, and the day is at hande, let us therfore cast away the dedes of darkenes, and put on the armour of light. *Rom.* 13

Christe Jesus is made of GOD, unto us wisedome, and righteousnes, and sanctifying, and redempcion, that (according as it is written) he whiche rejoyceth shoulde rejoyce in the Lorde.   1 *Cor.* 1

Knowe ye not that ye are the temple of GOD, and that the spirite of GOD dwelleth in you? If any manne defile the temple of GOD, him shall God destroy.   1 *Cor.* 3

Ye are derely bought, therfore glorifye God in your bodies, and in your spirites, for they belong to God.   1 *Cor.* 6

Be you folowers of God as deare children, and walke in love, even as

Christe loved us, and gave hymselfe for us an offeryng and a Sacrifyce of a sweete savoure to God. *Eph.* 5

Then the Priest shall geve thankes to God, in the name af all them that have communicated, turning him first to the people, and saying.

The Lorde be with you.
The aunswere. And with thy spirite.
The priest. Let us pray.

ALMIGHTYE and everlyvyng GOD,° we moste hartely thanke thee, for that thou hast vouchsafed to feede us in these holy Misteries, with the spirituall foode of the moste precious body and bloud of thy sonne, our saviour Jesus Christ, and haste assured us (duely receiving the same) of thy favour and goodnes toward us, and that we be very membres incorporate in thy Misticall bodye,° whiche is the blessed companye of all faythfull people: and heyres through hope of thy everlasting kingdome, by the merites of the most precious death and passion, of thy deare sonne. We therfore most humbly beseche thee, O heavenly father, so to assist us with thy grace, that we may continue in that holy felowship, and doe all suche good woorkes, as thou hast prepared for us to walke in, through Jesus Christe our Lorde, to whome with thee, and the holy goste, bee all honour and glory, world without ende.

Then the Priest turning hym to the people, shall let them depart with this blessing.

The peace of GOD° (which passeth all understanding) kepe your heartes and mindes in the knowledge and love of GOD, and of hys sonne Jesus Christe our lorde: And the blessing of God almightie, the father, the sonne, and the holy gost, be emonges you, and remayne with you alway.

Then the people shall aunswere.

Amen.

Where there are no clerkes, there the Priest shall say al thinges appoynted here for them to sing.

When the holy Communion is celebrate on the workeday, or in private howses: Then may be omitted, the Gloria in excelsis, the Crede, the Homily, and the exhortacion, beginning.

Dearely beloved, &c.

¶ *Collectes to bee sayed after the Offertory,° when there is no Communion, every such day one.*

ASSIST us mercifully, O Lord, in these our supplicacions and praiers, and dispose the way of thy servauntes, toward the attainement of everlasting salvacion, that emong all the chaunges and chaunces of thys mortall lyfe, they maye ever bee defended by thy moste gracious and readye helpe: throughe Christe our Lorde. Amen.

O ALMIGHTIE Lorde and everlyvyng GOD, vouchesafe, we beseche thee, to direct, sanctifye, and governe, both our heartes and bodies, in the wayes of thy lawes, and in the workes of thy commaundementes: that through thy most mightie proteccion, both here and ever, we may be preserved in body and soule: Through our Lorde and saviour Jesus Christ. Amen.

GRAUNT we beseche thee almightie god, that the wordes whiche we have hearde this day with our outwarde eares, may throughe thy grace, bee so grafted inwardly in our heartes, that they may bring foorth in us the fruite of good living, to the honour and prayse of thy name: Through Jesus Christe our Lorde. Amen.

PREVENT us, O lorde, in all our doinges, with thy most gracious favour, and further us with thy continuall helpe, that in al our woorkes begonne, continued and ended in thee: we may glorifye thy holy name, and finally by thy mercy obteine everlasting life. Through &c.

ALMIGHTIE God, the fountayn of all wisdome, which knowest our necessities beefore we aske, and our ignoraunce in asking: we beseche thee to have compassion upon our infirmities, and those thynges whiche for our unwoorthines we dare not, and for our blindnes we can not aske, vouchsave to geve us for the woorthines of thy sonne Jesu Christ our Lorde. Amen.

ALMIGHTIE god, which hast promised to heare the peticions of them that aske in thy sonnes name, we beseche thee mercifully to inclyne thyne eares to us that have made nowe our prayers and supplicacions unto thee, and graunte that those thynges whiche we have faythfullye asked accordyng to thy will, maye effectually bee obteyned to the reliefe of oure necessitye, and to the settyng foorth of thy glorye: Through Jesus Christ our Lorde.

For rayne.°

O GOD heavenly father, whiche by thy sonne Jesu Christ, hast promised to al them that seke thy kingdom, and the righteousnes therof, al thinges necessary to the bodely sustenaunce: send us (we beseche thee) in this our necessitie, such moderate rayne and showers, that we may receive the fruites of the earth, to our comfort and to thy honor: Through Jesus Christ our Lord.

For fayre wether.

O LORDE God, whiche for the sinne of manne, didst once drowne all the worlde, except eight persons, and afterwarde of thy great mercye, didste promise never to destroy it so agayn: We humbly beseche thee, that although we for oure iniquities have woorthelye deserved this plague of rayne and waters, yet upon our true repentaunce, thou wilt sende us suche wether wherby we may receive the fruites of the earth in due season, and learne both by thy punishment to amende our lives, and by the graunting of our peticion, to geve thee prayse and glory: Through Jesu Christ our Lorde.

¶ *Upon wednesdaies and frydaies, the English Letany shalbe said or song in all places, after suche forme as is appoynted by the kynges majesties Injunccions:° Or as is or shal bee otherwyse appoynted by his highnes. And thoughe there be none to communicate with the Prieste, yet these dayes (after the Letany ended) the Priest shall put upon him a playn Albe or surplesse, with a cope, and say al thinges at the Altar (appoynted to be sayde at the celebracyon of the lordes supper) untill after the offertory. And then shall adde one or two of the Collectes aforewritten, as occasion shall serve by his discrecion. And then turning him to the people shall let them depart with the accustomed blessing.*

And the same order shall be used all other dayes whensoever the people be customably assembled to pray in the churche, and none disposed to communicate with the Priest.

Lykewyse in Chapelles annexed,° and all other places, there shalbe no celebracion of the Lordes supper, except there be some to communicate with the Priest. And in suche Chapelles annexed where the people hath not bene accustomed to pay any holy bread, there they must either make some charitable provision for the bering of the charges of the Communion, or elles (for receyvying of the same) resort to theyr Parish Churche.

For advoyding of all matters and occasyon of dyscencyon, it is mete that the breade prepared for the Communion,° bee made, through all thys realme, after one sort and fashion: that is to say, unleavened, and rounde, as it was

afore, but without all maner of printe, and somethyng more larger and thicker
then it was, so that it may be aptly devided in divers pieces: and every one
shall be devided in two pieces, at the leaste, or more, by the discrecion of the
minister, and so distributed. And menne muste not thynke lesse to be receyved
in parte then in the whole, but in eache of them the whole body of our sæviour
Jesu Christ.°

And forsomuche as the Pastours and Curates within thys realme, shal continually fynd at theyr costes and charges in theyr cures, sufficient Breade and
Wyne for the holy Communion (as oft as theyr Parishioners shalbe disposed
for theyr spiritual comfort to receyve the same) it is therefore ordred, that in
recompence of suche costes and charges, the Parishioners of everye Parishe
shall offer every Sonday, at the tyme of the Offertory, the juste valour and
price of the holy lofe° (with all suche money, and other thinges as were wont
to be offered with the same) to the use of theyr Pastours and Curates, and
that in suche ordre and course, as they were woont to fynde and pay the sayd
holy lofe.

Also, that the receiving of the Sacrament of the blessed body and bloud of Christ,
may be most agreable to the institucion thereof, and to the usage of the prima-
tive Churche: In all Cathedrall and Collegiate Churches,° there shal alwaies
some Communicate with the Prieste that ministreth. And that the same may
bee also observed every where abrode in the countrey: Some one at the least
of that house in every Parishe to whome by course after the ordinaunce
herein made, it apperteyneth to offer for the charges of the Communion, or
some other whom they shall provide to offer for them, shall receive the holy
Communion with the Prieste: the whiche may be the better doen, for that
they knowe before, when theyr course commeth, and maie therfore dispose
themselves to the worthie receivyng of the Sacramente. And with hym or
them who doeth so offre the charges of the Communion: all other, who be
then Godly disposed thereunto, shall lykewyse receive the Communion. And
by this meanes the Minister hævyng alwaies some to communicate with him,
maie accordingly solempnise so high and holy misteries, with all the suffrages
and due ordre appoynted for the same. And the Priest on the weke daie, shall
forbeare to celebrate the Communion, excepte he have some that will communicate with hym.

Furthermore, every man and woman to be bound to heare and be at the divine
service, in the Parishe churche where they be resident, and there with devout
prayer, or Godlye silence and meditacion, to occupie themselves. There to
paie their dueties, to communicate once in the yeare at the least,° and there to
receyve, and take all other Sacramentes and rites, in this booke appoynted.
And whosoever willyngly upon no just cause, doeth absent themselves, or
doeth ungodly in the Parishe churche occupie themselves: upon profe therof,

*by the Ecelesiasticall lawes of the Realme to bee excommunicate, or suffre
other punishement, as shall to the Ecclesiastical judge (accordyng to his discrecion) seme convenient.*

*And although it bee redde in aunciente writers, that the people many yeares
past, received at the priestes handes, the Sacrament of the body of Christ in
theyr owne handes,° and no commaundement of Christ to the contrary: Yet
forasmuche as they many tymes conveyghed the same secretelye awaye, kept
it with them, and diversly abused it to supersticion and wickednes: lest any
suche thynge hereafter should be attempted, and that an uniformitie might
be used, throughoute the whole Realme: it is thought convenient the people
commonly receive the Sacrament of Christes body, in their mouthes, at the
Priestes hande.*

❧ The Letany and Suffrages.

O GOD the father of heaven: have mercy upon us° miserable synners.

O God the father of heaven: have mercy upon us miserable sinners.

O God the sonne, redemer of the world: have mercy upon us miserable sinners.

O God the sonne, redemer of the world: have mercy upon us miserable sinners.

O God the holy ghoste, procedyng from the father and the sonne: have mercy upon us miserable sinners.

O God the holy ghost, procedyng from the father and the sonne: have mercy upon us miserable sinners.

O holy, blessed, and glorious Trinitie,° three persons and one God: have mercye upon us miserable synners.

O holy, blessed, and glorious Trinitie, three persons and one God: have mercye upon us miserable synners.

Remember not lorde, our offences, nor the offences of our forefathers, neither take thou vengeaunce of our sinnes: spare us good lord, spare thy people, whom thou hast redemed with thy moost precious bloude, and be not angry with us for ever:

Spare us good Lorde.

From al evill and mischiefe,° from synne, from the craftes and assaultes of the devyll, from thy wrathe, and from everlastyng damnacion:

Good lorde deliver us.°

From blyndnes of heart, from pryde, vainglory, and Hypocrisy, from envy, hatred, and malice, and all uncharitablenes:

Good lorde deliver us.

From fornicacion, and all other deadlye synne, and from al the deceytes of the worlde, the fleshe, and the devill:

Good lorde deliver us.

From lightning and tempest, from plage, pestilence and famine, from battaile and murther, and from sodain death:

Good lorde deliver us.

From all sedicion and privye conspiracie, from the tyrannye of the bishop of Rome and all his detestable enormities,° from al false doctrine and herisy, from hardnes of heart, and contempte of thy word and commaundemente:

Good lorde deliver us.

By the mistery of thy holy incarnacion, by thy holy Nativitie and Circumcision, by thy Baptisme, fastyng, and temptacion:

Good lorde deliver us.

By thyne agony and bloudy sweate, by thy crosse and passion, by thy precious death and burial, by thy glorious resurreccion and ascencion, by the comming of the holy gost:

Good lorde deliver us.

In all tyme of our tribulacion, in all time of our wealth, in the houre of death, in the daye of judgement:

Good lorde deliver us.

We synners do beseche thee to heare us (O Lorde God) and that it maye please thee to rule and govern thy holy Churche universall in the right waye:

We beseche thee to heare us good lorde.

That it maye please thee to kepe Edward the .vi.° thy servaunt our kyng and governour:

We beseche thee to heare us good lorde.

That it maye please thee to rule his heart in thy faythe, feare, and love, that he maye alwayes have affiaunce in thee, and ever seke thy honour and glory:

We beseche thee to heare us good lorde.

That it maye please thee to be his defendour and keper, gevyng hym the victorye over all his enemyes:

We beseche thee to heare us good lorde.

That it maye please thee to illuminate all Bishops, pastours and ministers of the churche, with true knowlege and understandyng of thy word, and that bothe by theyr preachyng and living, they maye set it foorth and shewe it accordyngly:

We beseche thee to heare us good lorde.

That it may please thee to endue the Lordes of the counsaile, and all the nobilitie, with grace, wisedome, and understandyng:

We beseche thee to heare us good lorde.

That it may please thee to blesse and kepe the magistrates, gevyng them grace to execute justice, and to mayntayne trueth:

We beseche thee to heare us good lorde.

That it may please thee to blesse and kepe al thy people:

We beseche thee to heare us good lorde.

That it may please thee to geve to all nacions unitie, peace, and concorde:

We beseche thee to heare us good lorde.

That it may please thee to geve us an heart to love and dread thee, and diligently to lyve after thy commaundementes:

We beseche thee to heare us good lorde.

That it may please thee to geve all thy people increase of grace, to heare mekely thy worde, and to receyve it with pure affeccion, and to bryng forth the fruites of the spirite:

We beseche thee to heare us good lorde.

That it may please thee to bryng into the way of trueth all suche as have erred and are deceyved:

We beseche thee to heare us good lorde.

That it may please thee to strengthen suche as do stand, and to comfort and helpe the weake hearted, and to raise up them that fall, and finally to beate downe Sathan under our feete:

We beseche thee to heare us good lorde.

That it may please thee to succoure, helpe, and comfort all that be in daunger, necessitie, and tribulacion:

We beseche thee to heare us good lorde.

That it may please thee to preserve all that travayle by lande or by water, all women labouryng of chylde, all sicke persons and yong chyldren, and to shewe thy pytie upon all prisoners and captyves:

We beseche thee to heare us good lorde.

That it may please thee to defende and provide for the fatherles children and wyddowes, and all that be desolate and oppressed:

We beseche thee to heare us good lorde.

That it may please thee to have mercy upon all menne:

We beseche thee to heare us good lorde.

That it may please thee to forgeve our enemies, persecutours, and sclaunderers, and to turne their heartes:

We beseche thee to heare us good lorde.

That it may please thee to geve and preserve to our use the kyndly fruytes of the earth, so as in due tyme we may enjoy them:

We beseche thee to heare us good lorde.

That it may please thee to geve us true repentaunce, to forgeve us all our synnes, negligences, and ignoraunces, and to endue us with the grace of thy holy spirite, to amende our lyves accordyng to thy holy worde:

> *We beseche thee to heare us good lorde.*

Sonne of God: we beseche thee to heare us.

> *Sonne of God: we beseche thee to heare us.*

O lambe of God, that takest away the sinnes of the world:

> *Graunt us thy peace.*

O lambe of God, that takest away the sinnes of the world:

> *Have mercy upon us.*

O Christe heare us.

> *O Christe heare us.*

Lorde have mercy upon us.

> *Lorde have mercy upon us.*

Christe have mercy upon us.

> *Christe have mercy upon us.*

Lorde have mercy upon us.

> *Lorde have mercy upon us.*

Our father whiche art in heaven. [*With the residue of the Pater noster.*] And leade us not into temptacion.

> *But deliver us from evyll.*

The versicle. O Lorde, deale not with us after our synnes.

The aunswere. Neither rewarde us after our iniquities.

Let us praye.

O GOD mercifull father, that despisest not the syghyng of a contrite heart, nor the desire of such as be sorowfull, mercifully assyste our prayers, that we make before thee in all our troubles and adversities, when soever they oppresse us: And graciousely heare us, that those evyls, whiche the crafte and subteltie of the devyll or man worketh against us, be brought to nought, and by the providence of thy goodnes, they maye be dyspersed, that we thy servauntes, beyng hurte by no persecucions, maye evermore geve thankes unto thee, in thy holy churche, thorough Jesu Christe our Lorde.

> *O Lorde, aryse, helpe us, and delyver us for thy names sake.*

O God, we have heard with our eares,° and our fathers have declared unto us the noble workes that thou dyddest in theyr dayes, and in the olde tyme before them.

> *O Lorde, aryse, helpe us, and deliver us for thy honour.*

Glory be to the father, the sonne, and to the holy ghoste, as it was

in the begynning, is nowe, and ever shall be worlde with out ende.
Amen.

From our enemies defende us, O Chryste.

Graciously loke upon our afflyctions.

Pytifully beholde the sorowes of our heart.

Mercifully forgeve the synnes of thy people.

Favourably with mercy heare our prayers.

O sonne of David have mercy upon us.

Both nowe and ever vouchsafe to here us Christe.

Graciousely heare us, O Christ.

Graciousely heare us, O lord Christ.

The versicle. O Lorde, let thy mercy be shewed upon us.

The Aunswere. As we do put our truste in thee.

Let us praye.

WE humbly beseche thee,° O father, mercifully to loke upon our
infirmities, and for the glory of thy name sake, turne from us
all those evilles that we moste righteously have deserved: and graunte
that in all oure troubles we maye put our whole trust and confidence
in thy mercy, and evermore serve thee in purenes of livyng, to thy
honour and glory: through our onely mediator and advocate Jesus
Christ our Lorde. Amen.

ALMIGHTIE God, whiche hast geven us grace at this tyme
with one accorde to make our commune supplicacions
unto thee, and doest promise, that whan two or three
bee gathered in thy name, thou wylt graunt theyr
requestes: fulfill now, O lorde, the desires
and peticions of thy servauntes, as
maye bee moste expediente for them,
grauntyng us in this worlde knowlege of thy trueth, and in
the worlde to come
lyfe everlasting.
Amen.

❧ OF THE ADMINI- ❧
stracion of publyke Baptisme to
be used in the Churche.

*I*T *appeareth by auncient wryters, that the Sacramente of Baptisme in the*
olde tyme was not commonly ministred, but at two tymes in the yeare, at
Easter and whytsontyde, at whiche tymes it was openly mynistred in the pres-
ence of all the congregacion: Whiche custome (now beeyng growen out of use)
although it cannot for many consideracions be wel restored again, yet it is
thought good to folowe the same as nere as conveniently may be: Wherfore
the people are to bee admonished, that it is moste conveniente that baptisme
shoulde not be ministred but upon Sondayes and other holy dayes,° when the
most numbre of people maye come together. As well for that the congregacion
there presente may testifie the receyvyng of them, that be newly baptysed, into
the noumbre of Christes Churche, as also because in the Baptisme of Infantes,
every manne presente maye be put in remembraunce of his owne profession
made to God in his Baptisme. For whiche cause also, it is expediente that
Baptisme be ministred in the Englishe tounge. Neverthelesse (yf necessitie so
requyre) children ought at all tymes to be baptised, eyther at the churche or
els at home.

❧ PUBLIKE BAPTISME. ❧

When there are children to be Baptised upon the Sonday, or holy daye, the
parentes shall geve knowledge over nyght or in the mornyng, afore the begin-
ning of Mattens to the curate. And then the Godfathers, Godmothers, and
people, with the children muste be ready at the Church dore,° either imme-
diatly afore the laste Canticle at Mattens, or els immediatly afore the last
Canticle at Evensong, as the Curate by his discrecion shall appoynte. And
then standyng there, the prieste shall aske whether the chyldren be baptised or
no. If they aunswere. No. then shall the priest saye thus.

D EARE beloved,° forasmuche as all men bee conceyved and borne
in sinne, and that no manne borne in synne, can entre into the
kingdom of God (except he be regenerate, and borne a newe of water,
and the holy ghost) I beseche you to call upon God the father through
our Lord Jesus Christ, that of his bounteouse mercy he wil graunt to
these children that thing, which by nature they cannot have, that is

to saye, they may be baptised with the holy ghost, and receyved into Christes holy Church, and be made lyvely membres of the same.

¶ Then the prieste shall saye.

Let us praye.

ALMYGHTIE and everlastyng God,° whiche of thy justice dydest destroy by fluddes of water the whole worlde for synne, excepte .viii. persones, whome of thy mercy (the same tyme) thou didest save in the Arke: And when thou didest drowne in the read sea wycked kyng Pharao with al his armie, yet (at the same time) thou didest leade thy people the chyldren of Israel safely through the myddes therof: wherby thou didest fygure the washyng of thy holy Baptisme: and by the Baptisme of thy welbeloved sonne Jesus Christe, thou dydest sanctifie the fludde Jordan, and al other waters to this misticall washing away of synne: We beseche thee (for thy infinite mercies) that thou wilt mercifully looke upon these children, and sanctifie them with thy holy gost, that by this holesome laver of regeneracion, whatsoever synne is in them, may be washed cleane away, that they being delivered from thy wrathe, may be received into the arke of Christes churche, and so saved from peryshyng: and beeyng fervente in spirite, stedfaste in fayth, joyfull through hope, rooted in charitie, maye ever serve thee: And finally attayne to everlastyng lyfe, with all thy holy and chosen people. This graunte us we beseche thee, for Jesus Christes sake our Lorde. Amen.

¶ Here shall the priest aske what shall be the name of the childe, and when the Godfathers and Godmothers have tolde the name, then shall he make a crosse upon the childes forehead and breste,° saying.

¶ N. Receyve the signe of the holy Crosse, both in thy forehead, and in thy breste, in token that thou shalt not be ashamed to confesse thy fayth in Christe crucifyed, and manfully to fyght under his banner against synne, the worlde, and the devill, and to continewe his faythfull soldiour and servaunt unto thy lyfes ende. Amen.

And this he shall doe and saye to as many children as bee presented to be Baptised, one after another.

Let us praye.

ALMYGHTIE and immortall God,° the ayde of all that nede, the helper of all that flee to thee for succour, the life of them that beleve, and the resurreccion of the dead: we call upon thee for these

infantes, that they cummyng to thy holy Baptisme, may receyve
remission of theyr sinnes, by spirituall regeneracion. Receyve them
(o Lorde) as thou haste promysed by thy welbeloved sonne, saying:
Aske, and you shall have: seke and you shall fynde: knocke and it
shalbe opened unto you. So geve nowe unto us that aske: Lette us that
seke, fynde: open thy gate unto us that knocke: that these infantes
maye enjoy the everlastyng benediccion of thy heavenly washing, and
may come to the eternall kyngdome, whiche thou haste promysed, by
Christe our Lorde. Amen.

Then let the priest lokyng upon the chyldren, saye.

I COMMAUNDE thee, uncleane spirite,° in the name of the father, of
the sonne, and of the holy ghost, that thou come out, and departe
from these infantes, whom our Lord Jesus Christe hath vouchsaved,
to call to his holy Baptisme, to be made membres of his body, and
of his holy congregacion. Therfore thou cursed spirite, remembre
thy sentence, remembre thy judgemente, remembre the daye to be at
hande, wherin thou shalt burne in fyre everlasting, prepared for thee
and thy Angels. And presume not hereafter to exercise any tyrannye
towarde these infantes, whom Christe hathe bought with his precious
bloud, and by this his holy Baptisme calleth to be of his flocke.

Then shall the priest saye.

The Lorde be with you.
The people. And with thy spirite.
The Minister. ¶ Heare nowe the gospell written by S. Marke.°

A T a certayne tyme they brought children to Christe that he should
touche them, and hys disciples rebuked those that brought them.
But when Jesus sawe it, he was displeased, and sayed unto them:
Suffre lytle children to come unto me, and forbyd them not: for to
suche belongeth the kingdom of God. Verely I say unto you: whosoever doeth not receyve the kyngdom of God, as a lytle chylde: he shall
not entre therin. And when he had taken them up in his armes: he put
his handes upon them, and blessed them.   *Mark* 10

*After the gospell is red, the minister shall make this briefe exhortacion upon
the woordes of the gospell.*

F RENDES you heare in this gospell the woordes of our Saviour
Christe, that he commaunded the children to be brought unto him:
howe he blamed those that would have kept them from hym: howe he

exhorteth all men to folowe their innocencie. Ye perceyve howe by his outwarde gesture and dede, he declared his good wyll towarde them. For he embraced them in his armes, he layed his handes upon them, and blessed them: doubte ye not therfore, but earnestly beleve, that he wyll lykewyse favourably receyve these present infantes, that he wyll embrace them with the armes of his mercy, that he wyll geve unto them the blessyng of eternall lyfe: and make them partakers of his everlasting kingdome. Wherfore we beyng thus perswaded of the good wyll of our heavenly father towarde these infantes, declared by his sonne Jesus Christe: And nothyng doubtyng but that he favourably alloweth this charitable worke of ours, in bringing these children to his holy baptisme: let us faythfully and devoutly geve thankes unto him: And say the prayer° which the Lorde himselfe taught. And in declaracion of our fayth, let us also recyte the articles conteyned in our Crede.

Here the minister with the Godfathers, Godmothers, and people presente, shall saye.

Our father whiche art in heaven, halowed bee thy name. *&c.*

And then shall saye openly.

I beleve in God the father almightie. *&c.*

The priest shall adde also this prayer.

ALMIGHTIE and everlastyng God, heavenly father, we geve thee humble thankes, that thou haste vouchesaved to call us to knowledge of thy grace, and fayth in thee: Increase and confyrme this fayth in us evermore: Geve thy holy spirite to these infantes, that they may be borne agayne, and be made heyres of everlasting salvacion, through our Lord Jesus Christ: Who lyveth and reigneth with thee and the holy spirite, nowe and for ever. Amen.

Then let the priest take one of the children by the ryght hande,° the other being brought after him. And cumming into the Churche towarde the fonte, saye.

THE Lorde vouchesafe to receyve you into his holy housholde, and to kepe and governe you alwaye in the same, that you may have everlasting lyfe. Amen.

Then standyng at the fonte the priest shall speake° to the Godfathers and
Godmothers, on this wyse.

WELBELOVED frendes, ye have brought these children here to
bee Baptized, ye have prayed that our Lorde Jesus Christ would
vouchsafe to receyve them, to lay his handes upon them, to blesse
them, to release them of theyr sinnes, to geve them the kyngdome of
heaven, and everlastyng life. Ye have heard also that our Lorde Jesus
Christe hath promysed in his gospel, to graunte all these thynges that
ye have prayed for: whiche promyse he for his parte, will moste suerly
kepe and perfourme. Wherfore, after this promyse made by Christe,
these infantes muste also faythfully for theyr parte promise by you,
that be theyr sueries, that they wyll forsake the devyll and all his
workes, and constantly beleve Gods holy woorde, and obediently kepe
his commaundementes.

Then shall the priest demaunde of the childe (which shalbe first Baptized)
these questions folowing: first naming the childe, and saying.

N. Doest thou forsake the devill° and all his workes?
Aunswere. I forsake them.
Minister. Doest thou forsake the vaine pompe, and glory of the
worlde, with all the covetouse desyres of the same?
Aunswere. I forsake them.
Minister. Doest thou forsake the carnall desyres of the flesh, so that
thou wilt not folowe, nor be ledde by them?
Aunswere. I forsake them.
Minister. Doest thou beleve in God° the father almyghtie, maker of
heaven and earth?
Aunswere. I beleve.
Minister. Doest thou beleve in Jesus Christe his only begotten
sonne our Lorde, and that he was conceyved by the holy gost, borne
of the virgin Mary, that he suffered under Poncius Pilate, was crucified, dead, and buryed, that he went downe into hell, and also dyd
ryse agayne the thyrde daye: that he ascended into heaven, and sitteth
on the ryghthande of God the father almighty: And from thence shall
come agayne at the ende of the worlde, to judge the quicke and the
dead: Doest thou beleve this?
Aunswere. I beleve.
Minister. Doest thou beleve in the holy gost, the holy Catholike

Churche, the communion of Sainctes, remission of Sinnes, resurreccion of the fleshe, and everlastyng lyfe after death?

Aunswere. I beleve.

Minister. What doest thou desyre?

Aunswere. Baptisme.

Minister. Wilt thou be Baptized?

Aunswere. I wyll.

*Then the prieste shall take the childe in his handes, and aske the name.
And naming the childe, shall dyppe it in the water thryse.° First dypping
the ryght syde: Seconde the left syde: The thyrde tyme dippyng the face
towarde the fonte: So it be discretly and warely done, saying.*

N. I Baptize thee in the name of the father, and of the sonne, and
of the holy gost. Amen.

*And if the childe be weake, it shall suffice to powre water upon it, say-
ing the foresayed woordes. N. I baptize thee, &c. Then the Godfathers
and Godmothers shall take and lay theyr handes upon the childe, and
the minister shall put upon him his white vesture, commonly called the
Crisome:° And saye.*

TAKE this white vesture for a token of the innocencie, whiche by
Gods grace in this holy sacramente of Baptisme, is given unto
thee: and for a signe wherby thou art admonished, so long as thou
lyvest, to geve thy selfe to innocencie of living, that after this transit-
orye lyfe, thou mayst be partaker of the lyfe everlasting. Amen.

Then the prieste shall annoynt the infant upon the head,° saying.

ALMIGHTY God the father of our lorde Jesus Christ, who hath
regenerate thee by water and the holy gost, and hath geven unto
thee remission of al thy sinnes: he vouchsave to annoynte thee with
the unccion of his holy spirite, and bryng thee to the inheritaunce of
everlasting lyfe. Amen.

*When there are many to be Baptized, this ordre of demaunding, Baptizing, put-
tyng on the Crysome, and enoyntyng, shalbe used severally with every chylde.
Those that be firste Baptized departing from the fonte, and remaynyng in
some conveniente place within the Churche, untill all be Baptyzed. At the
laste ende, the priest calling the Godfathers and Godmothers together: shall
saye this shorte exhortacion folowing.*

FORASMUCH as these children have promised by you to forsake the
devill and al his workes, to beleve in God, and to serve him: you

must remembre that it is your partes and duetie to see that these infantes be taught, so soone as they shalbe able to learne, what a solemne vowe, promyse, and profession, they have made by you. And that they maye knowe these thynges the better: ye shall call upon them to heare sermons, and chiefly you shal provide that thei may learne the Crede, the Lordes prayer, and the ten commaundementes, in the englishe tounge: and all other thinges, which a christian manne ought to knowe and beleve to his soules health. And that these children may be vertuously brought up to leade a godly and christian life: remembring alwayes that Baptisme doeth represent unto us our profession, which is to folow the example of our Saviour Christe, and to be made lyke unto him, that as he dyed and rose againe for us: so should we (whiche are Baptised) dye from synne, and ryse agayne unto righteousnesse, continually mortifying all our evyll and corrupte affeccions, and dayly procedyng in all vertue and godlynesse of lyvyng.

The minister shall commaunde that the Crisomes be brought to the churche and delyvered to the priestes after the accustomed maner, at the purificacion of the mother of every chylde.° And that the children be brought to the Bushop to bee confirmed of hym, so soone as they can saye in theyr vulgare tounge the articles of the fayth, the Lordes prayer, and the ten commaundementes, and be further instructed in the Catechisme, set furth for that purpose, accordingly as it is there expressed.

And so lette the congregacion departe in the name of the Lorde.

¶ *Note that yf the numbre of children to be Baptised, and multitude of people presente bee so great that they cannot conveniently stand at the Churche doore: then let them stand within the Churche in some convenient place, nygh unto the Churche doore: And there all thynges be sayed and done, appoynted to be sayed and done at the Churche doore.*

ꜱ❧ OF THEM THAT BE ❧ꜱ

𝕭aptised in priuate houses° in tyme of necessitie.

¶ *The pastours amd curates shall oft admonyshe the people, that they differ not the Baptisme of infantes any longer then the Sondaye, or other holy daye, nexte after the chylde bee borne, onlesse upon a great and reasonable cause declared to the curate and by hym approved.*

And also they shal warne them that without great cause, and necessitie, they Baptise not children at home in theyr houses.° And when great nede shall compell them so to doe, that then they minister it on this fashion.

First let them that be present cal upon God for his grace, and saye the Lordes prayer, yf the tyme will suffre. And then one of them shal name the childe, and dippe him in the water, or poure water upon him, saying these woordes.

¶ *N.* I Baptise thee in the name of the father, and of the sonne and of the holy ghoste. Amen.

¶ *And let them not doubt, but that the childe so Baptised, is lawfully and suffi-ciently Baptised, and ought not to be Baptised againe, in the Churche. But yet neverthelesse, if the childe whiche is after this sorte Baptised, doe afterwarde lyve:° it is expedient that he be brought into the Churche, to the entente the prieste maye examine and trye, whether the childe be lawfully Baptised or no. And yf those that bryng any childe to the Churche doe aunswere that he is alreadye Baptised: Then shall the priest examin them, further.*

By whom the childe was Baptised?

Who was presente when the childe was baptised?

Whether they called upon God for grace and succoure in that necessitie?

With what thyng, or what matter they dyd Baptise the childe?

With what woordes the childe was Baptised?

Whether they thinke the childe to be lawfully and perfectly Baptised?

And if the minister shall prove by the aunswers of suche as brought the childe that all thynges were done, as they ought to be: Then shall not he christen the childe agayne, but shall receyve hym, as one of the flocke of the true christian people, saying thus.

I CERTIFIE you, that in this case ye have doen wel, and according unto due ordre concerning the baptising of this child, which being borne in original synne and in the wrathe of God, is nowe by the laver of regeneracion in Baptisme,° made the childe of God, and heire of everlastyng life: for oure Lorde Jesus Christe doeth not denye hys grace and mercie unto such infantes, but most lovingly doeth call them unto him. As the holy gospell doeth witnesse to our coumforte on this wyse.

AT a certaine time thei brought children unto Christ that he should touch them, and his disciples rebuked those that brought them. But when Jesus sawe it, he was displeased, and sayed unto them: Suffre lytle chyldren to come unto me, and forbidde them not, for to suche belongeth the kingdome of God. Verely I saye unto you, whosoever doeth not receyve the kingdom of God as a lytle chylde, he shall not enter therin. And when he had taken them up in his armes, he put his handes upon them, and blissed them. *Mark* 10

After the gospell is read: the minister shall make this exhortacion upon the woordes of the ghospell.

FRENDES ye heare in this gospell the woordes of our Saveoure Christ, that he commaunded the children to be brought unto him, how he blamed those that would have kept them from hym, howe he exhorted all men to folowe their innocencie: Ye perceive how by his outward gesture and dede he declared his good wyll towarde them, for he embraced them in his armes, he layed his handes upon them and blessed them. Doubt you not therfore, but earnestly beleve, that he hath lykewyse favourably receyved this presente infante, that he hath embraced him with the armes of his mercy, that he hath geven unto him the blessing of eternal lyfe, and made him partaker of his everlasting kingdom. Wherfore we beyng thus persuaded of the good will of oure heavenly father, declared by his sonne Jesus Christ towardes this infante: Let us faythfully and devoutly geve thankes unto him, and saye the prayer whiche the Lorde himselfe taught, and in declaracion of our fayth, let us also recyte the articles conteined in our Crede.

Here the minister with the Godfathers and Godmothers shall saye.

OUR father whiche arte in heaven, halowed be thy name. *&c.*

Then shall they saye the Crede, and then the prieste shall demaunde the name of the childe, whiche beyng by the Godfathers and Godmothers pronounced, the minister shall saye.

N. Doest thou forsake the devill and all his workes?

Aunswere. I forsake them.

Minister. Doest thou forsake the vaine pompe and glory of the worlde, with all the covetous desyres of the same?

Aunswere. I forsake them.

Minister. Doest thou forsake the carnall desyres of the flesh, so that thou wilt not folowe and be led by them?

Aunswere. I forsake them.

Minister. Doest thou beleve in God the father almyghtie, maker of heaven and yearth?

Aunswere. I beleve.

Minister. Doest thou beleve in Jesus Christe hys onely begotten sonne our lorde, and that he was conceyved by the holy Goste, borne of the virgin Marie, that he suffered under Pontius Pilate, was crucifyed, dead and buried, that he went downe into hel, and also did arise againe the third day, that he ascended into heaven, and sitteth on the righte hande of god the father almightie: And from thence shal come agayn at the ende of the world to judge the quicke and the dead, doest thou beleve thus?

Aunswere. I beleve.

Minister. Doest thou beleve in the holy goste, the holy catholyke Churche, the Communion of Saintes, Remission of sinnes, Resurreccion of the flesh, and everlasting life after deth?

Aunswere. I beleve.

Then the minister shal put the white vesture commonly colled the Crysome, upon the childe, saying.

TAKE thys whyte vesture for a token of the innocencie whiche by goddes grace in the holy sacramente of baptysme is geven unto thee, and for a signe wherby thou art admonished so long as thou shalt lyve, to geve thy selfe to innocencye of livyng, that after this transitory life, thou maiest be partaker of the life everlasting. Amen.

¶ Let us pray.

ALMIGHTIE and everlasting god heavenly father, wee geve thee humble thankes that thou hast vouchesafed to cal us to the knowlege of thy grace, and faith in thee: Increase and confirme this fayth in us evermore: Geve thy holy spirite to this infant, that he being borne agayne, and beeing made heyre of everlasting salvacion through our lord Jesus Christ, may continue thy servaunt, and attein thy promises through the same our lorde Jesus Christe thy sonne, who liveth and reigneth with thee in unitie of the same holy spirite everlastinglye. Amen.

Then shall the minister make this exhortacion, to the Godfathers, and Godmothers.

FORASMUCHE as this chylde hath promised by you to forsake the devil and al his workes, to beleve in god, and to serve him, you must remember that it is your partes and duetie to see that this infant be taught so sone as he shalbe able to learne, what a solemne vowe, promise, and profession he hath made by you, and that he may know these thinges the better, ye shall call upon hym to heare sermons: And chiefly ye shal provide that he may learne the Crede, the Lordes prayer, and the ten commaundementes in the english tong, and al other thinges which a christian man ought to know and beleve to his soules health, and that this childe may bee vertuously brought up, to leade a godly and a christian life. Remembring alway that baptisme doeth represent unto us our profession, which is to folow the example of our saviour Christe, and to be made like unto him, that as he died and rose again for us: so should we whiche are baptized, dye from sin, and ryse againe unto righteousnes, continually mortifying al our evil and corrupt affeccions, and dayly proceding in al vertue and godlines of living.

&c. As in Publike Baptisme.

¶ *But if they which bring the infantes to the church, do make an uncertain answere to the priestes questions, and say that they cannot tel what they thought, did, or sayde in that great feare and trouble of mynde (as oftentymes it chaunseth) Then let the priest Baptize him in forme above written, concernyng publyke Baptisme, sauyng that at the dyppyng of the childe in the fonte, he shall use this forme of woordes.*

IF thou be not Baptized already,° *N.* I Baptize thee in the name of the father, and of the sonne, and of the holy gost. Amen.

The water in the fonte° shalbe chaunged every moneth once at the lest, and afore any child be Baptized in the water so chaunged, the priest shall say at the font these prayers folowing.

O MOSTE mercifull god our savioure Jesu Christ, who hast ordeyned the element of water for the regeneracion of thy faythful people, upon whom beyng baptised in the river of Jordane, the holye ghoste came down in the likenesse of a doove: Sende down we beseche thee the same thy holye spirite to assiste us, and to bee present at this our invocacion of thy holy name: Sanctifie ✠ this fountaine of baptisme,° thou that art the sanctifier of al thynges, that by the power of thy worde, all those that shall be baptized therein, maye be spirituallye regenerated, and made the children of everlasting adopcion. Amen.

O mercifull God, graunte that the olde Adam, in them that shalbe baptized in this fountayne, maye so be buried, that the newe man may be raised up agayne. Amen.

Graunt that all carnal affeccions maie die in them: and that all thynges belongyng to the spirite maye live and growe in them. Amen.

Graunt to all them which at this fountayne forsake the devill and all his workes: that they maye have power and strength to have victorye and to triumph againste hym, the worlde and the fleshe. Amen.

Whosoever shal confesse thee, o lorde: recognise him also in thy kingdome. Amen.

Graunt that al sinne and vice here maie bee so extinct: that thei never have power to raigne in thy servauntes. Amen.

Graunte that whosoever here shall begynne to be of thy flocke: maie evermore continue in the same. Amen.

Graunt that all they which for thy sake in this life doe denie and forsake themselfes: may winne and purchase thee (o lord) which art everlasting treasure. Amen.

Graunt that whosoever is here dedicated to thee by our office and ministerie: maye also bee endewed with heavenly vertues, and everlastinglye rewarded through thy mercie, O Blessed lorde God, who doest live and governe al thinges world without ende. Amen.

The Lorde be with you.

Answere. And with thy spirite.

ALMIGHTYE everliving God, whose moste derely beloved sonne Jesus Christe, for the forgevenesse of our sinnes did shead out of his moste precious side bothe water and bloude, and gave commaundemente to his disciples that they shoulde goe teache all nacions, and baptise them in the name of the father, the sonne, and the holye ghoste: Regarde, we besche thee, the supplicacions of thy congregacion, and graunte that all thy servauntes which shall bee baptized in this water prepared for the mynystracion of thy holy sacrament, maye receive the fulnesse of thy grace, and ever remaine in the noumbre of thy faithful, and elect children, through Jesus Christ our Lord.

CONFIRMACION
wherin is conteined a Cathe-
chisme for children.

*T*O *the ende that confirmacion may be ministred to the more edifying of suche as shall receive it (according to Saint Paules doctrine, who teacheth that all thynges should be doen in the churche to the edificacion of the same) it is thought good that none hereafter shall be confirmed, but suche as can say in theyr mother tong,° the articles of the faith, the lordes prayer, and the tenne commaundementes: And can also aunswere to suche questions of this shorte Cathechisme, as the Busshop (or suche as he shall appoynte) shall by his discrecion appose them in. And this ordre is most convenient to be observed for divers consideracions.*

¶ *First, because that whan children come to the yeres of discrecion and have learned what theyr Godfathers and Godmothers promised for them in Baptisme, they may then themselfes with their owne mouth and with theyr owne consent, openly before the churche, ratifie and confesse the same, and also promise that by the grace of God, they will evermore endevour them-selves faithfully to observe and kepe such thinges, as they by theyre owne mouth and confession have assented unto.*

¶ *Secondly, for asmuch as confirmacion is ministred to them that be Baptised, that by imposicion of handes, and praier they may receive strength and defence against all temptacions to sin, and the assautes of the worlde, and the devill: it is most mete to be ministred, when children come to that age, that partly by the frayltie of theyr owne fleshe, partly by the assautes of the world and the devil, they begin to be in daungier to fall into sinne.*

¶ *Thirdly, for that it is agreeable with the usage of the churche in tymes past, wherby it was ordeined that confirmacion should bee ministred to them that were of perfecte age,° that they beyng instructed in Christes religion, should openly professe theyr owne fayth, and promise to be obedient unto the will of God.*

¶ *And that no manne shall thynke that anye detrimente shall come to children by differryng of theyr confirmacion: he shall knowe for trueth, that it is cer-tayn by Goddes woorde, that children beeyng Baptized (if they departe out of thys lyfe in theyr infancie) are undoubtedly saved.*

❧ A CATECHISME,° ❧
that is to say, an instruccion to bee learned of every childe, before he be brought to be confirmed of the Bushop.

Question. What is your name?°

Aunswere. N. or M.

Question. Who gave you this name?

Aunswere. My Godfathers and Godmothers in my Baptisme, wherein I was made a member of Christe, the childe of God, and an inheritour of the kingdome of heaven.

Question. What did your Godfathers and Godmothers then for you?

Aunswere. They did promise and vowe three thinges in my name. First, that I should forsake the devil and all his workes and pompes, the vanities of the wicked worlde, and all the sinnefull lustes of the fleshe. Secondly, that I should beleve all the articles of the Christian fayth. And thirdly, that I should kepe Goddes holy will and commaundementes, and walke in the same al the daies of my life.

Question. Dooest thou not thinke that thou arte bound to beleve, and to doe as they have promised for thee?

Aunswere. Yes verely. And by Gods helpe so I wil. And I hartily thanke our heavenlye father, that he hath called me to thys state of salvacion, through Jesus Christe our saveour. And I pray God to geve me hys grace, that I may continue in the same unto my lives ende.

Question. Rehearse the articles of thy beliefe.°

Aunswere.

I BELEVE in God the father almightie, maker of heaven and earth. And in Jesus Christ his only sonne our lord. Whiche was conceived by the holy gost, borne of the virgin Marie. Suffered under Ponce Pilate, was crucified, dead and buried, he descended into hel. The third day he rose agayn from the dead. He ascended into heaven, and sitteth on the right hande of God the father almightie. From thence shal he come to judge the quicke and the dead. I beleve in the holye goste. The holye catholike church. The communion of saintes. The forgevenes of sinnes. The resurreccion of the bodie. And the lyfe everlasting. Amen.

Question. What dooest thou chiefely learne in these articles of thy beliefe?

Aunswere. Firste, I learne to beleve in God the father, who hath made me and all the worlde.

Secondely, in God the sonne who hath redemed me and all mankinde.

Thirdly, in god the holy goste, who sanctifyeth me and all the electe people of god.

Question. You sayde that your Godfathers and Godmothers dyd promyse for you that ye should kepe Goddes commaundementes. Tell me how many there bee.

Aunswere. Tenne.

Question. Whiche be they?

Aunswere.

THOU shalte have none other Gods but me.

ii. Thou shalte not make to thy selfe anye graven image, nor the likenesse of any thyng° that is in heaven above, or in the earth beneath, nor in the water under the earth: thou shalt not bowe downe to them, nor wurship them.

iii. Thou shalt not take the name of the lord thy God in vayne.

iiii. Remember that thou kepe holy the Sabboth day.°

v. Honor thy father and thy mother.

vi. Thou shalt doe no murdre.

vii. Thou shalt not commit adultry.

viii. Thou shalt not steale.

ix. Thou shalt not beare false witnes against thy neighbour.

x. Thou shalt not covet thy neighbours wife, nor his servaunt, nor his mayde, nor his Oxe, nor his Asse, nor any thing that is his.

Question. What dooest thou chiefely learne by these commaundementes?

Aunswere. I learne two thinges: My duetie towardes god, and my duetie towardes my neighbour.

Question. What is thy duetie towardes god?

Aunswere. My duetie towardes God is, to beleve in him. To feare him. And to love him with al my hart, with al my mind, with al my soule, and with all my strength. To wurship him. To geve him thankes. To put my whole truste in hym. To call upon him. To honor his holy name and his word, and to serve him truely all the daies of my life.

Question. What is thy dutie towardes thy neighboure?

Answere. My duetie towardes my neighbour is: to love hym as my selfe. And to do to al men as I would they should do to me. To love, honour, and succoure my father and mother. To honour and obey the kyng, and his ministers. To submitte myselfe to all my governours, teachers, spirituall pastours, and maisters. To ordre myselfe lowlye and reverentelye to al my betters. To hurte no bodie by woorde nor dede. To bee true and just in al my dealing. To beare no malice nor hatred in my heart. To kepe my handes from picking and stealing, and my tongue from evill speaking, liyng, and slaundring. To kepe my body in temperaunce, sobreness, and chastitie. Not to covet nor desire other mennes goodes. But learne and laboure truely to geate my owne living, and to doe my duetie in that state of life: unto which it shal please God to cal me.

Question. My good sonne, knowe this, that thou arte not hable to do these thinges of thy self, nor to walke in the commaundementes of God and to serve him, without his speciall grace, which thou muste learne at all times to cal for by diligent prayer. Leat me heare therfore if thou canst say the Lordes prayer.

Answere.

O UR father whiche art in heaven, halowed bee thy name. Thy kyngdome come. Thy wil bee done in earth as it is in heaven. Geve us this day our dailye breade. And forgeve us our trespasses, as we forgeve them that trespasse againste us. And leade us not into temptacion, but deliver us from evil. Amen.

Question. What desireste thou of God in this prayer?

Answere. I desire my lord god our heavenly father, who is the gever of al goodnesse, to send his grace unto me, and to all people, that we may wurship him, serve hym, and obey him, as we ought to doe. And I praye unto God, that he will sende us al thynges that be nedeful both for our soules, and bodies: And that he wil bee mercifull unto us, and forgeve us our sinnes: And that it will please him to save and defende us in al daungers gostly and bodily: And that he wil kepe us from al sinne and wickednes, and from our gostly enemye, and from everlastyng death. And this I truste he wil doe of his mercie and goodnes, through our lorde Jesu Christe. And therefore I say, Amen. So be it.

¶ *So soone as the children can say in theyr mother tongue the articles of the faith, the lordes praier, the ten commaundementes, and also can aunswere to such questions of this short Cathechisme as the Bushop (or suche as he shall appointe) shal by hys discrecion appose them in: then shall they bee brought to the Bushop by one that shalbee his godfather or godmother, that everye childe maye have a wittenesse of hys confirmacion.*

¶ *And the Bushop shal confirme them on this wyse.*

Confirmacion.

Our helpe is in the name of the Lorde.°
Answere. Whiche hath made both heaven and yearth.
Minister. Blessed is the name of the lorde.
Answere. Henceforth worlde without ende.
Minister. The lorde be with you.
Answere. And with thy spirite.

Let us praye.

ALMIGHTY and everliving God, who hast vouchesafed to regenerate these thy servauntes of water and the holy goste: And haste geven unto them forgevenesse of all their sinnes: Sende downe from heaven we beseche thee (O lorde) upon them thy holy gost the coumforter, with the manifold giftes of grace, the spirite of wisdom and understandyng: The spirite of counsell and gostly strength: The spirite of knowledge and true godlinesse, and fulfil them (o lord) with the spirite of thy holy feare.
Aunswere. Amen.
Minister. Signe them (o lorde) and marke them to be thyne for ever, by the vertue of thy holye crosse and passion. Confirme and strength them with the inward unccion of thy holy gost, mercifully unto everlasting life. Amen.

Then the Bushop shal crosse them in the forehead,° and lay his handes upon theyr heades,° saying.

N. I signe thee with the signe of the crosse, and laye my hande upon thee. In the name of the father, and of the sonne, and of the holy gost. Amen.

And thus shall he doe to every childe one after another. And whan he hath layed hys hande upon every chylde, then shall he say.

The peace of the lorde abide with you.°
Aunswere. And with thy spirite.

¶ Let us pray.

ALMIGHTIE everliving god,° which makest us both to will and to doe those thinges that bee good and acceptable unto thy majestie: we make our humble supplicacions unto thee for these children, upon whome (after the example of thy holy Apostles) we have laied our handes, to certify them (by this signe) of thy favour and gracious goodnes toward them: leat thy fatherly hand (we beseche thee) ever be over them, let thy holy spirite ever bee with them, and so leade them in the knowledge and obedience of thy woord, that in the end they may obtein the life everlasting, through our lord Jesus Christ, who with thee and the holy goste liveth and reyneth one god world without ende. Amen.

Then shall the Busshop blisse the children, thus saying.

The blissing of god almightie,° the father, the sonne, and the holy goste, be upon you, and remayne with you for ever. Amen.

The curate of every parish once in sixe wekes at the least upon warnyng by him geven, shal upon some Soonday or holy day, half an houre before evensong openly in the churche instructe and examine so many children of his parish sent unto him, as the time wil serve, and as he shal thynke conveniente, in some parte of this Cathechisme. And all fathers, mothers, maisters, and dames, shall cause theyr children, servountes, and prentises (whiche are not yet confirmed) to come to the churche at the daie appoynted, and obediently heare and be ordered by the curate, untill suche time as they have learned all that is here appointed for them to learne.

¶ *And whansoever the Bushop shal geve knowlege for children to be brought afore him to any convenient place, for their confirmacion: Then shal the curate of every parish either bring or send in writing, the names of al those children of his parish which can say the articles of theyr faith, the lordes praier, and the ten commaundementes. And also how many of them can answere to the other questions conteined in this Cathechisme.*

¶ *And there shal none be admitted to the holye communion: until suche time as he be confirmed.*

❧ THE FORME OF ❦
Solemnizacion of
matrimonie.

¶ *First the bannes must be asked three several Soondaies° or holye dayes, in the*
service tyme, the people beeyng presente after the accustomed maner.

And if the persones that woulde bee maried dwel in divers parishes, the bannes
muste bee asked in bothe parishes, and the curate of the one parish shall not
solemnize matrimonie betwixt them, withoute a certificate of the bannes
beeyng thrise asked from the Curate of the other parishe.

At the daye appointed for Solemnizacion of matrimonie, the persones to be
maried shal come into the bodie of the churche,° with theyr frendes and neigh-
bours. And there the priest shal thus saye.

D EERELY beloved frendes, we are gathered together° here in
the syght of God, and in the face of his congregacion, to joyne
together this man and this woman in holy matrimonie, which is an
honorable estate instituted of God in paradise, in the time of mannes
innocencie,° signifiing unto us the misticall union that is betwixte
Christe and his Churche: whiche holy estate, Christe adorned and
beutified with his presence, and first miracle that he wrought in Cana
of Galile, and is commended of Sainct Paule to be honourable emong
all men, and therefore is not to bee enterprised, nor taken in hande
unadvisedlye, lightelye, or wantonly,° to satisfie mens carnal lustes
and appetites, like brute beastes that have no understanding: but rev-
erentely, discretely, advisedly, soberly, and in the feare of God. Duely
consideryng the causes for the whiche matrimonie was ordeined.°
One cause was the procreacion of children, to be brought up in the
feare and nurture of the Lord, and prayse of God. Secondly it was
ordeined for a remedie agaynst sinne, and to avoide fornicacion, that
suche persones as bee maried, might live chastlie in matrimonie, and
kepe themselves undefiled membres of Christes bodye. Thirdelye for
the mutuall societie, helpe, and coumfort,° that the one oughte to
have of the other, both in prosperitie and adversitie. Into the whiche
holy estate these two persones present, come nowe to be joyned.

Therefore if any man can shewe any just cause why they maie not lawfully be joyned so together: Leat him now speake, or els hereafter for ever hold his peace.°

And also speakyng to the persones that shalbe maried, he shall saie.

I REQUIRE and charge you (as you will aunswere at the dreadefull daye of judgemente, when the secretes of all hartes shalbee disclosed) that if either of you doe knowe any impedimente, why ye maie not bee lawfully joyned together in matrimonie, that ye confesse it. For be ye wel assured, that so manye as bee coupled together otherwaies then Goddes woord doeth allowe: are not joyned of God, neither is their matrimonie lawful.

At which daye of mariage yf any man doe allege any impediment why they maye not be coupled together in matrimonie: And will be bound, and sureties with hym, to the parties, or els put in a caution to the full value of suche charges as the persones to bee maried dooe susteyne, to prove his allegacion: then the Solemnizacion muste bee differred, unto suche tyme as the trueth bee tried. Yf no impedimente bee alleged, then shall the curate saye unto the man.

N. Wilte thou have this woman° to thy wedded wife, to live together after Goddes ordeinaunce in the holy estate of matrimonie? Wilt thou love her, coumforte her, honor and kepe her, in sickenesse and in health? And forsaking all other kepe thee only to her, so long as you both shall live?

The man shall aunswere.

I will.

Then shall the prieste saye to the woman.

N. Wilt thou have this man to thy wedded houseband, to live together after Goddes ordeinaunce, in the holy estate of matrimonie? Wilt thou obey° him, and serve him, love, honor and kepe him, in sickenes and in health? And forsaking al other kepe thee onely to him, so long as you bothe shall live?

The woman shall aunswere

I will.

Then shall the minister say.

Who geveth this woman° to be maried to this man?

*And the minister receiving the woman at her father or frendes handes: shall
cause the man to take the woman by the right hande, and so either to geve
their trouth to other: The man first saying.*

I N. take thee N. to my wedded wife, to have and to holde from
this day forwarde, for better, for wurse,° for richer, for poorer, in
sickenes, and in health, to love and to cherishe, til death us departe:
according to Goddes holy ordeinaunce:° And therto I plight thee my
trouth.

*Then shall they looce theyr handes,° and the woman taking again the man
by the right hande shall say.*

I N. take thee N. to my wedded husbande, to have and to holde from
this day forwarde, for better, for woorse, for richer, for poorer, in
sickenes and in health, to love, cherishe, and to obey,° till death us
departe: accordyng to Goddes holy ordeinaunce: And thereto I geve
thee my trouth.

*Then shall they agayne looce theyr handes, and the manne shall geve unto
the womanne a ring,° and other tokens of spousage,° as golde or silver,
laying the same upon the boke:° And the Priest taking the ring shall deliver
it unto the man: to put it upon the fowerth finger of the womans left hande.
And the man taught by the priest, shall say.*

¶ With thys ring I thee wed: Thys golde and silver I thee geve:
with my body I thee wurship:° and withal my worldly Goodes I thee
endowe. In the name of the father, and of the sonne, and of the holy
goste. Amen.

*Then the man leavyng the ring upon the fowerth finger of the womans left
hande, the minister shal say.*

¶ Let us pray.

O ETERNAL God creator and preserver of al mankinde, gever of al
spiritual grace, the author of everlasting life: Sende thy blessing
upon these thy servauntes, thys manne, and this woman, whome we
blesse in thy name, that as Isaac and Rebecca (after bracellets and
Jewels of golde° geven of the one to the other for tokens of their
matrimonie) lived faithfully together: So these persons may surely
perfourme and kepe the vowe and covenaunt betwixt them made,
wherof this ring geven, and received, is a token and pledge. And may
ever remayne in perfite love and peace together: And lyve accordyng
to thy lawes: through Jesus Christe our lorde. Amen.

Then shal the prieste joyne theyr ryght handes together, and say.

¶ Those whome god hath joyned together: let no man put a sundre.°

Then shall the minister speake unto the people.

F OR asmuche as *N.* and *N.* have consented together in holye
wedlocke, and have witnessed the same here before god and this
cumpany: And therto have geven and pledged theyr trouth eyther to
other, and have declared the same by gevyng and receyvyng golde
and sylver, and by joyning of handes: I pronounce that they bee man
and wyfe together. In the name of the father, of the sonne, and of the
holy gost. Amen.

And the minister shall adde this blessyng.

¶ God the father blesse you. ✠ God the sonne kepe you:° god the
holye gost lighten your understanding: The lorde mercifully with his
favour loke upon you, and so fil you with al spiritual benediction and
grace, that you may have remission of your sinnes in this life, and in
the worlde to come lyfe everlastyng. Amen.

*Then shal they goe into the quier,° and the ministers or clerkes shal saye or
syng, this psalme folowyng.*

Beati omnes.

B LESSED are al they that feare the lord, and walke in his wayes.
For thou shalte eate the laboure of thy handes: O wel is thee, and
happie shalt thou bee. *Ps.* 128

Thy wife shalbee as the fruitful vine, upon the walles of thy house.

Thy children like the olife braunches rounde about thy table.

Loe, thus shal the man be blessed, that feareth the lord.

The lord from out of Sion, shall so blesse thee : that thou shalt see
Hierusalem in prosperitie, al thy life long.

Yea that thou shalt see thy childers children: and peace upon Israel.

Glory to the father. *&c.*

As it was in the beginning. *&c.*

Or els this psalme° folowyng.

Deus misereatur nostri.

G OD be merciful unto us, and blesse us, and shew us the lighte of
his countenaunce: and bee mercifull unto us. *Ps.* 67

That thy waye maye bee knowen upon yearth, thy saving health
emong all nacions.

Leate the people praise thee (o god) yea leate all people prayse thee.

O leate the nacions rejoyce and bee glad, for thou shalte judge the folke righteously, and governe the nacions upon yearth.

Leat the people prayse thee (o god) leat al people prayse thee.

Then shal the yearth bring foorth her increase: and god, even our owne God, shal geve us his blessyng.

God shal blesse us, and all the endes of the worlde shall feare hym.

Glory to the father. *&c.*

As it was in the beginning. *&c.*

The psalme ended, and the manne and woman knelyng afore the aulter: the prieste standyng ot the aulter, and turnyng his face towarde them, shall saye.

Lorde have mercie upon us.

Answere. Christe have mercie upon us.

Minister. Lorde have mercie upon us.

¶ Our father whiche art in heaven. *&c.*

And leade us not into temptacion.

Answere. But deliver us from evill. Amen.

Minister. O lorde save thy servaunte, and thy handmaide.

Answere. Whiche put theyr truste in thee.

Minister. O lorde sende them helpe from thy holy place.

Answere. And evermore defende them.

Minister. Bee unto them a tower of strength.

Answere. From the face of their enemie.

Minister. O lorde heare my prayer.

Answere. And leate my crie come unto the.

The Minister. Leat us praye.

O GOD of Abraham, God of Isaac, God of Jacob, blesse these thy servauntes,° and sowe the seede of eternall life in their mindes, that whatsoever in thy holy woorde they shall profitablye learne: they may in dede fulfill the same. Looke, o Lord, mercifully upon them from heaven, and blesse them: And as thou diddest sende thy Aungell Raphaell to Thobie, and Sara, the daughter of Raguel, to their great comfort: so vouchsafe to send thy blessyng upon these thy servauntes, that thei obeyng thy wil, and alwaye beyng in safetie under thy proteccion: may abyde in thy love unto theyr lyves ende: throughe Jesu Christe our Lorde. Amen.

This prayer folowing shalbe omitted where the woman is past childe byrth.

O MERCIFUL Lord, and heavenly father, by whose gracious gifte mankind is increased: We beseche thee assiste with thy blessing these two persones, that they may both be fruictful in procreacion of children: and also live together so long in godlye love and honestie: that they may see their childers children, unto the thirde and fourth generacion, unto thy prayse and honour: through Jesus Christe our Lorde. Amen.

O GOD whiche by thy myghtye power° haste made all thinges of naughte, whiche also after other thinges set in order diddeste appoint that out of man (created after thine own image and simili-tude) woman should take her beginning: and knitting them together, diddest teache, that it should never be lawful to put a sondre those, whome thou by matrimonie haddeste made one: O god, whiche hast consecrated the state of matrimonie, to such an excellent misterie, that in it is signified and represented the spirituall mariage and unitie betwixte Christe and his churche: Loke mercifully upon these thy servauntes, that both this manne may love his wyfe, accordyng to thy woord (as Christ did love his spouse the churche, who gave himself for it, loving and cherishing it even as his own flesh:) And also that this woman may be loving and amiable to her houseband as Rachel, wise as Rebecca, faithful and obedient as Sara: And in al quietnes, sobrietie, and peace, bee a folower of holy and godlye matrones. O lorde blesse them bothe, and graunte them to inherite thy everlastyng kyngdome, throughe Jesu Christe oure Lorde. Amen.

Then shall the prieste blesse the man and the woman, saiyng.

A LMIGHTY god, which at the beginnyng did create oure firste parentes Adam and Eve, and dyd sanctifie and joyne them together in mariage: Powre upon you the rychesse of his grace, sanc-tifie and ✠ blisse you,° that ye may please hym bothe in bodye and soule: and live together in holy love, unto your lives ende. Amen.

Then shalbee sayed after the gospell a sermon, wherein ordinarily (so oft as there is any mariage) the office of man and wife shall bee declared, according to holy scripture. Or if there be no sermon, the minister shall reade this that foloweth.

Al ye whiche bee maried, or whiche entende to take the holye estate of matrimonie upon you: heare what holye scripture dooeth saye, as touchyng the duetye of housebandes towarde their wives, and wives towarde theyr housebandes.

Saincte Paule (in his epistle to the Ephesians the fyfth chapter) doeth geve this commaundement to al maried men.

Ye housebandes love your wives, even as Christ loved the churche, and hathe geven hymselfe for it, to sanctifie it, purgeyng it in the fountayne of water, throughe the word, that he might make it unto himself, a glorious congregacion, not having spot or wrincle, or any such thing, but that it should be holy and blameles. So men are bounde to love their owne wives as their owne bodies: he that loveth his owne wife, loveth himself. For never did any man hate his owne flesh, but nourisheth and cherisheth it, even as the lorde doeth the congregacion, for wee are membres of his bodie, of his fleshe, and of his bones. For this cause shal a man leave father and mother, and shalbe joyned unto his wife, and they two shalbe one fleshe. This mistery is great, but I speake of Christ, and of the congregacion. Neverthelesse let every one of you so love his owne wife, even as himselfe.   *Eph.* 5

Likewise the same Saint Paule (writing to the Colossians) speaketh thus to al menne that be maried: Ye men, love your wives and be not bitter unto them.   *Col.* 3

Heare also what saint Peter the apostle of Christ, (which was himselfe a maried man,) sayeth unto al menne that are maried. Ye husbandes, dwel with your wives according to knowledge: Gevyng honor unto the wife, as unto the weaker vessel, and as heyres together of the grace of lyfe, so that your prayers be not hindred.   1 *Pet.* 3

Hitherto ye have heard the duetie of the husbande towarde the wife.

Nowe lykewise, ye wives, heare and lerne your duetie toward your husbandes, even as it is playnely set furth in holy scripture.

Saint Paul (in the forenamed epistle to the Ephesians) teacheth you thus: Ye weomen submit yourselves unto your own husbandes as unto the lord: for the husband is the wives head, even as Christ is the head of the church: And he also is the saviour of the whole bodye. Therefore as the Churche, or congregacyon, is subjecte unto Christe: So lykewise let the wives also be in subjeccyon unto theyr owne husbandes in all thynges. And agayn he sayeth: Let the wife reverence her husbande.   *Eph.* 5

And (in his epistle to the Colossians) Saincte Paule geveth you this short lesson. Ye wives, submit yourselves unto your owne husbandes, as it is conveniente in the Lorde.   *Col.* 3

Saincte Peter also doeth instructe you very godly, thus saying: Let wives be subject to theyr owne husbandes, so that if any obey not the woorde, they may bee wonne without the woorde, by the conversacyon of the wives: Whyle they beholde your chaste conversacyon, coupled with feare, whose apparell let it not bee outwarde, with broyded heare, and trymmyng about with golde, either in putting on of gorgeous apparell: But leat the hyd man whiche is in the hearte, be without all corrupcion, so that the spirite be milde and quiete, which is a precious thing in the sight of god. For after this maner (in the olde tyme) did the holy women, which trusted in God, apparell themselves, beeing subjecte to theyr own husbandes: as Sara obeied Abraham calling him lorde, whose daughters ye are made, doing wel, and being not dismaied with any feare.   1 *Pet.* 3

The newe maried persones (the same daye of their mariage) must receive the
holy communion.°

❧ THE ORDER FOR ❧
the bisitacion of the sicke,
and the Communion
of the same.

¶ *The Prieste entring into the sicke persones house,°* *shall saye.*

Peace be in this house, and to all that dwell in it.

When he commeth into the sicke mannes presence, he shall saye this psalme.°

Domine exaudi.

HEARE my prayer (o lorde) and consider my desire: herken unto me for thy trueth and righteousnes sake.   *Ps.* 143

And entre not into judgemente with thy servaunt: for in thy sight shal no man living be justified.

For the enemie hath persecuted my soule: he hath smitten my life downe to the grounde: he hath laied me in the darkenesse, as the men that have bene long dead.

Therefore is my spirite vexed within me: and my harte within me is desolate.

Yet doe I remember the time paste, I muse upon all thy woorkes: yea, I exercise myselfe in the workes of thy handes.

I stretche forth mine handes unto thee: my soule gaspeth unto thee as a thyrstie lande.

Heare me (o lorde) and that soone: for my spirite weaxeth faint: hide not thy face from me, lest I be like unto them that goe downe into the pitte.

O leate me heare thy lovyng kyndenesse betimes in the morning, for in thee is my trust: shewe thou me the waie that I should walke in for I lift up my soule unto thee.

Deliver me (o lorde) from myne enemies: for I flye unto thee to hide me.

Teache me to dooe the thynge, that pleaseth thee, for thou art my god, leate thy loving spirite leade me foorth unto the lande of righteousnesse.

Quicken me (o lorde) for thy names sake, and for thy righteousnesse sake bring my soule out of trouble.

And of thy goodnesse slaie my enemies, and destroye all them that
vexe my soule, for I am thy servaunt.

Glory to the father and to the sonne. *&c.*

As it was in the beginning. *&c.*

¶ *With this antheme.*

Remember not Lord our iniquities,° nor the iniquities of our forefathers. Spare us good Lord, spare thy people, whom thou hast redemed
with thy most precious bloud, and be not angry with us forever.

Lorde have mercye upon us.

Christe have mercie upon us.

Lorde have mercie upon us.

Our father, whiche art in heaven. *&c.*

And leade us not into temptacion.

Answere. But deliver us from evill. Amen.

The Minister. O lorde save thy servaunte.°

Answere. Whiche putteth his trust in thee.

Minister. Sende hym helpe from thy holy place.

Answere. And evermore mightily defende hym.

Minister. Leat the enemie have none advauntage of hym.

Answere. Nor the wicked approche to hurte hym.

Minister. Bee unto hym, o lorde, a strong tower.

Answere. From the face of his enemie.

Minister. Lord heare my prayer.

Answer. And let my crye come unto thee.

Minister. Let us praye.

O LORD looke downe from heaven,° beholde, visite, and releve
this thy servaunte: Looke upon hym with the iyes of thy mercy,
geve hym coumforte, and sure confidence in thee: Defende him from
the daunger of the enemie, and kepe hym in perpetual peace, and
safetie: through Jesus Christe our Lorde. Amen.

HEARE us almightie and moste merciful God, and Saviour:
Extende thy accustomed goodnesse to this thy servaunt, which
is greved with sickenesse: Visite hym, o Lorde, as thou diddest visite
Peters wifes mother, and the Capitaines servaunt. And as thou preser-
vedest Thobie and Sara by thy Aungel from daunger: So restore unto

this sicke person his former helth (if it be thy will) or els geve hym grace so to take thy correccion: that after this painfull lyfe ended, he maye dwell with thee in lyfe everlastyng. Amen.

Then shall the Minister exhorte the sicke person° after this fourme, or other lyke.

D ERELY beloved, know this that almighty God is the Lorde over lyfe, and death, and over all thynges to them perteyning, as youth, strength, helth, age, weakenesse, and sickenesse. Wherfore, whatsoever your sickenes is, knowe you certaynly that it is Gods visitacion. And for what cause soever this sickenesse is sent unto you: whether it bee to trye your pacience for the example of other, and that your fayth may be founde, in the day of the Lorde, laudable, glorious and honourable, to the encrease of glory, and endelesse felicitie: Or els it be sent unto you to correcte and amende in you, whatsoever doeth offende the iyes of our heavenly father: knowe you certainly, that if you truely repent you of your synnes, and beare your sickenes paciently, trusting in Gods mercy, for his dere sonne Jesus Christes sake, and rendre unto him humble thankes for his fatherly visitacion, submytting your selfe wholy to his wil: it shal turne to your profite, and helpe you forewarde in the ryght waye that leadeth unto everlastyng lyfe.† Take therfore in good worthe, the chaste- † *If the person* ment of the lorde: For whom the lorde loveth he *visited   bee* chastiseth. Yea (as saincte Paul sayth) he scourgeth *very   sicke,* every sonne, which he receiveth: yf you indure chastise- *then the curate* ment, he offereth himselfe unto you as unto his owne *may end his* children. What sonne is he that the father chastiseth *exhortacion at* children. What sonne is he that the father chastiseth *this place.*

not? Yf ye be not under correccion (wherof all the true children are partakers), then are ye bastardes and not children. Therfore seyng that whan our carnal fathers doe correct us, we reverently obey them, shall we not now much rather be obedient to our spirituall father, and so live? And they for a fewe daies doe chastise us after theyr owne pleasure: but he doeth chastise us for our profite, to the entente he maye make us partakers of his holines. These wordes, good brother, are Gods wordes, and wryten in holy scripture for our coumfort and instruccion, that we should paciently and with thankesgevyng, beare our heavenly fathers correccion: whansoever by any maner of adversitie it shall please his gracious goodnesse to visite us. And there should be no greater coumfort to christian persons, then to be made lyke unto Christ, by sufferyng paciently adversities, troubles, and sickenesses. For he himselfe wente not up to joy, but firste he suffered payne: he entred not into his glory, before he was crucified. So truely our waye to eternall joy, is to suffre here with Christe, and our doore to entre into eternal life: is gladly to dye with Christe, that we may ryse againe from death, and dwell with him in everlasting life. Now therfore taking your sickenesse, which is thus profitable for you, paciently: I exhorte you in the name of God, to remembre the profession, which you made unto God in your Baptisme. And forasmuch as after this lyfe, there is accompte to be geven unto the ryghteous judge, of whom all must be judged without respecte of persons: I require you to examine yourselfe, and your state, both towarde God and man, so that accusyng and condemnyng yourselfe for your owne faultes, you may fynde mercy at our heavenly fathers hande, for Christes sake, and not be accused and condemned in that fearfull judgement. Therfore I shall shortely rehearse the articles of our fayth, that ye maye knowe whether you doe beleve as a christian manne should beleve, or no.

Here the minister shall rehearse the articles of the fayth° saying thus.

Doest thou beleve in God the father almyghtie?

And so forth as it is in Baptisme.

Then shall the minister examine whether he be in charitie with all the worlde. Exhortyng hym to forgeve from the botome of his herte al persons, that have offended hym, and yf he have offended other, to aske them forgevenesse: and where he hathe done injurye or wrong to any manne, that he make amendes to hys uttermoste power. And if he have not afore disposed his goodes, let him then make his will. (But men must be oft admonished that they set an ordre for theyr temporall goodes and landes whan they be in helth.) And also to declare his debtes, what he oweth, and what is owing to him: for discharging of his conscience, and quietnesse of his executours.† The minister may not forget, nor omitte to move the sicke person (and that moste earnestly) to lyberalitie towarde the poore.
† *This may be done before the minister begyn his prayers, as he shal see cause.*

¶ *Here shall the sicke person make a speciall confession, yf he fele his conscience troubled with any weightie matter. After which confession, the priest shall absolve hym after this forme: and the same forme of absolucion shalbe used in all pryvate confessions.°*

OUR Lord Jesus Christ, who hath lefte power to his Churche to absolve all sinners, which truely repent and beleve in hym: of his

great mercy forgeve thee thyne offences: and by his autoritie committed to me, I absolve thee from all thy synnes, in the name of the father,
and of the sonne, and of the holy gost. Amen.

And then the priest shall saye the collecte folowyng.

Let us praye.

O MOST mercifull God,° which according to the multitude of thy
mercies, doest so putte away the synnes of those which truely
repent, that thou remembrest them no more: open thy iye of mercy
upon this thy servaunt, who moste earnestly desireth pardon and forgevenesse: Renue in hym, moste lovyng father, whatsoever hath been
decayed by the fraude and malice of the devil, or by his owne carnall
wyll, and frailnesse: preserve and continue this sicke membre in the
unitie of thy Churche, consyder his contricion, accepte his teares,
aswage his payne, as shalbe seen to thee moste expedient for him. And
forasmuch as he putteth his full trust only in thy mercy: Impute not
unto him his former sinnes, but take him unto thy favour: through
the merites of thy moste derely beloved sonne Jesus Christe. Amen.

Then the minister shall saye this psalme.

In te Domine speravi.

I N thee, O Lorde have I put my trust, let me never be put to confusion, but ridde me, and deliver me into thy righteousnes: enclyne
thyne eare unto me, and save me.   *Ps. 71*

Be thou my strong holde (wherunto I may alwaye resorte) thou haste
promysed to helpe me: for thou art my house of defence and my castell.

Deliver me (O my God) out of the hande of the ungodly, out of the
hande of the unrighteous and cruell man.

For thou (O Lord God) art the thyng that I long for, thou art my
hope, even fro my youth.

Through thee have I been holden up ever since I was borne, thou
art he that tooke me out of my mothers wombe: my prayse shalbe
alwaye of thee.

I am become as it were a monster unto many: but my sure trust is
in thee.

Oh let my mouth be filled with thy prayse (that I may syng of thy
glory) and honour all the daye long.

Cast me not awaye in the tyme of age, forsake me not when my
strength fayleth me.

For mine enemies speake against me: and they that lay waite for my soule, take their cousayle together, saying: God hath forsaken hym, persecute hym and take hym, for there is none to delyver hym.

Goe not ferre fro me, O God: my God, haste thee to helpe me.

Let them be confounded and perishe, that are againste my soule: let them be covered with shame and dishonour, that seke to doe me evill.

As for me, I will paciently abyde alwaye, and wyll prayse thee more and more.

My mouth shall dayly speake of thy righteousnes and salvacion, for I knowe no ende therof.

I will goe forth in the strength of the Lorde God: and will make mencion of thy righteousnesse onely.

Thou (O God) haste taught me from my youth up until now, therfore wil I tel of thy wonderous workes.

Forsake me not (O God) in myne olde age, when I am gray headed, untill I have shewed thy strength unto this generacion, and thy power to all them that are yet for to come.

Thy righteousnesse (O God) is very high, and great thinges are they that thou haste doen: O God who is lyke unto thee?

O what great troubles and adversities hast thou shewed me? and yet diddest thou turne and refreshe me: yea, and broughtest me from the depe of the earth agayne.

Thou haste brought me to great honour, and coumforted me on every side.

Therfore will I prayse thee, and thy faithfulnes (O God) playing upon an instrument of musicke, unto thee will I syng upon the harpe, O thou holy one of Israel.

My lippes will be fayne, when I syng unto thee: and so will my soule whom thou haste delyvered.

My tounge also shall talke of thy righteousnesse all the daye long, for they are confounded and brought unto shame, that seke to doe me evyll.

Glory to the father. &c.

As it was in the beginnyng. &c.

Addyng this anthem.

O SAVEOUR of the world save us,° which by thy crosse and precious bloud hast redemed us, helpe us we beseche thee, O God.

Then shall the minister saye.

THE almighty Lord, whiche is a moste strong tower to all them that put their trust in hym, to whom all thynges in heaven, in earth, and under earth, doe bowe and obey: be now and evermore thy defence, and make thee knowe and fele, that there is no other name under heaven geven to man, in whom and through whom thou mayest receyue helth and salvacion, but only the name of our Lorde Jesus Christe. Amen.

¶ *If the sicke person desyre to be annoynted,° then shal the priest annoynte him upon the forehead or breast only, makyng the signe of the crosse, saying thus.*

AS with this visible oyle° thy body outwardly is annoynted: so our heavenly father almyghtye God, graunt of his infinite goodnesse, that thy soule inwardly may be annoynted with the holy gost, who is the spirite of al strength, coumforte, reliefe, and gladnesse. And vouchesafe for his great mercy (yf it be his blessed will) to restore unto thee thy bodely helth, and strength, to serve him, and sende thee release of al thy paines, troubles and diseases, both in body and minde. And howsoever his goodnesse (by his divyne and unserchable providence) shall dispose of thee: we, his unworthy ministers and servauntes, humbly beseche the eternall majestie, to doe with thee according to the multitude of his innumerable mercies, and to pardon thee all thy sinnes, and offences, committed by all thy bodily senses, passions, and carnall affeccions: who also vouchsafe mercifully to graunt unto thee gostely strength by his holy spirite, to withstand and overcome al temptacions and assaultes of thine adversarye, that in no wise he prevaile against thee, but that thou mayest have perfit victory and triumph against the devil, sinne, and death, through Christ our Lord: Who by his death hath overcome the Prince of death, and with the father, and the holy gost evermore liveth and reigneth God, worlde without ende. Amen.

Usque quo, Domine.

HOW long wilt thou forget me (O Lord) for ever? how long wilt thou hyde thy face from me?   *Ps.* 13

How long shall I seke counsell in my soule? and be so vexed in myne herte? how long shall myne enemye triumph over me?

Consydre, and heare me (O lord my God) lighten myne iyes, that I slepe not in death.

Leste myne enemy saye: I have prevayled against hym: for yf I be cast downe, they that trouble me will reioyce at it.

But my trust is in thy mercy: and my herte is joyfull in thy salvacion.

I will sing of the Lord, because he hath delte so lovingly with me.

Yea, I wyll prayse the name of the Lord the most highest.

Glory be to the &c.

As it was in the &c.

¶ The communion of the sicke.°

*F*ORASMUCHE *as all mortal men be subject to many sodaine perils, diseases, and sickenesses, and ever uncertaine what time they shall departe out of this lyfe: Therfore to the entente they may be alwayes in a readinesse to dye,° whensoever it shall please almighty God to call them: The curates shall diligently from tyme to tyme, but specially in the plague tyme, exhorte theyr paryshoners to the ofte receyvyng (in the churche) of the holy communion of the body and bloud of oure saviour Christe: whiche (yf they doe) they shall have no cause in theyr sodaine visitacion, to be unquyeted for lacke of the same. But if the sicke person be not hable to come to the churche, and yet is desirous to receyve the communion in his house, then he must geve knowlage over night, or els early in the morning to the curate, signifying also howe many be appoynted to communicate with hym. And yf the same daye there be a celebracion of the holy communion in the churche, then shall the priest reserve (at the open communion) so muche of the sacrament of the body and bloud, as shall serve the siche person, and so many as shall communicate with hym (yf there be any). And so soone as he conveniently may, after the open communion ended in the church, shall goe and minister the same, firste to those that are appoynted to communicate with the sicke (yf there be any) and last of all to the sicke person hymselfe. But before the curate distribute the holy communion:* the appoynted generall confession *must be made in the name of the communicantes,* the curate addyng the absolucion *with the* coumfortable sentences of scripture *folowyng in the open communion, and after the communion ended,* the collecte.

Almightie and everlyvyng God, we moste hertely thanke thee. &c.

¶ *But yf the daye be not appoynted for the open communion in the churche, then (upon convenient warning geven) the curate shal come and visite the sick person afore noone. And having a convenient place in the sicke mans house (where he may reverently celebrate) with all thinges necessary for the same, and not beyng otherwyse letted with the publike service. or any other just impediment: he shal there celebrate the holy communion after suche forme and sorte as hereafter is appoynted.*

❧ THE CELEBRA- ❧
cion of the holy communion for the sicke.

O PRAYSE the Lorde, all ye nacions, laude hym, all ye people: for his mercifull kyndenesse is confyrmed towarde us, and the trueth of the Lorde endureth for ever. Glory be to the father, *&c.*

Lord, have mercy upon us.
Christ, have mercy upon us. } *Without any more repeticion.*
Lord, have mercy upon us.

The Priest. The Lorde be with you.
Aunswere. And with thy spirite.

Let us pray.

A LMIGHTIE everlyving God, maker of mankynde, which doest correcte those whom thou doest love, and chastisest every one whome thou doest receyve: we beseche the to have mercy upon this thy servaunte visited with thy hande, and to graunt that he may take his sickenesse paciently, and recover his bodily helth (if it be thy gracious will) and whansoever his soule shall departe from the body, it may without spotte be presented unto thee: through Jesus Christe our Lord. Amen.

The Epistle. Heb. 12

M Y sonne despise not the correccion of the Lorde, neyther fainte when thou art rebuked of hym: for whom the Lorde loveth, hym he correcteth, yea and he scourgeth every sonne, whom he receyveth.

The gospell. John 5

V ERELY verely I saye unto you, he that heareth my woorde, and beleveth on hym that sente me, hath everlasting life, and shall not come unto damnacion, but he passeth from death unto life.

The Preface.

The Lorde be with you.
Aunswere. And with thy spirite.
Lifte up your hertes. *&c.*

Unto the ende of the Canon.°

¶ *At the tyme of the distribucion of the holy sacrament, the priest shall firste receyve the communion hymselfe, and after minister to them that be appoynted to communicate with the sicke (yf there be any) and then to the sicke person. And the sicke person shall all wayes desyre some, eyther of his owne house, or els of his neyghbours, to receyve the holy communion with hym, for that shall be to hym a singuler great coumforte, and of theyr parte a great token of charitie.*

¶ *And yf there be moe sicke persons to be visited the same day that the curate doth celebrate in any sicke mans house: then shall the curate (there) reserve so muche of the sacramente of the body and bloud: as shall serve the other sicke persons, and suche as be appoynted to communicate with them (yf there be any). And shall immediatly cary it, and minister it unto them.*

¶ *But yf any man eyther by reason of extremitie of sickenesse,° or for lacke of warnyng geven in due tyme, to the curate, or by any other just impedimente, doe not receyve the sacramente of Christes bodye and bloud: then the curate shall instruct hym, that yf he doe truely repent hym of his sinnes, and sted-fastly beleve that Jesus Christ hath suffered death upon the crosse for hym: and shed his bloud for his redempcion, earnestly remembring the benefites he hath therby, and geving hym hertie thankes therfore: he doeth eate and drynke spiritually the bodye and bloud of our sauioure Christe, profytably to his soules helth, although he doe not receyve the sacrament with his mouth.*

¶ *When the sicke persone is visited and receiveth the holy communion, all at one tyme: then the priest for more expedicion shall use this ordre at the visitacion.*

The Anthem.

Remembre not Lorde. *&c.*

Lorde have mercy upon us.

Christe have mercy upon us.

Lorde have mercy upon us.

¶ Our father whiche art in heaven. *&c.*

And leade us not into temptacion.

Aunswere. But deliver us from evyll. Amen.

Let us praye.

O Lorde looke downe from heaven. *&c.*

¶ *With the firste parte of the exhortacion and all other thynges unto the Psalme:*

In thee o Lorde have I put my trust. *&c.*

And yf the sicke desyre to be annoyncted, then shall the priest use the appoynted prayer without any Psalme.

❧ THE ORDRE FOR ❧
the buriall of the dead.

*The priest metyng the Corps at the Churche style, shall say: Or els the
priestes and clerkes shall sing, and so goe either into the Churche, or
towardes the grave.°*

I AM the resurreccion and the life° (sayth the Lord): he that beleveth
in me, yea though he were dead, yet shall he live. And whosoever
lyveth and beleveth in me: shall not dye for ever.   *John* 11

I KNOWE that my redemer lyveth,° and that I shall ryse out of the
yearth in the last daye, and shalbe covered again with my skinne,
and shall see God in my flesh: yea and I my selfe shall beholde hym,
not with other but with these same iyes.   *Job* 19

W E brought nothyng into this worlde, neyther may we carye any
thyng out of this worlde. The Lord geveth, and the Lord taketh
awaie. Even as it pleaseth the Lorde, so cummeth thynges to passe:
blessed be the name of the Lorde.   1 *Tim.* 6, *Job* 1

*When they come at the grave, whyles the Corps is made readie to be layed
into the earth,° the priest shall saye, or els the priest and clerkes shall syng.*

M AN that is borne of a woman,° hath but a shorte tyme to lyve,
and is full of miserye: he cummeth up and is cut downe lyke
a floure, he flyeth as it were a shadowe, and never continueth in one
staye.   *Job* 9

¶ In the myddest of lyfe we be in death, of whom may we seke for
succour but of thee, o Lorde, whiche for our synnes justly art moved:
yet o Lord God moste holy, o Lord moste mighty, o holy and moste mercifull saviour, delyver us not into the bitter paines of eternal death. Thou
knowest, Lord, the secretes of our hartes, shutte not up thy mercyfull
iyes to our praiers: But spare us Lord most holy, o God moste mighty,
o holy and mercifull saviour, thou moste worthy judge eternal, suffre
us not at our last houre for any paines of death, to fal from the.

Then the priest castyng earth upon the Corps,° shall saye.

I COMMENDE thy soule to God the father almighty,° and thy body to
the grounde, earth to earth, asshes to asshes, dust to dust, in sure

and certayne hope of resurreccion to eternall life, through our Lord Jesus Christ, who shall chaunge our vile body, that it may be lyke to his glorious body, accordyng to the myghtie workyng wherby he is hable to subdue all thynges to himselfe.

Then shalbe sayed or song.

I HEARDE a voyce from heaven saying unto me: Wryte, blessed are the dead whiche dye in the Lorde. Even so sayeth the spirite, that they rest from theyr labours.   *Rev.* 14

Let us praye.

W E commende into thy handes of mercy (moste mercifull father) the soule of this our brother departed, *N.* And his body we commit to the earth,° besechyng thyne infinite goodnesse, to geve us grace to lyve in thy feare and love, and to dye in thy favoure: that when the judgemente shall come which thou haste commytted to thy welbeloved sonne, both this our brother, and we, may be found acceptable in thy sight, and receive that blessing, whiche thy welbeloved sonne shall then pronounce to all that love and feare thee, saying: Come ye blessed children of my father: Receyve the kingdome prepared for you before the beginning of the worlde. Graunt this mercifull father for the honour of Jesu Christe our onely savior, mediator, and advocate. Amen.

This praier shall also be added.

A LMIGHTIE God, we geve thee hertie thankes for this thy servaunte, whom thou haste delyvered from the miseries of this wretched world, from the body of death and all temptacion. And, as we trust, hast brought his soule whiche he committed into thy holye handes, into sure consolacion and reste: Graunte we beseche thee, that at the daye of judgement his soule and all the soules of thy electe, departed out of this lyfe, may with us and we with them, fully receive thy promisses, and be made perfite altogether thorow the glorious resurreccion of thy sonne Jesus Christ our Lorde.

These psalmes with other suffrages folowyng,° are to be sayde in the churche, either before or after the buriall of the corps.

Dilexi quoniam.

I AM well pleased that the lorde hath hearde the voyce of my prayer. That he hath enclined his eare unto me, therefore wil I call upon him as long as I live.   *Ps.* 116

The snares of death compassed me round about, and the paynes of hel gatte holde upon me: I shal finde trouble and heavines, and I shal cal upon the name of the lorde: (O Lorde) I beseche thee deliver my soule.

Gracious is the lord, and righteous: yea, our god is mercifull.

The lord preserveth the simple: I was in misery and he helped me.

Turne agayn then unto thy rest, o my soule: for the lord hath rewarded thee.

And why? thou hast delivered my soule from death, mine iyes from teares, and my feete from fallyng.

I will walke before the lorde: in the lande of the living.

I beleved and therfore wil I speake, but I was sore troubled: I sayd in my haste, all menne are lyers.

What rewarde shall I geve unto the lorde: for al the benefites that he hath doen unto me?

I wil receive the cup of salvacion: and call upon the name of the lorde.

I will pay my vowes now in the presence of al his people: right dere in the sight of the lord is the death of hys Saintes.

Beholde (O lorde) how that I am thy servaunte: I am thy servaunt and the sonne of thy handmayde, thou hast broken my bondes in sunder.

I will offer to thee the sacrifice of thankes gevyng: and will call upon the name of the Lorde.

I will pay my vowes unto the lorde in the syghte of all his people: in the courtes of the lordes house, even in the middest of thee, o Hierusalem.

Glorie to the father. *&c*.

As it was in the beginning. *&c*.

Domine, probasti. °

O LORD, thou hast searched me out, and knowen me: Thou knowest my downsitting, and mine uprising: thou understandest my thoughtes long before.   *Ps.* 139

Thou art about my pathe, and about my bed: and spiest out al my waies.

For loe, there is not a woord in my toungue: but thou (o lorde) knoweste it altogether.

Thou hast fashioned me, behinde and before: and layed thine hande upon me.

Such knowelage is to woonderfull and excellente for me: I cannot attaine unto it.

Whither shall I goe then from thy spirite? or whither shal I goe then from thy presence?

If I clime up into heaven, thou art there: If I goe down to hel thou art there also.

If I take the winges of the morning: and remaine in the uttermoste partes of the sea.

Even there also shal thy hande leade me: and thy righte hande shall holde me.

If I saye, paradventure the darkenesse shall cover me: then shall my night bee turned to daye.

Yea the darkenesse is no darkenesse with thee: but the night is all clere as the daye, the darkenesse and lyghte to thee are bothe alike.

For my reynes are thine, thou hast covered me in my mothers wombe, I wyll geve thankes unto thee: for I am fearefully and woonderously made, mervailous are thy woorkes, and that my soule knoweth right well.

My bones are not hidde from thee: though I bee made secretely, and fashioned beneath in the yearth.

Thine eyes did see my substaunce, yet being unperfecte: and in thy booke were al my membres written.

Whiche daye by daye were fashioned: when as yet there was none of them.

Howe dere are thy councels unto me, O God? O howe greate is the summe of them?

If I tell them, they are moe in noumbre then the sande: when I wake up, I am present with thee.

Wilt thou not sley the wicked, O God? departe from me, ye bloudethristie men.

For they speake unrighteously againste thee: and thyne enemies take thy name in vaine.

Dooe not I hate them, O Lord, that hate thee? and am not I greved with those that ryse up against thee?

Yea I hate them righte sore: even as thoughe they were myne enemies.

Trye me, O God, and seeke the grounde of myne harte: prove me, and examine my thoughtes.

Looke well if there be any way of wickednes in me: and leade me in the waye everlasting.

Glory to the father. &c.

As it was in the beginning. &c.

Lauda, anima, mea.

PRAYSE the lorde, (o my soule) while I live wil I prayse the lorde: yea as long as I have any being, I wil sing prayses unto my god. *Ps.* 146

O put not your trust in princes, nor in any childe of man: for there is no helpe in them.

For when the breath of man goeth furth, he shall turne agayn to his yearth: and then all his thoughtes perish.

Blessed is he that hath the God of Jacob for hys helpe: and whose hope is in the lorde hys god.

Which made heaven and earth, the sea, and al that therein is: whiche kepeth his promise for ever.

Whiche helpeth them to right that suffer wrong: which feedeth the hungrie.

The lorde looseth men out of prieson: the Lorde geveth sight to the blynde.

The lorde helpeth them up that are fallen: the lorde careth for the righteous.

The lord careth for the straungers, he defendeth the fatherlesse and widdowe: as for the waye of the ungodly, he turneth it upsyde downe.

The lorde thy God, O Sion, shalbe kyng for evermore: and throughout all generacions.

Glory to the father. *&c.*

As it was in the beginning. *&c.*

Then shall folowe this lesson, taken out of the xv. Chapter to the
Corinthians, the firste Epistle.

CHRISTE is risen from the dead, and become the first fruictes of them that slepte. For by a man came death, and by a man came the resurreccion of the deade. For as by Adam all dye: even so by Christ shal al be made alive, but every manne in his owne ordre. The firste is Christe, then they that are Christes at hys comming. Then commeth the ende, when he hath delivered up the kyngdome to God the father, when he hath put downe al rule and al authoritie and power. For he must reygne til he have putte al his enemies under his feete. The laste enemie that shal bee destroyed, is death. For he hath putte all thinges under his feete. But when he sayeth al thinges are put under him, it is manifeste that he is excepted, whiche dyd putte all thinges under him. When all thynges are subdued unto hym, then shall the soonne also hymselfe bee subjecte unto hym that put all thinges under him, that god mai be all in all. Elles what doe they, whiche are baptized over the dead, if the dead ryse not at all? Why are they then baptized over them? Yea, and why stand we alway then in jeoperdie? By our rejoysing whiche I have in Christ Jesu oure lorde, I dye dayly. That I have fought with beastes at Ephesus after the maner of men, what avauntageth it me, if the dead ryse not agayn? Let us eate, and drynke, for to morowe we shall dye. Be not ye deceived: eivill wordes corrupt good maners. Awake truly out of slepe, and sinne not. For some have not the knowledge of God. I speake this to your shame. But some man will say: how aryse the dead? with what bodye shall they come? Thou foole, that whiche thou sowest, is not quickened except it dye. And what sowest thou? Thou sowest not that body that shall be: but bare corne, as of wheate, or of some other: but god geveth it a bodie at hys pleasure, to every seede his owne body. All fleshe is not one maner of fleshe: but there is one maner of fleshe of men, an other maner of fleshe of beastes, an other of fishes, an other of birdes. There are also celestiall bodies, and there are bodies terrestriall. But the glorye of the celestiall is one, and the glorye of the terrestrial is an other. There is one maner glory of the sonne, and an other glorye of the moone, and an other glorye of the sterres. For one sterre differeth from an other in glorie. So is the resurreccyon of the dead. It is sowen in corrupcion, it ryseth again in incorrupcion. It is sowen in dishonour, it ryscthe agayne in honour. It is sowen in weakenesse, it ryseth agayn in power. It is sowen a naturall bodie, it ryseth agayn a spirituall bodie. There is a naturall bodie, and there is a spirituall bodye: as it is also written: the firste manne Adam was made a living soule, and the last Adam was made a quickning spirite. Howebeit that is not firste which is spiritual: but that which is naturall, and then that whiche is spirituall. The firste man is of the earthe, yearthy: The seconde manne is the Lorde from heaven (heavenly). As is the earthy, such are they that are yearthy. And as is the heavenly, such are they that are heavenly. And as we have borne the image of the earthy, so shal we beare the image of the heavenly. This say I brethren, that fleshe and bloud can not enherite the kyngdome of God: Neyther doeth corrupcion inherite uncorrupcion. Behold, I shewe you a mistery. We shall not all slepe: but we shal al be chaunged, and that in a momente, in the twynkeling of an iye by the last trumpe. For the trumpe shall blowe, and the dead shall ryse incorruptible, and we shall be chaunged. For this corruptible must put on incorrupcion: and this mortall must put on immortalitie. When thys corruptible hath put on incorruption, and this mortall hath put on immortalitie: then shall bee brought to passe the saying that is written: Death is swalowed up in victorye: Death where is thy styng? Hell where is thy victorye? The styng of death is sinne: and the strength of sinne is the lawe. But thankes be unto god, whiche hath geven us victory, through our Lorde Jesus Christ. Therefore, my dere brethren, be ye stedfast and unmovable, alwaies ryche in the woorke of the lorde, forasmuch as ye know, how that your labour is not in vayne, in the lorde.

1 Cor. 15

The lesson ended then shall the priest say.

Lorde have mercie upon us.

Christe have mercie upon us.

Lorde have mercie upon us.

Our father whiche art in heaven. *&c.*

And leade us not into temptacion.

Aunswere. But deliver us from evil. Amen.

Priest. Entre not (o lorde) into judgement with thy servaunt.

Aunswere. For in thy sight no living creature shalbe justifyed.

Priest. From the gates of hell.°

Aunswere. Deliver theyr soules, o lorde.

Priest. I beleve to see the goodnes of the lorde.

Aunswere. In the lande of the living.

Prieste. O lorde, graciously heare my prayer.

Aunswere. And let my crye come unto thee.

Let us pray.

O LORDE, with whome dooe lyve the spirites of them that be dead:° and in whome the soules of them that bee elected, after they be delivered from the burden of the fleshe, be in joy and felicitie:° Graunte unto this thy servaunt, that the sinnes whiche he committed in this world be not imputed unto him, but that he escaping the gates of hell and paynes of eternall derkenes: may ever dwel in the region of lighte, with Abraham, Isaac, and Jacob, in the place where is no wepyng, sorowe, nor heavinesse: and when that dredeful day of the generall res-urreccion shall come, make him to ryse also with the just and righteous, and receive this bodie agayn to glory, then made pure and incorrupt-ible, set him on the right hand of thy sonne Jesus Christ, among thy holy and elect, that then he may heare with them these most swete and coumfortable wordes: Come to me ye blessed of my father, possesse the kingdome whiche hath bene prepared for you from the beginning of the worlde: Graunte thys we beseche thee, o mercifull father: through Jesus Christe our mediatour and redemer. Amen.

❧ THE CELEBRACION ❧
of the holy communion when
there is a burial of the dead.°

Quemadmodum.

LIKE as the hart desireth the water brookes: so longeth my soule after thee, o God.   *Ps.* 42

My soule is athirst for god, yea, even for the living god: when shal I come to appeare before the presence of god?

My teares have beene my meate day and nighte: whyle they dayly say unto me, where is now thy god?

Nowe when I thinke thereupon, I powre out my hart by my selfe: for I went with the multitude, and brought them furth unto the house of god, in the voyce of praise and thankesgeving, emong suche as kepe holy day.

Why art thou so full of heavines (O my soule): and why art thou so unquiete within me?

Put thy trust in god, for I wil yet geve him thankes: for the helpe of his countenaunce.

My God, my soule is vexed within me: therefore will I remember thee concerning the land of Jordane, and the litle hill of Hermon.

One deepe calleth an other, beecause of the noyse of thy water pypes: all thy waves and stormes are gone over me.

The lorde hath graunted his loving kyndenesse on the daye tyme: and in the nighte season dyd I syng of hym, and made my prayer unto the god of my lyfe.

I wil say unto the God of my strength, why haste thou forgotten me? why goe I thus hevelye, whyle the enemie oppresseth me?

My bones are smitten a soonder, whyle myne enemies (that trouble me) cast me in the teeth: namely while they say dayly unto me, where is nowe thy God?

Why art thou so vexed (O my soule): and why arte thou so disquieted within me?

O put thy trust in god, for I will yet thanke him which is the helpe of my countenaunce, and my God.

Glorie to the Father. *&c.*

As it was in the beginning. *&c.*

Collecte.

O MERCIFULL god the father of oure lorde Jesu Christ, who is the resurreccion and the life: In whom whosoever beleveth shall live thoughe he dye: And whosoever liveth, and beleveth in hym, shal not dye eternallye: who also hath taughte us (by his holye Apostle Paule) not to bee sory as men without hope for them that slepe in him: We mekely beseche thee (o father) to raise us from the death of sin, unto the life of righteousnes, that when we shall departe this lyfe, we maye slepe in him (as our hope is this our brother doeth) and at the general resurreccion in the laste daie, bothe we and this oure brother departed, receivyng agayne oure bodies, and rising againe in thy moste gracious favoure: maye with all thine elect Saynctes, obteine eternall joye. Graunte this, o Lorde god, by the meanes of our advocate Jesus Christ: which with thee and the holy ghoste, liveth and reigneth one God for ever. Amen.

The Epistle. 1 *Thess.* 4

I WOULDE not brethren that ye shoulde bee ignoraunt concernyng them which are fallen a slepe, that ye sorowe not as other doe, whiche have no hope. For if we beleve that Jesus dyed, and rose againe: even so them also whiche slepe by Jesus, will God bring again with him. For thys saye we unto you in the word of the Lorde: that we whiche shall lyve, and shal remain in the commyng of the Lord, shal not come ere they which slepe. For the Lorde himselfe shal descende from heaven with a shoute, and the voice of the Archangell and troump of God. And the deade in Christe shal arise first: then we whiche shall lyve (even wee whiche shal remayne) shal bee caughte up wyth them also in the cloudes, to meete the Lorde in the ayre. And so shall wee ever be with the Lorde. Wherefore coumforte youre selves one an other wyth these woordes.

¶ *The gospell.* John 6

JESUS saied to his disciples and to the Jewes: Al that the father geveth me, shall come to me: and he that commeth to me, I cast not away. For I came down from heaven: not to do that I wil, but that he wil, which hath sent me. And this is the fathers wyll whiche hath sente me, that of all whiche he hath geven me, I shal lose nothing: but raise them up again at the last day. And this is the wil of him that sent me: that every one which seeth the sonne and beleveth on him, have everlasting life. And I wil raise him up at the laste daye.

ᔒ THE ORDER OF THE ᔒ
Purificacion of weomen.

The woman shall come into the churche, and there shal kneele downe in some conveniente place, nygh unto the quier doore:° and the prieste standyng by her, shall saye these woordes or suche lyke, as the case shall require.

FOR asmuche as it hath pleased almightie god of hys goodnes to geve you safe deliveraunce: and your childe baptisme, and hath preserved you in the greate daunger of childebirth: ye shal therefore geve hartie thankes unto god, and pray.

Then shall the prieste say this psalme.

Levavi oculos.

I HAVE lifted up mine iyes° unto the hilles, from whence cummeth my helpe?   *Ps.* 121

My help cummeth even from the lord, which hath made heaven and earth.

He will not suffer thy foote to be moved, and he that kepeth thee wil not slepe.

Beholde he that kepeth Israel, shal neither slumber nor slepe.

The lorde himselfe is thy keper, the lorde is thy defence upon thy right hande.

So that the sonne shall not burne thee by daye, neyther the moone by nyght.

The lord shal preserve thee from al evil, yea it is even he that shal kepe thy soule.

The lord shal preserve thy going out, and thy cumming in, from this tyme furth for evermore.

Glorye to the father. *&c.*

As it was in the beginning. *&c.*

Lord have mercie upon us.

Christ have mercie upon us.

Lord have mercie upon us.

¶ Our father whiche art in heaven. *&c.*

And leade us not into temptacion.

Aunswere. But deliver us from evil. Amen.

Priest. O lord save this woman thy servaunt.

Aunswere. Whiche putteth her trust in thee.

Priest. Bee thou to her a strong tower.

Aunswere. From the face of her enemie.

Priest. O lord heare our prayer.

Aunswere. And let our crye come to thee.

Priest.

¶ Let us pray.

O ALMIGHTIE God, which hast delivered° this woman thy servaunt from the great payne and peril of childbirth: Graunt we beseche thee (most mercifull father) that she through thy helpe may both faithfully lyve, and walke in her vocacyon accordynge to thy will in thys lyfe presente: and also may be partaker of everlastyng glorye in the lyfe to come: through Jesus Christ our lorde. Amen.

The woman that is purifyed, must offer her Crysome, and other accustomed offeringes.° And if there be a communion,° it is convenient that she receive the holy communion.

The firste daie of lente com-
monly called Ashe-
wednisdaye.

¶ *After mattens ended, the people beeyng called together by the ryngyng of a bel,° and assembled in the churche: The inglyshe letanye shall be sayed after the accustomed maner: whiche ended, the prieste shal goe into the pulpitte and saye thus.*

B RETHREN, in the prymative churche° there was a godlye disci-plyne, that at the begynnyng of lente suche persones as were notorious synners, were put to open penaunce, and punished in this worlde, that theyr soules myght bee saved in the day of the lord. And that other, admonished by theyr example, might be more afrayed to offende. In the steede whereof until the saide disciplyne maye bee restored agayne: (whiche thynge is muche to bee wished) it is thoughte good that at thys tyme (in your presence) should bee read the general sentences of goddes cursyng agaynste impenitente sinners, gathered out of the xxvii. Chapter of Deuteronomie, and other places of scripture. And that ye shoulde aunswere to every sentence, Amen: To the entente that you beeyng admonished of the greate indignacion of God agaynste sinners: may the rather be called to earneste and true repentaunce, and maye walke more warely in these daungerous dayes, fleyng from such vices, for the whiche ye affirme with your owne mouthes: the curse of god to be due.

¶ Cursed is the man° that maketh any carved or molten image, an abominacion to the Lorde, the woorke of the handes of the craftes manne, and putteth it in a secrete place, to wurship it.

And the people shal aunswere, and saye.

Amen.

Minister. Cursed is he that curseth his father, and mother.

Aunswere. Amen.

Minister. Cursed is he that removeth alwaye the marke of hys neighbours land.

Aunswere. Amen.

Minister. Cursed is he that maketh the blinde to goe oute of hys waye.

Aunswere. Amen.

Minister. Cursed is he that letteth in judgemente the right of the straungier, of them that be fatherlesse, and of widdowes.

Aunswere. Amen.

Minister. Cursed is he that smiteth his neighbour secretely.

Aunswere. Amen.

Minister. Cursed is he that lieth with his neighbours wyfe.

Aunswere. Amen.

Minister. Cursed is he that taketh rewarde to slea the soule of innocent bloude.

Aunswere. Amen.

Minister. Cursed is he that putteth his truste in man, and taketh manne for his defence, and in his harte goeth from the Lorde.

Aunswere. Amen.

Minister. Cursed are the unmercifull, the fornicators and advouterers, the covetous persones, the wurshyppers of images, slaundreers, drunkardes, and extorcioners.

Aunswere. Amen.

The minister.

NOWE seeing that all they bee accursed° (as the Prophete David bearing witnesse) whiche doe erre and goe astray from the com-maundementes of God, let us (remembring the dredefull judgement hanging over our heades and beyng alwayes at hande) returne unto our lorde God, with all contricion and mekenes of heart, bewailing and lamenting our sinful life, knowlaging and confessing our offences, and seekyng to bring furth worthie fruites of penance. For even now is the axe put unto the roote of the trees, so that every tree whiche bryngeth not furth good fruite, is hewen downe and cast into the fyer. It is a fear-full thing to fall into the handes of the living God: he shal powre downe rayne upon the sinners, snares, fyer, and brimstone, storme and tem-pest: this shalbe theyr porcion to drynke. For loe the lorde is cummen out of his place, to visite the wickednes of such as dwell upon the earth. But who may abyde the daye of his cumming? who shalbee hable to endure whan he appeareth? His fanne is in his hande, and he wil pourge his floore, and gather his wheate into the barne, but he will burne the chaffe with unquenchable fier. The day of the lorde cummeth as a thiefe upon the night, and when men shall say peace, and all thynges are safe: then shall sodayne destruccion come upon them, as sorowe cometh upon a woman travaylyng with chylde, and they shall not escape: then shall appeare the wrathe of God in the daye of vengeaunce, whiche obstinate synners through the stubbernes of theyr hearte, have heaped unto themselfe, which despised the goodnesse, pacience and long suf-feraunce of god, when he called them continually to repentaunce. Then shall they cal upon me (sayth the lorde) but I wil not heare: they shal seke me early, but thei shal not finde me, and that because they hated knowlage, and received not the feare of the lord, but abhorred my coun-sell and despised my correccion: then shall it be to late to knocke, when the doore shalbe shut, and to late to cry for mercy, when it is the tyme of justice. O terrible voice of most just judgement, which shalbe pro-nounced upon them, when it shalbe sayde unto thee. Go ye cursed into the fyer everlasting, which is prepared for the devil and his angels. Therfore brethren take we hede by time, while the day of salvacion lasteth, for the night cometh when none can worke: but let us while we have the light, beleve in the light, and walke as the children of the light, that we be not cast into the utter derkenes, where is weping and gnash-ing of teeth. Let us not abuse the goodnes of god, whiche calleth us mercifully to amendement, and of his endlesse pitie, promiseth us

Ps. 118 [i.e. Ps. 119]

Matt. 3

Heb. 10

Ps. 10 [i.e. Ps. 11]

Isa. 26

Mal. 3

Matt. 3

1 Thess. 5

Rom. 2

Prov. 1

Matt. 25

2 Cor. 6
John 9

Matt. 25

forgevenes of that which is past: if (with a whole mind and a true hert)
we returne unto him: for though our sinnes be red as scarlet, they shalbe
as white as snowe, and though they be lyke purple, yet shall they be as
whyte as woolle. Turne you cleane (sayth the lord) from all your wick-   *Isa.* 1
ednes, and your synne shall not be your destruccion. Cast away from   *Ezek.* 18
you all your ungodlines that ye have doen, make you new hertes and
a new spirite: wherfore will ye dye, O ye house of Israel? seing I have no
pleasure in the death of him that dieth (sayth the Lord God). Turne you
then, and you shall lyve. Although we have sinned, yet have we an advocate with the father Jesus Christ the righteous, and he it is that obteyneth   *1 John* 2
grace for our sinnes, for he was wounded for our offences, and smitten
for our wickednes: let us therfore returne unto him, who is the merciful   *Isa.* 53
receiver of al true penitent sinners, assuring our selfe that he is ready to
receive us, and most willing to pardon us, if we come to him with faithful repentaunce: if we wil submit our selves unto him, and from henceforth walke in hys waies: if we wil take his easy yoke and light burden   *Matt.* 11
upon us to folowe him in lowlynesse, pacience, and charitie, and bee
ordred by the governaunce of his holy spirite, seking alwayes his glorye,
and serving him duely in our vocacion with thankes gevyng. This if we
doe, Christe wil deliver us from the curse of the law, and from the
extreme malediccion whiche shall lyght upon them that shalbee set on
the left hand: and he wyl sct us on his right hand, and geve us the blessed
benediccion of hys father, commaundyng us to take possession of hys
glorious kyngdome, unto the whiche he vouchsafe to bryng us al, for   *Matt.* 25
hys infinite mercye. Amen.

¶ *Then shall they all kneele upon theyr knees: And the prieste and clerkes*
kneelyng (where they are accustomed to saye the letanye) shall saye this psalme.

Miserere mei deus.°

HAVE mercye upon me (O God) after thy greate goodnesse:
according unto the multitude of thy mercies, do away mine
offences.   *Ps.* 51

Washe me throwly from my wickednes, and clense me from my synne.

For I knowlage my faultes, and my sinne is ever before me.

Agaynst thee only have I synned, and done this evyl in thy syght:
that thou myghtest bee justified in thy saying and clere when thou art
judged.

Behold, I was shapen in wickednes, and in synne hath my mother
conceived me.

But loe, thou requirest trueth in the inward partes, and shalte make me to understande wysdome secretelye.

Thou shalt pourge me with Isope, and I shall bee cleane: thou shalt washe me, and I shal bee whyter than snowe.

Thou shalte make me heare of joye and gladnesse, that the bones whiche thou haste broken, maye rejoyce.

Turne thy face from my synnes: and putte out all my mysdedes.

Make me a cleane herte (O God) and renue a ryght spyrite within me.

Caste me not a waye from thy presence, and take not thy holy spirite from me.

O geve me the coumforte of thy helpe agayne, and stablishe me wyth thy free spirite.

Then shal I teache thy waies unto the wicked, and sinners shal be converted unto thee.

Deliver me from bloud giltinesse (O God) thou that art the god of my health: and my toungue shall syng of thy righteousnesse.

Thou shalt open my lippes (O Lorde) my mouthe shal shewe thy prayse.

For thou desyreste no sacrifice, els would I geve it thee: but thou deliteste not in burnt offeryng.

The sacrifice of God is a troubled spirite, a broken and a contrite herte (O God) shalt thou not despise.

O bee favourable and gracious unto Syon, build thou the walles of Hierusalem.

Then shalt thou be pleased with the sacrifice of righteousnesse, wyth the burnt offeringes and oblacions: then shall they offre young bullockes upon thyne aultare.

> Glorye to the father. &c.
>
> As it was in the beginning. &c.

¶ Lorde have mercye upon us.

¶ Christe have mercye upon us.

¶ Lorde have mercye upon us.

¶ Our father whiche art in heaven. &c.

And leade us not into temptacion.

Aunswere. But deliver us from evyll. Amen.

Minister. O lorde save thy servauntes.

Aunswere. Whiche put theyr truste in thee.

Minister. Send unto them helpe from above.

Aunswere. And evermore mightily defende them.

Minister. Help us O God our saviour.

Aunswere. And for the glory of thy names sake delyver us, be mercifull unto us synners, for thy names sake.

Minister. O Lorde heare my prayer.

Aunswere. And let my crye come to thee.

Let us praye.

O LORD, we beseche thee° mercifully heare our prayers, and sparc all those which confesse theyr synnes to thee, that they (whose conscienses by synne are accused) by thy mercyfull pardon may be absolved, through Christe our Lorde. Amen.

O MOST mightie god° and mercifull father, which hast compassion of all menne, and hateste nothyng that thou haste made: whiche wouldeste not the deathe of a sinner, but that he shoulde rather turne from sinne and bee saved: mercifully forgeve us oure trespasses, receyve and coumforte us, whiche be grieved and weried with the burden of our sinne: Thy propertie is to have mercie, to thee onely it apperteineth to forgeve sinnes: spare us therfore, good Lorde, spare thy people whome thou hast redemed. Enter not into judgemente with thy servauntes, which be vile yearthe, and miserable sinners: But so turne thy ire from us, which mekely knowlage our vilenes, and truely repent us of our fautes: so make hast to helpe us in this worlde: that wee may ever live with thee in the worlde to come: through Jesus Christe our Lorde. Amen.

Then shal this antheme be sayed or song.°

T URNE thou us, good Lord, and so shall we be turned: bee favourable (O Lorde) bee favourable to thy people, whiche turne to thee in wepyng, fasting and praying: for thou art a mercifull God, full of compassion, long sufferyng, and of a great pietie. Thou sparest when we deserve punishemente, and in thy wrathe thykest upon mercy. Spare thy people, good Lorde, spare them, and lette not thy heritage bee brought to confusion: Heare us (O Lorde) for thy mercy is great, and after the multitude of thy mercyes looke upon us.

CERTAYNE NOTES
for the more playne explicacion and
decent ministracion of thinges, conteined
in thys booke.

*I*N *the saying or singing of Matens and Evensong, Baptizyng and Burying, the minister, in paryshe churches and chapels annexed to the same, shall use a Surples.° And in all Cathedral churches and Colledges, the archdeacons, Deanes, Provestes, Maisters, Prebendaryes, and fellowes, being Graduates, may use in the quiere, beside theyr Surplesses, such hoodes as pertaineth to their several degrees, which they have taken in any universitie within this realme. But in all other places, every minister shall be at libertie to use any Surples or no.° It is also seemely that Graduates, when they dooe preache, shoulde use such hoodes as pertayneth to theyr severall degrees.*

¶ *And whensoever the Bushop shall celebrate the holye communion in the churche, or execute any other publique minystracyon, he shall have upon hym, besyde his rochette,° a Surples or albe, and a cope or vestment, and also his pastorall staffe in his hande, or elles borne or holden by his chapeleyne.*

¶ *As touching kneeling,° crossing, holding up of handes, knocking upon the brest, and other gestures: they may be used or left as every mans devocion serveth without blame.*

¶ *Also upon Christmas day, Ester day, the Ascension daye, whit-soonday, and the feaste of the Trinitie, may bee used anye parte of holye scripture hereafter to be certaynly limited and appoynted, in the stede of the Letany.*

¶ *If there be a sermone, or for other greate cause, the Curate by his discretion may leave out the Letanye, Gloria in excelsis, the Crede, the homely, and the exhortation to the communion.*

The Kynges Majestie, by
the advyse of his moste deare uncle the Lorde Protector and other his highnes Counsell, streightly
chargeth and commaundeth, that no maner
of person do sell this present booke un-
bounde, above the price of .ii. Shyllynges the piece. And the same
bounde in paste or in boor-
des, not above the price
of three shyllynges
and foure pence
the piece.
God save the Kyng.

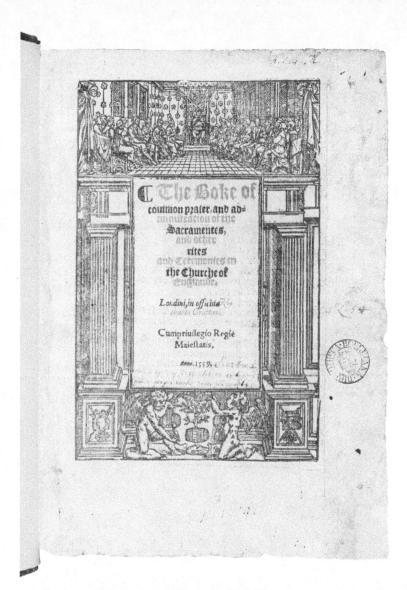

The boke of common praier (London: Richard Grafton, 1559), STC 16291, Title page. Oxford, Bodleian Library (shelf mark: CP. 1559 d.1). Reproduced with permission. A mid-seventeenth-century handwritten note adds: 'This is the very first Edition of the Comon-prayer booke vnder Elizabeth'.

❧ The contentes

of this booke.

¶ The ordre where mor-
ning and Evening prayer shalbe
used and sayde.

¶ *The Morning and Evening praier shalbe used in the accustomed place of the churche, chapel, or chauncell,° except it shalbe otherwise determined by the ordinarie of the place, and the chauncels shall remain as they have done in tymes past.*

And here is to be noted, that the Minister at the time of the communion, and at all other tymes in hys ministracion, shall use suche ornamentes in the church, as wer in use° by aucthoritie of parliament in the second yere of the reygne of king Edward the .vi. according to the acte of parliament set in the beginning of thys booke.

¶ An ordre for Morning prayer
dayly throughout the yere.

At the beginning both of Morning prayer, and lykewyse of Evening prayer, the Minister shall reade with a lowde voyce, some one of these sentences of the Scriptures that folowe.° And then he shall say that, which is written after the said sentences.

AT what tyme soever a synner doth repent him of his sinne from the botome of his harte, I wil put al his wickednes out of my remembraunce sayeth the Lord. *Ezek.* 18

I do know mine awne wickednes, and my syne is alwaies against me. *Ps.* 51

Turne thy face awaye from our sinnes (O lorde) and blotte out all our offences. *Ps.* 51

A sorowful spirite is a sacrifice to God: despise not (O Lorde) humble and contrite hartes. *Ps.* 51

Rende your hartes, and not your garmentes, and turne to the Lorde your God, because he is gentle and mercyful, he is pacient and of muche mercie, and such a one that is sory for your afflictions. *Joel* 2

To thee O Lorde God belongeth mercie and forgevenes, for we have gone away from thee, and have not harkened to thy voice, whereby we myght walcke in thy lawes, whiche thou hast appoincted for us. *Dan.* 9

Correcte us, O Lorde, and yet in thy judgement, not in thy furie, least we shoulde be consumed and brought to nothyng. *Jer.* 2

Amende your lives, for the kyngdome of GOD is at hande. *Matt.* 3

I will go to my father, and say to him, father I have sinned against heaven, and againste thee, I am no more worthy to be called thy sonne. *Luke* 15

Entre not in to judgement wyth thy servauntes, O Lorde, for no fleshe is rightous in thy sight. *Ps.* 142

If we saye that we have no synne, we deceyve ourselves, and there is no truthe in us. *1 John* 1

DERELY beloved Brethren, the Scripture moveth us in sondry places, to acknowledge and confesse° our manifolde sinnes and wickednes, and that we should not dissemble, nor cloke them before the face of almighty God our heavenly father, but confesse them wyth an humble, lowly, penitent, and obedient harte: to the ende that we maye obtaine forgevenes of the same by his infinite goodnesse and mercie. And although we ought at all tymes, humbly to knowlege our synnes before GOD, yet ought we moste chiefly so to doe, when we assemble and mete together, to rendre thankes for the greate benefites that we have received at his handes, to sette furth his moste worthie praise, to heare his moste holye worde, and to aske those thynges whiche be requisite and necessarie, aswel for the bodye as the soule. Wherfore I praye and beseche you, as many as be here presente, to accompany me wyth a pure harte and humble voice, unto the throne of the heauenly grace, saying after me.

A generall confession, to be saide of the whole congregacion after the minister, knelyng.°

ALMIGHTIE and moste merciful father, we have erred and straied from thy waies, lyke lost shepe. We have folowed to much the devises and desires of our owne hartes. We have offended against thy holy lawes. We have left undone those thinges whiche we ought to have done,° and we have done those thinges which we ought not to have done, and there is no health in us: but thou, O Lorde, have mercy upon us miserable offendours. Spare thou them O God, whiche confesse their faultes. Restore thou them that be penitent, accordyng to thy promises declared unto mankynde, in Christe Jesu our Lorde. And graunt, O moste merciful father, for his sake, that we may hereafter lyve a godly, ryghtuous, and sobre life, to the glory of thy holy name. Amen.

The absolution to be pronounced by the Minister alone.°

ALMIGHTY God, the father of our Lord Jesus Christ, which desireth not the deathe of a sinner, but rather that he maye turne from his wickednesse and lyve: and hath geven power and commaundement to hys Ministers, to declare and pronounce to his people beyng penitent, the absolution and remission of their synnes: he pardoneth and absolveth all them which truly repent, and unfeinedly beleve his holy gospel. Wherefore we beseche him to graunt us true repentaunce and hys holy spirite, that those thynges may please hym, whych we doe at thys present, and that the rest of our life hereafter may be pure and holy: so that at the last we may come to his eternall joye, through Jesus Christe our lorde. Amen.

The people shal aunswere.

Amen.

Then shall the Minister beginne the Lordes prayer° *with a loude voice.*

OUR Father whiche arte in heaven, hallowed be thy name. Thy kyngdom come. Thy will be done in earth as it is in heaven. Geve us this day our dayly breade. And forgeve us our trespasses, as we forgeve them that trespasse against us. And lead us not into temptacion. But deliver us from evil. Amen.

Then likewise he shall saye.

O Lord, open thou our lippes.°
Aunswere. And our mouthe shall shewe furth thy prayse.
Prieste. O God, make spede to save us.
Aunswere. O Lord make haste to helpe us.
Prieste. Glory be to the father, and to the sonne, and to the holye Ghoste.
As it was in the beginning, is nowe and ever shalbe. Worlde without ende. Amen.
Praise ye the Lorde.°

Then shalbe sayde or song, this Psalme folowyng.

Venite exultemus domino.

O COME let us syng unto the lord: let us hartely rejoyce in the strength of our salvacion.   *Ps.* 95

Let us come before his presence wyth thankesgevinge: and shewe oureselfe gladde in hym wyth Psalmes.

For the Lorde is a great god: and a greate Kynge, above all goddes.

In his hand are all the corners of the earth: and the strength of the hilles is his also.

The Sea is his, and he made it: and his handes prepared the drie lande.

O come, let us worshippe and fal doune: and knele before the lorde our maker.

For he is the Lorde our god: and we are the people of his pasture, and the shepe of his handes.

To day if ye wyl heare his voyce, harden not your hartes: as in the provocacion, and as in the daie of temptacion in the wildernesse.

When your fathers tempted me: proved me, and sawe my workes.

Fourtie yeres long was I greved with this generacion, and saide: it is a people that doe erre in their heartes, for they have not knowen my wayes.

Unto whom I sware in my wrath: that they shoulde not enter into my rest.

Glory be to the father, and to the sonne. *&c.*

As it was in the beginning, is now. *&c.*

¶ *Then shal folowe certeyn Psalmes in order, as they bene appoincted in a table made for that pourpose, excepte there be proper Psalmes appointed for that day, and at the end of everye Psalme throughout the yere, and likewise in the ende of* Benedictus, Benedicite, Magnificat, *and* Nunc Dimittis, *shal be repeated.*

Glory be to the father, and to the sonne. *&c.*

¶ *Then shalbe redde two Lessons distinctly with a loude voyce, that the people may heare. The first of the olde Testament, the seconde of the newe, Lyke as they be appointed by the Kalender, except there be proper Lessons, assigned for that daye: the Minister that readeth the Lesson, standyng and turning him so as he may best be heard of all such as be present. And before every lesson, the Minister shal saye thus, The fyrst, second, thyrd or fourth chapiter*

of Genesis, or Exodus, Mathewe, Marke, or other like, as is appoincted in the
Kalender. And in the end of everye chapiter, he shal saye,

Here endeth such a Chapiter of suche a Booke.

And (to the ende the people maye the better heare) in suche places where they
do synge, there shall the lessons be songe in a plaine tune after the maner of
distinct readinge: and likewise the Epystle and gospell.

After the firste lesson shall folowe, Te deum laudamus, *in Englyshe dayly*
throughe the whole yere.

Te Deum.

W E prayse thee, O God: we knoweledge thee to be the Lorde.
   All the earth doth worship thee, the Father everlastynge.

To thee al Aungels crye aloude: the heavens and all the powers therein.

To thee Cherubin, and Seraphin, continually do crye.

Holy, holy, holy, Lorde God of Sabaoth.

Heaven and earth are ful of° the majestye of thy glory.

The glorious company of the Apostles prayse thee.

The goodly felowship of the Prophetes prayse thee.

The noble armye of Martyrs prayse thee.

The holye Churche through out al the worlde dothe knowledge thee.

The father of an infinite Majestye.

Thy honourable true, and onely sonne.

Also the holy ghost the comforter.

Thou art the kyng of glory, O Christe.

Thou arte the everlastynge sonne of the father.

When thou tokest upon thee to deliver man, thou diddest not abhore the virgins wombe.

When thou haddeste overcome the sharpnes of death thou diddest open the kyngdome of heaven to al belevers.

Thou syttest on the ryght hand of God, in the glorye of the father.

We beleve that thou shalt come to be our judge.

We therefore pray thee, helpe thy servants whom thou hast redemed wyth thy precious bloude.

Make them to be numbred with thy saintes, in glorye everlasting.

O Lord save thy people: and blesse thine heritage.

Governe them and lifte them up for ever.

Day by day we magnifye thee.

And we worshyp thy name, ever world without ende.
Vouchsafe, O Lorde, to kepe us thys daye withoute synne.
O Lorde have mercy upon us, have mercie upon us.
O Lorde, let thy mercy lyghten upon us: as our trust is in thee.
O Lorde, in thee have I trusted: let me never be confounded.

Or this canticle, Benedicite° omnia opera Domini domino.

Benedicite.

O ALL ye worckes of the Lorde, blesse ye the Lorde: praise him, and magnify him for ever.

O ye Aungels of the Lord, blesse ye the Lorde: praise ye him, and magnifye him for ever.

O ye heavens, blesse ye the Lorde: prayse him and magnifye him for ever.

O ye waters that be above the firmamente, blesse ye the Lorde: prayse him and magnifye him for ever.

O all ye powers of the lord, blesse ye the Lorde: prayse hym, and magnifie him for ever.

O ye Sonne and Mone, blesse ye the Lorde: prayse hym and magnifie him for ever.

O ye starres of heaven, blesse ye the Lorde: praise him and magnifie him for ever.

O ye showers and dewe, blesse ye the Lorde: prayse him and magnifie him for ever.

O ye windes of God, blesse ye the Lorde: prayse him and magnifye him for ever.

O ye fyre and heate, blesse ye the Lord: praise him and magnifie him for ever.

O ye Winter and Sommer, blesse ye the Lorde: praise him and magnifie him for ever.

O ye dewes and frostes, blesse ye the Lorde: praise him and magnifie him for ever.

O ye froste and cold, blesse ye the Lord: praise him and magnify him for ever.

O ye Ise and Snowe, blesse ye the Lorde: praise him and magnifie him for ever.

O ye nightes and daies, blesse ye the Lord: praise him and magnifie him for ever.

O ye light and darknes, blesse ye the Lorde: prayse him and magnifie him for ever.

O ye lyghtenynges and cloudes, blesse ye the Lorde: praise him and magnifie him for ever.

O let the earth blesse the Lorde: yea, let it praise hym and magnify hym for ever.

O ye mountaynes and hils, blesse ye the Lorde: prayse hym and magnifie hym for ever.

O al ye grene thynges upon the earthe, blesse ye the Lord: praise him and magnifie hym for ever.

O ye welles, blesse ye the Lorde: praise him and magnifie hym for ever.

O ye Seas, and fluddes, blesse ye the Lorde: praise hym and magnifie hym for ever.

O ye whales, and all that move in the waters, blesse ye the Lorde: prayse him and magnifie him for ever.

O all ye foules of the aire, blesse ye the lord: praise him and magnifie him for ever.

O all ye beastes and cattell, blesse ye the Lorde: praise him and magnifye him for ever.

O ye children of men, blesse ye the Lord: praise him and magnifye him for ever.

O let Israel blesse the Lorde: praise him and magnify him for ever.

O ye prestes of the lord, blesse ye the Lord: prayse hym and magnifye him for ever.

O ye servauntes of the Lord, blesse ye the Lord: prayse him and magnifye him for ever.

O ye sprites and soules of the righteous, blesse ye the lord: prayse him and magnify him for ever.

O ye holy and humble men of herte, blesse ye the Lord: praise him and magnifye him for ever.

O Ananias, Azarias, and Misael, blesse ye the lord: prayse him and magnifye him for ever.

Glory be to the father, and to the Sonne, and to the holye Ghoste.

As it was in the begynninge, is nowe, and ever. *&c.*

And after the seconde lesson shalbe used and sayde Benedictus, *in Englyshe as foloweth.*

Benedictus.

BLESSED be the Lord GOD of Israell: for he hath visited and redemed his people.

And hath raised up a mighty salvacion for us: in the house of hys servaunt David.

As he spake by the mouth of his holy prophetes: which have bene sence the worlde began.

That we should be saved from our enemyes: and from the handes of al that hate us.

To performe the mercy promised to our forfathers: and to remember his holy covenant.

To perfourme the othe whiche he sware to our forefather Abraham: that he would geve us.

That we beyng delivered out of the handes of oure enemies: might serve him withoute feare.

In holynesse and ryghtuousnesse before hym: all the dayes of our lyfe.

And thou Chylde, shalt be called the Prophete of the hyghest: for thou shalt go before the face of the Lorde to prepare hys wayes.

To geve knowledge of salvacion unto hys people: for the remission of theyr synnes.

Through the tender mercie of our God: whereby the day spring from on hyghe, hath visited us.

To geve light to them that sitte in darckenes, and in the shadowe of death: and to guide our feete into the way of peace.

Glory be to the father, and to the sonne: and to the holy Goste.

As it was in the begynning, is now, and ever shalbe: worlde wythout ende. Amen.

Or the .C. Psalme.

Jubilate Deo.°

O BE joyfull in the Lorde (al ye landes): serve the Lorde wyth gladnes, and come before hys presence wyth a song. *Ps.* 100

Be ye sure that the Lord he is God: it is he that hath made us, and not we ourselves, we are hys people, and the shepe of his pasture.

O go your way into his gates wyth thankesgeving, and into his courtes wyth prayse: be thanckefull unto hym, and speake good of hys name.

For the Lorde is gracious, his mercy is everlastyng: and his truth endureth from generacion to generacyon.

Glory be to the Father, &c.

As it was in the beginning &c. Amen.

¶ *Then shal be sayd the Crede° by the Minister and the people standyng.*

I BELEVE in God the father almightie maker of heaven and earth. And in Jesus Christ hys onely sonne our Lorde. Which was conceived by the holy ghoste, borne of the Virgen Marie. Suffred under Ponce Pylate, was crucified dead and buried, he descended into Helle. The thirde daye he rose agayn from the deade. He ascended into heaven, and sitteth on the ryghte hande of God the Father almightie. From thence he shall come to judge the quicke and the deade. I beleve in the holy Ghoste. The holy Catholique Churche. The communion of sainctes. The forgevenesse of sinnes. The resurrection of the body. And the life everlasting. Amen.

And after that, these prayers folowyng, aswell at Evenyng praier, as at Mornyng prayer, al devoutlye knelyng. The Minister firste pronouncing with a loude voyce.

The Lorde be with you.

Answer. And with thy spirite.

Minister. Let us praie.

Lorde have mercy upon us.

   Christ have mercie upon us.

Lorde have mercy upon us.

¶ *Then the Minister, Clarkes, and people, shall saye the Lordes praier in Englyshe, with a loud voice.*

O URE father Which. &c.

¶ *Then the Minister standing up shal say.*

O lorde, shewe thy mercy upon us.

Aunswere. And graunte us thy salvacion.

Prieste. O Lorde save the Queene.°

Aunswere. And mercifully here us when we call upon thee.

Prieste. Endue thy ministers with rightuousnes.

Aunswere. And make thy chosen people joyful.

Prieste. O Lorde save thy people.

Aunswere. And blesse thyne enheritaunce.
Prieste. Geve peace in our tyme, O Lorde.
Aunswere. Because there is none other that fighteth for us, but onely thou, O God.
Prieste. O God make clene our hartes with in us.
Aunswere. And take not thy holy spirite from us.

¶ *Then shal folowe three Collectes. The firste of the daye, whiche shall be the same that is appoincted at the Communion. The seconde for peace. The thirde for grace to live wel. And the two laste Collectes shal never altre, but dayly be sayde at Mornyng praier, throughout al the yere, as foloweth.*

The seconde Collecte for Peace.

O GOD, whiche art authour of peace, and lover of concord, in knowledge of whom standeth our eternal lyfe, whose service is perfect fredom: defend us thy humble servaunts, in al assaultes of our enemies, that we surely trusting in thy defence, may not feare the power of any adversaries: through the might of Jesu Christ our lord. Amen.

The thirde Collecte for Grace.

O LORDE our heavenly father, almightie and everlastyng God, whiche hast safely broughte us to the begynnyng of thys day: defende us in the same wyth thy myghtye power, and graunte that this daie we fall into no synne, neither runne into any kinde of daunger, but that al our doinges may be ordred by thy governaunce to doe alwayes that is rightuous in thy sighte: through Jesus Christe our LORDE. Amen.

An order for evening
Praier throughout the yere.

The Priest shal saie.

OUR Father, which. *&c.*

¶ *Then likewise he shal saye.*

O Lord open thou our lippes.°
Aunswere. And our mouth shall shewe furth thy prayse.

Priest. O God make spede to save us.°

Aunswere. Lorde, make haste to helpe us.

Priest.

Glory be to the father, and to the sonne, and to the holy ghoste.

As it was in the beginninge, is nowe, and ever shal be: worlde wythout ende. Amen.

Praise ye the Lorde.

¶ *Then Psalmes in ordre, as they be appoincted in the Table for Psalmes, except there be propre Psalmes appointed for that day. Then a Lesson of the olde Testament, as is appointed likewise in the kalender, except there be propre lessons appointed for that day. After that,* Magnificat, *in Englishe, as foloweth.*

Magnificat.

M Y soule doeth magnifie the Lorde.   *Luke* 1
And my spirit hath rejoyced in god my saviour.

For he hath regarded the lowelines of his hand maiden.

For beholde from hencefurth al generacions shall call me blessed.

For he that is mightie hath magnified me: and holy is his name.

And his mercy is on them that feare him: throughout all generacions.

He hath shewed strength with his arme: he hath scatered the proude in the imagination of their hertes.

He hath put downe the mightye from theyr seate: and hath exalted the humble and meke.

He hath filled the hungry with good thinges: and the ryche he hath sent empty away.

He remembring his mercy, hath holpen his servaunte Israel: as he promysed to our forefathers,° Abraham and his sede for ever.

Glory be to the Father, and to the sonne, and to the holy Ghoste.

As it was in the beginninge, is nowe, and ever shalbe, world without ende. Amen.

Or the .xcviii. Psalme Cantate domino canticum novum.°

O SINGE unto the Lorde a newe songe: for he hath done marveilous thinges.   *Ps.* 98

With his owne right hande, and with his holy arme: hath he gotten him selfe the victorye.

The Lord declared his salvacion: his righteousnes hath he openly shewed in the syght of the Heathen.

He hath remembred his mercy and truthe towarde the house of Israell: and all the endes of the worlde haue sene the salvacion of our God.

Shewe yourselves joyfull unto the Lorde, all ye landes: synge, rejoyce, and geve thankes.

Prayse the Lorde upon the harpe: synge to the harp with a Psalme of thankesgeving.

With trumpettes also and shawmes: O shewe your selves joyfull before the Lord the kynge.

Let the Sea make a noyse, and all that therein is: the rounde worlde, and they that dwell therin.

Let the floudes clappe their handes, and let the hylles be joyful togyther before the Lord: for he is come to judge the earth.

With righteousnes shal he judge the worlde: and the people with equitie.

Glory be to the Father, and to the Sonne, and to the holy Ghoste. As it was in the beginninge, is nowe, and ever shalbe, worlde without ende. Amen.

¶ *Then a lesson of the new testament. And after that* (Nunc dimittis) *in Englyshe, as foloweth.*

L ORDE, nowe lettest thou thy servaunt departe in peace: according to thy worde.

For myne eyes have sene: thy salvacion.

Whiche thou haste prepared: before the face of all people.

To be a lyght to lyghten the Gentiles: and to be the glorye of thy people Israell.

Glorye be to the father, and to the sonne, and to the holye Ghoste.

As it was in the beginning, is nowe, and ever shall be, worlde withoute ende. Amen.

Or this Psalme, Deus misereatur nostri,° *in Englyshe.*

G OD be mercyfull unto us, and blesse us: and shewe us the lyghte of his countenaunce, and be mercyfull unto us.   *Ps.* 67

That thy way may be knowen upon earth: thy saving health among all nacions.

Let the people prayse thee, O GOD: yea, let all the people prayse thee.

O let the nacions rejoyce and be gladde: for thou shalt judge the folke righteouslye, and governe the Nacions upon earth.

Let the people prayse thee, O GOD: let all the people prayse thee.

Then shall the earthe bring forth her encrease: and God, even our owne God, shall geve us his blessynge.

God shall blesse us: and all the endes of the worlde shall feare him.

Glory be to the Father, and to the sonne, and to the holy Ghoste.

As it was in the beginninge, is nowe, and ever shalbe, worlde without ende. Amen.

¶ *Then shal folow the Crede,° with other prayers, as is before appoynted at Morning prayer, after* Benedictus. *And with thre Collectes: Fyrste of the day, the seconde of peace, the thyrde for ayde agaynste all peryls, as hereafter foloweth, whyche two last Collectes shalbe daylye sayde at Evenyng prayer wythout alteracion.*

¶ *The seconde Collect at Evenynge prayer.*

O GOD, from whome all holy desires, all good counsailes, and all juste woorkes do procede: geve unto thy servauntes that peace, whiche the worlde cannot geve: that bothe our hertes may be set to obey thy commaundementes, and also that by thee, we beynge defended from the feare of our enemies, may passe our time in rest and quietnes. Through the merites of Jesus Christ our saviour. Amen.

¶ *The thyrde Collecte for ayde against all peryls.*

LYGHTEN oure darckenesse, wee beseche thee (O LORDE) and by thy greate mercye defende us from all perils and daungers of this nyghte, for the love of thy onely sonne oure savioure Jesus Christe. Amen.

¶ *In the feastes of Christmas, the Epiphany, S. Mathye, Easter, the Ascencion, Pentecost, S. John Baptyst, S. James, S. Bartholomew, S. Mathew, S. Simon, and Jude, S. Andrew, and Trinitie Sonday: Shalbe songe or sayde, immediatly after* Benedictus, *thys confession of our Christen faythe.*

Quicunque vult.

WHOSOEVER wyll be saved: before all thynges, it is necessarye that he holde the catholyke faythe.

Whiche Faithe, excepte everye one dooe kepe holy and undefyled, withoute doubt he shall perysh everlastingly.

And the Catholyke Faythe is this: that we worshyp one God in Trinitie, and trinitie in unitie.

Neyther confounding the persons: nor devidinge the substaunce.

For there is one persone of the Father, an other of the Sonne: and another of the holy ghost.

But the Godhed of the Father, of the Sonne, and of the holy Ghost is al one: the glory equall, the majesty coeternall.

Suche as the Father is, such is the sonne: and suche is the holy ghost.

The father uncreate, the sonne uncreate: and the holy ghoste uncreate.

The Father incomprehensible, the sonne incomprehensyble: and the holye Ghoste incomprehensyble.

The father eternall, the sonne eternall: and the holye Ghoste eternall.

And yet they are not thre eternalles: but one eternall.

As also there be not thre incomprehensibles, nor thre uncreated: but one uncreated, and one incomprehensible.

So likewyse the Father is almighty, the sonne almighty, and the holy ghoste almighty.

And yet are not there thre Almightyes,° but one Almighty.

So the father is God, the sonne is God: and the holye Ghoste is God.

And yet are they not thre Gods, but one God.

So lykewyse the father is Lord, the sonne Lorde: and the holy ghoste Lorde.

And yet not thre Lordes, but one Lord.

For like as we be compelled by the Christian verity to acknowledge every person by hym selfe to be God, and Lorde.

So are we forbidden by the Catholique Religion, to say there be thre Gods, or thre Lordes.

The father is made of none, neyther created, nor begotten.

The sonne is of the Father alone: not made, nor created, but begotten.

The holye Ghoste is of the Father, and of the Sonne: neither made, nor created, nor begotten, but proceding.

So there is one father, not thre fathers, one sonne, not thre sonnes: one holy Ghost, not thre holy Ghostes.

And in this trinitie, none is afore, or after other: none is greater, nor lesse then an other.

But the whole thre persons: be coeternall together and coequall.

So that in all thinges as is aforesayde: the Unitye in Trinitie: and the Trinitie in unitie is to be worshypped.

He therefore that wil be saved: must thus thincke of the Trinitie.

Furthermore, it is necessarye to everlasting salvation: that he also beleve rightlye in the Incarnation of oure Lorde Jesu Christ.

For the right Faythe is, that we beleve and Confesse: that oure Lorde Jesus Christe the sonne of God, is God and Man.

GOD of the substaunce of the father, begotten before the worldes: and man of the substaunce of his mother, borne in the worlde.

Perfect god, and perfect man: of a reasonable Soule, and humaine flesh subsistynge.

Equal to the father as touching his godhead: and inferior to the father, touching his manhode.

Who although he be God and man: yet he is not two, but one Christ.

One, not by conversion of the Godhead into fleshe: but by taking of the manhode into God.

One altogether, not by confusion of Substaunce: but by unitie of person.

For as the reasonable soule and flesh is but one man: so God and man is but one Christe.

Who suffred for our salvation: descended into hell, rose againe the thirde day from the deade.

He ascended into heaven: he sitteth on the ryghte hand of the father, God Almighty, from whence he shall come to judge the quicke and the dead.

At whose comming al men shal rise againe with their bodies, and shall geve accompt for their owne worckes.

And they that have done good, shall go into life everlasting: and they that have done evel, into everlasting fyre.

This is the Catholike faith: whiche except a man beleve faithfully, he can not be saved.

Glory be to the father, and to the sonne: and to the holy Ghoste.

As it was in the beginninge, is nowe, and ever shalbe worlde without ende. Amen.

Thus endeth the order of Morning and Eveninge prayer through the whole yere.

Here foloweth the Letani
to be used upon Sondaies, Wednesdaies, and Fridayes,°
and at other tymes, when it shalbe commaun-
ded by the Ordinarye.

O GOD the father of heaven: have mercy upon us miserable synners.

O God the father of heaven: have mercy upon us miserable synners.

O God the sonne, redemer of the worlde: have mercye upon us miserable synners.

O God the sonne redemer of the worlde: have mercye upon us miserable synners.

O GOD the holye Ghoste, proceding from the father and the Sonne: have mercye upon us miserable synners.

O God the holy ghoste, proceding from the father and the Sonne: have mercye upon us miserable synners.

O holy, blessed, and glorious Trinitie, three persons and one god: have mercy upon us miserable synners.

O holy, blessed, and glorious trinitye, thre persons and one god: have mercy upon us miserable synners.

Remember not Lorde our offences, nor the offences of our fore-fathers, neyther take thou vengeaunce of oure synnes: spare us good Lorde, spare thy people whome thou haste redemed with thy moste precious bloude, and be not angry with us for ever.

Spare us good Lorde.

From all evil and mischief, from synne, from the craftes and assaul-tes of the Devil: from thy wrath, and from everlasting dampnation.

Good Lorde delyver us.

From all blyndnes of herte, from pride, vayne glorye, and hypoc-risy, from envy, hatred, and malice, and all uncharitablenes.

Good Lorde delyver us.

From fornicacion, and all other deadly Synne: and from all the deceiptes of the worlde, the Fleshe and the Devill.

Good Lorde delyver us.

From lightninges and tempestes, from plague, pestilence and fam-ine, from battayle and murther, and from soudeine deathe.°

Good Lorde delyver us.

From all sedicion and privey conspiracye, from all false doctrine and heresy, from hardnes of harte, and contempte of thy worde and commaundement.

   Good Lorde delyver us.

By the misterye of thy holye Incarnacion, by thy holy Nativitie and circumcision, by thy Baptysme, fastynge and temptacion.

   Good Lorde delyver us.

By thyne agonye and bloudy sweate, by thy crosse and passion, by thy precious deathe and buriall, by thy glorious resurrection, and ascencion, and by the commynge of the holy Ghoste.

   Good Lorde delyver us.

In al tyme of our tribulacion, in al tyme of our welth, in the houre of death, and in the daye of judgement.

   Good Lorde delyver us.

We synners do besche thee to heare us (O Lord God,) and that it may please thee to rule and governe thy holy Churche universally, in the right way.

   We besche thee to heare us good Lorde.

That it may please thee, to kepe and strengthen in the true wor-shipping of thee in righteousnes and holynes of lyfe,° thy servaunt Elizabeth our most gracious Quene and governour.°

   We besche thee to heare us good Lorde.

That it may please thee, to rule her harte in thy faith, feare, and love, that she may evermore have affiaunce in thee, and ever seke thy honoure and glory.

   We besche thee to heare us good Lorde.

That it may please thee to be her defender and keper, geving her the victory over al her enemyes.

   We besche thee to heare us good Lorde.

That it may please thee to illuminate all Byshoppes, Pastours, and ministers of the Church, with true knowledge, and understanding of thy worde, and that both by their preaching and livinge, they may sette it furth, and shewe it accordingly.

   We besche thee to heare us good Lorde.

That it maye please thee to endue the Lordes of the Counsayle, and all the nobilitie, with grace, wisedom, and understanding.

   We besche thee to heare us good Lorde.

That it may please thee to blesse and kepe the Magistrates, geving them grace to execute justice, and to maynteyne truthe.

We beseche thee to heare us good Lorde.

That it may please thee to blesse, and kepe al thy people.

We beseche thee to heare us good Lorde.

That it may please thee to geve to all nacions, unitie, peace and concorde.

We beseche thee to heare us good Lorde.

That it maye please thee to geve us an harte to love and dread thee, and diligently to lyve after thy commaundementes.

We beseche thee to heare us good Lorde.

That it maye please thee to gyve all thy people encrease of grace, to heare mekely thy worde, and to receyve it wyth pure affeccion, and to bring furthe the fruites of the spirit.

We beseche thee to heare us good Lorde.

That it may please thee to bring into the way of truth all suche as have erred, and are deceyved.

We beseche thee to heare us good Lorde.

That it maye please thee to strengthen suche as dooe stande, and to comforte and helpe the weake harted, and to rayse theym up that falle, and finally to beate downe Sathan under our feete.

We beseche thee to heare us good Lorde.

That it may please thee to succour, helpe, and comforte all that be in daunger, neccssitic, and tribulation.

We beseche thee to heare us good Lorde.

That it maye please thee to preserve all that travayle, by lande, or by water, al women labouringe of chylde, all sycke persons, and yonge chyldren, and to shew thy pitye upon all prisoners and captives.

We beseche thee to heare us good Lorde.

That it may please thee to defende and provide for the fatherles children and widowes, and all that be desolate and oppressed.

We beseche thee to heare us good Lorde.

That it may please thee to have mercy upon all men.

We beseche thee to heare us good Lorde.

That it may please thee to forgeve our enemies, persecutours, and slaunderers, and to turne theyr hertes.

We beseche thee to heare us good Lorde.

That it may please thee to geve and preserve to our use the kindly fruites of the earth, so as in due tyme we maye enjoye them.

We beseche thee to heare us good Lorde.

That it may please thee to geve us true repentaunce, to forgeve us

all our sinnes, negligences, and ignoraunces: and to endue us with the
grace of thy holy spirite, to amende our lyves, according to thy holy
worde.

We beseche thee to heare us good Lorde.

Sonne of God: we beseche thee to heare us.

Sonne of God: we beseche thee to heare us.

O Lambe of God that takest away the synnes of the worlde.

Graunt us thy peace.

O Lambe of God that takest awaye the synnes of the worlde.

Have mercy upon us.

O Christ heare us.

O Christe heare us.

Lorde have mercy upon us.

Lorde have mercy upon us.

Christe have mercy upon us.

Christe have mercy upon us.

Lorde have mercy upon us.

Lorde have mercy upon us.

Our father whiche art in heaven. *&c.*

And leade us not into temptation.

But delyver us from evyll. Amen.

¶ *The versycle.* O Lorde deale not with us after our synnes.

The Aunswere. Neither rewarde us after our iniquities.

¶ Let us praye.

O GOD mercifull father, that dispisest not the syghing of a contrite hart, nor the desyre of suche as be sorowfull, mercyfully
assiste our praiers, that we make before thee, in all our troubles, and
adversities, whensoever they oppresse us, and graciouslye heare us,
that those evelles, whiche the crafte and subtiltie of the devel, or man,
worketh against us, be broughte to noughte, and by the providence of
thy goodnesse, they may be dispersed, that we thy Servauntes beyng
hurt by no persecucions, may evermore geve thanckes to thee, in thy
holy Church, through Jesus Christ our Lorde.

O Lorde aryse, helpe us, and deliver us for thy names sake.

O GOD, we have hearde with our eares, and our fathers have
declared unto us the noble worckes that thou diddeste in their
dayes, and in the olde tyme before them.

O Lord aryse, helpe us, and delyver us for thyne honoure.

Glory be to the father, and to the sonne, and to the holye Goste.

As it was in the beginninge, is nowe, and ever shalbe worlde without ende. Amen.

From our enemues defende us, O Christ.

Graciously loke upon our afflictions.

Pitifully beholde the sorowes of our harte.

Mercifully forgeve the synnes of thy people.

Favourably with mercy heare our prayers.

O sonne of David have mercy upon us.

Bothe now and ever vouchesafe to heare us, O Christe.

Graciously heare us, O Christ,

Graciously heare us: O Lorde Christ.

The Versycle. O Lorde let thy mercy be shewed upon us.

The Aunswere. As we do put our trust in thee.

¶ Let us praye.

WE humbly beseche the, O father, mercifullye to loke upon oure infirmities, and for the glory of thy names sake, turne from us all those evilles that we moste righteously have deserved: and graunte that in all oure troubles we maye put our whole truste and confydence in thy mercye, and evermore serve thee in holynes and purenes of living, to thy honour and glory, throughe our onely mediatoure and advocate Jesus Christe our Lorde. Amen.

A prayer of the Quenes majesty.°

O LORD our hevenly father, high and mighty king of kynges, Lorde of Lordes, the onely ruler of princes, which doest from thy throne beholde all the dwellers upon earth, most hartely we beseche thee with thy favoure to beholde our mooste gracious soveraigne Lady Quene Elizabeth, and so replenyshe her with the grace of thy holy spirit, that she may alway incline to thy wil, and walcke in thy waye: Indue her plentifully wyth heavenly gifts: Graunt her in health and wealthe longe to live: strength her that she may vanquish and overcome al her enemies: And finally after this life, she may attaine everlasting joye and felicitie, thorowe Jesus Christ our Lorde. Amen.

ALMIGHTY and everlastinge God, whiche onely workest great mervailes, sende downe upon our Bishoppes and Curates, and al congregacions committed to their charge, the healthful spirit of thy grace, and that they may truely please thee, powre upon them the continuall deawe of thy blessinge: Graunte this, O Lorde, for the honour of our advocate and mediatoure Jesus Christ. Amen.

¶ *A Prayer of Chrisostome.*

A LMIGHTY God, which hast geven us grace at this tyme with one accorde, to make our common supplications unto thee, and doest promyse that when two or three be gathered together in thy name, thou wilt graunt their requestes: fulfyl nowe O Lorde, the desyres, and peticions of thy servauntes, as may be most expedient for them, graunting us in this world knowledge of thy truthe, and in the world to come lyfe everlasting. Amen.

¶ *.ii. Corin. xiii.*

T HE grace of oure Lorde Jesus Christe, and the love of God, and the felowship of the holye ghoste, bee wyth us all evermore. Amen.

¶ *For rayne, yf the tyme requyre.*°

O GOD heavenly father, whiche by thy Sonne Jesus Christe, haste promysed to all theim that seke thy kingdome, and the righteousnes therof, all thinges necessary to their bodelye sustenaunce: Sende us we beseche thee in this oure necessitie, such moderate raine and showers, that we may receyve the fruytes of the earthe to our comforte, and to thy honoure, throughe Jesus Christ our Lorde. Amen.

¶ *For fayre weather.*

O LORDE God, which for the synne of man diddest ones drowne al the world, excepte eyght persons, and afterward of thy great mercy diddest promise never to destroy it so againe: we humblye beseche the, that althoughe we for our iniquities have worthely deserved this Plague of raigne and waters: yet upon oure true repentaunce, thou wilt sende us suche wether, wherby we may receyve the fruites of the yearth in due season, and learne bothe by thy punishment to amende our lives, and for thy clemency to geve thee prayse and glorye, throughe Jesus Christ our Lorde. Amen.

¶ *In the tyme of dearth and famyne.*°

O GOD heavenly Father, whose gyft it is that the rayne dothe fall, the earth is frutefull, beastes encrease, and fyshes do multiply: Behold, we beseche thee, the afflictions of thy people, and graunte that the scarcitye and dearthe (which we do now moste justly suffer for our iniquitye) maye through thy goodnes be mercifully tourned into cheapnesse and plenty, for the love of Jesu Christ our Lorde, to whome with thee and the holye Ghoste be Prayse for ever. Amen.

¶ *In the tyme of Warre.*°

O ALMIGHTY God, king of al kinges, and governoure of al thinges, whose power no creature is hable to resiste, to whome it belongeth justly to punyshe synners, and to be mercyfull unto them that truely repente, Save, and deliver us (we humbly beseche thee) from the handes of our enemyes, abate their pryde, aswage theyr malyce, and confounde theyr devyses, that we beynge armed with thy defence, maye be preserved evermore from all peryls to glorifye thee, whiche art the onely gever of all victory, throughe the merites of thy onely sonne Jesus Christ our Lorde. Amen.

¶ *In the tyme of any common plague or syckenesse.*

O ALMIGHTYE God, whiche in thy wrathe, in the tyme of king David, didst slea with the plague of pestilence, thre score and ten thousande, and yet remembringe thy mercy, diddest save the rest: have pitie upon us miserable synners, that nowe are vysited with great sicknesse, and mortalitie, that like as thou diddest then commaunde thyne angel to cease from punishing: So it may now please thee to withdrawe from us this plague, and grevous syckenesse, throughe Jesus Christe oure Lorde. Amen.

¶ *And the Letany shal ever ende with thys Collecte folowyng.*

O GOD, whose nature and propertie is ever to have
and to forgeve, receyve our humble peticions: and
thoughe we be tyed and bounde with
the chayne of oure synnes, yet let
the pitifulnes of thy great mercy
lose us, for the honoure of
Jesus Christes sake,
our mediatoure
and advocate.
Amen.

¶ The ordre for the admi-
nistracion of the Lordes Supper, or
holy Communion.

So many as entend to be partakers of the holy Communion, shall signifie their names to the Curate over night: or els in the mornyng, afore the beginning of morning prayer or immediatly after.

And if any of those be an open and notorious evil liver, so that the congregacion by him is offended, or have done any wrong to hys neighbours by word or dede, the curate havyng knowledge therof, shal cal hym, and advertyse hym, in any wise not to presume to the Lordes table, until he have openly declared him self to have truely repented, and amended his former naughty lyfe, that the Congregation may therby be satisfyed, whych afore were offended, and that he have recompensed the parties, who he hath done wrong unto, or at the least declare him selfe° to be in full purpose so to doe, as sone as he conveniently may.

The same order shall the Curate use with those, betwixt whome he perceyveth malice and hatred to raigne, not suffering them to be partakers of the Lordes table untyll he know them to be reconciled. And if one of the parties so at variance, be content to forgeve from the botome of hys hart, all that the other hath trespassed agaynste him, and to make amends for that he hym self hath offended: and the other partye wyll not be perswaded to a godly unitye, but remain stil in his frowardnes and malice: The Minister in that case, ought to admit the penitent person to the holy Communyon, and not hym that is obstinate.

The table, havyng at the Communion tyme a fayre whyte linnen cloth° upon it, shall stand in the body of the churche,° or in the chauncell, where mornyng prayour and evenyng prayour be appointed to be sayd. And the priest stand-yng at the Northe syde of the table,° shal say the Lordes prayour wyth this collecte followyng.

ALMIGHTY God, unto whom al hartes be open, al desires knowen, and from whom no secretes are hyd: clense the thoughtes of our hartes by the inspiracion of thy holy spirite, that we may perfectly love thee, and worthily magnify thy holy name, through Christe our Lorde. Amen.

Then shal the Priest rehearse distinctly al the .x. Commaundementes,° and
the people knelyng shal after every Commaundemente aske Goddes mercye
for theyr transgressyon of the same, after thys sorte.

Minister. God spake these wordes and saide: I am the Lord thy
God, Thou shalt have none other Goddes but me.

People. Lorde have mercye upon us, and encline our hartes to kepe
this lawe.°

Minister.

THOU shalt not make to thy self any graven ymage, nor the likenes
of any thyng that is in heaven above, or in the earth beneth, or
in the water under the earth. Thou shalt not bow doune to them,
nor worshyppe them, for I the Lord thy God am a gelous God, and
visite the synne of the fathers uppon the children, unto the thyrde
and fourth generacyon of them that hate me, and shew mercie unto
thousandes in theim that love me, and keepe my commaundementes.

People. Lorde have mercye upon us, and encline our hartes to kepe
this lawe.

Minister. Thou shalt not take the name of the Lorde thy God in
vaine, for the Lorde wil not holde hym giltlesse that taketh his name
in vaine.

People. Lorde have mercie upon us, and encline our. *&c.*

Minister. Remembre that thou kepe holy the Sabboth daie, sixe
dayes shalt thou laboure, and doe all that thou haste to do, but the
seventh day is the Sabboth of the lorde thy God. In it thou shalt do
no maner of worke, thou and thy sonne and thy daughter, thy man
servaunt, and thy mayde servaunt, thy Catel, and the straunger that
is within thy gates: For in sixe daies the Lord made heaven and earth,
the Sea and all that in them is, and rested the seventh daye. Wherefore
the Lorde blessed the seventh daye and halowed it.

People. Lorde have mercie upon us, and encline our. *&c.*

Minister. Honour thy father and thy mother, that thy daies may be
long in the lande which the Lord thy God geveth thee.

People. Lorde have mercy upon us, and encline. *&c.*

The Minister. Thou shalt not do murther.

People. Lorde have mercy upon us, and encline. *&c.*

Minister. Thou shalt not committe adultery.

People. Lorde have mercy upon us, and encline. *&c.*

Minister. Thou shalt not steale.

People. Lorde have mercy upon us, *&c.*

Minister. Thou shalte not beare false wytnesse agaynste thy neyghboure.

People. Lorde have mercy upon us, and encline our hartes to kepe this lawe.

Minister. Thou shalt not covet thy neighbours house, Thou shalt not covet thy neighbours wife, nor his servaunt, nor his maide, nor his oxe, nor his asse, nor any thing that is his.

People. Lord have mercy upon us, and write al these thy lawes in our hartes we beseche thee.

¶ *Then shall folowe the Collect of the day, with one of these two Collectes folowyng for the Quene, the Priest standyng up and saying.*

Let us praye.

Priest.

A LMIGHTY God, whose kyngdom is everlasting, and power infinite: have mercy upon the whole congregacion, and so rule the hart of thy chosen servant Elizabeth our Quene and governoure that she (knowing whose minister she is) may above all thinges, seke thy honoure and glorye: and that we her subjectes (duly considering whose aucthority she hath) may faithfully serve, honour, and humblye obey her in thee, and for thee, according to thy blessed worde and ordinance: Through Jesus Christ our Lord, who with thee and the holye ghost, lyveth and reygneth ever one God, worlde without ende. Amen.

A LMIGHTY and everlastinge God, we be taughte by thy holy word, that the hartes of Princes are in thy rule and governaunce, and that thou doest dispose, and turne them as it semeth best to thy Godly wysedome: we humbly beseche thee, so to dispose and governe the harte of Elizabeth, thy servaunte, our Quene and governour, that in all her thoughtes, wordes, and workes she may ever seke thy honoure and glorye, and studye to preserve thy people committed to her charge, in welth, peace and godlynes. Graunt this O merciful father, for thy deare sonnes sake Jesus Christ our Lorde. Amen.

Immediatly after the Collectes, the Priest shall reade the Epystle, beginning thus.

The Epystle written in the [   ] Chapiter of [   ].

And the Epystle ended, he shal say the gospel, beginning thus.

The Gospell° wrytten in the [   ] Chapiter of [   ].

And the Epistle and Gospel being ended, shalbe said the Crede.

I BELEVE in one God, the father almighty, maker of heaven and earthe, and of all thynges visible and invisible. And in one Lorde Jesu Christe, the onely begotten sonne of God, begotten of his father before al worldes, god of God, lyghte of lyghte, verye God of verye God, gotten, not made, beynge of one substance wyth the father, by whome all thinges were made, who for us men, and for our salvacion, came doune from heaven, and was incarnate by the holy Ghoste, of the Virgine Mary, and was made man, and was crucified also for us, under Poncius Pilate. He suffered and was buried, and the thyrde day he rose againe accordinge to the Scriptures, and ascended into heaven, and sitteth at the right hande of the father. And he shal come againe with glory, to judge both the quicke and the deade, whose Kyngdome shall have none ende. And I beleve in the holye Ghoste, the Lorde and gever of life, who procedeth from the father and the sonne: who with the father and the sonne together is worshipped and glorified, who spake by the Prophetes. And I beleve one catholicke and Apostolicke Churche. I acknowledge one Baptisme, for the remission of synnes. And I loke for the resurreccion of the dead : and the lyfe of the worlde to come. Amen.

After the Crede yf there be no sermon, shall folowe one of the Homelies alredy set furth,° or hereafter to he set furth by commune aucthoritie.

After suche Sermon, homely, or exhortacion, the Curate shall declare unto the people,° whether there be anye holy daies or fastynge daies the weke folowyng, and earnestly exhorte theim to remembre the poore, saying one, or moe of these sentences followyng, as he thinketh most convenient by his discretion.

Let your light so shyne before men, that they maye see your good workes, and glorifye youre father whyche is in heaven.   *Matt.* 5

Laye not up youreselves treasure upon the earthe, where the ruste and motthe doeth corrupte, and where theeves breake through and steale: But lay up for youre selves treasures in heaven, where neyther rust, nor motthe doeth corrupt, and where theeves do not breake thorowe and steale.   *Matt.* 6

Whatsoever you woulde that menne shoulde do unto you, even so doe unto them, for this is the lawe and the Prophetes.   *Matt.* 7

Not every one that sayeth unto me Lord, Lord, shall entre into the Kingdome of heaven: but he that doeth the wyl of my father whiche is in heaven.   *Matt.* 7

Zache stode furthe, and sayde unto the Lorde, beholde Lord, the halfe of my goodes I gyve to the poore, and yf I have done any wronge to any man, I restore fourefolde.   *Luke* 19

Who goeth a warfare at any tyme of his owne coste? Who planteth a vyneyarde, and eateth not of the fruicte thereof? Or who feedeth a flocke, and eateth not of the mylke of the flocke?   1 *Cor.* 9

If we have sowen unto you spiritual thinges, is it a great matter, yf we shal reape your worldly thinges?   1 *Cor.* 9

Do ye not knowe, that they whiche minister aboute holy thinges, lyve of the sacrifyce? They whyche wayte of the aultare, are partakers with the aultare. Even so hath the Lorde also ordeyned: that they whiche preache the Gospell, shoulde lyve of the gospel.   1 *Cor.* 9

He which soweth lytle shal reape lytle: and he that soweth plente-ously, shal reape plenteously. Let every man doe accordynge as he is dysposed in his harte, not grudgynglye or of necessitie: for GOD loveth a cherefull gyver.   2 *Cor.* 9

Let hym that is taughte in the woorde, minister unto him that teacheth, in all good thinges. Be not deceived, God is not mocked: for whatsoever a man soweth, that shall he reape.   *Gal.* 6

Whyle we have tyme, let us do good unto al men, and specially unto them, whiche are of the householde of faythe.   *Gal.* 6

Godlynes is great ryches, yf a man be contente with that he hath: for we brought nothynge into the worlde, neyther may we cary any thing out.   1 *Tim.* 6

Charge them whyche are ryche in thys worlde, that they be ready to give, and glade to distribute, laying up in store for themselves a good foundacion, against the time to come, that they may attayne eternal lyfe.   1 *Tim.* 6

God is not unrighteous, that he wil forget your workes and laboure that procedeth of love, whiche love ye have shewed for his names sake, whiche have ministered unto sainctes, and yet do minister.   *Heb.* 6

To do good, and to distribute, forget not, for with such sacrifices God is pleased.   *Heb.* 13

Whoso hath thys worldes good, and seeth his brother have nede, and shutteth up his compassyon from hym, how dwelleth the love of God in hym?   1 *John* 3

Geve almose of thy goodes, and turne never thy face from any poore man, and then the face of the Lorde shall not be turned away from thee. *Tob.* 4

Be mercifull after thy power. If thou hast muche gyve plenteously: if thou hast litle, doe thy diligence gladly to geve of that litle, for so gatherest thou thy selfe a good rewarde in the day of necessitye.

Tob. 4

He that hath pitye upon the poore, lendeth unto the Lorde: and looke what he layeth out: it shalbe paied him agayne. *Pro.* 19

Blessed be the man that provydeth for the sycke, and nedy, the Lorde shall deliver him, in the time of trouble. *Ps.* 61

¶ *Then shal the Churche wardens, or some other by them appoyncted, gather the devocion of the people, and put the same into the poore mens boxe,° and upon the offeryng daies appoincted, every man and woman shal pay to the Curate the due and accustomed offeryngs: after whiche done, the Priest shal saie.*

Let us pray for the whole estate of Christes Churche militant° here in earth.

ALMIGHTYE and everlivyng God, whych by thy holye Apostle hast taughte us to make prayers and supplicacyons, and to geve thanckes for all men: We humbly beseche thee *If ther be no almes* moste mercifully (to accepte our almose and to) *geven unto the poore,* receyve these our prayers whyche of we offer unto *then shall the words* thy divine majestie, beseechyng thee to inspire *of accepting our* continually, the universall Churche wyth the *almes bee lefte out* *unsayd.* spiryte of truthe, unitye, and concorde: And graunt that all they that do confesse thy holy name, may agree in the truthe of thy holy woorde, and lyve in unytye and godlye love. We beseche thee also to save and defend alle Christyane Kynges, Pryncees, and Governours, and specially thy servaunt, Elysabeth our Quene that under her we may be godly and quietly governed: and graunt unto her whole Counsaill, and to all that be put in aucthoritye under her, that they may truely and indifferently minister justice, to the punishement of wyckednes and vice, and to the maintenaunce of goddes true religion and vertue. Give grace (O heavenly Father) to al Bishopes, Pastours, and Curates, that they may bothe by theyr life and doctrine set furth thy true and lively woorde and rightely and duely administer thy holy Sacramentes: and to all thy people gyve thy heavenlye grace, and especially to thys congregacion heare present, that with meke harte and due reverence, they may heare and receive thy holy worde, truely servyng thee in holines and ryghtuousnes all the dayes of theyr lyfe. And we moost humbly beseche thee of thy goodnes (O Lord) to comfort and succoure all theym whyche in thys transitory lyfe bee in trouble, sorowe, nede, sicknes, or any other adversity. Graunt this, O father, for Jesus Christes sake our onely Mediatour and advocate. Amen.

Then shal folowe this exhortacion, at certayne tymes when the Curate shal see the people negligent to come to the holy communyon.°

WE be come together at thys tyme derely beloved brethren,° to fede at the Lordes supper, unto the whyche in Goddes behalf I bydde you all that be heare present, and beseche you for the lorde Jesus Christes sake, that ye wyll not refuse to come thereto, beyng so lovyngly called, and bidden of God himselfe. Ye know howe grevous and unkynde a thing it is, when a manne hath prepared a riche feaste: decked his table with al kynde of provisyon, so that there lacketh nothinge but the gestes to site downe:° and yet they whych be called wythout anye cause, mooste unthankfully refuse to come. Whyche of you in suche a case woulde not be moved? Who woulde not thyncke a greate injurie and wrong done unto hym? Wherefore moste derely beloved in Christe, take ye good heede, lest ye wythdrawyng your selves from this holy supper, and provoke Goddes indignation against you. It is an easy matter for a man to say, I will not communicate, because I am otherwise letted with worldly busynes: but suche excuses be not so easily accepted and allowed before god. If any man say, I am a grevous sinner, and therefore am afrayed to come: wherefore then do ye not repent and amende? When god calleth you, be you not ashamed to say ye wil not come? when you should returne to god, wil you excuse your self, and say that you be not redy? Considre ernestly with your selves howe litle such feined excuses shall availe before GOD. They that refused the feaste in the Gospell, because they had bought a farme, or would trie their yokes of oxen, or because they were maried, were not so excused, but compted unworthy of the hevenly feast. I for my part am here present, and according to myne office, I bid you in the name of god, I cal you in Christes behalf, I exhort you, as you love your owne Salvation, that ye wil be partakers of this holy Communion. And as the sonne of God, did vouchesafe to yelde up his soule by death upon the crosse for your healthe, even so

it is youre duety to receyve the Communion together, in the remembraunce of his death as he hymselfe commaunded. Nowe, yf ye wyll
in no wise thus do, consider with your selves, how great injury ye
doe unto God, and howe sore punishment hangeth over your heades
for the same. And whereas ye offende God so sore in refusing this
holy banquet, I admonishe, exhorte, and beseche you, that unto this
unkyndenes ye wyll not adde any more. Whiche thing ye shall doe, yf
ye stande by as gasers and lokers of them that do Communicate, and
be no partakers° of the same your selves. For what thing can this be
accompted els, then a further contempt and unkindenes unto God?
Truly it is a greate unthankefulnes to saye naye when ye be called,
but the faulte is muche greater, when men stande by, and yet wyll
neyther eate, nor drincke this holye Communion with other. I praie
you what can this be elles but even to have the misteries of Christ
in derision? It is sayde unto al: Take ye and eate, take and drincke ye
al of this, do this in remembraunce of me. With what face then, or
with what countenaunce shal ye here these wordes? What wyl this be
els, but a neglecting, a despisyng, and mockynge of the Testament of
Christ? Wherfore rather then you shold so do, departe you hence, and
geve place to them that be Godly dysposed. But when you departe,
I beseche you pondre with yourselves, from whome ye departe: ye
departe from the Lordes Table: ye depart from your brethren, and
from the banket of most heavenly foode. These thynges yf ye earnestly consydre, ye shall by Goddes grace returne to a better mynde,
for the obteining wherof we shall make our humble peticions, while
we shal receive the holy Communion.

And some tyme shalbe said this also, at the discretion of the Curat.

DERELY beloved, for asmuche as our dutye is to rendre° to
almighty God our heavenly father most harty thanckes for that
he hathe geven his sonne our Sauiour Jesus Christ not onely to die
for us, but also to be oure Spirituall fode, and sustenaunce, as it is
declared unto us, aswel by Goddes worde, as by the holy sacramentes
of his blessed body and bloud, the which being so comfortable a thing
to them whiche receive it worthelye, and so daungerous to them that
wil presume to receyve it unworthely. My duty is to exhorte you to
considre the dignitie of the holy mistery, and the great peril of the
unworthy receiving therof, and so to searche, and examine youre
owne consciences, as you shold come holy and cleane to a moste godly

and hevenly feast, so that in no wise you come, but in the mariage garment required of God in holy scripture, and so come and be receyved as worthye partakers of suche a heavenly Table. The waye and meanes therto is:

First to examine your lives and conversation by the rule of Goddes commaundementes, and wherinsoeuer ye shall perceyve your selves to have offended eyther by wil, worde, or deede, there bewayle your owne synfull lives, confesse your selves to almighty God, with ful purpose of amendement of life. And yf ye shal perceive your offences to be such, as be not only against God, but also against your neighbours: then ye shal reconcyle youre selves unto them, ready to make restitution and satisfaction according to the uttermost of your powers for all injuries and wronges done by you to any other, and likewise being ready to forgeve other that have offended you, as you would have forgevenes of your offences at Goddes hande. For otherwyse the receiving of the holy Communion doth nothing els, but encrease your dampnation. And because it is requisite that no manne shoulde come to the holye Communion, but with a ful trust in goddes mercy, and with a quiet conscience: therfore yf there be any of you, which by the meanes aforesaid, can not quiet his owne conscience, but requireth further comforte or counsail, then let him come to me, or some other discrete and learned minister of gods word, and open his griefe, that he may receive suche ghostly counseil, advise, and comfort, as his conscience may be releved, and that by the ministery of Gods word, he may receyve comfort, and the benefyte of absolution, to the quieting of his conscience, and advoiding of all scruple and doubtfulnes.

¶ *Then shall the Priest say this exhortation.*

DERELY beloved in the Lorde: ye that mynde to come to the holye Communion° of the bodye and bloude of oure savioure Christe, must consyder what saincte Paule writeth unto the Corinthiens, howe he exhorteth all persones diligentlye to trye and examyne them selves before they presume to eate of that breade, and drincke of that cuppe. For as the benefyte is greate, yf wyth a trulye penitente herte and lyvely faith we receive that holy sacrament (for then we spiritually eate the fleshe of Christ, and drincke his blonde, then we dwell in Christe and Christe in us, we be one wyth Christ, and Christe with us) so is the daunger great, if we receyve the same unworthely. For

then we be gilty of the body and bloud of Christ our saviour.° We eate
and drincke our owne dampnation, not considering the lordes bodye.
We kindle Gods wrath against us. We provoke hym to plague us with
divers diseases, and sundrye kyndes of death. Therfore if any of you
be a blasphemer of god, an hinderer or slaunderer of his worde, an
adulterer, or be in malyce, or envye, or in anye other grevous crime,
bewaile your Sinnes, and come not to this holy table, lest after the
taking of that holy sacrament, the devil enter into you, as he entred
into Judas, and fil you full of al iniquities, and bring you to destruction both of bodye and soule. Judge therefore your selves (brethren)
that ye be not judged of the Lord. Repent you truly for your sinnes
past, have a lively and stedfast faithe in Christ our saviour. Amende
your lives, and be in perfect charitie wyth all men, so shall ye be mete
partakers of those holy misteries. And above al thinges ye must geve
most humble and herty thankes to God the father, the sonne, and
the holye ghost, for the redemption of the world by the deathe and
passion of our saviour Christ, bothe God and man, who did humble
him selfe even to the deathe, upon the crosse, for us miserable sinners which lay in darckenes, and shadowe of death, that he mighte
make us the children of God, and exalte us to everlasting life. And to
the ende that we should alwaie remembre the exceadinge greate love
of our master and onelie saviour Jesu Christ, thus diyng for us, and
the innumerable benefites (which by his precious bloud sheading) he
hath obteined to us, he hath instituted and ordeined holy misteries,
as pledges of his love, and continuall remembraunce of his death, to
our great and endles comfort. To him therfore with the father, and
the holye Ghost, let us geve (as we are moste bounden) continuall
thankes, submitting our selves wholy to his holie will and pleasure,
and studiyng to serve him in true holines and righteousnes, al the
daies of our life. Amen.

*Then shall the Priest saye to them that come to receyve the holy
Communion.*

YOU that do truly and ernestly repente you of youre sinnes, and
be in love and charite with your neighbors, and entende to lede
a newe lyfe, folowing the commaundementes of God, and walkynge
from hence furthe in his holy waies: Draw nere and take this holy
Sacrament to your comfort, make your humble confession to almighty

God, before this congregation here gathered together in his holye name, mekely knelynge upon your knees.

¶ *Then shall this generall confession be made,° in the name of all those, that are mynded to receyve this holy Communion, either by one of them, or els by one of the ministers, or by the priest hym selfe,° all kneling humbly upon their knees.*

ALMIGHTY God, father of oure Lorde Jesus Christe, maker of all thynges, Judge of all menne, we acknowledge and bewayle oure manifolde synnes and wyckednesse, whiche we from tyme to tyme moste grevously have committed, by thoughte, woorde and deede, against thy divine Majestie, provokynge mooste justlye thy wrathe and indignation againste us: we do earnestly repente, and bee hartely sorye for these oure misdoinges, the remembraunce of them is grevous unto us: the burthen of theim is intollerable: have mercy upon us, have mercye upon us, mooste mercyfull father, for thy sonne oure Lorde Jesus Christes sake, forgeve us all that is paste, and graunte that we may ever hereafter serve and please thee, in newenes of lyfe, to the honour and glorye of thy name throughe Jesus Christ our Lorde. Amen.

¶ *Then shall the priest or the Bishop (beyng present) stande up, and turning himself to the people shall say thus.*

ALMIGHTYE God, oure heavenly father, who of his great mercy, hathe promised forgevenes of sinnes to al them, whiche with hartye repentaunce and true faithe turne to hym: have mercye upon you, pardon and deliver you from all your sinnes, confirme, and strengthen you, in all goodnes, and bring you to everlastyng lyfe: through Jesus Christ our Lorde. Amen.

Then shall the Priest also saye.

¶ Here what comfortable wordes our saviour Christ saithe to all them that truly turne to him.

¶ Come unto me all that travaile and be heavy laden and I shal refreshe you. So God loved the world that he gave his onely begotten sonne, to the ende that al that beleve in him should not perishe, but have life everlastyng.

Heare also what S. Paule saithe.

¶ This is a true saieng, and worthy of all men to be receyved, that Jesus Christ came into the worlde to save synners.

Heare also what S. John saieth.

¶ If any manne sinne, we have an advocate with the father, Jesus Christ the righteous, and he is the propiciation for our sinnes.

After the whiche the priest shall procede saying.

Lift up your hartes.

Aunswere. We lyfte them up unto the Lorde.

Priest. Let us geve thanckes unto° our Lorde God.

Aunswere. It is mete and right so to do.

Priest.

¶ It is very mete, right, and our bounden duety that we should at all times, and in all places, geve thanckes to thee, O Lord holy father, almighty everlasting God.

Here shall folow the proper prefaces, according to the tyme, yf there be any specially appointed, or els immediatly shal folow:

Therfore with aungelles. &c.

Proper prefaces.

Upon Christmas day and seven dayes after.

BECAUSE thou dyddest geve Jesus Christ thyne onely Sonne, to be borne as this daye for us, who by the operation of the holy ghoste, was made very man of the substaunce of the vyrgin Mary his mother, and that without spot of synne, to make us clene from al sinne. Therefore with aungels. &c.

Upon Easter daye, and seven dayes after.

BUT chiefly are we bounde to praise thee for the glorious resurrection of thy sonne Jesus Christ our lord, for he is the very paschal lambe, whiche was offred for us, and hath taken awaye the sinne of the world, who by his death hath destroyed death, and by his rising to life againe, hath restored to us everlasting life. Therefore with aungels. &c.

Upon the Ascencion day, and seven dayes after.

THROUGH thy most deare beloved sonne Jesus Christ our Lorde, who after his moste glorious resurrection, manifestly appered to al his Apostles, and in their sight ascended up into heaven to prepare a place for us, that where he is, thether might we also ascende, and reigne with him in glory. Therfore with aungels. &c.

Upon Wytsonday, and six daies after.

THROUGH Jesu Christ our Lord, according to whose mooste true promyse, the holye ghoste came downe this daye from heaven, with a sodaine greate sounde, as it had bene a mighty wynde, in the lykenes of fiery tonges lightinge upon the Apostles, to teache them, and to leade them to all truth, geving them bothe the gyfte of divers languages, and also boldnes with fervent zeale, constantly to preache the gospel unto all nacions, whereby we are broughte out of darcknes and errour into the cleare light and true knowledge of thee, and of thy sonne Jesus Christ. Therefore with Aungels. &c.

Upon the feaste of Trinitie onely.

IT is very mete, right, and our bounden dutie, that we should at all times, and in all places, geve thankes to thee, O Lorde, almightie and everlasting God, which art one god, one lord, not one only person, but thre persons in one substaunce, for that whiche we beleve of the glorye of the father, the same we beleve of the sonne, and of the holy ghost, without any difference or inequalitie. Therfore. &c.

¶ *After which preface, shall folow immediatly.*

THERFORE with Aungelles, and Archangelles, and wyth all the company of heaven, we laude and magnify thy glorious name, evermore praising thee, and saying: Holy, holy, holy,° lord god of hostes, heven and earth are ful of thy glory, glory be to thee, O Lord most hyghe.

¶ *Then shall the priest, knelynge downe at Gods borde, say in the name of all them that shall receyve the communion, this prayer folowing.*

WE do not presume° to come to this thy table (O merciful Lorde) trustinge in oure owne rightuousnesse, but in thy manifolde and greate mercies, we be not worthy so muche as to gather up the crommes under thy Table, but thou arte the same Lord, whose property is alwaies to have mercy. Graunt us therefore gracious Lorde, so to eate the fleshe of thy deare sonne Jesus Christ, and to drinke his bloude,° that oure synful bodies may be made cleane by his body, and our soules washed through his most precious bloud, and that we may evermore dwell in him, and he in us.

Then the priest standing up, shal say as foloweth:

ALMIGHTY God our heavenly father whiche of thy tender mercye, diddest geve thine onely Sonne Jesus Christ to suffer death upon the Crosse for our redemption, who made ther (by his one oblation of himself once offered)° a ful, perfect and sufficient sacrifice, oblation, and satisfaction for the synnes of the whole worlde, and didde institute, and in his holy gospel commaunde us to continue a perpetual memory of that his precious deathe, untyll his comminge againe: Heare us O merciful father, we besech thee, and graunt that we receivyng these thy creatures of breade and wine,° accordinge to thy sonne our saviour Jesu Christes holy institution, in remembraunce of his death and passion, may be partakers of his moste blessed body and bloude: who in the same night that he was betraied,° toke bread, and when he had geven thankes, he brake it, and gave it to his disciples, saying: Take, eate, this is my bodie, which is geven for you. Doe this in remembraunce of me. Likewise after supper, he toke the cuppe, and when he had geven thankes, he gave it to them, saying: Drinke ye all of this, for this is my bloude of the new Testament, whiche is shedde for you and for many, for remission of sinnes: doe this as oft as ye shall drinke it, in remembraunce of me.

Then shall the minister fyrste receyve the Communion in bothe kyndes° him selfe, and next deliver it to other Ministers (yf any be there present, that they may helpe the chief minister) and after to the people in their handes° kneling. And when he delivereth the breade, he shall saye.

THE bodie of our lord Jesu Christ which was geven for thee,° preserve thy body and soule into everlastinge life, and take and eate this, in remembraunce that Christ died for thee, and feede on him in thine heart by faith with thankesgevynge.

And the minister that delivereth the cuppe shall saye.

THE bloude of our lorde Jesu Christ° which was shedd for thee, preserve thy body and soule into everlasting life. And drinke this in remembraunce that Christes bloude was shedde for thee, and be thankeful.

Then shall the priest say the Lordes prayer, the people repetynge after him every peticion. After shalbe sayde as foloweth.°

O LORDE and heavenly father, we thy humble servauntes, entierly desire thy fatherly goodnes mercifully to accept this our sacrifice of praise and thankesgevinge: moste humblye besechynge thee to graunte, that by the merites and death of thy sonne Jesus Christ and throughe faith in his bloude, we (and all thy whole church) may

obteine remission of our sinnes, and al other benefites of his passion. And here we offer and presente unto thee, O Lord, our selves,
our soules and bodies, to be a reasonable, holy, and lively sacrifice
unto thee, humblye beseching thee, that al we which be partakers of
this holye communion, may be fulfilled with thy grace and heavenly
benediction. And although we be unworthye throughe our manifolde sinnes, to offer unto thee any sacrifice, yet we beseche thee to
accept this our bounden duty and service, not weighing our merites,
but pardoning our offences, throughe Jesus Christ our Lord, by
whom, and with whom, in the unitie of the holy ghoste, all honour
and glorye be unto thee, O father almighty, world without ende.
Amen.

Or this.

A LMIGHTY and everlastinge God, we moste hartely thancke thee,°
for that thou doest vouchsafe to fede us, whiche have duly
received these holy misteries, with the spiritual fode of the moste
precious body and bloude of thy sonne, our saviour Jesus Christ, and
doest assure us therby of thy favour and goodnes towarde us, and
that we be very membres incorporate in thy mistical body, whiche is
the blessed company of al faithful people, and be also heyres through
hope of thy everlasting kingdom, by the merites of the most precious
death and passion of thy deare sonne. We now most humbly beseche
thee, o hevenly father, so to assist us with thy grace, that we may continue in that holy felowship, and do all suche good workes as thou
hast prepared for us to walke in, throughe Jesus Christe our Lord,
to whom with thee and the holy ghost be all honour and glory, world
without ende. Amen.

Then shalbe sayde or songe.

G LORYE be to GOD on hyghe.° And in earthe peace, good wyll
towardes men. We prayse thee, we blesse thee, we worshyppe
thee, we glorifye thee, wee geve thanckes to thee for thy greate glorye.
O LORDE GOD heavenlye Kynge. GOD the father Almyghtie.
O Lorde the onely begotten Sonne Jesu Christ. O Lord God, Lambe
of God, Sonne of the father, that takest awaye the sinnes of the
worlde, have mercye upon us: Thou that takest awaye the Sinnes of
the worlde, have mercy upon us.° Thou that takest away the synnes of
the worlde, receive our praier. Thou that syttest at the right hande of
God the Father, have mercy upon us. For thou onely art holy: Thou

only art the Lorde, thou only O Christe with the holy Ghost, art most highe in the Glory of God the father. Amen.

Then the Priest, or the Byshop, if he be present, shal let them depart with this blessing.

THE peace of God, which passeth all understanding, kepe youre hartes and mindes in the knowledge and love of God, and of his Sonne Jesu Christe, oure Lorde. And the blessing of God almyghty, the Father, the Sonne, and the holy Ghost, be among you, and remayne with you alwaies. Amen.

¶ *Collectes to be sayd after the offertory when there is no Communion: every suche daye one. And the same maye be sayde also° as often as occasion shall serve, after the Collectes, either of Morning and Evening Praier, Communion, or Letany, by the discretion of the Minister.*

ASSIST us mercifully, O Lorde, in these our Supplications and Praiers, and dispose the way of thy servauntes, towarde the attainement of everlasting salvation, that emong al the chaunges, and chaunces of this mortal lyfe, thei may ever be defended by thy moste gratious, and redy helpe: Through Christ our Lorde. Amen.

O ALMIGHTY Lorde, and everlivyng God, vouchesafe we beseche thee, to direct, sanctifie, and governe, bothe oure heartes, and bodies, in the wayes of thy lawes, and in the worckes of thy commaundementes, that through thy most mighty protection, both here and ever, we maye bee preserved in bodye, and Soule: throughe oure lorde and Savioure Jesus Christe. Amen.

GRAUNT we beseche thee almighty God, that the wordes which we have heard this daye with our outward eares, may through thi grace be so grafted inwardly in our hartes, that they may bring furth in us the fruite of good living, to the honour and praise of thy name: throughe Jesus Christ our Lorde. Amen.

PREVENTE us O Lorde in all our doynges, with thy most gratious favoure, and further us with thy continuall helpe, that in al our workes begonne, continued, and ended in thee: we may glorify thy holy name, and finally by thy mercy, obteine everlasting lyfe, Through Jesus Christ our Lorde. Amen.

ALMIGHTY God, the founteine of all wisedom, which knowest oure necessities before we aske, and our ignoraunce in asking, we beseche thee to have compassion upon our infirmities, and those thinges, which for our unworthiness we dare not, and for oure blindenes we cannot aske, vouchesafe to geve us for the worthines of thy sonne Jesus Christe our Lorde. Amen.

A LMIGHTY God, whiche haste promysed to here the peticions of them that aske in thy sonnes name, we beseche thee mercifully to encline thine Eares to us that have made nowe our praiers and supplications unto thee, and graunt that those thinges which we have faithfully asked, according to thy wil, may effectually be obteined to the relief of our necessitie, and to the setting furth of thy glory through Jesus Christ our Lorde. Amen.

Upon the holy daies (if there be no Communion) shalbe said al that is appointed at the Communion, untyll the ende of the homely, concluding with the generall praier, for the whole estate of Christes Churche militant here in earth, and one, or moe of these Collectes, before rehersed, as occasion shall serve.

¶ *And there shalbe no celebration of the lordes supper, except there be a good number to Communicate wyth the Priest, accordinge to his dyscretion.*

¶ *And yf there be not above .xx. persons in the Parish° of discretion to receyve the Communion, yet there shalbe no communion except foure or thre at the least communicate with the priest. And in Cathedral and collegiate churches, where be many Priestes and Deacons, they shall all receyve the communion with the minister every Sonday at the leaste, except they have a reasonable cause to the contrary.*

¶ *And to take awaye the superstition, whiche any person hath, or myghte have in the breade and wyne, it shall suffice that the breade be suche as is usual to be eaten at the table, with other meates, but the beste and purest wheate breade, that conveniently may be gotten.° And yf anye of the breade or wyne remaine, the Curate shall have it to hys owne use.°*

¶ *The bread and wyne for the Communion shalbe provyded by the Curate and the church wardenes, at the charges of the Paryshe, and the Paryshe shalbe discharged of suche summes of money, or other duties, which hitherto they have payed for the same by order of their houses every Sondaye.*

¶ *And note that every Parishioner shall communicate, at the leaste thre tymes in the yere, of whiche Easter to be one,° and shall also receyve the sacramentes, and other rytes, according to the order of this boke appoincted. And yerely at Easter, every Parishioner shall recon with his Parson, Vicar, or Curate, or his, or their deputie or deputies, and paye to them or hym, all ecclesiastical duties, accustomably due then, and at that tyme to be payed.*

The ministracion of
Baptisme to be used in the
Churche.

*I*T appeareth by auncient writers, that the Sacrament of Baptisme in the old *tyme, was not commonly Ministred, but at two times in the yeare, at Easter, and Whytsontide, at which tymes it was openly ministred in the presence of al the congregacion: which custome (now being growen out of use) although it can not for many consideracions bee well restored agayne, yet it is thought good to folow the same as nere as conveniently may be. Wherfore the people are to be admonished, that it is most convenient that Baptisme should not be ministred, but upon Sondayes, and other holy dayes when the most nombre of people may come together, aswel for that the congregacion there present maye testifie the receyving of them that be newly Baptized into the nomber of Christes Churche, as also because in the Baptisme of infants, everye man present may be put in remembraunce of his awne profession made to God in hys Baptisme. For which cause also, it is expedient that Baptisme be ministred in the English tongue. Nevertheles (if necessitie so require) children may at al tymes° be Baptized at home.*

Publique Baptysme.

When there are children to he Baptized upon the Sonday, or holy day, the parentes shal geve knowledge over nighte, or in the morning, afore the beginning of Mornyng prayour, to the curate. And then the Godfathers, Godmothers, and people with the children, must be ready at the Fonte,° eyther immediatly after the last Lesson at Morning prayour, or els immedi- atly after the last Lesson at Evening praiour, as the Curat by his discrecion shall appoincte. And then standinge there, the Priest shall aske whether the children be Baptised, or no. If they aunswer, No: Then shal the priest say thus.

DERELY beloved, forasmuche as al men be conceived and borne in synne, and that our saviour Christ saith, none can entre into the kingdom of God (except he be regenerate, and borne a new of water and the holy gost) I beseche you to cal upon God the father, throughe our lord Jesus Christ, that of his bounteous mercy, he wil graunt to these children, that thing which by nature thei can not have, that they may be baptised with water and the holy Ghost, and received into Christes holy churche, and be made lively membres of the same.

Then the Priest shall say.

Let us praye.

ALMIGHTIE and everlasting God, whiche of thy great mercy diddest save Noe and his familie° in the Arcke, from perishing by water, and also diddest saufly lead the children of Israel, thy people, through the redde Sea, figuring therby thy holy Baptisme: and by the Baptisme of thy welbeloved sonne Jesus Christe, diddest sanctifye the floude Jordane, and al other waters, to the mistical washinge away of synne: We beseche thee (for thine infinite mercies) that thou wilte mercifully loke upon these children, sanctify them and washe them with thy holy gost, that they beyng delivered from thy wrath, may be received into the Arcke of Christes churche, and beyng stedfast in faithe, joyfull throughe hope, and roted in charitie, may so passe the waves of this troublesome world,° that finally they may come to the lande of everlasting life, there to reigne with thee, worlde without ende, through Jesus Christ our Lorde. Amen.

ALMIGHTY and immortal God, the aide of al that nede, the helper of al that fly to thee for succour, the life of them that beleve, and the resurreccion of the deade, we cal upon thee for these infantes, that they comming to thy holy Baptisme, may receyve remission of their sinnes by spiritual regeneracion, receive them (O Lorde) as thou haste promised by thy welbeloved sonne, saiynge: Aske, and you shall have: seeke, and you shall fynde: knocke, and it shalbe opened unto you: So geve now unto us that aske. Let us that seeke, fynde, open thy gate unto us that knocke, that these infantes enjoy the everlasting benediction of thy heavenly wasshing, and may come to the eternal kingdome whiche thou haste promised by Christ our Lorde. Amen.°

¶ *Then shall the Priest saye.*

¶ Heare the words of the Gospel, written by Sainct Marke in the tenth Chapiter.

AT a certayne tyme they brought children to Christ that he should touche theim, and his Disciples rebuked those that brought them. But when Jesus sawe it, he was displeased, and sayde unto them. Suffre lytle children to come unto me, and forbydde them not: For to suche belongeth the Kyngdome of God. Verely, I saye unto you: whosoever doeth not receive the kingdome of GOD, as a lytle chylde: he shall not entre therin. And when he had taken them up in his armes: he put his handes upon them, and blessed them. *Mark* 10

¶ *After the Gospel is redde, the minister shal make this briefe exhortacion upon the wordes of the Gospell.*

FRENDES, ye heare in this Gospell the woordes of our saviour Christe, that he commaunded the chyldren to bee broughte unto him: howe he blamed those that woulde have kepte theym from hym, howe he exhorted all men to folowe their innocencye. Ye perceive how by his outward gesture and dede, he declared his good wil towarde them. For he embraced them in his armes, he laied his hands upon them, and blessed them: doubt not you therfore, but ernestly beleve that he wil likewise favourably receive these present infants, that he wil embrace them with the armes of his mercy, that he wil geve unto them the blessing of eternal life: and make them partakers of his everlasting kingdome. Wherfore we being thus perswaded of the good wyl of our heavenly father towardes these enfantes declared by his son Jesus Christ, and nothing doubting, but that he favourably alloweth this charitable woorke of ours, in bringing these children to his holye Baptisme: let us faithfully and devoutly geve thankes unto him, and saye.°

ALMIGHTY and everlasting God, heavenly Father, we geve thee humble thankes, that thou haste vouchsafed to call us to the knowledge of thy grace and fayth in thee, encrease this knowledge, and confirme this faith in us evermore: Geve thy holy spirit to these enfantes, that they may be borne againe, and be made heyres of everlasting salvacion, throughe our Lorde Jesus Christ. Who liveth and reigneth with thee, and the holy spirite, nowe and for ever. Amen.

Then the Priest shal speake unto the Godfathers and Godmothers, on this wyse.

WELBELOVED frendes, ye have broughte these children here to be baptised, ye have praied that our lord Jesus christ, would vouchesaufe to receive them, to lay his handes upon them, to blesse them, to release theim of their sinnes, to geve theim the kingdom of heaven, and everlasting lyfe. Ye have heard also that our Lord Jesus Christ hath promised in his Gospel, to graunt all these thinges that ye have praied for: which promise he for his part wil most surely kepe and performe. Wherfore after this promise made by Christ, these infants muste also faythfully for their part promise by you that be their sureties, that they wil forsake the divel and al his woorkes, and constantly beleve Gods holy word, and obediently kepe his commaundements.

¶ *Then shal the Priest demaunde of the Godfathers and Godmothers these questions.*

Doest thou forsake the devil and all his workes, the vaine pompe and glorye of the world, with al the covetous desires of the same, and the carnal desires of the flesh, so that thou wilt not folow, nor be led by them? *Aunswere.* I forsake them al.°

¶ *The Minister.* Doest thou beleve in god the father almighty, maker of heaven and earth? And in Jesus christ his only begotten sonne our Lord, and that he was conceived by the holy Ghost, borne of the virgin Mary: that he suffred under Poncius Pilate, was crucifyed, dead, and buried, that he went doune into hel, and also did rise againe the thirde day: that he ascended into heaven, and sitteth at the right hand of god the father almighty: and from thence shall come againe at the ende of the worlde, to judge the quicke and the dead? And doest thou beleve in the holy Ghoste, the holy Catholicque Churche, the communion of sainctes, the remission of synnes, the resurreccion of the fleshe, and everlasting lyfe after death? *Aunswere.* All this I stedfastly beleve.°

Ministre. Wylt thou be baptised° in this fayth? *Aunswere.* That is my desyre.

Then shal the Priest say.

O MERCIFUL God, graunte that the olde Adam in these children maye be so buried, that the newe man may be raysed up in them. Amen.

Graunte that all carnal affeccions maye dye in them, and that all thinges belonginge to the spirite may live and growe in them. Amen.

Graunte that they may have power and strength to have victory, and to triumphe against the Divel, the worlde and the flesh. Amen.

Graunt that whosoever is here dedicated to thee, by our office and ministerie, may also be endued with heavenly vertues, and everlastingly rewarded through thy mercy, O blessed Lord God, who doest live and governe al thinges worlde without ende. Amen.

A LMIGHTY everlyvyng God, whose most derely beloved son Jesus Christe, for the forgevenes of our sinnes did shed out his moste precious syde bothe water and bloude, and gave commaundement to his disciples that they should go teache al nacions, and baptise them in the name of the father, the sonne, and of the holy Ghost: Regard we beseche thee, the supplicacions of thy congregacion, and graunt that al thy servantes whiche shalbe baptised in this water, may receive the fulnes of thy grace, and ever remaine in the nombre of thy faithfull and elect chyldren, through Jesus Christ our Lord. Amen.

Then the Priest shal take the Childe in his handes, and aske the name: and naming the Childe, shal dippe it in the water,° so it be discretely and warely done, saying.

N. I Baptise thee in the name of the Father, and of the Sonne, and of the holy Ghost. Amen.

¶ *And yf the Childe be weake, it shall suffice to powre water upon it, saying the foresaid wordes.*

N. I Baptize thee° in the name of the Father, and of the sonne, and of the holy Ghost. Amen.

Then the Priest shall make a Crosse upon the Childes forehead,° saying:

WE receive this Childe into the congregacion of Christes flocke, and do sygne him with the signe of the crosse, in token that hereafter he shal not be ashamed to confesse the faith of Christ crucified, and manfully to fight under his banner against sinne, the worlde, and the devyll, and to continue Christes faithful souldiour and servaunt, unto his lives ende. Amen.

Then shal the Priest say.

SEYING now derely beloved Brethren that these children be regenerate and grafted into the bodye of christes congregacion, let us geve thankes unto God for these benefites,° and with one accorde make our praiours unto almighty God, that thei may lead the reste of their lyfe, according to this beginning.

Then shal be sayd.

OUR father which art. &c.

Then shal the Priest say,

WE yelde thee harty thankes most merciful father, that it hathe pleased thee to regenerate this enfant with thy holy spirite, to receyve him for thine owne childe by adoption, and to incorporate him into thy holy congregacion. And humbly we beseche thee to graunt that he being dead unto synne, and lyving unto righteousnes, and being buried with Christ in his death, maye crucify the old man, and utterly abolyshe the whole bodye of synne, that as he is made partaker of the deathe of thy sonne, so he maye be partaker of hys resurrection, so that finally with the residue of thy holy congregacion he may be inheritour of thine everlasting kingdome. Through Christ our Lord. Amen.

¶ *At the laste ende, the Priest calling the Godfathers and Godmothers together, shal say this shorte exhortation folowing.*

FORASMUCHE as these children have promysed by you to forsake the Devil and all his woorkes, to beleve in God, and to serve hym, you must remember that it is your parts and duties to see that these enfantes be taughte, so sone as they shalbe able to learne, what a solempne vowe, promyse, and profession, they have made by you. And that they may know these thinges the better: ye shal cal upon theim to heare Sermons, and chiefly you shal provide that they may learne the Crede, the Lordes praier, and the Ten Commaundementes in the English tongue: and al other thinges which a Christian man ought to know and beleve to his soules health. And that these children may be vertuously brought up, to leade a Godly and christian life, remembring alwaies that Baptisme doeth represent unto us our profession, which is to folow the example of our saviour Christ, and to be made like unto hym, that as he died and rose again for us: so should we (whiche are Baptised) dye from sinne, and ryse again unto rightuousnes, continually mortifiyng al our evyll and corrupt affections, and dailye procedynge in all vertue and godlynes of living.

¶ *The Minister shal commaunde that the chyldren be brought to the Byshop to be confyrmed of him, so sone as they can saye in theyr vulgare tongue the articles of the faythe, the Lordes praier, and the .x. Commaundementes, and be further instructed in the Catechisme set furth for that purpose, accordyngly as it is there expressed.*

Of them that be Bap-
tised in Private houses in
tyme of necessitie.°

¶ *The Pastours and Curates shal oft admonish the people, that they deferre not the Baptisme of enfantes any longer then the Sonday, or other holy day, next after the childe be borne, onlesse upon a great and reasonable cause declared to the Curate, and by him approved.*

And also they shal warne theim that without great cause, and necessity, they baptise not children at home in their houses, and when great nede shall compelle theim so to doe, that then they minister on this fassion.

Fyrste let theim that be present cal upon God for hys grace, and say the Lordes prayour, yf the time wil sufre. And then one of them shall name the childe, and dippe him in the water, or powre water upon him, saying these wordes.

N. I Baptise thee in the name of the Father, and of the Sonne, and of the holy Ghoste. Amen.

And let them not doubte, but that the childe so Baptised, is lawfully and sufficiently Baptised, and ought not to be Baptised agayne in the Church. But yet nevertheles, if the childe whyche is after this sorte Baptised, do afterwarde live, it is expediente that he be broughte into the Churche, to the entent the Priest may examyne and trie, whether the child be lawfully Baptised or no. And yf those that bryng any childe to the Churche do answere that he is alredy Baptised: Then shal the Priest examine them further.

¶ By whome the childe was Baptised?

¶ Who was present when the childe was Baptised?

¶ Whether they called upon God for grace and succour in that necessitie?

¶ Wyth what thing, or what matter they did Baptyse the Chylde?

¶ Wyth what wordes the childe was Baptised?

¶ Whether they thinke the childe to be lawfully and perfectly Baptised?

¶ *And yf the Minister shall prove by the aunswers of suche, as brought the childe, that all thinges were done as they oughte to be: Then shal not he Christen the childe againe, but shall receyve him, as one of the flocke of the true Christian people, saiynge thus.*

I CERTIFY you, that in this case ye have done wel, and accordinge unto due ordre concerning the Baptising of this childe, whiche beyng borne in Originall sinne, and in the wrathe of God, is nowe by the laver of regeneracion in Baptisme, received into the nomber of the children of God,° and heires of everlasting life, for our Lorde Jesus Christ doeth not deny his grace and mercy unto such infantes, but most lovingly doth cal them unto him: as the holy gospel doth witnes to our comfort on this wise.

The Gospell.

AT a certaine time they brought children unto Christ that he should touche them, and his dysciples rebuked those that brought them. But when Jesus saw it, he was displeased, and said unto them: Suffre litle children to come unto me, and forbid theim not, for to such belongeth the kingdome of God. Verely I say unto you, whosoever doth not receive the kingdom of God as a litle child, he shal not entre therin. And when he had taken them up in his armes, he put his handes upon them, and blessed them.   *Mark* 10

After the Gospel is redde, the minister shal make this exhortacion upon the wordes of the Gospel.

FRENDES, ye heare in this Gospell the wordes of oure saviour Christe, that he commaunded the chyldren to bee brought unto hym: howe he blamed those that woulde have kepte theym from him, howe he exhorted all men to folowe their innocencye: Ye perceive how by his outward gesture in dede, he declared his good wil toward them. For he embraced them in his armes, he laied his hands upon them, and blessed them, doubt not you therefore, but earnestly beleve, that he hath likewise favorably received this present infant, that he hathe embraced hym wyth the armes of hys mercy, that he hath geven unto him the blessing of eternal life: and made him partaker of his everlasting kingdom. Wherfore we beyng thus perswaded of the good wil of our hevenly father declared by his sonne Jesus Christ towards this infant, Let us faithfully and devoutly geve thankes unto him, and say the praier, which the lord him self taught, and in declaracion of our faith, let us recite the articles conteined in our Crede.

¶ *Here the Minister with the Godfathers, and Godmothers shall say.*

OUR Father which. *&c.*

¶ *Then the Priest shal demaund the name of the child, which beyng by the Godfathers, and Godmothers pronounced, the Minister shall say,*

¶ Doest thou in the name of this child° forsake the devil, and al his workes, the vaine pompe, and glory of the world, with al the covetous desires of the same, the carnal desires of the fleshe, and not to folowe and be ledde by them?

Aunswere. I forsake them al.

¶ *The Minister.* Doest thou in the name of this childe professe this faith: to beleve° in God the father almighty, maker of heaven and earth. And in Jesus Christ his only begotten son our Lord, and that he was conceived by the holy ghost, borne of the virgin Mary, that he suffered under Ponce Pilate, was crucified, dead, and buried, that he went doune into hel, and also did rise again the .iii. daye: that he ascended into heaven, and sytteth at the ryght hande of God the father almightye: and from thence he shal come again at the ende of the world, to judge the quicke and the dead? And do you in his name beleve in the holy gost, the holy Catholicque church, the communion of sainctes, the remission of sinnes, resurreccion of the fleshe, and everlasting life after death?

Aunswere. All this I steadfastly beleve.°

Let us pray.

ALMIGHTY and everlasting God, heavenly father, we geve thee humble thanckes, for that thou hast vouchsafed to call us to the knowledge of thy grace and faythe in thee: increase this knowledge, and confyrme this faythe in us evermore: Geve thy holye spirite to this infante, that he beynge borne agayne, and beynge made heyre of everlastynge salvacion through our Lord Jesus Christ, may continue thy servaunt, and atteine thy promise, through the same our Lorde Jesus Christ thy sonne, who liveth and reigneth with thee in the unitie of the same holy spirit everlasting. Amen.

¶ *Then shal the Minister make this exhortacion to the Godfathers and Godmothers.*

FORASMUCHE as this childe hath promised by you to forsake the devil, and al his workes, to beleve in God, and to serve him: you must remembre that it is your part and dutie, to see that this enfante be taught (so sone as he shalbe able to learne) what a solempne vowe, promise, and profession he hath made by you. And that he may know these thinges the better, ye shal call upon him to heare sermons. And chiefly ye shal provide that he may learne the Crede, the Lordes praier and the .x. Commaundementes in the English tongue, and al other thinges which a Christian man ought to know, and beleve to his soules health, and that this chyld may be vertuously brought up, to leade a godly, and a christian lyfe. Remembring alway that Baptisme doeth represent unto us our profession, which is to folow the example of our Saviour Christ, and be made like unto him, that as he died and rose againe for us, so shoulde we which are Baptized, dye from sinne, and rise againe unto righteousnes, continually mortifying all our evil and corrupt affections, and daily proceding in al vertue, and godlines of living. *&c. As in Publique Baptisme.*

¶ *But if they which bring the enfantes to the Church, do make an uncerteine aunswere to the Priestes questions, and say that they cannot tel what they thought, didde, or said, in that great feare, and trouble of minde (as often times it chaunseth) then let the Priest Baptise him in forme above written, concerning publique Baptisme, saving that at the dipping of the chylde in the Fonte, he shal use this forme of wordes.*

If thou be not Baptized al ready, *N.* I baptise thee in the name of the father, and of the Sonne, and of the holy ghoste. Amen.

Confirmacion wherin is conteined a Catechisme for children.

*T*O the ende that Confirmacion may be ministred to the more edifying of suche, as shal receive it (*according unto S. Paules doctrine, who teacheth that al things should he doen in the Church, to the edification of the same*) it is thought good that none herafter shalbe confyrmed but suche as can saie in their mother tongue the articles of the faith, the Lordes praier, and the .x. Commaundementes. And can also answere to suche questions of this short Cathechisme, as the Bishop (or suche as he shal appoinct) shal by hys discretion appose theim in. And this order is most convenient to be observed for divers consideracions.

First, because that when children come to the yeres of discrecion, and have learned what their godfathers, and godmothers promised for them in Baptisme, they may then themselves wyth their owne mouthe, and wyth their awne consent, openly before the Churche, ratifie and confyrme the same, and also promise that by the grace of God, they shall evermore endevour themselfes faithfully to observe and kepe suche thynges, as they by theyr owne mouth and confession have assented unto.

Secondly, forasmuche as Confirmacion is ministred to theym that be Baptised, that by imposition of handes, and prayer, they may receive strengthe and defence agaynst all temptacions to synne and the assaultes of the worlde and the Devill: it is most mete to be ministred when children come to that age, that partely by the frailtye of their awne fleshe, partely by the assaultes of the *worlde and the Devil, thei begyn to be in daunger to fal into sondry kyndes of synne.*°

Thirdly, for that it is agreable myth the usage of the Churche, in times paste, wherby it was ordeined that Confirmacion shoulde he mynistred to them that were of perfecte age, that they beyng instructed in Christes religion, should openly professe their awne faithe, and promise to be obedient unto the wyl of God.

And that no man shal thyncke that any detryment shall come to children by differring of their Confirmacyon: he shall knowe for truth, that it is certeine by Goddes worde, that children beyng Baptised, have all thynges necessarie for their salvacion:° *and be undoubtedly saved.*

¶ A Catechisme, that is to
say, an instruction to be learned of every childe,° before
he be brought to be confirmed of the Bishoppe.

Question. What is your name?
Aunswere. N. or *M.*
Question. Who gave you this name?
Aunswere. My Godfathers and Godmothers in my Baptisme, wherein I was made a membre of Christe, the childe of God, and an inheritour of the kingdome of heaven.
Question. What did your godfathers and godmothers then for you?
Aunswere. They did promise, and vowe .iii. thynges in my name. First, that I should forsake the devil, and all his workes and pompes, the vanities of the wicked worlde, and al the sinful lustes of the fleshe. Secondly, that I should beleve al the articles of the Christian faith. And thirdely, that I should kepe Goddes holy wil and Commaundementes, and walke in the same al the daies of my lyfe.
Question. Doest thou not thynke that thou art bounde to beleve and to do, as they have promised for thee?
Answere. Yes verely, and by Goddes helpe so I wil. And I hartely thanke our heavenly Father, that he hath called me to this state of salvation, through Jesus Christe our saviour. And I pray God to geve me his grace, that I may continue in the same unto my lyves ende.
Question. Reherse the Articles of thy belefe.

Aunswere.

I BELEVE in God the Father almighty, maker of heaven and of earth. And in Jesus Christ his onely Sonne our Lorde. Which was conceived of the holy Ghost. Borne of the Virgine Mary. Suffered under Ponce Pylate, was crucifyed, deade, and buried, he descended into hell. The thyrd day he rose agayne from the dead. He ascended into heven, and sitteth at the right hand of God the Father almighty. From thence he shal come to judge the quicke and the dead. I beleve in the Holy ghost. The holy catholike Churche. The Communion of saynctes. The forgivenes of synnes. The resurrection of the body. And the lyfe everlastinge. Amen.

Question. What doest thou chiefly learne in these artycles of thy beliefe?

Aunswere.

Firste, I learne to beleve in God the father, who hath made me and al the worlde.

Secondlye, in God the sonne, who hath redemed me and all mankinde.

Thirdly, in God the holy Ghost, who sanctifieth me, and all the elect people of God.

Question. You said, that your godfathers and godmothers dyd promise for you, that you shoulde kepe Gods commaundementes. Tell me how many there be?

Aunswere. Tenne.

Question. Whiche be they?

Aunswere.

THE same which God spake in the .xx. Chapter of Exodus,° saying: I am the Lord thy God whyche have brought thee out of the land of Egypt, oute of the house of bondage. Thou shalt have none other goddes but me.

ii. Thou shalt not make to thy selfe any graven Image nor the lykenes of any thyng that is in heaven above, or in the earthe beneth, nor in the water under the earthe: thou shalt not bow doune to them, nor worship them. For I the Lorde thy God am a gelous God,° and visyte the sinnes of the fathers upon the chyldren, unto the third and fourth generacion of them that hate me, and shewe mercye unto thousandes in them that love me, and kepe my commaundementes.

iii. Thou shalt not take the name of the Lord thy God in vaine, for the Lorde will not holde hym guiltles that taketh his name in vaine.

iiii. Remember thou kepe holy the Sabboth day. Syxe daies shalt thou laboure,° and do all that thou hast to do: but the seventh day is the Sabboth of the Lord thy God. In it thou shalt do no maner of worcke, thou and thy sonne, and thy daughter, thy manservaunt, and thy maydservaunt, thy cattel, and the straunger that is wythin thy gates: for in sixe daies the Lord made heaven and earth, the sea, and al that in them is, and rested the seventh day, wherfore the Lorde blessed the seventh day, and halowed it.

v. Honour thy father and thy mother, that thy daies may be long in the lande, whyche the Lorde thy God geveth thee.

vi. Thou shalt do no murther.

vii. Thou shalt not committe adultery.

viii. Thou shalt not steale.

ix. Thou shalt not beare false wytnes agaynste thy neighbour.

x. Thou shalt not covet thy neyghbours house,° thou shalt not covet thy neyghboures wyfe, nor hys servaunt, nor hys mayde, nor hys oxe, nor hys asse, nor any thyng that is hys.

Question. What doest thou chiefly learne by these commaunde-mentes?

Aunswere. I learne two thynges. My duty towardes God, and my dutye towardes my neighbour.

Question. What is thy dutye towardes God?

Aunswere. My dutye towardes God is, to beleve in hym, to feare him, and to love hym with all my harte, with al my mynde, with al my soule, and with all my strengthe. To worship hym. To geve hym thanckes. To putte my whole truste in hym. To call upon hym. To honour hys holy name, and hys woorde, and to serve hym truely all the dayes of my lyfe.

Question. What is thy dutye toward thy neighbour?

Aunswere. My dutye towardes my neyghbour is to love hym as my selfe: And to do to all men, as I would they should do unto me. To love, honour, and succour my father and mother. To honour and obey the Quene, and hir minysters. To submitte my selfe to al my gover-nours, teachers, spiritual Pastours, and Maisters. To order my selfe lowly and reverently to all my betters. To hurte no body by worde, nor dede. To be true and juste in all my dealyng. To beare no malice, nor hatred in my harte. To kepe my handes from pickyng and stealyng, and my tongue from evil speakyng, liyng and slaunderyng. To kepe my body in temperaunce, sobernes and chastitie. Not to covet nor desire other mennes goodes. But learne and labour truely to get myne awne livyng, and to do my dutye in that state of life, unto whiche it shal please God to cal me.

Question. My good child know this, that thou art not able to do these thinges of thy self, nor to walke in the commaundementes of God, and to serve hym, wythout hys specyall grace, whyche thou must learne at al tymes to cal for by diligent prayer. Let me heare therfore, if thou canst saye the Lordes praier?

Aunswere.

O UR father whiche art in heaven: Hallowed be thy name. Thy kyngdom come. Thy wil be done in earth, as it is in heaven. Geve us this day our daily bread. And forgeve us our trespasses, as we forgeve theim that trespasse against us. And leade us not into temptacion. But deliver us from evil. Amen.

Question. What desirest thou of God in this praier?

Aunswere. I desire my Lord God our heavenly Father, who is the gever of al goodnes, to send his grace unto me, and to all people, that we may worship hym, serve hym, and obeye hym as we ought to doe. And I pray unto God, that he will sende us all thynges that be nedefull, bothe for our soules and bodies. And that he will be merciful unto us, and forgeve us our sinnes: and that it wil please hym to save and defende us in al daungers ghostly and bodily: and that he wil kepe us from all synne and wikednes, and from our ghostly enemy, and from everlastyng death. And this I trust he wil do of his mercye and goodnes, throughe our lord Jesu Christ. And therfore I say. Amen. So be it.

¶ *So sone as the children can saye in theyr mother tongue, the articles of the faith, the Lordes prayer, the .x. commaundementes, and also can aunswere to such questyone of thys shorte Catechisme, as the Bishoppe (or suche as he shall appoinct) shal by hys discretyon appose them in, then shal they be brought to the Bysshop by one that shalbe hys godfather or godmother, that every childe may have a witnes of his Confirmacyon.*

¶ *And the Bishoppe shal confirme them on this wise.*

¶ Confirmacion.

Minister. Our helpe is in the name of the Lorde.
Aunswere. Whiche hath made bothe heaven and earth.
Minister. Blessed is the name of the Lorde.
Aunswere. Hencefurthe worlde without ende.
Minister. Lorde heare our prayer.
Aunswere. And let our crie come to thee.°

¶ Let us praie.

ALMIGHTYE and everlivyng God, whyche hast vouchsaufed to regenerate these thy servauntes by water and the holy Ghost: and hast geven unto them forgevenes of al theyr synnes: strengthen them we beseche thee (O Lorde) with the holy Ghoste the comforter, and daiely encrease in them thy manifolde giftes of grace, the spirite of wisedom, and understandyng: the spirite of counsail and ghostly strength, the spirite of knowledge and true godlinesse, and fulfyll them (O Lord) with the spirite of thy holy feare. Amen.

¶ *Then the Bishop shal laye hys hande upon every chylde° severally, saying.*

Defende, O Lorde, this childe with thy heavenly grace° that he may continue thine for ever, and daiely encrease in thy holy spirite more and more, untill he come unto thy everlastyng kingdome. Amen.

¶ *Then shal the Bishop saye.*

¶ Let us praie.

ALMIGHTIE everlivyng God, whiche makest us bothe to will, and to do those thynges that be good, and acceptable unto thy Majestie, we make our humble supplications unto thee for these children, upon whome (after the example of thy holy Apostles) we have laied our handes, to certifie theim (by thys signe) of thy favour and gracious goodnes toward them, let thy fatherly hande we beseche thee ever be over them, let thy holy spirite ever be with them, and so leade them in the knowledge and obedience of thy worde, that in the ende they may obtaine the everlasting lyfe: through our Lorde Jesus Christe, who with thee and the holy Ghost liveth and reigneth one God, worlde without ende. Amen.

¶ *Then the Bishop shal blesse the children, thus saying.*

¶ The blessyng of God almightye, the Father, the Sonne, and the Holy ghoste, be upon you, and remayne with you for ever. Amen.

The Curate of every paryshe, or some other at his appointement, shal diligently upon Sondayes and holy daies, halfe an houre before Evenyng prayer, openly in the Churche instruct and examyne so many children of his parish sent unto him, as the time wil serve and as he shal thinke convenient, in some part of this Cathechisme.

And al fathers, mothers, maisters, and dames, shal cause theyr children, servauntes, and prentises (whyche have not learned theyr Cathechysme)° to come to the Churche at the tyme appoyncted, and obediently to heare, and be ordred by the curate, untyll suche tyme as they have learned all that is here appoincted for theim to learne. And whensoever the Byshop shall geve knowledge for chyldren to be brought afore him to any convenyent place, for their confirmation: then shal the Curate of every Paryshe eyther bryng, or sende in wrytyng the names of all those children of hys Paryshe, whyche can say the Articles of their faith, the Lordes prayer, and the .x. Commaundementes, and also how many of them can answere to the other questions conteined in this Cathechisme.

¶ And there shall none be admitted to the holy communion: until suche tyme as he can saye the Cathechisme and be confirmed.

The fourme of solem-
pnization of Matrimonye.

¶ *First, the bannes must be asked thre severall Sondaies or holy daies, in the*
tyme of service, the people beyng present, after the accustomed maner.

¶ *And yf the persons that would be maryed dwell in diverse Paryshes, the*
bannes must be asked in both Parishes and the Curate of the one Paryshe
shall not solempnyze matrimonye betwyxt them, wythout a certifycate of the
bannes beyng thryse asked, from the Curate of the other Parysh. At the date
appoincted for solempnizacyon of Matrimonye,° the persones to be maryed
shal come into the body of the Churche, wyth theyr frendes and neighbours.°
And there the Pryest shall thus saye.

D EARELY beloved frendes, we are gathered together here in the
sight of God, and in the face of his congregacion, to joyne
together this man and this woman in holy matrimony, which is an
honorable state, instytuted of God in Paradise, in the time of mannes
innocencie, signifiyng unto us the mistical union that is betwixt
Christ and his Churche: which holy state Christe adourned and beautified with his presence and firste myracle that he wrought in Cana
of Galile, and is commended of sainct Paul to be honourable emong
all men, and therfore is not to be enterprised, nor taken in hande
unadvisedly, lightly, or wantonly, to satisfye mennes carnall lustes and
appetytes, lyke brute beastes that have no understandyng: but reverently, discretely, advisedly, soberly, and in the feare of God, duely
consideryng the causes for the which matrimonye was ordeined. One
was the procreation of children, to be brought up in the feare and
nurtoure of the Lorde, and praise of God. Secondly, it was ordeined
for a remedy agaynste synne and to avoide fornication, that suche
persones as have not the gifte of continencie° might marrye, and kepe
themselves undefiled membres of Christes body. Thirdly, for the
mutual societie, helpe, and comfort, that the one ought to have of the
other, bothe in prosperitye, and adversitye, into the whiche holy state,
these two persones present, come nowe to be joyned. Therefore if any
man can shewe any just cause, why thei may not lawfully be joyned
together, let hym now speake, or els hereafter for ever holde his
peace.

And also speakynge to the persons that shalbe maryed, he shall saie.

I require and charge you (as you wil aunswere at the dreadful day of judgement, when the secretes of all hartes shalbe disclosed) that if either of you doe knowe any impedyment,° why ye may not be lawfully joyned together in Matrimony, that ye confesse it. For be ye well assured, that so many as be coupled together, otherwyse then Goddes worde doeth allowe, are not joyned together by God, neither is their Matrimonye lawful.

At whyche day of Maryage, if any man do allege and declare any impediment, why they may not be coupled together in matrymony by Gods law, or the lawes of thys realme,° and wyll be bound, and sufficient sureties with him to the parties, or els put in a cautyon to the ful value of suche charges, as the persons to be maryed do susteine, to prove hys allegation: then the solempnization must be deferred unto suche tyme as the truthe be tried. If no impedyment be alledged, then shall the curate saye unto the man.

N. Wilt thou have thys woman to thy wedded wyfe, to lyve together after Goddes ordynaunce in the holye estate of Matrimony? Wylt thou love her, comforte her, honour, and kepe her, in sickenes, and in healthe? And forsakyng al other, kepe thee onely to her, so long as you both shall live?

The man shall aunswere.

I will.

Then shall the Priest saye to the woman.

N. Wilt thou have this man to thy wedded housband, to lyve together after Goddes ordynaunce, in the holy estate of matrimony? Wilt thou obey hym, and serve him, love, honour, and kepe him, in sycknes and in health? And forsakynge al other, kepe thee onely to him so long as ye bothe shal live?

The woman shall aunswere.

I will.

Then shall the Minister saie.

Who geveth this woman to be maried unto this man?

¶ *And the Minister receivyng the woman at her father or frendes handes, shall cause the man to take the woman by the right hand, and so either to geve their trouth to other, the man first saying.*

I *N.* take thee *N.* to my wedded wyfe, to have and to hold, from thys day forward, for better, for worse, for richer, for porer, in sickenes, and in healthe, to love and to cheryshe, tyll death us departe, accordynge to Gods holy ordinaunce: and therto I plight thee my trouth.

Then shall they loose their handes, and the woman takyng againe the man by the right hande, shall saie.

I *N.* take thee *N.* to my wedded husbande, to have and to holde, from this day forward, for better, for worse, for richer, for poorer, in sickenes, and in health, to love, cherish and to obey, till death us departe, accordynge to godes holy ordinaunce: and therto I geve thee my trouth.

Then shall they again loose theyr handes, and the man shal geve unto the woman a ring, laying the same upon the booke,° with the accustomed dutie to the Priest and Clerke.° And the Priest taking the ryng, shal deliver it unto the man, to put it upon the fourth finger of the womans left hand. And the man taught by the Priest shal say.

With this ring I thee wed: with my body I thee worship, and with all my worldly goodes, I thee endow. In the name of the Father, and of the Sonne, and of the holy Ghost. Amen.

Then the man leavyng the ryng upon the fourth finger of the womans left hande, the Minister shall saye.

¶ Let us praye.

O ETERNALL GOD, creatoure and preserver of all mankynd, giver of all spyrytuall grace, the aucthour of everlastyng life: send thy blessyng upon these thy servauntes, thys man and this woman, whom we blesse in thy name, that as Isaac and Rebecca lyved faithfully together: So these persons may surely performe and kepe the vow and covenaunt betwixte them made, wherof this ryng, geven and received, is a token and pledge, and may ever remain in perfect love and peace together, and live according unto thy lawes, thorough Jesus Christ our Lorde. Amen.

Then shal the Priest joyne their right handes together and say.

Those whome God hath joyned together, let no man put asonder.

Then shall the Minister speak unto the people.

For asmuche as *N.* and *N.* have consented together in holy wedlocke, and have witnessed the same before God, and thys company, and therto have geven and pledged their trouth eyther to other, and have declared the same by gevyng and receivyng of a ryng, and by joynyng of handes: I pronounce that thei be man and wife together. In the name of the father, of the sonne, and of the holy Ghost. Amen.

And the Minister shal adde this blessyng.

God the Father, God the Sonne, God the holy Ghost, blesse, preserve, and kepe you, the Lorde mercifully wyth his favour loke upon you, and so fil you with al spiritual benediction, and grace, that you may so lyve together in thys life,° that in the world to come, you may have life everlastyng. Amen.

¶ *Then the Ministers or Clerckes goyng to the Lordes table,° shall saie, or syng this Psalme folowyng,* Beati omnes.

B LESSED are all they that feare the Lorde, and walke in his waies. For thou shalt eate the labour of thy handes: O wel is thee, and happy shalt thou be.   *Ps.* 128

Thy wife shalbe as the fruitfull vine: upon the walles of thy house.

Thy children like the Olive braunches: rounde about thy table.

Lo thus shall the man be blessed: that feareth the lorde.

The Lorde from out of Sion shal blesse thee: that thou shalt see Hierusalem in prosperitie, al thy life long.

Yea, that thou shalt see thy childrens children: and peace upon Israel.

Glory be to the father. *&c.*

As it was in the beginning. *&c.*

¶ *Or elles this Psaime folowyng* Deus misereatur.

G OD be mercifull unto us, and blesse us: and shewe us the lyght of his countenaunce, and be merciful unto us.   *Ps.* 67

That thy waie maie be knowen upon the earth: thy savyng healthe among all nacions.

Let the people prayse thee (O God): yea, let all the people praise the.

O let the nacions rejoyce and be glad: for thou shalt judge the folke ryghteously, and governe the nacions upon the earth.

Let the people praise thee (O God): lette all the people praise thee.

Then shall the earthe bryng furthe her encrease: and God, even our God, shal geve us his blessyng.

God shall blesse us, and al the endes of the worlde shall feare him.

Glory be to the Father. *&c.*

As it was in the beginning. *&c.*

THE Psalme ended, and the man and the woman knelyng afore the Lordes table: The Priest standyng at the Table, and turnyng hys face towarde them, shal saie.

Lorde have mercie upon us.

Aunswere. Christe have mercie upon us.

Minister. Lorde have mercie upon us.

OUR FATHER whiche arte. *&c.*
And leade us not into temptation.

Aunswere. But deliver us from evil. Amen.

Minister. O Lorde save thy servaunt: and thy handmaide.

Aunswere. Whyche put their trust in thee.

Minister. O Lorde sende them helpe from thy holy place.

Aunswere. And ever more defende them.

Minister. Be unto them a towre of strength.

Aunswere. From the face of their enemie.

Minister. O Lorde heare our praier.

Aunswere. And let our crie come unto thee.

¶ *The Minister.*

O GOD of Abraham, God of Isaac, God of Jacob, blesse these thy servauntes, and sowe the sede of eternal life in their mindes, that whatsoever in thy holy worde they shal profitably learne, they may in dede fulfil the same. Loke, O Lorde, mercifully upon theim from heaven, and blesse them. And as thou diddest send thy blessing upon Abraham and Sara° to their greate comforte: so vouchesaufe to sende thy blessing upon these thy servauntes, that they obeiyng thy will, and alway beyng in saufetie under thy protection, may abide in thy love unto their lives ende, throughe Jesu Christe our Lorde. Amen.

¶ *This prayer next folowyng shal be omitted where the woman is past childe birth.*

O MERCIFULL Lorde, and heavenly Father, by whose gracious gifte mankynde is encreased, we beseche thee assiste with thy blessyng these two persones, that they may bothe be fruitefull in procreation of children, also live together so long in godly love and honestie, that they may see their childers children, unto the thirde and fourthe generacion, unto thy praise and honour: through Jesus Christe our Lorde. Amen.

O GOD whiche by thy mightie power hast made all thinges of naught, which also after other thinges set in ordre, diddest appoinct that out of man (created after thyne owne ymage and similitude) woman should take her beginning, and knitting them together, diddest teache that it shoulde never be lawfull to put asonder those whome thou by matrimonie haddest made one: O God which hast consecrated the state of matrimonie to suche an excellent misterie, that in it is signified and represented the spiritual mariage and unitie betwixte Christe and his Churche: Loke mercifully upon these thy servauntes, that both this man may love his wife, accordyng to thy worde (as Christe did love his spouse the Churche, who gave hymselfe for it, lovyng and cherishyng it, even as his owne fleshe). And also that this woman may be lovyng and amiable to her housband as Rachel, wise as Rebecca, faithfull and obedient as Sara, and in all quietnes, sobrietie, and peace, be a folower of holy and Godly matrones, O Lorde blesse them bothe, and graunt them to enherite thy everlastyng kyngdome: throughe Jesus Christe our Lorde. Amen.

¶ *Then shall the Priest saye.*

A LMIGHTIE God, which at the beginnyng did create our firste parentes Adam and Eve, and did sanctifie and joyne them together in mariage, powre upon you the richesse of his grace, sanctifie, and blesse you, that ye may please hym both in body and soule, and live together in holy love, unto your lives ende. Amen.

Then shal begyn the Communion,° and after the Gospel shalbe saied a Sermon, wherin ordinarily (so oft as there is any mariage) the office of a man and wife shalbe declared, accordyng to holy Scripture, or if there be no sermon, the Minister shal reade this that foloweth.

Al ye whiche be maried, or whiche entend to take the holy estate of Matrimonie upon you: heare what holy scripture doth say, as touchyng the dutie of housbandes towarde their wives, and wives toward their housbandes.

Saincte Paul (in his Epistle to the Ephesians, the .v. Chapiter) doeth geve this commaundement to all maried men.

Ye housbandes love your wives, even as Christ loved the Churche, and hath geven hymselfe for it, to sanctifie it, purgyng it in the fountaine of water, throughe the worde, that he might make it unto hym selfe a glorious congregacion, not havyng spot or wrincle, or any suche thyng, but that it shoulde be holy and blameles. So men are bounde to love their owne wyves, as their owne bodies. He that loveth his owne wife loveth hym selfe. For never did any man hate his owne fleshe, but nourisheth and cherisheth it, even as the Lorde doeth the congregacion, for we are membres of his body: of his flesh and of hys bones. *Eph.* 5

For this cause shall a man leave father and mother, and shalbe joined unto his wife, and thei two shalbe one flesh. This mistery is great, but I speake of Christe and of the congregacion. Neverthelesse, let every one of you so love his owne wyfe, even as hym selfe.

Likewise the same sainct Paule (wrytyng to the Collossians) speaketh thus to all men that be maried. Ye men, love your wyves, and be not bitter unto them. *Col.* 3

Heare also what saincte Peter the apostle of Christe, whiche was him selfe a maried man, saith unto al men that are maried. Ye housbandes, dwel with your wyves according to knowledge. Gevynge honour unto the wyfe as unto the weaker vessell, and as heires together of the grace of lyfe, so that your praiers be not hyndred. 1 *Pet.* 3

Hetherto ye have hearde the dutie of the housbande toward the wyfe.

Now likewise ye wyves heare and learne your dutie towarde your housbandes, even as it is plainely sette furth in holy scripture.

SAINCTE Paule (in the forenamed Epistle to the Ephesians) teacheth you thus: Ye women, submit youre selfes unto youre owne housbandes as unto the Lorde: for the housbande is the wyves headde, even as Christe is the headde of the Churche. And he is also the savioure of the whole bodye. Therefore as the Churche or congregacion, is subjecte unto Christe: so likewyse lette the wyves also be in subjection unto their owne housbandes in al thinges. And againe he sayeth: Let the wife reverence her housbande. *Eph.* 5

And (in his Epistle to the Collossians) Saynate Paule geveth you thys shorte lesson, Ye wyves submitte youre selves unto youre own housbandes as it is convenient in the Lorde. *Col.* 3

SAINCTE Peter also doeth instructe you verye godly, thus saiynge: Let wyves be subject to their owne housbandes, so that if anye obey not the woorde, they may be wonne withoute the woorde, by the conversacion of the wyves, whyle they beholde your chaste conversacion coupled with feare, whose apparell let it not be outward, with broided hayre and trymmyng about with golde, eyther in puttinge on of gorgeous apparell: but let the hidde manne, whiche is in the harte, be without all corruption, so that the spirite be milde and quiete, whiche is a precious thynge in the sighte of GOD. For after thys maner (in the olde tyme) did the holy women whiche trusted in God apparell them selves, beynge subject to their owne housbandes as Sara obeyed Abraham, callyng hym Lorde, whose daughters ye are made, doynge well, and beynge not dismayde with any feare.   1 *Pet.* 3

¶ *The newe maried persones (the same day of their mariage) must receyve the holy Communion.*

¶ 𝕿𝕳𝖊 𝕺𝖗𝖉𝖊𝖗 𝖋𝖔𝖗 𝖙𝖍𝖊
𝖛𝖎𝖘𝖎𝖙𝖆𝖈𝖎𝖔𝖓 𝖔𝖋 𝖙𝖍𝖊 𝕾𝖎𝖈𝖐𝖊.

¶ *The Priest entryng into the sicke persones house, shall saye.*

Peace be in this house, and to all that dwel in it.

¶ *When he commeth into the sicke mannes presence, he shall saye knelynge doune.*°

REMEMBRE not Lorde oure iniquities, nor the iniquities of our forefathers. Spare us good Lorde, spare thy people, whome thou hast redemed with thy most precious bloude, and bee not angry with us for ever.

Lorde have mercy upon us.

Christe have mercy upon us.

Lorde have mercy upon us.

¶ Our father whiche art in heaven. *&c.*

And leade us not into temptacion.

Aunswere. But deliver us from evel. Amen.

¶ *Minister.* O Lorde save thy servaunt.

¶ *Aunswere.* Whiche putteth his trust in thee.

¶ *Minister.* Sende him helpe from thy holy place.

¶ *Aunswere.* And evermore myghtely defende him.

¶ *Minister.* Let the enemy have none advauntage of him.

¶ *Aunswere.* Nor the wicked approche to hurte him.

¶ *Minister.* Be unto him O Lorde a strong Towre.

¶ *Aunswere.* From the face of his enemy.

¶ *Minister.* Lorde heare our praiers.

¶ *Aunswere.* And let our crie come unto thee.

¶ *Minister.*

O LORDE loke doune from Heaven, beholde, visite, and releve this thy servaunte. Loke uppon him with the eies of thy mercye, geve him comforte, and sure confidence in thee: defende him from the daunger of the enemy, and kepe him in perpetual peace, and saufety: Through Jesus Christe our Lorde. Amen.

H EARE us almighty and most mercifull God, and saviour. Extend thy accustomed goodnes to this thy servaunt whiche is greved with syckenesse, visit him O Lorde, as thou diddest visit Peters wifes mother, and the capiteines servaunt.° So visit and restore unto this sicke person his former health (if it bee thy wil) or els geve him grace so to take thy visitation,° that after this painful life ended, he may dwell with thee in life everlastyng. Amen.

¶ *Then shal the Minister exhorte the sicke person after this forme or other lyke.*

D ERELY beloved know this, that almighty god is the lorde of life and death, and over al thinges to theym perteinyng, as youthe, strength, helthe, age, weaknesse, and sicknes: wherfore, whatsoever your Syckenesse is, knowe you certainlye, that it is Goddes visitacion. And for what cause soever this sicknes is sent unto you: whether it bee to trie youre patience for the example of other, and that your faith may be founde in the daye of the lord laudable, glorious, and honorable, to the encrease of Glory, and endles felicitie: Or els it be sent unto you, to correct, and amende in you whatsoever dothe offende the eies of our heavenly father: knowe you certeinly, that yf you truly repent you of your sinnes, and beare your sickenes patiently, trustyng in Gods mercy, for his dere sonne Jesus Christes sake, and rendre unto him humble thankes for his fatherly visitacion, submittyng your selfe wholly to his will: it shall turne to your profite, and helpe you forwarde in the right waye that leadeth unto everlastyng life.

¶ Take therfore in good worthe, the chastemente of the lord, for whom the lord loveth he chastiseth. Yea, as S. Paul saith, he scourgeth every sonne which he receiveth. If you endure chastisement, he offereth himself unto you as unto his own *If the person visited be very sicke then the Curate may ende his exhortacion in thys place.* children. What sonne is he that the father chastiseth not? If ye be not under correction (whereof all true children are partakers) then are ye bastardes, and not children. Therfore seying, that when our carnal fathers do correct us, we reverently obey them, shal we not now muche rather be obedient to our spirituall father, and so live? And they for a few daies do chastise us after their owne pleasure, but he doth chastise us for our profit to the entent he maye make us partakers of his holines. These wordes good brother, are Gods wordes, and written in holy Scripture for our comforte and instruction, that we sholde paciently and with thankesgeving, beare our heavenly fathers Correction, whensoever by any maner of adversitie it shal please his gratious goodnes to visite us. And there shoulde be no greater comforte to Christian persons, than to be made like unto christ, by sufferyng patiently adversities, troubles, and Sickenesses. For he himselfe went not up to joye, but firste he suffered paine: hee entred not into his glorye, before he was crucified. So truly our way to eternall joye, is to suffer here with Christe, and our doore to entre into eternall life, is gladly to die with Christ, that we may ryse againe from death and dwell with him in everlastyng life. Nowe therfore, takyng your sickenesse, whiche is thus profitable for you paciently: I exhorte you in the name of God, to remembre the profession whiche you made unto God, in your Baptisme. And forasmuche as after this lyfe, there is accompte to be geven unto the rightuous judge, of whome all must be judged without respect of persons: I require you to examine your selfe, and your state, bothe towarde God and man, so that accusynge and condempnyng your self for your owne faultes, you may fynde mercy at our heavenly fathers hande, for Christes sake, and not be accused and condempned in that fearful judgement. Therfore I shal shortly rehearse the Articles of our faith, that ye may know whether you do beleve as a Christian man shoulde, or no.

Here the minister shall reherse the articles of the faith° saieng thus.

Doest thou beleve in God the father almighty?

And so furth, as it is in Baptisme

¶ *Then shal the minister examine whether he be in charitie, with all the worlde: exhortyng hym to forgive from the botome of his hart, al persons that have offended hym, and if he have offended other, to aske them forgevenesse: And wher he hathe done injury or wrong to any man, that he make amendes to the uttermost of his power. And if he have not afore* This may be done *disposed his goodes, let him then make his wil. (But men* before the minister *must be oft admonished that they set an order for their* begin his praiers *temporall goodes and landes, when they be in health.) And* as he shal se cause.

also to declare his debtes, what hee oweth, and what is owyng unto him, for discharging of his conscience, and quietnes of his executours. The minister may not forget, nor omitte to move the sicke person (and that most earnestly) to liberalitie towarde the poore.

¶ *Here shall the sicke persone make a speciall confession, if he feele hys conscience troubled with any weighty matter. After whiche confession the priest shall absolve him after this sorte.*

OUR Lorde Jesus Christ who hath left power to hys Churche to absolve all sinners, whiche truly repente and beleve in him: of hys greate mercie forgeve thyne offences, and by his aucthoritie committed to me, I absolve thee from al thy synnes. In the name of the father and of the sonne &c. Amen.

¶ *And then the priest shal say the Collect folowyng.*

¶ Let us praie.

O MOST merciful God, whiche accordyng to the multitude of thy mercies, dost so put away the sinnes of those whiche truly repent, that thou remembrest them no more, open thy eye of mercie upon this thy servant, who most earnestly desireth pardon, and forgevenes. Renue in him most lovying father, whatsoever hath been decaied by the fraud and malice of the devel, or by his owne carnall will and frailnes, preserve, and continue this sicke membre in the unitie of thy churche, consider his contricion, accept hys teares, asswage his paine, as shalbe sene to thee most expedient for him. And forasmuche as he putteth his full trust only in thy mercy, impute not unto him his former sinnes, but take him to thy favour, through the merites of thy moste derely beloved sonne Jesus Christ. Amen.

Then the Minister shal saie this Psalm.

In te, domine, speravi.

IN thee, Lorde have I put my trust, let me never bee put to confusion, but ridde me, and deliver me into thy ryghtuousnesse, encline thine eare unto me and save me.   *Ps.* 71

Be thou my strong holde, wherunto I may alway resorte: thou hast promysed to helpe me, for thou art my house of defence, and my Castel.

Deliver me o my God out of the hande of the ungodly: out of the hande of the unrighteous and cruell man.

For thou O lorde God, art the thyng that I long for: thou art my hope even from my youth.

Through thee have I ben holden up ever sence I was borne: thou art he that toke me out of my mothers wombe, my prayse shall alway be of thee.

I am become as it were a monster unto many: but my sure truste is in thee.

O let my mouth be filled with thy praise: (that I may sing of thy glory) and honor all the daie longe.

Cast me not away in the tyme of age: forsake me not when my strength faileth me.

For myne enemies speake againste me, and they that laye wayte for my soule, take their counsail together, saiynge: God hath forsaken hym, persecute hym, and take hym, for there is none to deliver hym.

Go not farre from me, O GOD: my GOD, haste thee to helpe me.

Let them be confounded and perishe, that are against my soule: let them be covered with shame and dishonoure that seke to do me evill.

As for me, I will paciently abide alwaie: and wil praise thee, more and more.

My mouthe shall dayely speake of thy righteousnes, and salvacion: for I knowe no ende therof.

I will go furth in the strength of the Lorde God: and will make mencion of thy righteousnesse onely.

Thou (O GOD) hast taughte me from my youthe up untill nowe: therefore I will tell of thy wonderous workes.

Forsake me not (O GOD) in myne olde age, when I am gray headed: until I have shewed thy strength unto this generacion, and thy power to all them that are yet for to come.

Thy righteousnesse (O GOD) is very hygh, and great thinges are they that thou hast done: O GOD, who is lyke unto thee?

O what great troubles and adversities hast thou shewed me? and yet diddest thou turne and refreshe me, yea, and broughtest me from the depe of the earth agayne.

Thou hast broughte me to great honour: and comforted me on every side.

Therfore will I prayse thee and thy faythefulnes (O GOD) plaiynge upon an instrument of Musicke: unto thee will I synge uppon the Harpe, O thou holy one of Israell.

My lippes will be faine, when I sing unto thee: and so will my soule whome thou hast delivered.

My tongue also shal talke of thy righteousnesse al the day long: for thei are confounded and brought unto shame, that seke to do me evill.

Glory be to the Father, and to the Sonne, and to the holy Ghoste.

As it was in the begynnynge, is nowe and ever shalbe worlde without ende. Amen.

Addyng thys.

O SAVIOUR of the worlde, save us, whyche by thy crosse and precious bloude hast redemed us, helpe us we beseche thee, O GOD.

¶ *Then shal the Minister saye.*

THE almightie Lord, whiche is a moste strong tower to all them that put their trust in him, to whom all thinges in heaven, in earthe, and under the earth doe bowe and obey: be nowe, and evermore thy defence, and make thee knowe and fele, that there is no other name under heaven geven to man, in whome, and throughe whome, thou mayest receyve healthe and salvacion, but onely the name of oure Lorde Jesus Christe.° Amen.

¶ 𝕿𝖍𝖊 𝕮𝖔𝖒𝖒𝖚𝖓𝖎𝖔𝖓
of 𝖙𝖍𝖊 𝕾𝖎𝖈𝖐𝖊.

*F*ORASMUCHE *as al mortal men be subjecte to many sodaine perilles, diseases, and sicknesses, and ever uncerteine what time they shal departe out of this lyfe: Therfore to the entent they may be alwaies in a readines to die, whensoever it shal please almightie GOD to cal them: The Curates shal diligently from tyme to tyme, but specially in the plague time, exhort their Parishioners to the oft receivyng in the Churche, of the holy Communion of the body and bloude of our sæviour Christ. Whiche (if thei do) thei shal have no cause in their sodaine visitation to be unquieted for lacke of the same. But if the sicke persone be not able to come to the Churche, and yet is desirous to receive the Communion in his house, then hee must give knowledge over night, or elles early in the Morning to the Curate, signifying also how many be appoincted to communicate with hym. And hævyng a convenient place in the sicke mans house, where the Curate may reverently minister, and a good nomber to receive the Communion with the sicke persone, with all thynges necessary for the same, he shal there minister the holy Communion.°*

The Collect.

ALMIGHTIE everlivyng GOD, maker of mankynde, whiche doest correcte those whom thou doest love, and chastisest every one whome thou doest receive, we besech thee to have mercie upon this thy servaunt, visited with thy hande, and to graunt that he may take his sickenesse paciently, and recover his bodily helth (yf it be thy gracious wil), and whensoever his soule shal depart from the body, it may bee without spot presented unto thee: Throughe Jesus Christe our Lorde. Amen.

The Epistle.   *Heb.* 12

MY sonne, despise not the correction of the Lorde, neither faint when thou art rebuked of hym. For whome the Lorde loveth, hym he correcteth: yea, and he scourgeth every sonne whom he receiveth.

The Gospel.   *John* 5

VERELY, verely I say unto you, he that heareth my worde, and beleveth on hym that sent me, hath everlastyng life, and shall not come unto dampnacion, but he passeth from death unto lyfe.

¶ *At the time of the distribucion of the holy Sacrament, the Priest shal first receive the Communion hymselfe, and after minister unto them that be appoincted to communicate with the sicke.*

¶ *But if any man, either by reason of extremitie of sickenes, or for lacke of warnyng in due time to the Curate, or for lacke of company to receive with hym, or by any other just impediment, do not receive the Sacrament of Christes body and bloud, then the Curate shall instruct hym, that if he do truely repent hym of his synnes, and stedfastly beleve that Jesus Christe hath suffred death upon the crosse for him, and shed his bloud for his redempcion, earnestly remembryng the benefites he hath therby, and geving him hartie thankes therfore, he doth eate and dryncke the body and bloude of our saviour Christe, profitably to his soules health, although he doe not receive the Sacrament with his mouthe.*

¶ *When the sicke person is visited, and receiveth the holy Communion al at one time, then the Priest, for more expedicion, shal cut off the fourme of the visitacion at the Psalme,* In thee, O Lorde have I put my trust, *and go streight to the Communion.*

¶ *In the time of plague, Swette, or such other like contagious tymes° of sickenesses or diseases, when none of the Parishe or neighbours can be gotten to communicate with the sicke in their houses, for feare of the infection, upon speciall request of the diseased, the minister may alonly communicate with hym.*

¶ The Order for the
Buriall of the dead.

¶ *The priest metyng the corps at the Church style, shal saye: Or els the priestes*
and clerkes shall syng, and so go eyther unto the churche, or towardes the
grave.

I AM the resurrection and the life (saith the Lord) he that beleveth
in me: yea, thoughe he were dead, yet shall he live. And whosoever
liveth, and beleveth in me, shall not dye for ever.   *John* 11

I KNOWE that my redemer lyveth, and that I shal rise out of the
earth in the last daye, and shalbe covered agayne with my skinne,
and shall se God in my flesh: yea, and I my selfe shall beholde hym,
not with other, but with these same eyes.   *Job* 19

WE brought nothinge into this worlde, neither may we cary any
thyng out of this worlde.   1 *Tim.* 6
The Lorde geveth, and the Lorde taketh awaye. Even as it hath
pleased the Lorde, so commeth thynges to passe: Blessed be the name
of the Lorde.   *Job* 1

¶ *When they come to the grave, whyles the corps is made redy to be layd*
into the earth, the priest shal say, or the priestes and clerkes shal sing.

MAN that is borne of a woman, hathe but a shorte tyme to lyve, and
is full of miserye: he commeth up, and is cut doune lyke a floure,
he flyeth as it were a shadow, and never continueth in one staye. In
the middest of lyfe we be in death, of whom may we seke for succour
but of thee, O Lorde, whiche for our sinnes justly arte displeased: yet
O Lorde God most holy, O Lorde moste mightye, O holy, and moste
mercifull Saviour, deliver us not into the bitter paynes of eternall
death. Thou knowest Lord the secretes of our hertes, shut not up thy
mercifull eyes to our prayers. But spare us Lorde moste holy, O God
moste mighty, O holy and mercifull Saviour, thou most worthy judge
eternall, suffer us not at our last houre for any paines of death to fall
from thee.

*¶ Then whyle the earth shalbe cast upon the body, by some standyng by,°
the priest shall saye.*

FORASMUCHE as it hath pleased almightie God° of his great mercy to take unto hym selfe the Soule of oure deare brother, here departed, we therfore committe hys bodye to the grounde,° earthe to earthe, ashes to ashes, dust to dust, in sure and certein hope of resurrection to eternall lyfe, throughe oure Lorde Jesus Christe, who shall chaunge oure vyle body that it may be lyke to his glorious body, according to the mighty workynge, whereby he is able to subdue al thynges to hymselfe.

Then shalbe sayde, or songe.

I HEARDE a voyce from heaven saiyng unto me, wryte from hence-furth, blessed are the dead whiche dye in the Lorde. Even so sayeth the spirite that they reste from their labours.°

*Then shall folowe this lesson, taken out of the .xv. Chapter to the
Corinthians, the first Epistle.*

CHRIST is rysen from the dead, and become the fyrst frutes of them that slept. For by a man came deth, and by a man came the resurreccion of the dead. For as by Adam al die, even so by Christ shal al be made alive, but every manne in his owne order. The fyrste is Christe, then they that are Christes at his comming. Then commeth the ende when he hathe delivered up the kyngedome to God the father, when he hath put doune all rule, and all aucthoritie, and power. For he must reygne till he have put hys enemies under hys fete. The laste enemye that shalbe destroyed is deathe. For he hath putte all thynges under his feete. But when he sayeth, all thynges are putte under hym, it is manifeste that hee is excepted, whyche dyd putte al thynges under hym. When al thinges are subdued unto him, then shall the sonne also hym selfe be subjecte unto him that put all thynges under hym, that God maye be al in all, elles what do they whyche are baptised over the deade, if the dead rise not at all? Why are they then baptised over them: yea, and why stande we alway then in jeopardye? By our rejoysinge which I have in Christ Jesu our Lorde, I dye daily. That I have foughte wyth beastes at Ephesus after the maner of men, what avauntageth it me, if the dead ryse not againe? Lette us eate and drincke, for to morow we shall dye. Be not ye deceyved: evil wordes corrupt good maners. Awake truly out of slepe and sinne not. For somme have not the knowledge of God. I speake this to your shame.

But some manne wyl say how aryse the dead? With what body shal they come? Thou foole, that whiche thou sowest is not quickened except it dye. And what sowest thou? thou sowest not that body that shalbe: but bare corne, as of wheate, or some other: but God geveth it a bodye at hys plesure, to everye sede his owne bodye. All fleshe is not one maner of flesh: but there is one maner of flesh of menne, another maner of flesh of beasts, another of fishes, another of byrdes. There are also celestial bodyes, and there are bodies terrestriall. But the glory of the celestiall is one, and the glory of the terrestrial is another. There is one maner glory of the Sonne, and another glory of the Moone, and another glory of the starres. For one starre differeth from another in glory: so is the resurrection of the deade. It is sowen in corrupcion, it riseth againe in incorrupcion. It is sowen in dishonoure, it riseth againe in honoure. It is sowen in weaknes, it riseth againe in power. It is sowen a natural body, it ryseth againe a spirituall bodye. There is a naturall body, and there is a spirituall body: as it is also wryten, the fyrst man Adam was made a lyvynge soule, and the laste Adam was made a quickeninge spyrite. How be it that is not fyrst whyche is spirituall: but that whiche is naturall, and then that whiche is spirytual. The first man is of the earth, earthye: The seconde manne is the Lord from Heaven (heavenlye). As is the earthy, suche are they that be earthy. And as is the heavenly, such are they that are heavenly. And as we have borne the ymage of the earthye, so shall we beare the ymage of the heavenly. Thys saye I brethren, that fleshe and bloude cannot enherite the kyngdome of God, neyther doth corruption enherite incorruption. Beholde, I shewe you a mysterye. We shall not all slepe: but we shall al be chaunged, and that in a momente, in the twynkelynge of an eye, by the last trumpe. For the trumpe shall blowe, and the deade shall rise incorruptible, and we shall be chaunged. For this corruptible must put on incorruption, and this mortall must put on immortalytye. When this corruptible hath put on incorruption, and this mortall hath put on immortalitye: then shall be broughte to passe the sayinge that is wrytten. Deathe is swallowed up in victory: Deathe where is thy stinge? Hell where is thy victory? The stynge of deathe is sinne, and the strengthe of sinne is the lawe. But thankes be unto God, whyche hathe geven us victory, through our Lord Jesus Christ. Therfore my deare brethren be ye stedfast and unmovable, alwaies rich in the worke of the lorde, for as much as ye knowe, howe that your laboure is not in vayne in the Lorde.

¶ *The Lesson ended, the Priest shall saye.*

Lorde have mercye upon us.

Christe have mercy upon us.

Lorde have mercye upon us.

Our Father whiche arte in heaven. *&c.*

And leade us not into temptation.

Aunswere. But deliver us from evil. Amen.

¶ *The Priest.*

ALMIGHTIE God, with whom do live the spirites° of them that depart hence in the lord, and in whome the soules of them that be elected, after they bee delivered from the burthen of the flesh, be in joye and felicitie. We geve thee hearty thankes for that it hath pleased thee to deliver this *N.* oure brother, out of the miseries of thys synneful worlde, beseching thee that it may please thee of thy gracious goodnes, shortelye to accomplishe the numbre of thyne electe, and to haste thy kyngedome, that we with thys oure brother, and all other departed in the true fayth of thy holy name, may have our perfect consummacion and blisse, bothe in bodye and soule in thy eternall and everlastynge glorie. Amen.°

¶ *The Collect.*

O MERCIFULL God, the father of our Lorde Jesus Christe, who is the Resurrection and the lyfe, in whom whosoever beleveth shall lyve, thoughe he dye, and whosoever lyveth and beleveth in hym, shall not dye eternally, who also taughte us (by hys holy Apostle Paule), not to be sory as men without hope, for them that slepe in hym: We mekely beseche thee (O Father) to rayse us from the deathe of sinne, unto the lyfe of righteousnes, that when we shall depart thys lyfe, we may rest in hym, as our hope is thys oure brother doeth, and that at the generall resurrection in the laste daye, we maye be founde acceptable in thy syghte, and receive that blessing which thy welbeloved sonne shall then pronounce to all that love and fear thee, saiynge: Come ye blessed children of my father, receyve the Kyngedome prepared for you frome the begynnynge of the worlde. Graunte thys, we beseche thee, O mercifull father, throughe Jesus Christe our mediatoure and redemer. Amen.

¶ The Thankesgevinge of women
after childe byrthe, communelye
called the Churchynge of women.

¶ *The woman shall come into the churche, and there shall knele downe in some convenient place, nyghe unto the place where the table standeth, and the priest standing by her, shal saie these wordes, or suche lyke, as the case shal require.*

FORASMUCHE as it hath pleased almyghtye God of hys goodnes to geve you safe delyveraunce, and hath preserved you in the great daunger of childbyrth: ye shal therfore geve heartye thankes unto God and praye.

Then shall the priest saye this Psalme.

I HAVE lyfted up myne eyes unto the hylles: from whence commeth my helpe.

My helpe commeth even from the Lord: whych hath made heaven and earth.

He wyll not suffre thy foote to be moved: and he that kepeth thee, wil not slepe.

Beholde, he that kepeth Israell: shall neyther slomber nor slepe.

The Lorde hym selfe is thy keper: the Lorde is thy defence upon thy ryght hande.

So that the sonne shall not burne thee by daye: neither the moone by night.

The Lorde shal preserve thee from al evil: yea, it is even he that shal kepe thy soule.

The Lorde shal preserve thy goinge out, and thy commynge in: from thys tyme forth for evermore.

Glory be to the Father, and to the Sonne &c.

As it was in the beginynge, is now &c.

Lorde have mercye upon us.

Christe have mercye upon us.

Lorde have mercye upon us.

OUR Father which arte &c.
And leade us not into temptation.

Aunswere. But deliver us from evil. Amen.

Priest. O Lorde save this woman thy servaunt.

Aunswere. Whiche putteth her trust in thee.

Priest. Be thou to her a strong Towre.

Aunswere. From the face of her enemy.

Priest. Lorde heare our praier.

Aunswere. And let our crie come unto thee.

Priest.

Let us praie.

O ALMIGHTY God, which hast delivered this woman thy servaunte from the great paine and peril of childe birthe: Graunt we beseche thee most mercifull Father, that she through thy help may bothe faithfully live, and walke in her vocation, accordyng to thy wil, in this lyfe present, and also may be partaker of everlastyng glory in the lyfe to come, Throughe Jesus Christ our Lorde. Amen.

¶ *The woman that commeth to give her thanckes,° muste offer accustomed offerynges, and if there be a Communion,° it is convenient that she receive the holy Communion.*

¶ 𝕬 Commination

against sinners, with certaine prayers, to be used

divers times in the yere.

A FTER *Mornyng prayer, the people beyng called together by the ringyng of a Bel, and assembled in the Churche, the english Letany shalbe saide after the accustomed maner, whyche ended the priest shal go into the pulpit and saie thus.*

B RETHREN, in the Prymatyve churche there was a godly discipline, that at the beginyng of Lent, suche personnes as were notory- ous Synners, were putte to open penaunce and punyshed in thys world, that their soules might be saved in the daie of the lord. And that others admonyshed by theyr example myght be more afrayde to offende. In the stede wherof (untill the sayde Discypline maye be restored agayne, whyche thynge is muche to be wyshed) it is thought good that at this time (in your presence) shoulde be redde the general sentences of goddes cursyng agaynst impenitent Synners, gathered out of the .xxvii. Chapiter of Deuteronomye, and other places of Scripture. And that ye shoulde aunswere to every sentence. Amen. To the yntent that you being admonished of the great indignation of God against Synners: may the rather be called to earnest and true repentaunce, and maye walke more warely in these daungerous daies, fleeing from suche vices, for the whyche ye affirme wyth your owne mouthes, the Curse of God to be due.

Cursed is the man that maketh any carved, or molten Image, an abhomination to the Lorde, the worke of the handes of the craftes man, and putteth it in a secrete place to worship it.

¶ And the people shal aunswere and saie.

Amen.

Minister. Cursed is he that cursethe his father, or mother.

Aunswere. Amen.

Minister. Cursed is hee that removeth away the marcke of hys neyghbours lande.

Aunswere. Amen.

Minister. Cursed is he that maketh the blynde to go oute of hys way.

Aunswere. Amen.

Minister. Cursed is he that letteth in judgement the right of the straunger, of them that be fatherles, and of widdowes.

Aunswere. Amen.

Minister. Cursed is he that smiteth his neighbour secretlye.

Aunswere. Amen.

Minister. Cursed is he that lieth with his neighbours wife.

Aunswere. Amen.

Minister. Cursed is he that taketh rewarde to slea the Soule of innocent bloude.

Aunswere. Amen.

Minister. Curseth is he that putteth hys trust in manne, and taketh manne for hys defence, and in hys harte goeth from the Lorde.

Aunswere. Amen.

Minister. Cursed are the unmerciful, the fornicatours, and adulterers, and the covetous persones, the worshippers of ymages, slaunderers, dronkardes, and extorcioners.

Aunswere. Amen.

The Minister.

N OWE seyng that all they be accursed (as the Prophete David
beareth wytnesse) whyche do erre, and go astraye from the commaundementes of GOD, let us remembring the dreadful judgemente
hanginge over our heddes, and beyng always at hande, returne unto
oure Lorde God, with all contricion and mekenes of hearte, bewail-
ynge and lamenting our synful lyfe, knowledging and confessing our
offences, and sekynge to brynge furth worthie fruictes of penaunce.
For nowe is the Axe put unto the roote of the trees, so that every tree
which bringeth not furth good fruict, is hewen downe and cast into
the fire. It is a fearfull thing to falle into the handes of the lyvinge
God: he shal poure doune raine upon the synners, Snares, fyre, and
brimstone, storme and tempeste, thys shalbe their portion to drincke.
For lo, the Lorde is comen out of his place, to visite the wickednesse
of suche as dwel upon the earth. But who may abyde the daye of his
comming? Who shalbe able to endure, when he apereth? His fanne is
in his hande, and he wyll pourge hys floore, and gather his wheate into
the barne, but he wyl burne the chaffe with unquenchable fyre. The
daye of the Lord commeth as a thefe upon the night, and when men
shall saye peace, and all thinges are saufe, then shal sodainely destruction come upon them, as sorowe commeth uppon a woman travailyng
with childe, and they shall not escape. Then shall appeare the wrathe
of God in the day of vengeance, which obstinate sinners, throughe the
stubburnnes of theyr hearte, have heaped unto them selfe, whyche
despysed the goodnes, pacyence, and longe sufferaunce of God, when
he called them continually to repentaunce. Then shall they call upon
me, sayeth the Lorde, but I wyll not heare: they shall seke me early,
but they shall not fynde me: and that because they hated knowledge,
and receyved not the feare of the Lorde, but abhorred my counsail,
and dispised my correcyon, then shall it be too late to knocke, when
the dore shalbe shutte, and too late to crye for mercye, when it is the
tyme of Justice. O terryble voyce of most just judgemente, whiche
shalbe pronounced upon them, when it shalbe sayde unto them: Go,
ye cursed, into the fyre everlastynge, whyche is prepared for the
devyll and hys Aungeles. Therfore brethren take we hede bytyme,
whyle the daie of salvacion lasteth, for the nyght commeth when none
can worke: but let us whyle we have the lyght, beleve in the lyghte,
and walke as the children of the lyght, that we be not caste into the
utter darckenes, where is wepyinge and gnasshynge of teeth. Lette us

Ps. 118
[i.e.
Ps. 119]

Matt. 3
Heb. 10
Ps. 10
[i.e.
Ps. 11]
Isa. 26
Mal. 3
Matt. 3

1 *Thess.* 5

Rom. 2

Prov. 1

Matt. 25

2 *Cor.* 6
John 9

Matt. 25

not abuse the goodnes of God, whyche calleth us mercyfully to amendement, and of hys endelesse pytye promysed us forgevenesse of that whyche is paste: If (wyth a whole mynde and true hearte) we returne unto hym. For though our synnes be red as scarlet, they shalbe as whyte as snowe, and thoughe they be lyke purple, yet shall they be as whyte as wolle. Turne you cleane (sayeth the Lorde) from *Isa. 1* all your wickednes, and your synne shal not be your destruction. Cast *Ezek. 18* awaye from you all your ungodlynes that ye have done: make you newe heartes, and a newe spiryte: wherfore wyll ye dye, O ye house of Israell? Seyng that I have no pleasure in the deathe of hym that dyeth (sayeth the Lorde God.) Turne you then, and you shall lyve. Although we have synned, yet have we an advocate wyth the Father, Jesus Christe the ryghteous, and he it is that obteyneth grace for our synnes, *1 John 2* for he was wounded for our offences, and smytten for our wyckednesse. Let us therfore returne unto hym, who is the mercifull receyver *Isa. 53* of all true penitent sinners, assuring oure selfe that he is ready to receyve us, and most willyng to pardone us, yf we come to him, with faythfull repentaunce. Yf we will submit our selves unto him, and from hencefurthe walke in his wayes. Yf we will take hys easy yoke, and lighte burthen upon us, to folowe hym in lowlines, pacience, and *Matt. 11* charitie, and be ordered by the governaunce of hys holy spirite, seking alwayes his glorie, and servyng hym duely in our vocation with thankesgevynge. This yf we do, Christ wil deliver us from the curse of the law, and from the extreme malediction, which shall light upon theym, that shalbe set on the left hand, and he wyll set us on hys ryght hande, and geve us the blessed benediction of hys father, commaundynge us to take possession of his gloryous kyngdome, unto the whiche *Matt. 25* he vouchesaufed to brynge us al, for hys infinite mercye.

¶ *Then shall they all knele upon theyr knees: And the Priestes and Clerckes knelynge (where they are accustomed to saye the Letany) shall say thys Psalme.*

Miserere mei Deus.

HAVE mercy upon me, O GOD after thy great goodnes: according to the multitude of thy mercyes, do away myne offences. *Ps. 51*
Washe me throughly from my wyckednes: and clense me from my synne.

For I acknowledge my faultes: and my synne is ever before me.

Against thee onely have I synned, and done this evyll in thy sight:

that thou mightest be justyfyed in thy sayeng, and cleare when thou art judged.

Beholde, I was shapen in wickednesse: and in synne hath my mother conceived me.

But lo, thou requirest trueth in inwarde parties: and shalt make me to understande wisedome secretlye.

Thou shalte purge me with hysoppe, and I shall be cleane: thou shalt washe me, and I shall be whyter then Snowe.

Thou shalt make me here of joy and gladnesse: that the bones whiche thou hast broken may rejoyce.

Turne thy face from my sinnes: and put oute all my misdedes.

Make me a cleane hearte (O God:) and renue a right spirite within me.

Cast me not away from thy presence: and take not thy holy spirite from me.

O geve me the comforte of thy helpe agayne: and stablysh me with thy free spirite.

Then shall I teache thy wayes unto the wicked: and sinners shalbe converted unto thee.

Deliver me from bloude giltines (O God) thou that art the God of my healthe: and my tonge shall synge of thy ryghteousnes.

Thou shalte open my lyppes (O Lord): my mouth shal shewe thy prayse.

For thou desirest no sacrifice, els woulde I geve it thee: but thou delightest not in burnt offerynge.

The sacrifice of God is a troubled spirite: a broken and a contrite hearte O God, shalte thou not despise.

O be favourable and gracious unto Sion: builde thou the walles of Jerusalem.

Then shalt thou be pleased with the sacrifice of rightuousnesse, with the burnt offerynges and oblations: then shall they offer yong bullockes upon thine aultare.

Glory bee to the Father, and to the Sonne, and to the holy Ghoste.

As it was in the beginning, is nowe, and ever shal be world without ende. Amen.

Lorde have mercy upon us.

Christ have mercy upon us.

Lorde have mercy upon us.

Our father which arte in heaven. &c.

And leade us not into temptacion.

Aunswere. But deliver us from evil. Amen.

Minister. O Lorde save thy servauntes.

Aunswere. Whiche put their trust in thee.

Minister. Sende unto them helpe from above.

Aunswere. And evermore mightely defende them.

Minister. Help us, O God our saviour.

Aunswere. And for the glorye of thy names sake deliver us, bee mercyfull unto us synners, for thy names sake.

The Minister. Lorde heare our praiers.

Aunswere. And let our crie come unto thee.

¶ Let us praye.

O LORD, we beseche thee, mercifully heare our prayers, and spare al those which confesse their sinnes to thee, that they (whose consciences by sin are accused) by thy merciful pardon may be absolved, throughe Christ our Lorde. Amen.

O MOSTE mighty GOD, and mercyfull father which haste compassion of al men, and hatest nothing that thou haste made: whiche wouldest not the deathe of a synner, but that he should rather turne from synne, and be saved: mercifully forgeve us oure trespasses, and comforte us, whiche be grieved and weryed with the burden of oure synne. Thy propertye is to have mercy, to thee onlye it apperteineth to forgeve synnes: spare us therefore good Lorde, spare thy people whom thou haste redemed. Enter not into judgement wyth thy servauntes, whiche be vyle earthe, and miserable synners, but so turne thyne yre from us whyche mekely knowledge oure vylenes, and trulye repente us of our faultes: so make haste to helpe us in this worlde, that we maye ever lyve wyth thee in the worlde to come, throughe Jesus Christe oure Lorde. Amen.

¶ *Then shall the people saye this that foloweth after the Minister.*

TURNE thou us, O good Lorde, and so shall we be turned: be favourable O Lord, bee favourable to thy people, whyche turne to thee, in wepynge, fastyng, and prayinge, for thou art a mercifull God, full of compassion, longe sufferynge, and of a great pitie. Thou sparest when we deserve punishment, and in thy wrathe thynkest upon mercye: spare thy people good Lorde, spare theym, and let not thy heritage be brought to confusion: heare us (O Lorde) for thy mercy is greate, and after the multitude of thy mercies, loke upon us.

The Book of Common-Prayer (London: John Bill and Christopher Barker, 1662), STC (Wing) B3622, Title page. Oxford, Bodleian Library (shelf mark: CP. 1662 b.4). Reproduced with permission. Two alternative title pages were made for the 1662 edition; some copies contain both. The engraving is by David Loggan (1634–92), after an original by J. B. Gaspars (1620–91).

The Book of Common-Prayer (London: John Bill and Christopher Barker, 1662), STC (Wing) B3622, Title page. Oxford, Bodleian Library (shelf mark: CP. 1662 b.5). Reproduced with permission. The engraving, as on the previous page, is an early work of Loggan.

THE
CONTENTS
OF THIS
BOOK.

AN ACT
FOR THE
UNIFORMITY
OF
COMMON PRAYER,
AND
Service in the CHURCH,
AND
Administration of the SACRAMENTS.

PRIMO ELIZABETHÆ.

WHERE at the death of our late Soveraign Lord King *Edward* the Sixth, there remained one uniform order of Common Service, and Prayer, and of the administration of Sacraments, Rites and Ceremonies of the Church of *England*, which was set forth in one Book, intituled, *The Book of Common Prayer, and Administration of Sacraments, and other Rites and Ceremonies in the Church of England*, Authorized by Act of Parliament holden in the fifth and sixth years of our said late Sovereign Lord King *Edward* the Sixth, intituled, *An Act for the Uniformity of Common Prayer, and Administration of the Sacraments*; The which was repealed, and taken away by Act of Parliament, in the first year of the Reign of our late Sovereign Lady Queen *Mary*, to the great decay of the due honour of God, and discomfort to the professors of the truth of Christs Religion:

Be it therefore enacted by the Authority of this present Parliament, That the said Statute of Repeal, and every thing therein contained, only concerning the said Book, and the Service, Administration of Sacraments, Rites, and Ceremonies contained or appointed in, or by the said Book, shall be void and of none effect, from and after the Feast of the Nativity of Saint *John Baptist* next coming: and That the said Book, with the Order of Service, and of the Administration of Sacraments, Rites and Ceremonies, with the alterations and additions therein added and appointed by this Statute, shall stand, and be, from, and after the said Feast of the Nativity of Saint *John Baptist*, in full force and effect, according to the tenour and effect of this

Statute: Any thing in the foresaid Statute of Repeal to the contrary notwithstanding.

And further be it Enacted by the Queens Highness, with the assent of the Lords and Commons of this present Parliament assembled, and by Authority of the same, That all, and singular Ministers in any Cathedral, or Parish-Church, or other place within this Realm of *England*, *Wales*, and the Marches of the same, or other the Queens Dominions, shall from and after the Feast of the Nativity of Saint *John Baptist* next coming, be bounden to say and use the Mattens, Evensong, celebration of the Lords Supper, and administration of each of the Sacraments, and all other Common and open Prayer, in such order and form as is mentioned in the said Book, so Authorized by Parliament in the said fifth and sixth year of the Reign of King *Edward* the Sixth, with one alteration, or addition° of certain Lessons to be used on every Sunday in the year, and the form of the Letany altered, and corrected, and two sentences only added in the delivery of the Sacrament to the Communicants, and none other, or otherwise: and, That if any manner of Parson, Vicar, or other whatsoever Minister, that ought or should sing, or say Common Prayer mentioned in the said Book, or minister the Sacraments, from, and after the Feast of the Nativity of Saint *John Baptist* next coming, refuse to use the said Common Prayers or to minister the Sacraments in such Cathedral, or Parish-Church, or other places, as he should use to minister the same, in such order and form, as they be mentioned, and set forth in the said Book, or shall wilfully, or obstinately standing in the same, use any other Rite, Ceremony, Order, Form, or Manner of celebrating of the Lords Supper openly, or privily, or Mattens, Evensong, administration of the Sacraments, or other open Prayers, than is mentioned, and set forth in the said Book, [*open Prayer in, and throughout this Act, is meant that Prayer, which is for other to come unto, or hear, either in Common Churches, or private Chappels, or Oratories, commonly called the Service of the Church*] or shall preach, declare, or speak anything in the derogation, or depraving of the said Book, or any thing therein contained, or of any part thereof, and shall be thereof lawfully convicted, according to the Laws of this Realm, by verdict of twelve men, or by his own confession, or by the notorious evidence of the fact; he shall lose, and forfeit to the Queens Highness, her Heirs, and Successors, for his first offence, the profit of all his Spiritual Benefices,° or Promotions, coming, or arising in one whole year next after his conviction: And also that the person so convicted shall for the same offence suffer imprisonment by the space of six moneths, without Bail or Mainprise:° And if any such person, once convict of any offence concerning the premisses, shall after his first conviction, eftsoons offend, and be thereof in form aforesaid lawfully convict; That then the same person shall for his second offence suffer imprisonment by the space of one whole year, and also shall therefore be deprived *ipso facto* of all his Spiritual Promotions; and That it shall be lawful to all Patrons, or Donors of all and singular the same Spiritual Promotions, or any of them, to present, or collate to the same, as though the person or persons so offending were dead: and That, if any such person, or persons, after he shall be twice convicted in form aforesaid, shall offend against any of the premisses the third time, and shall be thereof, in form aforesaid, lawfully convicted; That then the person so offending, and convicted the third time shall be deprived *ipso facto* of all his Spiritual Promotions, and also shall suffer imprisonment during his life: And if the person that shall offend, and be convict in form aforesaid, concerning any of the premisses, shall not be Beneficed, nor have any Spiritual Promotion; that then the same person, so offending, and convict, shall for the first offence suffer imprisonment during one whole year next after his said conviction, without Bail or Mainprise: And if any such person not having any Spiritual Promotion, after his first conviction, shall eftsoons offend in any thing concerning the premisses, and shall in form aforesaid be thereof lawfully convicted; That then the same person shall for his second offence suffer imprisonment during his life.

And it is Ordained, and Enacted by the Authority aforesaid, That if any person, or persons whatsoever, after the said Feast of the Nativity of Saint *John Baptist* next coming, shall in any Enterludes, Playes, Songs, Rimes, or by other open words° declare, or speak any thing in the derogation, depriving, or despising of the same Book, or of any thing therein contained, or any part thereof, or shall by open fact, deed, or by open threatenings compel, or cause, or otherwise procure, or maintain any Parson, Vicar, or other Minister in any Cathedral, or Parish-Church, or in Chappel, or in any other place, to sing, or say any Common or open Prayer, or to minister any Sacrament otherwise, or in any other manner, and form, than is mentioned in the said Book; or that by any of the said means shall unlawfully interrupt, or let any Parson, Vicar, or other Minister in any Cathedral, or Parish-Church,

Chappel, or any other place to sing or say Common and open Prayer, or to Minister the Sacraments, or any of them, in such manner, and form, as is mentioned in the said Book; That then every such person, being thereof lawfully convicted in form abovesaid, shall forfeit to the Queen our Sovereign Lady, her Heirs, and Successors for the first offence an hundred marks:° And if any person, or persons, being once convict of any such offence, eftsoons offend against any of the last recited offences, and shall in form aforesaid be thereof lawfully convict; That then the same person, so offending and convict, shall for the second offence forfeit to the Queen our Sovereign Lady, Her Heirs, and Successors, Four hundred marks: And if any person, after he in form aforesaid shall have been twice convict of any offence concerning any of the last recited offences, shall offend the third time, and be thereof in form abovesaid lawfully convict; That then every person so offending and convict, shall for his third offence, forfeit to our Sovereign Lady the Queen all his Goods and Chattels, and shall suffer imprisonment during his life: And if any person or persons, that for his first offence concerning the premisses, shall be convict in form aforesaid, do not pay the sum to be paid by vertue of his conviction, in such manner and form, as the same ought to be paid, within six weeks next after his conviction; That then every person so convict, and so not paying the same, shall for the same first offence, in stead of the said sum, suffer imprisonment by the space of six moneths, without Bail or Mainprise: And if any person, or persons, that for his second offence concerning the premisses shall be convict in form aforesaid, do not pay the said sum to be paid by vertue of his conviction, and this estatute, in such manner and form, as the same ought to be payed, within six weeks next after this said second conviction; That then every person so convicted, and not so paying the same, shall for the same second offence, in the stead of the said sum, suffer imprisonment during twelve moneths, without Bail or Mainprise: and, That from and after the said Feast of the Nativity of Saint *John Baptist* next coming, all, and every person and persons, inhabiting within this Realm, or any other the Queens Majesties Dominions, shall diligently, and faithfully, having no lawful, or reasonable excuse to be absent,° indeavour themselves to resort to their Parish-Church, or Chappel accustomed, or upon reasonable let thereof, to some usual place, where Common Prayer and such service of God shall be used in such time of let, upon every Sunday, and other days ordained and used to be kept as holy days, and then and there to abide orderly and soberly, during the time of Common Prayer, Preachings, or other Service of God there to be used and ministered, upon pain of punishment by the censures of the Church; and also upon pain, that every person so offending shall forfeit for every such offence twelve pence, to be levied by the Church-wardens of the Parish, where such offence shall be done, to the use of the poor of the same Parish, of the goods, lands, and tenements of such offender, by way of distress.

And for due execution hereof, the Queens most excellent Majesty, the Lords Temporal, and all the Commons in this present Parliament assembled, doth in Gods name earnestly require, and charge all the Archbishops, Bishops, and other Ordinaries, that they shall endeavor themselves to the uttermost of their knowledges, that the due and true execution hereof may be had throughout their Diocess and Charges, as they will answer before God for such evils and plagues, wherewith Almighty God may justly punish his people for neglecting his good and wholesom law. And for the Authority in this behalf, Be it further Enacted by the Authority aforesaid, That all and singular the same Archbishops, Bishops, and all other their officers, exercising Ecclesiastical jurisdiction, aswel in the place exempt, as not exempt, within their Diocess shall have full Power and Authority by this Act to reform, correct and punish by censures of the Church, all, and singular persons, which shall offend within any of their jurisdictions, or Diocess, after the said Feast of the Nativity of Saint *John Baptist* next coming, against this Act and Statute: Any other Law, Statute, Priviledge, Liberty, or Provision heretofore made, had, or suffered to the contrary notwithstanding.

And it is Ordained and Enacted by the Authority aforesaid, That all and every Justice of Oyer and Determiner, or Justise of Assize,° shall have full power and Authority in every of their open and general Sessions to enquire, hear and determine all and all manner of offences, that shall be committed, or done contrary to any Article contained in this present Act, within the limits of the Commission to them directed, and to make process for the execution of the same, as they may do against any person being indicted before them of trespass, or lawfully convicted thereof.

Provided always, and be it Enacted by the Authority aforesaid, That all and every Archbishop and Bishop, shall or may at all time and times at his liberty and pleasure, joyn and associate himself by vertue of this Act to the said Justices of Oyer and Determiner, or to the said Justices of Assise, at every of the said open and general Sessions, to be holden in any place within his Diocess, for and to the inquiry, hearing, and determining of the offences aforesaid.

Provided also, and be it Enacted by the Authority aforesaid, That the Books concerning the said Service shall at the costs and charges of the Parishioners of every Parish,° and Cathedral Church be attained, and gotten before the said Feast of the Nativity of Saint *John Baptist* next following, and that all such Parishes and Cathedral Churches, or other places, where the said Books shall be attained and gotten before the said Feast of the Nativity of Saint *John Baptist*, shall within three Weeks next after the said books so attained and gotten, use the said Service, and put the same in use according to this Act.

And be it further Enacted by the Authority aforesaid, that no person or persons shall be at any time hereafter impeached, or otherwise molested of or for any of the offences above mentioned, hereafter to be committed, or done contrary to this Act, unless he or they so offending be thereof indicted at the next general sessions to be holden before any such Justices of Oyer and Determiner, or Justices of Assise, next after any offence committed or done, contrary to the tenour of this Act.

Provided always, and be it Ordained, and Enacted by the Authority aforesaid, That all and singular Lords of the Parliament, for the third offence above mentioned, shall be tried by their peers.

Provided also, and be it Ordained, and Enacted by the Authority aforesaid, That the Mayor of *London*, and all other Mayors, Bayliffs, and other Head-officers of all, and singular Cities, Boroughs, and Towns-corporate within this Realm, *Wales*, and the Marches of the same, to the which Justices of Assise do not commonly repair, shall have full Power and Authority by vertue of this Act, to enquire, hear and determine the offences abovesaid, and every of them, yearly within fifteen Days after the Feasts of *Easter* and Saint *Michael* the *Archangel*, in like manner and form, as Justices of Assise and Oyer, and Determiner may do.

Provided always, and be it Ordained and Enacted by the Authority aforesaid, That all and singular Archbishops, and Bishops, and every of their Chancellors, Commissaries, Archdeacons, and other Ordinaries, having any peculiar Ecclesiastical jurisdiction, shall have full Power and Authority by vertue of this Act, aswel to enquire in their Visitation, Synods, or elsewhere within their jurisdiction, at any other time, and place, to take accusations, and informations of all, and every the things abovementioned, done, committed, or perpetrated within the limits of their jurisdiction and Authority, and to punish the same by admonition, excommunication, sequestration, or deprivation, or other censures and Processes, in like form, as heretofore hath been used in like cases by the Queens Ecclesiastical Laws.

Provided alwaies, and be it Enacted, That whatsoever person offending in the premisses shall for the first offence, receive punishment of the Ordinary, having a Testimonial thereof under the said Ordinaries seal, shall not for the same offence eftsoons be convicted before the Justices: and likewise receiving for the first said offence punishment by the Justices, he shall not for the same first offence eftsoons receive punishment of the Ordinary: Any thing contained in this Act to the contrary notwithstanding.

Provided always, and be it Enacted, That such ornaments of the Church and of the ministers thereof shall be retained, and be in use,° as was in this Church of *England*, by the Authority of Parliament in the second year of the reign of King *Edward* the Sixth, until other order shall be therein taken by Authority of the Queens Majesty, with the advice of her Commissioners, appointed and Authorized under the great seal of *England* for causes Ecclesiastical, or of the Metropolitan of this Realm: And also, That if there shall happen any Contempt, or irreverence to be used in the Ceremonies, or Rites of the Church, by the misusing of the Orders appointed in this Book; the Queens Majesty may by the like advice of the said Commissioners, or Metropolitan, ordain and publish such further Ceremonies, or Rites, as may be most for the advancement of Gods Glory, the edifying of his Church, and the due reverence of Christs holy Mysteries and Sacraments.

And be it further Enacted by the Authority aforesaid, That all Laws, Statutes, and Ordinances, wherein or whereby any other Service, Administration of Sacraments, or Common Prayer is limited, established, or set forth to be used within this Realm, or any other the Queens Dominions, and Countries, shall from henceforth utterly be void and of none effect.

AN ACT
FOR THE
UNIFORMITY
OF
PUBLICK PRAYERS;
AND

Administration of Sacraments, and other Rites and Ceremonies: And for the establishing the Form of Making, Ordaining, and Consecrating Bishops, Priests, and Deacons in the Church of *England*.

XIV. CAROLI II.

WHEREAS in the first year of the late Queen *Elizabeth* there was one Uniform Order of Common Service and Prayer, and of the Administration of Sacraments, Rites and Ceremonies in the Church of *England* (agreeable to the Word of God, and usage of the Primitive Church) compiled by the Reverend Bishops and Clergy, set forth in one Book, Entituled, *The Book of Common Prayer, and Administration of Sacraments, and other Rites and Ceremonies in the Church of England*, and enjoyned to be used by Act of Parliament, holden in the said First year of the said late Queen, Entituled, *An Act for the Uniformity of Common Prayer, and Service in the Church, and Administration of the Sacraments*, very comfortable to all good people desirous to live in Christian conversation, and most profitable to the Estate of this Realm, upon the which the Mercy, Favour and Blessing of Almighty God is in no wise so readily and plentifully poured, as by Common Prayers, due using of the Sacraments, and often Preaching of the Gospel, with devotion of the hearers: And yet this notwithstanding, a great number of people in divers parts of this Realm, following their own sensuality, and living without knowledge and due fear of God,° do wilfully and Schismatically abstain, and refuse to come to their Parish Churches and other Publick places where Common Prayer, Administration of the Sacraments, and Preaching of the Word of God is used upon the Sundays and other days ordained and appointed to be kept and observed as Holy days:

And whereas by the great and scandalous neglect of Ministers in using the said Order, or Liturgy so set forth and enjoyned as aforesaid, great mischiefs and inconveniences, during the times of the late unhappy troubles,° have arisen and grown; and many people have been led into Factions and Schisms, to the great decay and scandal of the Reformed Religion of the Church of *England*, and to the hazard of many souls: for prevention whereof in time to come, for settling the Peace of the Church, and for allaying the present distempers, which the indisposition of the time hath contracted, The Kings Majesty (according to His Declaration of the Five and twentieth of *October*, One thousand six hundred and sixty) granted His Commission under the great Seal of *England* to several Bishops and other Divines to review the Book of Common Prayer, and to prepare such Alterations and Additions, as they thought fit to offer; And afterwards the Convocations of both the Provinces of *Canterbury* and *York*, being by his Majesty called and assembled (and now sitting) His Majesty hath been pleased to Authorize and require the Presidents of the said Convocations, and other Bishops and Clergy of the same, to review the said Book of Common Prayer, and the Book of the Form and manner of the Making and Consecrating of Bishops, Priests and Deacons; And that after mature consideration, they should make such Additions and Alterations in the said Books respectively, as to them should seem meet and convenient; And should exhibit and present the same to His Majesty in writing, for his further allowance or confirmation; since which time, upon full and mature deliberation, they the said Presidents, Bishops, and Clergy of both Provinces have accordingly reviewed the said Books, and have made some Alterations which they think fit to be inserted° to the same; and some Additional Prayers to the said Book of Common-Prayer, to be used upon proper and emergent occasions; and have exhibited and presented the same unto his Majesty in writing, in one Book, Entituled, *The Book of Common Prayer, and Administration of the Sacraments, and other Rites and Ceremonies of the Church, according to the use of the Church of England, together with the Psalter, or Psalms of David, Pointed as they are to be sung or said in Churches; and the Form and Manner of Making, Ordaining, and Consecrating of Bishops, Priests, and Deacons*: All which His Majesty having duely considered hath fully approved and allowed the same, and recommended to this present Parliament, that the said Book of Common Prayer, and of the Form of Ordination and Consecration of Bishops, Priests, and Deacons, with the Alterations and Additions, which have been so made and presented to His Majesty by the said Convocations, be the Book, which shall be appointed to be used by all that Officiate in all Cathedral and Collegiate Churches and Chappels, and in all Chappels of Colledges and Halls in both the Universities, and the Colledges of *Eaton* and *Winchester*, and in all Parish-Churches and Chappels within the Kingdom of *England*, Dominion of *Wales*, and Town of *Berwick* upon *Tweed*, and by all that Make, or Consecrate Bishops, Priests or Deacons in any of the said Places, under such Sanctions and Penalties as the Houses of Parliament shall think fit: Now in regard that nothing conduceth more to the setling of the Peace of this Nation (which is desired of all good men) nor to the honour of our Religion, and the propagation thereof, than an Universal agreement in the Publick Worship of Almighty God; and to the intent that every person within this Realm, may certainly know the rule, to which he is to conform in Publick Worship, and Administration of Sacraments, and other Rites and Ceremonies of the Church of *England*, and the manner how, and by whom Bishops Priests and Deacons are, and ought to be Made, Ordained and Consecrated;

Be it Enacted by the Kings most Excellent Majesty, by the advice, and with the consent of the Lords Spiritual and Temporal, and of the Commons in this present Parliament assembled, and by the Authority of the same, That all and singular Ministers, in any Cathedral, Collegiate, or Parish-Church or Chappel, or other Place of Publick Worship within this Realm of *England*, Dominion of *Wales*, and Town of *Berwick* upon *Tweed*, shall be bound to say and use the Morning Prayer, Evening Prayer, Celebration and Administration of both the Sacraments, and all other the Publick, and Common Prayer, in such order and form as is mentioned in the said Book, annexed and joyned to this present Act,° and Entituled, *The Book of Common Prayer, and Administration of the Sacraments, and other Rites and Ceremonies of the Church, according to the use of the Church of England: together with the Psalter or Psalms of David, Pointed as they are to be sung or said in Churches; and the form or manner of Making, Ordaining, and Consecrating of Bishops, Priests and Deacons*: and That the Morning and Evening Prayers, therein contained, shall upon every Lords day, and upon all other days and occasions, and at the times therein appointed, be openly and solemnly read by all and every Minister or Curate in every Church, Chappel, or other place of Publick Worship within this Realm of *England*, and places aforesaid.

And to the end that Uniformity in the Publick Worship of God (which is so much desired) may be speedily effected, Be it further Enacted by the Authority aforesaid, That every Parson, Vicar, or other Minister whatsoever, who now hath, and enjoyeth any Ecclesiastical Benefice, or Promotion, within this Realm of *England*, or places aforesaid, shall in the Church, Chappel, or place of Publick Worship belonging to his said Benefice or Promotion, upon some Lords day before the Feast of Saint *Bartholomew*, which shall be in the year of our Lord God, One thousand six hundred sixty and two, openly, publickly, and solemnly read the Morning and Evening Prayer appointed to be read by, and according to the said Book of Common Prayer at the times thereby appointed, and after such reading thereof shall openly and publickly, before the Congregation there assembled, declare his unfeigned assent, and consent to the use of all things in the said Book contained and prescribed, in these words, and no other;

I *A. B.* Do here declare my unfeigned assent,° and consent to all, and every thing contained, and prescribed in, and by the Book intituled, *The Book of Common Prayer and Administration of the Sacraments, and other Rites, and Ceremonies of the Church, according to the use of the Church of England; together with the Psalter, or Psalms of David, Pointed as they are to be sung, or said in Churches, and the form, or manner of Making, Ordaining, and Consecrating of Bishops, Priests, and Deacons;*

And, That all and every such person, who shall (without some lawful Impediment, to be allowed and approved of by the Ordinary of the place) neglect or refuse to do the same within the time aforesaid, or (in case of such Impediment) within one Moneth after such Impediment removed, shall *ipso facto* be deprived of all his Spiritual Promotions; And that from thenceforth it shall be lawful to, and for all Patrons, and Donors of all and singular the said Spiritual Promotions, or of any of them, according to their respective Rights, and Titles, to present, or collate to the same; as though the person, or persons, so offending or neglected were dead.

And be it further Enacted by the Authority aforesaid, That every person, who shall hereafter be presented, or collated, or put into any Ecclesiastical Benefice, or Promotion within this Realm of *England* and places aforesaid, shall in the Church, Chappel, or Place of Publick Worship, belonging to his said Benefice or Promotion, within two Moneths next after that he shall be in the actual possession of the said Ecclesiastical Benefice or Promotion, upon some Lords day openly, publickly, and solemnly Read the Morning and Evening Prayers, appointed to be Read by, and according to the said Book of Common Prayer, at the times thereby appointed, and after such Reading thereof, shall openly, and publickly before the Congregation there assembled, declare his unfeigned assent, and consent to the use of all things therein contained and prescribed, according to the form before appointed: and That all and every such person, who shall (without some lawful Impediment, to be allowed and approved by the Ordinary of the place) neglect or refuse to do the same within the time aforesaid, or (in case of such Impediment) within one month after such Impediment removed shall *ipso facto* be deprived of all his said Ecclesiastical Benefices and Promotions; and That from thenceforth, it shall and may be lawful to, and for all Patrons, and Donors of all and singular the said Ecclesiastical Benefices and Promotions, or any of them (according to their respective Rights and Titles) to present, or collate to the same, as though the person or persons so offending, or neglecting, were dead.

And be it further Enacted by the Authority aforesaid, That in all places, where the proper Incumbent of any Parsonage, or Vicarage, or Benefice with Cure doth reside on his Living, and keep a Curate, the Incumbent himself in person (not having some lawful Impediment, to be allowed by the Ordinary of the place) shall once (at the least) in every month openly and publickly Read the Common prayers and Service, in, and by the said Book prescribed, and (if there be occasion) Administer each of the Sacraments and other Rites of the Church, in the Parish Church or Chappel, of, or belonging to the same Parsonage, Vicarage, or Benefice, in such order, manner and form, as in, and by the said Book is appointed, upon pain to forfeit the sum of Five pounds to the use of the poor of the Parish for every offence, upon conviction by confession, or proof of two credible Witnesses upon Oath, before two Justices of the Peace of the County, City, or Town-Corporate where the offence shall be committed, (which Oath the said Justices are hereby Impowred to Administer) and in default of payment within ten days, to be levied by distress, and sale of the goods and chattels of the Offender,° by the Warrant of the said Justices, by the Church-wardens, or Over-seers of the Poor of the said Parish, rendring the surplusage to the party.

And be it further Enacted by the Authority aforesaid, That every

Dean, Canon, and Prebendary of every Cathedral, or Collegiate Church, and all Masters, and other Heads, Fellows, Chaplains, and Tutors of, or in any Colledge, Hall, House of Learning, or Hospital, and every Publick Professor, and Reader in either of the Universities, and in every Colledge elsewhere, and every Parson, Vicar, Curate, Lecturer, and every other person in holy Orders, and every School-master keeping any publick, or private School, and every person Instructing, or Teaching any Youth in any House or private Family as a Tutor, or School-master, who upon the first day of *May*, which shall be in the year of our Lord God, One thousand six hundred sixty two, or at any time thereafter shall be Incumbent, or have possession of any Deanry, Canonry, Prebend, Mastership, Headship, Fellow-ship, Professors-place, or Readers place, Parsonage, Vicarage, or any other Ecclesiastical Dignity or Promotion, or of any Curates place, Lecture, or School; or shall instruct or teach any Youth as Tutor, or School-master, shall before the Feast-day of Saint *Bartholomew*, which shall be in the year of our Lord One thousand six hundred sixty two, or at or before his, or their respective admission to be Incumbent, or have possession aforesaid, subscribe the Declaration or Acknowledgement following, *Scilicet*,

I *A. B.* Do declare that it is not lawful upon any pretence whatsoever to take Arms against the King; and that I do abhor that Traiterous Position of taking Arms by His Authority against His Person, or against those that are Commissionated by him; and that I will conform to the Liturgy of the Church of England, as it is now by Law established. And I do declare that I do hold, there lies no Obligation upon me, or on any other person from the Oath, commonly called the *Solemn League and Covenant*,° to endeavor any change, or alteration of Government, either in Church, or State; and that the same was in itself an unlawful Oath, and imposed upon the Subjects of this Realm against the known Laws and Liberties of this Kingdom.

Which said Declaration and Acknowledgement shall be subscribed by every of the said Masters and other Heads, Fellows, Chaplains, and Tutors of, or in any Colledge, Hall, or House of Learning, and by every publick Professor and Reader in either of the Universities,° before the Vice-Chancellor of the respective Universities for the time being, or his Deputy; And the said Declaration or Acknowledgement shall be subscribed before the respective Arch-bishop, Bishop or Ordinary of the

Diocess, by every other person hereby injoyned to subscribe the same, upon pain, that all and every of the persons aforesaid, failing in such subscription, shall lose and forfeit such respective Deanry, Canonry, Prebend, Mastership, Headship, Fellowship, Professors place, Readers place, Parsonage, Vicarage, Ecclesiastical Dignity, or Promotion, Curates place, Lecture, and School, and shall be utterly disabled, and *ipso facto* deprived of the same; and that every such respective Deanry, Canonry, Prebend, Mastership, Headship, Fellowship, Professors place, Readers place, Parsonage, Vicarage, Ecclesiastical Dignity, or Promotion, Curates place, Lecture and School shall be void, as if such person so failing were naturally dead.

And if any Schoolmaster or other person, Instructing or teaching Youth in any private House or Family, as a Tutor or School-master, shall Instruct or Teach any Youth as a Tutor or School-master, before License obtained from his respective Archbishop, Bishop, or Ordinary of the Diocess, according to the Laws and Statutes of this Realm, (for which he shall pay twelve-pence onely) and before such subscription and acknowledgement made as aforesaid; Then every such School-master and other, Instructing and Teaching as aforesaid, shall for the first offence suffer three months Imprisonment without bail or main-prise; and for every second and other such offense shall suffer three months Imprisonment without bail or mainprise, and also forfeit to His Majesty the sum of five pounds.

And after such subscription made, every such Parson, Vicar, Curate, and Lecturer shall procure a certificate under the Hand and Seal of the respective Archbishop, Bishop, or Ordinary of the Diocess, (who are hereby enjoyned and required upon demand to make and deliver the same) and shall publickly and openly Read the same, together with the Declaration, or Acknowledgement aforesaid, upon some Lords day within three months then next following, in his Parish Church where he is to officiate, in the presence of the Congregation there assembled, in the time of Divine Service; upon pain that every person failing therein shall lose such Parsonage, Vicarage, or Benefice, Curates place, or Lecturers place respectively, and shall be utterly disabled, and *ipso facto* deprived of the same; And that the said Parsonage, Vicarage, or Benefice, Curates place, or Lecturers place shall be void, as if he was naturally dead.

Provided always that from and after the Twenty fifth day of *March*, which shall be in the year of our Lord God, One thousand six hundred eighty two, there shall be omitted in the said Declaration, or Acknowledgement so to be Subscribed and Read, these words following, *Scilicet,*

AND I do declare that I do hold, there lies no obligation on me, or on any other person from the Oath, commonly called the *Solemn League and Covenant,* to endeavour any change, or alteration of Government either in Church, or State; And that the same was in it self an unlawful Oath, and imposed upon the Subjects of this Realm against the known Laws and Liberties of this Kingdom;

So as none of the persons aforesaid shall from thenceforth be at all obliged to Subscribe or Read that part of the said Declaration or Acknowledgement.

Provided alwaies, and be it Enacted, That from and after the Feast of Saint *Bartholomew,* which shall be in the year of our Lord, One thousand six hundred sixty and two, no person, who now is Incumbent, and in possession of any Parsonage, Vicarage, or Benefice, and who is not already in holy Orders by Episcopal Ordination, or shall not before the said Feast-day of Saint *Bartholomew* be Ordained Priest, or Deacon, according to the form of Episcopal Ordination, shall have, hold, or enjoy the said Parsonage, Vicarage Benefice with Cure or other Ecclesiastical Promotion within this Kingdom of *England,* or the Dominion of *Wales,* or Town of *Berwick* upon *Tweed*; But shall be utterly disabled, and *ipso facto* deprived of the same; And all his Ecclesiastical Promotions shall be void, as if he was naturally dead.

And be it further Enacted by the Authority aforesaid, That no person whatsoever shall thenceforth be capable to be admitted to any Parsonage, Vicarage, Benefice, or other Ecclesiastical Promotion or Dignity whatsoever, nor shall presume to Consecrate and Administer the holy Sacrament of the Lords Supper, before such time as he shall be Ordained Priest, according to the form, and manner in, and by the said Book prescribed, unless he have formerly been made Priest by Episcopal Ordination,° upon pain to forfeit for every offence the sum of One hundred pounds; (one moyety thereof to the Kings Majesty, the other moyety thereof to be equally divided between the poor of the Parish where the offence shall be committed, and such person, or person as shall sue for the same by Action of Debt, Bill, Plaint, or Information in any of his Majesties Courts of Record, wherein no Essign, Protection, or Wager of Law shall be allowed) And to be disabled from taking, or being admitted into the Order of Priest, by the space of one whole year next following.

Provided that the Penalties of this Act shall not extend to the Foreiners or Aliens of the Forein Reformed Churches allowed, or to be allowed by the Kings Majesty, His Heirs and Successors, in *England*.

Provided always, That no title to confer, or present by lapse shall accrue by any avoidance, or deprivation *ipso facto* by vertue of this Statute, but after six months after notice of such voidance, or deprivation given by the Ordinary to the Patron, or such sentence of deprivation openly and publickly read in the Parish Church of the Benefice, Parsonage, or Vicarage becoming void, or whereof the Incumbent shall be deprived by vertue of this Act.

And be it further Enacted by the Authority aforesaid, That no Form, or Order of Common Prayers, Administration of Sacraments, Rites or Ceremonies, shall be openly used in any Church, Chappel, or other Publick place or in any Colledge, or Hall in either of the Universities, the Colledges of *Westminster*, *Winchester*, or *Eaton*, or any of them, other than what is prescribed and appointed to be used in and by the said Book; and That the present Governour, or Head of every Colledge and Hall in the said Universities, and of the said Colleges of *Westminster*, *Winchester*, and *Eaton*, within one month after the Feast of Saint *Bartholomew*, which shall be in the year of our Lord, One thousand six hundred sixty and two: And every Governour or Head of any of the said Colledges, or Halls, hereafter to be elected, or appointed, within one month next after his Election, or Collation, and Admission into the same Government, or Headship, shall openly and publickly in the Church, Chappel, or other Publick place of the same Colledge, or Hall, and in the presence of the Fellows and Scholars of the same, or the greater part of them then resident, Subscribe unto the Nine and thirty Articles of Religion,° mentioned in the Statute made in the thirteenth year of the Reign of the late Queen *Elizabeth*, and unto the said Book, and declare his unfeigned assent and consent unto, and approbation of the said Articles, and of the same Book, and to the use of all the Prayers, Rites, and Ceremonies, Forms, and Orders in the said Book prescribed, and contained according to the form aforesaid; and that all such Governours, or Heads of the said Colledges and Halls, or any of them as are, or shall be in holy Orders, shall once at least in every Quarter of the year (not having a lawful Impediment) openly and publickly Read the Morning Prayer, and

Service in and by the said Book appointed to be Read in the Church, Chappel, or other Publick place of the same Colledge or Hall, upon pain to lose, and be suspended of, and from all the Benefits and Profits belonging to the same Government or Headship, by the space of Six months, by the Visitor or Visitors of the same Colledge or Hall; And if any Governour or Head of any Colledge or Hall, Suspended for not Subscribing unto the said Articles and Book, or for not Reading of the Morning Prayer and Service as aforesaid, shall not at, or before the end of Six months next after such suspension, Subscribe unto the said Articles and Book, and declare his consent thereunto as aforesaid, or Read the Morning Prayer and Service as aforesaid, then such Government or Headship shall be *ipso facto* void.

Provided always, That it shall and may be lawful to use the Morning and Evening Prayer, and all other Prayers and Service prescribed in and by the said Book, in the Chappels or other Publick places of the respective Colledges and Halls in both the Universities, in the Colledges of *Westminster*, *Winchester*, and *Eaton*, and in the Convocations of the Clergies of either Province in Latine; Any thing in this Act contained to the contrary notwithstanding.

And be it further Enacted by the Authority aforesaid, That no person shall be, or be received as a Lecturer, or permitted, suffered, or allowed to Preach as a Lecturer, or to Preach, or Read any Sermon or Lecture in any Church, Chappel, or other place of Publick worship, within this Realm of *England*, or the Dominion of *Wales*, and Town of *Berwick* upon *Tweed*, unless he be first approved and thereunto Licensed by the Archbishop of the Province, or Bishop of the Diocess, or (in case the See be void) by the Guardian of the Spiritualties, under his Seal, and shall in the presence of the same Archbishop, or Bishop, or Guardian Read the Nine and thirty Articles of Religion, mentioned in the Statute of the Thirteenth year of the late Queen *Elizabeth*, with Declaration of his unfeigned assent to the same; and That every person, and persons who now is, or hereafter shall be Licensed, Assigned, Appointed, or Received as a Lecturer, to preach upon any day of the week in any Church, Chappel, or place of Publick worship within this Realm of *England*, or places aforesaid, the first time he Preacheth (before his Sermon) shall openly, publickly, and solemnly Read the Common Prayers and Service in and by the said Book appointed to be Read for that time of the day, and then and there publickly and openly declare his assent unto, and approbation of the said Book, and to the use of all the Prayers, Rites and Ceremonies, Forms and Orders therein contained and prescribed, according to the Form before appointed in this Act; And also shall upon the first Lecture-day of every month afterwards, so long as he continues Lecturer, or Preacher there, at the place appointed for his said Lecture or Sermon, before his said Lecture or Sermon, openly, publickly, and solemnly Read the Common Prayers and Service in and by the said Book appointed to be read for that time of the day, at which the said Lecture or Sermon is to be Preached, and after such Reading thereof, shall openly and publickly, before the Congregation there assembled, declare his unfeigned assent and consent unto, and approbation of the said Book, and to the use of all the Prayers, Rites and Ceremonies, Forms and Orders therein contained and prescribed, according to the form aforesaid; and, That all and every such person and persons who shall neglect or refuse to do the same, shall from thenceforth be disabled to Preach the said, or any other Lecture or Sermon in the said, or any other Church, Chappel, or place of Publick worship, until such time as he and they shall openly, publickly, and solemnly Read the Common-Prayers and Service appointed by the said Book, and Conform in all points to the things therein appointed and prescribed, according to the purport, true intent, and meaning of this Act.

Provided alwaies, that if the said Sermon or Lecture be to be Preached or Read in any Cathedral, or Collegiate Church or Chappel, it shall be sufficient for the said Lecturer openly at the time aforesaid, to declare his assent and consent to all things contained in the said Book, according to the form aforesaid.

And be it further Enacted by the Authority aforesaid, That if any person who is by this Act disabled to Preach any Lecture or Sermon, shall during the time that he shall continue and remain so disabled, Preach any Sermon or Lecture; That then for every such offence the person and persons so offending shall suffer Three months Imprisonment in the Common Gaol without Bail or mainprise, and that any two Justices of the Peace of any County of this Kingdom and places aforesaid, and the *May*or or other chief Magistrate of any City, or Town-Corporate, within the same, upon Certificate from the Ordinary of the place made to him or them of the offence committed, shall, and are hereby required to commit the person or persons so offending to the Gaol of the Same County, City, or Town Corporate accordingly.

Provided alwaies, and be it further Enacted by the Authority aforesaid, That at all and every time and times, when any Sermon or Lecture is to be Preached, the Common Prayers and Service in and by the said Book appointed to be Read for that time of the day, shall be openly, publickly, and solemnly Read by some Priest, or Deacon, in the Church, Chappel, or place of Publick worship, where the said Sermon or Lecture be Preached, before such Sermon or Lecture is to be Preached; And that the Lecturer then to Preach shall be present at the Reading thereof.

Provided nevertheless, That this Act shall not extend to the University-Churches° in the Universities of this Realm, or either of them, when or at such times as any Sermon or Lecture is Preached or Read in the same Churches, or any of them, for, or as the publick University-Sermon or Lecture; but that the same Sermons and Lectures may be Preached or Read in such sort and manner as the same have been heretofore Preached or Read; This Act, or any thing herein contained to the contrary thereof in any wise notwithstanding.

And be it further Enacted by the Authority aforesaid, That the several good Laws, and Statutes of this Realm, which have been formerly made, and are now in force for the Uniformity of Prayer and Administration of the Sacraments, within this Realm of *England*, and places aforesaid, shall stand in full force and strength to all intents and purposes whatsoever, for the establishing and confirming of the said Book; Entituled, *The Book of Common Prayer, and Administration of the Sacraments, and other Rites and Ceremonies of the Church, according to the use of the Church of England; together with the Psalter or Psalms of David, Pointed as they are to be sung or said in Churches; and the form or manner of Making, Ordaining, and Consecrating of Bishops, Priests and Deacons*; herein before mentioned to be joyned and annexed to this Act; and shall be applied, practised, and put in ure for the punishing of all offences contrary to the said Laws, with relation to the Book aforesaid, and no other.

Provided alwaies, and be it further Enacted by the Authority aforesaid, That in all those Prayers, Litanies, and Collects, which do any way relate to the King, Queen, or Royal Progeny, the Names be altered and changed from time to time, and fitted to the present occasion, according to the direction of lawful Authority.

Provided also, and be it Enacted by the Authority aforesaid, That a true Printed Copy of the said Book, Entituled, *The Book of Common Prayer, and Administration of the Sacraments, and other Rites and Ceremonies of the Church, according to the use of the Church of England; together with the Psalter or Psalms of David, Pointed as they are to be sung or said in Churches; and the form and manner of Making, Ordaining, and Consecrating of Bishops, Priests and Deacons,* shall at the costs and charges of the Parishioners of every Parish-Church, and Chappelry, Cathedral Church, Colledge, and Hall, be attained and gotten before the Feast-day of Saint *Bartholomew,* in the year of our Lord, One thousand six hundred sixty and two, upon pain of forfeiture of Three pounds by the months, for so long time as they shall then after be unprovided thereof, by every Parish, or Chappelry, Cathedral Church, Colledge, and Hall, making default therein.

Provided alwaies, and be it Enacted by the Authority aforesaid, That the Bishops of *Hereford,* Saint *Davids, Asaph, Bangor,* and *Landaff,* and their Successors shall take such order among themselves, for the souls health of the Flocks committed to their Charge within *Wales,* That the Book hereunto annexed be truly and exactly Translated° into the *Brittish* or *Welsh* Tongue, and that the same so Translated and being by them, or any three of them at the least viewed, perused, and allowed, be Imprinted to such number at least, so that one of the said Books so Translated and Imprinted may be had for every Cathedral, Collegiate, and Parish-Church, and Chappel of Ease in the said respective Dioceses, and places in *Wales,* where the *Welsh* is commonly spoken or used before the First day of *May,* One thousand six hundred sixty five; and, That from and after the Imprinting and publishing of the said Book so Translated, the whole Divine Service shall be used and said by the Ministers and Curates thoughout all *Wales* within the said Dioceses where the *Welsh* Tongue is commonly used, in the *Brittish,* or *Welsh* Tongue, in such manner and form as is prescribed according to the Book hereunto annexed to be used in the *English* Tongue, differing nothing in any Order or Form from the said *English* Book; for which Book, so Translated and Imprinted, the Church-wardens of every of the said Parishes shall pay out of the Parish-money in their hands for the use of the respective Churches, and be allowed the same on their Accompt; and, That the said Bishops and their Successors, or any Three of them, at the least, shall set and appoint the price, for which the said Book shall be sold; And one other Book of Common Prayer in the *English* Tongue shall be bought and had in every Church throughout *Wales,* in which the Book of Common Prayer in *Welsh* is to be had, by force of this Act, before the First day of *May*, One thousand six hundred sixty and four, and the same Book to remain in such convenient places, within the said Churches, that such as understand them may resort at all convenient times to read and peruse the same, and also such as do not understand the said Language, may by conferring both Tongues together, the sooner attain to the knowledge of the *English* Tongue; Any thing in this Act to the contrary notwithstanding; And until Printed Copies of the said Book so to be Translated may be had and provided, the Form of Common Prayer, established by Parliament before the making of this Act, shall be used as formerly in such parts of *Wales*, where the *English* Tongue is not commonly understood.

And to the end that the true and perfect Copies of this Act, and the said Book hereunto annexed may be safely kept, and perpetually preserved, and for the avoiding of all disputes for the time to come; Be it therefore Enacted by the Authority aforesaid, That the respective Deans and Chapters of every Cathedral, or Collegiate Church, within *England* and *Wales* shall at their proper costs and charges, before the twenty fifth day of *December*, One thousand six hundred sixty and two, obtain under the Great Seal of *England* a true and perfect Printed Copy of this Act, and of the said Book annexed hereunto, to be by the said Deans and Chapters, and their Successors kept and preserved in safety for ever, and to be also produced, and shewed forth in any Court of Record, as often as they shall be thereunto lawfully required; And also there shall be delivered true and perfect Copies of this Act, and of the same Book into the respective Courts at *Westminster*, and into the Tower of *London*, to be kept and preserved for ever among the Records of the said Courts, and the Records of the Tower, to be also produced and shewed forth in any Court as need shall require; which said Books so to be exemplified under the Great Seal of *England*, shall be examined by such persons as the Kings Majesty shall appoint under the Great Seal of *England* for that purpose, and shall be compared with the Original Book hereunto annexed, and shall have power to correct, and amend in writing any Error committed by the Printer in the printing of the same Book, or of any thing therein contained, and shall certifie in writing under their Hands and Seals, or the Hands and Seals of any Three of them at the end of the same Book, that they have examined and compared the same Book, and find it to be a true and perfect Copy; which said Books, and every one of them so exemplified under the Great

Seal of *England*, as aforesaid, shall be deemed, taken, adjudged, and expounded to be good, and available in the Law to all intents and purposes whatsoever, and shall be accounted as good Records as this Book it self hereunto annexed; Any Law or Custom to the contrary in any wise notwithstanding.

Provided also, That this Act or any thing therein contained shall not be prejudicial or hurtful unto the Kings Professor of the Law within the University of *Oxford*, for, or concerning the Prebend of *Shipton*, within the Cathedral Church of *Sarum*, united and annexed unto the place of the same Kings Professor for the time being, by the late King *James* of blessed memory.

Provided always, That whereas the Six and thirtieth Article of the Nine and thirty Articles agreed upon by the Arch-bishops, and Bishops of both Provinces, and the whole Clergy in the Convocation holden at *London*, in the year of our Lord, One thousand five hundred sixty two, for the avoiding of diversities of Opinions, and for establishing of consent, touching true Religion, is in these words following, *viz.*

That the Book of Consecration of Archbishops, and Bishops, and Ordaining of Priests and Deacons, lately set forth in the time of King Edward the Sixth, and confirmed at the same time by Authority of Parliament, doth contain all things necessary to such Consecration and Ordaining, neither hath it any thing that of it self is superstitious, and ungodly; And therefore whosoever are Consecrated or Ordered according to the Rites of that Book,° since the second year of the aforenamed King Edward unto this time, or hereafter shall be Consecrated or Ordered according to the same Rites; We decree all such to be rightly, orderly, and lawfully Consecrated and Ordered;

It be Enacted, and be it therefore Enacted by the Authority aforesaid, That all Subscriptions hereafter to be had or made unto the said Articles, by any Deacon, Priest, or Ecclesiastical person, or other person whatsoever, who by this Act or any other Law now in force is required to Subscribe unto the said Articles, shall be construed and taken to extend, and shall be applied (for and touching the said Six and thirtieth Article) unto the Book containing the form and manner of Making, Ordaining, and Consecrating of Bishops, Priests, and Deacons in this Act mentioned, in such sort and manner as the same did heretofore extend unto the Book set forth in the time of King *Edward* the Sixth, mentioned in the said Six and thirtieth Article;

Any thing in the said Article, or in any Statute, Act, or Canon heretofore had or made, to the contrary thereof in any wise notwithstanding.

Provided also, That the Book of Common Prayer, and Administration of the Sacraments and other Rites and Ceremonies of this Church of *England*, together with the form and manner of Ordaining, and Consecrating Bishops, Priests, and Deacons heretofore in use, and respectively established by Act of Parliament in the First and Eighth years of Queen *Elizabeth*, shall be still used and observed in the Church of *England*, until the Feast of Saint *Bartholomew*, which shall be in the year of our Lord God, One thousand six hundred sixty and two.

THE
PREFACE.

I T hath been the wisdom of the Church of *England*, ever since the first compiling of her publick Liturgy, to keep the mean between the two extremes,° of too much stiffness in refusing, and of too much easiness in admitting any variation from it. For, as on the one side common experience sheweth, that where a change hath been made of things advisedly established (no evident necessity so requiring) sundry inconveniences have thereupon ensued; and those many times more and greater than the evils, that were intended to be remedied by such change: So on the other side, the particular Forms of Divine worship, and the Rites and Ceremonies appointed to be used therein, being things in their own nature indifferent, and alterable,° and so acknowledged; it is but reasonable, that upon weighty and important considerations, according to the various exigency of times and occasions, such changes and alterations should be made therein, as to those that are in place of Authority should from time to time seem either necessary or expedient. Accordingly we find, that in the Reigns of several Princes of blessed memory since the Reformation, the Church, upon just and weighty considerations her thereunto moving, hath yielded to make such alterations in some particulars, as in their respective times were thought convenient: Yet so, as that the main Body and Essentials of it (as well in the chiefest materials, as in the frame and order thereof) have still continued the same unto this day, and do yet stand firm and unshaken, notwithstanding all the vain attempts and impetuous assaults° made against it, by such men as are given to change, and have always discovered a greater regard to their own private fancies and interests,° than to that duty they owe to the publick.

By what undue means, and for what mischievous purposes the use of the Liturgy (though enjoined by the Laws of the Land, and those Laws never yet repealed) came, during the late unhappy confusions, to be discontinued,° is too well known to the world, and we are not willing here to remember. But when, upon His Majesties happy Restoration, it seemed probable, that, amongst other things, the use of the Liturgy also would return of course (the same having never been legally abolished) unless some timely means were used to prevent it;

those men who under the late usurped powers had made it a great part of their business to render the people disaffected thereunto, saw themselves in point of reputation and interest concerned (unless they would freely acknowledge themselves to have erred, which such men are very hardly brought to do) with their utmost endeavours to hinder the restitution thereof. In order whereunto divers Pamphlets were published° against the Book of *Common Prayer*, the old Objections mustered up, with the addition of some new ones, more than formerly had been made, to make the number swell. In fine, great importunities were used to His Sacred Majesty, that the said Book might be revised, and such Alterations therein, and Additions thereunto made, as should be thought requisite for the ease of tender Consciences: whereunto His Majesty, out of his pious inclination to give satisfaction (so far as could be reasonably expected) to all his subjects of what persuasion soever, did graciously condescend.

In which review we have endeavoured to observe the like moderation, as we find to have been used in the like case in former times. And therefore of the sundry alterations proposed unto us, we have rejected all such as were either of dangerous consequence (as secretly striking at some established doctrine, or laudable practice of the Church of *England*, or indeed of the whole Catholick Church of Christ) or else of no consequence at all, but utterly frivolous and vain. But such alterations as were tendered to us, (by what persons, under what pretences, or to what purpose soever tendered) as seemed to us in any degree requisite or expedient, we have willingly, and of our own accord assented unto: not enforced so to do by any strength of Argument, convincing us of the necessity of making the said Alterations: For we are fully persuaded in our judgements (and we here profess it to the world) that the Book, as it stood before established by Law, doth not contain in it any thing contrary to the Word of God, or to sound Doctrine, or which a godly man may not with a good Conscience use and submit unto, or which is not fairly defensible against any that shall oppose the same; if it shall be allowed such just and favourable construction as in common equity ought to be allowed to all human Writings, especially such as are set forth by Authority, and even to the very best translations of the holy Scripture itself.

Our general aim therefore in this undertaking was, not to gratify this or that party in any their unreasonable demands; but to do that, which to our best understandings we conceived might most tend to the preservation of Peace and Unity in the Church; the procuring of Reverence, and exciting of Piety and Devotion in the publick Worship of God; and the cutting off occasion from them that seek occasion of cavil or quarrel against the Liturgy of the Church. And as to the several variations from the former Book, whether by Alteration, Addition, or otherwise, it shall suffice to give this general account. That most of the Alterations were made, either first, for the better direction of them that are to officiate in any part of Divine Service; which is chiefly done in the Kalendars and Rubricks: Or secondly, for the more proper expressing of some words or phrases of ancient usage in terms more suitable to the language of the present times, and the clearer explanation of some other words and phrases, that were either of doubtful signification, or otherwise liable to misconstruction: Or thirdly, for a more perfect rendering of such portions of holy Scripture, as are inserted into the Liturgy; which, in the Epistles and Gospels especially, and in sundry other places, are now ordered to be read according to the last Translation: and that it was thought convenient, that some Prayers and Thanksgivings, fitted to special occasions, should be added in their due places; particularly for those at Sea, together with an Office for the Baptism of such as are of Riper Years: which, although not so necessary when the former Book was compiled, yet by the growth of Anabaptism,° through the licentiousness of the late times crept in amongst us, is now become necessary, and may be always useful for the baptizing of Natives in our Plantations, and others converted to the Faith.° If any man, who shall desire a more particular account of the several Alterations in any part of the Liturgy, shall take the pains to compare the present Book with the former; we doubt not but the reason of the change may easily appear.

And having thus endeavoured to discharge our duties in this weighty affair, as in the sight of God, and to approve our sincerity therein (so far as lay in us) to the consciences of all men; although we know it impossible (in such variety of apprehensions, humours and interests, as are in the world) to please all; nor can expect that men of factious, peevish, and perverse spirits should be satisfied with any thing that can be done in this kind by any other than themselves: Yet we have good hope, that what is here presented, and hath been by the Convocations of both Provinces with great diligence examined and approved, will be also well accepted and approved by all sober, peaceable, and truly conscientious Sons of the Church of *England*.

Concerning the Service
of the CHURCH.

THERE was never any thing by the wit of man so well devised, or so sure established, which in continuance of time hath not been corrupted: As, among other things, it may plainly appear by the Common Prayers in the Church, commonly called *Divine Service*. The first original and ground whereof if a man would search out by the ancient Fathers, he shall find, that the same was not ordained but of a good purpose, and for a great advancement of godliness. For they so ordered the matter, that all the whole Bible (or the greatest part thereof) should be read over every year; intending thereby, that the Clergy, and especially such as were Ministers in the congregation, should (by often reading, and meditation in Gods word) be stirred up to godliness themselves and be more able to exhort others by wholesome Doctrine, and to confute them that were adversaries to the Truth; and further, that the people (by daily hearing of holy Scripture read in the Church) might continually profit more and more in the knowledge of God, and be the more inflamed with the love of his true Religion.

But these many years passed, this godly and decent order of the ancient Fathers hath been so altered, broken, and neglected, by planting in uncertain Stories, and Legends, with multitude of Responds, Verses, vain Repetitions, Commemorations, and Synodals; that commonly when any Book of the Bible was begun, after three or four Chapters were read out, all the rest were unread. And in this sort the Book of *Isaiah* was begun in *Advent*, and the Book of *Genesis* in *Septuagesima*; but they were only begun, and never read through: after like sort were other Books of holy Scripture used. And moreover, whereas St. *Paul* would have such language spoken to the people in the Church, as they might understand, and have profit by hearing the same; the service in this Church of *England* these many years hath been read in Latin to the people, which they understand not; so that they have heard with their ears only, and their heart, spirit and mind, have not been edified thereby. And furthermore, notwithstanding that the ancient Fathers have divided the *Psalms* into seven portions, whereof every one was called a *Nocturn*: now of late time a few of them have been daily said, and the rest utterly omitted. Moreover, the number and hardness of the Rules called the *Pie*, and the manifold changings of the service, was the cause, that to turn the book only was so hard and intricate a matter, that many times there was more business to find out what should be read, than to read it when it was found out.

These inconveniences therefore considered, here is set forth such an order, whereby the same shall be redressed. And for a readiness in this matter, here is drawn out a Kalendar for that purpose, which is plain and easy to be understood; wherein (so much as may be) the reading of holy Scripture is so set forth, that all things shall be done in order, without breaking one piece from another. For this cause be cut off Anthems, Responds, Invitatories, and such like things as did break the continual course of the reading of the Scripture.

Yet, because there is no remedy, but that of necessity there must be some Rules; therefore certain Rules are here set forth; which, as they are few in number, so they are plain and easy to be understood. So that here you have an Order for Prayer, and for the reading of the holy Scripture, much agreeable to the mind and purpose of the old Fathers, and a great deal more profitable and commodious, than that which of late was used. It is more profitable, because here are left out many things, whereof some are untrue, some uncertain, some vain and superstitious; and nothing is ordained to be read, but the very pure Word of God, the holy Scriptures, or that which is agreeable to the same; and that in such a language and order as is most easy and plain for the understanding both of the readers and hearers. It is also more commodious, both for the shortness thereof, and for the plainness of the order, and for that the rules be few and easy.

And whereas heretofore there hath been great diversity in saying and singing in Churches within this Realm; some following *Salisbury* Use, some *Hereford* Use, and some the Use of *Bangor,* some of *York,* some of *Lincoln*; now from henceforth all the whole Realm shall have but one Use.

And forasmuch as nothing can be so plainly set forth, but doubts may arise in the use and practice of the same; to appease all such diversity (if any arise) and for the resolution of all doubts, concerning the manner how to understand, do, and execute, the things contained in this Book; the parties that so doubt, or diversly take any thing, shall alway resort to the Bishop of the Diocess, who by his discretion shall take order for the quieting and appeasing of the same; so that the same order be not contrary to any thing contained in this Book. And if the Bishop of the Diocess be in doubt, then he may send for the resolution thereof to the Archbishop.

THOUGH it be appointed, that all things shall be read and sung in the Church in the *English* Tongue, to the end that the congregation may be thereby edified; yet it is not meant, but that when men say Morning and Evening Prayer privately, they may say the same in any language that they themselves do understand.

And all Priests and Deacons are to say daily the Morning and Evening Prayer either privately or openly, not being let by sickness, or some other urgent cause.

And the Curate that ministereth in every Parish-church or Chapel, being at home, and not being otherwise reasonably hindered, shall say the same in the Parish-church or Chapel where he ministereth, and shall cause a bell to be tolled thereunto a convenient time before he begin, that the people may come to hear Gods Word, and to pray with him.

❧ Of Ceremonies,

why some be abolished, and some retained.

OF such Ceremonies as be used in the Church, and have had their beginning by the institution of man, some at the first were of godly intent and purpose devised, and yet at length turned to vanity and superstition: some entered into the Church by undiscreet devotion, and such a zeal as was without knowledge; and for because they were winked at in the beginning, they grew daily to more and more abuses, which not only for their unprofitableness, but also because they have much blinded the people, and obscured the glory of God, are worthy to be cut away, and clean rejected: other there be, which although they have been devised by man, yet it is thought good to reserve them still, as well for a decent order in the Church, (for the which they were first devised) as because they pertain to edification, whereunto all things done in the Church (as the Apostle teacheth) ought to be referred.

And although the keeping or omitting of a Ceremony, in itself considered, is but a small thing; yet the wilful and contemptuous transgression and breaking of a common order and discipline is no small offence before God, *Let all things be done among you,* saith Saint *Paul, in a seemly and due order:* the appointment of the which order pertaineth not to private men; therefore no man ought to take in hand, nor presume to appoint or alter any publick or common Order in Christs Church, except he be lawfully called and authorized thereunto.

And whereas in this our time, the minds of men are so diverse, that some think it a great matter of conscience to depart from a piece of the least of their Ceremonies, they be so addicted to their old customs; and again on the other side, some be so newfangled, that they would innovate all things, and so despise the old, that nothing can like them, but that is new: it was thought expedient, not so much to have respect how to please and satisfy either of these parties, as how to please God, and profit them both. And yet lest any man should be offended, whom good reason might satisfy, here be certain causes rendered, why some of the accustomed Ceremonies be put away, and some retained and kept still.

Some are put away, because the great excess and multitude of them hath so increased in these latter days, that the burden of them was intolerable; whereof Saint *Augustine* in his time complained, that they were grown to such a number, that the estate of Christian people was in worse case concerning that matter, than were the Jews. And he counselled that such yoke and burden should be taken away, as time would serve quietly to do it. But what would Saint *Augustine* have said, if he had seen the Ceremonies of late days used among us; whereunto the multitude used in his time was not to be compared? This our excessive multitude of Ceremonies was so great, and many of them so dark, that they did more confound and darken, than declare and set forth Christs benefits unto us. And besides this, Christs Gospel is not a Ceremonial Law (as much of *Moses* Law was) but it is a Religion to serve God, not in bondage of the figure or shadow, but in the freedom of the Spirit;° being content only with those Ceremonies which do serve to a decent order and godly discipline, and such as be apt to stir up the dull mind of man to the remembrance of his duty to God, by some notable and special signification, whereby he might be edified. Furthermore, the most weighty cause of the abolishment of certain Ceremonies was, That they were so far abused, partly by the superstitious blindness of the rude and unlearned, and partly by the unsatiable avarice of such as sought more their own lucre, than the glory of God, that the abuses could not well be taken away, the thing remaining still.

But now as concerning those persons, which peradventure will be offended, for that some of the old Ceremonies are retained still: If they consider that without some Ceremonies it is not possible to keep any order, or quiet discipline in the Church, they shall easily perceive just cause to reform their judgements. And if they think much, that any of the old do remain, and would rather have all devised anew: then such men granting some Ceremonies convenient to be had, surely where the old may be well used, there they cannot reasonably reprove the old only for their age, without bewraying of their own folly. For in such a case they ought rather to have reverence unto them for their antiquity, if they will declare themselves to be more studious of unity and concord, than of innovations and new-fangleness, which (as much as may be with the true setting forth of Christs Religion) is always to be eschewed. Furthermore, such shall have no just cause with the Ceremonies reserved to be offended. For as those be taken away which were most abused, and did burden mens consciences without any cause; so the other that remain, are retained for a discipline and order, which (upon just causes) may be altered and changed, and therefore are not to be esteemed equal with Gods Law. And moreover, they be neither dark nor dumb Ceremonies, but are so set forth, that every man may understand what they do mean, and to what use they do serve. So that it is not like that they in time to come should be abused as other have been. And in these our doings we condemn no other nations, nor prescribe any thing but to our own people only: For we think it convenient that every country should use such Ceremonies as they shall think best to the setting forth of Gods honour and glory, and to the reducing of the people to a most perfect and godly living, without error or superstition; and that they should put away other things, which from time to time they perceive to be most abused, as in mens ordinances it often chanceth diversely in divers countries.

❧ The ORDER
how the Psalter is appointed to be read.

THE Psalter shall be read through once every Month, as it is there appointed, both for Morning and Evening Prayer. But in *February* it shall be read only to the Twenty eighth, or Twenty ninth day of the month.

And, whereas *January*, *March*, *May*, *July*, *August*, *October*, and *December* have One and thirty days apiece; It is ordered, that the same Psalms shall be read the last day of the said months, which were read the day before: so that the Psalter may begin again the first day of the next month ensuing.

And, whereas the CXIX Psalm is divided into XXII portions, and is overlong to be read at one time; It is so ordered, that at one time shall not be read above four or five of the said Portions.

And at the end of every Psalm, and of every such part of the CXIX Psalm, shall be repeated this Hymn,

Glory be to the Father, and to the Son: and to the Holy Ghost;

As it was in the beginning, is now, and ever shall be; world without end.
Amen.

Note, that the Psalter followeth the Division of the Hebrews, and the Translation of the great English Bible, set forth and used in the time of King *Henry* the Eighth and *Edward* the Sixth.

❧ The ORDER
how the rest of holy Scripture is appointed to be read.

THE Old Testament is appointed for the first Lessons at Morning and Evening Prayer, so as the most part thereof will be read every year once,° as in the Kalendar is appointed.

The New Testament is appointed for the second Lessons at Morning and Evening Prayer, and shall be read over orderly every year thrice, besides the Epistles and Gospels; except the Apocalyps, out of which there are only certain proper Lessons appointed upon divers feasts.

And to know what Lessons shall be read every day, look for the day of the month in the Kalendar following, and there ye shall find the Chapters that shall be read for the Lessons both at Morning and Evening Prayer; except only the Moveable Feasts, which are not in the Kalendar, and the Immovable, where there is a blanck left in the column of Lessons; the proper Lessons for all which days are to be found in the Table of the proper Lessons.

And note, that whensoever proper Psalms or Lessons are appointed; then the Psalms and Lessons of ordinary course appointed in the Psalter and Kalendar (if they be different) shall be omitted for that time.

Note also that the Collect, Epistle, and Gospel appointed for the Sunday shall serve all the week after, where it is not in this book otherwise ordered.

¶ Proper LESSONS to be Read at Morning and
Evening Prayer on the Sundays, and other Holidays throughout the year.

¶ *Lessons proper for Sundays.*

	Mattins	Evensong
Sundays of Advent		
The first	Isa. 1	Isa. 2
2	5	24
3	25	26
4	30	32
Sundays after Christmas		
The first	37	38
2	41	43
Sundays after the Epiphany		
The first	44	46
2	51	53
3	55	56
4	57	58
5	59	64
6	65	66
Septuagesima	Gen. 1	Gen. 2
Sexagesima	3	6
Quinquagesima	9.1–20	12
Lent		
First Sunday	19.1–30	22
2	27	34
3	39	42
4	43	45
5	Ex. 3	Ex. 5
6 1. Lesson	9	10
2. Lesson	Matt. 26	Heb. 5. 1–11

	Mattins	Evensong
Easter day		
1. Lesson	Ex. 12	Ex. 14
2. Lesson	Rom. 6	Acts 2. 1–22
Sundays after Easter		
The first	Num. 16	Num. 22
2	23, 24	25
3	Deut. 4	Deut. 5
4	6	7
5	8	9
Sunday after Ascension day	12	13
Whitsunday		
1. Lesson.	Deut. 16. 1–18	Isa. 11
2. Lesson.	Acts 10. 1–34	Acts 19. 1–21
Trinity Sunday		
1. Lesson	Gen. 1	Gen. 18
2. Lesson	Matt. 3	1 John 5
Sundays after Trinity		
The first	Josh. 10	Josh. 23
2	Judg. 4	Judg. 5
3	1 Sam. 2	1 Sam. 3
4	12	13
5	15	17
6	2 Sam. 12	2 Sam. 19
7	21	24

	Mattins	Evensong		Mattins	Evensong
Sundays after Trinity (cont.)			*Sundays after Trinity (cont.)*		
8	1 *Kings*	1 *Kings*	17	14	18
	13	17	18	20	24
9	18	19	19	*Dan.* 3	*Dan.* 6
10	21	22	20	*Joel* 2	*Mic.* 6
11	2 *Kings* 5	2 *Kings* 9	21	*Hab.* 2	*Prov.* 1
12	10	18	22	*Prov.* 2	3
13	19	23	23	11	12
14	*Jer.* 5	*Jer.* 22	24	13	14
15	35	36	25	15	16
16	*Ezek.* 2	*Ezek.* 13	26	17	19

¶ Lessons proper for Holidays.

	Mattins	Evensong		Mattins	Evensong
S. Andrew	*Prov.* 20	*Prov.* 21	*Conversion of S. Paul*		
S. Thomas the Apostle	23	24	1. Lesson	*Wisd.* 5	*Wisd.* 6
Nativity of CHRIST			2. Lesson	*Acts* 22.	*Acts* 26
1. Lesson	*Isa.* 9.	*Isa.* 7.		1–22	
	1–8	10–17	*Purification of the Virgin Mary*	*Wisd.* 9	*Wisd.* 12
2. Lesson	*Luke* 2.	*Tit.* 3.	*S. Matthias*	*Wisd.* 19	*Ecclus.* 1
	1–15	4–9	*Annunciation of our Lady*	*Ecclus.* 2	3
S. Steven			*Wednesday before Easter*		
1. Lesson	*Prov.* 28	*Ecc.* 4	1. Lesson	*Hos.* 13	*Hos.* 14
2. Lesson	*Acts* 6. 8. & 7. 1–30	*Acts* 7. 30–55	2. Lesson	*John* 11. 1–45	
S. John			*Thursday before Easter*		
1. Lesson	*Ecc.* 5	*Ecc.* 6	1. Lesson	*Dan.* 9.	*Jer.* 31
2. Lesson	*Rev.* 1	*Rev.* 22	2. Lesson	*John* 13	
Innocents Day	*Jer.* 31. 1–18	*Wisd.* 1	*Good Friday*		
Circumcision			1. Lesson	*Gen.* 22. 1–20	*Isa.* 53
1. Lesson	*Gen.* 17	*Deut.* 10. 1–12	2. Lesson	*John* 18	1 *Pet.* 2
2. Lesson	*Rom.* 2	*Col.* 2	*Easter Even*		
Epiphany			1. Lesson	*Zech.* 9	*Ex.* 13
1. Lesson	*Isa.* 60	*Isa.* 49	2. Lesson	*Luke* 23. 1–50	*Heb.* 4
2. Lesson	*Luke* 3. 1–23	*John* 2. 1–12			

	Mattins	Evensong
Munday in Easter week		
1. Lesson	Ex. 16	Ex. 17
2. Lesson	Matt. 28	Acts. 3
Tuesday in Easter week		
1. Lesson	Ex. 20	Ex. 32
2. Lesson	Luke 24.	1 Cor. 15
		1–13
S. Mark	Ecclus. 4	Ecclus. 5
S. Philip and S. James		
1. Lesson	7	
2. Lesson	John 1.	9
		1–43
Ascension day		
1. Lesson	Deut. 10	2 Kings 2
2. Lesson	Luke 24.	Eph. 4.
		1–44	1–17
Munday in Whitsun-week		
1. Lesson	Gen. 11.	Num. 11.
		1–10	16–30
2. Lesson	1 Cor. 12	1 Cor. 14.
		1–26
Tuesday in Whitsun-week		
1. Lesson	1 Sam. 19.	Deut. 30
		1–18
2. Lesson	1 Thess. 5.	1 John 4.
		12–24	1–14

	Mattins	Evensong
S. Barnabas		
1. Lesson	Ecclus. 10	Ecclus. 12
2. Lesson	Acts 14	Acts 15.
		1–36
S. John Baptist		
1. Lesson	Mal. 3	Mal. 4
2. Lesson	Matt. 3	Matt. 14.
		1–13
S. Peter		
1. Lesson	Ecclus. 15	Ecclus. 19
2. Lesson	Acts 3	Acts 4
S. James	Ecclus. 21	Ecclus. 22
S. Bartholomew	24	29
S. Matthew	35	38
S. Michael		
1. Lesson	Gen. 32	Dan. 10.
		1–5
2. Lesson	Acts 12.	Jude 6.
		1–20	1–16
S. Luke	Ecclus. 51	Job 1
S. Simon and S. Jude	Job 24, 25	42
All Saints		
1. Lesson	Wisd. 3.	Wisd. 5.
		1–10	1–17
2. Lesson	Heb. 11.	Rev. 19.
		33 & 12.	1–17
		1–7

¶ *Proper Psalms on certain days.*

	Mattins	Evensong
Christmas-day	Ps. 19	89
	45	110
	85	132
Ash-Wednesday	6	102
	32	130
	38	143
Good-Friday	22	69
	40	88
	54	

	Mattins	Evensong
Easter-day	2	113
	57	114
	111	118
Ascension-day	8	24
	15	47
	21	108
Whit-Sunday	48	104
	68	145

The Kalendar.

January hath 31 Days

The Moon hath 30

					Morning Prayer		Evening Prayer	
					1 Lesson	2 Lesson	1 Lesson	2 Lesson
2	1	*A.*	*Kalend.*	CIRCUMCISION OF OUR LORD				
	2	*B.*	4 *No.*		*Gen.* 1	*Matt.* 1	*Gen.* 2	*Rom.* 1
10	3	*C.*	3 *No.*		3	2	4	2
	4	*D.*	pr. *No.*		5	3	6	3
19	5	*E.*	*Nonæ*		7	4	8	4
8	6	*F.*	8 *Id.*	EPIPHANY OF OUR LORD				
	7	*G.*	7 *Id.*		9	5	12	5
16	8	*A.*	6 *Id.*	Lucian, Priest and Martyr	13	6	14	6
5	9	*B.*	5 *Id.*		15	7	16	7
	10	*C.*	4 *Id.*		17	8	18	8
13	11	*D.*	3 *Id.*		19	9	20	9
2	12	*E.*	pr. *Id.*		21	10	22	10
	13	*F.*	*Idus*	Hilary, Bishop & Confessor	23	11	24	11
10	14	*G.*	19 *Kl. Febr.*		25	12	26	12
	15	*A.*	18 *Kl.*		27	13	28	13
18	16	*B.*	17 *Kl.*		29	14	30	14
7	17	*C.*	16 *Kl.*		31	15	32	15
	18	*D.*	15 *Kl.*	Prisca, Roman Virgin & Martyr°	33	16	34	16
15	19	*E.*	14 *Kl.*		35	17	37	1 *Cor.* 1
4	20	*F.*	13 *Kl.*	Fabian, B. of Rome & M.	38	18	39	2
	21	*G.*	12 *Kl.*	Agnes, Rom. Virg. & Mart.	40	19	41	3
12	22	*A.*	11 *Kl.*	Vincent, Spanish Deacon & M.	42	20	43	4
1	23	*B.*	10 *Kl.*		44	21	45	5
	24	*C.*	9 *Kl.*		46	22	47	6
9	25	*D.*	8 *Kl.*	CONVERSION OF S. PAUL				
	26	*E.*	7 *Kl.*		48	23	49	7
17	27	*F.*	6 *Kl.*		50	24	*Ex.* 1	8
6	28	*G.*	5 *Kl.*		*Ex.* 2	25	3	9
	29	*A.*	4 *Kl.*		4	26	5	10
13	30	*B.*	3 *Kl.*	KING CHARLES MARTYR°	6. 1–14	27	7	11
3	31	*C.*	prid. *Kl.*		8	28	9	12

February hath 28 Days

The Moon hath 30

						Morning Prayer		Evening Prayer	
						1 Lesson	2 Lesson	1 Lesson	2 Lesson
	1	*D.*	*Kalend.*		*Fast*	*Ex.* 10	*Mark* 1	*Ex.* 11	1 *Cor.* 13
11	2	*E.*	4 *No.*	PURIFICATION OF MARY THE BLESSED VIRGIN			2		14
19	3	*F.*	3 *No.*			12	3	13	15
8	4	*G.*	*pr. No.*			14	4	15	16
	5	*A.*	*Nonæ*	*Agatha, a Sicilian V. & M.*		16	5	17	2 *Cor.* 1
16	6	*B.*	8 *Id.*			18	6	19	2
5	7	*C.*	7 *Id.*			20	7	21	3
	8	*D.*	6 *Id.*			22	8	23	4
13	9	*E.*	5 *Id.*			24	9	32	5
2	10	*F.*	4 *Id.*			33	10	34	6
	11	*G.*	3 *Id.*			*Lev.* 18	11	*Lev.* 19	7
10	12	*A.*	*pr. Id.*			20	12	26	8
	13	*B.*	*Idus*			*Num.* 11	13	*Num.* 12	9
18	14	*C.*	16 *Kl. Mart.*	*Valentine, Bishop & Martyr*		13	14	14	10
7	15	*D.*	15 *Kl.*			16	15	17	11
16	16	*E.*	14 *Kl.*			20	16	21	12
15	17	*F.*	13 *Kl.*			22	*Luke* 1. 1–39	23	13
4	18	*G.*	12 *Kl.*			24	1, 39–80	25	*Gal.* 1
	19	*A.*	11 *Kl.*			27	2	30	2
12	20	*B.*	10 *Kl.*			31	3	32	3
1	21	*C.*	9 *Kl.*			35	4	36	4
	22	*D.*	8 *Kl.*			*Deut.* 1	5	*Deut.* 2	5
9	23	*E.*	7 *Kl.*		*Fast*	3	6	4	6
	24	*F.*	6 *Kl.*	S. MATTHIAS, APOSTLE & M.			7		*Eph.* 1
17	25	*G.*	5 *Kl.*			5	8	6	2
6	26	*A.*	4 *Kl.*			7	9	8	3
	27	*B.*	3 *Kl.*			9	10	10	4
14	28	*C.*	*pr. Kl.*			11	11	12	5
	29	*D.*				13	*Matt.* 7	14	*Rom.* 12

March hath 31 days

The Moon hath 30

					Morning Prayer		Evening Prayer	
					1 Lesson	2 Lesson	1 Lesson	2 Lesson
3	1	D.	Kalend.	David, Archbishop of Menevia°	Deut. 15	Luke 12	Deut. 16	Eph. 6
	2	E.	6 No.	Cedde or Chad, Bishop of Litchfield	17	13	18	Phil. 1
11	3	F.	5 No.		19	14	20	2
	4	G.	4 No.		21	15	22	3
19	5	A.	3 No.		24	16	25	4
8	6	B.	pr. No.		26	17	27	Col. 1
	7	C.	Nonæ	Perpetua of Mauritania, Martyr	28	18	29	2
16	8	D.	8 Id.		30	19	31	3
5	9	E.	7 Id.		32	20	33	4
	10	F.	6 Id.		34	21	Josh. 1	1 Thess. 1
13	11	G.	5 Id.		Josh. 2	22	3	2
2	12	A.	4 Id.	Gregory, B. of Rome, & Confessor	4	23	5	3
	13	B.	3 Id.		6	24	7	4
10	14	C.	pr. Id.		8	John. 1	9	5
	15	D.	Idus		10	2	23	2 Thess. 1
18	16	E.	17 Kl. Apr.		14	3	Judg. 1	2
7	17	F.	16 Kl.		Judg. 2	4	3	3
	18	G.	15 Kl.	Edward K. of the West-Saxons°	4	5	5	1 Tim. 1
15	19	A.	14 Kl.		6	6	7	2, 3
4	20	B.	13 Kl.		8	7	9	4
	21	C.	12 Kl.	Benedict, Abbot	10	8	11	5
12	22	D.	11 Kl.		12	9	13	6
1	23	E.	10 Kl.		14	10	15	2 Tim. 1
	24	F.	9 Kl.	Fast	16	11	17	2
9	25	G.	8 Kl.	ANNUNCIATION OF MARY		12		3
	26	A.	7 Kl.		18	13	19	4
17	27	B.	6 Kl.		20	14	21	Tit. 1
6	28	C.	5 Kl.		Ruth 1	15	Ruth 2	2, 3
	29	D.	4 Kl.		3	16	4	Philem.
14	30	E.	3 Kl.		1 Sam. 1	17	1 Sam. 2	Heb. 1
3	31	F.	pr. Kl.		3	18	4	2

April hath 30 days
The Moon hath 29

					Morning Prayer		Evening Prayer	
					1 Lesson	2 Lesson	1 Lesson	2 Lesson
	1	G.	Kalend.		1 Sam. 5	John 19	1 Sam. 6	Heb. 3
9	2	A.	4 No.		7	20	8	4
	3	B.	3 No.	Richard, Bishop of Chichester	9	21	10	5
19	4	C.	pr. No.	Ambrose, Bishop of Milan	11	Acts 1	12	6
8	5	D.	Nonæ		13	2	14	7
16	6	E.	8 Id.		15	3	16	8
5	7	F.	7 Id.		17	4	18	9
	8	G.	6 Id.		19	5	20	10
13	9	A.	5 Id.		21	6	22	11
2	10	B.	4 Id.		23	7	24	12
	11	C.	3 Id.		25	8	26	13
10	12	D.	pr. Id.		27	9	28	Jas. 1
	13	E.	Idus		29	10	30	2
18	14	F.	18 Kl. Maij.		31	11	2 Sam. 1	3
7	15	G.	17 Kl.		2 Sam. 2	12	3	4
	16	A.	16 Kl.		4	13	5	5
15	17	B.	15 Kl.		6	14	7	1 Pet. 1
4	18	C.	14 Kl.		8	15	9	2
	19	D.	13 Kl.	Alphege, Archbishop of Canterbury	10	16	11	3
12	20	E.	12 Kl.		12	17	13	4
1	21	F.	11 Kl.		14	18	15	5
	22	G.	10 Kl.		16	19	17	2 Pet. 1
9	23	A.	9 Kl.	S. George, Martyr°	18	20	19	2
	24	B.	8 Kl.		20	21	21	3
17	25	C.	7 Kl.	S. MARK EVANGELIST & MARTYR		22		1 John 1
6	26	D.	6 Kl.		22	23	23	2
	27	E.	5 Kl.		24	24	1 Kings 1	3
14	28	F.	4 Kl.		1 Kings 2	25	3	4
3	29	G.	3 Kl.		4	26	5	5
	30	A.	pr. Kl.		6	27	7	2, 3 John

May hath 31 days

The Moon hath 30

					Morning Prayer		Evening Prayer	
					1 Lesson	2 Lesson	1 Lesson	2 Lesson
2	1	B.	Kalend.	S. PHILIP, & S. JAMES APOSTLE & M.				Jude
	2	C.	6 No.		1 Kings 8	Acts 28	1 Kings 9	Rom. 1
19	3	D.	5 No.	Invention of the Cross°	10	Mat. 1	11	2
8	4	E.	4 No.		12	2	13	3
	5	F.	3 No.		14	3	15	4
16	6	G.	pr. No.	S. John Evang. ante port. Latin.°	16	4	17	5
5	7	A.	Nonæ		18	5	19	6
	8	B.	8 Id.		20	6	21	7
13	9	C.	7 Id.		22	7	2 Kings 1	8
2	10	D.	6 Id.		2 Kings 2	8	3	9
	11	E.	5 Id.		4	9	5	10
10	12	F.	4 Id.		6	10	7	11
	13	G.	3 Id.		8	11	9	12
18	14	A.	pr. Id.		10	12	11	13
7	15	B.	Idus		12	13	13	14
	16	C.	17 Kl. Iunij.		14	14	15	15
15	17	D.	16 Kl.		16	15	17	16
4	18	E.	15 Kl.		18	16	19	1 Cor. 1
	19	F.	14 Kl.	Dunstan, Archbishop of Canterbury	20	17	21	2
12	20	G.	13 Kl.		22	18	23	3
1	21	A.	12 Kl.		24	19	25	4
	22	B.	11 Kl.		Ezra 1	20	Ezra 3	5
9	23	C.	10 Kl.		4	21	5	6
	24	D.	9 Kl.		6	22	7	7
17	25	E.	8 Kl.		9	23	Neh. 1	8
6	26	F.	7 Kl.	Augustine, first Archbishop of Canterbury	Neh. 2	24	4	9
	27	G.	6 Kl.	Venerable Bede, priest°	5	25	6	10
14	28	A.	5 Kl.		8	26	9	11
3	29	B.	4 Kl.	CHARLES II, NATIVITY AND RETURN°	10	27	13	12
	30	C.	3 Kl.		Esth. 1	28	Esth. 2	13
11	31	D.	pr. Kl.		3	Mark 1	4	14

June hath 30 days

The Moon hath 29

					Morning Prayer		Evening Prayer	
					1 Lesson	2 Lesson	1 Lesson	2 Lesson
	1	*E.*	*Kalend.*	Nicomede, Rom. Priest & Martyr	*Esth.* 5	*Mark* 2	*Esth.* 6	1 *Cor.* 15
19	2	*F.*	4 *No.*		7	3	8	16
8	3	*G.*	3 *No.*		9	4	*Job* 1	2 *Cor.* 1
16	4	*A.*	pr. *No.*		*Job* 2	5	3	2
5	5	*B.*	*Nonæ*	Boniface, B. of Mentz & Martyr	4	6	5	3
	6	*C.*	8 *Id.*		6	7	7	4
13	7	*D.*	7 *Id.*		8	8	9	5
2	8	*E.*	6 *Id.*		10	9	11	6
	9	*F.*	5 *Id.*		12	10	13	7
10	10	*G.*	4 *Id.*		14	11	15	8
	11	*A.*	3 *Id.*	S. BARNABAS APOSTLE & MARTYR				
18	12	*B.*	pr. *Id.*		16	12	17, 18	9
7	13	*C.*	*Idus*		19	13	20	10
	14	*D.*	18 *Kl. Iulii.*		21	14	22	11
15	15	*E.*	17 *Kl.*		23	15	24, 25	12
4	16	*F.*	16 *Kl.*		26, 27	16	28	13
	17	*G.*	15 *Kl.*	S. Alban Martyr	29	*Luke* 1	30	*Gal.* 1
12	18	*A.*	14 *Kl.*		31	2	32	2
1	19	*B.*	13 *Kl.*		33	3	34	3
	20	*C.*	12 *Kl.*	Translation of Edward K. of the W. Saxons	35	4	36	4
9	21	*D.*	11 *Kl.*		37	5	38	5
	22	*E.*	10 *Kl.*		39	6	40	6
17	23	*F.*	9 *Kl.*	*Fast*	41	7	42	*Eph.* 1
6	24	*G.*	8 *Kl.*	NATIVITY OF S. JOHN BAPTIST				
	25	*A.*	7 *Kl.*		*Prov.* 1	8	*Prov.* 2	2
14	26	*B.*	6 *Kl.*		3	9	4	3
3	27	*C.*	5 *Kl.*		5	10	6	4
	28	*D.*	4 *Kl.*	*Fast*	7	11	8	5
9	29	*E.*	3 *Kl.*	S. PETER APOSTLE & MARTYR				
	30	*F.*	pr. *Kl.*		9	12	10	6

July hath 31 days

The Moon hath 30

					Morning Prayer		Evening Prayer	
					1 Lesson	2 Lesson	1 Lesson	2 Lesson
19	1	G.	Kalend.		Prov. 11	Luke 13	Prov. 12	Phil. 1
8	2	A.	6 No.	Visitation of the Bl. Virgin Mary	13	14	14	2
	3	B.	5 No.		15	15	16	3
16	4	C.	4 No.	Translation of S. Martin B. & Confessor	17	16	18	4
5	5	D.	3 No.		19	17	20	Col. 1
	6	E.	pr. No.		21	18	22	2
13	7	F.	Nonæ		23	19	24	3
2	8	G.	8 Id.		25	20	26	4
	9	A.	7 Id.		27	21	28	1 Thes. 1
10	10	B.	6 Id.		29	22	31	2
	11	C.	5 Id.		Ecc. 1	23	Ecc. 2	3
18	12	D.	4 Id.		3	24	4	4
7	13	E.	3 Id.		5	John 1	6	5
	14	F.	pr. Id.		7	2	8	2 Thess. 1
15	15	G.	Idus	Swithun, B. of Winchester Translated	9	3	10	2
4	16	A.	17 Kl. Aug.		11	4	12	3
	17	B.	16 Kl.		Jer. 1	5	Jer. 2	1 Tim. 1
12	18	C.	15 Kl.		3	6	4	2, 3
1	19	D.	14 Kl.		5	7	6	4
	20	E.	13 Kl.	Margaret, Virgin & Martyr at Antioch	7	8	8	5
9	21	F.	12 Kl.	S. Mary Magdalen	9	9	10	6
	22	G.	11 Kl.		11	10	12	2 Tim. 1
17	23	A.	10 Kl.		13	11	14	2
6	24	B.	9 Kl.	Fast	15	12	16	3
	25	C.	8 Kl.	S. JAMES APOSTLE & MARTYR		13		4
14	26	D.	7 Kl.	S. Anne, mother to the Bl. Virgin Mary	17	14	18	Tit. 1
3	27	E.	6 Kl.		19	15	20	2, 3
	28	F.	5 Kl.		21	16	22	Philem.
9	29	G.	4 Kl.		23	17	24	Heb. 1
	30	A.	3 Kl.		25	18	26	2
19	31	B.	pr. Kl.		27	19	28	3

August hath 31 days

The Moon hath 30

					Morning Prayer		Evening Prayer	
					1 Lesson	2 Lesson	1 Lesson	2 Lesson
8	1	C.	Kalend.	Lammas day°	Jer. 29	John 20	Jer. 30	Heb. 4
16	2	D.	4 No.		31	21	32	5
5	3	E.	3 No.		33	Acts 1	34	6
	4	F.	pr. No.		35	2	36	7
13	5	G.	Nonæ		37	3	38	8
2	6	A.	8 Id.	Transfiguration of our Lord	39	4	40	9
	7	B.	7 Id.	Name of Jesus°	41	5	42	10
10	8	C.	6 Id.		43	6	44	11
	9	D.	5 Id.		45, 46	7	47	12
18	10	E.	4 Id.	S. Laurence, Archdeacon of Rome & Mart.	48	8	49	13
7	11	F.	3 Id.		50	9	51	Jas. 1
	12	G.	pr. Id.		52	10	Lam. 1	2
15	13	A.	Idus		Lam. 2	11	3	3
4	14	B.	19 Kl. Sept.		4	12	5	4
	15	C.	18 Kl.		Ezek. 2	13	Ezek. 3	5
12	16	D.	17 Kl.		6	14	7	1 Pet. 1
1	17	E.	16 Kl.		13	15	14	2
	18	F.	15 Kl.		18	16	33	3
9	19	G.	14 Kl.		34	17	Dan. 1	4
	20	A.	13 Kl.		Dan. 2	18	3	5
17	21	B.	12 Kl.		4	19	5	2 Pet. 1
6	22	C.	11 Kl.		6	20	7	2
	23	D.	10 Kl.	Fast	8	21	9	3
14	24	E.	9 Kl.	S. BARTHOLOMEW APOSTLE & MARTYR		22		1 John 1
3	25	F.	8 Kl.		10	23	11	2
	26	G.	7 Kl.		12	24	Hos. 1	3
11	27	A.	6 Kl.		Hos. 2, 3	25	4	4
	28	B.	5 Kl.	S. Augustine Bishop of Hippo, Confessor & Doctor	5, 6	26	7	5
19	29	C.	4 Kl.	Beheading of S. John Baptist	8	27	9	2, 3 John
8	30	D.	3 Kl.		10	28	11	Jude
	31	E.	pr. Kl.		12	Matt. 1	13	Rom. 1

September hath 30 days

The Moon hath 29

					Morning Prayer		Evening Prayer	
					1 Lesson	2 Lesson	1 Lesson	2 Lesson
16	1	F.	Kalend.	Giles, Abbot & Confessor	Hos. 14	Matt. 2	Joel 1	Rom. 2
5	2	G.	4 No.		Joel 2	3	3	3
	3	A.	3 No.		Amos 1	4	Amos 2	4
13	4	B.	pr. No.		3	5	4	5
2	5	C.	Nonæ		5	6	6	6
	6	D.	8 Id.		7	7	8	7
10	7	E.	7 Id.	Enurchus, Bishop of Orleans°	9	8	Obad.	8
	8	F.	6 Id.	Nativity of the Bl. Virgin Mary	Jon. 1	9	Jon. 2 3	9
18	9	G.	5 Id.		4	10	Mic. 1	10
7	10	A.	4 Id.		Mic. 2	11	3	11
	11	B.	3 Id.		4	12	5	12
15	12	C.	pr. Id.		6	13	7	13
4	13	D.	Idus		Nah. 1	14	Nah. 2	14
	14	E.	18 Kl. Octob.	Holy-Cross day°	3	15	Hab. 1	15
12	15	F.	17 Kl.		Hab. 2	16	3	16
1	16	G.	16 Kl.		Zeph. 1	17	Zeph. 2	1 Cor. 1
	17	A.	15 Kl.	Lambert, Bishop & Martyr	3	18	Hag. 1	2
9	18	B.	14 Kl.		Hag. 2	19	Zech. 1	3
	19	C.	13 Kl.		Zech. 2 3	20	4, 5	4
17	20	D.	12 Kl.	Fast	6	21	7	5
6	21	E.	11 Kl.	S. MATTHEW APOSTLE, EVANGELIST & MARTYR		22		6
	22	F.	10 Kl.		8	23	9	7
14	23	G.	9 Kl.		10	24	11	8
3	24	A.	8 Kl.		12	25	13	9
	25	B.	7 Kl.		14	26	Mal. 1	10
11	26	C.	6 Kl.	S. Cyprian, Archb. of Carthage & M.	Mal. 2	27	3	11
19	27	D.	5 Kl.		4	28	Tob. 1	12
	28	E.	4 Kl.		Tob. 2	Mark 1	3	13
8	29	F.	3 Kl.	S. MICHAEL, & ALL ANGELS°		2		14
	30	G.	pr. Kl.	S. Jerome, Priest, Confessor & Doctor	4	3	6	15

October hath 31 days

The Moon hath 30

					Morning Prayer		Evening Prayer	
					1 Lesson	2 Lesson	1 Lesson	2 Lesson
16	1	*A.*	*Kalend.*	Remigius, B. of Rhemes	*Tob.* 7	*Mark* 4	*Tob.* 8	1 *Cor.* 16
5	2	*B.*	6 *No.*		9	5	10	2 *Cor.* 1
13	3	*C.*	5 *No.*		11	6	12	2
2	4	*D.*	4 *No.*		13	7	14	3
	5	*E.*	3 *No.*		*Jud.* 1	8	*Jud.* 2	4
10	6	*F.*	*pr. No.*	Faith, Virgin & Martyr	3	9	4	5
	7	*G.*	*Nonæ*		5	10	6	6
18	8	*A.*	8 *Id.*		7	11	8	7
7	9	*B.*	7 *Id.*	S. Denys Areopagite, Bishop & M.	9	12	10	8
	10	*C.*	6 *Id.*		11	13	12	9
15	11	*D.*	5 *Id.*		13	14	14	10
4	12	*E.*	4 *Id.*		15	15	16	11
	13	*F.*	3 *Id.*	Translation of K. Edward Confessor	Wisd. 1	16	Wisd. 2	12
12	14	*G.*	*pr. Id.*		3	*Luke* 1. 1–39	4	13
1	15	*A.*	*Idus*		4	1.39–end	5	*Gal.* 1
	16	*B.*	17 *Kl. Nov.*		7	2	8	2
9	17	*C.*	16 *Kl.*	Etheldred, Virgin	9	3	10	3
	18	*D.*	15 *Kl.*	S. LUKE EVANGELIST		4		4
17	19	*E.*	14 *Kl.*		11	5	12	5
6	20	*F.*	13 *Kl.*		13	6	14	6
	21	*G.*	12 *Kl.*		15	7	16	*Eph.* 1
14	22	*A.*	11 *Kl.*		17	8	18	2
3	23	*B.*	10 *Kl.*		19	9	*Ecclus.* 1	3
	24	*C.*	9 *Kl.*		*Ecclus.* 2	10	3	4
11	25	*D.*	8 *Kl.*	Crispin, Martyr	4	11	5	5
19	26	*E.*	7 *Kl.*		6	12	7	6
	27	*F.*	6 *Kl.*	*Fast*	8	13	9	*Phil.* 1
8	28	*G.*	5 *Kl.*	S. SIMON & S. JUDE APOSTLES & M.		14		2
	29	*A.*	4 *Kl.*		10	15	11	3
16	30	*B.*	3 *Kl.*		12	16	13	4
5	31	*C.*	*pr. Kl.*	*Fast*	14	17	15	*Col.* 1

November hath 30 days

The Moon hath 29

					Morning Prayer		Evening Prayer	
					1 Lesson	2 Lesson	1 Lesson	2 Lesson
	1	D.	Kalend.	ALL SAINTS DAY				
13	2	E.	4 No.		Ecclus. 16	Luke 18	Ecclus. 17	Col. 2
2	3	F.	3 No.		18	19	19	3
	4	G.	pr. No.		20	20	21	4
10	5	A.	Nonæ	PAPISTS CONSPIRACY°	22	21	23	1 Thess. 1
	6	B.	8 Id.	Leonard, Confessor	24	22	25.1–13	2
18	7	C.	7 Id.		27	23	28	3
7	8	D.	6 Id.		29	24	30.1–18	4
	9	E.	5 Id.		31	John 1	32	5
15	10	F.	4 Id.		33	2	34	2 Thess. 1
4	11	G.	3 Id.	S. Martin, Bishop & Confessor	35	3	36	2
	12	A.	pr. Id.		37	4	38	3
12	13	B.	Idus	Britius, Bishop	39	5	40	1 Tim. 1
1	14	C.	18 Kl. Dec.		41	6	42	2, 3
	15	D.	17 Kl.	Machutus, Bishop	43	7	44	4
9	16	E.	16 Kl.		45	8	46.1–20	5
	17	F.	15 Kl.	Hugh, Bishop of Lincoln.°	47	9	48	6
17	18	G.	14 Kl.		49	10	50	2 Tim. 1
6	19	A.	13 Kl.		51	11	Bar. 1	2
	20	B.	12 Kl.	Edmund, King & Martyr	Bar. 2	12	3	3
14	21	C.	11 Kl.		4	13	5	4
3	22	D.	10 Kl.	Cecilia, Virgin & Martyr	6	14	Sus.	Titus 1
	23	E.	9 Kl.	S. Clement I, Bishop of Rome & Martyr	Bel & Dragon	15	Isa. 1	2, 3
11	24	F.	8 Kl.		Isa. 2	16	3	Philem.
19	25	G.	7 Kl.	Catherine, Virgin & Martyr	4	17	5	Heb. 1
	26	A.	6 Kl.		6	18	7	2
8	27	B.	5 Kl.		8	19	9	3
	28	C.	4 Kl.		10	20	11	4
16	29	D.	3 Kl.	Fast	12	21	13	5
5	30	E.	pr. Kl.	S. ANDREW APOSTLE & MARTYR		Acts 1		6

December hath 31 days

The Moon hath 30

					Morning Prayer		Evening Prayer	
					1 Lesson	2 Lesson	1 Lesson	2 Lesson
	1	F.	Kalend.		Isa. 14	Acts 2	Isa. 15	Heb. 7
13	2	G.	4 No.		16	3	17	8
2	3	A.	3 No.		18	4	19	9
10	4	B.	pr. No.		20, 21	5	22	10
	5	C.	Nonæ		23	6	24	11
18	6	D.	8 Id.	Nicholas, Bishop of Myra in Lycia	25	7.1–30	26	12
7	7	E.	7 Id.		27	7.30–end	28	13
	8	F.	6 Id.	Conception of the Bl. Virgin Mary	29	8	30	Jas. 1
15	9	G.	5 Id.		31	9	32	2
4	10	A.	4 Id.		33	10	34	3
	11	B.	3 Id.		35	11	36	4
12	12	C.	pr. Id.		37	12	38	5
1	13	D.	Idus	Lucy, Virgin & Martyr	39	13	40	1 Pet. 1
	14	E.	19 Kl. Ian.		41	14	42	2
9	15	F.	18 Kl.		43	15	44	3
	16	G.	17 Kl.	O Sapientia°	45	16	46	4
17	17	A.	16 Kl.		47	17	48	5
6	18	B.	15 Kl.		49	18	50	2 Pet. 1
	19	C.	14 Kl.		51	19	52	2
14	20	D.	13 Kl.	Fast	53	20	54	3
3	21	E.	12 Kl.	S Thomas Apostle & Martyr		21		1 John 1
	22	F.	11 Kl.		55	22	56	2
11	23	G.	10 Kl.		57	23	58	3
19	24	A.	9 Kl.	Fast	59	24	60	4
	25	B.	8 Kl.	Christmas day				
8	26	C.	7 Kl.	S. Stephen the first Martyr				
	27	D.	6 Kl.	S. John Apostle & Evangelist				
14	28	E.	5 Kl.	Innocents day		25		5
5	29	F.	4 Kl.		61	26	62	2 John
	30	G.	3 Kl.		63	27	64	3 John
13	31	A.	pr. Kl.	Silvester, Bishop of Rome	65	28	66	Jude

TABLES and RULES
FOR THE
Moveable, and Immoveable Feasts;
Together with the days of Fasting and Abstinence,
through the whole year.

RULES to know when the Moveable Feasts, and Holidays begin.

*E*ASTER-DAY (on which the rest depend)° is always the first Sunday after the first full Moon, which happens next after the One and twentieth day of *March*. And, if the Full Moon happens upon a Sunday, *Easter-day* is the Sunday after.

Advent-Sunday is always the nearest Sunday to the Feast of S. *Andrew*, whether before or after.

Septuagesima			Nine	
Sexagesima		Sunday is	Eight	weeks before
Quinquagesima			Seven	*Easter*.
Quadragesima			Six	

Rogation-Sunday			Five weeks	
Ascension-day		is	Forty days	after *Easter*.
Whitsunday			Seven weeks	
Trinity-Sunday			Eight weeks	

*Table of all the Feasts° that are to be observed in
the Church of* England *through the year.*

All Sundays in the Year

The Days of the Feasts of
- The Circumcision of our Lord JESUS CHRIST.
- The Epiphany.
- The Conversion of S. *Paul*.
- The Purification of the Blessed Virgin.
- S. *Matthias* the Apostle.
- The Annunciation of the Blessed Virgin.
- S. *Mark* the Evangelist.
- S. *Philip* and S. *James* the Apostles.
- The Ascension of our Lord JESUS CHRIST.
- S. *Barnabas*.
- The Nativity of S. *John Baptist*.
- S. *Peter* the Apostle.

The Days of the Feasts of
- S. *James* the Apostle
- S. *Bartholomew* the Apostle.
- S. *Matthew* the Apostle.
- S. *Michael*, and all Angels.
- S. *Luke* the Evangelist.
- S. *Simon* and S. *Jude* the Apostles.
- All Saints.
- S. *Andrew* the Apostle.
- S. *Thomas* the Apostle.
- The Nativity of our Lord.
- S. *Stephen* the Martyr.
- S. *John* the Evangelist.
- The Holy Innocents.

Monday
and   } in *Easter*-week.
Tuesday

Monday
and   } in *Whitsun*-week.
Tuesday

A Table of the Vigils, Fasts, and days of Abstinence,°
to be observed in the year.

The
Evens
or Vigils
before
{
The Nativity of our
  Lord.
The Purification of
  the Blessed Virgin *Mary*.
The Annunciation of
  the Blessed Virgin.
Easter-day.
Ascension-day.
Pentecost.
S. *Matthias*.
S. *John Baptist*.

The
Evens
or Vigils
before
{
S. *Peter*.
S. *James*.
S. *Bartholomew*.
S. *Matthew*.
S. *Simon* and S. *Jude*.
S. *Andrew*.
S. *Thomas*.
All Saints.

Note, that if any of these Feast-Days fall upon a Munday, then the Vigil or Fast-day shall
be kept upon the Saturday, and not upon the Sunday next before it.

Days of Fasting or Abstinence.

1. The Forty Days of Lent

2. The Ember-Days at the Four Seasons,
being the Wednesday, Friday, and
Saturday after . . . .
{
the First Sunday in Lent.
the Feast of *Pentecost*.
September 14.
December 13.

3. The Three Rogation-days, being the Munday, Tuesday, and
Wednesday, before Holy Thursday, or the Ascension of our Lord.

4. All the *Fridays* in the Year,° except *Christmas*-day.

Certain Solemn days, for which particular Services
are appointed.

1. The Fifth day of *November*, being the day of the Papists Conspiracy.

2. The thirtieth day of *January*, being the day of the Martyrdom of King
Charles the First.

3. The Nine and twentieth day of *May*, being the day of the Birth and
Return of King *Charles* the Second.

A TABLE of the Moveable Feasts

The year of our LORD	The Golden Number	The Epact	The Dominical Letter	Sundays after Epiphany	Septuagesima Sunday
1661	9	9	F	4	Feb. 10
1662	10	20	E	2	Jan. 26
1663	11	1	D	5	Feb. 15
1664	12	12	C B	4	Feb. 7
1665	13	23	A	2	Jan. 22
1666	14	4	G	5	Feb. 11
1667	15	15	F	3	Feb. 3
1668	16	26	E D	1	Jan. 19
1669	17	7	C	4	Feb. 7
1670	18	18	B	3	Jan. 30
1671	19	29	A	6	Feb. 19
1672	1	11	G F	4	Feb. 4
1673	2	22	E	2	Jan. 26
1674	3	3	D	5	Feb. 15
1675	4	14	C	3	Jan. 31
1676	5	25	B A	2	Feb. 23
1677	6	6	G	5	Feb. 11
1678	7	17	F	2	Jan. 27
1679	8	28	E	5	Feb. 16
1680	9	9	D C	4	Feb. 8
1681	10	20	B	3	Jan. 30
1682	11	1	A	5	Feb. 12
1683	12	12	G	4	Feb. 4
1684	13	23	F E	2	Jan. 27
1685	14	4	D	5	Feb. 15
1686	15	15	C	3	Jan. 31
1687	16	26	B	2	Jan. 23
1688	17	7	A G	5	Feb. 12
1689	18	18	F	2	Jan. 27
1690	19	29	E	5	Feb. 16
1691	1	11	D	4	Feb. 8
1692	2	22	C B	2	Jan. 24
1693	3	3	A	5	Feb. 12
1694	4	14	G	4	Feb. 4
1695	5	25	F	1	Jan. 20
1696	6	6	E D	4	Feb. 9
1697	7	17	C	3	Jan. 31
1698	8	28	B	6	Feb. 20
1699	9	9	A	4	Feb. 5
1700	10	20	G F	3	Jan. 28

calculated for Fourty years.°

The First Day of Lent	Easter-day	Rogation-Sunday	Ascension-day	Whit-sunday	Sundays after Trinity	Advent-Sunday
Feb. 27	Apr. 14	May 19	May 23	Jun. 2	24	Dec. 1
Feb. 12	Mar. 30	May 4	May 8	May 18	26	Nov. 30
Mar. 4	Apr. 19	May 24	May 28	Jun. 7	23	Nov. 29
Feb. 24	Apr. 10	May 15	May 19	May 29	24	Nov. 27
Feb. 8	Mar. 26	Apr. 30	May 4	May 14	27	Dec. 3
Feb. 28	Apr. 15	May 20	May 24	Jun. 3	24	Dec. 2
Feb. 20	Apr. 7	May 12	May 16	May 26	25	Dec. 1
Feb. 5	Mar. 22	Apr. 26	Apr. 30	May 10	27	Nov. 29
Feb. 24	Apr. 11	May 16	May 20	May 30	24	Nov. 28
Feb. 16	Apr. 3	May 8	May 12	May 22	25	Nov. 27
Mar. 8	Apr. 23	May 28	Jun. 1	Jun. 11	23	Dec. 3
Feb. 21	Apr. 7	May 12	May 16	May 26	25	Dec. 1
Feb. 12	Mar. 30	May 4	May 8	May 18	26	Nov. 30
Mar. 4	Apr. 19	May 24	May 28	Jun. 7	23	Nov. 29
Feb. 17	Apr. 4	May 9	May 13	May 23	25	Nov. 28
Feb. 9	Mar. 26	Apr. 30	May 4	May 14	27	Dec. 3
Feb. 28	Apr. 15	May 20	May 24	Jun. 3	24	Dec. 2
Feb. 13	Mar. 31	May 5	May 9	May 19	26	Dec. 1
Mar. 5	Apr. 20	May 25	May 29	Jun. 8	23	Nov. 30
Feb. 25	Apr. 11	May 16	May 20	May 30	24	Nov. 28
Feb. 16	Apr. 3	May 8	May 12	May 22	25	Nov. 27
Mar. 1	Apr. 16	May 21	May 25	Jun. 4	24	Dec. 3
Feb. 21	Apr. 8	May 13	May 17	May 27	25	Dec. 2
Feb. 13	Mar. 30	May 4	May 8	May 18	26	Nov. 30
Mar. 4	Apr. 19	May 24	May 28	Jun. 7	23	Nov. 29
Feb. 17	Apr. 4	May 9	May 13	May 23	25	Nov. 28
Feb. 9	Mar. 27	May 1	May 5	May 15	26	Nov. 27
Mar. 1	Apr. 15	May 20	May 24	Jun. 3	24	Dec. 2
Feb. 13	Mar. 31	May 5	May 9	May 19	26	Dec. 1
Mar. 5	Apr. 20	May 25	May 29	Jun. 8	23	Nov. 30
Feb. 25	Apr. 12	May 17	May 21	May 31	24	Nov. 29
Feb. 10	Mar. 27	May 1	May 5	May 15	26	Nov. 27
Mar. 1	Apr. 16	May 21	May 25	Jun. 4	24	Dec. 3
Feb. 21	Apr. 8	May 13	May 17	May 27	25	Dec. 2
Feb. 6	Mar. 24	Apr. 28	May 2	May 12	27	Dec. 1
Feb. 26	Apr. 12	May 17	May 21	May 31	24	Nov. 29
Feb. 17	Apr. 4	May 9	May 13	May 23	25	Nov. 28
Mar. 9	Apr. 24	May 29	Jun. 2	Jun. 12	22	Nov. 27
Feb. 22	Apr. 9	May 14	May 18	May 28	25	Dec. 3
Feb. 14	Mar. 31	May 5	May 9	May 19	26	Dec. 1

¶ To find *Easter* for ever.°

The Golden Number	A	B	C	D	E	F	G
1	April 9	10	11	12	6	7	8
2	March 26	27	28	29	30	31	April 1
3	April 16	17	18	19	20	14	15
4	April 9	3	4	5	6	7	8
5	March 26	27	28	29	23	24	25
6	April 16	17	11	12	13	14	15
7	April 2	3	4	5	6	March 31	April 1
8	April 23	24	25	19	20	21	22
9	April 9	10	11	12	13	14	8
10	April 2	3	March 28	29	30	31	April 1
11	April 16	17	18	19	20	21	22
12	April 9	10	11	5	6	7	8
13	March 26	27	28	29	30	31	25
14	April 16	17	18	19	13	14	15
15	April 2	3	4	5	6	7	8
16	March 26	27	28	22	23	24	25
17	April 16	10	11	12	13	14	15
18	April 2	3	4	5	March 30	31	April 1
19	April 23	24	18	19	20	21	22

¶ When ye have found the Sunday Letter in the upper-most Line, guide your eye downward from the same, till ye come right over against the Prime; and there is shewed both what Month, and what day of the Month *Easter* falleth that year. But note, that the name of the Month is set at the left Hand, or else just with the Figure, and followeth not, as in other Tables by descent, but collateral.

Note, that the supputation of the year of our Lord in the Church of *England* beginneth the Five and twentieth day of *March*.

The ORDER

FOR

Morning and Evening Prayer

daily to be said and used throughout the year.

THE Morning and Evening Prayer shall be used in the accustomed place of the Church, Chappel, or Chancel;° Except it shall be otherwise determined by the Ordinary of the place. And the Chancels shall remain as they have done in times past.

And here is to be noted, that such Ornaments of the Church° and of the Ministers thereof at all times of their Ministration, shall be retained and be in use as were in this Church of England by the Authority of Parliament, in the second year of the Reign of King Edward the Sixth.

THE

ORDER

FOR

Morning Prayer

Daily throughout the Year.

¶ *At the beginning of Morning Prayer the Minister shall read with a loud voice some one or more of these Sentences of the Scriptures, that follow. And then he shall say that which is written after the said Sentences.*

WHEN the wicked man turneth away° from his wickedness, that he hath committed, and doth that which is lawfull and right, he shall save his soul alive.   *Ezek.* 18.27

I acknowledge my transgressions, and my sin is ever before me

Ps. 51.3

Hide thy face from my sins, and blot out all mine iniquities.

Ps. 51.9

The sacrifices of God are a broken spirit: a broken, and a contrite heart, O God, thou wilt not despise.   *Ps.* 51.17

Rend your heart, and not your garments, and turn unto the Lord your God: for he is gracious, and merciful, slow to anger, and of great kindness, and repenteth him of the evil. *Joel* 2.13

To the Lord our God belong mercies, and forgivenesses, though we have rebelled against him: neither have we obeyed the voice of the Lord our God, to walk in his laws, which he set before us. *Dan.* 9.9–10

O Lord, correct me, but with judgment; not in thine anger, lest thou bring me to nothing. *Jer.* 10.24, *Ps.* 6.1

Repent ye; for the Kingdom of Heaven is at hand. *Matt.* 3.2

I will arise and go to my Father, and will say unto him; Father, I have sinned against Heaven, and before thee, and am no more worthy to be called thy son. *Luke* 15.18–9

Enter not into judgment with thy servant, O Lord; for in thy sight shall no man living be justified. *Ps.* 143.2

If we say, that we have no sin, we deceive our selves, and the truth is not in us. But, if we confess our sins, he is faithful and just to forgive us our sins, and to cleanse us from all unrighteousness. *1 John* 1.8–9

D EARLY beloved brethren, the Scripture moveth us in sundry places to acknowledge, and confess our manifold sins and wickedness, and that we should not dissemble nor cloak them before the face of Almighty God our heavenly Father, but confess them with an humble, lowly, penitent, and obedient heart; to the end, that we may obtain forgiveness of the same by his infinite goodness and mercy. And although we ought at all times humbly to acknowledge our sins before God, yet ought we most chiefly so to do, when we assemble, and meet together, to render thanks for the great benefits, that we have received at his hands, to set forth his most worthy praise, to hear his most holy word, and to ask those things, which are requisite, and necessary, as well for the body as the soul. Wherefore I pray, and beseech you as many as are here present, to accompany me with a pure heart, and humble voice unto the throne of the heavenly grace, saying after me.

¶ *A general Confession to be said of the whole Congregation after the Minister, all kneeling.*

A LMIGHTY, and most merciful Father; We have erred, and strayed from thy waies like lost sheep. We have followed too much the devices, and desires of our own hearts. We have offended against thy holy laws. We have left undone those things, which we ought to have done; And we have done those things, which we ought not to have done; And there is no health in us. But thou, O Lord, have mercy upon us, miserable offenders. Spare thou them, O God, which confess their faults. Restore thou them, that are penitent; According to thy promises declared unto mankind in Christ Jesu our Lord. And grant, O most merciful Father, for his sake; That we may hereafter live a godly, righteous, and sober life, To the glory of thy holy Name. Amen.

¶ *The Absolution or Remission of sins to be pronounced by the Priest alone, standing; the people still kneeling.*°

ALMIGHTY God, the Father of our Lord Jesus Christ, who desireth not the death of a sinner, but rather, that he may turn from his wickedness, and live; and hath given power, and commandment to his Ministers to declare and pronounce to his people, being penitent, the absolution and remission of their sins: He pardoneth, and absolveth all them, that truly repent, and unfeignedly believe his holy Gospel. Wherefore let us beseech him to grant us true repentance, and his Holy Spirit, that those things may please him, which we do at this present, and that the rest of our life hereafter may be pure, and holy, so that at the last we may come to his eternal joy, through Jesus Christ our Lord.

¶ *The people shall answer here, and at the end of all other prayers,*°

Amen.

¶ *Then the Minister shall kneel, and say the Lords Prayer with an audible voice; the People also kneeling, and repeating it with him,*° *both here, and wheresoever else it is used in Divine Service.*

OUR Father, which art in Heaven, Hallowed be thy Name. Thy Kingdom come. Thy will be done in Earth, As it is in Heaven. Give us this day our daily bread. And forgive us our trespasses, As we forgive them, that trespass against us. And lead us not into temptation: But deliver us from evil: For thine is the Kingdom, The Power, and the Glory, For ever and ever.° Amen.

¶ *Then likewise he shall say,*

O Lord, open thou our lips.
Answer. And our mouth shall shew forth thy praise.
Priest. O God, make speed to save us.
Answer. O Lord, make haste to help us.

¶ *Here all standing up,° the Priest shall say,*

Glory be to the Father, and to the Son: and to the Holy Ghost;
Answer. As it was in the beginning, is now, and ever shall be: world without end. Amen.

Priest. Praise ye the Lord.
Answer. The Lords Name be praised.°

¶ *Then shall be said, or sung° this Psalm following: Except on Easter day, upon which another Anthem is appointed: and on the Nineteenth day of every month it is not to be read here,° but in the ordinary course of the Psalms.*

Venite, exultemus Domino.

O COME, let us sing unto the Lord: let us heartily rejoyce in the strength of our salvation.   *Ps.* 95

Let us come before his presence with thanksgiving: and shew our selves glad in him with Psalms.

For the Lord is a great God: and a great King above all gods.

In his hand are all the corners of the earth: and the strength of the hills is his also.

The sea is his, and he made it: and his hands prepared the dry land.

O come, let us worship and fall down: and kneel before the Lord our Maker.

For he is the Lord our God: and we are the people of his pasture, and the sheep of his hand.

To day if ye will hear his voice, harden not your hearts: as in the provocation, and as in the day of temptation in the Wilderness;

When your fathers tempted me: proved me, and saw my works.

Forty years long was I grieved with this generation, and said: It is a people that do erre in their hearts, and they have not known my waies.

Unto whom I sware in my wrath: that they should not enter into my rest.

Glory be to the Father, and to the Son: and to the Holy Ghost;

As it was in the beginning, is now, and ever shall be: world without end. Amen.

¶ *Then shall follow the Psalms in order as they be appointed. And at the end of every Psalm throughout the year, and likewise at the end of Benedicite, Benedictus, Magnificat, and Nunc dimittis, shall be repeated,*

Glory be to the Father, and to the Son: and to the Holy Ghost;

Answer. As it was in the beginning, is now, and ever shall be: world without end. Amen.

¶ *Then shall be read distinctly with an audible voice° the First Lesson, taken out of the Old Testament, as is appointed in the Kalendar (except there be proper Lessons assigned for that day): He that readeth, so standing, and turning himself, as he may best be heard of all such as are present. And after that, shall be said, or sung in English the Hymn, called* Te Deum Laudamus, *daily throughout the Year.*

¶ *Note, that before every Lesson the Minister shall say,* Here beginneth such a Chapter, *or* Verse of such a Chapter, of such a Book: *And after every Lesson,* Here endeth the First, *or* the Second Lesson.

Te Deum Laudamus.

WE praise thee, O God: we acknowledge thee to be the Lord.
    All the earth doth worship thee: the Father everlasting.
To thee all Angels cry aloud: the Heavens, and all the Powers therein.
To thee Cherubin and Seraphin: continually do cry,
Holy, Holy, Holy: Lord God of Sabaoth.
Heaven, and Earth are full of the Majesty: of thy glory.
The glorious company of the Apostles: praise thee.
The goodly fellowship of the Prophets: praise thee.
The noble army of Martyrs: praise thee.
The holy Church throughout all the world: doth acknowledge thee;
The Father: of an infinite Majesty;
Thine honourable, true: and only Son;
Also the Holy Ghost: the Comforter.
Thou art the King of Glory: O Christ.
Thou art the everlasting Son: of the Father.
When thou tookest upon thee to deliver man: thou didst not abhor the Virgins womb.
When thou hadst overcome the sharpness of death: thou didst open the Kingdom of Heaven to all believers.
Thou sittest at the right hand of God: in the glory of the Father.
We believe that thou shalt come: to be our Judge.
We therefore pray thee, help thy servants: whom thou hast redeemed with thy precious blood.
Make them to be numbred with thy Saints: in glory everlasting.

O Lord, save thy people: and bless thine heritage.

Govern them: and lift them up for ever.

Day by day: we magnifie thee;

And we worship thy Name: ever world without end.

Vouchsafe, O Lord: to keep us this day without sin.

O Lord, have mercy upon us: have mercy upon us.

O Lord, let thy mercy lighten upon us: as our trust is in thee.

O Lord, in thee have I trusted: let me never be confounded.

¶ *Or this Canticle,*

Benedicite, omnia opera.

O ALL ye Works of the Lord, bless ye the Lord: praise him, and magnifie him for ever.

O ye Angels of the Lord, bless ye the Lord: praise him, and magnifie him for ever.

O ye Heavens, bless ye the Lord: praise him, and magnifie him for ever.

O ye Waters, that be above the Firmament, bless ye the Lord: praise him, and magnifie him for ever.

O all ye Powers of the Lord, bless ye the Lord: praise him, and magnifie him for ever.

O ye Sun and Moon, bless ye the Lord: praise him, and magnifie him for ever.

O ye Stars of heaven, bless ye the Lord: praise him, and magnifie him for ever.

O ye Showrs and Dew, bless ye the Lord: praise him, and magnifie him for ever.

O ye Winds of God, bless ye the Lord: praise him, and magnifie him for ever.

O ye Fire, and Heat, bless ye the Lord: praise him, and magnifie him for ever.

O ye Winter, and Summer, bless ye the Lord: praise him, and magnifie him for ever.

O ye Dews, and Frosts, bless ye the Lord: praise him, and magnifie him for ever.

O ye Frost, and Cold, bless ye the Lord: praise him, and magnifie him for ever.

O ye Ice, and Snow, bless ye the Lord: praise him, and magnifie him for ever.

O ye Nights, and Days, bless ye the Lord: praise him, and magnifie him for ever.

O ye Light, and Darkness, bless ye the Lord: praise him, and magnifie him for ever.

O ye Lightnings, and Clouds, bless ye the Lord: praise him, and magnifie him for ever.

O let the Earth bless the Lord: yea, let it praise him, and magnifie him for ever.

O ye Mountains, and Hills, bless ye the Lord: praise him, and magnifie him for ever.

O all ye Green Things upon the earth, bless ye the Lord: praise him, and magnifie him for ever.

O ye Wells, bless ye the Lord: praise him, and magnifie him for ever.

O ye Seas, and Floods, bless ye the Lord: praise him, and magnifie him for ever.

O ye Whales, and all that move in the waters, bless ye the Lord: praise him, and magnifie him for ever.

O all ye Fowls of the air, bless ye the Lord: praise him, and magnifie him for ever.

O all ye Beasts, and Cattel, bless ye the Lord: praise him, and magnifie him for ever.

O ye Children of men, bless ye the Lord: praise him, and magnifie him for ever.

O let Israel bless the Lord: praise him, and magnifie him for ever.

O ye Priests of the Lord, bless ye the Lord: praise him, and magnifie him for ever.

O ye Servants of the Lord, bless ye the Lord: praise him, and magnifie him for ever.

O ye Spirits, and Souls of the Righteous, bless ye the Lord: praise him, and magnifie him for ever.

O ye holy, and humble Men of heart, bless ye the Lord: praise him, and magnifie him for ever.

O Ananias, Azarias, and Misael, bless ye the Lord: praise him, and magnifie him for ever.

Glory be to the Father, and to the Son: and to the Holy Ghost;

As it was in the beginning, is now, and ever shall be: world without end. Amen.

¶ *Then shall be read in like manner the Second Lesson, taken out of the New Testament. And after that, the Hymn following; except when that shall happen to be read in the Chapter for the day, or for the Gospel on Saint* John Baptists *Day.*

Benedictus.

BLESSED be the Lord God of Israel: for he hath visited, and redeemed his people; *Luke* 1.68

And hath raised up a mighty salvation for us: in the house of his servant David;

As he spake by the mouth of his holy Prophets: which have been since the world began;

That we should be saved from our enemies: and from the hand of all that hate us;

To perform the mercy promised to our forefathers: and to remember his holy Covenant;

To perform the oath which he sware to our forefather Abraham: that he would give us;

That we being delivered out of the hand of our enemies: might serve him without fear;

In holiness, and righteousness before him: all the days of our life.

And thou, Childe, shalt be called the Prophet of the Highest: for thou shalt go before the face of the Lord to prepare his ways;

To give knowledge of salvation unto his people: for the remission of their sins,

Through the tender mercy of our God: whereby the Day-spring from on high hath visited us;

To give light to them that sit in darkness, and in the shadow of death: and to guide our feet into the way of peace.

Glory be to the Father, and to the Son: and to the Holy Ghost;

As it was in the beginning, is now, and ever shall be: world without end. Amen.

¶ *Or this Psalm,*

Jubilate Deo.

O BE joyful in the Lord all ye lands: serve the Lord with gladness, and come before his presence with a song. *Ps.* 100

Be ye sure that the Lord he is God: it is he that hath made us, and not we our selves, we are his people, and the sheep of his pasture.

O go your way into his gates with thanksgiving, and into his courts with praise: be thankful unto him, and speak good of his Name.

For the Lord is gracious, his mercy is everlasting: and his truth endureth from generation to generation.

Glory be to the Father, and to the Son: and to the Holy Ghost;

As it was in the beginning, is now, and ever shall be: world without end. Amen.

¶ *Then shall be sung, or said the Apostles Creed by the Minister, and the people standing.*° *Except only such daies as the Creed of Saint Athanasius is appointed to be read.*

I BELIEVE in God the Father Almighty, Maker of heaven and earth: And in Jesus Christ his only Son our Lord, Who was conceived by the holy Ghost, Born of the Virgin Mary, Suffered under Pontius Pilate, Was crucified, dead, and buried, He descended into hell; The third day he rose again from the dead, He ascended into Heaven, And sitteth on the right hand of God the Father Almighty; From thence he shall come to judge the quick and the dead.

I believe in the Holy Ghost; The holy Catholick Church; The Communion of Saints; The forgiveness of sins; The resurrection of the body, And the Life everlasting. Amen.

¶ *And after that, these Prayers following, all devoutly kneeling, the Minister first pronouncing with a loud voice,*

The Lord be with you.

Answer. And with thy spirit.

Minister. ¶ Let us pray.

Lord, have mercy upon us.

Christ, have mercy upon us.

Lord, have mercy upon us.

¶ *Then the Minister, Clerks, and people shall say the Lords Prayer with a loud voice.*

O UR Father, which art in heaven, Hallowed be thy Name. Thy kingdom come. Thy will be done in earth, As it is in heaven. Give us this day our daily bread. And forgive us our trespasses, As we forgive them, that trespass against us. And lead us not into temptation: But deliver us from evil. Amen.

¶ *Then the Priest standing up shall say,*

O Lord, shew thy mercy upon us.

Answer. And grant us thy salvation.

Priest. O Lord, save the King.

Answer. And mercifully hear us when we call upon thee.

Priest. Endue thy ministers with righteousness.

Answer. And make thy chosen people joyful.

Priest. O Lord, save thy people.

Answer. And bless thine inheritance.

Priest. Give peace in our time, O Lord.

Answer. Because there is none other that fighteth for us, but only thou, O God.

Priest. O God, make clean our hearts within us.

Answer. And take not thy holy Spirit from us.

¶ *Then shall follow three Collects; The first of the day, which shall be the same that is appointed at the Communion; The second for Peace; The third for grace to live well. And the two last Collects shall never alter, but daily be said at Morning Prayer throughout all the year, as followeth; all kneeling.*°

¶ *The second Collect, for Peace.*

O GOD, who art the author of peace and lover of concord, in know-ledge of whom standeth our eternal life, whose service is perfect freedom; defend us thy humble servants in all assaults of our enemies, that we surely trusting in thy defence, may not fear the power of any adversaries, through the might of Jesus Christ our Lord. *Amen*.

¶ *The third Collect, for Grace.*

O LORD our heavenly Father, Almighty and everlasting God, who hast safely brought us to the beginning of this day; defend us in the same with thy mighty power, and grant that this day we fall into no sin, neither run into any kind of danger; but that all our doings may be ordered by thy governance, to do always that is righteous in thy sight; through Jesus Christ our Lord. *Amen*.

¶ *In Quires and Places where they sing, here followeth the Anthem.*

¶ *Then these five Prayers following are to be read here,*° *except when the Litany is read; and then onely the two last are to be read, as they are there placed.*

¶ *A Prayer for the Kings Majesty.*°

O LORD, our heavenly Father, high and mighty, King of kings, Lord of lords, the onely Ruler of princes, who doest from thy throne behold all the dwellers upon earth; most heartily we beseech thee with thy favour to behold our most gracious Soveraign Lord King *CHARLES*, and so replenish him with the grace of thy Holy Spirit, that he may alway incline to thy will, and walk in thy way: Endue him plenteously with heavenly gifts, grant him in health and wealth long to live, strengthen him that he may vanquish and overcome all his enemies; and finally after this life, he may attain everlasting joy and felicity, through Jesus Christ our Lord. *Amen.*

¶ *A Prayer for the Royal Family.*°

ALMIGHTY God, the fountain of all goodness,° we humbly beseech thee to bless our gracious Queen *CATHERINE*, *Mary* the Queen-Mother, *James*, Duke of *York*, and all the Royal Family:° Endue them with thy holy Spirit; enrich them with thy heavenly grace; prosper them with all happiness; and bring them to thine ever-lasting kingdom, through Jesus Christ our Lord. *Amen.*

¶ *A Prayer for the Clergy and People.*

ALMIGHTY and everlasting God, who alone workest great marvels; send down upon our Bishops, and Curates, and all Congregations committed to their charge, the healthful Spirit of thy grace; and that they may truly please thee, pour upon them the continual dew of thy blessing. Grant this, O Lord, for the honour of our Advocate and Mediatour, Jesus Christ. *Amen.*

¶ *A Prayer of Saint* Chrysostom.

ALMIGHTY God, who hast given us grace at this time with one accord to make our common supplications unto thee, and dost promise, that when two or three are gathered together in thy Name, thou wilt grant their requests; Fulfill now, O Lord, the desires and petitions of thy servants, as may be most expedient for them; granting us in this world knowledge of thy truth, and in the world to come life everlasting. *Amen.*

2 Corinthians xiii.

THE grace of our Lord Jesus Christ, and the love of God, and the fellowship of the holy Ghost be with us all evermore. *Amen.*

Here endeth the Order of Morning Prayer throughout the year.

THE
ORDER
FOR
Evening Prayer
Daily throughout the Year.

¶ *At the beginning of Evening Prayer the Minister shall read with a loud voice*
some one, or more of these Sentences of the Scriptures,° that follow. And then
he shall say that which is written after the said Sentences.

WHEN the wicked man turneth away from his wickedness, that he
hath committed, and doeth that which is lawfull and right, he
shall save his soul alive. *Ezek.* 18.27

I acknowledge my transgressions, and my sin is ever before me.
Ps. 51.3

Hide thy face from my sins, and blot out all mine iniquities.
Ps. 51.9

The sacrifices of God are a broken spirit: a broken and a contrite
heart, O God, thou wilt not despise. *Ps.* 51.17

Rend your heart, and not your garments, and turn unto the Lord
your God: for he is gracious and merciful, slow to anger, and of great
kindness, and repenteth him of the evil. *Joel* 2.13

To the Lord our God belong mercies and forgivenesses, though
we have rebelled against him: neither have we obeyed the voice of the
Lord our God, to walk in his laws which he set before us. *Dan.* 9.9-10

O Lord, correct me, but with judgment; not in thine anger, lest
thou bring me to nothing. *Jer.* 10.24, *Ps.* 6.1

Repent ye; for the Kingdom of Heaven is at hand. *Matt.* 3.2

I will arise and go to my Father, and will say unto him; Father,
I have sinned against Heaven, and before thee, and am no more worthy to be called thy son. *Luke* 15.18-9

Enter not into judgment with thy servant, O Lord; for in thy sight
shall no man living be justified. *Ps.* 143.2

If we say that we have no sin, we deceive our selves, and the truth is
not in us. But if we confess our sins, he is faithful and just to forgive
us our sins, and to cleanse us from all unrighteousness. 1 *John* 1.8-9

D EARLY beloved brethren, the Scripture moveth us in sundry places, to acknowledge and confess our manifold sins and wickedness, and that we should not dissemble nor cloak them before the face of Almighty God our heavenly Father, but confess them with an humble, lowly, penitent, and obedient heart, to the end that we may obtain forgiveness of the same by his infinite goodness and mercy. And although we ought at all times humbly to acknowledge our sins before God, yet ought we most chiefly so to do, when we assemble and meet together, to render thanks for the great benefits that we have received at his hands, to set forth his most worthy praise, to hear his most holy word, and to ask those things which are requisite and necessary, as well for the body as the soul. Wherefore I pray and beseech you, as many as are here present, to accompany me with a pure heart and humble voice unto the throne of the heavenly grace, saying after me.

¶ *A general Confession to be said of the whole Congregation after the Minister, all kneeling.*

A LMIGHTY and most merciful Father; We have erred and strayed from thy waies like lost sheep. We have followed too much the devices and desires of our own hearts. We have offended against thy holy laws. We have left undone those things which we ought to have done; And we have done those things which we ought not to have done; And there is no health in us. But thou, O Lord, have mercy upon us, miserable offenders. Spare thou them, O God, which confess their faults. Restore thou them that are penitent; According to thy promises declared unto mankind in Christ Jesu our Lord. And grant, O most merciful Father, for his sake; That we may hereafter live a godly, righteous, and sober life, To the glory of thy holy Name. Amen.

¶ *The Absolution or Remission of sins to be pronounced by the Priest alone, standing; the people still kneeling.*

A LMIGHTY God, the Father of our Lord Jesus Christ, who desireth not the death of a sinner, but rather that he may turn from his wickedness, and live, and hath given power and commandment to his ministers to declare and pronounce to his people, being penitent, the absolution and remission of their sins: He pardoneth and absolveth all them that truly repent, and unfeignedly believe his holy Gospel. Wherefore beseech we him to grant us true repentance and his holy Spirit; that those things may please him which we do at this present, and that the rest of our life hereafter may be pure and holy, so that at the last we may come to his eternal joy, through Jesus Christ our Lord. *Amen.*

¶ *Then the Minister shall kneel, and say the Lords Prayer; the People also kneeling, and repeating it with him.*

OUR Father, which art in Heaven, Hallowed be thy Name. Thy Kingdom come. Thy will be done in Earth, As it is in Heaven. Give us this day our daily bread. And forgive us our trespasses, As we forgive them, that trespass against us. And lead us not into temptation; But deliver us from evil: For thine is the Kingdom, the Power, And the Glory, For ever and ever. Amen.

¶ *Then likewise he shall say,*

O Lord, open thou our lips.
Answer. And our mouth shall shew forth thy praise.
Priest. O God, make speed to save us.
Answer. O Lord, make haste to help us.

¶ *Here, all standing up, the Priest shall say,*

Glory be to the Father, and to the Son: and to the Holy Ghost;
Answer. As it was in the beginning, is now, and ever shall be: world without end. Amen.
Priest. Praise ye the Lord.
Answer. The Lords name be praised.

¶ *Then shall be said or sung the Psalms in order as they be appointed. Then a Lesson of the Old Testament, as is appointed: And after that* Magnificat (*or the Song of the blessed Virgin* Mary)° *in English as followeth.*

Magnificat.

MY soul doth magnifie the Lord: and my spirit hath rejoiced in God my Saviour. *Luke* 1

For he hath regarded: the lowliness of his hand-maiden.

For behold, from henceforth: all generations shall call me blessed.

For he that is mighty hath magnified me: and holy is his Name.

And his mercy is on them that fear him: throughout all generations.

He hath shewed strength with his arm: he hath scattered the proud in the imagination of their hearts.

He hath put down the mighty from their seat: and hath exalted the humble and meek.

He hath filled the hungry with good things: and the rich he hath sent empty away.

He remembring his mercy hath holpen his servant Israel: as he promised to our forefathers, Abraham and his seed for ever.

Glory be to the Father, and to the Son: and to the Holy Ghost.

As it was in the beginning, is now, and ever shall be: world without end. Amen.

¶ *Or else this Psalm; Except it be on the nineteenth day of the month, when it is read in the ordinary course of the Psalms.*

Cantate Domino.

O SING unto the Lord a new song: for he hath done marvellous things. *Ps.* 98

With his own right hand, and with his holy arm: hath he gotten himself the victory.

The Lord declared his salvation: his righteousness hath he openly shewed in the sight of the heathen.

He hath remembred his mercy and truth toward the house of Israel: and all the ends of the world have seen the salvation of our God.

Shew your selves joyful unto the Lord, all ye lands: sing, rejoyce, and give thanks.

Praise the Lord upon the harp: sing to the harp with a psalm of thanksgiving.

With trumpets also and shawms: O shew your selves joyful before the Lord the King.

Let the sea make a noise, and all that therein is: the round world, and they that dwell therein.

Let the flouds clap their hands, and let the hills be joyful together before the Lord: for he cometh to judge the earth.

With righteousness shall he judge the world: and the people with equity.

Glory be to the Father, and to the Son: and to the Holy Ghost.

As it was in the beginning, is now, and ever shall be: world without end. Amen.

¶ *Then a Lesson of the New Testament, as it is appointed: And after that* Nunc dimittis (*or the Song of* Simeon)° *in English, as followeth.*

Nunc dimittis.

LORD, now lettest thou thy servant depart in peace: according to thy word. *Luke 2.29*

For mine eyes have seen: thy salvation,

Which thou hast prepared: before the face of all people;

To be a light to lighten the Gentiles: and to be the glory of thy people Israel.

Glory be to the Father, and to the Son: and to the Holy Ghost;

As it was in the beginning, is now, and ever shall be: world without end. Amen.

¶ *Or else this Psalm; Except it be on the Twelfth day of the month.*

Deus misereatur.

GOD be merciful unto us, and bless us: and shew us the light of his countenance, and be merciful unto us. *Ps. 67*

That thy way may be known upon earth: thy saving health among all nations.

Let the people praise thee, O God: yea, let all the peoples praise thee.

O let the nations rejoice and be glad: for thou shalt judge the folk righteously, and govern the nations upon earth.

Let the people praise thee, O God: yea, let all the people praise thee.

Then shall the earth bring forth her increase: and God, even our own God, shall give us his blessing.

God shall bless us: and all the ends of the world shall fear him.

Glory be to the Father, and to the Son: and to the Holy Ghost;

As it was in the beginning, is now, and ever shall be: world without end. Amen.

¶ *Then shall be sung or said the Apostles Creed by the Minister and the people standing.*

I BELIEVE in God the Father Almighty, Maker of heaven and earth: And in Jesus Christ his only Son our Lord, Who was conceived by the holy Ghost, Born of the Virgin Mary, Suffered under Pontius Pilate, Was crucified, dead, and buried, He descended into hell; The third day he rose again from the dead, He ascended into heaven, And sitteth on the right hand of God the Father Almighty; From thence he shall come to judge the quick and the dead.

I believe in the Holy Ghost; The holy Catholick Church; The Communion of Saints; The forgiveness of sins; The resurrection of the body, And the life everlasting. Amen.

¶ *And after that, these Prayers following,° all devoutly kneeling, the Minister first pronouncing with a loud voice,*

The Lord be with you.

Answer. And with thy spirit.

Minister. ¶ Let us pray.

Lord have mercy upon us.

Christ have mercy upon us.

Lord have mercy upon us.

¶ *Then the Minister, Clerks, and people shall say the Lords Prayer with a loud voice.*

O UR Father, which art in heaven, Hallowed be thy Name. Thy Kingdom come. Thy will be done in earth, As it is in heaven. Give us this day our daily bread. And forgive us our trespasses, As we forgive them, that trespass against us. And lead us not into temptation: But deliver us from evil. Amen.

¶ *Then the Priest standing up shall say,*

O Lord, shew thy mercy upon us.

Answer. And grant us thy salvation.

Priest. O Lord, save the King.

Answer. And mercifully hear us when we call upon thee.

Priest. Endue thy ministers with righteousness.

Answer. And make thy chosen people joyful.

Priest. O Lord, save thy people.

Answer. And bless thine inheritance.

Priest. Give peace in our time, O Lord.

Answer. Because there is none other that fighteth for us, but only thou, O God.

Priest. O God, make clean our hearts within us.

Answer. And take not thy holy Spirit from us.

¶ *Then shall follow three Collects; The first of the day; The second for Peace; The third for aid against all perils, as hereafter followeth: Which two last Collects shall be daily said at Evening Prayer without alteration.*

¶ *The Second Collect at Evening Prayer.*

O GOD, from whom all holy desires, all good counsels, and all just works do proceed; Give unto thy servants that peace which the world cannot give, that both our hearts may be set to obey thy commandments, and also that by thee we being defended from the fear of our enemies, may pass our time in rest and quietness, through the merits of Jesus Christ our Saviour. *Amen.*

¶ *The Third Collect for aid against all perils.*

L IGHTEN our darkness, we beseech thee,° O Lord, and by thy great mercy defend us from all perils and dangers of this night, for the love of thy only Son, our Saviour Jesus Christ. *Amen.*

¶ *In Quires and Places where they sing, here followeth the Anthem.°*

¶ *A Prayer for the Kings Majesty.°*

O LORD, our heavenly Father, high and mighty, King of kings, Lord of lords, the onely Ruler of princes, who doest from thy throne behold all the dwellers upon earth; most heartily we beseech thee with thy favour to behold our most gracious Soveraign Lord King *CHARLES*, and so replenish him with the grace of thy Holy Spirit, that he may alway incline to thy will, and walk in thy way: Endue him plenteously with heavenly gifts, grant him in health and wealth long to live, strengthen him that he may vanquish and overcome all his enemies; and finally after this life, he may attain everlasting joy and felicity, through Jesus Christ our Lord. *Amen.*

¶ *A Prayer for the Royal Family.*

A LMIGHTY God, the fountain of all goodness, we humbly beseech thee to bless our gracious Queen *CATHERINE*, *Mary* the Queen-Mother, *James*, Duke of *York*, and all the Royal Family: Endue them with thy holy Spirit; enrich them with thy heavenly grace; prosper them with all happiness; and bring them to thine everlasting kingdom, through Jesus Christ our Lord. *Amen.*

¶ *A Prayer for the Clergy and People.*

A LMIGHTY and everlasting God, who alone workest great marvels; send down upon our Bishops, and Curates, and all Congregations committed to their charge, the healthful Spirit of thy grace; and that they may truly please thee, pour upon them the continual dew of thy blessing. Grant this, O Lord, for the honour of our Advocate and Mediatour, Jesus Christ. *Amen.*

¶ *A Prayer of Saint* Chrysostom.

ALMIGHTY God, who hast given us grace at this time with one accord to make our common supplications unto thee, and dost promise, that when two or three are gathered together in thy Name, thou wilt grant their requests; Fulfill now, O Lord, the desires and petitions of thy servants, as may be most expedient for them; granting us in this world knowledge of thy truth, and in the world to come life everlasting. *Amen.*

2 Corinthians xiii.

THE grace of our Lord Jesus Christ, and the love of God, and the fellowship of the Holy Ghost be with us all evermore. *Amen.*

Here endeth the Order of Evening Prayer throughout the year.

[The Creed of St. Athanasius.]

At Morning Prayer.

¶ *Upon these Feasts;* Christmas-*day, the* Epiphany, *Saint* Matthias, Easter-*day,* Ascension-*day,* Whitsun-*day, Saint* John Baptist, *Saint* James, *Saint* Bartholomew, *Saint* Matthew, *Saint* Simon *and Saint* Jude, *Saint* Andrew, *and upon* Trinity *Sunday shall be sung or said at Morning Prayer, instead of the Apostles Creed, this Confession of our Christian Faith, commonly called the Creed of Saint* Athanasius, *by the Minister and People standing.*°

Quicunque vult.

WHOSOEVER will be saved: before all things it is necessary that he hold the Catholick Faith.

Which Faith, except every one do keep whole and undefiled:° without doubt he shall perish everlastingly.

And the Catholick Faith is this: that we worship one God in Trinity, and Trinity in Unity;

Neither confounding the persons: nor dividing the substance.

For there is one person of the Father, another of the Son: and another of the Holy Ghost.

But the Godhead of the Father, of the Son, and of the Holy Ghost, is all one: the Glory equal, the Majesty co-eternal.

Such as the Father is, such is the Son: and such is the Holy Ghost.

The Father uncreate, the Son uncreate: and the Holy Ghost uncreate.

The Father incomprehensible, the Son incomprehensible: and the Holy Ghost incomprehensible.

The Father eternal, the Son eternal: and the Holy Ghost eternal.

And yet they are not three eternals: but one eternal.

As also there are not three incomprehensibles, nor three uncreated: but one uncreated, and one incomprehensible.

So likewise the Father is Almighty, the Son Almighty: and the Holy Ghost Almighty.

And yet they are not three Almighties: but one Almighty.

So the Father is God, the Son is God: and the Holy Ghost is God.

And yet they are not three Gods: but one God.

So likewise the Father is Lord, the Son Lord: and the Holy Ghost Lord;

And yet not three Lords: but one Lord.

For like as we are compelled by the Christian verity: to acknowledge every person by himself to be God and Lord;

So are we forbidden by the Catholick Religion: to say, There be three Gods, or three Lords.

The Father is made of none: neither created, nor begotten.

The Son is of the Father alone: not made, nor created, but begotten.

The Holy Ghost is of the Father, and of the Son: neither made, nor created, nor begotten, but proceeding.

So there is one Father, not three Fathers; one Son not three Sons: one Holy Ghost, not three Holy Ghosts.

And in this Trinity none is afore, or after other: none is greater, or less than another;

But the whole three persons are co-eternal together: and co-equal.

So that in all things, as is aforesaid: the Unity in Trinity, and the Trinity in Unity is to be worshipped.

He therefore, that will be saved: must thus think of the Trinity.

Furthermore, it is necessary to everlasting salvation: that he also believe rightly the Incarnation of our Lord Jesus Christ.

For the right Faith is, that we believe and confess: that our Lord Jesus Christ, the Son of God, is God, and Man;

God of the substance of the Father, begotten before the worlds: and Man of the substance of his Mother, born in the world;

Perfect God, and perfect Man: of a reasonable soul, and humane flesh subsisting;

Equal to the Father, as touching his Godhead: and inferior to the Father, as touching his Manhood;

Who, although he be God, and Man: yet he is not two, but one Christ;

One; not by conversion of the Godhead into flesh: but by taking of the Manhood into God;

One altogether; not by confusion of substance: but by unity of person.

For as the reasonable soul and flesh is one man: so God and Man is one Christ.

Who suffered for our salvation: descended into hell, rose again the third day from the dead.

He ascended into heaven, he sitteth at the right hand of the Father, God Almighty: from whence he shall come to judge the quick and the dead.

At whose coming all men shall rise again with their bodies: and shall give account for their own works.

And they that have done good shall go into life everlasting: and they that have done evil into everlasting fire.

This is the Catholick Faith: which except a man believe faithfully, he cannot be saved.

Glory be to the Father, and to the Son: and to the Holy Ghost;

As it was in the beginning, is now, and ever shall be: world without end. Amen.

The Litany.

¶ *Here followeth the Litany or General Supplication° to be sung or said after Morning Prayer upon Sundays, Wednesdays, and Fridays, and at other times when it shall be commanded by the Ordinary.*

O GOD the Father, of heaven: have mercy upon us miserable sinners.

O God the Father of heaven: have mercy upon us miserable sinners.

O God the Son, Redeemer of the world: have mercy upon us miserable sinners.

O God the Son, Redeemer of the world: have mercy upon us miserable sinners.

O God the Holy Ghost, proceeding from the Father, and the Son: have mercy upon us miserable sinners.

O God the Holy Ghost, proceeding from the Father, and the Son: have mercy upon us miserable sinners.

O holy, blessed and glorious Trinity, three Persons and one God: have mercy upon us miserable sinners.

O holy, blessed and glorious Trinity, three Persons and one God: have mercy upon us miserable sinners.

Remember not Lord, our offences, nor the offences of our forefathers; neither take thou vengeance of our sins: spare us, good Lord, spare thy people whom thou hast redeemed with thy most precious bloud, and be not angry with us for ever.

Spare us, good Lord.

From all evil and mischief, from sin, from the crafts and assaults of the devil, from thy wrath, and from everlasting damnation,

Good Lord, deliver us.

From all blindness of heart; from pride, vain-glory, and hypocrisie; from envy, hatred, and malice, and all uncharitableness,

Good Lord, deliver us.

From fornication, and all other deadly sin; and from all the deceits of the world, the flesh, and the devil,

Good Lord, deliver us.

From lightning and tempest; from plague, pestilence, and famine; from battel and murder, and from sudden death,°

Good Lord, deliver us.

From all sedition, privy conspiracy, and rebellion;° from all false doctrine, heresy, and schism;° from hardness of heart, and contempt of thy Word and Commandment,

Good Lord, deliver us.

By the mystery of thy holy Incarnation; by thy holy Nativity and Circumcision; by thy Baptism, Fasting, and Temptation,

Good Lord, deliver us.

By thine Agony and bloudy Sweat; by thy Cross and Passion; by thy precious Death and Burial, by thy glorious Resurrection and Ascension; and by the coming of the Holy Ghost,

Good Lord, deliver us.

In all time of our tribulation; in all time of our wealth; in the hour of death, and in the day of judgment,

Good Lord, deliver us.

We sinners do beseech thee to hear us, O Lord God, and that it may please thee to rule and govern thy holy Church universal in the right way;

We beseech thee to hear us, good Lord.

That it may please thee to keep and strengthen in the true worshipping of thee,° in righteousness and holiness of life, thy Servant *CHARLES*, our most gracious King and Governour;

We beseech thee to hear us, good Lord.

That it may please thee to rule his heart in thy faith, fear, and love, and that he may evermore have affiance in thee, and ever seek thy honour and glory;

We beseech thee to hear us, good Lord.

That it may please thee to be his defender and keeper, giving him the victory over all his enemies;

We beseech thee to hear us, good Lord.

That it may please thee to bless and preserve our gracious Queen *CATHERINE*, *Mary* the Queen-Mother, *James* Duke of *York*, and all the Royal Family;°

We beseech thee to hear us, good Lord.

That it may please thee to illuminate all Bishops, Priests, and Deacons° with true knowledge and understanding of thy Word, and that both by their preaching and living they may set it forth, and show it accordingly;

We beseech thee to hear us, good Lord.

That it may please thee to endue the Lords of the Council, and all the Nobility, with grace, wisdom, and understanding;

We beseech thee to hear us, good Lord.

That it may please thee to bless and keep the Magistrates, giving them grace to execute justice, and to maintain truth;

We beseech thee to hear us, good Lord.

That it may please thee to bless and keep all thy people;

We beseech thee to hear us, good Lord.

That it may please thee to give to all nations unity, peace, and concord;

We beseech thee to hear us, good Lord.

That it may please thee to give us an heart to love and dread thee, and diligently to live after thy commandments;

We beseech thee to hear us, good Lord.

That it may please thee to give to all thy people increase of grace, to hear meekly thy Word, and to receive it with pure affection, and to bring forth the fruits of the Spirit;

We beseech thee to hear us, good Lord.

That it may please thee to bring into the way of truth all such as have erred and are deceived;

We beseech thee to hear us, good Lord.

That it may please thee to strengthen such as do stand, and to comfort, and help the weak-hearted, and to raise up them that fall, and finally to beat down Satan under our feet;

We beseech thee to hear us, good Lord.

That it may please thee to succour, help, and comfort, all that are in danger, necessity, and tribulation;

We beseech thee to hear us, good Lord.

That it may please thee to preserve all that travel by land or by water, all women labouring of childe, all sick persons and young children, and to shew thy pity upon all prisoners and captives;

We beseech thee to hear us, good Lord.

That it may please thee to defend and provide for the fatherless children and widows, and all that are desolate and oppressed;

We beseech thee to hear us, good Lord.

That it may please thee to have mercy upon all men;

We beseech thee to hear us, good Lord.

That it may please thee to forgive our enemies, persecutors, and slanderers, and to turn their hearts;

We beseech thee to hear us, good Lord.

That it may please thee to give and preserve to our use the kindly fruits of the earth, so that in due time we may enjoy them;

We beseech thee to hear us, good Lord.

That it may please thee to give us true repentance, to forgive us all our sins, negligences, and ignorances, and to endue us with the grace of thy Holy Spirit, to amend our lives according to thy holy word;

We beseech thee to hear us, good Lord.

Son of God: we beseech thee to hear us.

Son of God: we beseech thee to hear us.

O Lamb of God: that takest away the sins of the world;
Grant us thy peace.
O Lamb of God: that takest away the sins of the world;
Have mercy upon us.
O Christ, hear us.
O Christ, hear us.
Lord, have mercy upon us.
Lord, have mercy upon us.
Christ, have mercy upon us.
Christ, have mercy upon us.
Lord, have mercy upon us.
Lord, have mercy upon us.

¶ *Then shall the Priest, and the people with him, say the Lords Prayer.*

OUR Father, which art in heaven, Hallowed be thy Name. Thy Kingdom come. Thy will be done in earth, As it is in heaven. Give us this day our daily bread. And forgive us our trespasses, As we forgive them, that trespass against us. And lead us not into temptation; But deliver us from evil. Amen.

Priest. O Lord, deal not with us after our sins.
Answer. Neither reward us after our iniquities.

¶ Let us pray.

OGOD, merciful Father, that despisest not the sighing of a contrite heart, nor the desire of such as be sorrowful; Mercifully assist our prayers that we make before thee in all our troubles and adversities, whensoever they oppress us; and graciously hear us, that those evils which the craft and subtilty of the devil or man worketh against us be brought to nought, and by the providence of thy goodness they may be dispersed, that we thy servants, being hurt by no persecutions, may evermore give thanks unto thee in thy holy Church, through Jesus Christ our Lord.

O Lord, arise, help us, and deliver us for thy Names sake.

OGOD, we have heard with our ears, and our fathers have declared unto us, the noble works that thou didst in their daies, and in the old time before them.

O Lord, arise, help us, and deliver us for thine honour.
Glory be to the Father, and to the Son: and to the holy Ghost;

As it was in the beginning, is now, and ever shall be: world without end. Amen.

From our enemies defend us, O Christ.

Graciously look upon our afflictions.

Pitifully behold the sorrows of our hearts.

Mercifully forgive the sins of thy people.

Favourably with mercy hear our prayers.

O Son of David, have mercy upon us.

Both now and ever vouchsafe to hear us, O Christ.

Graciously hear us, O Christ; graciously hear us, O Lord Christ.

Priest. O Lord, let thy mercy be shewed upon us;

Answer. As we do put our trust in thee.

Let us pray.

W E humbly beseech thee, O Father, mercifully to look upon our infirmities; and, for the glory of thy Name, turn from us all those evils that we most righteously have deserved; and grant, that in all our troubles we may put our whole trust and confidence in thy mercy, and evermore serve thee in holiness and pureness of living, to thy honour and glory, through our only Mediatour and Advocate, Jesus Christ our Lord. *Amen.*

¶ *A Prayer of Saint* Chrysostom.

A LMIGHTY God, who hast given us grace at this time with one accord to make our common supplications unto thee, and dost promise, that when two or three are gathered together in thy Name, thou wilt grant their requests; Fulfil now, O Lord, the desires and petitions of thy servants, as may be most expedient for them, granting us in this world knowledge of thy truth, and in the world to come life everlasting. *Amen.*

2 *Corinthians* 13

T HE grace of our Lord Jesus Christ, and the love of God, and the fellowship of the holy Ghost be with us all evermore. *Amen.*

Here endeth the Litany.

PRAYERS & THANKSGIVINGS

UPON

SEVERAL OCCASIONS.

To be used before the two final Prayers of the Litany, or of
Morning and Evening Prayer.

PRAYERS.

¶ *For Rain.*°

O GOD, heavenly Father, who by thy Son Jesus Christ hast promised to all them that seek thy Kingdom and the righteousness
thereof, all things necessary to their bodily sustenance; Send us, we
beseech thee, in this our necessity, such moderate rain and showrs,
that we may receive the fruits of the earth to our comfort, and to thy
honour; through Jesus Christ our Lord. *Amen.*

¶ *For Fair Weather.*

O ALMIGHTY Lord God, who for the sin of man didst once drown
all the world, except eight persons, and afterward of thy great
mercy didst promise never to destroy it so again; We humbly beseech
thee, that although we for our iniquities have worthily deserved
a plague of rain and waters, yet upon our true repentance thou wilt
send us such weather, as that we may receive the fruits of the earth in
due season, and learn both by thy punishment to amend our lives, and
for thy clemency to give thee praise and glory, through Jesus Christ
our Lord. *Amen.*

¶ *In Time of dearth and famine.*°

O GOD heavenly Father, whose gift it is that the rain doth fall, the
earth is fruitful, beasts increase, and fishes do multiply; Behold,
we beseech thee, the afflictions of thy people, and grant that the scarcity and dearth (which we do now most justly suffer for our iniquity)
may through thy goodness be mercifully turned into cheapness and
plenty, for the love of Jesus Christ our Lord; to whom with thee, and
the Holy Ghost be all honour and glory, now and for ever. *Amen.*

¶ *Or this.*

O GOD merciful Father, who in the time of Elisha the prophet didst suddenly in Samaria turn great scarcity and dearth into plenty and cheapness; Have mercy upon us, that we who are now for our sins punished with like adversity, may likewise find a seasonable relief: Increase the fruits of the earth by thy heavenly benediction; and grant that we, receiving thy bountiful liberality, may use the same to thy glory, the relief of those that are needy, and our own comfort, through Jesus Christ our Lord. *Amen.*

¶ *In the time of War and Tumults.*

O ALMIGHTY God, King of all kings, and Governour of all things, whose power no creature is able to resist, to whom it belongeth justly to punish sinners, and to be merciful to them that truly repent; Save and deliver us, we humbly beseech thee, from the hands of our enemies; abate their pride, asswage their malice, and confound their devices; that we, being armed with thy defence, may be preserved evermore from all perils, to glorifie thee, who art the only giver of all victory, through the merits of thy only Son Jesus Christ our Lord. *Amen.*

¶ *In the time of any common plague or Sickness.*

O ALMIGHTY God, who in thy wrath did send a plague upon thine own people in the wilderness for their obstinate rebellion against Moses and Aaron, and also in the time of king David didst slay with the plague of pestilence threescore and ten thousand, and yet remembring thy mercy didst save the rest; Have pity upon us miserable sinners, who now are visited with great sickness and mortality, that like as thou didst then accept of an atonement, and didst command the destroying Angel to cease from punishing; so it may now please thee to withdraw from us this plague and grievous sickness, through Jesus Christ our Lord. *Amen.*

¶ *In the Ember Weeks to be said every day,° for those that are to be admitted into holy Orders.*

A LMIGHTY God our heavenly Father, who hast purchased to thy self an universal Church, by the precious blood of thy dear Son; mercifully look upon the same, and at this time so guide and govern the minds of thy servants the Bishops and Pastours of thy flock, that they may lay hands suddenly on no man, but faithfully and wisely make choice of fit persons to serve in the sacred ministery of thy Church. And to those, which shall be Ordained to any holy function, give thy grace and heavenly benediction, that both by their life and doctrine they may set forth thy glory, and set forward the salvation of all men, through Jesus Christ our Lord. *Amen.*

¶ *Or this.*

ALMIGHTY God, the giver of all good gifts,° who of thy divine providence hast appointed divers orders in thy Church; Give thy grace, we humbly beseech thee, to all those, who are to be called to any office and administration in the same; and so replenish them with the truth of thy doctrine, and indue them with innocency of life, that they may faithfully serve before thee, to the glory of thy great Name, and the benefit of thy holy Church, through Jesus Christ our Lord. *Amen.*

¶ *A Prayer that may be said after any of the former.*

O GOD, whose nature and property is ever to have mercy° and to forgive, receive our humble petitions; and though we be tied and bound with the chain of our sins, yet let the pitifulness of thy great mercy loose us, for the honour of Jesus Christ our Mediatour and Advocate. *Amen.*

¶ *A Prayer for the High Court of Parliament,° to be read during their Session.*

MOST gracious God, we humbly beseech thee, as for this Kingdom in general, so especially for the High Court of Parliament, under our most religious and gracious King at this time assembled: That thou wouldest be pleased to direct and prosper all their consultations to the advancement of thy glory, the good of thy Church, the safety, honour, and welfare of our Soveraign and his Kingdoms; that all things may be so ordered and setled by their endeavours upon the best and surest foundations, that peace and happiness, truth and justice, religion and piety may be established among us for all generations. These and all other necessaries for them, for us, and thy whole Church we humbly beg in the Name and mediation of Jesus Christ our most blessed Lord and Saviour. *Amen.*

¶ *A Collect or Prayer for all conditions of men,° to be used at such times when the Litany is not appointed to be said.*

O GOD, the creator and preserver of all mankind, we humbly beseech thee for all sorts and conditions of men, that thou wouldest be pleased to make thy ways known unto them; thy saving health unto all nations. More especially we pray for the good estate of the Catholick Church;° that it may be so guided and governed by thy good Spirit, that all who profess and call themselves Christians,° may be led into the way of truth, and hold the faith in unity of spirit, in the bond of peace, and in righteousness of life. Finally, we commend to thy fatherly goodness all those who are any ways afflicted, or distressed in mind, body, or estate, [*especially those for whom our prayers are desired*]† that it may please thee to comfort and relieve them according to their several necessities, giving them patience under their sufferings, and a happy issue out of all their afflictions. And this we beg for Jesus Christ his sake. *Amen.*

† *This to be said when any desire the prayers of the congregation.*

THANKSGIVINGS.

¶ *A General Thanksgiving.*°

ALMIGHTY God, Father of all mercies, we thine unworthy servants do give thee most humble and hearty thanks for all thy goodness and loving kindness to us, and to all men; [*particularly to those who desire now to offer up their praises*° *and thanksgivings for thy late mercies vouchsafed unto them.*‡] We bless thee for our creation, preservation, and all the blessings of this life,° but above all for thine inestimable love in the redemption of the world by our Lord Jesus Christ; for the means of grace, and for the hope of glory. And we beseech thee give us that due sense of all thy mercies, that our hearts may be unfeignedly thankful, and that we shew forth thy praise, not only with our lips, but in our lives, by giving up ourselves to thy service, and by walking before thee in holiness and righteousness all our days, through Jesus Christ our Lord, to whom with thee and the holy Ghost be all honour and glory, world without end. *Amen.*

‡ *This to be said when any that have been prayed for, desire to return praise.*

¶ *For Rain.*°

O GOD our heavenly Father, who by thy gracious providence dost cause the former and the latter rain to descend upon the earth, that it may bring forth fruit for the use of man; we give thee humble thanks that it hath pleased thee in our great necessity to send us at the last a joyful rain upon thine inheritance, and to refresh it when it was dry, to the great comfort of us thy unworthy servants, and to the glory of thy holy Name, through thy mercies in Jesus Christ our Lord. *Amen.*

¶ *For Fair Weather.*

O LORD God, who hast justly humbled us by thy late plague of immoderate rain and waters, and in thy mercy hast relieved and comforted our souls by this seasonable and blessed change of weather; We praise and glorifie thy holy Name for this thy mercy, and will always declare thy loving kindness from generation to generation, through Jesus Christ our Lord. *Amen.*

¶ *For Plenty.*

O MOST merciful Father, who of thy gracious goodness hast heard the devout prayers of thy Church, and turned our dearth and scarcity into cheapness and plenty; We give thee humble thanks for this thy special bounty, beseeching thee to continue thy loving kindness unto us, that our land may yield us her fruits of increase, to thy glory and our comfort, through Jesus Christ our Lord. *Amen.*

¶ *For Peace, and deliverance from our enemies.*

O ALMIGHTY God, who art a strong tower of defence unto thy servants against the face of their enemies; We yield thee praise and thanksgiving for our deliverance from those great and apparent dangers wherewith we were compassed. We acknowledge it thy goodness that we were not delivered over as a prey unto them; beseeching thee still to continue such thy mercies towards us, that all the world may know that thou art our Saviour and mighty deliverer, through Jesus Christ our Lord. *Amen.*

¶ *For restoring publick peace at home.*°

O ETERNAL God our heavenly Father, who alone makest men to be of one mind in a house, and stillest the outrage of a violent and unruly people; We bless thy holy Name that it hath pleased thee to appease the seditious tumults which have been lately raised up amongst us; most humbly beseeching thee to grant to all of us grace, that we may henceforth obediently walk in thy holy commandments, and leading a quiet and peaceable life in all godliness and honesty, may continually offer unto thee our sacrifice of praise and thanksgiving for these thy mercies towards us; through Jesus Christ our Lord. *Amen.*

¶ *For deliverance from the Plague, or other common sickness.*

O LORD God, who hast wounded us for our sins, and consumed us for our transgressions by thy late heavy and dreadful visitation, and now, in the midst of judgment remembring mercy, hast redeemed our souls from the jaws of death; We offer unto thy fatherly goodness our selves, our souls and bodies, which thou hast delivered to be a living sacrifice unto thee, always praising and magnifying thy mercies in the midst of thy Church; through Jesus Christ our Lord. *Amen.*

¶ *Or this.*

WE humbly acknowledge before thee, O most merciful Father, that all the punishments which are threatened in thy law, might justly have fallen upon us by reason of our manifold transgressions and hardness of heart. Yet seeing it hath pleased thee of thy tender mercy upon our weak and unworthy humiliation, to asswage the contagious sickness, wherewith we lately have been sore afflicted, and to restore the voice of joy and health into our dwellings; we offer unto thy divine Majesty the sacrifice of praise and thanksgiving, lauding and magnifying thy glorious Name for such thy preservation and providence over us, through Jesus Christ our Lord. *Amen.*

THE

Collects, Epistles, and Gospels

to be used throughout the year.

¶ *Note that the Collect appointed for every Sunday, or for any Holiday that hath a Vigil or Eve, shall be said at the Evening Service next before.*

The first Sunday in Advent.

The Collect.°

ALMIGHTY God, give us grace that we may cast away the works of darkness, and put upon us the armour of light now in the time of this mortal life (in which thy Son Jesus Christ came to visit us in great humility;) that in the last day, when he shall come again in his glorious Majesty, to judge both the quick and the dead, we may rise to the life immortal, through him who liveth and reigneth with thee and the Holy Ghost, now and ever. *Amen.*

¶ *This Collect is to be repeated every day,° with the other Collects in Advent, until Christmas-Eve.*

The Epistle.   Rom. 13.8

OWE no man any thing, but to love one another: for he that loveth another hath fulfilled the law. For this, Thou shalt not commit adultery, Thou shalt not kill, Thou shalt not steal, Thou shalt not bear false witness, Thou shalt not covet; and if there be any other commandment, it is briefly comprehended in this saying, namely, Thou shalt love thy neighbour as thy self. Love worketh no ill to his neighbour, therefore love is the fulfilling of the law. And that, knowing the time, that now it is high time to awake out of sleep: for now is our salvation nearer than when we believed. The night is far spent, the day is at hand; let us therefore cast off the works of darkness, and let us put on the armour of light. Let us walk honestly as in the day, not in rioting and drunkenness, not in chambering and wantonness, not in strife and envying. But put ye on the Lord Jesus Christ, and make not provision for the flesh, to fulfil the lusts thereof.

The Gospel.°   Matt. 21.1

WHEN they drew nigh unto Jerusalem, and were come to Bethphage, unto the mount of Olives, then sent Jesus two disciples, saying unto them, Go into the village° over against you, and straightway ye shall find an ass tied, and a colt with her: loose them and bring them unto me. And if any man say ought unto you, ye shall say, The Lord hath need of them; and straightway he will send them. All this was done, that it might be fulfilled which was spoken by the Prophet, saying, Tell ye the daughter of Sion, Behold, thy King cometh unto thee, meek, and sitting upon an ass, and a colt the fole of an ass. And the disciples went, and did as Jesus commanded them, and brought the ass, and the colt, and put on them their clothes, and they set him thereon. And a very great multitude spread their garments in the way, others cut down branches from the trees and strawed them in the way. And the multitudes that went before, and that followed, cried, saying, Hosanna to the son of David: blessed is he that cometh in the name of the Lord, Hosanna in the highest. And when he was come into Jerusalem, all the city was moved, saying, Who is this? And the multitude said, This is Jesus the prophet of Nazareth of Galilee. And Jesus went into the temple of God; and cast out all them that sold and bought in the temple, and overthrew the tables of the monychangers, and the seats of them that sold doves, and said unto them, It is written, My house shall be called the house of prayer; but ye have made it a den of thieves.

The second Sunday in Advent.

The Collect.°

B LESSED Lord, who hast caused all holy Scriptures to be written for our learning; Grant that we may in such wise hear them, read, mark, learn, and inwardly digest them, that by patience and comfort of thy holy word, we may embrace, and ever hold fast the blessed hope of everlasting life, which thou hast given us in our Saviour Jesus Christ. *Amen.*

The Epistle.   Rom. 15.4

W HATSOEVER things were written aforetime, were written for our learning; that we through patience and comfort of the Scriptures might have hope. Now the God of patience and consolation, grant you to be like-minded one toward another, according to Christ Jesus: That ye may with one mind, and one mouth glorifie God, even the Father of our Lord Jesus Christ. Wherefore receive ye one another, as Christ also received us, to the glory of God. Now I say,

That Jesus Christ was a minister of the circumcision, for the truth of God, to confirm the promises made unto the fathers: And that the Gentiles might glorifie God for his mercy; as it is written, For this cause I will confess to thee among the Gentiles, and sing unto thy name. And again he saith, Rejoyce, ye Gentiles, with his people. And again, Praise the Lord, all ye Gentiles; and laud him, all ye people. And again Esaias saith, There shall be a root of Jesse, and he that shall rise to reign over the Gentiles, in him shall the Gentiles trust. Now the God of hope fill you with all joy and peace in believing, that ye may abound in hope, through the power of the Holy Ghost.

The Gospel.　　　　　　　　　*Luke* 21.25

A ND there shall be signs in the sun, and in the moon, and in the stars; and upon the earth distress of nations, with perplexity, the sea and the waves roaring; mens hearts failing them for fear, and for looking after those things, which are coming on the earth: for the powers of heaven shall be shaken. And then shall they see the Son of man coming in a cloud with power and great glory. And when these things begin to come to pass, then look up, and lift up your heads; for your redemption draweth nigh. And he spake to them a parable, Behold the fig-tree, and all the trees; When they now shoot forth, ye see and know of your own selves that summer is now nigh at hand. So likewise ye, when ye see these things come to pass, know ye that the kingdom of God is nigh at hand. Verily, I say unto you, This generation shall not pass away, till all be fulfilled: Heaven and earth shall pass away, but my words shall not pass away.

The third Sunday in Advent.

The Collect.°

O LORD Jesu Christ, who at thy first coming didst send thy messenger to prepare thy way before thee; Grant that the ministers and stewards of thy mysteries, may likewise so prepare and make ready thy way, by turning the hearts of the disobedient to the wisdom of the just, that at thy second coming to judge the world, we may be found an acceptable people in thy sight, who livest and reignest with the Father and the Holy Spirit, ever one God, world without end. *Amen.*

The Epistle.   1 *Cor.* 4.1

L ET a man so account of us, as of the ministers of Christ, and stewards of the mysteries of God. Moreover, it is required in stewards, that a man be found faithful. But with me it is a very small thing, that I should be judged of you, or of mans judgment: yea, I judge not mine own self. For I know nothing by my self, yet am I not hereby justified: but he that judgeth me, is the Lord. Therefore judge nothing before the time, until the Lord come, who both will bring to light the hidden things of darkness, and will make manifest the counsels of the hearts: and then shall every man have praise of God.

The Gospel.   *Matt.* 11.2

N OW when John had heard in the prison the works of Christ, he sent two of his disciples, and said unto him, Art thou he that should come, or do we look for another? Jesus answered and said unto them, Go and shew John again those things which ye do hear and see: The blind receive their sight, and the lame walk, the lepers are cleansed, and the deaf hear, the dead are raised up, and the poor have the gospel preached to them. And blessed is he whosoever shall not be offended in me. And as they departed, Jesus began to say unto the multitudes concerning John, What went ye out into the wilderness to see? A reed shaken with the wind? But what went ye out for to see? A man clothed in soft raiment? behold, they that wear soft clothing are in kings houses. But what went ye out for to see? A prophet? yea, I say unto you, and more than a prophet. For this is he of whom it is written, Behold, I send my messenger before thy face, which shall prepare thy way before thee.

The fourth Sunday in Advent.

The Collect.°

O LORD, raise up (we pray thee) thy power, and come among us, and with great might succour us; that whereas through our sins and wickedness, we are sore let and hindered in running the race that is set before us,° thy bountiful grace and mercy may speedily help and deliver us, through the satisfaction of thy Son our Lord; to whom with thee and the Holy Ghost be honour and glory, world without end. *Amen.*

REJOYCE in the Lord alway, and again I say, Rejoyce. Let your moderation be known unto all men. The Lord is at hand. Be careful for nothing: but in every thing by prayer and supplication with thanksgiving, let your requests be made known unto God. And the peace of God which passeth all understanding, shall keep your hearts and minds through Christ Jesus.

THIS is the record of John, when the Jews sent Priests and Levites from Jerusalem to ask him, Who art thou? And he confessed, and denied not; but confessed, I am not the Christ. And they asked him, What then? Art thou Elias? And he saith, I am not. Art thou that prophet? And he answered, No. Then said they unto him, Who art thou? that we may give an answer to them that sent us. What sayest thou of thy self? He said, I am the voice of one crying in the wilderness, Make straight the way of the Lord, as said the prophet Esaias. And they which were sent, were of the Pharisees. And they asked him, and said unto him, Why baptizest thou then, if thou be not that Christ, nor Elias, neither that prophet? John answered them saying, I baptize with water: but there standeth one among you, whom ye know not. He it is who coming after me, is preferred before me, whose shoes lachet I am not worthy to unloose. These things were done in Bethabara beyond Jordan, where John was baptizing.

᛭ *The Nativity of our Lord, or the Birth-day of Christ, commonly called* Christmas-day.°

The Collect.

ALMIGHTY God, who hast given us thy only begotten Son to take our nature upon him,° and as at this time° to be born of a pure Virgin; Grant that we being regenerate, and made thy children by adoption and grace, may daily be renewed by thy holy Spirit, through the same our Lord Jesus Christ, who liveth and reigneth with thee, and the same Spirit, ever one God, world without end. *Amen.*

GOD, who at sundry times, and in divers manners spake in time past unto the fathers by the prophets, hath in these last days spoken unto us by his Son, whom he hath appointed heir of all things, by whom also he made the worlds. Who being the brightness of his glory, and the express image of his person, and upholding all things by the word of his power, when he had by himself purged our sins, sat down on the right hand of the Majesty on high: Being made so much better than the angels, as he hath by inheritance obtained a more excellent name than they. For unto which of the angels said he at any time, Thou art my Son, this day have I begotten thee? And again, I will be to him a Father, and he shall be to me a Son? And again, when he bringeth in the first-begotten into the world, he saith, And let all the angels of God worship him. And of the angels, he saith, Who maketh his angels spirits, and his ministers a flame of fire. But unto the Son he saith, Thy throne, O God, is for ever and ever, a scepter of righteousness is the scepter of thy kingdom. Thou hast loved righteousness, and hated iniquity; therefore God, even thy God, hath anointed thee with the oyl of gladness above thy fellows. And, Thou Lord in the beginning hast laid the foundation of the earth; and the heavens are the works of thine hands. They shall perish; but thou remainest; and they all shall wax old as doth a garment; and as a vesture shalt thou fold them up, and they shall be changed: but thou art the same, and thy years shall not fail.

The Gospel.   *John.* 1.1

IN the beginning was the Word, and the Word was with God, and the Word was God. The same was in the beginning with God. All things were made by him, and without him was not any thing made, that was made. In him was life, and the life was the light of men. And the light shineth in darkness, and the darkness comprehended it not. There was a man sent from God, whose name was John. The same came for a witness to bear witness of the light, that all men through him might believe. He was not that light, but was sent to bear witness of that light. That was the true light, which lighteth every man that cometh into the world. He was in the world, and the world was made by him, and the world knew him not. He came unto his own, and his own received him not. But as many as received him, to them gave he power to become the sons of God, even to them that believe on his name: Which were born not of bloud, nor of the will of the flesh, nor of the will of man, but of God. And the Word was made flesh, and dwelt among us (and we beheld his glory, the glory as of the onely begotten of the Father) full of grace and truth.

S. Stephens day.

The Collect.°

GRANT, O Lord, that in all our sufferings here upon earth, for the testimony of thy truth, we may stedfastly look up to heaven, and by faith behold the glory that shall be revealed; and being filled with the Holy Ghost, may learn to love and bless our persecuters by the example of thy first Martyr Saint Stephen, who prayed for his murtherers to thee, O blessed Jesus, who standest at the right hand of God to succour all those that suffer for thee, our onely Mediatour and Advocate. *Amen.*

¶ *Then shall follow the Collect of the Nativity, which shall be said continually unto New-years Eve.*

For the Epistle.   *Acts* 7.55

STEPHEN being full of the holy Ghost, looked up stedfastly into heaven, and saw the glory of God, and Jesus standing on the right hand of God, And said, Behold, I see the heavens opened, and the Son of man standing on the right hand of God. Then they cryed out with a loud voice, and stopped their ears, and ran upon him with one accord, and cast him out of the city, and stoned him; and the witnesses laid down their clothes at a young mans feet, whose name was Saul. And they stoned Stephen calling upon God, and saying, Lord Jesus receive my spirit. And he kneeled down and cryed with a loud voice, Lord, lay not this sin to their charge. And when he had said this, he fell asleep.

The Gospel.   *Matt.* 23.34

BEHOLD, I send unto you prophets, and wisemen, and scribes: and some of them ye shall kill and crucifie; and some of them shall ye scourge in your synagogues, and persecute them from city to city; that upon you may come all the righteous bloud shed upon the earth, from the bloud of righteous Abel, unto the bloud of Zacharias, son of Barachias, whom ye slew between the temple and the altar. Verily I say unto you, All these things shall come upon this generation. O Jerusalem, Jerusalem, thou that killest the prophets, and stonest them which are sent unto thee; how often would I have gathered thy children together, even as a hen gathereth her chickens under her wings, and ye would not. Behold, your house is left unto you desolate.

For I say unto you, ye shall not see me henceforth, till ye shall say, Blessed is he that cometh in the name of the Lord.

S. John the Evangelists day.
The Collect.

M ERCIFUL Lord, we beseech thee to cast thy bright beams of light upon thy Church, that it being enlightned by the doctrine of thy blessed Apostle and Evangelist Saint John, may so walk in the light of thy truth,° that it may at length attain to the light of everlasting life, through Jesus Christ our Lord. *Amen.*

The Epistle.   1 *John* 1.1

T HAT which was from the beginning, which we have heard, which we have seen with our eyes, which we have looked upon, and our hands have handled of the word of life; (For the life was manifested, and we have seen it, and bear witness, and shew unto you that eternal life, which was with the Father, and was manifested unto us;) That which we have seen and heard, declare we unto you, that ye also may have fellowship with us; and truly our fellowship is with the Father, and with his Son Jesus Christ. And these things write we unto you, that your joy may be full. This then is the message which we have heard of him, and declare unto you, that God is light, and in him is no darkness at all. If we say that we have fellowship with him, and walk in darkness, we lie, and do not the truth: But if we walk in the light, as he is in the light, we have fellowship one with another, and the bloud of Jesus Christ his Son cleanseth us from all sin. If we say that we have no sin, we deceive our selves, and the truth is not in us. If we confess our sins, he is faithful and just to forgive us our sins, and to cleanse us from all unrighteousness. If we say that we have not sinned, we make him a liar, and his Word is not in us.

The Gospel.   *John* 21.19

J ESUS said unto Peter, Follow me. Then Peter turning about, seeth the disciple whom Jesus loved, following, which also leaned on his breast at supper, and said, Lord, which is he that betrayeth thee? Peter seeing him, saith to Jesus, Lord, and what shall this man do? Jesus saith unto him, If I will that he tarry till I come, what is that to thee? Follow thou me. Then went this saying abroad among the brethren, that that disciple should not die: yet Jesus said not unto him, He shall not die; but, If I will that he tarry till I come, what is that to thee? This is the disciple which testifieth of these things, and wrote these things: and we know that his testimony is true. And there are also many other things which Jesus did, the which if they should be written every one, I suppose, that even the world it self could not contain the books that should be written.

The Innocents day.

The Collect.°

O ALMIGHTY God, who out of the mouths of babes and suck-lings° hast ordained strength, and madest infants to glorifie thee by their deaths; mortifie and kill all vices in us, and so strengthen us by thy grace, that by the innocency of our lives, and constancy of our faith even unto death, we may glorifie thy holy Name, through Jesus Christ our Lord. *Amen.*

For the Epistle.   *Rev.* 14.1

I LOOKED, and lo, a Lamb stood on the mount Sion, and with him an hundred forty and four thousand, having his Fathers name written in their foreheads. And I heard a voice from heaven, as the voice of many waters, and as the voice of a great thunder: and I heard the voice of harpers harping with their harps: And they sung as it were a new song before the throne, and before the four beasts, and the elders; and no man could learn that song, but the hundred and forty and four thousand, which were redeemed from the earth. These are they which were not defiled with women, for they are virgins: these are they which follow the Lamb whithersoever he goeth: these were redeemed from among men, being the first fruits unto God, and to the Lamb. And in their mouth was found no guile; for they are without fault before the throne of God.

The Gospel.   *Matt.* 2.13

THE angel of the Lord appeareth to Joseph in a dream, saying, Arise, and take the young childe, and his mother, and flee into Egypt, and be thou there until I bring thee word; for Herod will seek the young child to destroy him. When he arose, he took the young child and his mother by night, and departed into Egypt, and was there until the death of Herod; that it might be fulfilled which was spoken of the Lord by the prophet, saying, Out of Egypt have I called my son. Then Herod when he saw that he was mocked of the wise-men, was exceeding wroth, and sent forth, and slew all the children that were in Bethlehem, and in all the coasts thereof, from two years old and under, according to the time which he had diligently enquired of the wise-men. Then was fulfilled that which was spoken by Jeremy the prophet, saying, In Rama was there a voice heard, lamentation, and weeping, and great mourning, Rachel weeping for her children, and would not be comforted, because they are not.

The Sunday after Christmas-day.

The Collect.

A LMIGHTY God, who hast given us thy only begotten Son to take our nature upon him,° and as at this time to be born of a pure Virgin; Grant that we being regenerate, and made thy children by adoption and grace, may daily be renewed by thy holy Spirit, through the same our Lord Jesus Christ, who liveth and reigneth with thee, and the same Spirit ever one God, world without end. *Amen.*

The Epistle.   *Gal.* 4.1

N OW I say, that the heir as long as he is a child, differeth nothing from a servant, though he be lord of all; but he is under tutours and governours, until the time appointed of the Father. Even so we, when we were children, were in bondage under the elements of the world: But when the fulness of the time was come, God sent forth his Son, made of a woman, made under the law, to redeem them that were under the law, that we might receive the adoption of sons. And because ye are sons, God hath sent forth the Spirit of his Son into your hearts, crying, Abba, Father. Wherefore thou art no more a serv-ant, but a son; and if a son, then an heir of God through Christ.

The Gospel.   *Matt.* 1.18

N OW the birth of Jesus Christ was on this wise: When as his mother Mary was espoused to Joseph, (before they came together) she was found with child of the Holy Ghost. Then Joseph her husband, being a just man, and not willing to make her a publick example, was minded to put her away privily. But while he thought on these things, behold, the angel of the Lord appeared unto him in a dream, saying, Joseph, thou son of David, fear not to take unto thee Mary thy wife; for that which is conceived in her, is of the Holy Ghost. And she shall bring forth a Son, and thou shalt call his name Jesus; for he shall save his people from their sins. (Now all this was done, that it might be fulfilled which was spoken of the Lord by the prophet, saying, Behold, a Virgin shall be with child, and shall bring forth a Son, and they shall call his name Emmanuel, which being interpreted, is, God with us.) Then Joseph being raised from sleep, did as the angel of the Lord had bidden him, and took unto him his wife: And knew her not till she had brought forth her first-born Son, and he called his name Jesus.

The Circumcision of Christ.°

The Collect.

ALMIGHTY God, who madest thy blessed Son to be circumcised, and obedient to the law for man; Grant us the true circumcision of the Spirit, that our hearts and all our members being mortified from all worldly and carnal lusts, we may in all things obey thy blessed will, through the same thy Son Jesus Christ our Lord. *Amen.*

The Epistle.   Rom. 4.8

BLESSED is the man to whom the Lord will not impute sin. Cometh this blessedness then upon the circumcision only, or upon the uncircumcision also? For we say, that faith was reckoned to Abraham for righteousness. How was it then reckoned? when he was in circumcision, or in uncircumcision? not in circumcision, but in uncircumcision. And he received the sign of circumcision, a seal of the righteousness of the faith, which he had yet being uncircumcised; that he might be the father of all them that believe, though they be not circumcised; that righteousness might be imputed unto them also: And the father of circumcision, to them who are not of the circumcision only, but who also walk in the steps of that faith of our father Abraham, which he had being yet uncircumcised. For the promise, that he should be the heir of the world, was not to Abraham or to his seed, through the law, but through the righteousness of faith. For if they which are of the law be heirs, faith is made void, and the promise made of none effect.

The Gospel.   Luke 2.15

AND it came to pass, as the angels were gone away from them into heaven, the shepherds said one to another, Let us now go even unto Bethlehem, and see this thing which is come to pass, which the Lord hath made known unto us. And they came with haste, and found Mary and Joseph, and the babe lying in a manger. And when they had seen it, they made known abroad the saying which was told them concerning this child. And all they that heard it, wondered at those things which were told them by the shepherds. But Mary kept all these things, and pondered them in her heart. And the shepherds returned, glorifying and praising God for all the things that they had heard and seen, as it was told unto them. And when eight days were accomplished for the circumcising of the child, his name was called JESUS, which was so named of the angel before he was conceived in the womb.

The same Collect, Epistle, and Gospel shall serve for every day after unto the Epiphany.°

The Epiphany, or the manifestation of Christ to the Gentiles.°

The Collect.

O GOD, who by the leading of a star didst manifest thy only begotten Son to the Gentiles: Mercifully grant, that we which know thee now by faith, may after this life have the fruition of thy glorious godhead, through Jesus Christ our Lord. *Amen.*

The Epistle.   *Eph.* 3. 1

FOR this cause, I Paul, the prisoner of Jesus Christ for you Gentiles; if ye have heard of the dispensation of the grace of God, which is given me to you-ward: How that by revelation he made known unto me the mystery (as I wrote afore in few words, whereby when ye reade ye may understand my knowledge in the mystery of Christ) which in other ages was not made known unto the sons of men, as it is now revealed unto his holy Apostles and Prophets by the Spirit; That the Gentiles should be fellow-heirs, and of the same body, and partakers of his promise in Christ, by the Gospel: Whereof I was made a minister, according to the gift of the grace of God given unto me by the effectual working of his power. Unto me, who am less than the least of all saints, is this grace given, that I should preach among the Gentiles the unsearchable riches of Christ; And to make all men see, what is the fellowship of the mystery, which from the beginning of the world hath been hid in God, who created all things by Jesus Christ: To the intent that now unto the principalities and powers in heavenly places, might be known by the Church the manifold wisdom of God, according to the eternal purpose which he purposed in Christ Jesus our Lord. In whom we have boldness, and access with confidence by the faith of him.

The Gospel.   *Matt.* 2.1

WHEN Jesus was born in Bethlehem of Judea in the days of Herod the king, behold, there came wise men from the east to Jerusalem, saying, Where is he that is born King of the Jews? for we have seen his star in the east, and are come to worship him. When Herod the king had heard these things, he was troubled, and all Jerusalem with him. And when he had gathered all the chief priests and scribes of the people together; he demanded of them, where Christ should be born. And they said unto him, In Bethlehem of Judea: For thus it is written by the prophet, And thou Bethlehem in the land of Juda, art not the least among the princes of Juda: For out of thee shall come a Governour that shall rule my people Israel. Then Herod when he had privily called the wise-men, enquired of them diligently what time the star appeared. And he sent them to Bethlehem, and said, Go, and search diligently for the young child, and when ye have found him, bring me word again, that I may come and worship him also. When they had heard the king, they departed; and lo, the star which they saw in the east went before them, till it came and stood over where the young child was. When they saw the star, they rejoiced with exceeding great joy. And when they were come into the house, they saw the young child with Mary his mother, and fell down and worshipped him: And when they had opened their treasures, they presented unto him gifts, gold, and frankincense, and myrrhe. And being warned of God in a dream, that they should not return to Herod, they departed into their own country another way.

The first Sunday after the Epiphany.

The Collect.

O LORD, we beseech thee mercifully to receive the prayers of thy people which call upon thee, and grant that they may both perceive, and know what things they ought to do, and also may have grace and power faithfully to fulfil the same, through Jesus Christ our Lord. *Amen.*

The Epistle.   Rom. 12.1

I BESEECH you therefore, brethren, by the mercies of God, that ye present your bodies a living sacrifice, holy, acceptable unto God, which is your reasonable service. And be not conformed to this world, but be ye transformed by the renewing of your mind, that ye may prove what is that good, and acceptable, and perfect, will of God. For I say, through the grace given unto me, to every man that is among you, not to think of himself more highly than he ought to think, but to think soberly, according as God hath dealt to every man the measure of faith. For as we have many members in one body, and all members have not the same office; so we being many are one body in Christ, and every one members one of another.

The Gospel.   Luke 2.41

NOW his parents went to Jerusalem every year at the feast of the passover. And when he was twelve years old, they went up to Jerusalem, after the custom of the feast. And when they had fulfilled the days, as they returned, the child Jesus tarried behind in Jerusalem, and Joseph and his mother knew not of it. But they supposing him to have been in the company, went a days journey, and they sought him among their kinsfolk and acquaintance. And when they found him not, they turned back again to Jerusalem, seeking him. And it came to pass, that after three days they found him in the temple, sitting in the midst of the doctors, both hearing them, and asking them questions. And all that heard him were astonished at his understanding and answers. And when they saw him, they were amazed: and his mother said unto him, Son, why hast thou thus dealt with us? behold thy father and I have sought thee sorrowing. And he said unto them, How is it, that ye sought me? wist ye not that I must be about my fathers business? And they understood not the saying which he spake unto them. And he went down with them, and came to Nazareth, and was subject unto them: but his mother kept all these sayings in her heart. And Jesus increased in wisdom and stature, and in favour with God and man.

The second Sunday after the Epiphany.

The Collect.

ALMIGHTY and everlasting God, who dost govern all things in heaven and earth, mercifully hear the supplications of thy

people, and grant us thy peace all the days of our life,° through Jesus
Christ our Lord. *Amen.*

The Epistle. Rom. 12.6

Having then gifts, differing according to the grace that is given to
us, whether prophesie, let us prophesie according to the proportion of faith; or ministry, let us wait on our ministring; or he that
teacheth, on teaching; or he that exhorteth on exhortation: he that
giveth let him do it with simplicity; he that ruleth with diligence; he
that sheweth mercy, with chearfulness. Let love be without dissimulation. Abhor that which is evil, cleave to that which is good. Be kindly
affectioned one to another with brotherly love, in honour preferring
one another: not slothful in business; fervent in spirit; serving the
Lord; rejoicing in hope; patient in tribulation; continuing instant in
prayer; distributing to the necessity of saints; given to hospitality.
Bless them which persecute you: bless and curse not. Rejoice with
them that do rejoyce, and weep with them that weep. Be of the same
mind one towards another. Mind not high things, but condescend to
men of low estate.

The Gospel. John 2.1

And the third day there was a marriage in Cana of Galilee, and
the mother of Jesus was there. And both Jesus was called and his
disciples to the marriage. And when they wanted wine, the mother
of Jesus saith unto him, They have no wine: Jesus saith unto her,
woman, what have I to do with thee? mine hour is not yet come. His
mother saith unto the servants, Whatsoever he saith unto you, do it.
And there were set there six water-pots of stone, after the manner of
the purifying of the Jews, containing two or three firkins apiece. Jesus
saith unto them, Fill the water-pots with water. And they filled them
up to the brim. And he saith unto them, Draw out now and bear unto
the governour of the feast. And they bare it. When the ruler of the
feast had tasted the water that was made wine, and knew not whence
it was: (but the servants which drew the water knew;) the governour
of the feast called the Bridegroom, And saith unto him, Every man
at the beginning doth set forth good wine, and when men have well
drunk, then that which is worse: but thou hast kept the good wine
until now. This beginning of miracles did Jesus in Cana of Galilee,
and manifested forth his glory, and his disciples believed on him.

The third Sunday after the Epiphany.

The Collect.

ALMIGHTY and everlasting God, mercifully look upon our infirmities, and in all our dangers and necessities, stretch forth thy
right hand to help and defend us, through Jesus Christ our Lord.
Amen.

The Epistle.   Rom. 12. 16

BE not wise in your own conceits. Recompense to no man evil for
evil. Provide things honest in the sight of all men. If it be possible,
as much as lieth in you, live peaceably with all men. Dearly beloved,
avenge not your selves, but rather give place unto wrath: for it is written, Vengeance is mine; I will repay, saith the Lord. Therefore if thine
enemy hunger, feed him; if he thirst, give him drink: for in so doing
thou shalt heap coals of fire on his head. Be not overcome of evil, but
overcome evil with good.

The Gospel.   Matt. 8. 1

WHEN he was come down from the mountain, great multitudes
followed him. And, behold, there came a leper and worshipped
him saying, Lord, if thou wilt, thou canst make me clean. And Jesus
put forth his hand and touched him, saying, I will, be thou clean. And
immediately his leprosie was cleansed. And Jesus saith unto him, See
thou tell no man, but go thy way, shew thyself to the priest, and offer
the gift that Moses commanded for a testimony unto them. And when
Jesus was entered into Capernaum, there came unto him a centurion
beseeching him, and saying, Lord my servant lieth at home sick of
the palsie, grievously tormented. And Jesus saith unto him, I will
come and heal him. The centurion answered and said, Lord I am not
worthy that thou shouldest come under my roof; but speak the word
only and my servant shall be healed. For I am a man under authority,
having soldiers under me: and I say unto this man, Go, and he goeth;
and to another, Come, and he cometh; and to my servant, Do this,
and he doth it. When Jesus heard it, he marvelled, and said to them
that followed, Verily I say unto you, I have not found so great faith,
no not in Israel. And I say unto you, that many shall come from the
east and west, and shall sit down with Abraham and Isaac, and Jacob
in the kingdom of heaven. But the children of the kingdom shall be

cast out into outer darkness: there shall be weeping and gnashing of teeth. And Jesus said unto the centurion, Go thy way, and as thou hast believed, so be it done unto thee. And his servant was healed in the self same hour.

The fourth Sunday after the Epiphany.

The Collect.

O GOD, who knowest us to be set in the midst of so many and great dangers, that by reason of the frailty of our nature we cannot always stand upright; Grant to us such strength and protection, as may support us in all dangers, and carry us through all temptations, through Jesus Christ our Lord. *Amen.*

The Epistle.   *Rom.* 13.1

LET every soul be subject unto the higher powers; for there is no power but of God: the powers that be are ordained of God. Whosoever therefore resisteth the power, resisteth the ordinance of God: and they that resist, shall receive to themselves damnation. For Rulers are not a terrour to good works, but to the evil. Wilt thou then not be afraid of the power? do that which is good, and thou shalt have praise of the same: for he is the minister of God to thee for good. But if thou do that which is evil, be afraid; for he beareth not the sword in vain: for he is the minister of God, a revenger to execute wrath upon him that doth evil. Wherefore ye must needs be subject, not onely for wrath, but also for conscience sake. For, for this cause pay you tribute also, for they are Gods ministers, attending continually upon this very thing. Render therefore to all their dues, tribute to whom tribute is due, custom to whom custom, fear to whom fear, honour to whom honour.

The Gospel.   *Matt.* 8.23

AND when he was entred into a ship, his disciples followed him. And, behold, there arose a great tempest in the sea, insomuch that the ship was covered with the waves: but he was asleep. And his disciples came to him, and awoke him, saying, Lord, save us, we perish. And he saith unto them, Why are ye fearful, O ye of little faith? Then he arose, and rebuked the winds and the sea, and there was a great calm. But the men marvelled, saying, What manner of man is this, that even the winds and the sea obey him? And when he was come to the other side into the country of the Gergesens, there met him two possessed with devils, coming out of the tombs, exceeding fierce, so that no man might pass by that way. And, behold, they cried out, saying, What have we to do with thee, Jesus thou Son of God? art thou come hither to torment us before the time? And there was a good way off from them an herd of many swine, feeding. So the devils besought him, saying, If thou cast us out, suffer us to go away into the herd of swine. And he said unto them, Go. And when they were come out, they went into the herd of swine: and behold, the whole herd of swine ran violently down a steep place into the sea, and perished in the waters. And they that kept them fled, and went their ways into the city, and told every thing, and what was befaln to the possessed of the devils. And behold the whole city came out to meet Jesus: and when they saw him, they besought him, that he would depart out of their coasts.

The fifth Sunday after the Epiphany.

The Collect.

O LORD, we beseech thee to keep thy Church and houshold continually in thy true religion, that they who do lean only upon the hope of thy heavenly grace, may evermore be defended by thy mighty power, through Jesus Christ our Lord. *Amen.*

The Epistle.   Col. 3.12

P UT on therefore (as the elect of God, holy and beloved) bowels of mercies, kindness, humbleness of mind, meekness, long-suffering, forbearing one another, and forgiving one another, if any man have a quarrel against any: even as Christ forgave you, so also do ye. And above all these things, put on charity, which is the bond of perfectness. And let the peace of God rule in your hearts, to the which also ye are called in one body; and be ye thankful. Let the word of Christ dwell in you richly in all wisdom, teaching and admonishing one another in psalms and hymns, and spiritual songs, singing with grace in your hearts to the Lord. And whatsoever ye do in word or deed, do all in the name of the Lord Jesus, giving thanks to God, and the Father by him.

The Gospel.   Matt. 13.24

T HE kingdom of heaven is likened unto a man, which sowed good seed in his field. But while men slept, his enemy came and sowed tares among the wheat, and went his way. But when the blade was sprung up, and brought forth fruit, then appeared the tares also. So the servants of the housholder came and said unto him, Sir, didst not thou sow good seed in thy field? from whence then hath it tares? He said unto them, An enemy hath done this. The servants said unto him, Wilt thou then that we go and gather them up? But he said, Nay; least while ye gather up the tares, ye root up also the wheat with them. Let both grow together until the harvest; and in the time of harvest I will say to the reapers, Gather ye together first the tares, and bind them in bundles to burn them: but gather the wheat into my barn.

The sixth Sunday after the Epiphany.

The Collect.°

O GOD, whose blessed Son was manifested, that he might destroy the works of the devil, and make us the sons of God, and heirs of eternal life; Grant us, we beseech thee, that having this hope, we may purifie our selves, even as he is pure; that when he shall appear again with power and great glory, we may be made like unto him in his eternal and glorious kingdom, where with thee, O Father, and thee, O holy Ghost, he liveth and reigneth ever one God world without end. *Amen.*

The Epistle.   1 *John* 3.1

B EHOLD, what manner of love the Father hath bestowed upon us, that we should be called the sons of God: therefore the world knoweth us not, because it knew him not. Beloved, now are we the Sons of God, and it doth not yet appear what we shall be: but we know that when he shall appear, we shall be like him; for we shall see him as he is. And every man that hath this hope in him, purifieth himself, even as he is pure. Whosoever committeth sin transgresseth also the law: for sin is the transgression of the law. And ye know that he was manifested to take away our sins; and in him is no sin. Whosoever abideth in him sinneth not: whosoever sinneth hath not seen him, neither known him. Little children, let no man deceive you: he that doth righteousness is righteous, even as he is righteous. He that committeth sin is of the devil: for the devil sinneth from the beginning. For this purpose the Son of God was manifested, that he might destroy the works of the devil.

The Gospel.   *Matt.* 24.23

THEN if any man shall say unto you, Lo here is Christ, or there: believe it not. For there shall arise false Christs and false prophets, and shall shew great signs and wonders; insomuch that (if it were possible) they shall deceive the very elect. Behold, I have told you before. Wherefore if they shall say unto you, Behold, he is in the desert, go not forth: behold, he is in the secret chambers, believe it not. For as the lightning cometh out of the east, and shineth even unto the west: so shall also the coming of the Son of man be. For wheresoever the carcase is, there will the eagles be gathered together. Immediately after the tribulation of those days, shall the sun be darkned, and the moon shall not give her light, and the stars shall fall from heaven, and the powers of the heavens shall be shaken. And then shall appear the sign of the Son of man in heaven: and then shall all the tribes of the earth mourn, and they shall see the Son of man coming in the clouds of heaven with power and great glory. And he shall send his angels with a great sound of a trumpet, and they shall gather together his elect from the four winds, from one end of heaven to the other.

The Sunday called Septuagesima,° or the third Sunday before Lent.

The Collect.

O LORD, we beseech thee favourably to hear the prayers of thy people, that we who are justly punished for our offences, may be mercifully delivered by thy goodness, for the glory of thy Name, through Jesus Christ our Saviour, who liveth and reigneth with thee and the Holy Ghost ever one God, world without end. *Amen.*

The Epistle.   1 *Cor.* 9.24

KNOW ye not that they which run in a race, run all, but one receiveth the prize? So run that ye may obtain. And every man that striveth for the mastery, is temperate in all things: Now they do it to obtain a corruptible crown, but we an incorruptible. I therefore so run, not as uncertainly; so fight I, not as one that beateth the air: But I keep under my body, and bring it into subjection, lest that by any means when I have preached to others, I my self should be a cast-away.

The Gospel.   Matt. 20.1

THE kingdom of heaven is like unto a man that is an housholder, which went out early in the morning to hire labourers into his vineyard. And when he had agreed with the labourers for a penny a day, he sent them into his vineyard. And he went out about the third hour, and saw others standing idle in the market-place, and said unto them, Go ye also into the vineyard, and whatsoever is right I will give you. And they went their way. Again he went out about the sixth and ninth hour, and did likewise. And about the eleventh hour he went out and found others standing idle, and saith unto them, Why stand ye here all the day idle? They say unto him, Because no man hath hired us. He saith unto them, Go ye also into the vineyard, and whatsoever is right, that shall ye receive. So when even was come, the Lord of the vineyard saith unto his steward, Call the labourers and give them their hire, beginning from the last unto the first. And when they came that were hired about the eleventh hour, they received every man a peny. But when the first came, they supposed that they should have received more, and they likewise received every man a peny. And when they had received it, they murmured against the good-man of the house, saying, These last have wrought but one hour, and thou hast made them equal unto us, which have borne the burden and heat of the day. But he answered one of them and said, Friend, I do thee no wrong: didst not thou agree with me for a peny? Take that thine is, and go thy way: I will give unto this last even as unto thee. Is it not lawful for me to do what I will with mine own? Is thine eye evil, because I am good? So the last shall be first, and the first last: for many be called, but few chosen.

The Sunday called Sexagesima, or the second Sunday before Lent.

The Collect.

O LORD God, who seest that we put not our trust in any thing that we do; Mercifully grant that by thy power° we may be defended against all adversity, through Jesus Christ our Lord. *Amen.*

The Epistle.   2 *Cor.* 11.19

YE suffer fools gladly, seeing ye your selves are wise. For ye suffer if a man bring you into bondage, if a man devour you, if a man take of you, if a man exalt himself, if a man smite you on the face. I speak as concerning reproach, as though we had been weak:

howbeit, whereinsoever any is bold (I speak foolishly) I am bold also. Are they Hebrews? so am I: are they Israelites? so am I: are they the seed of Abraham? so am I: are they ministers of Christ? (I speak as a fool) I am more: in labours more abundant; in stripes above measure; in prisons more frequent; in deaths oft. Of the Jews five times received I fourty stripes save one. Thrice was I beaten with rods. Once was I stoned. Thrice I suffered shipwrack. A night and a day I have been in the deep: in journeying often; in perils of waters; in perils of robbers; in perils by mine own countrey-men; in perils by the heathen; in perils in the city; in perils in the wilderness; in perils in the sea; in perils among false brethren; in weariness and painfulness; in watchings often; in hunger and thirst; in fastings often; in cold and nakedness; beside those things that are without, that which cometh upon me daily, the care of all the Churches. Who is weak, and I am not weak? who is offended, and I burn not? If I must needs glory, I will glory of the things which concern mine infirmities. The God and Father of our Lord Jesus Christ, which is blessed for evermore, knoweth that I lie not.

The Gospel.   Luke 8.4

WHEN much people were gathered together, and were come to him out of every city, he spake by a parable, A sower went out to sow his seed: and as he sowed, some fell by the way side, and it was trodden down, and the fowls of the air devoured it. And some fell upon a rock, and as soon as it was sprung up, it withered away, because it lacked moisture. And some fell among thorns, and the thorns sprang up with it, and choked it. And other fell on good ground and sprang up, and bare fruit an hundredfold. And when he had said these things, he cried, He that hath ears to hear let him hear. And his disciples asked him, saying, What might this parable be? And he said, Unto you it is given to know the mysteries of the kingdom of God: but to others in parables; that seeing they might not see, and hearing they might not understand. Now the parable is this; The seed is the word of God. Those by the way-side are they that hear; then cometh the devil, and taketh away the word out of their hearts, lest they should believe and be saved. They on the rock, are they, which when they hear, receive the word with joy; and these have no root, which for a while believe, and in time of temptation fall away. And that which fell among thorns, are they, which, when they have heard, go forth, and are choked with cares and riches, and pleasures of this life, and bring no fruit to perfection. But that on the good ground, are they, which in an honest and good heart, having heard the word, keep it, and bring forth fruit with patience.

The Sunday called *Quinquagesima*, or the next Sunday before Lent.

The Collect.°

O LORD, who hast taught us, that all our doings without charity are nothing worth; Send thy Holy Ghost, and pour into our hearts that most excellent gift of charity, the very bond of peace and of all vertues, without which whosoever liveth is counted dead before thee: Grant this for thine only Son Jesus Christs sake. *Amen.*

The Epistle. 　　　　　　　　　　　1 *Cor.* 13.1

THOUGH I speak with the tongues of men and of angels, and have not charity, I am become as sounding brass, or a tinckling cymbal. And though I have the gift of prophesie, and understand all mysteries, and all knowledge; and though I have all faith, so that I could remove mountains, and have no charity, I am nothing. And though I bestow all my goods to feed the poor, and though I give my body to be burned, and have not charity, it profiteth me nothing. Charity suffereth long, and is kind; charity envieth not; charity vaunteth not it self, is not puffed up, doth not behave it self unseemly, seeketh not her own, is not easily provoked, thinketh no evil, rejoyceth not in iniquity, but rejoyceth in the truth; beareth all things, believeth all things, hopeth all things, endureth all things. Charity never faileth, but whether there be prophesies, they shall fail; whether there be tongues, they shall cease; whether there be knowledge, it shall vanish away. For we know in part, and we prophesie in part. But when that which is perfect is come, then that which is in part shall be done away. When I was a child I spake as a child, I understood as a child, I thought as a child; but when I became a man, I put away childish things. For now we see through a glass darkly; but then face to face: now I know in part; but then shall I know even as also I am known. And now abideth faith, hope, charity, these three; but the greatest of these is charity.

The Gospel.   Luke 18.31

THEN Jesus took unto him the twelve and said unto them, Behold, we go up to Jerusalem, and all things that are written by the prophets concerning the Son of man shall be accomplished. For he shall be delivered unto the Gentiles, and shall be mocked, and spitefully entreated, and spitted on. And they shall scourge him, and put him to death; and the third day he shall rise again. And they understood none of these things: and this saying was hid from them, neither knew they the things which were spoken. And it came to pass, that as he was come nigh unto Jericho, a certain blind man sat by the way-side begging: And hearing the multitude pass by, he asked what it meant. And they told him, that Jesus of Nazareth passeth by. And he cried, saying, Jesus thou son of David, have mercy on me. And they which went before rebuked him, that he should hold his peace: but he cried so much the more, Thou son of David, have mercy on me. And Jesus stood and commanded him to be brought unto him: and when he was come near, he asked him, saying, What wilt thou that I should do unto thee? And he said, Lord, that I may receive my sight. And Jesus said unto him, Receive thy sight; thy faith hath saved thee. And immediately he received his sight, and followed him, glorifying God: and all the people when they saw it, gave praise unto God.

The first day of Lent, commonly called Ashwednesday.

The Collect.°

ALMIGHTY and everlasting God, who hatest nothing that thou hast made, and dost forgive the sins of all them that are penitent; Create and make in us new and contrite hearts, that we worthily lamenting our sins, and acknowledging our wretchedness, may obtain of thee, the God of all mercy, perfect remission and forgiveness, through Jesus Christ our Lord. *Amen.*

¶ *This Collect is to be read every day in Lent, after the Collect appointed for the day.*

For the Epistle.   Joel 2.12

TURN ye even to me saith the Lord, with all your heart, and with fasting, and with weeping, and with mourning. And rend your heart, and not your garments, and turn unto the Lord your God: for he is gracious and merciful, slow to anger, and of great kindness, and repenteth him of the evil. Who knoweth if he will return, and repent, and leave a blessing behind him, even a meat-offering and a drink-offering unto the Lord your God? Blow the trumpet in Zion, sanctifie a fast, call a solemn assembly, gather the people, sanctifie the congregation, assemble the elders, gather the children, and those that suck the breasts; let the bridegroom go forth of his chamber, and the bride out of her closet; let the priests, the ministers of the Lord, weep between the porch and the altar, and let them say, Spare thy people, O Lord, and give not thine heritage to reproach, that the heathen should rule over them: wherefore should they say among the people, Where is their God?

The Gospel.   *Matt.* 6.16

WHEN ye fast, be not as the hypocrites, of a sad countenance: for they disfigure their faces, that they may appear unto men to fast. Verily I say unto you, they have their reward. But thou, when thou fastest, anoint thine head, and wash thy face, that thou appear not unto men to fast, but unto thy Father which is in secret; and thy Father which seeth in secret, shall reward thee openly. Lay not up for your selves treasures upon earth, where moth and rust doth corrupt, and where thieves break through and steal. But lay up for your selves treasures in heaven, where neither moth nor rust doth corrupt, and where thieves do not break through nor steal. For where your treasure is, there will your heart be also.

The first Sunday in Lent.

The Collect.°

O LORD, who for our sake didst fast fourty days and fourty nights; Give us grace to use such abstinence, that our flesh being subdued to the Spirit; we may ever obey thy godly motions in righteousness and true holiness, to thy honour and glory, who livest and reignest with the Father and the holy Ghost, one God, world without end. *Amen.*

The Epistle.   2 *Cor.* 6.1

WE then as workers together with him, beseech you also, that ye receive not the grace of God in vain. (For he saith, I have heard thee in a time accepted, and in the day of salvation have I succoured thee: behold, now is the accepted time; behold, now is the day of salvation;) giving no offence in any thing, that the ministry be not blamed; but in all things approving our selves as the ministers of God, in much patience, in afflictions, in necessities, in distresses, in stripes, in imprisonments, in tumults, in labours, in watchings, in fastings; by pureness, by knowledge, by long-suffering, by kindness, by the holy Ghost, by love unfeigned, by the word of truth, by the power of God, by the armour of righteousness on the right hand, and on the left, by honour and dishonour, by evil report and good report: as deceivers, and yet true; as unknown, and yet well known; as dying, and, behold we live; as chastened, and not killed; As sorrowful, yet alway rejoycing; as poor, yet making many rich; as having nothing, and yet possessing all things.

The Gospel.   *Matt.* 4.1

THEN was Jesus led up of the spirit into the wilderness, to be tempted of the devil. And when he had fasted fourty days and fourty nights, he was afterward an hungred. And when the tempter came to him, he said, If thou be the Son of God, command that these stones be made bread. But he answered and said, It is written, Man shall not live by bread alone, but by every word that proceedeth out of the mouth of God. Then the devil taketh him up into the holy city, and setteth him on a pinnacle of the temple, and saith unto him, If thou be the Son of God, cast thy self down; for it is written, He shall give his angels charge concerning thee, and in their hands they shall bear thee up, lest at any time thou dash thy foot against a stone. Jesus said unto him, It is written again, Thou shalt not tempt the Lord thy God. Again the devil taketh him up into an exceeding high mountain, and sheweth him all the kingdoms of the world, and the glory of them; and saith unto him, All these things will I give thee, if thou wilt fall down and worship me. Then saith Jesus unto him, Get thee hence, Satan; for it is written, Thou shalt worship the Lord thy God, and him only shalt thou serve. Then the devil leaveth him, and behold, angels came and ministred unto him.

The second Sunday in Lent.

The Collect.°

ALMIGHTY God, who seest that we have no power of our selves to help our selves;° Keep us both outwardly in our bodies and inwardly in our souls, that we may be defended from all adversities which may happen to the body, and from all evil thoughts which may assault and hurt the soul, through Jesus Christ our Lord. *Amen.*

The Epistle. 1 *Thess.* 4.1

W E beseech you, brethren, and exhort you by the Lord Jesus, that as ye have received of us how ye ought to walk, and to please God, so ye would abound more and more. For ye know what commandments we gave you by the Lord Jesus. For this is the will of God, even your sanctification, that ye should abstain from fornication; that every one of you should know how to possess his vessel in sanctification and honour; not in the lust of concupiscence, even as the Gentiles which know not God: that no man go beyond, and defraud his brother in any matter, because that the Lord is the avenger of all such, as we also have forewarned you, and testified. For God hath not called us unto uncleanness, but unto holiness. He therefore that despiseth, despiseth not man, but God, who hath also given unto us his Holy Spirit.

The Gospel. *Matt.* 15.21

J ESUS went thence, and departed into the coasts of Tyre and Sidon. And behold, a woman of Canaan came out of the same coasts, and cried unto him, saying, Have mercy on me, O Lord, thou son of David, my daughter is grievously vexed with a devil. But he answered her not a word. And his disciples came and besought him, saying, Send her away, for she crieth after us. But he answered and said, I am not sent, but unto the lost sheep of the house of Israel. Then came she and worshipped him, saying, Lord help me. But he answered and said, It is not meet to take the childrens bread, and to cast it to dogs. And she said, Truth, Lord: yet the dogs eat of the crumbs which fall from their masters table. Then Jesus answered and said unto her, O woman, great is thy faith: be it unto thee even as thou wilt. And her daughter was made whole from that very hour.

The third Sunday in Lent.

The Collect.

W E beseech thee, Almighty God, look upon the hearty desires of thy humble servants, and stretch forth the right hand of thy Majesty, to be our defence against all our enemies, through Jesus Christ our Lord. *Amen.*

The Epistle.

Eph. 5.1

B E ye therefore followers of God, as dear children; and walk in love, as Christ also hath loved us, and hath given himself for us an offering and a sacrifice to God for a sweet-smelling savour. But fornication, and all uncleanness, or covetousness, let it not be once named among you, as becometh saints; neither filthiness, nor foolish talking, nor jesting, which are not convenient: but rather giving of thanks. For this ye know, that no whoremonger, nor unclean person, nor covetous man, who is an idolater, hath any inheritance in the kingdom of Christ, and of God. Let no man deceive you with vain words: for because of these things cometh the wrath of God upon the children of disobedience. Be not ye therefore partakers with them; For ye were sometimes darkness, but now are ye light in the Lord: walk as children of light; (for the fruit of the spirit is in all goodness, and righteousness, and truth) proving what is acceptable unto the Lord. And have no fellowship with the unfruitful works of darkness, but rather reprove them: For it is a shame even to speak of those things which are done of them in secret. But all things that are reproved, are made manifest by the light: for whatsoever doth make manifest, is light. Wherefore he saith, Awake thou that sleepest, and arise from the dead, and Christ shall give thee light.

The Gospel.

Luke 11.14

J ESUS was casting out a devil, and it was dumb. And it came to pass when the devil was gone out, the dumb spake; and the people wondred. But some of them said, He casteth out devils through Beelzebub, the chief of the devils. And other tempting him, sought of him a sign from heaven. But he knowing their thoughts, said unto them, Every kingdom divided against it self, is brought to desolation; and a house divided against a house, falleth. If Satan also be divided against himself, how shall his kingdom stand? because ye say that I cast out devils through Beelzebub. And if I by Beelzebub cast out devils, by whom do your sons cast them out? therefore shall they be your judges. But if I with the finger of God cast out devils, no doubt the kingdom of God is come upon you. When a strong man armed keepeth his palace, his goods are in peace; but when a stronger than he shall come upon him, and overcome him, he taketh from him all his armour wherein he trusted, and divideth his spoils. He that is not with me; is against me: and he that gathereth not with me, scattereth.

When the unclean spirit is gone out of a man, he walketh through dry places, seeking rest; and finding none, he saith, I will return unto my house, whence I came out. And when he cometh, he findeth it swept and garnished. Then goeth he, and taketh to him seven other spirits more wicked than himself, and they enter in, and dwell there; and the last state of that man is worse than the first. And it came to pass as he spake these things, a certain woman of the company lift up her voice, and said unto him, Blessed is the womb that bare thee, and the paps which thou hast sucked. But he said, Yea, rather blessed are they that hear the word of God, and keep it.

The fourth Sunday in Lent.

The Collect.

GRANT, we beseech thee, Almighty God, that we, who for our evil deeds do worthily deserve to be punished, by the comfort of thy grace may mercifully be relieved, through our Lord and Saviour Jesus Christ. *Amen.*

The Epistle.   Gal. 4.21

TELL me, ye that desire to be under the law, do ye not hear the law? For it is written, that Abraham had two sons, the one by a bond-maid, the other by a free-woman. But he who was of the bond-woman was born after the flesh; but he of the free-woman was by promise. Which things are an allegory: for these are the two covenants; the one from the mount Sinai, which gendereth to bondage, which is Agar. For this Agar is mount Sinai in Arabia, and answereth to Jerusalem which now is, and is in bondage with her children. But Jerusalem which is above is free; which is the mother of us all. For it is written, Rejoyce, thou barren that bearest not; break forth and cry, thou that travailest not: for the desolate hath many moe children than she which hath an husband. Now we, brethren, as Isaac was, are the children of promise. But as then, he that was born after the flesh, persecuted him that was born after the spirit, even so it is now. Nevertheless, what saith the scripture? Cast out the bond-woman and her son: for the son of the bond-woman shall not be heir with the son of the free-woman. So then, brethren, we are not children of the bond-woman, but of the free.

The Gospel.   *John* 6.1

J ESUS went over the sea of Galilee, which is the sea of Tiberias.
And a great multitude followed him, because they saw his miracles
which he did on them that were diseased. And Jesus went up into
a mountain, and there he sat with his disciples. And the passover,
a feast of the Jews, was nigh. When Jesus then lifted up his eyes, and
saw a great company come unto him, he saith unto Philip, Whence
shall we buy bread that these may eat? (And this he said to prove him;
for he himself knew what he would do.) Philip answered him, Two
hundred peny-worth of bread is not sufficient for them, that every
one of them may take a little. One of his disciples, Andrew, Simon
Peters brother, saith unto him, There is a lad here, which hath five
barley-loaves, and two small fishes: but what are they among so many?
And Jesus said, Make the men sit down. Now there was much grass in
the place. So the men sat down, in number about five thousand. And
Jesus took the loaves, and when he had given thanks, he distributed
to the disciples, and the disciples to them that were set down, and
likewise of the fishes as much as they would. When they were filled,
he said unto his disciples, Gather up the fragments that remain, that
nothing be lost. Therefore they gathered them together, and filled
twelve baskets with the fragments of the five barley-loaves, which
remained over and above unto them that had eaten. Then those men,
when they had seen the miracle that Jesus did, said, This is of a truth
that prophet that should come into the world.

The fifth Sunday in Lent.

The Collect.

W E beseech thee, Almighty God, mercifully to look upon thy
people; that by thy great goodness they may be governed and
preserved evermore, both in body and soul, through Jesus Christ our
Lord. *Amen.*

The Epistle.   *Heb.* 9.11

C HRIST being come an high priest of good things to come, by
a greater and more perfect tabernacle, not made with hands; that
is to say, not of this building; neither by the bloud of goats and calves;
but by his own bloud he entred in once into the holy place, having
obtained eternal redemption for us. For if the bloud of bulls, and of
goats, and the ashes of an heifer sprinkling the unclean, sanctifieth to

the purifying of the flesh; how much more shall the bloud of Christ, who through the eternal Spirit offered himself without spot to God, purge your conscience from dead works to serve the living God? And for this cause he is the Mediatour of the new testament, that by means of death, for the redemption of the transgressions that were under the first testament, they which are called might receive the promise of eternal inheritance.

The Gospel.　　　*John* 8.46

J ESUS said, Which of you convinceth me of sin? And if I say the truth, why do ye not believe me? He that is of God, heareth Gods words; ye therefore hear them not, because ye are not of God. Then answered the Jews, and said unto him, Say we not well, that thou art a Samaritan, and hast a devil? Jesus answered, I have not a devil; but I honour my Father, and ye do dishonour me. And I seek not mine own glory; there is one that seeketh and judgeth. Verily, verily, I say unto you, If a man keep my saying, he shall never see death. Then said the Jews unto him, Now we know that thou hast a devil. Abraham is dead, and the prophets; and thou saiest, If a man keep my saying, he shall never taste of death. Art thou greater than our father Abraham, which is dead: and the prophets are dead: whom makest thou thy self? Jesus answered, If I honour my self, my honour is nothing: it is my Father that honoureth me, of whom ye say, that he is your God; yet ye have not known him; but I know him: and if I should say, I know him not, I shall be a liar like unto you; but I know him, and keep his saying. Your Father Abraham rejoyced to see my day, and he saw it, and was glad. Then said the Jews unto him, Thou art not yet fifty years old, and hast thou seen Abraham? Jesus said unto them, Verily, verily, I say unto you, Before Abraham was, I am. Then took they up stones to cast at him: but Jesus hid himself, and went out of the temple.

The Sunday next before Easter.

The Collect.°

A LMIGHTY and everlasting God, who of thy tender love towards mankind, hast sent thy Son, our Saviour Jesus Christ, to take upon him our flesh, and to suffer death upon the cross, that all mankind should follow the example of his great humility; Mercifully grant that we may both follow the example of his patience, and also be made partakers of his resurrection, through the same Jesus Christ our Lord. *Amen.*

The Epistle.   *Phil.* 2. 5

L ET this mind be in you, which was also in Christ Jesus: who being in the form of God, thought it not robbery to be equal with God: but made himself of no reputation, and took upon him the form of a servant, and was made in the likeness of men: And being found in fashion as a man, he humbled himself, and became obedient unto death, even the death of the cross. Wherefore God also hath highly exalted him, and given him a Name, which is above every name; that at the name of Jesus every knee should bow, of things in heaven, and things in earth, and things under the earth; and that every tongue should confess that Jesus Christ is Lord, to the glory of God the Father.

The Gospel.°   *Matt.* 27. 1

W HEN the morning was come, all the chief priests and elders of the people took counsel against Jesus, to put him to death. And when they had bound him, they led him away, and delivered him to Pontius Pilate the governour. Then Judas who had betrayed him, when he saw that he was condemned, repented himself, and brought again the thirty pieces of silver to the chief priests and elders, saying, I have sinned, in that I have betrayed the innocent bloud. And they said, What is that to us? see thou to that. And he cast down the pieces of silver in the temple, and departed, and went and hanged himself. And the chief priests took the silver pieces, and said, It is not lawful for to put them into the treasury, because it is the price of bloud. And they took counsel, and bought with them the potters field, to bury strangers in. Wherefore that field was called, The field of bloud unto this day. (Then was fulfilled that which was spoken by Jeremy the prophet, saying, And they took the thirty pieces of silver, the price of him that was valued, whom they of the children of Israel did value, and gave them for the potters field, as the Lord appointed me.) And Jesus stood before the governour; and the governour asked him, saying, Art thou the King of the Jews? And Jesus said unto him, Thou sayest. And when he was accused of the chief priests and elders, he answered nothing. Then said Pilate unto him, Hearest thou not how many things they witness against thee? And he answered him to never a word, insomuch that the governour marvelled greatly. Now at that feast the governour was wont to release unto the people a prisoner, whom they would. And they had then a notable prisoner, called Barabbas. Therefore when they were gathered together, Pilate said unto them, Whom will ye that I release unto you? Barabbas or Jesus, which is called Christ? For he knew that for envy they had delivered him. When he was set down on the judgement seat, his wife sent unto him, saying, Have thou nothing to do with that just man: for I have suffered many things this day in a dream because of him. But the chief priests and elders perswaded the multitude that they should ask Barabbas, and destroy Jesus. The governour answered and said unto them, Whether of the twain will ye that I release unto you? They said, Barabbas. Pilate saith unto them, What shall I do then with Jesus, which is called Christ? They all say unto him, Let him be crucified. And the governour said, Why, what evil hath he done? But they cried out the more, saying, Let him be crucified. When Pilate saw that he could prevail nothing, but that rather a tumult was made, he took water, and washed his hands before the multitude, saying, I am innocent of the bloud of this just person: see ye to it. Then answered all the people, and said, His bloud be on us, and on our children. Then released he Barabbas unto them: and when he had scourged Jesus, he delivered him to be crucified. Then the souldiers of the governour took Jesus into the common hall, and gathered unto him the whole band of souldiers. And they stripped him, and put on him a scarlet robe. And when they had platted a crown of thorns, they put it upon his head, and a reed in his right hand: and they bowed the knee before him, and mocked him, saying, Hail, king of the Jews. And they spit upon him, and took the reed, and smote him on the head. And after that they had mocked him, they took the robe off from him, and put his own raiment on him, and led him away to crucifie him. And as they came out, they found a man of Cyrene, Simon by name: him they compelled to bear his cross. And when they were come unto a place called Golgotha, that is to say, a place of a skull, they gave him vineger to drink, mingled with gall: and when he had tasted thereof, he would not drink. And they crucified him, and parted his garments, casting lots: that it might be fulfilled, which was spoken by the prophet, They parted my garments among them, and upon my vesture did they cast lots. And sitting down they watched him there; And set up over his head his accusation written, *THIS IS JESUS THE KING OF THE JEWS*. Then were there two thieves crucified with him: one on the right hand, and another on the left. And they that passed by, reviled him, wagging their heads, and saying: Thou that destroyest the temple, and buildest it in three days, save thy self: if thou be the son of God, come down from the cross. Likewise also the chief priests mocking him, with the Scribes and elders, said, He saved others, himself he cannot save: if he be the King of Israel let him now come down from the cross, and we will believe him. He trusted in God; let him deliver him now if he will have him: for he said, I am the Son of God. The Thieves also which were crucified with him, cast the same in his teeth. Now from the sixth hour there was darkness over all the land, unto the ninth hour. And about the ninth hour, Jesus cried with a loud voice, saying, *Eli, Eli, lama sabachthani?* that is to say, My God, my God, why hast thou forsaken me? Some of them that stood there, when they heard that, said, This man calleth for Elias. And straightway one of them ran, and took a spunge and filled it with vineger, and put it on a reed, and gave him to drink. The rest said, Let be, let us see whether Elias will come to save him. Jesus when he had cried again with a loud voice yielded up the ghost. And behold, the vail of the temple was rent in twain from the top to the bottom, and the earth did quake, and the rocks rent, and the graves were opened, and many bodies of saints which slept, arose, and came out of the graves, after his resurrection, and went into the holy city, and appeared unto many. Now when the centurion, and they that were with him, watching Jesus, saw the earth-quake, and those things that were done, they feared greatly, saying, Truly this was the son of God.

Munday before Easter.

For the Epistle. *Isa.* 63. 1

WHO is this that cometh from Edom, with dyed garments from Bozrah? this that is glorious in his apparel, travelling in the greatness of his strength? I that speak in righteousness, mighty to save. Wherefore art thou red in thine apparel, and thy garments like him that treadeth in the wine-fat? I have trodden the wine-press alone, and of the people there was none with me: for I will tread them in mine anger, and trample them in my fury, and their bloud shall be sprinkled upon my garments, and I will stain all my raiment. For the day of vengeance is in mine heart, and the year of my redeemed is come. And I looked and there was none to help; and I wondred that there was none to uphold: therefore mine own arm brought salvation unto me, and my fury it upheld me. And I will tread down the people in mine anger, and make them drunk in my fury, and I will bring down their strength to the earth. I will mention the loving kindnesses of the Lord, and the praises of the Lord, according to all that the Lord hath bestowed on us, and the great goodness toward the house of Israel, which he hath bestowed on them, according to his mercies, and according to the multitude of his loving-kindnesses. For he said, Surely they are my people, children that will not lie: so he was their Saviour. In all their affliction, he was afflicted, and the angel of his presence saved them: in his love and in his pity he redeemed them, and he bare them, and carried them all the days of old. But they rebelled, and vexed his holy Spirit, therefore he was turned to be their enemy, and he fought against them. Then he remembred the days of old, Moses and his people, saying, Where is he that brought them up out of the sea with the shepherd of his flock? Where is he that put his holy spirit within him? that led them by the right hand of Moses with his glorious arm, dividing the water before them, to make himself an everlasting Name? That led them through the deep as an horse in the wilderness, that they should not stumble? as a beast goeth down into the valley, the spirit of the Lord caused him to rest: so didst thou lead thy people to make thy self a glorious Name. Look down from heaven, and behold from the habitation of thy holiness, and of thy glory: Where is thy zeal, and thy strength, the sounding of thy bowels, and of thy mercies towards me? are they restrained? Doubtless thou art our Father, though Abraham be ignorant of us, and Israel acknowledge us not: thou O Lord, art our father, our redeemer, thy Name is from everlasting. O Lord, Why hast thou made us to erre from thy waies? and hardned our hearts from thy fear? Return for thy servants sake, the tribes of thine inheritance. The people of thy holiness have possessed it but a little while: our adversaries have trodden down thy sanctuary. We are thine, thou never barest rule over them; they were not called by thy Name.

The Gospel.   Mark 14.1

AFTER two dayes was the feast of the passover, and of unleavened bread: and the chief priests and the Scribes sought how they might take him by craft, and put him to death. But they said, Not on the feast-day, lest there be an uprore of the people. And being in Bethany, in the house of Simon the leper, as he sat at meat, there came a woman, having an alabaster-box of ointment of spikenard, very precious, and she brake the box, and poured it on his head. And there were some that had indignation within themselves, and said, Why was this waste of the ointment made? For it might have been sold for more than three hundred pence, and have been given to the poor: and they murmured against her. And Jesus said, Let her alone; why trouble you her? she hath wrought a good work on me. For ye have the poor with you alwayes, and whensoever ye will, ye may do them good: but me ye have not alwayes. She hath done what she could: she is come aforehand to anoint my body to the burying. Verily I say unto you, Wheresoever this gospel shall be preached throughout the whole world, this also that she hath done shall be spoken of for a memorial of her. And Judas Iscariot, one of the twelve, went unto the chief priests, to betray him unto them. And when they heard it, they were glad, and promised to give him money. And he sought how he might conveniently betray him. And the first day of unleavened bread, when they killed the passover, his disciples said unto him, Where wilt thou that we go and prepare, that thou mayest eat the passover? And he sendeth forth two of his disciples, and saith unto them, Go ye into the city, and there shall meet you a man bearing a pitcher of water: follow him. And wheresoever he shall go in, say ye to the good-man of the house, The Master saith, Where is the guest-chamber, where I shall eat the passover with my disciples? And he will shew you a large upper room furnished, and prepared, there make ready for us. And his disciples went forth, and came into the city, and found as he had said unto them: and they made ready the passover. And in the evening he cometh with the twelve. And as they sat, and did eat, Jesus said, Verily I say unto you, One of you which eateth with me, shall betray me. And they began to be sorrowful, and to say unto him, one by one, Is it I? and another said, Is it I? And he answered and said unto them, It is one of the twelve that dippeth with me in the dish. The Son of man indeed goeth, as it is written of him: but wo to that man by whom the son of man is betrayed: good were it for that man if he had never been born. And as they did eat, Jesus took bread, and blessed, and brake it, and gave to them, and said, Take, eat: this is my body. And he took the cup, and when he had given thanks, he gave it to them: and they all drank of it. And he said unto them, This is my bloud of the new testament, which is shed for many. Verily I say unto you, I will drink no more of the fruit of the vine, until that day that I drink it new in the kingdom of God. And when they had sung an hymn, they went out into the mount of Olives. And Jesus saith unto them, All ye shall be offended because of me this night: for it is written, I will smite the shepherd, and the sheep shall be scattered. But after that I am risen, I will go before you into Galilee. But Peter said unto him, Although all shall be offended, yet will not I. And Jesus saith unto him; Verily I say unto thee, that this day, even in this night, before the cock crow twice, thou shalt deny me thrice. But he spake the more vehemently, If I should die with thee, I will not deny thee in any wise. Likewise also said they all. And they came to a place which was named Gethsemani, and he saith to his disciples, Sit ye here, while I shall pray. And he taketh with him Peter, and James, and John, and began to be sore amazed, and to be very heavy, and saith unto them, My soul is exceeding sorrowful unto death; tarry ye here, and watch. And he went forward a little, and fell on the ground, and prayed, that if it were possible the hour might pass from him. And he said, Abba, Father; All things are possible unto thee; take away this cup from me: nevertheless, not what I will, but what thou wilt. And he cometh and findeth them sleeping, and saith unto Peter, Simon, sleepest thou? couldst not thou watch one hour? Watch ye and pray, lest ye enter into temptation: The spirit truly is ready, but the flesh is weak. And again he went away, and prayed, and spake the same words. And when he returned, he found them asleep again, (for their eyes were heavy) neither wist they what to answer him. And he cometh the third time, and saith unto them, Sleep on now, and take your rest: it is enough, the hour is come; Behold the Son of man is betrayed into the hands of sinners. Rise up, let us go; lo, he that betrayeth me is at hand. And immediately, while he yet spake, cometh Judas, one of the twelve, and with him a great multitude with swords, and staves, from the chief Priests, and the Scribes, and the Elders. And he that betrayed him, had given them a token, saying, Whomsoever I shall kiss, that same is he; take him, and lead him away safely. And as soon as he was come, he goeth straightway to him, and saith, Master, master, and kissed him. And they laid their hands on him, and took him. And one of them that stood by, drew a sword, and smote a servant of the high Priest, and cut off his ear. And Jesus answered and said unto them, Are ye come out as against a thief, with swords and with staves, to take me? I was daily with you in the temple, teaching, and ye took me not: but the Scriptures must be fulfilled. And they all forsook him, and fled. And there followed him a certain young man having a linen cloth cast about his naked body, and the young men laid hold on him. And he left the linen cloth, and fled from them naked. And they led Jesus away to the high Priest, and with him were assembled all the chief Priests, and the Elders, and the Scribes; and Peter followed him afar off, even into the palace of the high Priest: and he sat with the servants, and warmed himself at the fire; and the chief Priests, and all the councel sought for witness against Jesus to put him to death, and found none. For many bare false witness against him, but their witness agreed not together. And there arose certain, and bare false witness against him, saying, We heard him say, I will destroy this temple that is made with hands, and within three dayes I will build another made without hands. But neither so did their witness agree together. And the high Priest stood up in the midst, and asked Jesus, saying, Answerest thou nothing? what is it which these witness against thee? But he held his peace, and answered nothing. Again the high Priest asked him, and said unto him, Art thou the Christ, the Son of the Blessed? And Jesus said, I am; and ye shall see the Son of man sitting on the right hand of power, and coming in the clouds of heaven. Then the high priest rent his clothes, and saith, What need we any further witnesses? ye have heard the blasphemy: what think ye? And they all condemned him to be guilty of death. And some began to spit on him, and to cover his face, and to buffet him, and to say unto him, Prophecy; and the servants did strike him with the palms of their hands. And as Peter was beneath in the palace, there cometh one of the maids of the high priest; and when she saw Peter warming himself, she looked upon him, and said, And thou also wast with Jesus of Nazareth. But he denied, saying, I know not, neither understand I what thou sayest. And he went out into the porch, and the cock crew. And a maid saw him again, and began to say to them that stood by, This is one of them. And he denied it again. And a little after, they that stood by said again to Peter, Surely thou art one of them; for thou art a Galilaean, and thy speech agreeth thereto. But he began to curse and to swear, saying, I know not this man of whom ye speak. And the second time the cock crew. And Peter called to mind the word that Jesus said unto him, Before the cock crow twice, thou shalt deny me thrice. And when he thought thereon, he wept.

Tuesday before Easter.

For the Epistle.   Isa. 50.5

THE Lord God hath opened mine ear, and I was not rebellious, neither turned away back. I gave my back to the smiters, and my cheeks to them that plucked off the hair: I hid not my face from shame and spitting. For the Lord God will help me, therefore shall I not be confounded: therefore have I set my face like a flint, and I know that I shall not be ashamed. He is near that justifieth me, who will contend with me? Let us stand together; who is mine adversary? let him come near to me. Behold, the Lord God will help me; who is he that shall condemn me? Lo, they all shall wax old as a garment: the moth shall eat them up. Who is among you that feareth the Lord, that obeyeth the voice of his servant, that walketh in darkness, and hath no light? let him trust in the Name of the Lord, and stay upon his God. Behold, all ye that kindle a fire, that compass your selves about with sparks; walk in the light of your fire, and in the sparks that ye have kindled. This shall ye have of mine hand; ye shall lie down in sorrow.

The Gospel.   Mark 15.1

AND straightway in the morning, the chief priests held a consultation with the elders and scribes, and the whole council, and bound Jesus, and carried him away, and delivered him to Pilate. And Pilate asked him, Art thou the king of the Jews? And he answering, said unto him, Thou saiest it. And the chief priests accused him of many things: but he answered nothing. And Pilate asked him again, saying, Answerest thou nothing? behold how many things they witness against thee. But Jesus yet answered nothing: so that Pilate marvelled. Now at that feast he released unto them one prisoner, whomsoever they desired. And there was one named Barabbas, which lay bound with them that had made insurrection with him, who had committed murder in the insurrection. And the multitude crying aloud, began to desire him to do as he had ever done unto them. But Pilate answered them, saying, Will ye that I release unto you the king of the Jews? (For he knew that the chief priests had delivered him for envy.) But the chief priests moved the people, that he should rather release Barabbas unto them. And Pilate answered, and said again unto them, What will ye then that I shall do unto him whom ye call the king of the Jews? and they cried out again, Crucifie him. Then Pilate said unto them, Why, what evil hath he done? and they cried out the more exceedingly, Crucifie him. And so Pilate, willing to content the people, released Barabbas unto them, and delivered Jesus, when he had scourged him, to be crucified. And the souldiers led him away into the hall, called Pretorium; and they call together the whole band. And they clothed him with purple, and platted a crown of thorns, and put it about his head. And began to salute him, Hail king of the Jews. And they smote him on the head with a reed, and did spit upon him, and bowing their knees worshipped him. And when they had mocked him, they took off the purple from him, and put his own clothes on him, and led him out to crucifie him. And they compel one Simon a Cyrenean, who passed by, coming out of the countrey, the father of Alexander, and Rufus, to bear his cross. And they bring him unto the place Golgotha, which is, being interpreted, The place of a scull. And they gave him to drink, wine mingled with myrrhe: but he received it not. And when they had crucified him, they parted his garments, casting lots upon them, what every man should take. And it was the third hour, and they crucified him. And the superscription of his accusation was written over, *THE KING OF THE JEWS*. And with him they crucifie two thieves, the one on his right hand, and the other on his left. And the Scripture was fulfilled, which saith, And he was numbred with the transgressors. And they that passed by, railed on him, wagging their heads, and saying, Ah, thou that destroyest the temple, and buildest it in three days, save thy self, and come down from the cross. Likewise also the chief priests mocking, said among themselves, with the scribes, He saved others, himself he cannot save. Let Christ the King of Israel descend now from the cross, that we may see and believe. And they that were crucified with him, reviled him. And when the sixth hour was come, there was darkness over the whole land, until the ninth hour. And at the ninth hour Jesus cried with a loud voice, saying, *Eloi, Eloi, lama sabachthani?* which is, being interpreted, My God, my God, why hast thou forsaken me? And some of them that stood by, when they heard it, said, Behold, he calleth Elias. And one ran and filled a spunge full of vineger, and put it on a reed, and gave him to drink, saying, Let alone; let us see whether Elias will come to take him down. And Jesus cried with a loud voice, and gave up the ghost. And the vail of the temple was rent in twain from the top to the bottom. And when the centurion which stood over against him, saw that he so cried out, and gave up the ghost, he said, Truly this man was the Son of God.

Wednesday before Easter.

The Epistle.   *Heb.* 9.16

W HERE a testament is, there must also of necessity be the
death of the testator: for a testament is of force after men are
dead; otherwise it is of no strength at all while the testator liveth.
Whereupon, neither the first testament was dedicated without bloud:
For when Moses had spoken every precept to all the people, according to the law, he took the bloud of calves, and of goats, with water
and scarlet wooll, and hyssop, and sprinkled both the book and all
the people, saying, This is the bloud of the testament, which God
hath enjoined unto you. Moreover, he sprinkled with bloud both the
tabernacle, and all the vessels of the ministry. And almost all things
are by the law purged with bloud; and without shedding of bloud is
no remission. It was therefore necessary that the patterns of things
in the heavens should be purified with these; but the heavenly things
themselves with better sacrifices than these. For Christ is not entred
into the holy places made with hands, which are the figures of the
truc; but into heaven it self, now to appear in the presence of God
for us; nor yet that he should offer himself often, as the high priest
entreth into the holy place every year with bloud of others; for then
must he often have suffered since the foundation of the world; but
now once in the end of the world, hath he appeared to put away sin by
the sacrifice of himself. And as it is appointed unto men once to die,
but after this the judgment: so Christ was once offered to bear the sins
of many; and unto them that look for him, shall he appear the second
time without sin unto salvation.

The Gospel.   *Luke* 22.1

N OW the feast of unleavened bread drew nigh, which is called
the passover. And the chief Priests and Scribes sought how they
might kill him; for they feared the people. Then entred Satan into
Judas surnamed Iscariot, being of the number of the twelve. And he
went his way, and communed with the chief Priests and captaines,
how he might betray him unto them. And they were glad, and cov-
enanted to give him money. And he promised, and sought opportunity to betray him unto them, in the absence of the multitude. Then
came the day of unleavened bread, when the passover must be killed.
And he sent Peter and John, saying, Go and prepare us the passover,

that we may eat. And they said unto him, Where wilt thou that we prepare? And he said unto them, Behold, when ye are entred into the city, there shall a man meet you, bearing a pitcher of water, follow him into the house where he entreth in. And ye shall say unto the good-man of the house, The master saith unto thee, Where is the guest-chamber, where I shall eat the passover with my disciples? And he shall shew you a large upper room furnished; there make ready. And they went, and found as he had said unto them: and they made ready the passover. And when the hour was come, he sat down and the twelve Apostles with him. And he said unto them, with desire I have desired to eat this passover with you before I suffer. For I say unto you, I will not any more eat thereof, until it be fulfilled in the kingdom of God. And he took the cup, and gave thanks, and said, Take this, and divide it among your selves. For I say unto you, I will not drink of the fruit of the vine, until the kingdom of God shall come. And he took bread, and gave thanks, and brake it, and gave unto them, saying, This is my body, which is given for you, this do in remembrance of me. Likewise also the cup after supper, saying, This cup is the new testament in my bloud, which is shed for you. But, behold, the hand of him that betrayeth me, is with me on the table. And truly the son of man goeth as it was determined; but wo unto that man, by whom he is betrayed. And they began to enquire among themselves, which of them it was that should do this thing. And there was also a strife among them, which of them should be accounted the greatest. And he said unto them, The kings of the Gentiles exercise lordship over them, and they that exercise authority upon them, are called benefactours. But ye shall not be so; but he that is greatest among you, let him be as the younger; and he that is chief, as he that doth serve. For whether is greater, he that sitteth at meat, or he that serveth? is not he that sitteth at meat? but I am among you, as he that serveth. Ye are they which have continued with me in my temptations. And I appoint unto you a kingdom, as my Father hath appointed unto me; that ye may eat and drink at my table in my kingdom, and sit on thrones, judging the twelve tribes of Israel. And the Lord said, Simon, Simon, behold, Satan hath desired to have you, that he may sift you as wheat: But I have prayed for thee, that thy faith fail not; and when thou art converted, strengthen thy brethren. And he said unto him, Lord, I am ready to go with thee both into prison and to death. And he said, I tell thee, Peter, the cock shall not crow this day, before that thou shalt thrice deny that thou knowest me. And he said unto them, When I sent you without purse, and scrip, and shoes, lacked ye any thing? And they said, Nothing. Then said he unto them, But now, he that hath a purse, let him take it, and likewise his scrip: and he that hath no sword, let him sell his garment, and buy one. For I say unto you, that this that is written must yet be accomplished in me, And he was reckoned among the transgressors: for the things concerning me have an end. And they said, Lord, behold, here are two swords. And he said unto them, It is enough. And he came out, and went, as he was wont, to the mount of Olives, and his disciples also followed him. And when he was at the place, he said unto them, Pray, that ye enter not into temptation. And he was withdrawn from them about a stones cast, and kneeled down, and prayed, Saying, Father, if thou be willing, remove this cup from me: nevertheless, not my will, but thine be done. And there appeared an angel unto him from heaven, strengthning him. And being in an agony, he prayed more earnestly; and his sweat was as it were great drops of bloud falling down to the ground. And when he rose up from prayer, and was come to his disciples, he found them sleeping for sorrow, and said unto them, Why sleep ye? rise and pray, lest ye enter into temptation. And while he yet spake, behold, a multitude, and he that was called Judas, one of the twelve, went before them, and drew near unto Jesus to kiss him. But Jesus said unto him, Judas, betrayest thou the Son of man with a kiss? When they which were about him, saw what would follow, they said unto him, Lord, shall we smite with the sword? And one of them smote the servant of the high Priest, and cut off his right ear. And Jesus answered and said, Suffer ye thus far. And he touched his ear, and healed him. Then Jesus said unto the chief Priests, and captains of the temple, and the Elders who were come to him, Be ye come out as against a thief, with swords and staves? When I was daily with you in the temple, ye stretched forth no hands against me: but this is your hour, and the power of darkness. Then took they him, and led him, and brought him into the high Priests house, and Peter followed afar off. And when they had kindled a fire in the midst of the hall, and were set down together, Peter sat down among them. But a certain maid beheld him, as he sat by the fire, and earnestly looked upon him, and said, This man was also with him. And he denied him, saying, Woman, I know him not. And after a little while another saw him, and said, Thou art also of them. And Peter said, Man, I am not. And about the space of one hour after, another confidently affirmed, saying, Of a truth this fellow also was with him; for he is a Galilaean. And Peter said, Man, I know not what thou sayest. And immediately while he yet spake, the cock crew. And the Lord turned, and looked upon Peter; and Peter remembred the word of the Lord, how he had said unto him, Before the cock crow, thou shalt deny me thrice. And Peter went out and wept bitterly. And the men that held Jesus mocked him, and smote him. And when they had blind-folded him, they struck him on the face, and asked him, saying, Prophesy, who is it that smote thee? And many other things blasphemously spake they against him. And as soon as it was day, the elders of the people, and the chief Priests, and the Scribes came together, and led him into their councel, saying, Art thou the Christ? tell us. And he said unto them, If I tell you, you will not believe. And if I also ask you, you will not answer me, nor let me go. Hereafter shall the son of man sit on the right hand of the power of God. Then said they all, Art thou then the Son of God? And he said unto them, Ye say that I am. And they said, What need we any further witness? for we our selves have heard of his own mouth.

Thursday before Easter.

The Epistle.

1 Cor. 11.17

IN this that I declare unto you, I praise you not; that you come together not for the better, but for the worse. For first of all, when ye come together in the Church, I hear that there be divisions among you, and I partly believe it. For there must be also heresies among you, that they who are approved, may be made manifest among you. When ye come together therefore into one place, this is not to eat the Lords supper: For in eating, every one taketh before other his own supper: and one is hungry, and another is drunken. What, have ye not houses to eat and to drink in? or despise ye the Church of God, and shame them that have not? What shall I say to you? shall I praise you in this? I praise you not: For I have received of the Lord that which also I delivered unto you, that the Lord Jesus, the same night in which he was betrayed took bread, and when he had given thanks, he brake it, and said, Take, eat, this is my body, which is broken for you: this do in remembrance of me. After the same manner also he took the cup, when he had supped, saying, This cup is the new testament in my bloud: this do ye as oft as ye drink it, in remembrance of me. For as often as ye eat this bread, and drink this cup, ye do shew the Lords death till he come. Wherefore, whosoever shall eat this bread, and drink this cup of the Lord unworthily, shall be guilty of the body and bloud of the Lord. But let a man examine himself, and so let him eat of that bread, and drink of that cup. For he that eateth, and drinketh unworthily, eateth and drinketh damnation to himself, not discerning the Lords body. For this cause many are weak and sickly among you, and many sleep. For if we would judge our selves, we should not be judged. But when we are judged, we are chastned of the Lord, that we should not be condemned with the world. Wherefore, my brethren, when ye come together to eat, tarry one for another. And if any man hunger, let him eat at home; that ye come not together unto condemnation. And the rest will I set in order when I come.

The Gospel.   *Luke* 23.1

THE whole multitude of them arose, and led him unto Pilate. And they began to accuse him, saying, We found this fellow perverting the nation, and forbidding to give tribute to Cesar, saying, that he himself is Christ a king. And Pilate asked him, saying, Art thou the King of the Jews? And he answered him and said, Thou saiest it. Then said Pilate to the chief priests, and to the people, I find no fault in this man. And they were the more fierce, saying, He stirreth up the people, teaching throughout all Jewry, beginning from Galilee to this place. When Pilate heard of Galilee, he asked whether the man were a Galilaean. And as soon as he knew that he belonged unto Herods jurisdiction, he sent him to Herod, who himself was also at Jerusalem at that time. And when Herod saw Jesus, he was exceeding glad; for he was desirous to see him of a long season, because he had heard many things of him, and he hoped to have seen some miracle done by him. Then he questioned with him in many words; but he answered him nothing. And the chief priests and scribes stood and vehemently accused him. And Herod with his men of war set him at naught, and mocked him, and arayed him in a gorgeous robe, and sent him again to Pilate. And the same day Pilate and Herod were made friends together; for before they were at enmity between themselves. And Pilate when he had called together the chief priests, and the rulers, and the people, said unto them, Ye have brought this man unto me, as one that perverteth the people; and, behold, I having examined him before you, have found no fault in this man touching those things whereof ye accuse him: No, nor yet Herod: for I sent you to him, and, lo, nothing worthy of death is done unto him. I will therefore chastise him, and release him. For of necessity he must release one unto them at the feast. And they cried out all at once, saying, Away with this man, and release unto us Barabbas: (Who for a certain sedition made in the city, and for murder was cast into prison.) Pilate therefore willing to release Jesus, spake again to them. But they cried, saying, Crucifie him, crucifie him. And he said unto them the third time, Why, what evil hath he done? I have found no cause of death in him: I will therefore chastise him and let him go. And they were instant with loud voices, requiring that he might be crucified: And the voices of them, and of the chief priests prevailed. And Pilate gave sentence, that it should be as they required. And he released unto them him that for sedition and murder was cast into prison, whom they had desired; but he delivered Jesus to their will. And as they led him away, they laid hold upon one Simon a Cyrenian, coming out of the country, and on him they laid the cross, that he might bear it after Jesus. And there followed him a great company of people, and of women, which also bewailed and lamented him. But Jesus turning unto them, said, Daughters of Jerusalem, weep not for me, but weep for your selves, and for your children. For behold, the daies are coming, in the which they shall say, Blessed are the barren, and the wombs that never bare, and the paps which never gave suck. Then shall they begin to say to the mountains, Fall on us; and to the hills, Cover us. For if they do these things in a green tree, what shall be done in the dry? And there were also two other malefactours led with him to be put to death. And when they were come to the place which is called Calvary, there they crucified him; and the malefactours, one on the right hand, and the other on the left. Then said Jesus, Father, forgive them, for they know not what they do. And they parted his raiment, and cast lots. And the people stood beholding; and the rulers also with them derided him, saying, He saved others, let him save himself, if he be Christ the chosen of God. And the souldiers also mocked him, coming to him, and offering him vineger, and saying, If thou be the king of the Jews, save thy self. And a superscription also was written over him in letters of Greek, and Latine, and Hebrew, *THIS IS THE KING OF THE JEWS*. And one of the malefactors which were hanged, railed on him, saying, If thou be Christ, save thy self and us. But the other answering, rebuked him, saying, Doest not thou fear God, seeing thou art in the same condemnation? And we indeed justly; for we receive the due reward of our deeds, but this man hath done nothing amiss. And he said unto Jesus, Lord, remember me when thou comest into thy kingdom. And Jesus said unto him, Verily I say unto thee, To day shalt thou be with me in paradise. And it was about the sixth hour. And there was a darkness over all the earth, until the ninth hour. And the sun was darkned, and the vail of the temple was rent in the midst. And when Jesus had cried with a loud voice, he said, Father, into thy hands I commend my spirit: and having said thus, he gave up the ghost. Now when the centurion saw what was done, he glorified God, saying, Certainly this was a righteous man. And all the people that came together to that sight, beholding the things that were done, smote their breasts, and returned. And all his acquaintance, and the women that followed him from Galilee, stood afar off, beholding these things.

Good Friday.

The Collects.°

A LMIGHTY God, we beseech thee graciously to behold this thy family, for which our Lord Jesus Christ was contented to be betrayed, and given up into the hands of wicked men, and to suffer death upon the cross, who now liveth and reigneth with thee and the holy Ghost, ever one God, world without end. *Amen.*

A LMIGHTY and everlasting God, by whose Spirit the whole body of the Church is governed and sanctified; Receive our supplications and prayers which we offer before thee for all estates of men in thy holy Church, that every member of the same in his vocation and ministry, may truly and godly serve thee, through our Lord and Saviour Jesus Christ. *Amen.*

O MERCIFUL God, who hast made all men, and hatest nothing that thou hast made, nor wouldest the death of a sinner, but rather that he should be converted and live; Have mercy upon all Jews, Turks, Infidels, and Hereticks, and take from them all ignorance, hardness of heart, and contempt of thy word; and so fetch them home, blessed Lord, to thy flock, that they may be saved among the remnant of the true Israelites, and be made one fold under one

Shepherd, Jesus Christ our Lord, who liveth and reigneth with thee and the holy Spirit, one God, world without end. *Amen.*

The Epistle.°   *Heb.* 10.1

THE law having a shadow of good things to come, and not the very image of the things, can never with those sacrifices which they offered year by year continually, make the comers thereunto perfect: for then would they not have ceased to be offered? because that the worshippers once purged, should have had no more conscience of sins. But in those sacrifices there is a remembrance again made of sins every year. For it is not possible that the bloud of bulls and of goats should take away sins: Wherefore when he cometh into the world, he saith, Sacrifice and offering thou wouldest not, but a body hast thou prepared me: In burnt-offerings, and sacrifices for sin thou hast had no pleasure: Then said I, Lo, I come (in the volume of the book it is written of me) to do thy will, O God. Above, when he said, Sacrifice and offering, and burnt-offerings and offering for sin thou wouldest not, neither hadst pleasure therein, which are offered by the law: Then said he, Lo, I come to do thy will, O God. He taketh away the first, that he may establish the second. By the which will we are sanctified, through the offering of the body of Jesus Christ once for all. And every priest standeth daily ministring, and offering oftentimes the same sacrifices which can never take away sins. But this man after he had offered one sacrifice for sins, for ever sat down on the right hand of God; from henceforth expecting till his enemies be made his foot-stool. For by one offering he hath perfected for ever them that are sanctified: Whereof the holy Ghost also is a witness to us: For after that he had said before, This is the covenant that I will make with them after those days, saith the Lord, I will put my laws into their hearts, and in their minds will I write them; and their sins and iniquities will I remember no more. Now where remission of these is, there is no more offering for sin. Having therefore, brethren, boldness to enter into the holiest by the bloud of Jesus, by a new and living way, which he hath consecrated for us, through the vail, that is to say, his flesh: And having an high Priest over the house of God; let us draw near with a true heart, in full assurance of faith, having our hearts sprinkled from an evil conscience, and our bodies washed with pure water. Let us hold fast the profession of our faith without wavering: (for he is faithful that promised) And let us consider one another to provoke unto love, and to good works; not forsaking the assembling of our selves together, as the manner of some is; but exhorting one another: and so much the more, as ye see the day approaching.

The Gospel.   *John* 19.1

PILATE therefore took Jesus, and scourged him. And the souldiers platted a crown of thorns, and put it on his head, and they put on him a purple robe, and said, Hail King of the Jews: And they smote him with their hands. Pilate therefore went forth again, and saith unto them, Behold, I bring him forth to you, that ye may know that I find no fault in him. Then came Jesus forth, wearing the crown of thorns, and the purple robe. And Pilate saith unto them, Behold the man. When the chief priests therefore, and officers saw him, they cried out, saying, Crucifie him, crucifie him. Pilate saith unto them, Take ye him, and crucifie him: for I finde no fault in him. The Jews answered him, We have a law, and by our law, he ought to die, because he made himself the Son of God. When Pilate therefore heard that saying, he was the more afraid; and went again into the judgement-hall, and saith unto Jesus, Whence art thou? But Jesus gave him no answer. Then saith Pilate unto him, Speakest thou not unto me? knowest thou not, that I have power to crucifie thee, and have power to release thee? Jesus answered, Thou couldest have no power at all against me, except it were given thee from above: therefore he that delivered me unto thee hath the greater sin. And from thence forth Pilate sought to release him: but the Jews cryed out, saying, If thou let this man go, thou art not Cesars friend: Whosoever maketh himself a king, speaketh against Cesar. When Pilate therefore heard that saying, he brought Jesus forth, and sate down in the judgement-seat, in a place that is called the Pavement, but in the Hebrew, Gabbatha. And it was the preparation of the passover, and about the sixth hour: and he saith unto the Jews, Behold your King. But they cried out, Away with him, away with him, crucifie him. Pilate saith unto them, Shall I crucifie your King? The chief priests answered, We have no king but Cesar. Then delivered he him therefore unto them to be crucified: and they took Jesus and led him away. And he bearing his cross, went forth into a place called the place of a scull, which is called in the Hebrew, Golgotha: Where they crucified him, and two other with him, on either side one, and Jesus in the midst. And Pilate wrote a title, and put it on the cross. And the writing was, *JESUS OF NAZARETH*

THE KING OF THE JEWS. This title then read many of the Jews: for the place where Jesus was crucified was nigh to the city: and it was written in Hebrew, and Greek, and Latine. Then said the chief priests of the Jews to Pilate, Write not, The King of the Jews; but that he said, I am the King of the Jews. Pilate answered, What I have written, I have written. Then the souldiers, when they had crucified Jesus, took his garments, (and made four parts, to every soldier a part) and also his coat: now the coat was without seam, woven from the top throughout. They said therefore among themselves, Let us not rend it, but cast lots for it, whose it shall be: that the Scripture might be fulfilled, which saith, They parted my raiment among them, and for my vesture they did cast lots. These things therefore the souldiers did. Now there stood by the cross of Jesus, his mother and his mothers sister, Mary, the wife of Cleophas, and Mary Magdalen. When Jesus therefore saw his mother, and the disciple standing by, whom he loved, he saith unto his mother, Woman, behold thy son. Then saith he to the disciple, Behold thy mother. And from that hour that disciple took her unto his own home. After this, Jesus knowing that all things were now accomplished, that the Scripture might be fulfilled, saith, I thirst. Now there was set a vessel full of vineger: and they filled a spunge with vineger, and put it upon hyssop, and put it to his mouth. When Jesus therefore had received the vineger, he said, It is finished: and he bowed his head, and gave up the ghost. The Jews therefore because it was the preparation, that the bodies should not remain upon the cross on the sabbath-day (for that sabbath-day was an high day) besought Pilate that their legs might be broken, and that they might be taken away. Then came the souldiers, and brake the legs of the first, and of the other which was crucified with him. But when they came to Jesus, and saw that he was dead already, they brake not his legs: But one of the souldiers with a spear pierced his side, and forthwith came there out bloud and water. And he that saw it bare record, and his record is true: and he knoweth that he saith true, that ye might believe. For these things were done that the Scripture should be fulfilled, A bone of him shall not be broken. And again, another Scripture saith, They shall look on him, whom they pierced.

Easter Even.

The Collect.°

GRANT, O Lord, that as we are baptized into the death of thy blessed Son our Saviour Jesus Christ; so by continual mortifying our corrupt affections, we may be buried with him, and that through the grave, and gate of death we may pass to our joyful resurrection, for his merits, who dyed, and was buried, and rose again for us, thy Son Jesus Christ our Lord. *Amen.*

The Epistle. 1 *Pet.* 3. 17

IT is better, if the will of God be so, that ye suffer for well-doing, then for evil-doing. For Christ also hath once suffered for sins, the just for the unjust; (that he might bring us to God) being put to death in the flesh, but quickened by the Spirit: By which also he went and preached unto the spirits in prison; which sometime were disobedient, when once the long-suffering of God waited in the dayes of Noah, while the ark was a preparing; wherein few, that is, eight souls, were saved by water. The like figure whereunto, even baptism, doth also now save us (not the putting away of the filth of the flesh, but the answer of a good conscience towards God) by the resurrection of Jesus Christ: Who is gone into heaven, and is on the right hand of God, angels, and authorities, and powers being made subject unto him.

The Gospel. *Matt.* 27. 57

WHEN the even was come, there came a rich man of Arimathaea, named Joseph, who also himself was Jesus disciple. He went to Pilate, and begged the body of Jesus. Then Pilate commanded the body to be delivered. And when Joseph had taken the body, he wrapped it in a clean linen cloth, and laid it in his own new tomb, which he had hewen out in the rock; and he rolled a great stone to the door of the sepulchre, and departed. And there was Mary Magdalene, and the other Mary, sitting over against the sepulchre. Now the next day that followed the day of the preparation, the chief priests and Pharisees came together unto Pilate, saying, Sir, we remember that that deceiver said, while he was yet alive, After three days I will rise again. Command therefore that the sepulchre be made sure until the third day, lest his disciples come by night and steal him away, and say unto the people, He is risen from the dead: so the last errour shall be worse than the first. Pilate said unto them, Ye have a watch, go your way, make it as sure as ye can. So they went and made the sepulchre sure, sealing the stone, and setting a watch.

Easter day.°

¶ *At Morning Prayer, instead of the Psalm,* O come let us, *&c. these Anthems shall be sung or said.*

C HRIST our passover is sacrificed for us: therefore let us keep the feast. Not with the old leaven nor with the leaven of malice and wickedness: but with the unleavened bread of sincerity and truth.

1 Cor. 5.7

C HRIST being raised from the dead dieth no more: death hath no more dominion over him. For in that he died, he died unto sin once: but in that he liveth, he liveth unto God. Likewise reckon ye also your selves to be dead indeed unto sin: but alive unto God through Jesus Christ our Lord.   *Rom.* 6.9

C HRIST is risen from the dead: and become the first-fruits of them that slept. For since by man came death: by man came also the resurrection of the dead. For as in Adam all die: even so in Christ shall all be made alive.   *1 Cor.* 15.20

Glory be to the Father, and to the Son: and to the Holy Ghost;

Answer. As it was in the beginning, is now, and ever shall be: world without end. Amen.

The Collect.

A LMIGHTY God, who through thine only-begotten Son Jesus Christ hast overcome death, and opened unto us the gate of everlasting life; We humbly beseech thee, that as by thy special grace preventing us, thou dost put into our minds good desires; so by thy continual help we may bring the same to good effect, through Jesus Christ our Lord, who liveth and reigneth with thee, and the holy Ghost, ever one God, world without end. *Amen.*

The Epistle.   *Col.* 3.1

I F ye then be risen with Christ, seek those things which are above, where Christ sitteth on the right hand of God. Set your affection on things above, not on things on the earth: For ye are dead, and your life is hid with Christ in God. When Christ who is our life, shall appear, then shall ye also appear with him in glory. Mortifie therefore your members which are upon the earth; fornication, uncleanness, inordinate affection, evil concupiscence, and covetousness, which is idolatry: For which things sake the wrath of God cometh on the children of disobedience: In the which ye also walked some time when ye lived in them.

The Gospel.   *John* 20.1

T HE first day of the week cometh Mary Magdalen early, when it was yet dark, unto the sepulchre, and seeth the stone taken away from the sepulchre. Then she runneth, and cometh to Simon Peter, and to the other disciple whom Jesus loved, and saith unto them, They have taken away the Lord out of the sepulchre, and we know not where they have laid him. Peter therefore went forth, and that other disciple, and came to the sepulchre. So they ran both together, and the other disciple did out-run Peter, and came first to the sepulchre; and he stooping down, and looking in, saw the linen clothes lying, yet went he not in. Then cometh Simon Peter following him, and went into the sepulchre, and seeth the linen clothes lie; and the napkin that was about his head, not lying with the linen clothes, but wrapped together in a place by it self. Then went in also that other disciple, which came first to the sepulchre, and he saw and believed. For as yet they knew not the Scripture, that he must rise again from the dead. Then the disciples went away again unto their own home.

Munday in Easter Week.°

The Collect.

A LMIGHTY God, who through thy only begotten Son Jesus Christ hast overcome death, and opened unto us the gate of everlasting life; We humbly beseech thee, that as by thy special grace preventing us, thou dost put into our minds good desires, so by thy continual help we may bring the same to good effect, through Jesus Christ our Lord, who liveth and reigneth with thee and the Holy Ghost ever one God, world without end. *Amen.*

For the Epistle.   *Acts* 10.34

P ETER opened his mouth, and said, Of a truth I perceive that God is no respecter of persons; but in every nation he that feareth him, and worketh righteousness, is accepted with him. The word which God sent unto the children of Israel, preaching peace by Jesus Christ (he is Lord of all) That word (I say) you know, which was published throughout all Judaea, and began from Galilee, after the baptism which John preached: How God anointed Jesus of Nazareth with the holy Ghost, and with power, who went about doing good, and healing all that were oppressed of the devil: for God was with him. And we are witnesses of all things which he did, both in the land of the Jews, and in Jerusalem, whom they slew, and hanged on a tree: Him God raised up the third day, and shewed him openly; not to all the people, but unto witnesses chosen before of God, even to us, who did eat and drink with him after he arose from the dead. And he commanded us to preach unto the people, and to testifie that it is he who was ordained of God, to be the judge of quick and dead. To him give all the prophets witness, that through his Name, whosoever believeth in him, shall receive remission of sins.

The Gospel.   Luke 24. 13

BEHOLD two of his disciples went that same day to a village called Emmaus, which was from Jerusalem about threescore furlongs. And they talked together of all these things which had happened. And it came to pass, that while they communed together, and reasoned, Jesus himself drew near, and went with them. But their eies were holden, that they should not know him. And he said unto them, What manner of communications are these that ye have one to another, as ye walk and are sad? And the one of them, whose name was Cleopas, answering, said unto him, Art thou only a stranger in Jerusalem, and hast not known the things which are come to pass there in these daies? And he said unto them, What things? And they said unto him, Concerning Jesus of Nazareth, who was a prophet mighty in deed and word, before God and all the people: And how the chief priests, and our rulers delivered him to be condemned to death, and have crucified him. But we trusted that it had been he, who should have redeemed Israel: and beside all this, to day is the third day since these things were done. Yea, and certain women also of our company made us astonished, who were early at the sepulchre; and when they found not his body, they came, saying, that they had also seen a vision of angels, which said that he was alive. And certain of them who were with us, went to the sepulchre, and found it even so as the women had said; but him they saw not. Then he said unto them, O fools, and slow of heart to believe all that the prophets have spoken: ought not

Christ to have suffered these things, and to enter into his glory? And beginning at Moses, and all the prophets, he expounded unto them in all the Scriptures, the things concerning himself. And they drew nigh unto the village, whither they went; and he made as though he would have gone further. But they constrained him, saying, Abide with us, for it is toward evening, and the day is far spent: and he went in to tarry with them. And it came to pass, as he sat at meat with them he took bread, and blessed it, and brake, and gave to them. And their eies were opened, and they knew him, and he vanished out of their sight. And they said one to another, Did not our heart burn within us, while he talked with us by the way, and while he opened to us the Scriptures? And they rose up the same hour, and returned to Jerusalem, and found the eleven gathered together, and them that were with them, saying, The Lord is risen indeed, and hath appeared to Simon. And they told what things were done in the way, and how he was known of them in breaking of bread.

Tuesday in Easter-Week.

The Collect.

A LMIGHTY God, who through thyne only begotten Son Jesus Christ hast overcome death, and opened unto us the gate of everlasting life; We humbly beseech thee, that as by thy special grace preventing us, thou doest put into our minds good desires, so by thy continual help we may bring the same to good effect, through Jesus Christ our Lord, who liveth and reigneth with thee, and the holy Ghost, ever one God world without end. *Amen.*

For the Epistle.   *Acts* 13.26

M EN, and brethren, children of the stock of Abraham, and whoso- ever among you feareth God, to you is the word of this salvation sent. For they that dwell at Jerusalem, and their rulers, because they knew him not, nor yet the voices of the prophets which are read every sabbath-day, they have fulfilled them in condemning him. And though they found no cause of death in him, yet desired they Pilate that he should be slain. And when they had fulfilled all that was written of him, they took him down from the tree, and laid him in a sepulchre. But God raised him from the dead: And he was seen many daies of them which came up with him from Galilee to Jerusalem, who are his witnesses unto the people. And we declare unto you glad tidings, how that the promise which was made unto the fathers, God hath fulfilled the same unto us their children, in that he hath raised up Jesus again, as it is also written in the second psalm, Thou art my Son, this day have I begotten thee. And as concerning that he raised him up from the dead, now no more to return to corruption, he said on this wise, I will give you the sure mercies of David. Wherefore he saith also in another psalm, Thou shalt not suffer thine holy one to see corruption. For David after he had served his own generation by the will of God, fell on sleep, and was laid unto his fathers, and saw corruption. But he whom God raised again, saw no corruption: Be it known unto you therefore, men, and brethren, that through this man is preached unto you the forgiveness of sins: And by him all that believe are justified from all things, from which ye could not be justified by the law of Moses. Beware therefore, lest that come upon you, which is spoken of in the prophets; Behold, ye despisers, and wonder, and perish: for I work a work in your daies, a work which you shall in no wise believe, though a man declare it unto you.

The Gospel.   *Luke* 24. 36

JESUS himself stood in the midst of them, and saith unto them, Peace be unto you. But they were terrified and affrighted, and supposed that they had seen a spirit. And he said unto them, Why are ye troubled, and why do thoughts arise in your hearts? Behold my hands and my feet, that it is I my self: handle me, and see; for a spirit hath not flesh and bones, as ye see me have. And when he had thus spoken, he shewed them his hands and his feet. And while they yet believed not for joy, and wondred, he said unto them, Have ye here any meat? And they gave him a piece of a broiled fish, and of an hony-comb. And he took it, and did eat before them. And he said unto them, These are the words which I spake unto you, while I was yet with you, that all things must be fulfilled, which were written in the law of Moses, and in the prophets, and in the psalms concerning me. Then opened he their understanding, that they might understand the Scriptures, and said unto them, Thus it is written, and thus it behoved Christ to suffer, and to rise from the dead the third day; and that repentance and remission of sins should be preached in his Name among all nations, beginning at Jerusalem. And ye are witnesses of these things.

The First Sunday after Easter.

The Collect.

ALMIGHTY Father, who has given thine only Son to die for our sins, and to rise again for our justification; Grant us so to put away the leaven of malice and wickedness, that we may alway serve thee in pureness of living and truth, through the merits of the same thy Son Jesus Christ our Lord. *Amen.*

The Epistle.   1 *John* 5.4

WHATSOEVER is born of God overcometh the world; and this is the victory that overcometh the world, even our faith. Who is he that overcometh the world, but he that believeth that Jesus is the Son of God? This is he that came by water and bloud, even Jesus Christ; not by water only, but by water and bloud: and it is the Spirit that beareth witness, because the Spirit is truth. For there are three that bear record in heaven, the Father, the Word, and the holy Ghost: and these three are one. And there are three that bear witness in earth, the spirit, and the water, and the bloud: and these three agree in one. If we receive the witness of men, the witness of God is greater: for this is the witness of God, which he hath testified of his Son. He that believeth on the Son of God, hath the witness in himself: he that believeth not God, hath made him a liar, because he believeth not the record that God gave of his Son. And this is the record, that God hath given to us eternal life; and this life is in his Son. He that hath the Son hath life, and he that hath not the Son hath not life.

The Gospel.   *John* 20.19

THE same day at evening, being the first day of the week, when the doors were shut, where the disciples were assembled for fear of the Jews, came Jesus and stood in the midst, and saith unto them, Peace be unto you. And when he had so said, he shewed unto them his hands and his side. Then were the disciples glad when they saw the Lord. Then said Jesus to them again, Peace be unto you: As my father hath sent me, even so send I you. And when he had said this, he breathed on them and saith unto them, Receive ye the holy Ghost. Whosesoever sins ye remit, they are remitted unto them; and whose-soever sins ye retain, they are retained.

The Second Sunday after Easter.

The Collect.°

ALMIGHTY God, who hast given thine onely Son to be unto us both a sacrifice for sin, and also an ensample of godly life; Give us grace that we may alwayes most thankfully receive that his inestimable benefit, and also daily endeavour our selves to follow the blessed steps of his most holy life, through the same Jesus Christ our Lord. *Amen.*

The Epistle.   1 *Pet.* 2.19

THIS is thank-worthy, if a man for conscience toward God endure grief, suffering wrongfully. For what glory is it, if when ye be buffeted for your faults, ye shall take it patiently? But if when ye do well, and suffer for it, ye take it patiently; this is acceptable with God. For even hereunto were ye called: because Christ also suffered for us, leaving us an example, that ye should follow his steps: Who did no sin, neither was guile found in his mouth: Who when he was reviled, reviled not again; when he suffered, he threatned not; but committed himself to him that judgeth righteously: Who his own self bare our sins in his own body on the tree, that we being dead to sins should live unto righteousness; by whose stripes ye were healed. For ye were as sheep going astray; but are now returned unto the shepherd, and Bishop of your souls.

The Gospel.   *John* 10.11

JESUS said I am the good shepherd: the good shepherd giveth his life for the sheep. But he that is an hireling, and not the shepherd, whose own the sheep are not, seeth the wolf coming, and leaveth the sheep, and fleeth; and the wolf catcheth them, and scattereth the sheep. The hireling fleeth, because he is an hireling, and careth not for the sheep. I am the good shepherd, and know my sheep, and am known of mine. As the Father knoweth me, even so know I the Father: and I lay down my life for the sheep. And other sheep I have which are not of this fold; them also I must bring, and they shall hear my voice; and there shall be one fold, and one shepherd.

The Third Sunday after Easter.

The Collect.

ALMIGHTY God, who shewest to them that be in errour the light of thy truth, to the intent that they may return into the way of righteousness; Grant unto all them that are admitted into the fellowship of Christs Religion, that they may eschew those things that are contrary to their profession, and follow all such things as are agreeable to the same, through our Lord Jesus Christ. *Amen.*

The Epistle.   1 *Pet.* 2.11

DEARLY beloved, I beseech you as strangers and pilgrims, abstain from fleshly lusts, which war against the soul; having your conversation honest among the Gentiles; that whereas they speak against you as evil-doers, they may by your good works which they shall behold, glorifie God in the day of visitation. Submit your selves to every ordinance of man for the Lords sake, whether it be to the king, as supreme; or unto governours, as unto them that are sent by him, for the punishment of evil-doers, and for the praise of them that do well. For so is the will of God, that with well doing ye may put to silence the ignorance of foolish men: as free, and not using your liberty for a cloak of maliciousness; but as the servants of God. Honour all men. Love the brotherhood. Fear God. Honour the King.

The Gospel.   *John* 16.16

JESUS said to his disciples, A little while and ye shall not see me; and again, a little while and ye shall see me, because I go to the Father. Then said some of his disciples among themselves, What is this that he saith unto us, A little while and ye shall not see me; and again, a little while and ye shall see me; and Because I go to the Father? They said therefore, What is this that he saith, A little while? we cannot tell what he saith. Now Jesus knew that they were desirous to ask him, and said unto them, Do ye enquire among your selves of that I said, A little while, and ye shall not see me; and again, a little while and ye shall see me? Verily, verily I say unto you, that ye shall weep and lament, but the world shall rejoice: and ye shall be sorrowful, but your sorrow shall be turned into joy. A woman when she is in travail, hath sorrow, because her hour is come: but as soon as she is delivered of the child, she remembreth no more the anguish, for joy that a man is born into the world. And ye now therefore have sorrow: but I will see you again, and your heart shall rejoyce, and your joy no man taketh from you.

The Fourth Sunday after Easter.

The Collect.°

O ALMIGHTY God, who alone canst order the unruly wills and affections of sinful men; Grant unto thy people, that they may love the thing which thou commandest, and desire that which thou dost promise, that so among the sundry, and manifold changes of the world, our hearts may surely there be fixed, where true joys are to be found, through Jesus Christ our Lord. *Amen.*

The Epistle.   Jas. 1.1

EVERY good gift, and every perfect gift is from above, and cometh down from the Father of lights, with whom is no variableness, neither shadow of turning. Of his own will begat he us with the word of truth, that we should be a kinde of first-fruits of his creatures. Wherefore, my beloved brethren, let every man be swift to hear, slow to speak, slow to wrath; for the wrath of man worketh not the righteousness of God. Wherefore lay apart all filthiness and superfluity of naughtiness, and receive with meekness the engrafted word, which is able to save your souls.

The Gospel.   John 16.5

JESUS said unto his disciples, Now I go my way to him that sent me, and none of you asketh me, Whither goest thou? But because I have said these things unto you sorrow hath filled your heart. Nevertheless, I tell you the truth, it is expedient for you that I go away: for if I go not away, the Comforter will not come unto you; but if I depart, I will send him unto you. And when he is come, he will reprove the world of sin, and of righteousness, and of judgment: Of sin, because they believe not on me: Of righteousness; because I go to my Father, and ye see me no more: Of judgment; because the prince of this world is judged. I have yet many things to say unto you, but ye cannot bear them now. Howbeit, when he, the Spirit of truth is come, he will guide you into all truth; for he shall not speak of himself; but whatsoever he shall hear, that shall he speak; and he will shew you things to come. He shall glorifie me: for he shall receive of mine, and shall shew it unto you. All things that the Father hath, are mine: therefore said I, that he shall take of mine, and shall shew it unto you.

The Fifth Sunday after Easter.

The Collect.

O LORD, from whom all good things do come; Grant to us thy humble servants, that by thy holy inspiration we may think those things that be good, and by thy merciful guiding may perform the same; through our Lord Jesus Christ. *Amen.*

The Epistle. *Jas.* 1.22

B E ye doers of the word, and not hearers onely, deceiving your own selves. For if any be a hearer of the word and not a doer, he is like unto a man beholding his natural face in a glass. For he beholdeth himself, and goeth his way, and straightway forgetteth what manner of man he was. But whoso looketh into the perfect law of liberty, and continueth therein; he being not a forgetful hearer, but a doer of the work, this man shall be blessed in his deed. If any man among you seem to be religious, and bridleth not his tongue, but deceiveth his own heart, this mans religion is vain. Pure religion, and undefiled before God and the Father, is this; To visit the fatherless and widows in their affliction, and to keep himself unspotted from the world.

The Gospel. *John* 16.23

V ERILY, verily, I say unto you, Whatsoever ye shall ask the Father in my name, he will give it you. Hitherto have ye asked nothing in my name: Ask, and ye shall receive, that your joy may be full. These things have I spoken unto you in proverbs: the time cometh when I shall no more speak unto you in proverbs, but I shall shew you plainly of the Father. At that day ye shall ask in my Name: and I say not unto you, that I will pray the Father for you; for the Father himself loveth you, because ye have loved me, and have believed that I came out from God. I came forth from the Father, and am come into the world: Again, I leave the world, and go to the Father. His disciples said unto him; Lo, now speakest thou plainly, and speakest no proverb. Now are we sure that thou knowest all things, and needest not that any man should ask thee: by this we believe that thou camest forth from God. Jesus answered them, Do ye now believe? Behold, the hour cometh, yea, is now come, that ye shall be scattered every man to his own, and shall leave me alone: and yet I am not alone, because the Father is with me. These things I have spoken unto you, that in me ye might have peace. In the world ye shall have tribulation; but be of good cheer, I have overcome the world.

The Ascension day.

The Collect.

GRANT, we beseech thee, Almighty God, that like as we do believe thy only begotten Son our Lord Jesus Christ to have ascended into the heavens; so we may also in heart and mind thither ascend, and with him continually dwell, who liveth and reigneth with thee, and the holy Ghost, one God, world without end. *Amen.*

For the Epistle.   *Acts* 1.1

THE former treatise have I made, O Theophilus, of all that Jesus began both to do and teach, until the day in which he was taken up, after that he through the holy Ghost had given commandments unto the Apostles whom he had chosen. To whom also he shewed himself alive after his passion, by many infallible proofs, being seen of them forty days, and speaking of the things pertaining to the kingdom of God: And being assembled together with them, commanded them that they should not depart from Jerusalem, but wait for the promise of the Father, which, saith he, ye have heard of me. For John truly baptized with water, but ye shall be baptized with the holy Ghost not many days hence. When they therefore were come together, they asked of him, saying, Lord, wilt thou at this time restore again the kingdom to Israel? And he said unto them, It is not for you to know the times, or the seasons, which the Father hath put in his own power. But ye shall receive power after that the holy Ghost is come upon you; and ye shall be witnesses unto me both in Jerusalem and in all Judaea, and in Samaria, and unto the uttermost part of the earth. And when he had spoken these things, while they beheld, he was taken up, and a cloud received him out of their sight. And while they looked stedfastly toward heaven, as he went up, behold, two men stood by them in white apparel; which also said, Ye men of Galilee, why stand ye gazing up into heaven? This same Jesus which is taken up from you into heaven, shall so come in like manner, as ye have seen him go into heaven.

The Gospel. *Mark* 16.14

JESUS appeared unto the eleven as they sat at meat, and upbraided them with their unbelief and hardness of heart, because they believed not them which had seen him after he was risen. And he said unto them, Go ye into all the world, and preach the Gospel to every creature. He that believeth and is baptized, shall be saved; but he that believeth not, shall be damned. And these signs shall follow them that believe: In my name shall they cast out devils, they shall speak with new tongues, they shall take up serpents, and if they drink any deadly thing, it shall not hurt them; they shall lay hands on the sick, and they shall recover. So then after the Lord had spoken unto them, he was received up into heaven, and sat on the right hand of God. And they went forth and preached every where, the Lord working with them, and confirming the word with signs following.

Sunday after Ascension-Day.

The Collect.°

O GOD the King of glory, who hast exalted thine only Son Jesus Christ with great triumph unto thy kingdom in heaven; We beseech thee leave us not comfortless; but send to us thine holy Ghost to comfort us, and exalt us unto the same place whither our Saviour Christ is gone before, who liveth and reigneth with thee, and the holy Ghost, one God, world without end. *Amen.*

The Epistle. 1 *Pet.* 4.7

THE end of all things is at hand; be ye therefore sober, and watch unto prayer. And above all things have fervent charity among your selves: for charity shall cover the multitude of sins. Use hospitality one to another without grudging. As every man hath received the gift, even so minister the same one to another, as good stewards of the manifold grace of God. If any man speak, let him speak as the oracles of God: If any man minister, let him do it, as of the ability which God giveth, that God in all things may be glorified through Jesus Christ, to whom be praise and dominion for ever and ever. Amen.

The Gospel.

John 15.26, *and part of Chapter* 16

WHEN the Comforter is come, whom I will send unto you from the Father, even the Spirit of truth, which proceedeth from the

Father, he shall testifie of me. And ye also shall bear witness, because ye have been with me from the beginning. These things have I spoken unto you, that ye should not be offended. They shall put you out of the synagogues: yea the time cometh, that whosoever killeth you will think that he doth God service. And these things will they do unto you, because they have not known the Father, nor me; but these things have I told you, that when the time shall come, ye may remember that I told you of them.

Whitsunday.°

The Collect.

G OD, who as at this time didst teach the hearts of thy faithful people by the sending to them the light of thy holy Spirit; Grant us by the same Spirit to have a right judgement in all things, and evermore to rejoyce in his holy comfort, through the merits of Christ Jesus our Saviour, who liveth and reigneth with thee, in the unity of the same Spirit, one God world without end. *Amen.*

For the Epistle.   *Acts* 2.1

W HEN the day of Pentecost was fully come, they were all with one accord in one place. And suddenly there came a sound from heaven, as of a rushing mighty wind, and it filled all the house where they were sitting. And there appeared unto them cloven tongues, like as of fire, and it sat upon each of them: And they were all filled with the holy Ghost, and began to speak with other tongues, as the Spirit gave them utterance. And there were dwelling at Jerusalem Jews, devout men, out of every nation under heaven. Now when this was noised abroad, the multitude came together, and were confounded, because that every man heard them speak in his own language. And they were all amazed, and marvelled, saying one to another, Behold, are not all these which speak, Galilaeans? And how hear we every man in our own tongue wherein we were born? Parthians, and Medes, and Elamites, and the dwellers in Mesopotamia, and in Judea, and Cappadocia, in Pontus and Asia, Phrygia, and Pamphilia, in Egypt, and in the parts of Libya, about Cyrene, and strangers of Rome, Jews and Proselytes, Cretes and Arabians, we do hear them speak in our tongues the wonderful works of God.

JESUS said unto his disciples, If ye love me keep my commandments. And I will pray the Father, and he shall give you another Comforter, that he may abide with you for ever; even the Spirit of truth, whom the world cannot receive, because it seeth him not, neither knoweth him; but ye know him; for he dwelleth with you, and shall be in you. I will not leave you comfortless; I will come to you. Yet a little while, and the world seeth me no more; but ye see me: because I live, ye shall live also. At that day ye shall know, that I am in my Father, and you in me, and I in you. He that hath my commandments, and keepeth them, he it is that loveth me; and he that loveth me shall be loved of my Father, and I will love him, and will manifest my self to him. Judas saith unto him, (not Iscariot) Lord, how is it that thou wilt manifest thy self unto us, and not unto the world? Jesus answered, and said unto him, If a man love me, he will keep my words: and my Father will love him, and we will come unto him, and make our abode with him. He that loveth me not, keepeth not my sayings: and the word which you hear, is not mine; but the Fathers which sent me. These things have I spoken unto you, being yet present with you. But the Comforter, which is the holy Ghost, whom the Father will send in my name, he shall teach you all things, and bring all things to your remembrance, whatsoever I have said unto you. Peace I leave with you, my peace I give unto you: not as the world giveth, give I unto you. Let not your heart be troubled, neither let it be afraid. Ye have heard how I said unto you, I go away and come again unto you. If ye loved me, ye would rejoyce, because I said, I go unto the Father: for my Father is greater than I. And now I have told you before it come to pass, that when it is come to pass ye might believe. Hereafter I will not talk much with you: for the prince of this world cometh, and hath nothing in me. But that the world may know that I love the Father; and as the Father gave me commandment, even so I do.

Munday in Whitsun Week.

The Collect.

GOD, who as at this time didst teach the hearts of thy faithful people, by the sending to them the light of thy holy Spirit; Grant us by the same Spirit to have a right judgment in all things, and evermore to rejoyce in his holy comfort, through the merits of Christ Jesu our Saviour, who liveth and reigneth with thee, in the unity of the same Spirit, one God world without end. *Amen.*

For the Epistle.   *Acts* 10.34

T HEN Peter opened his mouth, and said, Of a truth I perceive that God is no respecter of persons; but in every nation he that feareth him, and worketh righteousness, is accepted with him. The word which God sent unto the children of Israel, preaching peace by Jesus Christ (he is Lord of all;) That word, I say, you know, which was published throughout all Judea, and began from Galilee, after the baptism which John preached: How God anointed Jesus of Nazareth with the holy Ghost and with power, who went about doing good, and healing all that were oppressed of the devil: for God was with him. And we are witnesses of all things which he did, both in the land of the Jews, and in Jerusalem; whom they slew and hanged on a tree: Him God raised up the third day, and shewed him openly; not to all the people, but unto witnesses chosen before of God; even to us who did eat and drink with him after he rose from the dead. And he commanded us to preach unto the people, and to testifie that it is he which was ordained of God to be the judge of quick and dead. To him give all the prophets witness, that through his Name whosoever believeth in him, shall receive remission of sins. While Peter yet spake these words the holy Ghost fell on all them who heard the word. And they of the circumcision who believed, were astonished, as many as came with Peter, because that on the Gentiles also was poured out the gift of the holy Ghost. For they heard them speak with tongues, and magnifie God. Then answered Peter, Can any man forbid water, that these should not be baptized, who have received the holy Ghost as well as we? And he commanded them to be baptized in the Name of the Lord. Then prayed they him to tarry certain days.

The Gospel.   *John* 3.16

G OD so loved the world, that he gave his only begotten Son, that whosoever believeth in him, should not perish, but have ever-lasting life. For God sent not his Son into the world to condemn the world, but that the world through him might be saved. He that believeth on him, is not condemned: but he that believeth not is con-demned already, because he hath not believed in the Name of the only begotten Son of God. And this is the condemnation, that light is come into the world, and men loved darkness rather than light, because their deeds were evil. For every one that doth evil, hateth the light, neither cometh to the light, lest his deeds should be reproved. But he that doth truth, cometh to the light, that his deeds may be made manifest, that they are wrought in God.

Tuesday in whitsun week.

The Collect.

GOD, who as at this time didst teach the hearts of thy faithful people by sending to them the light of thy holy Spirit; Grant us by the same Spirit to have a right judgement in all things, and evermore to rejoyce in his holy comfort, through the merits of Christ Jesu our Saviour, who liveth, and reigneth with thee in the unity of the same Spirit, one God world without end. *Amen.*

For the Epistle.   *Acts* 8.14

WHEN the apostles who were at Jerusalem, heard that Samaria had received the word of God, they sent unto them Peter and John; who when they were come down, prayed for them, that they might receive the holy Ghost. (For as yet he was fallen upon none of them: onely they were baptized in the name of the Lord Jesus.) Then laid they their hands on them, and they received the holy Ghost.

The Gospel.   *John* 10.1

VERILY, verily I say unto you, He that entreth not by the door into the sheepfold, but climbeth up some other way, the same is a thief and a robber. But he that entreth in by the door, is the shepherd of the sheep. To him the porter openeth; and the sheep hear his voice, and he calleth his own sheep by name, and leadeth them out. And when he putteth forth his own sheep, he goeth before them, and the sheep follow him; for they know his voice. And a stranger will they not follow; but will flee from him; for they know not the voice of strangers. This parable spake Jesus unto them: but they understood not what things they were which he spake unto them. Then said Jesus unto them again; Verily, verily I say unto you, I am the door of the sheep. All that ever came before me are thieves and robbers; but the sheep did not hear them. I am the door; by me if any man enter in, he shall be saved, and shall go in and out, and find pasture. The thief cometh not but for to steal, and to kill, and to destroy: I am come that they might have life, and that they might have it more abundantly.

Trinity Sunday.°

The Collect.

ALMIGHTY, and everlasting God, who hast given unto us thy servants grace by the confession of a true faith to acknowledge the glory of the eternal Trinity, and in the power of the divine Majesty to worship the Unity; We beseech thee, that thou wouldst keep us stedfast in this faith, and evermore defend us from all adversities, who livest, and reignest one God world without end. *Amen.*

For the Epistle.   *Rev.* 4.1

AFTER this I looked, and, behold, a door was opened in heaven: and the first voice which I heard, was as it were of a trumpet talking with me; which said, Come up hither, and I will shew thee things which must be hereafter. And immediately I was in the Spirit; and behold, a throne was set in heaven, and one sat on the throne, and he that sat, was, to look upon, like a jasper, and a sardine stone: and there was a rainbow round about the throne, in sight like unto an emerald. And round about the throne were four and twenty seats; and upon the seats I saw four and twenty elders sitting, clothed in white raiment; and they had on their heads crowns of gold. And out of the throne proceeded lightnings, and thundrings, and voices. And there were seven lamps of fire burning before the throne, which are the seven spirits of God. And before the throne there was a sea of glass like unto crystal: and in the midst of the throne, and round about the throne were four beasts full of eyes before and behind. And the first beast was like a lion, and the second beast like a calf, and the third beast had a face as a man, and the fourth beast was like a flying eagle. And the four beasts had each of them six wings about him, and they were full of eyes within, and they rest not day and night, saying, Holy, holy, holy, Lord God Almighty, who was, and is, and is to come. And when those beasts give glory, and honour, and thanks to him that sat on the throne, who liveth for ever and ever, the four and twenty elders fall down before him that sat on the throne, and worship him that liveth for ever and ever, and cast their crowns before the throne, saying, Thou art worthy, O Lord, to receive glory, and honour, and power; for thou hast created all things, and for thy pleasure they are and were created.

The Gospel.   *John* 3.1

THERE was a man of the Pharisees, named Nicodemus, a ruler of the Jews. The same came to Jesus by night, and said unto him, Rabbi, we know that thou art a teacher come from God: For no man can do these miracles that thou doest, except God be with him. Jesus answered and said unto him, Verily, verily I say unto thee, Except a man be born again, he cannot see the kingdom of God. Nicodemus saith unto him, How can a man be born when he is old? can he enter the second time into his mothers womb, and be born? Jesus answered, Verily, verily I say unto thee, Except a man be born of water, and of the Spirit, he cannot enter into the kingdom of God. That which is born of the flesh, is flesh; and that which is born of the Spirit, is Spirit. Marvel not that I said unto thee, Ye must be born again. The wind bloweth where it listeth, and thou hearest the sound thereof; but canst not tell whence it cometh, and whither it goeth; so is every one that is born of the Spirit. Nicodemus answered and said unto him; How can these things be? Jesus answered and said unto him, Art thou a master of Israel, and knowest not these things? Verily, verily I say unto thee, We speak that we do know, and testifie that we have seen, and ye receive not our witness. If I have told you earthly things, and ye believe not; how shall ye believe if I tell you of heavenly things? And no man hath ascended up to heaven, but he that came down from heaven, even the Son of man, who is in heaven. And as Moses lifted up the serpent in the wilderness: even so must the Son of man be lifted up; that whosoever believeth in him, should not perish, but have eternal life.

The first Sunday after Trinity.

The Collect.°

O GOD, the strength of all them that put their trust in thee, mercifully accept our prayers; and because through the weakness of our mortal nature we can do no good thing without thee, grant us the help of thy grace, that in keeping of thy commandments we may please thee, both in will and deed, through Jesus Christ our Lord. *Amen.*

The Epistle.   1 *John* 4.7

BELOVED, let us love one another; for love is of God, and every one that loveth is born of God, and knoweth God. He that loveth not, knoweth not God; for God is love. In this was manifested the love of God towards us, because that God sent his only begotten Son into the world, that we might live through him. Herein is love, not that we loved God, but that he loved us, and sent his Son to be the propitiation for our sins. Beloved, if God so loved us, we ought also to love one another. No man hath seen God at any time. If we love one another, God dwelleth in us, and his love is perfected in us. Hereby know we that we dwell in him, and he in us, because he hath given us of his Spirit. And we have seen and do testifie, that the Father sent the Son to be the Saviour of the world. Whosoever shall confess that Jesus is the Son of God, God dwelleth in him, and he in God. And we have known and believed the love that God hath to us. God is love; and he that dwelleth in love, dwelleth in God, and God in him. Herein is our love made perfect, that we may have boldness in the day of judgment, because as he is, so are we in this world. There is no fear in love, but perfect love casteth out fear; because fear hath torment: He that feareth, is not made perfect in love. We love him, because he first loved us. If a man say, I love God, and hateth his brother, he is a liar: for he that loveth not his brother, whom he hath seen, how can he love God, whom he hath not seen? And this commandment have we from him, that he who loveth God, love his brother also.

The Gospel.   *Luke* 16.19

THERE was a certain rich man, who was clothed in purple, and fine linen, and fared sumptuously every day. And there was a certain beggar named Lazarus, who was laid at his gate full of sores; and desiring to be fed with the crumbs, which fell from the rich mans table: moreover the dogs came and licked his sores. And it came to pass that the begger died, and was carried by the angels into Abrahams bosom: the rich man also died and was buried. And in hell he lift up his eies being in torments, and seeth Abraham afar off, and Lazarus in his bosom. And he cried, and said, Father Abraham, have mercy on me, and send Lazarus that he may dip the tip of his finger in water, and cool my tongue, for I am tormented in this flame. But Abraham said, Son, remember, that thou in thy life time receivedst thy good things, and likewise Lazarus evil things: but now he is comforted, and thou art tormented. And beside all this, between us and you there is a great gulf fixed: so that they who would pass from hence to you, cannot; neither can they pass to us, that would come from thence. Then he said, I pray thee therefore, father, that thou wouldest send him to my fathers house: For I have five brethren; that he may testifie unto them, lest they also come into this place of torment. Abraham saith unto him, They have Moses and the prophets; let them hear them. And he said, Nay, father Abraham; but if one went unto them from the dead, they will repent. And he said unto him, If they hear not Moses and the prophets, neither will they be perswaded, though one rose from the dead.

The second Sunday after Trinity.

The Collect.

O LORD, who never failest to help and govern them who thou dost bring up in thy stedfast fear and love; Keep us, we beseech thee, under the protection of thy good providence, and make us to have a perpetual fear and love of thy holy Name, through Jesus Christ our Lord. *Amen.*

The Epistle.   1 *John* 3.13

MARVEL not, my brethren, if the world hate you. We know that we have passed from death unto life, because we love the brethren: He that loveth not his brother abideth in death. Whosoever hateth his brother, is a murderer; and ye know that no murderer hath eternal life abiding in him. Hereby perceive we the love of God, because he laid down his life for us: and we ought to lay down our lives for the brethren. But whoso hath this worlds good, and seeth his brother have need, and shutteth up his bowels of compassion from him; how dwelleth the love of God in him? My little children, let us not love in word, neither in tongue; but in deed, and in truth. And hereby we know that we are of the truth, and shall assure our hearts before him. For if our heart condemn us, God is greater than our heart, and knoweth all things. Beloved, if our heart condemn us not, then have we confidence towards God. And whatsoever we ask, we receive of him, because we keep his commandments, and do those things that are pleasing in his sight. And this is his commandment, that we should believe on the Name of his Son Jesus Christ, and love one another as he gave us commandment. And he that keepeth his commandments dwelleth in him, and he in him: and hereby we know that he abideth in us, by the Spirit which he hath given us.

The Gospel.   Luke 14.16

A CERTAIN man made a great supper, and bade many; And sent his servant at supper time to say to them that were bidden, Come, for all things are now ready. And they all with one consent began to make excuse: The first said unto him, I have bought a piece of ground, and I must needs go and see it; I pray thee have me excused. And another said, I have bought five yoke of oxen, and I go to prove them; I pray thee have me excused. And another said, I have married a wife, and therefore I cannot come. So that servant came, and shewed his Lord these things. Then the master of the house being angry said to his servant, Go out quickly into the streets and lanes of the city, and bring in hither the poor, and the maimed, and the halt, and the blind. And the servant said, Lord, it is done as thou hast commanded, and yet there is room. And the Lord said unto the servant, Go out into the high-ways, and hedges, and compel them to come in, that my house may be filled. For I say unto you, that none of those men which were bidden, shall taste of my Supper.

The third Sunday after Trinity.
The Collect.

O LORD, we beseech thee mercifully to hear us; and grant that we, to whom thou hast given an hearty desire to pray, may by thy mighty aid be defended and be comforted in all dangers and adversities, through Jesus Christ our Lord. *Amen.*

The Epistle.   1 Pet. 5.5

A LL of you be subject one to another, and be clothed with humility: for God resisteth the proud, and giveth grace to the humble. Humble your selves therefore under the mighty hand of God, that he may exalt you in due time; casting all your care upon him, for he careth for you. Be sober, be vigilant; because your adversary the devil, as a roaring lion, walketh about seeking whom he may devour. Whom resist stedfast in the faith, knowing that the same afflictions are accomplished in your brethren that are in the world. But the God of all grace, who hath called us unto his eternal glory by Christ Jesus, after that ye have suffered a while, make you perfect, stablish, strengthen, settle you. To him be glory and dominion for ever and ever. *Amen.*

The Gospel. Luke 15.1

THEN drew near unto him all the publicans and sinners for to hear him. And the Pharisees and Scribes murmured, saying, This man receiveth sinners, and eateth with them. And he spake this parable unto them, saying, What man of you having an hundred sheep, if he lose one of them, doth not leave the ninety and nine in the wilderness, and go after that which is lost, until he find it? And when he hath found it, he laieth it on his shoulders, rejoycing. And when he cometh home, he calleth together his friends and neighbours saying unto them, Rejoyce with me, for I have found my sheep which was lost. I say unto you, that likewise joy shall be in heaven over one sinner that repenteth, more than over ninety and nine just persons, which need no repentance. Either what woman, having ten pieces of silver, if she lose one piece, doth not light a candle, and sweep the house, and seek diligently till she find it? And when she hath found it, she calleth her friends and her neighbours together, saying, Rejoyce with me; for I have found the piece which I had lost. Likewise I say unto you, There is joy in the presence of the angels of God, over one sinner that repenteth.

The fourth Sunday after Trinity.

The Collect.

O GOD, the protectour of all that trust in thee, without whom nothing is strong, nothing is holy; Encrease and multiply upon us thy mercy, that thou being our ruler and guide, we may so pass through things temporal, that we finally lose not the things eternal: Grant this, O heavenly Father, for Jesus Christs sake our Lord. *Amen.*

The Epistle. Rom. 8.18

I RECKON that the sufferings of this present time are not worthy to be compared with the glory which shall be revealed in us. For the earnest expectation of the creature waiteth for the manifestation of the sons of God. For the creature was made subject to vanity, not willingly, but by reason of him who hath subjected the same in hope: Because the creature it self also shall be delivered from the bondage of corruption into the glorious liberty of the children of God. For we know that the whole creation groaneth, and travaileth in pain together until now. And not only they, but our selves also, which have the first-fruits of the spirit, even we our selves groan within our selves, waiting for the adoption, to wit, the redemption of our body.

The Gospel. *Luke* 6.36

BE ye therefore merciful, as your Father also is merciful. Judge not, and ye shall not be judged: condemn not, and ye shall not be condemned: forgive, and ye shall be forgiven: give, and it shall be given unto you: good measure, pressed down, and shaken together, and running over shall men give into your bosom. For with the same measure that ye mete withall, it shall be measured to you again. And he spake a parable unto them, Can the blind lead the blind? shall they not both fall into the ditch? The disciple is not above his master; but every one that is perfect shall be as his master. And why beholdest thou the mote that is in thy brothers eye, but perceivest not the beam that is in thine own eye? Either how canst thou say to thy brother, Brother, let me pull out the mote that is in thine eye, when thou thy self beholdest not the beam that is in thine own eye? Thou hypocrite, cast out first the beam out of thine own eye, and then shalt thou see clearly to pull out the mote that is in thy brothers eye.

The fifth Sunday after Trinity.

The Collect.

GRANT, O Lord, we beseech thee, that the course of this world may be so peaceably ordered by thy governance, that thy Church may joyfully serve thee in all godly quietness, through Jesus Christ our Lord. *Amen.*

The Epistle. *1 Pet.* 3.8

BE ye all of one minde, having compassion one of another, love as brethren, be pitiful, be courteous: not rendring evil for evil, or railing for railing; but contrarywise blessing; knowing that ye are thereunto called, that ye should inherit a blessing. For he that will love life, and see good daies, let him refrain his tongue from evil, and his lips that they speak no guile. Let him eschew evil, and do good; let him seek peace, and ensue it. For the eyes of the Lord are over the righteous, and his ears are open unto their prayers: but the face of the Lord is against them that do evil. And who is he that will harm you, if ye be followers of that which is good? But and if ye suffer for righteousness sake, happy are ye, and be not afraid of their terrour, neither be troubled; but sanctifie the Lord God in your hearts.

The Gospel.					*Luke* 5.1

IT came to pass, that, as the people pressed upon him to hear the word of God, he stood by the lake of Gennesareth; and saw two ships standing by the lake: but the fisher-men were gone out of them, and were washing their nets. And he entred into one of the ships, which was Simons, and prayed him that he would thrust out a little from the land: and he sat down and taught the people out of the ship. Now when he had left speaking, he said unto Simon, Launch out into the deep, and let down your nets for a draught. And Simon answering, said unto him, Master, we have toiled all the night, and have taken nothing; nevertheless at thy word, I will let down the net. And when they had this done, they enclosed a great multitude of fishes, and their net brake. And they beckned unto their partners which were in the other ship, that they should come and help them. And they came and filled both the ships, so that they began to sink. When Simon Peter saw it, he fell down at Jesus knees, saying, Depart from me, for I am a sinful man, O Lord. For he was astonished, and all that were with him at the draught of the fishes which they had taken: And so was also James, and John, the sons of Zebedee, who were partners with Simon. And Jesus said unto Simon, Fear not, from henceforth thou shalt catch men. And when they had brought their ships to land, they forsook all, and followed him.

The sixth Sunday after Trinity.
The Collect.

O GOD, who hast prepared for them that love thee, such good things as pass mans understanding; Pour into our hearts such love toward thee, that we, loving thee above all things, may obtain thy promises, which exceed all that we can desire, through Jesus Christ our Lord. *Amen.*

The Epistle.					*Rom.* 6.3

KNOW ye not, that so many of us as were baptized into Jesus Christ, were baptized into his death? Therefore we are buried with him by baptism into death, that like as Christ was raised up from the dead by the glory of the Father; even so we also should walk in newness of life. For if we have been planted together in the likeness of his death, we shall be also in the likeness of his resurrection: Knowing this, that our old man is crucified with him, that the body of sin might be destroyed, that henceforth we should not serve sin. For he that is dead, is freed from sin. Now if we be dead with Christ, we believe that we shall also live with him; knowing, that Christ being raised from the dead, dieth no more; death hath no more dominion over him. For in that he died, he died unto sin once: but in that he liveth, he liveth unto God. Likewise reckon ye also your selves to be dead indeed unto sin: but alive unto God, through Jesus Christ our Lord.

The Gospel.   Matt. 5.20

JESUS said unto his disciples, Except your righteousness shall exceed the righteousness of the Scribes and Pharisees, ye shall in no case enter into the kingdom of heaven. Ye have heard, that it was said by them of old time, Thou shalt not kill: and whosoever shall kill, shall be in danger of the judgement. But I say unto you, that whosoever is angry with his brother without a cause shall be in danger of the judgement: and whosoever shall say to his brother, Racha, shall be in danger of the councel: but whosoever shall say, Thou fool, shall be in danger of hell fire. Therefore if thou bring thy gift to the altar, and there remembrest that thy brother hath ought against thee; leave there thy gift before the altar, and go thy way, first be reconciled to thy brother, and then come and offer thy gift. Agree with thine adversary quickly, whiles thou art in the way with him; lest at any time the adversary deliver thee to the judge, and the judge deliver thee to the officer, and thou be cast into prison. Verily I say unto thee, thou shalt by no means come out thence, till thou hast paid the uttermost farthing.

The seventh Sunday after Trinity.

The Collect.

LORD of all power and might, who art the author and giver of all good things; Graft in our hearts the love of thy Name, increase in us true religion, nourish us with all goodness, and of thy great mercy keep us in the same, through Jesus Christ our Lord. *Amen.*

The Epistle.   Rom. 6.19

I SPEAK after the manner of men, because of the infirmity of your flesh: for as ye have yielded your members servants to uncleanness, and to iniquity, unto iniquity; even so now yield your members servants to righteousness, unto holiness. For when ye were the servants of sin, ye were free from righteousness. What fruit had ye then in those things, whereof ye are now ashamed? for the end of those things is death. But now being made free from sin, and become servants to God, ye have your fruit unto holiness, and the end everlasting life. For the wages of sin is death: but the gift of God is eternal life, through Jesus Christ our Lord.

The Gospel.   *Mark* 8.1

I N those days the multitude being very great, and having nothing to eat, Jesus called his disciples unto him, and saith unto them, I have compassion on the multitude, because they have now been with me three daies, and have nothing to eat: And if I send them away fasting to their own houses, they will faint by the way: for divers of them came from far. And his disciples answered him, From whence can a man satisfie these men with bread here in the wilderness? And he asked them, How many loaves have ye? And they said, Seven. And he commanded the people to sit down on the ground. And he took the seven loaves, and gave thanks, and brake, and gave to his disciples to set before them, and they did set them before the people. And they had a few small fishes, and he blessed and commanded to set them also before them. So they did eat and were filled: And they took up of the broken meat that was left, seven baskets. And they that had eaten were about four thousand. And he sent them away.

The eighth Sunday after Trinity.

The Collect.

O GOD, whose never-failing providence ordereth all things both in heaven and earth; We humbly beseech thee to put away from us all hurtful things, and to give us those things which be profitable for us, through Jesus Christ our Lord. *Amen.*

The Epistle.   *Rom.* 8.12

B RETHREN, we are debters, not to the flesh, to live after the flesh: For if ye live after the flesh, ye shall die: but if ye through the Spirit do mortifie the deeds of the body, ye shall live. For as many as are led by the Spirit of God, they are the sons of God. For ye have not received the spirit of bondage again to fear: but ye have received the

Spirit of adoption, whereby we cry, Abba, Father. The Spirit it self beareth witness with our spirit, that we are the children of God. And if children, then heirs: heirs of God, and joynt-heirs with Christ: if so be that we suffer with him, that we may be also glorified together.

The Gospel.　　　　　*Matt.* 7.15

BEWARE of false prophets, which come to you in sheeps clothing, but inwardly they are ravening wolves. Ye shall know them by their fruits: Do men gather grapes of thorns, or figs of thistles? Even so every good tree bringeth forth good fruit; but a corrupt tree bringeth forth evil fruit. A good tree cannot bring forth evil fruit; neither can a corrupt tree bring forth good fruit. Every tree that bringeth not forth good fruit, is hewen down, and cast into the fire. Wherefore by their fruits ye shall know them. Not every one that saith unto me, Lord, Lord, shall enter into the kingdom of heaven: but he that doth the will of my Father who is in heaven.

The ninth Sunday after Trinity.

The Collect.

GRANT to us, Lord, we beseech thee, the Spirit to think and do always such things as be rightful; that we who can not do any thing that is good without thee, may by thee be enabled to live according to thy will, through Jesus Christ our Lord. *Amen.*

The Epistle.　　　　　1 *Cor.* 10.1

BRETHREN, I would not that ye should be ignorant, how that all our fathers were under the cloud, and all passed through the sea; and were all baptized unto Moses in the cloud, and in the sea; and did all eat the same spiritual meat, And did all drink the same spiritual drink: (for they drank of that spiritual rock that followed them; and that rock was Christ). But with many of them God was not well pleased; for they were overthrown in the wilderness. Now these things were our examples, to the intent we should not lust after evil things, as they also lusted. Neither be ye idolaters, as were some of them; as it is written, The people sat down to eat and drink, and rose up to play. Neither let us commit fornication, as some of them committed, and fell in one day three and twenty thousand. Neither let us tempt Christ, as some of them also tempted, and were destroyed of serpents. Neither murmure ye, as some of them also murmured, and were destroyed of the destroyer. Now all these things happened unto them for ensamples: and they are written for our admonition, upon whom the ends of the world are come. Wherefore let him that thinketh he standeth, take heed lest he fall. There hath no temptation taken you, but such as is common to man: but God is faithful, who will not suffer you to be tempted above that ye are able; but will with the temptation also make a way to escape, that ye may be able to bear it.

The Gospel.   *Luke* 16.1

JESUS said unto his disciples, There was a certain rich man who had a steward, and the same was accused unto him, that he had wasted his goods. And he called him, and said unto him, How is it that I hear this of thee? Give an account of thy stewardship; for thou mayest be no longer steward. Then the steward said within himself, What shall I do? for my Lord taketh away from me the stewardship: I cannot dig; to beg I am ashamed. I am resolved what to do, that when I am put out of the stewardship, they may receive me into their houses. So he called every one of his lords debtors unto him, and said unto the first, How much owest thou unto my lord? And he said, An hundred measures of oyl. And he said unto him, Take thy bill, and sit down quickly, and write fifty. Then said he to another, And how much owest thou? And he said, An hundred measures of wheat. And he said unto him, Take thy bill, and write fourscore. And the Lord commended the unjust steward, because he had done wisely: for the children of this world are in their generation wiser than the children of light. And I say unto you, Make to your selves friends of the Mammon of unrighteousness, that when ye fail, they may receive you into everlasting habitations.

The tenth Sunday after Trinity.

The Collect.

LET thy merciful ears, O Lord, be open to the prayers of thy humble servants; and that they may obtain their petitions, make them to ask such things as shall please thee; through Jesus Christ our Lord. *Amen.*

The Epistle.   1 *Cor.* 12.1

CONCERNING spiritual gifts, brethren, I would not have you ignorant. Ye know that ye were Gentiles carried away unto these dumb idols, even as ye were led. Wherefore I give you to understand, that no man speaking by the Spirit of God, calleth Jesus accursed; and that no man can say that Jesus is the Lord, but by the holy Ghost. Now there are diversities of gifts, but the same Spirit. And there are differences of administrations, but the same Lord. And there are diversities of operations, but it is the same God, who worketh all in all. But the manifestation of the Spirit is given to every man to profit withall. For to one is given by the Spirit the word of wisdom; to another the word of knowledge by the same Spirit; to another faith by the same Spirit; to another the gifts of healing by the same Spirit; to another the working of miracles; to another prophecy; to another discerning of spirits; to another divers kinds of tongues; to another the interpretation of tongues: But all these worketh that one and the self same Spirit, dividing to every man severally as he will.

The Gospel.   *Luke* 19.41

A ND when he was come near, he beheld the city, and wept over it, saying, If thou hadst known, even thou, at least in this thy day, the things which belong unto thy peace! but now they are hid from thine eyes. For the days shall come upon thee, that thine enemies shall cast a trench about thee, and compass thee round, and keep thee in on every side, and shall lay thee even with the ground, and thy children within thee: and they shall not leave in thee one stone upon another, because thou knewest not the time of thy visitation. And he went into the temple, and began to cast out them that sold therein, and them that bought, saying unto them, It is written, My house is the house of prayer, but ye have made it a den of thieves. And he taught daily in the temple.

The eleventh Sunday after Trinity.

The Collect.

O GOD, who declarest thy Almighty power, most chiefly in shew- ing mercy and pity; Mercifully grant unto us such a measure of thy grace, that we running the way of thy commandments, may obtain thy gracious promises, and be made partakers of thy heavenly treasure, through Jesus Christ our Lord. *Amen.*

The Epistle.   1 *Cor.* 15.1

B RETHREN, I declare unto you the Gospel which I preached unto you, which also ye have received, and wherein ye stand. By which also ye are saved, if ye keep in memory what I preached unto you, unless ye have believed in vain. For I delivered unto you first of all that which I also received, how that Christ died for our sins, according to the Scriptures; and that he was buried; and that he rose again the third day according to the Scriptures; and that he was seen of Cephas, then of the twelve: After that he was seen of above five hundred brethren at once; of whom the greater part remain unto this present; but some are faln asleep. After that he was seen of James; then of all the Apostles; and last of all he was seen of me also, as of one born out of due time: for I am the least of the Apostles, that am not meet to be called an Apostle, because I persecuted the Church of God. But by the grace of God I am what I am: and his grace which was bestowed upon me, was not in vain; but I laboured more abundantly then they all; yet not I, but the grace of God which was with me: Therefore whether it were I or they, so we preach, and so ye believed.

The Gospel.   *Luke* 18.9

JESUS spake this parable unto certain which trusted in themselves, that they were righteous, and despised others; Two men went up into the temple to pray; the one a Pharisee, and the other a Publican. The Pharisee stood and prayed thus with himself, God, I thank thee, that I am not as other men are, extortioners, unjust, adulterers, or even as this Publican. I fast twice in the week, I give tithes of all that I possess. And the Publican standing afar off, would not lift up so much as his eyes unto heaven, but smote upon his breast, saying, God be merciful to me a sinner. I tell you, this man went down to his house justified rather than the other: for every one that exalteth himself, shall be abased; and he that humbleth himself, shall be exalted.

The twelfth Sunday after Trinity.

The Collect.

ALMIGHTY and everlasting God, who art always more ready to hear, than we to pray, and art wont to give more than either we desire, or deserve; Pour down upon us the abundance of thy mercy, forgiving us those things whereof our conscience is afraid, and giving us those good things which we are not worthy to ask, but through the merits and mediation of Jesus Christ thy Son our Lord. *Amen.*

The Epistle.   2 *Cor.* 3.4

SUCH trust have we through Christ to God-ward. Not that we are sufficient of ourselves to think any thing as of ourselves; but our sufficiency is of God. Who also hath made us able ministers of the new Testament; not of the letter, but of the Spirit: for the letter killeth, but the Spirit giveth life. But if the ministration of death written and engraven in stones was glorious; so that the children of Israel could not stedfastly behold the face of Moses for the glory of his countenance, which glory was to be done away; How shall not the ministration of the Spirit be rather glorious? For if the ministration of condemnation be glory, much more doth the ministration of righteousness exceed in glory.

The Gospel.   *Mark* 7.31

JESUS departing from the coasts of Tyre and Sidon, came unto the sea of Galilee, through the midst of the coasts of Decapolis. And they bring unto him one that was deaf, and had an impediment in his speech; and they beseech him to put his hand upon him. And he took him aside from the multitude, and put his fingers into his ears, and he spit, and touched his tongue; and looking up to heaven, he sighed, and saith unto him, *Ephphatha*, that is, Be opened. And straitway his ears were opened, and the string of his tongue was loosed, and he spake plain. And he charged them that they should tell no man; but the more he charged them, so much the more a great deal they published it, and were beyond measure astonished, saying, He hath done all things well; he maketh both the deaf to hear, and the dumb to speak.

The thirteenth Sunday after Trinity.

The Collect.

ALMIGHTY and merciful God, of whose only gift it cometh, that thy faithful people do unto thee true and laudable service; Grant, we beseech thee, that we may so faithfully serve thee in this life, that we fail not finally to attain thy heavenly promises, through the merits of Jesus Christ our Lord. *Amen.*

The Epistle.   *Gal.* 3.16

TO Abraham and his seed were the promises made. He saith not, And to seeds, as of many; but as of one; And to thy seed, which is Christ. And this I say, that the covenant that was confirmed before of God in Christ, the law which was four hundred and thirty years after, cannot disannul; that it should make the promise of none effect. For if the inheritance be of the law, it is no more of promise; but God gave it to Abraham by promise. Wherefore then serveth the law? It was added because of transgressions, till the seed should come, to whom the promise was made; and it was ordained by angels in the hand of a mediatour. Now a mediatour is not a mediatour of one, but God is one. Is the law then against the promises of God? God forbid: for if there had been a law given, which could have given life, verily righteousness should have been by the law. But the scripture hath concluded all under sin, that the promise by faith of Jesus Christ might be given to them that believe.

The Gospel.   *Luke* 10.23

BLESSED are the eyes which see the things that ye see. For I tell you, that many prophets and kings have desired to see those things which ye see, and have not seen them; and to hear those things which ye hear, and have not heard them. And behold, a certain lawyer stood up, and tempted him, saying, Master, what shall I do to inherit eternal life? He said unto him, What is written in the law? how readest thou? And he answering said, Thou shalt love the Lord thy God with all thy heart, and with all thy soul, and with all thy strength, and with all thy mind, and thy neighbour as thy self. And he said unto him, Thou hast answered right; this do, and thou shalt live. But he willing to justifie himself, said unto Jesus, And who is my neighbour? And Jesus answering said, A certain man went down from Jerusalem to Jericho, and fell among thieves, which stripped him of his raiment, and wounded him, and departed leaving him half dead. And by chance there came down a certain priest that way, and when he saw him, he passed by on the other side. And likewise a Levite, when he was at the place, came and looked on him, and passed by on the other side. But a certain Samaritan, as he journeyed, came where he was; and when he saw him, he had compassion on him, and went to him, and bound up his wounds, pouring in oyl, and wine, and set him on his own beast, and brought him to an inn, and took care of him. And on the morrow when he departed, he took out two pence, and gave them to the host, and said unto him, Take care of him, and whatsoever thou spendest more, when I come again I will repay thee. Which now of these three, thinkest thou, was neighbour unto him that fell among the thieves? And he said, He that shewed mercy on him. Then said Jesus unto him, Go and do thou likewise.

The fourteenth Sunday after Trinity.

The Collect.

A LMIGHTY and everlasting God, give unto us the increase of faith, hope, and charity; and, that we may obtain that which thou dost promise, make us to love that which thou dost command, through Jesus Christ our Lord. *Amen.*

The Epistle.   *Gal.* 5.16

I SAY then, Walk in the Spirit, and ye shall not fulfil the lust of the flesh. For the flesh lusteth against the Spirit, and the Spirit against the flesh; and these are contrary the one to the other; so that ye cannot do the things that ye would. But if ye be led of the Spirit, ye are not under the law. Now the works of the flesh are manifest, which are these, Adultery, fornication, uncleanness, lasciviousness, idolatry, witchcraft, hatred, variance, emulations, wrath, strife, seditions, heresies, envyings, murders, drunkenness, revellings, and such like: of the which I tell you before, as I have also told you in time past, that they who do such things shall not inherit the kingdom of God. But the fruit of the Spirit is love, joy, peace, long-suffering, gentleness, goodness, faith, meekness, temperance: against such there is no law. And they that are Christs have crucified the flesh with the affections and lusts.

The Gospel.   *Luke* 17.11

A ND it came to pass, as Jesus went to Jerusalem, that he passed through the midst of Samaria, and Galilee. And as he entred into a certain village, there met him ten men that were lepers, which stood afar off. And they lifted up their voices, and said, Jesus master, have mercy on us. And when he saw them, he said unto them, Go shew your selves unto the priests. And it came to pass, that as they went, they were cleansed. And one of them, when he saw that he was healed, turned back, and with a loud voice glorified God, and fell down on his face at his feet, giving him thanks; and he was a Samaritan. And Jesus answering, said, Were there not ten cleansed? but where are the nine? There are not found that returned to give glory to God, save this stranger. And he said unto him, Arise, go thy way, thy faith hath made thee whole.

The fifteenth Sunday after Trinity.

The Collect.

K EEP, we beseech thee, O Lord, thy Church with thy perpetual mercy. And because the frailty of man without thee cannot but fall, keep us ever by thy help from all things hurtful, and lead us to all things profitable to our salvation, through Jesus Christ our Lord. *Amen.*

The Epistle.   *Gal.* 6.11

Y E see how large a letter I have written unto you with mine own hand. As many as desire to make a fair shew in the flesh, they constrain you to be circumcised; only lest they should suffer persecution for the cross of Christ. For neither they themselves who are circumcised keep the law; but desire to have you circumcised, that they may glory in your flesh. But God forbid that I should glory, save in the cross of our Lord Jesus Christ, by whom the world is crucified unto me, and I unto the world. For in Christ Jesus neither circumcision availeth any thing, nor uncircumcision, but a new creature. And as many as walk according to this rule, peace be on them, and mercy, and upon the Israel of God. From henceforth let no man trouble me, for I bear in my body the marks of the Lord Jesus. Brethren, the grace of our Lord Jesus Christ be with your spirit. *Amen.*

The Gospel.   *Matt.* 6.24

N O man can serve two masters: for either he will hate the one, and love the other; or else he will hold to the one, and despise the other. Ye cannot serve God and Mammon. Therefore I say unto you, Take no thought for your life, what ye shall eat, or what ye shall drink; nor yet for your body, what ye shall put on: Is not the life more than meat, and the body than raiment? Behold the fowls of the air; for they sow not, neither do they reap, nor gather into barns; yet your heavenly Father feedeth them: Are ye not much better than they? Which of you by taking thought can add one cubit unto his stature? And why take ye thought for raiment? Consider the lilies of the field how they grow: they toil not, neither do they spin: And yet I say unto you, That even Solomon in all his glory was not arayed like one of these. Wherefore if God so clothe the grass of the field, which to day is, and to morrow is cast into the oven; shall he not much more clothe you, O ye of little faith? Therefore take no thought, saying, What shall we eat? or what shall we drink? or wherewithal shall we be clothed? (for after all these things do the Gentiles seek) for your heavenly Father knoweth that ye have need of all these things. But seek ye first the kingdom of God, and his righteousness, and all these things shall be added unto you. Take therefore no thought for the morrow; for the morrow shall take thought for the things of it self: sufficient unto the day is the evil thereof.

The sixteenth Sunday after Trinity.

The Collect.

O LORD, we beseech thee, let thy continual pity cleanse and defend thy church; and because it cannot continue in safety without thy succour, preserve it evermore by thy help and goodness, through Jesus Christ our Lord. *Amen.*

The Epistle.   Eph. 3. 13

I DESIRE that ye faint not at my tribulations for you, which is your glory. For this cause I bow my knees unto the Father of our Lord Jesus Christ, of whom the whole family in heaven and earth is named, that he would grant you according to the riches of his glory, to be strengthened with might by his Spirit in the inner man: That Christ may dwell in your hearts by faith; that ye being rooted and grounded in love, may be able to comprehend with all saints, what is the breadth, and length, and depth, and height; and to know the love of Christ, which passeth knowledge, that ye might be filled with all the fulness of God. Now unto him that is able to do exceeding abundantly above all that we ask or think, according to the power that worketh in us, unto him be glory in the Church by Christ Jesus, throughout all ages, world without end. *Amen.*

The Gospel.   Luke 7. 11

A ND it came to pass the day after, that Jesus went into a city called Nain, and many of his disciples went with him, and much people. Now when he came nigh to the gate of the city, behold, there was a dead man carried out, the only son of his mother, and she was a widow; and much people of the city was with her. And when the Lord saw her, he had compassion on her, and said unto her, Weep not.

And he came and touched the biere, (and they that bare him stood still) and he said, Young man, I say unto thee, Arise. And he that was dead, sat up, and began to speak: and he delivered him to his mother. And there came a fear on all, and they glorified God, saying, That a great Prophet is risen up among us, and that God hath visited his people. And this rumour of him went forth throughout all Judaea, and throughout all the region round about.

The seventeenth Sunday after Trinity.

The Collect.

LORD, we pray thee, that thy grace may always prevent and follow us; and make us continually to be given to all good works, through Jesus Christ our Lord. *Amen.*

The Epistle.   *Eph.* 4.1

I THEREFORE, the prisoner of the Lord, beseech you that ye walk worthy of the vocation wherewith ye are called, with all lowliness, and meekness, with long-suffering, forbearing one another in love; endeavouring to keep the unity of the spirit in the bond of peace. There is one body, and one Spirit, even as ye are called in one hope of your calling; one Lord, one faith, one baptism, one God and Father of all, who is above all, and through all, and in you all.

The Gospel.   *Luke* 14.1

IT came to pass, as Jesus went into the house of one of the chief Pharisees to eat bread on the sabbath-day, that they watched him. And behold, there was a certain man before him which had the drop-sie. And Jesus answering, spake unto the lawyers and Pharisees, saying, Is it lawful to heal on the sabbath-day? And they held their peace. And he took him, and healed him, and let him go; and answered them, saying, Which of you shall have an ass, or an ox fallen into a pit, and will not straight-way pull him out on the sabbath-day? And they could not answer him again to these things. And he put forth a parable to those who were bidden, when he marked how they chose out the chief rooms, saying unto them, When thou art bidden of any man to a wedding, sit not down in the highest room, lest a more hon-ourable man than thou be bidden of him: And he that bade thee and him, come and say to thee, Give this man place; and thou begin with shame to take the lowest room. But when thou art bidden, go and sit down in the lowest room, that when he that bade thee, cometh, he may say unto thee, Friend, go up higher: then shalt thou have worship in the presence of them that sit at meat with thee. For whosoever exalteth himself, shall be abased; and he that humbleth himself, shall be exalted.

The eighteenth Sunday after Trinity.

The Collect.

LORD, we beseech thee, grant thy people grace to withstand the temptations of the world, the flesh, and the devil, and with pure hearts and minds to follow thee the only God, through Jesus Christ our Lord. *Amen.*

The Epistle.   1 *Cor.* 1.4

I THANK my God always on your behalf, for the grace of God which is given you by Jesus Christ; that in every thing ye are enriched by him, in all utterance, and in all knowledge, even as the testimony of Christ was confirmed in you: So that ye come behind in no gift; waiting for the coming of our Lord Jesus Christ, who shall also confirm you unto the end, that ye may be blameless in the day of our Lord Jesus Christ.

The Gospel.   *Matt.* 22.34

WHEN the Pharisees had heard that Jesus had put the Sadduces to silence, they were gathered together. Then one of them, who was a lawyer, asked him a question, tempting him, and saying, Master, which is the great commandment in the law? Jesus said unto him, Thou shalt love the Lord thy God with all thy heart, and with all thy soul, and with all thy mind. This is the first and great commandment. And the second is like unto it, Thou shalt love thy neighbour as thy self. On these two commandments hang all the law and the prophets. While the Pharisees were gathered together, Jesus asked them, saying, What think ye of Christ? whose son is he? They say unto him, The son of David. He saith unto them, How then doth David in spirit call him Lord, saying, The Lord said unto my Lord, Sit thou on my right hand, till I make thine enemies thy footstool? If David then call him Lord, how is he his Son? And no man was able to answer him a word, neither durst any man (from that day forth) ask him any moe questions.

The nineteenth Sunday after Trinity.

The Collect.

O GOD, for as much as without thee we are not able to please thee; Mercifully grant, that thy holy Spirit may in all things direct, and rule our hearts, through Jesus Christ our Lord. *Amen.*

The Epistle.   *Eph.* 4.17

THIS I say therefore, and testifie in the Lord, that ye henceforth walk not as other Gentiles walk in the vanity of their mind; having the understanding darkned, being alienated from the life of God through the ignorance that is in them, because of the blindness of their heart: who being past feeling, have given themselves over unto lasciviousness, to work all uncleanness with greediness. But ye have not so learned Christ: If so be that ye have heard him, and have been taught by him, as the truth is in Jesus: That ye put off concerning the former conversation, the old man, which is corrupt according to the deceitful lusts; and be renewed in the spirit of your mind; and that ye put on the new man, which after God is created in righteousness and true holiness. Wherefore putting away lying, speak every man truth with his neighbour; for we are members one of another. Be ye angry and sin not. Let not the sun go down upon your wrath: Neither give place to the devil. Let him that stole, steal no more; but rather let him labour, working with his hands the thing which is good, that he may have to give to him that needeth. Let no corrupt communication proceed out of your mouth, but that which is good to the use of edifying, that it may minister grace unto the hearers. And grieve not the holy Spirit of God, whereby ye are sealed unto the day of redemption. Let all bitterness, and wrath, and anger, and clamour, and evil-speaking, be put away from you, with all malice. And be ye kind one to another, tender-hearted, forgiving one another, even as God for Christs sake hath forgiven you.

The Gospel.   *Matt.* 9.1

JESUS entred into a ship, and passed over, and came into his own city. And behold, they brought to him a man sick of the palsie, lying on a bed. And Jesus seeing their faith, said unto the sick of the palsie, Son, be of good cheer: thy sins be forgiven thee. And behold, certain of the scribes said within themselves, This man blasphemeth.

And Jesus knowing their thoughts said, Wherefore think ye evil in your hearts? For whether is easier to say, Thy sins be forgiven thee? or to say, Arise, and walk? But that ye may know that the Son of man hath power on earth to forgive sins, (then saith he to the sick of the palsie) Arise, take up thy bed, and go unto thine house. And he arose, and departed to his house. But when the multitude saw it, they marvelled, and glorified God, which had given such power unto men.

The twentieth Sunday after Trinity.

The Collect.

O ALMIGHTY and most merciful God, of thy bountiful goodness keep us, we beseech thee, from all things that may hurt us; that we being ready both in body and soul, may cheerfully accomplish those things that thou wouldest have done, through Jesus Christ our Lord. *Amen.*

The Epistle.   *Eph.* 5.15

SEE then that ye walk circumspectly, not as fools, but as wise, redeeming the time, because the days are evil. Wherefore be ye not unwise, but understanding what the will of the Lord is. And be not drunk with wine, wherein is excess; but be filled with the Spirit; speaking to your selves in psalms, and hymns, and spiritual songs; singing and making melody in your heart to the Lord; giving thanks always for all things unto God, and the Father, in the Name of our Lord Jesus Christ; submitting your selves one to another in the fear of God.

The Gospel.   *Matt.* 22.1

JESUS said, The kingdom of heaven is like unto a certain king, who made a marriage for his son; and sent forth his servants to call them that were bidden to the wedding; and they would not come. Again, he sent forth other servants, saying, Tell them which are bidden, Behold, I have prepared my dinner; my oxen and my fatlings are killed, and all things are ready, come unto the marriage. But they made light of it, and went their ways, one to his farm, another to his merchandise: And the remnant took his servants, and entreated them spitefully, and slew them. But when the king heard thereof he was wroth; and he sent forth his armies, and destroyed those murderers, and burnt up their city. Then saith he to his servants, The wedding is ready, but they who were bidden were not worthy. Go ye therefore into the high-ways, and as many as ye shall find, bid to the marriage. So those servants went out into the high-ways, and gathered together all as many as they found, both bad and good; and the wedding was furnished with guests. And when the king came in to see the guests, he saw there a man who had not on a wedding garment. And he saith unto him, Friend, how camest thou in hither, not having a wedding garment? And he was speechless. Then said the king to the servants, Bind him hand and foot, and take him away, and cast him into outer darkness: There shall be weeping and gnashing of teeth. For many are called, but few are chosen.

The one and twentieth Sunday after Trinity.

The Collect.

G RANT, we beseech thee, merciful Lord, to thy faithful people pardon and peace, that they may be cleansed from all their sins, and serve thee with a quiet mind, through Jesus Christ our Lord. *Amen.*

The Epistle.   *Eph.* 6.10

M Y brethren, be strong in the Lord, and in the power of his might. Put on the whole armour of God, that ye may be able to stand against the wiles of the devil. For we wrestle not against flesh and bloud, but against principalities, against powers, against the rulers of the darkness of this world, against spiritual wickedness in high places. Wherefore take unto you the whole armour of God, that ye may be able to withstand in the evil day, and having done all, to stand. Stand therefore having your loins girt about with truth, and having on the breast-plate of righteousness; and your feet shod with the preparation of the gospel of peace; Above all taking the shield of faith, wherewith ye shall be able to quench all the fiery darts of the wicked. And take the helmet of salvation, and the sword of the Spirit, which is the word of God: Praying always with all prayer and supplication in the Spirit, and watching thereunto with all perseverance and supplication for all saints; and for me, that utterance may be given unto me, that I may open my mouth boldly, to make known the mystery of the gospel; for which I am an ambassador in bonds, that therein I may speak boldly, as I ought to speak.

The Gospel.   *John* 4.46

THERE was a certain noble man, whose son was sick at Capernaum. When he heard that Jesus was come out of Judea into Galilee, he went unto him, and besought him, that he would come down, and heal his son; for he was at the point of death. Then said Jesus unto him, Except ye see signs and wonders, ye will not believe. The noble man saith unto him, Sir, come down ere my child die. Jesus saith unto him, Go thy way, thy son liveth. And the man believed the word that Jesus had spoken unto him, and he went his way. And as he was now going down, his servants met him, and told him, saying, Thy son liveth. Then enquired he of them the hour when he began to amend: And they said unto him, Yesterday at the seventh hour the fever left him. So the father knew that it was at the same hour, in the which Jesus said unto him, Thy son liveth; and himself believed, and his whole house. This is again the second miracle that Jesus did when he was come out of Judea into Galilee.

The two and twentieth Sunday after Trinity.

The Collect.

LORD, we beseech thee to keep thy houshold the Church in continual godliness, that through thy protection it may be free from all adversities, and devoutly given to serve thee in good works to the glory of thy Name, through Jesus Christ our Lord. *Amen.*

The Epistle.   *Phil.* 1.3

I THANK my God upon every remembrance of you, (always in every prayer of mine for you all, making request with joy) for your fellowship in the gospel from the first day until now; being confident of this very thing, that he who hath begun a good work in you, will perform it until the day of Jesus Christ; even as it is meet for me to think this of you all, because I have you in my heart, inasmuch as both in my bonds, and in the defence and confirmation of the gospel, ye all are partakers of my grace. For God is my record, how greatly I long after you all in the bowels of Jesus Christ. And this I pray, that your love may abound yet more and more in knowledge, and in all judgement: That ye may approve things that are excellent, that ye may be sincere, and without offence till the day of Christ: Being filled with the fruits of righteousness, which are by Jesus Christ, unto the glory and praise of God.

The Gospel. Matt. 18.21

PETER said unto Jesus, Lord, how oft shall my brother sin against me, and I forgive him? till seven times? Jesus saith unto him, I say not unto thee, until seven times; but until seventy times seven. Therefore is the kingdom of heaven likened unto a certain king, who would take account of his servants. And when he had begun to reckon, one was brought unto him, who owed him ten thousand talents. But forasmuch as he had not to pay, his lord commanded him to be sold, and his wife and children, and all that he had, and payment to be made. The servant therefore fell down and worshipped him, saying, Lord, have patience with me, and I will pay thee all. Then the lord of that servant was moved with compassion, and loosed him, and forgave him the debt. But the same servant went out, and found one of his fellow-servants, who owed him an hundred pence; and he laid hands on him, and took him by the throat, saying, Pay me that thou owest. And his fellow-servant fell down at his feet, and besought him, saying, Have patience with me, and I will pay thee all. And he would not; but went and cast him into prison, till he should pay the debt. So when his fellow-servants saw what was done, they were very sorry, and came and told unto their lord all that was done. Then his lord after that he had called him, said unto him, O thou wicked servant, I forgave thee all that debt, because thou desiredst me: Shouldest not thou also have had compassion on thy fellow-servant, even as I had pity on thee? And his lord was wroth, and delivered him to the tormenters, till he should pay all that was due unto him. So likewise shall my heavenly Father do also unto you, if ye from your hearts forgive not every one his brother their trespasses.

The three and twentieth Sunday after Trinity.

The Collect.

O GOD, our refuge and strength, who art the authour of all godliness, be ready we beseech thee, to hear the devout prayers of thy church; and grant that those things which we ask faithfully, we may obtain effectually, through Jesus Christ our Lord. *Amen.*

The Epistle. Phil. 3.17

BRETHREN, be followers together of me, and mark them which walk so, as ye have us for an ensample. (For many walk, of whom I have told you often, and now tell you even weeping, that they are the enemies of the cross of Christ; whose end is destruction, whose god is their belly, and whose glory is in their shame, who mind earthly things.) For our conversation is in heaven, from whence also we look for the Saviour, the Lord Jesus Christ; who shall change our vile body, that it may be fashioned like unto his glorious body, according to the working whereby he is able even to subdue all things unto himself.

The Gospel.   *Matt.* 22.15

THEN went the Pharisees and took counsel how they might intangle him in his talk. And they sent out unto him their disciples with the Herodians, saying, Master, we know that thou art true, and teachest the way of God in truth, neither carest thou for any man: for thou regardest not the person of men. Tell us therefore, What thinkest thou? Is it lawful to give tribute unto Caesar, or not? But Jesus perceived their wickedness, and said, Why tempt ye me, ye hypocrites? Shew me the tribute-mony. And they brought unto him a peny. And he saith unto them, Whose is this image and superscription? They say unto him, Cesars. Then saith he unto them, Render therefore unto Cesar the things which are Cesars; and unto God, the things that are Gods. When they had heard these words, they marvelled, and left him, and went their way.

The four and twentieth Sunday after Trinity.

The Collect.

O LORD, we beseech thee, absolve thy people from their offences; that through thy bountiful goodness we may all be delivered from the bands of those sins, which by our frailty we have committed: Grant this, O heavenly Father, for Jesus Christs sake, our blessed Lord and Saviour. *Amen.*

The Epistle.   *Col.* 1.3

WE give thanks to God, and the Father of our Lord Jesus Christ, praying always for you, since we heard of your faith in Christ Jesus, and of the love which ye have to all the saints; for the hope which is laid up for you in heaven, whereof ye heard before in the word of the truth of the Gospel; which is come unto you, as it is in all the world, and bringeth forth fruit, as it doth also in you, since the day ye heard of it, and knew the grace of God in truth. As ye also learned of Epaphras our dear fellow-servant, who is for you a faithful minister of Christ; who also declared unto us your love in the Spirit. For this cause we also, since the day we heard it, do not cease to pray for you, and to desire that ye might be filled with the knowledge of his will in all wisdom and spiritual understanding. That ye might walk worthy of the Lord unto all pleasing, being fruitful in every good work, and increasing in the knowledge of God; strengthened with all might, according to his glorious power, unto all patience and long-suffering with joyfulness; giving thanks unto the Father, who hath made us meet to be partakers of the inheritance of the saints in light.

The Gospel.   *Matt.* 9.18

WHILE Jesus spake these things unto Johns disciples, behold, there came a certain ruler and worshipped him, saying, My daughter is even now dead; but come and lay thy hand upon her, and she shall live. (And Jesus arose, and followed him, and so did his disciples. And behold, a woman, who was diseased with an issue of bloud twelve years, came behind him, and touched the hem of his garment: For she said within her self, If I may but touch his garment, I shall be whole. But Jesus turned him about, and when he saw her, he said, Daughter, be of good comfort, thy faith hath made thee whole. And the woman was made whole from that hour.) And when Jesus came into the rulers house, and saw the minstrels and the people making a noise, he said unto them, Give place: for the maid is not dead, but sleepeth. And they laughed him to scorn. But when the people were put forth, he went in, and took her by the hand, and the maid arose. And the fame hereof went abroad into all that land.

The twentyfifth Sunday after Trinity.

The Collect.°

STIR up, we beseech thee, O Lord, the wills of thy faithful people, that they plenteously bringing forth the fruit of good works, may of thee be plenteously rewarded, through Jesus Christ our Lord. *Amen.*

For the Epistle.   *Jer.* 23.5

BEHOLD, the days come, saith the Lord, that I will raise unto David a righteous branch, and a King shall reign, and prosper, and shall execute judgement and justice in the earth. In his days Judah shall be saved and Israel shall dwel safely: and this is his Name whereby he shall be called, THE LORD OUR RIGHTEOUSNESS. Therefore behold, the days come, saith the Lord, that they shall no more say, The Lord liveth who brought up the children of Israel out of the land of Egypt; but the Lord liveth, who brought up and who led the seed of the house of Israel out of the north-countrey, and from all countreys whither I had driven them, and they shall dwell in their own land.

The Gospel.   *John* 6. 5

WHEN Jesus then lift up his eyes, and saw a great company come unto him, he saith unto Philip, Whence shall we buy bread that these may eat? (And this he said to prove him: for he himself knew what he would do.) Philip answered him, Two hundred peny-worth of bread is not sufficient for them, that every one of them may take a little. One of his disciples, Andrew, Simon Peters brother, saith unto him, There is a lad here, who hath five barley loaves, and two small fishes; but what are they among so many? And Jesus said, Make the men sit down. Now there was much grass in the place. So the men sat down, in number about five thousand. And Jesus took the loaves, and when he had given thanks, he distributed to the disciples, and the disciples to them that were set down, and likewise of the fishes as much as they would. When they were filled, he said unto his disciples, Gather up the fragments that remain, that nothing be lost. Therefore they gathered them together, and filled twelve baskets with the fragments of the five barley-loaves, which remained over and above unto them that had eaten. Then those men, when they had seen the miracle that Jesus did, said, This is of a truth that Prophet that should come into the world.

¶ *If there be any moe Sundays before Advent-Sunday, the Service of some of those Sundays that were omitted after the Epiphany, shall be taken in to supply so many as are here wanting. And if there be fewer, the overplus may be omitted: Provided that this last Collect, Epistle, and Gospel shall always be used upon the Sunday next before Advent.*

Saint Andrews Day.

The Collect.°

ALMIGHTY God, who didst give such grace unto thy holy Apostle Saint Andrew, that he readily obeyed the calling of thy Son Jesus Christ, and followed him without delay; Grant unto us all, that we being called by thy holy word, may forthwith give up our selves obediently to fulfil thy holy commandments, through the same Jesus Christ our Lord. *Amen.*

The Epistle.   *Rom.* 10.9

IF thou shalt confess with thy mouth the Lord Jesus, and shalt believe in thine heart, that God hath raised him from the dead, thou shalt be saved. For with the heart man believeth unto righteousness, and with the mouth confession is made unto salvation. For the scripture saith, Whosoever believeth on him shall not be ashamed. For there is no difference between the Jew and the Greek: for the same Lord over all is rich unto all that call upon him. For whosoever shall call upon the Name of the Lord shall be saved. How then shall they call on him in whom they have not believed? And how shall they believe in him of whom they have not heard? and how shall they hear without a preacher? And how shall they preach, except they be sent? as it is written, How beautiful are the feet of them that preach the Gospel of peace, and bring glad tidings of good things! But they have not all obeyed the Gospel. For Esaias saith, Lord, who hath believed our report? So then, faith cometh by hearing, and hearing by the word of God. But I say, Have they not heard? Yes verily, their sound went into all the earth, and their words unto the ends of the world. But I say, Did not Israel know? First Moses saith, I will provoke you to jealousie by them that are no people, and by a foolish nation I will anger you. But Esaias is very bold, and saith, I was found of them that sought me not; I was made manifest unto them that asked not after me. But to Israel he saith, All day long I have stretched forth my hands unto a disobedient and gain-saying people.

The Gospel.   *Matt.* 4.18

JESUS walking by the sea of Galilee, saw two brethren, Simon called Peter, and Andrew his brother, casting a net into the sea (for they were fishers). And he saith unto them, Follow me and I will make you fishers of men. And they straitway left their nets, and followed him. And going on from thence, he saw other two brethren, James the son of Zebedee, and John his brother in a ship with Zebedee their father, mending their nets; and he called them. And they immediately left the ship and their father, and followed him.

Saint Thomas the Apostle.

The Collect.°

ALMIGHTY and everliving God, who for the more confirmation of the faith didst suffer thy holy Apostle Thomas to be doubtful in thy Sons resurrection; Grant us so perfectly, and without all doubt to believe in thy Son Jesus Christ, that our faith in thy sight may never be reproved. Hear us, O Lord, through the same Jesus Christ, to whom with thee and the holy Ghost be all honour and glory now and for evermore. *Amen.*

The Epistle.   Eph. 2.19

NOW therefore ye are no more strangers and foreiners, but fellow-citizens with the saints, and of the houshold of God; and are built upon the foundation of the Apostles and Prophets, Jesus Christ himself being the chief corner-stone; in whom all the building fitly framed together groweth unto an holy temple in the Lord; in whom ye also are builded together for an habitation of God through the Spirit.

The Gospel.   John 20.24

THOMAS, one of the twelve, called Didymus, was not with them when Jesus came. The other disciples therefore said unto him, We have seen the Lord. But he said unto them, Except I shall see in his hands the print of the nails, and put my finger into the print of the nails, and thrust my hand into his side, I will not believe. And after eight days again his disciples were within, and Thomas with them: then came Jesus, the doors being shut, and stood in the midst, and said, Peace be unto you. Then saith he to Thomas, Reach hither thy finger, and behold my hands; and reach hither thy hand, and thrust it into my side, and be not faithless, but believing. And Thomas answered and said unto him, My Lord, and my God. Jesus saith unto him, Thomas, because thou hast seen me, thou hast believed; blessed are they that have not seen, and yet have believed. And many other signs truly did Jesus in the presence of his disciples, which are not written in this book. But these are written that ye might believe that Jesus is the Christ, the Son of God; and that believing ye might have life through his Name.

The Conversion of Saint Paul.

The Collect.°

O GOD, who through the preaching of the blessed Apostle Saint Paul hast caused the light of the Gospel to shine throughout the world; Grant, we beseech thee, that we having his wonderful conversion in remembrance, may shew forth our thankfulness unto thee for the same, by following the holy doctrine which he taught, through Jesus Christ our Lord. *Amen.*

For the Epistle. *Acts* 9.1

AND Saul yet breathing out threatnings and slaughter against the disciples of the Lord, went unto the high priest, and desired of him letters to Damascus to the synagogues, that if he found any of this way, whether they were men or women, he might bring them bound unto Jerusalem. And as he journeyed he came near Damascus, and suddenly there shined round about him a light from heaven. And he fell to the earth, and heard a voice saying unto him, Saul, Saul, why persecutest thou me? And he said, Who art thou, Lord? And the Lord said, I am Jesus whom thou persecutest: it is hard for thee to kick against the pricks. And he trembling and astonished, said, Lord, what wilt thou have me to do? And the Lord said unto him, Arise, and go into the city, and it shall be told thee what thou must do. And the men which journeyed with him stood speechless, hearing a voice, but seeing no man. And Saul arose from the earth, and when his eyes were opened, he saw no man; but they led him by the hand, and brought him into Damascus. And he was three days without sight, and neither did eat nor drink. And there was a certain disciple at Damascus, named Ananias, and to him said the Lord in a vision, Ananias. And he said, Behold, I am here, Lord. And the Lord said unto him, Arise, and go into the street which is called Straight, and enquire in the house of Judas for one called Saul, of Tarsus: for behold, he prayeth, and hath seen in a vision a man named Ananias, coming in, and putting his hand on him, that he might receive his sight. Then Ananias answered, Lord, I have heard by many of this man, how much evil he hath done to thy saints at Jerusalem; and here he hath authority from the chief priests to bind all that call on thy Name. But the Lord said unto him, Go thy way; for he is a chosen vessel unto me, to bear my Name before the Gentiles, and kings, and the children of Israel.

For I will shew him how great things he must suffer for my Names sake. And Ananias went his way, and entred into the house; and putting his hands on him, said, Brother Saul, the Lord (even Jesus that appeared unto thee in the way as thou camest) hath sent me, that thou mightest receive thy sight, and be filled with the holy Ghost. And immediately there fell from his eyes as it had been scales; and he received sight forthwith, and arose, and was baptized. And when he had received meat, he was strengthened. Then was Saul certain days with the disciples which were at Damascus. And straitway he preached Christ in the synagogues, that he is the Son of God. But all that heard him were amazed, and said, Is not this he that destroyed them which called on this Name in Jerusalem, and came hither for that intent, that he might bring them bound unto the chief priests? But Saul increased the more in strength, and confounded the Jews which dwelt at Damascus, proving that this is very Christ.

The Gospel.　　　　　　　　　　　　　　　*Matt.* 19.27

PETER answered and said unto Jesus, Behold, we have forsaken all and followed thee, what shall we have therefore? And Jesus said unto them, Verily I say unto you, that ye which have followed me in the regeneration when the Son of man shall sit in the throne of his glory, ye also shall sit upon twelve thrones, judging the twelve tribes of Israel. And every one that hath forsaken houses, or brethren, or sisters, or father, or mother, or wife, or children, or lands for my Names sake shall receive an hundred fold, and shall inherit everlasting life. But many that are first shall be last, and the last shall be first.

The Presentation of Christ in the temple,° commonly called, The Purification of Saint Mary the Virgin.

The Collect.

ALMIGHTY and everliving God, we humbly beseech thy Majesty, that as thy only begotten Son was this day presented in the temple in substance of our flesh; so we may be presented unto thee with pure and clean hearts, by the same thy Son Jesus Christ our Lord. *Amen.*

For the Epistle.　　　　　　　　　　　　　　*Mal.* 3.1

BEHOLD, I will send my messenger, and he shall prepare the way before me: and the Lord whom ye seek, shall suddenly come to his temple; even the messenger of the covenant, whom ye delight in; behold, he shall come, saith the Lord of hosts. But who may abide the day of his coming? and who shall stand when he appeareth? for he is like a refiners fire, and like fullers sope. And he shall sit as a refiner and purifier of silver; and he shall purifie the sons of Levi, and purge them as gold and silver, that they may offer unto the Lord an offering in righteousness. Then shall the offerings of Judah and Jerusalem be pleasant unto the Lord, as in the days of old, and as in former years. And I will come near to you to judgement, and I will be a swift witness against the sorcerers, and against the adulterers, and against false swearers, and against those that oppress the hireling in his wages, the widow and the fatherless, and that turn aside the stranger from his right, and fear not me, saith the Lord of hosts.

The Gospel.   *Luke* 2.22

A ND when the days of her purification, according to the law of Moses, were accomplished, they brought him to Jerusalem to present him to the Lord (as it is written in the law of the Lord, Every male that openeth the womb, shall be called holy to the Lord). And to offer a sacrifice according to that which is said in the law of the Lord, A pair of turtle-doves, or two young pigeons. And behold, there was a man in Jerusalem, whose name was Symeon; and the same man was just and devout, waiting for the consolation of Israel: and the holy Ghost was upon him. And it was revealed unto him by the holy Ghost, that he should not see death, before he had seen the Lords Christ. And he came by the Spirit into the temple, and when the parents brought in the child Jesus, to do for him after the custom of the law, then took he him up in his arms, and blessed God, and said, Lord, now lettest thou thy servant depart in peace, according to thy word. For mine eyes have seen thy salvation; which thou hast prepared before the face of all people, a light to lighten the Gentiles, and the glory of thy people Israel. And Joseph and his mother marvelled at those things which were spoken of him. And Symeon blessed them, and said unto Mary his mother, Behold, this child is set for the fall and rising again of many in Israel; and for a sign which shall be spoken against (Yea, a sword shall pierce through thy own soul also) that the thoughts of many hearts may be revealed. And there was one Anna a prophetess, the daughter of Phanuel, of the tribe of Aser; she was of a great age, and had lived with an husband seven years from her virginity. And she was a widow of about fourscore and four years; which departed not from the temple, but served God with fastings and prayers night and day. And she coming in that instant gave thanks likewise unto the Lord, and spake of him to all them that looked for redemption in Jerusalem. And when they had performed all things according to the law of the Lord, they returned into Galilee to their own city Nazareth. And the child grew, and waxed strong in spirit, filled with wisdom; and the grace of God was upon him.

Saint Matthias day.

The Collect.°

O ALMIGHTY God, who into the place of the traitor Judas didst choose thy faithful servant Matthias to be of the number of the twelve Apostles; Grant that thy Church being alway preserved from false Apostles, may be ordered and guided by faithful and true pastours, through Jesus Christ our Lord. *Amen.*

For the Epistle.   *Acts* 1.15

IN those days Peter stood up in the midst of the disciples, and said (the number of the Names together were about an hundred and twenty), Men and brethren, this Scripture must needs have been fulfilled, which the holy Ghost by the mouth of David spake before concerning Judas, which was guide to them that took Jesus: for he was numbered with us, and had obtained part of this ministry. Now this man purchased a field with the reward of iniquity, and falling headlong he burst asunder in the midst, and all his bowels gushed out. And it was known unto all the dwellers at Jerusalem, insomuch as that field is called in their proper tongue, Aceldama, that is to say, The field of bloud. For it is written in the book of Psalms, Let his habitation be desolate, and let no man dwell therein; and his bishoprick let another take. Wherefore of these men which have companied with us all the time that the Lord Jesus went in and out among us; beginning from the baptism of John, unto that same day that he was taken up from us, must one be ordained to be a witness with us of his resurrection. And they appointed two, Joseph called Barsabas, who was sirnamed Justus, and Matthias. And they prayed, and said, Thou Lord, which knowest the hearts of all men, shew whether of these two thou hast chosen; that he may take part of this ministry and apostleship, from which Judas by transgression fell, that he might go to his own place.

And they gave forth their lots; and the lot fell upon Matthias, and he was numbred with the eleven Apostles.

The Gospel. *Matt.* 11.25

AT that time Jesus answered and said, I thank thee, O Father, Lord of heaven and earth, because thou hast hid these things from the wise and prudent, and hast revealed them unto babes. Even so, Father: for so it seemed good in thy sight. All things are delivered unto me of my Father: and no man knoweth the Son but the Father; neither knoweth any man the Father save the Son, and he to whomsoever the Son will reveal him. Come unto me all ye that labour and are heavy laden, and I will give you rest. Take my yoke upon you, and learn of me, for I am meek and lowly in heart, and ye shall find rest unto your souls. For my yoke is easy and my burden is light.

The Annunciation of the blessed Virgin Mary.

The Collect.°

WE beseech thee, O Lord, pour thy grace into our hearts, that as we have known the incarnation of thy Son Jesus Christ by the message of an angel; so by his cross and passion we may be brought unto the glory of his resurrection, through the same Jesus Christ our Lord. *Amen.*

For the Epistle. *Isa.* 7.10

MOREOVER, the Lord spake again unto Ahaz, saying, Ask thee a sign of the Lord thy God; ask it either in the depth, or in the height above. But Ahaz said, I will not ask, neither will I tempt the Lord. And he said, Hear ye now, O house of David, Is it a small thing for you to weary men, but will ye weary my God also? Therefore the Lord himself shall give you a sign, Behold, a virgin shall conceive and bear a Son, and shall call his name Immanuel. Butter and honey shall he eat, that he may know to refuse the evil, and choose the good.

The Gospel. *Luke* 1.26

AND in the sixth month the angel Gabriel was sent from God unto a city of Galilee, named Nazareth, to a virgin espoused to a man whose name was Joseph, of the house of David; and the virgins name was Mary. And the angel came in unto her, and said, Hail, thou that art highly favoured, the Lord is with thee; blessed art thou among women. And when she saw him, she was troubled at his saying, and cast in her mind what manner of salutation this should be. And the angel said unto her, Fear not, Mary; for thou hast found favour with God. And behold, thou shalt conceive in thy womb, and bring forth a Son, and shalt call his Name Jesus. He shall be great, and shall be called the Son of the Highest; and the Lord God shall give unto him the throne of his father David. And he shall reign over the house of Jacob for ever, and of his kingdom there shall be no end. Then said Mary unto the angel, How shall this be, seeing I know not a man? And the angel answered and said unto her, The Holy Ghost shall come upon thee, and the power of the Highest shall overshadow thee: therefore also that holy thing which shall be born of thee, shall be called the Son of God. And, behold, thy cosin Elizabeth, she hath also conceived a son in her old age; and this is the sixth month with her who was called barren. For with God nothing shall be unpossible. And Mary said, Behold the hand-maid of the Lord; be it unto me according to thy word. And the angel departed from her.

Saint Marks day.

The Collect.

O ALMIGHTY God, who hast instructed thy holy Church with the heavenly doctrine of thy Evangelist Saint Mark; Give us grace, that being not like children carried away with every blast of vain doctrine, we may be established in the truth of thy holy Gospel, through Jesus Christ our Lord. *Amen.*

The Epistle.　　　　　　　　　　　　　　　　Eph. 4.7

UNTO every one of us is given grace according to the measure of the gift of Christ. Wherefore he saith, When he ascended up on high, he led captivity captive, and gave gifts unto men. (Now that he ascended, what is it but that he also descended first into the lower parts of the earth? He that descended is the same also that ascended up far above all heavens, that he might fill all things.) And he gave some apostles, and some prophets, and some evangelists, and some pastours and teachers; for the perfecting of the saints, for the work of the ministry, for the edifying of the body of Christ; till we all come in the unity of the faith, and of the knowledge of the Son of God, unto a perfect man, unto the measure of the stature of the fulness of Christ; that we henceforth be no more children tossed to and fro, and carried about with every wind of doctrine, by the sleight of men, and cunning craftiness, whereby they lie in wait to deceive; but speaking the truth in love, may grow up into him in all things, which is the head, even Christ. From whom the whole body fitly joyned together, and compacted by that which every joynt supplieth, according to the effectual working in the measure of every part, maketh increase of the body, unto the edifying of it self in love.

The Gospel.   *John* 15.1

I AM the true vine, and my Father is the husbandman. Every branch in me that beareth not fruit, he taketh away; and every branch that beareth fruit, he purgeth it, that it may bring forth more fruit. Now ye are clean through the word which I have spoken unto you. Abide in me, and I in you. As the branch cannot bear fruit of it self, except it abide in the vine; no more can ye, except ye abide in me. I am the vine, ye are the branches: He that abideth in me, and I in him, the same bringeth forth much fruit; for without me ye can do nothing. If a man abide not in me, he is cast forth as a branch, and is withered; and men gather them, and cast them into the fire, and they are burned. If ye abide in me, and my words abide in you, ye shall ask what ye will, and it shall be done unto you. Herein is my Father glorified, that ye bear much fruit; so shall ye be my disciples. As the Father hath loved me, so have I loved you; continue ye in my love. If ye keep my commandments, ye shall abide in my love; even as I have kept my Fathers commandments, and abide in his love. These things have I spoken unto you, that my joy might remain in you, and that your joy might be full.

Saint Philip and Saint James Day.

The Collect.

O ALMIGHTY God, whom truly to know is everlasting life; grant us perfectly to know thy Son Jesus Christ to be the way, the truth, and the life, that following the steps of thy holy Apostles, saint Philip and saint James, we may stedfastly walk in the way that leadeth to eternal life, through the same thy Son Jesus Christ our Lord. *Amen.*

The Epistle.   *Jas.* 1.1

J AMES a servant of God, and of the Lord Jesus Christ, to the twelve tribes which are scattered abroad, greeting. My brethren, count it all joy when ye fall into divers temptations; knowing this, that the trying of your faith worketh patience. But let patience have her perfect work, that ye may be perfect and entire, wanting nothing. If any of you lack wisdom, let him ask of God, that giveth to all men liberally, and upbraideth not; and it shall be given him. But let him ask in faith, nothing wavering; for he that wavereth is like a wave of the sea, driven with the wind, and tossed. For let not that man think that he shall receive any thing of the Lord. A double-minded man is unstable in all his ways. Let the brother of low degree rejoyce in that he is exalted; but the rich in that he is made low; because as the flower of the grass he shall pass away. For the sun is no sooner risen with a burning heat, but it withereth the grass, and the flower thereof falleth, and the grace of the fashion of it perisheth: so also shall the rich man fade away in his ways. Blessed is the man that endureth temptation; for when he is tryed, he shall receive the crown of life, which the Lord hath promised to them that love him.

The Gospel.   John 14.1

AND Jesus said unto his disciples, Let not your heart be troubled; ye believe in God, believe also in me. In my Fathers house are many mansions; if it were not so, I would have told you. I go to prepare a place for you: And if I go and prepare a place for you, I will come again, and receive you unto my self, that where I am, there ye may be also. And whither I go, ye know, and the way ye know. Thomas saith unto him, Lord, we know not whither thou goest, and how can we know the way? Jesus saith unto him, I am the way, the truth, and the life; no man cometh unto the Father but by me. If ye had known me, ye should have known my Father also; and from henceforth ye know him, and have seen him. Philip saith unto him, Lord, shew us the Father, and it sufficeth us. Jesus saith unto him, Have I been so long time with you, and yet hast thou not known me, Philip? He that hath seen me, hath seen the Father; and how sayest thou then, Shew us the Father? Believest thou not that I am in the Father, and the Father in me? the words that I speak unto you, I speak not of my self; but the Father that dwelleth in me, he doth the works. Believe me, that I am in the Father, and the Father in me; or else believe me for the very works sake. Verily, verily I say unto you, He that believeth on me, the works that I do, shall he do also, and greater works than these shall he do; because I go unto my Father. And whatsoever ye shall ask in my Name, that will I do, that the Father may be glorified in the Son. If ye shall ask any thing in my Name, I will do it.

Saint Barnabas the Apostle.

The Collect.

O LORD God Almighty, who didst endue thy holy apostle Barnabas with singular gifts of the Holy Ghost; Leave us not, we beseech thee, destitute of thy manifold gifts, nor yet of grace to use them alway to thy honour and glory, through Jesus Christ our Lord. *Amen.*

For the Epistle.   *Acts* 11.22

TIDINGS of these things came unto the ears of the Church which was in Jerusalem; and they sent forth Barnabas, that he should go as far as Antioch. Who when he came, and had seen the grace of God, was glad, and exhorted them all that with purpose of heart they would cleave unto the Lord. For he was a good man, and full of the holy Ghost, and of faith; and much people was added unto the Lord. Then departed Barnabas to Tarsus for to seek Saul. And when he had found him, he brought him unto Antioch. And it came to pass, that a whole year they assembled themselves with the Church, and taught much people; and the disciples were called Christians first in Antioch. And in these days came prophets from Jerusalem unto Antioch. And there stood up one of them named Agabus, and signified by the Spirit, that there should be great dearth throughout all the world; which came to pass in the days of Claudius Cesar. Then the disciples, every man according to his ability, determined to send relief unto the brethren which dwelt in Judea. Which also they did, and sent it to the elders by the hands of Barnabas and Saul.

The Gospel.   *John* 15.12

THIS is my commandment, that ye love one another, as I have loved you. Greater love hath no man than this, that a man lay down his life for his friends. Ye are my friends, if ye do whatsoever I command you. Henceforth I call you not servants; for the servant knoweth not what his Lord doth: but I have called you friends; for all things that I have heard of my Father, I have made known unto you. Ye have not chosen me, but I have chosen you, and ordained you, that ye should go and bring forth fruit, and that your fruit should remain; that whatsoever ye shall ask of the Father in my Name, he may give it you.

Saint John Baptist.

The Collect.°

ALMIGHTY God, by whose providence thy servant John Baptist was wonderfully born, and sent to prepare the way of thy Son our Saviour by preaching of repentance; Make us so to follow his doctrine and holy life, that we may truly repent according to his preaching, and after his example constantly speak the truth, boldly rebuke vice, and patiently suffer for the truths sake, through Jesus Christ our Lord. *Amen.*

For the Epistle.   *Isa.* 40.1

COMFORT ye, comfort ye my people, saith your God. Speak ye comfortably to Jerusalem, and cry unto her, that her warfare is accomplished, that her iniquity is pardoned; for she hath received of the Lords hand double for all her sins. The voice of him that cryeth in the wilderness, Prepare ye the way of the Lord, make strait in the desert a high way for our God. Every valley shall be exalted, and every mountain and hill shall be made low; and the crooked shall be made strait, and the rough places plain. And the glory of the Lord shall be revealed, and all flesh shall see it together; for the mouth of the Lord hath spoken it. The voice said, Cry. And he said, What shall I cry? All flesh is grass, and all the goodliness thereof is as the flower of the field. The grass withereth, the flower fadeth, because the spirit of the Lord bloweth upon it: surely the people is grass. The grass withereth, the flower fadeth, but the word of our God shall stand for ever. O Zion, that bringest good tidings, get thee up into the high mountain: O Jerusalem, that bringest good tidings, lift up thy voice with strength; lift it up, be not afraid: say unto the cities of Judah, Behold your God. Behold, the Lord God will come with strong hand, and his arm shall rule for him; behold, his reward is with him, and his work before him. He shall feed his flock like a shepherd, he shall gather the lambs with his arm, and carry them in his bosom, and shall gently lead those that are with young.

The Gospel.   *Luke* 1.57

ELIZABETHS full time came that she should be delivered; and she brought forth a son. And her neighbours and her cosins heard how the Lord had shewed great mercy upon her, and they rejoyced with her. And it came to pass, that on the eighth day they came to circumcise the child, and they called him Zacharias, after the name of his father. And his mother answered and said, Not so; but he shall be called John. And they said unto her, There is none of thy kindred that is called by this name. And they made signs to his father, how he would have him called. And he asked for a writing-table, and wrote, saying, His name is John. And they marvelled all. And his mouth was opened immediately, and his tongue loosed, and he spake and praised God. And fear came on all that dwelt round about them; and all these sayings were noised abroad throughout all the hill-countrey of Judea. And all they that heard them, laid them up in their hearts, saying, What manner of child shall this be? And the hand of the Lord was with him. And his father Zacharias was filled with the holy Ghost, and prophesied, saying, Blessed be the Lord God of Israel, for he hath visited and redeemed his people, and hath raised up an horn of salvation for us in the house of his servant David; as he spake by the mouth of his holy prophets, which have been since the world began; that we should be saved from our enemies, and from the hand of all that hate us; to perform the mercy promised to our fathers, and to remember his holy covenant; the oath which he sware to our father Abraham, that he would grant unto us, that we, being delivered out of the hand of our enemies, might serve him without fear, in holiness and righteousness before him all the days of our life. And thou child, shalt be called the prophet of the Highest; for thou shalt go before the face of the Lord to prepare his ways; to give knowledge of salvation unto his people by the remission of their sins, through the tender mercy of our God, whereby the Day-spring from on high hath visited us; to give light to them that sit in darkness, and in the shadow of death, to guide our feet into the way of peace. And the child grew, and waxed strong in spirit; and was in the deserts till the day of his shewing unto Israel.

Saint Peters Day.°

The Collect.

O ALMIGHTY God, who by thy Son Jesus Christ didst give to thy Apostle saint Peter many excellent gifts, and commandest him earnestly to feed thy flock; Make, we beseech thee, all bishops and pastours diligently to preach thy holy word, and the people obediently to follow the same, that they may receive the crown of everlasting glory, through Jesus Christ our Lord. *Amen.*

For the Epistle.   *Acts* 12.1

ABOUT that time Herod the king stretched forth his hands to vex certain of the church. And he killed James the brother of John with the sword. And because he saw it pleased the Jews, he proceeded further to take Peter also. (Then were the days of unleavened bread.) And when he had apprehended him, he put him in prison, and delivered him to four quaternions of souldiers to keep him, intending after Easter to bring him forth to the people. Peter therefore was kept in prison; but prayer was made without ceasing of the Church unto God for him. And when Herod would have brought him forth, the same night Peter was sleeping between two souldiers, bound with two chains; and the keepers before the door kept the prison. And behold, the angel of the Lord came upon him, and a light shined in the prison; and he smote Peter on the side, and raised him up, saying, Arise up quickly. And his chains fell off from his hands. And the angel said unto him, Gird thy self, and bind on thy sandals: and so he did. And he saith unto him, Cast thy garment about thee, and follow me. And he went out and followed him, and wist not that it was true which was done by the angel; but thought he saw a vision. When they were past the first and the second ward, they came unto the iron gate that leadeth unto the city, which opened to them of his own accord; and they went out, and passed on through one street, and forthwith the angel departed from him. And when Peter was come to himself, he said, Now I know of a surety, that the Lord hath sent his angel, and hath delivered me out of the hand of Herod, and from all the expectation of the people of the Jews.

The Gospel.   *Matt.* 16.13

WHEN Jesus came into the coasts of Cesarea Philippi, he asked his disciples, saying, Whom do men say, that I, the Son of man, am? And they said, Some say that thou art John the Baptist, some Elias, and others Jeremias, or one of the prophets. He saith unto them, But whom say ye that I am? And Simon Peter answered and said, Thou art Christ, the Son of the living God. And Jesus answered and said unto him, Blessed art thou, Simon Barjona: for flesh and bloud hath not revealed it unto thee, but my Father which is in heaven. And I say also unto thee, that thou art Peter, and upon this rock I will build my

Church; and the gates of hell shall not prevail against it. And I will give unto thee the keys of the kingdom of heaven: and whatsoever thou shalt bind on earth, shall be bound in heaven; and whatsoever thou shalt loose on earth, shall be loosed in heaven.

Saint James the Apostle.

The Collect.

GRANT, O merciful God, that as thine holy Apostle Saint James, leaving his father and all that he had, without delay was obedient unto the calling of thy Son Jesus Christ, and followed him; so we forsaking all worldly and carnal affections, may be evermore ready to follow thy holy commandments, through Jesus Christ our Lord. *Amen.*

For the Epistle.　　　　　　　　　　　*Acts* 11.27

IN these days came prophets from Jerusalem unto Antioch. And there stood up one of them named Agabus, and signified by the Spirit, that there should be great dearth throughout all the world; which came to pass in the days of Claudius Cesar. Then the disciples, every man according to his ability, determined to send relief unto the brethren which dwelt in Judea. Which also they did, and sent it to the elders by the hands of Barnabas and Saul. Now about that time, Herod the king stretched forth his hands to vex certain of the Church. And he killed James the brother of John with the sword. And because he saw it pleased the Jews, he proceeded further to take Peter also.

The Gospel.　　　　　　　　　　　　*Matt.* 20.20

THEN came to him the mother of Zebedees children with her sons, worshipping him, and desiring a certain thing of him. And he said unto her, What wilt thou? She saith unto him, Grant that these my two sons may sit, the one on thy right hand, and the other on the left, in thy kingdom. But Jesus answered and said, Ye know not what ye ask. Are ye able to drink of the cup that I shall drink of, and to be baptized with the baptism that I am baptized with? They say unto him, We are able. And he saith unto them, Ye shall drink indeed of my cup, and be baptized with the baptism that I am baptized with: but to sit on my right hand, and on my left, is not mine to give, but it shall be given to them for whom it is prepared of my Father. And when the ten heard it, they were moved with indignation against the two brethren.

But Jesus called them unto him, and said, Ye know that the princes
of the Gentiles exercise dominion over them, and they that are great
exercise authority upon them. But it shall not be so among you: but
whosoever will be great among you, let him be your minister; and
whosoever will be chief among you, let him be your servant: Even as
the Son of man came not to be ministered unto, but to minister, and
to give his life a ransome for many.

Saint Bartholomew the Apostle.

The Collect.

O ALMIGHTY and everlasting God, who didst give to thine
Apostle Bartholomew grace truly to believe and to preach thy
word; Grant, we beseech thee, unto thy Church to love that word
which he believed, and both to preach and receive the same; through
Jesus Christ our Lord. *Amen.*

For the Epistle.   *Acts* 5.12

B Y the hands of the apostles were many signs and wonders wrought
among the people, (and they were all with one accord in Solomons
porch. And of the rest durst no man joyn himself to them: but the
people magnified them. And believers were the more added to the
Lord, multitudes both of men and women). Insomuch that they
brought forth the sick into the streets, and laid them on beds and
couches, that at the least the shadow of Peter passing by might overshadow some of them. There came also a multitude out of the cities
round about unto Jerusalem, bringing sick folks, and them which
were vexed with unclean spirits, and they were healed every one.

The Gospel.   *Luke* 22.24

A ND there was also a strife among them, which of them should be
accounted the greatest. And he said unto them, The kings of the
Gentiles exercise lordship over them; and they that exercise authority
upon them, are called benefactors. But ye shall not be so: but he that
is greatest among you, let him be as the younger; and he that is chief,
as he that doth serve. For whether is greater, he that sitteth at meat,
or he that serveth? is not he that sitteth at meat? but I am among
you as he that serveth. Ye are they which have continued with me in
my temptations. And I appoint unto you a kingdom, as my Father

hath appointed unto me; that ye may eat and drink at my table in my kingdom, and sit on thrones judging the twelve tribes of Israel.

Saint Matthew the Apostle.

The Collect.

O ALMIGHTY God, who by thy blessed Son didst call Matthew from the receit of custom to be an Apostle and Evangelist; Grant us grace to forsake all covetous desires and inordinate love of riches, and to follow the same thy Son Jesus Christ, who liveth and reigneth with thee and the Holy Ghost, one God, world without end. *Amen.*

The Epistle.   2 *Cor.* 4.1

T HEREFORE seeing we have this ministry, as we have received mercy we faint not; but have renounced the hidden things of dishonesty, not walking in craftiness, nor handling the word of God deceitfully, but by manifestation of the truth, commending our selves to every mans conscience in the sight of God. But if our Gospel be hid, it is hid to them that are lost: In whom the God of this world hath blinded the minds of them which believe not, lest the light of the glorious Gospel of Christ, who is the image of God, should shine unto them. For we preach not our selves, but Christ Jesus the Lord; and our selves your servants for Jesus sake. For God who commanded the light to shine out of darkness, hath shined in our hearts, to give the light of the knowledge of the glory of God, in the face of Jesus Christ.

The Gospel.   *Matt.* 9.9

A ND as Jesus passed forth from thence, he saw a man named Matthew, sitting at the receit of custom: and he saith unto him, Follow me. And he arose, and followed him. And it came to pass, as Jesus sat at meat in the house, behold, many Publicans and sinners came and sat down with him and his disciples. And when the Pharisees saw it, they said unto his disciples, Why eateth your Master with Publicans and sinners? But when Jesus heard that, he said unto them, They that be whole need not a Physician, but they that are sick. But go ye and learn what that meaneth, I will have mercy, and not sacrifice; for I am not come to call the righteous, but sinners to repentance.

Saint Michael and all Angels.

The Collect.°

O EVERLASTING God, who hast ordained and constituted the services of Angels and men in a wonderful order; Mercifully grant, that as thy holy Angels alway do thee service in heaven; so by thy appointment they may succour and defend us on earth, through Jesus Christ our Lord. *Amen.*

For the Epistle.   *Rev.* 12.7

THERE was war in heaven: Michael and his Angels fought against the dragon, and the dragon fought and his angels; and prevailed not, neither was their place found any more in heaven. And the great dragon was cast out, that old serpent, called the devil and Satan, which deceiveth the whole world; he was cast out into the earth, and his angels were cast out with him. And I heard a loud voice saying in heaven, Now is come salvation, and strength, and the kingdom of our God, and the power of his Christ: for the accuser of our brethren is cast down, which accused them before our God day and night. And they overcame him by the bloud of the Lamb, and by the word of their testimony; and they loved not their lives unto the death. Therefore rejoyce, ye heavens, and ye that dwell in them. Woe to the inhabiters of the earth and of the sea: for the devil is come down unto you, having great wrath, because he knoweth that he hath but a short time.

The Gospel.   *Matt.* 18.1

AT the same time came the disciples unto Jesus, saying, Who is the greatest in the kingdom of heaven? And Jesus called a little child unto him, and set him in the midst of them, and said, Verily I say unto you, Except ye be converted, and become as little children, ye shall not enter into the kingdom of heaven. Whosoever therefore shall humble himself as this little child, the same is greatest in the kingdom of heaven. And whoso shall receive one such little child in my Name, receiveth me. But whoso shall offend one of these little ones which believe in me, it were better for him that a mil-stone were hanged about his neck, and that he were drowned in the depth of the sea. Wo unto the world, because of offences: for it must needs be that offences come; but wo to that man by whom the offence cometh. Wherefore if thy hand or thy foot offend thee, cut them off, and cast them from thee: it is better for thee to enter into life halt or maimed, rather than having two hands or two feet to be cast into everlasting fire. And if thine eye offend thee pluck it out, and cast it from thee: it is better for thee to enter into life with one eye, rather than having two eyes to be cast into hell fire. Take heed that ye despise not one of these little ones; for I say unto you, That in heaven their angels do always behold the face of my Father which is in heaven.

Saint Luke the Evangelist.

The Collect.

A LMIGHTY God, who calledst Luke the Physician, whose praise is in the Gospel, to be an Evangelist, and Physician of the soul; May it please thee, that by the wholesom medicines of the doctrine delivered by him, all the diseases of our souls may be healed, through the merits of thy Son Jesus Christ our Lord. *Amen.*

The Epistle.   2 *Tim.* 4. 5

W ATCH thou in all things, endure afflictions, do the work of an Evangelist, make full proof of thy ministery. For I am now ready to be offered, and the time of my departure is at hand. I have fought a good fight, I have finished my course, I have kept the faith. Henceforth there is laid up for me a crown of righteousness, which the Lord the righteous judge shall give me at that day: and not to me onely, but unto all them also that love his appearing. Doe thy diligence to come shortly unto me: For Demas hath forsaken me, having loved this present world, and is departed unto Thessalonica; Crescens to Galatia, Titus unto Dalmatia. Only Luke is with me. Take Mark and bring him with thee: for he is profitable to me for the ministery. And Tychicus have I sent to Ephesus. The cloak that I left at Troas with Carpus, when thou comest bring with thee, and the books, but especially the parchments. Alexander the coppersmith did me much evil: the Lord reward him according to his works. Of whom be thou ware also, for he hath greatly withstood our words.

The Gospel.   *Luke* 10. 1

T HE Lord appointed other seventy also, and sent them two and two before his face into every city and place whither he himself would come. Therefore said he unto them, The harvest truly is great, but the labourers are few; pray ye therefore the Lord of the harvest that he would send forth labourers into his harvest. Go your wayes, behold, I send you forth as lambs among wolves. Carry neither purse, nor scrip, nor shoes, and salute no man by the way. And into whatsoever house ye enter, first say, Peace be to this house. And if the son of peace be there, your peace shall rest upon it: if not, it shall turn to you again. And in the same house remain, eating and drinking such things as they give: for the labourer is worthy of his hire.

Saint Simon and Saint Jude Apostles.

The Collect.

O ALMIGHTY God, who hast built thy Church upon the foundation of the Apostles and Prophets, Jesus Christ himself being the head corner-stone; Grant us so to be joyned together in unity of spirit by their doctrine, that we may be made an holy temple acceptable unto thee, through Jesus Christ our Lord. *Amen.*

The Epistle.   Jude 1

J UDE the servant of Jesus Christ, and brother of James, to them that are sanctified by God the Father, and preserved in Jesus Christ, and called: Mercy unto you, and peace, and love be multiplyed. Beloved, when I gave all diligence to write unto you of the common salvation, it was needful for me to write unto you, and exhort you, that ye should earnestly contend for the faith which was once delivered unto the saints. For there are certain men crept in unawares, who were before of old ordained to this condemnation; ungodly men, turning the grace of our God into lasciviousness, and denying the onely Lord God, and our Lord Jesus Christ. I will therefore put you in remembrance, though ye once knew this, how that the Lord, having saved the people out of the land of Egypt, afterward destroyed them that believed not. And the angels which kept not their first estate, but left their own habitation, he hath reserved in everlasting chains under darkness unto the judgement of the great day. Even as Sodom and Gomorrha, and the cities about them in like manner giving themselves over to fornication, and going after strange flesh, are set forth for an example, suffering the vengeance of eternal fire. Likewise also these filthy dreamers defile the flesh, despise dominion, and speak evil of dignities.

The Gospel. *John* 15.17

THESE things I command you, that ye love one another. If the world hate you, ye know that it hated me, before it hated you. If ye were of the world, the world would love his own: but because ye are not of the world, but I have chosen you out of the world, therefore the world hateth you. Remember the word that I said unto you, The servant is not greater than his Lord: if they have persecuted me, they will also persecute you; if they have kept my saying, they will keep yours also. But all these things will they do unto you for my Names sake, because they know not him that sent me. If I had not come and spoken unto them, they had not had sin: but now they have no cloak for their sin. He that hateth me, hateth my Father also. If I had not done among them the works which none other man did, they had not had sin; but now have they both seen, and hated both me and my Father. But this cometh to pass that the word might be fulfilled that is written in their law, They hated me without a cause. But when the Comforter is come, whom I will send unto you from the Father, even the Spirit of truth, which proceedeth from the Father, he shall testifie of me. And ye also shall bear witness, because ye have been with me from the beginning.

All Saints day.

The Collect.

O ALMIGHTY God, who hast knit together thine elect in one communion and fellowship, in the mystical body of thy Son Christ our Lord; Grant us grace so to follow thy blessed Saints° in all vertuous and godly living, that we may come to those unspeakable joys, which thou hast prepared for them that unfeignedly love thee, through Jesus Christ our Lord. *Amen.*

For the Epistle. *Rev.* 7.2

AND I saw another angel ascending from the east, having the seal of the living God; and he cried with a loud voice to the four angels, to whom it was given to hurt the earth, and the sea, saying, Hurt not the earth, neither the sea, nor the trees, till we have sealed the servants of our God in their foreheads. And I heard the number of them which were sealed; and there were sealed an hundred and forty and four thousand, of all the tribes of the children of Israel.

Of the tribe of Juda were sealed twelve thousand.

Of the tribe of Reuben were sealed twelve thousand.

Of the tribe of Gad were sealed twelve thousand.
Of the tribe of Aser were sealed twelve thousand.
Of the tribe of Nephthalim were sealed twelve thousand.
Of the tribe of Manasses were sealed twelve thousand.
Of the tribe of Simeon were sealed twelve thousand.
Of the tribe of Levi were sealed twelve thousand.
Of the tribe of Isachar were sealed twelve thousand.
Of the tribe of Zabulon were sealed twelve thousand.
Of the tribe of Joseph were sealed twelve thousand.
Of the tribe of Benjamin were sealed twelve thousand.

After this I beheld, and, lo, a great multitude which no man could number, of all nations, and kinreds, and people, and tongues, stood before the throne, and before the Lamb, clothed with white robes, and palms in their hands: And cried with a loud voice, saying, Salvation to our God, which sitteth upon the throne, and unto the Lamb. And all the angels stood round about the throne, and about the elders, and the four beasts, and fell before the throne on their faces, and worshipped God, saying, Amen; Blessing, and glory, and wisdom, and thanksgiving, and honour, and power, and might be unto our God for ever and ever. *Amen.*

The Gospel.   Matt. 5.1

JESUS seeing the multitudes, went up into a mountain; and when he was set, his disciples came unto him. And he opened his mouth, and taught them, saying, Blessed are the poor in spirit: for theirs is the kingdom of heaven. Blessed are they that mourn: for they shall be comforted. Blessed are the meek: for they shall inherit the earth. Blessed are they which do hunger and thirst after righteousness: for they shall be filled. Blessed are the merciful: for they shall obtain mercy. Blessed are the pure in heart: for they shall see God. Blessed are the peace-makers: for they shall be called the children of God. Blessed are they which are persecuted for righteousness sake: for theirs is the kingdom of heaven. Blessed are ye when men shall revile you, and persecute you, and shall say all manner of evil against you falsly for my sake. Rejoyce and be exceeding glad; for great is your reward in heaven: for so persecuted they the prophets which were before you.

The Order
for the Administration of the Lords Supper,
or Holy Communion.

¶ *So many as intend to be partakers of the holy Communion shall signifie their names to the Curate at least sometime the day before.*°

¶ *And if any of those be an open and notorious evil liver, or have done any wrong to his neighbours by word or deed, so that the Congregation be thereby offended; the Curate having knowledge thereof, shall call him and advertise him, that in any wise he presume not to come to the Lords Table, until he hath openly declared himself to have truly repented and amended his former naughty life, that the Congregation may thereby be satisfied, which before were offended; and that he hath recompensed the parties to whom he hath done wrong, or at least declare himself to be in full purpose so to do, as soon as he conveniently may.*

¶ *The same order shall the Curate use with those betwixt whom he perceiveth malice and hatred to reign; not suffering them to be partakers of the Lords Table, until he know them to be reconciled. And if one of the parties so at variance be content to forgive from the bottom of his heart all that the other hath trespassed against him, and to make amends for that he himself hath offended; and the other party will not be perswaded to a godly unity, but remain still in his frowardness and malice: the Minister in that case ought to admit the penitent person to the holy Communion, and not him that is obstinate. Provided that every Minister so repelling any,*° *as is specified in this, or the next precedent Paragraph of this Rubrick, shall be obliged to give an account of the same to the Ordinary within fourteen dayes after at the farthest. And the Ordinary shall proceed against the offending person according to the Canon.*

¶ *The Table at the Communion time having a fair white linen cloth upon it, shall stand in the body of the Church, or in the Chancel, where Morning and Evening Prayer are appointed to be said. And the Priest standing at the north side of the Table shall say the Lords Prayer, with the Collect following, the people kneeling.*°

OUR Father which art in heaven; Hallowed be thy Name. Thy Kingdom come. Thy will be done in earth, As it is in heaven. Give us this day our daily bread. And forgive us our trespasses, As we forgive them that trespass against us. And lead us not into temptation, But deliver us from evil. *Amen.*

The Collect

ALMIGHTY God, unto whom all hearts be open, all desires known, and from whom no secrets are hid; Cleanse the thoughts of our hearts by the inspiration of thy holy Spirit, that we may perfectly love thee, and worthily magnifie thy holy Name, through Christ our Lord. *Amen.*

¶ *Then shall the Priest, turning to the people,° rehearse distinctly all the TEN COMMANDMENTS; and the people still kneeling, shall after every Commandment ask God mercy for their transgression thereof for the time past, and grace to keep the same for the time to come, as followeth.*

Minister.

GOD spake these words and said, I am the Lord thy God: Thou shalt have none other Gods but me.

People. Lord, have mercy upon us, and incline our hearts to keep this law.

Minister. Thou shalt not make to thy self any graven image, nor the likeness of any thing that is in heaven above, or in the earth beneath, or in the water under the earth. Thou shalt not bow down to them, nor worship them: for I the Lord thy God am a jealous God, and visit the sins of the fathers upon the children unto the third and fourth generation of them that hate me, and shew mercy unto thousands in them that love me, and keep my commandments.

People. Lord, have mercy upon us, and incline our hearts to keep this law.

Minister. Thou shalt not take the Name of the Lord thy God in vain: for the Lord will not hold him guiltless that taketh his Name in vain.

People. Lord, have mercy upon us, and incline our hearts to keep this law.

Minister. Remember that thou keep holy the Sabbath day. Six dayes shalt thou labour, and do all that thou hast to do; but the seventh day is the Sabbath of the Lord thy God. In it thou shalt do no manner of work, thou, and thy son, and thy daughter, thy man-servant, and thy maid-servant, thy cattel, and the stranger that is within thy gates. For in six dayes the Lord made heaven and earth, the sea, and all that in them is, and rested the seventh day: wherefore the Lord blessed the seventh day, and hallowed it.

People. Lord, have mercy upon us, and incline our hearts to keep this law.

Minister. Honour thy father and thy mother, that thy dayes may be long in the land which the Lord thy God giveth thee.

People. Lord, have mercy upon us, and incline our hearts to keep this law.

Minister. Thou shalt do no murder.

People. Lord, have mercy upon us, and incline our hearts to keep this law.

Minister. Thou shalt not commit adultery.

People. Lord, have mercy upon us, and incline our hearts to keep this law.

Minister. Thou shalt not steal.

People. Lord, have mercy upon us, and incline our hearts to keep this law.

Minister. Thou shalt not bear false witness against thy neighbour.

People. Lord, have mercy upon us, and incline our hearts to keep this law.

Minister. Thou shalt not covet thy neighbours house, thou shalt not covet thy neighbours wife, nor his servant, nor his maid, nor his ox, nor his ass, nor any thing that is his.

People. Lord, have mercy upon us, and write all these thy laws in our hearts, we beseech thee.

¶ *Then shall follow one of these two Collects for the King, the Priest standing as before, and saying,*

Let us pray.

ALMIGHTY God, whose kingdom is everlasting, and power infinite; Have mercy upon the whole Church, and so rule the heart of thy chosen servant *Charles*, our King and Governour, that he (knowing whose minister he is) may above all things seek thy honour and glory; and that we and all his subjects (duly considering whose authority he hath) may faithfully serve, honour, and humbly obey him, in thee, and for thee, according to thy blessed word and ordinance, through Jesus Christ our Lord, who with thee and the holy Ghost, liveth and reigneth ever one God, world without end. *Amen.*

¶ *Or,*

ALMIGHTY and everlasting God, we are taught by thy holy Word, that the hearts of kings are in thy rule and governance, and that thou dost dispose and turn them as it seemeth best to thy godly wisdom; We humbly beseech thee so to dispose and govern the heart of *CHARLES* thy Servant, our King and Governour, that in all his thoughts, words and works, he may ever seek thy honour and glory, and study to preserve thy people committed to his charge, in wealth, peace and godliness: Grant this, O merciful Father, for thy dear Sons sake Jesus Christ our Lord. *Amen.*

¶ *Then shall be said the Collect of the day.° And immediately after the Collect the Priest shall read the Epistle, saying,* The Epistle [or, The portion of Scripture appointed for the Epistle] is written in the —— Chapter of —— beginning at the —— verse. *And the Epistle ended, he shall say,* Here endeth the Epistle. *Then shall he read the Gospel (the people all standing up) saying,* The holy Gospel is written in the —— Chapter of —— beginning at the —— verse. *And the Gospel ended, shall be sung or said the Creed following, the people still standing, as before.*

I BELIEVE in one God the Father Almighty, Maker of heaven and earth, And of all things visible and invisible:

And in one Lord Jesus Christ, the only begotten son of God, Begotten of his Father before all worlds, God of God, Light of Light, Very God of very God, Begotten, not made, Being of one substance with the Father, By whom all things were made: Who for us men, and for our salvation came down from heaven, And was incarnate by the holy Ghost of the Virgin Mary, And was made man, And was crucified also for us under Pontius Pilate. He suffered and was buried, And the third day he rose again according to the Scriptures, And ascended into heaven, And sitteth on the right hand of the Father. And he shall come again with glory to judge both the quick and the dead: Whose kingdom shall have no end.

And I believe in the holy Ghost, The Lord and giver of life, Who proceedeth from the Father and the Son, Who with the Father and the Son together is worshipped and glorified, Who spake by the prophets. And I believe one Catholick and Apostolick Church. I acknowledge one Baptism for the remission of sins, And I look for the Resurrection of the dead, And the life of the world to come. Amen.

¶ *Then the Curate shall declare unto the people what holy-dayes, or fasting-dayes, are in the week following to be observed. And then also (if occasion be) shall notice be given of the Communion;° and the banns of Matrimony published; and Briefs, Citations, and Excommunications read. And nothing shall be proclaimed or published in the Church,° during the time of Divine Service, but by the Minister: Nor by him any thing, but what is prescribed in the Rules of this Book, or enjoyned by the King, or by the Ordinary of the place.*

¶ *Then shall follow the Sermon, or one of the Homilies already set forth, or hereafter to be set forth by Authority.*

¶ *Then shall the Priest return to the Lords Table,° and begin the Offertory, saying one or more of these Sentences following, as he thinketh most convenient in his discretion.*

L ET your light so shine before men, that they may see your good works, and glorifie your Father which is in heaven.   *Matt.* 5

Lay not up for your selves treasure upon the earth, where the rust and moth doth corrupt, and where thieves break through and steal: but lay up for your selves treasures in heaven, where neither rust nor moth doth corrupt, and where thieves do not break through and steal.
                                                                                          Matt. 6

Whatsoever ye would that men should doe unto you, even so doe unto them; for this is the law and the prophets.   *Matt.* 7

Not every one that saith unto me, Lord, Lord, shall enter into the kingdom of heaven, but he that doth the will of my Father which is in heaven.   *Matt.* 7

Zaccheus stood forth, and said unto the Lord, Behold, Lord, the half of my goods I give to the poor, and if I have done any wrong to any man, I restore four fold.   *Luke* 19

Who goeth a warfare at any time of his own cost? Who planteth a vineyard, and eateth not of the fruit thereof? Or who feedeth a flock, and eateth not of the milk of the flock?   1 *Cor.* 9

If we have sown unto you spiritual things, is it a great matter if we shall reap your worldly things?   1 *Cor.* 9

Do ye not know, that they who minister about holy things, live of the sacrifice? and they who wait at the altar, are partakers with the altar? Even so hath the Lord also ordained, that they who preach the Gospel should live of the Gospel.   1 *Cor.* 9

He that soweth little, shall reap little: and he that soweth plenteously, shall reap plenteously. Let every man do according as he is disposed in his heart, not grudgingly, or of necessity; for God loveth a cheerful giver.   2 *Cor.* 9

Let him that is taught in the word, minister unto him that teacheth in all good things. Be not deceived, God is not mocked: for whatsoever a man soweth that shall he reap.   *Gal.* 6

While we have time let us do good unto all men, and specially unto them that are of the houshold of faith.   *Gal.* 6

Godliness is great riches, if a man be content with that he hath: for we brought nothing into the world, neither may we carry any thing out.   1 *Tim.* 6

Charge them who are rich in this world, that they be ready to give, and glad to distribute, laying up in store for themselves a good foundation against the time to come, that they may attain eternal life.   1 *Tim.* 6

God is not unrighteous, that he will forget your works and labour that proceedeth of love; which love ye have shewed for his Names sake, who have ministered unto the saints, and yet do minister. *Heb.* 6

To do good, and to distribute, forget not; for with such sacrifices God is pleased.   *Heb.* 13

Whoso hath this worlds good, and seeth his brother have need, and shutteth up his compassion from him, how dwelleth the love of God in him?   1 *John* 3

Give alms of thy goods, and never turn thy face from any poor man; and then the face of the Lord shall not be turned away from thee.   *Tob.* 4

Be merciful after thy power. If thou hast much, give plenteously. If thou hast little, do thy diligence gladly to give of that little: for so gatherest thou thy self a good reward in the day of necessity.   *Tob.* 4

He that hath pity upon the poor, lendeth unto the Lord: and look what he laieth out, it shall be paid him again.   *Prov.* 19

Blessed be the man that provideth for the sick and needy: the Lord shall deliver him in the time of trouble.   *Ps.* 41

¶ *Whilst these Sentences are in reading, the Deacons, Church-wardens, or other fit person appointed for that purpose, shall receive the alms for the poor, and other devotions of the people, in a decent basin, to be provided by the Parish° for that purpose; and reverently bring it to the Priest, who shall humbly present and place it upon the holy Table.*

¶ *And when there is a Communion, the Priest shall then place upon the Table so much Bread and Wine, as he shall think sufficient.° After which done the Priest shall say,*

Let us pray for the whole state of Christs Church militant here in earth.

Almighty and everliving God, who by thy holy Apostle hast taught us to make prayers and supplications, and to give thanks for all men; We humbly beseech thee most mercifully [† *to accept our alms and oblations, and*] to receive these our prayers, which we offer unto thy divine Majesty, beseeching thee to inspire continually the universal Church with the spirit of truth, unity, and concord: And grant, that all they

† *If there be no alms or oblations, then the words* [of accepting our alms and oblations]° *be left out unsaid.*

that do confess thy holy Name, may agree in the truth of thy holy word, and live in unity and godly love. We beseech thee also to save and defend all Christian kings, princes, and governours; and specially thy servant *CHARLES* our King, that under him we may be godly and quietly governed: and grant unto his whole Council, and to all that are put in authority under him, that they may truly and indifferently minister justice, to the punishment of wickedness and vice, and to the maintenance of thy true religion and vertue. Give grace, O heavenly Father, to all Bishops, and Curates, that they may both by their life and doctrine set forth thy true and lively word, and rightly and duly administer thy holy Sacraments: And to all thy people give thy heavenly grace; and especially to this congregation here present, that with meek heart and due reverence they may hear, and receive thy holy word, truly serving thee in holiness and righteousness all the dayes of their life. And we most humbly beseech thee of thy goodness, O Lord, to comfort and succour all them who in this transitory life are in trouble, sorrow, need, sickness, or any other adversity. And we also bless thy holy Name, for all thy servants departed this life in thy faith and fear;° beseeching thee to give us grace so to follow their good examples, that with them we may be partakers of thy heavenly kingdom. Grant this, O Father, for Jesus Christs sake our only Mediatour and Advocate. *Amen.*

¶ *When the Minister giveth warning for the celebration of the holy Communion,* ° (*which he shall alwayes do upon the Sunday or some holy-day immediately preceding*) *After the Sermon, or Homily ended, he shall read this exhortation following.*

Dearly beloved, on —— day next I purpose, through Gods assistance to administer to all such as shall be religiously and devoutly disposed, the most comfortable Sacrament of the Body and Bloud of Christ, to be by them received in remembrance of his meritorious cross and passion, whereby alone we obtain remission of our sins, and are made partakers of the kingdom of heaven. Wherefore it is our duty to render most humble and hearty thanks to Almighty God our heavenly Father, for that he hath given his Son our Saviour Jesus Christ, not only to die for us, but also to be our spiritual food and sustenance in that holy Sacrament. Which being so divine and comfortable a thing to them who receive it worthily, and so dangerous to them that will presume to receive it unworthily; my duty is to exhort you in the mean season to consider the dignity of that holy mystery, and the great peril of the unworthy receiving thereof, and so to search and examine your owne consciences, (and that not lightly, and after the manner of dissemblers with God; but so) that ye may come holy and clean to such a heavenly feast, in the marriage-garment required by God in holy Scripture, and be received as worthy partakers of that holy Table.

The way and means thereto is; First, to examine your lives and conversations by the rule of Gods commandments; and wherein soever ye shall perceive yourselves to have offended, either by will, word, or deed, there to bewail your own sinfulness, and to confess your selves to Almighty God, with full purpose of amendment of life. And if ye shall perceive your offences to be such as are not onely against God, but also against your neighbours, then ye shall reconcile your selves unto them, being ready to make restitution and satisfaction according to the uttermost of your powers, for all injuries and wrongs done by you to any other; and being likewise ready to forgive others that have offended you, as ye would have forgiveness of your offences at Gods hand: for otherwise the receiving of the holy Communion doth nothing else but increase your damnation. Therefore if any of you be a blasphemer of God,° an hinderer or slanderer of his Word, an adulterer, or be in malice, or envie, or in any other grievous crime; Repent you of your sins, or else come not to that holy Table, lest after the taking of that holy Sacrament, the devil enter into you, as he entred into Judas, and fill you full of all iniquities, and bring you to destruction both of body and soul.

And because it is requisite, that no man should come to the holy Communion, but with a full trust in Gods mercy, and with a quiet conscience; therefore if there be any of you, who by this means cannot quiet his own conscience herein, but requireth further comfort or counsel; let him come to me, or to some other discreet and learned

Minister of Gods Word, and open his grief, that by the ministery of Gods holy word he may receive the benefit of absolution, together with ghostly counsel and advice, to the quieting of his conscience, and avoiding of all scruple and doubtfulness.

¶ *Or in case he shall see the people negligent° to come to the holy Communion, in stead of the former, he shall use this exhortation.*

DEARLY beloved brethren, on —— I intend, by Gods grace, to celebrate the Lords Supper: unto which, in Gods behalf, I bid you all that are here present, and beseech you, for the Lord Jesus Christs sake, that ye will not refuse to come thereto, being so lovingly called and bidden by God himself. Ye know how grievous and unkind a thing it is, when a man hath prepared a rich feast, decked his table with all kind of provision, so that there lacketh nothing but the guests to sit down, and yet they who are called (without any cause) most unthankfully refuse to come. Which of you in such a case would not be moved? Who would not think a great injury and wrong done unto him? Wherefore, most dearly beloved in Christ, take ye good heed, lest ye withdrawing your selves from this holy Supper, provoke Gods indignation against you. It is an easie matter for a man to say, I will not communicate, because I am otherwise hindred with worldly business. But such excuses are not so easily accepted and allowed before God. If any man say, I am a grievous sinner, and therefore am afraid to come: wherefore then do ye not repent and amend? When God calleth you, are ye not ashamed to say you will not come? When ye should return to God, will ye excuse your selves, and say ye are not ready? Consider earnestly with your selves, how little such feigned excuses will avail before God. They that refused the feast in the Gospel, because they had bought a farm, or would try their yokes of oxen, or because they were married, were not so excused, but counted unworthy of the heavenly feast. I for my part shall be ready, and according to mine office, I bid you in the Name of God, I call you in Christs behalf, I exhort you, as ye love your own salvation, that ye will be partakers of this holy Communion. And as the Son of God did vouchsafe to yield up his soul by death upon the Cross for your salvation: so it is your duty to receive the Communion, in remembrance of the sacrifice of his death, as he himself hath commanded: Which if ye shall neglect to do, consider with your selves how great injury ye do unto God, and how sore punishment hangeth over your heads for the same; when ye wilfully abstain° from the Lords Table, and separate from your brethren, who come to feed on the banquet of that most heavenly food. These things if ye earnestly consider, ye will by Gods grace return to a better mind: for the obtaining whereof we shall not cease to make our humble petitions unto Almighty God our heavenly Father.

¶ *At the time of the Celebration of the Communion the Communicants being conveniently placed° for the receiving of the holy Sacrament, the Priest shall say this Exhortation.*

D EARLY beloved in the Lord, ye that mind to come to the holy Communion of the body and bloud of our Saviour Christ, must consider how Saint Paul exhorteth all persons diligently to try and examine themselves, before they presume to eat of that Bread, and drink of that Cup. For as the benefit is great, if with a true penitent heart and lively faith we receive that holy Sacrament (for then we spiritually eat the flesh of Christ, and drink his bloud; then we dwell in Christ, and Christ in us; we are one with Christ, and Christ with us): So is the danger great, if we receive the same unworthily. For then we are guilty of the body and bloud of Christ our Saviour; we eat and drink our own damnation, not considering the Lords Body; we kindle Gods wrath against us; we provoke him to plague us with divers diseases, and sundry kinds of death. Judge therefore your selves, brethren, that ye be not judged of the Lord; repent you truely for your sins past; have a lively and stedfast faith in Christ our Saviour; amend your lives, and be in perfect charity with all men, so shall ye be meet partakers of those holy mysteries. And above all things ye must give most humble and hearty thanks to God the Father, the Son, and the holy Ghost, for the redemption of the world by the death and passion of our Saviour Christ, both God and man, who did humble himself even to the death upon the Cross, for us miserable sinners, who lay in darkness and the shadow of death, that he might make us the children of God, and exalt us to everlasting life. And to the end that we should alway remember the exceeding great love of our Master, and onely Saviour, Jesus Christ, thus dying for us, and the innumerable benefits which by his precious bloud-shedding he hath obtained to us; he hath instituted and ordained holy mysteries, as pledges of his love, and for a continual remembrance of his death, to our great and endless comfort. To him therefore with the Father, and the holy Ghost, let us give (as we are most bounden) continual thanks, submitting our selves wholly to his holy will and pleasure, and studying to serve him in true holiness and righteousness all the dayes of our life. *Amen.*

¶ *Then shall the Priest say to them that come to receive the holy Communion,*

YE that do truly and earnestly repent you of your sins, and are in love and charity with your neighbours, and intend to lead a new life, following the commandments of God, and walking from henceforth in his holy wayes; Draw near with faith,° and take this holy Sacrament to your comfort; and make your humble confession to Almighty God, meekly kneeling upon your knees.

¶ *Then shall this general confession be made, in the name of all those that are minded to receive the holy Communion, by one of the Ministers, both he and all the people kneeling humbly upon their knees, and saying,*°

ALMIGHTY God, Father of our Lord Jesus Christ, Maker of all things, Judge of all men; We acknowledge° and bewail our manifold sins and wickedness, Which we from time to time most grievously have committed, By thought, word, and deed, Against thy divine Majesty, Provoking most justly thy wrath and indignation against us. We do earnestly repent, And are heartily sorry for these our misdoings, The remembrance of them is grievous unto us; The burthen of them is intolerable. Have mercy upon us, Have mercy upon us, most merciful Father; For thy Son our Lord Jesus Christs sake, Forgive us all that is past, And grant that we may ever hereafter Serve and please thee In newness of life, To the honour and glory of thy Name, Through Jesus Christ our Lord. Amen.

¶ *Then shall the Priest (or the Bishop being present) stand up, and turning himself to the people, pronounce this Absolution.*°

ALMIGHTY God our heavenly Father, who of his great mercy hath promised forgiveness of sins to all them that with hearty repentance and true faith turn unto him; Have mercy upon you, pardon and deliver you from all your sins, confirm and strengthen you in all goodness, and bring you to everlasting life, through Jesus Christ our Lord. *Amen.*

¶ *Then shall the Priest say,*

Hear what comfortable words our Saviour Christ saith unto all that truly turn to him.

COME unto me all that travail and are heavy laden, and I will refresh you. *Matt.* 11.28

So God loved the world, that he gave his onely begotten Son, to the end that all that believe in him should not perish, but have everlasting life. *John* 3.16

Hear also what Saint Paul saith.

This is a true saying, and worthy of all men to be received, that Jesus Christ came into the world to save sinners. 1 *Tim.* 1.15

Hear also what Saint John saith.

If any man sin, we have an Advocate with the Father, Jesus Christ the righteous, and he is the propitiation for our sins. 1 *John* 2.1

¶ *After which the Priest shall proceed, saying,*

Lift up your hearts.

Answer. We lift them up unto the Lord.

Priest. Let us give thanks unto our Lord God.

Answer. It is meet and right so to do.

¶ *Then shall the Priest turn to the Lords Table,° and say,*

IT is very meet, right, and our bounden duty, that we should at all times, and in all places give thanks unto thee, O Lord, †holy Father, Almighty, everlasting God.

† *These words* [holy Father] *must be omitted on* Trinity Sunday.

¶ *Here shall follow the proper Preface, according to the time, if there be any specially appointed: or else immediately shall follow,*

THEREFORE with Angels and Archangels, and with all the company of heaven we laud and magnify thy glorious Name, evermore praising thee, and saying, Holy, holy, holy, Lord God of hosts, Heaven and earth are full of thy glory. Glory be to thee, O Lord most High. *Amen.*

¶ *Proper Prefaces*

¶ *Upon Christmas day, and seven dayes after.*

BECAUSE thou didst give Jesus Christ thine only Son to be born as at this time° for us, who by the operation of the holy Ghost was made very man of the substance of the Virgin Mary his mother, and that without spot of sin, to make us clean from all sin. Therefore with Angels, &c.

¶ *Upon Easter day, and seven dayes after,*

BUT chiefly are we bound to praise thee for the glorious resurrection of thy Son Jesus Christ our Lord: for he is the very Paschal Lamb which was offered for us, and hath taken away the sin of the world; who by his death hath destroyed death, and by his rising to life again hath restored to us everlasting life. Therefore with Angels, *&c.*

¶ *Upon Ascension day, and seven dayes after.*

THROUGH thy most dearly beloved Son Jesus Christ our Lord, who after his most glorious resurrection manifestly appeared to all his Apostles, and in their sight ascended up into heaven to prepare a place for us; that where he is, thither we might also ascend, and reign with him in glory. Therefore with Angels, *&c.*

¶ *Upon Whitsunday, and six dayes after.*

THROUGH Jesus Christ our Lord; according to whose most true promise the holy Ghost came down as at this time from heaven with a sudden great sound, as it had been a mighty wind, in the likeness of fiery tongues, lighting upon the Apostles, to teach them, and to lead them to all truth, giving them both the gift of divers languages, and also boldness with fervent zeal, constantly to preach the Gospel unto all nations, whereby we have been brought out of darkness and errour into the clear light and true knowledge of thee, and of thy Son Jesus Christ. Therefore with Angels, *&c.*

¶ *Upon the Feast of Trinity only.*

WHO art one God, one Lord; not one onely person, but three persons in one substance. For that which we believe of the glory of the Father, the same we believe of the Son, and of the holy Ghost, without any difference or inequality. Therefore with Angels, *&c.*

¶ *After each of which Prefaces, shall immediately be sung or said,*

THEREFORE with Angels and Archangels, and with all the company of heaven, we laud and magnifie thy glorious Name, evermore praising thee, and saying, Holy, holy, holy, Lord God of hosts, heaven and earth are full of thy glory. Glory be to thee, O Lord most High. *Amen.*

¶ *Then shall the Priest kneeling down at the Lords Table say in the name of all them that shall receive the Communion, this Prayer following.*

WE do not presume to come to this thy Table, O merciful Lord, trusting in our own righteousness, but in thy manifold and great mercies. We are not worthy so much as to gather up the crumbs under thy Table. But thou art the same Lord, whose property is alwayes to have mercy; Grant us therefore, gracious Lord, so to eat the flesh of thy dear Son Jesus Christ, and to drink his bloud, that our sinful bodies may be made clean by his body, and our souls washed through his most precious bloud, and that we may evermore dwell in him, and he in us. *Amen.*

¶ *When the Priest, standing before the Table,° hath so ordered the Bread and Wine, that he may with the more readiness and decency break the Bread before the people, and take the Cup into his hands, he shall say the Prayer of Consecration, as followeth.*

ALMIGHTY God, our heavenly Father, who of thy tender mercy didst give thine onely Son Jesus Christ to suffer death upon the cross for our redemption, who made there (by his one oblation of himself once offered) a full, perfect, and sufficient sacrifice, oblation and satisfaction for the sins of the whole world, and did institute, and in his holy Gospel command us to continue a perpetual memory of that his precious death, until his coming again; Hear us, O merciful Father, we most humbly beseech thee, and grant that we receiving these thy creatures of bread and wine, according to thy Son our Saviour Jesus Christs holy institution, in remembrance of his death and passion, may be partakers of his most blessed body and bloud: Who in the same night that he was betrayed, *took bread, and when he had given thanks, †he brake it, and gave it to his disciples, saying, Take, eat, ‡this is my body which is given for you, do this in remembrance of me. Likewise after supper he §took the cup, and when he had given thanks, he gave it to them, saying, Drink ye all of this, for this ‖is my bloud of the New Testament, which is shed for you and for many for the remission of sins: Doe this, as oft as ye shall drink it, in remembrance of me. *Amen.*°

* *Here the priest is to take the Paten into his hands.*

† *And here to break the bread.°*

‡ *And here to lay his hand upon all the bread.*

§ *Here he is to take the cup into his hand.*

‖ *And here to lay his hand upon every vessel (be it Chalice or Flagon) in which there is any wine to be consecrated.*

¶ *Then shall the Minister first receive the Communion in both kinds himself,*
and then proceed to deliver the same to the Bishops, Priests, and Deacons in
like manner (if any be present) and after that to the people also in order, into
their hands, all meekly kneeling.° And when he delivereth the bread to any
one, he shall say,

THE body of our Lord Jesus Christ,° which was given for thee,
preserve thy body and soul unto everlasting life. Take and eat this
in remembrance that Christ died for thee, and feed on him in thy
heart by faith with thanksgiving.

¶ *And the Minister that delivereth the cup to any one, shall say,*

THE bloud of our Lord Jesus Christ, which was shed for thee,
preserve thy body and soul unto everlasting life. Drink this in
remembrance that Christs bloud was shed for thee, and be thankful.

¶ *If the consecrated bread or wine be all spent before all have communicated;°*
the Priest is to consecrate more according to the form before prescribed:
Beginning at [Our Saviour Christ in the same night, &c.] for the blessing
of the bread; and at [Likewise after Supper, &c.] for the blessing of the cup.

¶ *When all have communicated, the Minister shall return to the Lords Table,*
and reverently place upon it what remaineth of the consecrated Elements,°
covering the same with a fair linen cloth.

¶ *Then shall the Priest say the Lords Prayer, the people repeating after*
him every Petition.

OUR Father which art in heaven; Hallowed be thy Name. Thy
kingdom come. Thy will be done in earth, As it is in heaven.
Give us this day our daily bread. And forgive us our trespasses, As we
forgive them that trespass against us. And lead us not into temptation: But deliver us from evil. For thine is the kingdom, The power,
and the glory, For ever and ever. Amen.

¶ *After shall be said as followeth.*

O LORD and heavenly Father, we thy humble servants entirely
desire thy Fatherly goodness, mercifully to accept this our sacrifice of praise and thanksgiving; most humbly beseeching thee to grant,
that by the merits and death of thy Son Jesus Christ, and through
faith in his blood, we and all thy whole Church may obtain remission
of our sins, and all other benefits of his passion. And here we offer
and present unto thee, O Lord, our selves, our souls and bodies, to be

a reasonable, holy, and lively sacrifice unto thee; humbly beseeching thee, that all we who are partakers of this holy Communion, may be fulfilled with thy grace and heavenly benediction. And although we be unworthy through our manifold sins to offer unto thee any sacrifice; yet we beseech thee to accept this our bounden duty and service; not weighing our merits, but pardoning our offences, through Jesus Christ our Lord; by whom, and with whom, in the unity of the holy Ghost, all honour and glory be unto thee, O Father Almighty, world without end. *Amen.*

¶ *Or this.*

ALMIGHTY and everliving God, we most heartily thank thee, for that thou dost vouchsafe to feed us, who have duly received these holy mysteries, with the spiritual food of the most precious body and bloud of thy Son our Saviour Jesus Christ; and dost assure us thereby of thy favour and goodness towards us; and that we are very members incorporate in the mystical body of thy Son, which is the blessed company of all faithful people; and are also heirs through hope of thy everlasting kingdom, by the merits of the most precious death and passion of thy dear Son. And we most humbly beseech thee, O heavenly Father, so to assist us with thy grace, that we may continue in that holy fellowship, and do all such good works as thou hast prepared for us to walk in, through Jesus Christ our Lord, to whom with thee and the holy Ghost be all honour and glory world without end. *Amen.*

¶ *Then shall be said or sung,*

GLORY be to God on high, and in earth peace, good will towards men. We praise thee, we bless thee, we worship thee, we glorifie thee, we give thanks to thee for thy great glory, O Lord God, heavenly King, God the Father Almighty.

O Lord, the onely begotten Son Jesu Christ; O Lord God, Lamb of God, Son of the Father, that takest away the sins of the world, have mercy upon us. Thou that takest away the sins of the world, have mercy upon us. Thou that takest away the sins of the world, receive our prayer. Thou that sittest at the right hand of God the Father, have mercy upon us.

For thou only art holy, thou only art the Lord, thou only, O Christ, with the holy Ghost, art most high in the glory of God the Father. *Amen.*

¶ *Then the Priest (or Bishop if he be present) shall let them depart with
this blessing.*

T HE peace of God which passeth all understanding, keep your
hearts and minds in the knowledge and love of God, and of his
son Jesus Christ our Lord: And the blessing of God Almighty, the
Father, the Son, and the holy Ghost, be amongst you, and remain
with you alwayes. *Amen.*

¶ *Collects to be said after the Offertory, when there is no Communion, every
such day one, or more; and the same may be said also, as often as occasion shall serve, after the Collects either of Morning or Evening Prayer,
Communion, or Litany, by the discretion of the Minister.*

A SSIST us mercifully, O Lord, in these our supplications and
prayers, and dispose the way of thy servants, towards the attain-
ment of everlasting salvation; that, among all the changes and chances
of this mortal life, they may ever be defended by thy most gracious
and ready help, through Jesus Christ our Lord. *Amen.*

O ALMIGHTY Lord, and everlasting God, vouchsafe, we beseech
thee, to direct, sanctifie, and govern both our hearts and bodies
in the wayes of thy laws, and in the works of thy commandments,
that through thy most mighty protection, both here and ever, we may
be preserved in body and soul, through our Lord and Saviour Jesus
Christ. *Amen.*

G RANT, we beseech thee, Almighty God, that the words which
we have heard this day with our outward ears, may through thy
grace be so grafted inwardly in our hearts, that they may bring forth
in us the fruit of good living, to the honour and praise of thy Name,
through Jesus Christ our Lord. *Amen.*

P REVENT us, O Lord, in all our doings, with thy most gracious
favour, and further us with thy continual help, that in all our works
begun, continued and ended in thee, we may glorifie thy holy Name,
and finally by thy mercy obtain everlasting life, through Jesus Christ
our Lord. *Amen.*

A LMIGHTY God, the fountain of all wisdom, who knowest our
necessities before we ask, and our ignorance in asking; We

beseech thee to have compassion upon our infirmities; and those things which for our unworthiness we dare not, and for our blindness we cannot ask, vouchsafe to give us for the worthiness of thy Son Jesus Christ our Lord. *Amen.*

A LMIGHTY God, who hast promised to hear the petitions of them that ask in thy Sons Name; We beseech thee mercifully to incline thine ears to us that have made now our prayers and supplications unto thee, and grant that those things which we have faithfully asked according to thy will, may effectually be obtained, to the relief of our necessity, and to the setting forth of thy glory, through Jesus Christ our Lord. *Amen.*

¶ *U* PON *the Sundaies and other holy days (if there be no Communion)°
shall be said all that is appointed at the Communion, until the end of
the general Prayer* [For the whole state of Christs Church militant here
in earth] *together with one or more of these Collects last before rehearsed,
concluding with the Blessing.*

¶ *And there shall be no celebration of the Lords Supper, except there be a convenient number to communicate with the Priest, according to his discretion.*

¶ *And if there be not above twenty persons in the Parish of discretion to receive
the Communion; yet there shall be no Communion, except four (or three at
the least) communicate with the Priest.*

¶ *And in Cathedral and Collegiate Churches and Colledges, where there are
many Priests and Deacons, they shall all receive the Communion with the
Priest every Sunday at the least, except they have a reasonable cause to the
contrary.*

¶ *And to take away all occasion of dissension, and superstition, which any
Person hath or might have concerning the Bread and Wine, it shall suffice
that the Bread be such as is usual to be eaten; but the best and purest Wheat
Bread that conveniently may be gotten.*

¶ *And if any of the Bread and Wine remain unconsecrated, the Curate shall
have it to his own use: but if any remain of that which was consecrated, it
shall not be carried out of the Church, but the Priest and such other of the
Communicants as he shall then call unto him, shall immediately after the
Blessing, reverently eat and drink the same.*

¶ *The Bread and Wine for the Communion shall be provided by the Curate and the Church-wardens, at the charges of the Parish.*

¶ *And note, that every Parishioner shall communicate at the least three times in the year, of which Easter to be one.° And yearly at Easter every Parishioner shall reckon with the Parson, Vicar, or Curate; or his or their Deputy, or Deputies, and pay to them or him all Ecclesiastical duties, accustomably due, then and at that time to be paid.*

¶ *After the Divine Service ended, the money given at the Offertory° shall be disposed of to such pious and charitable uses, as the Minister and Church-wardens shall think fit. Wherein if they disagree, it shall be disposed of as the Ordinary shall appoint.*

---

*W*HEREAS *it is ordained in this Office for the Administration of the Lords Supper, that the Communicants should receive the same Kneeling;° (which Order is well meant, for a signification of our humble and grateful acknowledgment of the benefits of Christ therein given to all worthy Receivers, and for the avoiding of such profanation, and disorder in the holy Communion, as might otherwise ensue). Yet, lest the same Kneeling should by any persons, either out of ignorance and infirmity, or out of malice and obstinacy, be misconstrued and depraved; It is hereby declared, that thereby no Adoration is intended, or ought to be done, either unto the Sacramental bread or wine, there bodily received, or unto any Corporal Presence of Christs natural Flesh, and Bloud.° For the Sacramental bread and wine remain still in their very Natural Substances, and therefore may not be adored, (for that were Idolatrie, to be abhorred of all faithful Christians). And the natural body and bloud of our Saviour Christ are in Heaven, and not here; it being against the truth of Christs Natural body, to be at one time in more places than one.*

THE
MINISTRATION
OF
Publick Baptism of *INFANTS*
to be used in the Church.

¶ *THE people are to be admonished,° that it is most convenient that Baptism should not be administered but upon Sundays and other holy-dayes, when the most number of people come together: as well for that the Congregation there present may testifie the receiving of them that be newly baptized into the number of Christs Church; as also because in the Baptism of Infants, every man present may be put in remembrance of his own profession made to God in his Baptism. For which cause also it is expedient that Baptism be ministered in the vulgar tongue. Nevertheless (if necessity so require) children may be baptized upon any other day.°*

¶ *And note, that there shall be for every male child to be baptized two Godfathers and one Godmother:° and for every female, one Godfather and two Godmothers.*

¶ *When there are children to be baptized, the Parents shall give knowledge thereof over night, or in the morning before the beginning of morning Prayer to the Curate. And then the Godfathers and Godmothers, and the People, with the Children must be ready at the Font, either immediately after the last Lesson at Morning Prayer, or else immediately after the last Lesson at Evening Prayer, as the Curate by his discretion shall appoint. And the Priest coming to the Font (which is then to be filled with pure water)° and standing there, shall say,*

Hath this Child been already baptized, or no?

¶ *If they answer, No: Then shall the Priest proceed as followeth.*

DEARLY beloved, forasmuch as all men are conceived and born in sin, and that our Saviour Christ saith, None can enter into the kingdom of God, except he be regenerate and born anew of water and of the holy Ghost; I beseech you to call upon God the Father, through our Lord Jesus Christ, that of his bounteous mercy he will grant to *this child* that thing which by nature *he* cannot have, that *he* may be baptized with water and the holy Ghost, and received into Christs holy Church, and be made *a lively member* of the same.

¶ *Then shall the Priest say,*

Let us pray.

ALMIGHTY and everlasting God, who of thy great mercy didst save Noah and his family in the ark from perishing by water, and also didst safely lead the children of Israel thy people through the Red Sea, figuring thereby thy holy baptism; and by the baptism of thy wel-beloved Son Jesus Christ in the river Jordan didst sanctifie water to the mystical washing away of sin;° We beseech thee for thine infinite mercies° that thou wilt mercifully look upon *this Child*; wash *him* and sanctifie *him* with the holy Ghost, that *he* being delivered from thy wrath, may be received into the ark of Christs Church; and being stedfast in faith, joyful through hope, and rooted in charity, may so pass the waves of this troublesome world, that finally *he* may come to the land of everlasting life; there to reign with thee world without end, through Jesus Christ our Lord. *Amen.*

ALMIGHTY and immortal God, the aid of all that need, the helper of all that flee to thee for succour, the life of them that believe, and the resurrection of the dead; We call upon thee for *this infant*, that *he* coming to thy holy baptism, may receive remission of *his* sins by spiritual regeneration. Receive *him*, O Lord, as thou hast promised by thy wel-beloved Son, saying, Ask, and ye shall have; seek, and ye shall finde; knock, and it shall be opened unto you: So give now unto us that ask; let us that seek finde; open the gate unto us that knock; that *this infant* may enjoy the everlasting benediction of thy heavenly washing, and may come to the eternal kingdom which thou hast promised, by Christ our Lord. *Amen.*

¶ *Then shall the people stand up,° and the Priest shall say,*

Hear the words of the Gospel, written by Saint *Mark*, in the tenth chapter, at the thirteenth verse.

THEY brought young children to Christ, that he should touch them; and his disciples rebuked those that brought them. But when Jesus saw it, he was much displeased, and said unto them, Suffer the little children to come unto me, and forbid them not; for of such is the kingdom of God. Verily I say unto you, Whosoever shall not receive the kingdom of God as a little child, he shall not enter therein. And he took them up in his arms, put his hands upon them, and blessed them.   *Mark* 10.13

¶ *After the Gospel is read, the Minister shall make this brief exhortation upon the words of the Gospel.*

BELOVED, ye hear in this Gospel the words of our Saviour Christ, that he commanded the children to be brought unto him; how he blamed those that would have kept them from him; how he exhorteth all men to follow their innocency. Ye perceive how by his outward gesture and deed he declared his good will toward them; for he embraced them in his arms, he laid his hands upon them, and blessed them. Doubt ye not therefore, but earnestly believe, that he will likewise favourably receive *this* present *Infant*, that he will embrace *him* with the arms of his mercy, that he will give unto *him* the blessing of eternal life, and make *him* partaker of his everlasting kingdome. Wherefore we being thus perswaded of the good will of our heavenly Father towards *this Infant*, declared by his Son Jesus Christ, and nothing doubting but that he favourably alloweth this charitable work of ours, in bringing *this Infant* to his holy baptism, let us faithfully and devoutly give thanks unto him, and say,

ALMIGHTY and everlasting God, heavenly Father, we give thee humble thanks, that thou hast vouchsafed to call us to the knowledge of thy grace, and faith in thee: Increase this knowledge, and confirm this faith in us evermore. Give thy Holy Spirit to *this Infant*, that *he* may be born again, and be made *an heir* of everlasting salvation, through our Lord Jesus Christ, who liveth and reigneth with thee and the holy Spirit, now and for ever. *Amen.*

¶ *Then shall the Priest speak unto the Godfathers and Godmothers on this wise.*

DEARLY beloved, ye have brought *this child* here to be baptized, ye have prayed that our Lord Jesus Christ would vouchsafe to receive *him*, to release *him* of *his* sins, to sanctifie him with the holy Ghost,° to give *him* the kingdom of heaven, and everlasting life. Ye have heard also that our Lord Jesus Christ hath promised in his Gospel to grant all these things that ye have prayed for: which promise he for his part will most surely keep and perform. Wherefore, after this promise made by Christ, *this Infant* must also faithfully for *his* part, promise by you that are *his* sureties (until *he* come of age to take it upon *himself*)° that *he* will renounce the devil and all his works, and constantly believe Gods holy word, and obediently keep his commandments.

I demand therefore,

DOST thou, in the name of this child renounce the devil° and all his works, the vain pomp and glory of the world, with all covetous desires of the same, and the carnal desires of the flesh, so that thou wilt not follow nor be led by them?

Answer. I renounce them all.

Minister.

DOST thou believe in God the Father Almighty, Maker of heaven and earth?

And in Jesus Christ his onely begotten Son our Lord? And that he was conceived by the holy Ghost; born of the Virgin Mary; that he suffered under Pontius Pilate, was crucified, dead, and buried; that he went down into hell, and also did rise again the third day; that he ascended into heaven, and sitteth at the right hand of God the Father Almighty; and from thence shall come again at the end of the world, to judge the quick and the dead?

And dost thou believe in the Holy Ghost; the holy Catholick Church; the Communion of saints; the remission of sins; the resurrection of the flesh; and everlasting life after death?

Answer. All this I stedfastly believe.

Minister.

WILT thou be baptized in this faith?
Answer. That is my desire.

Minister.

WILT thou then obediently keep Gods holy will° and commandments, and walk in the same all the dayes of thy life?
Answer. I will.

¶ *Then shall the Priest say,*

O MERCIFUL God, grant that the old Adam in *this child* may be so buried, that the new man may be raised up in *him*. *Amen.*

Grant that all carnal affections may die in *him*, and that all things belonging to the Spirit may live and grow in *him*. *Amen.*

Grant that *he* may have power and strength to have victory, and to triumph against the devil, the world, and the flesh. *Amen.*

Grant that whosoever is here dedicated to thee by our office and ministry, may also be indued with heavenly vertues, and everlastingly rewarded, through thy mercy, O blessed Lord God, who dost live and govern all things, world without end. *Amen.*

ALMIGHTY everliving God, whose most dearly beloved Son Jesus Christ, for the forgiveness of our sins, did shed out of his most precious side both water and bloud, and gave commandment to his disciples, that they should go teach all nations, and baptize them in the Name of the Father, and of the Son, and of the holy Ghost; Regard, we beseech thee, the supplications of thy congregation; sanctifie this water to the mystical washing away of sin:° and grant that *this child* now to be baptized therein, may receive the fulness of thy grace, and ever remain in the number of thy faithful and elect children, through Jesus Christ our Lord. *Amen.*

¶ *Then the Priest shall take the child into his hands, and shall say to the Godfathers and Godmothers,*

Name this Child.

And then naming it after them (if they shall certifie him that the child may well endure it) he shall dip it in the water discreetly and warily, saying,

N. I baptize thee in the Name of the Father, and of the Son, and of the holy Ghost. *Amen.*

¶ *But if they certifie that the childe is weak, it shall suffice to pour water upon it,° saying the foresaid words,*

N. I baptize thee in the Name of the Father, and of the Son, and of the holy Ghost. *Amen.*

¶ *Then the Priest shall say,*

WE receive this Child into the congregation of Christs flock,° † and do signe *him* with the signe of the cross, in token that hereafter *he* shall not be ashamed to confess the faith of Christ crucified, and manfully to fight under his banner,° against sin, the world, and the devil, and to continue Christs faithful souldier and servant unto *his* lives end. Amen.

† *Here the Priest shall make a cross° upon the childs forehead.*

¶ *Then shall the Priest say,*

SEEING now, dearly beloved brethren, that *this child is* regenerate and grafted into the body of Christs Church, let us give thanks unto Almighty God for these benefits, and with one accord make our prayers unto him, that *this child* may lead the rest of *his* life according to this beginning.

¶ *Then shall be said, all kneeling;*

OUR Father which art in heaven; Hallowed be thy Name. Thy kingdom come. Thy will be done in earth, As it is in heaven. Give us this day our daily bread. And forgive us our trespasses, As we forgive them that trespass against us. And lead us not into temptation; But deliver us from evil. *Amen.*

¶ *Then shall the Priest say,*

WE yield thee hearty thanks, most merciful Father, that it hath pleased thee to regenerate *this infant* with thy holy Spirit, to receive *him* for thine own *child* by adoption, and to incorporate *him* into thy holy Church.° And humbly we beseech thee to grant, that *he* being dead unto sin, and living unto righteousness, and being buried with Christ in his death, may crucifie the old man, and utterly abolish the whole body of sin, and that as *he is* made *partaker* of the death of thy Son, *he* may also be *partaker* of his resurrection; so that finally with the residue of thy holy Church, *he* may be an *inheritour* of thine everlasting kingdom, through Christ our Lord. *Amen.*

¶ *Then all standing up, the Priest shall say to the Godfathers and Godmothers this exhortation following.*

FORASMUCH as *this child* hath promised by you *his* sureties to renounce the devil and all his works, to believe in God, and to serve him; ye must remember that it is your parts and duties to see that *this infant* be taught, so soon as *he* shall be able to learn, what a solemn vow, promise and profession *he hath* here made by you. And that *he* may know these things the better, ye shall call upon *him* to hear Sermons, and chiefly ye shall provide that *he* may learn the Creed, the Lords Prayer, and the ten Commandments in the vulgar tongue, and all other things which a Christian ought to know and believe to his souls health; and that *this child* may be vertuously brought up to lead a godly and a Christian life; remembring alwayes that baptism doth represent unto us our profession, which is, to follow the example of our Saviour Christ, and to be made like unto him; that as he died and rose again for us; so should we who are baptized, die from sin, and rise again unto righteousness, continually mortifying all our evil and corrupt affections, and daily proceeding in all vertue and godliness of living.

¶ *Then shall he adde and say,*

YE are to take care that *this child* be brought to the Bishop to be confirmed by him, so soon as *he* can say the Creed, the Lords Prayer, and the ten Commandments in the vulgar tongue, and be further instructed in the Church-Catechism set forth for that purpose.

IT is certain by Gods word, that children which are baptized, dying before they commit actual sin,° are undoubtedly saved.

TO take away all scruple concerning the use of the signe of the Cross° in Baptism; the true Explication thereof, and the just reasons for the retaining of it may be seen in the thirtieth Canon, first published in the Year 1604.

THE
MINISTRATION
OF
Private Baptism of *CHILDREN*
in Houses.

¶ *THE Curates of every parish shall often admonish the people, that they deferre not the Baptism of their children longer than the first or second Sunday next after their birth, or other holy-day falling between, unless a great and reasonable cause, to be approved by the Curate.*

¶ *And also they shall warn them, that without like great cause and necessity they procure not their Children to be baptized at home in their houses. But when need shall compel them so to do, then Baptism shall be administered on this fashion.*

¶ *First let the Minister of the Parish (or in his absence, any other lawful Minister that can be procured) with them that are present call upon God, and say the Lords Prayer, and so many of the Collects appointed to be said before in the Form of Publick Baptism, as the time and present exigence will suffer. And then, the child being named by some one that is present, the Minister shall pour water upon it, saying these words;*

N. I baptize thee in the Name of the Father, and of the Son, and of the Holy Ghost. Amen.

¶ *Then all kneeling down, the Minister shall give thanks unto God, and say,*

WE yield thee hearty thanks, most merciful Father, that it hath pleased thee to regenerate *this infant* with thy holy Spirit; to receive *him* for thine own child by adoption, and to incorporate him into thy holy Church. And we humbly beseech thee to grant, that as *he is* now made *partaker* of the death of thy Son, so *he* may be also of his resurrection: And that finally with the residue of thy Saints *he* may inherit thine everlasting kingdom, through the same thy Son Jesus Christ our Lord. *Amen.*

¶ *And let them not doubt, but that the Child so baptized is lawfully and sufficiently baptized, and ought not to be baptized again. Yet nevertheless, if the child which is after this sort Baptized, do afterward live, it is expedient that it be brought into the Church, to the intent that if the Minister of the same Parish did himself Baptize that Child, the Congregation may be certified of the true form of Baptism, by him privately before used: In which case he shall say thus,*

I CERTIFIE you, that according to the due and prescribed order of the Church, *at such a time*, and *at such a place*, before divers witnesses I baptized this Child.

¶ *B*UT *if the Child were baptized by any other lawful Minister, then the Minister of the Parish where the child was born or christned, shall examine and try whether the child be lawfully baptized,° or no. In which case, if those that bring any child to the Church, do answer that the same child is already baptized, then shall the Minister examine them further, saying,*

BY whom was this Child baptized?
  Who was present when this Child was baptized?
Because some things essential to this sacrament may happen to be omitted through fear or haste, in such times of extremity; therefore I demand further of you,
  With what matter was this child baptized?
  With what words was this child baptized?

¶ *And if the Minister shall find by the answers of such as bring the child, that all things were done as they ought to be; then shall not he christen the child again, but shall receive him as one of the flock of true Christian people, saying thus,*

I CERTIFIE you, that in this case all is well done, and according unto due order, concerning the baptizing of this child; who being born in original sin, and in the wrath of God, is now, by the laver of Regeneration in Baptism received into the number of the children of God, and heirs of everlasting life: For our Lord Jesus Christ doth not deny his grace and mercy unto such infants, but most lovingly doth call them unto him, as the holy Gospel doth witness to our comfort on this wise.

THEY brought young children to Christ, that he should touch them; and his disciples rebuked those that brought them. But when Jesus saw it, he was much displeased, and said unto them, Suffer the little children to come unto me, and forbid them not; for of such is the kingdom of God. Verily I say unto you, Whosoever shall not receive the kingdom of God as a little child, he shall not enter therein. And he took them up in his arms, put his hands upon them, and blessed them.   *Mark* 10.13

¶ *After the Gospel is read, the Minister shall make this brief exhortation upon the words of the Gospel.*

BELOVED, ye hear in this Gospel the words of our Saviour Christ, that he commanded the children to be brought unto him; how he blamed those that would have kept them from him; how he exhorted all men to follow their innocency. Ye perceive how by his outward gesture and deed he declared his good will toward them; for he embraced them in his arms, he laid his hands upon them, and blessed them. Doubt ye not therefore, but earnestly believe, that he hath likewise favourably received *this* present *infant*, that he hath embraced *him* with the arms of his mercy, and (as he hath promised in his holy word) will give unto *him* the blessing of eternal life, and make *him* partaker of his everlasting kingdome. Wherefore we being thus perswaded of the good will of our heavenly Father, declared by his Son Jesus Christ towards *this infant*, let us faithfully and devoutly give thanks unto him, and say the Prayer which the Lord himself taught us.

OUR Father which art in heaven; Hallowed be thy Name. Thy kingdom come. Thy will be done in earth, As it is in heaven. Give us this day our daily bread. And forgive us our trespasses, As we forgive them that trespass against us. And lead us not into temptation; But deliver us from evil. Amen.

A LMIGHTY and everlasting God, heavenly Father, we give thee humble thanks, that thou hast vouchsafed to call us to the knowledge of thy grace, and faith in thee; Increase this knowledge, and confirm this faith in us evermore. Give thy holy Spirit to *this Infant*, that *he* being born again, and being made *an heir* of everlasting salvation, through our Lord Jesus Christ, may continue thy servant, and attain thy promise, through the same our Lord Jesus Christ thy Son, who liveth and reigneth with thee and the holy Spirit, now and for ever. *Amen.*

¶ *Then shall the Priest demand the Name of the child; which being by the Godfathers and Godmothers pronounced, the Minister shall say,*

D OST thou in the name of this child renounce the devil and all his works, the vain pomp and glory of this world, with all covetous desires of the same, and the carnal desires of the flesh, so that thou wilt not follow nor be led by them?

Answer. I renounce them all.

Minister.

D OST thou believe in God the Father Almighty, maker of heaven and earth?

And in Jesus Christ his onely begotten Son our Lord? And that he was conceived by the holy Ghost; born of the Virgin Mary; that he suffered under Pontius Pilate, was crucified, dead, and buried; that he went down into hell, and also did rise again the third day; that he ascended into heaven, and sitteth at the right hand of God the Father Almighty; and from thence shall come again at the end of the world to judge the quick and the dead?

And dost thou believe in the holy Ghost; the holy Catholick Church; the Communion of saints; the remission of sins; the resurrection of the flesh; and everlasting life after death?

Answer. All this I stedfastly believe.

Minister.

W ILT thou then obediently keep Gods holy will and commandments, and walk in the same all the dayes of thy life?

Answer. I will.

¶ *Then shall the Priest say,*

WE receive this child into the congregation of Christs flock,
† and do signe *him* with the signe of the cross,   † *The Priest*
in token that hereafter *he* shall not be ashamed to con-   *shall make a*
fess the faith of Christ crucified, and manfully to fight   *cross°   upon*
under his banner, against sin, the world, and the devil;   *the childs fore-*
and to continue Christs faithful souldier and servant   *head.*
unto *his* lives end. Amen.

¶ *Then shall the Priest say,*

SEEING now, dearly beloved brethren, that *this child is* by Baptism
regenerate and grafted into the body of Christs Church, let us give
thanks unto Almighty God for these benefits, and with one accord
make our prayers unto him, that *he* may lead the rest of *his* life according to this beginning.

¶ *Then shall the Priest say,*

WE yield thee most hearty thanks, most merciful Father, that it
hath pleased thee to regenerate *this infant* with thy holy Spirit,
to receive *him* for thine own child by adoption, and to incorporate *him*
into thy holy Church. And humbly we beseech thee to grant, that *he*
being dead unto sin, and living unto righteousness, and being buried
with Christ in his death, may crucifie the old man, and utterly abolish
the whole body of sin, and that as *he is* made *partaker* of the death of
thy Son, *he* may also be *partaker* of his resurrection; so that finally
with the residue of thy holy Church, *he* may be *an inheritour* of thine
everlasting kingdom, through Jesus Christ our Lord. *Amen.*

¶ *Then all standing up, the Minister shall make this exhortation to the*
Godfathers and Godmothers.

FORASMUCH as *this child* hath promised by you *his* sureties to
renounce the devil and all his works, to believe in God, and to
serve him; ye must remember that it is your parts and duties to see
that *this infant* be taught, so soon as *he* shall be able to learn, what
a solemn vow, promise, and profession *he hath* made by you. And that
he may know these things the better, ye shall call upon *him* to hear
Sermons, and chiefly ye shall provide that *he* may learn the Creed,
the Lords Prayer, and the ten Commandments in the vulgar tongue,
and all other things which a Christian ought to know and believe to
his souls health; and that this child may be vertuously brought up

to lead a godly and a Christian life; remembring alway, that Baptism doth represent unto us our profession, which is, to follow the example of our Saviour Christ, and to be made like unto him; that as he died and rose again for us; so should we who are baptized die from sin, and rise again unto righteousness, continually mortifying all our evil and corrupt affections, and daily proceeding in all vertue and godliness of living.

¶ *But if they which bring the infant to the Church do make such uncertain answers to the Priests questions, as that it cannot appear that the child was baptized with water,* In the Name of the Father, and of the Son, and of the Holy Ghost (*which are essential parts of Baptism*) *then let the Priest baptize it in the form before appointed for Publick Baptism of infants; saving that at the dipping of the child in the Font, he shall use this form of words.*

I F thou art not already baptized, *N.* I baptize thee in the name of the Father, and of the Son, and of the holy Ghost. Amen.

THE
MINISTRATION
OF
BAPTISM to such as are of riper years,
and able to answer for themselves.

¶ *When any such persons as are of riper years are to be baptized, timely notice shall be given to the Bishop, or whom he shall appoint for that purpose, a week before at the least, by the Parents, or some other discreet persons; that so due care may be taken for their examination, whether they be sufficiently instructed in the principles of the Christian Religion; and that they may be exhorted to prepare themselves with prayers and fasting for the receiving of this holy Sacrament.*

¶ *And if they shall be found fit, then the Godfathers and Godmothers (the people being assembled upon the Sunday or Holy-day appointed) shall be ready to present them at the Font immediately after the second Lesson, either at Morning or Evening Prayer, as the Curate in his discretion shall think fit.*

¶ *And standing there, the Priest shall ask whether any of the persons here presented be baptized or no: If they shall answer,* No, *then shall the Priest say thus,*

D EARLY beloved; Forasmuch as all men are conceived and born in sin, (and that which is born of the flesh is flesh) and they that are in the flesh cannot please God, but live in sin, committing many actual transgressions; and that our Saviour Christ saith, None can enter into the kingdom of God, except he be regenerate and born anew of water and of the holy Ghost; I beseech you to call upon God the Father, through our Lord Jesus Christ, that of his bounteous goodness he will grant to *these persons* that which by nature *they* cannot have; that *they* may be baptized with water and the holy Ghost, and received into Christs holy Church, and be made lively *members* of the same.

¶ *Then shall the Priest say,*

Let us pray.

(¶ *And here all the Congregation shall kneel.*)

A LMIGHTY and everlasting God, who of thy great mercy didst save Noah and his family in the ark from perishing by water, and also didst safely lead the children of Israel thy people through the Red Sea, figuring thereby thy holy baptism; and by the baptism of thy wel-beloved Son Jesus Christ in the river Jordan didst sanctifie the element of water to the mystical washing away of sin; We beseech thee for thine infinite mercies, that thou wilt mercifully look upon *these* thy *servants*; wash *them* and sanctifie *them* with the holy Ghost, that *they* being delivered from thy wrath may be received into the ark of Christs Church; and being stedfast in faith, joyful through hope, and rooted in charity, may so pass the waves of this troublesom world, that finally *they* may come to the land of everlasting life, there to reign with thee world without end, through Jesus Christ our Lord. *Amen.*

A LMIGHTY and immortal God, the aid of all that need, the helper of all that flee to thee for succour, the life of them that believe, and the resurrection of the dead; We call upon thee for *these persons*, that *they* coming to thy holy baptism, may receive remission of *their* sins by spiritual regeneration. Receive *them*, O Lord, as thou hast promised by thy wel-beloved Son, saying, Ask, and ye shall receive; seek, and ye shall find; knock, and it shall be opened unto you; So give now unto us that ask; let us that seek find; open the gate unto us that knock; that *these persons* may enjoy the everlasting benediction of thy heavenly washing, and may come to the eternal kingdom which thou hast promised by Christ our Lord. *Amen.*

¶ *Then shall the people stand up, and the Priest shall say,*

Hear the words of the Gospel, written by Saint John, in the third Chapter beginning at the first Verse.

THERE was a man of the Pharisees, named Nicodemus, a ruler of the Jews. The same came to Jesus by night, and said unto him, Rabbi, we know that thou art a teacher come from God; for no man can do these miracles that thou dost, except God be with him. Jesus answered and said unto him, Verily, verily I say unto thee, Except a man be born again, he cannot see the kingdom of God. Nicodemus saith unto him, How can a man be born when he is old? Can he enter the second time into his mothers womb, and be born? Jesus answered, Verily, verily I say unto thee, Except a man be born of water and of the Spirit he cannot enter into the kingdom of God. That which is born of the flesh is flesh; and that which is born of the Spirit is spirit. Marvel not that I said unto thee, Ye must be born again. The wind bloweth where it listeth, and thou hearest the sound thereof; but canst not tell whence it cometh, and whither it goeth: so is every one that is born of the Spirit. *John* 3.1

¶ *After which he shall say this exhortation following.*

BELOVED, ye hear in this Gospel the express words of our Saviour Christ, that except a man be born of water and of the Spirit, he cannot enter into the kingdom of God. Whereby ye may perceive the great necessity of this Sacrament, where it may be had. Likewise immediately before his ascension into heaven, (as we read in the last Chapter of Saint Marks Gospel) he gave command to his disciples, saying, Go ye into all the world, and preach the Gospel to every creature. He that believeth and is baptized shall be saved; but he that believeth not shall be damned. Which also sheweth unto us the great benefit we reap thereby. For which cause Saint Peter the Apostle, when upon his first preaching of the Gospel many were pricked at the heart, and said to him and the rest of the Apostles, Men and brethren, what shall we doe? replyed and said unto them, Repent and be baptized every one of you for the remission of sins, and ye shall receive the gift of the holy Ghost. For the promise is to you and your children, and to all that are afar off, even as many as the Lord our God shall call. And with many other words exhorted he them, saying, Save your selves from this untoward generation. For (as the same Apostle testifieth in another place) even Baptism doth also now save us (not the putting away of the filth of the flesh, but the answer of a good conscience towards God) by the resurrection of Jesus Christ. Doubt ye not therefore, but earnestly believe that he will favourably receive *these* present *persons*, truly repenting and coming unto him by faith, that he will grant *them* remission of *their* sins, and bestow upon *them* the holy Ghost; that he will give *them* the blessing of eternal life, and make *them partakers* of his everlasting kingdom.

Wherefore we being thus perswaded of the good will of our heavenly Father towards *these persons*, declared by his Son Jesus Christ; let us faithfully and devoutly give thanks to him and say,

A LMIGHTY and everlasting God, heavenly Father, we give thee humble thanks, for that thou hast vouchsafed to call us to the knowledge of thy grace, and faith in thee; Increase this knowledge, and confirm this faith in us evermore: Give thy holy Spirit to *these persons*, that *they* may be born again and be made *heirs* of everlasting salvation, through our Lord Jesus Christ, who liveth and reigneth with thee and the holy Spirit, now and for ever. *Amen.*

¶ *Then the Priest shall speak to the* persons *to be baptized on this wise.*

W ELL beloved, who are come hither desiring to receive holy Baptism, *ye* have heard how the congregation hath prayed that our Lord Jesus Christ would vouchsafe to receive you and bless you, to release you of your sins, to give you the kingdom of heaven and everlasting life. *Ye* have heard also that our Lord Jesus Christ hath promised in his holy word to grant all those things that we have prayed for; which promise he for his part will most surely keep and perform.

Wherefore, after this promise made by Christ, *ye* must also faithfully for your part promise in the presence of these your witnesses, and this whole congregation, that ye will renounce the devil and all his works, and constantly believe Gods holy word, and obediently keep his commandments.

¶ *Then shall the Priest demand of each of the persons to be baptized severally these questions following.*

Question.

D OST thou renounce the devil and all his works, the vain pomp and glory of the world, with all covetous desires of the same, and the carnal desires of the flesh, so that thou wilt not follow, nor be led by them?

Answer. I renounce them all.

Question.

D OST thou believe in God the Father Almighty, maker of heaven and earth?

And in Jesus Christ his only begotten Son our Lord? And that he was conceived by the holy Ghost; born of the Virgin Mary; that he suffered under Pontius Pilate, was crucified, dead, and buried; that he went down into hell, and also did rise again the third day; that he ascended into heaven, and sitteth at the right hand of God the Father Almighty; and from thence shall come again at the end of the world to judge the quick and the dead?

And dost thou believe in the holy Ghost; the holy Catholick Church; the Communion of saints; the remission of sins; the resurrection of the flesh; and everlasting life after death?

Answer. All this I stedfastly believe.

Question.

W ILT thou be baptized in this faith?
Answer. That is my desire.

Question.

W ILT thou then obediently keep Gods holy will and commandments, and walk in the same all the days of thy life?

Answer. I will endeavour so to do, God being my helper.

¶ *Then shall the Priest say,*

O MERCIFUL God, grant that the old Adam in *these persons* may be so buried, that the new man may be raised up in *them. Amen.*

Grant that all carnal affections may die in *them,* and that all things belonging to the Spirit, may live and grow in *them. Amen.*

Grant that *they* may have power and strength to have victory, and to triumph against the devil, the world, and the flesh. *Amen.*

Grant that *they* being here dedicated to thee by our office and ministry, may also be indued with heavenly vertues, and everlastingly rewarded through thy mercy, O blessed Lord God, who dost live and govern all things, world without end. *Amen.*

ALMIGHTY everliving God, whose most dearly beloved Son Jesus Christ, for the forgiveness of our sins did shed out of his most precious side both water and bloud, and gave commandment to his disciples, that they should go teach all nations, and baptize them In the Name of the Father, and of the Son, and of the holy Ghost; Regard, we beseech thee, the supplications of this congregation; sanctifie this water to the mystical washing away of sin: and grant that *the persons* now to be baptized therein, may receive the fulness of thy grace, and ever remain in the number of thy faithful and elect children, through Jesus Christ our Lord. *Amen.*

¶ *Then shall the Priest take each person to be baptized by the right hand, and placing him conveniently by the Font, according to his discretion, shall ask the Godfathers and Godmothers the Name; and then shall dip him in the water, or pour water upon him, saying,*

N. I baptize thee In the Name of the Father, and of the Son, and of the Holy Ghost. *Amen.*

¶ *Then shall the Priest say,*

WE receive this person into the congregation of Christs flock; † and do signe *him* with the signe of the cross, in token that hereafter *he* shall not be ashamed to confess the faith of Christ crucified, and manfully to fight under his banner against sin, the world, and the devil; and to continue Christs faithful souldier and servant unto *his* lives end. *Amen.*

† *Here the Priest shall make a cross upon the persons forehead.*

¶ *Then shall the Priest say,*

SEEING now, dearly beloved brethren, that *these persons are* regenerate and grafted into the body of Christs Church, let us give thanks unto Almighty God for these benefits, and with one accord make our prayers unto him, that *they* may lead the rest of *their* life according to this beginning.

¶ *Then shall be said the Lords Prayer, all kneeling.*

OUR Father which art in heaven; Hallowed be thy Name. Thy kingdom come. Thy will be done in earth, As it is in heaven. Give us this day our daily bread. And forgive us our trespasses, As we forgive them that trespass against us. And lead us not into temptation; But deliver us from evil. *Amen.*

W E yield thee humble thanks, O heavenly Father, that thou hast vouchsafed to call us to the knowledge of thy grace, and faith in thee; Increase this knowledge, and confirm this faith in us evermore. Give thy holy Spirit to *these persons*, that being now born again, and made *heirs* of everlasting salvation through our Lord Jesus Christ, *they* may continue thy *servants*, and attain thy promises, through the same Lord Jesus Christ thy Son, who liveth and reigneth with thee in the unity of the same holy Spirit everlastingly. *Amen.*

¶ *Then, all standing up, the Priest shall use this exhortation following; speaking to the Godfathers and Godmothers first.*

F ORASMUCH as *these persons* have promised in your presence to renounce the devil and all his works, to believe in God, and to serve him; ye must remember that it is your part and dutie to put *them* in mind what a solemn vow, promise and profession *they have* now made before this congregation, and especially before you *their* chosen witnesses. And ye are also to call upon *them* to use all diligence to be rightly instructed in Gods holy word, that so *they* may grow in grace, and in the knowledge of our Lord Jesus Christ, and live godly, righteously and soberly in this present world.

(¶ *And then, speaking to the new baptized* persons, *he shall proceed, and say,*)

A ND as for you, who have now by Baptism put on Christ, it is your part and duty also, being made the children of God, and of the light by faith in Jesus Christ, to walk answerably to your Christian calling, and as becometh the children of light: remembring alwayes that Baptism representeth unto us our profession; which is, to follow the example of our Saviour Christ, and to be made like unto him; that as he died, and rose again for us; so should we who are baptized, die from sin, and rise again unto righteousness, continually mortifying all our evil and corrupt affections, and daily proceeding in all vertue and godliness of living.

¶ *It is expedient that every person thus baptized should be confirmed by the Bishop so soon after his Baptism as conveniently may be; that so he may be admitted to the holy Communion.*

¶ *If any persons not baptized in their infancy shall be brought to be baptized before they come to years of discretion to answer for themselves; it may suffice to use the Office for Publick Baptism of infants, or (in case of extreme danger) the Office for Private Baptism, only changing the word* [Infant] *for* [Child or Person] *as occasion requireth.*

A CATECHISM,

That is to say,
an Instruction to be learned of every person,
before he be brought to be confirmed
by the Bishop.

Question.

WHAT is your Name?
 Answer. N. or *M.*

Question. Who gave you this Name?

Answer. My Godfathers and Godmothers in my Baptism, wherein I was made a member of Christ, the child of God, and an inheritor of the Kingdom of heaven.

Question. What did your Godfathers and Godmothers then for you?

Answer. They did promise and vow three things in my name. First, that I should renounce the devil and all his works, the pomps and vanity of this wicked world, and all the sinful lusts of the flesh. Secondly, that I should believe all the articles of the Christian faith. And thirdly, that I should keep Gods holy will and commandments, and walk in the same all the dayes of my life.

Question. Dost thou not think that thou art bound to believe, and to doe, as they have promised for thee?

Answer. Yes verily; and by Gods help so I will. And I heartily thank our heavenly Father, that he hath called me to this state of salvation, through Jesus Christ our Saviour. And I pray unto God to give me his grace, that I may continue in the same unto my lives end.

Catechist

Rehearse the Articles of thy belief.

Answer.

I BELIEVE in God the Father Almighty, Maker of heaven and earth: And in Jesus Christ his only Son our Lord, Who was conceived by the holy Ghost, Born of the Virgin Mary, Suffered under Pontius Pilate, Was crucified, dead and buried, He descended into hell, The third day he rose again from the dead, He ascended into heaven, And sitteth at the right hand of God the Father Almighty: From thence he shall come to judge the quick and the dead.

I believe in the holy Ghost; The holy Catholick Church; The Communion of saints; The forgiveness of sins; The resurrection of the body; And the life everlasting. Amen.

Question. What dost thou chiefly learn in these Articles of thy belief?

Answer. First, I learn to believe in God the Father, who hath made me, and all the world.

Secondly, in God the Son, who hath redeemed me, and all mankind.

Thirdly, in God the holy Ghost, who sanctifieth me, and all the elect people of God.

Question.

YOU said that your Godfathers and Godmothers did promise for you, that you should keep Gods commandments. Tell me how many there be?

Answer. Ten.

Question. Which be they?

Answer.

THE same which God spake in the twentieth Chapter of Exodus, saying, I am the Lord thy God, who brought thee out of the land of Egypt, out of the house of bondage.

I. Thou shalt have none other gods, but me.

II. Thou shalt not make to thy self any graven image,° nor the likeness of any thing that is in heaven above, or in the earth beneath, or in the water under the earth. Thou shalt not bow down to them, nor worship them. For I the Lord thy God am a jealous God, and visit the sins of the fathers upon the children unto the third and fourth generation of them that hate me, and shew mercy unto thousands in them that love me, and keep my commandments.

III. Thou shalt not take the Name of the Lord thy God in vain: for the Lord will not hold him guiltless that taketh his Name in vain.

IV. Remember that thou keep holy the Sabbath day.° Six dayes shalt thou labour, and do all that thou hast to doe; but the seventh day is the Sabbath of the Lord thy God. In it thou shalt doe no manner of work, thou, and thy son, and thy daughter, thy man-servant and thy maid-servant, thy cattel and the stranger that is within thy gates. For in six dayes the Lord made heaven and earth, the sea, and all that in them is, and rested the seventh day; wherefore the Lord blessed the seventh day, and hallowed it.

V. Honour thy father and thy mother, that thy dayes may be long in the land which the Lord thy God giveth thee.

VI. Thou shalt do no murder.

VII. Thou shalt not commit adultery.

VIII. Thou shalt not steal.

IX. Thou shalt not bear false witness against thy neighbour.

X. Thou shalt not covet thy neighbours house, thou shalt not covet thy neighbours wife, nor his servant, nor his maid, nor his ox, nor his ass, nor any thing that is his.

Question.

What dost thou chiefly learn by these commandments?

Answer. I learn two things: my duty towards God, and my duty towards my neighbour.

Question. What is thy duty towards God?

Answer. My duty towards God, is to believe in him, to fear him, and to love him with all my heart, with all my mind, with all my soul, and with all my strength; to worship him, to give him thanks, to put my whole trust in him, to call upon him, to honour his holy Name and his Word, and to serve him truly all the days of my life.

Question. What is thy duty towards thy neighbour?

Answer. My duty towards my neighbour, is to love him as my self, and to do to all men, as I would they should do unto me. To love, honour, and succour my father and mother. To honour and obey the King, and all that are put in authority under him. To submit my self to all my governours, teachers, spiritual pastours and masters. To order my self lowly and reverently to all my betters. To hurt no body by word, or deed. To be true and just in all my dealing. To bear no malice nor hatred in my heart. To keep my hands from picking and stealing, and my tongue from evil speaking, lying and slandering. To keep my body in temperance, soberness, and chastity. Not to covet nor desire other mens goods; but to learn and labour truly to get mine own living, and to do my duty in that state of life, unto which it shall please God to call me.

Catechist

My good child, know this, that thou art not able to do these things of thy self, nor to walk in the Commandments of God, and to serve him without his special grace, which thou must learn at all times to call for by diligent prayer. Let me hear therefore if thou canst say the Lords Prayer.

Answer.

OUR Father which art in heaven; Hallowed be thy Name. Thy kingdom come. Thy will be done in earth, As it is in heaven. Give us this day our daily bread. And forgive us our trespasses, As we forgive them that trespass against us. And lead us not into temptation: But deliver us from evil. Amen.

Question. What desirest thou of God in this Prayer?

Answer. I desire my Lord God our heavenly Father, who is the giver of all goodness, to send his grace unto me, and to all people, that we may worship him, serve him, and obey him as we ought to do. And I pray unto God, that he will send us all things that be needful both for our souls and bodies; and that he will be merciful unto us, and forgive us our sins; and that it will please him to save and defend us in all dangers ghostly and bodily; and that he will keep us from all sin and wickedness and from our ghostly enemy, and from everlasting death. And this I trust he will doe of his mercy and goodness, through our Lord Jesus Christ. And therefore I say, Amen. So be it.

Question.

HOW many Sacraments hath Christ ordained in his Church?°
Answer. Two only, as generally necessary to salvation, that is to say, Baptism, and the Supper of the Lord.

Question. What meanest thou by this word *Sacrament?*

Answer. I mean an outward and visible signe of an inward and spiritual grace,° given unto us, ordained by Christ himself, as a means whereby we receive the same, and a pledge to assure us thereof.

Question. How many parts are there in a Sacrament?

Answer. Two: the outward visible signe, and the inward spiritual grace.

Question. What is the outward visible signe or form in Baptism?

Answer. Water: wherein the person is baptized, *In the Name of the Father, and of the Son, and of the Holy Ghost.*

Question. What is the inward and spiritual grace?

Answer. A death unto sin, and a new birth unto righteousness: for being by nature born in sin, and the children of wrath, we are hereby made the children of grace.

Question. What is required of persons to be baptized?

Answer. Repentance, whereby they forsake sin; and faith, whereby they stedfastly believe the promises of God, made to them in that Sacrament.

Question. Why then are infants baptized, when by reason of their tender age they cannot perform them?

Answer. Because they promise them both by their sureties:° which promise, when they come to age, themselves are bound to perform.

Question. Why was the Sacrament of the Lords Supper ordained?

Answer. For the continual remembrance of the sacrifice of the death of Christ, and of the benefits which we receive thereby.

Question. What is the outward part or signe of the Lords Supper?

Answer. Bread and wine, which the Lord hath commanded to be received.

Question. What is the inward part, or thing signified?

Answer. The body and bloud of Christ, which are verily and indeed taken and received by the faithful in the Lords Supper.

Question. What are the benefits whereof we are partakers thereby?

Answer. The strengthening and refreshing of our souls by the body and bloud of Christ, as our bodies are by the bread and wine.

Question. What is required of them who come to the Lords Supper?

Answer. To examine themselves, whether they repent them truly of their former sins, stedfastly purposing to lead a new life; have a lively faith in Gods mercy through Christ, with a thankful remembrance of his death; and be in charity with all men.

¶ *The Curate of every Parish shall diligently upon Sundayes and Holydayes, after the second Lesson at Evening Prayer openly in the Church instruct and examine so many Children of his Parish sent unto him, as he shall think convenient, in some part of this Catechism.*

¶ *And all Fathers, Mothers, Masters and Dames, shall cause their children, servants and prentices (which have not learned their Catechism) to come to the Church at the time appointed, and obediently to hear, and be ordered by the Curate, until such time as they have learned all that is here appointed for them to learn.*

¶ *So soon as Children are come to a competent age, and can say in their Mother tongue the Creed, the Lords Prayer, and the ten Commandments; and also can answer to the other questions of this short Catechism; they shall be brought to the Bishop. And every one shall have a Godfather, or a Godmother, as a witness of their Confirmation.*

¶ *And whensoever the Bishop shall give knowledge for children to be brought*
unto him for their Confirmation, the Curate of every Parish shall either
bring, or send in writing, with his hand subscribed thereunto, the names of
all such persons within his Parish, as he shall think fit to be presented to the
Bishop to be confirmed. And, if the Bishop approve of them, he shall confirm
them in manner following.

The ORDER

OF

Confirmation

OR

Laying on of hands upon those that are baptized
and come to years of discretion.

¶ *Upon the day appointed all that are to be then confirmed, being placed, and*
standing in Order before the Bishop; he (or some other Minister appointed by
him) shall read this Preface following.

To the end that Confirmation may be ministered° to the more
edifying of such as shall receive it, the Church hath thought good
to order, That none hereafter shall be Confirmed, but such as can
say the Creed, the Lords Prayer, and the ten Commandments; and
can also answer to such other questions, as in the short Catechism
are contained: Which Order is very convenient to be observed, to the
end that children, being now come to the years of discretion,° and
having learned what their Godfathers and Godmothers promised for
them in Baptism, they may themselves with their own mouth and
consent openly before the Church ratifie and confirm the same; and
also promise that by the grace of God they will evermore endeavour
themselves faithfully to observe such things as they by their own confession have assented unto.

¶ *Then shall the Bishop say,*

Do ye here in the presence of God° and of this congregation renew
the solemn promise and vow that was made in your name at your
Baptism; ratifying and confirming the same in your own persons,
and acknowledging your selves bound to believe and to doe all those

things, which your Godfathers and Godmothers then undertook for you?

¶ *And every one shall audibly answer,*

I doe.

The Bishop

O UR help is in the Name of the Lord;
    Answer. Who hath made heaven and earth.
Bishop. Blessed be the Name of the Lord.
Answer. Henceforth world without end.
Bishop. Lord, hear our prayers.
Answer. And let our cry come unto thee.

The Bishop.

Let us pray.

A LMIGHTY and everliving God, who hast vouchsafed to regenerate these thy servants by water and the holy Ghost, and hast given unto them forgiveness of all their sins: Strengthen them, we beseech thee, O Lord, with the holy Ghost the Comforter, and daily increase in them thy manifold gifts of grace; the spirit of wisdom and under-standing; the spirit of counsel and ghostly strength; the spirit of knowledge and true godliness; and fill them, O Lord, with the spirit of thy holy fear, now and for ever. *Amen.*

¶ *Then all of them in order kneeling before the Bishop,°* he shall lay his
hand upon the head of every one severally, saying,

D EFEND, O Lord, this thy Child [*or* this thy Servant] with thy heavenly grace, that *he* may continue thine for ever: and daily increase in thy holy Spirit more and more, until *he* come unto thy everlasting kingdom. Amen.

¶ *Then shall the Bishop say,*

The Lord be with you.
Answer. And with thy spirit.

¶ *And (all kneeling down) the Bishop shall add,*

Let us pray.

O UR Father which art in heaven;° Hallowed be thy Name. Thy kingdom come. Thy will be done in earth, As it is in heaven. Give us this day our daily bread. And forgive us our trespasses, As we forgive them that trespass against us. And lead us not into temptation: But deliver us from evil. Amen.

¶ *And this Collect.*

ALMIGHTY and everliving God, who makest us both to will and to do those things that be good and acceptable unto thy divine Majesty; We make our humble supplications unto thee for these thy servants, upon whom (after the example of thy holy Apostles) we have now laid our hands, to certifie them (by this sign) of thy favour and gracious goodness towards them. Let thy Fatherly hand, we beseech thee, ever be over them; let thy holy Spirit ever be with them; and so lead them in the knowledge and obedience of thy word, that in the end they may obtain everlasting life, through our Lord Jesus Christ, who with thee and the holy Ghost liveth and reigneth, ever one God, world without end. *Amen.*

O ALMIGHTY Lord, and everlasting God,° vouchsafe, we beseech thee, to direct, sanctifie and govern both our hearts and bodies in the ways of thy laws, and in the works of thy commandments, that through thy most mighty protection, both here and ever, we may be preserved in body and soul, through our Lord and Saviour Jesus Christ. *Amen.*

¶ *Then the Bishop shall bless them, saying thus,*

THE Blessing of God Almighty, the Father, the Son, and the holy Ghost, be upon you, and remain with you for ever. *Amen.*

¶ *And there shall none be admitted to the holy Communion, until such time as he be confirmed, or be ready and desirous to be confirmed.*

THE FORM
OF
SOLEMNIZATION
OF
MATRIMONY.

¶ *F*IRST *the Banns of all that are to be married together, must be published in the Church three several Sundaies or Holy-daies, in the time of Divine Service, immediately before the sentences for the Offertory;° the Curate saying after the accustomed manner,*

I publish the Banns of marriage° between *M*. of — and *N*. of —. If any of you know cause or just impediment,° why these two persons should not be joyned together in holy matrimony, ye are to declare it: This is the first [*second*, or *third*] time of asking.

¶ *And if the persons that are to be married, dwell in divers Parishes, the Banns must be asked in both Parishes; and the Curate of the one Parish shall not solemnize Matrimony betwixt them, without a Certificate of the Banns being thrice asked, from the Curate of the other Parish.*

¶ *At the day and time appointed for solemnization of Matrimony, the persons to be married shall come into the body of the Church with their friends and neighbours: and there standing together, the man on the right hand,° and the woman on the left, the Priest shall say,*

D EARLY beloved, we are gathered together here in the sight of God, and in the face of this congregation, to joyn together this man and this woman in holy Matrimony, which is an honourable estate instituted of God in the time of mans innocency, signifying unto us the mystical union that is betwixt Christ and his Church; which holy estate Christ adorned and beautified with his presence, and first miracle that he wrought in Cana of Galilee, and is commended of Saint Paul to be honourable among all men; and therefore is not by any to be enterprized, nor taken in hand unadvisedly, lightly, or wantonly, to satisfie mens carnal lusts and appetites, like brute beasts that have no understanding; but reverently, discreetly, advisedly, soberly, and in the fear of God, duly considering the causes for which matrimony was ordained.

First, it was ordained for the procreation of children, to be brought up in the fear and nurture of the Lord, and to the praise of his holy Name.°

Secondly, it was ordained for a remedy against sin, and to avoid fornication, that such persons as have not the gift of continency, might marry, and keep themselves undefiled members of Christs body.

Thirdly, It was ordained for the mutual society, help and comfort that the one ought to have of the other, both in prosperity and adversity: Into which holy estate these two persons present come now to be joyned. Therefore if any man can shew any just cause why they may not lawfully be joyned together, let him now speak, or else hereafter for ever hold his peace.

¶ *And also, speaking unto the persons that shall be married, he shall say,*

I REQUIRE and charge you both° (as ye will answer at the dreadful day of judgement, when the secrets of all hearts shall be disclosed) that if either of you know any impediment, why ye may not be lawfully joyned together in matrimony, ye do now confess it. For be ye well assured, that so many as are coupled together otherwise than Gods Word doth allow, are not joyned together by God, neither is their Matrimony lawful.

¶ *At which day of marriage, if any man do alledge and declare any impediment why they may not be coupled together in matrimony, by Gods law, or the Laws of this Realm, and will be bound, and sufficient sureties with him, to the parties, or else put in a caution (to the full value of such charges as the persons to be married do thereby sustain) to prove his allegation: Then the solemnization must be deferred until such time as the truth be tryed.*

¶ *If no impediment be alledged, then shall the Curate say unto the man,*

N. WILT thou have this woman to thy wedded wife, to live together after Gods ordinance, in the holy estate of matrimony? Wilt thou love her, comfort her, honour and keep her in sickness and in health, and forsaking all other, keep thee only unto her, so long as ye both shall live?

¶ *The man shall answer,*

I will.

¶ *Then shall the Priest say unto the woman,*

N. WILT thou have this man to thy wedded husband, to live together after Gods ordinance, in the holy estate of matrimony? Wilt thou obey him, and serve him, love, honour and keep him in sickness and in health, and forsaking all other, keep thee only unto him, so long as ye both shall live?

¶ *The Woman shall answer,*

I will.

¶ *Then shall the Minister say,*

Who giveth this woman to be married to this man?

¶ *Then shall they give their troth to each other in this manner.*

¶ *The Minister receiving the woman at her fathers or friends hands, shall cause the man with his right hand to take the woman by her right hand, and to say after him as followeth,°*

I N. take thee N. to my wedded wife, to have and to hold from this day forward, for better for worse, for richer for poorer, in sickness and in health, to love and to cherish, till death us do part, according to Gods holy ordinance; and thereto I plight thee my troth.

¶ *Then shall they loose their hands, and the woman with her right hand taking the man by his right hand, shall likewise say after the Minister,*

I N. take thee N. to my wedded husband, to have and to hold from this day forward, for better for worse, for richer for poorer, in sickness and in health, to love, cherish, and to obey, till death us do part,° according to Gods holy ordinance; and thereto I give thee my troth.

¶ *Then shall they again loose their hands, and the man shall give unto the woman a ring, laying the same upon the book, with the accustomed duty to the Priest and Clerk. And the Priest taking the ring, shall deliver it unto the man, to put it upon the fourth finger of the womans left hand. And the man holding the ring there,° and taught by the Priest, shall say,*

WITH this ring I thee wed, with my body I thee worship,° and with all my worldly goods I thee endow: In the Name of the Father, and of the Son, and of the holy Ghost. Amen.

¶ *Then the man leaving the ring upon the fourth finger of the womans left hand, they shall both kneel down,° and the Minister shall say,*

Let us pray.

O ETERNAL God, creatour and preserver of all mankind, giver of all spiritual grace, the author of everlasting life; Send thy blessing upon these thy servants, this man and this woman, whom we bless in thy Name; that, as Isaac and Rebecca lived faithfully together, so these persons may surely perform and keep the vow and covenant betwixt them made, (whereof this ring given and received is a token and pledge) and may ever remain in perfect love and peace together, and live according to thy laws, through Jesus Christ our Lord. *Amen.*

¶ *Then shall the Priest join their right hands together, and say,*

Those whom God hath joyned together, let no man put asunder.

¶ *Then shall the Minister speak unto the people.*

F ORASMUCH as *N.* and *N.* have consented together in holy wedlock, and have witnessed the same before God and this company, and thereto have given and pledged their troth either to other, and have declared the same by giving and receiving of a ring, and by joyning of hands; I pronounce that they be man and wife together, In the Name of the Father, and of the Son, and of the holy Ghost. Amen.

¶ *And the Minister shall add this blessing.*

G OD the Father, God the Son, God the holy Ghost, bless, preserve and keep you, the Lord mercifully with his favour look upon you; and so fill you with all spiritual benediction and grace, that ye may so live together in this life, that in the world to come ye may have life everlasting. *Amen.*

¶ *Then the Minister or Clerks going to the Lords table, shall say or sing this Psalm following.*

Beati omnes.

B LESSED are all they that fear the Lord: and walk in his ways. For thou shalt eat the labour of thine hands: O well is thee, and happy shalt thou be.　　　　　　　　　　　　　　　　　*Ps.* 128
　　Thy wife shall be as the fruitful vine: upon the walls of thyne house.
　　Thy children like the olive-branches: round about thy table.
　　Lo, thus shall the man be blessed: that feareth the Lord.

The Lord from out of Sion shall so bless thee: that thou shalt see Jerusalem in prosperity all thy life long;

Yea, that thou shalt see thy childrens children: and peace upon Israel.

Glory be to the Father, and to the Son: and to the holy Ghost;

As it was in the beginning, is now, and ever shall be: world without end. Amen.

¶ *Or this Psalm.*

Deus misereatur.

G OD be merciful unto us, and bless us: and shew us the light of his countenance, and be merciful unto us.   *Ps.* 67

That thy way may be known upon earth: thy saving health among all nations.

Let the people praise thee, O God: yea, let all the people praise thee.

O let the nations rejoyce and be glad: for thou shalt judge the folk righteously, and govern the nations upon earth.

Let the people praise thee, O God: yea, let all the people praise thee.

Then shall the earth bring forth her increase: and God, even our own God shall give us his blessing.

God shall bless us: and all the ends of the world shall fear him.

Glory be to the Father, and to the Son: and to the holy Ghost;

As it was in the beginning, is now, and ever shall be: world without end. Amen.

¶ *The Psalm ended, and the man and the woman kneeling before the Lords Table, the Priest standing at the Table, and turning his face towards them, shall say,*

Lord, have mercy upon us.

Answer. Christ, have mercy upon us.

Minister. Lord, have mercy upon us.

O UR Father which art in heaven, Hallowed be thy Name. Thy kingdom come. Thy will be done in earth, As it is in heaven. Give us this day our daily bread. And forgive us our trespasses, As we forgive them that trespass against us. And lead us not into temptation: But deliver us from evil. Amen.

Minister. O Lord, save thy servant, and thy handmaid;

Answer. Who put their trust in thee.

Minister. O Lord, send them help from thy holy place;

Answer. And evermore defend them.

Minister. Be unto them a tower of strength;

Answer. From the face of their enemy.

Minister. O Lord, hear our prayer.

Answer. And let our cry come unto thee.

Minister.

O GOD of Abraham, God of Isaac, God of Jacob, bless these thy servants, and sow the seed of eternal life in their hearts, that whatsoever in thy holy Word they shall profitably learn, they may in deed fulfil the same. Look, O Lord, mercifully upon them from heaven, and bless them. And as thou didst send thy blessing upon Abraham and Sarah, to their great comfort; so vouchsafe to send thy blessing upon these thy servants, that they obeying thy will, and alway being in safety under thy protection, may abide in thy love unto their lives end, through Jesus Christ our Lord. *Amen.*

¶ *This Prayer next following shall be omitted, where the woman is past child-bearing.*

O MERCIFUL Lord and heavenly Father, by whose gracious gift mankind is increased; We beseech thee assist with thy blessing these two persons, that they may both be fruitful in procreation of children, and also live together so long in godly love and honesty, that they may see their children Christianly and vertuously brought up,° to thy praise and honour, through Jesus Christ our Lord. *Amen.*

O GOD, who by thy mighty power hast made all things of nothing, who also (after other things set in order) didst appoint that out of man (created after thine own image and similitude) woman should take her beginning; and knitting them together, didst teach that it should never be lawful to put asunder those whom thou by matrimony hadst made one: O God, who hast consecrated the state of matrimony to such an excellent mystery, that in it is signified and represented the spiritual marriage and unity betwixt Christ and his Church; Look mercifully upon these thy servants, that both this man may love his wife, according to thy Word, as Christ did love his spouse the Church, who gave himself for it, loving and cherishing it even as his own flesh, and also that this woman may be loving and amiable, faithful and obedient to her husband, and in all quietness, sobriety, and peace, be a follower of holy and godly matrons. O Lord, bless them both, and grant them to inherit thy everlasting kingdom, through Jesus Christ our Lord. *Amen.*

¶ *Then shall the Priest say,*

ALMIGHTY God who at the beginning did create our first parents, Adam and Eve, and did sanctifie and joyn them together in marriage; Pour upon you the riches of his grace, sanctifie and bless you, that ye may please him both in body and soul, and live together in holy love unto your lives end. *Amen.*

¶ *After which, if there be no Sermon declaring the duties of man and wife, the Minister shall read as followeth.*

ALL ye that are married, or that intend to take the holy estate of matrimony upon you, hear what the holy Scripture doth say as touching the duty of husbands towards their wives, and wives towards their husbands.

Saint Paul in his Epistle to the Ephesians, the Fifth Chapter, doth give this commandment to all married men, Husbands, love your wives, even as Christ also loved the Church, and gave himself for it, that he might sanctifie and cleanse it with the washing of water, by the word; that he might present it to himself a glorious Church, not having spot or wrinkle, or any such thing; but that it should be holy and without blemish. So ought men to love their wives as their own bodies: He that loveth his wife, loveth himself. For no man ever yet hated his own flesh, but nourisheth and cherisheth it, even as the Lord the Church: For we are members of his body, of his flesh, and of his bones. For this cause shall a man leave his father and mother, and shall be joyned unto his wife, and they two shall be one flesh. This is a great mystery; but I speak concerning Christ and the Church. Nevertheless, let every one of you in particular, so love his wife, even as himself.

Likewise the same Saint Paul writing to the Colossians, speaketh thus to all men that are married, Husbands, love your wives, and be not bitter against them.

Hear also what Saint Peter the Apostle of Christ, who was himself a married man, saith unto them that are married, Ye husbands, dwell with your wives according to knowledge, giving honour unto the wife, as unto the weaker vessel, and as being heirs together of the grace of life, that your prayers be not hindred.

Hitherto ye have heard the duty of the husband toward the wife. Now likewise, ye wives, hear and learn your duties toward your husbands, even as it is plainly set forth in holy Scripture.

Saint Paul in the aforenamed Epistle to the Ephesians, teacheth you thus; Wives, submit your selves unto your own husbands, as unto the Lord. For the husband is the head of the wife, even as Christ is the head of the Church: and he is the Saviour of the body. Therefore as the Church is subject unto Christ, so let the wives be to their own husbands in every thing. And again he saith, Let the wife see that she reverence her husband.

And in his Epistle to the Colossians, Saint Paul giveth you this short lesson, Wives, submit your selves unto your own husbands, as it is fit in the Lord.

Saint Peter also doth instruct you very well, thus saying, Ye wives, be in subjection to your own husbands; that if any obey not the word, they also may without the word be won by the conversation of the wives; while they behold your chaste conversation coupled with fear. Whose adorning let it not be that outward adorning of plaiting the hair, and of wearing of gold, or of putting on of apparel; but let it be the hidden man of the heart, in that which is not corruptible, even the ornament of a meek and quiet spirit, which is in the sight of God of great price. For after this manner in the old time, the holy women also who trusted in God, adorned themselves, being in subjection unto their own husbands; even as Sarah obeyed Abraham, calling him Lord; whose daughters ye are as long as ye do well, and are not afraid with any amazement.

¶ *It is convenient that the new married persons should receive the holy Communion° at the time of their marriage, or at the first opportunity after their marriage.*

The ORDER
For the
VISITATION OF THE SICK.

¶ *When any person is sick, notice shall be given thereof to the Minister° of the Parish; who, coming into the sick persons house, shall say,*

PEACE be to this house, and to all that dwell in it.

¶ *When he cometh into the sick mans presence he shall say,*
kneeling down,

REMEMBER not, Lord, our iniquities, nor the iniquities of our fore-fathers: Spare us, good Lord, spare thy people whom thou hast redeemed with thy most precious bloud, and be not angry with us for ever.

Answer. Spare us, good Lord.°

¶ *Then the Minister shall say,*
Let us pray.

Lord, have mercy upon us.
Christ, have mercy upon us.
Lord, have mercy upon us.

OUR Father which art in heaven, Hallowed be thy Name. Thy kingdom come. Thy will be done in earth, As it is in heaven. Give us this day our daily bread. And forgive us our trespasses, As we forgive them that trespass against us. And lead us not into temptation: But deliver us from evil. Amen.

Minister. O Lord, save thy servant;
Answer. Which putteth *his* trust in thee.
Minister. Send *him* help from thy holy place;
Answer. And evermore mightily defend *him.*
Minister. Let the enemy have no advantage of *him*;
Answer. Nor the wicked approach to hurt *him.*
Minister. Be unto *him*, O Lord, a strong tower;
Answer. From the face of *his* enemy.
Minister. O Lord, hear our prayers.
Answer. And let our cry come unto thee.

Minister.

O LORD, look down from heaven, behold, visit and relieve this thy servant. Look upon *him* with the eyes of thy mercy, give *him* comfort and sure confidence in thee, defend *him* from the danger of the enemy, and keep *him* in perpetual peace and safety, through Jesus Christ our Lord. *Amen.*

HEAR us, Almighty and most merciful God and Saviour; extend thy accustomed goodness to this thy servant who is grieved with sickness. Sanctifie, we beseech thee, this thy fatherly correction to *him*;° that the sense of *his* weakness may add strength to *his* faith, and seriousness to *his* repentance. That if it shall be thy good pleasure to restore *him* to *his* former health, *he* may lead the residue of *his* life in thy fear, and to thy glory: or else give *him* grace so to take thy visitation, that, after this painful life ended *he* may dwell with thee in life everlasting, through Jesus Christ our Lord. *Amen.*

¶ *Then shall the Minister exhort the sick person after this form,*
or other like.

DEARLY beloved, know this, that Almighty God is the Lord of life and death, and of all things to them pertaining, as youth, strength, health, age, weakness, and sickness. Wherefore, whatsoever your sickness is, know you certainly that it is Gods visitation. And for what cause soever this sickness is sent unto you, whether it be to try your patience for the example of others, and that your faith may be found in the day of the Lord laudable, glorious, and honourable, to the increase of glory and endless felicity; or else it be sent unto you to correct and amend in you whatsoever doth offend the eyes of your heavenly Father; know you certainly that if you truly repent you of your sins, and bear your sickness patiently, trusting in Gods mercy, for his dear Son Jesus Christs sake, and render unto him humble thanks for his fatherly visitation, submitting yourself wholly unto his will, it shall turn to your profit, and help you forward in the right way that leadeth unto everlasting life.

¶ *If the person visited be very sick, then the Curate may end his exhort-*
ation in this place, or else proceed.

TAKE therefore in good part the chastisement of the Lord: For (as Saint Paul saith in the twelfth Chapter to the Hebrews) whom the Lord loveth he chastneth, and scourgeth every son whom he receiveth. If ye endure chastning, God dealeth with you as with sons; for what son is he whom the father chastneth not? But if ye be without chastisement, whereof all are partakers, then are ye bastards, and not sons. Furthermore, we have had fathers of our flesh, which corrected us, and we gave them reverence: shall we not much rather be in subjection unto the Father of Spirits, and live? For they verily for a few days chastned us after their own pleasure; but he for our profit, that we might be partakers of his holiness. These words, good *brother*, are written in holy Scripture for our comfort and instruction, that we should patiently, and with thanksgiving bear our heavenly Fathers correction, whensoever by any manner of adversity it shall please his gracious goodness to visit us. And there should be no greater comfort to Christian persons, than to be made like unto Christ, by suffering patiently adversities, troubles, and sicknesses. For he himself went not up to joy, but first he suffered pain; he entred not into his glory before he was crucified. So truly our way to eternal joy is to suffer here with Christ; and our door to enter into eternal life is gladly to die with Christ; that we may rise again from death, and dwell with him in everlasting life. Now therefore taking your sickness, which is thus profitable for you, patiently, I exhort you, in the Name of God, to remember the profession which you made unto God in your baptism. And for as much as after this life there is an account to be given unto the righteous Judge, by whom all must be judged without respect of persons; I require you to examine yourself and your estate, both toward God and man; so that accusing and condemning your self for your own faults, you may find mercy at our heavenly Fathers hand for Christs sake, and not be accused and condemned in that fearful judgement. Therefore I shall rehearse to you the Articles of our Faith, that you may know whether you do believe as a Christian man should, or no.

¶ *Here the Minister shall rehearse the Articles of the Faith, saying thus,*

Dost thou believe in God the Father Almighty, maker of heaven and earth?

And in Jesus Christ his only begotten Son our Lord? And that he was conceived by the holy Ghost, born of the Virgin Mary; that he suffered under Pontius Pilate, was crucified, dead and buried; that he went down into hell, and also did rise again the third day; that he ascended into heaven, and sitteth at the right hand of God the Father

Almighty, and from thence shall come again at the end of the world to judge the quick and the dead?

And dost thou believe in the holy Ghost; the holy Catholick Church; the Communion of saints; the remission of sins; the resurrection of the flesh; and everlasting life after death?

¶ *The sick person shall answer,*

All this I stedfastly believe.°

¶ *Then shall the Minister examine whether he repent him truly of his sins,° and be in charity with all the world; exhorting him to forgive from the bottom of his heart all persons that have offended him, and if he hath offended any other, to ask them forgiveness; and where he hath done injury or wrong to any man, that he make amends to the uttermost of his power. And if he hath not before disposed of his goods, let him then be admonished to make his will, and to declare his debts, what he oweth, and what is owing unto him, for the better discharging of his conscience, and the quietness of his executors. But men should often be put in remembrance° to take order for the settling of their temporal estates, whilst they are in health.*

¶ *These words before rehearsed, may be said before the Minister begin his prayer, as he shall see cause.*

¶ *The Minister should not omit earnestly to move such sick persons as are of ability, to be liberal to the poor.*

¶ *Here shall the sick person be moved to make a special confession of his sins, if he feel his conscience troubled with any weighty matter. After which confession, the Priest shall absolve him (if he humbly and heartily desire it)° after this sort.*

OUR Lord Jesus Christ, who hath left power to his Church to absolve all sinners who truly repent and believe in him, of his great mercy forgive thee thine offences: And by his authority committed to me, I absolve thee from all thy sins, In the Name of the Father, and of the Son, and of the holy Ghost. Amen.

¶ *And then the Priest shall say the Collect following.*

Let us pray.

O MOST merciful God, who according to the multitude of thy mercies, dost so put away the sins of those who truly repent, that thou remembrest them no more; Open thine eye of mercy upon this thy servant, who most earnestly desireth pardon and forgiveness. Renew in *him* (most loving Father) whatsoever hath been decayed by the fraud and malice of the devil, or by *his* own carnal will and frailness;

preserve and continue this sick member in the unity of the Church; consider *his* contrition, accept *his* tears, asswage *his* pain, as shall seem to thee most expedient for *him*. And forasmuch as *he* putteth *his* full trust only in thy mercy, impute not unto *him his* former sins; but strengthen *him* with thy blessed Spirit,° and when thou art pleased to take *him* hence, take *him* unto thy favour, through the merits of thy most dearly beloved Son Jesus Christ our Lord. *Amen.*

¶ *Then shall the Minister say this Psalm,*

In te, Domine, speravi.

IN thee, O Lord, have I put my trust, let me never be put to confusion: but rid me and deliver me in thy righteousness; incline thine ear unto me, and save me.   *Ps.* 71

Be thou my strong hold, whereunto I may alway resort: thou hast promised to help me, for thou art my house of defence, and my castle.

Deliver me, O my God, out of the hand of the ungodly: out of the hand of the unrighteous and cruel man.

For thou, O Lord God, art the thing that I long for: thou art my hope even from my youth.

Through thee have I been holden up ever since I was born: thou art he that took me out of my mothers womb; my praise shall alway be of thee.

I am become as it were a monster unto many: but my sure trust is in thee.

O let my mouth be filled with thy praise: that I may sing of thy glory and honour all the day long.

Cast me not away in the time of age: forsake me not when my strength faileth me.

For mine enemies speak against me, and they that lay wait for my soul, take their counsel together, saying: God hath forsaken him, persecute him, and take him; for there is none to deliver him.

Go not far from me, O God: my God, haste thee to help me.

Let them be confounded and perish that are against my soul: let them be covered with shame and dishonour, that seek to do me evil.

As for me, I will patiently abide alway: and will praise thee more and more.

My mouth shall daily speak of thy righteousness and salvation: for I know no end thereof.

I will go forth in the strength of the Lord God: and will make mention of thy righteousness only.

Thou, O God, hast taught me from my youth up until now: therefore will I tell of thy wondrous works.

Forsake me not, O God, in mine old age, when I am gray-headed: until I have shewed thy strength unto this generation, and thy power to all them that are yet for to come.

Thy righteousness, O God,° is very high, and great things are they that thou hast done: O God, who is like unto thee?

Glory be to the Father, and to the Son: and to the Holy Ghost;

As it was in the beginning, is now and ever shall be: world without end. Amen.

¶ *Adding this.*

O SAVIOUR of the world, who by thy Cross and precious bloud hast redeemed us, save us and help us, we humbly beseech thee, O Lord.

¶ *Then shall the Minister say,*

THE Almighty Lord, who is a most strong tower to all them that put their trust in him, to whom all things in heaven, in earth and under the earth, do bow and obey, be now and evermore thy defence, and make thee know and feel, that there is none other name under heaven given to man, in whom, and through whom thou mayest receive health and salvation, but only the Name of our Lord Jesus Christ. Amen.

¶ *And after that shall say,*

UNTO Gods gracious mercy and protection° we commit thee. The Lord bless thee and keep thee. The Lord make his face to shine upon thee, and be gracious unto thee. The Lord lift up his countenance upon thee, and give thee peace, both now and evermore. *Amen.*

¶ *A Prayer for a sick Child.*°

O ALMIGHTY God and merciful Father, to whom alone belong the issues of life and death; Look down from heaven, we humbly beseech thee, with the eyes of mercy upon this child now lying upon the bed of sickness: Visit *him*, O Lord, with thy salvation; deliver *him* in thy good appointed time from *his* bodily pain, and save *his* soul for thy mercies sake. That if it shall be thy pleasure to prolong *his* days here on earth, *he* may live to thee, and be an instrument of thy glory, by serving thee faithfully, and doing good in *his* generation; or else receive *him* into those heavenly habitations, where the souls of them that sleep in the Lord Jesus enjoy perpetual rest and felicity. Grant this, O Lord, for thy mercies sake, in the same thy Son our Lord Jesus Christ, who liveth and reigneth with thee and the holy Ghost, ever one God, world without end. *Amen.*

¶ *A Prayer for a sick person, when there appeareth small hope of recovery.*

O FATHER of mercies, and God of all comfort, our only help in time of need; We flie unto thee for succour in behalf of this thy servant, here lying under thy hand in great weakness of body. Look graciously upon *him*, O Lord; and the more the outward man decayeth, strengthen *him*, we beseech thee, so much the more continually with thy grace and holy Spirit in the inner man. Give *him* unfeigned repentance for all the errours of *his* life past, and stedfast faith in thy Son Jesus, that *his* sins may be done away by thy mercy, and *his* pardon sealed in heaven, before *he* go hence, and be no more seen. We know, O Lord, that there is no word impossible with thee; and that if thou wilt, thou canst even yet raise *him* up, and grant *him* a longer continuance amongst us. Yet, forasmuch as in all appearance the time of *his* dissolution draweth near, so fit and prepare *him*, we beseech thee, against the hour of death, that after *his* departure hence in peace and in thy favour, *his* soul may be received into thine everlasting kingdom, through the merits and mediation of Jesus Christ thine only Son, our Lord and Saviour. *Amen.*

¶ *A commendatory Prayer for a sick person at the point of departure.*

O ALMIGHTY God, with whom do live the spirits of just men made perfect, after they are delivered from their earthly prisons; We humbly commend the soul of this thy servant, our dear *brother*, into thy hands, as into the hands of a faithful Creatour, and most merciful Saviour; most humbly beseeching thee that it may be precious in thy sight. Wash it, we pray thee, in the bloud of that immaculate Lamb that was slain to take away the sins of the world; that whatsoever defilements it may have contracted in the midst of this miserable and naughty world, through the lusts of the flesh, or the wiles of Satan, being purged and done away, it may be presented pure and without spot before thee. And teach us who survive, in this and other like daily spectacles of mortality, to see how frail and uncertain our own condition is, and so to number our days, that we may seriously apply our hearts to that holy and heavenly wisdom, whilst we live here, which may in the end bring us to life everlasting, through the merits of Jesus Christ thine only Son our Lord. *Amen.*

¶ *A Prayer for persons troubled in mind or in conscience.*

O BLESSED Lord, the Father of mercies, and the God of all comforts, we beseech thee look down in pity and compassion upon this thy afflicted servant. Thou writest bitter things against *him*, and makest *him* to possess his former iniquities; thy wrath lieth hard upon *him*, and *his* soul is full of trouble: But, O merciful God, who hast written thy holy word for our learning, that we through patience and comfort of thy holy Scriptures might have hope; give *him* a right understanding of *himself*, and of thy threats and promises, that *he* may neither cast away *his* confidence in thee, nor place it any where but in thee. Give *him* strength against all *his* temptations, and heal all *his* distempers. Break not the bruised reed, nor quench the smoking flax. Shut not up thy tender mercies in displeasure; but make *him* to hear of joy and gladness, that the bones which thou hast broken may rejoyce. Deliver *him* from fear of the enemy, and lift up the light of thy countenance upon him, and give *him* peace, through the merits and mediation of Jesus Christ our Lord. *Amen.*

The COMMUNION of the Sick.

¶ *F*ORASMUCH *as all mortal men be subject to many sudden perils, diseases and sicknesses, and ever uncertain what time they shall depart out of this life; therefore, to the intent they may be always in a readiness to die whensoever it shall please Almighty God to call them, the Curates shall diligently from time to time (but especially in the time of pestilence, or other infectious sickness)° exhort their Parishioners to the often receiving of the holy Communion of the body and bloud of our Saviour Christ, when it shall be publickly administred in the Church; that so doing, they may in case of sudden visitation, have the less cause to be disquieted for lack of the same. But if the sick person be not able to come to the Church, and yet is desirous to receive the Communion in his house; then he must give timely notice to the Curate, signifying also how many there are to communicate with him (which shall be three, or two at the least)° and having a convenient place in the sick mans house, with all things necessary so prepared, that the Curate may reverently minister, he shall there celebrate the holy Communion, beginning with the Collect, Epistle and Gospel here following.*

The Collect

ALMIGHTY everliving God, maker of mankind, who dost correct those whom thou dost love, and chastise every one whom thou dost receive; We beseech thee to have mercy upon this thy servant visited with thine hand, and to grant that *he* may take *his* sickness patiently, and recover *his* bodily health (if it be thy gracious will) and whensoever *his* soul shall depart from the body, it may be without spot presented unto thee, through Jesus Christ our Lord. *Amen.*

The Epistle. Heb. 12.5

MY son, despise not thou the chastning of the Lord, nor faint when thou art rebuked of him. For whom the Lord loveth, he chastneth; and scourgeth every son whom he receiveth.

The Gospel. John 5.24

VERILY, verily I say unto you, He that heareth my word, and believeth on him that sent me, hath everlasting life, and shall not come into condemnation; but is passed from death unto life.

¶ *After which the Priest shall proceed according to the form before prescribed for the holy Communion, beginning at these words* [Ye that do truly, &c.]

¶ *At the time of the distribution of the holy Sacrament, the Priest shall first receive the Communion himself, and after minister unto them that are appointed to communicate with the sick, and last of all to the sick person.*

¶ *But if a man, either by reason of extremity of sickness, or for want of warning in due time to the Curate, or for lack of company to receive with him, or by any other just impediment, do not receive the Sacrament of Christs body and bloud, the Curate shall instruct him, that if he do truly repent him of his sins, and stedfastly believe that Jesus Christ both suffered death upon the cross for him, and shed his bloud for his redemption, earnestly remembering the benefits he hath thereby, and giving him hearty thanks therefore, he doth eat and drink the body and bloud of our Sæviour Christ profitably to his souls health, although he do not receive the Sacrament with his mouth.*

¶ *When the sick person is visited, and receiveth the holy Communion all at one time, then the Priest, for more expedition, shall cut off the form of the Visitation at the Psalm* [In thee, O Lord, have I put my trust] *and go straight to the Communion.*

¶ *In the time of the plague, sweat, or such other like contagious times of sickness or diseases, when none of the Parish or neighbours can be gotten to communicate with the sick in their houses, for fear of the infection, upon special request of the diseased, the Minister may only communicate with him.*

The ORDER

For the

BURIAL of the DEAD.

¶ *Here is to be noted, that the Office ensuing is not to be used for any that die*
unbaptized, or excommunicate, or have laid violent hands upon themselves.°

¶ *The Priest and Clerks meeting the corps at the entrance of the Church-*
yard,° *and going before it, either into the Church, or towards the grave,*
shall say, or sing,

I AM the resurrection and the life, saith the Lord: he that believeth
in me, though he were dead, yet shall he live. And whosoever liveth
and believeth in me, shall never die.   *John* 11.25–6

I KNOW that my Redeemer liveth, and that he shall stand at the latter day upon the earth. And though after my skin worms destroy
this body, yet in my flesh shall I see God: whom I shall see for myself,
and mine eyes shall behold, and not another.   *Job* 19.25–7

W E brought nothing into this world, and it is certain we can carry
nothing out. The Lord gave, and the Lord hath taken away;
blessed be the Name of the Lord.   1 *Tim.* 6.7; *Job* 1.21

¶ *After they are come into the Church, shall he read one or both of these*
Psalms° *following.*

Dixi, custodiam.

I SAID, I will take heed to my ways: that I offend not in my tongue.
        I will keep my mouth as it were with a bridle: while the ungodly
is in my sight.   *Ps.* 39
        I held my tongue, and spake nothing: I kept silence, yea, even from
good words; but it was pain and grief to me.
        My heart was hot within me, and while I was thus musing, the fire
kindled: and at the last I spake with my tongue.
        Lord, let me know myne end, and the number of my days: that
I may be certified how long I have to live.
        Behold, thou hast made my days as it were a span long: and mine
age is even as nothing in respect of thee, and verily every man living
is altogether vanity.

For man walketh in a vain shadow, and disquieteth himself in vain: he heapeth up riches, and cannot tell who shall gather them.

And now, Lord, what is my hope: truly my hope is even in thee.

Deliver me from all mine offences: and make me not a rebuke unto the foolish.

I became dumb and opened not my mouth: for it was thy doing.

Take thy plague away from me: I am even consumed by means of thy heavy hand.

When thou with rebukes dost chasten man for sin, thou makest his beauty to consume away, like as it were a moth fretting a garment: every man therefore is but vanity.

Hear my prayer, O Lord, and with thine ears consider my calling: hold not thy peace at my tears.

For I am a stranger with thee: and a sojourner as all my fathers were.

O spare me a little, that I may recover my strength: before I go hence, and be no more seen.

Glory be to the Father, and to the Son: and to the holy Ghost;

As it was in the beginning, is now, and ever shall be: world without end. Amen.

Domine, refugium.

LORD, thou hast been our refuge: from one generation to another.

Before the mountains were brought forth, or ever the earth and the world were made: thou art God from everlasting, and world without end.   *Ps.* 90

Thou turnest man to destruction: again thou saist, Come again, ye children of men.

For a thousand years in thy sight are but as yesterday: seeing that is past as a watch in the night.

As soon as thou scatterest them, they are even as a sleep: and fade away suddenly like the grass.

In the morning it is green, and groweth up: but in the evening it is cut down, dryed up, and withered.

For we consume away in thy displeasure: and are afraid at thy wrathful indignation.

Thou hast set our misdeeds before thee: and our secret sins in the light of thy countenance.

For when thou art angry all our days are gone: we bring our years to an end, as it were a tale that is told.

The days of our age are threescore years and ten, and though men be so strong that they come to fourscore years: yet is their strength then but labour and sorrow; so soon passeth it away, and we are gone.

But who regardeth the power of thy wrath: for even thereafter as a man feareth, so is thy displeasure.

O teach us to number our days: that we may apply our hearts unto wisdom.

Turn thee again, O Lord, at the last: and be gracious unto thy servants.

O satisfie us with thy mercy, and that soon: so shall we rejoyce and be glad all the days of our life.

Comfort us again, now after the time that thou hast plagued us: and for the years wherein we have suffered adversity.

Shew thy servants thy work: and their children thy glory.

And the glorious Majesty of the Lord our God be upon us: prosper thou the work of our hands upon us, O prosper thou our handy-work.

Glory be to the Father, and to the Son: and to the holy Ghost;

As it was in the beginning, is now, and ever shall be: world without end. Amen.

¶ *Then shall follow the Lesson° taken out of the fifteenth Chapter of the former Epistle of Saint Paul to the Corinthians.*

Now is Christ risen from the dead, and become the first-fruits of them that slept. For since by man came death, by man came also the resurrection of the dead. For as in Adam all die, even so in Christ shall all be made alive. But every man in his own order: Christ the first-fruits; afterward they that are Christs, at his coming. Then cometh the end, when he shall have delivered up the kingdom to God, even the Father; when he shall have put down all rule, and all authority and power. For he must reign till he hath put all enemies under his feet. The last enemy that shall be destroyed is death: For he hath put all things under his feet. But when he saith all things are put under him, it is manifest that he is excepted which did put all things under him. And when all things shall be subdued unto him, then shall the Son also himself be subject unto him that put all things under him, that God may be all in all. Else what shall they do which are baptized for the dead, if the dead rise not at all? why are they then baptized for the dead? And why stand we in jeopardy every hour? I protest by your rejoycing, which I have in Christ Jesus our Lord, I die daily. If after the manner of men I have fought with beasts at Ephesus, what advantageth it me, if the dead rise not? Let us eat and drink, for to morrow we die. Be not deceived; evil communications corrupt good manners. Awake to righteousness, and sin not; for some have not the knowledge of God. I speak this to your shame. But some man will say, How are the dead raised up? and with what body do they come? Thou fool, that which thou sowest is not quickened, except it die. And that which thou sowest, thou sowest not that body that shall be, but bare grain, it may chance of wheat, or of some other grain. But God giveth it a body, as it hath pleased him, and to every seed his own body. All flesh is not the same flesh, but there is one kind of flesh of men, another flesh of beasts, another of fishes, and another of birds. There are also celestial bodies, and bodies terrestrial; but the glory of the celestial is one, and the glory of the terrestrial is another. There is one glory of the sun, and another glory of the moon, and another glory of the stars; for one star differeth from another star in glory. So also is the resurrection of the dead; It is sown in corruption; it is raised in incorruption: It is sown in dishonour; it is raised in glory: It is sown in weakness; it is raised in power: It is sown a natural body; it is raised a spiritual body. There is a natural body, and there is a spiritual body. And so it is written, The first man Adam was made a living soul, the last Adam was made a quickning Spirit. Howbeit, that was not first which is spiritual; but that which is natural, and afterward that which is spiritual. The first man is of the earth, earthy: the second man is the Lord from heaven. As is the earthy, such are they that are earthy: and as is the heavenly, such are they also that are heavenly. And as we have borne the image of the earthy, we shall also bear the image of the heavenly. Now this I say, brethren, that flesh and bloud cannot inherit the kingdom of God; neither doth corruption inherit incorruption. Behold, I shew you a mystery. We shall not all sleep, but we shall all be changed in a moment, in the twinkling of an eye, at the last trump; (for the trumpet shall sound and the dead shall be raised incorruptible, and we shall be changed.) For this corruptible must put on incorruption, and this mortal must put on immortality. So when this corruptible shall have put on incorruption, and this mortal shall have put on immortality, then shall be brought to pass the saying that is written, Death is swallowed up in victory. O death, where is thy sting? O grave, where is thy victory? The sting of death is sin, and the strength of sin is the law. But thanks be to God which giveth us the victory, through our Lord Jesus Christ. Therefore, my beloved brethren, be ye stedfast, unmoveable, always abounding in the work of the Lord, forasmuch as ye know that your labour is not in vain in the Lord.   1 *Cor.* 15.20

¶ *When they come to the grave, while the corps is made ready to be laid into the earth, the Priest shall say, or the Priest and Clerks shall sing,*

MAN that is born of a woman, hath but a short time to live, and is full of misery. He cometh up, and is cut down like a flower; he fleeth as it were a shadow, and never continueth in one stay.

In the midst of life we are in death: of whom may we seek for succour, but of thee, O Lord, who for our sins art justly displeased?

Yet, O Lord God most holy, O Lord most mighty, O holy and most merciful Saviour, deliver us not into the bitter pains of eternal death.

Thou knowest, Lord, the secrets of our hearts; shut not thy merciful ears to our prayer; but spare us, Lord most holy, O God most mighty, O holy and merciful Saviour, thou most worthy Judge eternal, suffer us not at our last hour for any pains of death to fall from thee.

¶ *Then while the earth shall be cast upon the body by some standing by, the Priest shall say,*

FORASMUCH as it hath pleased Almighty God of his great mercy to take unto himself the soul of our dear *brother* here departed, we therefore commit *his* body to the ground; earth to earth, ashes to ashes, dust to dust, in sure and certain hope of the resurrection° to eternal life, through our Lord Jesus Christ, who shall change our vile body, that it may be like unto his glorious body, according to the mighty working, whereby he is able to subdue all things to himself.

¶ *Then shall be said or sung,*

I HEARD a voice from heaven, saying unto me, Write; From henceforth blessed are the dead which die in the Lord: even so saith the Spirit; for they rest from their labours.

¶ *Then the Priest shall say,*

Lord, have mercy upon us.
  Christ, have mercy upon us.
Lord, have mercy upon us.

Our Father which art in heaven, Hallowed be thy Name. Thy kingdom come. Thy will be done in earth, As it is in heaven. Give us this day our daily bread. And forgive us our trespasses, As we forgive them that trespass against us. And lead us not into temptation: But deliver us from evil. Amen.

¶ *Priest.*

Almighty God, with whom do live the spirits of them that depart hence in the Lord, and with whom the souls of the faithful,° after they are delivered from the burden of the flesh, are in joy and felicity; We give thee hearty thanks, for that it hath pleased thee to deliver this our *brother* out of the miseries of this sinful world; beseeching thee that it may please thee of thy gracious goodness, shortly to accomplish the number of thine elect, and to hasten thy kingdom, that we, with all those that are departed in the true faith of thy holy Name, may have our perfect consummation and bliss, both in body and soul, in thy eternal and everlasting glory, through Jesus Christ our Lord. *Amen.*

The Collect

O merciful God, the Father of our Lord Jesus Christ, who is the resurrection and the life; in whom whosoever believeth, shall live, though he die; and whosoever liveth and believeth in him, shall not die eternally; who also hath taught us (by his holy Apostle Saint Paul) not to be sorry, as men without hope, for them that sleep in him; We meekly beseech thee, O Father, to raise us from the death of sin unto the life of righteousness; that when we shall depart this life, we may rest in him, as our hope is this our *brother* doth, and that at the general resurrection in the last day we may be found acceptable in thy sight, and receive that blessing which thy well-beloved Son shall then pronounce to all that love and fear thee, saying, Come, ye blessed children of my Father, receive the kingdom prepared for you from the beginning of the world. Grant this, we beseech thee, O merciful Father, through Jesus Christ our mediatour and redeemer. *Amen.*

The grace of our Lord Jesus Christ,° and the love of God, and the fellowship of the holy Ghost, be with us all evermore. *Amen.*

The Thanksgiving of Women after Child-birth,

Commonly called

The Churching of Women.

¶ *The woman at the usual time after her delivery,° shall come into the Church decently apparelled,° and there shall kneel down in some convenient place,° as hath been accustomed, or as the Ordinary shall direct: And then the Priest shall say unto her,*

FORASMUCH as it hath pleased Almighty God of his goodness to give you safe deliverance, and hath preserved you in the great danger of child-birth, you shall therefore give hearty thanks unto God, and say,

(¶ *Then shall the Priest say the 116th Psalm.*)°

Dilexi quoniam.

I AM well pleased: that the Lord hath heard the voice of my prayer.

That he hath inclined his ear unto me: therefore will I call upon him as long as I live.

The snares of death compassed me round about: and the pains of hell gat hold upon me.

I found trouble and heaviness, and I called upon the Name of the Lord: O Lord, I beseech thee, deliver my soul.

Gracious is the Lord, and righteous: yea, our God is merciful.

The Lord preserveth the simple: I was in misery, and he helped me.

Turn again then unto thy rest, O my soul: for the Lord hath rewarded thee.

And why? thou hast delivered my soul from death: mine eyes from tears, and my feet from falling.

I will walk before the Lord: in the land of the living.

I believed, and therefore will I speak, but I was sore troubled: I said in my haste, All men are lyars.

What reward shall I give unto the Lord: for all the benefits that he hath done unto me?

I will receive the cup of salvation: and call upon the Name of the Lord.

I will pay my vows now in the presence of all his people: in the courts of the Lords house, even in the midst of thee, O Jerusalem. Praise the Lord.

Glory be to the Father, and to the Son: and to the holy Ghost;

As it was in the beginning, is now, and ever shall be: world without end. Amen.

¶ *Or, Psalm 127.*

Nisi Dominus.

EXCEPT the Lord build the house: their labour is but lost that build it.

Except the Lord keep the city: the watchman waketh but in vain.

It is but lost labour that ye haste to rise up early, and so late take rest, and eat the bread of carefulness: for so he giveth his beloved sleep.

Lo, children and the fruit of the womb: are an heritage and gift that cometh of the Lord.

Like as the arrows in the hand of the giant: even so are the young children.

Happy is the man that hath his quiver full of them: they shall not be ashamed when they speak with their enemies in the gate.

Glory be to the Father, and to the Son: and to the holy Ghost;

As it was in the beginning, is now, and ever shall be: world without end. Amen.

¶ *Then the Priest shall say,*

Let us pray.

Lord, have mercy upon us.

Christ, have mercy upon us.

Lord, have mercy upon us.

OUR Father which art in heaven, Hallowed be thy Name. Thy kingdom come. Thy will be done in earth, As it is in heaven. Give us this day our daily bread. And forgive us our trespasses, As we forgive them that trespass against us. And lead us not into temptation: But deliver us from evil. For thine is the kingdom,° the power, and the glory, for ever and ever. Amen.

Minister. O Lord, save this woman thy servant;

Answer. Who putteth her trust in thee.

Minister. Be thou to her a strong tower;

Answer. From the face of her enemy.

Minister. Lord, hear our prayer.

Answer. And let our cry come unto thee.

Minister. Let us pray.

O ALMIGHTY God, we give thee humble thanks for that thou hast vouchsafed to deliver this woman thy servant from the great pain and peril of child-birth; Grant, we beseech thee, most merciful Father, that she through thy help may both faithfully live and walk according to thy will in this life present, and also may be partaker of everlasting glory in the life to come, through Jesus Christ our Lord. *Amen.*

¶ *The woman that cometh to give her thanks, must offer accustomed offerings; and if there be a Communion, it is convenient that she receive the holy Communion.*

A COMMINATION,

OR

Denouncing of Gods anger and judgements against sinners, With certain prayers to be used on the first day of Lent, and at other times, as the Ordinary shall appoint.

¶ *After Morning Prayer, the Litany ended according to the accustomed manner, the Priest shall in the reading Pew° or Pulpit, say,*

B RETHREN, in the primitive Church there was a godly discipline, that at the beginning of Lent, such persons as stood convicted of notorious sin, were put to open penance, and punished in this world, that their souls might be saved in the day of the Lord; and that others admonished by their example, might be the more afraid to offend.

Instead whereof (until the said discipline may be restored again, which is much to be wished) it is thought good, that at this time (in the presence of you all) should be read the general sentences of Gods cursing against impenitent sinners, gathered out of the seven and twentieth Chapter of Deuteronomy, and other places of Scripture; and that ye should answer to every sentence, *Amen*: To the intent that being admonished of the great indignation of God against sinners, ye may the rather be moved to earnest and true repentance, and may walk more warily in these dangerous days; fleeing from such vices, for which ye affirm with your own mouths the curse of God to be due.

C URSED is the man that maketh any carved or molten image,° to worship it.

¶ *And the people shall answer and say,*

Amen.

Minister. Cursed is he that curseth his father or mother.
Answer. Amen.
Minister. Cursed is he that removeth his neighbours landmark.
Answer. Amen.
Minister. Cursed is he that maketh the blind to go out of his way.
Answer. Amen.
Minister. Cursed is he that perverteth the judgement° of the stranger, the fatherless, and widow.
Answer. Amen.
Minister. Cursed is he that smiteth his neighbour secretly.
Answer. Amen.
Minister. Cursed is he that lieth with his neighbours wife.
Answer. Amen.
Minister. Cursed is he that taketh reward to slay the innocent.
Answer. Amen.
Minister. Cursed is he that putteth his trust in man, and taketh man for his defence, and in his heart goeth from the Lord.
Answer. Amen.
Minister. Cursed are the unmerciful, fornicators, and adulterers, covetous persons, idolaters,° slanderers, drunkards, and extortioners.
Answer. Amen.

Minister.

N OW seeing that all they are accursed (as the prophet David beareth witness) who do erre and go astray from the command- ments of God, let us (remembering the dreadful judgement hanging over our heads, and always ready to fall upon us) return unto our Lord God with all contrition and meekness of heart; bewailing and lamenting our sinful life, acknowledging and confessing our offences, and seeking to bring forth worthy fruits of penance. For now is the ax put unto the root of the trees, so that every tree that bringeth not forth good fruit, is hewn down and cast into the fire. It is a fearful thing to fall into the hands of the living God: he shall pour down rain

Ps.
119.21

Matt.
3.10
Heb.
10.31

upon the sinners, snares, fire and brimstone, storm and tempest; this *Ps.* 11.6
shall be their portion to drink. For lo, the Lord is come out of his *Isa.*
place to visit the wickedness of such as dwell upon the earth. But who 26.21
may abide the day of his coming? Who shall be able to endure when
he appeareth? His fan is in his hand, and he will purge his floor, and *Mal.* 3.2
gather his wheat into the barn, but he will burn the chaff with *Matt.*
unquenchable fire. The day of the Lord cometh as a thief in the night: 3.12
and when men shall say, Peace, and all things are safe, then shall sudden destruction come upon them, as sorrow cometh upon a woman *1 Thess.*
travailing with child, and they shall not escape. Then shall appear the 5.2–3
wrath of God in the day of vengeance, which obstinate sinners,
through the stubbornness of their heart, have heaped unto themselves, which despised the goodness, patience, and long-sufferance of *Rom.*
God, when he calleth them continually to repentance. Then shall they 2.4–5
call upon me (saith the Lord) but I will not hear; they shall seek me *Prov.*
early, but they shall not find me, and that because they hated knowl- 1.28–9
edge, and received not the fear of the Lord, but abhorred my counsel,
and despised my correction. Then shall it be too late to knock when *Matt.*
the door shall be shut; and too late to cry for mercy when it is the time 25.10–12
of justice. O terrible voice of most just judgement which shall be
pronounced upon them, when it shall be said unto them, Go ye
cursed into the fire everlasting, which is prepared for the devil and his
angels. Therefore, brethren, take we heed betime, while the day of *John*
salvation lasteth; for the night cometh, when none can work: but let 9.4–5
us, while we have the light, believe in the light, and walk as children *2 Cor.* 6.2
of the light, that we be not cast into utter darkness, where is weeping *Matt.*
and gnashing of teeth. Let us not abuse the goodness of God, who 25.30
calleth us mercifully to amendment, and of his endless pity promiseth
us forgiveness of that which is past, if with a perfect and true heart we
return unto him. For though our sins be as red as scarlet, they shall be
made white as snow: and though they be like purple, yet they shall be
made white as wooll. Turn ye (saith the Lord) from all your wicked- *Isa.* 1.18
ness, and your sin shall not be your destruction. Cast away from you *Ezek.*
all your ungodliness that ye have done, make you new hearts, and 18.30
a new spirit: Wherefore will ye die, O ye house of Israel, seeing that
I have no pleasure in the death of him that dieth, saith the Lord God?
Turn ye then, and ye shall live. Although we have sinned, yet have we *1 John*
an advocate with the Father, Jesus Christ the righteous, and he is the 2.1–2
propitiation for our sins.° For he was wounded for our offences, and

Isa. 53.5 smitten for our wickedness. Let us therefore return unto him, who is the merciful receiver of all true penitent sinners; assuring our selves that he is ready to receive us, and most willing to pardon us, if we come unto him with faithful repentance; if we will submit our selves *Matt.* unto him, and from henceforth walk in his ways; if we will take his *11.29–30* easy yoke, and light burden upon us, to follow him in lowliness, patience, and charity, and be ordered by the governance of his holy Spirit; seeking always his glory, and serving him duly in our vocation with thanksgiving. This if we do, Christ will deliver us from the curse of the law, and from the extream malediction which shall light upon them that shall be set on the left hand; and he will set us on his right *Matt.* hand, and give us the gracious benediction of his Father, command-*25.33–4* ing us to take possession of his glorious kingdom: unto which he vouchsafe to bring us all, for his infinite mercy. Amen.

¶ *Then shall they all kneel upon their knees, and the Priest and Clerks kneeling (in the place where they are accustomed to say the Litany)° shall say this Psalm.*

Miserere mei, Deus.

HAVE mercy upon me, O God, after thy great goodness: according to the multitude of thy mercies, do away mine offences.   *Ps.* 51

Wash me throughly from my wickedness: and cleanse me from my sin.

For I acknowledge my faults: and my sin is ever before me.

Against thee only have I sinned, and done this evil in thy sight: that thou mightest be justified in thy saying, and clear when thou art judged.

Behold, I was shapen in wickedness: and in sin hath my mother conceived me.

But lo, thou requirest truth in the inward parts: and shalt make me to understand wisdom secretly.

Thou shalt purge me with hyssop, and I shall be clean: thou shalt wash me, and I shall be whiter than snow.

Thou shalt make me hear of joy and gladness: that the bones which thou hast broken, may rejoyce.

Turn thy face away from my sins: and put out all my misdeeds.

Make me a clean heart, O God: and renew a right spirit within me.

Cast me not away from thy presence: and take not thy holy Spirit from me.

O give me the comfort of thy help again: and stablish me with thy free Spirit.

Then shall I teach thy ways unto the wicked: and sinners shall be converted unto thee.

Deliver me from bloud-guiltiness, O God, thou that art the God of my health: and my tongue shall sing of thy righteousness.

Thou shalt open my lips, O Lord: and my mouth shall shew thy praise.

For thou desirest no sacrifice, else would I give it thee: but thou delightest not in burnt-offerings.

The sacrifice of God is a troubled spirit: a broken and contrite heart, O God, shalt thou not despise.

O be favourable and gracious unto Sion: build thou the walls of Jerusalem.

Then shalt thou be pleased with the sacrifice of righteousness, with the burnt-offerings, and oblations: then shall they offer young bullocks upon thine altar.

Glory be to the Father, and to the Son: and to the holy Ghost;

Answer. As it was in the beginning, is now, and ever shall be: world without end. Amen.

Lord, have mercy upon us.

Christ, have mercy upon us.

Lord, have mercy upon us.

O UR Father which art in heaven, Hallowed be thy Name. Thy kingdom come. Thy will be done in earth, As it is in heaven. Give us this day our daily bread. And forgive us our trespasses, As we forgive them that trespass against us. And lead us not into temptation: But deliver us from evil. Amen.

Minister. O Lord, save thy servants;

Answer. That put their trust in thee.

Minister. Send unto them help from above.

Answer. And evermore mightily defend them.

Minister. Help us, O God our Saviour.

Answer. And for the glory of thy Name deliver us; be merciful to us sinners for thy Names sake.

Minister. O Lord, hear our prayer.

Answer. And let our cry come unto thee.

Minister. Let us pray.

O LORD, we beseech thee mercifully hear our prayers, and spare all those who confess their sins unto thee, that they whose consciences by sin are accused, by thy merciful pardon may be absolved, through Christ our Lord. *Amen.*

O MOST mighty God, and merciful Father, who hast compassion upon all men, and hatest nothing that thou hast made, who wouldest not the death of a sinner, but that he should rather turn from his sin, and be saved; Mercifully forgive us our trespasses; receive and comfort us, who are grieved and wearied with the burthen of our sins. Thy property is always to have mercy; to thee only it appertaineth to forgive sins. Spare us therefore, good Lord, spare thy people whom thou hast redeemed; enter not into judgement with thy servants, who are vile earth, and miserable sinners; but so turn thine anger from us,° who meekly acknowledge our vileness, and truly repent us of our faults; and so make haste to help us in this world, that we may ever live with thee in the world to come, through Jesus Christ our Lord. *Amen.*

¶ *Then shall the people say this that followeth, after the Minister.*

TURN thou us, O good Lord, and so shall we be turned. Be favourable, O Lord, Be favourable to thy people, Who turn to thee in weeping, fasting, and praying. For thou art a merciful God, Full of compassion. Long-suffering, and of great pity. Thou sparest when we deserve punishment, And in thy wrath thinkest upon mercy. Spare thy people, good Lord, spare them, And let not thine heritage be brought to confusion. Hear us, O Lord, for thy mercy is great, And after the multitude of thy mercies look upon us, Through the merits and mediation of thy blessed Son,° Jesus Christ our Lord. Amen.

¶ *Then the Minister alone shall say,*

THE Lord bless us, and keep us; the Lord lift up the light of his countenance upon us, and give us peace now and for evermore. *Amen.*

THE
Psalms of David.

Day 1. *Morning Prayer.*

Psalm 1

Beatus vir, qui non abiit.°

BLESSED is the man that hath not walked in the counsel of the ungodly, nor stood° in the way of sinners: and hath not sat in the seat of the scornful.

2 But his delight is in the law of the Lord: and in his law will he exercise himself day and night.

3 And he shall be like a tree planted by the water-side: that will bring forth his fruit in due season.

4 His leaf also shall not wither: and look, whatsoever he doth, it shall prosper.

5 As for the ungodly it is not so with them: but they are like the chaff which the wind scattereth away from the face of the earth.

6 Therefore the ungodly shall not be able to stand in the judgment: neither the sinners in the congregation of the righteous.

7 But the Lord knoweth the way of the righteous: and the way of the ungodly shall perish.

Psalm 2

Quare fremuerunt gentes?

WHY do the heathen so furiously rage together: and why do the people imagine a vain thing?

2 The kings of the earth stand up, and the rulers take counsel together: against the Lord, and against his anointed.

3 Let us break their bonds asunder: and cast away their cords from us.

4 He that dwelleth in heaven, shall laugh them to scorn: the Lord shall have them in derision.

5 Then shall he speak unto them in his wrath: and vex them in his sore displeasure.

6 Yet I have set my king: upon my holy hill of Sion.

7 I will preach the law, whereof the Lord hath said unto me: Thou art my Son, this day have I begotten thee.

8 Desire of me, and I shall give thee the heathen for thine inheritance: and the utmost parts of the earth for thy possession.

9 Thou shalt bruise them with a rod of iron: and break them in pieces like a potters vessel.

10 Be wise now therefore, O ye kings: be learned, ye that are judges of the earth.

11 Serve the Lord in fear: and rejoyce unto him with reverence.

12 Kiss the Son, lest he be angry, and so ye perish from the right way: if his wrath be kindled (yea, but a little) blessed are all they that put their trust in him.

Psalm 3

Domine, quid multiplicati?

LORD, how are they increased that trouble me: many are they that rise against me.

2 Many one there be that say of my soul: There is no help for him in his God.

3 But thou, O Lord, art my defender: thou art my worship, and the lifter up of my head.

4 I did call upon the Lord with my voice: and he heard me out of his holy hill.

5 I laid me down and slept, and rose up again: for the Lord sustained me.

6 I will not be afraid for ten thousands of the people: that have set themselves against me round about.

7 Up Lord, and help me, O my God: for thou smitest all mine enemies upon the cheekbone; thou hast broken the teeth of the ungodly.

8 Salvation belongeth unto the Lord: and thy blessing is upon thy people.

Psalm 4

Cum invocarem.

HEAR me when I call, O God of my righteousness: thou hast set me at liberty when I was in trouble; have mercy upon me, and hearken unto my prayer.

2 O ye sons of men, how long will ye blaspheme mine honour: and have such pleasure in vanity, and seek after leasing?

3 Know this also, that the Lord hath chosen to himself the man that is godly: when I call upon the Lord, he will hear me.

4 Stand in awe, and sin not: commune with your own heart, and in your chamber, and be still.

5 Offer the sacrifice of righteousness: and put your trust in the Lord.

6 There be many that say: Who will shew us any good?

7 Lord, lift thou up: the light of thy countenance upon us.

8 Thou hast put gladness in my heart: since the time that their corn and wine and oyl increased.

9 I will lay me down in peace, and take my rest: for it is thou, Lord, only that makest me dwell in safety.

Psalm 5

Verba mea auribus.

PONDER my words, O Lord: consider my meditation.

2 O hearken thou unto the voice of my calling, my King, and my God: for unto thee will I make my prayer.

3 My voice shalt thou hear betimes, O Lord: early in the morning will I direct my prayer unto thee, and will look up.

4 For thou art the God that hast no pleasure in wickedness: neither shall any evil dwell with thee.

5 Such as be foolish shall not stand in thy sight: for thou hatest all them that work vanity.

6 Thou shalt destroy them that speak leasing: the Lord will abhor both the bloud-thirsty and deceitful man.

7 But as for me, I will come into thine house, even upon the multitude of thy mercy: and in thy fear will I worship toward thy holy temple.

8 Lead me, O Lord, in thy righteousness, because of mine enemies: make thy way plain before my face.

9 For there is no faithfulness in his mouth: their inward parts are very wickedness.

10 Their throat is an open sepulchre: they flatter with their tongue.

11 Destroy thou them, O God; let them perish through their own

imaginations: cast them out in the multitude of their ungodliness; for they have rebelled against thee.

12 And let all them that put their trust in thee rejoyce: they shall ever be giving of thanks, because thou defendest them; they that love thy Name, shall be joyful in thee;

13 For thou, Lord, wilt give thy blessing unto the righteous: and with thy favourable kindness wilt thou defend him as with a shield.

Day 1. *Evening Prayer.*

Psalm 6

Domine, ne in furore.

O LORD, rebuke me not in thine indignation: neither chasten me in thy displeasure.

2 Have mercy upon me, O Lord, for I am weak: O Lord, heal me, for my bones are vexed.

3 My soul also is sore troubled: but, Lord, how long wilt thou punish me?

4 Turn thee, O Lord, and deliver my soul: O save me for thy mercies sake.

5 For in death no man remembreth thee: and who will give thee thanks in the pit?

6 I am weary of my groaning, every night wash I my bed: and water my couch with my tears.

7 My beauty is gone for very trouble: and worn away because of all mine enemies.

8 Away from me, all ye that work vanity: for the Lord hath heard the voice of my weeping.

9 The Lord hath heard my petition: the Lord will receive my prayer.

10 All mine enemies shall be confounded, and sore vexed: they shall be turned back, and put to shame suddenly.

Psalm 7

Domine, Deus meus.

O LORD my God, in thee have I put my trust: save me from all them that persecute me, and deliver me;

2 Lest he devour my soul like a lion, and tear it in pieces: while there is none to help.

3 O Lord my God, if I have done any such thing: or if there be any wickedness in my hands;

4 If I have rewarded evil unto him that dealt friendly with me: yea, I have delivered him that without any cause is mine enemy;

5 Then let mine enemy persecute my soul, and take me: yea, let him tread my life down upon the earth, and lay mine honour in the dust.

6 Stand up, O Lord, in thy wrath, and lift up thy self, because of the indignation of mine enemies: arise up for me in the judgment that thou hast commanded.

7 And so shall the congregation of the people come about thee: for their sakes therefore lift up thy self again.

8 The Lord shall judge the people; give sentence with me, O Lord: according to my righteousness, and according to the innocency that is in me.

9 O let the wickedness of the ungodly come to an end: but guide thou the just.

10 For the righteous God: trieth the very hearts and reins.

11 My help cometh of God: who preserveth them that are true of heart.

12 God is a righteous judge, strong and patient: and God is provoked every day.

13 If a man will not turn, he will whet his sword: he hath bent his bow, and made it ready.

14 He hath prepared for him the instruments of death: he ordaineth his arrows against the persecutours.

15 Behold, he travaileth with mischief: he hath conceived sorrow, and brought forth ungodliness.

16 He hath graven and digged up a pit: and is faln himself into the destruction that he made for other.

17 For his travail shall come upon his own head: and his wickedness shall fall on his own pate.

18 I will give thanks unto the Lord, according to his righteousness: and I will praise the Name of the Lord most High.

Psalm 8

Domine, Dominus noster.

O LORD our governour, how excellent is thy Name in all the world: thou hast set thy glory above the heavens!

2 Out of the mouth of very babes and sucklings hast thou ordained strength, because of thine enemies: that thou mightest still the enemy and the avenger.

3 For I will consider thy heavens, even the works of thy fingers: the moon and the stars which thou hast ordained.

4 What is man, that thou art mindful of him: and the son of man, that thou visitest him?

5 Thou madest him lower than the angels: to crown him with glory and worship.

6 Thou makest him to have dominion of the works of thy hands: and thou hast put all things in subjection under his feet;

7 All sheep and oxen: yea, and the beasts of the field;

8 The fowls of the air, and the fishes of the sea: and whatsoever walketh through the paths of the seas.

9 O Lord our governour: how excellent is thy Name in all the world!

Day 2. *Morning Prayer.*

Psalm 9

Confitebor tibi.

I WILL give thanks unto thee, O Lord, with my whole heart: I will speak of all thy marvellous works.

2 I will be glad and rejoyce in thee: yea, my songs will I make of thy Name, O thou most Highest.

3 While mine enemies are driven back: they shall fall and perish at thy presence.

4 For thou hast maintained my right, and my cause: thou art set in the throne that judgest right.

5 Thou hast rebuked the heathen, and destroyed the ungodly: thou hast put out their name for ever and ever.

6 O thou enemy, destructions are come to a perpetual end: even as

the cities which thou hast destroyed; their memorial is perished with them.

7 But the Lord shall endure for ever: he hath also prepared his seat for judgment.

8 For he shall judge the world in righteousness: and minister true judgment unto the people.

9 The Lord also will be a defence for the oppressed: even a refuge in due time of trouble.

10 And they that know thy Name, will put their trust in thee: for thou, Lord, hast never failed them that seek thee.

11 O praise the Lord which dwelleth in Sion: shew the people of his doings.

12 For when he maketh inquisition for bloud, he remembreth them: and forgetteth not the complaint of the poor.

13 Have mercy upon me, O Lord, consider the trouble which I suffer of them that hate me: thou that liftest me up from the gates of death.

14 That I may shew all thy praises within the ports of the daughter of Sion: I will rejoyce in thy salvation.

15 The heathen are sunk down in the pit that they made: in the same net which they hid privily, is their foot taken.

16 The Lord is known to execute judgment: the ungodly is trapped in the work of his own hands.

17 The wicked shall be turned into hell: and all the people that forget God.

18 For the poor shall not alway be forgotten: the patient abiding of the meek shall not perish for ever.

19 Up, Lord, and let not man have the upper hand: let the heathen be judged in thy sight.

20 Put them in fear, O Lord: that the heathen may know themselves to be but men.

Psalm 10

Ut quid, Domine?

WHY standest thou so far off, O Lord: and hidest thy face in the needful time of trouble?

2 The ungodly for his own lust doth persecute the poor: let them be taken in the crafty wiliness that they have imagined.

3 For the ungodly hath made boast of his own hearts desire: and speaketh good of the covetous whom God abhorreth.

4 The ungodly is so proud, that he careth not for God; neither is God in all his thoughts.

5 His ways are always grievous: thy judgments are far above out of his sight, and therefore defieth he all his enemies.

6 For he hath said in his heart, Tush, I shall never be cast down: there shall no harm happen unto me.

7 His mouth is full of cursing, deceit, and fraud: under his tongue is ungodliness and vanity.

8 He sitteth lurking in the thievish corners of the streets: and privily in his lurking dens doth he murther the innocent; his eyes are set against the poor.

9 For he lieth waiting secretly, even as a lion lurketh he in his den: that he may ravish the poor.

10 He doth ravish the poor: when he getteth him into his net.

11 He falleth down and humbleth himself: that the congregation of the poor may fall into the hands of his captains.

12 He hath said in his heart, Tush, God hath forgotten: he hideth away his face, and he will never see it.

13 Arise, O Lord God, and lift up thine hand: forget not the poor.

14 Wherefore should the wicked blaspheme God: while he doth say in his heart, Tush, thou God carest not for it.

15 Surely thou hast seen it: for thou beholdest ungodliness and wrong.

16 That thou mayest take the matter into thy hand: the poor committeth himself unto thee; for thou art the helper of the friendless.

17 Break thou the power of the ungodly and malicious: take away his ungodliness, and thou shalt find none.

18 The Lord is King for ever and ever: and the heathen are perished out of the land.

19 Lord, thou hast heard the desire of the poor: thou preparest their heart, and thine ear hearkeneth thereto.

20 To help the fatherless and poor unto their right: that the man of the earth be no more exalted against them.

Psalm 11

In Domino confido.

IN THE Lord put I my trust: how say ye then to my soul, that she should flee as a bird unto the hill?

2 For lo, the ungodly bend their bow, and make ready their arrows within the quiver: that they may privily shoot at them which are true of heart.

3 For the foundations will be cast down: and what have the righteous done?

4 The Lord is in his holy temple: the Lords seat is in heaven.

5 His eyes consider the poor: and his eye-lids try the children of men.

6 The Lord alloweth the righteous: but the ungodly, and him that delighteth in wickedness, doth his soul abhor.

7 Upon the ungodly he shall rain snares, fire and brimstone, storm, and tempest: this shall be their portion to drink.

8 For the righteous Lord loveth righteousness: his countenance will behold the thing that is just.

Day 2. *Evening Prayer.*

Psalm 12

Salvum me fac.

HELP me, Lord, for there is not one godly man left: for the faithful are minished from among the children of men.

2 They talk of vanity every one with his neighbour: they do but flatter with their lips, and dissemble in their double heart.

3 The Lord shall root out all deceitful lips: and the tongue that speaketh proud things.

4 Which have said, With our tongue will we prevail: we are they that ought to speak, who is Lord over us?

5 Now for the comfortless troubles sake of the needy: and because of the deep sighing of the poor;

6 I will up, saith the Lord: and will help every one from him that swelleth against him, and will set him at rest.

7 The words of the Lord are pure words: even as the silver, which from the earth is tryed, and purified seven times in the fire.

8 Thou shalt keep them, O Lord: thou shalt preserve him from this generation for ever.

9 The ungodly walk on every side: when they are exalted, the children of men are put to rebuke.

Psalm 13

Usque quo, Domine?

HOW long wilt thou forget me, O Lord, for ever: how long wilt thou hide thy face from me?

2 How long shall I seek counsel in my soul, and be so vexed in my heart: how long shall mine enemies triumph over me?

3 Consider and hear me, O Lord my God: lighten mine eyes, that I sleep not in death.

4 Lest mine enemy say, I have prevailed against him: for if I be cast down, they that trouble me, will rejoyce at it.

5 But my trust is in thy mercy: and my heart is joyful in thy salvation.

6 I will sing of the Lord, because he hath dealt so lovingly with me: yea, I will praise the name of the Lord most Highest.

Psalm 14

Dixit insipiens.

THE fool hath said in his heart: There is no God.

2 They are corrupt, and become abominable in their doings: there is none that doth good, no not one.

3 The Lord looked down from heaven upon the children of men: to see if there were any that would understand, and seek after God.

4 But they are all gone out of the way, they are altogether become abominable: there is none that doth good, no not one.

5 Their throat is an open sepulchre, with their tongues have they deceived: the poison of asps is under their lips.

6 Their mouth is full of cursing, and bitterness: their feet are swift to shed bloud.

7 Destruction, and unhappiness is in their ways, and the way of peace have they not known: there is no fear of God before their eyes.

8 Have they no knowledge, that they are all such workers of mischief: eating up my people as it were bread, and call not upon the Lord?

9 There were they brought in great fear, even where no fear was: for God is in the generation of the righteous.

10 As for you, ye have made a mock at the counsel of the poor: because he putteth his trust in the Lord.

11 Who shall give salvation unto Israel out of Sion? When the Lord turneth the captivity of his people: then shall Jacob rejoyce, and Israel shall be glad.

Day 3. *Morning Prayer*.

Psalm 15

Domine, quis habitabit?

LORD, who shall dwell in thy tabernacle: or who shall rest upon thy holy hill?

2 Even he, that leadeth an uncorrupt life: and doth the thing which is right, and speaketh the truth from his heart.

3 He that hath used no deceit in his tongue, nor done evil to his neighbour: and hath not slandred his neighbour.

4 He that setteth not by himself, but is lowly in his own eyes: and maketh much of them, that fear the Lord.

5 He that sweareth unto his neighbour, and disappointeth him not: though it were to his own hindrance.

6 He that hath not given his money upon usury: nor taken reward against the innocent.

7 Whoso doth these things: shall never fall.

Psalm 16

Conserva me, Domine.

PRESERVE me, O God: for in thee have I put my trust.

2 O my soul, thou hast said unto the Lord: Thou art my God, my goods are nothing unto thee.

3 All my delight is upon the saints, that are in the earth: and upon such, as excel in virtue.

4 But they, that run after another god: shall have great trouble.

5 Their drink-offerings of bloud will I not offer: neither make mention of their names within my lips.

6 The Lord himself is the portion of mine inheritance, and of my cup: thou shalt maintain my lot.

7 The lot is fallen unto me in a fair ground: yea, I have a goodly heritage.

8 I will thank the Lord for giving me warning: my reins also chasten me in the night-season.

9 I have set God always before me: for he is on my right hand, therefore I shall not fall.

10 Wherefore my heart was glad, and my glory rejoyced: my flesh also shall rest in hope.

11 For why? thou shalt not leave my soul in hell: neither shalt thou suffer thy holy One to see corruption.

12 Thou shalt shew me the path of life; in thy presence is the fulness of joy: and at thy right hand there is pleasure for evermore.

Psalm 17

Exaudi, Domine.

Hear the right, O Lord, consider my complaint: and hearken unto my prayer, that goeth not out of feigned lips.

2 Let my sentence come forth from thy presence: and let thine eyes look upon the thing that is equal.

3 Thou hast proved, and visited mine heart in the night season; thou hast tryed me, and shalt find no wickedness in me: for I am utterly purposed, that my mouth shall not offend.

4 Because of mens works, that are done against the words of thy lips: I have kept me from the ways of the destroyer.

5 O hold thou up my goings in thy paths: that my footsteps slip not.

6 I have called upon thee, O God, for thou shalt hear me: incline thine ear to me, and hearken unto my words.

7 Shew thy marvellous loving kindness, thou that art the Saviour of them, which put their trust in thee: from such as resist thy right hand.

8 Keep me as the apple of an eye: hide me under the shadow of thy wings.

9 From the ungodly, that trouble me: mine enemies compass me round about to take away my soul.

10 They are inclosed in their own fat: and their mouth speaketh proud things.

11 They lie waiting in our way on every side: turning their eyes down to the ground.

12 Like of a lion that is greedy of his prey: and as it were a lions whelp, lurking in secret places.

13 Up, Lord, disappoint him, and cast him down: deliver my soul from the ungodly, which is a sword of thine.

14 From the men of thy hand, O Lord, from the men, I say, and from the evil world: which have their portion in this life, whose bellies thou fillest with thy hid treasure.

15 They have children at their desire: and leave the rest of their substance for their babes.

16 But as for me, I will behold thy presence in righteousness: and when I awake up after thy likeness, I shall be satisfied with it.

Day 3. *Evening Prayer.*

Psalm 18

Diligam te, Domine.

I WILL love thee, O Lord, my strength; the Lord is my stony rock, and my defence: my Saviour, my God, and my might, in whom I will trust, my buckler, the horn also of my salvation, and my refuge.

2 I will call upon the Lord, which is worthy to be praised: so shall I be safe from mine enemies.

3 The sorrows of death compassed me: and the overflowings of ungodliness made me afraid.

4 The pains of hell came about me: the snares of death overtook me.

5 In my trouble I will call upon the Lord: and complain unto my God.

6 So shall he hear my voice out of his holy temple: and my complaint shall come before him, it shall enter even into his ears.

7 The earth trembled, and quaked: the very foundations also of the hills shook, and were removed, because he was wroth.

8 There went a smoke out in his presence: and a consuming fire out of his mouth, so that coals were kindled at it.

9 He bowed the heavens also, and came down: and it was dark under his feet.

10 He rode upon the Cherubins, and did flie: he came flying upon the wings of the wind.

11 He made darkness his secret place: his pavilion round about him with dark water, and thick clouds to cover him.

12 At the brightness of his presence his clouds removed: hail-stones, and coals of fire.

13 The Lord also thundred out of heaven, and the Highest gave his thunder: hail-stones, and coals of fire.

14 He sent out his arrows, and scattered them: he cast forth lightnings, and destroyed them.

15 The springs of water were seen, and the foundations of the round world were discovered, at thy chiding, O Lord: at the blasting of the breath of thy displeasure.

16 He shall send down from on high to fetch me: and shall take me out of many waters.

17 He shall deliver from me my strongest enemy, and from them, which hate me: for they are too mighty for me.

18 They prevented me in the day of my trouble: but the Lord was my upholder.

19 He brought me forth also into a place of liberty: he brought me forth, even because he had a favour unto me.

20 The Lord shall reward me after my righteous dealing: according to the cleanness of my hands shall he recompense me.

21 Because I have kept the waies of the Lord: and have not forsaken my God, as the wicked doth.

22 For I have an eye unto all his laws: and will not cast out his commandments from me.

23 I was also uncorrupt before him: and eschewed mine own wickedness.

24 Therefore shall the Lord reward me after my righteous dealing: and according unto the cleanness of my hands in his eye-sight.

25 With the holy thou shalt be holy: and with a perfect man thou shalt be perfect.

26 With the clean thou shalt be clean: and with the froward thou shalt learn frowardness.

27 For thou shalt save the people, that are in adversity: and shalt bring down the high looks of the proud.

28 Thou also shalt light my candle: the Lord my God shall make my darkness to be light.

29 For in thee I shall discomfit an host of men: and with the help of my God I shall leap over the wall.

30 The way of God is an undefiled way: the word of the Lord also is tried in the fire; he is the defender of all them, that put their trust in him.

31 For who is God, but the Lord: or who hath any strength, except our God?

32 It is God, that girdeth me with strength of war: and maketh my way perfect.

33 He maketh my feet like harts feet: and setteth me up on high.

34 He teacheth mine hands to fight: and mine arms shall break even a bow of steel.

35 Thou hast given me the defence of thy salvation: thy right hand also shall hold me up, and thy loving correction shall make me great.

36 Thou shalt make room enough under me for to go: that my footsteps shall not slide.

37 I will follow upon mine enemies, and overtake them: neither will I turn again till I have destroyed them.

38 I will smite them, that they shall not be able to stand: but fall under my feet.

39 Thou hast girded me with strength unto the battle: thou shalt throw down mine enemies under me.

40 Thou hast made mine enemies also to turn their backs upon me: and I shall destroy them, that hate me.

41 They shall cry, but there shall be none to help them: yea even unto the Lord shall they cry, but he shall not hear them.

42 I will beat them as small as the dust before the wind: I will cast them out as the clay in the streets.

43 Thou shalt deliver me from the strivings of the people: and thou shalt make me the head of the heathen.

44 A people, whom I have not known: shall serve me.

45 As soon as they hear of me they shall obey me: but the strange children shall dissemble with me.

46 The strange children shall fail: and be afraid out of their prisons.

47 The Lord liveth, and blessed be my strong helper: and praised be the God of my salvation.

48 Even the God, that seeth that I be avenged: and subdueth the people unto me.

49 It is he, that delivereth me from my cruel Enemies, and setteth me up above mine Adversaries: thou shalt rid me from the wicked man.

50 For this cause will I give thanks unto thee, O Lord, among the Gentiles: and sing praises unto thy Name.

51 Great prosperity giveth he unto his King: and sheweth loving kindness unto David his Anointed, and unto his Seed for evermore.

Day 4. *Morning Prayer.*
Psalm 19
Caeli enarrant.

THE Heavens declare the glory of God: and the Firmament sheweth his handy-work.

2 One day telleth another: and one night certifieth another.

3 There is neither speech, nor language: but their voices are heard among them.

4 Their sound is gone out into all lands: and their words into the ends of the world.

5 In them hath he set a tabernacle for the Sun: which cometh forth as a Bridegroom out of his chamber, and rejoyceth as a Giant to run his course.

6 It goeth forth from the uttermost part of the Heaven, and runneth about unto the end of it again: and there is nothing hid from the heat thereof.

7 The law of the Lord is an undefiled law, converting the soul: the testimony of the Lord is sure, and giveth wisdom unto the simple.

8 The statutes of the Lord are right, and rejoyce the heart: the commandment of the Lord is pure, and giveth light unto the eyes.

9 The fear of the Lord is clean, and endureth for ever: the judgements of the Lord are true, and righteous altogether.

10 More to be desired are they than gold, yea, than much fine gold: sweeter also than honey, and the honey-comb.

11 Moreover by them is thy Servant taught: and in keeping of them there is great reward.

12 Who can tell how oft he offendeth: O cleanse thou me from my secret faults.

13 Keep thy servant also from presumptuous sins, lest they get the dominion over me: so shall I be undefiled, and innocent from the great offence.

14 Let the words of my mouth, and the meditation of my heart: be alway acceptable in thy sight,

15 O Lord: my strength, and my redeemer.

Psalm 20
Exaudiat te Dominus.

THE Lord hear thee in the day of trouble: the Name of the God of Jacob defend thee.

2 Send thee help from the Sanctuary: and strengthen thee out of Sion.

3 Remember all thy offerings: and accept thy burnt Sacrifice.

4 Grant thee thy hearts desire: and fulfil all thy mind.

5 We will rejoyce in thy salvation, and triumph in the Name of the Lord our God: the Lord perform all thy petitions.

6 Now know I, that the Lord helpeth his Anointed, and will hear him from his holy Heaven: even with the wholesom strength of his right hand.

7 Some put their trust in Chariots, and some in Horses: but we will remember the Name of the Lord our God.

8 They are brought down, and faln: but we are risen, and stand upright.

9 Save, Lord, and hear us, O King of Heaven: when we call upon thee.

Psalm 21
Domine, in virtute tua.

THE King shall rejoyce in thy strength, O Lord: exceeding glad shall he be of thy salvation.

2 Thou hast given him his hearts desire: and hast not denied him the request of his lips.

3 For thou shalt prevent him with the blessings of goodness: and shalt set a crown of pure gold upon his head.

4 He asked life of thee, and thou gavest him a long life: even for ever, and ever.

5 His honour is great in thy salvation: glory, and great worship shalt thou lay upon him.

6 For thou shalt give him everlasting felicity: and make him glad with the joy of thy countenance.

7 And why? because the King putteth his trust in the Lord: and in the mercy of the most Highest he shall not miscarry.

8 All thine enemies shall feel thyne hand: thy right hand shall find out them that hate thee.

9 Thou shalt make them like a fiery oven in time of thy wrath: the Lord shall destroy them in his displeasure, and the fire shall consume them.

10 Their fruit shalt thou root out of the earth: and their seed from among the children of men.

11 For they intended mischief against thee: and imagined such a device as they are not able to perform.

12 Therefore shalt thou put them to flight: and the strings of thy bow shalt thou make ready against the face of them.

13 Be thou exalted, Lord, in thine own strength: so will we sing, and praise thy power.

Day 4. *Evening Prayer.*

Psalm 22

Deus, Deus meus.

M Y GOD, my God, look upon me, why hast thou forsaken me: and art so far from my health, and from the words of my complaint?

2 O my God, I cry in the day time, but thou hearest not: and in the night season also I take no rest.

3 And thou continuest holy: O thou worship of Israel.

4 Our fathers hoped in thee: they trusted in thee, and thou didst deliver them.

5 They called upon thee, and were holpen: they put their trust in thee, and were not confounded.

6 But as for me, I am a worm, and no man: a very scorn of men, and the out-cast of the people.

7 All they that see me, laugh me to scorn: they shoot our their lips, and shake their heads, saying,

8 He trusted in God, that he would deliver him: let him deliver him, if he will have him.

9 But thou art he, that took me out of my mothers womb: thou wast my hope, when I hanged yet upon my mothers brests.

10 I have been left unto thee ever since I was born: thou art my God even from my mothers womb.

11 O go not from me, for trouble is hard at hand: and there is none to help me.

12 Many oxen are come about me: fat bulls of Basan close me in on every side.

13 They gape upon me with their mouths: as it were a ramping and a roaring lion.

14 I am poured out like water, and all my bones are out of joynt: my heart also in the midst of my body is even like melting wax.

15 My strength is dryed up like a potsherd, and my tongue cleaveth to my gums: and thou shalt bring me into the dust of death.

16 For many dogs are come about me: and the council of the wicked layeth siege against me.

17 They pierced my hands, and my feet, I may tell all my bones: they stand staring, and looking upon me.

18 They part my garments among them: and cast lots upon my vesture.

19 But be not thou far from me, O Lord: thou art my succour, haste thee to help me.

20 Deliver my soul from the sword: my darling from the power of the dog.

21 Save me from the lions mouth: thou hast heard me also from among the horns of the unicorns.

22 I will declare thy name unto my brethren: in the midst of the congregation will I praise thee.

23 O praise the Lord, ye that fear him: magnifie him, all ye of the seed of Jacob, and fear him, all ye seed of Israel.

24 For he hath not despised, nor abhorred the low estate of the poor: he hath not hid his face from him, but when he called unto him he heard him.

25 My praise is of thee in the great congregation: my vows will I perform in the sight of them that fear him.

26 The poor shall eat, and be satisfied: they that seek after the Lord shall praise him; your heart shall live for ever.

27 All the ends of the world shall remember themselves, and be turned unto the Lord: and all the kindreds of the nations shall worship before him.

28 For the kingdom is the Lords: and he is the governour among the people.

29 All such as be fat upon earth: have eaten, and worshipped.

30 All they, that go down into the dust, shall kneel before him: and no man hath quickned his own soul.

31 My seed shall serve him: they shall be counted unto the Lord for a generation.

32 They shall come, and the heavens shall declare his righteousness: unto a people that shall be born, whom the Lord hath made.

Psalm 23

Dominus regit me.

THE Lord is my shepherd: therefore can I lack nothing.

2 He shall feed me in a green pasture: and lead me forth beside the waters of comfort.

3 He shall convert my soul: and bring me forth in the paths of righteousness for his Names sake.

4 Yea, thou I walk through the valley of the shadow of death, I will fear no evil: for thou art with me, thy rod and thy staff comfort me.

5 Thou shalt prepare a table before me against them, that trouble me: thou hast anointed my head with oil, and my cup shall be full.

6 But thy loving kindness and mercy shall follow me all the days of my life: and I will dwell in the house of the Lord for ever.

Day 5. *Morning Prayer.*

Psalm 24

Domini est terra.

THE earth is the Lords, and all that therein is: the compass of the world, and they that dwell therein.

2 For he hath founded it upon the seas: and prepared it upon the flouds.

3 Who shall ascend into the hill of the Lord: or who shall rise up in his holy place?

4 Even he, that hath clean hands, and a pure heart: and that hath not lift up his mind unto vanity, nor sworn to deceive his neighbour.

5 He shall receive the blessing from the Lord: and righteousness from the God of his salvation.

6 This is the generation of them that seek him: even of them that seek thy face, O Jacob.

7 Lift up your heads, O ye gates, and be ye lift up, ye everlasting doors: and the King of glory shall come in.

8 Who is the King of glory: it is the Lord strong and mighty, even the Lord mighty in battel.

9 Lift up your heads, O ye gates, and be ye lift up, ye everlasting doors: and the King of glory shall come in.

10 Who is the King of glory: even the Lord of hosts, he is the King of glory.

Psalm 25

Ad te, Domine, levavi.

UNTO thee, O Lord, will I lift up my soul, my God, I have put my trust in thee: O let me not be confounded, neither let mine enemies triumph over me.

2 For all they that hope in thee shall not be ashamed: but such as transgress without a cause shall be put to confusion.

3 Shew me thy waies, O Lord: and teach me thy paths.

4 Lead me forth in thy truth, and learn me: for thou art the God of my salvation; in thee hath been my hope all the day long.

5 Call to remembrance, O Lord, thy tender mercies: and thy loving kindnesses, which have been ever of old.

6 O remember not the sins and offences of my youth: but according to thy mercy think thou upon me, O Lord, for thy goodness.

7 Gracious and righteous is the Lord: therefore will he teach sinners in the way.

8 Them that are meek shall he guide in judgement: and such as are gentle, them shall he learn his way.

9 All the paths of the Lord are mercy, and truth: unto such as keep his covenant, and his testimonies.

10 For thy Names sake, O Lord: be merciful unto my sin, for it is great.

11 What man is he, that feareth the Lord: him shall he teach in the way, that he shall choose.

12 His soul shall dwell at ease: and his seed shall inherit the land.

13 The secret of the Lord is among them, that fear him: and he will shew them his covenant.

14 Mine eyes are ever looking unto the Lord: for he shall pluck my feet out of the net.

15 Turn thee unto me, and have mercy upon me: for I am desolate, and in misery.

16 The sorrows of my heart are inlarged: O bring thou me out of my troubles.

17 Look upon my adversity, and misery: and forgive me all my sin.

18 Consider mine enemies how many they are: and they bear a tyrannous hate against me.

19 O keep my soul, and deliver me: let me not be confounded, for I have put my trust in thee.

20 Let perfectness and righteous dealing wait upon me: for my hope hath been in thee.

21 Deliver Israel, O God: out of all his troubles.

Psalm 26

Judica me, Domine.

B E THOU my judge, O Lord, for I have walked innocently: my trust hath been also in the Lord, therefore shall I not fall.

2 Examine me, O Lord, and prove me: try out my reins, and my heart.

3 For thy loving kindness is ever before mine eyes: and I will walk in thy truth.

4 I have not dwelt with vain persons: neither will I have fellowship with the deceitfull.

5 I have hated the congregation of the wicked: and will not sit among the ungodly.

6 I will wash my hands in innocency, O Lord: and so will I go to thine altar;

7 That I may shew the voice of thanksgiving: and tell of all thy wondrous works.

8 Lord, I have loved the habitation of thy house: and the place where thine honour dwelleth.

9 O shut not up my soul with the sinners: nor my life with the bloud-thirsty.

10 In whose hands is wickedness: and their right hand is full of gifts.

11 But as for me, I will walk innocently: O deliver me, and be merciful unto me.

12 My foot standeth right: I will praise the Lord in the congregations.

Day 5. *Evening Prayer.*

Psalm 27

Dominus illuminatio.

THE Lord is my light, and my salvation; whom then shall I fear: the Lord is the strength of my life; of whom then shall I be afraid?

2 When the wicked, even mine enemies and my foes, came upon me to eat up my flesh: they stumbled and fell.

3 Though an host of men were laid against me, yet shall not my heart be afraid: and though there rose up war against me, yet will I put my trust in him.

4 One thing have I desired of the Lord, which I will require: even that I may dwell in the house of the Lord all the daies of my life, to behold the fair beauty of the Lord, and to visit his temple.

5 For in the time of trouble he shall hide me in his tabernacle: yea, in the secret place of his dwelling shall he hide me, and set me up upon a rock of stone.

6 And now shall he lift up mine head: above mine enemies round about me.

7 Therefore will I offer in his dwelling an oblation with great gladness: I will sing, and speak praises unto the Lord.

8 Hearken unto my voice, O Lord, when I cry unto thee: have mercy upon me, and hear me.

9 My heart hath talked of thee, Seek ye my face: thy face, Lord, will I seek.

10 O hide not thou thy face from me: nor cast thy servant away in displeasure.

11 Thou hast been my succour: leave me not, neither forsake me, O God of my salvation.

12 When my Father and my Mother forsake me: the Lord taketh me up.

13 Teach me the way, O Lord: and lead in the right way, because of mine enemies.

14 Deliver me not over into the will of mine adversaries: for there are false witnesses risen up against me, and such as speak wrong.

15 I should utterly have fainted: but that I believe verily to see the goodness of the Lord in the land of the living.

16 O tarry thou the Lords leasure: be strong, and he shall comfort thine heart, and put thou thy trust in the Lord.

Psalm 28

Ad te, Domine.

UNTO thee will I cry, O Lord my strength: think no scorn of me, lest if thou make as though thou hearest not, I become like them, that go down into the pit.

2 Hear the voice of my humble petitions, when I cry unto thee: when I hold up my hands towards the mercy-seat of thy holy temple.

3 O pluck me not away, neither destroy me with the ungodly, and wicked doers: which speak friendly to their neighbours, but imagine mischief in their hearts.

4 Reward them according to their deeds: and according to the wickedness of their own inventions.

5 Recompense them after the work of their hands: pay them that they have deserved.

6 For they regard not in their mind the works of the Lord, nor the operation of his hands: therefore shall he break them down, and not build them up.

7 Praised be the Lord: for he hath heard the voice of my humble petitions.

8 The Lord is my strength, and my shield, my heart hath trusted in him, and I am helped: therefore my heart danceth for joy, and in my song will I praise him.

9 The Lord is my strength: and he is the wholesom defence of his Anointed.

10 O save thy people, and give thy blessing unto thine inheritance: feed them, and set them up for ever.

Psalm 29

Afferte Domino.

BRING unto the Lord, O ye mighty, bring young rams unto the Lord: ascribe unto the Lord worship, and strength.

2 Give the Lord the honour due unto his Name: worship the Lord with holy worship.

3 It is the Lord, that commandeth the waters: it is the glorious God, that maketh the thunder.

4 It is the Lord, that ruleth the Sea; the voice of the Lord is mighty in operation: the voice of the Lord is a glorious voice.

5 The voice of the Lord breaketh the Cedar-trees: yea, the Lord breaketh the Cedars of Libanus.

6 He maketh them also to skip like a calf: Libanus also and Sirion, like a young unicorn.

7 The voice of the Lord divideth the flames of fire, the voice of the Lord shaketh the wilderness: yea, the Lord shaketh the wilderness of Cades.

8 The voice of the Lord maketh the hinds to bring forth young, and discovereth the thick bushes: in his temple doth every man speak of his honour.

9 The Lord sitteth above the water-floud: and the Lord remaineth a King for ever.

10 The Lord shall give strength unto his people: the Lord shall give his people the blessing of peace.

Day 6. *Morning Prayer.*

Psalm 30

Exaltabo te, Domine.

I WILL magnifie thee, O Lord, for thou hast set me up: and not made my foes to triumph over me.

2 O Lord my God, I cryed unto thee: and thou hast healed me.

3 Thou, Lord, hast brought my soul out of hell: thou hast kept my life from them, that go down to the pit.

4 Sing praises unto the Lord, O ye saints of his: and give thanks unto him for a remembrance of his holiness.

5 For his wrath endureth but the twinkling of an eye, and in his pleasure is life: heaviness may endure for a night, but joy cometh in the morning.

6 And in my prosperity I said, I shall never be removed: thou, Lord, of thy goodness hast made my hill so strong.

7 Thou didst turn thy face from me: and I was troubled.

8 Then cried I unto thee, O Lord: and gat me to my Lord right humbly.

9 What profit is there in my bloud: when I go down to the pit?

10 Shall the dust give thanks unto thee: or shall it declare thy truth?

11 Hear, O Lord, and have mercy upon me: Lord, be thou my helper.

12 Thou hast turned my heaviness into joy: thou hast put off my sack-cloth, and girded me with gladness.

13 Therefore shall every good man sing of thy praise without ceasing: O my God, I will give thanks unto thee for ever.

Psalm 31

In te, Domine, speravi.

IN THEE, O Lord, have I put my trust: let me never be put to confusion, deliver me in thy righteousness.

2 Bow down thine ear to me: make haste to deliver me.

3 And be thou my strong rock, and house of defence: that thou mayest save me.

4 For thou art my strong rock, and my castle: be thou also my guide, and lead me for thy Names sake.

5 Draw me out of the net, that they have laid privily for me: for thou art my strength.

6 Into thy hands I commend my spirit: for thou hast redeemed me, O Lord, thou God of truth.

7 I have hated them, that hold of superstitious vanities: and my trust hath been in the Lord.

8 I will be glad, and rejoyce in thy mercy: for thou hast considered my trouble, and hast known my soul in adversities.

9 Thou hast not shut me up into the hand of the enemy: but hast set my feet in a large room.

10 Have mercy upon me, O Lord, for I am in trouble: and mine eye is consumed for very heaviness; yea, my soul, and my body.

11 For my life is waxen old with heaviness: and my years with mourning.

12 My strength faileth me, because of mine iniquity: and my bones are consumed.

13 I became a reproof among all mine enemies, but especially among my neighbours: and they of mine acquaintance were afraid of me, and they, that did see me without, conveyed themselves from me.

14 I am clean forgotten, as a dead man out of mind: I am become like a broken vessel.

15 For I have heard the blasphemy of the multitude: and fear is on

every side, while they conspire together against me, and take their counsel to take away my life.

16 But my hope hath been in thee, O Lord: I have said, Thou art my God.

17 My time is in thy hand, deliver me from the hand of mine enemies: and from them, that persecute me.

18 Shew thy servant the light of thy countenance: and save me for thy mercies sake.

19 Let me not be confounded, O Lord, for I have called upon thee: let the ungodly be put to confusion, and be put to silence in the grave.

20 Let the lying lips be put to silence: which cruelly, disdainfully, and despitefully speak against the righteous.

21 O how plentiful is thy goodness which thou hast laid up for them, that fear thee: and that thou hast prepared for them, that put their trust in thee, even before the sons of men!

22 Thou shalt hide them privily by thine own presence from the provoking of all men: thou shalt keep them secretly in thy tabernacle from the strife of tongues.

23 Thanks be to the Lord: for he hath shewed me marvellous great kindness in a strong city.

24 And when I made haste, I said: I am cast out of the sight of thine eyes.

25 Nevertheless thou heardest the voice of my prayer: when I cryed unto thee.

26 O love the Lord, all ye his saints: for the Lord preserveth them, that are faithful, and plenteously rewardeth the proud doer.

27 Be strong, and he shall establish your heart: all ye, that put your trust in the Lord.

Day 6. *Evening Prayer.*

Psalm 32

Beati, quorum.

Blessed is he, whose unrighteousness is forgiven: and whose sin is covered.

2 Blessed is the man unto whom the Lord imputeth no sin: and in whose spirit there is no guile.

3 For while I held my tongue: my bones consumed away through my daily complaining.

4 For thy hand is heavy upon me day and night: and my moisture is like the drought in summer.

5 I will acknowledge my sin unto thee: and mine unrighteousness have I not hid.

6 I said, I will confess my sins unto the Lord: and so thou forgavest the wickedness of my sin.

7 For this shall every one that is godly make his prayer unto thee, in a time when thou mayest be found: but in the great water-flouds they shall not come nigh him.

8 Thou art a place to hide me in, thou shalt preserve me from trouble: thou shalt compass me about with songs of deliverance.

9 I will inform thee, and teach thee in the way, wherein thou shalt go: and I will guide thee with mine eye.

10 Be ye not like to horse and mule, which have no understanding: whose mouths must be held with bit and bridle, lest they fall upon thee.

11 Great plagues remain for the ungodly: but whoso putteth his trust in the Lord, mercy embraceth him on every side.

12 Be glad, O ye righteous, and rejoyce in the Lord: and be joyful, all ye that are true of heart.

Psalm 33

Exultate, justi.

REJOYCE in the Lord, O ye righteous: for it becometh well the just to be thankful.

2 Praise the Lord with harp: sing praises unto him with the lute, and instrument of ten strings.

3 Sing unto the Lord a new song: sing praises lustily unto him with a good courage.

4 For the word of the Lord is true: and all his works are faithful.

5 He loveth righteousness, and judgement: the earth is full of the goodness of the Lord.

6 By the word of the Lord were the heavens made: and all the hosts of them by the breath of his mouth.

7 He gathereth the waters of the sea together, as it were upon an heap: and laieth up the deep, as in a treasure-house.

8 Let all the earth fear the Lord: stand in awe of him, all ye that dwell in the world.

9 For he spake, and it was done: he commanded, and it stood fast.

10 The Lord bringeth the counsel of the heathen to nought: and maketh the devices of the people to be of none effect, and casteth out the counsels of Princes.

11 The counsel of the Lord shall endure for ever: and the thoughts of his heart from generation to generation.

12 Blessed are the people, whose God is the Lord Jehovah: and blessed are the folk, that he hath chosen to him to be his inheritance.

13 The Lord looked down from heaven, and beheld all the children of men: from the habitation of his dwelling he considereth all them, that dwell on the earth.

14 He fashioneth all the hearts of them: and understandeth all their works.

15 There is no king, that can be saved by the multitude of an host: neither is any mighty man delivered by much strength.

16 A horse is counted but a vain thing to save a man: neither shall he deliver any man by his great strength.

17 Behold, the eye of the Lord is upon them, that fear him: and upon them, that put their trust in his mercy.

18 To deliver their soul from death: and to feed them in the time of dearth.

19 Our soul hath patiently tarried for the Lord: for he is our help, and our shield.

20 For our heart shall rejoyce in him: because we have hoped in his holy name.

21 Let thy merciful kindness, O Lord, be upon us: like as we do put our trust in thee.

Psalm 34

Benedicam Domino.

I WILL alway give thanks unto the Lord: his praise shall ever be in my mouth.

2 My soul shall make her boast in the Lord: the humble shall hear thereof, and be glad.

3 O praise the Lord with me: and let us magnifie his Name together.

4 I sought the Lord, and he heard me: yea, he delivered me out of all my fear.

5 They had an eye unto him, and were lightened: and their faces were not ashamed.

6 Lo, the poor crieth, and the Lord heareth him: yea, and saveth him out of all his troubles.

7 The Angel of the Lord tarrieth round about them that fear him: and delivereth them.

8 O taste, and see, how gracious the Lord is: blessed is the man, that trusteth in him.

9 O fear the Lord, ye that are his Saints: for they that fear him, lack nothing.

10 The lions do lack, and suffer hunger: but they, who seek the Lord, shall want no manner of thing, that is good.

11 Come, ye children, and hearken unto me: I will teach you the fear of the Lord.

12 What man is he, that lusteth to live: and would fain see good daies?

13 Keep thy tongue from evil: and thy lips, that they speak no guile.

14 Eschew evil, and do good: seek peace, and ensue it.

15 The eyes of the Lord are over the righteous: and his ears are open unto their prayers.

16 The countenance of the Lord is against them, that do evil: to root out the remembrance of them from the earth.

17 The righteous cry, and the Lord heareth them: and delivereth them out of all their troubles.

18 The Lord is nigh unto them, that are of a contrite heart: and will save such, as be of an humble spirit.

19 Great are the troubles of the righteous: but the Lord delivereth him out of all.

20 He keepeth all his bones: so that not one of them is broken.

21 But misfortune shall slay the ungodly: and they that hate the righteous, shall be desolate.

22 The Lord delivereth the souls of his servants: and all they, that put their trust in him, shall not be destitute.

Day 7. *Morning Prayer.*

Psalm 35

Judica, Domine.

PLEAD thou my cause, O Lord, with them that strive with me: and fight thou against them, that fight against me.

2 Lay hand upon the shield and buckler: and stand up to help me.

3 Bring forth the spear, and stop the way against them that persecute me: say unto my soul, I am thy salvation.

4 Let them be confounded and put to shame, that seek after my soul: let them be turned back, and brought to confusion, that imagine mischief for me.

5 Let them be as the dust before the wind: and the Angel of the Lord scattering them.

6 Let their way be dark, and slippery: and let the Angel of the Lord persecute them.

7 For they have privily laid their net to destroy me without a cause: yea, even without a cause have they made a pit for my soul.

8 Let a sudden destruction come upon him unawares, and his net, that he hath laid privily, catch himself: that he may fall into his own mischief.

9 And, my soul, be joyful in the Lord: it shall rejoyce in his salvation.

10 All my bones shall say, Lord, who is like unto thee, who deliverest the poor from him that is too strong for him: yea, the poor, and him that is in misery, from him that spoileth him?

11 False witnesses did rise up: they laid to my charge things, that I knew not.

12 They rewarded me evil for good: to the great discomfort of my soul.

13 Nevertheless, when they were sick, I put on sackcloth, and humbled my soul with fasting: and my prayer shall turn into mine own bosom.

14 I behaved my self as though it had been my friend, or my brother: I went heavily, as one that mourneth for his mother.

15 But in mine adversity they rejoyced, and gathered themselves together: yea, the very abjects came together against me unawares, making mouthes at me, and ceased not.

16 With the flatterers were busie mockers: who gnashed upon me with their teeth.

17 Lord, how long wilt thou look upon this: O deliver my soul from the calamities, which they bring on me, and my darling from the lions.

18 So will I give thee thanks in the great congregation: I will praise thee among much people.

19 O let not them that are mine enemies triumph over me ungodly: neither let them wink with their eyes, that they hate me without a cause.

20 And why? their communing is not for peace: but they imagine deceitful words against them, that are quiet in the land.

21 They gaped upon me with their mouths, and said: Fie on thee, fie on thee, we saw it with our eyes.

22 This thou hast seen, O Lord: hold not thy tongue then, go not far from me, O Lord.

23 Awake and stand up to judge my quarrel: avenge thou my cause, my God, and my Lord.

24 Judge me, O Lord my God, according to thy righteousness: and let them not triumph over me.

25 Let them not say in their hearts, There, there, so would we have it: neither let them say, We have devoured him.

26 Let them be put to confusion and shame together, that rejoyce at my trouble: let them be clothed with rebuke and dishonour, that boast themselves against me.

27 Let them be glad and rejoyce, that favour my righteous dealing: yea, let them say alway, Blessed be the Lord, who hath pleasure in the prosperity of his servant.

28 And as for my tongue, it shall be talking of thy righteousness: and of thy praise all the day long.

Psalm 36

Dixit injustus.

MY HEART sheweth me the wickedness of the ungodly: that there is no fear of God before his eyes.

2 For he flattereth himself in his own sight: until his abominable sin be found out.

3 The words of his mouth are unrighteous, and full of deceit: he hath left off to behave himself wisely, and to do good.

4 He imagineth mischief upon his bed, and hath set himself in no good way: neither doth he abhor any thing that is evil.

5 Thy mercy, O Lord, reacheth unto the heavens: and thy faithfulness unto the clouds.

6 Thy righteousness standeth like the strong mountains: thy judgements are like the great deep.

7 Thou, Lord, shalt save both man and beast; How excellent is thy mercy, O God: and the children of men shall put their trust under the shadow of thy wings.

8 They shall be satisfied with the plenteousness of thy house: and thou shalt give them drink of thy pleasures, as out of the river.

9 For with thee is the well of life: and in thy light shall we see light.

10 O continue forth thy loving kindness unto them, that know thee: and thy righteousness unto them, that are true of heart.

11 O let not the foot of pride come against me: and let not the hand of the ungodly cast me down.

12 There are they faln, all that work wickedness: they are cast down, and shall not be able to stand.

Day 7. *Evening Prayer*.

Psalm 37

Noli aemulari.

FRET not thyself because of the ungodly: neither be thou envious against the evil doers.

2 For they shall soon be cut down like the grass: and be withered even as the green herb.

3 Put thou thy trust in the Lord, and be doing good: dwell in the land, and verily thou shalt be fed.

4 Delight thou in the Lord: and he shall give thee thy hearts desire.

5 Commit thy way unto the Lord, and put thy trust in him: and he shall bring it to pass.

6 He shall make thy righteousness as clear as the light: and thy just dealing as the noon-day.

7 Hold thee still in the Lord, and abide patiently upon him: but grieve not thy self at him, whose way doth prosper, against the man that doth after evil counsels.

8 Leave off from wrath, and let go displeasure: fret not thy self, else shalt thou be moved to do evil.

9 Wicked doers shall be rooted out: and they, that patiently abide the Lord, those shall inherit the land.

10 Yet a little while, and the ungodly shall be clean gone: thou shalt look after his place, and he shall be away.

11 But the meek-spirited shall possess the earth: and shall be refreshed in the multitude of peace.

12 The ungodly seeketh counsel against the just: and gnasheth upon him with his teeth.

13 The Lord shall laugh him to scorn: for he hath seen that his day is coming.

14 The ungodly have drawn out the sword, and have bent their bow: to cast down the poor and needy, and to slay such, as are of a right conversation.

15 Their sword shall go through their own heart: and their bow shall be broken.

16 A small thing that the righteous hath: is better than great riches of the ungodly.

17 For the arms of the ungodly shall be broken: and the Lord upholdeth the righteous.

18 The Lord knoweth the days of the godly: and their inheritance shall endure for ever.

19 They shall not be confounded in the perillous time: and in the days of dearth they shall have enough.

20 As for the ungodly, they shall perish, and the enemies of the Lord shall consume as the fat of lambs: yea, even as the smoke shall they consume away.

21 The ungodly borroweth, and payeth not again: but the righteous is merciful and liberal.

22 Such as are blessed of God shall possess the land: and they, that are cursed of him, shall be rooted out.

23 The Lord ordereth a good mans going: and maketh his way acceptable to himself.

24 Though he fall, he shall not be cast away: for the Lord upholdeth him with his hand.

25 I have been young, and now am old: and yet saw I never the righteous forsaken, nor his seed begging their bread.

26 The righteous is ever merciful, and lendeth: and his seed is blessed.

27 Flee from evil, and do the thing that is good: and dwell for evermore.

28 For the Lord loveth the thing that is right: he forsaketh not his that be godly, but they are preserved for ever.

29 The unrighteous shall be punished: as for the seed of the ungodly, it shall be rooted out.

30 The righteous shall inherit the land: and dwell therein forever.

31 The mouth of the righteous is exercised in wisdom: and his tongue will be talking of judgement.

32 The law of his God is in his heart: and his goings shall not slide.

33 The ungodly seeth the righteous: and seeketh occasion to slay him.

34 The Lord will not leave him in his hand: nor condemn him when he is judged.

35 Hope thou in the Lord, and keep his way, and he shall promote thee, that thou shalt possess the land: when the ungodly shall perish, thou shalt see it.

36 I my self have seen the ungodly in great power: and flourishing like a green bay-tree.

37 I went by, and lo, he was gone: I sought him, but his place could no where be found.

38 Keep innocency, and take heed unto the thing that is right: for that shall bring a man peace at the last.

39 As for the transgressours, they shall perish together: and the end of the ungodly is, they shall be rooted out at the last.

40 But the salvation of the righteous cometh of the Lord: who is also their strength in the time of trouble.

41 And the Lord shall stand by them, and save them: he shall deliver them from the ungodly, and shall save them, because they put their trust in him.

Day 8. *Morning Prayer.*

Psalm 38

Domine, ne in furore.

Put me not to rebuke, O Lord, in thine anger: neither chasten me in thy heavy displeasure.

2 For thine arrows stick fast in me: and thy hand presseth me sore.

3 There is no health in my flesh, because of thy displeasure: neither is there any rest in my bones, by reason of my sin.

4 For my wickednesses are gone over my head: and are like a sore burthen, too heavy for me to bear.

5 My wounds stink, and are corrupt: through my foolishness.

6 I am brought into so great trouble, and misery: that I go mourning all the day long.

7 For my loins are filled with a sore disease: and there is no whole part in my body.

8 I am feeble, and sore smitten: I have roared for the very disquietness of my heart.

9 Lord, thou knowest all my desire: and my groaning is not hid from thee.

10 My heart panteth, my strength hath failed me: and the sight of mine eyes is gone from me.

11 My lovers and my neighbours did stand looking upon my trouble: and my kinsmen stood afar off.

12 They also, that sought after my life, laid snares for me: and they, that went about to do me evil, talked of wickedness, and imagined deceit all the day long.

13 As for me, I was like a deaf man, and heard not: and as one that is dumb, who doth not open his mouth.

14 I became even as a man, that heareth not: and in whose mouth are no reproofs.

15 For in thee, O Lord, have I put my trust: thou shalt answer for me, O Lord my God.

16 I have required that they, even mine enemies, should not triumph over me: for when my foot slipt, they rejoyced greatly against me.

17 And I, truly, am set in the plague: and my heaviness is ever in my sight.

18 For I will confess my wickedness: and be sorry for my sin.

19 But mine enemies live, and are mighty: and they, that hate me wrongfully, are many in number.

20 They also, that reward evil for good, are against me: because I follow the thing that good is.

21 Forsake me not, O Lord my God: be not thou far from me.

22 Haste thee to help me: O Lord God of my salvation.

Psalm 39
Dixi, custodiam.

I SAID, I will take heed to my waies: that I offend not in my tongue.

2 I will keep my mouth as it were with a bridle: while the ungodly is in my sight.

3 I held my tongue, and spake nothing: I kept silence, yea, even from good words; but it was pain, and grief to me.

4 My heart was hot within me, and while I was thus musing, the fire kindled: and at the last I spake with my tongue.

5 Lord, let me know myne end, and the number of my daies: that I may be certified how long I have to live.

6 Behold, thou hast made my days as it were a span long: and mine age is even as nothing in respect of thee, and verily every man living is altogether vanity.

7 For man walketh in a vain shadow, and disquieteth himself in vain: he heapeth up riches, and cannot tell who shall gather them.

8 And now, Lord, what is my hope: truly my hope is even in thee.

9 Deliver me from all mine offences: and make me not a rebuke unto the foolish.

10 I became dumb, and opened not my mouth: for it was thy doing.

11 Take thy plague away from me: I am even consumed by the means of thy heavy hand.

12 When thou with rebukes dost chasten man for sin, thou makest his beauty to consume away, like as it were a moth fretting a garment: every man therefore is but vanity.

13 Hear my prayer, O Lord, and with thine ears consider my calling: hold not thy peace at my tears.

14 For I am a stranger with thee, and a sojourner: as all my fathers were.

15 O spare me a little, that I may recover my strength: before I go hence, and be no more seen.

Psalm 40

Expectans expectavi.

I WAITED patiently for the Lord: and he inclined unto me, and heard my calling.

2 He brought me also out of the horrible pit, out of the mire and clay: and set my feet upon the rock, and ordered my goings.

3 And he hath put a new song in my mouth: even a thanksgiving unto our God.

4 Many shall see it, and fear: and shall put their trust in the Lord.

5 Blessed is the man, that hath set his hope in the Lord: and turned not unto the proud, and to such as go about with lies.

6 O Lord my God, great are the wondrous works, which thou hast done, like as be also thy thoughts, which are to us-ward: and yet there is no man, that ordereth them unto thee.

7 If I should declare them, and speak of them: they should be moe than I am able to express.

8 Sacrifice, and meat-offering thou wouldest not: but mine ears hast thou opened.

9 Burnt-offerings, and sacrifice for sin hast thou not required: then said I, Lo, I come.

10 In the volume of the book it is written of me, that I should fulfil thy will, O my God: I am content to do it, yea, thy law is within my heart.

11 I have declared thy righteousness in the great congregation: lo, I will not refrain my lips, O Lord, and that thou knowest.

12 I have not hid thy righteousness within my heart: my talk hath been of thy truth, and of thy salvation.

13 I have not kept back thy loving mercy, and truth: from the great congregation.

14 Withdraw not thou thy mercy from me, O Lord: let thy loving kindness and thy truth alway preserve me.

15 For innumerable troubles are come about me, my sins have taken such hold upon me, that I am not able to look up: yea, they are moe in number than the hairs of my head, and my heart hath failed me.

16 O Lord, let it be thy pleasure to deliver me: make haste, O Lord, to help me.

17 Let them be ashamed and confounded together, that seek after

my soul to destroy it: let them be driven backward, and put to rebuke, that wish me evil.

18 Let them be desolate, and rewarded with shame: that say unto me, Fie upon thee, fie upon thee.

19 Let all those that seek thee be joyful, and glad in thee: and let such as love thy salvation say alway, The Lord be praised.

20 As for me, I am poor and needy: but the Lord careth for me.

21 Thou art my helper, and redeemer: make no long tarrying, O my God.

Day 8. *Evening Prayer.*

Psalm 41

Beatus qui intelligit.

B LESSED is he, that considereth the poor and needy: the Lord shall deliver him in the time of trouble.

2 The Lord preserve him, and keep him alive, that he may be blessed upon earth: and deliver not thou him into the will of his enemies.

3 The Lord comfort him, when he lieth sick upon his bed: make thou all his bed in his sickness.

4 I said, Lord, be merciful unto me: heal my soul, for I have sinned against thee.

5 Mine enemies speak evil of me: When shall he die, and his name perish?

6 And if he come to see me, he speaketh vanity: and his heart conceiveth falshood within himself, and when he cometh forth he telleth it.

7 All mine enemies whisper together against me: even against me do they imagine this evil.

8 Let the sentence of guiltiness proceed against him: and now that he lieth, let him rise up no more.

9 Yea, even mine own familiar friend, whom I trusted: who did also eat of my bread, hath laid great wait for me.

10 But be thou merciful unto me, O Lord: raise thou me up again, and I shall reward them.

11 By this I know thou favourest me: that mine enemy doth not triumph against me.

12 And when I am in my health, thou upholdest me: and shalt set me before thy face for ever.

13 Blessed be the Lord God of Israel: world without end. Amen.

Psalm 42

Quemadmodum.

LIKE as the hart desireth the water-brooks: so longeth my soul after thee, O God.

2 My soul is athirst for God, yea, even for the living God: when shall I come to appear before the presence of God?

3 My tears have been my meat day and night: while they daily say unto me, Where is now thy God?

4 Now when I think thereupon, I pour out my heart by my self: for I went with the multitude, and brought them forth into the house of God;

5 In the voice of praise and thanksgiving: among such as keep holy-day.

6 Why art thou so full of heaviness, O my soul: and why art thou so disquieted within me?

7 Put thy trust in God: for I will yet give him thanks for the help of his countenance.

8 My God, my soul is vexed within me: therefore will I remember thee concerning the land of Jordan, and the little hill of Hermon.

9 One deep calleth another, because of the noise of the water-pipes: all thy waves and storms are gone over me.

10 The Lord hath granted his loving kindness on the day-time: and in the night-season did I sing of him, and made my prayer unto the God of my life.

11 I will say unto the God of my strength, Why hast thou forgotten me: why go I thus heavily, while the enemy oppresseth me?

12 My bones are smitten asunder as with a sword: while mine enemies that trouble me cast me in the teeth;

13 Namely, while they say daily unto me: Where is now thy God?

14 Why art thou so vexed, O my soul: and why art thou so disquieted within me?

15 O put thy trust in God: for I will yet thank him, which is the help of my countenance, and my God.

Psalm 43

Judica me, Deus.

GIVE sentence with me, O God, and defend my cause against the ungodly people: O deliver me from the deceitful and wicked man.

2 For thou art the God of my strength, why hast thou put me from thee: and why go I so heavily, while the enemy oppresseth me?

3 O send out thy light and thy truth, that they may lead me: and bring me unto thy holy hill, and to thy dwelling.

4 And that I may go unto the altar of God, even unto the God of my joy and gladness: and upon the harp I will give thanks unto thee, O God, my God.

5 Why art thou so heavy, O my soul: and why art thou so disquieted within me?

6 O put thy trust in God: for I will yet give him thanks, which is the help of my countenance, and my God.

Day 9. *Morning Prayer.*

Psalm 44

Deus, auribus.

WE HAVE heard with our ears, O God, our fathers have told us: what thou hast done in their time of old.

2 How thou hast driven out the heathen with thy hand, and planted them in: how thou hast destroyed the nations, and cast them out.

3 For they gat not the land in possession through their own sword: neither was it their own arm that helped them.

4 But thy right hand, and thine arm, and the light of thy countenance: because thou hadst a favour unto them.

5 Thou art my King, O God: send help unto Jacob.

6 Through thee will we overthrow our enemies: and in thy Name will we tread them under, that rise up against us.

7 For I will not trust in my bow: it is not my sword that shall help me.

8 But it is thou that savest us from our enemies: and puttest them to confusion that hate us.

9 We make our boast of God all day long: and will praise thy Name for ever.

10 But now thou art farr off, and puttest us to confusion: and goest not forth with our armies.

11 Thou makest us to turn our backs upon our enemies: so that they, which hate us, spoil our goods.

12 Thou lettest us be eaten up like sheep: and hast scattered us among the heathen.

13 Thou sellest thy people for nought: and takest no money for them.

14 Thou makest us to be rebuked of our neighbours: to be laughed to scorn, and had in derision of them that are round about us.

15 Thou makest us to be a by-word among the heathen: and that the people shake their heads at us.

16 My confusion is daily before me: and the shame of my face hath covered me;

17 For the voice of the slanderer, and blasphemer: for the enemy, and avenger.

18 And though all this be come upon us, yet do we not forget thee: nor behave our selves frowardly in thy covenant.

19 Our heart is not turned back: neither our steps gone out of thy way;

20 No, not when thou hast smitten us into the place of dragons: and covered us with the shadow of death.

21 If we have forgotten the Name of our God, and holden up our hands to any strange God: shall not God search it out? for he knoweth the very secrets of the heart.

22 For thy sake also are we killed all the day long: and are counted as sheep appointed to be slain.

23 Up, Lord, why sleepest thou: awake, and be not absent from us for ever.

24 Wherefore hidest thou thy face: and forgettest our misery and trouble?

25 For our soul is brought low, even unto the dust: our belly cleaveth unto the ground.

26 Arise, and help us: and deliver us for thy mercies sake.

Psalm 45

Eructavit cor meum.

M Y HEART is inditing of a good matter: I speak of the things which I have made unto the King.

2 My tongue is the pen: of a ready writer.

3 Thou art fairer than the children of men: full of grace are thy lips, because God hath blessed thee for ever.

4 Gird thee with thy sword upon thy thigh, O thou most mighty: according to thy worship, and renown.

5 Good luck have thou with thine honour: ride on, because of the word of truth, of meekness and righteousness, and thy right hand shall teach thee terrible things.

6 Thy arrows are very sharp, and the people shall be subdued unto thee: even in the midst among the kings enemies.

7 Thy seat, O God, endureth for ever: the scepter of thy kingdom is a right scepter.

8 Thou hast loved righteousness, and hated iniquity: wherefore God, even thy God, hath anointed thee with the oil of gladness above thy fellows.

9 All thy garments smell of Myrrh, Aloes, and Cassia: out of the ivory palaces, whereby they have made thee glad.

10 Kings daughters were among thy honourable women: upon thy right hand did stand the Queen in a vesture of gold, wrought about with divers colours.

11 Hearken, O daughter, and consider, encline thine ear: forget also thine own people, and thy fathers house.

12 So shall the King have pleasure in thy beauty: for he is thy Lord God, and worship thou him.

13 And the daughter of Tyre shall be there with a gift: like as the rich also among the people shall make their supplication before thee.

14 The Kings daughter is all glorious within: her clothing is of wrought gold.

15 She shall be brought unto the King in raiment of needle-work: the virgins, that be her fellows, shall bear her company, and shall be brought unto thee.

16 With joy and gladness shall they be brought: and shall enter into the Kings palace.

17 Instead of thy fathers thou shalt have children: whom thou mayest make princes in all lands.

18 I will remember thy Name from one generation to another: therefore shall the people give thanks unto thee, world without end.

Psalm 46

Deus noster refugium.

G OD is our hope and strength: a very present help in trouble.

2 Therefore will we not fear though the earth be moved: and though the hills be carried into the midst of the sea.

3 Though the waters thereof rage, and swell: and though the mountains shake at the tempest of the same.

4 The rivers of the floud thereof shall make glad the city of God: the holy place of the tabernacle of the most Highest.

5 God is in the midst of her, therefore shall she not be removed: God shall help her, and that right early.

6 The heathen make much ado, and the kingdoms are moved: but God hath shewed his voice, and the earth shall melt away.

7 The Lord of hosts is with us: the God of Jacob is our refuge.

8 O come hither, and behold the works of the Lord: what destruction he hath brought upon the earth.

9 He maketh wars to cease in all the world: he breaketh the bow, and knappeth the spear in sunder, and burneth the chariots in the fire.

10 Be still then, and know that I am God: I will be exalted among the heathen, and I will be exalted in the earth.

11 The Lord of hosts is with us: the God of Jacob is our refuge.

Day 9. *Evening Prayer.*

Psalm 47

Omnes gentes, plaudite.

O CLAP your hands together, all ye people: O sing unto God with the voice of melody.

2 For the Lord is high, and to be feared: he is the great King upon all the earth.

3 He shall subdue the people under us: and the nations under our feet.

4 He shall choose out an heritage for us: even the worship of Jacob, whom he loved.

5 God is gone up with a merry noise: and the Lord with the sound of the trump.

6 O sing praises, sing praises unto our God: O sing praises, sing praises unto our King.

7 For God is the King of all the earth: sing ye praises with understanding.

8 God reigneth over the heathen: God sitteth upon his holy seat.

9 The princes of the people are joyned unto the people of the God of Abraham: for God, which is very high exalted, doth defend the earth, as it were with a shield.

Psalm 48

Magnus Dominus.

GREAT is the Lord, and highly to be praised: in the city of our God, even upon his holy hill.

2 The hill of Sion is a fair place, and the joy of the whole earth: upon the north-side lieth the city of the great King; God is well known in her palaces as a sure refuge.

3 For lo, the kings of the earth: are gathered, and gone by together.

4 They marvelled to see such things: they were astonished, and suddenly cast down.

5 Fear came there upon them, and sorrow: as upon a woman in her travail.

6 Thou shalt break the ships of the sea: through the east-wind.

7 Like as we have heard, so have we seen in the city of the Lord of hosts; in the city of our God: God upholdeth the same for ever.

8 We wait for thy loving kindness, O God: in the midst of thy temple.

9 O God, according to thy Name, so is thy praise unto the worlds end: thy right hand is full of righteousness.

10 Let the mount Sion rejoyce, and the daughter of Judah be glad: because of thy judgments.

11 Walk about Sion, and go round about her: and tell the towers thereof.

12 Mark well her bulwarks, set up her houses: that ye may tell them that come after.

13 For this God is our God for ever, and ever: he shall be our guide unto death.

Psalm 49

Audite haec, omnes.

O HEAR ye this, all ye people: ponder it with your ears, all ye, that dwell in the world.

2 High and low, rich and poor: one with another.

3 My mouth shall speak of wisdom: and my heart shall muse of understanding.

4 I will incline mine ear to the parable: and shew my dark speech upon the harp.

5 Wherefore should I fear in the dayes of wickedness: and when the wickedness of my heels compasseth me round about?

6 There be some that put their trust in their goods: and boast themselves in the multitude of their riches.

7 But no man may deliver his brother: nor make agreement unto God for him;

8 For it cost more to redeem their souls: so that he must let that alone for ever;

9 Yea, though he live long: and see not the grave.

10 For he seeth that wise men also die, and perish together: as well as the ignorant and foolish, and leave their riches for other.

11 And yet they think that their houses shall continue for ever: and that their dwelling places shall endure from one generation to another, and call the lands after their own names.

12 Nevertheless, man will not abide in honour: seeing he may be compared unto the beasts that perish; this is the way of them.

13 This is their foolishness: and their posterity praise their saying.

14 They lie in the hell like sheep, death gnaweth upon them, and the righteous shall have domination over them in the morning: their beauty shall consume in the sepulchre out of their dwelling.

15 But God hath delivered my soul from the place of hell: for he shall receive me.

16 Be not thou afraid, though one be made rich: or if the glory of his house be increased;

17 For he shall carry nothing away with him, when he dieth: neither shall his pomp follow him.

18 For while he lived, he counted himself an happy man: and so long as thou doest well unto thy self, men will speak good of thee.

19 He shall follow the generation of his fathers: and shall never see light.

20 Man being in honour hath no understanding: but is compared unto the beasts that perish.

Day 10. *Morning Prayer.*

Psalm 50

Deus deorum.

THE Lord, even the most mighty God hath spoken: and called the world, from the rising up of the sun, unto the going down thereof.

2 Out of Sion hath God appeared: in perfect beauty.

3 Our God shall come, and shall not keep silence: there shall go before him a consuming fire, and a mighty tempest shall be stirred up round about him.

4 He shall call the heaven from above: and the earth, that he may judge his people.

5 Gather my saints together unto me: those that have made a covenant with me with sacrifice.

6 And the heavens shall declare his righteousness: for God is Judge himself.

7 Hear, O my people, and I will speak: I my self will testifie against thee, O Israel; for I am God, even thy God.

8 I will not reprove thee because of thy sacrifices, or for thy burnt-offerings: because they were not alway before me.

9 I will take no bullock out of thine house: nor he-goat out of thy folds.

10 For all the beasts of the forest are mine: and so are the cattel upon a thousand hills.

11 I know all the fowls upon the mountains: and the wilde beasts of the field are in my sight.

12 If I be hungry, I will not tell thee: for the whole world is mine, and all that is therein.

13 Thinkest thou, that I will eat bulls flesh: and drink the bloud of goats?

14 Offer unto God thanksgiving: and pay thy vows unto the most Highest.

15 And call upon me in the time of trouble: so will I hear thee, and thou shalt praise me.

16 But unto the ungodly said God: Why dost thou preach my laws, and takest my covenant in thy mouth;

17 Whereas thou hatest to be reformed: and hast cast my words behind thee?

18 When thou sawest a thief, thou consentedst unto him: and hast been partaker with the adulterers.

19 Thou hast let thy mouth speak wickedness: and with thy tongue thou hast set forth deceit.

20 Thou satest, and spakest against thy brother: yea, and hast slandered thine own mothers son.

21 These things hast thou done, and I held my tongue, and thou thoughtest wickedly, that I am even such a one as thy self: but I will reprove thee, and set before thee the things that thou hast done.

22 O consider this, ye that forget God: lest I pluck you away, and there be none to deliver you.

23 Whoso offereth me thanks and praise, he honoureth me: and to him, that ordereth his conversation right, will I shew the salvation of God.

Psalm 51

Miserere mei, Deus.

HAVE mercy upon me, O God, after thy great goodness: according to the multitude of thy mercies do away mine offences.

2 Wash me throughly from my wickedness: and cleanse me from my sin.

3 For I knowledge my faults: and my sin is ever before me.

4 Against thee onely have I sinned, and done this evil in thy sight: that thou mightest be justified in thy saying, and clear, when thou art judged.

5 Behold, I was shapen in wickedness: and in sin hath my mother conceived me.

6 But lo, thou requirest truth in the inward parts: and shalt make me to understand wisdom secretly.

7 Thou shalt purge me with hyssop, and I shall be clean: thou shalt wash me, and I shall be whiter than snow.

8 Thou shalt make me hear of joy, and gladness: that the bones, which thou hast broken, may rejoyce.

9 Turn thy face from my sins: and put out all my misdeeds.

10 Make me a clean heart, O God: and renew a right spirit within me.

11 Cast me not away from thy presence: and take not thy holy Spirit from me.

12 O give me the comfort of thy help again: and stablish me with thy free Spirit.

13 Then shall I teach thy wayes unto the wicked: and sinners shall be converted unto thee.

14 Deliver me from blood-guiltiness, O God, thou that art the God of my health: and my tongue shall sing of thy righteousness.

15 Thou shalt open my lips, O Lord: and my mouth shall shew thy praise.

16 For thou desirest no sacrifice, else would I give it thee: but thou delightest not in burnt-offerings.

17 The sacrifice of God is a troubled spirit: a broken and contrite heart, O God, shalt thou not despise.

18 O be favourable, and gracious unto Sion: build thou the walls of Jerusalem.

19 Then shalt thou be pleased with the sacrifice of righteousness, with the burnt-offerings and oblations: then shall they offer young bullocks upon thine altar.

Psalm 52

Quid gloriaris?

WHY boastest thou thy self, thou tyrant: that thou canst do mischief;

2 Whereas the goodness of God: endureth yet daily?

3 Thy tongue imagineth wickedness: and with lies thou cuttest like a sharp rasour.

4 Thou hast loved unrighteousness, more than goodness: and to talk of lies more than righteousness.

5 Thou hast loved to speak all words, that may do hurt: O thou false tongue.

6 Therefore shall God destroy thee for ever: he shall take thee, and pluck thee out of thy dwelling, and root thee out of the land of the living.

7 The righteous also shall see this, and fear: and shall laugh him to scorn.

8 Lo, this is the man, that took not God for his strength: but trusted unto the multitude of his riches, and strengthned himself in his wickedness.

9 As for me, I am like a green olive-tree in the house of God: my trust is in the tender mercy of God for ever, and ever.

10 I will alwayes give thanks unto thee for that thou hast done: and I will hope in thy Name, for thy saints like it well.

Day 10. *Evening Prayer*.

Psalm 53

Dixit insipiens.

THE foolish body hath said in his heart: There is no God.

2 Corrupt are they, and become abominable in their wickedness: there is none, that doth good.

3 God looked down from heaven upon the children of men: to see if there were any, that would understand, and seek after God.

4 But they are all gone out of the way, they are altogether become abominable: there is also none that doth good, no not one.

5 Are not they without understanding, that work wickedness: eating up my people as if they would eat bread? they have not called upon God.

6 They were afraid where no fear was: for God hath broken the bones of him, that besieged thee; thou hast put them to confusion, because God hath despised them.

7 O that the salvation were given unto Israel out of Sion: O that the Lord would deliver his people out of captivity!

8 Then should Jacob rejoyce: and Israel should be right glad.

Psalm 54

Deus, in nomine.

SAVE me, O God, for thy Names sake: and avenge me in thy strength.

2 Hear my prayer, O God: and hearken unto the words of my mouth.

3 For strangers are risen up against me: and tyrants, which have not God before their eyes, seek after my soul.

4 Behold, God is my helper: the Lord is with them that uphold my soul.

5 He shall reward evil unto mine enemies: destroy thou them in thy truth.

6 An offering of a free heart will I give thee, and praise thy Name, O Lord: because it is so comfortable.

7 For he hath delivered me out of all my trouble: and mine eye hath seen his desire upon mine enemies.

Psalm 55

Exaudi, Deus.

Hear my prayer, O God: and hide not thy self from my petition.

2 Take heed unto me, and hear me: how I mourn in my prayer, and am vexed.

3 The enemy crieth so, and the ungodly cometh on so fast: for they are minded to do me some mischief, so maliciously are they set against me.

4 My heart is disquieted within me: and the fear of death is fallen upon me.

5 Fearfulness and trembling are come upon me: and an horrible dread hath overwhelmed me.

6 And I said, O that I had wings like a dove: for then would I flee away and be at rest.

7 Lo, then would I get me away far off: and remain in the wilderness.

8 I would make haste to escape: because of the stormy wind and tempest.

9 Destroy their tongues, O Lord, and divide them: for I have spied unrighteousness, and strife in the city.

10 Day and night they go about within the walls thereof: mischief also, and sorrow are in the midst of it.

11 Wickedness is therein: deceit and guile go not out of their streets.

12 For it is not an open enemy, that hath done me this dishonour: for then I could have borne it.

13 Neither was it mine adversary, that did magnifie himself against me: for then peradventure I would have hid my self from him.

14 But it was even thou, my companion: my guide, and mine own familiar friend.

15 We took sweet counsel together: and walked in the house of God as friends.

16 Let death come hastily upon them, and let them go down quick into hell: for wickedness is in their dwellings, and among them.

17 As for me, I will call upon God: and the Lord shall save me.

18 In the evening, and morning, and at noon day will I pray, and that instantly: and he shall hear my voice.

19 It is he that hath delivered my soul in peace, from the battle that was against me: for there were many with me.

20 Yea, even God, that endureth for ever, shall hear me, and bring them down: for they will not turn, nor fear God.

21 He laid his hands upon such as be at peace with him: and he brake his covenant.

22 The words of his mouth were softer than butter, having war in his heart: his words were smoother than oil, and yet be they very swords.

23 O cast thy burden upon the Lord, and he shall nourish thee: and shall not suffer the righteous to fall for ever.

24 And as for them: thou, O God, shalt bring them into the pit of destruction.

25 The bloud-thirsty and deceitful men shall not live out half their dayes: nevertheless, my trust shall be in thee, O Lord.

Day 11. *Morning Prayer.*

Psalm 56

Miserere mei, Deus.

BE MERCIFUL unto me, O God, for man goeth about to devour me: he is daily fighting, and troubling me.

2 Mine enemies are daily in hand to swallow me up: for they be many, that fight against me, O thou most Highest.

3 Nevertheless, though I am sometime afraid: yet put I my trust in thee.

4 I will praise God, because of his word: I have put my trust in God, and will not fear what flesh can do unto me.

5 They daily mistake my words: all that they imagine is to do me evil.

6 They hold all together, and keep themselves close: and mark my steps, when they lay wait for my soul.

7 Shall they escape for their wickedness: thou, O God, in thy displeasure shalt cast them down.

8 Thou tellest my flittings; put my tears into thy bottle: are not these things noted in thy book?

9 Whensoever I call upon thee, then shall mine enemies be put to flight: this I know; for God is on my side.

10 In Gods word will I rejoyce: in the Lords word will I comfort me.

11 Yea, in God have I put my trust: I will not be afraid what man can do unto me.

12 Unto thee, O God, will I pay my vows: unto thee will I give thanks.

13 For thou hast delivered my soul from death, and my feet from falling: that I may walk before God in the light of the living.

Psalm 57

Miserere mei, Deus.

BE MERCIFUL unto me, O God, be merciful unto me, for my soul trusteth in thee: and under the shadow of thy wings shall be my refuge, until this tyranny be over-past.

2 I will call unto the most high God: even unto the God, that shall perform the cause which I have in hand.

3 He shall send from heaven: and save me from the reproof of him, that would eat me up.

4 God shall send forth his mercy, and truth: my soul is among lions.

5 And I lie even among the children of men, that are set on fire: whose teeth are spears and arrows, and their tongue a sharp sword.

6 Set up thy self, O God, above the heavens: and thy glory above all the earth.

7 They have laid a net for my feet, and pressed down my soul: they have digged a pit before me, and are faln into the midst of it themselves.

8 My heart is fixed, O God, my heart is fixed: I will sing, and give praise.

9 Awake up, my glory; awake, lute, and harp: I my self will awake right early.

10 I will give thanks unto thee, O Lord, among the people: and I will sing unto thee among the nations.

11 For the greatness of thy mercy reacheth unto the heavens: and thy truth unto the clouds.

12 Set up thy self, O God, above the heavens: and thy glory above all the earth.

Psalm 58
Si vere utique.

Are your minds set upon righteousness, O ye congregation: and do ye judge the thing that is right, O ye sons of men?

2 Yea, ye imagine mischief in your heart upon the earth: and your hands deal with wickedness.

3 The ungodly are froward, even from their mothers womb: as soon as they are born, they go astray, and speak lies.

4 They are as venomous as the poison of a serpent: even like the deaf adder, that stoppeth her ears.

5 Which refuseth to hear the voice of the charmer: charm he never so wisely.

6 Break their teeth, O God, in their mouths; smite the jaw-bones of the lions, O Lord: let them fall away like water that runneth apace, and when they shoot their arrows let them be rooted out.

7 Let them consume away like a snail, and be like the untimely fruit of a woman: and let them not see the sun.

8 Or ever your pots be made hot with thorns: so let indignation vex him,° even as a thing that is raw.

9 The righteous shall rejoyce when he seeth the vengeance: he shall wash his footsteps in the bloud of the ungodly.

10 So that a man shall say, Verily there is a reward for the righteous: doubtless there is a God that judgeth the earth.

Day 11. *Evening Prayer.*

Psalm 59
Eripe me de inimicis.

Deliver me from mine enemies, O God: defend me from them that rise up against me.

2 O deliver me from the wicked doers: and save me from the blood-thirsty men.

3 For lo, they lie waiting for my soul: the mighty men are gathered against me without any offence or fault of me, O Lord.

4 They run and prepare themselves without my fault: arise thou therefore to help me, and behold.

5 Stand up, O Lord God of hosts, thou God of Israel, to visit all the heathen: and be not merciful unto them that offend of malicious wickedness.

6 They go to and fro in the evening: they grin like a dog, and run about through the city.

7 Behold, they speak with their mouth, and swords are in their lips: for who doth hear?

8 But thou, O Lord, shalt have them in derision: and thou shalt laugh all the heathen to scorn.

9 My strength will I ascribe unto thee: for thou art the God of my refuge.

10 God sheweth me his goodness plenteously: and God shall let me see my desire upon mine enemies.

11 Slay them not, lest my people forget it: but scatter them abroad among the people, and put them down, O Lord our defence.

12 For the sin of their mouth, and for the words of their lips they shall be taken in their pride: and why? their preaching is of cursing and lies.

13 Consume them in thy wrath, consume them, that they may perish: and know that it is God that ruleth in Jacob, and unto the ends of the world.

14 And in the evening they will return: grin like a dog, and will go about the city.

15 They will run here and there for meat: and grudge if they be not satisfied.

16 As for me, I will sing of thy power, and will praise thy mercy betimes in the morning: for thou hast been my defence and refuge in the day of my trouble.

17 Unto thee, O my strength, will I sing: for thou, O God, art my refuge and my merciful God.

Psalm 60

Deus, repulisti nos.

O GOD, thou hast cast us out, and scattered us abroad: thou hast also been displeased, O turn thee unto us again.

2 Thou hast moved the land and divided it: heal the sores thereof, for it shaketh.

3 Thou hast shewed thy people heavy things: thou hast given us a drink of deadly wine.

4 Thou hast given a token for such as fear thee: that they may triumph because of the truth.

5 Therefore were thy beloved delivered: help me with thy right hand, and hear me.

6 God hath spoken in his holiness, I will rejoyce, and divide Sichem: and mete out the valley of Succoth.

7 Gilead is mine, and Manasses is mine: Ephraim also is the strength of my head; Judah is my law-giver.

8 Moab is my washpot, over Edom will I cast out my shoe: Philistia be thou glad of me.

9 Who will lead me into the strong city: who will bring me into Edom?

10 Hast not thou cast us out, O God: Wilt not thou, O God, go out with our hosts?

11 O be thou our help in trouble: for vain is the help of man.

12 Through God will we do great acts: for it is he that shall tread down our enemies.

Psalm 61

Exaudi, Deus.

HEAR my crying, O God: give ear unto my prayer.

2 From the ends of the earth will I call upon thee: when my heart is in heaviness.

3 O set me up upon the rock that is higher than I: for thou hast been my hope, and a strong tower for me against the enemy.

4 I will dwell in thy tabernacle for ever: and my trust shall be under the covering of thy wings.

5 For thou, O Lord, hast heard my desires: and hast given an heritage unto those that fear thy Name.

6 Thou shalt grant the King a long life: that his years may endure throughout all generations.

7 He shall dwell before God for ever: O prepare thy loving mercy and faithfulness, that they may preserve him.

8 So will I always sing praise unto thy Name: that I may daily perform my vows.

Day 12. *Morning Prayer.*

Psalm 62

Nonne Deo?

M Y SOUL truly waiteth still upon God: for of him cometh my salvation.

2 He verily is my strength and my salvation: he is my defence, so that I shall not greatly fall.

3 How long will ye imagine mischief against every man: ye shall be slain all the sort of you; yea, as a tottering wall shall ye be, and like a broken hedge.

4 Their device is onely how to put him out whom God will exalt: their delight is in lies, they give good words with their mouth, but curse with their heart.

5 Nevertheless, my soul, wait thou still upon God: for my hope is in him.

6 He truly is my strength and my salvation: he is my defence, so that I shall not fall.

7 In God is my health and my glory: the rock of my might, and in God is my trust.

8 O put your trust in him alway, ye people: pour out your hearts before him, for God is our hope.

9 As for the children of men, they are but vanity: the children of men are deceitful upon the weights, they are altogether lighter than vanity it self.

10 O trust not in wrong and robbery, give not your selves unto vanity: if riches increase, set not your heart upon them.

11 God spake once, and twice I have also heard the same: That power belongeth unto God;

12 And that thou Lord, art merciful: for thou rewardest every man according to his work.

Psalm 63

Deus, Deus meus.

O GOD, thou art my God: early will I seek thee.

2 My soul thirsteth for thee, my flesh also longeth after thee: in a barren and dry land where no water is.

3 Thus have I looked for thee in holiness: that I might behold thy power and glory.

4 For thy loving kindness is better than the life it self: my lips shall praise thee.

5 As long as I live will I magnifie thee on this manner: and lift up my hands in thy Name.

6 My soul shall be satisfied even as it were with marrow and fatness: when my mouth praiseth thee with joyful lips.

7 Have I not remembred thee in my bed: and thought upon thee when I was waking?

8 Because thou hast been my helper: therefore under the shadow of thy wings will I rejoyce.

9 My soul hangeth upon thee: thy right hand hath upholden me.

10 These also, that seek the hurt of my soul: they shall go under the earth.

11 Let them fall upon the edge of the sword: that they may be a portion for foxes.

12 But the King shall rejoyce in God; all they also, that swear by him, shall be commended: for the mouth of them, that speak lies, shall be stopped.

Psalm 64

Exaudi, Deus.

HEAR my voice, O God, in my prayer: preserve my life from fear of the enemy.

2 Hide me from the gathering together of the froward: and from the insurrection of wicked doers.

3 Who have whet their tongue like a sword: and shoot out their arrows, even bitter words.

4 That they may privily shoot at him that is perfect: suddenly do they hit him, and fear not.

5 They incourage themselves in mischief: and commune among themselves, how they may lay snares, and say, that no man shall see them.

6 They imagine wickedness, and practise it: that they keep secret among themselves, every man in the deep of his heart.

7 But God shall suddenly shoot at them with a swift arrow: that they shall be wounded.

8 Yea, their own tongues shall make them fall: insomuch that who so seeth them shall laugh them to scorn.

9 And all men, that see it, shall say, This hath God done: for they shall perceive that it is his work.

10 The righteous shall rejoyce in the Lord, and put his trust in him: and all they, that are true of heart, shall be glad.

Day 12. *Evening Prayer.*

Psalm 65

Te decet hymnus.

THOU, O God, art praised in Sion: and unto thee shall the vow be performed in Jerusalem.

2 Thou that hearest the prayer: unto thee shall all flesh come.

3 My misdeeds prevail against me: O be thou merciful unto our sins.

4 Blessed is the man, whom thou choosest, and receivest unto thee: he shall dwell in thy court, and shall be satisfied with the pleasures of thy house, even of thy holy temple.

5 Thou shalt shew us wonderful things in thy righteousness, O God of our salvation: thou, that art the hope of all the ends of the earth, and of them that remain in the broad sea.

6 Who in his strength setteth fast the mountains: and is girded about with power.

7 Who stilleth the raging of the sea: and the noise of his waves, and the madness of the people.

8 They also, that dwell in the uttermost parts of the earth, shall be afraid at thy tokens: thou, that makest the out-goings of the morning and evening to praise thee.

9 Thou visitest the earth, and blessest it: thou makest it very plenteous.

10 The river of God is full of water: thou preparest their corn, for so thou providest for the earth.

11 Thou waterest her furrows, thou sendest rain into the little valleys thereof: thou makest it soft with the drops of rain, and blessest the increase of it.

12 Thou crownest the year with thy goodness: and thy clouds drop fatness.

13 They shall drop upon the dwellings of the wilderness: and the little hills shall rejoyce on every side.

14 The folds shall be full of sheep: the valleys also shall stand so thick with corn, that they shall laugh and sing.

Psalm 66

Jubilate Deo.

O BE joyful in God, all ye lands: sing praises unto the honour of his Name, make his praise to be glorious.

2 Say unto God, O how wonderful art thou in thy works: through the greatness of thy power shall thine enemies be found liars unto thee.

3 For all the world shall worship thee: sing of thee, and praise thy Name.

4 O come hither, and behold the works of God: how wonderful he is in his doing toward the children of men.

5 He turned the sea into dry land: so that they went through the water on foot; there did we rejoyce thereof.

6 He ruleth with his power for ever, his eyes behold the people: and such, as will not believe, shall not be able to exalt themselves.

7 O praise our God, ye people: and make the voice of his praise to be heard;

8 Who holdeth our soul in life: and suffereth not our feet to slip.

9 For thou, O God, hast proved us: thou also hast tried us, like as silver is tried.

10 Thou broughtest us into the snare: and laidst trouble upon our loins.

11 Thou sufferedst men to ride over our heads: we went through fire and water, and thou broughtest us out into a wealthy place.

12 I will go into thine house with burnt-offerings: and will pay thee my vows, which I promised with my lips, and spake with my mouth, when I was in trouble.

13 I will offer unto thee fat burnt-sacrifices, with the incense of rams: I will offer bullocks and goats.

14 O come hither, and hearken, all ye that fear God: and I will tell you, what he hath done for my soul.

15 I called unto him with my mouth: and gave him praises with my tongue.

16 If I incline unto wickedness with mine heart: the Lord will not hear me.

17 But God hath heard me: and considered the voice of my prayer.

18 Praised be God, who hath not cast out my prayer: nor turned his mercy from me.

Psalm 67

Deus misereatur.

G OD be merciful unto us, and bless us: and shew us the light of his countenance, and be merciful unto us:

2 That thy way may be known upon earth: thy saving health among all nations.

3 Let the people praise thee, O God: yea, let all the people praise thee.

4 O let the Nations rejoyce, and be glad: for thou shalt judge the folk righteously, and govern the nations upon earth.

5 Let the people praise thee, O God: let all the people praise thee.

6 Then shall the earth bring forth her increase: and God, even our own God, shall give us his blessing.

7 God shall bless us: and all the ends of the world shall fear him.

Day 13. *Morning Prayer.*

Psalm 68

Exurgat Deus.

L ET God arise, and let his enemies be scattered: let them also, that hate him, flee before him.

2 Like as the smoke vanisheth, so shalt thou drive them away: and like as wax melteth at the fire, so let the ungodly perish at the presence of God.

3 But let the righteous be glad and rejoyce before God: let them also be merry, and joyful.

4 O sing unto God, and sing praises unto his Name: magnifie him, that rideth upon the heavens, as it were upon an horse; praise him in his Name yea and rejoyce before him.

5 He is a father of the fatherless, and defendeth the cause of the widows: even God in his holy habitation.

6 He is the God, that maketh men to be of one minde in an house,

and bringeth the prisoners out of captivity: but letteth the runagates continue in scarceness.

7 O God, when thou wentest forth before the people: when thou wentest through the wilderness.

8 The earth shook, and the heavens dropped at the presence of God: even as Sinai also was moved at the presence of God, who is the God of Israel.

9 Thou, O God, sentest a gracious rain upon thine inheritance: and refreshedst it when it was weary.

10 Thy congregation shall dwell therein: for thou, O God, hast of thy goodness prepared for the poor.

11 The Lord gave the word: great was the company of the preachers.

12 Kings with their armies did flee, and were discomfited: and they of the houshold divided the spoil.

13 Though ye have lien among the pots, yet shall ye be as the wings of a dove: that is covered with silver wings, and her feathers like gold.

14 When the Almighty scattered kings for their sake: then were they as white as snow in Salmon.

15 As the hill of Basan, so is Gods hill: even an high hill, as the hill of Basan.

16 Why hop ye so, ye high hills? this is Gods hill, in the which it pleaseth him to dwell: yea, the Lord will abide in it for ever.

17 The chariots of God are twenty thousand, even thousands of Angels: and the Lord is among them, as in the holy place of Sinai.

18 Thou art gone up on high, thou hast led captivity captive, and received gifts for men: yea, even for thine enemies, that the Lord God might dwell among them.

19 Praised be the Lord daily: even the God who helpeth us, and poureth his benefits upon us.

20 He is our God, even the God of whom cometh salvation: God is the Lord, by whom we escape death.

21 God shall wound the head of his enemies: and the hairy scalp of such a one as goeth on still in his wickedness.

22 The Lord hath said, I will bring my people again, as I did from Basan: mine own will I bring again, as I did sometime from the deep of the sea.

23 That thy foot may be dipped in the bloud of thine enemies: and that the tongue of thy dogs may be red through the same.

24 It is well seen, O God, how thou goest: how thou, my God and King, goest in the sanctuary.

25 The singers go before, the minstrels follow after: in the midst are the damsels playing with the timbrels.

26 Give thanks, O Israel, unto God the Lord in the congregations: from the ground of the heart.

27 There is little Benjamin their ruler, and the princes of Judah their counsel: the princes of Zabulon, and the princes of Nephthali.

28 Thy God hath sent forth strength for thee: stablish the thing, O God, that thou hast wrought in us,

29 For thy temples sake at Jerusalem: so shall kings bring presents unto thee.

30 When the company of the spear-men and multitude of the mighty are scattered abroad among the beasts of the people, so that they humbly bring pieces of silver: and when he hath scattered the people that delight in war.

31 Then shall the princes come out of Egypt: the Morians land shall soon stretch out her hands unto God.

32 Sing unto God, O ye kingdoms of the earth: O sing praises unto the Lord.

33 Who sitteth in the heavens over all from the beginning: lo, he doth send out his voice, yea, and that a mighty voice.

34 Ascribe ye the power to God over Israel: his worship and strength is in the clouds.

35 O God, wonderful art thou in thy holy places: even the God of Israel; he will give strength and power unto his people; blessed be God.

Day 13. *Evening Prayer.*

Psalm 69

Salvum me fac.

SAVE me, O God: for the waters are come in, even unto my soul.

2 I stick fast in the deep mire, where no ground is: I am come into deep waters, so that the flouds run over me.

3 I am weary of crying; my throat is dry: my sight faileth me for waiting so long upon my God.

4 They, that hate me without a cause, are more than the hairs of

my head: they, that are mine enemies, and would destroy me guiltless, are mighty.

5 I paid them the things that I never took: God, thou knowest my simpleness, and my faults are not hid from thee.

6 Let not them, that trust in thee, O Lord God of hosts, be ashamed for my cause: let not those, that seek thee, be confounded through me, O Lord God of Israel.

7 And why? for thy sake have I suffered reproof: shame hath covered my face.

8 I am become a stranger unto my brethren: even an alien unto my mothers children.

9 For the zeal of thine house hath even eaten me: and the rebukes of them, that rebuked thee, are faln upon me.

10 I wept, and chastned my self with fasting: and that was turned to my reproof.

11 I put on sackcloth also: and they jested upon me.

12 They, that sit in the gate, speak against me: and the drunkards make songs upon me.

13 But, Lord, I make my prayer unto thee: in an acceptable time.

14 Hear me, O God, in the multitude of thy mercy: even in the truth of thy salvation.

15 Take me out of the mire, that I sink not: O let me be delivered from them that hate me, and out of the deep waters.

16 Let not the water-floud drown me, neither let the deep swallow me up: and let not the pit shut her mouth upon me.

17 Hear me, O Lord, for thy loving kindness is comfortable: turn thee unto me according to the multitude of thy mercies.

18 And hide not thy face from thy servant, for I am in trouble: O haste thee and hear me.

19 Draw nigh unto my soul and save it: O deliver me because of mine enemies.

20 Thou hast known my reproof, my shame, and my dishonour: mine adversaries are all in thy sight.

21 Thy rebuke hath broken my heart, I am full of heaviness: I looked for some to have pity on me, but there was no man, neither found I any to comfort me.

22 They gave me gall to eat: and when I was thirsty, they gave me vinegar to drink.

23 Let their table be made a snare to take themselves withal: and let

the things, that should have been for their wealth, be unto them an occasion of falling.

24 Let their eyes be blinded that they see not: and ever bow thou down their backs.

25 Pour out thine indignation upon them: and let thy wrathful displeasure take hold of them.

26 Let their habitation be void: and no man to dwell in their tents.

27 For they persecute him whom thou hast smitten: and they talk how they may vex them whom thou hast wounded.

28 Let them fall from one wickedness to another: and not come into thy righteousness.

29 Let them be wiped out of the book of the living: and not be written among the righteous.

30 As for me, when I am poor and in heaviness: thy help, O God, shall lift me up.

31 I will praise the name of God with a song: and magnifie it with thanksgiving.

32 This also shall please the Lord: better than a bullock that hath horns and hoofs.

33 The humble shall consider this and be glad: seek ye after God and your soul shall live.

34 For the Lord heareth the poor: and despiseth not his prisoners.

35 Let heaven and earth praise him: the sea and all that moveth therein.

36 For God will save Sion, and build the cities of Juda: that men may dwell there, and have it in possession.

37 The posterity also of his servants shall inherit it: and they, that love his name, shall dwell therein.

Psalm 70

Deus, in adjutorium.

HASTE thee, O God, to deliver me: make haste to help me, O Lord.
2 Let them be ashamed and confounded, that seek after my soul: let them be turned backward and put to confusion, that wish me evil.

3 Let them for their reward be soon brought to shame: that cry over me, There, there.

4 But let all those, that seek thee, be joyful and glad in thee: and let all such as delight in thy salvation, say alway, The Lord be praised.

5 As for me, I am poor and in misery: haste thee unto me, O God.

6 Thou art my helper and my Redeemer: O Lord, make no long tarrying.

Day 14. *Morning Prayer.*

Psalm 71

In te, Domine, speravi.

I N THEE, O Lord, have I put my trust, let me never be put to confusion: but rid me, and deliver me in thy righteousness; incline thine ear unto me and save me.

2 Be thou my strong hold, whereunto I may alway resort: thou hast promised to help me, for thou art my house of defence and my castle.

3 Deliver me, O my God, out of the hand of the ungodly: out of the hand of the unrighteous and cruel man.

4 For thou, O Lord God, art the thing that I long for: thou art my hope, even from my youth.

5 Through thee have I been holden up ever since I was born: thou art he that took me out of my mothers womb, my praise shall be alwaies of thee.

6 I am become as it were a monster unto many: but my sure trust is in thee.

7 O let my mouth be filled with thy praise: that I may sing of thy glory and honour all the day long.

8 Cast me not away in the time of age: forsake me not when my strength faileth me.

9 For mine enemies speak against me, and they, that lay wait for my soul, take their counsel together, saying: God hath forsaken him, persecute him and take him, for there is none to deliver him.

10 Go not far from me, O God: my God, haste thee to help me.

11 Let them be confounded and perish, that are against my soul: let them be covered with shame and dishonour, that seek to do me evil.

12 As for me, I will patiently abide alway: and will praise thee more and more.

13 My mouth shall daily speak of thy righteousness and salvation: for I know no end thereof.

14 I will go forth in the strength of the Lord God: and will make mention of thy righteousness only.

15 Thou, O God, hast taught me from my youth up until now: therefore will I tell of thy wondrous works.

16 Forsake me not, O God, in mine old age, when I am gray-headed: until I have shewed thy strength unto this generation, and thy power to all them that are yet for to come.

17 Thy righteousness, O God, is very high: and great things are they that thou hast done; O God, who is like unto thee?

18 O what great troubles and adversities hast thou shewed me! and yet didst thou turn and refresh me: yea, and broughtest me from the deep of the earth again.

19 Thou hast brought me to great honour: and comforted me on every side.

20 Therefore will I praise thee and thy faithfulness, O God, playing upon an instrument of musick: unto thee will I sing upon the harp, O thou holy One of Israel.

21 My lips will be fain when I sing unto thee: and so will my soul whom thou hast delivered.

22 My tongue also shall talk of thy righteousness all the day long: for they are confounded and brought unto shame, that seek to do me evil.

Psalm 72

Deus, judicium.

GIVE the King thy judgments, O God: and thy righteousness unto the Kings son.

2 Then shall he judge thy people according unto right: and defend the poor.

3 The mountains also shall bring peace: and the little hills righteousness unto the people.

4 He shall keep the simple folk by their right: defend the children of the poor, and punish the wrong-doer.

5 They shall fear thee, as long as the sun and moon endureth: from one generation to another.

6 He shall come down like the rain into a fleece of wooll: even as the drops that water the earth.

7 In his time shall the righteous flourish: yea, and abundance of peace, so long as the moon endureth.

8 His dominion shall be also from the one sea to the other: and from the floud unto the worlds end.

9 They, that dwell in the wilderness, shall kneel before him: his enemies shall lick the dust.

10 The kings of Tharsis, and of the Isles shall give presents: the kings of Arabia and Saba shall bring gifts.

11 All kings shall fall down before him: all nations shall do him service.

12 For he shall deliver the poor, when he cryeth: the needy also, and him that hath no helper.

13 He shall be favourable to the simple and needy: and shall preserve the souls of the poor.

14 He shall deliver their souls from falshood and wrong: and dear shall their bloud be in his sight.

15 He shall live, and unto him shall be given of the gold of Arabia: prayer shall be made ever unto him, and daily shall he be praised.

16 There shall be an heap of corn in the earth, high upon the hills: his fruit shall shake like Libanus, and shall be green in the city like grass upon the earth.

17 His name shall endure for ever, his name shall remain under the sun among the posterities: which shall be blessed through him, and all the heathen shall praise him.

18 Blessed be the Lord God, even the God of Israel: which only doeth wondrous things;

19 And blessed be the name of his Majesty for ever: and all the earth shall be filled with his Majesty. Amen, Amen.

Day 14. *Evening Prayer.*

Psalm 73

Quam bonus Israel.

TRULY God is loving unto Israel: even unto such as are of a clean heart.

2 Nevertheless, my feet were almost gone: my treadings had well-nigh slipt.

3 And why? I was grieved at the wicked: I do also see the ungodly in such prosperity.

4 For they are in no peril of death: but are lusty and strong.

5 They come in no misfortune like other folk: neither are they plagued like other men.

6 And this is the cause that they are so holden with pride: and overwhelmed with cruelty.

7 Their eyes swell with fatness: and they do even what they lust.

8 They corrupt other, and speak of wicked blasphemy: their talking is against the most High.

9 For they stretch forth their mouth unto the heaven: and their tongue goeth through the world.

10 Therefore fall the people unto them: and thereout suck they no small advantage.

11 Tush, say they, how should God perceive it: is there knowledge in the most High?

12 Lo, these are the ungodly, these prosper in the world, and these have riches in possession: and I said, Then have I cleansed my heart in vain, and washed mine hands in innocency.

13 All the day long have I been punished: and chastened every morning.

14 Yea, and I had almost said even as they: but lo, then I should have condemned the generation of thy children.

15 Then thought I to understand this: but it was too hard for me.

16 Until I went into the sanctuary of God: then understood I the end of these men;

17 Namely, how thou dost set them in slippery places: and castest them down, and destroyest them.

18 O how suddenly do they consume: perish, and come to a fearful end!

19 Yea, even like as a dream when one awaketh: so shalt thou make their image to vanish out of the city.

20 Thus my heart was grieved: and it went even through my reins.

21 So foolish was I, and ignorant: even as it were a beast before thee.

22 Nevertheless, I am alway by thee: for thou hast holden me by my right hand.

23 Thou shalt guide me with thy counsel: and after that receive me with glory.

24 Whom have I in heaven but thee: and there is none upon earth, that I desire in comparison of thee.

25 My flesh, and my heart faileth: but God is the strength of my heart, and my portion for ever.

26 For lo, they that forsake thee, shall perish: thou hast destroyed all them that commit fornication against thee.

27 But it is good for me to hold me fast by God, to put my trust in the Lord God: and to speak of all thy works in the gates of the daughter of Sion.

Psalm 74

Ut quid, Deus?

O GOD, wherefore art thou absent from us so long: why is thy wrath so hot against the sheep of thy pasture?

2 O think upon thy congregation: whom thou hast purchased, and redeemed of old.

3 Think upon the tribe of thine inheritance: and mount Sion, wherein thou hast dwelt.

4 Lift up thy feet, that thou maiest utterly destroy every enemy: which hath done evil in thy sanctuary.

5 Thine adversaries roar in the midst of thy congregations: and set up their banners for tokens.

6 He that hewed timber afore out of the thick trees: was known to bring it to an excellent work.

7 But now they break down all the carved work thereof: with axes and hammers.

8 They have set fire upon thy holy places: and have defiled the dwelling-place of thy Name, even unto the ground.

9 Yea, they said in their hearts, Let us make havock of them altogether: thus have they burnt up all the houses of God in the land.

10 We see not our tokens, there is not one prophet more: no, not one is there among us, that understandeth any more.

11 O God, how long shall the adversary do this dishonour: how long shall the enemy blaspheme thy Name, for ever?

12 Why withdrawest thou thy hand: why pluckest thou not thy right hand out of thy bosom to consume the enemy?

13 For God is my King of old: the help, that is done upon earth, he doth it himself.

14 Thou didst divide the sea through thy power: thou brakest the heads of the dragons in the waters.

15 Thou smotest the heads of Leviathan in pieces: and gavest him to be meat for the people in the wilderness.

16 Thou broughtest out fountains, and waters out of the hard rocks: thou driedst up mighty waters.

17 The day is thine, and the night is thine: thou hast prepared the light and the sun.

18 Thou hast set all the borders of the earth: thou hast made summer and winter.

19 Remember this, O Lord, how the enemy hath rebuked: and how the foolish people hath blasphemed thy Name.

20 O deliver not the soul of thy turtle-dove unto the multitude of the enemies: and forget not the congregation of the poor for ever.

21 Look upon the covenant: for all the earth is full of darkness, and cruel habitations.

22 O let not the simple go away ashamed: but let the poor and needy give praise unto thy Name.

23 Arise, O God, maintain thine own cause: remember how the foolish man blasphemeth thee daily.

24 Forget not the voice of thine enemies: the presumption of them that hate thee encreaseth ever more and more.

Day 15. *Morning Prayer.*

Psalm 75

Confitebimur tibi.

UNTO thee, O God, do we give thanks: yea, unto thee do we give thanks.

2 Thy Name also is so nigh: and that do thy wondrous works declare.

3 When I receive the congregation: I shall judge according unto right.

4 The earth is weak, and all the inhabiters thereof: I bear up the pillars of it.

5 I said unto the fools, Deal not so madly: and to the ungodly, Set not up your horn.

6 Set not up your horn on high: and speak not with a stiff neck.

7 For promotion cometh neither from the east, nor from the west: nor yet from the south.

8 And why? God is the judge: he putteth down one, and setteth up another.

9 For in the hand of the Lord there is a cup, and the wine is red: it is full mixt, and he poureth out of the same.

10 As for the dregs thereof: all the ungodly of the earth shall drink them, and suck them out.

11 But I will talk of the God of Jacob: and praise him for ever.

12 All the horns of the ungodly also will I break: and the horns of the righteous shall be exalted.

Psalm 76

Notus in Judaea.

I N JEWRY is God known: his Name is great in Israel.
2 At Salem is his tabernacle: and his dwelling in Sion.

3 There brake he the arrows of the bow: the shield, the sword, and the battel.

4 Thou art of more honour and might: than the hills of the robbers.

5 The proud are robbed, they have slept their sleep: and all the men, whose hands were mighty, have found nothing.

6 At thy rebuke, O God of Jacob: both the chariot and horse are faln.

7 Thou, even thou art to be feared: and who may stand in thy sight, when thou art angry?

8 Thou didst cause thy judgement to be heard from heaven: the earth trembled, and was still;

9 When God arose to judgement: and to help all the meek upon earth.

10 The fierceness of man shall turn to thy praise: and the fierceness of them shalt thou refrain.

11 Promise unto the Lord your God, and keep it, all ye that are round about him: bring presents unto him that ought to be feared.

12 He shall refrain the spirit of Princes: and is wonderful among the kings of the earth.

Psalm 77

Voce mea ad Dominum.

I WILL cry unto God with my voice: even unto God will I cry with my voice, and he shall hearken unto me.

2 In the time of my trouble I sought the Lord: my sore ran, and ceased not in the night-season; my soul refused comfort.

3 When I am in heaviness, I will think upon God: when my heart is vexed, I will complain.

4 Thou holdest mine eyes waking: I am so feeble, that I cannot speak.

5 I have considered the daies of old: and the years that are past.

6 I call to remembrance my song: and in the night I commune with mine own heart, and search out my spirits.

7 Will the Lord absent himself for ever: and will he be no more intreated?

8 Is his mercy clean gone for ever: and is his promise come utterly to an end for evermore?

9 Hath God forgotten to be gracious: and will he shut up his loving kindness in displeasure?

10 And I said, It is mine own infirmity: but I will remember the years of the right hand of the most Highest.

11 I will remember the works of the Lord: and call to mind thy wonders of old time.

12 I will think also of all thy works: and my talking shall be of thy doings.

13 Thy way, O God, is holy: who is so great a God, as our God?

14 Thou art the God that doth wonders: and hast declared thy power among the people.

15 Thou hast mightily delivered thy people: even the sons of Jacob and Joseph.

16 The waters saw thee, O God, the waters saw thee, and were afraid: the depths also were troubled.

17 The clouds poured out water, the air thundred: and thine arrows went abroad.

18 The voice of thy thunder was heard round about: the lightnings shone upon the ground, the earth was moved and shook withal.

19 Thy way is in the sea, and thy paths in the great waters: and thy footsteps are not known.

20 Thou leddest thy people like sheep: by the hand of Moses and Aaron.

Day 15. *Evening Prayer.*

Psalm 78

Attendite, popule.

HEAR my law, O my people: incline your ears unto the words of my mouth.

2 I will open my mouth in a parable: I will declare hard sentences of old;

3 Which we have heard and known: and such as our fathers have told us;

4 That we should not hide them from the children of the generations to come: but to shew the honour of the Lord, his mighty and wonderful works that he hath done.

5 He made a covenant with Jacob, and gave Israel a law: which he commanded our forefathers to teach their children;

6 That their posterity might know it: and the children which were yet unborn;

7 To the intent, that when they came up: they might shew their children the same;

8 That they might put their trust in God: and not to forget the works of God, but to keep his commandments;

9 And not to be as their forefathers, a faithless and stubborn generation: a generation that set not their heart aright, and whose spirit cleaveth not stedfastly unto God;

10 Like as the children of Ephraim: who being harnessed, and carrying bows, turned themselves back in the day of battel.

11 They kept not the covenant of God: and would not walk in his law;

12 But forgat what he had done: and the wonderful works that he had shewed for them.

13 Marvellous things did he in the sight of our forefathers, in the land of Egypt: even in the field of Zoan.

14 He divided the sea, and let them go through: he made the waters to stand on an heap.

15 In the day-time also he led them with a cloud: and all the night through with a light of fire.

16 He clave the hard rocks in the wilderness: and gave them drink thereof, as it had been out of the great depth.

17 He brought waters out of the stony rock: so that it gushed out like the rivers.

18 Yet for all this they sinned more against him: and provoked the most Highest in the wilderness.

19 They tempted God in their hearts: and required meat for their lust.

20 They spake against God also, saying: Shall God prepare a table in the wilderness?

21 He smote the stony rock indeed, that the water gushed out, and the streams flowed withal: but can he give bread also, or provide flesh for his people?

22 When the Lord heard this, he was wroth: so the fire was kindled in Jacob, and there came up heavy displeasure against Israel;

23 Because they believed not in God: and put not their trust in his help.

24 So he commanded the clouds above: and opened the doors of heaven.

25 He rained down Manna also upon them for to eat: and gave them food from heaven.

26 So man did eat Angels food: for he sent them meat enough.

27 He caused the east-wind to blow under heaven: and through his power he brought in the south-west-wind.

28 He rained flesh upon them as thick as dust: and feathered fowls like as the sand of the sea.

29 He let it fall among their tents: even round about their habitation.

30 So they did eat, and were well filled, for he gave them their own desire: they were not disappointed of their lust.

31 But while the meat was yet in their mouths, the heavy wrath of God came upon them, and slew the wealthiest of them: yea, and smote down the chosen men that were in Israel.

32 But for all this they sinned yet more: and believed not his wondrous works.

33 Therefore their days did he consume in vanity: and their years in trouble.

34 When he slew them, they sought him: and turned them early, and enquired after God.

35 And they remembered that God was their strength: and that the high God was their redeemer.

36 Nevertheless, they did but flatter him with their mouth: and dissembled with him in their tongue.

37 For their heart was not whole with him: neither continued they stedfast in his covenant.

38 But he was so merciful, that he forgave their misdeeds: and destroyed them not.

39 Yea, many a time turned he his wrath away: and would not suffer his whole displeasure to arise.

40 For he considered that they were but flesh: and that they were even a wind that passeth away, and cometh not again.

41 Many a time did they provoke him in the wilderness: and grieved him in the desert.

42 They turned back and tempted God: and moved the holy One in Israel.

43 They thought not of his hand: and of the day when he delivered them from the hand of the enemy;

44 How he had wrought his miracles in Egypt: and his wonders in the field of Zoan.

45 He turned their waters into bloud: so that they might not drink of the rivers.

46 He sent lice among them, and devoured them up: and frogs to destroy them.

47 He gave their fruit unto the caterpillar: and their labour unto the grasshopper.

48 He destroyed their vines with hailstones: and their mulberry-trees with the frost.

49 He smote their cattel also with hailstones: and their flocks with hot thunder-bolts.

50 He cast upon them the furiousness of his wrath, anger, displeasure and trouble: and sent evil angels among them.

51 He made a way to his indignation, and spared not their soul from death: but gave their life over to the pestilence.

52 And smote all the first-born in Egypt: the most principal and mightiest in the dwellings of Ham.

53 But as for his own people, he led them forth like sheep: and carried them in the wilderness like a flock.

54 He brought them out safely, that they should not fear: and over-whelmed their enemies with the sea.

55 And brought them within the borders of his sanctuary: even to his mountain which he purchased with his right hand.

56 He cast out the heathen also before them: caused their land to

be divided among them for an heritage, and made the tribes of Israel to dwell in their tents.

57   So they tempted and displeased the most high God: and kept not his testimonies;

58   But turned their backs, and fell away like their forefathers: starting aside like a broken bow.

59   For they grieved him with their hill-altars: and provoked him to displeasure with their images.

60   When God heard this, he was wroth: and took sore displeasure at Israel.

61   So that he forsook the tabernacle in Silo: even the tent that he had pitched among men.

62   He delivered their power into captivity: and their beauty into the enemies hand.

63   He gave his people over also unto the sword: and was wroth with his inheritance.

64   The fire consumed their young men: and their maidens were not given to marriage.

65   Their priests were slain with the sword: and there were no widows to make lamentation.

66   So the Lord awaked as one out of sleep: and like a giant refreshed with wine.

67   He smote his enemies in the hinder parts: and put them to a perpetual shame.

68   He refused the tabernacle of Joseph: and chose not the tribe of Ephraim;

69   But chose the tribe of Judah: even the hill of Sion which he loved.

70   And there he built his temple on high: and laid the foundation of it like the ground which he hath made continually.

71   He chose David also his servant: and took him away from the sheep-folds.

72   As he was following the ewes great with young ones he took him: that he might feed Jacob his people, and Israel his inheritance.

73   So he fed them with a faithful and true heart: and ruled them prudently with all his power.

Day 16. *Morning Prayer.*

Psalm 79

Deus, venerunt.

O GOD, the heathen are come into thine inheritance: thy holy temple have they defiled, and made Jerusalem an heap of stones.

2 The dead bodies of thy servants have they given to be meat unto the fowls of the air: and the flesh of thy saints unto the beasts of the land.

3 Their bloud have they shed like water on every side of Jerusalem: and there was no man to bury them.

4 We are become an open shame to our enemies: a very scorn and derision unto them that are round about us.

5 Lord, how long wilt thou be angry: shall thy jealousy burn like fire for ever?

6 Pour out thine indignation upon the heathen that have not known thee: and upon the kingdoms that have not called upon thy Name.

7 For they have devoured Jacob: and laid waste his dwelling place.

8 O remember not our old sins, but have mercy upon us, and that soon: for we are come to great misery.

9 Help us, O God of our salvation, for the glory of thy Name: O deliver us and be merciful unto our sins for thy Names sake.

10 Wherefore do the heathen say: Where is now their God?

11 O let the vengeance of thy servants bloud that is shed: be openly shewed upon the heathen in our sight.

12 O let the sorrowful sighing of the prisoners come before thee: according to the greatness of thy power, preserve thou those that are appointed to die.

13 And for the blasphemy wherewith our neighbours have blasphemed thee: reward thou them, O Lord, seven fold into their bosom.

14 So we, that are thy people and sheep of thy pasture, shall give thee thanks for ever: and will alway be shewing forth thy praise from generation to generation.

Psalm 80

Qui regis Israel.

HEAR, O thou shepherd of Israel, thou that leadest Joseph like a sheep: shew thy self also, thou that sittest upon the Cherubims.

2 Before Ephraim, Benjamin, and Manasses: stir up thy strength, and come, and help us.

3 Turn us again, O God: shew the light of thy countenance, and we shall be whole.

4 O Lord God of hosts: how long wilt thou be angry with thy people that prayeth?

5 Thou feedest them with the bread of tears: and givest them plenteousness of tears to drink.

6 Thou hast made us a very strife unto our neighbours: and our enemies laugh us to scorn.

7 Turn us again, thou God of hosts: shew the light of thy countenance, and we shall be whole.

8 Thou hast brought a vine out of Egypt: thou hast cast out the heathen and planted it.

9 Thou madest room for it: and when it had taken root it filled the land.

10 The hills were covered with the shadow of it: and the boughs thereof were like the goodly cedar-trees.

11 She stretched out her branches unto the sea: and her boughs unto the river.

12 Why hast thou then broken down her hedge: that all they that go by pluck off her grapes?

13 The wild boar out of the wood doth root it up: and the wild beasts of the field devour it.

14 Turn thee again, thou God of hosts, look down from heaven: behold, and visit this vine;

15 And the place of the vineyard that thy right hand hath planted: and the branch that thou madest so strong for thy self.

16 It is burnt with fire and cut down: and they shall perish at the rebuke of thy countenance.

17 Let thy hand be upon the man of thy right hand: and upon the son of man, whom thou madest so strong for thine own self.

18 And so will not we go back from thee: O let us live, and we shall call upon thy Name.

19 Turn us again, O Lord God of hosts: shew the light of thy countenance, and we shall be whole.

Psalm 81

Exultate Deo.

SING we merrily unto God our strength: make a cheerful noise unto the God of Jacob.

2 Take the psalm, bring hither the tabret: the merry harp with the lute.

3 Blow up the trumpet in the new-moon: even in the time appointed, and upon our solemn feast-day.

4 For this was made a statute for Israel: and a law of the God of Jacob.

5 This he ordained in Joseph for a testimony: when he came out of the land of Egypt, and had heard a strange language.

6 I eased his shoulder from the burden: and his hands were delivered from making the pots.

7 Thou calledst upon me in troubles, and I delivered thee: and heard thee what time as the storm fell upon thee.

8 I proved thee also: at the waters of strife.

9 Hear, O my people, and I will assure thee, O Israel: if thou wilt hearken unto me,

10 There shall no strange god be in thee: neither shalt thou worship any other god.

11 I am the Lord thy God, who brought thee out of the land of Egypt: open thy mouth wide, and I shall fill it.

12 But my people would not hear my voice: and Israel would not obey me.

13 So I gave them up unto their own hearts lusts: and let them follow their own imaginations.

14 O that my people would have hearkned unto me: for if Israel had walked in my ways,

15 I should soon have put down their enemies: and turned my hand against their adversaries.

16 The haters of the Lord should have been found liars: but their time should have endured for ever.

17 He should have fed them also with the finest wheat-flour: and with honey out of the stony rock should I have satisfied thee.

Day 16. *Evening Prayer*.

Psalm 82

Deus stetit.

GOD standeth in the congregation of princes: he is a judge among gods.

2 How long will ye give wrong judgement: and accept the persons of the ungodly?

3 Defend the poor and fatherless: see that such as are in need and necessity have right.

4 Deliver the out-cast and poor: save them from the hand of the ungodly.

5 They will not be learned nor understand, but walk on still in darkness: all the foundations of the earth are out of course.

6 I have said, Ye are gods: and ye are all the children of the most Highest.

7 But ye shall die like men: and fall like one of the princes.

8 Arise, O God, and judge thou the earth: for thou shalt take all heathen to thine inheritance.

Psalm 83

Deus, quis similis?

HOLD not thy tongue, O God, keep not still silence: refrain not thy self, O God.

2 For lo, thine enemies make a murmuring: and they that hate thee have lift up their head.

3 They have imagined craftily against thy people: and taken counsel against thy secret ones.

4 They have said, Come, and let us root them out, that they be no more a people: and that the name of Israel may be no more in remembrance.

5 For they have cast their heads together with one consent: and are confederate against thee;

6 The tabernacles of the Edomites and the Ismaelites: the Moabites and Hagarenes;

7 Gebal, and Ammon, and Amalech: the Philistines, with them that dwell at Tyre.

8 Assur also is joined with them: and have holpen the children of Lot.

9 But do thou to them as unto the Madianites: unto Sisera, and unto Jabin at the brook of Kison;

10 Who perished at Endor: and became as the dung of the earth.

11 Make them and their princes like Oreb and Zeb: yea, make all their princes like as Zeba and Salmana;

12 Who say, Let us take to our selves: the houses of God in possession.

13 O my God, make them like unto a wheel: and as the stubble before the wind;

14 Like as the fire that burneth up the wood: and as the flame that consumeth the mountains.

15 Persecute them even so with thy tempest: and make them afraid with thy storm.

16 Make their faces ashamed, O Lord: that they may seek thy Name.

17 Let them be confounded and vexed evermore and more: let them be put to shame and perish.

18 And they shall know that thou whose Name is Jehovah: art only the most Highest over all the earth.

Psalm 84

Quam dilecta!

O HOW amiable are thy dwellings: thou Lord of hosts!
　　2 My soul hath a desire and longing to enter into the courts of the Lord: my heart and my flesh rejoyce in the living God.

3 Yea, the sparrow hath found her an house, and the swallow a nest, where she may lay her young: even thy altars, O Lord of hosts, my King and my God.

4 Blessed are they that dwell in thy house: they will be alway praising thee.

5 Blessed is the man whose strength is in thee: in whose heart are thy ways.

6 Who going through the vale of misery, use it for a well: and the pools are filled with water.

7 They will go from strength to strength: and unto the God of gods appeareth every one of them in Sion.

8 O Lord God of hosts, hear my prayer: hearken, O God of Jacob.

9 Behold, O God our defender: and look upon the face of thine anointed.

10 For one day in thy courts: is better than a thousand.

11 I had rather be a door-keeper in the house of my God: than to dwell in the tents of ungodliness.

12 For the Lord God is a light and defence: the Lord will give grace and worship, and no good thing shall he withhold from them that live a godly life.

13 O Lord God of hosts: blessed is the man that putteth his trust in thee.

Psalm 85

Benedixisti, Domine.

LORD, thou art become gracious unto thy land: thou hast turned away the captivity of Jacob.

2 Thou hast forgiven the offence of thy people: and covered all their sins.

3 Thou hast taken away all thy displeasure: and turned thy self from thy wrathful indignation.

4 Turn us then, O God our Saviour: and let thine anger cease from us.

5 Wilt thou be displeased at us for ever: and wilt thou stretch out thy wrath from one generation to another?

6 Wilt thou not turn again and quicken us: that thy people may rejoyce in thee?

7 Shew us thy mercy, O Lord: and grant us thy salvation.

8 I will hearken what the Lord God will say concerning me: for he shall speak peace unto his people, and to his saints, that they turn not again.

9 For his salvation is nigh them that fear him: that glory may dwell in our land.

10 Mercy and truth are met together: righteousness and peace have kissed each other.

11 Truth shall flourish out of the earth: and righteousness hath looked down from heaven.

12 Yea, the Lord shall shew loving kindness: and our land shall give her increase.

13 Righteousness shall go before him: and he shall direct his going in the way.

Day 17. *Morning Prayer.*

Psalm 86

Inclina, Domine.

Bow down thine ear, O Lord, and hear me: for I am poor, and in misery.

2 Preserve thou my soul, for I am holy: my God, save thy servant that putteth his trust in thee.

3 Be merciful unto me, O Lord: for I will call daily upon thee.

4 Comfort the soul of thy servant: for unto thee, O Lord, do I lift up my soul.

5 For thou, Lord, art good and gracious: and of great mercy unto all them that call upon thee.

6 Give ear, Lord, unto my prayer: and ponder the voice of my humble desires.

7 In the time of my trouble I will call upon thee: for thou hearest me.

8 Among the gods there is none like unto thee, O Lord: there is not one that can do as thou dost.

9 All nations whom thou hast made shall come and worship thee, O Lord: and shall glorifie thy Name.

10 For thou art great, and dost wondrous things: thou art God alone.

11 Teach me thy way, O Lord, and I will walk in thy truth: O knit my heart unto thee, that I may fear thy Name.

12 I will thank thee, O Lord my God, with all my heart: and will praise thy Name for evermore.

13 For great is thy mercy toward me: and thou hast delivered my soul from the nethermost hell.

14 O God, the proud are risen against me: and the congregations of naughty men have sought after my soul, and have not set thee before their eyes.

15 But thou, O Lord God, art full of compassion and mercy: long-suffering, plenteous in goodness and truth.

16 O turn thee then unto me, and have mercy upon me: give thy strength unto thy servant, and help the son of thine handmaid.

17 Shew some token upon me for good, that they who hate me may see it and be ashamed: because thou, Lord, hast holpen me and comforted me.

Psalm 87

Fundamenta ejus.

H ER foundations are upon the holy hills: the Lord loveth the gates of Sion more than all the dwellings of Jacob.

2 Very excellent things are spoken of thee: thou city of God.

3 I will think upon Rahab and Babylon: with them that know me.

4 Behold ye the Philistines also: and they of Tyre, with the Morians, lo, there was he born.

5 And of Sion it shall be reported that he was born in her: and the most High shall stablish her.

6 The Lord shall rehearse it when he writeth up the people: that he was born there.

7 The singers also and trumpeters shall he rehearse: All my fresh springs shall be in thee.

Psalm 88

Domine Deus

O LORD God of my salvation, I have cryed day and night before thee: O let my prayer enter into thy presence, encline thine ear unto my calling.

2 For my soul is full of trouble: and my life draweth nigh unto hell.

3 I am counted as one of them that go down into the pit: and I have been even as a man that hath no strength.

4 Free among the dead, like unto them that are wounded, and lie in the grave: who are out of remembrance, and are cut away from thy hand.

5 Thou hast laid me in the lowest pit: in a place of darkness and in the deep.

6 Thine indignation lieth hard upon me: and thou hast vexed me with all thy storms.

7 Thou hast put away mine acquaintance far from me: and made me to be abhorred of them.

8 I am so fast in prison: that I cannot get forth.

9 My sight faileth for very trouble: Lord, I have called daily upon thee, I have stretched forth my hands unto thee.

10 Dost thou shew wonders among the dead: or shall the dead rise up again, and praise thee?

11 Shall thy loving kindness be shewed in the grave: or thy faithfulness in destruction?

12 Shall thy wondrous works be known in the dark: and thy righteousness in the land where all things are forgotten?

13 Unto thee have I cryed, O Lord: and early shall my prayer come before thee.

14 Lord, why abhorrest thou my soul: and hidest thou thy face from me?

15 I am in misery, and like unto him that is at the point to die: even from my youth up thy terrours have I suffered with a troubled mind.

16 Thy wrathful displeasure goeth over me: and the fear of thee hath undone me.

17 They came round about me daily like water: and compassed me together on every side.

18 My lovers and friends hast thou put away from me: and hid mine acquaintance out of my sight.

Day 17. *Evening Prayer.*

Psalm 89

Misericordias Domini.

M Y SONG shall be alway of the loving kindness of the Lord: with my mouth will I ever be shewing thy truth from one generation to another.

2 For I have said, Mercy shall be set up for ever: thy truth shalt thou stablish in the heavens.

3 I have made a covenant with my chosen: I have sworn unto David my servant,

4 Thy seed will I stablish for ever: and set up thy throne from one generation to another.

5 O Lord, the very heavens shall praise thy wondrous works: and thy truth in the congregation of the saints.

6 For who is he among the clouds: that shall be compared unto the Lord?

7 And what is he among the gods: that shall be like unto the Lord?

8 God is very greatly to be feared in the councel of the saints: and to be had in reverence of all them that are round about him.

9 O Lord God of hosts, who is like unto thee: thy truth, most mighty Lord, is on every side.

10 Thou rulest the raging of the sea: thou stillest the waves thereof when they arise.

11 Thou hast subdued Egypt and destroyed it: thou hast scattered thine enemies abroad with thy mighty arm.

12 The heavens are thine, the earth also is thine: thou hast laid the foundation of the round world, and all that therein is.

13 Thou hast made the north and the south: Tabor and Hermon shall rejoyce in thy Name.

14 Thou hast a mighty arm: strong is thy hand, and high is thy right hand.

15 Righteousness and equity are the habitation of thy seat: mercy and truth shall go before thy face.

16 Blessed is the people, O Lord, that can rejoyce in thee: they shall walk in the light of thy countenance.

17 Their delight shall be daily in thy Name: and in thy righteousness shall they make their boast.

18 For thou art the glory of their strength: and in thy loving kindness thou shalt lift up our horns.

19 For the Lord is our defence: the holy One of Israel is our King.

20 Thou spakest sometime in visions unto thy saints, and saidst: I have laid help upon one that is mighty, I have exalted one chosen out of the people.

21 I have found David my servant: with my holy oil have I anointed him.

22 My hand shall hold him fast: and my arm shall strengthen him.

23 The enemy shall not be able to do him violence: the son of wickedness shall not hurt him.

24 I will smite down his foes before his face: and plague them that hate him.

25 My truth also and my mercy shall be with him: and in my Name shall his horn be exalted.

26 I will set his dominion also in the sea: and his right hand in the flouds.

27 He shall call me, Thou art my Father: my God, and my strong salvation.

28 And I will make him my first-born: higher than the kings of the earth.

29 My mercy will I keep for him for evermore: and my covenant shall stand fast with him.

30 His seed also will I make to endure for ever: and his throne as the daies of heaven.

31 But if his children forsake my law: and walk not in my judgements;

32 If they break my statutes, and keep not my commandments: I will visit their offences with the rod, and their sin with scourges.

33 Nevertheless, my loving kindness will I not utterly take from him: nor suffer my truth to fail.

34 My covenant will I not break, nor alter the thing that is gone out of my lips: I have sworn once by my holiness, that I will not fail David.

35 His seed shall endure for ever: and his seat is like as the sun before me.

36 He shall stand fast for evermore as the moon: and as the faithful witness in heaven.

37 But thou hast abhorred, and forsaken thine Anointed: and art displeased at him.

38 Thou hast broken the covenant of thy servant: and cast his crown to the ground.

39 Thou hast overthrown all his hedges: and broken down his strong holds.

40 All they that go by, spoil him: and he is become a reproach to his neighbours.

41 Thou hast set up the right hand of his enemies: and made all his adversaries to rejoyce.

42 Thou hast taken away the edge of his sword: and givest him not victory in the battel.

43 Thou hast put out his glory: and cast his throne down to the ground.

44 The dayes of his youth hast thou shortned: and covered him with dishonour.

45 Lord, how long wilt thou hide thy self, for ever: and shall thy wrath burn like fire?

46 O remember how short my time is: wherefore hast thou made all men for nought?

47 What man is he that liveth, and shall not see death: and shall he deliver his soul from the hand of hell?

48 Lord, where are thy old loving kindnesses: which thou swarest unto David in thy truth?

49 Remember, Lord, the rebuke, that thy servants have: and how I do bear in my bosom the rebukes of many people;

50 Wherewith thine enemies have blasphemed thee, and slandered the footsteps of thine Anointed: praised be the Lord for evermore. Amen, and Amen.

Day 18. *Morning Prayer.*

Psalm 90

Domine, refugium.

LORD, thou hast been our refuge: from one generation to another.

2 Before the mountains were brought forth, or ever the earth and the world were made: thou art God from everlasting, and world without end.

3 Thou turnest man to destruction: again thou sayest, Come again, ye children of men.

4 For a thousand years in thy sight are but as yesterday: seeing that is past as a watch in the night.

5 As soon as thou scatterest them, they are even as a sleep: and fade away suddenly like the grass.

6 In the morning it is green, and groweth up: but in the evening it is cut down, dried up, and withered.

7 For we consume away in thy displeasure: and are afraid at thy wrathful indignation.

8 Thou hast set our misdeeds before thee: and our secret sins in the light of thy countenance.

9 For when thou art angry, all our dayes are gone: we bring our years to an end, as it were a tale that is told.

10 The days of our age are threescore years and ten, and though men be so strong, that they come to fourscore years: yet is their strength then but labour, and sorrow; so soon passeth it away, and we are gone.

11 But who regardeth the power of thy wrath: for even thereafter as a man feareth, so is thy displeasure.

12 So teach us to number our dayes: that we may apply our hearts unto wisdom.

13 Turn thee again, O Lord, at the last: and be gracious unto thy servants.

14 O satisfie us with thy mercy, and that soon: so shall we rejoyce and be glad all the dayes of our life.

15 Comfort us again now after the time that thou hast plagued us: and for the years wherein we have suffered adversity.

16 Shew thy servants thy work: and their children thy glory.

17 And the glorious Majesty of the Lord our God be upon us: prosper thou the work of our hands upon us, O prosper thou our handy-work.

Psalm 91

Qui habitat.

WHOSO dwelleth under the defence of the most High: shall abide under the shadow of the Almighty.

2 I will say unto the Lord, Thou art my hope, and my strong hold: my God, in him will I trust.

3 For he shall deliver thee from the snare of the hunter: and from the noisome pestilence.

4 He shall defend thee under his wings, and thou shalt be safe under his feathers: his faithfulness and truth shall be thy shield and buckler.

5 Thou shalt not be afraid for any terrour by night: nor for the arrow that flieth by day;

6 For the pestilence that walketh in darkness: nor for the sickness that destroyeth in the noon-day.

7 A thousand shall fall beside thee, and ten thousand at thy right hand: but it shall not come nigh thee.

8 Yea, with thine eyes shalt thou behold: and see the reward of the ungodly.

9 For thou, Lord, art my hope: thou hast set thine house of defence very high.

10 There shall no evil happen unto thee: neither shall any plague come nigh thy dwelling.

11 For he shall give his angels charge over thee: to keep thee in all thy wayes.

12 They shall bear thee in their hands: that thou hurt not thy foot against a stone.

13 Thou shalt go upon the lion and adder: the young lion and the dragon shalt thou tread under thy feet.

14 Because he hath set his love upon me, therefore will I deliver him: I will set him up, because he hath known my Name.

15 He shall call upon me, and I will hear him: yea, I am with him in trouble; I will deliver him, and bring him to honour.

16 With long life will I satisfie him: and shew him my salvation.

Psalm 92

Bonum est confiteri.

IT IS a good thing to give thanks unto the Lord: and to sing praises unto thy Name, O most Highest;

2 To tell of thy loving kindness early in the morning: and of thy truth in the night-season.

3 Upon an instrument of ten strings, and upon the lute: upon a loud instrument, and upon the harp.

4 For thou, Lord, hast made me glad through thy works: and I will rejoyce in giving praise for the operations of thy hands.

5 O Lord, how glorious are thy works: thy thoughts are very deep.

6 An unwise man doth not well consider this: and a fool doth not understand it.

7 When the ungodly are green as the grass, and when all the workers of wickedness do flourish: then shall they be destroyed for ever; but thou, Lord, art the most Highest for evermore.

8 For lo, thine enemies, O Lord, lo, thine enemies shall perish: and all the workers of wickedness shall be destroyed.

9 But mine horn shall be exalted like the horn of an unicorn: for I am anointed with fresh oil.

10 Mine eye also shall see his lust of mine enemies: and mine ear shall hear his desire of the wicked that arise up against me.

11 The righteous shall flourish like a palm-tree: and shall spread abroad like a Cedar in Libanus.

12 Such as are planted in the house of the Lord: shall flourish in the courts of the house of our God.

13 They also shall bring forth more fruit in their age: and shall be fat and well liking.

14 That they may shew how true the Lord my strength is: and that there is no unrighteousness in him.

Day 18. *Evening Prayer.*

Psalm 93

Dominus regnavit.

THE Lord is King, and hath put on glorious apparel: the Lord hath put on his apparel, and girded himself with strength.

2 He hath made the round world so sure: that it cannot be moved.

3 Ever since the world began hath thy seat been prepared: thou art from everlasting.

4 The flouds are risen, O Lord, the flouds have lift up their voice: the flouds lift up their waves.

5 The waves of the sea are mighty, and rage horribly: but yet the Lord, who dwelleth on high, is mightier.

6 Thy testimonies, O Lord, are very sure: holiness becometh thine house for ever.

Psalm 94

Deus ultionum.

O LORD God, to whom vengeance belongeth: thou God, to whom vengeance belongeth, shew thy self.

2 Arise, thou Judge of the world: and reward the proud after their deserving.

3 Lord, how long shall the ungodly: how long shall the ungodly triumph?

4 How long shall all wicked doers speak so disdainfully: and make such proud boasting?

5 They smite down thy people, O Lord: and trouble thine heritage.

6 They murder the widow, and the stranger: and put the fatherless to death.

7 And yet they say, Tush, the Lord shall not see: neither shall the God of Jacob regard it.

8 Take heed, ye unwise among the people: O ye fools, when will ye understand?

9 He that planted the ear, shall he not hear: or he that made the eye, shall he not see?

10 Or he that nurtureth the heathen: it is he that teacheth man knowledge, shall not he punish?

11 The Lord knoweth the thoughts of man: that they are but vain.

12 Blessed is the man whom thou chastenest, O Lord: and teachest him in thy law.

13 That thou mayest give him patience in time of adversity: until the pit be digged up for the ungodly.

14 For the Lord will not fail his people: neither will he forsake his inheritance;

15 Until righteousness turn again unto judgement: all such as are true in heart shall follow it.

16 Who will rise up with me against the wicked: or who will take my part against the evil doers?

17 If the Lord had not helped me: it had not failed but my soul had been put to silence.

18 But when I said, My foot hath slipped: thy mercy, O Lord, held me up.

19 In the multitude of the sorrows that I had in my heart: thy comforts have refreshed my soul.

20 Wilt thou have any thing to do with the stool of wickedness: which imagineth mischief as a law?

21 They gather them together against the soul of the righteous: and condemn the innocent bloud.

22 But the Lord is my refuge: and my God is the strength of my confidence.

23 He shall recompense them their wickedness, and destroy them in their own malice: yea, the Lord our God shall destroy them.

Day 19. *Morning Prayer.*

Psalm 95

Venite, exultemus.

O COME let us sing unto the Lord: let us heartily rejoyce in the strength of our salvation.

2 Let us come before his presence with thanksgiving: and shew our selves glad in him with psalms.

3 For the Lord is a great God: and a great King above all gods.

4 In his hand are all the corners of the earth: and the strength of the hills is his also.

5 The sea is his, and he made it: and his hands prepared the dry land.

6 O come, let us worship and fall down: and kneel before the Lord our maker.

7 For he is the Lord our God: and we are the people of his pasture, and the sheep of his hand.

8 To day if ye will hear his voice, harden not your hearts: as in the provocation, and as in the day of temptation in the wilderness;

9 When your fathers tempted me: proved me, and saw my works.

10 Forty years long was I grieved with this generation, and said: It is a people that do erre in their hearts, for they have not known my wayes;

11 Unto whom I sware in my wrath: that they should not enter into my rest.

Psalm 96

Cantate Domino.

O SING unto the Lord a new song: sing unto the Lord, all the whole earth.

2 Sing unto the Lord, and praise his Name: be telling of his salvation from day to day.

3 Declare his honour unto the heathen: and his wonders unto all people.

4 For the Lord is great, and cannot worthily be praised: he is more to be feared than all gods.

5 As for all the gods of the heathen, they are but idols: but it is the Lord that made the heavens.

6 Glory and worship are before him: power and honour are in his sanctuary.

7 Ascribe unto the Lord, O ye kindreds of the people: ascribe unto the Lord worship and power.

8 Ascribe unto the Lord the honour due unto his Name: bring presents, and come into his courts.

9 O worship the Lord in the beauty of holiness: let the whole earth stand in awe of him.

10 Tell it out among the heathen that the Lord is King: and that it is he who hath made the round world so fast that it cannot be moved, and how that he shall judge the people righteously.

11 Let the heavens rejoyce, and let the earth be glad: let the sea make a noise, and all that therein is.

12 Let the field be joyful, and all that is in it: then shall all the trees of the wood rejoyce before the Lord.

13 For he cometh, for he cometh to judge the earth: and with righteousness to judge the world, and the people with his truth.

Psalm 97

Dominus regnavit.

THE Lord is King, the earth may be glad thereof: yea, the multitude of the isles may be glad thereof.

2 Clouds and darkness are round about him: righteousness and judgement are the habitation of his seat.

3 There shall go a fire before him: and burn up his enemies on every side.

4 His lightnings gave shine unto the world: the earth saw it, and was afraid.

5 The hills melted like wax at the presence of the Lord: at the presence of the Lord of the whole earth.

6 The heavens have declared his righteousness: and all the people have seen his glory.

7 Confounded be all they that worship carved images, and that delight in vain gods: worship him, all ye gods.

8 Sion heard of it, and rejoyced: and the daughters of Juda were glad, because of thy judgements, O Lord.

9 For thou, Lord, art higher than all that are in the earth: thou art exalted far above all gods.

10 O ye, that love the Lord, see that ye hate the thing which is evil: the Lord preserveth the souls of his saints; he shall deliver them from the hand of the ungodly.

11 There is sprung up a light for the righteous: and joyful gladness for such as are true-hearted.

12 Rejoyce in the Lord, ye righteous: and give thanks for a remembrance of his holiness.

Day 19. *Evening Prayer.*

Psalm 98

Cantate Domino.

O SING unto the Lord a new song: for he hath done marvellous things.

2 With his own right hand, and with his holy arm: hath he gotten himself the victory.

3 The Lord declared his salvation: his righteousness hath he openly shewed in the sight of the heathen.

4 He hath remembered his mercy and truth toward the house of Israel: and all the ends of the world have seen the salvation of our God.

5 Shew your selves joyful unto the Lord, all ye lands: sing, rejoyce and give thanks.

6 Praise the Lord upon the harp: sing to the harp with a psalm of thanksgiving.

7 With trumpets also and shawms: O shew your selves joyful before the Lord the King.

8 Let the sea make a noise, and all that therein is: the round world, and they that dwell therein.

9 Let the flouds clap their hands, and let the hills be joyful together before the Lord: for he is come to judge the earth.

10 With righteousness shall he judge the world: and the people with equity.

Psalm 99

Dominus regnavit.

THE Lord is King, be the people never so unpatient: he sitteth between the cherubims, be the earth never so unquiet.

2 The Lord is great in Sion: and high above all people.

3 They shall give thanks unto thy Name: which is great, wonderful, and holy.

4 The kings power loveth judgement, thou hast prepared equity: thou hast executed judgment, and righteousness in Jacob.

5 O magnifie the Lord our God: and fall down before his footstool, for he is holy.

6 Moses and Aaron among his priests, and Samuel among such as call upon his Name: these called upon the Lord, and he heard them.

7 He spake unto them out of the cloudy pillar: for they kept his testimonies, and the law that he gave them.

8 Thou heardest them, O Lord our God: thou forgavest them, O God, and punishedst their own inventions.

9 O magnifie the Lord our God, and worship him upon his holy hill: for the Lord our God is holy.

Psalm 100

Jubilate Deo.

O BE joyful in the Lord, all ye lands: serve the Lord with gladness, and come before his presence with a song.

2 Be ye sure that the Lord he is God: it is he that hath made us, and not we our selves; we are his people, and the sheep of his pasture.

3 O go your way into his gates with thanksgiving, and into his courts with praise: be thankful unto him, and speak good of his Name.

4 For the Lord is gracious, his mercy is everlasting: and his truth endureth from generation to generation.

Psalm 101

Misericordiam et judicium.

M Y SONG shall be of mercy and judgement: unto thee, O Lord, will I sing.

2 O let me have understanding: in the way of godliness.

3 When wilt thou come unto me: I will walk in my house with a perfect heart.

4 I will take no wicked thing in hand; I hate the sins of unfaithfulness: there shall no such cleave unto me.

5 A froward heart shall depart from me: I will not know a wicked person.

6 Whoso privily slandereth his neighbour: him will I destroy.

7 Whoso hath also a proud look and high stomack: I will not suffer him.

8 Mine eyes look upon such as are faithful in the land: that they may dwell with me.

9 Whoso leadeth a godly life: he shall be my servant.

10 There shall no deceitful person dwell in my house: he that telleth lies, shall not tarry in my sight.

11 I shall soon destroy all the ungodly that are in the land: that I may root out all wicked doers from the city of the Lord.

Day 20. *Morning Prayer.*

Psalm 102

Domine, exaudi.

HEAR my prayer, O Lord: and let my crying come unto thee.

2 Hide not thy face from me in the time of my trouble: incline thine ear unto me when I call; O hear me, and that right soon.

3 For my dayes are consumed away like smoke: and my bones are burnt up as it were a fire-brand.

4 My heart is smitten down, and withered like grass: so that I forget to eat my bread.

5 For the voice of my groaning: my bones will scarce cleave to my flesh.

6 I am become like a pelican in the wilderness: and like an owl that is in the desert.

7 I have watched, and am even as it were a sparrow: that sitteth alone upon the house-top.

8 Mine enemies revile me all the day long: and they, that are mad upon me, are sworn together against me.

9 For I have eaten ashes as it were bread: and mingled my drink with weeping;

10 And that because of thine indignation and wrath: for thou hast taken me up, and cast me down.

11 My days are gone like a shadow: and I am withered like grass.

12 But thou, O Lord, shalt endure for ever: and thy remembrance throughout all generations.

13 Thou shalt arise, and have mercy upon Sion: for it is time that thou have mercy upon her, yea, the time is come.

14 And why? thy servants think upon her stones: and it pitieth them to see her in the dust.

15 The heathen shall fear thy Name, O Lord: and all the kings of the earth thy Majesty;

16 When the Lord shall build up Sion: and when his glory shall appear;

17 When he turneth him unto the prayer of the poor destitute: and despiseth not their desire.

18 This shall be written for those that come after: and the people which shall be born shall praise the Lord.

19 For he hath looked down from his Sanctuary: out of the heaven did the Lord behold the earth;

20 That he might hear the mournings of such as are in captivity: and deliver the children appointed unto death;

21 That they may declare the Name of the Lord in Sion: and his worship at Jerusalem;

22 When the people are gathered together: and the kingdoms also to serve the Lord.

23 He brought down my strength in my journey: and shortned my dayes.

24 But I said, O my God, take me not away in the midst of mine age: as for thy years they endure throughout all generations.

25 Thou, Lord, in the beginning hast laid the foundation of the earth: and the heavens are the work of thy hands.

26 They shall perish, but thou shalt endure: they all shall wax old as doth a garment,

27 And as a vesture shalt thou change them, and they shall be changed: but thou art the same, and thy years shall not fail.

28 The children of thy servants shall continue: and their seed shall stand fast in thy sight.

Psalm 103

Benedic, anima mea.

PRAISE the Lord, O my soul: and all that is within me praise his holy Name.

2 Praise the Lord, O my soul: and forget not all his benefits;

3 Who forgiveth all thy sin: and healeth all thine infirmities;

4 Who saveth thy life from destruction: and crowneth thee with mercy and loving-kindness;

5 Who satisfieth thy mouth with good things: making thee young and lusty as an eagle.

6 The Lord executeth righteousness and judgement: for all them that are oppressed with wrong.

7 He shewed his wayes unto Moses: his works unto the children of Israel.

8 The Lord is full of compassion and mercy: long suffering, and of great goodness.

9 He will not alway be chiding: neither keepeth he his anger for ever.

10 He hath not dealt with us after our sins: nor rewarded us according to our wickednesses.

11 For look how high the heaven is in comparison of the earth: so great is his mercy also toward them that fear him.

12 Look how wide also the east is from the west: so far hath he set our sins from us.

13 Yea, like as a father pitieth his own children: even so is the Lord merciful unto them that fear him.

14 For he knoweth whereof we are made: he remembreth that we are but dust.

15 The dayes of man are but as grass: for he flourisheth as a flower of the field.

16 For as soon as the wind goeth over it, it is gone: and the place thereof shall know it no more.

17 But the merciful goodness of the Lord endureth for ever and ever upon them that fear him: and his righteousness upon childrens children;

18 Even upon such as keep his covenant: and think upon his commandments to do them.

19 The Lord hath prepared his seat in heaven: and his kingdom ruleth over all.

20 O praise the Lord, ye Angels of his, ye that excell in strength: ye that fulfil his commandment, and hearken unto the voice of his words.

21 O praise the Lord, all ye his hosts: ye servants of his that do his pleasure.

22 O speak good of the Lord, all ye works of his, in all places of his dominion: praise thou the Lord, O my soul.

Day 20. *Evening Prayer.*

Psalm 104

Benedic, anima mea.

PRAISE the Lord, O my soul: O Lord my God, thou art become exceeding glorious, thou art clothed with majesty and honour.

2 Thou deckest thy self with light as it were with a garment: and spreadest out the heavens like a curtain.

3 Who layeth the beams of his chambers in the waters: and maketh the clouds his chariot, and walketh upon the wings of the wind.

4 He maketh his Angels spirits: and his ministers a flaming fire.

5 He laid the foundations of the earth: that it never should move at any time.

6 Thou coveredst it with the deep like as with a garment: the waters stand in the hills.

7 At thy rebuke they flee: at the voice of thy thunder they are afraid.

8 They go up as high as the hills, and down to the valleys beneath: even unto the place which thou hast appointed for them.

9 Thou hast set them their bounds which they shall not pass: neither turn again to cover the earth.

10 He sendeth the springs into the rivers: which run among the hills.

11 All beasts of the field drink thereof: and the wilde asses quench their thirst.

12 Beside them shall the fowls of the air have their habitation: and sing among the branches.

13 He watereth the hills from above: the earth is filled with the fruit of thy works.

14 He bringeth forth grass for the cattel: and green herb for the service of men.

15 That he may bring food out of the earth, and wine that maketh glad the heart of man: and oil to make him a chearful countenance, and bread to strengthen mans heart.

16 The trees of the Lord also are full of sap: even the cedars of Libanus which he hath planted.

17 Wherein the birds make their nests: and the firre-trees are a dwelling for the stork.

18 The high hills are a refuge for the wild goats: and so are the stony rocks for the conies.

19 He appointed the moon for certain seasons: and the sun knoweth his going down.

20 Thou makest darkness that it may be night: wherein all the beasts of the forest do move.

21 The lions roaring after their prey: do seek their meat from God.

22 The sun ariseth, and they get them away together: and lay them down in their dens.

23 Man goeth forth to his work, and to his labour: until the evening.

24 O Lord, how manifold are thy works: in wisdom hast thou made them all, the earth is full of thy riches.

25 So is the great and wide sea also: wherein are things creeping innumerable, both small and great beasts.

26 There go the ships, and there is that Leviathan: whom thou hast made to take his pastime therein.

27 These wait all upon thee: that thou mayest give them meat in due season.

28 When thou givest it them, they gather it: and when thou openest thy hand, they are filled with good.

29 When thou hidest thy face, they are troubled: when thou takest away their breath, they die, and are turned again to their dust.

30 When thou lettest thy breath go forth, they shall be made: and thou shalt renew the face of the earth.

31 The glorious Majesty of the Lord shall endure for ever: the Lord shall rejoyce in his works.

32 The earth shall tremble at the look of him: if he do but touch the hills, they shall smoak.

33 I will sing unto the Lord as long as I live: I will praise my God while I have my being.

34 And so shall my words please him: my joy shall be in the Lord.

35 As for sinners they shall be consumed out of the earth, and the ungodly shall come to an end: praise thou the Lord, O my soul, praise the Lord.

Day 21. *Morning Prayer.*

Psalm 105

Confitemini Domino.

O GIVE thanks unto the Lord, and call upon his Name: tell the people what things he hath done.

2 O let your songs be of him, and praise him: and let your talking be of all his wondrous works.

3 Rejoyce in his holy Name: let the heart of them rejoyce that seek the Lord.

4 Seek the Lord and his strength: seek his face evermore.

5 Remember the marvellous works that he hath done: his wonders and the judgments of his mouth;

6 O ye seed of Abraham his servant: ye children of Jacob his chosen.

7 He is the Lord our God: his judgements are in all the world.

8 He hath been alway mindful of his covenant and promise: that he made to a thousand generations;

9 Even the covenant that he made with Abraham: and the oath that he sware unto Isaac;

10 And appointed the same unto Jacob for a law: and to Israel for an everlasting testament.

11 Saying, Unto thee will I give the land of Canaan: the lot of your inheritance.

12 When there were yet but a few of them: and they strangers in the land;

13 What time as they went from one nation to another: from one kingdom to another people;

14 He suffered no man to do them wrong: but reproved even kings for their sakes.

15 Touch not mine Anointed: and do my prophets no harm.

16 Moreover he called for a dearth upon the land: and destroyed all the provision of bread.

17 But he had sent a man before them: even Joseph, who was sold to be a bond-servant;

18 Whose feet they hurt in the stocks: the iron entred into his soul;

19 Until the time came that his cause was known: the word of the Lord tried him.

20 The king sent, and delivered him: the prince of the people let him go free.

21 He made him lord also of his house: and ruler of all his substance;

22 That he might inform his princes after his will: and teach his senatours wisdom.

23 Israel also came into Egypt: and Jacob was a stranger in the land of Ham.

24 And he increased his people exceedingly: and made them stronger than their enemies;

25 Whose heart turned so, that they hated his people: and dealt untruly with his servants.

26 Then sent he Moses his servant: and Aaron whom he had chosen.

27 And these shewed his tokens among them: and wonders in the land of Ham.

28 He sent darkness, and it was dark: and they were not obedient unto his word.

29 He turned their waters into bloud: and slew their fish.

30 Their land brought forth frogs: yea, even in their kings chambers.

31 He spake the word, and there came all manner of flies: and lice in all their quarters.

32 He gave them hailstones for rain: and flames of fire in their land.

33 He smote their vines also and fig-trees: and destroyed the trees that were in their coasts.

34 He spake the word, and the grasshoppers came, and caterpillars innumerable: and did eat up all the grass in their land, and devoured the fruit of their ground.

35 He smote all the first-born in their land: even the chief of all their strength.

36 He brought them forth also with silver and gold: there was not one feeble person among their tribes.

37 Egypt was glad at their departing: for they were afraid of them.

38 He spread out a cloud to be a covering: and fire to give light in the night-season.

39 At their desire he brought quails: and he filled them with the bread of heaven.

40 He opened the rock of stone, and the waters flowed out: so that rivers ran in the dry places.

41 For why? he remembred his holy promise: and Abraham his servant.

42 And he brought forth his people with joy: and his chosen with gladness;

43 And gave them the lands of the heathen: and they took the labours of the people in possession;

44 That they might keep his statutes: and observe his laws.

Day 21. *Evening Prayer.*

Psalm 106

Confitemini Domino.

O GIVE thanks unto the Lord, for he is gracious: and his mercy endureth for ever.

2 Who can express the noble acts of the Lord: or shew forth all his praise?

3 Blessed are they that alway keep judgement: and do righteousness.

4 Remember me, O Lord, according to the favour that thou bearest unto thy people: O visit me with thy salvation;

5 That I may see the felicity of thy chosen: and rejoyce in the gladness of thy people, and give thanks with thine inheritance.

6 We have sinned with our fathers: we have done amiss, and dealt wickedly.

7 Our fathers regarded not thy wonders in Egypt, neither kept they thy great goodness in remembrance: but were disobedient at the sea, even at the Red sea.

8 Nevertheless, he helped them for his Names sake: that he might make his power to be known.

9 He rebuked the Red sea also, and it was dried up: so he led them through the deep, as through a wilderness.

10 And he saved them from the adversaries hand: and delivered them from the hand of the enemy.

11 As for those that troubled them, the waters overwhelmed them: there was not one of them left.

12 Then believed they his words: and sang praise unto him.

13 But within a while they forgat his works: and would not abide his counsel.

14 But lust came upon them in the wilderness: and they tempted God in the desert.

15 And he gave them their desire: and sent leanness withall into their soul.

16 They angred Moses also in the tents: and Aaron the saint of the Lord.

17 So the earth opened, and swallowed up Dathan: and covered the congregation of Abiram.

18 And the fire was kindled in their company: the flame burnt up the ungodly.

19 They made a calf in Horeb: and worshipped the molten image.

20 Thus they turned their glory: into the similitude of a calf that eateth hay.

21 And they forgat God their Saviour: who had done so great things in Egypt;

22 Wondrous works in the land of Ham: and fearful things by the Red sea.

23 So he said, he would have destroyed them, had not Moses his chosen stood before him in the gap: to turn away his wrathful indignation, lest he should destroy them.

24 Yea, they thought scorn of that pleasant land: and gave no credence unto his word.

25 But murmured in their tents: and hearkned not unto the voice of the Lord.

26 Then lift he up his hand against them: to overthrow them in the wilderness;

27 To cast out their seed among the nations: and to scatter them in the lands.

28 They joined themselves unto Baal-peor: and ate the offerings of the dead.

29 Thus they provoked him to anger with their own inventions: and the plague was great among them.

30 Then stood up Phinees and prayed: and so the plague ceased.

31 And that was counted unto him for righteousness: among all posterities for evermore.

32 They angred him also at the waters of strife: so that he punished Moses for their sakes;

33 Because they provoked his spirit: so that he spake unadvisedly with his lips.

34 Neither destroyed they the heathen: as the Lord commanded them;

35 But were mingled among the heathen: and learned their works.

36 Insomuch that they worshipped their idols, which turned to their own decay: yea, they offered their sons and their daughters unto devils,

37 And shed innocent bloud, even the bloud of their sons and of their daughters: whom they offered unto the idols of Canaan, and the land was defiled with bloud.

38 Thus were they stained with their own works: and went a whoring with their own inventions.

39 Therefore was the wrath of the Lord kindled against his people: insomuch that he abhorred his own inheritance.

40 And he gave them over into the hand of the heathen: and they, that hated them, were lords over them.

41 Their enemies oppressed them: and had them in subjection.

42 Many a time did he deliver them: but they rebelled against him with their own inventions, and were brought down in their wickedness.

43 Nevertheless when he saw their adversity: he heard their complaint.

44 He thought upon his covenant, and pitied them, according unto the multitude of his mercies: yea, he made all those that led them away captive, to pity them.

45 Deliver us, O Lord our God, and gather us from among the heathen: that we may give thanks unto thy holy Name, and make our boast of thy praise.

46 Blessed be the Lord God of Israel from everlasting, and world without end: and let all the people say, Amen.

Day 22. *Morning Prayer.*

Psalm 107

Confitemini Domino.

O GIVE thanks unto the Lord, for he is gracious: and his mercy endureth for ever.

2 Let them give thanks whom the Lord hath redeemed: and delivered from the hand of the enemy;

3 And gathered them out of the lands, from the east, and from the west: from the north and from the south.

4 They went astray in the wilderness out of the way: and found no city to dwell in;

5 Hungry and thirsty: their soul fainted in them.

6 So they cried unto the Lord in their trouble: and he delivered them from their distress.

7 He led them forth by the right way: that they might go to the city where they dwelt.

8 O that men would therefore praise the Lord for his goodness: and declare the wonders that he doth for the children of men;

9 For he satisfieth the empty soul: and filleth the hungry soul with goodness;

10 Such as sit in darkness and in the shadow of death: being fast bound in misery and iron.

11 Because they rebelled against the words of the Lord: and lightly regarded the counsel of the most Highest;

12 He also brought down their heart through heaviness: they fell down, and there was none to help them.

13 So when they cried unto the Lord in their trouble: he delivered them out of their distress.

14 For he brought them out of darkness, and out of the shadow of death: and brake their bonds in sunder.

15 O that men would therefore praise the Lord for his goodness: and declare the wonders that he doth for the children of men;

16 For he hath broken the gates of brass: and smitten the bars of iron in sunder.

17 Foolish men are plagued for their offence: and because of their wickedness.

18 Their soul abhorred all manner of meat: and they were even hard at deaths door.

19 So when they cried unto the Lord in their trouble: he delivered them out of their distress.

20 He sent his word, and healed them: and they were saved from their destruction.

21 O that men would therefore praise the Lord for his goodness: and declare the wonders that he doth for the children of men;

22 That they would offer unto him the sacrifice of thanksgiving: and tell out his works with gladness.

23 They that go down to the sea in ships: and occupy their business in great waters,

24 These men see the works of the Lord: and his wonders in the deep.

25 For at his word the stormy wind ariseth: which lifteth up the waves thereof.

26 They are carried up to the heaven, and down again to the deep: their soul melteth away because of the trouble.

27 They reel to and fro, and stagger like a drunken man: and are at their wits end.

28 So when thy cry unto the Lord in their trouble: he delivereth them out of their distress.

29 For he maketh the storm to cease: so that the waves thereof are still.

30 Then are they glad, because they are at rest: and so he bringeth them unto the haven where they would be.

31 O that men would therefore praise the Lord for his goodness: and declare the wonders that he doth for the children of men!

32 That they would exalt him also in the congregation of the people: and praise him in the seat of the elders!

33 Who turneth the flouds into a wilderness: and drieth up the water-springs.

34 A fruitful land maketh he barren: for the wickedness of them that dwell therein.

35 Again he maketh the wilderness a standing water: and water-springs of a dry ground.

36 And there he setteth the hungry: that they may build them a city to dwell in.

37 That they may sow their land, and plant vineyards: to yield them fruits of increase.

38 He blesseth them, so that they multiply exceedingly: and suffereth not their cattel to decrease.

39 And again, when they are minished and brought low: through oppression, through any plague or trouble;

40 Though he suffer them to be evil intreated through tyrants: and let them wander out of the way in the wilderness;

41 Yet helpeth he the poor out of misery: and maketh him housholds like a flock of sheep.

42 The righteous will consider this and rejoyce: and the mouth of all wickedness shall be stopped.

43 Whoso is wise will ponder these things: and they shall understand the loving kindness of the Lord.

Day 22. *Evening Prayer.*

Psalm 108

Paratum cor meum.

O GOD, my heart is ready, my heart is ready: I will sing and give praise with the best member that I have.

2 Awake, thou lute and harp: I my self will awake right early.

3 I will give thanks unto thee, O Lord, among the people: I will sing praises unto thee among the nations.

4 For thy mercy is greater than the heavens: and thy truth reacheth unto the clouds.

5 Set up thy self, O God, above the heavens: and thy glory above all the earth.

6 That thy beloved may be delivered: let thy right hand save them, and hear thou me.

7 God hath spoken in his holiness: I will rejoyce therefore and divide Sichem, and mete out the valley of Succoth.

8 Gilead is mine and Manasses is mine: Ephraim also is the strength of my head.

9 Juda is my law-giver, Moab is my wash-pot: over Edom will I cast out my shoe; upon Philistia will I triumph.

10 Who will lead me into the strong city: and who will bring me into Edom?

11 Hast not thou forsaken us, O God: and wilt not thou, O God, go forth with our hosts?

12 O help us against the enemy: for vain is the help of man.

13 Through God we shall do great acts: and it is he that shall tread down our enemies.

Psalm 109

Deus, laudem.

HOLD not thy tongue, O God of my praise: for the mouth of the ungodly, yea, the mouth of the deceitful is opened upon me.

2 And they have spoken against me with false tongues: they compassed me about also with words of hatred, and fought against me without a cause.

3 For the love that I had unto them, lo, they take now my contrary part: but I give my self unto prayer.

4 Thus have they rewarded me evil for good: and hatred for my good will.

5 Set thou an ungodly man to be ruler over him: and let Satan stand at his right hand.

6 When sentence is given upon him, let him be condemned: and let his prayer be turned into sin.

7 Let his dayes be few: and let another take his office.

8 Let his children be fatherless: and his wife a widow.

9 Let his children be vagabonds, and beg their bread: let them seek it also out of desolate places.

10 Let the extortioner consume all that he hath: and let the stranger spoil his labour.

11 Let there be no man to pity him: nor to have compassion upon his fatherless children.

12 Let his posterity be destroyed: and in the next generation let his name be clean put out.

13 Let the wickedness of his fathers be had in remembrance in the sight of the Lord: and let not the sin of his mother be done away.

14 Let them alway be before the Lord: that he may root out the memorial of them from off the earth;

15 And that, because his mind was not to do good: but persecuted the poor helpless man, that he might slay him that was vexed at the heart.

16 His delight was in cursing, and it shall happen unto him: he loved not blessing, therefore shall it be far from him.

17 He clothed himself with cursing, like as with a raiment: and it shall come into his bowels like water, and like oil into his bones.

18 Let it be unto him as the cloke that he hath upon him: and as the girdle that he is alway girded withal.

19 Let it thus happen from the Lord unto mine enemies: and to those that speak evil against my soul.

20 But deal thou with me, O Lord God, according unto thy Name: for sweet is thy mercy.

21 O deliver me, for I am helpless and poor: and my heart is wounded within me.

22 I go hence like the shadow that departeth: and am driven away as the grasshopper.

23 My knees are weak through fasting: my flesh is dried up for want of fatness.

24 I became also a reproach unto them: they that looked upon me, shaked their heads.

25 Help me, O Lord my God: O save me according to thy mercy.

26 And they shall know, how that this is thy hand: and that thou, Lord, hast done it.

27 Though they curse, yet bless thou: and let them be confounded that rise up against me; but let thy servant rejoyce.

28 Let mine adversaries be clothed with shame: and let them cover themselves with their own confusion as with a cloak.

29 As for me, I will give great thanks unto the Lord with my mouth: and praise him among the multitude.

30 For he shall stand at the right hand of the poor: to save his soul from unrighteous judges.

Day 23. *Morning Prayer*.

Psalm 110

Dixit Dominus.

THE Lord said unto my Lord: Sit thou on my right hand, until I make thine enemies thy footstool.

2 The Lord shall send the rod of thy power out of Sion: be thou ruler, even in the midst among thine enemies.

3 In the day of thy power shall the people offer thee free-will offerings with an holy worship: the dew of thy birth is of the womb of the morning.

4 The Lord sware, and will not repent: Thou art a priest for ever after the order of Melchisedech.

5 The Lord upon thy right hand: shall wound even kings in the day of his wrath.

6 He shall judge among the heathen; he shall fill the places with the dead bodies: and smite in sunder the heads over divers countries.

7 He shall drink of the brook in the way: therefore shall he lift up his head.

Psalm 111

Confitebor tibi.

I WILL give thanks unto the Lord with my whole heart: secretly among the faithful, and in the congregation.

2 The works of the Lord are great: sought out of all of them that have pleasure therein.

3 His work is worthy to be praised and had in honour: and his righteousness endureth for ever.

4 The merciful and gracious Lord hath so done his marvellous works: that they ought to be had in remembrance.

5 He hath given meat unto them that fear him: he shall ever be mindful of his covenant.

6 He hath shewed his people the power of his works: that he may give them the heritage of the heathen.

7 The works of his hands are verity and judgement: all his commandments are true.

8 They stand fast for ever and ever: and are done in truth and equity.

9 He sent redemption unto his people: he hath commanded his covenant for ever; holy and reverend is his Name.

10 The fear of the Lord is the beginning of wisdom: a good understanding have all they that do thereafter; the praise of it endureth for ever.

Psalm 112

Beatus vir.

B LESSED is the man that feareth the Lord: he hath great delight in his commandments.

2 His seed shall be mighty upon earth: the generation of the faithful shall be blessed.

3 Riches and plenteousness shall be in his house: and his righteousness endureth for ever.

4 Unto the godly there ariseth up light in the darkness: he is merciful, loving, and righteous.

5 A good man is merciful, and lendeth: and will guide his words with discretion.

6 For he shall never be moved: and the righteous shall be had in everlasting remembrance.

7 He will not be afraid of any evil tidings: for his heart standeth fast, and believeth in the Lord.

8 His heart is established, and will not shrink: until he see his desire upon his enemies.

9 He hath dispersed abroad, and given to the poor: and his righteousness remaineth for ever; his horn shall be exalted with honour.

10 The ungodly shall see it, and it shall grieve him: he shall gnash with his teeth and consume away; the desire of the ungodly shall perish.

Psalm 113

Laudate, pueri.

PRAISE the Lord, ye servants: O praise the Name of the Lord.

2 Blessed be the Name of the Lord: from this time forth for evermore.

3 The Lords Name is praised: from the rising up of the sun, unto the going down of the same.

4 The Lord is high above all heathen: and his glory above the heavens.

5 Who is like unto the Lord our God that hath his dwelling so high: and yet humbleth himself to behold the things that are in heaven and earth?

6 He taketh up the simple out of the dust: and lifteth the poor out of the mire.

7 That he may set him with the princes: even with the princes of his people.

8 He maketh the barren woman to keep house: and to be a joyful mother of children.

Day 23. *Evening Prayer.*

Psalm 114

In exitu Israel.

WHEN Israel came out of Egypt: and the house of Jacob from among the strange people,

2 Juda was his sanctuary: and Israel his dominion.

3 The sea saw that and fled: Jordan was driven back.

4 The mountains skipped like rams: and the little hills like young sheep.

5 What aileth thee, O thou sea, that thou fleddest: and thou Jordan that thou wast driven back?

6 Ye mountains that ye skipped like rams: and ye little hills like young sheep?

7 Tremble thou earth at the presence of the Lord: at the presence of the God of Jacob.

8 Who turned the hard rock into a standing water: and the flint-stone into a springing well.

Psalm 115

Non nobis, Domine.

NOT unto us, O Lord, not unto us, but unto thy name give the praise: for thy loving mercy, and for thy truths sake.

2 Wherefore shall the heathen say: where is now their God?

3 As for our God, he is in heaven: he hath done whatsoever pleased him.

4 Their idols are silver and gold: even the work of mens hands.

5 They have mouths and speak not: eyes have they and see not.

6 They have ears and hear not: noses have they and smell not.

7 They have hands and handle not, feet have they and walk not: neither speak they through their throat.

8 They that make them are like unto them: and so are all such as put their trust in them.

9 But thou house of Israel, trust thou in the Lord: he is their succour and defence.

10 Ye house of Aaron, put your trust in the Lord: he is their helper and defender.

11 Ye that fear the Lord, put your trust in the Lord: he is their helper and defender.

12 The Lord hath been mindfull of us, and he shall bless us: even he shall bless the house of Israel, he shall bless the house of Aaron.

13 He shall bless them that fear the Lord: both small and great.

14 The Lord shall increase you more and more: you and your children.

15 Ye are the blessed of the Lord: who made heaven and earth.

16 All the whole heavens are the Lords: the earth hath he given to the children of men.

17 The dead praise not thee, O Lord: neither all they that go down into silence.

18 But we will praise the Lord: from this time forth for evermore. Praise the Lord.

Day 24. *Morning Prayer.*

Psalm 116

Dilexi, quoniam.

I AM well pleased: that the Lord hath heard the voice of my prayer.

2 That he hath enclined his ear unto me: therefore will I call upon him as long as I live.

3 The snares of death compassed me round about: and the pains of hell gat hold upon me.

4 I shall find trouble and heaviness, and I will call upon the Name of the Lord: O Lord, I beseech thee, deliver my soul.

5 Gracious is the Lord and righteous: yea, our God is merciful.

6 The Lord preserveth the simple: I was in misery, and he helped me.

7 Turn again then unto thy rest, O my soul: for the Lord hath rewarded thee.

8 And why? thou hast delivered my soul from death: mine eyes from tears, and my feet from falling.

9 I will walk before the Lord: in the land of the living.

10 I believed, and therefore will I speak, but I was sore troubled: I said in my haste, All men are liars.

11 What reward shall I give unto the Lord: for all the benefits that he hath done unto me?

12 I will receive the cup of salvation: and call upon the Name of the Lord.

13 I will pay my vows now in the presence of all his people: right dear in the sight of the Lord is the death of his saints.

14 Behold, O Lord, how that I am thy servant: I am thy servant, and the son of thine handmaid, thou hast broken my bonds in sunder.

15 I will offer to thee the sacrifice of thanksgiving: and will call upon the Name of the Lord.

16 I will pay my vows unto the Lord, in the sight of all his people: in the courts of the Lords house, even in the midst of thee, O Jerusalem. Praise the Lord.

Psalm 117

Laudate Dominum.

O PRAISE the Lord, all ye heathen: praise him, all ye nations.

2 For his merciful kindness is ever more and more towards us: and the truth of the Lord endureth for ever. Praise the Lord.

Psalm 118

Confitemini Domino.

O GIVE thanks unto the Lord, for he is gracious: because his mercy endureth for ever.

2 Let Israel now confess, that he is gracious: and that his mercy endureth for ever.

3 Let the house of Aaron now confess: that his mercy endureth for ever.

4 Yea, let them now that fear the Lord, confess: that his mercy endureth for ever.

5 I called upon the Lord in trouble: and the Lord heard me at large.

6 The Lord is on my side: I will not fear what man doth unto me.

7 The Lord taketh my part with them that help me: therefore shall I see my desire upon mine enemies.

8 It is better to trust in the Lord: than to put any confidence in man.

9 It is better to trust in the Lord: than to put any confidence in princes.

10 All nations compassed me round about: but in the Name of the Lord will I destroy them.

11 They kept me in on every side, they kept me in, I say, on every side: but in the Name of the Lord will I destroy them.

12 They came about me like bees, and are extinct even as the fire among the thorns: for in the Name of the Lord I will destroy them.

13 Thou hast thrust sore at me, that I might fall: but the Lord was my help.

14 The Lord is my strength and my song: and is become my salvation.

15 The voice of joy and health is in the dwellings of the righteous: the right hand of the Lord bringeth mighty things to pass.

16　The right hand of the Lord hath the preeminence: the right hand of the Lord bringeth mighty things to pass.

17　I shall not die, but live: and declare the works of the Lord.

18　The Lord hath chastened and corrected me: but he hath not given me over unto death.

19　Open me the gates of righteousness: that I may go in to them, and give thanks unto the Lord.

20　This is the gate of the Lord: the righteous shall enter into it.

21　I will thank thee, for thou hast heard me: and art become my salvation.

22　The same stone which the builders refused: is become the head-stone in the corner.

23　This is the Lords doing: and it is marvellous in our eyes.

24　This is the day which the Lord hath made: we will rejoyce and be glad in it.

25　Help me now, O Lord: O Lord, send us now prosperity.

26　Blessed be he that cometh in the Name of the Lord: we have wished you good luck , ye that are of the house of the Lord.

27　God is the Lord who hath shewed us light: bind the sacrifice with cords, yea, even unto the horns of the altar.

28　Thou art my God, and I will thank thee: thou art my God, and I will praise thee.

29　O give thanks unto the Lord, for he is gracious: and his mercy endureth for ever.

Day 24. *Evening Prayer.*

Psalm 119

Beati immaculati.

B LESSED are those that are undefiled in the way: and walk in the law of the Lord.

2　Blessed are they that keep his testimonies: and seek him with their whole heart.

3　For they who do no wickedness: walk in his wayes.

4　Thou hast charged: that we shall diligently keep thy commandments.

5　O that my wayes were made so direct: that I might keep thy statutes.

6 So shall I not be confounded: while I have respect unto all thy commandments.

7 I will thank thee with an unfeigned heart: when I shall have learned the judgements of thy righteousness.

8 I will keep thy ceremonies: O forsake me not utterly.

In quo corriget?

WHEREWITHALL shall a young man cleanse his way: even by ruling himself after thy word.

10 With my whole heart have I sought thee: O let me not go wrong out of thy commandments.

11 Thy words have I hid within my heart: that I should not sin against thee.

12 Blessed art thou, O Lord: O teach me thy statutes.

13 With my lips have I been telling: of all the judgements of thy mouth.

14 I have had as great delight in the way of thy testimonies: as in all manner of riches.

15 I will talk of thy commandments: and have respect unto thy wayes.

16 My delight shall be in thy statutes: and I will not forget thy word.

Retribue servo tuo.

O DO well unto thy servant: that I may live and keep thy word.

18 Open thou mine eyes: that I may see the wondrous things of thy law.

19 I am a stranger upon earth: O hide not thy commandments from me.

20 My soul breaketh out for the very fervent desire: that it hath alway unto thy judgements.

21 Thou hast rebuked the proud: and cursed are they that do erre from thy commandments.

22 O turn from me shame and rebuke: for I have kept thy testimonies.

23 Princes also did sit and speak against me: but thy servant is occupied in thy statutes.

24 For thy testimonies are my delight: and my counsellors.

Adhaesit pavimento.

M Y SOUL cleaveth to the dust: O quicken thou me according to thy word.

26 I have knowledged my wayes, and thou heardest me: O teach me thy statutes.

27 Make me to understand the way of thy commandments: and so shall I talk of thy wondrous works.

28 My soul melteth away for very heaviness: comfort thou me according unto thy word.

29 Take from me the way of lying: and cause thou me to make much of thy law.

30 I have chosen the way of truth: and thy judgements have I laid before me.

31 I have stuck unto thy testimonies: O Lord, confound me not.

32 I will run the way of thy commandments: when thou hast set my heart at liberty.

Day 25. *Morning Prayer.*

Legem pone.

T EACH me, O Lord, the way of thy statutes: and I shall keep it unto the end.

34 Give me understanding, and I shall keep thy law: yea, I shall keep it with my whole heart.

35 Make me to go in the path of thy commandments: for therein is my desire.

36 Incline my heart unto thy testimonies: and not to covetousness.

37 O turn away mine eyes, lest they behold vanity: and quicken thou me in thy way.

38 O stablish thy word in thy servant: that I may fear thee.

39 Take away the rebuke that I am afraid of: for thy judgements are good.

40 Behold, my delight is in thy commandments: O quicken me in thy righteousness.

Et veniat super me.

L ET thy loving mercy come also unto me, O Lord: even thy salvation, according unto thy word.

42 So shall I make answer unto my blasphemers: for my trust is in thy word.

43 O take not the word of thy truth utterly out of my mouth: for my hope is in thy judgements.

44 So shall I alway keep thy law: yea, for ever and ever.

45 And I will walk at liberty: for I seek thy commandments.

46 I will speak of thy testimonies also, even before kings: and will not be ashamed.

47 And my delight shall be in thy commandments: which I have loved.

48 My hands also will I lift up unto thy commandments, which I have loved: and my study shall be in thy statutes.

Memor esto servi tui.

O THINK upon thy servant, as concerning thy word: wherein thou hast caused me to put my trust.

50 The same is my comfort in my trouble: for thy word hath quickned me.

51 The proud have had me exceedingly in derision: yet have I not shrinked from thy law.

52 For I remembred thine everlasting judgements, O Lord: and received comfort.

53 I am horribly afraid: for the ungodly that forsake thy law.

54 Thy statutes have been my songs: in the house of my pilgrimage.

55 I have thought upon thy Name, O Lord, in the night-season: and have kept thy law.

56 This I had: because I kept thy commandments.

Portio mea, Domine.

THOU art my portion, O Lord: I have promised to keep thy law.

58 I made my humble petition in thy presence with my whole heart: O be merciful unto me, according to thy word.

59 I called mine own wayes to remembrance: and turned my feet unto thy testimonies.

60 I made haste, and prolonged not the time: to keep thy commandments.

61 The congregations of the ungodly have robbed me: but I have not forgotten thy law.

62 At midnight I will rise to give thanks unto thee: because of thy righteous judgements.

63 I am a companion of all them that fear thee: and keep thy commandments.

64 The earth, O Lord, is full of thy mercy: O teach me thy statutes.

Bonitatem fecisti.

O LORD, thou hast dealt graciously with thy servant: according unto thy word.

66 O learn me true understanding and knowledge: for I have believed thy commandments.

67 Before I was troubled, I went wrong: but now have I kept thy word.

68 Thou art good and gracious: O teach me thy statutes.

69 The proud have imagined a lie against me: but I will keep thy commandments with my whole heart.

70 Their heart is as fat as brawn: but my delight hath been in thy law.

71 It is good for me that I have been in trouble: that I may learn thy statutes.

72 The law of thy mouth is dearer unto me: than thousands of gold and silver.

Day 25. *Evening Prayer.*

Manus tuae fecerunt me.

THY hands have made me and fashioned me: O give me under-standing, that I may learn thy commandments.

74 They that fear thee will be glad when they see me: because I have put my trust in thy word.

75 I know, O Lord, that thy judgements are right: and that thou of very faithfulness hast caused me to be troubled.

76 O let thy merciful kindness be my comfort: according to thy word unto thy servant.

77 O let thy loving mercies come unto me, that I may live: for thy law is my delight.

78 Let the proud be confounded, for they go wickedly about to destroy me: but I will be occupied in thy commandments.

79 Let such as fear thee, and have known thy testimonies: be turned unto me.

80 O let my heart be sound in thy statutes: that I be not ashamed.

Defecit anima mea.

M Y SOUL hath longed for thy salvation: and I have a good hope because of thy word.

82 Mine eyes long sore for thy word: saying, O when wilt thou comfort me?

83 For I am become like a bottle in the smoke: yet do I not forget thy statutes.

84 How many are the dayes of thy servant: when wilt thou be avenged of them that persecute me?

85 The proud have digged pits for me: which are not after thy law.

86 All thy commandments are true: they persecute me falsely; O be thou my help.

87 They had almost made an end of me upon earth: but I forsook not thy commandments.

88 O quicken me after thy loving kindness: and so shall I keep the testimonies of thy mouth.

In aeternum, Domine

O LORD, thy word: endureth for ever in heaven.

90 Thy truth also remaineth from one generation to another: thou hast laid the foundation of the earth, and it abideth.

91 They continue this day according to thine ordinance: for all things serve thee.

92 If my delight had not been in thy law: I should have perished in my trouble.

93 I will never forget thy commandments: for with them thou hast quickned me.

94 I am thine, O save me: for I have sought thy commandments.

95 The ungodly laid wait for me, to destroy me: but I will consider thy testimonies.

96 I see that all things come to an end: but thy commandment is exceeding broad.

Quomodo dilexi!

L ORD, what love have I unto thy law: all the day long is my study in it.

98 Thou through thy commandments hast made me wiser than mine enemies: for they are ever with me.

99 I have more understanding than my teachers: for thy testimonies are my study.

100 I am wiser than the aged: because I keep thy commandments.

101 I have refrained my feet from every evil way: that I may keep thy word.

102 I have not shrunk from thy judgements: for thou teachest me.

103 O how sweet are thy words unto my throat: yea, sweeter than honey unto my mouth.

104 Through thy commandments I get understanding: therefore I hate all evil wayes.

Day 26. *Morning Prayer*.

Lucerna pedibus meis.

THY word is a lantern unto my feet: and a light unto my paths.

106 I have sworn and am stedfastly purposed: to keep thy righteous judgements.

107 I am troubled above measure: quicken me, O Lord, according to thy word.

108 Let the free-will offerings of my mouth please thee, O Lord: and teach me thy judgements.

109 My soul is alway in my hand: yet do I not forget thy law.

110 The ungodly have laid a snare for me: but yet I swerved not from thy commandments.

111 Thy testimonies have I claimed as mine heritage for ever: and why? they are the very joy of my heart.

112 I have applyed my heart to fulfil thy statutes alway: even unto the end.

Iniquos odio habui.

I HATE them that imagine evil things: but thy law do I love.

114 Thou art my defence and shield: and my trust is in thy word.

115 Away from me, ye wicked: I will keep the commandments of my God.

116 O stablish me according to thy word, that I may live: and let me not be disappointed of my hope.

117 Hold thou me up, and I shall be safe: yea, my delight shall be ever in thy statutes.

118 Thou hast trodden down all them that depart from thy statutes: for they imagine but deceit.

119 Thou puttest away all the ungodly of the earth like dross: therefore I love thy testimonies.

120 My flesh trembleth for fear of thee: and I am afraid of thy judgements.

Feci judicium.

I DEAL with the thing that is lawful and right: O give me not over unto mine oppressours.

122 Make thou thy servant to delight in that which is good: that the proud do me no wrong.

123 Mine eyes are wasted away with looking for thy health: and for the word of thy righteousness.

124 O deal with thy servant according unto thy loving mercy: and teach me thy statutes.

125 I am thy servant, O grant me understanding: that I may know thy testimonies.

126 It is time for thee, Lord, to lay to thine hand: for they have destroyed thy law.

127 For I love thy commandments: above gold and precious stone.

128 Therefore hold I strait all thy commandments: and all false wayes I utterly abhor.

Mirabilia.

THY testimonies are wonderful: therefore doth my soul keep them.

130 When thy word goeth forth: it giveth light and understanding unto the simple.

131 I opened my mouth, and drew in my breath: for my delight was in thy commandments.

132 O look thou upon me, and be merciful unto me: as thou usest to do unto those that love thy Name.

133 Order my steps in thy word: and so shall no wickedness have dominion over me.

134 O deliver me from the wrongful dealings of men: and so shall I keep thy commandments.

135 Shew the light of thy countenance upon thy servant: and teach me thy statutes.

136 Mine eyes gush out with water: because men keep not thy law.

Justus es, Domine.

R IGHTEOUS art thou, O Lord: and true is thy judgement.
138 The testimonies that thou hast commanded: are exceeding righteous and true.

139 My zeal hath even consumed me: because mine enemies have forgotten thy words.

140 Thy word is tried to the uttermost: and thy servant loveth it.

141 I am small, and of no reputation: yet do I not forget thy commandments.

142 Thy righteousness is an everlasting righteousness: and thy law is the truth.

143 Trouble and heaviness have taken hold upon me: yet is my delight in thy commandments.

144 The righteousness of thy testimonies is everlasting: O grant me understanding, and I shall live.

Day 26. *Evening Prayer.*

Clamavi in toto corde meo.

I CALL with my whole heart: hear me, O Lord, I will keep thy statutes.

146 Yea, even unto thee do I call: help me, and I shall keep thy testimonies.

147 Early in the morning do I cry unto thee: for in thy word is my trust.

148 Mine eyes prevent the night-watches: that I might be occupied in thy words.

149 Hear my voice, O Lord, according unto thy loving kindness: quicken me according as thou art wont.

150 They draw nigh that of malice persecute me: and are farre from thy law.

151 Be thou nigh at hand, O Lord: for all thy commandments are true.

152 As concerning thy testimonies, I have known long since: that thou hast grounded them for ever.

Vide humilitatem.

O CONSIDER mine adversity, and deliver me: for I do not forget thy law.

154 Avenge thou my cause, and deliver me: quicken me according to thy word.

155 Health is farre from the ungodly: for they regard not thy statutes.

156 Great is thy mercy, O Lord: quicken me as thou art wont.

157 Many there are that trouble me, and persecute me: yet do I not swerve from thy testimonies.

158 It grieveth me when I see the transgressors: because they keep not thy law.

159 Consider, O Lord, how I love thy commandments: O quicken me according to thy loving kindness.

160 Thy word is true from everlasting: all the judgements of thy righteousness endure for evermore.

Principes persecuti sunt.

PRINCES have persecuted me without a cause: but my heart standeth in awe of thy word.

162 I am as glad of thy word: as one that findeth great spoils.

163 As for lies, I hate and abhor them: but thy law do I love.

164 Seven times a day do I praise thee: because of thy righteous judgements.

165 Great is the peace that they have who love thy law: and they are not offended at it.

166 Lord, I have looked for thy saving health: and done after thy commandments.

167 My soul hath kept thy testimonies: and loved them exceedingly.

168 I have kept thy commandments and testimonies: for all my wayes are before thee.

Appropinquet deprecatio.

LET my complaint come before thee, O Lord: give me understanding according to thy word.

170 Let my supplication come before thee: deliver me, according to thy word.

171 My lips shall speak of thy praise: when thou hast taught me thy statutes.

172 Yea, my tongue shall sing of thy word: for all thy commandments are righteous.

173 Let thine hand help me: for I have chosen thy commandments.

174 I have longed for thy saving health, O Lord: and in thy law is my delight.

175 O let my soul live, and it shall praise thee: and thy judgements shall help me.

176 I have gone astray like a sheep that is lost: O seek thy servant, for I do not forget thy commandments.

Day 27. *Morning Prayer.*

Psalm 120

Ad Dominum.

WHEN I was in trouble, I called upon the Lord: and he heard me.
2 Deliver my soul, O Lord, from lying lips: and from a deceitful tongue.

3 What reward shall be given or done unto thee, thou false tongue: even mighty and sharp arrows, with hot burning coals.

4 Wo is me, that I am constrained to dwell with Mesech: and to have my habitation among the tents of Kedar.

5 My soul hath long dwelt among them: that are enemies unto peace.

6 I labour for peace, but when I speak unto them thereof: they make them ready to battel.

Psalm 121

Levavi oculus.

I WILL lift up mine eyes unto the hills: from whence cometh my help.

2 My help cometh even from the Lord: who hath made heaven and earth.

3 He will not suffer thy foot to be moved: and he that keepeth thee will not sleep.

4 Behold, he that keepeth Israel: shall neither slumber nor sleep.

5 The Lord himself is thy keeper: the Lord is thy defence upon thy right hand;

6 So that the sun shall not burn thee by day: neither the moon by night.

7 The Lord shall preserve thee from all evil: yea, it is even he that shall keep thy soul.

8   The Lord shall preserve thy going out and thy coming in: from this time forth for evermore.

Psalm 122

Laetatus sum.

I was glad when they said unto me: We will go into the house of the Lord.

2   Our feet shall stand in thy gates: O Jerusalem.

3   Jerusalem is built as a city: that is at unity in it self.

4   For thither the tribes go up, even the tribes of the Lord: to testifie unto Israel, to give thanks unto the Name of the Lord.

5   For there is the seat of judgement: even the seat of the house of David.

6   O pray for the peace of Jerusalem: they shall prosper that love thee.

7   Peace be within thy walls: and plenteousness within thy palaces.

8   For my brethren and companions sakes: I will wish thee prosperity.

9   Yea, because of the house of the Lord our God: I will seek to do thee good.

Psalm 123

Ad te levavi oculos meos.

U nto thee lift I up mine eyes: O thou that dwellest in the heavens.

2   Behold, even as the eyes of servants look unto the hand of their masters, and as the eyes of a maiden unto the hand of her mistress: even so our eyes wait upon the Lord our God, until he have mercy upon us.

3   Have mercy upon us, O Lord, have mercy upon us: for we are utterly despised.

4   Our soul is filled with the scornful reproof of the wealthy: and with the despitefulness of the proud.

Psalm 124

Nisi quia Dominus.

I f the Lord himself had not been on our side, now may Israel say: if the Lord himself had not been on our side, when men rose up against us;

2 They had swallowed us up quick: when they were so wrathfully displeased at us.

3 Yea, the waters had drowned us: and the stream had gone over our soul.

4 The deep waters of the proud: had gone even over our soul.

5 But praised be the Lord: who hath not given us over for a prey unto their teeth.

6 Our soul is escaped even as a bird out of the snare of the fowler: the snare is broken, and we are delivered.

7 Our help standeth in the Name of the Lord: who hath made heaven and earth.

Psalm 125

Qui confidunt.

THEY that put their trust in the Lord, shall be even as the mount Sion: which may not be removed, but standeth fast for ever.

2 The hills stand about Jerusalem: even so standeth the Lord round about his people, from this time forth for evermore.

3 For the rod of the ungodly cometh not into the lot of the righteous: lest the righteous put their hand unto wickedness.

4 Do well, O Lord: unto those that are good and true of heart.

5 As for such as turn back unto their own wickedness: the Lord shall lead them forth with the evil doers; but peace shall be upon Israel.

Day 27. *Evening Prayer.*

Psalm 126

In convertendo.

WHEN the Lord turned again the captivity of Sion: then were we like unto them that dream.

2 Then was our mouth filled with laughter: and our tongue with joy.

3 Then said they among the heathen: the Lord hath done great things for them.

4 Yea, the Lord hath done great things for us already: whereof we rejoyce.

5 Turn our captivity, O Lord: as the rivers in the south.

6 They that sowe in tears: shall reap in joy.

7 He that now goeth on his way weeping, and beareth forth good

seed: shall doubtless come again with joy, and bring his sheaves with him.

Psalm 127

Nisi Dominus.

EXCEPT the Lord build the house: their labour is but lost that build it.

2 Except the Lord keep the city: the watchman waketh but in vain.

3 It is but lost labour that ye haste to rise up early, and so late take rest, and eat the bread of carefulness: for so he giveth his beloved sleep.

4 Lo, children and the fruit of the womb: are an heritage and gift that cometh of the Lord.

5 Like as the arrows in the hand of the giant: even so are the young children.

6 Happy is the man that hath his quiver full of them: they shall not be ashamed when they speak with their enemies in the gate.

Psalm 128

Beati omnes.

BLESSED are all they that fear the Lord: and walk in his wayes.

2 For thou shalt eat the labours of thine hands: O well is thee, and happy shalt thou be.

3 Thy wife shall be as the fruitful vine: upon the walls of thine house.

4 Thy children like the olive-branches: round about thy table.

5 Lo, thus shall the man be blessed: that feareth the Lord.

6 The Lord from out of Sion shall so bless thee: that thou shalt see Jerusalem in prosperity all thy life long.

7 Yea, that thou shalt see thy childrens children: and peace upon Israel.

Psalm 129

Saepe expugnaverunt.

MANY a time have they fought against me from my youth up: may Israel now say.

2 Yea, many a time have they vexed me from my youth up: but they have not prevailed against me.

3 The plowers plowed upon my back: and made long furrows.

4 But the righteous Lord: hath hewen the snares of the ungodly in pieces.

5 Let them be confounded and turned backward: as many as have evil will at Sion.

6 Let them be even as the grass growing upon the house-tops: which withereth afore it be plucked up.

7 Whereof the mower filleth not his hand: neither he, that bindeth up the sheaves, his bosome.

8 So that they who go by say not so much as, The Lord prosper you: we wish you good luck in the Name of the Lord.

Psalm 130

De profundis.

OUT of the deep have I called unto thee, O Lord: Lord, hear my voice.

2 O let thine ears consider well: the voice of my complaint.

3 If thou, Lord, wilt be extreme to mark what is done amiss: O Lord, who may abide it?

4 For there is mercy with thee: therefore shalt thou be feared.

5 I look for the Lord, my soul doth wait for him: in his word is my trust.

6 My soul fleeth unto the Lord: before the morning watch, I say, before the morning watch.

7 O Israel, trust in the Lord, for with the Lord there is mercy: and with him is plenteous redemption.

8 And he shall redeem Israel: from all his sins.

Psalm 131

Domine, non est.

LORD, I am not high-minded: I have no proud looks.

2 I do not exercise myself in great matters: which are too high for me.

3 But I refrain my soul, and keep it low, like as a child that is weaned from his mother: yea, my soul is even as a weaned child.

4 O Israel, trust in the Lord: from this time forth for evermore.

Day 28. *Morning Prayer.*

Psalm 132

Memento, Domine.

LORD, remember David: and all his trouble.

2 How he sware unto the Lord: and vowed a vow unto the Almighty God of Jacob;

3 I will not come within the tabernacle of mine house: nor climb up into my bed;

4 I will not suffer mine eyes to sleep, nor mine eye-lids to slumber: neither the temples of my head to take any rest,

5 Until I find out a place for the temple of the Lord: an habitation for the mighty God of Jacob.

6 Lo, we heard of the same at Ephrata: and found it in the wood.

7 We will go into his tabernacle: and fall low on our knees before his footstool.

8 Arise, O Lord, into thy resting place: thou, and the ark of thy strength.

9 Let thy priests be clothed with righteousness: and let thy saints sing with joyfulness.

10 For thy servant Davids sake: turn not away the presence of thine Anointed.

11 The Lord hath made a faithful oath unto David: and he shall not shrink from it;

12 Of the fruit of thy body: shall I set upon thy seat.

13 If thy children will keep my covenant, and my testimonies that I shall learn them: their children also shall sit upon thy seat for evermore.

14 For the Lord hath chosen Sion to be an habitation for himself: he hath longed for her.

15 This shall be my rest for ever: here will I dwell, for I have a delight therein.

16 I will bless her victuals with increase: and will satisfie her poor with bread.

17 I will deck her priests with health: and her saints shall rejoyce and sing.

18 There shall I make the horn of David to flourish: I have ordained a lantern for mine Anointed.

19 As for his enemies, I shall clothe them with shame: but upon himself shall his crown flourish.

Psalm 133

Ecce, quam bonum.

B EHOLD, how good and joyful a thing it is: brethren to dwell together in unity.

2 It is like the precious ointment upon the head, that ran down unto the beard: even unto Aarons beard, and went down to the skirts of his clothing.

3 Like as the dew of Hermon: which fell upon the hill of Sion.

4 For there the Lord promised his blessing: and life for evermore.

Psalm 134

Ecce nunc.

B EHOLD now, praise the Lord: all ye servants of the Lord;

2 Ye that by night stand in the house of the Lord: even in the courts of the house of our God.

3 Lift up your hands in the sanctuary: and praise the Lord.

4 The Lord that made heaven and earth: give thee blessing out of Sion.

Psalm 135

Laudate Nomen.

O PRAISE the Lord, laud ye the Name of the Lord: praise it, O ye servants of the Lord;

2 Ye that stand in the house of the Lord: in the courts of the house of our God.

3 O praise the Lord, for the Lord is gracious: O sing praises unto his Name, for it is lovely.

4 For why? the Lord hath chosen Jacob unto himself: and Israel for his own possession.

5 For I know that the Lord is great: and that our Lord is above all gods.

6 Whatsoever the Lord pleased, that did he in heaven and in earth: and in the sea, and in all deep places.

7 He bringeth forth the clouds from the ends of the world: and

sendeth forth lightnings with the rain, bringing the winds out of his treasures.

8 He smote the first-born of Egypt: both of man and beast.

9 He hath sent tokens and wonders into the midst of thee, O thou land of Egypt: upon Pharaoh, and all his servants.

10 He smote divers nations: and slew mighty kings;

11 Sehon king of the Amorites, and Og the king of Basan: and all the kingdoms of Canaan;

12 And gave their land to be an heritage: even an heritage unto Israel his people.

13 Thy Name, O Lord, endureth for ever: so doth thy memorial, O Lord, from one generation to another.

14 For the Lord will avenge his people: and be gracious unto his servants.

15 As for the images of the heathen, they are but silver and gold: the work of mens hands.

16 They have mouths, and speak not: eyes have they, but they see not.

17 They have ears, and yet they hear not: neither is there any breath in their mouths.

18 They that make them are like unto them: and so are all they that put their trust in them.

19 Praise the Lord, ye house of Israel: praise the Lord, ye house of Aaron.

20 Praise the Lord, ye house of Levi: ye that fear the Lord, praise the Lord.

21 Praised be the Lord out of Sion: who dwelleth at Jerusalem.

Day 28. *Evening Prayer.*

Psalm 136

Confitemini.

O GIVE thanks unto the Lord, for he is gracious: and his mercy endureth for ever.

2 O give thanks unto the God of all gods: for his mercy endureth for ever.

3 O thank the Lord of all lords: for his mercy endureth for ever.

4 Who only doth great wonders: for his mercy endureth for ever.

5 Who by his excellent wisdom made the heavens: for his mercy endureth for ever.

6 Who laid out the earth above the waters: for his mercy endureth for ever.

7 Who hath made great lights: for his mercy endureth for ever;

8 The sun to rule the day: for his mercy endureth for ever;

9 The moon and the stars to govern the night: for his mercy endureth for ever.

10 Who smote Egypt with their first-born: for his mercy endureth for ever;

11 And brought out Israel from among them: for his mercy endureth for ever;

12 With a mighty hand and stretched-out arm: for his mercy endureth for ever.

13 Who divided the Red sea in two parts: for his mercy endureth for ever;

14 And made Israel to go through the midst of it: for his mercy endureth for ever.

15 But as for Pharaoh and his host, he overthrew them in the Red sea: for his mercy endureth for ever.

16 Who led his people through the wilderness: for his mercy endureth for ever.

17 Who smote great kings: for his mercy endureth for ever;

18 Yea, and slew mighty kings: for his mercy endureth for ever;

19 Sehon king of the Amorites: for his mercy endureth for ever;

20 And Og the king of Basan: for his mercy endureth for ever;

21 And gave away their land for an heritage: for his mercy endureth for ever;

22 Even for an heritage unto Israel his servant: for his mercy endureth for ever.

23 Who remembered us when we were in trouble: for his mercy endureth for ever;

24 And hath delivered us from our enemies: for his mercy endureth for ever.

25 Who giveth food to all flesh: for his mercy endureth for ever.

26 O give thanks unto the God of heaven: for his mercy endureth for ever.

27 O give thanks unto the Lord of lords: for his mercy endureth for ever.

Psalm 137

Super flumina.

BY THE waters of Babylon we sat down and wept: when we remembred thee, O Sion.

2 As for our harps, we hanged them up: upon the trees that are therein.

3 For they that led us away captive, required of us then a song and melody in our heaviness: Sing us one of the songs of Sion.

4 How shall we sing the Lords song: in a strange land?

5 If I forget thee, O Jerusalem: let my right hand forget her cunning.

6 If I do not remember thee, let my tongue cleave to the roof of my mouth: yea, if I prefer not Jerusalem in my mirth.

7 Remember the children of Edom, O Lord, in the day of Jerusalem: how they said, Down with it, down with it, even to the ground.

8 O daughter of Babylon, wasted with misery: yea, happy shall he be that rewardeth thee as thou hast served us.

9 Blessed shall he be, that taketh thy children: and throweth them against the stones.

Psalm 138

Confitebor tibi.

I WILL give thanks unto thee, O Lord, with my whole heart: even before the gods will I sing praise unto thee.

2 I will worship toward thy holy temple, and praise thy Name, because of thy loving kindness and truth: for thou hast magnified thy Name, and thy word above all things.

3 When I called upon thee, thou heardest me: and enduedst my soul with much strength.

4 All the kings of the earth shall praise thee, O Lord: for they have heard the words of thy mouth.

5 Yea, they shall sing in the wayes of the Lord: that great is the glory of the Lord.

6 For though the Lord be high, yet hath he respect unto the lowly: as for the proud, he beholdeth them afar off.

7 Though I walk in the midst of trouble, yet shalt thou refresh

me: thou shalt stretch forth thy hand upon the furiousness of mine enemies, and thy right hand shall save me.

8 The Lord shall make good his loving kindness toward me: yea, thy mercy, O Lord, endureth for ever; despise not then the works of thine own hands.

Day 29. *Morning Prayer.*

Psalm 139

Domine, probasti.

O LORD, thou hast searched me out, and known me: thou knowest my down-sitting and mine up-rising, thou understandest my thoughts long before.

2 Thou art about my path, and about my bed: and spiest out all my wayes.

3 For lo, there is not a word in my tongue: but thou, O Lord, knowest it altogether.

4 Thou hast fashioned me behind and before: and laid thine hand upon me.

5 Such knowledge is too wonderful and excellent for me: I cannot attain unto it.

6 Whither shall I go then from thy Spirit: or whither shall I go then from thy presence?

7 If I climb up into heaven, thou art there: if I go down to hell, thou art there also.

8 If I take the wings of the morning: and remain in the uttermost parts of the sea;

9 Even there also shall thy hand lead me: and thy right hand shall hold me.

10 If I say, Peradventure the darkness shall cover me: then shall my night be turned to day.

11 Yea, the darkness is no darkness with thee, but the night is as clear as the day: the darkness and light to thee are both alike.

12 For my reins are thine: thou hast covered me in my mothers womb.

13 I will give thanks unto thee, for I am fearfully and wonderfully made: marvellous are thy works, and that my soul knoweth right well.

14 My bones are not hid from thee: though I be made secretly, and fashioned beneath in the earth.

15 Thine eyes did see my substance, yet being unperfect: and in thy book were all my members written;

16 Which day by day were fashioned: when as yet there was none of them.

17 How dear are thy counsels unto me, O God: O how great is the summe of them!

18 If I tell them, they are moe in number than the sand: when I wake up, I am present with thee.

19 Wilt thou not slay the wicked, O God: depart from me ye bloud-thirsty men.

20 For they speak unrighteously against thee: and thine enemies take thy Name in vain.

21 Do not I hate them, O Lord, that hate thee: and am not I grieved with those that rise up against thee?

22 Yea, I hate them right sore: even as though they were mine enemies.

23 Try me, O God, and seek the ground of my heart: prove me, and examine my thoughts.

24 Look well if there be any way of wickedness in me: and lead me in the way everlasting.

Psalm 140

Eripe me, Domine.

DELIVER me, O Lord, from the evil man: and preserve me from the wicked man.

2 Who imagine mischief in their hearts: and stir up strife all the day long.

3 They have sharpned their tongues like a serpent: adders poison is under their lips.

4 Keep me, O Lord, from the hands of the ungodly: preserve me from the wicked men, who are purposed to overthrow my goings.

5 The proud have laid a snare for me, and spread a net abroad with cords: yea, and set traps in my way.

6 I said unto the Lord, Thou art my God: hear the voice of my prayers, O Lord.

7 O Lord God, thou strength of my health: thou hast covered my head in the day of the battel.

8 Let not the ungodly have his desire, O Lord: let not his mischievous imagination prosper, lest they be too proud.

9 Let the mischief of their own lips fall upon the head of them: that compass me about.

10 Let hot burning coals fall upon them: let them be cast into the fire, and into the pit, that they never rise up again.

11 A man full of words shall not prosper upon the earth: evil shall hunt the wicked person to overthrow him.

12 Sure I am, that the Lord will avenge the poor: and maintain the cause of the helpless.

13 The righteous also shall give thanks unto thy Name: and the just shall continue in thy sight.

Psalm 141

Domine, clamavi.

LORD, I call upon thee, haste thee unto me: and consider my voice, when I cry unto thee.

2 Let my prayer be set forth in thy sight as the incense: and let the lifting up of my hands be an evening-sacrifice.

3 Set a watch, O Lord, before my mouth: and keep the door of my lips.

4 O let not mine heart be inclined to any evil thing: let me not be occupied in ungodly works, with the men that work wickedness, lest I eat of such things as please them.

5 Let the righteous rather smite me friendly: and reprove me.

6 But let not their precious balms break my head: yea, I will pray yet against their wickedness.

7 Let their judges be overthrown in stony places: that they may hear my words, for they are sweet.

8 Our bones lie scattered before the pit: like as when one breaketh and heweth wood upon the earth.

9 But mine eyes look unto thee, O Lord God: in thee is my trust, O cast not out my soul.

10 Keep me from the snare that they have laid for me: and from the traps of the wicked doers.

11 Let the ungodly fall into their own nets together: and let me ever escape them.

Day 29. *Evening Prayer.*

Psalm 142

Voce mea ad Dominum.

I CRIED unto the Lord with my voice: yea, even unto the Lord did I make my supplication.

2 I poured out my complaints before him: and shewed him of my trouble.

3 When my spirit was in heaviness, thou knewest my path: in the way wherein I walked have they privily laid a snare for me.

4 I looked also upon my right hand: and saw there was no man that would know me.

5 I had no place to flee unto: and no man cared for my soul.

6 I cried unto thee, O Lord, and said: Thou art my hope and my portion in the land of the living.

7 Consider my complaint: for I am brought very low.

8 O deliver me from my persecutors: for they are too strong for me.

9 Bring my soul out of prison, that I may give thanks unto thy Name: which thing if thou wilt grant me, then shall the righteous resort unto my company.

Psalm 143

Domine, exaudi.

HEAR my prayer, O Lord, and consider my desire: hearken unto me for thy truth and righteousness sake.

2 And enter not into judgement with thy servant: for in thy sight shall no man living be justified.

3 For the enemy hath persecuted my soul, he hath smitten my life down to the ground: he hath laid me in the darkness, as the men that have been long dead.

4 Therefore is my spirit vexed within me: and my heart within me is desolate.

5 Yet do I remember the time past, I muse upon all thy works: yea, I exercise my self in the works of thy hands.

6 I stretch forth my hands unto thee: my soul gaspeth unto thee as a thirsty land.

7 Hear me, O Lord, and that soon, for my spirit waxeth faint:

hide not thy face from me, lest I be like unto them that go down into the pit.

8   O let me hear thy loving kindness betimes in the morning, for in thee is my trust: shew thou me the way that I should walk in, for I lift up my soul unto thee.

9   Deliver me, O Lord, from mine enemies: for I flee unto thee to hide me.

10   Teach me to do the thing that pleaseth thee, for thou art my God: let thy loving Spirit lead me forth into the land of righteousness.

11   Quicken me, O Lord, for thy Names sake: and for thy righteousness sake bring my soul out of trouble.

12   And of thy goodness slay mine enemies: and destroy all them that vex my soul, for I am thy servant.

Day 30. *Morning Prayer*.

Psalm 144

Benedictus Dominus.

B LESSED be the Lord my strength: who teacheth my hands to war, and my fingers to fight;

2   My hope and my fortress, my castle and deliverer, my defender, in whom I trust: who subdueth my people that is under me.

3   Lord, what is man, that thou hast such respect unto him: or the son of man, that thou so regardest him?

4   Man is like a thing of nought: his time passeth away like a shadow.

5   Bow thy heavens, O Lord, and come down: touch the mountains, and they shall smoke.

6   Cast forth thy lightning and tear them: shoot out thine arrows and consume them.

7   Send down thine hand from above: deliver me, and take me out of the great waters, from the hand of strange children;

8   Whose mouth talketh of vanity: and their right hand is a right hand of wickedness.

9   I will sing a new song unto thee, O God: and sing praises unto thee upon a ten-stringed lute.

10   Thou hast given victory unto kings: and hast delivered David thy servant from the peril of the sword.

11   Save me, and deliver me from the hand of strange children:

whose mouth talketh of vanity, and their right hand is a right hand of iniquity.

12 That our sons may grow up as the young plants: and that our daughters may be as the polished corners of the temple.

13 That our garners may be full and plenteous with all manner of store: that our sheep may bring forth thousands, and ten thousands in our streets.

14 That our oxen may be strong to labour, that there be no decay: no leading into captivity, and no complaining in our streets.

15 Happy are the people that are in such a case: yea, blessed are the people who have the Lord for their God.

Psalm 145

Exaltabo te, Deus.

I WILL magnifie thee, O God, my King: and I will praise thy Name for ever and ever.

2 Every day will I give thanks unto thee: and praise thy Name for ever and ever.

3 Great is the Lord, and marvellous, worthy to be praised: there is no end of his greatness.

4 One generation shall praise thy works unto another: and declare thy power.

5 As for me, I will be talking of thy worship: thy glory, thy praise and wondrous works;

6 So that men shall speak of the might of thy marvellous acts: and I will also tell of thy greatness.

7 The memorial of thine abundant kindness shall be shewed: and men shall sing of thy righteousness.

8 The Lord is gracious and merciful: long-suffering, and of great goodness.

9 The Lord is loving unto every man: and his mercy is over all his works.

10 All thy works praise thee, O Lord: and thy saints give thanks unto thee.

11 They shew the glory of thy kingdom: and talk of thy power;

12 That thy power, thy glory, and mightiness of thy kingdom: might be known unto men.

13 Thy kingdom is an everlasting kingdom: and thy dominion endureth throughout all ages.

14　The Lord upholdeth all such as fall: and lifteth up all those that are down.

15　The eyes of all wait upon thee, O Lord: and thou givest them their meat in due season.

16　Thou openest thine hand: and fillest all things living with plenteousness.

17　The Lord is righteous in all his wayes: and holy in all his works.

18　The Lord is nigh unto all them that call upon him: yea, all such as call upon him faithfully.

19　He will fulfil the desire of them that fear him: he also will hear their cry, and will help them.

20　The Lord preserveth all them that love him: but scattereth abroad all the ungodly.

21　My mouth shall speak the praise of the Lord: and let all flesh give thanks unto his holy Name for ever and ever.

Psalm 146

Lauda, anima mea.

PRAISE the Lord, O my soul, while I live will I praise the Lord: yea, as long as I have any being, I will sing praises unto my God.

2　O put not your trust in princes, nor in any child of man: for there is no help in them.

3　For when the breath of man goeth forth, he shall turn again to his earth: and then all his thoughts perish.

4　Blessed is he that hath the God of Jacob for his help: and whose hope is in the Lord his God.

5　Who made heaven and earth, the sea and all that therein is: who keepeth his promise for ever.

6　Who helpeth them to right that suffer wrong: who feedeth the hungry.

7　The Lord looseth men out of prison: the Lord giveth sight to the blind.

8　The Lord helpeth them that are fallen: the Lord careth for the righteous.

9　The Lord careth for the strangers, he defendeth the fatherless and widow: as for the way of the ungodly, he turneth it upside down.

10　The Lord thy God, O Sion, shall be King for evermore: and throughout all generations.

Day 30. *Evening Prayer.*

Psalm 147

Laudate Dominum.

O PRAISE the Lord, for it is a good thing to sing praises unto our God: yea, a joyful and pleasant thing it is to be thankful.

2 The Lord doth build up Jerusalem: and gather together the outcasts of Israel.

3 He healeth those that are broken in heart: and giveth medicine to heal their sickness.

4 He telleth the number of the stars: and calleth them all by their names.

5 Great is our Lord, and great is his power: yea, and his wisdom is infinite.

6 The Lord setteth up the meek: and bringeth the ungodly down to the ground.

7 O sing unto the Lord with thanksgiving: sing praises upon the harp unto our God.

8 Who covereth the heaven with clouds, and prepareth rain for the earth: and maketh the grass to grow upon the mountains, and herb for the use of men.

9 Who giveth fodder unto the cattel: and feedeth the young ravens that call upon him.

10 He hath no pleasure in the strength of an horse: neither delighteth he in any mans legs.

11 But the Lords delight is in them that fear him: and put their trust in his mercy.

12 Praise the Lord, O Jerusalem: praise thy God, O Sion.

13 For he hath made fast the bars of thy gates: and hath blessed thy children within thee.

14 He maketh peace in thy borders: and filleth thee with the flour of wheat.

15 He sendeth forth his commandment upon earth: and his word runneth very swiftly.

16 He giveth snow like wooll: and scattereth the hoar-frost like ashes.

17 He casteth forth his ice like morsels: who is able to abide his frost?

18 He sendeth out his word, and melteth them: he bloweth with his wind, and the waters flow.

19 He sheweth his word unto Jacob: his statutes and ordinances unto Israel.

20 He hath not dealt so with any nation: neither have the heathen knowledge of his laws.

Psalm 148

Laudate Dominum.

O PRAISE the Lord of heaven: praise him in the height.
    2 Praise him, all ye angels of his: praise him, all his host.

3 Praise him, sun and moon: praise him, all ye stars and light.

4 Praise him, all ye heavens: and ye waters, that are above the heavens.

5 Let them praise the Name of the Lord: for he spake the word, and they were made, he commanded, and they were created.

6 He hath made them fast for ever and ever: he hath given them a law which shall not be broken.

7 Praise the Lord upon earth: ye dragons and all deeps;

8 Fire and hail, snow and vapours: wind and storm, fulfilling his word;

9 Mountains and all hills: fruitful trees and all cedars;

10 Beasts and all cattel: worms and feathered fowls;

11 Kings of the earth and all people: princes and all judges of the world;

12 Young men and maidens, old men and children, praise the Name of the Lord: for his Name only is excellent, and his praise above heaven and earth.

13 He shall exalt the horn of his people, all his saints shall praise him: even the children of Israel, even the people that serveth him.

Psalm 149

Cantate Domino.

O SING unto the Lord a new song: let the congregation of saints praise him.

    2 Let Israel rejoyce in him that made him: and let the children of Sion be joyful in their King.

3 Let them praise his Name in the dance: let them sing praises unto him with tabret and harp.

4 For the Lord hath pleasure in his people: and helpeth the meek-hearted.

5 Let the saints be joyful with glory: let them rejoice in their beds.

6 Let the praises of God be in their mouth: and a two-edged sword in their hands;

7 To be avenged of the heathen: and to rebuke the people;

8 To bind their kings in chains: and their nobles with links of iron.

9 That they may be avenged of them, as it is written: Such honour have all his saints.

Psalm 150

Laudate Dominum.

O PRAISE God in his holiness: praise him in the firmament of his power.

2 Praise him in his noble acts: praise him according to his excellent greatness.

3 Praise him in the sound of the trumpet: praise him upon the lute and harp.

4 Praise him in the cymbals and dances: praise him upon the strings and pipe.

5 Praise him upon the well-tuned cymbals: praise him upon the loud cymbals.

6 Let every thing that hath breath: praise the Lord.

Forms of Prayer
to be used at
SEA.

¶ *The Morning and Evening Service to be used daily at Sea, shall be the same which is appointed in the Book of Common Prayer.*

¶ *These two following Prayers are to be also used in his Majesties Navy every day.*

O ETERNAL Lord God, who alone spreadest out the heavens, and rulest the raging of the sea; who hast compassed the waters with bounds until day and night come to an end; Be pleased to receive into thy Almighty and most gratious protection the persons of us thy servants, and the Fleet in which we serve. Preserve us from the dangers of the sea, and from the violence of the enemy, that we may be a safe-guard unto our most gratious soveraign lord, King *CHARLES* and his kingdoms, and a security for such as pass on the seas upon their lawful occasions; that the inhabitants of our Island may in peace and quietness serve thee our God, and that we may return in safety to enjoy the blessings of the land, with the fruits of our labours; and with a thankfull remembrance of thy mercies to praise and glorifie thy holy Name, through Jesus Christ our Lord. *Amen.*

The Collect.

P REVENT us, O Lord, in all our doings, with thy most gracious favour, and further us with thy continual help; that in all our works begun, continued, and ended in thee, we may glorifie thy holy Name, and finally by thy mercy obtain everlasting life, through Jesus Christ our Lord. *Amen.*

Prayers to be used in Storms at Sea.

O MOST powerful and glorious Lord God, at whose command the winds blow, and lift up the waves of the sea, and who stillest the rage thereof; We thy creatures, but miserable sinners, do in this our great distress cry unto thee for help: save, Lord, or else we perish. We confess, when we have been safe, and seen all things quiet about us, we have forgot thee our God, and refused to hearken to the still voice of thy Word, and to obey thy commandments: But now we see how terrible thou art in all thy works of wonder; the great God to be feared above all: And therefore we adore thy divine Majesty, acknowledging thy power, and imploring thy goodness. Help, Lord, and save us for thy mercies sake in Jesus Christ thy Son, our Lord. *Amen.*

Or this,

O MOST glorious and gracious Lord God, who dwellest in heaven, but beholdest all things below; Look down, we beseech thee, and hear us, calling out of the depth of misery, and out of the jaws of this death, which is ready now to swallow us up: Save Lord, or else we perish. The living, the living shall praise thee. O send thy word of command to rebuke the raging winds, and the roaring sea, that we being delivered from this distress may live to serve thee, and to glorifie thy Name all the daies of our life. Hear, Lord, and save us, for the infinite merits of our blessed Saviour, thy Son, our Lord Jesus Christ. *Amen.*

The Prayer to be said before a Fight at Sea against any Enemy.

O MOST powerful and glorious Lord God, the Lord of hosts, that rulest and commandest all things; Thou sittest in the throne judging right; and therefore we make our address to thy divine Majesty in this our necessity, that thou wouldest take the cause into thine own hand, and judge between us, and our enemies. Stir up thy strength, O Lord, and come and help us; for thou givest not alway the battel to the strong, but canst save by many or by few. O let not our sins now cry against us for vengeance, but hear us thy poor servants begging mercy, and imploring thy help, and that thou wouldst be a defence unto us against the face of the enemy. Make it appear that thou art our Saviour and mighty deliverer, through Jesus Christ our Lord. *Amen.*

Short Prayers for single persons, that cannot meet to joyn in Prayer with others by reason of the Fight, or Storm.

General Prayers.

L ORD, be merciful to us sinners, and save us for thy mercies sake.
Thou art the great God, that hast made and rulest all things: O deliver us for thy Names sake.

Thou art the great God to be feared above all: O save us, that we may praise thee.

Special Prayers with respect to the Enemy.

Tʜᴏᴜ, O Lord, art just and powerful; O defend our cause against the face of the enemy.

O God, thou art a strong tower of defence to all that flee unto thee: O save us from the violence of the enemy.

O Lord of hosts, fight for us, that we may glorifie thee.

O suffer us not to sink under the weight of our sins, or the violence of the enemy.

O Lord, arise, help us, and deliver us for thy Names sake.

Short Prayers in respect of a Storm.

Tʜᴏᴜ, O Lord, that stillest the raging of the sea, hear, hear us, and save us, that we perish not.

O blessed Saviour, that didst save thy disciples ready to perish in a storm, hear us and save us, we beseech thee.

Lord, have mercy upon us.

Christ, have mercy upon us.

Lord, have mercy upon us.

O Lord, hear us.

O Christ, hear us.

God the Father, God the Son, God the Holy Ghost, have mercy upon us, save us now and evermore. Amen.

Oᴜʀ Father which art in heaven, Hallowed be thy Name. Thy kingdom come. Thy will be done in earth, As it is in heaven. Give us this day our daily bread. And forgive us our trespasses, As we forgive them that trespass against us. And lead us not into temptation: But deliver us from evil: For thine is the Kingdom, the Power, and the Glory, For ever and ever. Amen.

¶ *When there shall be imminent danger, as many as can be spared from necessary service in the Ship, shall be called together, and make an humble Confession of their sin to God: In which every one ought seriously to reflect upon those particular sins of which his Conscience shall accuse him: Saying as followeth,*

The Confession.

Aʟᴍɪɢʜᴛʏ God, Father of our Lord Jesus Christ, maker of all things, judge of all men; We acknowledge and bewail our manifold sins and wickedness, which we from time to time most grievously have committed, by thought, word, and deed, against thy divine majesty, provoking most justly thy wrath and indignation against us. We do earnestly repent, and be heartily sorry for these our misdoings; the remembrance of them is grievous unto us; the burden of them is intolerable. Have mercy upon us, have mercy upon us, most merciful Father; for thy Son our Lord Jesus Christ's sake,° forgive us all that is past, and grant, that we may ever hereafter serve and please thee in newness of life, to the honour and glory of thy Name, through Jesus Christ our Lord. Amen.

¶ *Then shall the Priest, if there be any in the Ship, pronounce this Absolution.*

ALMIGHTY God, our heavenly Father, who of his great mercy hath promised forgiveness of sins to all them that with hearty repentance and true faith turn unto him; Have mercy upon you, pardon and deliver you from all your sins; confirm and strengthen you in all goodness, and bring you to everlasting life, through Jesus Christ our Lord. *Amen.*

Thanksgiving after a Storm.

Jubilate Deo.

O BE joyful in God, all ye lands: sing praises unto the honour of his name, make his praise to be glorious.   *Ps.* 66

Say unto God, O how wonderful art thou in thy works: through the greatness of thy power shall thine enemies be found liars unto thee.

For all the world shall worship thee: sing of thee, and praise thy Name.

O come hither, and behold the works of God: how wonderful he is in his doing towards the children of men.

He turned the sea into dry land: so that they went through the water on foot; there did we rejoyce thereof.

He ruleth with his power for ever, his eies behold the people: and such as will not believe shall not be able to exalt themselves.

O praise our God, ye people: and make the voice of his praise to be heard;

Who holdeth our soul in life: and suffereth not our feet to slip.

For thou, O God, hast proved us: thou also hast tried us, like as silver is tried.

Thou broughtest us into the snare: and laidst trouble upon our loins.

Thou sufferedst men to ride over our heads: we went through fire and water, and thou broughtest us out into a wealthy place.

I will go into thine house with burnt-offerings: and wilt pay thee my vows which I promised with my lips, and spake with my mouth when I was in trouble.

I will offer unto thee fat burnt-sacrifices, with the incense of ramms: I will offer bullocks and goats.

O come hither and hearken, all ye, that fear God: and I will tell you what he hath done for my soul.

I called unto him with my mouth: and gave him praises with my tongue.

If I incline unto wickedness with myne heart: the Lord will not hear me.

But God hath heard me: and considered the voice of my prayer.

Praised be God, who hath not cast out my prayer: nor turned his mercy from me.

Glory be to the Father, and to the Son, and to the Holy Ghost;

As it was in the beginning, is now, and ever shall be, world without end. Amen.

Confitemini Domino.

O GIVE thanks unto the Lord, for he is gracious: and his mercy endureth for ever.   *Ps.* 107

Let them give thanks whom the Lord hath redeemed: and delivered from the hand of the enemy;

And gathered them out of the lands, from the east and from the west: from the north and from the south.

They went astray in the wilderness out of the way: and found no city to dwell in;

Hungry and thirsty: their soul fainted in them.

So they cryed unto the Lord in their trouble: and he delivered them from their distress.

He led them forth by the right way: that they might go to the city where they dwelt.

O that men would therefore praise the Lord for his goodness: and declare the wonders that he doeth for the children of men.

For he satisfieth the empty soul: and filleth the hungry soul with goodness.

Such as sit in darkness, and in the shadow of death: being fast bound in misery and iron;

Because they rebelled against the words of the Lord: and lightly regarded the counsel of the most high;

He also brought down their heart through heaviness: they fell down, and there was none to help them.

So when they cryed unto the Lord in their trouble: he delivered them out of their distress.

For he brought them out of darkness, and out of the shadow of death: and brake their bonds in sunder.

O that men would therefore praise the Lord for his goodness: and declare the wonders that he doth for the children of men.

For he hath broken the gates of brass: and smitten the barrs of iron in sunder.

Foolish men are plagued for their offence: and because of their wickedness.

Their soul abhorred all manner of meat: and they were even hard at deaths door.

So when they cryed unto the Lord in their trouble: he delivered them out of their distress.

He sent his word and healed them: and they were saved from their destruction.

O that men would therefore praise the Lord for his goodness: and declare the wonders that he doth for the children of men.

That they would offer unto him the sacrifice of thanksgiving: and tell out his works with gladness.

They that go down to the sea in ships: and occupy their business in great waters;

These men see the works of the Lord: and his wonders in the deep.

For at his word the stormy wind ariseth: which lifteth up the waves thereof.

They are carried up to the heaven, and down again to the deep: their soul melteth away because of the trouble.

They reel to and fro, and stagger like a drunken man: and are at their wits end.

So when they cry unto the Lord in their trouble: he delivereth them out of their distress.

For he maketh the storm to cease: so that the waves thereof are still.

Then are they glad, because they are at rest: and so he bringeth them unto the haven where they would be.

O that men would therefore praise the Lord for his goodness: and declare the wonders that he doth for the children of men.

That they would exalt him also in the congregation of the people: and praise him in the seat of the elders;

Who turneth the flouds into a wilderness: and drieth up the water-springs.

A fruitful land maketh he barren: for the wickedness of them that dwell therein.

Again he maketh the wilderness a standing water: and water-springs of a dry ground.

And there he setteth the hungry: that they may build them a city to dwell in;

That they may sow their land, and plant vineyards: to yield them fruits of increase.

He blesseth them, so that they multiply exceedingly: and suffereth not their cattel to decrease.

And again, when they are minished and brought low: through oppression, through any plague or trouble,

Though he suffer them to be evil-entreated through tyrants:and let them wander out of the way in the wilderness;

Yet helpeth he the poor out of misery: and maketh him housholds like a flock of sheep.

The righteous will consider this, and rejoyce: and the mouth of all wickedness shall be stopped.

Who so is wise, will ponder these things: and they shall understand the loving kindness of the Lord.

Glory be to the Father, and to the Son, and to the Holy Ghost;

As it was in the beginning, is now, and ever shall be, world without end. Amen.

Collects of Thanksgiving.

O MOST blessed and glorious Lord God, who art of infinite goodness and mercy, we thy poor creatures, whom thou hast made and preserved, holding our souls in life, and now rescuing us out of the jaws of death, humbly present our selves again before thy divine Majesty, to offer a sacrifice of praise and thanksgiving, for that thou heardest us, when we called in our trouble, and didst not cast out our prayer, which we made before thee in our great distress; even, when we gave all for lost, our ship, our goods, our lives, then didst thou mercifully look upon us, and wonderfully command a deliverance; for which, we now being in safety, do give all praise and glory to thy holy Name, through Jesus Christ our Lord. *Amen.*

Or, this:

O MOST mighty and gracious good God, thy mercy is over all thy works, but in special manner hath been extended toward us, whom thou hast so powerfully and wonderfully defended. Thou hast shewed us terrible things, and wonders in the deep, that we might see how powerful and gracious a God thou art; how able and ready to help them that trust in thee. Thou hast shewed us, how both winds and seas obey thy command, that we may learn even from them, hereafter to obey thy voice, and to do thy will. We therefore bless and glorifie thy Name for this thy mercy in saving us, when we were ready to perish. And we beseech thee, make us as truly sensible now of thy mercy, as we were then of the danger: And give us hearts alwayes ready to express our thankfulness, not only by words, but also by our lives, in being more obedient to thy holy commandments. Continue, we beseech thee, this thy goodness to us, that we, whom thou hast saved, may serve thee in holiness and righteousness, all the days of our life, through Jesus Christ our Lord and Saviour. *Amen.*

A Hymn of Praise and Thanksgiving after a dangerous Tempest.

O COME, let us give thanks unto the Lord, for he is gracious: and his mercy endureth for ever.

Great is the Lord, and greatly to be praised; let the redeemed of the Lord say so: whom he hath delivered from the merciless rage of the sea.

The Lord is gratious and full of compassion: slow to anger, and of great mercy.

He hath not dealt with us according to our sins: neither rewarded us according to our iniquities.

But as the heaven is high above the earth: so great hath been his mercy towards us.

We found trouble and heaviness: we were even at deaths door;

The waters of the sea had well nigh covered us: the proud waters had well nigh gone over our soul;

The sea roared: and the stormy wind lifted up the waves thereof;

We were carried, up as it were, to heaven, and then down again into the deep: our soul melted within us, because of trouble;

Then cryed we unto thee, O Lord: and thou didst deliver us out of our distress.

Blessed be thy name, who didst not despise the prayer of thy servants: but didst hear our cry, and hast saved us.

Thou didst send forth thy commandment: and the windy storm ceased, and was turn'd into a calm.°

O let us therefore praise the Lord for his goodness: and declare the wonders that he hath done, and still doth for the children of men.

Praised be the Lord daily: even the Lord that helpeth us, and poureth his benefits upon us.

He is our God, even the God of whom cometh salvation: God is the Lord, by whom we have escaped death.

Thou, Lord, hast made us glad through the operation of thy hands: and we will triumph in thy praise.

Blessed be the Lord God: even the Lord God, who only doth wondrous things;

And blessed be the Name of his majesty for ever: and let every one of us say, Amen, Amen.

Glory be to the Father, and to the Son, and to the Holy Ghost;

As it was in the beginning, is now, and ever shall be, world without end. Amen.

2 *Cor.* 13

THE grace of our Lord Jesus Christ, and the love of God, and the fellowship of the holy Ghost, be with us all evermore. *Amen.*

After Victory or Deliverance from an Enemy.

A Psalm or Hymn of praise and thanksgiving after Victory.

IF the Lord had not been on our side, now may we say: if the Lord himself had not been on our side, when men rose up against us;

They had swallowed us up quick: when they were so wrathfully displeased at us.

Yea the waters had drowned us, and the stream had gone over our soul: the deep waters of the proud had gone over our soul.

But praised be the Lord: who hath not given us over as a prey unto them.

The Lord hath wrought: a mighty salvation for us.

We gat not this by our own sword, neither was it our own arm that saved us: but thy right hand, and thine arm, and the light of thy countenance, because thou hadst a favour unto us.

The Lord hath appeared for us: the Lord hath covered our heads, and made us to stand in the day of battel.

The Lord hath appeared for us: the Lord hath overthrown our enemies, and dashed in pieces those that rose up against us;

Therefore not unto us, O Lord, not unto us: but unto thy Name be given the glory.

The Lord hath done great things for us: the Lord hath done great things for us, for which we rejoyce.

Our help standeth in the Name of the Lord: who hath made heaven and earth.

Blessed be the Name of the Lord: from this time forth for evermore.

Glory be to the Father, and to the Son, and to the Holy Ghost;

As it was in the beginning, is now, and ever shall be, world without end. Amen.

¶ *After this Hymn may be sung the* Te Deum.

¶ *Then this Collect.*

O ALMIGHTY God, the soveraign commander of all the world, in whose hand is power and might which none is able to withstand; We bless and magnifie thy great and glorious Name for this happy victory, the whole glory whereof we do ascribe to thee, who art the only giver of victory. And, we beseech thee, give us grace to improve this great mercy to thy glory, the advancement of thy Gospel, the honour of our Soveraign, and, as much as in us lieth, to the good of all mankind. And, we beseech thee, give us such a sense of this great mercy, as may engage us to a true thankfulness, such as may appear in our lives by an humble, holy, and obedient walking before thee all our dayes, through Jesus Christ our Lord: To whom with thee, and the holy Spirit, as for all thy mercies, so in particular for this victory and deliverance, be all glory and honour world without end. *Amen.*

2 *Cor.* 13

THE grace of our Lord Jesus Christ, and the love of God, and the fellowship of the holy Ghost, be with us all evermore. *Amen.*

At the Burial of their Dead at Sea.

¶ *T*HE *Office in the Common Prayer-book may be used; only instead of these words* [We therefore commit his body to the ground, earth to earth, &c.] *say,*

WE therefore commit his body to the Deep, to be turned into corruption, looking for the resurrection of the body, (when the sea shall give up her dead,) and the life of the world to come, through our Lord Jesus Christ; who at his coming shall change our vile body, that it may be like his glorious body, according to the mighty working, whereby he is able to subdue all things to himself.

THE

FORM AND MANNER

OF

MAKING, ORDAINING, and CONSECRATING

OF

BISHOPS, PRIESTS and DEACONS,

According to the Order of the CHURCH OF ENGLAND.

The Preface.

IT is evident unto all men diligently reading holy Scripture and ancient Authors, that from the Apostles time there have been these Orders of Ministers° in Christs Church; Bishops, Priests, and Deacons.° Which Offices were evermore had in such reverend estimation, that no man might presume to execute any of them, except he were first called, tried, examined, and known to have such qualities° as are requisite for the same; and also by publick prayer, with imposition of hands, were approved and admitted thereunto by lawful Authority. And therefore, to the intent that these Orders may be continued, and reverently used and esteemed in the Church of *England*; No man shall be accounted or taken to be a lawful Bishop, Priest, or Deacon, in the Church of *England*, or suffered to execute any of the said Functions, except he be called, tryed, examined and admitted thereunto, according to the Form hereafter following, or hath had formerly Episcopal Consecration, or Ordination.

And none shall be admitted a Deacon, except he be Twenty-three years of age, unless he have a Faculty. And every man which is to be admitted a Priest,° shall be full Four and twenty years old. And every man which is to be Ordained or Consecrated Bishop, shall be fully Thirty years of age.

And the Bishop knowing either by himself, or by sufficient testimony, any person to be a man of vertuous conversation, and without crime, and after examination and tryal, finding him learned in the Latine Tongue, and sufficiently instructed in holy Scripture, may at the times appointed in the Canon or else, on urgent occasion, upon some other Sunday or Holy-day, in the face of the Church, admit him a Deacon, in such manner and form as hereafter followeth.

THE

Form and Manner of Making of
DEACONS.

¶ *When the day appointed by the Bishop is come, after Morning Prayer is ended, there shall be a Sermon or Exhortation, declaring the Duty and Office of such as come to be admitted Deacons; how necessary that Order is in the Church of Christ; and also, how the people ought to esteem them in their Office.*

¶ *First the Arch-Deacon° or his Deputy shall present unto the Bishop (sitting in his chair near to the holy Table) such as desire to be ordained Deacons (each of them being decently habited)° saying these words,*

R EVEREND Father in God, I present unto you these persons present to be admitted Deacons.

The Bishop.

T AKE heed that the persons whom ye present unto us, be apt and meet, for their learning and godly conversation, to exercise their Ministry duly, to the honour of God, and the edifying of his Church.

The Arch-Deacon shall answer,

I HAVE inquired of them, and also examined them, and think them so to be.

¶ *Then the Bishop shall say unto the people,*

B RETHREN, if there be any of you° who knoweth any impediment or notable crime in any of these persons presented to be ordered Deacons, for the which he ought not to be admitted to that Office, let him come forth in the Name of God, and shew what the crime or impediment is.

¶ *And if any great crime or impediment be objected, the Bishop shall surcease from Ordering that person, until such time as the party accused shall be found clear of that crime.*

¶ *Then the Bishop (commending such as shall be found meet to be Ordered, to the prayers of the congregation) shall, with the Clergy and people present, sing or say the Litany,° with the Prayers, as followeth.*

The Litany and Suffrages

O GOD the Father of heaven: have mercy upon us miserable sinners.
O God the Father of heaven: have mercy upon us miserable sinners.

O God the Son, Redeemer of the world: have mercy upon us miserable sinners.

O God the Son, Redeemer of the world: have mercy upon us miserable sinners.

O God the Holy Ghost, proceeding from the Father, and the Son: have mercy upon us miserable sinners.

O God the Holy Ghost, proceeding from the Father, and the Son: have mercy upon us miserable sinners.

O holy, blessed and glorious Trinity, three persons and one God: have mercy upon us miserable sinners.

O holy, blessed and glorious Trinity, three persons and one God: have mercy upon us miserable sinners.

Remember not Lord our offences, nor the offences of our forefathers, neither take thou vengeance of our sins: spare us, good Lord, spare thy people whom thou hast redeemed with thy most precious bloud, and be not angry with us for ever.

Spare us, good Lord.

From all evil and mischief, from sin, from the crafts and assaults of the devil, from thy wrath, and from everlasting damnation,

Good Lord, deliver us.

From all blindness of heart; from pride, vain-glory, and hypocrisie; from envy, hatred, and malice, and all uncharitableness,

Good Lord, deliver us.

From fornication, and all other deadly sin; and from all the deceits of the world, the flesh, and the devil,

Good Lord, deliver us.

From lightning and tempest; from plague, pestilence, and famine; from battel and murder, and from sudden death,

Good Lord, deliver us.

From all sedition, privy conspiracy, and rebellion; from all false doctrine, heresie, and schism; from hardness of heart, and contempt of thy Word and Commandment,

Good Lord, deliver us.

By the mystery of thy holy Incarnation; by thy holy Nativity and Circumcision; by thy Baptism, Fasting, and Temptation,

Good Lord, deliver us.

By thine Agony and bloudy Sweat; by thy Cross and Passion; by thy precious Death and Burial; by thy glorious Resurrection and Ascension, and by the coming of the Holy Ghost,

Good Lord, deliver us.

In all time of our tribulation; in all time of our wealth; in the hour of death, and in the day of judgment,

Good Lord, deliver us.

We sinners do beseech thee to hear us, O Lord God, and that it may please thee to rule and govern thy holy Church universal in the right way;

We beseech thee to hear us, good Lord.

That it may please thee to keep and strengthen in the true worshipping of thee, in righteousness and holiness of life, thy servant *CHARLES*, our most gracious King and Governour;

We beseech thee to hear us, good Lord.

That it may please thee to rule his heart in thy faith, fear, and love, and that he may evermore have affiance in thee, and ever seek thy honour and glory;

We beseech thee to hear us, good Lord.

That it may please thee to be his defender and keeper, giving him the victory over all his enemies;

We beseech thee to hear us, good Lord.

That it may please thee to bless and preserve our gracious Queen *CATHERINE*, *Mary* the Queen Mother, *James* Duke of *York*, and all the Royal Family;

We beseech thee to hear us, good Lord.

That it may please thee to illuminate all Bishops, Priests, and Deacons,° with true knowledge and understanding of thy Word, and that both by their preaching and living they may set it forth, and shew it accordingly;

We beseech thee to hear us, good Lord.

That it may please thee to bless these thy servants, now to be admitted to the Order of Deacons, [or *Priests*] and to pour thy grace upon them; that they may duly execute their Office, to the edifying of thy Church, and the glory of thy holy Name;

We beseech thee to hear us, good Lord.

That it may please thee to endue the Lords of the Council, and all the Nobility, with grace, wisdom and understanding;

We beseech thee to hear us, good Lord.

That it may please thee to bless and keep the Magistrates, giving them grace to execute justice, and to maintain truth;

We beseech thee to hear us, good Lord.

That it may please thee to bless and keep all thy people;
We beseech thee to hear us, good Lord.

That it may please thee to give to all nations unity, peace, and concord;
We beseech thee to hear us, good Lord.

That it may please thee to give us an heart to love and dread thee, and diligently to live after thy commandments;
We beseech thee to hear us, good Lord.

That it may please thee to give to all thy people increase of grace, to hear meekly thy Word, and to receive it with pure affection, and to bring forth the fruits of the Spirit;
We beseech thee to hear us, good Lord.

That it may please thee to bring into the way of truth all such as have erred and are deceived;
We beseech thee to hear us, good Lord.

That it may please thee to strengthen such as do stand, and to comfort and help the weak-hearted, and to raise up those that fall, and finally to beat down Satan under our feet;
We beseech thee to hear us, good Lord.

That it may please thee to succour, help, and comfort, all that are in danger, necessity, and tribulation;
We beseech thee to hear us, good Lord.

That it may please thee to preserve all that travel by land or by water, all women labouring of childe, all sick persons and young children, and to shew thy pity upon all prisoners and captives;
We beseech thee to hear us, good Lord.

That it may please thee to defend and provide for the fatherless children and widows, and all that be desolate and oppressed;
We beseech thee to hear us, good Lord.

That it may please thee to have mercy upon all men;
We beseech thee to hear us, good Lord.

That it may please thee to forgive our enemies, persecutors, and slanderers, and to turn their hearts;
We beseech thee to hear us, good Lord.

That it may please thee to give and preserve to our use the kindly fruits of the earth, so as in due time we may enjoy them;
We beseech thee to hear us, good Lord.

That it may please thee to give us true repentance, to forgive us all our sins, negligences and ignorances, and to endue us with the grace of thy holy Spirit, to amend our lives according to thy holy word;

>*We beseech thee to hear us, good Lord.*

Son of God: we beseech thee to hear us.

>*Son of God: we beseech thee to hear us.*

O Lamb of God: that takest away the sins of the world;

>*Grant us thy peace.*

O Lamb of God: that takest away the sins of the world;

>*Have mercy upon us.*

O Christ, hear us.

>*O Christ, hear us.*

Lord, have mercy upon us.

>*Lord, have mercy upon us.*

Christ, have mercy upon us.

>*Christ, have mercy upon us.*

Lord, have mercy upon us.

>*Lord, have mercy upon us.*

¶ *Then shall the Priest, and the people with him, say the Lords Prayer.*

OUR Father, which art in heaven, Hallowed be thy Name. Thy kingdom come. Thy will be done in earth, As it is in heaven. Give us this day our daily bread. And forgive us our trespasses, As we forgive them, that trespass against us. And lead us not into temptation, But deliver us from evil. Amen.

Priest. O Lord, deal not with us after our sins.

Answer. Neither reward us after our iniquities.

Let us pray.

O GOD, merciful Father, that despisest not the sighing of a contrite heart, nor the desire of such as be sorrowful; Mercifully assist our prayers that we make before thee in all our troubles and adversities, whensoever they oppress us; and graciously hear us, that those evils which the craft and subtilty of the devil or man worketh against us, may be brought to nought, and by the providence of thy goodness they may be dispersed, that we thy servants, being hurt by no persecutions, may evermore give thanks unto thee in thy holy Church, through Jesus Christ our Lord.

>*O Lord, arise, help us, and deliver us for thy Names sake.*

O GOD, we have heard with our ears, and our fathers have declared unto us the noble works that thou didst in their daies, and in the old time before them.

O Lord, arise, help us, and deliver us for thine honour.

Glory be to the Father, and to the Son: and to the holy Ghost;

As it was in the beginning, is now, and ever shall be: world without end. Amen.

From our enemies defend us, O Christ.

Graciously look upon our afflictions.

Pitifully behold the sorrows of our hearts.

Mercifully forgive the sins of thy people.

Favourably with mercy hear our prayers.

O Son of David, have mercy upon us.

Both now and ever vouchsafe to hear us, O Christ.

Graciously hear us, O Christ; graciously hear us, O Lord Christ.

Priest. O Lord, let thy mercy be shewed upon us;

Answer. As we do put our trust in thee.

Let us pray.

WE humbly beseech thee, O Father, mercifully to look upon our infirmities; and for the glory of thy Name, turn from us all those evils that we most righteously have deserved; and grant, that in all our troubles we may put our whole trust and confidence in thy mercy, and evermore serve thee in holiness and pureness of living, to thy honour and glory, through our only Mediatour and Advocate, Jesus Christ our Lord. *Amen.*

¶ *Then shall be sung or said the Service for the Communion,*° *with the Collect, Epistle, and Gospel, as followeth.*

The Collect.

ALMIGHTY God, who by thy divine providence hast appointed divers Orders of Ministers in thy Church, and didst inspire thine Apostles to choose into the Order of Deacons the first Martyr Saint Steven, with others; Mercifully behold these thy servants now called to the like Office and Administration. Replenish them so with the truth of thy doctrine, and adorn them with innocency of life, that both by word and good example, they may faithfully serve thee in this Office, to the glory of thy Name, and the edification of thy

Church,° through the merits of our Saviour Jesus Christ, who liveth and reigneth with thee and the holy Ghost now and for ever. *Amen.*

The Epistle.

L IKEWISE must the Deacons be grave, not double-tongued, not given to much wine, not greedy of filthy lucre, holding the mystery of the faith in a pure conscience. And let these also first be proved, then let them use the Office of a Deacon, being found blameless. Even so must their wives be grave, not slanderers, sober, faithful in all things. Let the Deacons be the husbands of one wife, ruling their children and their own houses well. For they that have used the Office of a Deacon well, purchase to themselves a good degree, and great boldness in the faith which is in Christ Jesus.   1 *Tim.* 3.8

¶ *Or else this out of the sixth of the Acts of the Apostles.*

T HEN the twelve called the multitude of the disciples unto them, and said, It is not reason that we should leave the word of God, and serve tables. Wherefore, brethren, look ye out among you seven men of honest report, full of the holy Ghost and wisdom, whom we may appoint over this business. But we will give our selves continually to prayer, and to the ministry of the word. And the saying pleased the whole multitude. And they chose Steven, a man full of faith, and of the holy Ghost, and Philip, and Prochorus, and Nicanor, and Timon, and Parmenas, and Nicolas, a proselyte of Antioch: Whom they set before the Apostles, and when they had prayed, they laid their hands on them. And the word of God encreased, and the number of the Disciples multiplied in Jerusalem greatly, and a great company of the Priests were obedient to the faith.   *Acts* 6.2

¶ *And before the Gospel, the Bishop sitting in his Chair shall cause the Oath of the Kings Supremacy,° and against the power and authority of all foreign Potentates to be ministred unto every one of them that are to be Ordered.*

The Oath of the Kings Supremacy

I A.B. do utterly testifie and declare in my conscience, That the Kings Highness is the only Supream Governour of this Realm, and of all other His Highnesses Dominions and Countries, as well in all Spiritual or Ecclesiastical things, or causes, as Temporal: And that no foreign Prince, Person, Prelate, State, or Potentate hath, or ought to have any jurisdiction, power, superiority, preeminence or authority Ecclesiastical or Spiritual within this Realm. And therefore I do utterly renounce and forsake all foreign jurisdictions, powers, superiorities and authorities; and do promise, That from henceforth I shall bear faith and true allegiance to the Kings Highness, His Heirs and lawful Successors, and to my power shall assist and defend all jurisdictions, privileges, preeminences and authorities granted or belonging to the Kings Highness, His Heirs and Successors, or united and annexed to the Imperial Crown of this Realm. So help me God, and the Contents of this Book.

¶ *Then shall the Bishop examine every one of them° that are to be Ordered, in the presence of the people, after this manner following*

DO you trust that you are inwardly moved by the holy Ghost, to take upon you this Office and Ministration, to serve God for the promoting of his glory, and the edifying of his people?
Answer. I trust so.

The Bishop.

DO you think that you are truly called according to the will of our Lord Jesus Christ, and the due Order of this Realm, to the Ministry of the Church?
Answer. I think so.

The Bishop.

DO you unfeignedly believe all the Canonical Scriptures of the Old and New Testament?
Answer. I do believe them.

The Bishop.

WILL you diligently read the same unto the people assembled in the Church where you shall be appointed to serve?
Answer. I will.

The Bishop.

IT appertaineth to the Office of a Deacon in the Church where he shall be appointed to serve, to assist the Priest in Divine service, and specially when he ministreth the holy Communion, and to help him in the distribution thereof, and to read holy Scriptures and Homilies in the Church; and to instruct the youth in the Catechism; in the absence of the Priest to Baptize infants, and to Preach, if he be admitted thereto by the Bishop. And furthermore, it is his Office, where provision is so made, to search for the sick, poor and impotent people of the Parish, to intimate their estates, names, and places where they dwell, unto the Curate, that by his exhortation they may be relieved with the alms of the Parishioners or others. Will you do this gladly and willingly?

Answer. I will so do by the help of God.

The Bishop.

WILL you apply all your diligence to frame and fashion your own lives, and the lives of your families, according to the doctrine of Christ, and to make both your selves and them, as much as in you lieth, wholsome examples of the flock of Christ?

Answer. I will so do, the Lord being my helper.

The Bishop.

WILL you reverently obey your Ordinary, and other chief Ministers of the Church, and them to whom the charge and government over you is committed, following with a glad mind and will their godly admonitions?

Answer. I will endeavour my self, the Lord being my helper.

¶ *Then the Bishop, laying his hands severally upon the head of every one of them,° humbly kneeling before him, shall say,*

TAKE thou Authority to execute the Office of a Deacon in the Church of God committed unto thee; In the Name of the Father, and of the Son, and of the holy Ghost. *Amen.*

¶ *Then shall the Bishop deliver to every one of them the New Testament,° saying,*

TAKE thou Authority to read the Gospel in the Church of God, and to preach the same, if thou be thereto licensed by the Bishop himself.

¶ *Then one of them, appointed by the Bishop, shall read*
The Gospel.

LET your loins be girded about, and your lights burning; and ye your selves like unto men that wait for their lord, when he will return from the wedding; that when he cometh and knocketh, they may open unto him immediately. Blessed are those servants, whom the Lord when he cometh, shall find watching: Verily I say unto you, that he shall gird himself, and make them to sit down to meat, and will come forth and serve them. And if he shall come in the second

watch, or come in the third watch, and find them so, blessed are those
servants.   *Luke* 12.35

¶ *Then shall the Bishop proceed in the Communion, and all that are Ordered,*
shall tarry and receive the holy Communion the same day with the Bishop.

¶ *The Communion ended, after the last Collect, and immediately before the*
Benediction shall be said these Collects following.

ALMIGHTY God, giver of all good things,° who of thy great goodness
hast vouchsafed to accept and take these thy servants unto the
Office of Deacons in thy Church; Make them, we beseech thee,
O Lord, to be modest, humble, and constant in their Ministration,
to have a ready will to observe all spiritual discipline; that they having always the testimony of a good conscience, and continuing ever
stable and strong in thy Son Christ, may so well behave themselves in
this inferiour Office, that they may be found worthy to be called unto
the higher Ministries in thy Church, through the same thy Son our
Saviour Jesus Christ, to whom be glory and honour world without
end. *Amen.*

PREVENT us, O Lord, in all our doings with thy most gracious
favour, and further us with thy continual help; that in all our
works begun, continued and ended in thee, we may glorifie thy holy
Name, and finally by thy mercy obtain everlasting life, through Jesus
Christ our Lord. *Amen.*

THE Peace of God which passeth all understanding keep your
hearts and minds in the knowledge and love of God, and of his
Son Jesus Christ our Lord. And the Blessing of God Almighty, the
Father, the Son, and the holy Ghost be amongst you, and remain with
you alwaies. *Amen.*

¶ *And here it must be declared unto the Deacon, that he must continue in that*
Office of a Deacon the space of a whole year (except for reasonable causes it
shall otherwise seem good unto the Bishop) to the intent he may be perfect,
and well expert in the things appertaining to the Ecclesiastical administra-
tion. In executing whereof, if he be found faithful and diligent, he may be
admitted by his Diocesan to the Order of Priesthood, at the times appointed in
the Canon; or else on urgent occasion, upon some other Sunday or Holy-day,
in the face of the Church, in such manner and form as hereafter followeth.

¶ The Form and Manner of Ordering of PRIESTS.

¶ *When the day appointed by the Bishop is come, after Morning Prayer is ended, there shall be a Sermon or Exhortation, declaring the Duty and Office of such as come to be admitted Priests; how necessary that Order is in the Church of Christ; and also how the people ought to esteem them in their Office.*

¶ *First the Arch-Deacon, or, in his absence, one appointed in his stead, shall present unto the Bishop sitting in his chair near to the Holy Table, all them that shall receive the Order of Priesthood that day (each of them being decently habited) and say,*

REVEREND Father in God, I present unto you these persons present, to be admitted to the Order of Priesthood.

¶ The Bishop.

TAKE heed that the persons whom ye present unto us be apt and meet, for their learning and godly conversation, to exercise their Ministry duely, to the honour of God and the edifying of his Church.

¶ The Arch-Deacon shall answer,

I HAVE enquired of them, and also examined them, and think them so to be.

¶ Then the Bishop shall say unto the people,

GOOD People, these are they whom we purpose, God willing, to receive this day unto the holy Office of Priesthood: For after due examination we find not to the contrary, but that they be lawfully called to their Function and Ministry, and that they be persons meet for the same. But yet if there be any of you who knoweth any impediment, or notable crime in any of them, for the which he ought not to be received into this holy Ministry, let him come forth in the Name of God, and shew what the crime or impediment is.

¶ *And if any great crime or impediment be objected, the Bishop shall surcease from Ordering that person, until such time as the party accused shall be found clear of that crime.*

¶ *Then the Bishop (commending such, as shall be found meet to be Ordered, to the prayers of the congregation) shall, with the Clergy and People present, sing or say the Litany, with the prayers, as is before appointed in the Form of Ordering Deacons; save only that in the proper Suffrage there added, the word* [Deacons] *shall be omitted, and the word* [Priests] *inserted instead of it.*

¶ *Then shall be sung or said the Service for the Communion with the Collect, Epistle, and Gospel, as followeth.*

The Collect.

ALMIGHTY God, giver of all good things, who by thy holy Spirit hast appointed divers Orders of Ministers in thy Church, Mercifully behold these thy servants now called to the Office of Priesthood, and replenish them so with the truth of thy doctrine, and adorn them with innocency of life, that, both by word and good example they may faithfully serve thee in this Office, to the glory of thy Name, and the edification of thy Church, through the merits of our Saviour Jesus Christ, who liveth and reigneth with thee and the holy Ghost, world without end. *Amen.*

The Epistle.°

UNTO every one of us is given grace, according to the measure of the gift of Christ. Wherefore he saith, When he ascended up on high, he led captivity captive, and gave gifts unto men. (Now that he ascended, what is it, but that he also descended first into the lower parts of the earth? He that descended, is the same also that ascended up far above all heavens, that he might fill all things.) And he gave some Apostles, and some Prophets, and some Evangelists, and some Pastors and Teachers, for the perfecting of the saints, for the work of the ministry, for the edifying of the body of Christ; till we all come in the unity of the faith, and of the knowledge of the Son of God, unto a perfect man, unto the measure of the stature of the fulness of Christ. *Eph.* 4.7

¶ *After this shall be read for the Gospel° part of the Ninth Chapter of Saint Matthew, as followeth.*

WHEN Jesus saw the multitudes, he was moved with compassion on them, because they fainted, and were scattered abroad, as sheep having no shepherd. Then saith he unto his disciples, The harvest truly is plenteous, but the labourers are few. Pray ye therefore the Lord of the harvest, that he will send forth labourers into his harvest. *Matt.* 9.36

¶ *Or else this that followeth out of the Tenth Chapter of Saint John.*

VERILY verily I say unto you, He that entreth not by the door into the sheep-fold, but climbeth up some other way, the same is a thief and a robber. But he that entreth in by the door, is the shepherd of the sheep. To him the porter openeth, and the sheep hear his voice; and he calleth his own sheep by name, and leadeth them out. And when he putteth forth his own sheep, he goeth before them, and the sheep follow him; for they know his voice. And a stranger will they not follow, but will flee from him; for they know not the voice of strangers. This parable spake Jesus unto them, but they understood not what things they were which he spake unto them. Then said Jesus unto them again, Verily verily I say unto you, I am the door of the sheep. All that ever came before me are thieves and robbers, but the sheep did not hear them. I am the door, by me if any man enter in, he shall be saved, and shall go in and out, and find pasture. The thief cometh not but for to steal, and to kill, and to destroy: I am come that they might have life, and that they might have it more abundantly. I am the good Shepherd: the good Shepherd giveth his life for the sheep. But he that is an hireling and not the shepherd, whose own the sheep are not, seeth the wolf coming, and leaveth the sheep, and fleeth; and the wolf catcheth them, and scattereth the sheep. The hireling fleeth because he is an hireling, and careth not for the sheep. I am the good Shepherd, and know my sheep, and am known of mine. As the Father knoweth me, even so know I the Father; and I lay down my life for the sheep. And other sheep I have which are not of this fold: them also I must bring, and they shall hear my voice; and there shall be one fold, and one shepherd. *John* 10.1

¶ *Then the Bishop sitting in his Chair shall minister unto every one of them the Oath concerning the Kings Supremacy, as it is before set forth in the Form for the Ordering of Deacons.*

¶ *And that done, he shall say unto them as hereafter followeth.*

YOU have heard, brethren,° as well in your private examination, as in the exhortation which was now made to you, and in the holy Lessons taken out of the Gospel, and the writings of the Apostles, of what dignity, and of how great importance this Office is, whereunto ye are called. And now again we exhort you, in the Name of our Lord Jesus Christ, that you have in remembrance into how high a dignity, and to how weighty an office and charge ye are called: That is to say, to be messengers, watchmen, and stewards of the Lord; to teach and to premonish, to feed and provide for the Lords family; to seek for Christs sheep that are dispersed abroad, and for his children who are in the midst of this naughty world, that they may be saved through Christ for ever.

Have always therefore printed in your remembrance, how great a treasure is committed to your charge. For they are the sheep of Christ, which he bought with his death, and for whom he shed his bloud. The Church and Congregation whom you must serve, is his spouse, and his body. And if it shall happen the same Church, or any member thereof, to take any hurt or hindrance by reason of your negligence, ye know the greatness of the fault, and also the horrible punishment that will ensue. Wherefore consider with your selves the end of your ministry towards the children of God, towards the spouse and body of Christ; and see that you never cease your labour, your care and diligence, until you have done all that lieth in you, according to your bounden duty, to bring all such as are or shall be committed to your charge, unto that agreement in the faith and knowledge of God, and to that ripeness and perfectness of age in Christ, that there be no place left among you, either for errour in Religion, or for viciousness in Life.

Forasmuch then as your Office is both of so great excellency, and of so great difficulty, ye see with how great care and study ye ought to apply your selves, as well that ye may shew your selves dutiful and thankful unto that Lord who hath placed you in so high a dignity; as also to beware that neither you your selves offend, nor be occasion that others offend. Howbeit ye cannot have a mind and will thereto of your selves; for that will and ability is given of God alone: Therefore ye ought, and have need to pray earnestly for his holy Spirit. And seeing that you cannot by any other means compass the doing of so weighty a work, pertaining to the salvation of man, but with doctrine and exhortation taken out of the holy Scriptures, and with a life agreeable to the same; consider how studious ye ought to be in reading and learning the Scriptures, and in framing the manners both of your selves, and of them that specially pertain unto you, according to the rule of the same Scriptures: And for this self-same cause, how ye ought to forsake and set aside (as much as you may) all worldly cares and studies.

We have good hope that you have well weighed and pondered these things with your selves, long before this time; and that you have clearly determined, by Gods grace, to give your selves wholly to this Office, whereunto it hath pleased God to call you: So that as much as lieth in you, you will apply your selves wholly to this one thing, and draw all your cares and studies this way; and that you will continually pray to God the Father, by the mediation of our onely Saviour Jesus Christ, for the heavenly assistance of the holy Ghost; that, by daily reading and weighing of the Scriptures, ye may wax riper and stronger in your ministry, and that ye may so endeavour your selves from time to time, to sanctifie the lives of you and yours, and to fashion them after the rule and doctrine of Christ, that ye may be wholsome and godly examples and patterns for the people to follow.

And now that this present congregation of Christ here assembled, may also understand your minds and wills in these things, and that this your promise may the more move you to do your duties; ye shall answer plainly to these things, which we in the Name of God, and of his Church, shall demand of you touching the same.

D O you think in your heart that you be truly called, according to the will of our Lord Jesus Christ, and the Order of this Church of England, to the Order and Ministry of Priesthood?

Answer. I think it.

The Bishop.

A RE you perswaded that the holy Scriptures contain sufficiently all Doctrine required of necessity for eternal salvation through faith in Jesus Christ? And are you determined out of the said Scriptures to instruct the people committed to your charge and to teach nothing (as required of necessity to eternal salvation) but that which you shall be perswaded may be concluded and proved by the Scripture?

Answer. I am so perswaded, and have so determined by Gods grace.

The Bishop.

W ILL you then give your faithful diligence always so to minister the Doctrine and Sacraments, and the Discipline of Christ, as the Lord hath commanded, and as this Church and Realm hath received the same, according to the Commandments of God; so that you may teach the people committed to your Cure and Charge, with all diligence to keep and observe the same?

Answer. I will so do by the help of the Lord.

The Bishop.

WILL you be ready with all faithful diligence to banish and drive away all erroneous and strange doctrines, contrary to Gods word; and to use both publick and private monitions and exhortations, as well to the sick, as to the whole within your Cures, as need shall require, and occasion shall be given?

Answer. I will, the Lord being my helper.

The Bishop.

WILL you be diligent in prayers, and in reading of the holy Scriptures, and in such studies as help to the knowledge of the same, laying aside the study of the world and the flesh?

Answer. I will endeavour my self so to do, the Lord being my helper.

The Bishop.

WILL you be diligent to frame and fashion your own selves and your families, according to the Doctrine of Christ; and to make both your selves and them, as much as in you lieth, wholsome examples and patterns to the flock of Christ?

Answer. I will apply my self thereto, the Lord being my helper.

The Bishop.

WILL you maintain and set forwards, as much as lieth in you, quietness, peace and love among all Christian people, and especially among them that are or shall be committed to your charge?

Answer. I will so do, the Lord being my helper.

The Bishop.

WILL you reverently obey your Ordinary, and other chief Ministers, unto whom is committed the charge and government over you; following with a glad mind and will their godly admonitions, and submitting your selves to their godly judgements?

Answer. I will so do, the Lord being my helper.

¶ *Then, shall the Bishop standing up, say,*

ALMIGHTY God, who hath given you this will to do all these things, Grant also unto you strength and power to perform the same; that he may accomplish his work which he hath begun in you, through Jesus Christ our Lord. *Amen.*

¶ *After this the Congregation shall be desired, secretly in their prayers to make their humble supplications to God for all these things: For the which prayers there shall be silence kept for a space.*

¶ *After which shall be sung or said by the Bishop (the persons to be Ordained Priests, all kneeling)* Veni, Creator Spiritus; *the Bishop beginning, and the Priests and others that are present, answering by Verses, as followeth.*

COME, holy Ghost, our souls inspire,°
   And lighten with celestial fire.
Thou the anointing Spirit art,
   Who dost thy sevenfold gifts impart.
Thy blessed Unction from above,
   Is comfort, life, and fire of love.
Enable with perpetual light
   The dulness of our blinded sight.
Anoint and cheer our soiled face
   With the abundance of thy grace.
Keep far our foes, give peace at home:
   Where thou art guide, no ill can come.
Teach us to know the Father, Son,
   And thee, of both, to be but one.
That through the ages all along,
   This may be our endless song;
      Praise to thy eternal merit,
      Father, Son, and Holy Spirit.

¶ *Or this:*

COME, holy Ghost, eternal God,°
   proceeding from above,
Both from the Father and the Son,
   the God of peace and love.

Visit our minds, into our hearts
   thy heavenly grace inspire,
That truth and godliness we may
   pursue with full desire.

Thou art the very Comforter
   in grief and all distress;
The heavenly gift of God most high,
   no tongue can it express.

The fountain and the living spring
   of Joy celestial:
The fire so bright, the love so sweet,
   the Unction spiritual.

Thou in thy gifts art manifold,
   by them Christs Church doth stand:
In faithful hearts thou writ'st thy law,
   the finger of Gods hand.

According to thy promise, Lord,
   thou givest speech with grace,
That through thy help Gods praises may
   resound in every place.

O holy Ghost, into our minds
   Send down thy heavenly light;
kindle our hearts with fervent zeal,
   to serve God day and night.

Our weakness strengthen and confirm
   (for Lord, thou knowst us frail)
That neither devil, world nor flesh,
   against us may prevail.

Put back our enemy far from us,
   and help us to obtain
Peace in our hearts with God and man
   (the best, the truest gain;)

And grant that thou being, O Lord,
   our leader and our guide,
We may escape the snares of sin,
   and never from thee slide.

Such measures of thy powerful grace
   grant, Lord, to us, we pray,
That thou maist be our comforter
   at the last dreadful day.

Of strife and of dissension
dissolve, O Lord, the bands,
And knit the knots of peace and love,
throughout all Christian lands.

Grant us the grace that we may know
the Father of all might,
That we of his beloved Son
may gain the blisful sight,

And that we may with perfect faith
ever acknowledge thee,
The Spirit of Father, and of Son,
one God in persons three.

To God the Father, laud and praise,
and to his blessed Son,
And to the holy Spirit of grace,
Co-equal Three in One.

And pray we, that our only Lord
would please his spirit to send
On all that shall profess his Name,
from hence to the worlds end.

Amen.

¶ *That done, the Bishop shall pray in this wise, and say,*

Let us pray.

ALMIGHTY God and heavenly Father,° who, of thine infinite love
and goodness towards us, hast given to us thy only and most
dearly beloved Son Jesus Christ, to be our Redeemer, and the Authour
of everlasting life; who after he had made perfect our Redemption by
his death, and was ascended into heaven, sent abroad into the world
his Apostles, Prophets, Evangelists, Doctors and Pastors, by whose
labour and ministry he gathered together a great flock in all the parts
of the world, to set forth the eternal praise of thy holy Name: For
these so great benefits of thy eternal goodness, and for that thou hast

vouchsafed to call these thy servants here present, to the same Office and Ministry appointed for the salvation of mankind, we render unto thee most hearty thanks, we praise and worship thee; and we humbly beseech thee by the same thy blessed Son, to grant unto all, which either here or elsewhere call upon thy holy Name, that we may continue to shew our selves thankful unto thee for these and all other thy benefits, and that we may daily encrease and go forwards in the knowledge and faith of thee and thy Son, by the Holy Spirit. So that as well by these thy Ministers, as by them over whom they shall be appointed thy Ministers, thy holy Name may be for ever glorified, and thy blessed Kingdom enlarged, through the same thy Son Jesus Christ our Lord, who liveth and reigneth with thee in the unity of the same holy Spirit, world without end. *Amen.*

¶ *When this Prayer is done, the Bishop, with the Priests present, shall lay their hands severally upon the head of every one° that receiveth the Order of Priesthood; the receivers humbly kneeling upon their knees, and the Bishop saying,*

RECEIVE the holy Ghost° for the Office and work of a Priest in the Church of God, now committed unto thee by the Imposition of our hands. Whose sins thou dost forgive, they are forgiven; and whose sins thou dost retain, they are retained. And be thou a faithful Dispenser of the Word of God, and of his holy Sacraments; in the Name of the Father, and of the Son, and of the holy Ghost. Amen.

¶ *Then the Bishop shall deliver to every one of them kneeling the Bible°
into his hand, saying,*

TAKE thou Authority to preach the Word of God, and to minister the holy Sacraments in the Congregation, where thou shalt be lawfully appointed thereunto.

¶ *When this is done, the Nicene Creed shall be sung or said, and the Bishop shall after that go on in the Service of the Communion, which all they that receive Orders shall take together, and remain in the same place where hands were laid upon them, until such time as they have received the Communion.*

¶ *The Communion being done, after the last Collect, and immediately before the Benediction, shall be said these Collects.*

MOST merciful Father, we beseech thee to send upon these thy servants, thy heavenly blessing, that they may be clothed with righteousness, and that thy word spoken by their mouths, may have such success, that it may never be spoken in vain. Grant also that we may have grace to hear and receive what they shall deliver out of thy most holy Word, or agreeable to the same, as the means of our salvation; that in all our words and deeds we may seek thy glory, and the increase of thy Kingdom; through Jesus Christ our Lord. *Amen.*

PREVENT us, O Lord, in all our doings with thy most gracious favour, and further us with thy continual help, that in all our works begun, continued, and ended in thee, we may glorifie thy holy Name, and finally by thy mercy obtain everlasting life, through Jesus Christ our Lord. *Amen.*

THE Peace of God which passeth all understanding, keep your hearts and minds in the knowledge and love of God, and of his Son Jesus Christ our Lord. And the blessing of God Almighty, the Father, the Son, and the holy Ghost be amongst you, and remain with you always. *Amen.*

¶ *And if on the same day the Order of Deacons be given to some, and the Order of Priesthood to others; The Deacons shall be first presented, and then the Priests: and it shall suffice that the Litany be once said for both. The Collects shall both be used; first that for Deacons, then that for Priests. The Epistle shall be* Ephesians iv. 7–13, *as before in this Office. Immediately after which, they that are to be made Deacons, shall take the Oath of Supremacy, and be Examined and Ordained, as is above prescribed. Then one of them having read the Gospel (which shall be either out of* St. Matthew ix. 36–38, *as before in this Office; or else* St. Luke xii. 35–38, *as before in the Form for the Ordering of Deacons) they that are to be made Priests shall likewise take the Oath of Supremacy, and be Examined and Ordained, as is in this Office before appointed.*

The Form of Ordaining or Consecrating of an
ARCH-BISHOP, or BISHOP;
Which is always to be performed upon some
Sunday or Holy-day.

¶ *When all things are duly prepared in the Church, and set in Order; after*
Morning Prayer is ended, the Arch-Bishop (or some other Bishop appointed)
shall begin the Communion-Service; in which this shall be

The Collect.

ALMIGHTY God, who by thy Son Jesus Christ° didst give to thy
holy Apostles many excellent gifts, and didst charge them to feed
thy flock; Give grace, we beseech thee, to all Bishops, the Pastors
of thy Church, that they may diligently preach thy Word, and duly
administer the godly Discipline thereof; and grant to the people, that
they may obediently follow the same, that all may receive the crown of
everlasting glory, through Jesus Christ our Lord. *Amen.*

And another Bishop shall read the Epistle.

THIS is a true saying, If a man desire the Office of a Bishop, he
desireth a good work. A Bishop then must be blameless, the husband of one wife, vigilant, sober, of good behaviour, given to hospitality, apt to teach, not given to wine, no striker, not greedy of filthy
lucre; but patient, not a brawler, not covetous; one that ruleth well
his own house, having his children in subjection with all gravity; (For
if a man know not how to rule his own house, how shall he take care
of the church of God?) Not a novice, lest being lifted up with pride,
he fall into the condemnation of the devil. Moreover, he must have
a good report of them which are without, lest he fall into reproach,
and the snare of the devil. *1 Tim.* 3.1

¶ *Or this, for the Epistle.°*

FROM Miletus Paul sent to Ephesus, and called the elders of the
church. And when they were come to him, he said unto them,
Ye know from the first day that I came into Asia, after what manner
I have been with you at all seasons, serving the Lord with all humility
of mind, and with many tears and temptations which befell me by
the lying in wait of the Jews: And how I kept back nothing that was

profitable unto you, but have shewed you, and have taught you publickly, and from house to house, testifying both to the Jews, and also to
the Greeks repentance toward God, and faith toward our Lord Jesus
Christ. And now behold, I go bound in the Spirit unto Jerusalem, not
knowing the things that shall befall me there; save that the holy Ghost
witnesseth in every city, saying, That bonds and afflictions abide me.
But none of these things move me, neither count I my life dear unto
my self, so that I might finish my course with joy, and the ministry
which I have received of the Lord Jesus, to testifie the Gospel of
the grace of God. And now behold, I know that ye all among whom
I have gone preaching the Kingdom of God, shall see my face no
more. Wherefore I take you to record this day, that I am pure from
the bloud of all men. For I have not shunned to declare unto you all
the counsel of God. Take heed therefore unto your selves, and to all
the flock, over the which the holy Ghost hath made you Overseers,
to feed the Church of God, which he hath purchased with his own
bloud. For I know this, that after my departing, shall grievous wolves
enter in among you, not sparing the flock. Also of your own selves
shall men arise, speaking perverse things, to draw away disciples after
them. Therefore watch, and remember, that by the space of three
years I ceased not to warn every one night and day with tears. And
now, brethren, I commend you to God, and to the word of his grace,
which is able to build you up, and to give you an inheritance among
all them which are sanctified. I have coveted no mans silver or gold,
or apparel, yea, you your selves know, that these hands have ministred
unto my necessities, and to them that were with me. I have shewed
you all things, how that so labouring ye ought to support the weak,
and to remember the words of the Lord Jesus, how he said, It is more
blessed to give than to receive.   *Acts* 20.17

¶ *Then another Bishop shall read*°
The Gospel.

J ESUS saith to Simon Peter, Simon, son of Jonas, lovest thou me
more than these? He saith unto him, Yea, Lord, thou knowest that
I love thee. He saith unto him, Feed my lambs. He saith to him again
the second time, Simon, son of Jonas, lovest thou me? He said unto
him, Yea, Lord, thou knowest that I love thee. He saith unto him,
Feed my sheep. He saith unto him the third time, Simon, son of
Jonas, lovest thou me? Peter was grieved because he said unto him

the third time, Lovest thou me? And he said unto him, Lord, thou knowest all things; thou knowest that I love thee. Jesus saith unto him, Feed my sheep. *John* 21.15

¶ *Or else this.*

THE same day at evening, being the first day of the week, when the doors were shut, where the disciples were assembled for fear of the Jews, came Jesus and stood in the midst, and saith unto them, Peace be unto you. And when he had so said, he shewed unto them his hands and his side. Then were the disciples glad, when they saw the Lord. Then saith Jesus to them again, Peace be unto you: As my Father hath sent me, even so send I you. And when he had said this, he breathed on them, and saith unto them, Receive ye the holy Ghost. Whose soever sins ye remit, they are remitted unto them; and whose soever sins ye retain, they are retained. *John* 20.19

¶ *Or this.*

JESUS came and spake unto them, saying, All power is given unto me in heaven and in earth. Go ye therefore, and teach all nations, baptizing them in the Name of the Father, and of the Son, and of the holy Ghost: teaching them to observe all things whatsoever I have commanded you: And lo I am with you alway, even unto the end of the world. *Matt.* 28.18

¶ *After the Gospel, and the Nicene Creed, and the Sermon are ended, the Elected Bishop (vested with his Rotchet)° shall be presented by two Bishops unto the Arch-Bishop of that Province (or to some other Bishop appointed by lawful commission) the Arch-Bishop sitting in his chair near the holy Table,° and the Bishops that present him, saying,*

MOST REVEREND Father in God, we present unto you this godly and well-learned man, to be Ordained and Consecrated Bishop.

¶ *Then shall the Arch-Bishop demand the Kings Mandate for the Consecration, and cause it to be read. And the Oath touching the acknowledgement of the Kings Supremacy, shall be ministred to the persons Elected, as it is set down before in the Form for the Ordering of Deacons. And then shall also be ministred unto them the Oath of due obedience to the Arch-Bishop,° as followeth.*

The Oath of due obedience to the Archbishop

IN the Name of God, Amen. I, *N.*, chosen Bishop of the Church and See of *N.* do profess and promise all due reverence and obedience to the Archbishop, and to the Metropolitical Church of *N.* and to their Successors; So help me God, through Jesus Christ.

¶ *This Oath shall not be made at the Consecration of an Archbishop.*

¶ *Then the Archbishop shall move the Congregation present to pray, saying thus to them,*

BRETHREN, it is written in the Gospel of St. Luke, That our Saviour Christ continued the whole night in prayer, before he did choose and send forth his twelve Apostles. It is written also in the Acts of the Apostles, That the Disciples who were at Antioch, did fast and pray before they laid hands on Paul and Barnabas, and sent them forth. Let us, therefore, following the example of our Saviour Christ and his Apostles, first fall to prayer, before we admit and send forth this person presented unto us, to the work whereunto we trust the holy Ghost hath called him.

¶ *And then shall be said the Litany, as before, in the Form of Ordering Deacons, Save only, that after this place,* That it may please thee to illuminate all Bishops, &c., *the proper Suffrage there following, shall be omitted, and this inserted in stead of it;*

THAT it may please thee to bless this our brother Elected, and to send thy grace upon him, that he may duly execute the Office whereunto he is called, to the edifying of thy Church, and to the honour, praise and glory of thy Name.

Answer. We beseech thee to hear us, good Lord.

¶ *Then shall be said this Prayer following.*

ALMIGHTY God, giver of all good things, who by thy holy Spirit hast appointed divers Orders of Ministers in thy Church, mercifully behold this thy servant now called to the work and Ministry of a Bishop, and replenish him so with the truth of thy doctrine, and adorn him with innocency of life, that both by word and deed, he may faithfully serve thee in this Office, to the glory of thy Name, and the edifying and well governing of thy Church, through the merits of our Saviour Jesus Christ, who liveth and reigneth with thee and the same holy Ghost, world without end. *Amen.*

¶ *Then the Archbishop sitting in his chair, shall say to him that is to be Consecrated,*

BROTHER, forasmuch as the holy Scripture, and the ancient Canons command, that we should not be hasty in laying on hands, and admitting any person to government in the Church of Christ, which he hath purchased with no less price than the effusion of his own bloud; before I admit you to this Administration, I will examine you in certain Articles, to the end that the Congregation present may have a trial, and bear witness how you be minded to behave your self in the Church of God.

A RE you perswaded that you be truly called to this Ministration, according to the will of our Lord Jesus Christ, and the order of this Realm?

Answer. I am so perswaded.

The Archbishop.

A RE you perswaded that the holy Scriptures contain sufficiently all doctrine required of necessity for eternal salvation through faith in Jesus Christ? And are you determined out of the same holy Scriptures to instruct the people committed to your charge; and to teach or maintain nothing as required of necessity to eternal salvation, but that which you shall be perswaded may be concluded and proved by the same?

Answer. I am so perswaded and determined by Gods grace.

The Archbishop.

W ILL you then faithfully exercise your self in the same holy Scriptures, and call upon God by prayer, for the true understanding of the same; so as ye may be able by them to teach and exhort with wholsome doctrine, and to withstand and convince the gain-sayers?

Answer. I will so do, by the help of God.

The Archbishop.

B E you ready with all faithful diligence to banish and drive away all erroneous and strange Doctrine, contrary to Gods Word; and both privately and openly to call upon, and encourage others to the same?

Answer. I am ready, the Lord being my helper.

The Archbishop.

W ILL you deny all ungodliness and worldly lusts, and live soberly, righteously, and godly in this present world, that you may shew your self in all things an example of good works unto others, that the adversary may be ashamed, having nothing to say against you?

Answer. I will so do, the Lord being my helper.

The Archbishop.

WILL you maintain and set forward, as much as shall lie in you, quietness, love, and peace among all men; and such as be unquiet, disobedient, and criminous within your Diocess, correct and punish, according to such authority as you have by Gods Word, and as to you shall be committed by the Ordinance of this Realm?

Answer. I will so do, by the help of God.

The Archbishop.

WILL you be faithful in ordaining, sending, or laying hands upon others?

Answer. I will so be, by the help of God.

The Archbishop.

WILL you shew your self gentle, and be merciful for Christs sake to poor and needy people, and to all strangers destitute of help?

Answer. I will so shew my self, by Gods help.

Then the Archbishop standing up, shall say,

ALMIGHTY God, our heavenly Father, who hath given you a good will to do all these things, grant also unto you strength and power to perform the same; that he accomplishing in you the good work which he hath begun, you may be found perfect and irreprehensible at the latter day, through Jesus Christ our Lord. *Amen.*

¶ *Then shall the Bishop Elect put on the rest of the Episcopal habit, and kneeling down,* Veni, Creator Spiritus *shall be sung or said over him, the Archbishop beginning, and the Bishops, with others that are present, answering by Verses, as followeth.*

COME, Holy Ghost, our souls inspire,
  And lighten with celestial fire.
Thou the anointing Spirit art,
  Who dost thy sevenfold gifts impart.
Thy blessed Unction from above,
  Is comfort, life, and fire of love.
Enable with perpetual light
  The dulness of our blinded sight.
Anoint and cheer our soiled face
  With the abundance of thy grace.
Keep far our foes, give peace at home;
  Where thou art guide, no ill can come.

Teach us to know the Father, Son,
And thee, of both, to be but One;
That, through the ages all along,
This may be our endless song;
Praise to thy eternal merit,
Father, Son, and holy Spirit.

¶ *Or this.*

COME, Holy Ghost, eternal God, &c.

as before in the Form for Ordering Priests.

¶ *That ended, the Archbishop shall say,*

Lord, hear our prayer.
Answer. And let our cry come unto thee.

Let us pray.

ALMIGHTY God, and most merciful Father, who, of thine infinite goodness hast given thy only and dearly beloved Son Jesus Christ, to be our Redeemer, and the author of everlasting life; who after that he had made perfect our redemption by his death, and was ascended into heaven, poured down his Gifts abundantly upon men, making some Apostles, some Prophets, some Evangelists, some Pastors and Doctors, to the edifying and making perfect his Church; Grant, we beseech thee, to this thy servant such grace, that he may evermore be ready to spread abroad thy Gospel, the glad tidings of reconciliation with thee, and use the authority given him, not to destruction, but to salvation; not to hurt, but to help; so that as a wise and faithful servant, giving to thy family their portion in due season, he may at last be received into everlasting joy; through the same Jesus Christ our Lord, who, with thee and the Holy Ghost, liveth and reigneth, one God, world without end. *Amen.*

¶ *Then the Archbishop and Bishops present shall lay their hands upon the head of the Elected Bishop, kneeling before them upon his knees, the Archbishop saying,*

RECEIVE the holy Ghost, for the Office and work of a Bishop in the Church of God, now committed unto thee by the Imposition of our hands; In the Name of the Father, and of the Son, and of the holy Ghost. Amen. And remember that thou stir up the grace of God which is given thee by this Imposition of our hands: for God hath not given us the spirit of fear, but of power, and love, and soberness.

¶ *Then the Archbishop shall deliver him the Bible, saying,*

GIVE heed unto reading, exhortation and doctrine. Think upon the things contained in this Book. Be diligent in them, that the encrease coming thereby may be manifest unto all men. Take heed unto thy self, and to doctrine, and be diligent in doing them: for by so doing, thou shalt both save thyself and them that hear thee. Be to the flock of Christ a shepherd, not a wolf; feed them, devour them not. Hold up the weak, heal the sick, bind up the broken, bring again the outcasts, seek the lost. Be so merciful that ye be not too remiss; so minister discipline, that you forget not mercy, that when the chief Shepherd shall appear, ye may receive the never-fading crown of glory,° through Jesus Christ our Lord. *Amen.*

¶ *Then the Archbishop shall proceed in the Communion-Service; with whom the new Consecrated Bishop (with others) shall also communicate.*

¶ *And for the last Collect, immediately before the Benediction, shall be said these Prayers.*

MOST merciful Father, we beseech thee to send down, upon this thy servant thy heavenly blessing, and so endue him with thy holy Spirit, that he preaching thy Word, may not only be earnest to reprove, beseech, and rebuke with all patience and doctrine; but also may be to such as believe, a wholsome example in word, in conversation, in love, in faith, in chastity, and in purity; that faithfully fulfilling his course, at the latter day he may receive the crown of righteousness laid up by the Lord, the righteous judge, who liveth and reigneth one God with the Father and the holy Ghost, world without end. *Amen.*

PREVENT us, O Lord, in all our doings, with thy most gracious favour, and further us with thy continual help; that in all our works begun, continued and ended in thee, we may glorifie thy holy Name, and finally by thy mercy obtain everlasting life, through Jesus Christ our Lord. *Amen.*

THE Peace of God, which passeth all understanding, keep your hearts and minds in the knowledge and love of God, and of his Son Jesus Christ our Lord, And the blessing of God Almighty, the Father, the Son, and the holy Ghost be amongst you, and remain with you always. *Amen.*

A

Form of prayer with

Thanksgiving to be used yearly upon the Fifth day of
November. For the happy deliverance of the King, and
the Three Estates of the Realm, from the most Traiterous
and Bloudy intended Massacre by Gun-Powder.

¶ *The Service shall be the same with the usual Office for Holidays in all things;*
Except where it is hereafter otherwise appointed.

¶ *If this day shall happen to be a Sunday, only the Collect proper for that*
Sunday, shall be added to this Office in its place.

¶ *Morning Prayer shall begin with these Sentences*

TURN thy face away from our sins, O lord; and blot out all our
offences. *Ps.* 51.9

Correct us, O Lord, but with judgment, not in thine anger; lest
thou bring us to nothing. *Jer.* 10.14

I will go to my father, and will say unto him; Father, I have sinned
against heaven, and before thee; and am no more worthy to be called
thy son. *Luke* 15.18–19

¶ *Proper Psalms.* 35, 64, 124, 129.

¶ *Proper Lessons.* { *The first,* 2 Sam. 22
{ *The second,* Acts 23

¶ *In the Suffrages after the Creed, these shall be inserted and used for the*
King.

Priest. O Lord, save the King;
People. Who putteth his trust in thee.
Priest. Send him help from thy holy place.
People. And evermore mightily defend him.
Priest. Let his enemies have no advantage against him.
People. Let not the wicked approach to hurt him.

¶ *Instead of the First Collect at Morning Prayer, shall these two be used.*

ALMIGHTY God, who hast in all ages shewed thy power and mercy
in the miraculous and gracious deliverance of thy Church,
and in the protection of righteous and religious Kings and States,°
professing thy holy and eternal truth, from the wicked conspiracies,

and malicious practises of all the enemies thereof; We yield thee our unfeigned thanks and praise, for the wonderful and mighty deliverance of our late gracious Sovereign King *James*, the Queen, the Prince, and all the Royal Branches, with the Nobility, Clergy, and Commons of this Realm, then assembled in Parliament, by Popish treachery appointed as sheep to the slaughter, in a most barbarous, and savage manner, beyond the examples of former ages. From this unnatural conspiracy, not our merit, but thy mercy; not our foresight, but thy providence delivered us:° And therefore, not unto us, O Lord, not unto us; but unto thy Name be ascribed all honour and glory in all Churches of the saints, from generation to generation, through Jesus Christ our Lord. *Amen.*

O LORD, who didst this day discover the snares of death that were laid for us, and didst wonderfully deliver us from the same; Be thou still our mighty Protector, and scatter our enemies that delight in blood. Infatuate and defeat their counsels, abate their pride, asswage their malice, and confound their devices. Strengthen the hands of our gracious King *Charles*, and all that are put in authority under him, with Judgment and justice, to cut off all such workers of iniquity, as turn religion into rebellion,° and faith into faction; that they may never prevail against us, or triumph in the ruine of thy Church among us: But that our gracious Soveraign and his Realms, being preserved in thy true Religion, and by thy merciful goodness protected in the same, we may all duly serve thee, and give thee thanks in thy holy congregation, through Jesus Christ our Lord. *Amen.*

¶ *In the end of the Litany* (*which shall always this day be used*) *after the Collect* [We humbly beseech thee, O Father, &c.], *shall this be said which followeth.*

A LMIGHTY God, and heavenly Father, who of thy gracious providence, and tender mercy towards us, didst prevent the malice and imaginations of our enemies, by discovering and confounding their horrible and wicked enterprise, plotted, and intended this day to be executed against the King, and whole State of this Realm, for the subversion of the Government, and Religion established amongst us; We most humbly praise and magnifie thy glorious Name for this thine infinite gracious goodness towards us. We confess, it was thy mercy, thy mercy alone, that we were not then consumed. For our sins cried to heaven against us; and our iniquities justly called for vengeance upon us. But thou hast not dealt with us after our sins, nor rewarded us after our iniquities; nor given us over, as we deserved, to be a prey to our enemies; but didst in mercy deliver us from their malice, and preserve us from death and destruction. Let the consideration of this thy goodness, O Lord, work in us true repentance, that iniquity may not be our ruine. And increase in us more and more a lively faith, and fruitful love in all holy obedience, that thou maist continue thy favour, with the light of thy Gospel to us and our posterity for evermore; and that for thy dear Sons sake, Jesus Christ our only Mediatour and Advocate. *Amen.*

¶ *In the Communion Service, instead of the Collect for the Day, shall this which followeth, be used.*

ETERNAL God, and our most mighty protector, we thy unworthy servants do humbly present our selves before thy Majesty, acknowledging thy power, wisdom, and goodness in preserving the King, and the three Estates of this Realm assembled in Parliament,° from the destruction this day intended against them. Make us, we beseech thee, truly thankful for this thy great mercy towards us. Protect and defend our Soveraign Lord the King, and all the Royal Family from all treasons and conspiracies: Preserve them in thy faith, fear, and love; prosper his Reign with long happiness here on earth; and crown him with everlasting glory hereafter in the kingdom of heaven; through Jesus Christ our only Saviour and Redeemer. *Amen.*

The Epistle.   *Rom.* 13.1

LET every soul be subject unto the higher powers. For there is no power but of God: the powers that be, are ordained of God. Whosoever therefore resisteth the power, resisteth the ordinance of God: and they that resist, shall receive to themselves damnation. For rulers are not a terrour to good works, but to the evil. Wilt thou then not be afraid of the power? do that which is good, and thou shalt have praise of the same: For he is the minister of God to thee for good. But if thou do that which is evil, be afraid; for he beareth not the sword in vain: for he is the minister of God, a revenger to execute wrath upon him that doth evil. Wherefore ye must needs be subject, not only for wrath, but also for conscience sake. For, for this cause pay you tribute also: for they are Gods ministers, attending continually upon this very thing. Render therefore to all their dues; tribute to whom tribute is due, custom to whom custom, fear to whom fear, honour to whom honour.

The Gospel. *Matt.* 27.1

W HEN the morning was come, all the chief priests and elders of the people took counsel against Jesus to put him to death. And when they had bound him, they led him away, and delivered him to Pontius Pilate the governour. Then Judas which had betrayed him, when he saw that he was condemned, repented himself, and brought again the thirty pieces of silver to the chief priests and elders, saying, I have sinned, in that I have betrayed the innocent bloud. And they said, What is that to us? see thou to that. And he cast down the pieces of silver in the temple, and departed, and went and hanged himself. And the chief priests took the silver pieces, and said, It is not lawful for to put them into the treasury, because it is the price of bloud. And they took counsel, and bought with them the potters field, to bury strangers in. Wherefore that field was called, The field of bloud unto this day. Then was fulfilled that which was spoken by Jeremy the prophet, saying, And they took the thirty pieces of silver, the price of him that was valued, whom they of the children of Israel did value; and gave them for the potters field, as the Lord appointed me.

¶ *After the Creed, if there be no Sermon, shall be read one of the six Homilies against Rebellion.°*

¶ *This Sentence is to be read at the Offertory.*

W HATSOEVER ye would that men should do to you, do ye even so to them; for this is the law, and the prophets. *Matt.* 7.12

A
Form of Common Prayer,

to be used yearly upon the 30. day of *January*,
being the day of the Martyrdom of
K. CHARLES the First.

¶ *If this day shall happen to be Sunday, this Form of Service shall be used the next day following.*

¶ *The Service shall be the same with the usual Office for Holidays in all things; except where it is hereafter otherwise appointed.*

The Order for Morning Prayer.

¶ *He that ministreth, shall begin with one of these sentences.*

CORRECT us, O Lord, but with judgement, not in thine anger: lest thou bring us to nothing. *Jer.* 10.24

Rend your heart, and not your garments, and turn to the Lord your God: for he is gracious and merciful; slow to anger, and of great kindness; and repenteth him of the evil. *Joel* 2.13

It is of the Lords mercies that we are not consumed; because his compassions fail not. *Lam.* 3.22

¶ *Instead of* Venite Exultemus° *shall this Psalm following be used, one verse by the Priest, and another by the Clerk and People.*

O COME, let us worship, and fall down: and kneel before the Lord our maker. *Ps.* 95.6

Let us repent, and turn from our wickedness: and our sins shall be forgiven us. *Acts* 3.19

Let us turn every one from his evil way: and the Lord will turn from fierce anger, and we shall not perish. *Jonah* 3.8, 9

We acknowledge our faults: and our sins are ever before us. *Ps.* 51.3

We have provoked thine anger, O Lord: but there is mercy with thee, therefore shalt thou be feared. *Lam.* 3.42; *Ps.* 130.4

O shut not up our souls with sinners: nor our life with the blood-thirsty. *Ps.* 26.9

Thou hast promised, O Lord, that before we call, thou wilt answer: and whiles we are yet speaking, thou wilt hear. *Is.* 65.24

And now in the anguish of our souls we cry unto thee: Hear, Lord, and have mercy. *Bar.* 3.1

O Lord, rebuke us not in thine indignation: neither chasten us in thy displeasure. *Ps.* 6.1

For thy Names sake be merciful to our sin: for it is great. *Ps.* 25.10

Turn thy face from our sins: and put out all our misdeeds.

Make us clean hearts, O God: and renew a right spirit within us.

Deliver us from bloud-guiltiness, O God: thou that art the God of our salvation. *Ps.* 51.9, 10, 14

O deliver us, and be merciful to our sins: for thy Names sake. *Ps.* 79.9

O be favourable and gracious unto Sion: build thou the walls of Jerusalem. *Ps.* 51.18

So we that are thy people, and sheep of thy pasture, shall give thee

*thanks for ever: and will alway be shewing forth thy praise from gener-
ation to generation.* Ps. 79.14

Glory to the Father, and to the Son: and to the holy Ghost;

*As it was in the beginning, is now, and ever shall be: world without
end. Amen.*

¶ *Proper Psalms.* 7, 9, 10, 11

¶ *Proper Lessons.* { The first, 2 Sam. 1
The second, Matt. 27

¶ *Instead of the first Collect at Morning Prayer, this which followeth shall be
used.*

O MOST mighty God, terrible in thy judgments, and wonderful in
thy doings towards the children of men, who in thy heavy displeasure didst suffer the life of our late gracious Soveraign to be this
day taken away by wicked hands; We, thy unworthy servants, humbly
confess, that the sins of this Nation have been the cause° which hath
brought this heavy judgment upon us. But, O gracious God, when
thou makest inquisition for bloud, lay not the guilt of this innocent
bloud, (the shedding whereof nothing but the bloud of thy Son can
expiate) lay it not to the charge of the people of this Land, nor let it
ever be required of us, or our posterity. Be merciful, be merciful unto
thy people, whom thou hast redeemed; and be not angry with us for
ever; but pardon us for thy mercies sake, through the merits of thy
Son our Lord Jesus Christ. *Amen.*

¶ *In the end of the Litany* (*which shall always on this day be used*) *after the
Collect* [We humbly beseech thee, O Father, &c.] *These three Collects are
to be used.*

O LORD, we beseech thee, mercifully hear our prayers, and spare
all those who confess their sins unto thee, that they whose consciences by sin are accused, by thy merciful pardon may be absolved,
through Christ our Lord. *Amen.*

O MOST mighty God, and merciful Father, who hast compassion
upon all men, and hatest nothing that thou hast made, who
wouldest not the death of a sinner, but that he would rather turn from
his sin, and be saved; Mercifully forgive us our trespasses, receive and
comfort us, who are grieved and wearied with the burthen of our sins.
Thy property is always to have mercy, to thee only it appertaineth to
forgive sins; Spare us therefore good Lord, spare thy people whom

thou hast redeemed; enter not into judgment with thy servants, who are vile earth, and miserable sinners: but so turn thine anger from us, who meekly acknowledge our vileness, and truly repent us of our faults; and so make haste to help us in this world, that we may ever live with thee in the world to come, through Jesus Christ our Lord. *Amen.*

¶ *Then shall the people say this that followeth, after the Minister.*

TURN thou us, O good Lord, and so shall we be turned: Be favourable, O Lord, Be favourable to thy people, Who turn to thee in weeping, fasting and praying: For thou art a merciful God, Full of compassion, Long-suffering, and of great pity. Thou sparest, when we deserve punishment, And in thy wrath thinkest upon mercy. Spare thy people, good Lord, spare them, And let not thine heritage be brought to confusion. Hear us, O Lord, for thy mercy is great, And after the multitude of thy mercies look upon us: Through the merits and mediation of thy blessed Son Jesus Christ our Lord. *Amen.*

¶ *In the Communion-Service, immediately after the Commandments shall this Collect be used.*

O ALMIGHTY Lord, and everlasting God; Vouchsafe, we beseech thee, to direct, sanctifie, and govern both our hearts and bodies in the ways of thy laws, and in the works of thy commandments; that through thy most mighty protection both here and ever, we may be preserved in body and soul; through our Lord and Saviour Jesus Christ. *Amen.*

¶ *Then shall follow the Prayer for the King,* [Almighty God, whose Kingdom is everlasting, &c.] *And after that, these two collects instead of that for the day.*

BLESSED Lord, in whose sight the death of thy saints is precious; We magnifie thy Name for that abundant grace bestowed upon our late Martyred Soveraign; by which he was enabled so chearfully to follow° the steps of his blessed Master and Saviour, in a constant meek suffering of all barbarous indignities, and at last resisting unto bloud; and even then, according to the same pattern, praying for his murtherers. Let his memory, O Lord, be ever blessed among us, that we may follow the example of his patience, and charity: And grant, that this our Land may be freed from the vengeance of his bloud,° and thy mercy glorified in the forgiveness of our sins; and all for Jesus Christ his sake. *Amen.*

G RANT, Lord, we beseech thee, that the course of this world may be so peaceably ordered by thy governance, that thy Church may joyfully serve thee in all godly quietness, through Jesus Christ. *Amen.*

The Epistle. 1 *Pet.* 2.13

S UBMIT your selves to every ordinance of man for the Lords sake; whether it be to the King, as supream; or unto governours, as unto them that are sent by him for the punishment of evil doers, and for the praise of them that do well. For so is the will of God, that with wel-doing ye may put to silence the ignorance of foolish men: As free, and not using your liberty for a cloak of maliciousness, but as the servants of God. Honour all men. Love the brotherhood. Fear God. Honour the King. Servants be subject to your masters with all fear, not only to the good and gentle, but also to the froward. For this is thank-worthy, if a man for conscience toward God endure grief, suffering wrongfully. For what glory is it, if when ye be buffeted for your faults, ye shall take it patiently? but if when ye do well, and suffer for it, ye take it patiently; this is acceptable with God. For even hereunto were ye called; because Christ also suffered for us, leaving us an example, that ye should follow his steps;° who did no sin, neither was guile found in his mouth.

The Gospel. *Matt.* 21.33

T HERE was a certain housholder which planted a vineyard, and hedged it round about, and digged a wine-press in it, and built a tower, and let it out to husbandmen, and went into a far countrey. And when the time of the fruit drew near, he sent his servants to the husbandmen, that they might receive the fruits of it. And the husbandmen took his servants, and beat one, and killed another, and stoned another. Again, he sent other servants, moe than the first: and they did unto them likewise. But last of all, he sent unto them his son, saying, They will reverence my son. But when the husbandmen saw the son, they said among themselves, This is the heir, come, let us kill him, and let us seize on his inheritance. And they caught him, and cast him out of the vineyard, and slew him. When the lord therefore of the vineyard cometh, what will he do unto those husbandmen? They say unto him, He will miserably destroy those wicked men, and will let out his vineyard unto other husbandmen, which shall render him the fruits in their seasons.

¶ *After the Prayer,* [For the whole state of Christs Church, &c.] *this Collect shall be used.*

O LORD, our heavenly Father, who dost not punish us as our sins have deserved, but hast in the midst of judgment remembred mercy; We acknowledge it thy special favour, that though for our many and great provocations thou didst suffer thine Anointed to fall this day into the hands of violent and bloud-thirsty men,° and barbarously to be murthered by them; yet thou didst not leave us for ever as sheep without a shepherd, but by thy gracious providence didst miraculously preserve the undoubted heir of his Crown, our most gracious Soveraign King *CHARLES* the Second, from his bloudy enemies, hiding him under the shadow of thy wings, until their tyranny was overpast, and bringing him back in thy good appointed time to sit in peace upon the throne of his Father, and to exercise that authority over us, which of thy special grace thou hadst committed unto him. For these thy great and unspeakable mercies we render thee most humble thanks from the bottom of our hearts, beseeching thee still to continue thy gracious protection over him, and to grant him a long and happy reign over us: So we that are thy people, will give thee thanks for ever, and will alway be shewing forth thy praise from generation to generation, through Jesus Christ our Lord. *Amen.*

The Order for Evening Prayer.

Proper Psalms. 38, 64, 143

¶ *Proper Lessons.* { *The First, Jer.* 41.9 *or Dan.* 9.1–22
{ *The Second, Heb.* 11.32 *to* 12.7

¶ *Instead of the first Collect of Evening Prayer, use the two which follow.*

O BLESSED Lord God, who by thy wisdom not only guidest and orderest all things most suitably to thine own justice, but also performest thy pleasure in such a manner, that we cannot but acknowledge thee to be righteous in all thy ways, and holy in all thy works; We thy sinful people fall down before thee, confessing that thy judgments were right in permitting cruel men, sons of Belial,° this day to imbrue their hands in the bloud of thine Anointed; we having drawn down the same upon our selves, by the great and long provocations of our sins against thee; For which we do therefore here humble our selves before thee, imploring thy mercy for the pardon of them all; and that thou wouldst deliver this Nation from bloud-guiltiness° (that of this day especially) and turn from us and our posterity all those judgments which we by our sins have deserved: Grant this for the all-sufficient merits of thy Son, our Saviour Jesus Christ. *Amen.*

B LESSED God, just, and powerful, who didst permit thy dear servant, our late dread Soveraign, to be this day given up to the violent outrages of wicked men, to be despightfully used, and at last murthered by them; Though we cannot reflect upon so foul an act but with horrour and astonishment; yet do we most gratefully commemorate the glories of thy grace, which then shined forth in thine Anointed, whom thou wert pleased, even at the hour of death, to endue with an eminent measure of exemplary patience, meekness, and charity, before the face of his cruel enemies. And albeit, thou didst suffer them to proceed to such a height of violence against him, as to kill his person, and take possession of his throne; yet didst thou in great mercy preserve his son, whose right it was, and at length by a wonderful providence bring him back, and set him thereon, to restore thy true Religion, and to settle peace among us: For which, we glorifie thy Name, through Jesus Christ our blessed Saviour. *Amen.*

¶ *Immediately before the Prayer of Chrysostom, shall this Collect be used.*

A LMIGHTY and everlasting God, whose righteousness is like the strong mountains, and thy judgments like the great deep; and who, by that barbarous murder this day committed upon the sacred person of thine Anointed, our late Soveraign, hast taught us, that neither the greatest of kings, nor the best of men are more secure from violence, than from natural death; Teach us also hereby so to number our days, that we may apply our hearts unto wisdom. And grant that neither the splendour of any thing that is great, nor the conceit of any thing that is good in us, may any way withdraw our eyes from looking upon our selves as sinful dust and ashes; but that (according to the example of this thy blessed Martyr) we may press forward towards the prize of the high calling that is before us, in faith and patience, humility and meekness, mortification and self-denial, charity and constant perseverance unto the end: And all this for thy Son our Lord Jesus Christs sake; To whom, with thee, and the holy Ghost be all honour and glory, world without end. *Amen.*

A Form of PRAYER with THANKSGIVING

To be used yearly on the 29. day of *May*
Being the day of His Majesties Birth, and happy
Return to His Kingdoms.

¶ *The Service shall be the same with the usual Office for Holidays in all things; except where it is hereafter otherwise appointed.*

¶ *If this day shall happen to be Ascension-day, Whitsunday, or Trinity-Sunday, only the Collects of this Office are to be added to the several Services for those Festivals in their proper places. If it shall happen to be any other Sunday, or to be Munday, or Tuesday in Whitsun-week, the Collects shall be used as before, and also the proper Psalms here appointed, instead of those of ordinary course, and all the rest of this office omitted.*

¶ *Morning Prayer shall begin with this Sentence*

I EXHORT that, first of all supplications, prayers, intercessions, and giving of thanks be made for all men; for kings, and all that are in Authority, that we may lead a quiet and peaceable life in all godliness and honesty; For this is good and acceptable in the sight of God our Saviour. *1 Tim. 2.1, 2, 3*

¶ *Instead of* Venite Exultemus, *shall be said or sung the Hymn following; one Verse by the Priest, and another by the Clerk and people.*

O COME let us sing unto the Lord: let us heartily rejoyce in the strength of our salvation. *Ps. 95.1*

Let us come before his presence with thanksgiving: and shew our selves glad in him with psalms. 2

For the Lord is a great God: and a great King above all gods. 3

With his own right hand, and with his holy arm: hath he gotten himself the victory. *Ps. 98.2*

The Lord declared his salvation: his righteousness hath he openly shewed in the sight of the heathen. 3

He hath remembered his mercy and truth towards the house of Israel: and all the ends of the world have seen the salvation of our God. 4

For he hath found David his servant: with his holy oyl hath he anointed him. *Ps. 89.21*

His hand hath held him fast: and his arm hath strengthned him. 22

The enemy hath not been able to do him violence: the son of wickedness hath not hurt him. 23

He hath smitten down his foes before his face: and plagued them that hated him. 24

His truth also, and his mercy hath been with him: and in his Name is his horn exalted. 25

He hath set his dominion also in the sea: and his right hand in the flouds. 26

Therefore all the Kings of the earth shall praise thee, O Lord: for they have heard the words of thy mouth. *Ps.* 138.4

Yea, they shall sing in the ways of the Lord: that great is the glory of the Lord. 5

My mouth also shall speak the praise of the Lord: and let all flesh give thanks unto his holy name for ever and ever. *Ps.* 145.21

Glory to the Father, and to the Son: and to the Holy Ghost;

As it was in the beginning, is now, and ever shall be: world without end. Amen.

¶ *Proper Psalms, 20, 21, 85, 118*

¶ *Proper Lessons.* { *The First, 2 Sam.* 19.9
{ *The Second, Rom.* 13

¶ *In the Suffrages after the Creed there shall be inserted and used for the King.*

Priest. O Lord, save the King.

People. Who putteth his trust in thee.

Priest. Send him help from thy holy place.

People. And evermore mightily defend him.

Priest. Let his enemies have no advantage against him.

People. Let not the wicked approach to hurt him.

¶ *Instead of the first Collect for Morning Prayer these two shall be used.*

O LORD God of our salvation, who hast been exceedingly gracious unto this land, and by thy miraculous providence hast delivered us out of our late miserable confusions,° by restoring to us our dread Soveraign Lord, thy servant, King *CHARLES*; We are now here before thee with all due thankfulness to acknowledge thine unspeakable goodness this day shewed unto us, and to offer up our sacrifices of praise unto thy glorious Name; humbly beseeching thee to accept this our unfeigned, though unworthy oblation of our selves; vowing all holy obedience in thought, word, and work unto thy divine Majesty; and promising in thee, and for thee all loyal and dutiful allegiance to thine Anointed servant, and to his heirs after him: whom we beseech thee to bless with all encrease of grace, honour, and happiness in this world, and to crown with immortality and glory in the world to come; for Jesus Christ his sake, our only Lord and Saviour. *Amen.*

O GOD, who by thy divine providence and goodness didst this day first bring into this world, and didst this day also bring back and restore to us,° and to his own just and undoubted rights our most gracious Soveraign Lord thy servant King *CHARLES*; Preserve his life, and establish his throne, we beseech thee. Be unto him a helmet of salvation against the face of his enemies, and a strong tower of defence in the time of trouble. Let his Reign be prosperous, and his days many. Let justice, truth, and holiness; let peace, and love, and all Christian vertues flourish in his time. Let his people serve him with honour and obedience; and let him so duly serve thee on earth, that he may hereafter everlastingly reign with thee in heaven, through Jesus Christ our Lord. *Amen.*

¶ *In the end of the Litany (which shall always this day be used) after the Collect* [We humbly beseech thee, O Father, &c.] *shall this be said which followeth.*

O LORD God, most merciful Father, who of thine especial grace and favour didst this day bring home unto us thy servant King *CHARLES* our Soveraign, and place him in the throne of this Kingdom, thereby restoring to us the publick and free profession of thy true Religion and worship,° to the great comfort and joy of our hearts; We thine unworthy servants, here assembled together to celebrate the memory of this thy mercy, most humbly beseech thee to grant us grace, that we may always shew our selves truly and unfeignedly thankful unto thee for the same: And that our gracious King may through thy mercy continue his Reign over us in all vertue, godliness, and honour, many, and many years; and that we dutifully obeying him, as faithful and loyal subjects, may long enjoy him with the continuance of thy great blessings, which by him thou hast vouchsafed unto us, through Jesus Christ our Lord. *Amen.*

¶ *Immediately before the Prayer of Chrysostom, use the Collect of Thanksgiving,* [for Peace, and Deliverance from our enemies].

O ALMIGHTY God, who art a strong tower of defence unto thy servants against the face of their enemies; We yield thee praise and thanksgiving for our deliverance from those great and apparent dangers wherewith we were compassed. We acknowledge it thy goodness that we were not delivered over as a prey unto them; beseeching thee still to continue such thy mercies towards us, that all the world may know that thou art our Saviour and mighty deliverer, through Jesus Christ our Lord. *Amen.*

¶ *In the Communion Service between the Commandments and the Epistle, shall these two Collects be used, instead of the Collect for the King, and that of the day.*

O MOST gracious God, and merciful Father, who hast by thy infinite power and goodness safely and quietly, after so many and great troubles and adversities, setled thy servant our Soveraign Lord King *CHARLES* in the throne of his Fathers, (notwithstanding all the power and malice of his enemies) restoring unto us with him, and by him the free profession of thy sacred truth and Gospel, together with our former peace and prosperity; We beseech thee to grant him the defence of thy salvation, and to shew forth thy loving kindness, and mercy to him; and to stir up continually in our hearts all faithful duty and loyalty towards him, with a religious obedience, and thankfulness unto thee for these and all other thy mercies, through Jesus Christ our Lord. *Amen.*

GRANT, we beseech thee, Almighty God, that our Soveraign Lord the King, whom thou didst this day happily bring home, and restore to us, may be a mighty protector of his people, a religious defender of thy sacred Faith, and of thy holy Church among us, a glorious conquerour over all his enemies, a gracious governour unto all his subjects, and a happy father of many children to rule this Nation by succession in all ages, through Jesus Christ our Lord. *Amen.*

The Epistle 1 *Pet.* 2.11

DEARLY beloved, I beseech you as strangers and pilgrims, abstain from fleshly lusts, which war against the soul; having your conversation honest among the Gentiles: that whereas they speak against you as evil-doers, they may by your good works which they shall behold, glorifie God in the day of visitation. Submit your selves to every ordinance of man for the Lords sake; whether it be to the King, as supream; or unto governours, as unto them that are sent by him for the punishment of evil-doers, and for the praise of them that do well. For so is the will of God, that with well-doing ye may put to silence the ignorance of foolish men: As free, and not using your liberty for a cloak of maliciousness, but as the servants of God. Honour all men. Love the brotherhood. Fear God. Honour the King.

The Gospel   Matt. 22.16

A ND they sent out unto him their disciples, with the Herodians, saying, Master, we know that thou art true, and teachest the way of God in truth, neither carest thou for any man; for thou regardest not the person of men. Tell us therefore, What thinkest thou? Is it lawful to give tribute unto Cesar, or not? But Jesus perceived their wickedness, and said, Why tempt ye me, ye hypocrites? Shew me the tribute-money. And they brought unto him a peny. And he saith unto them, Whose is this image and superscription? They say unto him, Cesars. Then saith he unto them, Render therefore unto Cesar, the things which are Cesars; and unto God, the things that are Gods. When they had heard these words, they marvelled, and left him, and went their way.

¶ *After the Prayer* [For the whole state of Christs Church, &c.] *this Collect following shall be used.*

O LORD our God, who upholdest and governest all things in heaven and earth; Receive our humble prayers with our thanks-givings for our Soveraign Lord *CHARLES*, set over us by thy grace and providence to be our King: And so, together with him, bless the whole Royal Family with the dew of thy heavenly Spirit, that they, ever trusting in thy goodness, protected by thy power, and crowned with thy gracious and endless favour, may continue before thee in health, peace, joy, and honour, a long and happy life upon earth, and after death obtain everlasting life and glory in the kingdom of heaven, by the merits and mediation of Christ Jesus our Saviour; who with the Father, and the holy Spirit, liveth and reigneth ever one God, world without end. *Amen.*

FINIS.

APPENDIX A

From *THE BOKE OF COMMON PRAYER* (1552)

'The Black Rubric'

[from *The order for the administracion of the Lordes supper, or holye Communion*]

*A*LTHOUGH *no ordre can be so perfectlye devised, but it may be of some, eyther for theyr ignoraunce and infermitie, or els of malice and obstinacie, misconstrued, depraved, and interpreted in a wrong part:°And yet because brotherly charitie willeth, that so much as conveniently may be, offences shoulde be taken awaye: therefore we willing to doe the same. Whereas it is ordeyned in the booke of common prayer, in the administracion of the Lordes Supper, that the Communicants knelyng shoulde receyve the holye Communion:° whiche thynge beyng well mente, for a sygnificacion of the humble and gratefull acknowledgyng of the benefites of Chryst, geven unto the woorthye receyver, and to avoyde the prophanacion and dysordre, which about the holy Communion myght els ensue: Leste yet the same kneelyng myght be thought or taken otherwyse, we dooe declare that it is not ment thereby, that any adoracion is doone, or oughte to bee doone,° eyther unto the Sacramentall bread or wyne there bodily receyved, or unto anye reall and essencial presence there beeyng of Christes naturall fleshe and bloude.° For as concernynge the Sacramentall bread and wyne, they remayne styll in theyr verye naturall substaunces, and therefore may not be adored, for that were Idolatrye to be abhorred of all faythfull christians. And as concernynge the naturall body and blood of our saviour Christ, they are in heaven and not here. For it is agaynst the trueth of Christes true natural bodye, to be in moe places then in one, at one tyme.*

APPENDIX B

ADDITIONAL ORDERS OF SERVICE, ARTICLES, AND TABLES, 1662–1685

AT THE HEALING

The Gospel.   *Mark* 16.14

JESUS appeared unto the Eleven as they sat at meat, and cast in their teeth their unbelief and hardness of heart, because they believed not them which had seen that he was risen again from the dead. And he said unto them, Go ye into all the world, and preach the Gospel to all Creatures: He that Believeth and is Baptized, shall be Saved; but he that believeth not, shall be damned. And these Tokens shall follow them that believe: In my Name shall they cast out devils, they shall speak with new tongues, they shall drive away serpents, and if they drink any deadly thing, it shall not hurt them: †*They shall lay their hands on the Sick, and they shall recover.* So when the Lord had spoken unto them, he was received into heaven, and is on the right hand of God: And they went forth, and preached every where, the Lord working with them, and confirming the word with miracles following.

† *Here the infirm persons are presented to the King upon their knees, and the King layeth his hands upon them.*

The Gospel.   *John* 1.1

IN the beginning was the Word, and the Word was with God, and God was the Word. The same was in the beginning with God. All things were made by it, and without it was made nothing that was made. In it was life, and the life was the light of men, and the Light shined in the darkness, and the darkness comprehended it not. There was sent from God a man whose name was JOHN. The same came as a witness, to bear witness of the Light, that all men through him might believe. He was not that Light, but was sent to bear witness of the Light. ‡*That Light was the true Light, which lighteth every man that cometh into the world.* He was in the World, and the World was made by him, and the World knew him not. He

‡ *Here they are again presented unto the King upon their knees, and the King putteth his Gold about their necks.*°

came among his own, and his own received him not. But as many as received him, to them gave he power to be made the Sons of God, even them that believed on his Name: which were born not of blood, nor of the will of the flesh, nor yet of the will of man, but of God. And the same Word became Flesh, and dwelt among us, and we saw the Glory of it, as the glory of the only begotten Son of the Father, full of grace and truth.

The Prayers.

Verse. Lord have mercy upon us.
Response. Lord have mercy upon us.
Verse. Christ have mercy upon us.
Response. Christ have mercy upon us.
Verse. Lord have mercy upon us.
Response. Lord have mercy upon us.

OUR Father which art in heaven, Hallowed be thy Name. Thy kingdom come. Thy will be done on earth, As it is in heaven. Give us this day our daily bread. And forgive us our trespasses, As we forgive them that trespass against us. And lead us not into temptation: But deliver us from evil. Amen.

Verse. O Lord save thy Servants.
Response. Which put their trust in thee.†   † *These Answers are*
Verse. Send help unto them from above.   *to be made by them*
                                             that come to be healed.
Response. And evermore mightily defend them.
Verse. Help us, O God our Saviour.
Response. And for the glory of thy Name deliver us, be merciful unto us sinners for thy Names sake.
Verse. O Lord hear our Prayer.
Response. And let our cry come unto thee.

O ALMIGHTY God, who art the Giver of all health, and the Ayd of them that seek to Thee for succour, we call upon thee for thy help and goodness mercifully to be shewed unto these thy servants, that they being healed of their infirmity, may give thanks unto thee, in thy holy Church, through Jesus Christ our Lord. *Amen.*

THE GRACE of our Lord Jesus Christ, and the love of God, and the fellowship of the holy Ghost, be with us evermore. Amen.

Forms of Prayer

to be used yearly on the second of *September*,
for the dreadful fire of *London*.

*The service shall be the same with the usual office for holy days in all things,
except where it is hereafter otherwise appointed.*

The Order for Morning Prayer.

¶ *Let him that ministreth read with a loud voice these sentences of
Scripture.*

To the Lord God belong mercies and forgivenesses, though we
have rebelled against him: neither have we obeyed the voice of
the Lord our God, to walk in his laws which he set before us.
Dan. 9.9–10

O Lord correct us, but with judgment; not in thine anger, lest thou
bring us to nothing. *Jer.* 10.24

¶ *Instead of* [Venite, exultemus], *shall be sung or said this Hymn following; one verse by the Priest, and another by the Clerk and People.*

O COME let us humble our selves, and fall down before the Lord:
with reverence and fear. *Ps.* 95.6–7

*For he is the Lord our God: and we are the people of his pasture, and
the sheep of his hand.*

Come, therefore, let us turn again unto our Lord: for he hath smitten us, and he will heal us. *Hos.* 6.1

*Let us repent and turn from our wickedness: and our sins shall be for-
given us.* *Acts* 3

Let us turn, and the Lord will turn from his heavy wrath: and will
pardon us, and we shall not perish. *John* 3

*We acknowledge indeed, that our punishments are less then our deserv-
ings: but yet of thy mercy, O Lord, correct us to amendment, and plague
us not to our destruction.* *Job* 11.6; *Wisd.* 11.23

We have provoked thine anger, thy wrath is waxed hot: and thy
heavy displeasure is sore kindled against us. *Lam.* 3

*How doth the city sit solitary, that was full of thy people? how is she
become as a widow, she that was great among the nations, and Princess
among the provinces?* *Lam.* 1.1

How hath the Lord covered the daughter of Sion with a cloud in his anger: and cast down from heaven unto the earth the beauty of Israel, and remembred not his footstool in the day of his anger.   *Lam.* 2.1

He hath cut off in his fierce anger the horn of Israel, and consumed all that was pleasant to the eye: in the tabernacle of the daughter of Sion he poured out his fury like fire.   *Lam.* 2.4

The Lord was an enemy; he hath swallowed up Israel, he hath swallowed up all her palaces: he hath destroyed his strong holds; and hath increased in the daughter of Judah mourning and lamentations.   *Lam.* 2.5

But thy hand is not shortned that thou canst not help: neither is thy goodness abated, that thou wilt not hear.   *Isa.* 59.1

Thou hast promised, O Lord, that before we cry, thou wilt hear us: whilst we are yet speaking thou wilt have mercy upon us.

Isa. 65.24; *Job* 5.18

For thou art the only Lord, who woundest and dost heal again: thou killest and revivest; bringest even to hell, and bringest back again. *Hos.* 6.2

Thou forgivest all our sins: and healest all our infirmities. *Ps.* 103.3

Thou savest our life from destruction: and crownest us with mercy and loving kindness.   *Ps.* 103.4

Our fathers hoped in thee: they trusted in thee, and thou didst deliver them.   *Ps.* 22.4

They called upon thee and were holpen: they put their trust in thee, and were not confounded.   *Ps.* 22.5

And now in the vexation of our spirits, and the anguish of our souls we cry unto thee: hear, Lord, and have mercy.   *Bar.* 3.1–2

For many troubles are come about us: our sins have taken such hold upon us, that we are not able to look up.   *Ps.* 50.15

O remember not our sins, and our offences: but according to thy mercy think thou upon us, O Lord, for thy goodness.   *Ps.* 25.6

Hide not thy face from us in the time of our trouble: encline thine ears unto us when we call; O hear us, and that right soon.   *Ps.* 102.2

For thine own sake, and for thy holy names sake, encline thine ear: and hear, O merciful Lord.   *Dan.* 9.18–9

For we do not present our supplications before thee, trusting in our own righteousness: but in thy manifold and great mercies.

Help us, O God of our salvation, for the glory of thy name: O deliver us, and be merciful unto our sins, for thy names sake.   *Ps.* 79.9

So we that are thy people, and sheep of thy pasture, shall give thee

thanks for ever: and will always be shewing forth thy praise from gener-
ation to generation.   *Ps.* 79.14

Glory be to the Father and to the Son: and to the holy Ghost.

As it was in the beginning, is now and ever shall be: world without end.
Amen.

Proper Psalms; 25, 77, 86.

The first Lesson is, Isaiah the first chapter.

¶ *After the first lesson shall follow* Te Deum laudamus *in English.*

The second Lesson is S. Luke 21.

¶ *After the second Lesson shall follow* Benedictus *in English.*

¶ *Instead of the first Collect at morning prayer, shall be used the Collect for*
Ashwednesday.

¶ *After the Litany (which is always to be used on this day) the Priest and Clerk,*
or he that ministers (still kneeling in the place where they are accustomed
to say or sing the Litany) shall there repeat Psalm 51 *and then shall be*
used the suffrages, and prayers (all but the last) immediately following the
Commination.

L OOK down, O Lord, in the bowels of thy mercy, upon the sorrows
and distresses of thy servants, who in the depest sense of thy
amazing judgments, and our own manifold provocations, lie prostrate
in the dust before thee.

To thee, O God, holy, and true, belong mercy and forgiveness; but
unto us confusion of face as it is this day: For we are that incorrigible
nation who have resisted thy judgments, and abused thy mercies; we
have despised the chastisements of the Lord; and turned his grace
into wantonness.

What shall we then say unto thee, O thou preserver of men? thou
hast found out the iniquity of thy servants, and discovered our nakedness and pollution, in a vengeance suited and answerable to our
grievous crying sins. Our pride, oppression, and fulness of bread, had
made us like to Sodom, and thou hast afflicted us as Gomorrha. We
would not be reclaimed by thy exemplary punishments upon others
or our selves, and thou hast made us a terrour and astonishment to all
that are round about us.

And now, O Lord, thou art most just in all that is come upon us;
for thou hast done right, but we have done very wickedly; yet behold
we are all thy people, though an unthankful and a rebellious people:

suffer us therefore to implore thy pity, and the sounding of thy bowels, and for thy names sake, and for thy mercies sake; for Christ Jesus sake encline thine ear to us and save us.

Above all, we beseech thee, abandon us not to our selves; but by what method soever it shall please thee to reduce us, though to this bitter cup of trembling thou shalt add more and more grievous afflictions, by any the severest course, subdue us unto thy self, and make us see the things belonging to our peace, before they be hid from our eyes, that being duely humbled under thy mighty hand, We may be capable of being relieved and exalted in thy due time, through Christ our Lord. *Amen.*

In the Communion Service, in stead of the Collect for the day, shall be used the Collect for Ash-wednesday.

The Epistle 1 *Corinthians* 10 *verse* 1 *to* 14.

The Gospel. S. Luke 17. *verse* 26.

After the Sermon shall follow these Sentences.

L ET your light so shine before men, that they may see your good works, and glorifie your Father which is in heaven. *Matt.* 5.16

Blessed be the man that provideth for the sick, and needy: the Lord shall deliver him in the time of trouble. *Ps.* 41.1

After the Prayer [For the whole state of Christs Church, &c.]
this Collect shall be used.

W E bless and magnifie thy name, O Lord, for that wonderful mercy thou hast vouchsafed us in the midst of thy just and dreadful judgments. It is of thy goodness that we are not consumed; That when we had provoked thee to give us all up to utter ruine and desolation, and thy hand was stretched out to execute thy whole displeasure upon us: yet thou hast preserved a remnant, and plucked us as a brand out of the fire, that we should not utterly perish in our sins. Add, we beseech thee, this one mercy to all that thou hast hitherto so unsuccessfully cast away upon us: by thy mighty convincing spirit awaken our sleepy consciences, soften and melt our hard hearts, that being humbled by thy chastisements, we may by thy goodness be led to repentance, and sin no more, lest a worse thing happen unto us; but contrariwise may faithfully improve this respite and relief, with all its precious advantages and opportunities, to a thankful, humble, profitable walking before thee, that so thy Name may be glorified, the Gospel credited, and our souls saved in the day of the Lord: Grant this, O Father, for Jesus Christs sake our onely Mediatour and Redeemer. *Amen.*

¶ *Here may be added the Collects for the second and fourth Sunday in Lent, one, or both together, with the Collect* [Almighty God, who hath promised, *&c.*] *at the end of the Communion Service, and then the Priest shall let them depart with this blessing, The peace of God, &c.*

The thirty nine Articles of Religion.

1. *Of faith in the Holy Trinity.*

THERE is but one living and true God, everlasting, without body, parts, or passions; of infinite power, wisdom, and goodness; the maker and preserver of all things both visible and invisible. And in unity of this Godhead there be three persons, of one substance, power, and eternity; the Father, the Son, and the Holy Ghost.

2. *Of the Word or Son of God, which was made very man.*

THE Son, which is the Word of the Father, begotten from everlasting of the Father, the very and eternal God of one substance with the Father, took mans nature in the Womb of the blessed Virgin, of her substance: so that two whole and perfect natures, that is to say, the Godhead and manhood, were joyned together in one person, never to be divided, whereof is one Christ, very God and very man, who truly suffered, was crucified, dead and buried, to reconcile his Father to us, and to be a sacrifice, not only for original guilt, but also for actual sins of men.

3. *Of the going down of Christ into Hell.*

AS Christ died for us, and was buried so also is it to be believed, that he went down into hell.

4. *Of the resurrection of Christ.*

CHRIST did truly rise again from death, and took again his body, with flesh, bones, and all things appertaining to the perfection of mans nature, wherewith he ascended into heaven, and there sitteth, until he return to judge all men at the last day.

5. *Of the Holy Ghost.*

THE Holy Ghost, proceeding from the Father and the Son, is of one Substance, Majesty, and Glory, with the Father and the Son, very and eternal God.

6. *Of the sufficiency of the holy Scriptures for salvation.*

HOLY Scriptures containeth all things necessary to salvation: so that whatsoever is not read therein, nor may be proved thereby, is not to be required of any man, that it should be believed as an article of the faith, or be thought requisite or necessary to salvation. In the name of holy Scripture, we do understand those Canonical books of the Old and New Testament, of whose authority was never any doubt in the Church.

Of the Names and Number of the Canonical Books.

Genesis.	*The* 1. *book of Chronicles.*
Exodus.	*The* 2. *book of Chronicles.*
Leviticus.	*The* 1. *book of Esdras.*
Numeri.	*The* 2. *book of Esdras.*
Deuteronomium.	*The book of Hester.*
Josue.	*The book of Job.*
Judges.	*The Psalms.*
Ruth.	*The Proverbs.*
The 1. *book of Samuel.*	*Ecclesiastes, or the Preacher.*
The 2. *book of Samuel.*	*Cantica, or Songs of Solomon.*
The 1. *book of Kings.*	*Four Prophets the Greater.*
The 2. *book of Kings.*	*Twelve Prophets the Less.*

And the other books (as *Hierom* saith) the Church doth read for example of life and instruction of manners; but yet doth it not apply them to establish any Doctrine; such are these following:

The 3. *book of Esdras.*	*Baruch the Prophet.*
The 4. *book of Esdras.*	*The song of the three Children.*
The book of Tobias.	*The story of Susanna.*
The book of Judith.	*Of Bel and the Dragon.*
The rest of the book of Hester.	*The Prayer of Manasses.*
The book of Wisdom.	*The* 1. *book of Maccabees.*
Jesus the son of Sirach.	*The* 2. *book of Maccabees.*

All the books of the New Testament, as they are commonly received, we do receive and account them Canonical.

7. *Of the Old Testament.*

THE Old Testament is not contrary to the New: for both in the Old and New Testament, everlasting life is offered to mankind by Christ, who is the only Mediator between God and man, being both God and man. Wherefore they are not to be heard, which feign that the old Fathers did look only for transitory promises. Although the law given from God by Moses, as touching Ceremonies and Rites, do not bind Christian men, nor the civil Precepts thereof ought of necessity to be received in any Commonwealth; yet notwithstanding, no Christian man whatsoever is free from the obedience of the Commandments which are called Moral.

8. *Of the three Creeds.*

THE three Creeds, *Nicene* Creed, *Athanasius* Creed, and that which is commonly called the *Apostles* Creed, ought thoroughly to be received and believed: for they may be proved by most certain warrants of Holy Scripture.

9. *Of Original or Birth Sin.*

ORIGINAL sin standeth not in the following of *Adam* (as the Pelagians do vainly talk) but it is the fault and corruption of the nature of every man, that naturally is engendered of the off-spring of *Adam*, whereby man is very far gone from original righteousness, and is of his own nature inclined to evil, so that the flesh lusteth always contrary to the spirit; and therefore in every person born into this world, it deserveth Gods wrath and damnation. And this infection of nature doth remain, yea, in them that are regenerated, whereby the lust of the flesh, called in Greek φρόνημα σαρκὸς, which some do expound the wisdom, some sensuality, some the affection, some the desire of the flesh, is not subject to the law of God. And although there is no condemnation for them that believe and are baptized, yet the Apostle doth confess, that concupiscence and lust hath of it self the nature of sin.

10. *Of Free-Will.*

THE condition of man after the fall of *Adam* is such, that he cannot turn and prepare himself by his own natural strength and good works to faith and calling upon God: wherefore we have no power to do good works pleasant and acceptable to God, without the grace of God by Christ preventing us, that we may have a good will, and working with us when we have that good will.

11. *Of the Justification of man.*

WE are accounted righteous before God, only for the merit of our Lord and Saviour Jesus Christ by faith, and not for our own works, or deservings. Wherefore, that we are justified by faith only, is a most wholsom Doctrine, and very full of comfort, as more largely is expressed in the Homily of Justification.

12. *Of good Works.*

ALBEIT that good works, which are the fruits of faith, and follow after Justification, cannot put away our sins, and endure the severity of Gods judgment, yet are they pleasing and acceptable to God in Christ, and do spring out necessarily of a true and lively faith, insomuch that by them a lively faith may be as evidently known, as a tree discerned by the fruit.

13. *Of Works before Justification.*

WORKS done before the grace of Christ and the inspiration of his Spirit, are not pleasant to God, forasmuch as they spring not of Faith in Jesus Christ, neither do they make men meet to receive grace, or (as the School-authors say) deserve grace of congruity: yea, rather for that they are not done as God hath willed and commanded them to be done, we doubt not but they have the nature of sin.

14. *Of Works of Supererogation.*

VOLUNTARY Works besides, over and above Gods Commandments, which they call Works of Supererogation, cannot be taught without arrogancy and impiety. For by them men do declare, That they do not only render unto God as much as they are bound to do, but that they do more for his sake than of bounden duty is required: Whereas Christ saith plainly, When ye have done all that are commanded to you, say, We are unprofitable servants.

15. *Of Christ alone without Sin.*

CHRIST in the truth of our nature, was made like unto us in all things (sin only except), from which he was clearly void, both in his flesh and in his spirit. He came to be a lamb without spot, Who by sacrifice of himself once made, should take away the sins of the world: and sin, as St. *John* saith, was not in him. But all we the rest (although baptized and born again in Christ) yet offend in many things, and if we say we have no sin, we deceive our selves, and the truth is not in us.

16. *Of Sin after Baptism.*

NOT every deadly sin willingly committed after Baptism, is sin against the Holy Ghost, and unpardonable. Wherefore the grant of repentance is not to be denied to such as fall into sin after Baptism. After we have received the Holy Ghost, we may depart from Grace given, and fall into sin, and by the grace of God (we may) arise again, and amend our lives. And therefore they are to be condemned, which say they can no more sin as long as they live here, or deny the place of forgiveness to such as truly repent.

17. *Of Predestination and Election.*

PREDESTINATION to life, is the everlasting purpose of God, whereby (before the foundations of the world were laid) he hath constantly Decreed by his Counsel, secret to us, to deliver from curse and damnation, those whom he hath chosen in Christ out of mankind, and to bring them by Christ to everlasting salvation, as vessels made to honour. Wherefore they which be endued with so excellent a benefit of God, be called according to Gods purpose by his Spirit working in due season: they through grace obey the calling: they be justified freely: they be made sons of God by adoption: they be made like the image of his only begotten Son Jesus Christ: they walk religiously in good works: and at length by Gods mercy they attain to everlasting felicity.

As the godly consideration of Predestination and our Election in Christ, is full of sweet, pleasant, and unspeakable comfort to godly persons, and such as feel in themselves the working of the Spirit of Christ, mortifying the works of the flesh, and their earthly members, and drawing up their mind to high and heavenly things, as well because it doth greatly establish and confirm their faith of eternal salvation, to be enjoyed through Christ, as because it doth fervently kindle their love towards God: so for curious and carnal persons, lacking the Spirit of Christ, to have continually before their eyes the sentence of Gods Predestination, is a most dangerous downfal, whereby the devil doth thrust them either into desperation, or into wretchlessness of most unclean living, no less perilous than desperation.

Furthermore, we must receive Gods promises in such wise as they be generally set forth to us in holy Scripture: and in our doings, that will of God is to be followed, which we have expressly declared unto us in the word of God.

18. *Of obtaining eternal Salvation only by the name of Christ.*

THEY also are to be had accursed that presume to say, that every man shall be saved by the law or sect which he professeth, so that he be diligent to frame his life according to that law, and the light of nature. For holy Scripture doth set out to us only the name of Jesus Christ, whereby men must be saved.

19. *Of the Church.*

THE visible Church of Christ is a Congregation of faithful men, in the which the pure word of God is Preached and the Sacraments be duly Ministred, according to Christs Ordinance, in all those things that of necessity are requisite to the same.

As the Church of *Jerusalem, Alexandria,* and *Antioch* have erred: so also the Church of *Rome* hath erred, not only in their living and manner of Ceremonies, but also in matters of Faith.

20. *Of the Authority of the Church.*

THE Church hath power to decree Rites or Ceremonies and Authority in Controversies of Faith: and yet it is not lawful for the Church to ordain any thing contrary to Gods word written, neither may it so expound one place of Scripture, that it be repugnant to another. Wherefore although the Church be a witness and a keeper of Holy Writ, yet, as it ought not to Decree any thing against the same; so besides the same ought it not to enforce anything to be believed for necessity of salvation.

21. *Of the authority of General Councels.*

GENERAL Councels may not be gathered together without the commandment and will of Princes. And when they be gathered together (forasmuch as they be an assembly of men, whereof all be not governed with the Spirit and Word of God) they may err, and sometime have erred, even in things pertaining unto God. Wherefore things ordained by them as necessary to salvation, have neither strength nor authority, unless it may be declared that they be taken out of holy Scripture.

22. *Of Purgatory.*

THE Romish Doctrine concerning Purgatory, Pardons, Worshipping and Adoration as well of Images, as of Reliques, and also Invocation of Saints, is a fond thing, vainly invented, and grounded upon no warranty of Scripture, but rather repugnant to the word of God.

23. *Of ministring in the Congregation.*

IT is not lawful for any man to take upon him the Office of publick Preaching or Ministring the Sacraments in the Congregation, before he be lawfully called, and sent to execute the same. And those we ought to judge lawfully called and sent, which be chosen and called to this work by men who have publick Authority given unto them in the Congregation, to call and send Ministers into the Lords Vineyard.

24. *Of speaking in the Congregation, in such a Tongue as the people understandeth.*

IT is a thing plainly repugnant to the word of God, and the custom of the Primitive Church, to have publick Prayer in the Church, or to minister the Sacraments in a Tongue not understood of the people.

25. *Of the Sacraments.*

SACRAMENTS ordained of Christ, be not only badges or tokens of Christian mens profession: but rather they be certain sure witnesses, and effectual signs of grace, and Gods good will towards us, by the which He doth work invisibly in us, and doth not only quicken, but also strengthen and confirm our faith in Him.

There are two Sacraments ordained of Christ our Lord in the Gospel, that is to say, Baptism and the Supper of the Lord.

Those five commonly called Sacraments, that is to say, Confirmation, Penance, Orders, Matrimony, and Extreme Unction, are not to be counted for Sacraments of the Gospel, being such as have grown, partly of the corrupt following of the Apostles, partly are states of life allowed in the Scriptures: but yet have not the like nature of Sacraments with Baptism and the Lords Supper, for that they have not any visible sign or ceremony ordained of God.

The Sacraments were not ordained of Christ to be gazed upon, or to be carried about, but that we should duly use them. And in such only as worthily receive the same, they have a wholsom Effect or Operation: but they that receive them unworthily, purchase to themselves damnation, as St. *Paul* saith.

26. *Of the unworthiness of the Ministers, which hinders not the effect of the Sacraments.*

ALTHOUGH in the visible Church the evil be ever mingled with the good, and sometime the evil have chief authority in the ministration of the word and Sacraments; yet forasmuch as they do not the same in their own name, but in Christs, and do minister by His commission and authority, we may use their Ministry, both in hearing the word of God, and in the receiving of the Sacraments. Neither is the effect of Christs ordinance taken away by their wickedness, nor the grace of Gods gifts diminished from such, as by faith, and rightly do receive the Sacraments ministred unto them, which be effectual, because of Christs Institution and Promise, although they be ministred by evil men.

Nevertheless, it appertaineth to the discipline of the Church, that enquiry be made of evil Ministers, and that they be accused by those that have knowledge of their offences: and finally being found guilty, by just judgment be deposed.

27. *Of Baptism.*

BAPTISM is not only a sign of Profession, and mark of Difference, whereby Christian men are discerned from other that be not Christened: but it is also a sign of Regeneration or New Birth, whereby, as by an Instrument, they that receive Baptism rightly, are grafted into the church: the promises of the forgiveness of sin, and of our adoption to be the sons of God, by the holy Ghost, are visibly signed and sealed; faith is confirmed, and grace increased by vertue of prayer unto God. The Baptism of young children is in any wise to be retained in the Church, as most agreeable with the Institution of Christ.

28. *Of the Lords Supper.*

THE Supper of the Lord is not only a sign of the love that Christians ought to have among themselves one to another: but rather it is a Sacrament of our Redemption by Christs death: Insomuch that to such as rightly, worthily, and with faith receive the same, the Bread which we break, is a partaking of the Body of Christ: and likewise the Cup of blessing, is a partaking of the Blood of Christ.

Transubstantiation (or the change of the substance of Bread and Wine) in the Supper of the Lord, cannot be proved by holy Writ: but is repugnant to the plain words of Scripture, overthroweth the nature of a Sacrament, and hath given occasion to many superstitions.

The Body of Christ is given, taken, and eaten in the Supper only after an heavenly and spiritual manner. And the mean whereby the Body of Christ is received and eaten in the Supper, is Faith.

The Sacrament of the Lords Supper was not by Christs ordinance reserved, carried about, lifted up, or worshipped.

29. *Of the wicked which do not eat the body of Christ in the use of the Lords Supper.*

THE wicked and such as be void of a lively faith, although they do carnally and visibly press with their teeth (as St. *Augustine* saith) the Sacrament of the Body and Blood of Christ: yet in no wise are they partakers of Christ, but rather to their condemnation do eat and drink the Sign or Sacrament of so great a thing.

30. *Of both kinds.*

THE Cup of the Lord is not to be denied to the Lay-people: For both parts of the Lords Sacrament, by Christs Ordinance and Commandment, ought to be ministred to all Christian men alike.

31. *Of the one oblation of Christ finished upon the Cross.*

THE offering of Christ once made, is the perfect redemption, propitiation, and satisfaction for all the sins of the whole world, both original and actual, and there is none other satisfaction for sin, but that alone. Wherefore the Sacrifices of Masses, in the which it was commonly said that the priests did offer Christ for the quick and the dead, to have remission of pain or guilt, were blasphemous fables, and dangerous deceits.

32. *Of the Marriage of Priests.*

BISHOPS, Priests, and Deacons are not commanded by Gods Law, either to vow the estate of single life, or to abstain from marriage: therefore it is lawful for them, as for all other Christian men, to marry at their own discretion, as they shall judge the same to serve better to godliness.

33. *Of Excommunicate persons, how they are to be avoided.*

THAT person which by open denunciation of the Church, is rightly cut off from the unity of the Church, and excommunicated, ought to be taken of the whole multitude of the faithful, as an heathen and Publican, until he be openly reconciled by Penance, and received into the Church by a Judge that hath authority thereunto.

34. *Of the Traditions of the Church.*

IT is not necessary that Traditions and Ceremonies be in all places one, or utterly like; for at all times they have been divers, and may be changed according to the diversity of Countries, Times, and mens Manners, so that nothing be ordained against Gods word. Whosoever through his private judgment willingly and purposely doth openly break the Traditions and Ceremonies of the Church, which be not repugnant to the word of God, and be ordained and approved by common Authority, ought to be rebuked openly that other may fear to do the like, as he that offendeth against common Order of the Church, and hurteth the authority of the Magistrate, and woundeth the Consciences of the weak Brethren.

Every Particular or National Church hath authority to ordain, change, and abolish Ceremonies or Rites of the Church ordained only by mans Authority, so that all things be done to edifying.

35. *Of Homilies.*

THE second Book of Homilies, the several Titles whereof we have joyned under this Article, doth contain a godly and wholsom Doctrine, and necessary for these Times, as doth the former Book of Homilies, which were set forth in the time of *Edward* the Sixth, and therefore we judge them to be read in Churches by the Ministers diligently and distinctly, that they may be understood of the people.

Of the Names of the Homilies.

1. *Of the right Use of the Church.*
2. *Against peril of Idolatry.*
3. *Of the repairing and keeping clean of Churches.*
4. *Of good Works, first of Fasting.*
5. *Against Gluttony and Drunkenness.*
6. *Against excess of Apparel.*
7. *Of Prayer.*
8. *Of the place and time of Prayer.*
9. *That Common Prayers and Sacraments ought to be ministred in a known tongue.*
10. *Of the reverent estimation of Gods Word.*
11. *Of Alms-doing.*
12. *Of the Nativity of Christ.*
13. *Of the Passion of Christ.*
14. *Of the Resurrection of Christ.*
15. *For the worthy receiving of the Sacrament of the Body and Blood of Christ.*
16. *Of the Gifts of the Holy Ghost.*
17. *For the Rogation days.*
18. *Of the state of Matrimony.*
19. *Of Repentance.*
20. *Against Idleness.*
21. *Against Rebellion*

36. *Of Consecration of Bishops and Ministers.*

THE Book of Consecration of Archbishops and Bishops, and ordering of Priests and Deacons, lately set forth in the time of *Edward* the Sixth, and confirmed at the same time by Authority of Parliament, doth contain all things necessary to such Consecration and Ordering: neither hath it any thing that of it self is superstitious and ungodly. And therefore whosoever are Consecrate or Ordered according to the Rites of that book, since the second year of the aforenamed King *Edward*, unto this time, or hereafter shall be Consecrated or Ordered according to the same Rites, we decree all such to be rightly, orderly, and lawfully Consecrated and Ordered.

37. *Of the Civil Magistrates.*

THE Queens Majesty hath the chief Power in this Realm of *England* and other her Dominions, unto whom the chief Government of all Estates of this Realm, whether they be Ecclesiastical or Civil, in all Causes doth appertain, and is not, nor ought to be subject to any Foreign Jurisdiction.

Where we attribute to the Queens Majesty the chief Government, by which Titles we understand the minds of some slanderous folks to be offended: we give not to our Princes the ministring either of Gods Word, or of the Sacraments, the which thing the Injunctions also lately set forth by *Elizabeth* our Queen do most plainly testifie: but that only Prerogative which we see to have been given always to all godly Princes in holy Scriptures by God himself, *that is*, that they should rule all Estates and Degrees committed to their charge by God, whether they be Ecclesiastical or Temporal, and restrain with the Civil Sword the stubborn and evil doers.

The Bishop of *Rome* hath no jurisdiction in this realm of *England*.

The Laws of a Realm may punish Christian men with death for heinous and grievous offences.

It is lawful for Christian men, at the commandment of the Magistrate, to wear weapons, and serve in the wars.

38. *Of Christian mens goods, which are not common.*

THE Riches and Goods of Christians are not common, as touching the Right, Title, and Possession of the same, as certain Anabaptists do falsely boast: Notwithstanding, every man ought of such things as he possesseth, liberally to give Alms to the Poor, according to his ability.

39. *Of a Christian mans Oath.*

AS we confess that vain and rash swearing is forbidden Christian men by our Lord Jesus Christ, and *James* his Apostle: So we judge that Christian Religion doth not prohibit, but that a man may swear when the magistrate requireth, in a cause of faith and charity, so it be done according to the Prophets teaching, in Justice, Judgment, and Truth.

The Ratification.

*T*HIS *Book of Articles before rehearsed, is again approved, and allowed to be holden and executed within the Realm, by the assent and consent of our Sovereign Lady ELIZABETH, by the grace of God, of England, France, and* Ireland, *Queen, Defender of the Faith, &c. Which Articles were deliberately read, and confirmed again by the Subscription of the hand of the Archbishop and Bishops of the Upper House, and by the subscription of the whole Clergy of the Nether House in their Convocation, in the year of our Lord, 1571.*

A Table of Kindred and Affinity,

wherein whosoever are related, are forbidden in Scripture, and Our Laws to Marry together.

A Man may not marry his

1. *Grandmother,*
2. *Grandfathers wife.*
3. *Wives grandmother.*
4. *Fathers sister.*
5. *Mothers sister.*
6. *Fathers brothers wife.*
7. *Mothers brothers wife.*
8. *Wives fathers sister.*
9. *Wives mothers sister.*
10. *Mother.*
11. *Step-mother.*
12. *Wives mother.*
13. *Daughter.*
14. *Wives daughter.*
15. *Sons wife.*
16. *Sister.*
17. *Wives sister.*
18. *Brothers wife.*
19. *Sons daughter.*
20. *Daughters daughter.*
21. *Sons sons wife.*
22. *Daughters sons wife.*
23. *Wives sons daughter.*
24. *Wives daughters daughter.*
25. *Brothers daughter.*
26. *Sisters daughter.*
27. *Brothers sons wife.*
28. *Sisters sons wife.*
29. *Wives brothers daughter.*
30. *Wives sisters daughter.*

A Woman her

1. *Grandfather.*
2. *Grandmothers husband.*
3. *Husbands grandfather.*
4. *Fathers brother.*
5. *Mothers brother.*
6. *Fathers sisters husband.*
7. *Mothers sisters husband.*
8. *Husbands fathers brother.*
9. *Husbands mothers brother.*
10. *Father.*
11. *Step-father,*
12. *Husbands father.*
13. *Son.*
14. *Husbands son.*
15. *Daughters husband.*
16. *Brother.*
17. *Husbands brother.*
18. *Sisters husband.*
19. *Sons son.*
20. *Daughters son.*
21. *Sons daughters husband.*
22. *Daughters daughters husband.*
23. *Husbands sons son.*
24. *Husbands daughters son.*
25. *Brothers son.*
26. *Sisters son.*
27. *Brothers daughters husband.*
28. *Sisters daughters husband.*
29. *Husbands brothers son.*
30. *Husbands sisters son.*

EXPLANATORY NOTES

ABBREVIATIONS

BCP	*Book of Common Prayer*; individual versions are represented by the year in italics, e.g. *1549*, *1662*, etc.
BL	British Library
Blunt	J. H. Blunt, *The Annotated Book of Common Prayer*, rev. edn. (London: Rivingtons, 1872)
Breviarium	*Breviarium ad usum Sarum*, ed. F. Procter and C. Wordsworth, 3 vols. (Cambridge: Cambridge University Press, 1879–86) [text based on the 1531 printed ed. of Sarum]
Brightman	F. E. Brightman, *The English Rite*, 2 vols. (London: Rivingtons, 1915)
Canons (1604)	*Constitutions and Canons Ecclesiastical 1604*, ed. H. A. Wilson (Oxford: Clarendon Press, 1923)
Censura	*Martin Bucer and the Book of Common Prayer*, ed. E. C. Whitaker (Great Wakering: Alcuin Club, 1974)
Conferences	Edward Cardwell, *A History of Conferences Connected with the Revision of the Book of Common Prayer 1558–1690* (Oxford: Oxford University Press, 1861)
Cressy	David Cressy, *Birth, Marriage and Death: Ritual, Religion and the Life-Cycle in Tudor and Stuart England* (Oxford: Oxford University Press, 1997)
Duffy	Eamon Duffy, *The Stripping of the Altars: Traditional Religion in England 1400–1580* (New Haven and London: Yale University Press, 1992)
Durham Book	*The Durham Book: Being the First Draft of the Revision of the Book of Common Prayer in 1661*, ed. G. J. Cuming, University of Durham Publications (Oxford: Oxford University Press, 1961)
English Church Architecture	Francis Bond, *An Introduction to English Church Architecture*, 2 vols. (Oxford: Oxford University Press, 1913)
English Church Furniture	J. C. Cox and A. Harvey, *English Church Furniture* (London: Methuen, 1907)
Fincham and Tyacke	Kenneth Fincham and Nicholas Tyacke, *Altars Restored: The Changing Face of English Religious Worship, 1547–c.1700* (Oxford: Oxford University Press, 2007)
Gelasian Sacramentary	*The Gelasian Sacramentary: Liber Sacramentorum Romanae Ecclesiae*, ed. H. A. Wilson (Oxford: Clarendon Press, 1894)

Godly Order	*The Godly Order: Texts and Studies Relating to the Book of Common Prayer*, ed. Geoffrey Cuming, Alcuin Club (London: SPCK, 1983)
Green, *Christian's ABC*	Ian Green, *The Christian's ABC: Catechisms and Catechizing in England c.1530–1740* (Oxford: Clarendon Press, 1996)
Gregorian Sacramentary	*The Gregorian Sacramentary under Charles the Great*, ed. H. A. Wilson, Henry Bradshaw Society, 49 (London, 1915)
Hermann, *Consultation*	Hermann von Wied, *A simple and religious consultation of us Herman Archebishop of Colone* (London: John Day, 1548)
Hooper, *Early Writings*	John Hooper, *Early Writings*, ed. S. Carr, Parker Society (Cambridge: Cambridge University Press, 1843)
Hooper, *Later Writings*	John Hooper, *Later Writings*, ed. C. Nevinson, Parker Society (Cambridge: Cambridge University Press, 1852)
Hunt, 'Lay Baptism'	Arnold Hunt, 'The Debate on Lay Baptism in Early Modern England', *Past and Present* (forthcoming, 2011)
Hunt, 'Lord's Supper'	Arnold Hunt, 'The Lord's Supper in Early Modern England', *Past and Present*, 161 (1998), 39–83
KJV	King James Bible (the Authorized Version of 1611)
L & P	*Letters and Papers, Foreign and Domestic, of the Reign of Henry VIII*, ed. J. S. Brewer, J. Gairdner, and R. H. Brodie (London: HMSO, 1862–1932)
MacCulloch, *Cranmer*	Diarmaid MacCulloch, *Thomas Cranmer: A Life* (New Haven and London: Yale University Press, 1996)
Maltby	Judith Maltby, *Prayer Book and People in Elizabethan and Early Stuart England* (Cambridge: Cambridge University Press, 1998)
Manuale	*Manuale ad usum percelebris ecclesie Sarisburiensis*, ed. A. Jefferies Collins, Henry Bradshaw Society, vol. 91 (1960)
Marshall	Peter Marshall, *Beliefs and the Dead in Reformation England* (Oxford: Oxford University, 2002)
Mirk, *Festial*	John Mirk, *Festial: A Collection of Homilies*, ed. T. Erbe, Early English Texts Society (London, 1905)
Mirk, *Instructions*	John Mirk, *Instructions for Parish Priests*, ed. E. Peacock, Early English Texts Society (London, 1868)
Missale	*The Sarum Missal, Edited from Three Early Manuscripts*, ed. J. Wickham Legg (Oxford: Clarendon Press, 1916)
Original Letters	*Original Letters Relative to the English Reformation*, ed. H. Robinson, 2 vols. (Cambridge: Parker Society, 1846–7)
Processionale	*Processionale ad usum insignis ac praeclarae ecclesiae Sarum*, ed. W. G. Henderson (Leeds: McCorquodale, 1882)

Procter and Frere	F. Procter and W. H. Frere, *A New History of the Book of Common Prayer* (London: Macmillan, 1901)
Roodscreens and Roodlofts	F. B. Bond and Dom Bede Camm, *Roodscreens and Roodlofts*, 2 vols. (London: Pitman, 1909)
Statutes of the Realm	*The Statutes of the Realm: From Original Records and Authentic Manuscripts*, ed. A. Luders and others, 12 vols. (London: 1810–28)
Stow, Memoranda	John Stow, *Historical Memoranda*, Camden Society (London, 1880)
Stow, Survey	John Stow, *Survey of London*, ed. J. L. Kingsland, 2 vols. (Oxford: Clarendon Press, 1908)
Synodalia	Edward Cardwell, *A Collection of Articles of Religion, Canons, and Proceedings of Convocations 1547–1717* (Oxford: Oxford University Press, 1862)
Troubles	*Troubles Connected with the Prayer Book of 1549*, ed. N. Pocock, Camden Society, NS 37 (1884)
TRP	*Tudor Royal Proclamations*, ed. P. Hughes and J. Larkin, 3 vols. (New Haven: Yale University Press, 1964–9)
VAI	*Visitation Articles and Injunctions of the Period of the Reformation*, ed. W. H. Frere, 3 vols., Alcuin Club, 14–16 (London: Longmans, 1910)

THE BOOK OF COMMON PRAYER, 1549

The origins and printing of *1549* are traced in the Introduction, pp. xxii–xxxi, and the Note on the Texts, pp. liii–liv.

PREFACE

Cranmer's Preface is based on the preface to the reformed breviary by Cardinal Francisco Quiñones, undertaken on the order of Pope Clement VII and first printed in 1535. Cranmer's Latin draft of the Preface survives in his first (undated) attempt at a daily office, the *Festivale et horarum canonicarum series*, in BL MS Royal 7B.IV (*Cranmer's Liturgical Projects*, ed. J. Wickham Legg, Henry Bradshaw Society (London, 1915)). Cranmer contrives to borrow the authority of the Roman rite while also surreptitiously undermining it. The English version in the BCP is abridged from this draft (*Cranmer's Liturgical Projects*, 15–17) and tones down some of Cranmer's more outspoken adaptations of Quiñones.

    4 *hath not been corrupted*: Cranmer reverses the sense in Quiñones (which is a defence of church tradition in liturgy combined with a justification for revising it), and uses the idea of revision to mount an attack on the 'uncertein stories, Legendes, Respondes, Verses, vaine repeticions' (these terms are not in Cranmer's Latin draft, p. 15) that he claims have been allowed to adhere to scriptural sources.

4 *daily hearyng of holy scripture read in the Churche*: Cranmer's Latin draft for a reformed Prayer Book provided for the order of holy scripture to be presented in sequence 'entire and unbroken' through the year, with a scheme for reciting all 150 Psalms in each month. Two lessons are assigned for both Matins and Evensong, the OT beginning at Genesis in both cases, the NT at Matthew in Matins and at Romans in Evensong. The Psalter was printed in 1549 in editions for use in churches by Whitchurch, Grafton, and Oswen. Not until the Elizabethan period was a Psalter published to be bound in with a BCP.

in Latin to the people, whiche they understoode not: Cranmer began experimenting with the idea of English forms of service in the late 1530s (see Introduction, p. xxii). A single Primer in English was proposed under Henry VIII in 1545. A proclamation of 6 May 1545 (*TRP* i. 248) desired that 'our people and subjects which have no understanding in the Latin tongue . . . may pray in the vulgar tongue'.

a nocturne: a unit of psalms and lessons from the Bible (and other sources) used in Matins; the term is derived from the practice of saying this office at midnight in monasteries.

5 *the rules called the pie*: a term for a medieval Latin Ordinal (a book giving the order of rituals in the year), so called because it was printed in black-and-white ('magpie'), not in red.

here is drawen out a Kalendar: the Calendar in the medieval liturgy set out the sequence of scriptural readings through the church year, including major festivals and saints' days. The *1549* Kalendar greatly diminished the number of saints' days from the Roman rite, leaving the apostles and evangelists and other figures from the New Testament (see pp. 752–3).

some folowyng Salsbury use: by the sixteenth century the use of Salisbury ('Sarum'), a variant of the Roman rite, was by far the most common in English use: its relative importance can be gauged by the fact that printed editions of Sarum outnumbered the other uses by around ten to one.

the whole realme shall have but one use: an Act of Parliament of January 1549 prescribed 'Unyformytie of Service and Admynistracion of the Sacramentes throughout the Realme' (2 & 3 Ed. VI c.1, *Statutes of the Realm*, iv. 37). A proclamation of 25 December 1549 (*TRP* i. 353) ordered that all service books following the use of Sarum, Lincoln, York, Bangor, Hereford, and elsewhere should be turned in and destroyed, to reinforce the 'godly and uniform order which by a common consent is now set forth'.

MORNING PRAYER

The BCP orders for Matins and Evensong comprise a unit which corresponds to the Latin Breviary, the book which contained the divine Office (or 'hours'). Cranmer's scheme for a daily office of worship worked by collapsing five of the medieval hours into two forms of service, for morning and evening.

Duplications between the medieval hours were rationalized, and the 'little hours' of Terce, Sext, and Nones were removed. The vernacular Order for Morning Prayer merged the medieval hours of Matins (the monastic 'Vigils'), Lauds, and Prime. By 1549, practically every word used in this service was already in print in a variety of primers and occasional orders.

7 *The Priest beeyng in the quier*: the rubric was open to different interpretations in terms of vestments and the bodily movement and gesture of the priest; Bishop John Hooper's expressions of disapproval in his fourth sermon on Jonah in 1550 shows that many (perhaps most) priests kept to former practices (Hooper, *Early Writings*, 491–2). Martin Bucer in his *Censura* of the BCP in 1551 objected to the position of the priest in the choir as separating the clergy from the laity, being both 'anti-Christian' and hard to hear.

the Pater noster: the Latin name for the Lord's Prayer, being the first words, 'Our Father'. The practice of opening Morning Prayer with the *Pater noster* dates back at least to the ninth century, and appears in Sarum (*Breviarium*, ii. 1). The full English wording here follows the text of Matt. 6 in the King's Primer of 1545, although many phrases are older: e.g. 'Our Father' originates in Anglo-Saxon ('Fæder ure þu þe eart on heofonum'); and 'halwid be þi name' appears in the fourteenth-century Wyclifite Bible. The precise phraseology varied considerably in Primers in the 1530s; a list of variants is given in C. C. Butterworth, *The English Primers (1529–1545)* (Philadelphia: University of Pennsylvania Press, 1953), 301–3. The BCP form of the prayer (repeated in all services) effectively standardized usage until the 1960s. The vernacular term 'lordes prayer' is first found replacing the Latin *Pater noster* in a Primer in 1537 (ibid. 235). Thomas Cromwell's Injunctions of 1536 ordered instruction in the Lord's Prayer in English, along with the Ten Commandments and the Creed. However, vernacular versions of all three had been staple elements in catechism since the fourteenth century. The *Lay Folk's Catechism* was reissued by Wolsey in 1518 (Duffy, 54). As throughout *1549*, the source for much of Matins is in the Roman Office. However, the significance often lies as much in what is left out as what is left in. In the Sarum breviary, the *Pater noster* was an inaudible internal prayer, in *1549* it is uttered loudly. In Sarum it is followed by the *Ave Maria* (*Breviarium*, ii. 2); this is omitted in *1549*.

hallowed by thy name: the use of the pronoun 'thou/thy' in relation to God is for many modern readers the most distinctive feature of the archaism of BCP language. In modern contexts the word is associated with formality and old-fashionedness, qualities at odds with its former meaning. As a general rule, as in modern French *tu*, 'thou' in fact signified familiarity, intimacy (or even sometimes disrespect), as opposed to the more formal 'you'. However, this general rule is subject to complex social valencies. As any reader of Shakespeare knows, the sixteenth century was prone to pronoun-switching, by which one register could be exchanged for another. Using 'thou' could be a habit of a more powerful or senior person to a junior one; but it could also be used affectionately or to convey ease. In the case of God, using 'thou' was established by long precedent in Middle English devotional material, as in the Lord's Prayer (see above). On the use in the BCP, see Stella Brook, *The Language of the Book of Common Prayer* (London: Deutsch, 1965), 53–7.

7 *O Lorde, open thou my lippes*: these versicles are from Sarum, originating from Pss. 51 and 70.

Alleluya: the Hebrew word הללו יה ('Praise God') was retained as a superlative expression of thanksgiving and triumph in early Christian liturgies in Greek, Syriac, and Latin, and was used in the Roman rite for the Mass as well as the Office. Its use was especially prominent in Easter rituals, and was commonly excluded from liturgical performance during Lent.

without any Invitatori: a refrain sung before the *Venite* in the medieval Office, and repeated after each verse. The use of antiphons is pared down almost entirely in *1549*, creating a much simpler structure of psalms and lessons.

Venite exultemus: Ps. 95 has been sung at the opening of the Office in the Western church since the earliest times, and is mentioned in St Benedict's *Regula* (sixth century). The pointing of Ps. 95 is here regularized with the rest of the Psalter; in the medieval church it had its own chant.

8 *certaine Psalmes in ordre as they been appointed in a table*: set out in the Table following the Preface. See *1662*, pp. 217 ff., which reproduces the order in *1549* exactly. The Psalter was distributed in the breviary through different hours, and varied considerably with the pattern of festival liturgy. In the BCP the order is made a logical sequence divided between Morning and Evening Prayer.

shalbe read ii. lessons distinctely with a loude voice: the lessons from the Old and New Testaments are set out in the Table with the Psalms (see *1662*, pp. 219 ff.). The service is now structured around these formal readings, with the singing of the hymns designed to frame the scriptural centrepiece, in accordance with Reformed devotional discipline. In the Sarum breviary, portions of scripture were broken up and alternated with antiphons and responds.

9 *shall the lessons be songe in a playne tune after the maner of distincte readyng*: referring to the argument (expressed explicitly by Cranmer) that musical performance should assist meaning rather than conceal it, by making one syllable correspond to one note.

Te Deum laudamus in Englyshe: this hymn (and the following, the *Benedicite*) are the only sources prescribed in *1549* which are not from canonical scripture. By legend the *Te Deum* was first sung, under inspiration, at the baptism of St Augustine by St Ambrose in Milan at the Easter vigil in 387. The first documentary record is in St Benedict's *Regula*, but it was probably in common use before then. In Sarum it is used at Matins on Sundays and Festivals (*Breviarium*, ii. 27–8). The *1549* order for its use daily except in Lent (where it is replaced by the *Benedicite*) was altered in *1552*, where the *Benedicite* is retained as an alternative canticle. Both canticles were included in English versions in the *Hortulus animae* (1530) and in Primers up to the King's Primer of 1545; *1549* draws on these versions but is considerably revised, showing how close the textual supervision of the final text was; Whitchurch's later issues in June 1549 show further small changes after the first printing (*Godly Order*, 30).

noumbred with thy sainctes: 'numbered' translates *numerari* in the 1531 printed text of Sarum (*Breviarium*, ii. 28), a mistranscription of *munerari* ('rewarded') in the older MSS. However, the omission of the idea of reward is also theological: Protestants rejected the idea of 'works' and insisted on the primacy of faith.

10 *Benedicite*: an ancient hymn, part of the Greek addition to the third chapter of Daniel, is an exposition of Ps. 148 and was used in early Jewish liturgies. Some patristic writers thought it to be of equivalent value to scripture. It was used on Sundays in the medieval hour of Lauds, which followed Matins.

11 *O Ananias, Asarias, and Misael*: the three youths chosen with Daniel and taken captive with him after they refused the extravagant lifestyle of Nebuchadnezzar (Dan. 1).

Benedictus dominus deus Israel: the prophetic prayer or 'gospel canticle' of Zacharias from Luke 1: 68–79 was the daily climax of the hour of Lauds.

12 *Lorde, have mercie upon us*: this standard sequence of intercessional prayers (*preces*) is translated directly from the breviary. The words *Kyrie eleison* and *Christe eleison* were left in Greek in the Latin service out of reverence (compare *Alleluia* above). The prayers 'Lorde have mercie' and 'Christe have mercie', in *1549* as in Sarum, were repeated three times.

the Crede and the Lordes praier: the 'Crede' (from the first word in Latin, *credo*, 'I believe') was originally a statement of profession used in Baptism. The text of the Apostles' Creed (used here) dates to the fourth century; it was sung in Prime and Compline, where it appears in Sarum. The English version was made standard in the King's Book of 1543. The instruction that the priest alone says these parts of the service was dropped in *1552* when 'the people' joined in. For the six major feasts of the year, the Apostles' Creed was replaced by the Athanasian Creed; the text is placed after *Evening Prayer* (see p. 16).

O Lorde, shewe thy mercie upon us: these are 'suffrages' or set forms of intercession with responses, and are found throughout the BCP. Their origin is very old in Christian liturgy and they are commonplace throughout the various offices of the medieval church. They perform many kinds of function, not only theological or ritual; they create a distinctive rhythm, an interplay of dramatic voices, and often mark a transition from one part of the liturgy to another. This particular set of bidding prayers in Matins was known as the 'Lesser Litany'.

13 *three Collectes*: the first Collect 'of the daie' is shared with the order for Communion, usually associated with the theme of the Gospel and Epistle set out for that occasion. The second and third Collects are translations of very old prayers dating back to the *Liber sacramentorum Romanae ecclesiae* (the 'Gelasian sacramentary', eighth century? or earlier). The collect 'for peace' *Deus auctor pacis et amator* (*Gelasian Sacramentary*, 272) was later used in Sarum at the Lauds of the Blessed Virgin; that 'for grace', *Domine Sancte Pater omnipotens aeterne Deus*, was used at Prime (*Breviarium*, ii. 54).

EVENING PRAYER

The Order for Evening Prayer was formed by fusing Vespers with Compline. The 'little hours' from the medieval Latin liturgy, Terce, Sext, and Nones, were thus discarded. The structure is made to be uniform with Morning Prayer, and the two services are presented as a continuous design. Evening Prayer is even more pared down and altered from the breviary than Morning. While both services are based on Latin sources, they are very different from their originals. Like Matins, Evensong was established in printed form before the BCP and in widespread use in the early part of the reign of Edward.

15 *Psalmes in ordre as they bee appointed in the Table*: as for Morning Prayer. See *1662*, pp. 217 ff.

Magnificat: the hymn of Mary from Luke 1: 46–55. Its use in different churches was very ancient. It appears in the Office of Aurelian (sixth century); in the Benedictine *Regula* it is sung at Vespers, a position retained in the Roman (and Sarum) rite (*Breviarium*, ii. 221). There are several versions in Middle English. The version here is that of the King's Primer of 1545, which follows Tyndale's NT quite closely, with some rhythmical alteration (Butterworth, *The English Primers*, 265). In the Eastern church the *Magnificat* was also used in Morning Prayer.

Nunc Dimittis: the 'Song of Simeon' from Luke 2: 29–32, like the *Magnificat*, is one of the oldest forms of Christian liturgy, being mentioned in the Apostolical Constitutions (early fifth century). It was in use in Compline in the Roman rite perhaps by the time of St Gregory the Great (sixth century); the position in Sarum (*Breviarium*, ii. 225) is followed by BCP. There are several versions in Middle English. This is the version as fixed in the King's Primer in 1545.

16 *seconde Collecte at Evensong*: an old prayer (*Deus a quo sancta desideria*), dating back to the *Gelasian sacramentary* (p. 271), and used in the Sarum Vespers for the Virgin and in prayers before Mass (*Missale*, 210). The BCP wording is a good example of Cranmer's close reworking of material, including the Redman Primer of 1535, which had already gone through several revisions in the primers of 1541 and 1545 (MacCulloch, *Cranmer*,

418–19); the opening phrase, however, is already strikingly present in a version in a fourteenth-century English primer ('God of whom bin hooli desiris, ri3t councels and iust werkis').

thirde Collect: another very old prayer from the order for Compline in Sarum. The language is paraphrased from the Psalms.

shalbe song or sayd immediatly: the Athanasian creed was commonly sung by the priest in medieval liturgy.

Quicunque vult: the 'Creed of Athanasius', although named after the fourth-century bishop of Alexandria (opponent of the Arian heresy and one of the four doctors of the Eastern church), is neither a creed nor the work of Athanasius: it is probably Latin in origin; the earliest written trace is sixth-century in a commentary by Venantius Fortunatus. It was used in the English medieval office as a kind of Christian psalm, following the psalms in Prime. In Quiñones's reformed breviary it was prescribed for use on Sundays only. Here, although placed in the order for Evensong, it is directed for use in Morning Prayer on the six major Christian festivals of the year as a public profession of faith.

holy and undefyled: 'holy' is an error, possibly a scribal mistake for 'hole'; the correct reading 'whole' (translating the Latin *integram*) was not adopted until the 1637 Scottish BCP.

18 *Thus endeth the ordre of Matyns and Evensong*: after the order for Morning and Evening Prayer in *1549* are placed the 'Collectes, Epistles, and Gospels' for use in holy Communion on Sundays and festivals throughout the year. The readings are taken from the Great Bible of 1540. The order of the readings can be found to a great degree by using the text in *1662*, pp. 271 ff., although the texts there follow the KJV of 1611.

COMMUNION

The Order for Communion is the equivalent of the Ordinary and Canon of the Roman Mass, which had formed the centrepiece of English liturgy for centuries. The Sarum Missal (or Mass book) consisted of the Ordinary and Canon of the Mass, which set out the invariable elements of the service; along with the *Temporale*, which provided the requirements for Sundays and ferial (non-feast) days through the church year; and the *Sanctorale*, the portions for saints' days. (The *Temporale* and *Sanctorale* are covered by the 'Collectes, Epistles, and Gospels', see above.)

The term *Supper of the Lorde* is taken from 1 Cor. 11: 20, where Paul refers to the *Agape* or Eucharistic love-feasts of the early church; but is not part of the vocabulary of the Roman Mass. The term is used in pre-Reformation liturgical texts such as *The Mirror of Love* (1530); and in Daye's translation of Hermann's German reformed liturgy (English version printed in 1547). It came to be preferred by English Protestants to the common vernacular term 'Mass', although it created a confusion with the Last Supper (whereas the first sacrament took place strictly *after* supper).

The use of 'Communion' as a term for the sacrament derives from the Vulgate text of 1 Cor. 10: 16 (*communicatio sanguinis Christi*). In the Great Bible this word is rendered 'partakynge' (following Tyndale and Coverdale). The word 'communion' is found widely in pre-Reformation English but is not a synonym for 'Mass' (which means the whole service). In medieval usage (e.g. 'hooly communyon' in Caxton's translation of the *Golden Legend* (1483)) it means only the taking of the Eucharistic elements during Mass.

The use of three alternative titles by Cranmer ('supper . . . holy Communion . . . commonly called the Masse') signals that this is the most controversial part of the divine service in *1549*. In post-Reformation use the word 'Mass' (from the Latin *missa*, meaning a 'message', originally used of any liturgy but later exclusively for the sacrament of the Eucharist) came under increasing suspicion as unscriptural and redolent of Catholic doctrine. From *1552* it was excised from the BCP.

19 *the Curate*: the parish priest.

> *an open and notorious evill liver*: following the example of the German and Swiss Reformers, this disciplinary rubric attempts to exclude the ungodly from worship. It was confirmed in the Catechism of 1553, which provided for 'Brotherly correction and excommunication, or banishing those out of the Church that will not amend their lives'. See also Article 33 in *1662*, p. 682. Practical measures for such acts of outcasting were less forthcoming; see Hunt, 'Lord's Supper'.

> *reconciled*: primarily the sense of 'reconcile' here is to 'bring back, restore, or readmit to the Church' (*OED* 4a) but the word has overtones with Catholic doctrines of penance and absolution (see notes to pp. 25, 75, and 104). Although absolution as a sacrament was controversial among Reformers, this sense of 'reconcile' is current in early sixteenth-century Bible translations (e.g. Ps. 51: 7 (Coverdale) and Lev. 6: 30 (Great Bible)).

> *a white Albe plain, with a vestement or Cope*: the dress of the priest is further specified in 'Certayne notes', see p. 98. Over his cassock or long tunic a priest put on an 'albe' or close-fitting white robe, a 'stole' or narrow scarf, and the 'vestement', also known as a 'cope' or 'chasuble', a short cloak reaching to the knees and gathered up at the arms, forming an oval. The chasuble was the characteristic robe for the Eucharist throughout Western Europe, but became highly controversial post-Reformation. Vestments were among the items noted by Bucer in his *Censura* of the BCP in 1551 as being too much in accordance with idolatrous ritual (*retenta vestigia idolatriae*); his account may give some sense of how the *1549* Communion was put into practice: 'there are people who endeavour to represent that Mass of theirs, which we can never sufficiently execrate, with all the outward show they can, with vestments and lights, with bowings and crossings, with washing the chalice and other gestures from the missal, with breathing over the bread and chalice of the eucharist, with moving the book on the table from the right side of it to the left, with setting the table in the same place where the altar used to stand, with

displaying the bread and chalice' (*Censura*, 138–9). The cope was more acceptable because also used by the laity. Vestments came more openly into controversy when Hooper gave a series of court sermons on the book of Jonah during Lent in 1550. Here he decried the vestments of the Mass as unnecessary, since the word of God alone was sufficient, and they were 'rather the habit and vesture of Aaron and the gentiles, than of the ministers of Christ' (Hooper, *Early Writings*, 479; see also p. 554). Hooper repeatedly drew an analogy between unreformed liturgy and the 'Aaronic' practice of the Jewish law, overturned by Christ. Stipulations for priestly dress were excised from *1552* as part of a systematic desacralization of liturgical performance.

20 *afore the middes of the Altar*: altars or places of sacrifice are found frequently in the OT, and the word θυσιαστήριον appears twenty-four times in the NT, e.g. Heb. 13: 10. It referred both to the sacrifice made by Christ and later to the physical place where the Eucharist took place in recognition of Christ's sacrifice. Altars were generally wooden in the Eastern church, while in the West stone always replaced wood. In the Reformation both the physical make-up and the position of the altar became controversial. Reformers argued for the use of a wooden 'table', perhaps of a portable kind, to correspond to the table at the Last Supper. The word 'altar' was removed in *1552* and replaced with 'the Lord's Table'. From 1551 there was a campaign against physical altars in English parish churches led by Hooper (e.g. in his visitation articles in the diocese of Gloucester, *Later Writings*, 128). See also the 'Black Rubric' of *1552* (printed as Appendix A in this edition).

this Collect: this prayer (*Deus cui omne cor*), which is translated from the introductory prayers of the celebrant in the Sarum Ordinary (*Missale*, 216), was not part of the Roman missal. Cranmer follows the Latin closely but omits the reference to human merit (*mereamur*) in his phrase 'worthely magnifie thy holy name' (MacCulloch, *Cranmer*, 419). Cranmer was meticulous in eliminating references which implied the doctrine of salvation through good works.

the introite: the term for an antiphon or psalm sung while the priest approached the altar to celebrate Mass (from Latin *introitus*, 'an entrance').

Lorde have mercie upon us: the *Kyrie* formed the first of the key elements of the Latin Mass (*Missale*, 210), sometimes sung in elaborate expanded forms in festival services.

standyng at Goddes borde: the Communion table in a church. It is a common phrase in Middle English (e.g. William Bond, *Pilgrimage of Perfection* (1526), 10).

Glory be to God on high: the *Gloria in excelsis*, known in the East as the 'great doxology', is a very old hymn, appearing in the Apostolical Constitutions and cited in the works of Athanasius and Chrysostom. In liturgical use the *Gloria* came early in the Mass, after the *Kyrie*, a position retained here in *1549* but abandoned in *1552*, when it was used as a post-Communion thanksgiving (see *1559*, p. 138).

20 *the priest shall turne him to the people*: the position of the priest throughout the service, and his facing the altar or the people, was highly significant to the laity in indicating sacred processes; such physical questions were also highly controversial.

21 *Collectes folowynge for the kyng*: these two collects were composed for *1549*, although the second uses phrases from the *Missa pro rege* and the coronation rite of Henry VIII (*Deus in cuius manu sunt corda regum*, 'God in whose hand are the hearts of kings', Blunt, 27). It is not clear why there are two, although superfluity is a safe policy where a monarch is concerned.

Epistle . . . Gospel: the readings are set out in a separate section of BCP along with the collects; the order of the readings largely followed Sarum but using the Great Bible English text.

22 *I beleve in one God*: the recitation of the Nicene Creed (named after the first ecumenical council of the church in 325; revised in 381) in the public performance of the Mass was established in the fifth century; the Third Council of Toledo of 589 recommended its value as an antidote to the Arian heresy, which rejected the Trinity. It was an essential part of sacramental liturgies on solemn days (often sung or else chanted by the priest). The *Lay Folk's Mass-Book* (*c*.1450) suggested its readers say the shorter Apostles' Creed in English while the choir sang the Latin text (as also for the *Gloria*).

the Sermon or Homely: the sermon precedes the Offertory, following the Lutheran order as against the Latin missal, where the Offertory comes first. The prescription that a sermon or homily be delivered every Sunday implies a poor reflection on pre-Reformation preaching practice, often criticized in Protestant polemic. However, the surviving 200 pre-Reformation pulpits in English parish churches, mostly fifteenth-century, suggest otherwise (Duffy, 57). The cult of the Name of Jesus was a focus for new forms of late medieval preaching; see Susan Wabuda, *Preaching During the English Reformation* (Cambridge: Cambridge University Press, 2002), 147–77. John Mirk's fourteenth-century *Festial*, a collection of homilies for use throughout the year, was widely copied in MS and printed in several early sixteenth-century editions. Nonetheless, the Reformation placed a new and forcible emphasis on preaching (ibid. 81–106).

one of the Homelyes: for occasions when a new sermon could not be given, a book of set sermons, *Certayne Homelies*, was published in 1547, so that 'all curates, of what learnyng soever they be, may have some godly and fruitfull lessons in readines to reade and declare unto their parishioners, for their edifying, instruction and comfort' (ed. Bond, pp. 55–6). The book contained twelve sermons, many already in print, reflecting the political theology of Cromwell and Cranmer. The first concerns the reading of scripture; others deal with doctrinal questions such as faith and works;

others are moral, condemning swearing, comforting 'against the feare of deathe', and recommending marriage in preference to 'whoredom, and adultery'. *Certayne Homelies* was often bound in with copies of the BCP and sometimes published with it (e.g. Oswen's 1549 quarto).

exhortacion: this was introduced as part of the *Order of the Communion* of 1548.

if with a truly penitent heart: the sacrament of penance was required of every Christian at least once a year at the Fourth Lateran Council of 1215. Nobody could make their first Communion without first going to confession. Confessional manuals, often in the vernacular, were highly popular in the middle ages. Penance was among the earliest issues debated at the Reformation. Luther's attack on papal 'indulgences' in 1517 had at its heart a dispute about the system of pardons mediated by the church as acts of contrition. Luther countered that the only penitence that mattered was in the heart of the believer, rather than physical actions or 'works'; justification took place 'by faith alone' (*sola fide*). Following Luther, the Reformers questioned the sacramental nature of penance; however, this exhortation shows that a connection is retained in *1549* between penitence and Communion, but is no longer dependent on specific acts of confession.

spiritually eate: a phrase used by English Reformers (for example John Frith, in the 1530s) to distinguish themselves from Catholic doctrine on the sacrament. We eat 'spiritually' in Communion, that is, we do not eat the body of Christ in fact. Thomas More glossed (and disputed) this meaning of 'spiritual eating' as: 'he goth about to take awaye from vs y⁰ very lytterall trewth, of the very eatynge and bodely receyuynge of Chrystes owne very flesshe & bloud' (*The answere to the fyrst parte of the poysened booke* (1533), sig. 6ʳ). Reformers took a variety of positions on the 'real presence' of Christ in the Eucharistic elements (see Introduction, pp. xxv–xxvii). Luther defended the idea of the literal interpretation of *hoc est corpus meum* at Marburg in 1529. Zwingli argued Christ meant the phrase only metaphorically. In addition, Zwingli stated that the Communion gives spiritual benefit only to the faithful, and was followed in this by Calvin and (by the 1540s) by Cranmer. Zwingli ('On the Lord's Supper') called the real presence 'bread-worship'.

24 *the mariage garment required of God in scripture*: see Matt. 22: 11–12.

charitie: Christian love, from *caritas* in Vulgate, translating ἀγάπη in NT. Here in the sense of fellow-feeling for others: 'Haue cherité with herte fyne . . . that eche man loue wel othere' (*Lay Folks' Mass Book* (*c.*1450)).

25 *conscience*: in medieval and sixteenth-century usage a rational faculty conveying inner awareness, often figured in popular culture as a worm biting inwardly, the 'gnawyng with-in of conscience' (*The Prick of Conscience* (*c.*1340)).

the auriculer and secret confession to the Priest: the careful wording shows

how controversial the subject of penance and confession is; this exhortation approves general confession but allows for private confession, following the traditional practice. Indeed the wording assumes a traditional
view of the priest's role in absolution, rejected in *1552*. Most people in
most medieval parishes confessed once a year in Lent; the more devout, or
learned, or leisured, confessed more regularly. Instructions for priests in
conducting confessions were structured around the Ten Commandments
and the seven deadly sins (see e.g. Mirk, *Instructions*, 24–46); but they
also included more detailed practical inquiries into neighbourly quarrels, backbiting and tale-telling, and (among the young) 'temptacyons
carnalles' (Duffy, 60, citing a fifteenth-century MS). Confession was
time-consuming in the run-up to Easter, and these secret interviews may
have been brief; a font at Walsoken in Norfolk (dated 1544) shows queues
forming behind a penitent (Duffy, pl. 20).

25 *the Offertory*: the term refers to the verses sung after the Creed in the
Roman and Sarum rite; the second main phase of the medieval Mass.

Sentences of holy scripture: a Reformed version of the offertory antiphons.
The sacrificial prayers of the offertory are, however, excised.

27 *the poore mennes boxe*: a collection-box for money or other gifts to be distributed to the poor.

the women on the other syde: this division by gender in the Mass follows
medieval practice (Margaret Aston, 'Segregation in Church', in W. J.
Sheils and Diana Wood (eds.), *Women in the Church, Studies in Church
History* (Oxford: Blackwell, 1990), 237–41). The Reformation made no
difference, and segregation was explicitly endorsed in Lutheran services:
ibid. 281.

the breade upon the corporas: a cloth on which the consecrated elements
were placed during the Mass (and which was used to cover the remnants
after the celebration). The purpose was to prevent crumbs of consecrated
bread being mislaid; it was rejected in *1552*.

or els in the paten: a plate or shallow dish (often silver or gold), on which the
host was laid during the Eucharist.

Lift up your heartes: the *Sursum corda* is referred to as early as St Cyprian
in the third century.

28 *Propre Prefaces*: in addition to these alternative prefaces proper to the five
major festivals of the Christian year, the Sarum missal contained several
more, including for Epiphany, for Ash-Wednesday, the saints' days of the
evangelists and some apostles, and the feast of the Blessed Virgin (*Missale*,
211–15).

29 *Holy, holy, holy*: the *Sanctus* is one of the oldest elements in the Mass,
referred to by St Cyril of Jerusalem in the fourth century. It incorporates
a text from scripture, the song of the Seraphim (Isa. 6: 3). Cranmer translates from Sarum (*Missale*, 220).

Osanna in the highest: הושענא (*Hoshana*) is a Hebrew word meaning 'save' or 'help'. The Greek transcription ὡσαννά was carried verbatim into the words *Hosanna in excelsis*, which concluded the *Sanctus* throughout the Middle Ages. The use of the Hebrew word (conveying special reverence) was dropped in *1552*.

Blessed is he: the *Benedictus* consists of the song of welcome for Christ on Palm Sunday (Matt. 21: 9). This, too, was excised in *1552*, perhaps because of the tradition of turning to the altar and making the sign of the cross at this point in the liturgy.

the Priest turnyng hym to the Altar, shall saye or syng: this key physical gesture by the priest marks the beginning of the Canon of the Mass, the third and most solemn part of the Roman rite. Its employment here in *1549* was disputed in the House of Lords in December 1548 in advance of publication, and it was cut in *1552*. Luther brought out the German tract *On the Abomination of the Canon of the Mass* in 1525. Continental Reformed liturgies (from Luther to Hermann) retained only Christ's words of institution from the gospels, read as a lesson, sometimes facing the Lord's Table. Cranmer follows the order of the Canon, while transposing its six prayers (each marked by *Amen*) into three long paragraphs. Sometimes he translates literally, sometimes he paraphrases using material from Hermann; sometimes he chooses his words with extreme theological care.

30 *commemoracion*: replaces the word *sacrificium* from Sarum (*Missale*, 221); 'commemoracion' articulates Zwingli's doctrine of Communion as a memorial re-enactment, rather than a renewed performance, of the original sacrifice of Christ. He declared this in his *67 Articles* of 1523 (*Opera omnia* (1829), i. 264).

all thy sainctes: while the list of individual named saints from Sarum is cut (*Missale*, 221), the reference here to the Virgin, apostles, martyrs, and the departed gives them a prominence suppressed elsewhere in the BCP. Mutual participation with the dead in the Mass was emphasized in the medieval rite, and was equally frowned upon by Reformers.

all other thy servauntes, which are departed: Calvin wrote to Protector Somerset in October 1549, warning that this reference to the departed was unsuitable in the holy context of Communion (Marshall, 110).

a full, perfect, and sufficient sacrifyce, oblacion, and satysfaccyon: no six words in *1549* were more dearly bought. 'Oblation' (the offering presented to God in the elements of the Eucharist) was a central feature of the Roman Canon (*Quam oblationem*; *Missale*, 222), and the word was rejected at the committee of bishops preceding the formulation of BCP. Cranmer here retains the vocabulary of the Roman theology while attributing it only to Christ's action on the cross. He thus conforms to the letter of the doctrine later set out in Article 31 (see p. 682), which explicitly denied that Christ was offered in 'the sacrifices of Masses' by the priest, while perhaps allowing those parishioners who believed in the traditional view to continue to practise it. The 'sacrifice' of the Mass was the first of the Eucharistic doctrines to be rejected by the Reformers. Luther called the sacrificial concept of the Mass 'the worst of abuses' in a sermon of 1519, and developed the argument in his widely influential tract, *The Babylonian Captivity of the Church* (1520): it is safer to reject all the sayings of the church fathers 'than to admit that the Mass is a work and a sacrifice' (WA 6.524). This was one point on which Lutherans and Zwinglians still agreed in 1529.

30 *to bl✠esse and sanc✠tifie*: the medial crosses imitate the form used in printed Sarum missals (and earlier manuscript versions) to signify the mysterious acts conjured by the words. The primary function is to signify the manual acts of the priest in performing the rite (e.g. in making a sign of the cross). But more than this, perhaps, it implies the performative function of utterance, the ability of words to transform things. This typographical feature, also used in the *1549* orders for Baptism and Matrimony, shows a continuing sense of the physical power of words to effect things; it was dropped in *1552*.

31 *Here the priest must take the bread into his handes*: in general, the instructions for the bodily actions of the priest during Communion in *1549* are unspecific when compared with the Sarum rite. Gestures are neither enjoined nor forbidden (with some exceptions, such as the elevation, below); perhaps a variation in performance is allowed.

without any elevacion, or shewing the Sacrament to the people: from the twelfth century the priest would lift the host above his head immediately after the words *Hoc est enim corpus meum*, signalling the miracle of the transubstantiation (*Hic elevet alcius corpus ut videatur ab omnibus*; *Missale*, 222). Lights were provided for the laity to aid 'seeing the host', the highpoint of the whole rite. This practice was also the focus of Reformed objection to the 'idolatry' of the Roman Mass. By forbidding the elevation the BCP eliminated participation in the Mass as it was popularly understood, and also removed its spiritual benefit; one belief held seeing the elevation as a protection against sudden death for the rest of the day.

Instytucyon: Christ's words after the Last Supper (Matt. 26: 26–8; Mark 14: 22–4; Luke 22: 19–20) provided the central moment in the consecration.

holy Tabernacle: in the OT, the dwelling-place of Jehovah, or of God; in medieval usage it was also an ornamented receptacle for the pyx containing the consecrated host (*OED*). Nonetheless the significance of the holy body and blood are here diminished in *1549* in favour of the 'prayers and supplicacions' of the people.

32 *thys generall Confession*: this element in the service, while a novelty, was based on old sources. A form of verbal confession is used at Compline in the Sarum breviary and also in the introduction to the missal, spoken by the Priest *privatim* ('privately') in the sanctuary of the choir. Cranmer here also used Hermann's *Consultation*; where the priest 'shall make

a confession in the name of the whole congregation' (2E4ᵛ). The form is transposed in *1549* so that the whole congregation gives voice to communal confession, combining the formal act of the priest with a personal performance of humility and critical self-analysis.

we knowlege and bewaile our manyfold synnes and wyckednes: adapted from Hermann, *Consultation*: 'we acknowledge, and we lament, that we were conceived and borne in sinnes, and that therefore we be prone to al evils' (2E4ᵛ).

by thought, word and dede: translating the words *cogitatione, locutione, et opere* from the Sarum breviary.

33 *comfortable woordes*: these three texts of scripture are cited together as part of a group of five in Hermann, *Consultation*, 2E5ʳ⁻ᵛ; the phrase, 'comfortable wordes' is Cranmer's (based on Hermann, 'Hören den Evangelischen trost', where German *trost* = 'consolation, comfort').

shall the Priest, turnyng him to gods boord, knele down: both of these gestures were the focus of evangelical disapproval in relation to *1549*.

We do not presume: this version of the 'prayer of humble access' was included in *The Order of the Communion* (1548). Although based on the Sarum prayer *da nobis hoc corpus*, Cranmer creates a cento of scriptural texts of great beauty, especially perhaps the touching reference to Mark 7: 28 ('neverthelesse, the whelpes [puppies] also eat under the table of the chyldrens cromes' (*Great Bible*)).

34 *dwell in hym, and he in us*: 'that so we maye daily more and more abide, and lyve in hym, and he in us' (Hermann, *Consultation*, 2E1ʳ).

Communion in both kindes: from the twelfth century it became commonplace for the chalice containing the wine to be administered to the priest alone. Restoring Communion 'in both kinds' was a rallying-point of the Reformation from the beginning; Luther, while a conservative on the theology of the real presence, insisted on it in his revised missal, the *Formula Missae et Communionis* (1523).

preserve thy bodye and soule unto everlasting lyfe: the oldest form of wording in the delivery of the elements, mentioned in a sermon of St Ambrose, was *Corpus Christi*, 'The Body of Christ'. Various formulae were added later; *1549* translates word for word the standard English pre-Reformation form, *custodiat corpus tuum et animam tuam in vitam aeternam* (*Missale*, 131).

O lambe of god: the *Agnus Dei* was the last of the invariable elements of the Roman rite, beginning as a chant; its form with a triple repetition and the change of the third refrain was fixed by the twelfth century (*Missale*, 225). It was dropped from *1552*.

then shall the Clarkes syng the post Communion: the post-Communion antiphon in Sarum was a fragment from a psalm. Sentences now replace in

1549 the prayer following the administration of the Eucharist, *Deus cujus misericordiae* (*Missale*, 460) in the Roman Mass.

36 *Almightye and everlyvyng God*: this prayer of thanksgiving has no source in the Latin Mass; it is similar to a prayer written in 1542 by Thomas Becon, Cranmer's chaplain (MacCulloch, *Cranmer*, 417).

very membres incorporate in thy Misticall bodye: owes its phrasing to Bond's *The Pilgrimage of Perfection* (1526): 'to be incorporate in him as one of the members of his mystical body.'

The peace of God: the *pax* (or kiss of peace) in the Roman Mass preceded Communion. In the later middle ages an implement of gold, silver, ivory, or wood, often with a decorated handle depicting the crucifixion, was kissed by the celebrating priest and then by the other participants. The *pax* is now removed to the end of the service in this beautiful prayer of benediction.

37 *Collectes to bee sayed after the Offertory*: the first, second, and fourth were ancient prayers; the fifth and sixth are new compositions, the last derived from the prayer of St Chrysostom.

38 *For rayne*: both this prayer, and the following, 'For fayre wether', were special, or it might be said quintessential, English compositions for the BCP.

the kynges majesties Injunccions: the 1547 Injunctions were a considerable enforcement of what is now known as the second Reformation, with strong measures against the use of images and other so-called 'idolatrous' practices.

in Chapelles annexed: in parish churches, also in cathedrals and abbey churches, chapels were usually annexed in the recesses on the sides of the aisles.

the breade prepared for the Communion: the stipulation that the Communion bread be 'unleavened, and rounde', and yet without a stamp such as a cross upon it, is a classic compromise. Wafers were in widespread use in the late medieval church. Markings on the wafers suggested idolatry to some Reformers, who argued for the use of ordinary loaves, which were allowed in *1552*.

39 *but in eache of them the whole body of our saviour Jesu Christ*: the doctrine of the real presence here receives a clear endorsement, excised in *1552*.

the juste valour and price of the holy lofe: this replaced the holy loaf rota (see Duffy, p. 125) in medieval parishes.

Collegiate Churches: a church where the office of worship is maintained by a college of canons (a community of clergy, organized as a self-governing corporate body).

to communicate once in the yeare at the least: formal rules on frequency of Communion varied; the Fourth Lateran Council of 1215 stipulated that all receive Communion once a year at Easter. Some Protestants argued for more frequent worship, with scripture and sermon, and less emphasis on Communion with its association with Catholicism. Calvin's services in Geneva, following his return there in 1541, provided for confession, prayer for pardon, psalms, prayers, sermon, readings, and intercession, ending with the Lord's Prayer. If Communion was taken, it followed intercession.

40 *in theyr owne handes*: this final rubric once again reflects conflict over the material and mystical benefits of the host. Holy bread was used in a variety of apotropaic rituals to ward off disasters or troubles of many kinds. Communication directly into the mouth prevented the stealing of the host. The practice was abominated by Reformers as smacking of idolatry in the refusal to allow the hands to touch the host.

LITANY

A λιτανεία in Classical Greek referred to any form of solemn entreaty. The term was used for penitential services as early as the fourth century in the Eastern church. In the pre-Reformation English church its use was universal as part of the elaborate system of medieval processional (for which there was a separate book of Offices). The Litany was used in the blessing of the font on Easter eve; at the ordination of deacons and priests; during Lent after Terce; and as an independent processional on Rogation days and other occasions of public prayer. Cranmer took its use very seriously. The Litany was the first vernacular service to be authorized officially in England and was published on 27 May 1544. Each clause was prescribed to be repeated by the choir. Cranmer entertained hopes of producing an independent English processional as a whole, and produced a detailed draft for Henry VIII with his own formal experiments and with some proposals for musical reform. While this plan was never realized, the 1544 service was carried over into the 1545 King's Primer, and with small alterations into BCP. In *1549* in early printings it was issued as an appendix, but later copies, as here, placed the Litany after the Communion, although this does not indicate its liturgical position. By this time the Royal Injunctions of 1547 had banned any kind of processional, and the BCP Litany is static. The processional element of Sarum is displaced into a form which manages to remove the cult of the saints, and concentrates instead on public, communal worship, including prayers of national and political incorporation. Much of Cranmer's Litany is translated directly from the Sarum rite (*Breviarium*, ii. 249–59), with the invocation of saints removed, and only Mary mentioned by name. Its eclectically chosen sources also include Luther, and a Latin translation of St Chrysostom. Even in this patchwork of derivation Cranmer was not original: he drew on William Marshall's *Godly Primer* of 1535.

41 *have mercy upon us*: the early refrains in the English text are based on the *Kyrie*, as they are in Latin versions of the Litany (*Breviarium*, ii. 250).

O holy, blessed, and glorious Trinitie: as in the Latin litany, invocations of the Trinity follow the *Kyrie*. After this the Reformed version differs, leaving out the invocation of the saints completely, even removing Mary, the angels and archangels, and the 'prophets, apostles, martyrs, confessors, and virgins', who remained in the litany for the King's Primer (1545).

41 *From al evill and mischiefe*: here begin the Deprecations, based in outline on the Penitential Psalms. While the Latin litany uses mainly single clauses, Cranmer groups them together, with rhythmic skill and gravity.

Spare us good Lorde . . . Good lorde deliver us: again, following the Latin formulae of response, such as *Parce nobis Domine* and *Libera nos Domine* (*Breviarium*, ii. 251–2).

from the tyrannye of the bishop of Rome and all his detestable enormities: this clause, not surprisingly, was removed from the English Litany published under Mary I (*God the Father in Heaven* (1554?) (STC 16453)), and was not restored in *1559* under Elizabeth I.

42 *to kepe Edward the .vi.*: in the Intercessions, the order departs from the Latin example and shows the influence of the Lutheran litany in placing the temporal powers next after the church, and before 'pastours and ministers of the churche'.

44 *we have heard with our eares*: adapted from Ps. 44.

45 *We humbly beseche thee*: a final Collect is adapted from a litany for the last of the Rogation Days, an odd example of the survival of medieval processional in the BCP.

BAPTISM

The remainder of the BCP consists almost entirely of services from the Latin Manual (also known as the Sacerdotal), the compendium of occasional services administered by the priest.

Baptism had some claim to be as old as the gospels, being prescribed by Christ in Matt. 28: 19. Its outline form was extremely ancient, consisting of renunciation of Satan, profession of faith, and baptism by water. Already by the third century elaborate baptismal customs existed: candidates were selected with great care; the preparation (with teaching and exorcism) took forty days; the baptism (by total triple immersion) occurred at night, as part of the Easter vigil. A large patristic literature of these ceremonies exists, including in Tertullian (d. 220), alongside famous later narratives such as the baptism of St Augustine in Milan in 387. As Western Europe Christianized, however, baptism transferred largely to infants, although treated as adults. The rite itself developed into a miniature imitation of the ancient practice: baptism in the Sarum Manual in a single service combined the expulsion of the devil with the spiritual transformation of the infant, providing a series of bodily acts: the priest breathing on the candidate at the door of the church; salt placed in the mouth to remove the corruption of sin; exorcising; anointing the ears and lips with spittle (following Christ's healing of the dumb man in Mark 7: 33–4, the *ephphatha*, after Jesus's word in Aramaic, הפתח, 'be opened'); the white robe;

the signing of the infant on the hand; unction with oil on breast and back; and the giving of a candle or taper.

Baptism presented a dilemma for the Reformed liturgy, as it was clearly scriptural but the plethora of bodily performances in Sarum were anathema. The English service swept away almost all the physical actions, yet for the laity these were often the most functional parts of the ritual. Holy words and gestures held objective power; the baptismal water was kept separate, and was considered to have magical powers; the chrisom or cloth for the anointment of the child was to be retained by the priest; godparents washed their hands to ensure none of the holy oil used in blessing the baptismal water remained. While *1549* placed didactic emphasis on scripture and the verbal promise of baptism, its central action involved a transformation by water, and it retained some other physical aspects, such as signing of the forehead, exorcism, chrisom, and unction, which were to remain controversial up to *1662*.

46 *baptisme shoulde not be ministred but upon Sondayes and other holy dayes*: the 6th Article of the Devon and Cornwall rebels in 1549 specifically objected to this clause, arguing that 'the infants may at any day or hour be baptized as oft as any case of necessity requireth' (*Troubles*, 164).

ready at the Church dore: the exhortation at the door represents a residual sense of the elaborate Latin order of preparation (the 'making of the catechumen', *Manuale*, 25), as does the enquiry to the parents and godparents.

Deare beloved: from Luther's German baptismal rite of 1523, showing a strong emphasis on the doctrine of original sin.

47 *Almyghtie and everlastyng God*: from Hermann's *Consultation*, Y7ʳ.

a crosse upon the childes forehead and breste: this physical action, although also used in the Cologne Reformed rite (Hermann, *Consultation*, Y5ᵛ), was dropped in *1552*.

Almyghtie and immortall God: from the Sarum office (*Manuale*, 27), where it is one of the prayers of exorcism.

48 *I commaunde thee, uncleane spirite*: this is the formal exorcism from the Sarum rite (*Exorcizo te immunde spiritus*, *Manuale*, 28). In the Sarum version the cross that is marked on the forehead is said to be a physical barrier against the devil's entrance (*Manuale*, 29).

the gospell written by S. Marke: this was the scriptural passage favoured in Germany and used in Hermann; Sarum used the corresponding version in Matt. 19.

49 *And say the prayer*: the short homily here is based on Hermann (Y8ᵛ–2A1ʳ). This point in the service is a good example of the gradual effacement of the Roman rite: the gospel in Sarum (*Manuale*, 29–30) preceded the *ephphatha* (dropped in *1549*), which leads into the recital of the Lord's Prayer and Creed by the sponsors (which in turn was dropped in *1552*).

49 *let the priest take one of the children by the ryght hande*: the introductory service at the church door now ends, as the children enter the church.

50 *standyng at the fonte the priest shall speake*: this marks the beginning of the rite proper, the *Ritus baptizandi* as it was known in the Roman church.

Doest thou forsake the devill: the three-part renunciation of the devil is retained from Sarum (*Manuale*, 36), although the anointing is omitted.

Doest thou beleve in God: in Sarum (*Manuale*, 36), three short credal propositions are presented, to which the candidate replies, *credo*. In *1549* the second proposition is expanded into a fuller version of the Apostles' Creed.

51 *dyppe it in the water thryse*: triple immersion, with rubrics to ensure the whole body is covered, follows the Roman rite in Sarum (*Manuale*, 36); a single act of water is used in *1552*.

white vesture, commonly called the Crisome: white robe, put on the child at baptism as a sign of innocence; sometimes merely a headcloth, to stop the unguent ('chrism') being rubbed off (*OED*).

annoynt the infant upon the head: the unction was dropped in *1552*.

52 *at the purificacion of the mother of every chylde*: the chrisom was tradition-ally returned by the mother to the priest at her churching as an offering (see Churching of Women, p. 91), at which point the priest would burn it or keep it 'for the uses of the church' (Duffy, 280); like the unction and the chrisom, the offering was dropped in *1552*.

in private houses: as the rubric indicates, this separate service provides for baptism in cases of emergency. By the fourteenth century baptism was expected to take place within a few days of birth. The fate of the unbaptized infant, while theologically sensitive, was widely assumed to be damnation; communities therefore found various improvisatory means of conferring baptism if a child was in mortal danger, including lay baptism (Hunt, 'Lay Baptism'). The *1549* service inherits these problematic trad-itions, and makes intricate suggestions for emergency practice. Much of the service is identical with public baptism.

53 *Baptise not children at home in theyr houses*: the rubric allowing for baptism by the laity in cases of necessity remained controversial, and after the accession of James I was removed in *1604*. See note to p. 146.

if the childe whiche is after this sorte Baptised, doe afterwarde lyve: this con-voluted rubric both assures that a valid baptism takes place and prevents a duplicate ritual.

nowe by the laver of regeneracion in Baptisme: the wording shows more clearly than in the rite for public baptism the doctrine that the rite itself effects the benefits of salvation, a point disputed by some Protestants and later controversial to Puritans.

56 *If thou be not Baptized already*: the strange counter-factual form of the sentence testifies to the sense of a sacred action that cannot be repeated.

Luther had rejected 'conditional baptism', since how could divine grace be conditional? *1549*, however, instead follows the medieval formula.

The water in the fonte: in the Sarum rite the consecration of the font was a separate ritual performed as part of the Easter vigil. The retention of a simplified version here, and the renewing of the water at least once a month, shows a continuing reverence for physical things, and a persistent popular belief in the power of holy water, like holy bread. This act was dropped in *1552*.

57 *Sanctifie* ✠ *this fountaine of baptisme*: the typographical use of the cross, identical to that in the consecration of the elements of the Communion (see above, p. 30), envisages a manual act of blessing by the priest, and shows a special status of material objects as sacred things. It was removed in *1552*.

CONFIRMATION

The rite of Confirmation is linked to Baptism in the NT, where in Acts 8: 14–17 a group of baptized submit to a laying on of hands by the apostles Peter and John, conveying the action of the Holy Spirit. Similar processes in the NT are referred to as 'sealing' or 'anointing'. In the early church the two rites might be consecutive, but after the practice of infant baptism became commonplace, Confirmation became a separate initiation by which a person already baptized at birth is renewed in the faith at the age of reason. In the Sarum rite Confirmation took place where possible by the age of 3; by postponing it until the child could recite the catechism, Cranmer moved decisively to make confirmation an adolescent rite of passage. However, he continued to view it as an exclusively episcopal rite. Confirmation was one of the seven sacraments of the medieval church, and the liturgy follows Baptism in the Sarum Manual. The Reformers disputed the sacramental status of Confirmation, which is declared in Article 25 (see p. 680) 'not to be counted for Sacraments of the Gospel'. However, the opportunity for instruction in the faith which it entailed was valued in the Protestant confessions from Luther onwards.

58 *suche as can say in theyr mother tong*: the Injunctions of 1536 and 1538 ordered curates to teach the people the Lord's Prayer, the Creed, and the Ten Commandments, sentence by sentence, on Sundays and holy days; these orders were repeated in the Injunctions of 1547 under Edward VI.

of perfecte age: the 'ages of man' were proverbial: 'one man in his time plays many parts, | His acts being seven ages'; Shakespeare, *As You Like It*, II. vii. 142–3.

59 *A Catechisme*: the word derives from the Greek κατήχησις, instruction by 'word of mouth'. It is the verb used in Luke 1: 4 for instruction in the faith, and manuals for such practices date back to St Cyril of Jerusalem (347) and St Augustine (400). Catechetical material abounds in late medieval religious literature in England. Luther wrote a *Small Catechism* for younger children and a *Large Catechism* (1529), intended for instructors

and parents, for the education of those with a capacity to understand for themselves. He required that 'young people . . . may hear it explained and may learn to understand what every part contains, so as to be able to recite it as they have heard it, and, when asked, may give a correct answer, so that the preaching may not be without profit and fruit'.

59 *What is your name?*: the English catechism for BCP eschews the sophisticated material of the Lutheran *Large Catechism* or even Calvin's more direct catechism for use in Geneva (1541; rev. 1545) in favour of brief questions and answers of a formulaic kind. This does not imply a lack of interest in doctrinal education; the BCP catechism was supplemented by frequently reprinted works such as *The ABC with the catechisme* and *The primer and catechisme* (Green, *Christian's ABC*, 65).

the articles of thy beliefe: the rehearsal of the Creed, Ten Commandments, and Lord's Prayer, which follow, clearly follows the bare outline of the educational aspirations of the Injunctions.

60 *anye graven image, nor the likenesse of any thyng*: this commandment was the spur and sanction for the widespread outbreaks of iconoclasm in Edwardian churches, often officially authorized.

kepe holy the Sabboth day: while the English medieval church taught that Sunday was a day of devotion, dancing and games after Mass were commonplace. Protestant views were varied: Lee's Injunctions in York in 1538 asked clergy to 'instruct their flock . . . they must utterly withdraw themselves from all worldly and fleshly business' (*VAI* ii. 51); whereas the Royal Injunctions of 1547 permitted 'labour upon holy and festival days' and advised against 'scrupulosity or grudge of conscience' on the matter (*VAI* ii. 125). Sabbatarianism, which became typical of seventeenth-century Puritanism, was a later phenomenon.

62 *Our helpe is in the name of the Lorde*: the beginning of the rite of Confirmation is a translation of the Sarum rite (*Adiutorium nostrum in nomine domini*; Brightman, ii. 792).

shal crosse them in the forehead: as in Baptism, this ritual act (which follows Sarum) was retained in *1549* and dropped in *1552*. In a classic form of compromise, the unction with the chrism (in the same rubric in Sarum) was excised from *1549*.

lay his handes upon theyr heades: this physical action, being mentioned frequently in scripture, escaped the strictures of the Protestants.

The peace of the lorde abide with you: the *Pax tibi* in the medieval service was accompanied by a mild striking of the cheek to signify that the person confirmed was a soldier of Christ, ready to suffer blows for his sake.

63 *Almightie everliving god*: this collect was taken from a longer collect in Hermann.

The blissing of god almightie: the final benediction is from Sarum (Brightman, ii. 796).

MATRIMONY

Mention of a marriage being sanctioned by a Christian bishop goes back to a letter of St Ignatius of Antioch to St Polycarp (early second century). The earliest rites followed Roman pagan custom, which comprised the *sponsalia* or betrothal, consisting of four ceremonies—the giving of presents in recognition of the compact, the kiss, the ring, and the joining of hands; followed by the wedding itself, in which the bride was veiled and a sacrificial cake was shared. Nuptial Masses replacing the pagan sacrifices are recorded in Tertullian; the three early sacramentaries also provide for a special nuptial benediction. These forms are present in Sarum, which has a *sponsalia* followed by a Benediction followed by the nuptial Mass. There was more variation among the medieval English uses (such as Hereford and York) on matrimony than for other services; and this rite was also unusual in containing large parts in the vernacular. While Cranmer is commonly cited as the author of the famous wording of English wedding vows, only the phrase 'to love and to cherish' can properly be said to be his; yet these words make a distinctive contribution, in insisting on an emotional and companionate language as central to the ceremony. This service freely mixes the ritual elements of Sarum and York with the continental Reformed moral and social doctrine of Hermann's *Consultation*.

64 *the bannes must be asked three several Soondaies*: the Synod of Westminster in 1200 asserted that no marriage could take place without banns published three times in church. The banns in the medieval church were a prevention against clandestine marriages or ones that broke canon law. Following *1549*, they are part of an attempt to bring marriage within a statutory legal framework, breaking down the distinction between ecclesiastical and secular law.

into the bodie of the churche: pre-Reformation weddings began at the church porch, on the threshold of divine space rather than in its midst. Mirk's *Instructions for Parish Priests* enjoined the couple: 'So openlyche at the church dore | Lete hem eyther wedde othere.' This division of holy place may be compared with the preparation of the catechumen in the rite of baptism. The vows and the giving of rings took place outside, and the couple only moved inside for the Mass and the blessing. *1549* began baptism at the church door, but marriage was thrown straight into the nave, in an act of full public witness.

we are gathered together: the introduction follows the medieval rite; indeed, the wording of the opening of the York Manual is in the vernacular and *1549* is verbally close: 'Lo brethren we are comen here before God and his angels and all his halowes in the face and presence of our moder holy Chyrche for to couple and to knyt these two bodyes togyder' (BL MS Royal 2A.XXI).

an honorable estate instituted of God in paradise, in the time of mannes innocencie: 'considre firste, howe holie a kinde of lyfe, and howe acceptable to God matrimonie is. For . . . God him selfe instituted holye wedlocke, and that in paradise man being yet perfecte, and holye' (Hermann, *Consultation*, 2I1ᵛ).

64 *nor taken in hande unadvisedlye, lightelye, or wantonly*: 'how unsemelye a thinge it is for Christian menne, to contracte matrimonie, the right holie copulacion of men, secretely, and rashely' (Hermann, *Consultation*, 2I7ʳ).

the causes for the whiche matrimonie was ordeined: this moralizing analysis is original to *1549*, although it is loosely based on the introduction to the marriage service in Hermann, *Consultation*, 2I1ᵛ–2I2ᵛ.

the mutuall societie, helpe, and coumfort: this third cause of marriage is an innovation, reflecting the ethic of 'companionate marriage' adopted among the Reformers, especially the Germans Luther and Bucer. The word 'mutually' is used in Hermann, *Consultation*, 2I2ʳ. Bucer, who like Luther and Cranmer was married himself, suggested in 1551 that it be placed as the first of the causes.

65 *Leat him now speake, or els hereafter for ever hold his peace*: these heavy warnings against impediments to marriage or the solemnization of improper weddings are similar to those used in the ordination of priests and bishops and go back to ancient sources. The York use asks of the couple: 'yf there be any thinge done pryuely or openly betwene yourselfe, or that ye know any lawfull letting why ye may not be wedded togyder at this tyme say it nowe, er we do any more to this mater.' The BCP rubric, however, ensures that the marriage is legal; part of the attempt to use the church service to regulate social practice.

Wilte thou have this woman: the wedding vows were in the vernacular in most manuscripts of the Sarum and other uses, and are among the oldest examples of liturgical text in English. The wording varies; this is from a copy of the York Manual: 'Wilt thou haue this woman to thy wife: and loue her and kepe her in syknes and in helthe, and in all other degrees so be to her as a husbande sholde be to his wife, and all other forsake for her: and holde thee only to her, to thy lyues ende?' The form of the Middle English response is: 'I wyll.' In Shakespeare's *As You Like It*, IV. i. 120–5, Celia's reluctance to say the words of the priest during the performance of the vows in the mock-marriage of Rosalind and Orlando shows the illocutionary power felt to be invested in the verbal promise 'I will'.

obey: the wording for the wife differs in the injunction to 'obey'. This, too, follows the medieval rite (Sarum 'obeye to him'; York 'serue him'). York also requires that she 'be buxum to him'.

Who geveth this woman: this marks how the wedding ceremony incorporated a betrothal. The woman passes from dependence on her father (or family) to dependence on her husband.

66 *for better, for wurse*: the plighting of troths follows the wording in the York rite: 'for better: for wors: for richere: for poorer ['for fairer for fowler' added sometimes in Sarum, *Manuale*, 48]: in sykenesse and in hele: tyl dethe us departe.'

to Goddes holy ordeinaunce: altered from the emphasis on the mediation of the church in the medieval rite, 'if holy chyrche it woll ordeyne'.

looce theyr handes: the rubrics allow for considerable physical detail in an elaborate dance of gestures somewhat at odds with the restraint shown in other parts of BCP.

to love, cherishe, and to obey: these words replace the reading in the York Manual: 'to be bonere and buxum in bedde and at the borde.' The phrase 'love and cherish' is Cranmer's innovation in this context, although it is proverbial, and occurs in several texts of Caxton e.g. the translation of *Dictes or sayengis of the philosophres* (1477).

geve unto the womanne a ring: traditionally on the fourth finger of the woman's left hand, explained in the Latin Manual: 'a certain vein . . . runs from thence as far as the heart' (*usque ad cor*; *Manuale*, 49). Cressy cites a seventeenth-century source which repeats this touching anatomy of love (Cressy, 342). Rings were a pre-Christian mark of marriage and the subject of much symbolic analysis: 'The ring is rounde aboute and hath non ende in token that ther loue shulde be endles: and no thynge depart theim but deth alone' (*Dives and Pauper* (London: Richard Pynson, 1493), vi. 2).

other tokens of spousage: dowry gifts are retained in *1549* but were dropped in *1552*.

laying the same upon the boke: the rubric draws attention to the special status of the ring as a material object endowing a change in physical status upon its wearer. The ceremony of the giving of the rings was the most dramatic visual moment of the service in BCP, but in medieval marriages it was the clasping of hands and not the exchange of rings that was seen as the sacramental moment akin to seeing the elevation of the host in the Mass, or the anointing and chrisom in baptism. Rings in the medieval rite were sprinkled with holy water and prayers were said over them. Reformers objected to such practices, as they did to similar acts of consecration in relation to the physical book, such as kissing or elevating the gospel before readings and during processions.

with my body I thee wurship: 'honour'; as in the Wyclifite translation (1387) of Matt. 19: 19: 'worschipe thi fadir and modir.'

bracellets and Jewels of golde: the reference to the wedding gifts in Gen. 24: 53 justifies the 'tokens of spousage' above; the reference was dropped in *1552* along with the tokens.

67 *let no man put a sundre*: Matt. 19: 6. The prayer and the accompanying gesture of joining of hands is taken from Hermann (*Consultation*, 2I3ᵛ), although the line appears in the gospel reading for the *Missa sponsalium*. In other countries the hands were tied together with the priest's stole.

God the father blesse you. ✠ *God the sonne kepe you*: the third instance of a typographical indication of the sacred power of words in *1549*, indicating

the manual action of the priest in giving the sign of the cross while blessing. Like the others it was removed in *1552*.

67 *Then shal they goe into the quier*: this marks the transition into the second
part of the service, in medieval terms the wedding proper, consisting of
the Benediction and the nuptial Mass. The psalm is used processionally to
allow for the physical movement into the choir of the church.

Or els this psalme: the alternative is provided for women beyond the age of
child-bearing.

68 *blesse these thy servauntes*: this and the following two Collects form the
equivalent to the Benediction in the medieval marriage rite (*Manuale*, 50).
The first is a conflation of two Latin prayers.

69 *O God whiche by thy myghtye power*: this prayer was moved from a position
after the Canon in the nuptial Mass. In the medieval ceremony a veil was
held over the bride and groom.

sanctifie and ✠ *blisse you*: the final instance of the typographical cross, also
removed in *1552*.

71 *must receive the holy communion*: the rubric while compulsory is also
ambiguous. It marks the traditional association of the wedding with
a Communion (in the medieval rite, the Mass of the Trinity); but here
the Communion is no longer part of the ceremony (which was itself
a sacrament), but a separate obligation enjoining devout behaviour on the
couple.

VISITATION OF THE SICK

The service follows closely the medieval *Ordo visitandi* in the Sarum Manual,
although in abridged form. It was not (Blunt, 275) 'a mere piece of civility or
neighbourly kindness', but a religious rite, with scriptural authority. In Jas. 5:
14–15 the elders of the church are instructed to visit the sick, pray over them,
and anoint them with oil; the act is associated with healing and also with the
forgiveness of sins.

72 *Prieste entring into the sicke persones house*: in the medieval rite the priest
entered holding a crucifix before him (Duffy, 314). Julian of Norwich
describes this event as marking the beginning of her visions, when the
priest visited her on the third day in the extremity of her sickness: 'The
persone [parson] sette the crosse before my face, and sayd: Dowȝtter,
I have brought the the ymage of thy sauioure' (*A Book of Showings to
the Anchoress Julian of Norwich*, ed. Edmund Colledge and James Walsh,
2 vols., Studies and Texts, 35 (Toronto: Pontifical Institute of Medieval
Studies, 1978), Shorter Version, ch. 2; I, 208; see also Longer Version,
ch. 3; II, 291).

saye this psalme: all seven Penitential Psalms were prescribed in the medieval Order, of which only one is used here.

73 *Remembre not Lord our iniquities*: this prayer was followed in Sarum by the sprinkling of holy water on the sick person (*Manuale*, 99), here omitted.

O lorde save thy servaunte: these suffrages are used throughout the occasional offices with minor variations according to circumstance; they are taken from Pss. 86, 20, 89, 61, and 102.

looke downe from heaven: this and the following collect are translated in heavily abbreviated form from Sarum (*Respice domine de celo* and *Exaudi nos omnipotens*; *Manuale*, 99–100), where nine Collects are used in all.

74 *exhorte the sicke person*: the next part of the service is penitential, combining a rationalization of the causes of sickness with exhortations to patience, self-analysis, and faith. This follows the example of Sarum but is considerably rewritten.

75 *the articles of the fayth*: a renewal of the baptismal vows (see pp. 54–5).

shalbe used in all pryvate confessions: covering the provision for private confession already made in the order for Communion (see p. 25 and note). The issue is discussed at length in Hermann's *Consultation* (2G7ʳ–2H1ʳ). The wording of the absolution, while based on a Latin original going back to the Gelasian sacramentary, had been through several stages of composition, in the English version of Hermann's *Consultation*, and in the *Order of the Communion* of 1548. In *1552* the reference to private confession was excised.

76 *O most mercifull God*: this prayer of the 'reconciliation of a penitent near death' marks the beginning of the rite for extreme unction (*Manuale*, 106–7).

77 *O saveour of the world save us*: a unique case of an antiphon being used in its original form in the BCP, that is, a verse appended to a psalm in order to draw out its meaning or adapt its purpose to the occasion in hand.

78 *If the sicke person desyre to be annoynted*: the rite of unction is retained, but is made optional according to the wishes of the sick person. A single anointing on forehead or breast replaces the medieval practice of anointing in turn the eyes, ears, lips, limbs, and heart (*Manuale*, 108–9). Anointing with oil was dropped in *1552*.

As with this visible oyle: this prayer and the psalm following adhere to the rite of extreme unction in Sarum, which nonetheless is heavily abbreviated.

79 *The communion of the sicke*: in the pre-Reformation church the sacrament was kept reserved for the sick according to usual custom, and administered in a simple fashion following the unction. In *1549* the rubric allows for different alternatives: on a day when Communion has already been celebrated, and the elements consecrated, a shortened service of confession, absolution, distribution, and thanksgiving takes place. If Communion has to be provided specially for the sick, a reduced rite takes place with

a *Kyrie*, Epistle, and Gospel, followed by the Canon, at which the elements are consecrated.

79 *alwayes in a readinesse to dye*: the *ars moriendi* or 'art of dying' was a popular tradition throughout Europe in the fifteenth century. Men and women from all walks of life were encouraged to consider their own death and to prepare ahead. Texts advising how to help friends and neighbours on their deathbeds, including penitential interrogatories and prayers, were widely copied; printed versions by Caxton and Wynkyn de Worde disseminated them into the sixteenth century (Duffy, 315).

80 *Unto the ende of the Canon*: this rubric is notable for the use of the word 'Canon' in relation to the Mass, not mentioned in the text of the order for Communion itself, and controversial in debates before and after the introduction of the BCP (see p. 701 above).

81 *by reason of extremitie of sickenesse*: as in the Sarum rite, provision is made, where taking the sacrament is impossible, for the sick person to make a spiritual communion.

BURIAL OF THE DEAD

The medieval church provided for the dead, as for the dying, a rich array of spiritual comforts. A round of prayer in last sickness preceded psalms and litanies as death approached, and a last farewell in the name of the Trinity, the angels, and saints. After death came a service of commendation, with psalms and antiphons, as the body was prepared for burial. There were psalms to accompany the corpse to church. All of this was a prelude to the *Officium pro defunctis*, with an evening vigil or dirge, and a separate Matins and Lauds. Then came the Requiem Mass, and the censing and sprinkling of the body with holy water, before finally the actual burial. Beyond the grave there were memorial Offices and Masses in the month following death, and on anniversaries after.

The theology of death was controversial at the Reformation, for a number of reasons: the doctrine of purgatory, of the continued labour of souls after death towards salvation, was first disputed and then abolished; the system of Masses for the dead was strongly associated not only with purgatory but with the cult of saints; the Lutheran view of justification held that salvation came through the personal interaction of faith with God. One of the earliest sets of proposals of the English Reformation, promulgated by Thomas Cromwell in 1534, argued that 'the prayers of men that be here living can in no wise be profitable for the souls of them that be dead' (Marshall, 65). Purgatory as much as the Mass was the focus of the first wave of Protestant polemic in the 1530s. This extended in the 1540s to a physical attack on 'tabernacles, tombs, and sepulchres' for the dead, which were interpreted as idolatry (*VAI*, ii. 284–5). In April 1549 the chapel and charnel house of the Pardon Churchyard at St Paul's were pulled down by order of Somerset, so that only bare ground remained (Stow, *Survey*, i. 327–30). The service for burial in the Cologne rite allows for the singing of a psalm while the corpse is carried (Hermann, *Consultation*, 218ᵛ), but otherwise consists of exhortations and scriptural readings. By containing elements of procession and suffrage, *1549* represents both a radical departure from the medieval liturgy of death and yet at the same time its lingering farewell.

82 *so goe either into the Churche, or towardes the grave*: the introductory sentences represent a residual form of procession to the church or grave, especially when sung as anthems by the choir.

I am the resurreccion and the life: this beautiful processional anthem was part of the medieval *Inhumatio defuncti* (*Manuale*, 160).

I knowe that my redemer lyveth: part of the Sarum dirge or *Vigiliae mortuorum* (*Manuale*, 137); vernacular versions existed in fourteenth-century Primers ('I believe that my aȝenbiere lyueth').

the Corps is made readie to be layed into the earth: this marks the transition from the procession to the office of burial.

Man that is borne of a woman: a series of scriptural citations forms a textual (and usually musical) sequence which is unique to the Sarum *Manuale* (p. 138); it does not appear in the Roman rite. The section 'In the myddest of lyfe we be in death' formed an anthem by the ninth-century poet Notker, which was adapted for use as a dirge all over Germany through the middle ages. Luther wrote a popular hymn on the basis of it, 'Mitten wir im Leben sind'. This was translated into English and included in Coverdale's *Ghostly Psalms*, providing the source for *1549*.

castyng earth upon the Corps: a custom which precedes Christianity (Horace, *Odes* 1.28.35); the instruction for performance by the priest follows Sarum (*Manuale*, 158).

I commende thy soule to God the father almighty: as in Sarum, these words of committal are addressed to the corpse (*Commendo animam tuam*; *Manuale*, 158). This is a remarkable feature of *1549* and was altered in *1552*, where the words are addressed instead to the congregation.

83 *his body we commit to the earth*: this follows the service of burial in the medieval Manual.

psalmes with other suffrages folowyng: after the burial, this part of the service forms the function of the medieval *Officium defuncti*. In the medieval Office ten different psalms, along with the seven Penitential Psalms in addition (or instead of them the *De profundis*, Ps. 130) were indicated. Not all were presumably used at every burial. *1549* provides for some flexibility while also allowing for a process of some time and dignity, with three psalms, a long lesson, and suffrages of the type used for all of the occasional services.

84 *Domine, probasti*: the ordering of the following two psalms is reversed in Whitchurch's March printing; it has been corrected here in line with the editions from later in the year.

88 *From the gates of hell*: as in the committal, this sequence of responses

includes an unequivocal prayer for the souls of the dead ('Deliver theyr soules, o lorde'). This was at odds with the theology of the Reformers and was excised in *1552*.

88　*O lorde, with whome dooe lyve the spirites of them that be dead*: the final prayer of the office of the dead is taken partly from a Gregorian prayer (*Deus apud quem mortuorum spiritus vivunt*; *Gregorian Sacramentary*, 211). This appears in the Sarum *Manuale* (p. 158); while the ending comes from the Sarum Requiem Mass (Brightman, ii. 874). The awkward grammar of 'of them that be dead' (rather than 'of the dead') perhaps shows some uncertainty about how to express the physical status of the dead in the new theology.

　　be in joy and felicitie: this passage shows some confusion due to the pressure of different kinds of theology. Having just prayed for the soul of the corpse to escape hell, this prayer now at first assumes that the dead person is in heaven; but then falters, and prays that the sins of mortal life will not be imputed. The issue of the salvation of the deceased remained controversial up to *1662*. The wording of this prayer seems still to be trying to make use of the moral subtlety of the doctrine of purgatory, while having formally discarded it. As in the Canon of Communion, Cranmer is on thin ice.

89　*holy communion when there is a burial of the dead*: this special Eucharist retains the outward character of the medieval *Missa pro defunctis*, if in a much-truncated form; while at the same time denying its central function, of interceding on behalf of the dead. The Communion at burial is denied to be a 'work' which can benefit the dead spiritually, such as in Masses for the dead which limited the time spent in purgatory. In this new form, Ps. 42, *Quemadmodum*, forms an introit, and a special Collect, Epistle, and Gospel are provided. This forms the last remains of the principle enshrined in the medieval liturgy of the community of the living with the dead, but new tensions between the two realms are evident.

CHURCHING OF WOMEN

The origins of this service were traced back to the Jewish rite of purification referred to in Lev. 12: 2–8. It marked the return of women to church after childbirth. The English service followed closely the Latin rite in the Manual.

　　nygh unto the quier doore: in the medieval rite, 'churching' was linked to the Mass, into which the new mother was reincorporated.

　　I have lifted up mine iyes: Ps. 121 is used in Sarum (*Manuale*, 43).

92　*O almightie God, which hast delivered*: *1549* follows the form of the Sarum rite (*Manuale*, 44) in the suffrages (which follow the standard form for the occasional services), and this prayer, but omits the ceremony in which the mother was sprinkled and blessed with holy water.

　　must offer her Crysome, and other accustomed offeringes: the chrisom from the anointment at baptism is given to the priest, following medieval practice; candles were often offered as well, to be placed before images of the Blessed Virgin. The usual fee to the priest in cash or kind is intended here, since the offering of candles was forbidden in the Injunctions of 1547.

if there be a communion: the Mass was the invariable culmination of the pre-Reformation service, indeed the whole point; this rubric therefore has an oddly perfunctory sound.

COMMINATION

The public penance of the medieval rite for the beginning of Lent originally included the Penitential Psalms, a set of suffrages, and six Collects, followed by a solemn public absolution; by the end of the middle ages the act of penitence consisted mainly of the blessing and distribution of ashes, in which the cross was marked with ash on the forehead of all the people. In the BCP, the sacramental nature of penance is suppressed, and is replaced with a new liturgical form, with a homiletic and moral emphasis, consisting of a formal species of devotional denunciation aimed both at the self and at the community. The word 'commination' (from Latin, meaning a 'threatening') became a vogue term in Protestant literature (beginning with *The Glasse of Truth* in 1532) for ritualized cursing, and in *1552* was made the title for this service.

92   *the ryngyng of a bel*: this is the only mention in the text of *1549* of the ringing of a bell, an intrinsic part of medieval church life. Church bells date back to the Norman conquest, and were among the most expensive part of a church's inventory. They were used in monasteries to sound the hours of prayer, and in parishes to announce the *Ave Maria*, Matins and Evensong, or the Mass of the dead. The 'chime' or 'peal' summoned worshippers to church; the 'passing-bell' called them to pray for the departed; the 'death knell' was used to signal a death in the parish. Muffled bells at funerals were as much a part of the synaesthetic of religious feeling as wedding bells at marriages. The lack of textual record in the BCP is not, for once, a sign of physical suppression, although it may indicate some controversy in Reformed opinion. Bells continued to be part of everyday church life, and were used to indicate the beginnings and other key moments of the divine services. Surviving bell inscriptions in the vernacular in the sixteenth century and later show that the 'passing bell' was still used at funerals to summon to the grave, despite changes in theology in the burial service itself. The full number of bells in a church tower was eight (although five or six were sufficient), and was used to create a comprehensive musical effect. In the seventeenth century Protestant England became the home of 'change ringing', an elaborate bell-ringing practice symbolic of the life of a church in the community up to the present day.

Brethren, in the prymative churche: the origin of this preamble is in the Gelasian Sacramentary. The term 'open penaunce' refers to the practice of formally expelling notorious penitents in the presence of the officiating archdeacon or priest; those ejected on Ash Wednesday were readmitted on Maundy Thursday.

93 *Cursed is the man*: this part of the service was known as the 'maledictions'. Cursings against sinners were not part of the medieval rite but the practice of reading out anathema against individual sins is mentioned in Mirk, *Instructions*, 21–4 ('we accursen al them'), and was recommended on two or three occasions a year, with tolling of bells and extinction of lights. This formal cursing of sinners seems to have attracted itself to a Reformed sense of devotion and is adapted to create the structure of the new service.

94 *Nowe seeing that all they bee accursed*: the homily is made up largely of a tissue of denunciatory scriptural texts.

95 *Miserere mei deus*: Ps. 51 is the only one of the Penitential Psalms maintained for the vernacular service from the Latin version, which used all seven. It was the best-known of the seven, routinely used in preparation for confession, and with the dying.

97 *O lord, we beseche thee*: this translates the Collect *Exaudi quaesumus* from Sarum.

   O most mightie god: the beginning of this prayer is taken from the blessing of the ashes in the medieval rite; of the ashes themselves no trace remains.

   Then shal this antheme be sayed or song: a residual part of the processional aspect of the medieval form for Ash Wednesday, taken from the anthem indicated in the Sarum *Manuale* for the distribution of the ashes (*Processionale*, 29); it is unusual for Cranmer to prescribe such a long text for singing; in *1552* it is said, not sung. In the medieval rite there then followed a Mass, which may also have been the implied intention here.

CERTAIN NOTES

This section followed Of Ceremonies in *1549*. That text was reprinted in all editions of the BCP, and so is found in this edition in *1662* (pp. 214–16). Of Ceremonies provides a necessary context (and even commentary) on the practical use of *1549*, and should be read here. Certain Notes was not reprinted in any subsequent BCP, and so is included in this edition of *1549*.

98 *a Surples*: a 'surplice' is a loose vestment of white linen with wide sleeves, sometimes reaching to the feet, worn over a cassock (*OED*).

   to use any Surples or no: the contrary stipulation of freedom of dress testifies to the problematic status of vestments among Reformers. No issue caused more continuous animosity, not even crossing or kneeling. For some, following Hooper, the use of vestments implied creating a sacerdotal class separate from the people, and endowed with magical powers. This was anathema. For others, ministerial dress implied precisely a proper sense of the sacred, and of the sacred acts they were required to perform. This latter view became more prominent in the Jacobean period and later, among Laudians, where vestments and other ornaments are seen as part and parcel of a fully realized spirituality. This group took heart from the way that the BCP seemed in some places explicitly to endorse the use of vestments. See also Of Ceremonies, originally printed in *1549* directly before Certain Notes, and in this edition included in *1662*. The line adopted by Cranmer, however, seems to be that ornaments, including vestments, are neither necessary to faith nor incompatible with it. They are part of what was known as the *adiaphora* of doctrine—things which are not needed for salvation but can be helpful in conducting a good Christian life.

his rochette: a 'rochet' is a special vestment like a surplice, worn by bishops (*OED*).

As touching kneeling: sensitivity to gestures of body and the use of material objects in divine service can be seen throughout *1549*. This note attempts to patch up a consensus, but the royal Injunctions of 1547, and the promulgation of the BCP itself, hardly provoked either tolerance or conformity. Bodily ritual remained controversial through all the versions of the BCP represented in this edition.

THE BOOK OF COMMON PRAYER, 1559

Movements to reform the 1549 Book of Common Prayer began almost as soon as it was printed. Different parties, often arguing vociferously, divided over points of ceremony and doctrine. By December 1549 Bishop Hooper was rejoicing over the destruction of the altars in planned acts of iconoclasm, even though the use of altars was directed in the text of *1549*. To manage criticism, continental divines including Peter Martyr Vermigli and Martin Bucer were invited to comment on the new liturgy. Revision was discussed at Convocation in December 1550. Bucer's *Censura*, a full-scale book on the BCP, was delivered in January 1551. Discussion continued for a year. The Act to promulgate the second BCP was passed on 14 April 1552 and a deadline set for its production of All Saints' Day (1 November). Whitchurch and Grafton retained their monopoly on the printing of the BCP. *1552* made substantial alterations to *1549* throughout, with significant changes including adding confession and absolution to Morning and Evening Prayer, turning these services into a collective act of penitential Protestant devotion; a radical transformation of Communion, with the Canon removed, reference to the real presence of Christ in the Eucharist severely reduced, and stone altars replaced by a wooden 'Lord's table'; the excision of anointing and other bodily actions in Baptism and the Visitation of the Sick; and a drastic reduction in the Burial of the Dead. Vestments and ceremonies were reduced or effaced throughout.

After Edward's death in June 1553, his sister Mary restored the Catholic religion and abolished the BCP. The Latin Mass and other rites returned, along with the church year of the cult of the saints, and images, roods, etc. On Elizabeth's succession on 17 November 1558 all of the places of ecclesiastical power were therefore occupied by Catholics, and there was good hope in that party that the Roman rites would remain. While a decision on religious polity stalled, a private committee of Protestants gathered in the house of Sir Thomas

Smith to discuss revisions to the BCP. This committee included returning exiles from Geneva and elsewhere, as well as divines loyal foremost to the queen. At this point there was support both for *1549* and *1552*. There was a debate at Westminster in March 1559 which considered, *inter alia*, whether authority in matters of faith belonged only to the clergy; whether liturgy should be in the vernacular; vestments and ceremonies; the church calendar; and details of doctrine, especially concerning the nature of sacraments, the sacrifice of the Mass, and the real presence (*Conferences*, 23–9; documents, pp. 55–92). The result of these debates was decided by the queen finding in favour of the Protestants; the Act of Uniformity of April 1559 (see p. 186), however, was still only narrowly passed. It restored the BCP and prescribed a fine of 12*d*. (equivalent to £11 in 2010) for failure to attend church on Sundays. Matthew Parker was made archbishop of Canterbury. The printing history of *1559* is as confused as the religious settlement which provoked it. John Cawood, the royal printer under Mary, was eventually retained by Elizabeth, in conjunction with Richard Jugge, who had printed a NT in 1550. In the meantime Grafton, one of the two main printers of *1549* and *1552*, seems to have attempted to reclaim his position as royal printer by beginning work on *1559*. Imprints survive of *1559* bearing both his mark and that of Jugge and Cawood; one copy of Grafton has the names of the other printers pasted in on an error slip. Jugge and Cawood in due course assumed a monopoly of the printing of BCP, but Grafton's edition is the only one of *1559* to incorporate all of the decisions of the 1559 Act of Uniformity and is used here. In haste, the word 'King' was used in *1559* editions.

1559 is a close relation to *1552*, with small yet significant changes, e.g. to the words of distribution of the Eucharist and to the Litany. The Explanatory Notes for *1559* comment on the changes between *1549* and *1552* as well as these alterations in *1559*. The 'Black Rubric', part of the text for *1552* that was eliminated in *1559*, is included in Appendix A as a separate text. The Explanatory Notes for *1549* may also usefully be consulted in relation to the following.

MORNING PRAYER

In the reign of Elizabeth the services of Morning and Evening Prayer were already becoming the most familiar aspects of religious life using the new liturgy. There were complex reasons for this. In late medieval religion the Mass was the central experience of worship, yet it was common to take Communion only once a year at Easter; on other occasions seeing the host was sufficient. Among Protestants, although the desire of the clergy and the godly was for parishioners to take regular Communion, congregations were culturally reluctant to do so. Since the elevation of the host was now forbidden, Communion required the taking of the elements of bread and wine; this must have taken place regularly only in larger churches and cathedrals. In smaller parishes Morning Prayer took on the character of the major service on Sundays. This may be reflected in some of the additions to Morning Prayer in *1552*.

102 *in the accustomed place of the churche, chapel, or chauncell*: the initial rubric for *1549* had been cursory, directing only that the priest should be in the

choir, and begin the service 'with a loude voyce'. In *1552* complex instructions were introduced. Following criticisms in Bucer's *Censura* (p. 15) that the congregation was separated from the priest, the minister was told to place himself anywhere in the church (and at such an angle) 'as yᵉ people maye best heare' the word of God. Even so, the *1552* rubric, in case there might be 'any controversie therein', referred the matter to the bishop for final adjudication, and allowed for the use of the chancel as in times past. In *1559* the rubric was further altered to remove the note of controversy and to allow for a variety of practice, relying on custom in individual churches.

suche ornamentes in the church, as wer in use: in *1552* a prohibitive rubric was introduced that the priest, in the Communion as well as Matins, 'shall use neither albe, vestment, nor cope' but 'shall have and wear a surplice onely'. Bucer (*Censura*, 19) recommended that the special vestments be abolished, not because they were 'wicked' (*impii*) in themselves, but because, in the absence of good teaching in church, they encouraged 'superstitious belief'. In 1559 the Act of Uniformity, backed up with Visitation Injunctions, drew a rough line in the rubble of argument and counter-argument, between the iconoclasts who were destroying altars at will and demanding the barest ecclesiastical dress, and those (including the queen) who did not wish to be forced into Puritan practice. The *1559* rubric restores the letter of regulation in line with *1549*, thus giving permission for more traditional customs to prevail without insisting on uniform practice. This did not prevent the continued devastation of chancel furnishings in churches where Reformers took a more determined attitude. The Royal Orders on 10 October 1561, moderating destructive zeal, show the degree of continued physical violence to the internal decoration of some churches. The 1569 Visitation Articles at Norwich indicate that in some churches the priest was given a seat in the body of the church (in large churches) or outside the chancel door (in smaller ones), for use throughout the divine service. The *1559* rubric also implies that vestments were no longer enforced according to the *1552* strictures, but defiance was shown on both sides. In 1559 even the Royal Chapel at one point had the crucifix, candles, and vestments removed; but they had been restored by October. In 1562–3 appeals were made to Convocation to remove the necessity of vestments, but this was defeated. Parker's efforts to enforce conformity led to an outbreak of public protest in 1566. Stow records how the minister of St Magnus-the-Martyr, who had earlier preached against vestments but had now conformed and was wearing a surplice, was attacked by women who threw stones at him, pulled him out of the pulpit, tore his surplice, and scratched his face (Stow, *Memoranda*, p. 139). Robert Crowley's clandestinely published *A Briefe Discourse Against the Outwarde Apparel of the Popishe Church* (1566) led to a literary war on the subject. The 'Vestiarian Controversy' was never resolved and remained the source of tension for a century and more. This so-called 'Ornaments Rubric' of

1559, upholding the position of *1549*, was confirmed in *1662* (see note to p. 239).

102 *some one of these sentences of the Scriptures that folowe*: these penitential sentences were prefixed to the Morning Service in *1552*, perhaps reflecting the full transition from the medieval Office based on monastic practice (including regular mental disciplines of penance) to the needs of a mixed congregation.

103 *the Scripture moveth us in sondry places, to acknowledge and confesse*: this exhortation was newly composed in *1552* in line with Reformed principles of penitence as a lay practice enjoined by scripture and public morality.

A generall confession, to be saide of the whole congregacion after the minister, knelyng: another original composition of *1552*, although modelled on older confessional formularies. A general form of confession was introduced in the *1549* Communion, but is here regularized as a language of daily discipline, the forms of private confession having been removed. It is prescribed to be said 'after the minister', traditionally clause by clause (although this is not the only possible interpretation of the rubric). Adding the confession to Morning Prayer may reflect the way in which it was taking on some of the functions of Communion in regular Sunday worship.

We have left undone those thinges whiche we ought to have done: see Rom. 7: 15. This chapter of Paul lies behind the structure of the whole of the *1552* general confession.

104 *The absolution to be pronounced by the Minister alone*: forms of absolution had been prescribed in both the *1549* Communion and Visitation of the Sick, but the text here is once again a new composition of *1552*, using material from the medieval hours of Prime and Compline. At the 1604 Hampton Court Conference it was declared that the priest's absolution conferred remission of sins, although it is clear that this was not the theological intention of the wording here, which avoids the Latin formula *te absolvo* translated literally in the *1549* Visitation of the Sick (p. 76).

the Lordes Prayer: this rubric signals a return to the text of the *1549* Matins, following the confessional interpolations of *1552*. There are two minute verbal changes: the 'priest' is now referred to as 'the Minister'; and the Lord's Prayer is no longer, unlike in *1549*, referred to by the familiar Latin tag *Pater noster*.

O Lord, open thou our lippes: changed from 'my lippes' in *1549*.

Praise ye the Lorde: the 'Alleluya' prescribed in *1549* from Easter to Trinity Sunday is omitted in *1552* and *1559*, as also in Evensong.

106 *Heaven and earth are ful of*: a retranslation of *Te Deum*, line 10 (*Pleni sunt coeli et terra*) correcting the awkward reading 'replenyshed with' of *1549*.

107 *Or this canticle, Benedicite*: now simply an alternative to *Te Deum*, rather than, as in *1549*, prescribed during Lent.

109 *Jubilate Deo*: this psalm, which was the second of the fixed psalms at Lauds

on a Sunday, was adopted as an alternative canticle in *1552* because the *Benedictus* is sometimes the lesson or Gospel of the day (i.e. 18 February, 17 June, 24 June (St John the Baptist's Day), and 15 October).

110 *the Crede*: the saying of the Apostles' Creed now precedes the prayers rather than, as in *1549*, following them.

O Lorde save the Queene: the first occurrence of the change in the gender of the monarch within the suffrages, revised throughout *1559* from *1552*, and of course altered back in *1604*. Individual copies of older BCPs, surviving into a new reign, are often altered by hand to reflect the change in monarch.

EVENING PRAYER

As with Morning Prayer, this service established itself as a central part of regular worship. Diaries written in the late sixteenth century (such as that of the gentlewoman Margaret Hoby) indicate frequent attendance at both Morning and Evening Prayer on the same Sunday.

111 *O Lord open thou our lippes*: the opening versicle and response was introduced in *1552*, borrowed from the order for Morning Prayer.

112 *O God make spede to save us*: as in Morning Prayer, the plural form is preferred over the singular used by the priest in *1549*.

our forefathers: the attention to detail in the *1552* revision is shown by this small preference in translating τους πατέρας ημών in Luke 1: 55.

Or the xcviii. Psalme Cantate domino canticum novum: the prescription of this Ps. 98 as an alternative responsory may reflect Reformers' anxiety over the Marian connotations of the *Magnificat*; alternatively, it may simply provide for the alternation of OT and NT material.

113 *Or this Psalme, Deus misereatur nostri*: as after the *Magnificat*, an alternative responsory is suggested from the psalms; in this case, the use of Ps. 67 goes back to Lauds, and also to the bidding prayers used every Sunday in the medieval rite.

114 *Then shal folow the Crede*: the use of the Creed was introduced in *1552*, mirroring the order for Morning Prayer. This is another indication of the way that these two services were acquiring something of the status of staple forms of worship equal to (and in practice more regularly attended than) Communion.

115 *And yet are not there thre Almightyes*: the reading here differs from that in the Jugge and Cawood printing in the same year, 'And yet thei are not thre Almightyes'. The latter reading is in line with the Whitchurch printing of *1549* used in this edition and his edition of *1552*; and with later printings from *1564* onwards. The alternative reading 'are not there' was used by Grafton in his printing of *1549* and *1552*, and its use here is one of the indications that Grafton was involved in the printing of this text of *1559*,

while he was still attempting (unsuccessfully) to renew his rights as a royal printer of Prayer Books. See Note on the Texts, pp. lix–lx.

LITANY

The final function of the Litany in the BCP was only established in *1552*. In *1549* its status was still ambiguous, and Cranmer for some time seems to have hoped to create a separate English processional. In *1552* it was moved in the contents of the BCP to this place before Communion, where it is set as a solitary and stationary performance before the Eucharist. Apart from a tiny procession on Easter Day, and the service for Ash-Wednesday, this is all that now remained from the medieval Processional, a whole extra service book which provided a panoply of communal processions for Sundays, feast days, and Rogation days, along with music. The Litany was, however, static; its process is entirely mental.

117 *to be used upon Sondaies, Wednesdaies, and Fridayes*: the 1559 Injunctions connected the Litany with the Communion. In 1571, in his Visitation at York, Edmund Grindal required that there should be no pause between Morning Prayer, Litany, and Communion, and that all three services be said without intermission, so that the people would stay continually in prayer and the hearing of the word of God.

and from soudeine deathe: the clause against 'the tyrannye of the bishop of Rome and all his detestable enormities' (see p. 41 and note), which had been removed in Mary I's Litany, reappeared in early printings of the independent Elizabethan Litany, but was removed in *1559*.

118 *and strengthen in the true worshipping of thee in righteousnes and holynes of lyfe*: these words were added in *1559* to the shorter intercession set for the monarch in *1549* and *1552*. Prayers for the consort of the monarch, and for the monarch's children, were added as appropriately in *1604* and after *1625*.

Elizabeth our most gracious Quene and governour: copies of the BCP were frequently corrected by hand by subsequent owners to mark the change of monarch in this set prayer. Thus in the BL copy of the 1554 Litany (shelf mark C.25.b.10) published separately under Mary I (the only part of the BCP to be reissued between 1553 and 1558), 'Phylyp and Mary' are later crossed out and 'elizabeth' added in MS; then in another hand, 'Quene' is crossed out, and 'James' and 'gracious King' are inserted.

121 *A Prayer for the Quenes Majesty*: this prayer for the monarch originated in two books of private prayers in 1545 and 1547. It was also used in the 1553 Primer. It was moved to this position at the end of the Litany in *1559*. A prayer for kings is sanctioned by 1 Tim. 2: 2; a *Missa pro rege* is found as early as the sixth century in Gregorian Sacramentaries; and prayers for the king were included in a similar form of Mass in the Sarum missal. Cf. also the Collects for the king (or queen) in Communion.

122 *For rayne, yf the tyme requyre*: this and the prayer for 'fayre weather' were

transposed here in *1552* from the Collects at the end of Communion in *1549*.

In the tyme of dearth and famyne: this prayer was included for the first time in *1552*, along with a second alternative prayer for the same purpose, which was left out in *1559* and in *1604*, although it is found in some editions and was restored in *1662* (p. 266).

123 *In the tyme of Warre*: this prayer was introduced in *1552*, along with the prayer 'In the tyme of any common plague or syckenesse'. On plague, see note to p. 170. The final prayer was added in *1559*.

COMMUNION

The second Edwardian BCP of *1552* made radical changes throughout this service. The vernacular Canon of *1549*, achieved at such cost, was split in three; the first part, the intercession, was placed earlier in the service; the central consecration was altered and ended abruptly; the third, the oblation, was removed until after the Communion of the people. In addition, there were further changes to almost all of the other invariable elements in the old Mass, including the *Kyrie*, *Gloria*, *Sanctus*, and *Agnus Dei*. As significant as these verbal changes were alterations to vestments and ornaments and even to the furniture of the church, altars in many cases being replaced by a wooden table in the midst of the church. It was a revolution in ritual as dramatic as the initial introduction of the vernacular service in *1549*. In addition, the use of the Communion service was adapted to parish needs. There remained a reluctance to take the elements (i.e. bread and wine), and encouraging regular attendance at the new service proved difficult. The Protestant view was that Communion was only valid if the elements were taken, whereas in the medieval Mass seeing the host was the central experience for the laity. Priests who remained sympathetic to traditional beliefs may have used the new service in the same way as the old; those who were more Reformed probably held Communion very irregularly, with Morning Prayer becoming the standard Sunday service (see pp. xxxviii–xl). Parish accounts, which include charges for bread and wine, are clear evidence of infrequency of Communion services. Hunt, 'The Lord's Supper', discusses periodic attempts to hold monthly (or more frequent) Communion.

The *1552* text remained the basis for the *1559* version, although the 'Black Rubric' (Appendix A, see p. 667 and note) was removed and the words of consecration were altered.

The word 'masse' was removed from the title-heading of the service in *1552*, leaving 'the Lordes Supper, or holy Communion'.

124 *or at the least declare him selfe*: this phrase, distinguishing between an intention to amend a naughty life, and the declaration of such an intention, was added in *1552*. Bucer (*Censura*, 19) called these directions of the 'greatest value', as ensuring that the devotion of the communicant was worthy of the seriousness of religious worship.

The table, havyng at the Communion tyme a fayre whyte linnen cloth: the forcible removal of stone altars took place in an indiscriminate fashion during the iconoclasm of the reign of Edward VI. Wooden Communion tables were noticed in London in 1549 (Fincham and Tyacke, 19). The Elizabethan Injunctions of 1559 insisted neither on destruction nor on a ban on destruction; provided 'the Sacrament be duly and reverently administered', it was 'no matter of great moment' whether the altar was stone or not. If an altar was removed, it was stipulated 'no riotous or disordered manner to be used'. If a wooden table was provided it should be 'decently made' and 'commonly covered, as thereto belongeth' with a cloth. Stone altars remained in the royal chapels and in several cathedrals. But tables were now the rule, and visitations enforced this (Fincham and Tyacke, 21–3). A number of Elizabethan altar tables survive, usually with bulbous bossed 'melon' legs and sometimes with ornamental sculpture on the rails or with inscribed carvings of the name of the donor or of a devotional message (for examples see *English Church Furniture*, 12–17).

124 *shall stand in the body of the churche*: the replacing of the table in the midst of the church is the most striking visual image of the religious changes wrought on the post-Reformation parish church. Instead of the Mass taking place at the end of the building in hallowed privacy, the Communion table was placed in the middle of the chancel, its axis east–west. Archbishop Holgate instituted this rule in York diocese in June 1551; Salisbury followed in 1553 (Fincham and Tyacke, 23). Surviving tables are large in size and would have dominated the view. There is a nineteenth-century photograph of Hailes in Gloucestershire (see Diarmaid MacCulloch, *Tudor Church Militant: Edward VI and the Protestant Reformation* (London: Allen Lane, 1999), 159–60), taken before the Victorian liturgical reforms, showing such a table, with ranks of benches for communicants occupying the position of the old altar.

standyng at the Northe syde of the table: the table would usually be housed along the east wall but brought into the body of the church for Communion. The bodily position of the priest on the north side of the table, facing half of his congregation, instead of the sacrament at the altar, was an equally dramatic statement of religious change.

125 *Then shal the Priest rehearse distinctly al the .x. Commaundementes*: this replaces the psalm used as an introit in *1549*, and the *Kyrie*, and marks the dominance of the verbal over the visual in the new rite. In 1547, according to the *Chronicle of Grey Friars*, there was a general demolition of rood-screens and images in churches, and in their place, 'alle churches new whyte-lymed, with the Commandments written on the walles'. Under Mary I new images were made and scriptural texts often washed out in turn (for instance, in Ashburton there is a 1554 payment for 'Strykynge out of the Scriptur upon the Rode Lofte'). In 1559 the reversals began again, indiscriminately, until a 1561 Royal Order prescribed some uniformity of architecture, the upper parts of the wooden vaults always removed, but screens often retained or reformed, creating 'a comely partition' between

chancel and church'. Such orders were nonetheless resisted in many parts of the country sympathetic to Catholic tradition, and patchily observed.

Lorde have mercye upon us, and encline our hartes to kepe this lawe: the element of catechism in Communion is an innovation, and emphasizes its role as a doctrinal and devotional reinforcement. MacCulloch (*Cranmer*, 505–6) suggests a possible influence from Valerand Poullain's French refugee congregation set up by Somerset in Glastonbury, although there the recitation and response of the Commandments was metrical. Here, the words of the *Kyrie* are incorporated into the responses, assimilating the older Latin practice. Protestantization of churches was textual in form. A letter of 1561 to the dean and chapter of Bristol ordered a wooden board to be inscribed with the Ten Commandments 'in large characters' and placed on the east wall of the choir where the Communion table stood; under King James it was required (*Canons* (1604), LXXXII) that the Commandments be set upon the east wall of every church, and other sentences to be written in convenient places (*Roodscreens and Roodlofts*, i. 109). Scriptural texts on walls whitewashed of their paintings of saints, or sometimes in the identical position of the old rood-screen, made the church into a three-dimensional representation of scripture. However, paintings of apostles and prophets were sometimes allowed to remain, and an example of a new image of Moses and Aaron survives at Croydon, commissioned to accompany the Commandments (Fincham and Tyacke, 89–90).

127 *The Gospell*: the acclamation of the gospel in *1549* ('Glory be to thee, O Lorde', following the Latin *Gloria tibi domine*) was removed in *1552*.

one of the Homelies alredy set furth: in 1563 a new expanded edition of *Certain Homilies* was issued, now with twenty homilies (instead of the twelve published in 1547). The additions concentrate on moral discipline. In 1570 the homily on rebellion was added, making twenty-one in all. The homilies are listed in Article 35 (see p. 683).

the Curate shall declare unto the people: these notices follow the sermon, and immediately precede the Offertory. The Exhortations to the faithful to attend Communion, which followed at this point in the *1549* order, are postponed until after the intercession in *1552*. The sermon now occupied a principal role in the service, and the pulpit rather than the altar was the focus of visual attention. Bucer (*Censura*, 47) expresses the desire of many for the universities to provide pastors sufficiently learned to write their own sermons containing edifying instruction. However, the small number of surviving Elizabethan pulpits, compared with the reigns of James I and Charles I, implies both slow progress on this front and continued use of medieval pulpits, either in the nave of the church (the now preferred position), or a transitional tolerance of the alternative site in the rood-loft.

129 *gather the devocion of the people, and put the same into the poore mens boxe*: the Edwardian government ordered a poorbox to collect alms to be placed in

every church. This reinforced the order that charity was not to be aimed at Masses for the departed but towards the needs of the living. Bucer defined the offerings as the true meaning of the 'sacrifice' or 'oblation' of the Mass (*Censura*, 39), in clear contradiction of the Roman missal; this new view was reinforced through the seventeenth century (see note to p. 395).

129 *Let us pray for the whole estate of Christes Churche militant*: the intercession was moved to this early point in the service in *1552* from its place in the Canon in *1549*. This was a highly significant change, removing intercession from its position as part of the ritual Mass of the faithful, living and departed, and making it instead a separate form of devotional supplication. The prayers themselves follow the same order as in *1549*, for the monarch; then for the bishops, pastors, and curates; then for the present congregation; and for those suffering 'trouble, sorowe, nede, sicknes, or any other adversity'. The prayers for the departed, which followed in *1549*, were eliminated in *1552*. Bucer (*Censura*, 51–3) disputed even ancient authorities on prayers for the dead, and recommended omission.

130 *the people negligent to come to the holy communyon*: the first exhortation, placed now after the offertory and intercession rather than before, and thus leading straight into Communion, begins with a warning note. Bucer in his *Censura* (p. 147) commented adversely on the practice of coming but rarely to Communion ('ut in anno vix plures quam ter aut quater'; 'in a year no more than three or four times'). Bucer, however, had himself found it difficult to encourage frequent Communion in Strassburg; and Calvin also in Geneva.

We be come together at thys tyme derely beloved brethren: this exhortation was written new for the *1552* service.

so that there lacketh nothinge but the gestes to site downe: despite the initial admonitory tone, this exhortation contains the kernel of a new form of devotional and affective language for the Eucharist, adopting the medieval concept of the feast but turning it to a domestic sentiment of a familiar meal. The idea of the family of Christians 'lovyngly called' enters into the religious idiom of the Church of England, as can be seen in George Herbert's celebratory Eucharistic poem 'Love (III)', where the allegorical figure of love 'Drew nearer to me, sweetly questioning, | If I lack'd any thing. | | A guest, I answer'd, worthy to be here'.

131 *yf ye stande by as gasers and lokers of them that do Communicate, and be no partakers*: the criticism recalls (and rebukes) the late medieval devotion surrounding 'seeing the host' at the moment that it is raised to the view of the parishioners. It also reveals the quandary of the practical reception of the new liturgy, as it defined 'partaking' through the taking of the elements; while most parishioners retained the traditional reluctance to do so more than once a year.

Derely beloved, for asmuche as our dutye is to rendre: this is based on the second of the exhortations in *1549*, although considerably rewritten (see

p. 24). In particular, it omits reference to making charitable restitution of goods to a neighbour who has been cheated in any way; and to 'auriculer and secret confession to the Priest' for any communicant who feels the general confession is insufficient to expiate the penitent conscience.

132 *ye that mynde to come to the holye Communion*: the third exhortation is adapted from the first exhortation in *1549*. The rubric requiring those who do not intend to partake to retire out of the choir is now omitted.

133 *For then we be gilty of the body and bloud of Christ our saviour*: these words are inscribed round the frame of a Communion table at Ombersley, Worcestershire, probably donated by Lord Sandys in 1572 (*English Church Furniture*, 13).

134 *Then shall this generall confession be made*: the invitation and confession are largely identical to *1549*, but are moved in *1552* to this place before Consecration, thus implying that the salving of conscience takes place as part of the preparation for worthy receiving of the Communion, rather than as part of the rite.

   either by one of them, or els by one of the ministers, or by the priest hym selfe: this rubric proved controversial among Puritans, who objected to the idea of words of faith being said on behalf of another person.

135 *geve thanckes unto*: an example of a tiny verbal alteration in *1552* (for 'geve thankes to'), adopted in other places and retained thereafter, providing a more subtle aural rhythm.

136 *Holy, holy, holy*: the Hebraic formula 'Osanna in the highest' is omitted from the *Sanctus* in *1552*.

   We do not presume: the prayer of humble access was moved here as a preface to the consecration in *1552*, instead of its previous place after the Canon, perhaps to emphasize the participation of the laity in the performance of Communion.

   to drinke his bloude: the additional words in *1549*, 'in these holy Misteries', are excised; Archbishop William Laud later suggested their revival.

137 *his one oblation of himself once offered*: there are two small changes in the initial part of the institution, one concerning the problematic word 'oblation', the occasion of so much theological controversy, and here defined as Christ's own sacrifice 'of himself'. The other is the replacement of the phrase 'to celebrate a perpetuall memory' (*1549*) with 'to continue a perpetual memory' (*1552*). Both changes subtly adjust the relationship between Communion as the repeated re-celebration of a sacrifice in the here and now, and the memorial of a sacrifice made once by Christ in the past and now devoutly remembered. The difference creates a fault-line between the idea of the Mass as a physical action altering things in the world, with Christ actually present (the Catholic view, but also retained in some form in some versions of Protestantism, when interpreted spiritually); and Communion as a form of spiritual edification for the godly,

recalling Christ's actions and maintaining faith in him (the Zwinglian view, at the root of much Protestant thinking and reviled by Catholics). Cranmer had come to accept the latter version, and this is reflected in *1549* and *1552*; but he also tolerated some language of 'oblation' which implied the former version. Calvinists would interpret this, however, as a spiritual action and not a physical one.

137 *graunt that we receivyng these thy creatures of breade and wine*: the syntax of this prayer, now using the modal auxiliary 'may', modulates and downplays the directness of the ritual speech act in *1549*, 'vouchsafe to bl✠esse'; in *1552* the typographical cross, signalling the moment of bodily performance and transformation, is also removed, along with the marginal indications of accompanying gestures, such as '*Here the priest must take the bread into his handes*'. This was in accord with the comment by Bucer (*Censura*, 61), who rejected the practice of priests in bowing to the bread and wine and breathing on them as they said the words of institution ('inclinantes se ad panem, & vinum, & in haec inspirantes dicunt'). Such actions, and muttering over the bread, implied, he said, that the priest was talking to the bread and not to the congregation; and that 'by the pronunciation of these words some change was to take place in the elements'. Christ, in distributing the bread and wine to the disciples, did not suggest he was 'himself making himself from the bread and wine' (*se effecisse de pano ipse, & vino per se*), but intended only to arouse thanksgiving in the disciples, and to encourage them to do the same for others. The following section of the Canon, in which the priest turned to the altar in *1549*, is also partly excised, and partly removed to the post-Communion.

who in the same night that he was betraied: the recitation of the gospel narrative is instructional rather than a re-enactment of the change in the elements.

receyve the Communion in bothe kyndes: expenditure on wine shows a far greater incidence of taking Communion at Easter than at other times. In some parishes two grades of wine were purchased; the smaller portions of Muscat were presumably for the minister and upper-class members of the congregation (Hunt, 'Lord's Supper', 49).

after to the people in their handes: not, that is, directly into the mouth. This is to emphasize a lack of physical alteration in the elements; the desire of the communicant not to touch sacred things is taken to be a superstition. Bucer recommended the change (*Censura*, 35), since it implied a 'false honour' (*falsi honoris*) tended to the sacrament, and encouraged the arrogance of the priesthood, in thinking themselves to have 'a sanctity greater than that of the people of Christ'.

The bodie of our lord Jesu Christ which was geven for thee: in *1549* the formula for delivering the elements was, 'The body of our Lorde Jesus Christe whiche was geven for thee, preserve thy bodye and soule unto everlasting lyfe'. This was replaced in *1552* with a completely novel formula reduced to the simple clause, 'Take and eate this, in remembraunce that Christ died for thee, and fede on him in thy heart by faith, with thankesgevyng', thus removing any inference of calling the bread the body (or the wine the blood). There is no known source for this, a drastic reduction in sacramental action in favour of doctrinal statement. It is based on Zwingli's concept of 'memorialism'; that is, the taking of the elements is a reminder of a previous action, not an action in itself (see note to p. 30). In *1559*, in the single most important revision to the Communion service in the Elizabethan BCP, the two formulae of *1549* and *1552* were simply combined, paying scant attention to grammatical sense, but allowing either interpretation.

The bloude of our lorde Jesu Christ: as above, the two clauses of the formula, the first from *1549*, the second from *1552*, are juxtaposed in *1559*.

After shalbe sayde as foloweth: the post-Communion begins with textual material taken from the *1549* Canon (p. 31), in the form of the traditional prayer of oblation ('we offer and presente unto thee, O Lord, our selves, our soules and bodies, to be a reasonable, holy, and lively sacrifice unto thee'), derived from Rom. 12: 1.

138 *Almighty and everlastinge God, we moste hartely thancke thee*: the alternative prayer brings the service back in line with the *1549* post-Communion thanksgiving (p. 36).

Glorye be to God on hyghe: the *Gloria* is replaced here from its position at the beginning of the medieval Office, where it had remained in *1549*.

Thou that takest awaye the Sinnes of the worlde, have mercy upon us: the repetition of this phrase, new in *1552*, seems to be a recompense for the removal of the *Agnus Dei* from the *1552* post-Communion.

139 *And the same maye be sayde also*: this rubric was added in *1552*. The Collects are identical to those in *1549*, except that the Collects for rain and for fair weather were now placed in *1552* and *1559* with the other special prayers at the end of the Litany.

140 *And yf there be not above .xx. persons in the Parish*: this rubric was added in *1552*.

the beste and purest wheate breade, that conveniently may be gotten: this rubric, following Protestant preference (e.g. in Calvin) for everyday bread, replaces in *1552* the rubric ordering 'unleavened, and rounde' wafers in *1549*. Bucer (*Censura*, 23) said the shape and type of bread was indifferent; the bread is significant, after all, only as a symbol ('vero tantum symboli gratia'). Yet the Yorkshire minister Robert Parkyn (in the 1560s) insisted on bread 'such as men use in their houses with meate'. In practice there was considerable ambiguity on this matter. The Elizabethan Injunctions of 1559 insisted on wafers, 'heretofore named singing cakes'. Archbishop Mathew Parker, consulted repeatedly on the issue, temporized that where wafers were unavailable, or where a minister feared superstition in the use of wafers, ordinary (but good-quality) bread was to be used. He tolerated different practices, and demurred only from excessive dissension on loaf-bread.

140 *the Curate shall have it to hys owne use*: tradition allowed the clergy to 'live by the altar' and take any unconsecrated bread for their own use. The wording in *1559*, however, following the revision of *1552*, makes it unclear whether this also applies to consecrated bread; the radical Reformed rejected the idea that the bread had changed into 'holy' form. Bucer (*Censura*, 41) called the belief that 'something spiritual or holy inhered of itself in this bread and wine' a *superstitio*; equally, for others the mundane consumption of holy bread was an appalling sacrilege.

at the leaste thre tymes in the yere, of whiche Easter to be one: changed from 'once in the yeare at least' in *1549*. Bucer called refusing to take Communion an 'insult (*contumelia*) to Christ our Saviour' (*Censura*, 27). He argued that people should take Communion as often as it was offered in the holy assembly (p. 31). But this was a pious hope in practice. At the Middle Temple in 1580 members were ordered to take Communion three times a year; in 1614 the rule was changed to twice; and soon afterwards to once (Hunt, 'Lord's Supper', 41). This reflected the truth that most people received Communion only at Easter. In some parishes there are records of payments for bread and wine on three occasions per year (Whitsun, Christmas, and Easter). In other parishes the Easter Communion was staggered over several weeks up to Whitsun. In the early seventeenth century there was a trend towards more frequent Communion, such as monthly, especially in London churches (ibid. 55).

BAPTISM

The order for Baptism was one of the most controversial in the late Tudor and early Stuart periods. This is reflected in the simplification of the *1549* rite in *1552*, and in the removal of rituals such as exorcism and blessing the font. Bucer (*Censura*, 87) somewhat snobbishly commented on the delight of the common people for 'theatrical actions' and 'outward signs'. He wished to see removed both the white robe ('chrisom') and the anointing with chrism (oil mixed with balm). However, the crossing of the forehead, which was retained in *1552*, remained the object of Puritan ire, and the English church continued to divide between seeing baptism as a sacred rite of transformation or as a covenantal 'seal' (Calvin's term) of incorporation within the Christian faith. An additional anxiety surrounded the practice of lay baptism in circumstances of emergency. Catholic custom allowed this, the desire for the salvation of the newly born taking precedence here over the sacerdotal primacy of the priest. Luther encouraged the principle of lay baptism, in line with his theory of the 'priesthood of all believers'; Calvin, however, rejected lay baptism since only the disciples had scriptural authority to perform baptism. On this point Cranmer showed more of a Lutheran sentiment rather than the more radical view, and *1552* continued in line with *1549* (Hunt, 'Lay Baptism'). The position was left unchanged in *1559*, but this is an issue where clerical practice and lay feeling often ran ahead of the text of the BCP. Rubrics in the BCP continued to provoke these differences of opinion and feeling over a century and more.

141 *may at al tymes*: altered from 'ought' in *1549*, thus implying permission rather than encouragement or enforcement. Baptism at home remained contentious throughout the Elizabethan and Jacobean reigns. Aquinas had expressed the view (*Summa theologiae*, 3a. q.67, a.3–6) that a child should not be deprived of heaven for want of some water or a person able to administer some words. Midwives were the most likely persons to be available, and were expected to know the right verbal formulae. Despite arguments among different Protestant confessional positions, this remained the view in Cranmer's BCP. See below, and Hunt, 'Lay Baptism'.

must be ready at the Fonte: no longer at the church door, as in *1549*. The change in location breaks the link with the separate medieval rite of the preparation of the catechumen, which took place outside the church (see p. 46 and note); but the concentration of the whole service at the font also gave it unity and simplicity.

142 *diddest save Noe and his familie*: the altered wording here shows how the *1552* revisers worked to give the narrative message of the scriptural basis of baptism more clarity.

so passe the waves of this troublesome world: this peroration was added to the opening exhortation in *1552*.

by Christ our Lorde. Amen: the exorcism which followed at this point in Sarum and in *1549* was omitted in *1552*.

143 *geve thankes unto him, and saye*: the recitation of the Lord's Prayer and Creed by the godparents is omitted from *1549*. Thus the last remnant of the *ephphatha* (see notes to p. 46 and 49) was removed. Since the whole ceremony now takes place at the font, the procession into the body of the church at this point is removed as redundant.

144 *Aunswere. I forsake them al*: in *1549* the renunciation of Satan is made three times. In *1552* the mantric element of ritual repetition is eliminated in favour of a single statement of intent.

All this I stedfastly beleve: once again, the triple profession of faith is reduced to one statement; the word 'stedfastly' is also added to the response in *1552*.

Wylt thou be baptised: the blessing of the font at this point in *1549* is cut from the service in *1552*. Like many changes in *1552*, this reflects a criticism made in the *Censura* of Bucer (p. 89), who objected to the sense that 'some kind of sanctifying power was imparted to the water'.

145 *shal dippe it in the water*: only once, rather than thrice as in the medieval rite and in *1549*. Alexander Nowell's *Catechism* of 1570 explained that the baptismal water 'signified' forgiveness and regeneration but did not ensure it. The unbelieving could refuse the promises offered by God;

Nowell nonetheless added, without explanation, 'do they not thereby make the sacraments lose their force and nature'.

145 *N. I Baptize thee*: in one small but significant alteration, the *1552* service makes the moment of baptism the first location of the calling of the child's name.

the Priest shall make a Crosse upon the Childes forehead: at this point in *1549* baptism is followed by a laying on of hands and the putting on of the chrisom. Both practices were done away with in *1552*, and replaced with the signing with the cross, transferred here from the exorcism. Crossing was the last of the elaborate series of sanctified gestures from the medieval rite using cloth, hands, oil, or spittle, otherwise successively excised in *1549* and *1552*. Bucer recommended retaining it (*Censura*, 91), as a simple reminder of the cross of Christ. Although glossed within the following prayer in symbolic terms as a 'token that hereafter he shal not be ashamed to confesse the faith of Christ crucified', Puritans continued to object to it as a remnant of Catholic idolatry. A proposal at the Canterbury Convocation in 1563 to remove the sign of the cross at baptism, 'as tending to superstition', lost by one vote. The use of the practice was confirmed in the Jacobean *Canons* (1604), XXX. Maltby (pp. 52–6) records a case where a Puritan minister refused to make the sign of the cross, so that the parents worried whether the baptism had been correctly performed. She interprets this as popular attachment to the BCP; Hunt points out that it could equally show the survival of Catholic beliefs. Cressy (p. 105) lists similar cases.

let us geve thankes unto God for these benefites: the element of thanksgiving after baptism was new to the service in *1552*, and follows a parallel development in Communion. The Lord's Prayer was moved here from its place at the end of the exorcism in *1549*.

146 *in Private houses in tyme of necessitie*: lay persons (including women) were allowed in the medieval church to baptize in the case of an emergency, provided the correct formulae were used. This permission continued in *1549* through to *1552* and *1559*. Although most theologians were reluctant to endorse explicitly Augustine's conclusion that unbaptized infants were condemned to the fires of hell, the common view was that they were at least deprived of heaven. However, Calvin argued that since salvation was already determined before birth, baptism itself did not confer grace but only provided a 'seal' (or confirmation) of its action. Puritans usually rejected lay baptism as unnecessary and illogical (Hunt, 'Lay Baptism'). Elizabethan orthodoxy, despite its Calvinist leanings, was less doctrinaire. In 1567 Archbishop Parker authorized the licensing of midwives to perform baptisms where there was no alternative. Yet in the same year Bishop Grindal of London collected opinions from continental divines which forthrightly rejected the idea of women baptizing. In 1576 Convocation voted to interpret the rubric as meaning that the baptism could only be administered by a minister called to the purpose, but the queen did not

give her assent. Lay baptism remained permitted in BCP while 'disowned by many of the bishops' (ibid.). Archbishop Whitgift took the view that it was tolerated but not authorized by the church. The BCP may here be allowing for lay beliefs which persisted in thinking, whatever Reformed theology said, that baptism was necessary for an infant to be accepted by God. Not all midwives felt able to perform the act: a survey in Chichester in 1579 records forty-two midwives serving 120 parishes, of whom only three had performed baptisms (Cressy, 120). At the 1604 Hampton Court Conference King James gave his view that he 'utterly disliked' baptism by those who were not ministers, and when the subject of women performing the act was broached, 'his highness grew somewhat earnest'. An ape, he said, was as likely to be able to baptize as a woman (William Barlow, *The summe and substance of the conference which it pleased his excellent Majestie to have with the lords bishops, and other of his clergie ... at Hampton Court* (London: John Windet, 1604), P1ʳ). In the *1604* BCP a clause was added that private baptism was to be conducted only 'by the Minister of the parish, or any other lawful Minister that can be procured'. The revisions to Baptism are the most significant change to the text of the BCP between *1559* and *1662*. The insistence on the presence and action of the minister in turn created anxiety for parents, and complaints when, for example, a Puritan minister refused to attend on a weekday (see Maltby, 52–6). However, there is evidence that increased emphasis on the saving sacramental power of baptism among ministers also seems to have accorded with popular feelings (Hunt, 'Lay Baptism').

147 *received into the nomber of the children of God*: the addition of these words testifies to continued controversy over the fate of the unbaptized soul. Richard Hooker argued that 'grace is not absolutely tyed unto sacramentes' (*Laws of Ecclesiastical Polity*, V. 60. 6). In practice, children who died before baptism were usually given burial in the churchyard.

148 *Doest thou in the name of this child*: this clause was added in *1552*, covering Reformed uncertainty about declarations of faith produced vicariously on behalf of others. Forsaking the devil takes place only once rather than thrice, as in public baptism.

149 *professe this faith: to beleve*: the profession of faith is made only once, not thrice, in *1552*.

All this I steadfastly beleve: these words were added in *1552*.

CONFIRMATION

The order for confirmation, being already in line with reformed doctrine and belief, was changed only minimally in *1552*. Bucer (*Censura*, 101), however, warned that it was crucial that a person being confirmed should not merely recite the words of the profession, but understand them and feel them in the heart. He therefore recommended proper instruction. In 1553 a more advanced form of catechism was published in Latin and in English, for use by school students and others, giving instruction in Christian religion, but it did not succeed in replacing the catechisms of continental humanists and Reformers such as Erasmus (whose catechism had been adopted by John Colet for St Paul's School in its foundation statutes in 1509), Heinrich Bullinger, and Calvin. The bishops commissioned a uniform version for use in schools, which culminated in Alexander Nowell's *Catechism* (1570), which appeared in at least fifty-six editions in a variety of forms, large, small, or middle in size, in Latin or English. This book, though, proved unsuitable for regular use in church, and a range of other material was produced, supplemented by the efforts of clergy to catechize orally (Green, *Christian's ABC*, 143).

151 *to fal into sondry kyndes of synne*: 'sondry kyndes' added in *1552*.

have all thynges necessarie for their salvacion: this clause was added in *1552*.

an instruction to be learned of every childe: there is abundant written evidence of the detailed concerns of clergy in Elizabethan and Jacobean England that knowledge of doctrine be encouraged (and if necessary examined) not only among children but also regularly throughout parish life. From 1610 onwards over a hundred different printed expositions of the BCP catechism survive, often in multiple editions (Green, *Christian's ABC*, 149).

152 *The same which God spake in the .xx. Chapter of Exodus*: added in *1552*; in *1549* the Commandments were repeated without any gloss. The change represents the increasing emphasis on the Ten Commandments, also reflected in placing the scriptural text on boards on the east wall of the church in place of the rood or doom (see notes to p. 125). *Canons* (1604), LIX stipulated that clergy examine 'young and ignorant persons' in the Ten Commandments (see *Synodalia*, 280).

For I the Lorde thy God am a gelous God: this clause was also added in *1552*, bolstering the case against idolatry and justifying iconoclasm.

Syxe daies shalt thou laboure: the rest of this paragraph added in *1552*, reflecting Reformers' concern with the keeping of the sabbath. Plays and bear-baitings typically occurred on Sundays as late as 1579, but later were banned by Puritan authorities. Sabbatarianism was growing in the late sixteenth century; in 1595 Nicholas Bownde in *The Doctrine of the Sabbath* claimed for the Christian Sunday all the authority of the Jewish sabbath of Saturday. Yet even among the gentry, who could afford Sunday leisure, evidence is mixed. The devoutly Puritan Lady Margaret Hoby attended church on forty-seven Sundays out of fifty-two in 1600, and on forty-two of them attended twice; the remaining five she was prevented by a toothache or severe cough (*The Diary of Lady Margaret Hoby 1599–1605*, ed. Dorothy Meads (London: Routledge, 1930), 96). But she also wrote letters on Sundays, entertained tenants for dinner, and took the boat when in London.

153 *Thou shalt not covet thy neyghbours house*: this concern with property was added in *1552*.

154 *And let our crie come to thee*: these last two versicles were added in *1552*, replacing the *Dominus vobiscum*.

155 *laye hys hande upon every childe*: from *1552* the bishop no longer crosses them on the forehead as in *1549*.

Defende, O Lorde, this childe with thy heavenly grace: this prayer was added in *1552*, in place of words signifying ritual enactment. The Peace was also omitted.

(whyche have not learned theyr Cathechysme): added in *1552*. Visitation articles in the 1580s show bishops concerned to ensure that clergy reinforce use of the BCP catechism through oral exposition. Bishop Aylmer in London in 1586 specified enquiry not only into learning by rote but 'the understanding thereof' (Green, *Christian's ABC*, 146).

MATRIMONY

The marriage service remained almost entirely unchanged from *1549* in *1552* and *1559* and throughout the seventeenth century and even beyond, despite some distaste among Puritans for the elements of bodily ritual such as the exchanging of rings.

157 *the date appoincted for solempnizacyon of Matrimonye*: although in principle humans are mammals that can be sexually active at any time of year, the church calendar had for centuries prohibited marriage at any time of fasting and devotion, such as Lent, Rogation and Ember days, or Advent. This was one respect where the Puritan faction in the Reformed churches felt bound to tradition. Cressy (p. 299) calculates that there were 144 prohibited days out of the 365 in the year (40 per cent). However, the prohibition was not absolute, and payment for a licence could persuade a vicar to be lenient to impatient couples; leading to James Calfhill's description of marriage licences in 1565 as 'the milk cow that yieldeth so large a meal of spiritual extortion'. In the seventeenth century there was some movement to divide between 'times sacred, and common'; March weddings remained rare right through the seventeenth century (continuing the view, 'marry in Lent, you'll soon repent'); but December weddings gradually increased, and in Stuart times the prohibition at Rogation largely disappeared.

wyth theyr frendes and neighbours: the purpose of this is not social festivity but a marked reworking of church weddings as an instrument of social control. Common-law marriage was widespread; a marriage was considered viable if a couple were cohabiting with some sense of public propriety: the key determinant in law was a complex set of rules concerning promises given either *per verba de praesenti*, interpreted as a full act of consent embodying a legal contract; or else *de futuro* (as a betrothal) which expressed only a future intention, but which was considered an equal form of contract *cum copula*, when confirmed by consummation. The plots of several Shakespeare plays, such as *Measure for Measure* and *All's Well That Ends Well*, turn on this ambiguity over what constitutes a sexual contract. The Elizabethan marriage was partly an attempt to kick common-law marriage into the long grass and solemnize all sexual union within the confines of church law. The presence of neighbours provides legal witnesses to the binding contract of the ceremony. Despite this, bridal pregnancy (measured by the interval between marriage and baptism according to parish registers) remained high, even though depressed somewhat in the early seventeenth century.

157 *suche persones as have not the gifte of continencie*: these brittle words of puritanical admonition were added in *1552* to the causes of marriage.

158 *you doe knowe any impedyment*: this covered the rules of consanguinity, in varying degrees of incest, which were published separately in 1560 (see Table of Kindred and Affinity, Appendix B, and note on p. 796). But it also covered the problem of pre-contract, by which if someone was already contracted to another, he or she could not marry. The declaring of an impediment now seems the stuff of fiction, familiar to most only from the pages of Charlotte Bronte's *Jane Eyre* (1847): 'when a distinct and near voice said:—"The marriage cannot go on: I declare the existence of an *impediment*".' Yet it was a common issue in sixteenth-century church court proceedings; as when Agnes Nevill in 1583 attempted to stop the marriage of George Hien in Banbury, on the grounds that he 'had once had carnal knowledge of her'. He admitted fornication but denied pre-contract on the basis that there had been no verbal promise. His wedding proceeded; Agnes had a child outside marriage. In *Much Ado About Nothing* there is a reference to this tightening (and internalization) of the interpretation of marriage law: 'If either of you know any inward impediment why you should not be conjoined, I charge you on your souls to utter it' (IV. i. 10–12)—one of the clearest cases of direct quotation from the BCP in Shakespeare.

or the lawes of thys realme: added in *1552*.

159 *and the man shal geve unto the woman a ring, laying the same upon the booke*: the use of the ring became one of the most vivid forms of controversy between different wings of the church in Tudor and Stuart England. Hooker justified it as 'nothing more fit to serve as a token of our purposed endless continuance in that which we never ought to revoke'. The minister Henry Smith claimed that the fit of a ring to the finger showed the success of the marriage: if it was too tight 'it will pinch, and if it be wider than the finger it will fall off; but if it be fit, it neither pincheth nor slippeth'. Rings not only had sexual significance, they were widely felt to have physical powers; a wedding ring could fight disease or ward off devils. Wedding rings could be costly and were sometimes inscribed: Thomas Whythorne, a musician who wrote an early form of autobiography, paid for this inscription in his: 'The eye doth find, the heart doth choose, and love doth bind till death doth loose.' Puritans increasingly disapproved. The *Admonition to Parliament*, the presbyterian manifesto of 1572, declared 'the use of the ring in marriage is foolish'. An attempt was made to ban

wedding rings at the Hampton Court Conference in 1604; but King James 'confessed that he was married withal, and added that he thought they would prove to be scarce well married who are not married with a ring'. Nonconformist practice in the seventeenth century increasingly refused the BCP prescription in favour of rings, and after 1645 wearing a wedding ring could be taken as a sign of covert royalism and episcopalianism.

with the accustomed dutie to the Priest and Clerke: added in *1552*.

160 *you may so lyve together in thys life*: the reference to 'remission of your sinnes' in *1549* (see above, p. 67) is altered to a prayer of steadfastness within the married state. Divorce was not an option in the early modern church; the only release from marriage was death. Widowhood was, however, commonplace, and remarriage of widows a favoured topic among moralists and satirists; Whythorne wrote: 'He that wooeth a widow must not carry quick eels in his codpiece.'

the Lordes table: throughout this service, references to actions in the choir or at the altar are replaced in *1552* with a position at the wooden table used for Communion, to reflect a more austere relationship to religious space in the body of the church.

161 *upon Abraham and Sara*: references to the book of Tobit in the Apocrypha were here cut in *1552*.

162 *Then shal begyn the Communion*: the nuptial Communion was retained in *1552*. However, there is evidence it was often omitted (Hunt, 'The Lord's Supper', 65).

VISITATION OF THE SICK

This service, with its connotation of the medieval sacrament of extreme unction, came under attack during the Edwardian 'second Reformation'. The revised version of *1552* was little more than half the length of *1549*. It omitted the provision for anointing, a practice Bucer dismissed as *praepostera* ('absurd') in *Censura* (p. 125). But whereas Bucer wished the whole service to be abolished, a view supported by radical bishops such as Hooper, it was retained. Part of the sentiment behind this was the reorganization in Elizabethan England of the handling of the sick; but also, despite Reformist attacks, there was a continuing respect for traditions of the *ars moriendi*, the idea of 'dying well'. This was retained on all wings, from even radical writers such as Thomas Becon in his *Sick Man's Salve* (1561), to Laudian revivalists such as Jeremy Taylor in his *Rules and Exercises of Holy Dying* (1651). John Donne's *Devotions upon Emergent Occasions* (1623), written after he had unexpectedly survived an attack of typhoid fever, describes devotional treatments (such as imagining one's own death) side by side with medical ones (such as tying pigeons to his feet). Each part of the work is divided between 'meditations' on the subject of dying, 'expostulations' addressed internally to the soul to prepare for the Lord, and 'prayers' appealing to God for mercy and salvation.

164 *he shall saye knelynge doune*: the Penitential Psalm used in *1549* is omitted.

A residual sense of sacramental performance is retained in the new rubric that the priest be kneeling.

165 *and the capiteines servaunt*: the NT stories of the healing of the apostle Peter's wife's mother (Matt. 8: 14–15, Mark 1: 29–31, and Luke 4: 38–41) and the centurion's servant (Matt. 8: 5–13 and Luke 7: 1–10) are retained, but the reference to the Apocryphal account of the intervention of the angel Raphael (Tob. 11: 7–8) is omitted.

take thy visitation: 'visitation' replaces 'correction' in *1549*, reducing the element of penance.

166 *the articles of the faith*: the exhortation of the sick and the rehearsal of the catechism now form the central core of the service of visitation.

169 *oure Lorde Jesus Christe*: in *1549* at this point the option of unction is retained; in *1552* it was removed, in line with the rigorous replacement of a sacramental rite with a reinforcement of faith in the believer approaching death.

he shal there minister the holy Communion: in *1552* and *1559* the communion of the sick follows straight from the catechism; however, the complex provisions for the reservation of the sacrament from consecration at ordinary Communion, or else for the consecration in the sick person's house, are omitted.

170 *the time of plague, Swette, or such other like contagious tymes*: this provision for times of plague was added in *1552*. Plague was an increasing problem in Tudor England. In 1563, in London alone, over 80,000 people died of the disease, somewhere between a quarter and a third of the total Elizabethan London population. Elizabeth moved her court to Windsor Castle, and ordered that anyone coming from London was to be hanged. The import of goods was prohibited as a measure to prevent the spread of plague to the court. There were further major outbreaks in 1578, 1582, 1592, 1603, and 1607. 'Sweating sickness', perhaps a virulent form of influenza, was also endemic in England in the 1550s.

BURIAL OF THE DEAD

One of the services most visibly changed in *1552* from *1549*. An immediate indication is how far it has been cut—the text is less than half the size. The processional element was entirely removed; the Office of the Dead was eliminated; there was no Mass, even of the residual kind allowed in *1549*; and there were no prayers at the graveside. It was an office embodying the bare minimum of a proper removal of the corpse to the earth. The rest was left to God. Nevertheless, in practice, in surviving accounts of Elizabethan funerals processions seem to have taken place. In the funeral of Sir Philip Sidney, of which an engraving survives, banners are carried by members of the family and a white pall covers the coffin; his friends (including Fulke Greville) hold the four corners; all these mourners are dressed in cowls with hoods. Although an unusually elaborate funeral, it also shows a continuing form of processional.

The ringing of bells was also prescribed in *Canons* (1604), LXVII, 'when any is passing out of this life, a Bell shall bee tolled', with another short peal before the burial, and one after.

172 *the earth shalbe cast upon the body, by some standing by*: this action was performed by the priest in *1549*. Flowers or herbs (such as rosemary) were often strewn on the coffin at the same time; cf. Gertrude at Ophelia's funeral in *Hamlet*, V. i. 226.

Forasmuche as it hath pleased almightie God: this new wording, introduced in *1552*, was taken from Hermann's *Consultation*, echoing the sentiment in Ecc. 12: 7, and emphasizing God's sovereignty in the passage from life to death.

we therfore committe hys bodye to the grounde: the priest's role is further diminished by the omission of the first-person singular 'I commende' from *1549*; while the body is committed, the soul is no longer commended.

reste from their labours: at this point the whole of the *1549* service up to the scriptural lesson is omitted. The medieval *Officium defuncti* is thus given up, along with the psalms and suffrages. A form of this service was retained, however, in the Elizabethan Primer of 1559, and was used at the 'Memorial Service' at the death of King Henri II of France on 8 September 1559, where Matthew Parker, the new archbishop of Canterbury, officiated in surplice and hood (*Private Prayers Put Forth by Authority During the Reign of Queen Elizabeth*, ed. W. Clay (Cambridge: Parker Society, 1851)). The Latin Prayer Book of 1560 contains prayers for the deceased, and a service of commemoration for the monarch and for the benefactors of Oxford and Cambridge colleges. In 1570 an English form of this service for benefactors was prescribed by royal sanction for colleges in Cambridge and for the companions of the Order of the Garter every quarter at St George's Chapel, Windsor.

174 *Almightie God, with whom do live the spirites*: this collect once again is altered to exclude direct prayers for the departed. The celebration of holy Communion which followed the collect in *1549* is removed. A form of Communion was retained in the 1560 Latin Prayer Book.

in thy eternall and everlastynge glorie. Amen: the psalms used in *1549* are omitted and the service proceeds straight to the final Collect. Robert Parkyn, the Yorkshire curate, commented how there were no more dirges and devout prayers sung and said for the dead: 'Why? Be cawsse ther sowlles were immediattlye in blisse and joy after the departtynge from the bodies, and therefore they nedyde no prayer' (Marshall, 111).

CHURCHING OF WOMEN

This service was little altered in *1552*, except for the alternative title, 'The Thankesgevinge of women'; 'purification' was considered dubious by Puritans. 'Churching' was a neutral term for any religious service.

176 *The woman that commeth to give her thanckes*: changed from 'is purifyed' (*1549*); the offering of the baptismal chrisom is removed.

and if there be a Communion: in practice this seems hardly ever to have been observed (Hunt, 'Lord's Supper', 45).

COMMINATION

The service (Ash-Wednesday) was not altered from *1549* save for the title, made at the suggestion of Bucer, with the additional rubric recommending its use at 'divers times in the yere': the evidence of Grindal's Visitation Articles suggests that in the Elizabethan period the service was sometimes used on the three Sundays before Easter, and on one of the two Sundays immediately before both Pentecost and Christmas.

THE BOOK OF COMMON PRAYER, 1662

The progress towards the revised version of the BCP after the Restoration is described in the Introduction, pp. xiii–xvi and xli–xlvi. The Civil War took away bishops, deans, cathedral chapters, and traditional feast days, as well as the BCP. A fifth of clergy were deprived of their livings; although in a contrary direction, many that remained covertly used the BCP. In the summer of 1660 the presbyterian *classes* (synods) were disbanded, and episcopacy was reintroduced. Churchwardens' accounts show that around half of the nation's parishes purchased the pre-war Prayer Book in the first 18 months of the new regime (Ronald Hutton, *The Restoration* (Oxford: Clarendon Press, 1986), 172). In rural parishes old copies could readily be dusted down, but in London, more severely presbyterian, only one copy is recorded in the inventories of 1659. In the autumn following the introduction of *1662*, the bishops' visitations show a patchy progress in its reinstitution: in Buckinghamshire 79 of 183 parishes had no surplice, and 25 no BCP; whereas in the whole province of York the majority had no surplice or book of homilies or Canons, and a third no Prayer Book. Many churches were still in ruin, and churchwardens did not always reply. Up to a quarter of parishes reported continuing nonconformism (ibid. 177–8).

ACT FOR THE UNIFORMITY OF COMMON PRAYER (1559)

Acts of Parliament have been used to promulgate the BCP since *1549*, and every edition since has been authorized by a new Act. To this day, the BCP is a statutory artefact, and its copyright belongs directly to royal prerogative. The authority invested in the book combined regulation of religious practice in conjunction with textual monopoly. The first Act of Uniformity (2 & 3 Edw. VI c. 1) ordered 'one convenient and meet order, rite, and fashion of common and open prayer and administration of the sacraments to be had and used in his Majesty's realm of England and in Wales' (*Statutes of the Realm*, iv. 37). All of this is contained 'in the said book and none other or otherwise'. In *1552* the second Act of Uniformity was printed in the BCP (5 & 6 Edw. VI c. 1).

This was replaced in *1559* with the 1559 Act (1 Eliz. I c. 2), which remained in all subsequent editions of the BCP up to the Civil Wars (in preference to subsequent Acts under the Stuart kings). It was retained with pride of place in *1662*, as the Act which provided unbroken statutory authority (Edward VI's Acts having been repealed by Mary I in 1553) in matters of religion.

187 *with one alteration, or addition*: the 1559 Act here lists the principal changes made in *1559* to the text of *1552*.

the profit of all his Spiritual Benefices: ecclesiastical benefices were the dues and fees provided for clergy through lay donations; effectively the source of income for ministers. This and the following penalties outlawed the ministering of Catholic ritual in England, laws pursued with even greater rigour in the 1580s and after.

188 *without Bail or Mainprise*: money or person standing surety for a person's appearance in court on a specified day (*OED*).

in any Enterludes, Playes, Songs, Rimes, or by other open words: one of a variety of statutory attempts at censorship of religious dissent in popular culture (as well as in print publication) which were a feature of Tudor and Stuart law, beginning with the Act for the Advancement of Religion in 1543 (34 & 35 Hen. VIII, c. 1).

189 *for the first offence an hundred marks*: the mark was a monetary unit equivalent to two-thirds of a troy pound of pure silver or two-thirds of a pound sterling (13*s*. 8*d*.). The measure was used especially in determining exact legal fines (*OED*).

having no lawful, or reasonable excuse to be absent: religious conformity was thus protected by a simple test of attendance in church, rather than any more difficult or dubious legal definition of doctrine or belief. Parishioners as well as clergy made charges against their neighbours, who were examined in the church courts. As well as attendance, a charge could concern failure to take Communion or failure to use the ceremonies of the BCP correctly (Maltby, 20–1). Those who failed to attend church became known from the 1570s onwards as 'recusants', used mostly of Catholics who thus refused to take what they considered unlawful sacraments; but Puritans and other dissenters were also thus covered by the Act.

190 *every Justice of Oyer and Determiner, or Justise of Assize*: 'oyer and terminer' (law-French, 'to hear and determine') is the authority to hold a court in English law; an 'assize' is a sitting or session of a legal body (*OED*).

191 *shall at the costs and charges of the Parishioners of every Parish*: responsibility for the procurement of copies of the BCP was thus laid at the door of the people not the state.

192 *such ornaments of the Church and of the ministers thereof shall be retained, and be in use*: this controversial statement was invoked up to 1662 (and beyond) to justify the use of all kinds of vestment, artefact, and ceremony in the performance of the liturgy, although its precise meaning was consistently

disputed in almost every respect. At the heart of the controversy is what actions or words are required for salvation, and what the limits are of the state in adjudicating and regulating their observance.

ACT FOR THE UNIFORMITY OF PUBLICK PRAYERS

This new Act of Uniformity (14 Chas. II, c. 4) restored the 'one uniform order' of common religion in the state and once again embodied the BCP as the living instrument for 'settling the peace of the Church, and for allaying the present distempers which the indisposition of the time hath contracted'. It resumed the terms for revising the BCP through a commission of bishops and divines (first set out in the Worcester House Declaration of 1660), and approved the new edition of the BCP which had resulted. As in *1559*, the presence of the new Act within the covers of *1662* represents a kind of mutually binding textual authority. The BCP provides the divine testimony which gives validity to the Act of Parliament which in turn gives the BCP political legitimacy. In effect, the Act is the Book, and the Book is the Act.

193 *following their own sensuality, and living without knowledge and due fear of God*: the second Act of Uniformity in 1552 already condemned the 'sensuality' of those who 'wilfully and damnably' refuse the sacraments ordained in the BCP. The new Act extends this reference to the large number of sects which grew up in the political turmoil of the 1640s and 1650s, including (as well as the presbyterians) independents, Baptists, familists, Quakers, 'Ranters', Muggletonians, and so on.

194 *during the times of the late unhappy troubles*: a direct reference to the Civil Wars and the Commonwealth of 1649–60. 'Troubles' was a commonplace post-1660 euphemism.

have made some Alterations which they think fit to be inserted: rather than the risk of a wholly new edition, authority was preserved by making the new BCP strictly a revised version of the old, instead of a new, book.

195 *the said Book, annexed and joyned to this present Act*: the authorized version of the BCP is thus neither the book printed for the use of the revisers in 1661 nor the one printed under royal authority in 1662, but the individual copies known as 'Sealed Books' (see Introduction, p. xlv) corrected in manuscript and preserved in parliament and in the great cathedrals under seal.

196 *I A. B. Do here declare my unfeigned assent*: oaths were used throughout the early modern period in England to signify public subscription to authority. See also the Ordinal, p. 629.

197 *sale of the goods and chattels of the Offender*: in law, 'goods and chattels' is a comprehensive phrase for all kinds of personal property forfeit when a previous legal penalty is unpaid (*OED*).

198 *commonly called the Solemn League and Covenant*: this was an agreement made in 1643 between the Scottish Covenanters and the leaders of the English parliamentarians in the first Civil War. It laid out common

principles in the practice of religion, broadly in line with presbyterian-
ism (although not formally defined as such) and virulently opposed to
'popery' and 'prelacy'—thus including the BCP as well as Catholicism. It
was approved by the Long Parliament and used as a form of subscription
to the parliamentary army (although some radicals, such as John Lilburne,
refused to take the oath). The exiled Charles II signed the Covenant at the
Treaty of Breda (1650) in order to gain Scottish support for his fight to
regain the kingdom; in the Sedition Act (1661) the Covenant was declared
unlawful and was publicly burned.

every publick Professor and Reader in either of the Universities: conformity in religion by means of the BCP had been established in Oxford and
Cambridge from Elizabeth's reign onwards.

200 *unless he have formerly been made Priest by Episcopal Ordination*: this clause
attempts to remove any ambiguity about the status of the ministry created
by the years of the Civil Wars, in which many incumbents were removed
from their parishes or barred from taking services.

201 *the Nine and thirty Articles of Religion*: the Thirty-Nine Articles of Religion
were established in 1563 by Act of Parliament as the defining statements
on doctrine in the Church of England (and remain in use today). A variety of doctrinal statements were issued under Henry VIII, including
the Ten Articles of 1536, the Six Articles of 1539, and the King's Book
of 1543, which took a variety of more and less Reformed positions. In
1553, under Edward VI, the Forty-Two Articles written under Cranmer
produced a distinctively Reformed statement in line with the continental Reformations, but the articles were quickly superseded by the king's
death and repealed under Mary I. The Thirty-Nine Articles revised some
of the most Calvinist formulae of 1553 and were again revised in 1571;
they were often printed with the BCP after 1662, although not formally
part of it (see Appendix B, p. 674).

204 *this Act shall not extend to the University-Churches*: the universities were
consistently allowed certain exemptions from the rule of uniformity in
parishes; from the time of Elizabeth they were allowed to use a Latin order
of service, and to perform special rites such as the commemoration of
benefactors, including prayers for the dead (see note to p. 172).

205 *be truly and exactly Translated*: the status of the BCP is thus varied to
include the authentic representation of the text in other languages,
increasingly a feature of the life of the BCP with imperial expansion and
the widening ministry of the Anglican communion particularly in the
eighteenth and nineteenth centuries (see Introduction, pp. xlviii–xlix).

207 *whosoever are Consecrated or Ordered according to the Rites of that Book*:
the Ordinal (see note to p. 622) had previously been a separate (although
parallel) book of services used in conjunction with the BCP; it is now
incorporated within the one book of liturgy.

PREFACE

This new preface was added in *1662*, alongside Cranmer's *1549* Preface (which had been used in all editions up to *1660*). The writer was Robert Sanderson, bishop of Lincoln. Convocation instructed him to take into account 'satisfying all the dissenting brethren and other'; the tone is self-consciously irenic, and parallels in some ways the secular ends of the Act of Oblivion and Indemnity of 1660 (12 Chas. II, c. 11), which had declared 'a hearty and pious Desire to put an end to all Suits and Controversies that by occasion of the late Distractions have arisen and may arise between all His [Majesty's] Subjects'.

209 *the mean between the two extremes*: the idea of the Church of England as a 'middle way' between the Catholic and Reformed traditions was increasingly common in the mid-seventeenth century. Edward Stillingfleet, later bishop of Worcester, used the phrase *via media* in his *Irenicum* (1659), an attempt to reconcile the divisions in English Christianity at the end of the Interregnum.

things in their own nature indifferent, and alterable: a classic distinction existed in theology between doctrines 'necessary' to salvation (which all Christians must uphold), and the *adiaphora*, doctrines or practices which, while edifying and beneficial, are not essential. Stillingfleet had described no church order as 'unalterable'. Article 34 (see p. 684) considered 'Traditions and Ceremonies' to 'have been divers, and may be changed according to the diversity of Countries, Times, and mens Manners'. Laudians had argued that ceremonies are nonetheless central to Christian holiness.

vain attempts and impetuous assaults: a reference to the continuing campaign of the presbyterians. Some hoped still that a version of the *Directory*, which had replaced the BCP after 1645, might yet win out; Richard Baxter used his position at the Savoy Conference to continue to promote the idea of replacing the BCP rather than revising it.

their own private fancies and interests: these are highly-charged words in mid-seventeenth-century English, often implying a negative connotation. Jeremy Taylor, in *The second part of the dissuasive from popery* (1667), described Catholic sentiment as characterized by 'private fancy', a term often applied to the religion of opponents. On the other hand, ministers who had been turned out of their parishes in the 1640s and 1650s were sometimes accused of looking to their 'private interest' in their hope to reclaim lost benefices.

came, during the late unhappy confusions, to be discontinued: the BCP was abolished by parliament in 1645, and no editions were printed again until 1660.

210 *divers Pamphlets were published*: more than ten pamphlets attacking the BCP appeared in 1660 alone, including *Erastus Junior* and *The Common Prayer Unmasked*; there was an equal number of replies, including the

Aristophanic satire *An Anti-Brekekekex-Coax-Coax, or, A throat-hapse for the frogges and toades that lately crept abroad, croaking against the Common-prayer book.*

211 *by the growth of Anabaptism*: the 'anabaptists', a variety of sects that limited baptism to adults capable of making a profession of faith, were among the most widespread radical groupings of the Reformation, and among the most bitterly persecuted. 'Anabaptist' is a deliberately polemical term: it connoted ancient forms of heresy, although in practice the sixteenth-century anabaptist movements such as the Mennonites were no longer current in seventeenth-century England. Here, the 'Baptists' were an offcut of Calvinism, an increasingly widespread group in the Civil Wars known for mass public adult baptisms (hence the name 'Dippers'). Like the Quakers, the origins of Baptist groups lie in revolutionary sectarian nonconformism, which animates this section of the Preface. These groups should be distinguished from their later descendants in movements of the same name in the eighteenth and nineteenth centuries. Evidence for the deep-rooted hold of Baptist beliefs was provided by Grant's *Observations on the Bills of Mortality* (1665), which reported that during the plague it was harder than expected to keep proper records of age at death, because christening rates had been so low.

the baptizing of Natives in our Plantations, and others converted to the Faith: the question of the baptizing of populations with no knowledge of Christ had been widely debated in medieval theology, not least in Dante's *Divina Commedia*. In one of the earliest English texts promoting the benefits of colonization, Richard Hakluyt's *Reasons for Colonization* (1585), he places first 'The glory of God by planting of religion among those infidels'. Thomas Hariot's *Brief and True Report of the New Found Land of Virginia* (1590) declared that 'Manie times and in every towne where I came, according as I was able, I made declaration of the contentes of the Bible; that therein was set foorth the true and onelie GOD, and his mightie woorkes, that therein was contayned the true doctrine of salvation through Christ'. The languages of America were examined for divine concepts: an early word-list for Algonquin lists an equivalent for 'God'. The first translation of the BCP into a North American language was an abridged version in Mohawk (Iroquois) in 1715.

CONCERNING THE SERVICE OF THE CHURCH

This is Cranmer's Preface to *1549*. It is reprinted verbatim except for a small number of minor changes mostly involving archaisms in grammar; the replacement of the word 'congregation' with 'Church' (see note to p. 412); and the omission of two sentences about parish curates needing no other books for divine service than the Bible and the BCP. Cosin (or Overall in Cosin's hand?) adds in his First Notes the bookish comment: 'sure ye more books, ye more solemne wold Gods service be'.

OF CEREMONIES

Written by Cranmer for *1549* and placed as an appendix to the BCP just before Certain Notes (see note to p. 98). In *1552* Certain Notes was redistributed into two rubrics at the beginning of Morning Prayer, and this section was removed to its present position as an additional preface. It explains the attitude to old ceremonies within the BCP. The abolition of some is defended, both on practical and doctrinal grounds; the retention of others is justified on the grounds that some form of ceremonial is intrinsic to liturgy, and old ceremonies are better than new ones.

Like many parts of the BCP, this text was as complex in its afterlife as it was in its composition. While initially conceived perhaps as a rebuff to traditional Catholics and a vindication of Reformed attitudes in the sixteenth century, in the seventeenth it became the manifesto of the Laudians in defending the use of ceremonies as an essential part of Christian faith and practice. Cranmer's literary even-handedness was now employed for purposes he might have winced at.

215 *not in bondage of the figure or shadow, but in the freedom of the Spirit*: the distinction between body and spirit, and between literal and figurative, sums up the problem of 'ceremonies' in the Protestant liturgical controversies. Cranmer worries that undue deference to the body in ritual creates 'superstitious blindness', or (switching metaphors) that undue fixation on ceremony is a kind of 'dumb' figure without true meaning. Yet he also sticks to the view that a spiritual life can only find an expression in a bodily performance. After the Restoration the paradox was resolved by an argument in favour of ceremony as the 'outward' or 'speaking' sign of an inward religious reality (see note to p. 429), summed up by Thomas Bisse in *The Beauty of Holiness in the Common-prayer* (1716). In the intelligible difference between standing for the Gospel and sitting for the Epistle, the one expresses the proper attitude of the body to the 'words of the master', the other to 'the words of his servants'. Typically, Anglicanism came to imagine ritual in terms appropriate to social order.

THE ORDER HOW THE PSALTER IS APPOINTED TO BE READ

Included first in *1549* and reprinted unchanged over the next century; in *1662* there are some small clarifications but no substantial changes; the version of the Psalms used remains the Great Bible of 1540 rather than the KJV used for the Epistles and Gospels. Other scriptural citations and sentences in *1662* are intermittently revised in line with KJV.

217 *so as the most part thereof will be read every year once*: in *1549* this reads: 'shal bee redde through every yere once, except certain bokes and Chapiters, whiche bee least edifying, and might best be spared, and therfore are left unred.' This decidedly quirky sentence was queried by Matthew Wren, who commented it would 'rather incite the quarrelsome to a comparison' as to which parts of scripture were more or less edifying. Wren and Cosin

also noticed that the stipulation to read all scripture through once a year was impossible to uphold using the BCP system; while Wren wished to suppress this awkward fact, Cosin prevailed, with the pedantic rider, 'the most part thereof' (Durham Book, 22).

PROPER LESSONS

A lectionary had been provided in the medieval church in a variety of forms, some devised for monastic use (such as the Benedictine rule) and some for the secular clergy to use in church on a daily basis. These systems differed but were all based on the liturgical year, with sequences of readings chosen as appropriate to the narratives implied in the annual pattern of festivals. The BCP followed this principle of a pattern of lessons for Sundays and holidays (and often followed directly the sequence in Sarum, although with many adjustments). At the same time, a second parallel lectionary was introduced in the Calendar for a system of daily reading of lessons following the civil year, in a simple numerical order of biblical books and chapters. This latter innovation was motivated by the needs of the laity, as opposed to the clergy (as in the medieval lectionary); it may also reflect the convenience of the format of printed bibles for daily usage.

CALENDAR

The origins of the Calendar lie in the early church, indeed followed on in some sense from the divisions of the Jewish year. The anniversaries of the crucifixion and resurrection were kept from apostolic times, and were closely associated with the Jewish Passover (beginning with Seder, סֶדֶר). Christmas was introduced in the second century. From scripture a wide array of days emerged to mark the rhythms of the liturgical year. As a preparation for Easter, the forty days of Lent, with fasting and penitence, stretched back to Ash-Wednesday; Advent, a mirroring period of reflection before Christmas, lasted four Sundays. Punctuating the year between these major periods were the commemorations of scriptural events such as Epiphany or the Annunciation; festival days of martyrs and other saints; and an increasing number of more abstract commemorations of the Trinity, or the Mass ('Corpus Christi'), or the Holy Cross ('Holyrood'). Vigils of fasting often preceded these days; and major festivals spread out to their 'Octave', a full week of celebration. The Christian year was more than a list of church events or of holidays; it formed the social and cultural framework of everyday life. It encompassed varying rhythms of penitence and festivity, often acutely juxtaposed, and took in the weather and the body and the life of the countryside and the soil as well as the spirit. Many of these occasions had roots well before Christianity: the four 'Ember Weeks' corresponded to the pagan festivals of the seasons, of sowing, reaping, and harvest, neatly transferred over time to correlate Christian observances (Lent, Pentecost, the September festival of Holy Cross, and St Lucy's Day in midwinter) with the passing of the annual changes, as in a medieval rhyme: 'Fasting days and Emberings be | Lent, Whitsun, Holyrood, and Lucie.' The Rogation days or 'Litanies', on 25 April and for three days at Ascension were additional markings of communal penance and included rituals involving prayers and sacrifices for the safe-keeping of crops. For three weeks after Rogation Sunday no weddings would take place; and on the days themselves there was a 'beating of the bounds', in which priest and congregation hiked in procession around the entire boundaries of the parish with prayers for protection in the coming year.

The earliest calendars developed in Rome and emphasized local saints—the days of popes and the early Roman martyrs. At the Synod of Cloveshoo in 747 the English church adopted the Roman calendar, which transferred these Roman customs to new shores; they were gradually added to with the observation of local favourites such as St Alban and St Augustine of Canterbury, until papal authority became more systematically involved in the creation of new festivals from the twelfth century onwards. The Sarum Calendar inherited these traditions and added new ones gradually, reflecting new trends in devotion such as for St Anne (after 1383), the Transfiguration (in 1480), and the Sweet Name of Jesus (early sixteenth century).

In the case of some parts of the continental Reformation the calendar was abolished completely. In England some cursory deletions were made under Henry VIII, such as the erasure of the feast of St Thomas (Becket) of Canterbury. Cranmer, however, in his drafts of services devised first a calendar with a reduced number of saints but including the biblical ones and twelve doctors of the church and a similar number from Sarum; in a second version he idiosyncratically added a large number of new OT saints' days (Abel, Noah, Abraham, Sara, etc.) to make up for omissions created by removing medieval saints. In the BCP in *1549* there was a classic compromise. Clarity was introduced by distinguishing between 'red-letter' and 'black-letter' days (distinguished indeed by typography), the former consisting of twenty-five major festivals—Christmas, Easter, the apostles, evangelists, other major NT figures, along with Holy Innocents, All Saints, Michaelmas, and just two (the Purification and the Annunciation) of the many medieval festivals devoted to the Virgin Mary. Of these, St Mary Magdalene was dropped in *1552*, leaving twenty-four as the number of red-letter days in *1662* (the Magdalene came back as a black-letter day under Elizabeth, but never as a red). Red-letter feasts had variants provided for their services (and individualized Collects, Epistles, and Gospels), although the BCP minimized the variation in liturgy between festivals and created a coherent (if rather prosaic) uniformity of ritual action through the year. Black-letter days, on the other hand, involved no change of service at all, and were of rather ambiguous significance. Vigils and Ember and Rogation days were retained, but not observed as holy days; a slightly arbitrary selection of saints was left in place, sometimes with inaccuracies of date; these were even added to after *1552*, with Enurchus (an obscure saint, probably in reality called Evurtius) added in *1604*, and St Alban and the Venerable Bede in *1662*. The logic of this was often wanting: while St George was revived as a national figure in the sixteenth century, nobody knows why St Cuthbert was suppressed but St Blaise left in. St Clement was introduced in *1552* and then dropped in *1559*; St Barnabas was dropped in *1552* and restored in *1559*. Ronald Hutton (*The Rise and Fall of Merry England: The Ritual Year 1400–1700*

(Oxford: Oxford University Press, 1994), 93) points out that the textual reforms should not be confused with emotion and practice on the ground, which often persisted in older traditions. Indeed, this may explain some of the textual animosity, anxiety, and recidivism in the BCP towards yearly church ritual. The church in Scotland abolished the calendar, which was another reason why the 1637 Scottish BCP was reviled (including local saints such as Mungo and Columba). The 'Root and Branch' petition of December 1640 demanded a reduction in the number of holy days (ibid. 202). In January 1645 the English parliament banned festivals and holy days, keeping only monthly fasts. In reply, the bishops at the Savoy Conference justified the observation of saints' days as being 'not feasting, but the exercise of holy duties' (*Conferences*, 340). Puritans consistently complained of the Calendar that it encouraged superstition, in the form of popular traditions of 'lucky days' and 'dog days', good and bad occasions for arranging events or going on long journeys. A Lambeth Palace copy of *1549* indeed shows how the BCP could be used in this way: 14 July is marked by hand, 'dog daies begynne', and 6 September is heralded, 'dog daies ende'. In the contrary direction, in *1662* part of the motivation for keeping the black-letter days seems to have been to put the Puritans in their place. At Savoy the practice was justified to the effect that they were not holy days, 'but they are useful for the preservation of their memories' in remembering good Christian deeds, and were socially benign in the making of leases and other legal documents, or for determining legal and scholastic term dates (*Conferences*, 341).

Protestant English attitudes towards the church calendar are, in short, full of ambiguity (for sixteenth- and early seventeenth-century examples, see Maltby, 38–40). Even under the Commonwealth, when the BCP was banned and notoriously even Christmas was not safe, actual practice was inconsistent. Throughout the seventeenth century Puritans preferred the term 'Christtide'. The date of Christmas had no scriptural authority, but objection was more vociferous towards open merrymaking and the ancillary holy days of the Christmas season which involved shutting shops, feasting, and dancing. Yet in the 1650s there was more success in stopping religious services (such as John Evelyn's famously interrupted Communion of 1657; see Introduction, p. xli) than in ending merriment. Often the full twelve days of Christmas continued to be observed, if with some effort at concealment. Other church festivals, such as Rogation days, were useful in teaching local youngsters the parish boundaries (which were walked on that day). See Hutton, *Merry England*, on the survival of holidays and holiday festivity in the early modern period.

Each monthly table in the Calendar contains nine columns, as follows: (1) The 'Golden Number', for determining the lunar cycle (see note to p. 234); (2) the day of the month; (3) the 'Sunday Letter', showing the sequence of the week (if A is a Sunday, B will represent Monday, etc.; (4) the day of the month using the Roman system of Kalends, Nones, and Ides; (5) the Feast Day, where applicable; (6) and (7) the readings at Morning Prayer; (8) and (9) the readings at Evening Prayer. (1) and (3) are used in conjunction with the Tables and Rules which follow (see p. 234). (6) to (9) present the whole of the biblical corpus to be read through the year in canonical sequence, regardless of the liturgical year.

This provides a Reformed lay equivalent to the medieval monastic lectionary. The OT and Apocrypha is read in the first lesson at both Matins and Evensong; the Gospels and Acts in the second reading in Matins; and the Epistles in the second at Evensong. The cycle of the NT is repeated when it finishes (and read three times through in the year as a whole); that of the OT appears only once, ending (in a single gesture to liturgical appropriateness) with Isaiah in December in the run-up to Christmas.

In this edition red-letter days are represented in small capitals and black-letter days in italic. *Abbreviations*: B = Bishop, K = King, M = Martyr, V = Virgin.

222 *Prisca, Roman Virgin & Martyr*: an example of the residual bias in BCP from the earliest Roman calendars.

   King Charles Martyr: added in *1662*. See the State Services, note to p. 655.

224 *David, Archbishop of Menevia*: the patron of Wales was added to the Sarum Calendar in 1415 (along with Chad, or Ceadda); Menevia (or Mynyw) is a legendary ascription.

   Edward K. of the West-Saxons: an example of the local affiliations of the Sarum Calendar inherited in BCP.

225 *S. George, Martyr*: St George is a striking case of the equivocal fortune of the saints in the Reformed church of the sixteenth century. While the indubitably historical St Thomas Becket was subject to material censorship, his name crossed out in Latin missals and breviaries under Henry VIII and his tomb in Canterbury desecrated (along with that of St Cuthbert in Durham), St George, whose peculiar legendary story (complete with dragon) might seem to make him liable to Protestant scorn, survived and even grew in fortune. It was in fact only in the sixteenth century that he achieved his full national cult as an Englishman (despite increasing awareness of his Slavic origins), perhaps as a form of Tudor ideological compensation for the loss of so many other local heroes. In 1552 special permission was granted for the Knights of the Garter to observe his feast day. His name was first introduced in the BCP Calendar in *1559*; he was suspended for a while in *1561* but later restored. His image was widely used by printers, including for the woodcut of the Redcrosse knight in Book I of Edmund Spenser's *Faerie Queene*.

226 *Invention of the Cross*: the finding of the true cross by Helena, mother of Constantine.

   S. John Evang. ante port. Latin.: Tertullian recorded how the evangelist was delivered from a terrible death in a cauldron of boiling oil *ante portam Latinam* ('in front of the Latin gate') in Rome.

   Venerable Bede, priest: the theologian, poet, polymath, monk of Jarrow, and classic historian of the early English church was added to the BCP Kalendar in *1662*.

   Charles II, Nativity and Return: like his father, Charles Stuart was added to the Kalendar in *1662*. See the State Services, note on p. 793.

229 *Lammas day*: the blessing of the 'first fruits' of the harvest, derived from *Loaf-mass*, also known as Vincula-mass, since the day was also the feast of the dedication of the church of St Peter ad Vincula in Rome, where one of the apostle's chains (*vincula*) was preserved.

Name of Jesus: a late medieval cult officially sanctioned by the Borgia pope, Alexander VI (1493–1503), one of the newest traditions preserved in the BCP Kalendar, which in general suppressed the more recent cults.

230 *Enurchus, Bishop of Orleans*: a fourth-century martyr, oddly elevated to fame in the Kalendar in *1604*. His obscurity is only enhanced by the fact that he is a misprint; the name is a mistranscription (perhaps from the York Breviary) of Evurtius, corrected in nineteenth-century editions of the BCP. The explanation is more devious: 7 September was the day of the nativity of the late Queen Elizabeth. Her cult continued to rise posthumously, and also formed a covert form of criticism of the new monarch James I: see David Cressy, *Bonfires and Bells: National Memory and the Protestant Calendar in Elizabethan and Stuart England*, rev. edn. (London: The History Press, 2004). The discreet placing of a black-letter day with the initial letter 'E' may have been a bishop's way of keeping her flame alive, unnoticed by a jealous successor. A possible culprit is Richard Bancroft, bishop of London from 1591 and archbishop of Canterbury from 1604.

Holy-Cross day: 14 September 335 was the date of the dedication of the emperor Constantine's basilica in Jerusalem, during which a portion of the 'true cross' was discovered. Over a hundred churches in England were dedicated to the Holy Cross, a highly popular and visible cult.

S. Michael, & all Angels: the status of angels was a further example of tension between the Puritans and 'prayer book Christians'. Michaelmas had wider social significance in the secular calendar: it marked one of the four 'quarters' in the business year, and the beginning of a new term in the lawcourts and at Oxford and Cambridge.

232 *Papists Conspiracy*: the 'powder plot' of Guy Fawkes; nevertheless an anomalous entry in the Kalendar, otherwise restricted to memorializing godliness. Special prayers were ordered to mark the day on the first anniversary, which was in *1662* given a place in printed editions of the BCP; see State Services, p. 652. Popular celebrations such as bonfires marked the day by the reign of Charles I, when it became the focus for further anti-Catholic fervour associated with the marriage to Henrietta Maria; it was the only festival not banned by parliament in 1647. In 1673, after the conversion to Catholicism of James, duke of York, John Evelyn recorded in his diary seeing city youths setting fire to an effigy of the pope.

Hugh, Bishop of Lincoln: this was also the accession day of Queen Elizabeth; in Lincolnshire especially the accession day was often called 'St Hugh's', and was a covert way of continuing the celebration of the saint's cult during her reign (Hutton, *Merry England*, 150). After her death this day was then revived in a reverse process (Cressy, *Bonfires and Bells*, 130–40) as part of the posthumous cult of Elizabeth (see note to p. 230, *St Enurchus*).

233 *O Sapientia*: this was the first of the seven antiphons of the *Magnificat*, which were sung at Vespers on the days leading up to Christmas. An alternative erroneous tradition thought this was the name of a saint, one of the 11,000 virgins who suffered with St Ursula.

TABLES AND RULES FOR THE MOVEABLE, AND IMMOVEABLE FEASTS

'Moveable feasts' are points in the church calendar which change from year to year, the principal of which is Easter, which is calculated by the lunar calendar and varies in date between 22 March and 24 April. On this variation also depends a great deal of the rest of the church year; from Septuagesima (nine weeks before Easter) to Trinity Sunday. 'Immoveable feasts' are, by contrast, fixed in date; Christmas Day is of course the principal of these, although the day of the week on which Christmas falls alters a number of festivals around it, including determining the first Sunday in Advent. An Almanack for finding Easter in the immediately following years was first included in *1552*, and then in *1559*; more elaborate tables were introduced in *1604*, and in *1662* are increased with gusto.

234 *Easter-day (on which the rest depend)*: while Easter was always calculated by the lunar calendar, the astronomy of the problem caused difficulties for centuries. At the Nicene Council (325) a solution was proposed using 21 March as the vernal equinox, and fixing Easter to the first Sunday after the first full moon following that, corresponding to the full moon of the month Nisan in the Jewish calendar. At the synod of Whitby in 664 it was determined that the English Easter be calculated following the Roman custom rather than that of Iona, a principle maintained after the Reformation.

A Table of all the Feasts: first found in MS of 'Second Notes' and copied into the 'Durham Book'; it was Cosin's desire that the BCP should give a more prominent and comprehensive guide to the Christian year.

235 *Table of the Vigils, Fasts, and days of Abstinence*: this table originally appeared in Cosin's *Devotions*, and was first included in the BCP in *1662*.

All the Fridays in the Year: fasting was one of the most traditional elements in the observation of holy days, but while fiercely disputed by Puritans in relation to the cult of the saints, was happily practised elsewhere. Fasting was common at times of political stress or bad weather to ward off the effects of divine providence; see Alexandra Walsham, *Providence in Early Modern England* (Oxford: Oxford University Press, 1999), 143–7. 'Days of humiliation' were declared in parliament (Hutton, *Merry England*, 208).

237 *A TABLE of the Moveable Feasts calculated for Fourty years*: this and the following table have been a favourite for those with lower attention spans

during sermons since early times. They are lovingly updated in subsequent editions of the BCP to the present day.

238 *To find Easter for ever*: a promise not strictly true, since the mathematics changed at the year 1899, for complex reasons beyond the purview of this edition. In 1752 the BCP was emended to take account of this problem. The 'golden numbers' from 1 to 19 provide a key which, when collated with the 'Sunday letter' (a code to find the day on which a Sunday will fall in any given year), produces a date for Easter.

MORNING PRAYER

For all of the divine services that follow, it will be useful to consult also the Explanatory Notes for *1549* and *1559*.

While the texts of Morning and Evening Prayer remained almost stable from *1552* onwards, the rubrics continued to cause sticking-points, and these are the main source of change in *1662*. Matins and Evensong were by now the staple services of Sunday worship. Visitations ensured that these services were regularly performed; parishioners sometimes complained when a service went missing (Maltby, 36–8). Pepys's diary shows how it was customary to attend both as part of the rhythm of the day; he refers frequently to the singing of psalms and canticles, in a variety of churches of different sizes around London.

In the divine services for *1662*, it is to be noted that while the revisers were ultimately enjoined to retain the version of *1552* as far as possible, its significance had been transformed over the previous century. Thus while *1552* represented at the time a victory for the Puritan party, and vigorously opposed many traditional Catholic elements of ritual remaining in *1549*, in the 1640s Puritan pamphlets often cited the BCP (largely the same as *1552*) as a bastion of 'popish' Catholicism. Somewhat improbably, it was a Puritan claim that 'the book of common prayer was the invention of the pope of Rome' (Essex Record Office assize files, 35/84: 1641/13). While rejecting this charge, defenders of the BCP, in the 'Prayer Book petitions' of 1641–2, and also after 1660, used the latitude of the rubrics, and of the variations possible through the application of the idea of 'ceremonies', to interpret *1552* in a far more ritualized and sacramental fashion than that envisaged by its original composers (on the 'petitions', see Maltby, and Michael Braddick, *God's Fury, England's Fire* (London: Penguin Books, 2008), 152–3). This is a good instance of the capacity of the BCP to take on variable meanings over time. With *1662* the BCP became the embodiment of 'established' religion—the religion of the national church, and of priestly and episcopal (and therefore monarchical) authority, as opposed to the evangelical (and dissident) religion of nonconformism.

239 *the accustomed place of the Church, Chappel, or Chancel*: by the time of the Restoration this referred to the 'pew' (a term which could mean any boxed area, and is used by Milton to refer to sheep-pens and Pepys to opera boxes) situated on either side of the chancel and used by the clergy and singers.

such Ornaments of the Church: the exuberantly incoherent rubric of *1559*

(p. 102), now also historically arcane, was retained in *1662* despite considerable discussion. It confirmed the arrangements of the second year of the reign of Edward VI, 120 years old, partly in order to avoid any new precise formulation. In practice, the issue of ornaments had for some time been superseded by bishops' injunctions for their particular dioceses, which in the Laudian period were often highly specific and exacting.

239 *When the wicked man turneth away*: the minister declares 'one or more' rather than only one of the Sentences first introduced in *1552*. The text is regularized in line with the KJV and two Sentences are changed from *1559* to emphasize the penitential character.

241 *the Priest alone, standing; the people still kneeling*: the words 'Remission of sins' are added to clarify the authority of the priest in absolving. Some clergy performed this function kneeling, but the *1662* rubric confirms the view of Bishop Andrewes that he must stand since he speaks 'in the name of Christ and his Church'.

and at the end of all other prayers: the rubrics in *1662* in general are amplified to clarify practice which in earlier editions had been left unspecific or ambiguous.

the People also kneeling, and repeating it with him: this injunction providing for the people to join in the saying of the Lord's Prayer at the opening of Morning Prayer was introduced in *1662* at the suggestion of Bishop Cosin, to create a communal opening to a collective service of worship.

For thine is the Kingdom . . . For ever and ever: the 'doxology' which ends the Lord's Prayer in Matt. 6: 13 does not appear in Luke 11: 2–4. Many commentators believed that it was a later liturgical interpolation and should not be included in the prayer as such. It was introduced here in *1661*, and despite Cosin's 'Directions to be given to the printer' that the text should finish 'deliver us from evil', it was retained in *1662* and was not altered after.

242 *Here all standing up*: this gesture was introduced in *1662*.

The Lords Name be praised: this answer was first introduced in the Scottish Prayer Book of 1637, when the words 'Praise ye the Lord' were reassigned from the people to the priest.

shall be said, or sung: sung in places where there is a choir; read aloud where there is none.

it is not to be read here: to clarify that the *Venite* is not to be repeated when it is already the ordinary psalm for that day in the sequence just following.

243 *an audible voice*: replacing 'loud' in earlier editions. After the Restoration, at St Paul's there were usually organ voluntaries before the first lesson at Morning and Evening Prayer; presumably this was also the case at other churches where there was an organ. Organ music provided a common embellishment of the *1662* BCP; Thomas Tomkins was a prolific composer of such music for church use, mostly written in the 1640s and 1650s.

247 *Then shall be sung, or said the Apostles Creed by the Minister, and the people standing*: the chanting of the Creed is permitted in a change from *1559*. In the seventeenth century it also became common for the congregation to face east (i.e. towards the altar) during the profession of faith, and to bow at the name of Jesus; the latter practice was recommended in *Canons* (1604), XVIII: 'due and lowly reverence shall be done by all persons present, as it hath been accustomed; testifying by these outward ceremonies and gestures their inward humility, Christian resolution, and due acknowledgement of the Lord Jesus Christ.' Visitation articles in the 1620s and 1630s (e.g. in London, Bristol, Rochester) routinely inquire whether bowing has been observed (Kenneth Fincham (ed.), *Visitation Articles and Injunctions of the Early Stuart Church* (Woodbridge: Boydell & Brewer, 1998), 20, 56, 80). Nonetheless, the word 'bowing' never occurs in any rubric even of *1662*. Eleazar Duncon defended bowing towards the altar in Cambridge in 1634. His work was published in Latin in 1660, producing a storm as much against as in favour (Fincham and Tyacke, 310).

248 *all kneeling*: as elsewhere, a bodily gesture is textually reinforced in *1662*.

these five Prayers following are to be read here: the curious verb 'read', also used in relation to the *Venite* above, is a mid-seventeenth-century usage to distinguish formal prayer from the 'extemporary' prayers of the dissenters who had opposed the use of BCP during the Interregnum. Extemporary prayer is frequently cited as a perverse Puritan practice in petitions defending the BCP in 1641–2, and again in visitations enquiring into nonconformism in the autumn of 1662.

A Prayer for the Kings Majesty: these prayers, all (except the second) part of the Litany since *1559*, were inserted here in *1662*.

249 *A Prayer for the Royal Family*: this prayer was added to the Collects at the end of Litany in *1604*, approved by Archbishop Whitgift and possibly composed by him. Praying for the royal spouse and children had not been necessary for either Edward VI or Elizabeth, for obvious reasons.

the fountain of all goodness: these words were introduced into the prayer in *1627*, after the marriage of Charles I to Henrietta Maria, as appropriate to a sovereign now wedded but as yet without issue.

all the Royal Family: some controversy was caused under Archbishop Laud when the names of the monarch's children were omitted from specific prayers; the new catch-all phrase avoided continually adding to the language of the prayer.

EVENING PRAYER

Morning and Evening Prayer were the staple services of Sunday worship in *1662*, more than Communion. The form of this service was by now well established and well loved. As well as Sundays, Evening Prayer was frequently observed on weekdays (Maltby, 38).

250 *one, or more of these Sentences of the Scriptures*: the Sentences, exhortation, confession, and absolution were printed as part of the service for the first time in *1662*, although their use was assumed since *1552*.

252 *the Song of the blessed Virgin Mary*: the alternative title, while a clarification of the Latin name for the song, is a striking phrasing in relation to Puritan sensitivities. The *Magnificat* and the *Nunc dimittis* were habitually sung in cathedrals and larger churches; they were collected in Clifford's *Divine Services and Anthems* (1663; 2nd edn. 1664), which collected music dating back to the time of Tallis. New settings were common in the eighteenth century.

253 *the Song of Simeon*: the alternative title is added in *1662* as for the *Magnificat*.

255 *after that, these Prayers following*: the Suffrages and Lesser Litany are here copied from Matins for the first time in Evensong in *1662*.

256 *Lighten our darkness, we beseech thee*: to meet objections of superstition, Cosin wrote a revised version into the Durham Book, p. 82: 'Lighten the darkness of our hearts, we beseech thee, O Lord.' For *1662* the old version was restored.

   here followeth the Anthem: this rubric was added in *1662*. In the late seventeenth and early eighteenth centuries the practice grew of using a metrical psalm or one of the new body of hymns at this point.

   A Prayer for the Kings Majesty: these prayers, as in Matins, were added in *1662* from the Litany.

CREED OF ST. ATHANASIUS

This was now given a separate heading and its use clarified. In the medieval English church it had been used in the daily Office; in the Reformed breviary of Quiñones its use was reduced to weekly, on Sundays; in the Church of England its recitation was now in effect prescribed monthly, on six major festivals and seven saint's days. See p. 695 above, note to p. 16.

257 *by the Minister and People standing*: this rubric was added in *1662*. In the Durham Book (p. 82), Cosin experimented with a form of verse and response alternating between priest and people, or when sung by a choir, between the alternating sides. This was now dropped in favour of unison performance.

   every one do keep whole and undefiled: the reading 'whole' was corrected from 'holy' for the first time in the 1637 Scottish BCP and is adopted in *1662*.

LITANY

By the mid-seventeenth century the Litany had completed its transition from the processional of the medieval church to a supplicatory (and stationary) form of service. The Injunctions of Edward VI and of Elizabeth stipulated 'the midst of the church' for its performance. Cosin followed the Injunctions in setting out a formal pattern in his *Notes on the Common Prayer*: 'The priest goeth from out his seat into the body of the church, and at a low desk before the chancel door, called the faldstool, kneels, and says or sings the Litany.' Bishop Andrewes had a 'faldstool' (folding stool) in his chapel, and Cosin enquired, on becoming archdeacon of the East Riding in 1627, whether one was available 'with some decent carpet over it, in the middle alley of the church, whereat the Litany may be said'. As well as Sunday use, *Canons* (1604), XV required the Litany to be read every Wednesday and Friday, announced beforehand by the ringing of the church bell.

259 *or General Supplication*: this gloss added in *1662* also better explains the function of the service within the Church of England rite.

260 *and from sudden death*: Puritans consistently objected to this phrase up to the Savoy Conference of 1661. Writing in 1603, even Archbishop Whitgift wondered at its propriety, since 'we ought so to live, that death should never find us unprepared'.

   privy conspiracy, and rebellion: the words 'and rebellion' were added in *1662*; this was the standard term to refer to the events between 1642 and 1660.

   heresy, and schism: the words 'and schism' were also added in *1662*; 'schism' was used to refer to the many nonconformist groups which had grown up in the 1640s and 1650s.

261 *to keep and strengthen in the true worshipping of thee*: this is an expanded form of the already embellished form of *1559*; compare the very brief prayer for the sovereign in *1549* and *1552*.

   and all the Royal Family: a prayer for the consort Queen Katherine and for Prince Edward had been included in the Litany of 1544, but had been redundant in versions under Edward and Elizabeth. A form for the whole royal family was first instituted under James I in *1604*.

   all Bishops, Priests, and Deacons: changed from earlier versions, e.g. *1559*: 'all Byshoppes, Pastours, and ministers . . .'

PRAYERS AND THANKSGIVINGS

This compilation of special prayers and thanksgivings was added to Morning and Evening Prayer in *1662*, combining material from the old BCPs, from more recent special services, and new compositions. Some derive from medieval occasional rites: a printed missal of 1514 (owned by Cosin) contained a *Missa tempore belli* ('Mass in time of war') and a prayer *contra aëreas tempestates* ('to ward off storms'). Two occasional prayers appear in *1549* among the Collects at the end of Communion; four more were added in *1552* and all six placed at the end of the Litany. The Thanksgivings corresponding to these six prayers were added in *1604*. Cosin revised all this material in *1662* along with the introduction of newer material.

265 *For Rain*: this and the prayer 'For Fair Weather' are from *1549*, where they were part of Communion; in *1552* they were moved to the Litany.

265 *In Time of dearth and famine*: the two prayers with this title and the two following are from the Litany in *1552*.

266 *In the Ember Weeks to be said every day*: the first of the Ember Collects was published in Cosin's *Collection of Private Devotions* (1627), and seems to be his own composition.

267 *Almighty God, the giver of all good gifts*: the second Ember Collect is taken from the Ordinal, and was inserted at the end of the Litany in the 1637 Scottish BCP.

O God, whose nature and property is ever to have mercy: this prayer, originally from the 1544 Litany but excluded in *1549* and *1552*, was placed at the end of the Litany in *1559* and moved here in *1662*.

A Prayer for the High Court of Parliament: this prayer, for both the House of Commons and the House of Lords, and for the Convocation of Bishops, originates in a special *Form of Common Prayer* published in 1625, and appears to have been written by William Laud, then bishop of St David's. In *1662* it may have been intended for use only at parliament, but the wording did not preclude its use elsewhere whenever parliament seemed in particular need of intercession.

A Collect or Prayer for all conditions of men: composed by Peter Gunning, Master of St John's College, Cambridge, perhaps specially for *1662*, although based on the Collects for Good Friday (see pp. 317–18). Gunning was a prominent presence among the revisers.

268 *for the good estate of the Catholick Church*: these words were added by Cosin.

all who profess and call themselves Christians: a reference to the nonconformist groups of the Civil War period.

A General Thanksgiving: composed (or compiled) by Edward Reynolds, who was unusual among the Restoration bishops in having been a presbyterian during the Civil War who had preached before parliament in 1657 and 1659, while joining himself to the cause of 'moderation' after the death of Oliver Cromwell. The presbyterians at the Savoy Conference in 1661 (of whom Reynolds was one) objected to the Collects on the grounds that they were too short; the General Thanksgiving may be considered a form of concession to these concerns for the BCP to allow longer forms of prayer.

those who desire now to offer up their praises: this and the 'Prayer for all conditions of men' offer opportunities for the kind of extemporary prayer favoured by the Puritans, who were now being encouraged back into the Church of England.

for our creation, preservation, and all the blessings of this life: the wording here appears to be borrowed from a prayer attributed to Queen Elizabeth (*Liturgies and Occasional Forms of Prayer Set Forth in the Reign of Queen Elizabeth*, ed. W. K. Clay (Cambridge: Parker Society, 1847), 667).

For Rain: the 'occasional thanksgivings' (apart from the one for 'publick peace') were placed at the end of the Litany after the Hampton Court Conference in *1604*.

269 *For restoring publick peace at home*: this prayer appears in Cosin's handwriting in the margin of the Durham Book (p. 98), and seems to be his own composition. It is written in reaction to the Civil Wars, being originally entitled (in the Durham Book) 'For Victory over Rebells'; some of the references in the original manuscript version ('Madness of a raging and unreasonable people') have been toned down in *1662*.

COLLECTS, EPISTLES, AND GOSPELS

This is the variable part of the BCP, providing material to be used in the different orders of service that changes at least once a week and, during the major festivals, on a daily basis. In *1549* Introits were also printed in this section, derived from the Psalms; in *1552* and subsequent editions these were dropped. After *1662* hymns were increasingly used in their place. The form of the Collect dates back to the sixth-century sacramentaries, and may be older still; its name is thought to derive from the idea that the priest in it speaks on collective behalf of the people (as opposed to the verses and responses, where the people themselves have a voice). A Collect usually consists of a single grammatical period, containing a single petition, usually referring to Christ's mediation in the life of the congregation, and often ending in a statement of praise. In the Roman liturgy Collects almost always began with an introductory reference to the event or day commemorated, followed by a single central prayer. The English primers before 1549 contained a variety of often clumsy versions of the Latin Collects. Cranmer undertook a full-scale revision of these, sometimes translating literally from the Latin, sometimes adapting, and sometimes making new compositions (there are twenty-four of these, mostly for saints' days, which provoked an obvious need for doctrinal alteration). Cranmer's Collects are usually considered the pinnacle of his liturgical writing. *1662* takes over Cranmer's compilations with some revision. Of the eighty-three Collects in *1662*, seventy-seven are largely Cranmer's; fifty-nine are derived originally from Sarum; four are new Collects written by Cosin.

The Epistles and Gospels in *1662* follow, almost entirely, the order and shape of the readings supplied in *1549* and in many cases are identical to the medieval lectionary. In the first half of the Christian year, from Advent to Trinity, the readings follow the events of the life of Christ, chronologically and doctrinally, from incarnation to ascension. In the second part of the year, from Trinity onwards, the readings from the Epistles are sequential, and the Gospels chosen to strike a chord with them. The texts for the readings are supplied in *1662* from the KJV of 1611, replacing the Great Bible of 1540 which was used in *1549*, *1559*, and after. Matthew Wren, in his *Advices* on the BCP, written in imprisonment in the Tower of London between 1641 and 1660, commented: 'It must here be well considered and determined, in what Translation they shall now be read: For the Old Translation in very many places is much amiss.' Wren also expressed concern about mistakes in the KJV; despite periodic movements for revision, this remained the official version in BCP.

271 *The Collect*: this Collect for the first Sunday in Advent is word for word the same as in Cranmer's version. This is one of Cranmer's original compositions, and is a good example of his method, taking its lead from the Epistle to create a balanced syntax based upon an antithesis of the first and the second coming of Christ.

This Collect is to be repeated every day: the instruction that the first Advent Collect be repeated as a subsidiary Collect after the main Collect of the day up until Christmas was first made by Matthew Wren in his *Advices* on the BCP, and then adopted by Cosin in the Durham Book.

The Gospel: Cranmer extended the reading from that prescribed in Sarum to include the section 'And Jesus went into the temple of God', which Reformers took to be a reference to their own cause.

272 *Go into the village*: the capitalization here indicates the beginning of direct speech, a typographical convention observed throughout the Epistles and Gospels.

The Collect: that for the second Sunday in Advent is another of Cranmer's compositions, derived from the Epistle. It contains an epitome of Protestant piety in its insistence on lay reading and 'inward digestion' of scripture; and (in the final clause) on the embodiment of Christ 'in' scripture, rather than his mediation 'through' scripture as the instrument of the church. At Wren's suggestion the collective response 'Amen' was added to all the Collects in *1662*, whereas in *1549* it only occurs intermittently.

273 *The Collect*: that for the third Sunday in Advent was written by Cosin, replacing the translation of the short Sarum collect in *1549*. It is similar in style to that for the sixth Sunday after Epiphany (p. 289), another of Cosin's compositions, and as there he draws equally on Epistle and Gospel, following his own rule that Collect should be closely matched ('relateth') to the readings. This may be contrasted with Cranmer's practice where, of twenty-four original Collects, eight are drawn from the Epistle, four from the Gospel, and twelve from neither (while freely adapting other scriptural material).

274 *The Collect*: this, for the fourth Sunday in Advent, is the only one of the Advent Collects to be translated from the familiar sequence in Sarum which all began with the word *Excita* ('raise up'), although here, too, Cranmer improvised freely at the end of the Collect to improve the rhythm and embellish the relationship between sinfulness and grace.

in running the race that is set before us: these words are added in *1662* to clarify the sense.

275 *Christmas-day*: in the Latin rite there were three separate Masses for the nativity, and another for the vigil which preceded them. In *1549* provision

was made for Collects, Epistle, and Gospels for two separate Communion services, while the vigil was dropped. In *1552* this was reduced to one service, the practice adopted in *1662*.

take our nature upon him: see Heb. 2: 1, 'Wee ought to bee obedient to Christ Jesus ... because he vouchsafed to take our nature upon him'. The incarnation is turned into a literal embodiment of the sanctification of the individual Christian.

and as at this time: altered from 'this daye' in *1549* and subsequent versions. Puritans objected to the idea that Christ's nature was different on one day from another, even at Christmas, and the *Exceptions* required the phrase to be omitted. Cosin and the bishops complied, but for a different, liturgical reason: this Collect was repeated for the week following Christmas (the 'octave'), so that the wording was confusing.

277 *The Collect*: for St Stephen's Day, almost certainly written by Cosin, building on the shorter version in *1549*. The reference to 'all our sufferings here upon earth', bringing the congregation into sympathy with the first martyr, presumably alludes to the recent struggles of the Civil Wars, including Cosin's own exile for seventeen years in France.

278 *may so walk in the light of thy truth*: these words were added to the Collect for St John the Evangelist's Day in *1662*, drawing on the Epistle.

279 *The Collect*: in the Collect for Innocents' Day the epithet 'Holy' was first added to 'Innocents' by Cosin in the Durham Book and then crossed out.

out of the mouths of babes and sucklings: these words from Ps. 8: 2 (also cited in Matt. 21: 16) were added in *1662*, perhaps suggested by the psalm used on this day in the Latin rite.

280 *to take our nature upon him*: Cosin added a note in the margin of the Durham Book that this is 'most proper to say' on this day and at Christmas, 'for that is ἐπιλαμβάνεσθαι ['to assume'] the manhood into God'.

281 *The Circumcision of Christ*: this feast had more prominence in the BCP than in the Latin rite, where it formed the octave of Christmas. Cranmer composed a new Collect, and an Epistle was added, both alluding to the obedience of Christ to the law. Cosin raised here and elsewhere the problem of what to do when this feast fell upon a Sunday, since this Collect is 'inconsistent' with the one for the Sunday after Christmas.

282 *every day after unto the Epiphany*: replacing *1552*, where provision was made only if a Sunday intervened; in *1552* it was assumed that Communion would not take place daily. The new rubric implies at least the desirability of more frequent Communion during the holiday season. The 'twelve days of Christmas' were, however, anathema to Puritans.

Epiphany, or the manifestation of Christ to the Gentiles: the explanatory phrase was added by Cosin.

285 *all the days of our life*: a good example of Cranmer's felicity in translating from Sarum *nostris temporibus*, implying not only 'in our time' but

throughout the period of our mortality. He borrows the phrase from his version of the *Benedictus* (see p. 12).

289   *The Collect*: variations in the position of Easter in the calendar year ensured that different provision for the numbering of Sundays was needed in different years. As there is rarely a sixth Sunday after Epiphany, in *1549* the material for this Sunday was copied from that for the fifth Sunday. In creating an independent service, Cosin added a new collect of his own; his phrase 'purifie our selves' shows the Catholic leanings of his soteriology.

290   *Septuagesima*: the theme of Collects and readings now alters from the joy of Christmas to a preparation for the fasting and humility of Lent.

291   *by thy power*: Cranmer excised the reference here in Sarum (retained in the Roman missal) to the special protection of St Paul on Sexagesima, making Christ the only defence in adversity.

293   *The Collect*: the Collect for Quinquagesima is one of Cranmer's new compositions in *1549*, based on the Epistle.

294   *The Collect*: this Collect for Ash-Wednesday was written by Cranmer and incorporates material (heavily reduced) from the old Latin prayer for blessing the ashes which were applied in the Latin rite to the forehead of the penitent, a ceremony otherwise cut out from BCP. The instruction 'to be read every day in Lent' was added at Wren's suggestion, which he may have found in Sarum.

295   *The Collect*: unlike all of the subsequent Collects in Lent, which are closely based on Sarum, Cranmer rewrote this for the first Sunday in close proximity to the Gospel.

296   *The Collect*: while based on Sarum, in the Collect for the second Sunday in Lent Cranmer draws out the antithesis between the Latin words *interius* and *exterius* to create a full comparison of the realms of soul and body.

         of our selves to help our selves: these added words are a good example of Cranmer's free reworking of the Latin to create a psychological drama.

301   *The Collect*: in the Collect for the Sunday before Easter the phrase 'of thy tender love towards mankind' is added by Cranmer.

302   *The Gospel*: a rare example of a change of reading from *1549*, which provided Matt. 26 and 27 in sequence. To make the reading shorter, *1662* cuts Matt. 26 and places it as a proper reading for Matins instead. The readings for the week leading up to Easter were subject to small but painstaking changes in sequence to create a careful narrative order, incorporating the different versions in the synoptic gospels, each reading having its own crescendo and proper climax. The readings in some places were cut from *1549* in order to restrict all reference to the burial of Christ to Easter Even.

317   *The Collects*: the provision of three separate Collects for Good Friday is a residual gesture towards the peculiar Latin Office of Good Friday, which contained elaborate processions, lessons, collects, and intercessions. No

direction is given as to whether the Eucharist is to be withheld on this day and Easter Even, as it was in the Roman rite.

318 *The Epistle*: Hebrews 10 replaced in *1549* the passage from Exodus used in the Latin rite.

321 *The Collect*: there was no service on Easter Even in the medieval church, awaiting the special rites for the Easter vigil. In *1549* provision was made for a service, commemorating the events of the day but without any reference to the vigil. There was no Collect, and the version in *1662* is based on the one written for the 1637 Scottish BCP.

322 *Easter day*: in *1549* an element of the medieval processional had been retained in a series of initial anthems and psalms, and a second Communion service with a separate Collect and readings. This was reduced to two anthems in *1552*, with the alleluyas omitted, and the second Communion was dropped. In *1662* a new first anthem was added to Matins; otherwise the form since *1552* was retained, except that the Collect for the second Communion was moved to the first Sunday after Easter.

323 *Munday in Easter Week*: the Latin rite has special Masses for every day in Easter week. In the BCP this was reduced to two days; the readings were enlarged to take in the material missing from the other services.

328 *The Collect*: the Collect for the second Sunday after Easter was a new composition by Cranmer in *1549*. The words 'onely son' read 'holy son' in *1549*, a misprint corrected in *1596*.

330 *The Collect*: the Bishops' *Reply* to the Puritans' *Exceptions* in 1661 asked that the Collects after Easter be altered; in this case, the words 'who alone canst order the unruly wills and affections of sinful men' were added at Convocation.

333 *The Collect*: the Collect for the Sunday after Ascension Day is one of Cranmer's compositions in *1549*.

334 *Whitsunday*: as in other parts of northern Europe, Pentecost is called 'White Sunday', perhaps because it was frequently used for baptisms. The corruption *whit* created a confusion with 'wit', and it was sometimes said that 'wit' was given to the apostles on this day.

338 *Trinity Sunday*: in the early church the first Sunday after Pentecost was celebrated merely as an octave. The celebration of a festival of the Trinity, summing up the teaching of the first half of the Christian year, arose in the eleventh century; in England it was formalized by Thomas Becket at his consecration as archbishop of Canterbury in 1162.

339 *The Collect*: Cranmer's new compositions for the Collects are concentrated in the early part of the year; all of the Collects after Trinity are translated or adapted from the Latin rite.

365 *The Collect*: the final rubric for this service ensures that the material here, which anticipates Advent, is retained for the last Sunday before Advent, even if there are more than twenty-five weeks after Trinity. The phrase,

'Stir up, we beseech thee', makes clear (against the implication of the Latin original) that human works occur only through divine intervention; this Sunday was popularly known as 'Stir up Sunday' as a result. Some used this name as an injunction to begin the preparation of plum pudding for the following Christmas, leaving a month for the development of flavours. Recipes survive from the seventeenth century.

366 *The Collect*: the phrasing 'readily obeyed the calling of thy Son Jesus Christ' was used in *1552* to replace a reference in *1549* to the traditional (but non-scriptural) story of the martyrdom of Andrew on a cross.

368 *The Collect*: the Collect for St Thomas's Day was composed by Cranmer in *1549*. The theme of doubt becoming the occasion for the confirmation of faith is a centrally Protestant notion, in which Cranmer shows the influence of Luther.

369 *The Collect*: Cranmer's version of the Collect for the Conversion of St Paul was amplified by Cosin in *1662* with the words 'hast caused the light of the Gospel to shine throughout the world'.

370 *The Presentation of Christ in the temple*: Cosin introduced this alternative title in *1662*.

372 *The Collect*: composed by Cranmer in *1549*; as with many of the Latin collects for the saints' days, the original wording consisted only in a form of intercession to the saint, inadmissible to the Reformers.

373 *The Collect*: for the Annunciation is taken from the post-Communion in Sarum, rather than the collect for the day, which included a Marian framework unacceptable to the Reformers.

378 *The Collect*: the word 'repentance' in *1662* replaces 'penaunce' in all earlier versions; Cosin commented in 1660 that the latter word 'is now abused by the Papists'.

379 *St Peters Day*: the feast of St Mary Magdalene, which appeared in *1549*, was dropped in *1552* from its place between St Peter and St James.

384 *The Collect*: the phrase 'thy holy Angels' was added in *1662*.

387 *to follow thy blessed Saints*: 'blessed' replaces 'holy Saints', said by Wren to be 'very improper speech'. This feast was sensitive to Protestant fears about the cult of saints, and Cranmer's language carefully departs from Sarum by elucidating the doctrine of election.

COMMUNION

Communion was at the heart of the devotion of prominent revisers such as Cosin, as much in terms of practice and emotion as in theology. Yet this emphasis among the Laudians competed against the continuing cultural trend of irregular Communion among the laity. Some Puritans, on the other hand, referred contemptuously to Communion as 'the Mass', and to the BCP as 'mass-books' (Bodleian MS Rawlinson D 158, fo. 43r). In conscious defiance,

Evelyn's diary is one piece of evidence that royalist loyalists and exiles held to the Communion in particular as a way of maintaining the BCP. Cosin worked on sacramental ideas during his Paris years. As in other respects, the initial instinct in revising the Communion after 1660 was to restore the version of *1549*. The *1549* version had been the ideal of the Laudians and even before them of Andrewes and Overall (the latter being Cosin's patron and master). In the Scottish BCP of 1637 this had been realized in the virtual restoration of the *1549* Canon (see note to p. 29), and in the repositioning of the Lord's Prayer and 'We do not presume'. Initially these revisions were incorporated in the Durham Book, but were rejected at a late stage by the bishops at Ely House, probably in November 1661. In *1662* the 'back to 1549' movement became diluted, and *1552* is the model, although many revisions were made.

389 *sometime the day before*: Wren and Cosin both commented that the old rubric, which asked for notification before or after Matins, was now problematic, since it was the custom in most churches for Communion (when it occurred) to follow immediately from Morning Prayer.

Provided that every Minister so repelling any: Cosin (*Particulars*, fo. 6ʳ) remarked on the vague wording in the old BCP of the refusal to grant Communion to 'an open & notorious Evill liver', and in order to avoid 'disputes, doubts, & contentions' recommended bringing this into line with *Canons* (1604), XXVI. There was a considerable literature about the benefits and perils of enforcing godliness by withholding Communion (Hunt, 'The Lord's Supper', 62 f.). It was difficult in practice to turn parishioners away; and it might even harden them in their wicked ways.

the people kneeling: added in *1662*.

390 *the Priest, turning to the people*: Cosin's 'First Notes' to the BCP are more explicit about the performative aspects of his intention for this part of the service: the priest makes a low adoration to the altar and reads the Commandments while they lie prostrate to the end.

392 *Then shall be said the Collect of the day*: now placed after, rather than before, the Collects for the monarch. This alteration was later often criticized into the twentieth century; Cosin's reason was that the collect of the day was designed to comment on the Epistle and Gospel which now followed directly.

also (if occasion be) shall notice be given of the Communion: the notices were transferred here to the beginning of the sermon in *1662*. In 1753, Act 26 Geo. II, c. 33, provision was made for the banns of marriage to be said when there was no morning service.

And nothing shall be proclaimed or published in the Church: this injunction was suggested by Wren to articulate the renewed authority of the priesthood after the Restoration.

393 *Then shall the Priest return to the Lords Table*: at Cosin's suggestion; in his Visitation articles in the East Riding in 1626 he was already querying the movement of the priest at this point of the liturgy, showing the

delicacy of such questions in confessional disputes. Communion tables began to be replaced back at the east wall, at the top of the chancel, during the early seventeenth century, and the Laudian *Constitutions and Canons Ecclesiasticall* (1640), VII, gave retrospective authority for this move (Fincham and Tyacke, 176). They were also often railed off. After the Restoration some Laudian survivors such as Wren attempted to reintroduce railed altars, although churchwardens' accounts and vestry minutes demonstrate little enthusiasm (Hutton, *Restoration*, 177). On the other hand, in the royal chapels altars were covered with a carpet of velvet with white and gold satin, flagons and candlesticks atop, and the BCP resting on a cushion. Cathedrals also adopted elaborate decoration; Edmund Hickeringill said that in St Paul's, apart from the English language, he might be back in Catholic Portugal or Spain (Fincham and Tyacke, 312–15). The issue continued to cause difference of practice. By the 1680s Christopher Wren's new City churches often had railed altars. In Kent in 1683, at St Mary's, Dover, the Communion table was moved to the east end, forcibly removing the mayor and aldermen from their pew of choice, which was at the top of the chancel (ibid. 333).

394 *in a decent basin, to be provided by the Parish*: in *1549* and later versions the receptacle for the alms of the people was the 'poore mennes boxe'. Cosin observed in 1660 that this was now hardly ever observed, and that it was preferable for the priest to gather the collection at the altar. The direction here for the use of a 'basin' for this purpose was taken from the Scottish BCP of 1637.

so much Bread and Wine, as he shall think sufficient: this restored the rubric of *1549*.

395 *our alms and oblations*: a curious wording, later disputed in the nineteenth century. 'Oblation' had been one of the most controversial words in the *1549* Communion; here it may signify either (in the interpretation of Wren) the sacrifice of alms in charitable giving; or else the elements of the sacrament which have just been placed on the altar.

for all thy servants departed this life in thy faith and fear: added in *1662*. Praying for the dead during the Mass had been eliminated from *1552*. The Elizabethan Injunctions of 1559 had allowed a form of bidding prayer praising God for the lives of those who have departed in the faith of Christ, but *1559* left out such a prayer at this point, according to Wren, 'that the Vulgar might not thinck, they did either pray to the Dead, or for the Dead'. Cosin recommended restoring such a prayer, using the wording in the Scottish BCP of 1637 as a template (Durham Book, 148).

When the Minister giveth warning for the celebration of the holy Communion: this exhortation was carefully revised by Cosin in *1662* in accordance with *Canons* (1604), XXII ('every Minister to give warning to his parishioners publickly in the Church at Morning Prayer, the Sunday before every time of his administering that holy Sacrament'). In the process he restored some of the distinctive sacramental language of *1549* ('in remembrance of his meritorious cross and passion') which had been cut in *1552*.

396 *Therefore if any of you be a blasphemer of God*: Cosin argued in 1660 (*Particulars*, fo. 8ʳ) that this requirement should be placed here and not later, since a blasphemer or adulterer was hardly likely 'suddenly' to stand up and leave in the middle of the preparation for Communion.

397 *Or in case he shall see the people negligent*: this exhortation now comes in a later position from its place in *1552* and *1559*. The passage about the ill effects of 'gazing' at the host was excised in *1662*, being crossed out by Sancroft, the secretary of the Committee.

398 *ye wilfully abstain*: the wording here is clarified from *1552* and *1559*.

conveniently placed: reviving the rubric in *1549*, which required that all who do not intend to take Communion depart out of the choir at this point.

399 *Draw near with faith*: expanded from 'Draw nere' (*1559*); Cosin (*Particulars*, fo. 8ʳ) pointed out that in the sixteenth century, when the Lord's Table had been placed in the middle of the church, this implied a physical movement. In the late seventeenth century, when in many cases the congregation would already be physically close to the sacrament, the movement is mental and spiritual.

kneeling humbly upon their knees, and saying: while retaining the rubric that the confession is said by the priest 'in the name of' the congregation, the words 'and saying' were intended to reinforce the view that the people join in by repeating after him. This was clarified by the bishops in 1661. Kneeling at the general confession was enforced in visitations (Fincham, *Visitation Articles*, e.g. 15, 54, 120).

We acknowledge: an example of an archaism (*1619*: 'We knowledge') amended at the suggestion of Wren and Sanderson (although the change had been made in Grafton's text of *1559*, used here, it was not followed in later Elizabethan versions).

pronounce this Absolution: these words, formalizing the action of the priest, were added in the Scottish BCP in 1637. The word 'Absolution' was often suspected by Puritans of a 'popish' ring, and the term 'remission' preferred; the objection was summed up thus in 1610: 'Absolution implyeth forgiving of sins with authority, Remission only by declaration' (Ambrose Fisher, *A Defence of the Liturgie of the Church of England*).

400 *Then shall the Priest turn to the Lords Table*: this action was added in *1662* following a suggestion by Wren.

born as at this time: on a number of occasions in *1662*, as here, this phrase is substituted for 'on this daye' as being only applicable precisely on Christmas Day itself.

402 *When the Priest, standing before the Table*: this careful note on the position of the priest so that he is both in full view of the congregation and freely able

to perform the sacramental action with visual as well as verbal clarity was added in *1662*, collating together different pieces of text from the Scottish BCP of 1637, from Wren's *Advice*, and Cosin's *Particulars* of 1660. The physical design of the cup continued to cause emotion on both sides; Bryan Spinks, *Sacraments, Ceremonies and Stuart Divines* (Aldershot: Ashgate, 2002), 183–4, illustrates some seventeenth-century examples. The word 'Consecration' was an innovation in *1662*; it was carefully avoided in the Edwardian BCP to avoid the taint of transubstantiation.

402 *And here to break the bread*: the physical actions for administering the bread and wine were the source of much discussion by Cosin in his *Particulars* of 1660 and then in the Durham Book (p. 166). Noting that the direction for the breaking of the bread, included in *1549*, had been cut from subsequent versions, he proposed much more explicit manual actions: the priest should physically break the bread, and then 'hold his hands over it' (changed in a second thought to 'lay his hands upon it'). In a rare moment of unity over ritual practice, the *Exceptions* (1661) also approved 'the Ministers breaking of the bread', in order to reinforce, however, the scriptural narrative rather than the priestly sacrament. The wording from *1549* and from the Scottish BCP of 1637 was therefore adapted in *1662* to form a precise series of performable accompaniments to the words of Institution. However, the initial intention (in the Durham Book) to restore the words of the epiclesis ('blesse and sanctifie') from *1549* (as had been used in the Scottish BCP of 1637) was not incorporated in *1662*.

Amen: Jeremy Taylor and Hamon L'Estrange had first suggested this corroboration by the congregation of the sacred action.

403 *all meekly kneeling*: the position of the minister and the requirement to kneel (by either him or the congregation) had been a continual cause of controversy among Puritans and was justified at length by Cosin (Durham Book, 171). To presbyterians, kneeling during reception of Communion was idolatry, because it signified adoration; conformists by contrast defended kneeling as 'an act of reverence' (Spinks, *Sacraments, Ceremonies and the Stuart Divines*, 121 and 151). Kneeling at reception was perhaps the clearest visible signal of conformism versus nonconformism: no other rubric is enquired into more frequently in early seventeenth-century visitations (see the index to Fincham, *Visitation Articles*, 287).

The body of our Lord Jesus Christ: this form of words was first added in *1559*. There was some dispute as to whether the communicant should say 'Amen' on receiving; some felt that the affirmation might give to Roman Catholics 'some Colour of their fancy of Transubstantiation'. Although approved by Andrewes and Cosin, and used in the Scottish BCP of 1637, it was omitted in *1662*. Theologians in the 1660s debated vigorously the presence of Christ in the sacrament: Herbert Thorndike indicated that while 'the bodily substance of bread and wine is not abolished nor ceaseth', Christ is present 'mystically and spiritually and sacramentally'. As to the precise process, he affirmed that Christ is present ' "in", and "with", and "under" ' the elements, but declined to say what the prepositions meant, saying that he was 'not obliged to declare the manner of that which must be mystical, when I have said what I can say to declare it' (quoted in Spinks, *Sacraments, Ceremonies and the Stuart Divines*, 155).

If the consecrated bread or wine be all spent before all have communicated: such a rubric had been included in the *Order of the Communion* of 1548 but excluded from *1549* and *1552*. The new wording builds on several suggested versions in Wren and Cosin (Durham Book, 185–7).

what remaineth of the consecrated Elements: this rubric conceals some controversy. In the 'First Notes' on the BCP (in Cosin's hand but perhaps authored by his master Overall) the orthodox position is declared to be that, 'upon the words of consecration the body and blood of Christ is really and substantially present' in the elements, and the Calvinists are reproached for teaching that Christ is present only 'in the act of eating'. Some believed that it was a profanation that in *1552* the curate is allowed to keep any bread and wine remaining for his own use. Later, however, Cosin took the view that the consecration does not 'remain longer than the holy action itself remains', and that when it is over the elements 'return to their former use again'. The division in *1662* between the distribution of remaining unconsecrated and consecrated elements is therefore a compromise.

406 *Upon the Sundaies and other holy days (if there be no Communion)*: this implies a form of service for use when there were not sufficient communicants; a useful provision, despite attempts to instil more regular taking of Communion.

407 *every Parishioner shall communicate at the least three times in the year, of which Easter to be one*: the thrice-yearly rule was frequently repeated in visitations but not frequently observed. At King's Sutton in Oxfordshire in 1619 it was estimated only half the parish observed the rule (Hunt, 'Lord's Supper', 41). This may have been unusually high. Bishop Montagu's visitation in Norwich in 1638 wryly comments that frequency of Communion has been in decline since the early church, and that 'in latter times, devotion slaking', three times a year was optimistic, and most came 'especially' at Easter, 'which is the limitation in our church' (Fincham, *Visitation Articles*, 204). The situation did not change with the Restoration; indeed, it may be that Puritans had attended Communion more regularly, and so attendance declined once they left the churches. A vicar in Bedfordshire reported to his bishop in 1691 that only ten of his several hundred parishioners regularly attended Communion.

the money given at the Offertory: the Scottish BCP of 1637 provided that one half of the money should be used to purchase books of divinity for the minister; the Durham Book at first kept this rubric; *1662* adopts a more open formula.

should receive the same Kneeling: this peculiar rubric sums up over a century of frantic argument. It was written into the revision of *1662* at a late stage by hand in the manuscript, having been discussed in Privy Council on 21 and 24 February 1662 (the main text of the BCP had already been agreed by 20 December). The wording is based closely on the 'Black Rubric' (see Appendix A, p. 667) that had been inserted into some copies of *1552*, but which was removed from *1559* and subsequent editions. In the meantime the practice of kneeling had become one of the cardinal aspects of Laudianism; and thus had also come into fierce criticism from Puritans in the Civil War period. The inclusion of this rubric may have been suggested by John Gauden, bishop of Worcester, who had tried to satisfy both sides during the Civil War, and while upholding the benefit of the BCP tried to accommodate presbyterian criticisms.

407 *unto any Corporal Presence of Christs natural Flesh, and Bloud*: the wording here is carefully revised from the version in *1552*: 'unto anye reall and essencial presence there beeyng of Christes naturall fleshe and bloude.' The new version distinguished itself from the Catholic doctrine of transubstantiation without denying the real presence.

BAPTISM

Like Communion, baptism was the cause of continual controversy throughout the seventeenth century. Radical Puritans, such as the Particular Baptists, objected to infant baptism on the grounds that the child was incapable of making a serious profession of faith; many more Puritans also objected to what they saw as superstition in its performance. These bodily rituals were championed to the same degree among defenders of the BCP, who campaigned instead for greater emphasis on sacramentalism.

408 *The people are to be admonished*: in *1662* the introduction to this rubric, with its short history of baptism written in *1549* (p. 46), was removed.

upon any other day: replacing 'at home' in *1559*. King James's personal horror in 1604 at the idea of home baptism, and especially at the prospect of 'baptizing by women and laikes' (William Barlow, *Summe and Substance of the Conference*, 8), had become the focus for maintaining the uniqueness of priestly authority in conferring the rite. There is a case for believing that Catholics practised lay baptism at home using Catholic rituals and then presented their children for public baptism afterwards; there were sharp fines for failure to concur with this stipulation. However, firm evidence on this point is naturally hard to find.

two Godfathers and one Godmother: although these figures were stipulated as early as the Synod of Worcester in 1240, earlier editions of BCP had not mentioned a number. Cosin at first (in the Durham Book, p. 196) used the formula 'three at least', possibly in riposte to Puritan dislike of any use of sponsors.

which is then to be filled with pure water: Cosin added this practical rubric in *1662*. The position and ornamentation of fonts was a source of renewed interest in the 1660s; some were provided with a drain to collect the baptismal water.

409 *didst sanctifie water to the mystical washing away of sin*: the Scottish BCP of 1637 contained at this point a prayer to 'sanctifie this fountaine', in imitation of a similar act of blessing in *1549*; Cosin, in the Durham Book (p. 192), first proposed this prayer and then crossed it out.

thine infinite mercies: as on several occasions in *1662*, emended from 'thy', despite the general decline in the seventeenth century of 'thine' as the usage before a vowel. This is one instance of a general preference in *1662* for a certain archaic grandeur in language.

Then shall the people stand up: added in *1662*, following a suggestion in Wren.

410 *to sanctifie him with the holy Ghost*: added in *1662*.

until he come of age to take it upon himself: added in *1662*.

411 *renounce the devil*: 'renounce' preferred to 'foresake' here and in the following, in an emendation first suggested by Jeremy Taylor.

Wilt thou then obediently keep Gods holy will: added in *1662*, taken from the Catechism in *1549*.

412 *sanctifie this water to the mystical washing away of sin*: in *1662* the act of blessing the water is restored, which had been abolished in *1552*. This perhaps accords with popular beliefs, and also reflects a trend back towards endowing physical materials with spiritual properties through ritual. The Durham Book (p. 196) includes a prayer of blessing the water, then crossed out: 'wch we here blesse in thy name, & dedicate to this holy action' (using the wording of the Scottish BCP of 1637); the *1662* text includes the idea of blessing implicit in the grammar, without specifying an accompanying action.

it shall suffice to pour water upon it: Taylor specified that the priest should 'sprinkle water on the face'.

the congregation of Christs flock: Cosin objected to 'congregation', first used in *1552*, on the grounds that the word appears in no previous liturgy or ancient writer; he proposed 'Church of Christ', but the bishops did not concur. The word 'congregation' as an alternative to 'church' had been a controversial point in English theological language since William Tyndale and Sir Thomas More in 1528–32. It brought together at least three historical frameworks: the OT sense of the 'congregation of the Lord' (e.g. Num. 1: 2); the NT word ἐκκλησία, as translated by Tyndale to rid the word of association with the Roman church; and the Lutheran sense of the German *Gemeinde*, the Christian community of believers. Only in the eighteenth century did the modern predominant meaning, 'a body of persons assembled for religious worship', become prevalent.

make a cross: this was a controversial legacy of *1552*, which had eliminated all other bodily processes in baptism apart from the use of water itself.

William Juxon, Laud's successor as bishop of London, enforced the use of the cross in baptism as one of two defining principles of uniformity. Puritans hated this oppression above any other. 'It is the mark of the beast', an Essex man declared; several incidents in that county record the child being snatched from the priest's hands, or the face being covered with a cloth, or even the curate's hand being twisted behind his back, to prevent the ritual taking place (John Walter, 'Confessional Politics in Pre-Civil War Essex', *Historical Journal*, 44 (2001), 683). Despite Puritan objections to crossing, *1662* emphasizes the ritual action by clarifying its performance. Wren put in a physical mark (✠), but this was not adopted. See notes to pp. 30, 57, 67, 69 and 137, for the process by which this sign was used and then removed.

412 *manfully to fight under his banner*: in an early and unexpected venture in inclusive language, Archbishop William Laud, baptizing the Princess Royal on 4 November 1631, varied this phrase 'bycause it appertaynes not naturally, to the Female Sexe'.

413 *into thy holy Church*: replaces 'congregation' in *1559*.

414 *children which are baptized, dying before they commit actual sin*: this rubric dates back originally to the Ten Articles of 1536 and the Bishops' Book of 1537; it also appeared in *1549* in the introductory rubric to Confirmation. As to the fate of infants dying without baptism, neither the *Canons* (1604) nor those of 1640 made provision, but Sanderson (one of the bishops involved in the revision of *1662*) commented in an unpublished treatise around 1625 that God may 'supply unto Infants unbaptized some other way, by the immediate work of his holy and almighty spirit, without the use of the outward means of the word and sacraments' (*Pax Ecclesiae*, included in the 1678 edition of Izaak Walton's *Life of Sanderson*, 71).

all scruple concerning the use of the signe of the Cross: this rubric addressed to the Puritans was added in *1662*; it was first proposed in 1641 in response to the fall of Laud.

PRIVATE BAPTISM OF CHILDREN IN HOUSES

This practice continued to cause vexation throughout the period. In line with the view of King James in 1604, the sacramental act was limited to the performance of the priest. However some bishops, including Overall and Samuel Harsnett, continued to tolerate baptism by midwives in cases of necessity (Hunt, 'Lay Baptism'). The Laudian view may have been to take the BCP rubric as not covering such cases, although the 1604 revision was written precisely to exclude baptism by the laity in any circumstances. At the same time Laudians leaned heavily to the sacramental idea of the necessity of baptism for the fulfilment of grace and salvation. *1662* follows the letter of *1604* on this point, while also continuing to insist on the functional presence of the minister. Indeed, *1662* in general formalizes prayers and actions so as to make their liturgical function clear even within the home. This accorded with a general principle in *1662* to limit the use of extemporary prayer popular among nonconformists.

Yet this formal propriety fought with social trends which made the necessity of emergency baptism more likely: in later Stuart times the median interval between birth and baptism was eight days—and became longer in the eighteenth century (Cressy, 101). Fear over the fate of unbaptized children was often expressed (see Sanderson above), down to Thomas Hardy's *Tess of the d'Urbervilles* (1891); the plot of that novel, where Tess agonizes whether her baby Sorrow can be given Christian burial, because she (and not a priest) has baptized him (ch. 14), would have been obviated if the rule in *1549* and *1559* had been maintained in preference to that of *1604* and *1662*.

415 *shall examine and try whether the child be lawfully baptized*: Cosin (Durham Book, 205) was concerned particularly that a child be baptized again, 'when only a *Midwife* or some *other such* hath baptized it before'. However, there was the opposite worry of not repeating for a second time a lawful sacrament. Conditional baptism had been controversial since Calvin.

418 *shall make a cross*: this procedure was omitted in the *1549* and *1559* forms for private baptism, but is included in *1662* as part of the process of making the rite as much like the church service as possible.

BAPTISM OF RIPER YEARS

Sanderson's Preface (see p. 211) stated that this service was necessitated in *1662* 'by the growth of Anabaptism, through the licentiousness of the late times crept in among us'. It was also considered necessary for the 'baptizing of natives in our plantations and others converted to the faith'. Adult baptism was rumoured, in often sensational reports in the 1640s and 1650s, to take place with mixed sexes and in naked immersion in the open air in rivers and other places. Lawrence Clarkson, in his autobiographical *The Lost Sheep Found* (1660), commented drily that inclement weather made the truth of these reports unlikely. However, the idea that only adults could make a true profession for baptism was increasingly widespread, and attracted converts. Tewkesbury is one example of a Baptist chapel of the seventeenth century with a trench in the middle with steps leading down to it for the purposes of complete adult immersion; a trap-door enabled the floor to be used for other purposes. The new service in BCP was commissioned in May 1661 by Convocation and completed within the month; its purpose was to readmit dissenters who had previously delayed baptism. This is one case of a rapprochement with Puritan beliefs within the Church of England; the rite follows the procedures and wording, including catechism, as for infants, substituting the word 'persons' for 'children'.

CATECHISM

Now taken out of Confirmation and given a separate heading. The form follows that in *1559*, but is expanded in line with the additions first introduced in the BCP in *1604*. Reynolds expressed the Puritan wish for a longer form of catechism at the Hampton Court Conference of January 1604; radical Protestants campaigned for this throughout the seventeenth century (see Green, *Christian's ABC*). *Canons* (1604), LIX prescribed that 'fathers, mothers, masters and mistresses, shall cause their children, servants and apprentices . . . to come to the Church at the time appointed, obediently to hear, and to be ordered by the Minister, until they have learned the same'. Penalties were applied to ministers who neglected this duty.

427 *any graven image*: iconoclasm had been a revived feature of radical religion during the Civil War years.

thou keep holy the Sabbath day: while this part of the Catechism remained unchanged from *1559*, Sabbatarian controversy was an open sore in the religion of the 1640s and 1650s, and a rallying-cry for Puritanism.

429 *How many Sacraments hath Christ ordained in his Church?*: this passage was introduced in *1604* as part of the longer catechism. Cosin reported that this expanded form was the work of Overall, dean of St Paul's, but if so it was compiled from a variety of sources, including Nowell's expanded catechism of 1570 and an old Latin catechism used at St Paul's School.

an outward and visible signe of an inward and spiritual grace: the concept of the 'outward and visible sign' is a medieval scholastic commonplace, found in Peter Lombard's *Sentences* (twelfth century). The Homily of 1562 described a sacrament as 'a visible sign of an invisible grace'.

430 *Because they promise them both by their sureties*: the presbyterians objected at the Savoy Conference that the baptismal vows could not express 'a really actual faith and repentance of their own' (*Conferences*, 326).

CONFIRMATION

The beginning of this service is reshaped due to the separation of the Catechism. Cosin designed the revision. His first draft, preserved in the Durham Book, was more elaborate.

431 *To the end that Confirmation may be ministered*: the opening preface is repeated from the order in *1549* onwards.

being now come to the years of discretion: a precise age was not determined, but *Canons* (1604), LXI required a child to have reached a stage of intelligent analysis, 'as can render an account of their faith'.

Do ye here in the presence of God: Cosin here creates a renewed version of the baptismal vows, including the same formulae used by the godparents at that service. In the Durham Book (p. 222) he included a longer form of admonition based on the rubric to the Lyons Pontifical, using his researches into older Latin liturgical history (Blunt, 441).

432 *Then all of them in order kneeling before the Bishop*: in Sarum there was a ritual use of oil at this point, as the act of confirmation began. In *1549* unction was dropped but signing with the cross was retained; in *1552* the action was reduced to the laying on of hands. However, an episcopal visitation in Oxford in 1619 shows that the sign of the cross was later revived in many churches, sometimes using the *1549* formula as justification. The visitation recommended that it be left to the discretion of

the bishop performing the rite, and it may be that the revision of *1662* also felt it prudent not to make explicit a practice that was nonetheless allowed. Kneeling, here included in the rubric for the first time, in any case registers a new sacramental spirit in the service.

Our Father which art in heaven: the Lord's Prayer was introduced into the service in *1662*. The *Pax tibi*, used in *1549* but dropped in *1552*, was not reintroduced.

433 *O almighty Lord, and everlasting God*: this second Collect was added in *1662* as a prayer for the general congregation, as opposed to the first, which is for the confirmed.

MATRIMONY

The service for marriage was largely unchanged in *1662*, and indeed is one of the most stable parts of the BCP; however, certain ceremonies, for example the use of rings and arrangements for a nuptial Communion, continued to aggravate presbyterians. These aspects of the service were especially fraught since many nonconformists attended church for marriage who otherwise never came across the BCP. If not married in the Church of England their children would be regarded as legally illegitimate. See Cressy (p. 332), on marriages 'without banns or licence'.

434 *immediately before the sentences for the Offertory*: the point in the divine service for notices is prescribed for the first time in *1662*; publication of banns was confirmed in statute in the Marriage Acts of George II and George IV.

I publish the Banns of marriage: the formula of the banns was inserted into the service by Cosin (Durham Book, 230).

cause or just impediment: defined in the Durham Book (p. 230) as prior contract to another; consanguinity (see the Table, p. 686); divorce from a spouse yet living; being under-age; or wanting instruction in the catechism or confirmation order.

the man on the right hand: Cosin took this rubric from Sarum (*vir autem stet a dextra mulieris*), transcribing the Latin in his 'Second Notes' on the BCP. However, the Hereford Manual placed the couple in the opposite positions, interpreting 'on the right hand' as meaning 'of the priest' (as is the case in Jewish marriages).

435 *his holy Name*: altered from 'God' (in *1559*) in the Durham Book.

I require and charge you both: the word 'both' was included at the suggestion of Sanderson, presumably as implying the onus is on the woman as well as the man.

436 *to say after him as followeth*: in *1662* it is stipulated for the first time that the vows be said in repetition after the minister.

till death us do part: 'do part' replaced 'depart' from *1559*, one of the archaisms objected to as 'improperly used' in the presbyterian *Exceptions* of 1661.

436 *the man holding the ring there*: the manual gesture emphasizes the ritual significance of the wedding ring, in the face of long-standing Puritan objections. In the Durham Book, Cosin added the *1549* reference to further gifts of gold, silver, or bracelets, but then crossed it out. In his 'Third Notes' on the BCP he noted that Bucer approved of these additional marriage tokens, and that they were still customary in the north of England.

with my body I thee worship: the word 'worship' was a source of consistent objection among Puritans. When Reynolds criticized the word at the Hampton Court Conference in 1604, King James was reported smilingly to have answered, 'if you had a good wife your selfe, all the honour and worshippe you could doe her, were well bestowed'; there was initial agreement at the Conference to the mitigating addition, 'worship and honour'. In 1641 the committee of the House of Lords on church reform proposed 'I give thee power over my body'.

437 *they shall both kneel down*: added in *1662*; first suggested by Wren.

439 *see their children Christianly and vertuously brought up*: replacing the reference to grandchildren to the third and fourth generations; a concession to the presbyterians.

441 *It is convenient that the new married persons should receive the holy Communion*: replacing 'must' in *1552*. This was a concession to the presbyterians, who objected that this forced people unprepared for Communion either to remain unmarried or to take Communion in a state of sin. Cosin's word 'convenient' implies 'suitable' but not 'mandatory'. In some churches the custom was retained at this point for the groom to kiss the bride, following a note in Sarum. John Marston's *The Insatiate Countess* (1613) refers to the tradition: 'the kisse thou gav'st me in the church', V. i (sig. I1ᵛ). Feasting, and accompanying the couple to bed, followed the formal rituals in social acts which were enjoyed by Puritans as well as conformists. Oliver Cromwell gave his daughter a wedding gift of a chest inlaid with erotic scenes from Ovid's *Metamorphoses* (now in the National Museum of Ireland (Collins Barracks), Dublin).

VISITATION OF THE SICK

This service, which had been altered considerably in *1552*, was left largely unchanged in *1662*, except for the addition of set prayers for the sick.

notice shall be given thereof to the Minister: Cosin's visitation articles from the East Riding in 1626 suggest that this new rubric arises from his experience as a parish priest.

Answer. Spare us, good Lord: Cosin introduces the response in line with the Litany.

443 *Sanctifie, we beseech thee, this thy fatherly correction to him*: this passage of moral commentary was substituted in *1662* in place of the NT allusions

in *1559*. The variations for gender throughout the service were added in *1662*.

445 *All this I stedfastly believe*: the response (and the catechistic material spoken by the minister) are regularized in accordance with the order for Baptism.

repent him truly of his sins: added in *1662*.

But men should often be put in remembrance: added in *1662*.

(*if he humbly and heartily desire it*): this clause added in *1662* in accordance with presbyterian concerns that absolution should be dependent on repentance not on priestly authority.

446 *strengthen him with thy blessed Spirit*: added in *1662*. Puritans had long been concerned that prayers in the case of sudden death were futile except where a person was prepared through repentance.

447 *Thy righteousness, O God*: after this verse, the last five verses of Ps. 71 are omitted in *1662* as inappropriate to the occasion.

Unto Gods gracious mercy and protection: this is an old form of Jewish benediction, written in Cosin's handwriting into the margin of the Durham Book (p. 244), derived from his research into old liturgies, possibly from an Anglo-Saxon mass-book.

A Prayer for a sick Child: this and the following three prayers appended to Visitation were added in *1662*. In the Durham Book there is an additional rubric (p. 246) that the names of the sick be left at the minister's reading-desk and read out after the final Collect at Morning or Evening Prayer. The rubric was not adopted in *1662* but reflects common practice, since it also appears in Wren's *Advice*.

449 *the time of pestilence, or other infectious sickness*: altered from 'the plague time' (*1559*). The continued relevance of the rubric was brought into sharp relief by the bubonic plague of 1665, at which point elaborate guidance was created for ministers dealing with afflicted houses.

(*which shall be three, or two at the least*): the number was specified for the first time in *1662*.

BURIAL OF THE DEAD

Among the Puritan complaints against the Laudians was a revival of prayers for the dead (Marshall, 186–7). Cosin's book of private devotions in 1627 was singled out for this criticism. The service was amplified and clarified in *1662*. It was substantially the work of Sanderson, rebuilding and amplifying the order of service after the radical cuts of *1552*, without entirely following the original principles of *1549*. Funeral rites were the cause of heightened sensitivity among those who had been exiled in France during the Interregnum. Cosin was shocked to find that Catholic tolerance of Anglicans ended at death: 'they will allow us no other burial of our dead than the burial of a dog' (*Godly Order*, 137).

451 *any that die unbaptized, or excommunicate, or have laid violent hands upon*

themselves: in line with *Canons* (1604), LXVIII, which forbade the minister to refuse burial on any other grounds, with a penalty of suspension from the ministry. The refusal to bury the excommunicated had been explicit in medieval canon law and applied throughout the history of the BCP; Ophelia in *Hamlet*, V. i. 213, is given 'maimed rites' because of the suspicion of suicide at her death.

451 *the entrance of the Church-yard*: replacing 'stile', in *1662* considered an archaism. Cosin originally provided an alternative rubric to allow sermons to be delivered over the corpse in the middle of the church; although excluded from *1662*, the practice was evidently common.

shall be read one or both of these Psalms: processional psalms, which characterized the medieval Office of the Dead, had been excised from *1552* following Bucer's misgivings about prayers for the dead. The element of ritual is here restored, but takes place within the church rather than in procession towards it.

453 *Then shall follow the Lesson*: placed here in *1662*, instead of its position after the committal in *1552*.

455 *in sure and certain hope of the resurrection*: this was one of a number of phrases objected to by the presbyterians at the Savoy Conference as taking for granted the salvation of a person; which, they added caustically, 'had ecclesiastical discipline been truly and vigorously executed . . . might be better supposed, but . . . cannot now be rationally admitted'. In the Durham Book (p. 250), Cosin suggested as a concession, 'in hope of our generall & joyfull reurrection', using a phrase from the Collect for Easter Even. Sanderson supplied the alternative 'in hope of a resurrection', but in the event the original phrase was allowed.

456 *the souls of the faithful*: this phrase replaces 'them that be elected' in *1559*.

The grace of our Lord Jesus Christ: added in *1662*.

CHURCHING OF WOMEN

457 *at the usual time after her delivery*: added in *1662*; Cosin's first draft read 'a month after her delivery being recovered'.

decently apparelled: this is not an etiquette of dress code, but refers to the common practice of wearing a veil for this service; Cosin's first draft read 'decently vayled'. Puritans, however, considered wearing the veil a sin, as an unnecessary ceremony; the veil also revealed the origins of the service as a form of ritual purification, rather than a thanksgiving (as in the changed wording of *1552*).

some convenient place: in the medieval rite this was the church door; in *1549* it was altered to the entrance to the choir; in *1552* to near the Lord's Table. The key point was to establish some liminal place signifying readmission to divine worship. Wren's visitation articles in Norwich in 1636 required the woman to kneel near the Communion table and to wear a veil but with no hat (Fincham, *Visitation Articles*, 204). In some churches a 'churching stool' was used.

the 116th Psalm: replacing Ps. 121 in *1549* and *1559*.

458 *For thine is the kingdom*: the doxology was added in *1662*; using the doxology in every instance of the Lord's Prayer was one of the demands of the presbyterians at Savoy.

COMMINATION

The gloss to the title, 'Denouncing of Gods anger', was added by Wren.

459 *reading Pew*: the chancel pew or stalls occupied by the clergy and singers; a change suggested first in the Memorandum of 1641 at the fall of Archbishop Laud. Not to be confused with the enclosed 'pews' increasingly favoured by the gentry, sometimes with screens and even locks (Pepys found himself once unable to enter his pew because the sexton had locked it). They were often frowned upon by clergy, who considered them a hiding-place for falling asleep during services, or even worse vices.

460 *Cursed is the man that maketh any carved or molten image*: although the admonition of idolatry from the Second Commandment is retained, it is reduced from *1552* and its iconoclastic relish is softened. The iconoclasm of the Civil Wars was a horrific memory to Restoration bishops like Cosin. The responses which follow are from Deut. 27: 15–25.

perverteth the judgement: altered from the archaic phrasing in *1559*.

idolaters: replaces 'worshippers of ymages' in *1559*.

461 *the propitiation for our sins*: replaces 'that obteyneth grace for our synnes' in *1559*.

462 *(in the place where they are accustomed to say the Litany)*: see note to p. 259.

464 *turn thine anger from us*: replacing 'ire' (now felt to be archaic) in *1559*.

Through the merits and mediation of thy blessed Son: this note of hope, and the blessing which followed, were added in *1662*.

PSALMS

The Psalter was not printed as part of the same book as the BCP until *1662*, but its use was intrinsic to all previous versions. Cranmer envisaged from the beginning of his proposals for a vernacular order of worship a recitation of the Psalms entire each month, repeated through the year. Whitchurch, Grafton, and Oswen all produced imprints of the Psalter which are found bound in with copies of *1549*, and from 1552 (in quarto) and 1564 (in folio) complementary imprints were issued by the same printer of BCP and Psalter together. The English version used was Miles Coverdale's, first printed in 1535 and included in the Great Bible of 1540. Indeed, despite the replacement of all the Gospels and Epistles with the KJV in *1662*, the Psalter remains that of the Great Bible. The discrepancy was noted by Wren; but the older version was hallowed by long use and its pointing for sung use would have required a wholesale revision to accommodate the KJV version for the purposes of chant. The only alteration to the text of the Psalter in the history of the BCP was to introduce verse numbers (which took place in 1620, although the Latin Prayer Book of 1572 already contained them). Verse numbers were first introduced into bibles in Robert Estienne's Geneva polyglot Bible of 1551, and were immediately adopted in Calvin's commentaries, and thereafter in Catholic Europe as well.

Liturgical use of the Psalms is mentioned in the OT (1 Chr. 16: 7), and was an established part of Jewish ritual practice for centuries before the time of Jesus and the apostles, who refer to them frequently in the NT. Use of the Psalter was likely the earliest form of Christian worship as well, often in the Septuagint translation into Greek. A Latin version existed at a very early date; this formed the basis of Jerome's first version of the Psalms, a revision of this text being used in liturgy in the Vatican and in San Marco in Venice up to the twentieth century. His third version (translated directly from the Hebrew) was never used in divine service; it was his second (known as the Gallican, translated from the Septuagint) that was used in the Western church throughout the middle ages. A pattern was set out for the use of the Psalter by St Benedict (sixth century), and this formed the basis for the English pre-Reformation liturgical performance, in which all the psalms were chanted in a single week, spread over the eight Hours of the divine office, in an elaborate pattern (although not in sequence). While this pattern was used in religious orders, in parish churches a large number of psalms were set for festival use, so that the ferial psalms used in regular services comprised about half the total. This led Cranmer (somewhat disingenuously, in view of the central part of the Psalter in the religious life of the late middle ages) in his *1549* Preface (p. 4) to complain that 'now of late tyme a fewe of them have been dailye sayed (and ofte repeated) and the rest utterly omitted' (a point he takes from Quiñones and applies polemically).

His own plan, retained intact in *1662*, divides the 150 psalms so that they are performed in exact sequence over Morning and Evening Prayer in a thirty-day pattern. In a month with thirty-one days, the thirtieth day is repeated the next day. Ps 119, being 176 verses long, was divided into twenty-two portions and sung over several days.

Medieval chant for the Psalter was elaborate and survives in thousands of local examples. Three main forms of chanting psalms developed: *cantus directus*, where the psalm was sung straight through by the whole choir; *cantus antiphonalis*, in which the choir divided into two sides, *cantoris* and *decani*, each singing alternate verses; and *cantus responsarius*, where the precentor sang the verses with uneven numbers and the choir or congregation those with even numbers. In the Church of England all three practices have prevailed. While music was not printed in the BCP, except for *The booke of common praier noted* (1550), individual cathedrals and churches formulated their own chant books, in use to the present day. These followed the punctuation of the BCP (hence 'Pointed as shall be sung or said in churches', as on the title-page, see p. 184). See the Note on Music.

The Psalms were traditionally ascribed to the single authorship of the biblical King David, although increasingly this was shown to be unlikely; modern biblical scholars attribute them to a variety of periods over several hundred years. Pss. 1–41 and 51–72 are regarded as belonging in some sense to the reign of David.

In the margin the Psalter is divided into sections, a group of Psalms for each set of Morning and Evening Prayer through the month.

465 *Beatus vir, qui non abiit*: the Latin titles were given for the psalms from *1549* onwards, forming a standard form of reference used also in the text of the BCP where psalms are set for other liturgical purposes.

    nor stood: a rare example of an emendation in *1662* by Cosin of the archaic preterite verb-form 'stand'.

518 *so let indignation vex him*: out of the whole Psalter, this was the one verse Cosin suggested for a substantial emendation; the revisers rejected the new reading.

PRAYERS TO BE USED AT SEA

These prayers were written for *1662*, and were authored by Sanderson, according to Izaak Walton's *Life* of the bishop. The origins of this unusual liturgical form lie in the Civil War. In 1645 parliament issued *A Supply of Prayer for the Ships of this Kingdom, that want Ministers to pray with them*. This was a supplement to the *Directory for the Public Worship of God*, the Calvinist alternative liturgy which supplanted the banned BCP after 1645. Parliament was concerned that sailors at sea were using old copies of BCP and so issued a short form of worship with prayers and psalms. This included 'a prayer particularly fitted for those that travell upon the seas' and 'a prayer in a storm'. The navy expanded radically under Cromwell, and in *1662* these occasional forms were supplemented by a confession and absolution for situations of 'imminent danger', similar in motivation to the Visitation of the Sick. British interests overseas made the new prayers in the BCP popular in the eighteenth and nineteenth centuries. The American Prayer Book later included them while omitting reference to 'his Majesty'; the Irish edition excised all reference to the British navy.

615 *for thy Son our Lord Jesus Christ's sake*: the only instance of the use of an apostrophe in *1662*.

620 *and was turn'd into a calm*: the punctuation marking an elision once again is unique in *1662* (apart from one example in the Ordinal). The explanation in both cases is that this material was newly written and thus set fresh, presumably in this instance by a new compositor.

ORDINAL

Forms of service for the ordination of holy orders survive from the sixth century onwards; two different traditions, the Roman and the Gallican, were fused in the later medieval period to form the Pontifical, the liturgical book of rites performed by a bishop (which also included confirmation). The Sarum Pontifical contained an elaborate rite for ordaining priests and deacons and other minor orders (including acolytes, exorcists, readers, etc.), which

contained the essential elements of the oldest services which were incorporated
into a form of Mass including special features: the litany, the laying on of
hands, bidding prayers, a consecratory prayer, and the hymn *Veni creator*; along
with the 'tradition of elements'—the conferring of the objects used in priestly
actions, such as the Bible, chalice, vestments, etc.—a ceremony defined by Pope
Eugenius IV in 1439 as the essential feature of ordination (and confirmed as
such by Cardinal Pole in the English Catholic Counter-Reformation in 1556).

The Reformers in 1550 composed a revised form of ordination service known
as the Ordinal which was printed in a separate edition by Grafton alongside the
BCP. The German Reformers had already wrestled with the question of the
function of priests, and Bucer produced a draft service in Latin for the benefit
of his English colleagues. Nevertheless, the 1550 service was based primarily
on Sarum, with a holy Communion incorporating the litany, the laying on of
hands, bidding collects, consecration, *Veni creator*, and even a residual form
of 'tradition of elements' in the conferring of the Bible. They gave to the new
order a visual coherence in which the laying on of hands was central, along with
the verbal formula 'Receive the holy ghost'; they also placed renewed emphasis
on the examination of the ordained person to certify competence in doctrine
and some learning.

The Ordinal continued to be printed separately alongside the BCP in its various revisions in *1552, 1559, 1604*, and later, and largely conserved its central
structure and wording, despite controversies about the nature of the priesthood
throughout the period. Elizabethan Puritanism divided between those who followed Calvinist doctrine but accepted episcopal structures of hierarchy, and
those (increasingly persecuted) who felt that Calvinist doctrine also required
reform of ecclesiastical authority along Calvin's lines. The Ordinal therefore
became a special litmus of religious and political party. In the Commonwealth
the removal of the Ordinal was as much an occasion of triumph as that of the
BCP. After 1660, when only nine bishops survived, the role of priests and
bishops was debated anew, and the restoration of the episcopacy was a crucial
element in the enforcement of a new ecclesiastical order, however outwardly
committed to 'toleration' of dissenting views. In *1662* a revised Ordinal was for
the first time incorporated inside the BCP, based very closely on the 1550 order.
Cosin annotated his own copy of *1552* to prepare his revision. Although placed
at the end of the book, it defined the whole as 'episcopalian' in character, with
a strong emphasis on the oaths of allegiance to the monarch, since all of the
preceding orders of service were dependent on the initial authorization of the
priest, embodied in this service, to perform all those subsequent acts.

622 *from the Apostles time there have been these Orders of Ministers*: the origin of ministry in the NT was the crucial point of doctrinal argument
between all parties, but it was also unfailingly complex. Christ's mission
to the apostles was set out in a series of passages in the gospels, and after
Pentecost this is extended to others (Acts 6: 6), whose personnel and function are described in a variety of ways throughout Acts and the epistles.

Bishops, Priests, and Deacons: the English word 'Bishop' (ME 'Biscop') was a corruption of the Latin transliteration (*episcopus*) of the Greek ἐπίσκοπος (lit. 'overseer') used in the NT. There it is virtually a synonym for πρεσβύτερος, a word (lit. 'the senior of two people') which is used frequently in the NT to describe the 'elders' or officials in the emergent church. In Latin this latter term was sometimes translated literally as *senior* (or *maior*), or more occasionally—as when the office is authorized or 'ordained' by an apostle, as at Acts 14: 23—as *presbyterus*, the origin of the English word 'priest'. Church historians viewed the rank of bishop as dating back to the second century, when the chief centres of Christianity began to be headed by an official of a different and higher rank than a 'priest'; however, James Ussher (1581–1656), archbishop of Armagh, had recently disputed some of this evidence. There was also a third level of official, the 'deacon' (from NT Greek διάκονος, lit. a 'servant'), who came to have an assistant role to the priest. The post-Reformation English church carried over this distinction of formal roles from the medieval church, but only in the wake of considerable philological and political argument. The earliest English Protestant version of the NT, by William Tyndale, aggressively used the word 'senior' in place of priest (which he defended in a vituperative semantic quarrel with Sir Thomas More), although he retained 'bisshoppe' (Tit. 1: 7); and Calvin's new form of ecclesiastical authority rigorously enforced NT distinctions on linguistic lines, ordaining 'presbyters' (hence 'presbyterian' to describe a distinctive form of church authority deriving from a meeting of the clergy or 'presbytery') and abandoning 'bishops' as a misreading of NT Greek usage. The BCP, however, derived its whole structure from the authority of bishops to ordain priests who could then perform the functions of the various services. The 1979 BCP of the Episcopal Church of the United States clarifies (or muddies) the question by referring to 'presbyters, or ordained elders, in subsequent times generally known as priests'.

except he were first called, tried, examined, and known to have such qualities: this clause reflects the desire in 1550 to emphasize the doctrinal and catechistical functions of the priesthood alongside the sacerdotal performance of ritual embodied in 'the tradition of elements'.

And every man which is to be admitted a Priest: the minimum age was specified in *Canons* (1604), XXXIV, which also required that he must have taken a degree 'in either of the . . . Universities' or else be able to demonstrate some ability in Latin and to expound the scriptures; and have some testimony of his 'good life and conversation'.

623 *the Arch-Deacon*: dioceses in England were divided into archdeaconries from the eleventh century onwards; the archdeacon acted as the bishop's representative with the duty of supervising parish priests and churches.

decently habited: in 1550 this is specified as 'a playne Albe', a requirement dropped in *1552*; in *1662* a surplice was the minimum indication of holy orders. Priestly garb had been a major bone of contention in the Civil War period: in Essex in 1640 a clerk was forced to hand over his surplice, which was then ripped to shreds (Walter, 'Confessional Politics', *Historical Journal*, 44 (2001), 682).

623　*Brethren, if there be any of you*: this inquiry follows closely the Latin text for ordination written by Bucer for the English church and printed in 1549.

　　The Litany: its use here is found in English Pontificals as early as the tenth century.

625　*to illuminate all Bishops, Priests, and Deacons*: replaces 'Bisshops, Pastours and Ministers of the Churche' in *1552*. The change in vocabulary marks a tightening of ecclesiological terminology in the seventeenth century.

628　*Then shall be sung or said the Service for the Communion*: the service for ordination traditionally formed part of a Mass, a practice unchanged in the BCP. The Collect which forms the introduction to this in *1662* was transferred here from a prayer after the Litany in previous versions.

629　*the edification of thy Church*: changed in *1662* from 'profyte of the congregacion' (*Ordinal*, 1552), a subtle but significant alteration reflecting the concerns of the Restoration revision.

　　The Oath of the Kings Supremacy: the form of this oath changed throughout the sixteenth and seventeenth centuries. An oath of allegiance was one of the first forms of enforcement of the Reformation under Henry VIII. In the *Ordinals* of 1550 and 1552 the oath used included a disavowal to 'utterly renounce, refuse, relinquishe, and forsake the Bysshop of Rome, and hys authoritie, power and jurisdiction'. Its renewal in *1662* was not without irony; it was noted by satirists between the 1660s and 1680s that subjects had been required to swear to God so many contradictory things by the authority of this or that king or commonwealth over the last two generations that they were now inveterate perjurers. Despite, or perhaps because of this political stress, *The Whole Duty of Man* (1658), which became the bible of Anglican morality down to the nineteenth century, devoted chapter 4 to the binding nature of oaths and the sinfulness of swearing an unlawful one. The reference to the monarch as 'Supream Governour' was (temporarily) removed under William III and Mary. Oaths became newly controversial with the Jacobite quarrels over the line of succession. In 1865 (in the Clerical Subscription Act) the oath was moved to a more discreet and private act taken before the service begins.

630　*Then shall the Bishop examine every one of them*: these formularies of doctrinal questioning follow closely the pattern suggested in Bucer's Latin Ordinal.

631　*Then the Bishop, laying his hands severally upon the head of every one of them*: the ritual action originates in Acts 8: 17, 'Then laid they their hands on them, and they received the holy Ghost'. It is referred to as part of the ordination ritual in the Fourth Council of Carthage (fourth century).

Then shall the Bishop deliver to every one of them the New Testament: this corresponds to the 'tradition of elements' in Sarum.

632 *Almighty God, giver of all good things*: this is translated from the medieval Pontifical.

ORDERING OF PRIESTS

The first part of this form of the service is identical to that for deacons, but in *1662* is printed out separately for ease of use. In 1550 Ps. 40 was sung as an Introit to the Communion, but this was dropped in 1552 and not revived in *1662*.

634 *The Epistle*: this reading replaced the whole of Acts 20, used in 1550 and 1552 onwards.

After this shall be read for the Gospel: the first Gospel is again changed from previous editions, where Matt. 28 was used. The second reading remained unchanged.

635 *You have heard, brethren*: this exhortation again follows, often literally, Bucer's Latin Ordinal, as do the Examinations which follow.

639 *Come, holy Ghost, our souls inspire*: the hymn *Veni creator spiritus* has been used in the ordination of priests since at least the eleventh century. The short version here is by Cosin, and first appeared in his *Private Devotions* (1627).

Come, holy Ghost, eternal God: this is the version used in 1550 and afterwards.

641 *Almighty God and heavenly Father*: the prayer of consecration is taken from the Sarum version of the medieval Pontifical.

642 *shall lay their hands severally upon the head of every one*: as in the Making of Deacons (p. 631), the laying on of hands, the oldest part of the ritual, is made central to the visual spectacle.

Receive the holy Ghost: the first words of the act of ordination are taken from John 20: 22; the rest of this sentence, beginning 'for the Office and work of a Priest', was added in *1662*.

Then the Bishop shall deliver to every one of them kneeling the Bible: in 1550 the chalice was also delivered by the bishop into the hands of the new priest, in a more complete form of 'tradition of elements'. This was dropped in 1552. The requirement that the priest be kneeling at this point was added in *1662*.

CONSECRATING A BISHOP

644 *Almighty God, who by thy Son Jesus Christ*: the Collect is that for St Peter's Day, omitting his name.

Or this, for the Epistle: this reading was previously set for the Ordering of Priests, as are also the alternative readings for the Gospel.

645 *Then another Bishop shall read*: three bishops are thus required to perform the service.

646 *(vested with his Rotchet)*: in the Sarum Pontifical the new bishop is still dressed in his priest's robe. In 1550 he was required to wear a surplice and cope, the same garb as the presenting bishops. In 1552 all indication of dress was removed. The 'rotchet', which was prescribed for the use of bishops at the Fourth Lateran Council (1215), was like an albe in reaching below the knees, but differed from a surplice in having straight sleeves.

the Arch-Bishop sitting in his chair near the holy Table: the archbishop's position is first specified in *1662*.

the Oath of due obedience to the Arch-Bishop: the oath of allegiance to a superior bishop is first recorded in the seventh century.

651 *the never-fading crown of glory*: 'never-fading' is a felicitous revision of the reading 'immarcessible' (for Lat. *immarcescibiles*) in the 1550 Ordinal, a rare example of Cranmer committing a Latin sin against the English language (MacCulloch, *Cranmer*, 421).

STATE SERVICES

In the Calendar of *1662* three new red-letter days were included, 30 January ('King Charles Martyr'), 29 May ('Charles II, Nativity and Return'), and 5 November ('Papists Conspiracy'). Although not included in the 'Sealed Book', a manuscript note prescribes that services are to be provided for each occasion in the printed BCP. A licence was signed by Charles II and presented to Convocation in 1662 annexing them to the BCP (*Conferences*, 383). In *1662* they duly appear after the Ordinal, and a royal warrant at the beginning of every new reign renewed this status until 1859, when they were officially excluded, and replaced with a single service for the accession day of every subsequent monarch. Alterations were made to these services from time to time, such as the prayers of thanksgiving composed for the 5 November service under William III after his safe landing from the Netherlands, which also took place on the same date in 1688.

There is a similar structure for each of the services: special opening sentences from scripture, picking out some of the direst warnings against disobedience; alternative Collects are used at Morning Prayer in place of the Collect of the day; the Litany is said; special suffrages used in the preparation for Communion; a special Epistle and Gospel; and there are other additional prayers. The new Collects are longer and more complex in form than the proper BCP collects, and include sometimes wordy diatribes against the enemies of the Stuarts.

Services commemorating the accession of the monarch date back to the Elizabethan period, where a form of prayer of thanksgiving for the life of the queen was incorporated into Morning Prayer in 1576. This was the model and inspiration for later accession services. Beginning in the reign of Anne (1702–14), this service was included in the BCP, continuing after the revision of 1859 with an enlarged service for Victoria, right up to Elizabeth II in the 1952 BCP. However, since it was not part of any service book in the reign of

Charles II (for whom there was already the 29 May service), it is not included here.

In the American Prayer Book a parallel to the state services (which were themselves, of course, excluded) was introduced to commemorate 4 July, Independence Day; similar services are found in other versions of the BCP around the world.

GUNPOWDER PLOT

A quarto of Prayers and thankesgivings to be used for the happy deliverance from the intended massacre the 5 of November 1605 was first published in 1606 by the King's Printer, Robert Barker; it was reissued regularly up to 1640. See also Calendar, p. 232.

652 *in the protection of righteous and religious Kings and States*: in his speech to parliament in 1610 James I declared that 'prayers and tears' are the only weapons a subject may use against a monarch. This collect is shot through with the absolutist theory of monarchy favoured by James in his own political works such as *The True Law of Free Monarchies* (1596).

653 *thy providence delivered us*: the doctrine of providence was often invoked in absolutist attacks on what was known as 'resistance theory', the justification of rebellion against a tyrant. Divine providence can always be trusted to take the right side in politics, it was averred.

all such workers of iniquity, as turn religion into rebellion: a clear reference not only to the Catholic conspiracy of the Gunpowder Plot, but also to other kinds of religious enemy in the Civil Wars.

654 *the three Estates of this Realm assembled in Parliament*: the commons, lords, and bishops.

655 *one of the six Homilies against Rebellion*: the homilies published in the reign of Elizabeth continued to be reprinted after the Restoration, indeed in increasing numbers as late as *Certain sermons or homilies appointed to be read in churches in the time of Queen Elizabeth of famous memory and now reprinted for the use of private families* (1687). They were regarded as having a similar authority in determining the tradition of the Church of England as the BCP, the Articles of Religion, and the 1604 Canons of the Church.

MARTYRDOM OF CHARLES I

This service was written for *1662* by a committee appointed on 8 May 1661 by Convocation; it included bishops Warner, King, Morley, and Reynolds.

656 *Instead of Venite Exultemus . . .*: this cento of psalms is a symptom of the beginnings of a new aesthetic of hymn-singing which became highly popular in the eighteenth century; see also the Birth and Happy Return of Charles II (p. 662).

657 *the sins of this Nation have been the cause*: the phrase 'sins of the Nation' became a cliché in polemic on both sides of the Civil Wars; King Charles

used the phrase frequently himself: the 'sins of the Nation, the obstin-
acie of the other partie cannot be overcome; but that his Majestie and his
People must yet be further scourged by Gods afflicting hand of war': *The
Kings answer to the propositions for peace* (1645).

658 *our late Martyred Soveraign; by which he was enabled so chearfully to follow*:
pamphlets describing Charles as 'Martyr King' appeared immediately
after his execution at Banqueting House, including *An elegie upon the
death of our dread soveraign Lord King Charls the martyr* (1649) and *The
life and death of King Charles the martyr, parallel'd with our saviour in all his
sufferings. Who was murdered (before His own palace at Whitehall) the 30th
of Jan. 1648. With some observations upon his cruel and bloudy persecutors*
(1649).

grant, that this our Land may be freed from the vengeance of his bloud: while
the language here is scriptural, especially from the Psalms (e.g. Pss. 58: 9;
79: 11), it had already been appropriated for the example of Charles since
the sensational appearance of the best-selling *Eikon basilike: the portraic-
ture of His sacred Majestie in his solitudes and svfferings* (1649), where the
condemned king is represented as praying to God before death: 'When
they have destroyed Me, (for I know not how farre *God* may permit the
malice and cruelty of My Enemies to proceed, and such apprehensions
some mens words and actions have already given Me) as I doubt not but
My bloud will crie aloud for vengeance to heaven' (Q3ʳ).

659 *Christ also suffered for us, leaving us an example, that ye should follow his
steps*: the identification of Charles's execution with Christ's passion was
also a commonplace in royalist literature, and is found in *Eikon basilike*: 'If
I must suffer a violent death with my Saviour; it is but mortality crowned
with martyrdome' (R2ʳ).

660 *thou didst suffer thine Anointed to fall this day into the hands of violent and
bloud-thirsty men*: Charles is described as God's anointed in *Eikon basilike*: 'Thou seest how mine Enemies use all means to cloud mine Honor,
to pervert my purposes, and to slander the footsteps of thine Annointed'
(N1ᵛ). It was a standard part of the vocabulary of divine-right theory
expounded by James I, such as in royal proclamations for the dissolution
of parliament.

confessing that thy judgments were right in permitting cruel men, sons of Belial:
Belial is one of the four princes of hell, referred to several times in the
Apocrypha and once in the NT (2 Cor. 6: 15). The name was frequently
invoked in the literature of the Civil Wars, on both sides, not least in
Milton's *Paradise Lost*, where he is one of the debating fallen angels.

661 *deliver this Nation from bloud-guiltiness*: the mortality rates in the Civil
Wars caused both anguish and further contention as to which side was the
more guilty for the violence. Milton, in *Eikonoklastes* (1650), a polemical
counterblast to *Eikon basilike*, replied to the outrage at Charles's violent
end: 'there hath bin more Christian blood shed by the Commission,

approbation, and connivance of King Charles, and his Father James in the latter end of thir raigne, then in the Ten Roman Persecutions' (M3ʳ).

BIRTH AND HAPPY RETURN OF CHARLES II

This service was written for *1662* by a committee appointed on 8 May 1661 by Convocation; it included bishops Wren, Skinner, Laney, and Henchman; it was completed by 18 May.

663 *by thy miraculous providence hast delivered us out of our late miserable confusions*: a conventional trope of the return of Charles II; see *The most humble address of the ministers of the word of God in the County of Lincoln* (1660): 'These things were to us as the dawning of the day of Salvation, which God after a dark night of Confusion hath now (not by an ordinary working of providence) caused to shine upon us.' Dryden's *Astraea Redux* (1660) presented the king as the instrument of providence.

664 *didst this day also bring back and restore to us*: the term 'Restoration' was applied immediately: e.g. in the subtitle of Dryden's panegyric *Astraea Redux: A Poem On the Happy Restoration & Return Of His Sacred Majesty Charles the Second*. The biblical connotation (cf. Ps. 23: 3) of this word was emphasized everywhere.

the publick and free profession of thy true Religion and worship: religious toleration was a concept inherited from the Netherlands (the first expression in English is in an Amsterdam publication of 1614; the fact that the book was not published in England is itself a commentary on the problem). Cromwellian and Restoration England both claimed a version of it, although what was usually meant was an enforcement of history for the victors, and Catholicism continued to be excluded by both sides. At the Declaration of Breda (April 1660), immediately before his return, Charles II announced 'a liberty to tender consciences'. For examples of practical intolerance in relation to the 1662 Act, see Alexandra Walsham, *Charitable Hatred: Tolerance and Intolerance in England 1500–1700* (Manchester: Manchester University Press, 2006), 117. In effect, as here in the BCP, what is meant is peaceful adherence to the established order. Defenders of the Restoration settlement argued, however, that dissent was not itself criminal in England, and this made England a less tyrannical place than many others.

APPENDIX A: THE 'BLACK RUBRIC', 1552

The 'Black Rubric' was inserted into *1552* at the last minute on the eve of publication. The story, and still more the meaning, of the rubric is complex. John Knox was invited at the behest of the duke of Northumberland to assist in the final revisions to the Prayer Book. He attacked kneeling at Communion at a sermon before the king in September, as reported with approval by Jan Uttenhove of the Dutch Stranger church. Grafton was asked to delay printing of *1552* while this issue was sorted. In October Knox wrote to the lord chancellor asking for a Declaration to be added to the BCP 'touching the kneeling at the receiving of the Communion' (Council Book, 27 October 1552), in accordance with the draft Articles of Religion. Cranmer intervened, wittily disputing Knox's insistence on an entirely scriptural approach by stating that in that case Communion should be taken lying down, since this was how dinner was served in NT times, 'like Tartars and Turks today'. The Declaration as adopted was by no means the victory for Knox that has often been claimed. He wished to abolish kneeling, while the Declaration allows it; the rubric rather attempts to constrain, rather awkwardly, the feelings people experience while kneeling. It adds some venture into Eucharistic doctrine which is entirely in accord with Cranmer's mature opinion. The rubric did not appear in some of the earliest copies; it was subsequently tipped in, in later copies, into the binding between fo. O1 and fo. O2, after Communion. It is called 'black' somewhat confusingly, since while some rubrics were in red, most, like this late addition, were printed in black. The correct place for it can be found after the last rubric on p. 140 of Communion in *1559* (from which edition it was removed). For its subsequent history in *1662*, see p. 407 and note.

667 *misconstrued, depraved, and interpreted in a wrong part*: the word 'misconstrued' is rare before the sixteenth century, and is much stronger than in modern English; this sentence is couched in the oppressive language of Tudor censorship. Compare, in a defence of the real presence, Stephen Gardiner, *A Detection of the Devils Sophistry* (London, 1546), I6ʳ: 'scripture, is lykewise misconstrued and crokedly expounded.'

the Communicants knelyng shoulde receyve the holye Communion: Bucer (*Censura*, 43) commented on the variety of customs appertaining to kneeling: 'genuflections, making the sign of the cross in the air, raising their hands, beating their breasts'; he wished instead for 'suitable and moderate (*moderati*) gestures', such as 'can serve the pure religion of Christ'. Humanist decorum, as well as avoidance of idolatry, was part of his motivation.

any adoracion is doone, or oughte to bee doone: the Royal Injunctions of 1547 contained a wide range of anxieties about any implication of idolatry involved in religious practice, especially concerning the use of the body to indicate the worship of objects or beings. Hooper was the bishop most zealous in seeking out such practices. On the Communion, he stated; 'The outward behaviour and gesture of the receiver should want all kind of suspicion, show, or inclination of idolatry. Wherefore seeing kneeling is a show and external sign of honouring and worshipping, and heretofore hath grievous and damnable idolatry been committed by the honouring of the Sacrament, I would wish it were commanded by the magistrates that the communicators and receivers should do it standing or sitting.'

anye reall and essencial presence there beeyng of Christes naturall fleshe and bloude: this contentious polemic against the doctrine of transubstantiation nonetheless represents it inaccurately as asserting that the real presence implied the presence of the natural body of Christ; a view specifically rejected in Thomas Aquinas, *Super Sententiis*, IV, 10 q.2, a.2; q.3 ad.4.

APPENDIX B: ADDITIONAL ORDERS OF SERVICE, ARTICLES, AND TABLES, 1662–1685

Forms of special service have appeared throughout the history of the BCP, beginning with a prayer for victory and peace in 1548, and continuing with various thanksgivings for the end of plague under Elizabeth, and almost routine warnings and comminations against rebellion under the Stuarts. Sometimes these were bound in with copies of the BCP. The Gunpowder Plot service was first issued in this way, before being incorporated in *1662* as one of the State Services. At the Healing and Fire of London were temporarily included in some issues of the BCP, virtually if not in fact as State Services, and so are included here. Two other items, the Articles of Religion and Table of Kindred and Affinity, have been included in numerous editions of the BCP since 1681 down to the present day, although they are not formally part of it.

AT THE HEALING

The disease of *scrofula*, a bacterial form of tuberculosis affecting the neck, came to be known as 'the King's Evil', due to the belief that it could be cured by the touch of the monarch. The practice was revived under the Stuarts as part of the demonstration of the divine right of kingship. Single-page sheets in black-letter of this rite began to be bound in to individual copies of the BCP from 1633; several survive from the reign of Charles II. A longer version used under James II, *The ceremonies for the Healing of them that be diseased with the Kings evil* (London: Henry Hills, 1686), is never found in a BCP. Dropped under William and Mary, the tradition was revived under Queen Anne, who was said to have touched the infant Samuel Johnson. Johnson 'had, he said, a confused, but somehow a sort of solemn recollection of a lady in diamonds, and a long black hood' (Hesther Lynch Piozzi, *Anecdotes of Samuel Johnson* (1786), 10). The last printings occurred as late as 1721 under George I, although he repudiated the rite. Jacobites held that the touch still resided in the male Stuart line; this was rejected fiercely by Whigs. See G. MacDonald Ross, 'The Royal Touch and the Book of Common Prayer', *Notes & Queries*, 30 (1983), 433–5.

Text edited from *Book of Common Prayer* (London: John Bill, Thomas Newcomb, and Henry Hills, 1680), Wing B3659, British Library shelf mark 3406.f.9; compared with a copy dated 1672 in the James R. Page Collection in the Huntington Library, shelf mark HN: 438000:27. In each case a single undated sheet has been tipped in to an edition of the BCP.

668 *the King putteth his Gold about their necks*: this citation from Gen. 41: 42 (also found in Dan. 5: 7 and 5: 16) is used as a ritual action of healing by the king to enact the cure.

FIRE OF LONDON

The conflagration of September 1666, described vividly by Pepys, Evelyn, and others, destroyed the homes of 70,000 of the city's 80,000 inhabitants, as well as St Paul's Cathedral and eighty-seven parish churches. Following on from the plague of 1665, it was variously interpreted as a divine punishment for the rebellion against Charles I or for the libidinous lifestyle of his son. Its cultural interpretation became the object of government concern along with the practical business of rebuilding. Christopher Wren's Monument, incorporating symbolism of the phoenix rising from the ashes, was erected on the site of the fire between 1671 and 1677. This service follows a similar ideology of penitence and humility in the face of God's sovereignty.

Text edited from *Book of Common Prayer* (Oxford: at the Theatre, 1681), Wing 3663A, British Library shelf mark C.48.l.4. Printed as part of the same volume, on the verso of the *Birth and Happy Return*.

THE THIRTY-NINE ARTICLES OF RELIGION

Among the last acts of the government of Edward VI was to request articles of faith to cement the Reformation in formal terms. Cranmer submitted forty-two articles to the Privy Council in November 1552, but they were not authorized until shortly before the king's terminal illness in 1553. They nonetheless formed the basis of the Thirty-Nine Articles passed by Act of Parliament in 1563. From 1571 clergy in England were required to subscribe to them.

The history and interpretation of the Articles lie beyond the scope of this volume, but they may be divided into five groups: (1) the nature of God (arts. 1–5); (2) Scripture and the creeds (arts. 6–8); (3) salvation and the individual, including the doctrines of justification and predestination (arts. 9–18); (4) salvation and the church, including the ministry and the sacraments (arts. 19–31); (5) miscellaneous, including church discipline and excommunication (arts. 31–9).

Text (as for Fire of London), edited from *Book of Common Prayer*, British Library shelf mark C.48.l.4. Printed as part of the same volume, following Fire of London, in same typeface.

TABLE OF KINDRED AND AFFINITY

First published as a broadsheet by Archbishop Matthew Parker, *An admonition to all such as shall intend hereafter to enter the state of matrimonie* (1560), based on the laws set out in Lev. 18.

Text (as for Fire of London), edited from *Book of Common Prayer*, British Library shelf mark C.48.l.4. Printed as part of the same volume, following Articles of Religion, in same typeface.

GLOSSARY

THE abbreviation *MED* refers to the *Middle English Dictionary*, University of Michigan, http://quod.lib.umich.edu/m/med/

a newe anew

a so(/u)ndre asunder; apart, separate

a waye away

abhor(re) to regard with horror, reject

absoluc(/t)ion (1) (*theol.*) REMISSION or forgiveness of sins; (2) a formula declaring sins to be remitted, e.g. within the liturgy, and thus enacted by the priest; this sense controversial in BCP, see notes to pp. 104 and 399

accompte account

accustomably habitually, customarily

Advent the season of preparation for Christmas; originally a period of FAST

advertise to call the attention of (another); to give notice, notify

advouterer adulterer

affecc(/t)ion mental state; emotion, passion, feeling

affiaunce faith, trust

affinity relationship by marriage

afrayed afraid

alb(e) robe made of white linen, the length of a cassock. See note to p. 19

almanac(k) an annual table containing a calendar of months and days

almose ALMS

alms charitable relief of the poor; charity; a charitable donation

a(u)lta(/e)r(e), altar the structure consecrated to the celebration of the EUCHARIST (in *medieval* usage always of stone; *post-Reformation* usually of wood, and called the 'LORD'S TABLE'). See notes to pp. 20 and 124

alwai(/y)(es) always

annunciation the announcing of the incarnation made by the angel Gabriel to the Virgin Mary; the FESTIVAL commemorating this

an(n)oi(/y)n(c)t to apply or pour on oil as a religious ceremony

anointed a consecrated person (*esp.* of Christ)

anthem(e) originally synonymous with ANTIPHON; later (and esp. in BCP) any piece of sacred vocal music performed during divine service, but not part of the liturgy

antiphon a versicle or sentence sung by one choir in response to another; used particularly of phrases sung before and after each psalm

apostolic(/k)(e) of, or belonging to, or contemporary with the apostles (the twelve witnesses to Christ in the NT)

apparel(l) dress

appoi(/y)nted fixed by authority; ordained

appose to examine, interrogate, question

archbishop the chief BISHOP; the highest dignitary in an episcopal church

archdeacon a rank of minister above priest and below bishop; in the Church of England an archdeacon is appointed by, and gives assistance to, the BISHOP, superintending the rural DEANS

ark (1) the wooden coffer containing the tables of the Jewish law, kept in the TABERNACLE; (2) the boat of Noah

article each of the separate clauses or statements of a summary of faith

ascencion FESTIVAL of the ascent of Christ to heaven on the fortieth day after the resurrection

Ash(-)wednesday the first day of LENT

assau(l)t(e) an attack by spiritual enemies; a temptation to evil

assertei(g)n(e) to make (a thing) certain to the mind

assone as soon

athirst thirsty

aungell angel

aunswere answer

auricula(/e)r addressed to the ear; told privately in the ear (specifically in CONFESSION). See note to p. 25

autho(u)r the person who originates or gives existence to anything; the Creator

au(c)t(h)oriti(/y)(e) authority

avai(/y)l(e) to be effectual, serviceable, or of use

awaie away

awne own

ayd(e) aid, help

banket banquet

ban(n)(e)s public notice given in church of an intended marriage

baptism(e) immersion of a person in water, or application of water by pouring or sprinkling, as a religious rite. See notes to pp. 46 and 51

batta(/e)(i)le battle

bee; be(e)n(e) (*past tense*) be

begotten procreated

benedicc(/t)ion the utterance of a BLESSING; devout expression of a wish for the prosperity of another; God's blessing or SALVATION

Benedicite a CANTICLE; see note to p. 10

Benedictus (1) a part of the MASS or COMMUNION; see note to p. 29; (2) the hymn of Zacharias, used as a CANTICLE in Morning Prayer in BCP; see note to p. 11

benefice the right to enjoy the fruits (pecuniary or in kind) of an ECCLE-SIASTICAL OFFICE

be(a)r(e); bare (*past tense*) bear

bese(e)ch(e) to supplicate, entreat, implore

be(/y)times early

beutify to beautify, make beautiful

bewai(/y)l(e) to bewail; to express great sorrow for something; to lament loudly, mourn

bewray betray

bi(/u)s(c)(h)op(p)(e) a clergyman consecrated for the spiritual government of a 'diocese,' ranking beneath an ARCHBISHOP and above a PRIEST (from Gk. ἐπίσκοπος, 'overseer')

blessing (1) authoritative declaration of divine favour, or the form of words used in this declaration; (2) bestowal of divine favour

blisse bless

bloud(e) blood

bo(o)rd(e) board; table ('Goddes borde', the LORD'S TABLE)

bounden under obligation

bowel compassion, mercy ('bowels of mercies')

breviary the book containing the divine OFFICE for each day

brief a letter licensing collections in churches for a charitable purpose

broided platted

burthen burden

Canon (1) a rule, law, or decree of the church; (2) the portion of the MASS included between the Preface and the *Pater noster*, and containing the words of consecration; see notes to pp. 29 and 80; (3) a species of musical composition in which the different parts take up the same subject one after another; (4) the collection or list of books of the Bible accepted by the Christian Church as genuine and inspired; (5) a clergyman living with others in a clergy-house (*claustrum*), or within the precinct or close of a cathedral or COLLEGIATE CHURCH

canticle song, hymn

carnal(l) of the body; esp. as seat of passions and appetites; sensual

catechism an elementary treatise for instruction in the principles of the Christian religion, often in the form of question and answer. See note to p. 59

catell 'A collective name for live animals held as property, or reared to serve as food'; hence 'property, article of property (*goods and chattel*)' (*OED*)

cathedral principal church of a DIOCESE, the seat (Lat. *cathedra*) of a bishop

Catholi(/y)c(/k)(e) universal; hence esp. of the church, the whole body of Christians; sometimes used post-Reformation to distinguish the church of Rome from the CHURCH OF ENGLAND; sometimes to include the Church of England within a universal concept of the church

caution security, guarantee, legal pledge

celebrant the PRIEST who officiates at the EUCHARIST

ceremony 'An outward rite or observance, religious or held sacred' (*OED*). See notes to pp. 98 and 214

chaff(e) the husks of grain separated by threshing; also figuratively in a spiritual sense, of the unregenerate

chalice the cup in which the wine is administered in the celebration of the EUCHARIST

chambering sexual indulgence

chancel the part of a church, usually at the east end and often separated by a screen or rails, where parts of the service such as the SACRAMENTS are performed

Chapel(l)(e) (1) a sanctuary or place of Christian worship, not the church; (2) hence, a compartment of a CATHEDRAL or large church (usually in the aisle), separately dedicated and containing its own ALTAR (*annexed*)

chap(e)la(/e)i(/y)n(e), chaplain a clergyman who conducts religious services in the private chapel of a monarch, lord, or BISHOP

chapter (1) passage of scripture read in divine service; (2) general meeting or assembly of the CANONS of a COLLEGIATE or CATHEDRAL church

chariti(/y)(e) Christian love; the Christian state of love and right feeling towards one's fellow Christians

chastement chastisement; means of amendment, punishment

chaunse chance

cherish to hold dear, treat with tenderness and affection

Cherubim(/n) (*plural*) being of a celestial or angelic order (excelling in knowledge)

choir (1) the body of singers in cathedral or church service; (2) the part of a church reserved for the singers (specifically east of the nave) in which services are performed, often separated by a screen; (3) the CHANCEL

chrism oil mingled with balm, consecrated for use as an unguent in the administration of SACRAMENTS. See notes to pp. 51 and 62

christen baptize; see BAPTISM

Church(e) of England a phrase used in medieval usage to describe the CATHOLIC church within the realm of England; adopted in 1534 by Henry VIII in establishing himself as its 'supreme head' (e.g. Act of Supremacy, 26 Hen. VIII, c. 1) and increasingly used as a term to describe the post-Reformation church

Church(e)(-)warden(e) a LAY officer of a PARISH or district church

citation a summons in an ecclesiastical court

clense cleanse

cle(a)rgie, clergy 'The clerical order; the body set apart by ordination for religious service; opposed to *laity*' (*OED*). From OT/NT Gk. κλῆρος; and Lat. *clerus* (Tertullian, second cent.)

clerk(e) (1) a man ordained to the ministry of the Christian church; (2) a layman who performs such offices in CATHEDRALS, churches, or CHAPELS; (3) in BCP, a CHOIR man; (4) the lay officer of a parish church, who has charge of the church and assists the CLERGY

clime climb

coeternal(l) equally eternal; existing with another eternally

Collect(e) a short prayer, condensed in form, usually consisting of a single point or combination of two related points, used in Western Christianity since early times; applied particularly to the prayer, varying with the day, week, or octave, said before the Epistle in the MASS, and in the BCP also in Morning and Evening Prayer, called the 'collect of the day'. See notes to pp. 13 and 271

colle(d)ge (1) a foundation within a university; (2) a COLLEGIATE CHURCH

collegiate church a church endowed for a CHAPTER, but without a bishop's SEE

comfortable strengthening or supporting (morally or spiritually)

co(u)mforter a title of the Holy Spirit, translating Gk. παράκλητος (e.g. John 14: 16), lit. 'advocate'; often left untranslated as 'paraclete'

comma(u)nd(e)ment(e) an authoritative order or injunction; (in *plural* with specific sense) the Ten Commandments or precepts of the Decalogue of Moses in Exod. 20: 2–17 and Deut. 5: 6–21

comminac(/t)ion 'denunciation'; from Lat. *comminari* ('to threaten with')

commodious convenient, handy

common prayer a familiar term in medieval usage for collective worship in church; e.g. in the fifteeth-cent. *Dives and Pauper*: 'Comon prayer is the prayer of the ministres of hooly churche and of comon persones in holy churche.'

communicant a person who partakes of or receives COMMUNION on a particular occasion

communicate to take COMMUNION

Communion (1) the fellowship or mutual relationship between members of the church; (2) the EUCHARIST as a religious observance ('holy Communion'); (3) either or both of the consecrated elements administered in the Eucharist (to 'take Communion'). See Introduction, pp. xxv–xxvii

compline the last service of the day, completing the canonical HOURS

comprehend to include, take in

conceit conception, thought, idea; the faculty of having the same

concord(e) agreement or harmony between things; a state of peace

concupiscence eager desire, esp. (in Bible) desire for CARNAL things

condescend to seek willingly an equal level with social inferiors

confession the acknowledging of sin or sinfulness; esp. in set form in public worship

confound(e) to defeat utterly, destroy, bring to ruin; to discomfort, confuse

congregac(/t)ion synonymous with 'the people'; sometimes only of 'the baptised' (cf. Art. 19); sometimes (in controversial usage) as strict translation of ἐκκλησία, the NT Gk. word often translated as 'church' (and in Lutheran Ger. as *Gemeinde*)

consecrac(/t)ion the giving of the sacramental character to the eucharistic ELEMENTS of bread and wine; the actions in the liturgy in which this takes place. See notes to pp. 34 and 402

considre consider

contei(/y)gn(e) contain

continewe continue

contric(/t)ion sorrow or affliction of mind for an injury done; PENITENCE for sin

convenient appropriate

conveygh convey

convocation a synod of clergy called by statute to determine ecclesiastical matters in the Church in England, pre- and post-Reformation

cope large cloak, semicircular in shape. See note to p. 19

corporas a cloth, usually of linen, upon which the consecrated ELEMENTS are placed during the celebration of Communion

corps corpse

counsai(/y)l(l)(e) counsel; advice

countrey country

covena(u)nt a mutual agreement; hence a 'promise of legal validity' or 'contract under seal'; in biblical sense, usually between God and mankind

coveto(u)s(e) having an excessive desire for anything

craft (in *special* sense) deceit, guile, fraud

Cre(e)d(e) a summary of the things to be believed; also the form of words used in such a formula; originally a set of baptismal oaths, subsequently codified in three main forms as the Apostles' Creed, the Nicene, and the Athanasian. See note to p. 12

c(h)risom(e) a white robe, put on a child at baptism

crome crumb

cubit an ancient measure of length derived from the forearm.

cu(m)m come

curate the priest who has the 'care' (Lat. *cura*) of souls in a particular area, usually the parish

cure care, charge; spiritual charge

customably according to custom

daie day

dalmatic an ecclesiastical VESTMENT, with a slit on each side of the skirt, and wide sleeves, and marked with two stripes

daung(i)er danger

Dean The head of the CHAPTER or body of CANONS of a COLLEGIATE or CATHEDRAL church; 'rural dean', a priest having jurisdiction over a division of an archdeaconry

de(a)con a member of the third order of the MINISTRY, ranking below BISHOPS and PRIESTS, having the functions of assisting the priest in divine service

dedication ('dedication festival') annual commemoration of the consecration of a church, usually the feast day of the PATRONAL saint.

delite delight

delivera(u)nce (1) liberation, release; esp. divine, e.g. of Moses or through divine grace; (2) bringing forth of offspring, delivery

depart(e) separate

dere dear

di(y)(e); diying(c) die; dying

differ (1) differ; (2) defer

diocese the district under the pastoral care of a BISHOP

di(/y)p(p)(e) to let down or plunge into liquid; to immerse during BAPTISM

di(/y)scipline (1) instruction, teaching; (2) the system or method by which order is maintained in a church

discrec(/t)ion liberty or power of deciding

dispose to regulate or govern in an orderly way; to order, control, direct

dissimuler dissembler

distinct(e)-ly clear, plain, definite; *hence* without confusion or obscurity

diversiti(/y)(e) divers manners or sorts

dooe; do(o)en (*past tense*) do

doove dove

doune down

doxology a short formula of praise to God used in liturgy, e.g. at the end of the Lord's Prayer. See notes to pp. 241 and 458

dread(e)ful(l) inspiring dread, terror, or reverence

dyscensyon dissent

dyscrete discreet, judicious, prudent

ecclesiastical of or pertaining to the church

edifi(/y)e to build up (the church, the soul) in faith and holiness

eftsoons a second time

eie eye

elect(e) chosen by God, esp. for salvation or eternal life

elements the bread and wine used in the EUCHARIST

elevac(/t)ion the lifting up of the HOST for the adoration of the people

Elias the prophet Elijah

Ember Days, Weeks festivals of the seasons, with 'Ember Days' falling on the Wednesday, Friday, and Saturday in the four 'Ember Weeks': between 3 and 4 ADVENT, between 1 and 2 LENT, between PENTECOST and TRINITY SUNDAY, and the week after Holy Cross (14 September). Originating in pagan agricultural festivals corresponding to winter sowing, summer reaping, and autumn vintage, a fourth was added to balance the whole Christian year; they were the recognized time for ORDINATION of priests

emonges amongst

enclyne incline

encrease increase

end(e) in specific senses, (1) intended result of an action; (2) death

enoynt anoint

ensample example

entende intend

enterprise to take in hand, undertake

entiere entire

entituled entitled

Epact the difference between the last day of the lunar year and the last day of the solar; used in calculating Easter and other dates

ephphatha a touch with a moistened finger used as a ritual act in BAPTISM (from Gk. transcription of Aramaic 'be opened', Mark 7: 34)

epiclesis a part of the prayer of CONSECRATION in which the holy spirit is invoked to bless the Eucharistic ELEMENTS

epi(/y)phani(/y)(e) FESTIVAL commemorating the appearance of Christ to the gentiles in the persons of the Magi; observed on 6 January, the twelfth day after Christmas (hence 'Twelfth Night')

Epistle an extract (usually from one of the apostolic letters in the NT) read as part of divine service

Esai(a)(e)(s) the prophet Isaiah

estate condition

Eucharist the SACRAMENT of the Lord's Supper; the COMMUNION (from Gk. εὐχαριστία, 'thanksgiving'). See Introduction, pp. xxv–xxvii

evensong Evening Prayer

everlivyng that lives or will live for ever

e(i)vi(/y)ll evil

excommunicate to cut off from COMMUNION; to exclude from participation in the SACRAMENTS and services of the church

executour a person appointed by a testator to carry into effect his will after his decease

exhortac(/t)ion formal address in a religious observance or rite

exigence necessity

expedic(/t)ion speedy performance

expedient conducive to advantage; fit, proper

faln past tense of 'fall'

fast a day or season appointed for fasting; abstaining from food as an act of religious observance.

faut fault

feast(e) a religious anniversary to be observed with rejoicing (opposed to a FAST), in commemoration of an event or in honour of a person

fede feed

fellow a member of a college or COLLEGIATE foundation

felowshyp, fellowship 'the condition of being in company with another or others'; *also* 'the spirit that binds companions or friends together'; hence 'the Christian community' (*MED*)

Ferial any day which is not a Sunday or a holy day

ferre far

Festival of or pertaining to a FEAST or a feast-day

fi(/y)er fire

fi(/y)gure to represent; be an image, symbol of

fi(/y)rmament(e) the arch or vault of heaven overhead; the sky or heavens

first(-)fruit the first produce of the season, customarily offered to God

flock(e) in spiritual sense, of a body or the whole body of Christians

fl(o)ud(d)(es) water (as opposed to land); a river; a violent outpouring of water, inundation

fode food

folow(eth) follow(s)

font 'A receptacle, usually of stone, for the water used in the sacrament of baptism' (*OED*)

foorth forth

forbi(/y)d (1) to command not to do something; (2) to refuse someone something

forein foreign

forgeve forgive

fornicac(/t)ion voluntary sex between a man and an unmarried woman; adultery

forsake to break off from or renounce esp. an evil practice or sin

foule(s) any feathered vertebrate animal

fourme form

fowerth fourth

fre(e)dom(e) (1) the state of being free from servitude; (2) liberation from the bondage or dominating influence of sin, etc.; (3) in a particular Christian sense an overriding liberty of self derived from God

frend(e) friend

frowardnes(se) 'froward' quality or condition, i.e. perversity, unacceptable behaviour

fuller one whose occupation is to gather or pleat cloth

furth(e) forth

fyre fire

gain-say to deny, contradict

gelous jealous

gender to give rise to, bring about, engender

general (1) a collective unity; (2) relating or applicable to a whole class of objects

Gentile any or all of the nations other than the Jewish (often in plural)

ge(a)t(e) get

geve; geve knowlege give; give notice

gi(/y)lti(/y)(e) guilty

Gloria (1) (*Gloria patri*) the doxology ('Glory be to the Father') following the psalms and CANTICLES; (2) (*Gloria in excelsis*), a hymn forming part of the COMMUNION; see note to p. 20

G(/g)oddes (1) plural of God; (2) possessive pronoun ('God's')

godhead the character or quality of being God or a god

godli(/y)(nes)(s)(e) devoutly observant of the laws of God; religious, pious; sometimes used to distinguish the saved; or those of the correct religious beliefs

good-man chief householder

Gospel(l)(e) an extract from one of the four gospels in the NT read as part of divine service

gost(e) ghost (e.g. 'holy ghost', the holy spirit)

g(h)ostli(/y)(e) spiritual

governa(u)nce the action or manner of governing; control, sway, mastery

grace (in special sense) 'The free and unmerited favour of God as manifested in the salvation of sinners and the bestowing of blessings' (*OED*)

gra(u)nt to agree, consent; to consent to fulfil (a request, prayer, wish, etc.); to bestow or confer as a favour, or in answer to a request (often used of God in prayer in relation to his sovereign power)

graven sculptured, hewn

greve grieve

habilitie ability

hal(l)ow(ed) sanctify, bless; 'to honour (God, his name, etc.) as holy' (*MED*).

hand(e)maiden female servant

hardnes(s)(e) inflexibility; obduracy, obstinacy

hart(e) heart

harti(/y)(e) hearty

hast(e) second-person sing. of 'have'

hear(e) (1) to hear; (2) hair

hel hell

Herford Hereford

herisy heresy

heritage inheritance

hevelye heavily

heyr(e) heir

Hierusalem Jerusalem

holden past tense of 'hold'

holesome wholesome

holi(/y)e(-)dai(/y)(e), holiday any FESTIVAL day apart from Sundays

holpen past tense of 'help'

home(/i)ly a religious discourse addressed to a congregation; a sermon; in Church of England specifically applied to the *Book of Homilies* published in 1547 and 1563

hood(e) covering for the head worn as a mark of dignity by ecclesiastics and university graduates

horn(e) (in biblical sense): an emblem of power and might; a means of defence or resistance

Hosanna an exclamation, meaning 'Save now!' from Ps. 118: 25, used frequently in Jewish (and thence Christian) liturgy

host (1) (*pl.*) the multitude of angels that attend upon God (as in the 'Lord of Hosts', a frequent title for Jehovah); (2) a man who lodges another in his house; (3) the bread consecrated in the EUCHARIST, regarded as the body of Christ; a consecrated wafer; sometimes also the wafer before consecration

hours in medieval liturgy the prayers or OFFICES appointed to be said at the eight times of the day allotted to prayer

hous(e)band(e) husband

houshold household

howr hour

humayne human

husbandman a man who tills or cultivates the soil

hymn a religious song

hyssop 'A plant, the twigs of which were used for sprinkling in Jewish rites' (*OED*)

idolatry the worship of idols or images

ignora(u)nce (*pl.*) an act due to want of knowledge; an offence or sin caused by ignorance

impediment hindrance, obstruction

imposic(/t)ion the laying on of hands in blessing, ORDINATION, confirmation

impute (*theol.*) to attribute or ascribe (righteousness, guilt) to a person

in the ste(e)de instead

incarnac(/t)ion embodiment in flesh, i.e. of Christ

incomprehensible that cannot be contained or circumscribed within limits; illimitable, boundless, infinite

incorporate united in one body

incorrupc(/t)ion freedom from physical corruption or decay

incumbent the holder of a parochial benefice, whether rector, vicar, or curate

indifferent(ly) not inclined to prefer one person or thing to another; unbiased, impartial

indue 'to invest with a power or quality, a spiritual gift, etc.' (*OED*)

indure endure

inglyshe English

inherita(u)nce something obtained by right or divine grant; birthright. In biblical sense applied to persons, esp. God's chosen people, as his possession, and to blessings (material or spiritual) enjoyed by such people (*OED*)

injuncc(/t)ion an authoritative or emphatic order; a common technical term in Tudor and Stuart politics and religion

insti(/y)c(/t)ution 'The establishment of a sacrament, *esp.* the eucharist, by Christ. Hence, that part of the office of baptism, and of the prayer of consecration in the eucharist, which consists in reciting the words used in institution' (*OED*)

intercession the action of pleading on behalf of another; in liturgy, an intercessory prayer

introit an ANTIPHON or psalm sung while the priest approaches the altar to celebrate MASS or holy COMMUNION

invention discovery; specifically the reputed finding of the 'true cross' by Helena, mother of the emperor Constantine

invitatory(/i) antiphonal form of Ps. 95 sung at NOCTURNS

inward(e) (1) situated within; mental or spiritual; (2) heartfelt, deeply felt

Israel the Jewish or Hebrew nation or people; hence 'the chosen people of God'

iye(s) eye(s)

jeoperdie jeopardy

justify (1) to show (a person or action) to be just or in the right; (2) (*theol.*) to declare free from the penalty of sin on the ground of Christ's righteousness (*OED*)

Kalendar 'A table showing the division of a given year into its months and days; also indicating ecclesiastical festivals' (*OED*). See note to p. 236

kepe(r) keep(er)

kindred relationship by blood or descent

knowla(/e)ge (in special sense) acknowledge

kyndle kindle

kyng(e) king

la(t)chet a shoelace

Lammas 1 August, originally observed as a harvest festival, at which loaves of bread were consecrated ('loaf mass')

last(e) last; aforementioned

laver the baptismal font; the spiritual 'washing' of baptism

lay a person not of the clergy

leaven a substance added to dough to produce fermentation; used figuratively to mean the unregenerate part of man.

Lent(e) the period of forty weekdays from Ash-Wednesday to Easter Eve, observed as a time of fasting and penitence in commemoration of Jesus's temptation in the wilderness

lesson portion of scripture or other sacred writing read at divine service

le(a)t (1) to leave; to allow to pass; (2) to hinder, prevent, obstruct

letani(/y)(e), litany a form of public prayer with a penitential character. See note to p. 41

li(/y)beraliti(/y)(e) generosity

lie with to have sexual intercourse with

lighteninge(s) lightning

lively expressing or conveying spiritual or eternal life

liver a living creature

lofe loaf

loke look

looce loose

Lord(e)s Table the table on which the elements are placed for holy COMMUNION; often (in sixteenth and seventeenth centuries) used in deliberate opposition to ALTAR

low(e)liness(e) low state or condition; poverty; meekness, humility

lyer liar

lyve live

magistrate a civil officer charged with the administration of the law

Magnificat the hymn of the Virgin Mary used as a CANTICLE at EVENSONG; see note to p. 15

magnifie to praise highly; to glorify, extol

maie may

maister master

maledicc(/t)ion curse; God's rejection of wickedness (see BENEDICTION)

Mammon inordinate desire for wealth or possessions

mani(/y)fold(e) numerous, varied; of many kinds

mansion an apartment within a large house

Mari Mary

Mass(e) the liturgical celebration of the EUCHARIST. See note to p. 19

Mat(t)e(/i)ns originally the form of service used in VIGILS in monasteries and performed at night; over time, as monks slept in later, a form of morning office: in *1549* (and later) a synonym for Morning Prayer

mediato(u)r an intermediary between God and mankind, specifically Jesus

menne(s) men('s)

mete meet; appropriate or worthy

middes middle

minister (1) a servant, attendant; (2) a member of the clergy, often in BCP synonymous with PRIEST, but increasingly used by Puritans in preference to that term

ministery ministry

ministracion the action or an act of ministering

misdoing(e) wrongdoing, evildoing

mistery mystery

misticall mystical

mo(e) more

moneth month

mony money

mortify to bring the body or its appetites into subjection through self-denial

Munday Monday
murther murder
myght power; (*gramm.*) might
mynd(e) intend
myne mine

nacion a people or group of peoples
name (in special senses): (1) the designation of a divine being invoking the power of that being; (2) a good or distinguished reputation
naughtie morally bad, wicked
negligence a negligent act; a careless omission
nocturn(e) an office, used at MATINS (i.e. originally at night), consisting both of psalms (each with an ANTIPHON), and of lessons (each with a RESPOND)
Noe Noah
no(u)mbre number
nought nothing
Nunc dimittis the Song of Simeon used as a CANTICLE at EVENSONG; see note to p. 15

oblac(/t)ion (1) an offering or sacrifice; esp. the EUCHARIST understood as sacrifice; (2) the presentation of money, goods, property, etc., to the church. See notes to p. 30 and p. 395
obteign obtain
occasional The OFFICES in the BCP for specific occasions (such as baptism, matrimony, etc.)
octave in the Roman liturgy, the eighth day (inclusively) after a FEAST, i.e. falling on the same day of the week as the feast itself; from Lat. *octava* ('eighth'). The term also meant the whole period of these eight days
offence a breach of law; transgression, sin
offertory (1) (in Roman MASS) a short ANTHEM immediately after the CREED, while the offerings of the people were being received; (2) (in BCP) the scriptural sentences in the corresponding part of COMMUNION; (3) the part of the EUCHARIST, during which the offerings of the congregation (orig. bread and wine) are placed on the altar; (4) a collection taken of ALMS during the Eucharist, or the alms themselves
Office (1) an authorized form of divine service or worship; (2) (in the medieval church) the daily service of the BREVIARY for each of the canonical hours; (3) the service of the MASS or COMMUNION, esp. the INTROIT sung at the beginning of this service (also called the 'Office of the Mass'); (4) in BCP, any special liturgy for a particular occasion; (5) a duty attaching to a person's station or position
olife olive

onely only

onlesse unless

ordeyned ordained

ordinal (1) (pre-Reformation) a book detailing the order of church services at different times of the ecclesiastical year; (2) (in BCP) a book containing the form of service to be used in the ORDINATION of DEACONS and PRIESTS and the consecration of BISHOPS

ordina(u)nce an authoritative direction, decree, or command, esp. of God

Ordinary spiritual jurisdiction, with the authority to act in a certain geographical area; e.g. a BISHOP within a DIOCESE, or his appointed deputy such as an ARCHDEACON

ordination the action of conferring holy ORDERS; the ritual for such

ordre, order (1) a stated form of liturgical service, or of administration of a rite or CEREMONY, prescribed by ecclesiastical authority; (2) a grade or rank in the Christian ministry. In plural (frequently as 'holy orders'), the rank or status of an ordained minister; (3) a religious society or fraternity; (4) in general sense: the condition in which everything has its correct or appropriate place; (5) an appointed sequence

ornament (*pl.*) 'The accessories or furnishings of a church; the sacred vessels, vestments, etc., used in religious worship' (*OED*)

Osanna HOSANNA

othe oath

otherwaies otherwise

outward of or relating to the body or its outer surface

oyl oil

painfull performed with or involving great care or diligence

Palm Sunday the Sunday before Easter

pap a woman's breast

pardon (*theol.*) the forgiveness of a sin or sins; in Catholic doctrine, full restitution: this sense denied by Protestants

parish 'an area or district having its own priest, parson, or other incumbent under the jurisdiction of a bishop; a territorial subdivision of a diocese' (*OED*)

part(e) a person's share in some action; a duty

Pascall Paschal; of or relating to Easter; used in Easter celebrations; of or relating to PASSOVER ('paschal lamb')

passion Jesus's suffering and death on the cross

passover (1) the Jewish spring festival commemorating the liberation of the people of Israel from Egyptian bondage; (2) the lamb eaten at the festival

pasto(u)r a person who has the spiritual care of a body of Christians

paten 'A plate or shallow dish (usually silver or gold), on which the host is laid during the eucharist, and which may also serve as a cover for the chalice' (*OED*)

Patriarchs Adam and his male descendants down to Noah

patron saint under whose name a church is dedicated

penance (1) the performance of some act of self-mortification or the undergoing of some penalty as an expression of sorrow for sin; (2) repentance; (3) a sacrament in the medieval church, including CONTRITION, CONFESSION, SATISFACTION, and ABSOLUTION

penitent (1) (*adj.*) that REPENTS with sincere desire to amend the sin, repentant, contrite; (2) (*noun*) a person who repents

Pentecost FESTIVAL of the seventh Sunday after Easter, commemorating Acts 2 where the Holy Spirit is reported to have descended upon the disciples during the Jewish festival of Pentecost

peny penny

perfect(e) ('perfect age'): the age at which a person is considered to be mature or adult

perfite perfect

person(e)s (in special sense) the individual members of the TRINITY.

pie a term for the medieval ORDINAL, fr. Lat. *pica* ('magpie'), i.e. because predominantly with rubrics in black, not coloured

plage plague

plaines plainness: 'honesty or straightforwardness (of conduct); directness or frankness (of language)' (*OED*)

plight to give in pledge.

potsherd a broken piece of pottery

powre pour

prai(y)se 'In religious contexts: the expression of admiration, gratitude, etc., or the acknowledgement of glory and honour, performed as an act of worship' (*OED*)

Prebend the estate or portion of land from which a stipend is derived to support a CANON of a CATHEDRAL or COLLEGIATE church (hence 'Prebendary')

prentise apprentice; person learning a trade or profession from an employer

preserve to keep safe from injury or harm

presume to dare or venture

prevent of God, God's GRACE, etc.: to go before (a person) with spiritual guidance and help

prick a goad for driving oxen (cf. 'to kick against the pricks')

priest an ordained minister ranking above a DEACON and below a BISHOP, having authority to administer the SACRAMENTS

prima(/i)tive the period of the early church

pri(/y)mer a prayer book or devotional manual for the use of LAY people; a book of HOURS

print(e) the impression or imprint made by the impact of a stamp

profession a declaration of belief in and obedience to religion

properti(/y)(e) the characteristic quality of a person or thing

prophesy(/y)e (1) to speak by divine inspiration, sometimes in foretelling the future; (2) to interpret the Bible

prophet(e) a divinely inspired interpreter, revealer, or teacher; in plural, the prophetic writers of the OT and their books

propitiac(/t)ion (of Christ): 'offered or sacrificed for the purpose of appeasement or expiation' (*OED*)

propre/proper those parts of a service which vary with the day, season, or occasion

proselyte a convert; (in special sense) a gentile who has converted to Judaism

providence 'The foreknowing and protective care of God; divine direction, control, or guidance' (*OED*)

Provost head of an ecclesiastical CHAPTER or religious community

pryest PRIEST

public(k)(e) public

publican a tax-gatherer in ancient Judaea; regarded as traitorous because of service to Rome

pulpit(t)(e) a raised, enclosed platform in a church from which the priest conducts the service or gives a sermon or LESSON

p(o)urge to make pure or clean; also figuratively, in spirit, thought, or morals; to rid of sin

purificac(/t)ion the action of making ceremonially or ritually clean

pytie pity

quaternion a Roman officer in charge of four soldiers

quick(e) living, endowed with life, animate

quiet(yng) 'To subdue (the sense of feeling or moving)' (*MED*)

quietness(e) the condition of being quiet; calmness, tranquillity

Quinquagesima the Sunday before LENT (from Lat. *quinquaginta*, 'fifty', i.e. fifty days before Easter)

quire CHOIR

Raguel the father of Sarah, wife of Tobias in the Book of Tobit

read(e) (1) read; (2) red

reasonable (in special sense) proportionate

red(e) (1) red; (2) read

rede(e)me(d) lit. 'To pay off a debt'; hence (*theol.*) 'to deliver (a person, a soul, etc.) from sin or damnation'

regenerate spiritually reborn

rejoyse rejoice

remaigne remain

remission forgiveness or pardon granted for sins; the cancelling of, or deliverance from, the guilt and penalties of sin

renue renew

repent 'To feel contrition or regret for something one has done or omitted to do; (*esp.* in religious contexts) to acknowledge the sinfulness of past action or conduct by showing remorse and undertaking reform' (*OED*)

replenyshed 'to be provided or filled (with riches, goods, animals, etc.)' (*MED*)

respond(e) a form of ANTIPHON

reyn (1) reign; (2) rein

risi(/y)ng (in special sense) resurrection

ro(t)chet(t)(e) an ecclesiastical VESTMENT similar to a SURPLICE, typically of white linen and chiefly worn by a BISHOP

Rogation days the three days preceding ASCENSION, on which SUPPLICA-TIONS and the litany is said; see note to p. 236

rood a crucifix, esp. one stationed above the middle of a rood-screen. See note to p. 125

rubric(k) a direction for the conduct of divine service inserted in liturgical books, originally written or printed in red (Lat. *ruber*)

rychesse wealth, riches; spiritual wealth

ryghthande 'right hand'; to sit to the immediate right of a host, *trad.* the place of honour

Sabaoth (Lord of) Heb. (lit. 'armies', 'hosts'), retained untranslated in the English NT (as in the Gk. Septuagint and the Lat. Vulgate) and the *Te Deum*; lit. 'The Lord of Hosts'

sabba(/o)th (1) the seventh day of the week (Saturday), considered a day of rest in Jewish practice; (2) (post-Reformation) the first day of the week (Sunday) held by Protestants to be subject to the same law; (3) a synonym for Sunday

sacrament common name for certain solemn ceremonies or religious acts belonging to the institutions of the Christian church; there were seven in the medieval church, only two post-Reformation (BAPTISM and COMMUNION)

Sadduce(e)s a religious party within ancient Judaism

sainct saint

salvac(/t)ion 'the deliverance from sin, and admission to eternal bliss, wrought by the atonement of Christ' (*OED*)

sanctify to make (a person) holy, to purify or free from sin; to cause to undergo sanctification

Sanctus a hymn forming part of the COMMUNION; see note to p. 29

Sarum (Lat.) 'of Salisbury' (esp. 'USE of Sarum')

Sathan Satan

satisfacc(/t)ion (1) performance by a penitent of the penalties required after CONFESSION of sins; (2) the atonement made by Christ for sin, equivalent to the penalties due for the sins of the world

save (in specialized sense): 'To deliver (a person, the soul) from sin and its consequences; to admit to eternal bliss' (*OED*)

scater scatter

sclaunder slander

scribe (*biblical*) a member of the class of professional interpreters of the Jewish law

scrip a small bag or wallet

scruple a thought or circumstance that troubles the mind or conscience; a doubt, uncertainty or hesitation

see the seat or diocese held by a bishop

seed(e) (1) that which is sown; (2) the germ or latent beginning of some growth or development, esp. religious sense of fulfilment; (3) offspring, progeny

seke seek

sene past tense of 'see'

sentence a short passage of scripture used in liturgy

Septuagesima the third Sunday before LENT

Seraphim(/n) (*pl.*) being of a celestial or angelic order (excelling in love)

sermon 'a discourse, usually delivered from a pulpit and based upon a text of Scripture, for the purpose of religious instruction or exhortation' (*OED*)

Sexagesima the second Sunday before LENT

sharpenesse severity, acuteness (of pain or sorrow)

shew(e); shewed (*past tense*) show

sixt sixth

slea(/y) slay

smite to strike with a weapon, slay; to visit with death or destruction (e.g. through God's will or action)

societi(/y)(e) companionship, fellowship, company

sodain sudden

solem(p)nis(/z)e to honour by CEREMONIES; celebrate

sond(e)ry sundry

song past tense of 'sing'

sope soap

sorowe sorrow

sory sorry

souldier soldier

speciallye especially

spikenard an aromatic substance obtained from a plant

spirit(e) (1) the animating or vital principle in man; (2) incorporeal or immaterial being, as opposed to body or matter; (3) the soul of a person, e.g. at death; (4) a supernatural, incorporeal, rational being or personality (sometimes with qualifying terms, as 'evil spirit'); (5) the Spirit of God (or the Lord), the active essence or essential power of God, e.g. 'the holy spirit'; (6) the active or essential principle or power of some emotion, etc.

spot stain, taint (esp. in moral sense)

spousage marriage

spunge sponge

stablish(e) establish

sterre star

stoare store

straungier stranger

straw; strawed (*past tense*) strew, scatter loosely

strength strengthen

style stile

substa(u)nce 'Essential nature, essence; *esp. theol.*, with regard to the being of God, the divine nature or essence in respect of which the three persons of the Trinity are one' (*OED*)

suff(e)r(e) (1) to endure pain; (2) to be subject to something; (3) to tolerate or allow

suffrage (often in collective plural) prayers, esp. intercessory prayers, intercessions

superstic(/t)ious 'having an irrational religious belief or practice founded on fear or ignorance' (*OED*); a common word in the fifteenth cent. used habitually in the sixteenth to describe pre-Reformation concepts and feelings

supplicac(/t)ion humble or earnest petition or entreaty

supre(a)m(e) ('supreme head' or 'governour') the position of the sovereign as the paramount authority in the CHURCH OF ENGLAND

surple(/i)c(/s)(s)(e), surplice a loose VESTMENT of white linen with wide sleeves sometimes reaching to the feet, worn (usually over a cassock) by clerics, choristers, and others taking part in church services. See note to p. 98

su(e)r(e)ti(/y)(e) (1) a sponsor at a baptism; (2) legal guarantee

sware past tense of 'swear'

swette a fever characterized by profuse sweating; fatal epidemics occurred frequently in England in the fifteenth and sixteenth centuries

syckenes sickness

synne sin

synodal(le) a FESTIVAL peculiar to a particular diocese

Syon Zion, i.e. Jerusalem as holy centre and by extension the heavenly city

tabernacle (1) the curtained tent, containing the Ark of the Covenant; a temple; (2) a dwelling, place of abode; (3) applied to the human body regarded as the temporary abode of the soul or of life (*OED*)

tare an injurious weed among corn (from Lat. *zizania*)

tary tarry, delay

testament (1) a will made before death; (2) a COVENANT; (3) one of the two divisions of the Bible

thank(e)sge(/i)ve(/i)ng, thankes geving the act of giving thanks, esp. to God; a form of words, or prayer, for this purpose

thei they

Thobie Tobias

th(o)row (1) through; (2) thorough

thryse thrice

to morowe tomorrow

toke past tense of 'take'

to(u)ng(u)e (in special sense) language

transfiguration the change in the appearance of Christ on the mountain (Matt. 7, Mark 9, Luke 9); the FESTIVAL commemorating this

translation removal (1) of a bishop from one see to another; (2) of the body or relics of a saint from one place to another

travai(/y)l(e) synonymous with TRAVEL

travel(l)(e) (1) travel; (2) travail; to suffer affliction; to labour, toil; (3) to suffer in childbirth, to be in labour

trespac(/ss)e 'To violate God's laws, etc.; commit a sinful act, do evil, sin' (*MED*)

tri(/y)(e) test; put to trial

Triniti(/y)(e) (1) a (post-biblical) doctrine applied to the existence of one God in three persons, Father, Son, and Holy Spirit; (2) the Sunday next after WHIT-SUNDAY, observed as a FESTIVAL in honour of the Trinity; (3) the season of twenty-five Sundays following Trinity before the Christian year begins again at ADVENT

troth solemn promise or engagement

trouth troth

tuna(/i)cle a vestment resembling the DALMATIC, worn by sub-deacons over the alb

tush a mild swear-word indicating contempt

tutour tutor

tyrannye violent or lawless action

unc(c)(/t)ion the action of anointing with oil as a religious rite

unclean(e) morally impure or defiled

uncreate(d) not brought into existence by a special act of creation; of a self-existent or eternal nature

undefyled not rendered morally foul or impure; unpolluted

unfained unfeigned; sincere, genuine

unleavened unfermented

unpossible impossible

unquyet disquiet; disturbance of mind

untoward unruly, perverse

ure use

use the distinctive ritual and liturgy that prevailed in a particular church, province, diocese, community, etc. (e.g. 'use of Sarum')

usury the practice of lending money at interest

vail, veil (in special sense) the piece of cloth separating the sanctuary from the body of the TABERNACLE

valour value

variaunce disagreement

veritie truth

vertue virtue

very true

Vespers the sixth of the canonical HOURS of the BREVIARY, celebrated towards evening; (in BCP, EVENSONG)

vestment garment worn by a priest on the occasion of divine service

vesture clothing

vigil the eve of a FESTIVAL, an occasion of religious observance

visitation (1) the practice of visiting sick or distressed persons as a work of charity; (2) a visit to examine into the state of a DIOCESE, PARISH, religious institution, etc.; in special sense a visit of inspection by a BISHOP or ARCHDEACON

vocac(/t)i(/y)on calling by God, to salvation or else to any action or function

vouchsaf(/v)e to show a gracious readiness or willingness, to grant readily

vulgar(e) vernacular

waie way

waiyng weighing

wantonly (1) recklessly, unadvisedly; (2) lasciviously, luxuriously

warely warily

warfare ('goeth a warfare') goes to war

weax wax; to grow

weke week

wel(l)beloved dearly loved

whale(s) any large marine creature; incl. mammals of the order *Cetacea*

whan when

whi(/y)les whilst

Whitso(/u)n(day)(e) the FESTIVAL day or season of PENTECOST

whoremonger fornicator, lecher

wont to be accustomed

wooll wool

woord(e) word

wo(o)rk(e)s deeds; actions; often in sense 'morally upright'

world without end(e) endlessly, for ever; used as translation of Lat. *in secula seculorum*, 'for ever and ever' (*OED*)

worthely according to merit; with due devotion or reverence

wrastle wrestle

wrinc(/k)le moral stain or blemish

wurse worse

wyne wine

yearth(e) earth

yere year

yf if

yong young

yse ice

Zache the prophet Zechariah

INDEX AND CONCORDANCE OF SERVICES AND ORDERS

The Oxford World's Classics Website

www.worldsclassics.co.uk

- Browse the full range of Oxford World's Classics online

- Sign up for our monthly e-alert to receive information on new titles

- Read extracts from the Introductions

- Listen to our editors and translators talk about the world's greatest literature with our Oxford World's Classics audio guides

- Join the conversation, follow us on Twitter at OWC_Oxford

- Teachers and lecturers can order inspection copies quickly and simply via our website

www.worldsclassics.co.uk